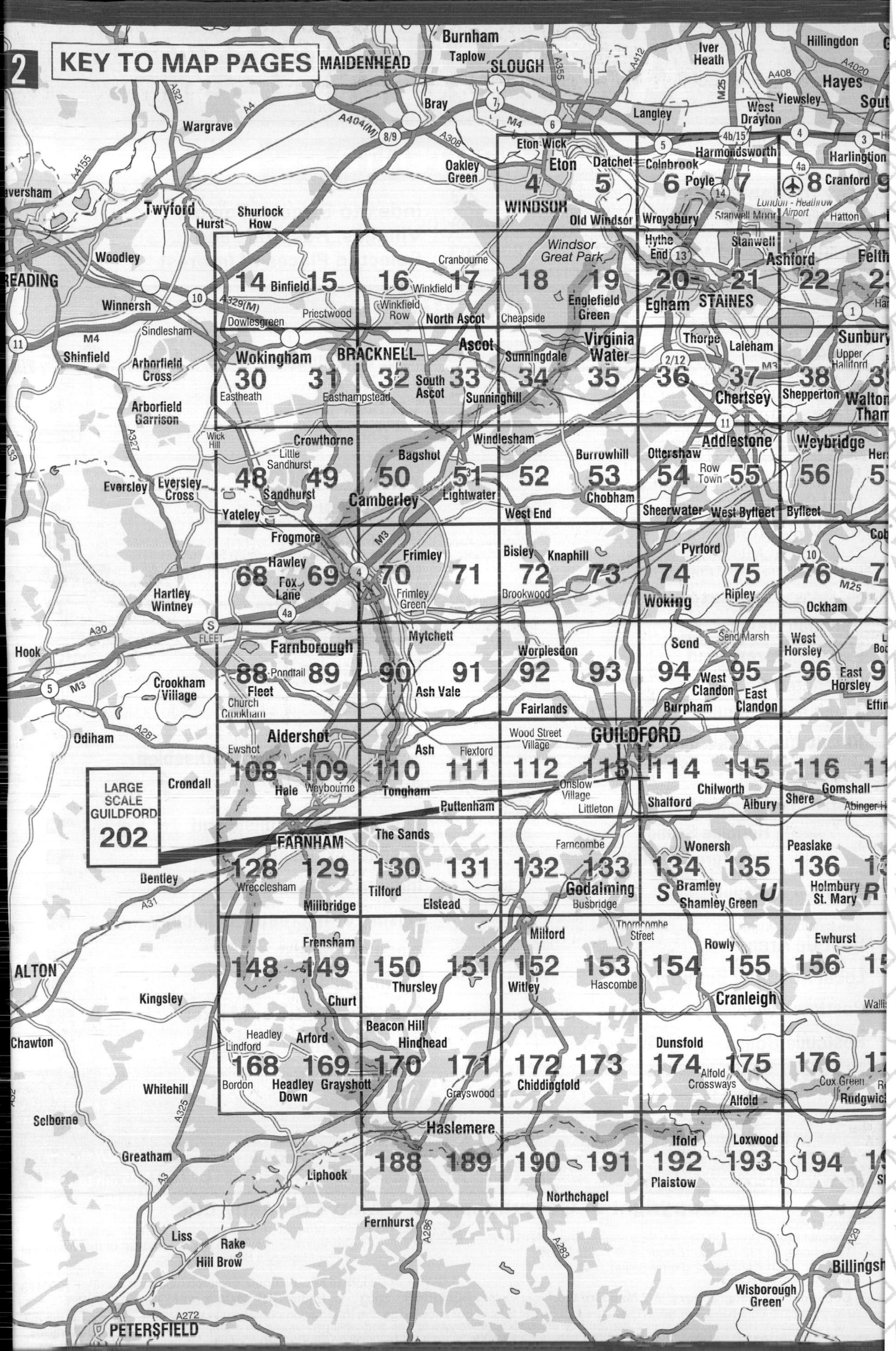

30119 024 336 093

D0183085

London Borough of Sutton

PUBLIC LIBRARIES

PER ARDUA   IN FIDE   SERVITE DEO

REFERENCE LIBRARY

A-Z SURREY

CONTENTS

REFERENCE

Motorway	M3
A Road	A246
Under Construction	
Proposed	
B Road	B3430
Dual Carriageway	
One-Way Street	
Traffic flow on A Roads is indicated by a heavy line on the driver's left	
Large Scale Pages Only	
Junction Name	APEX CORNER
Pedestrianized Road	
Restricted Access	
Track and Footpath	
Residential Walkway	
Railway	Tunnel / Level Crossing
Stations: National Rail Network	
Heritage Station	
Underground Station	is the registered trade mark of Transport for London
Croydon Tramlink	Tunnel / Stop
The boarding of Tramlink trams at stops may be limited to a single direction, indicated by the arrow	
Built-Up Area	HIGH STREET
Local Authority Boundary	
Posttown Boundary	
Postcode Boundary (within Posttown)	

Map Continuation	80
Car Park (Selected)	
Park & Ride	P+
Church or Chapel	
Fire Station	
Hospital	
House Numbers A & B Roads only	51 22
Information Centre	
National Grid Reference	
Police Station	
Post Office	
Toilet	
with Facilities for the Disabled	
Viewpoint	
Educational Establishment	
Hospital or Hospice	
Industrial Building	
Leisure or Recreational Facility	
Place of Interest	
Public Building	
Shopping Centre or Market	
Other Selected Buildings	

SCALE

Map Pages 4-199 1:20,267	Map Pages 200-203 1:9051
0 ¼ ½ Mile	0 ⅛ ¼ Mile
0 250 500 750 Metres	0 100 200 300 400 Metres
approx. 3 inches (7.94cm) to 1 mile 4.93 cm to 1 km	7 inches (17.78 cm) to 1 mile 11.05 cm to 1

Copyright of Geographers' A-Z Map Company Ltd.

Head Office:
Fairfield Road, Borough Green, Sevenoaks, Kent TN15 8PP
Telephone: 01732 781000 (Enquiries & Trade Sales)
01732 783422 (Retail Sales)
www.a-zmaps.co.uk

Ordnance Survey®

This product includes mapping data licensed fr Ordnance Survey® with the permission of the C of Her Majesty's Stationery Office.

Copyright © Geographers' A-Z Map Co. Ltd.

© Crown Copyright 2002. All rights reserved   Licence number

Edition 4   2002   Edition 4B   2004 (part revision)

Every possible care has been taken to ensure that, to the best of our knowledge, the information contained in this atlas is accurate at of publication. However, we cannot warrant that our work is entirely error free and whilst we would be grateful to learn of any inaccu we do not accept any responsibility for loss or damage resulting from reliance on information contained within this publication

LONDON BOROUGH OF SUTTON
LIBRARY SERVICE

02433609 3	
Askews	Dec-2006
912.4221	

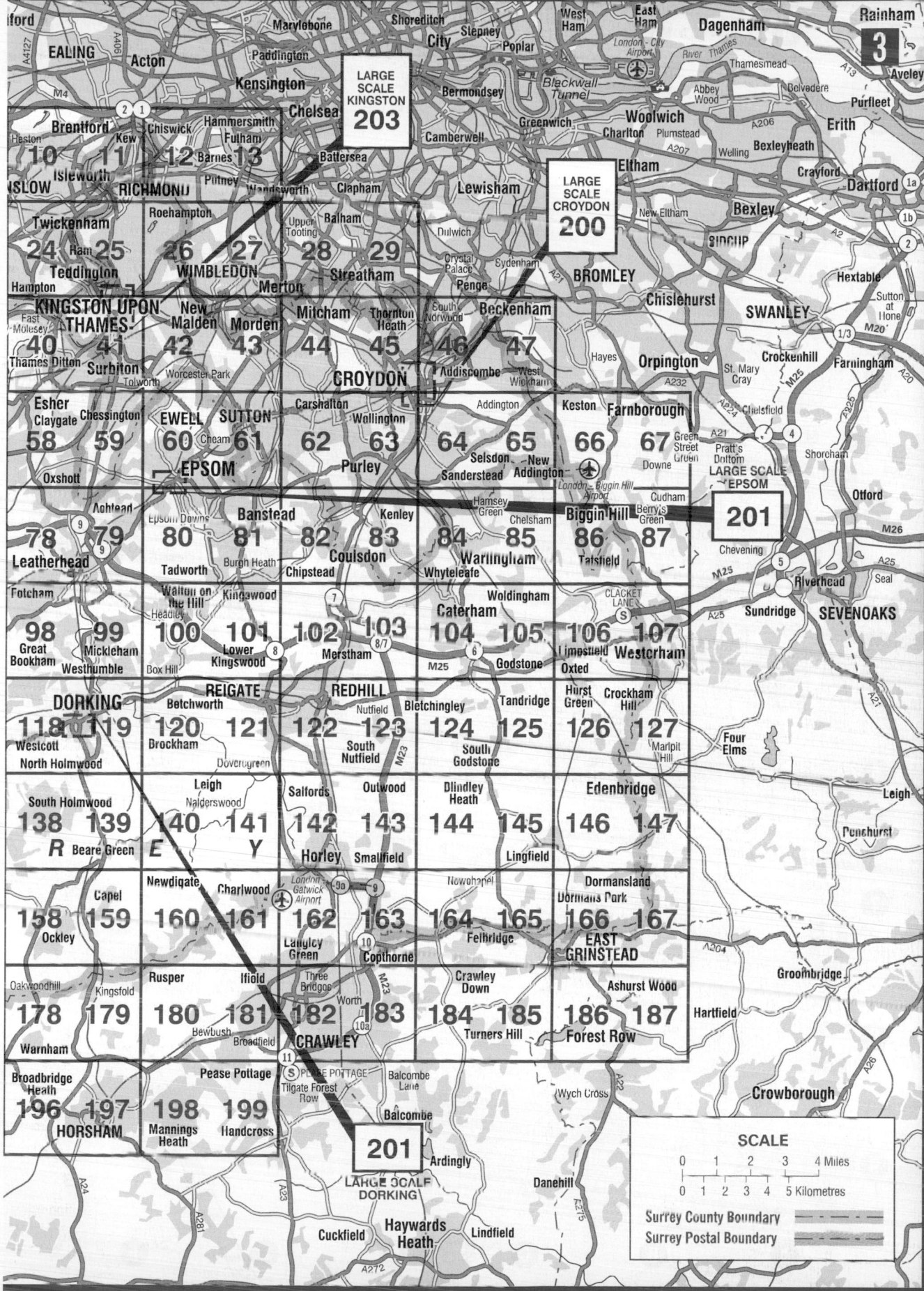

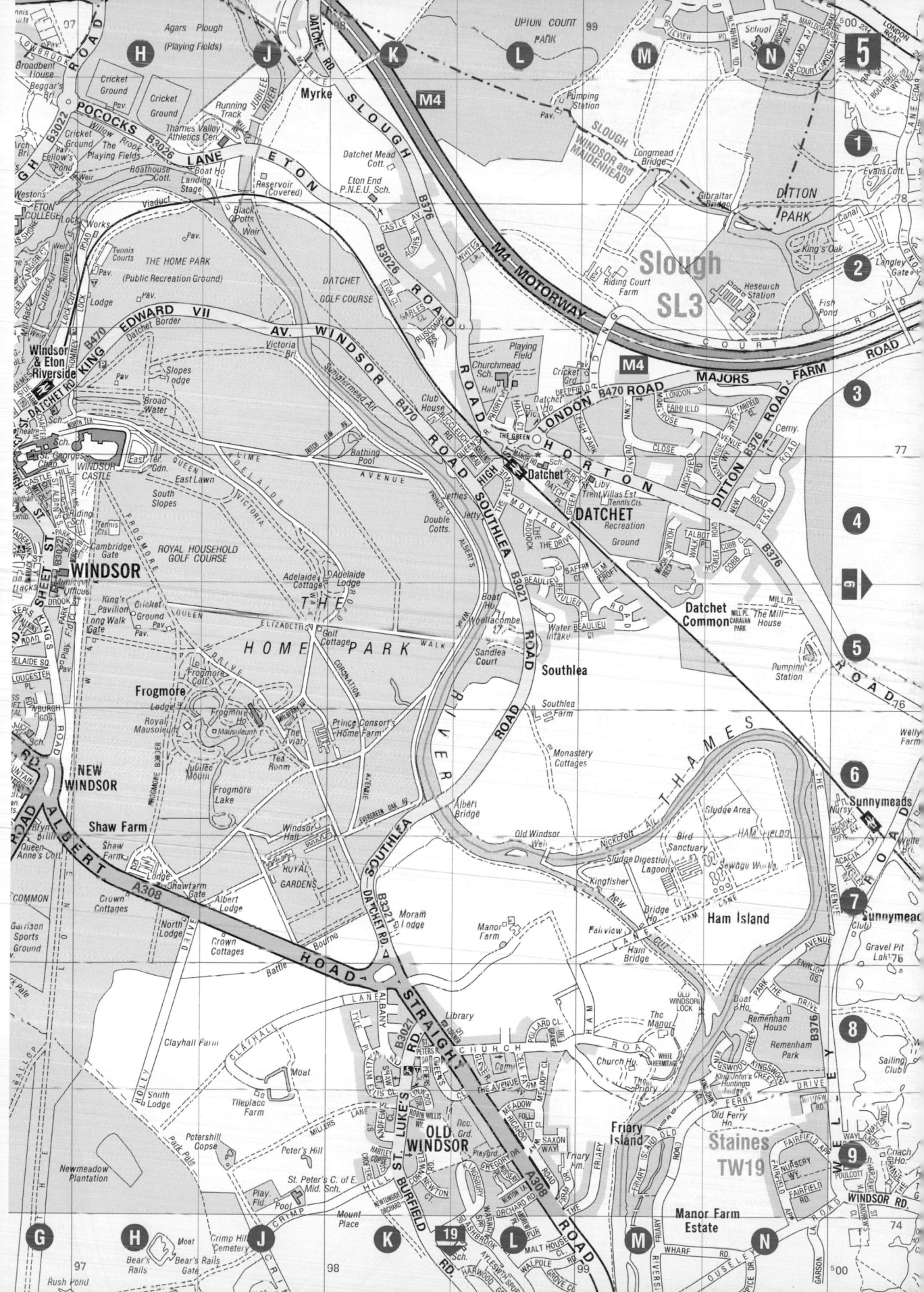

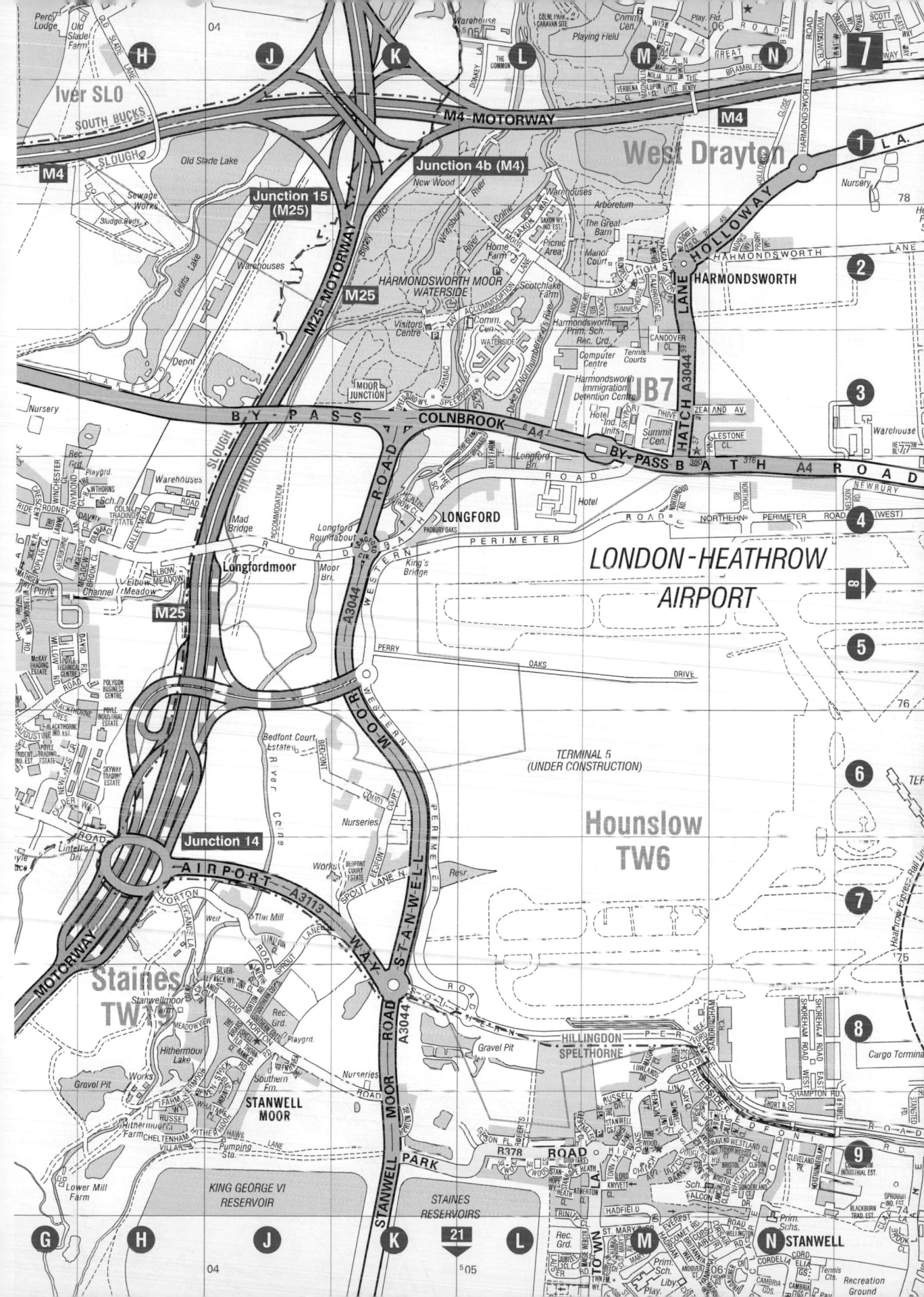

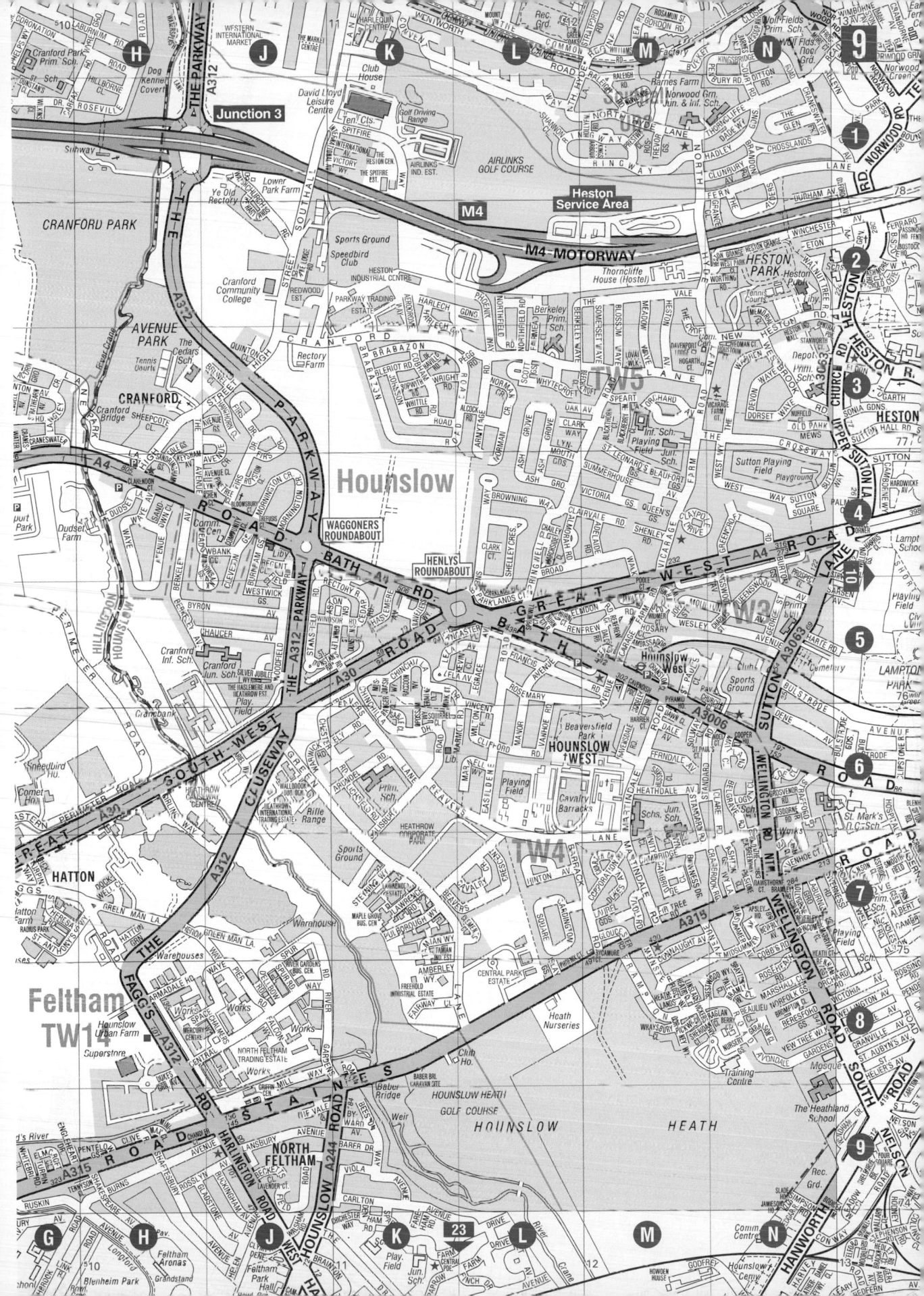

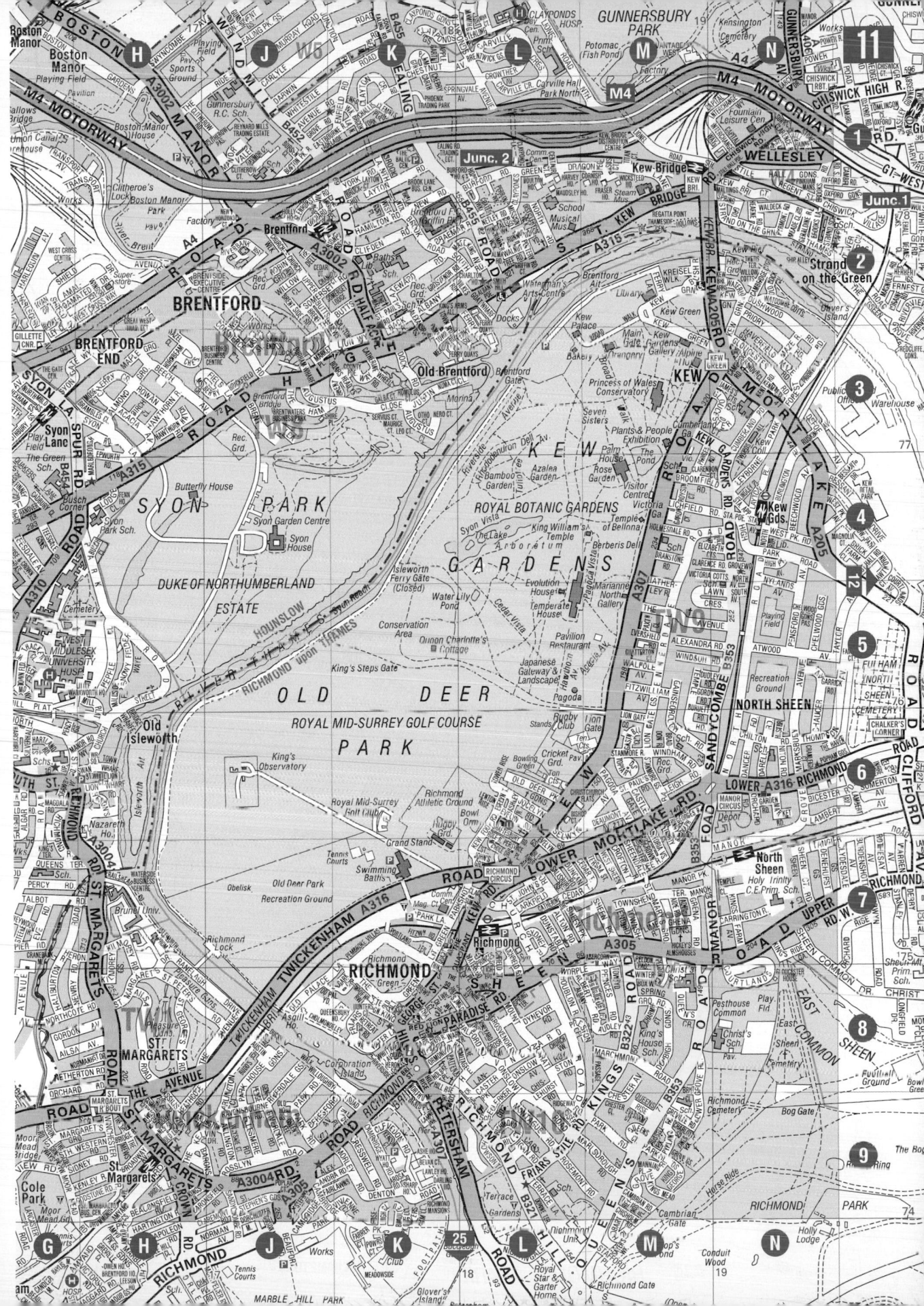

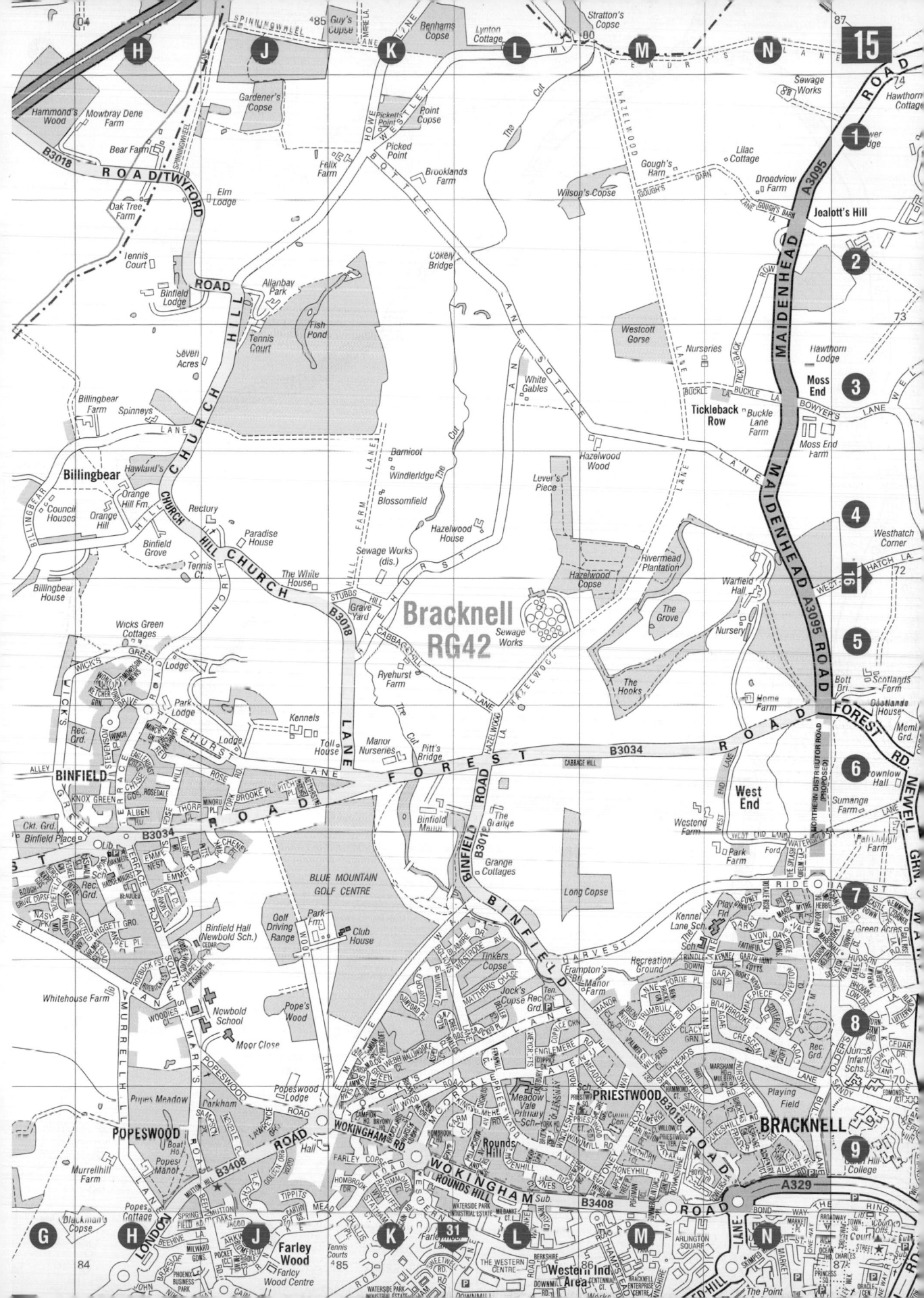

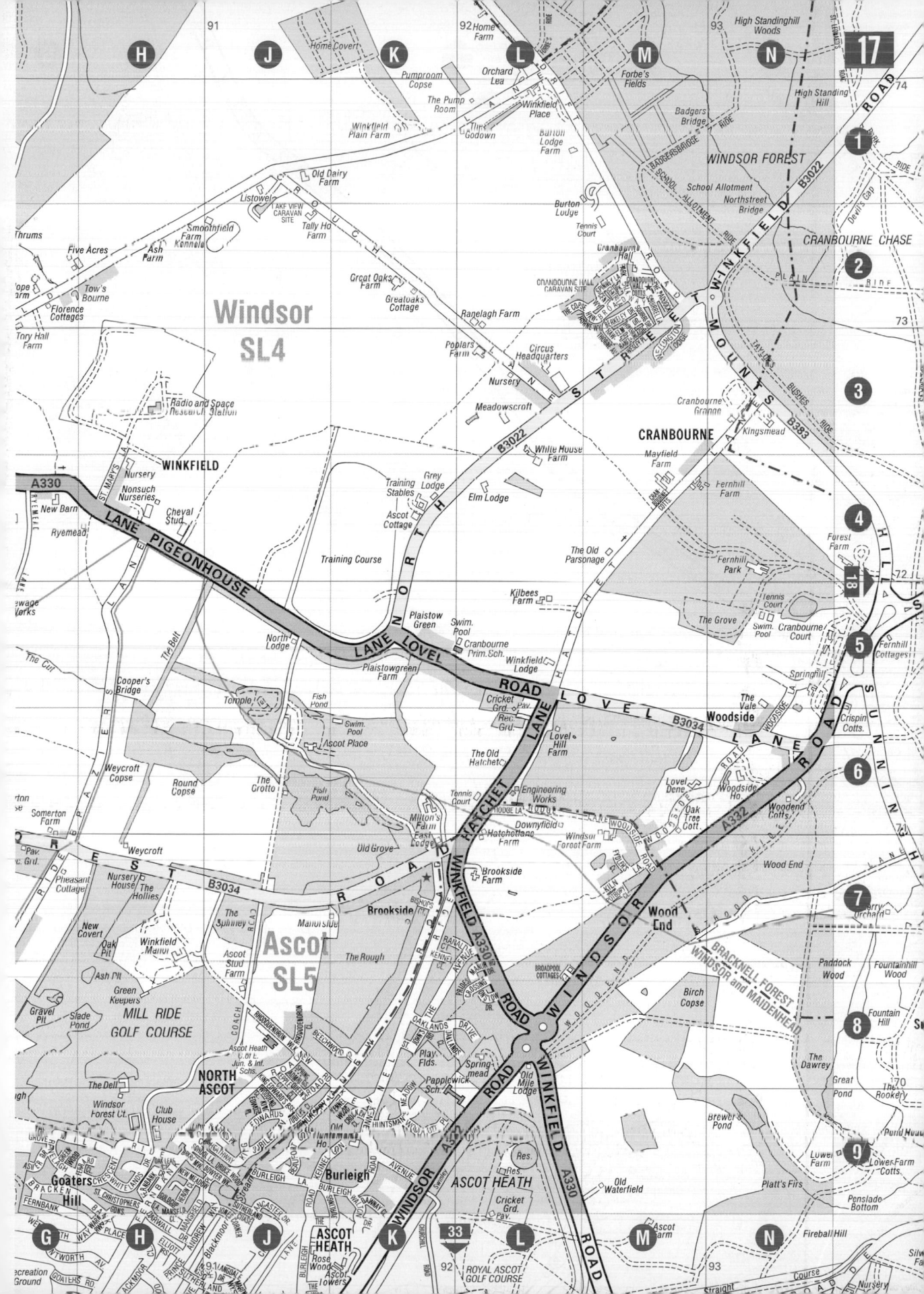

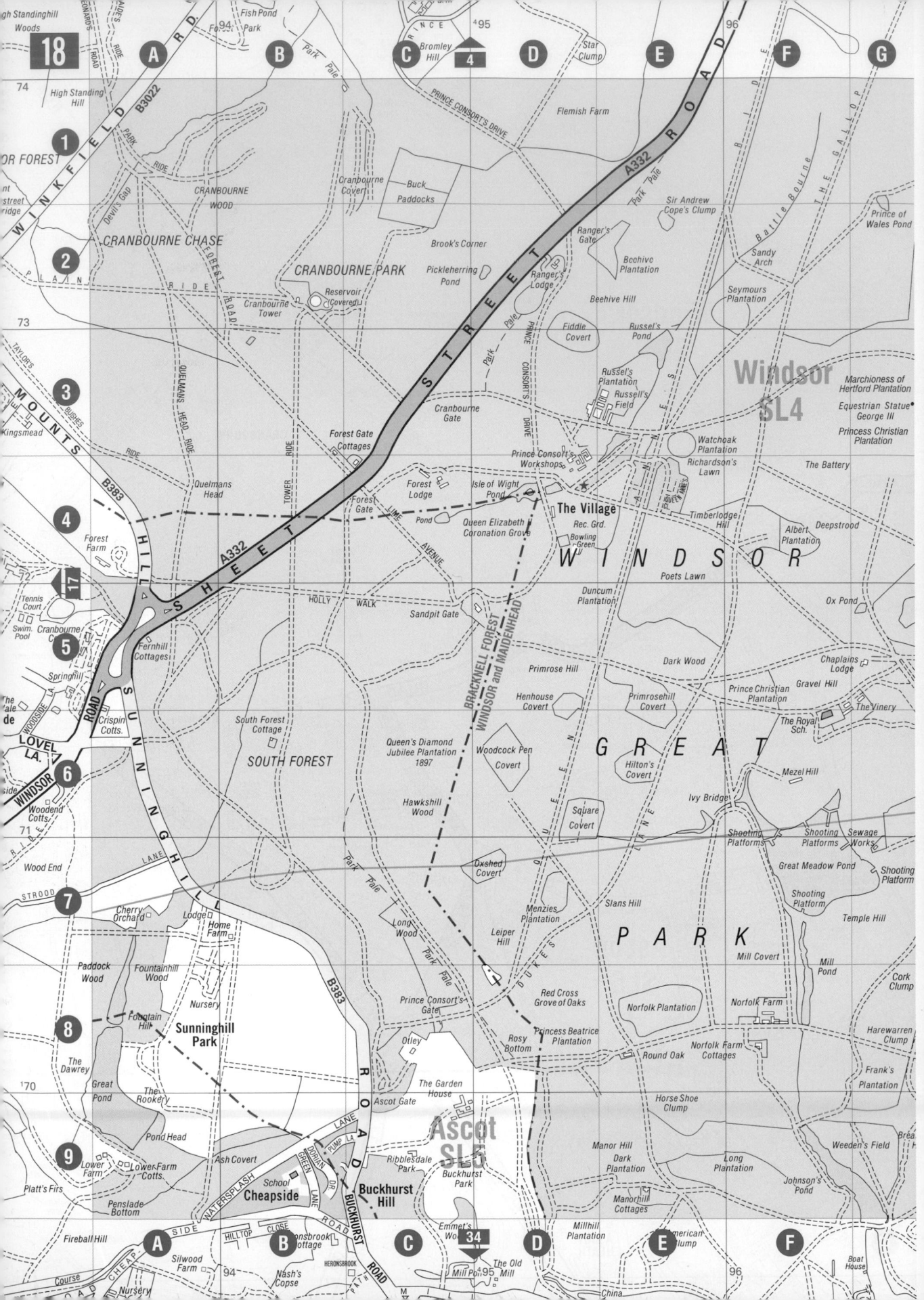

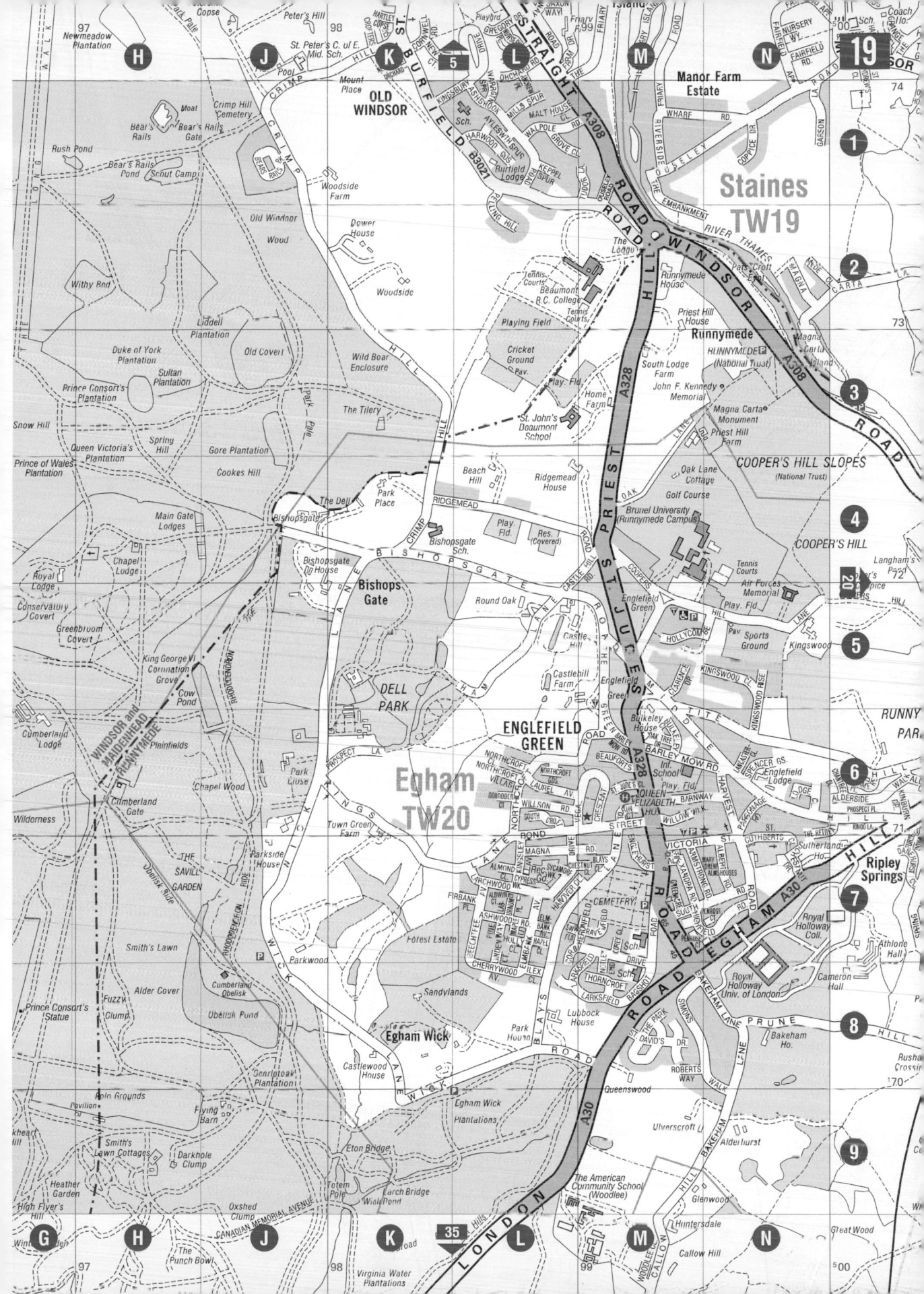

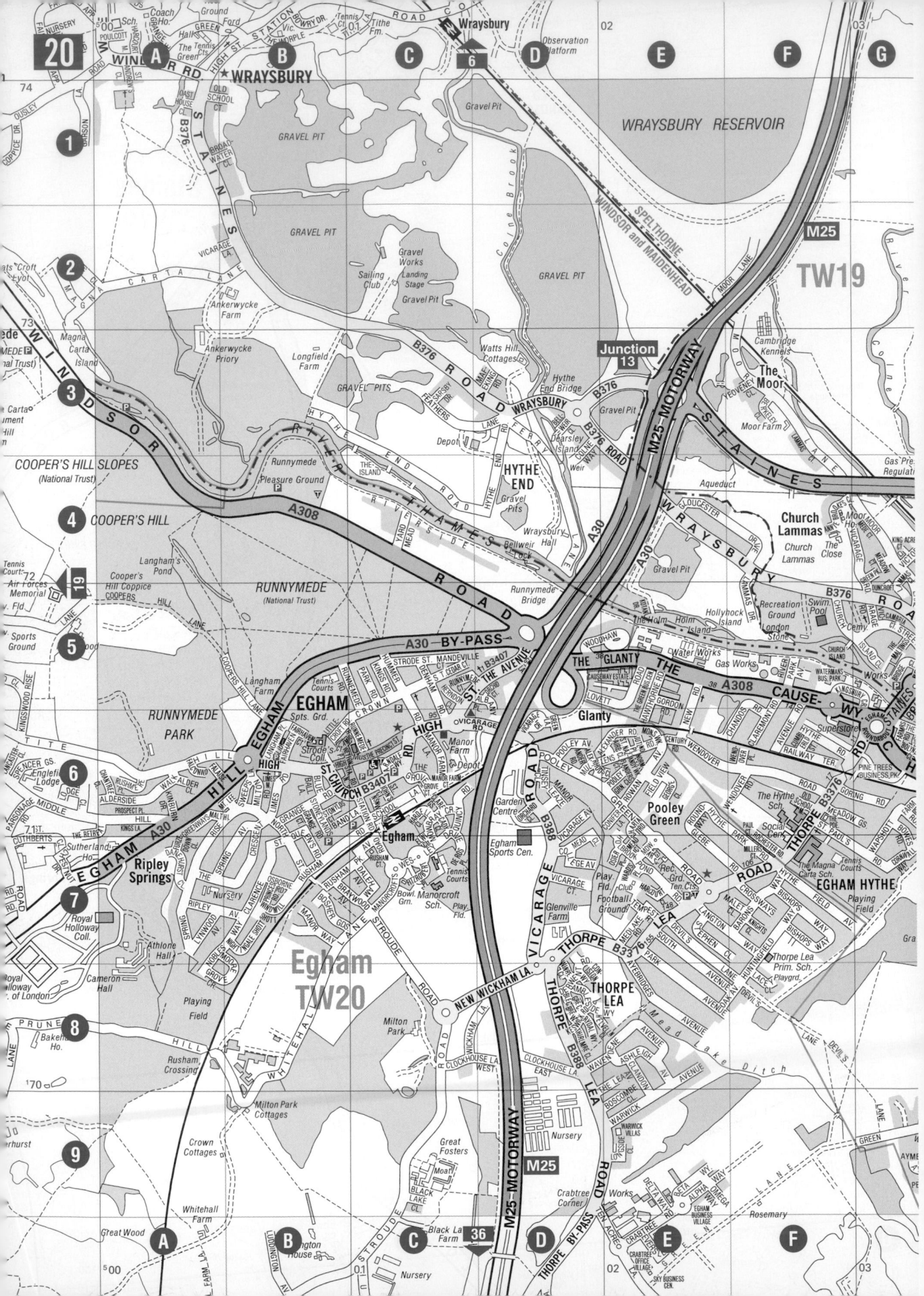

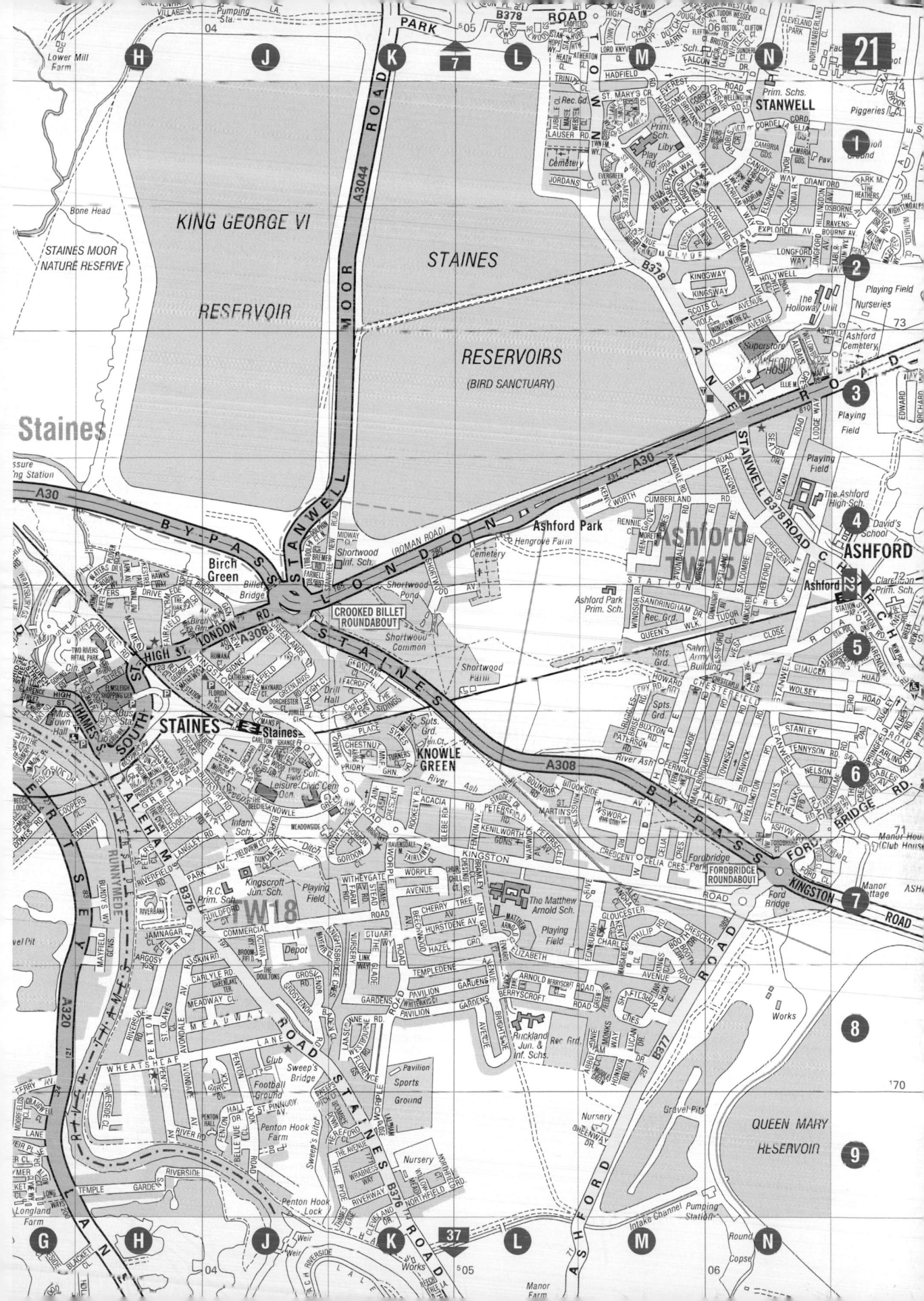

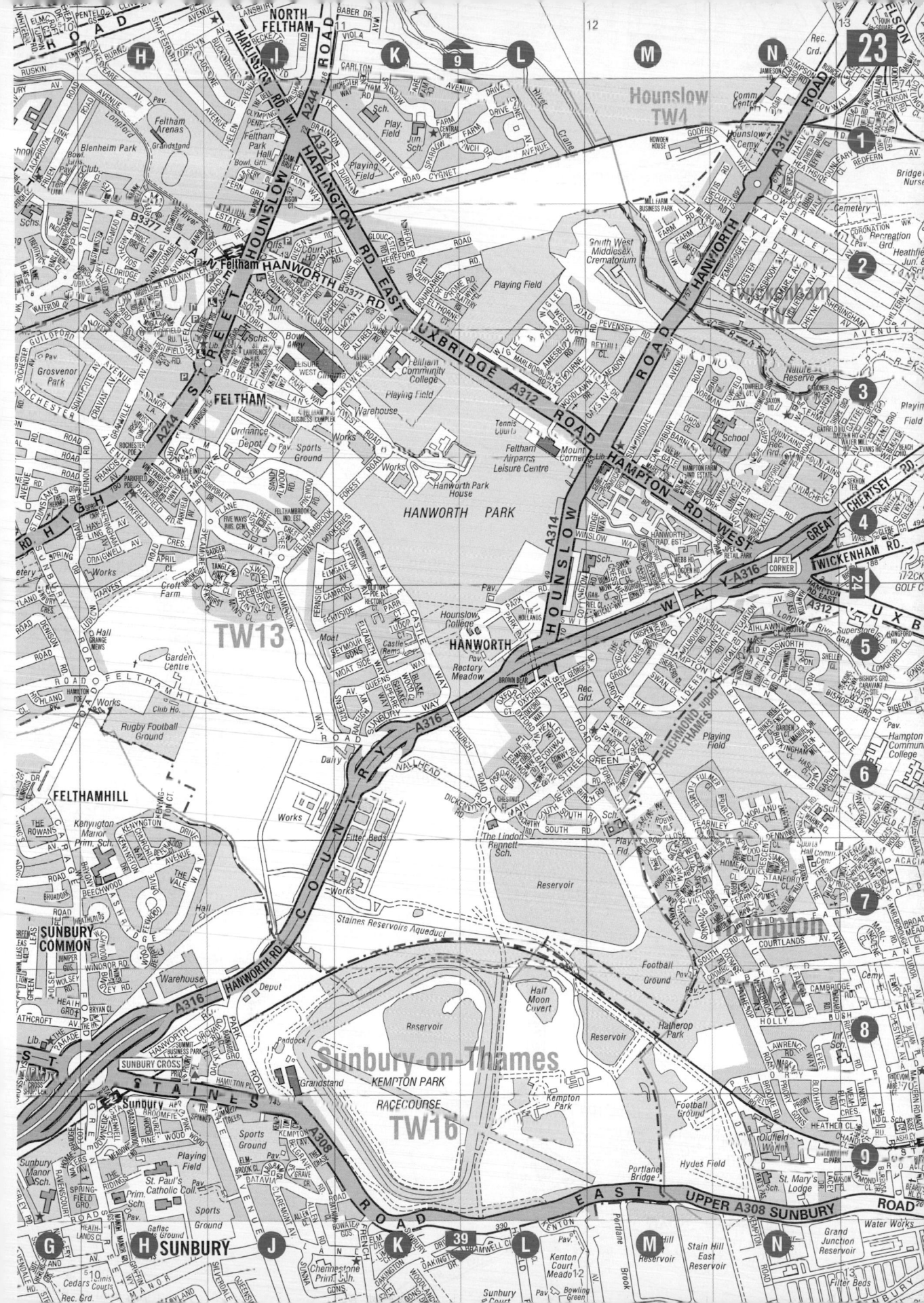

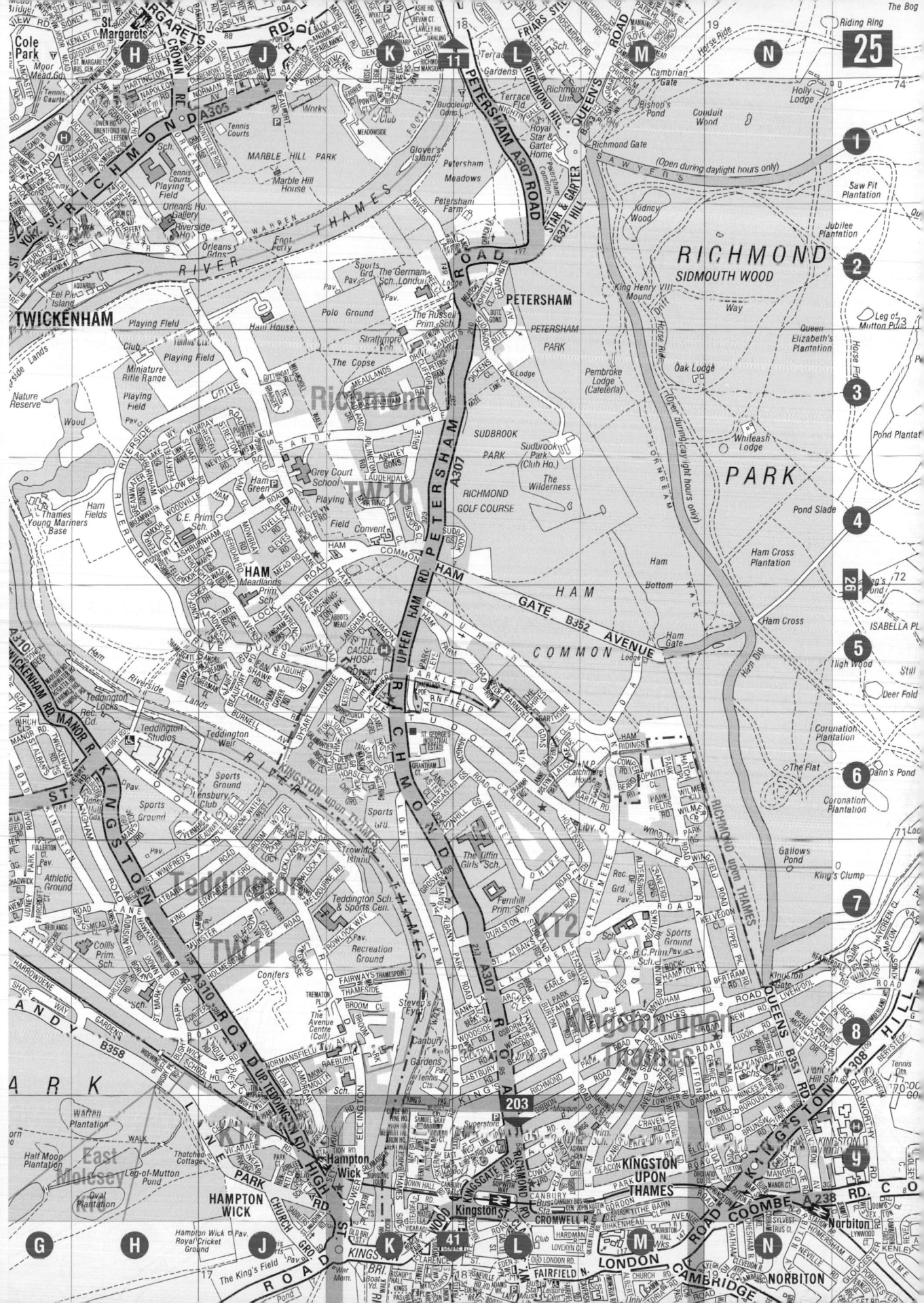

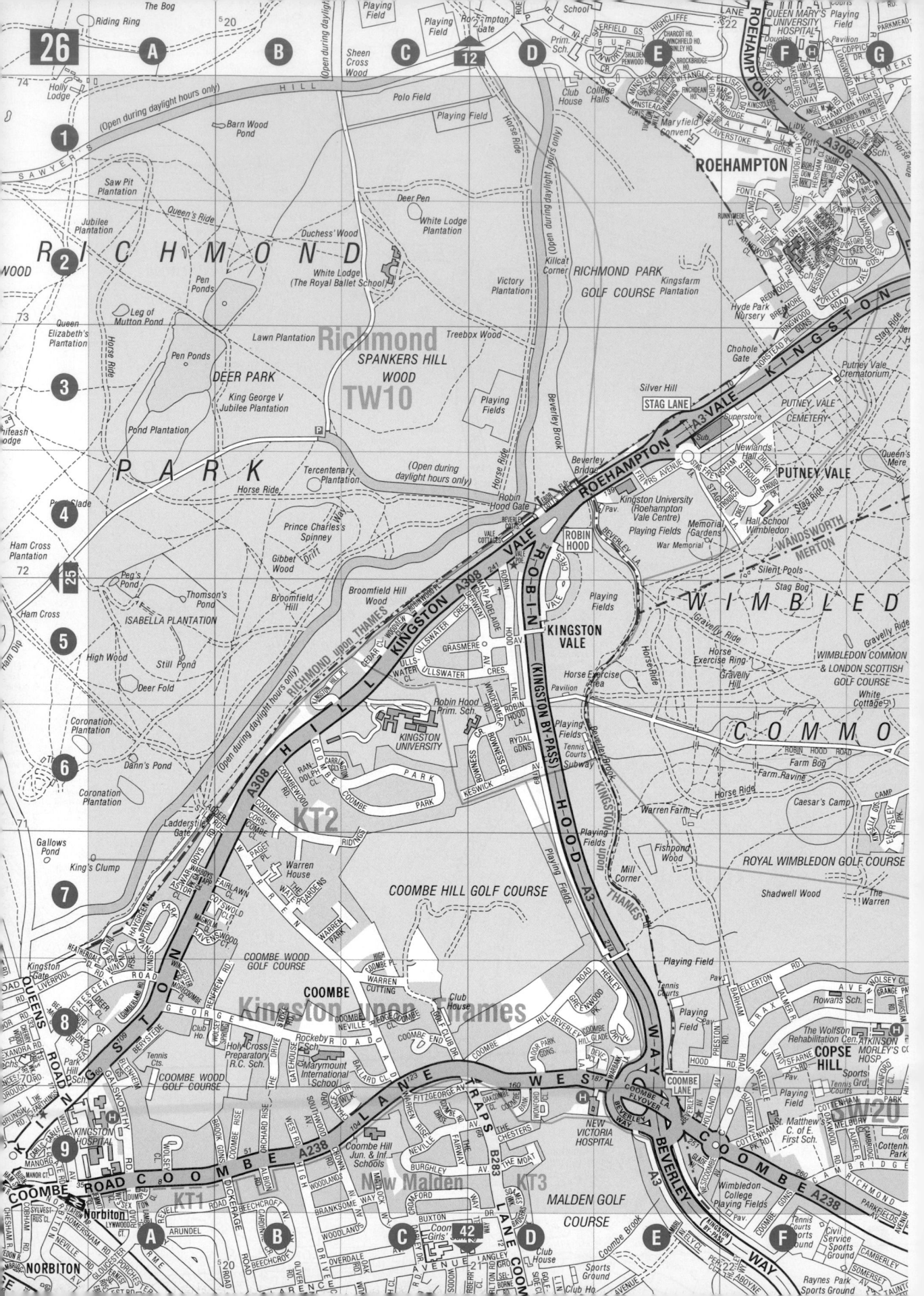

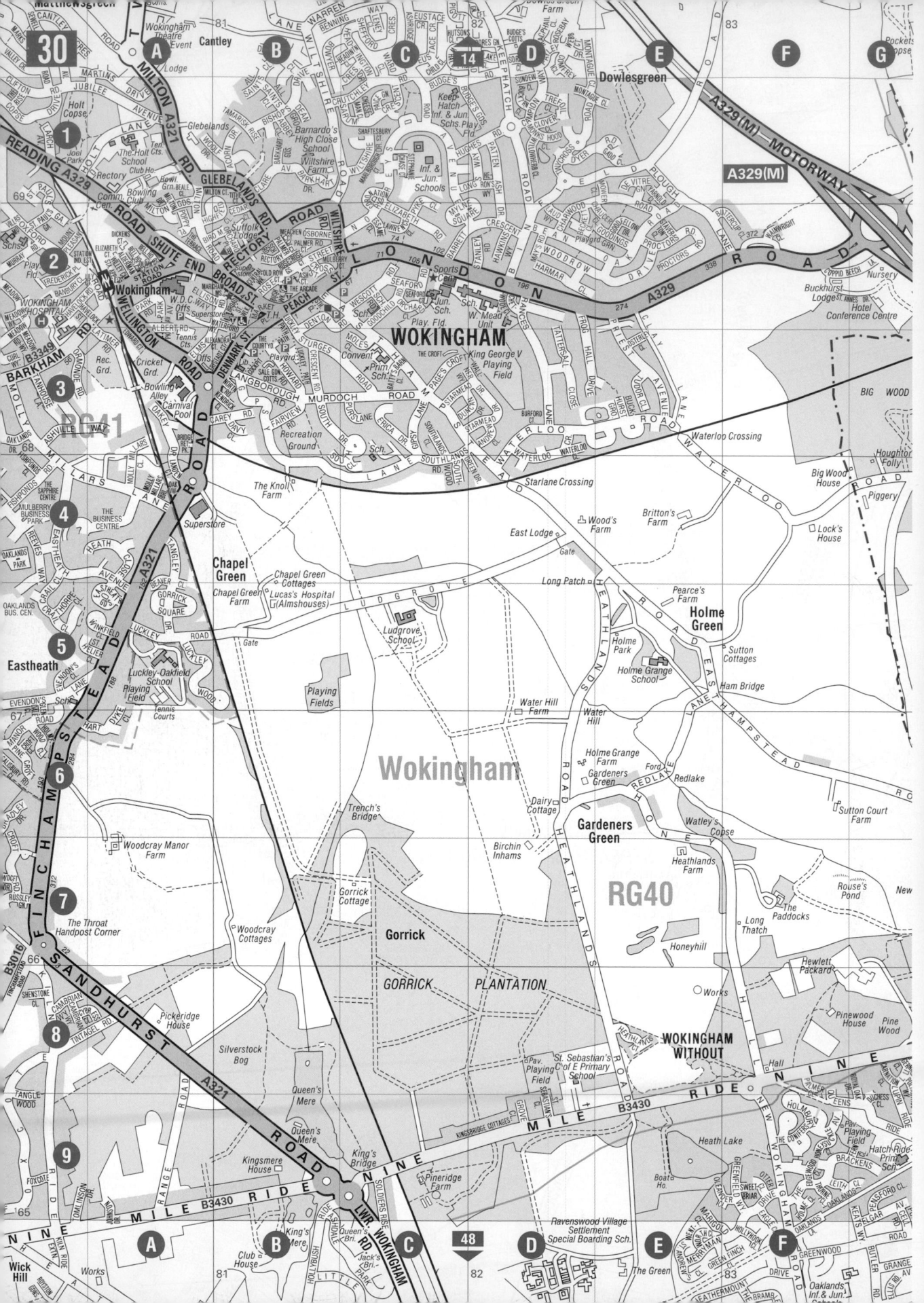

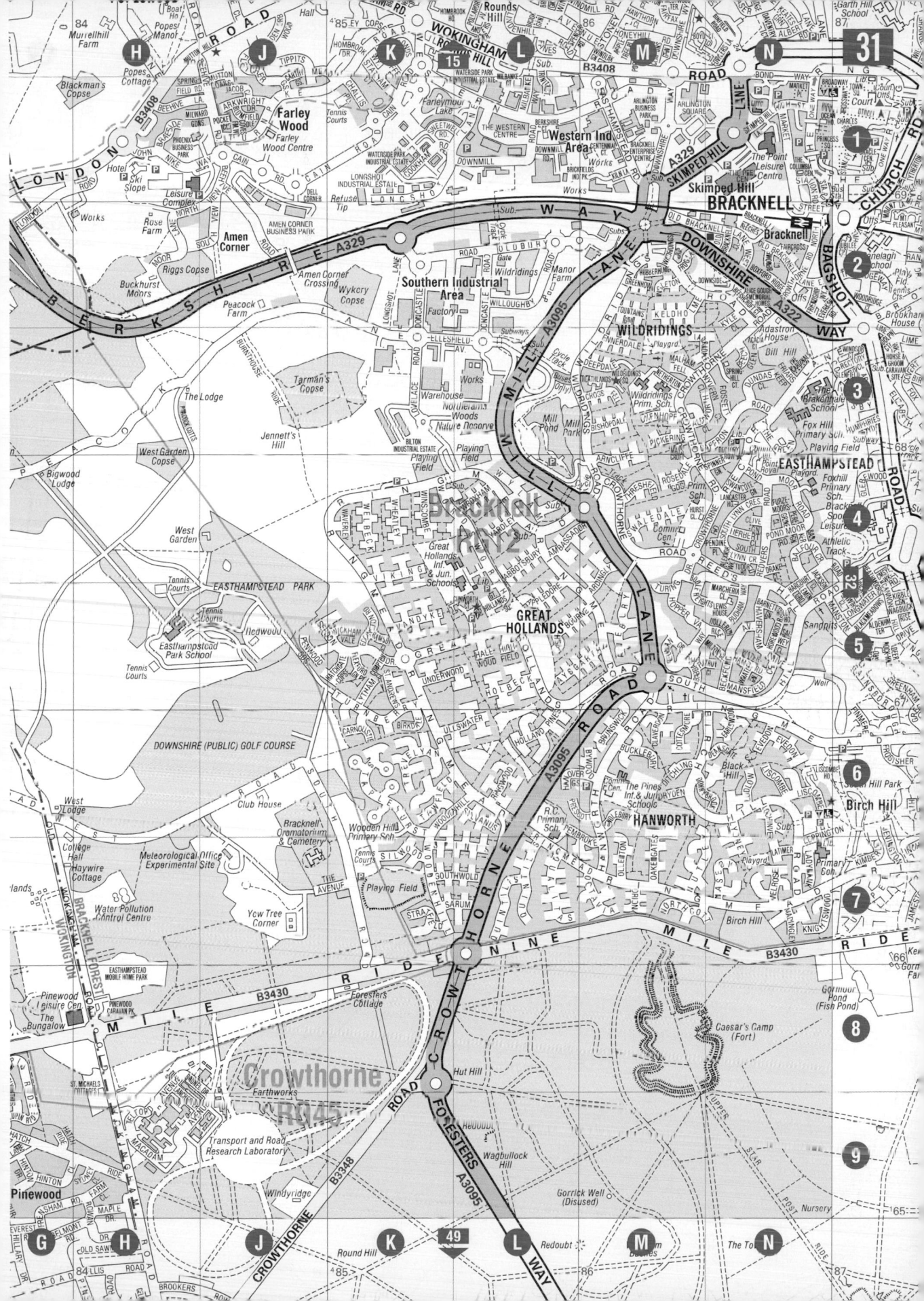

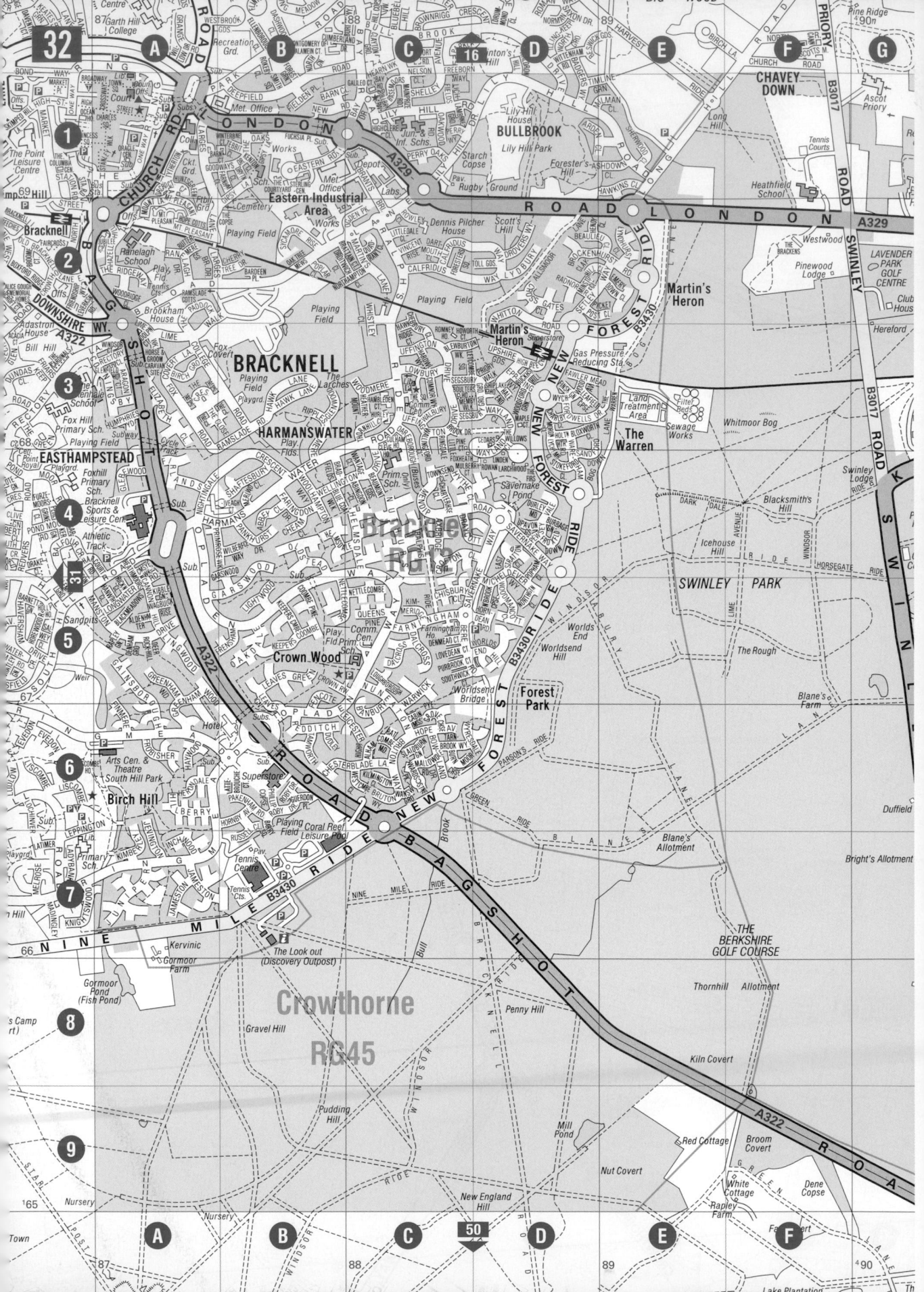

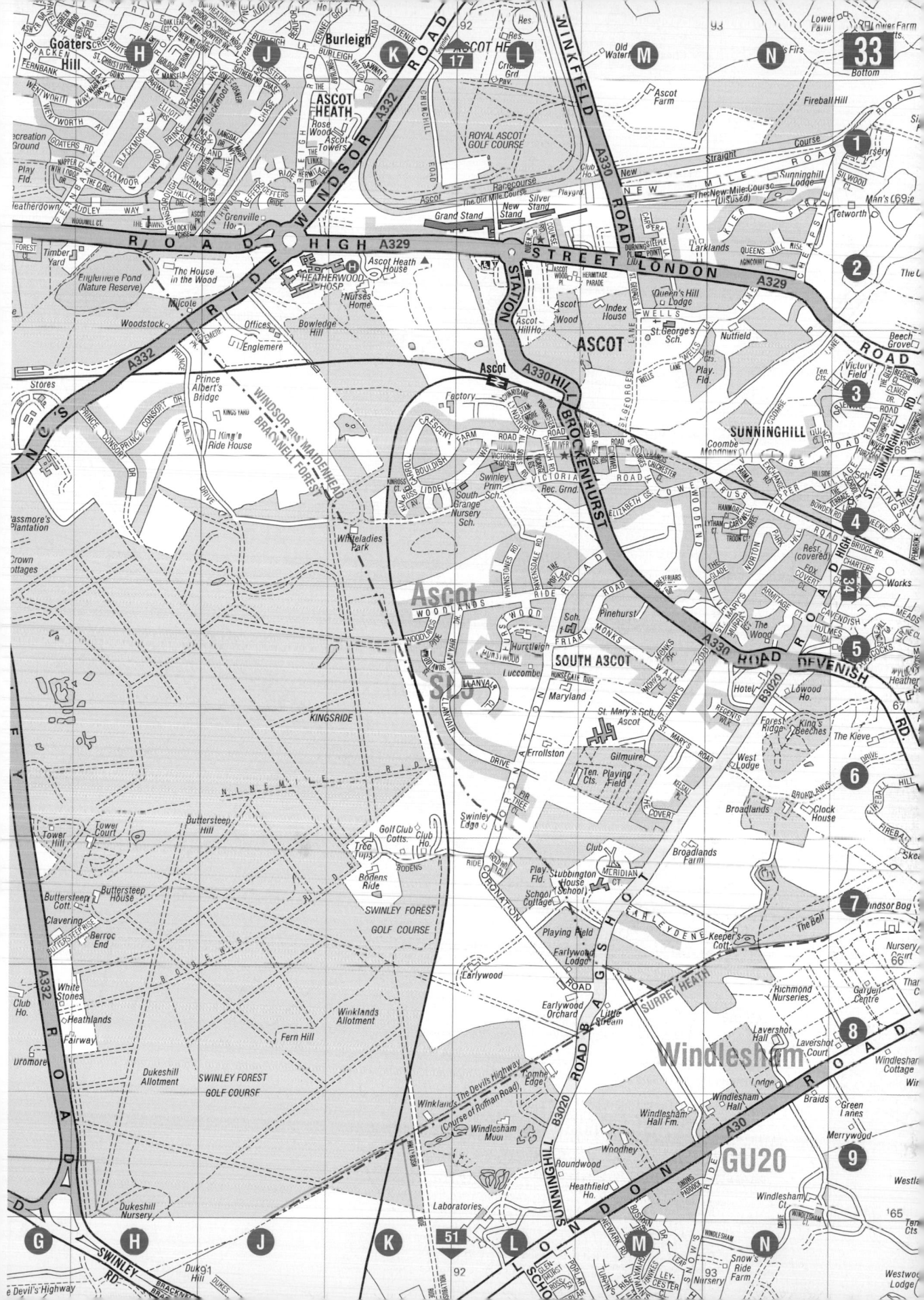

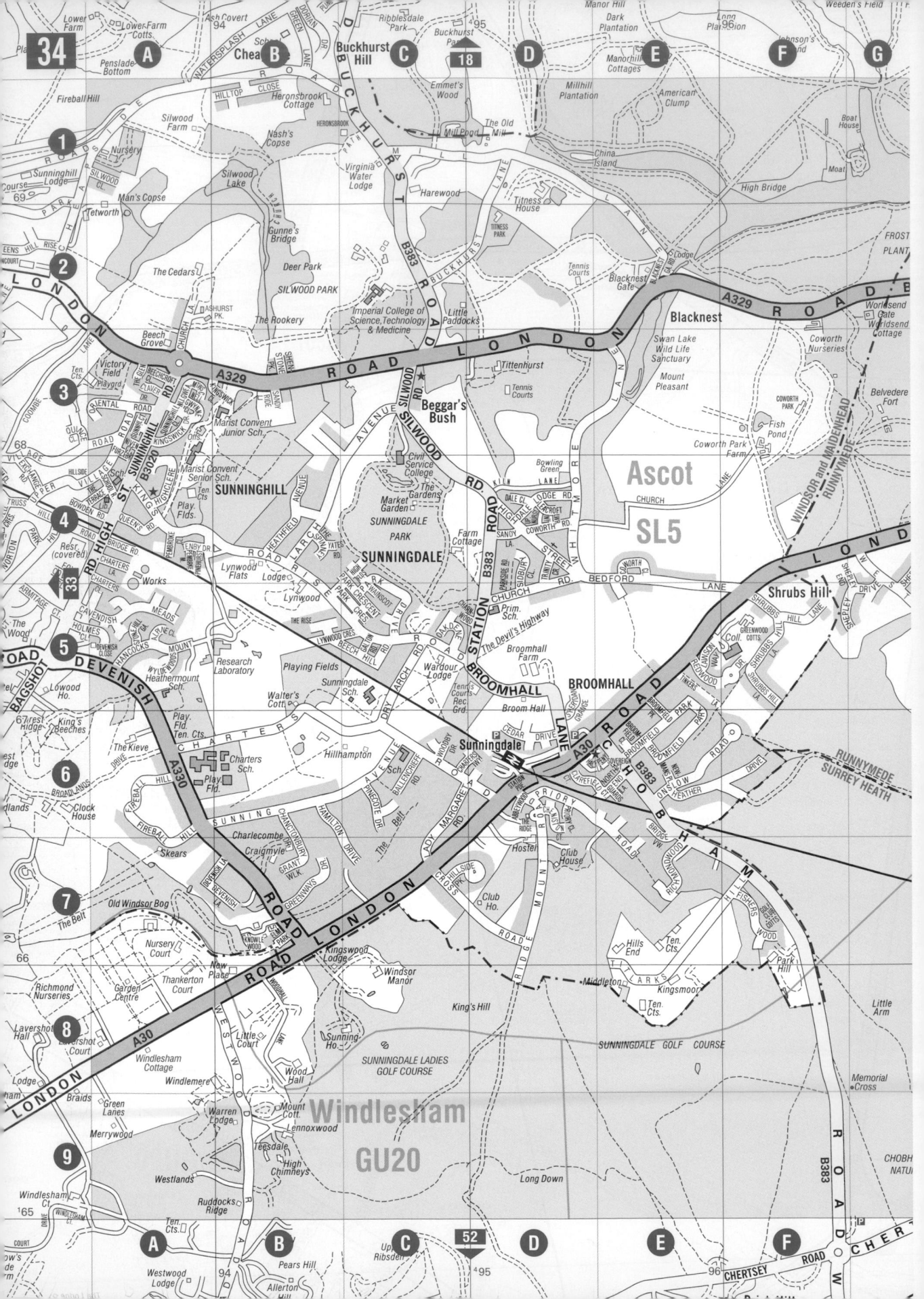

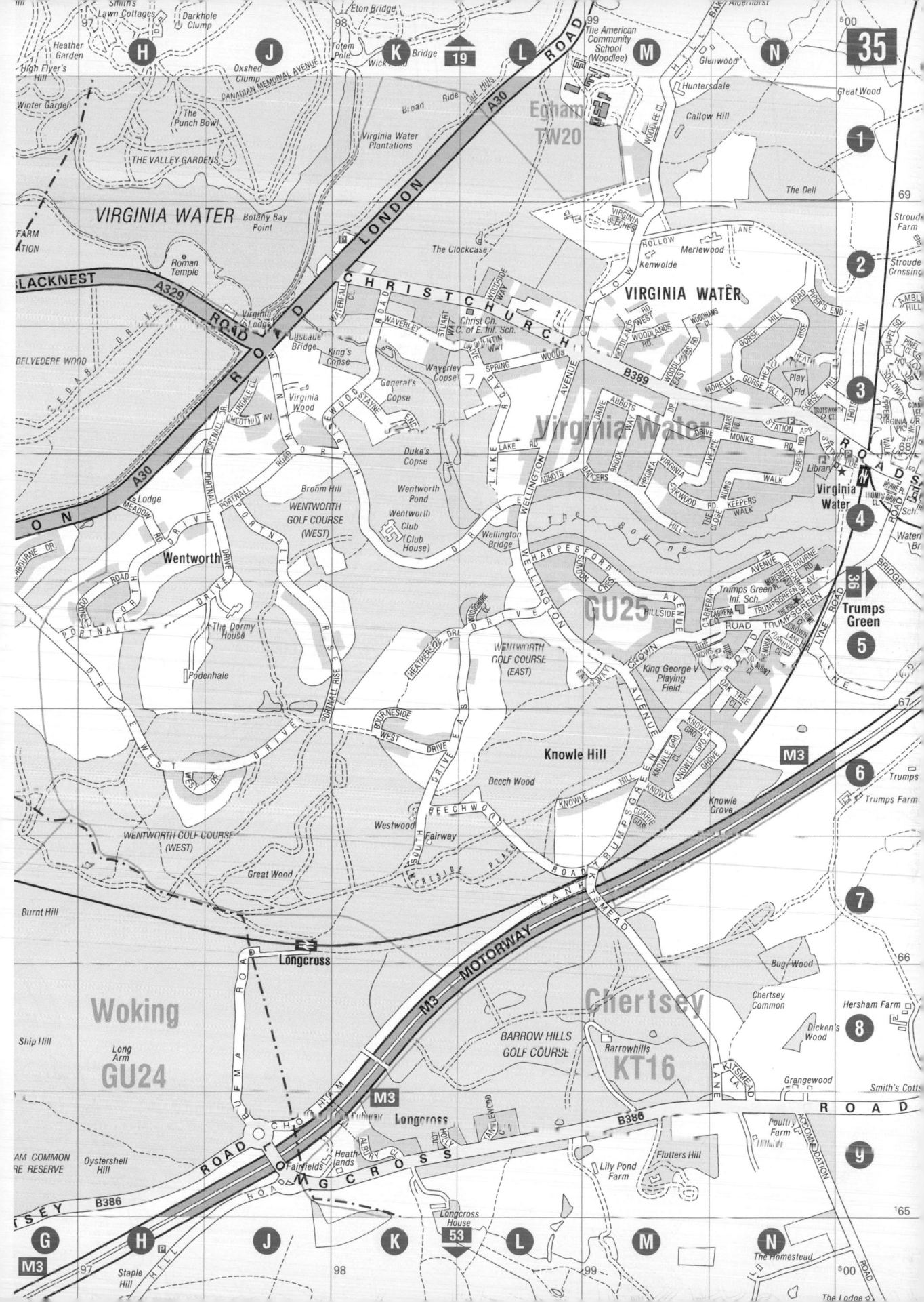

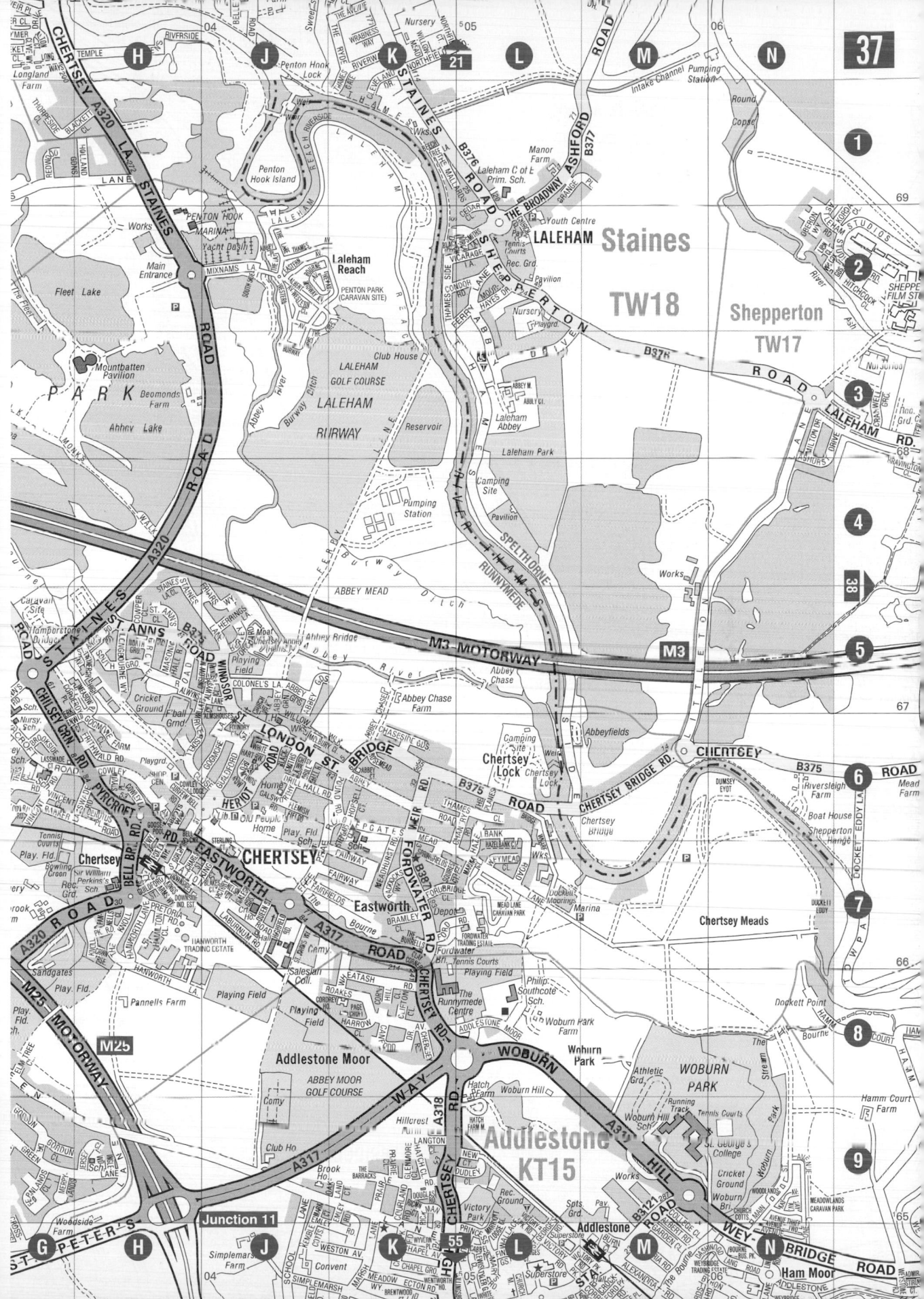

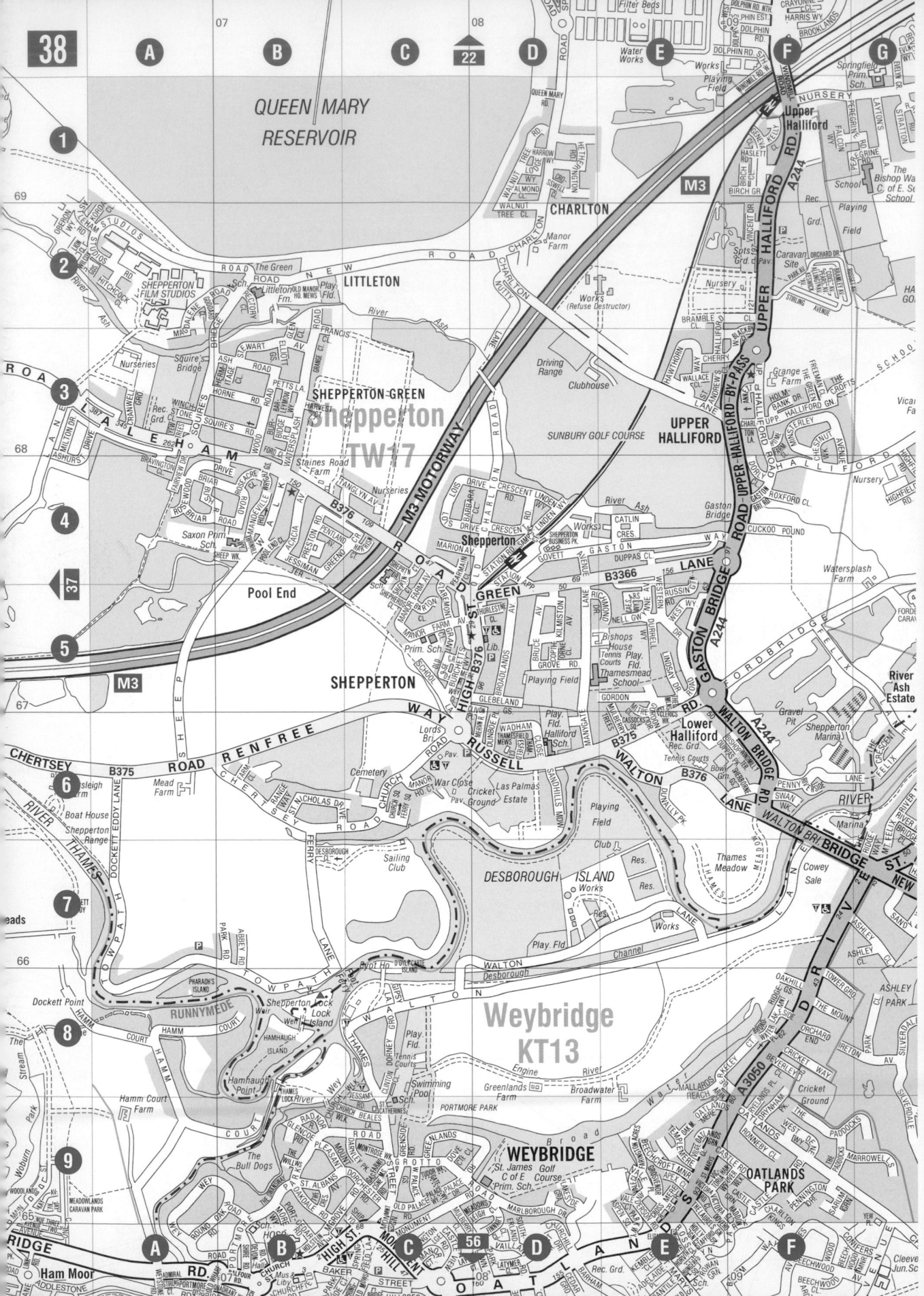

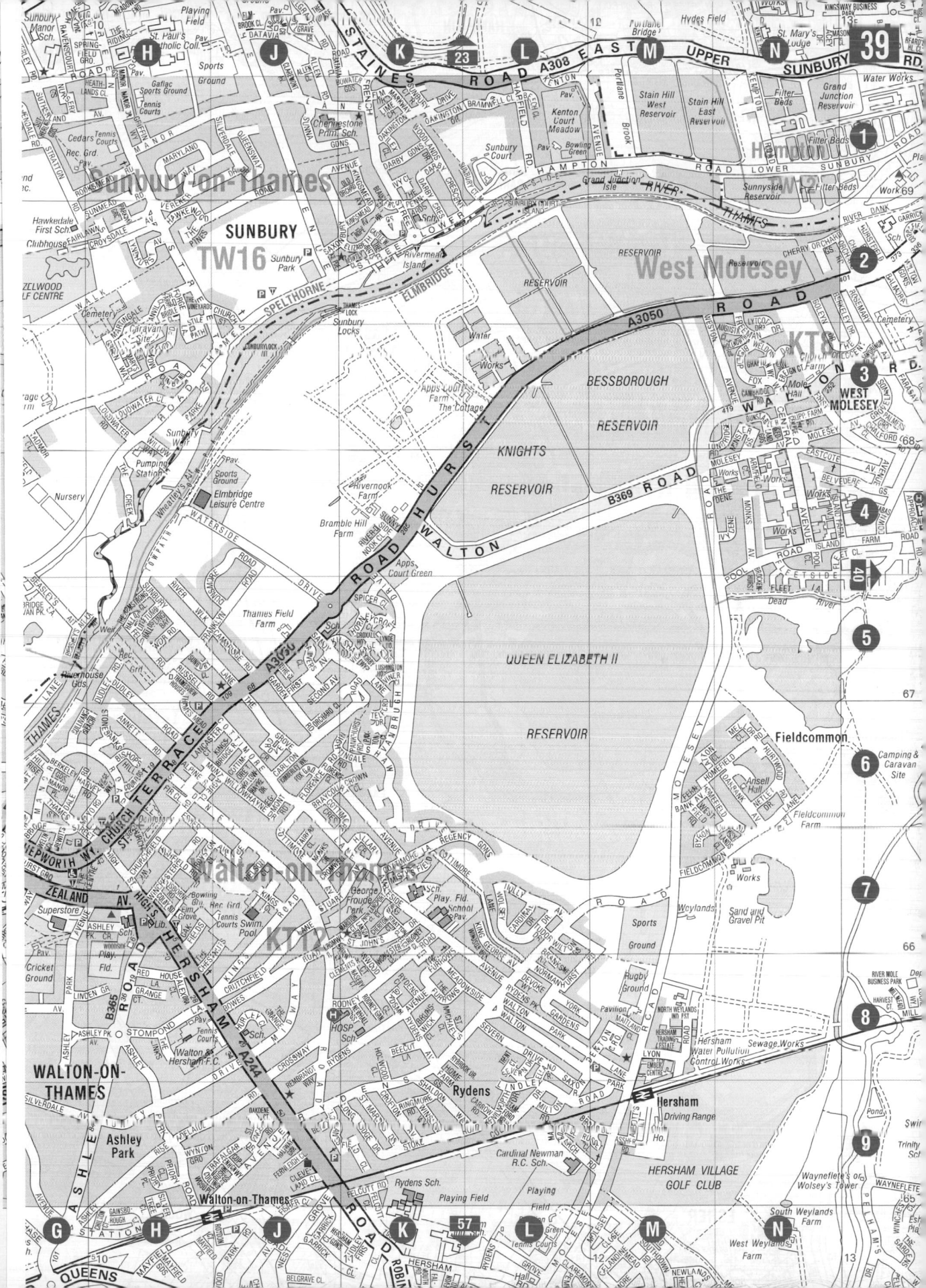

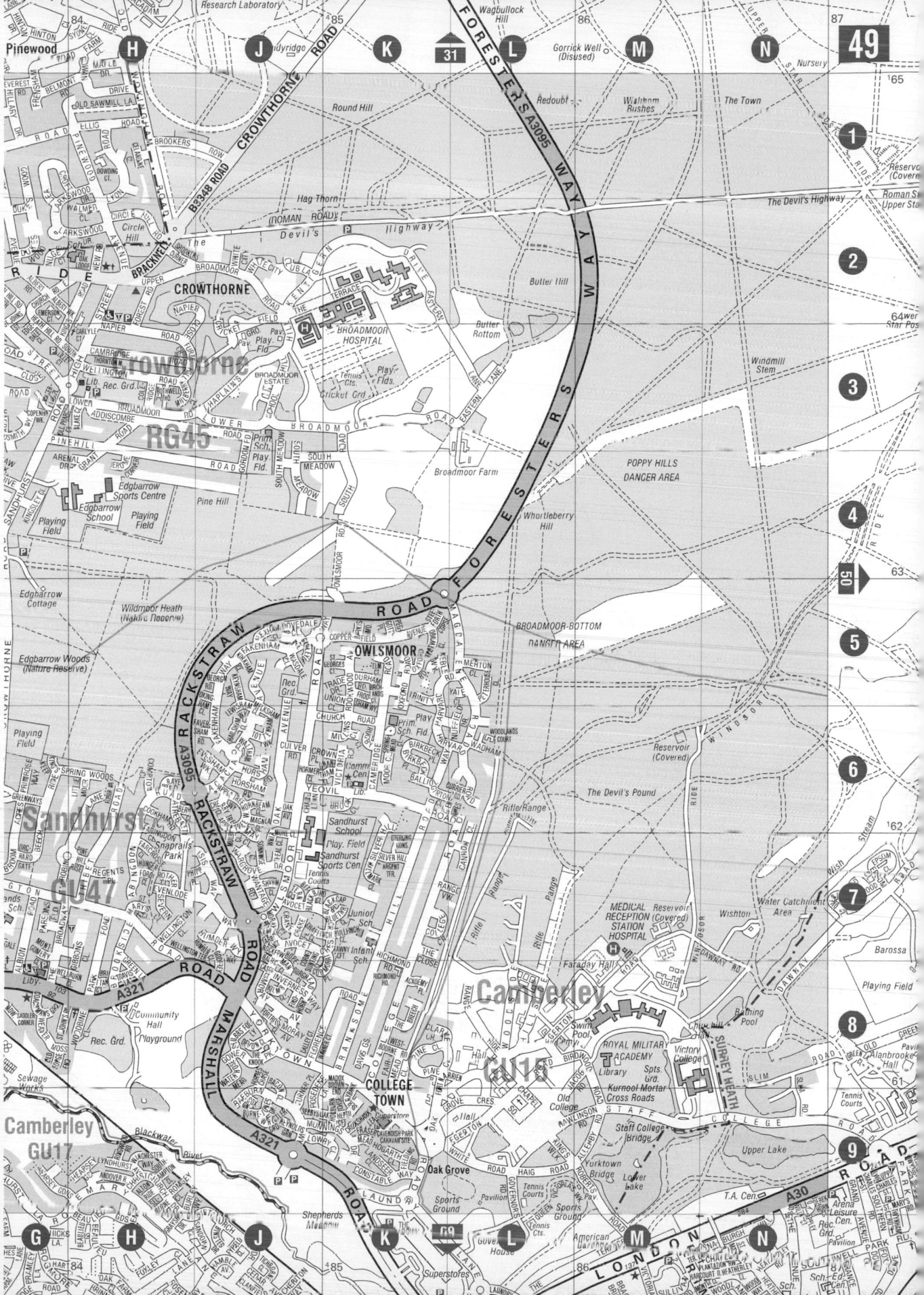

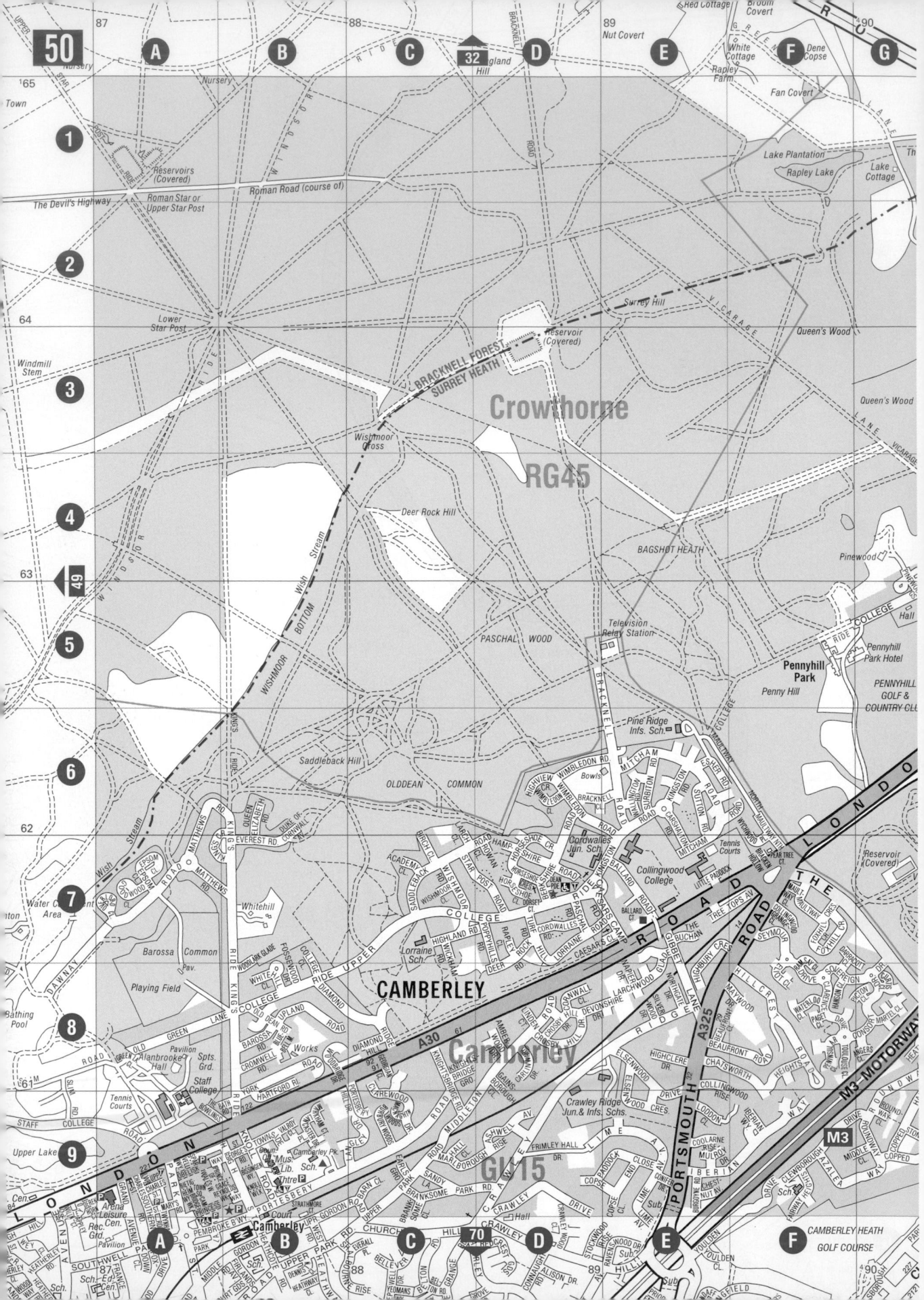

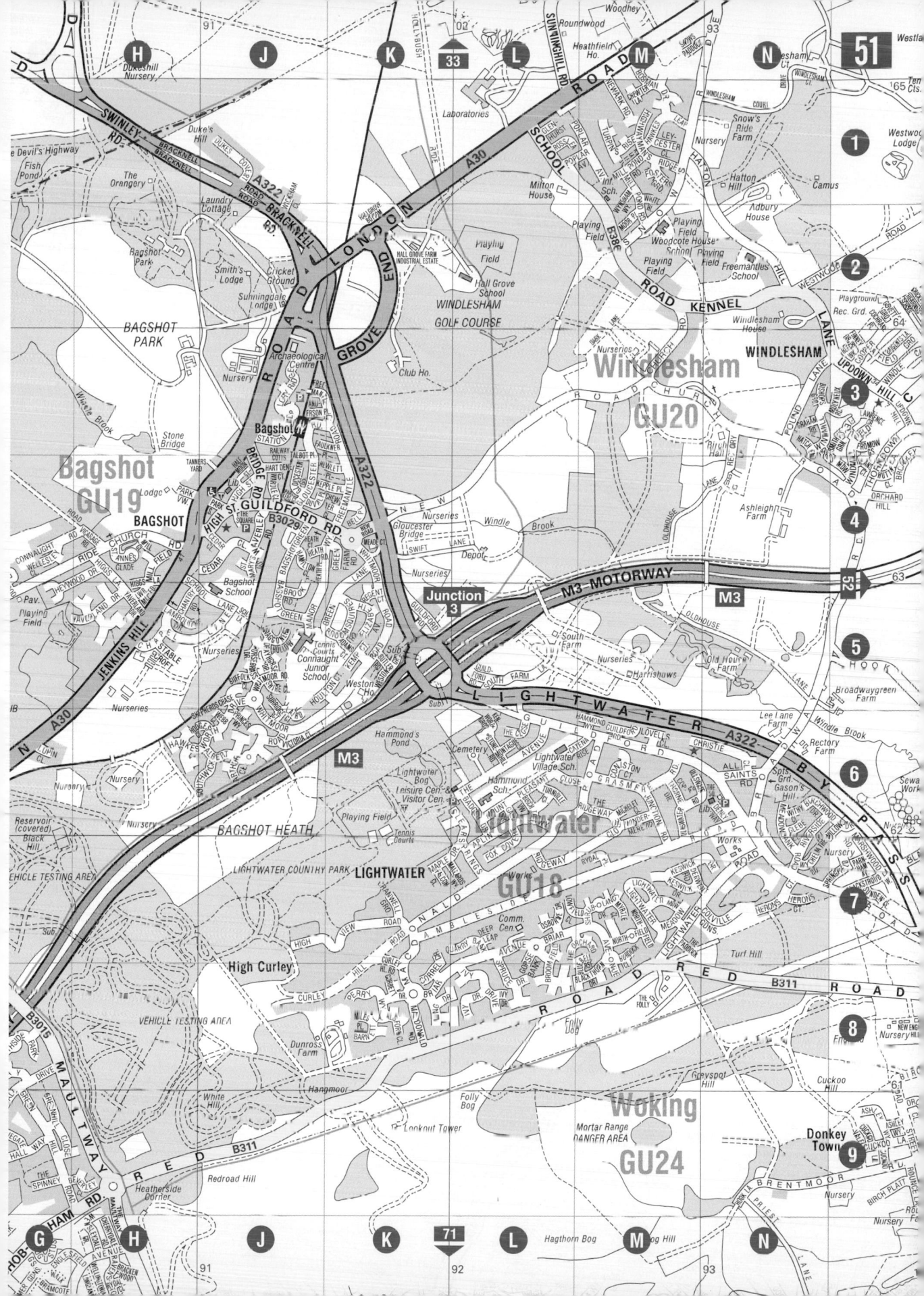

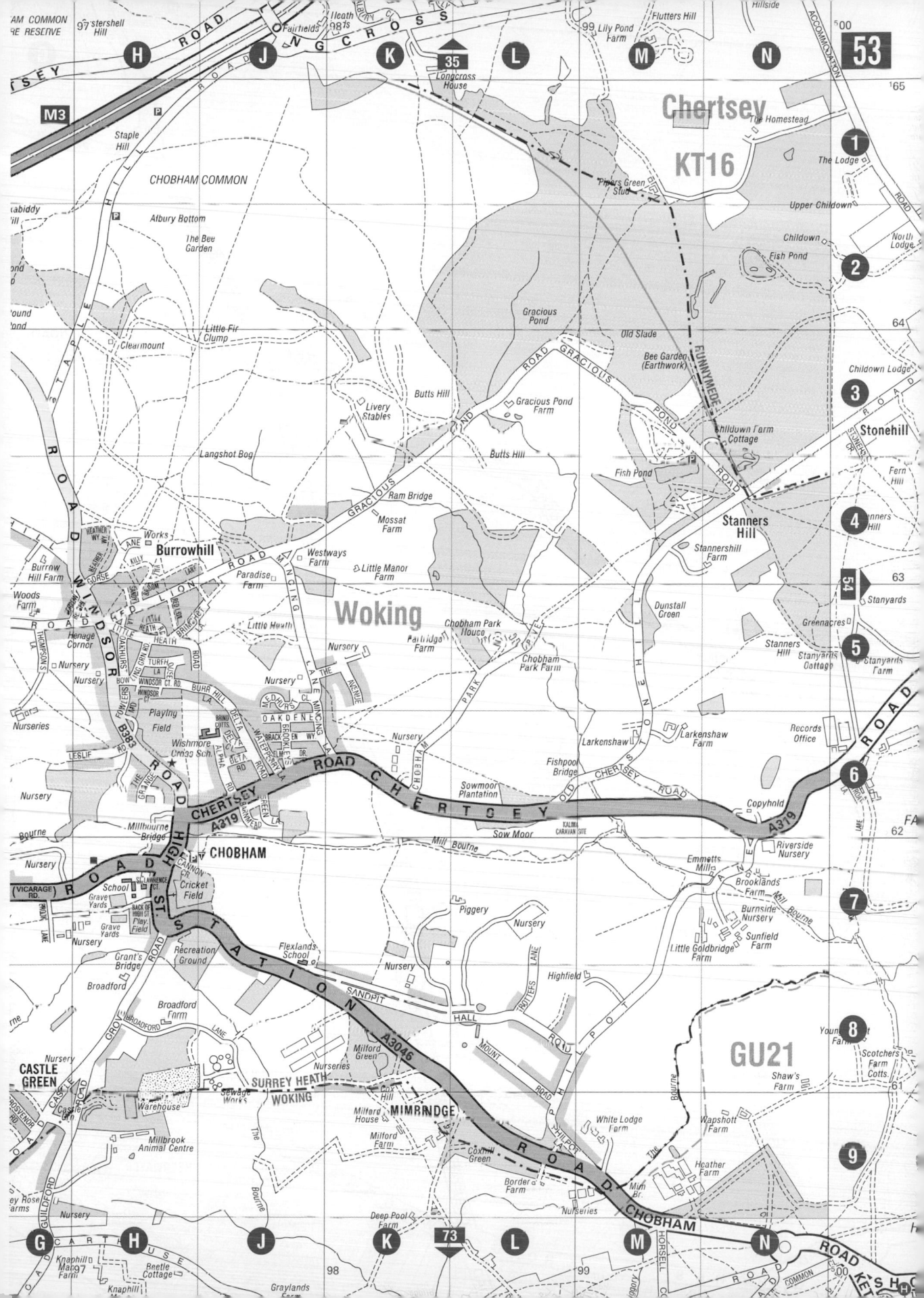

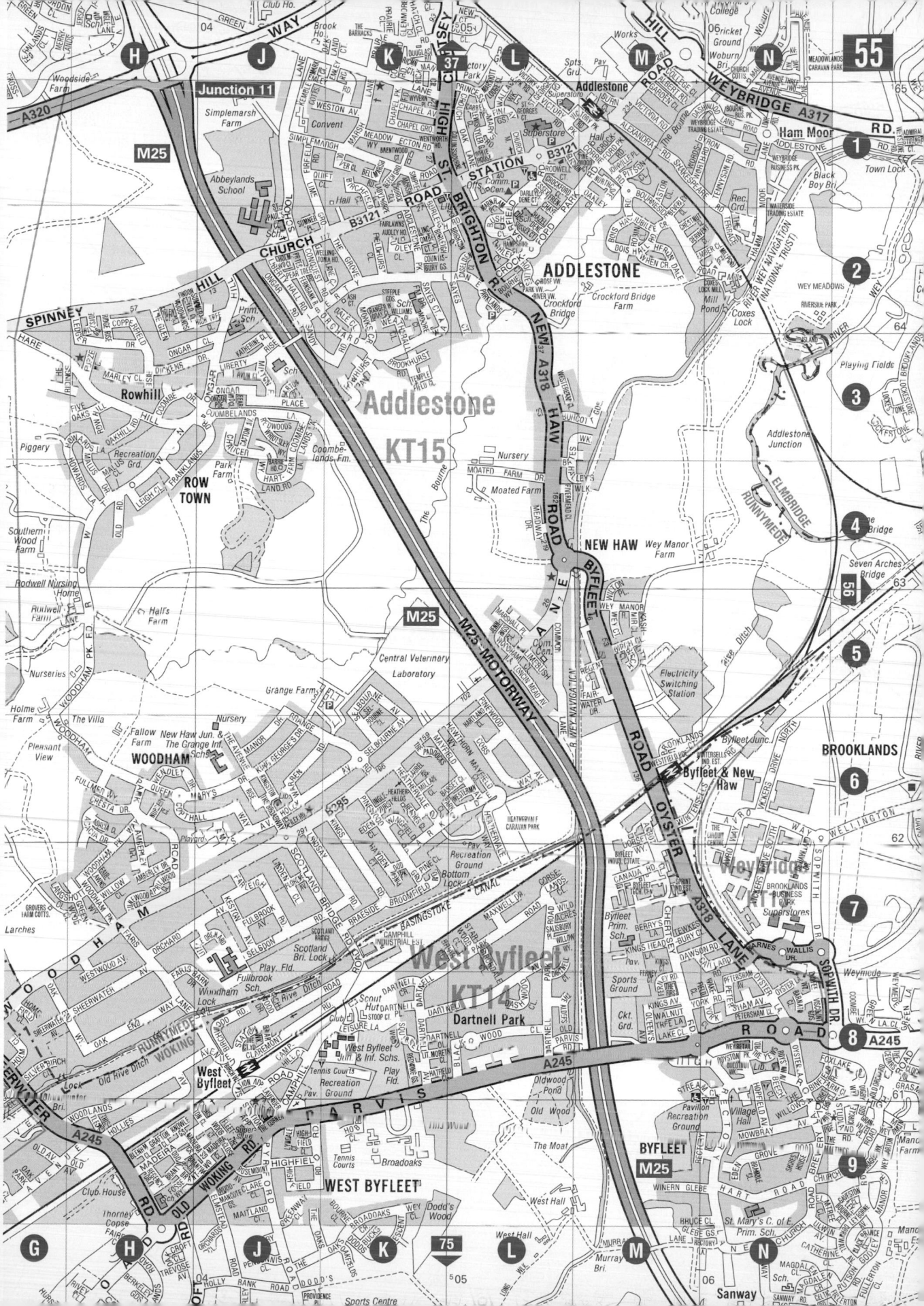

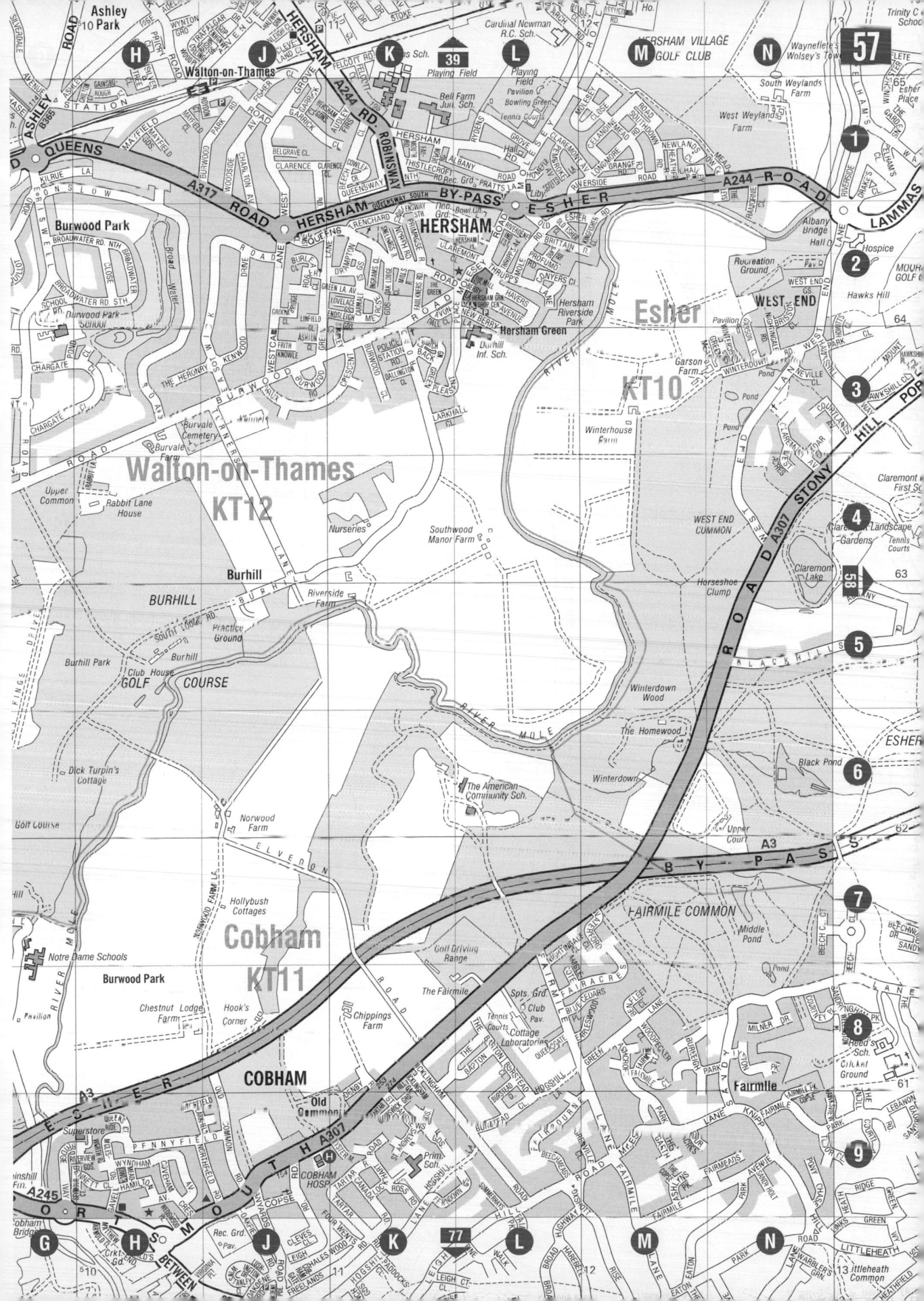

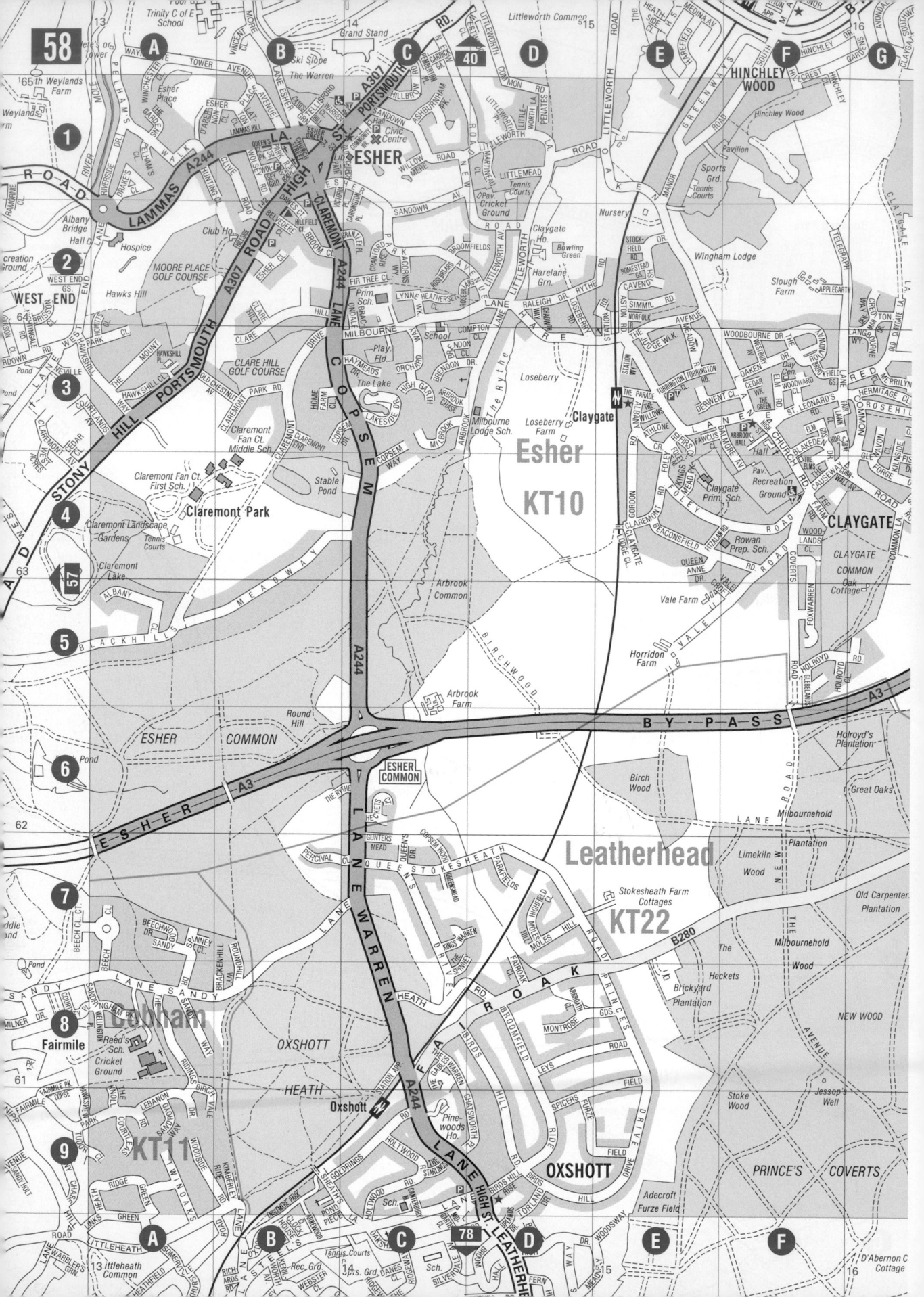

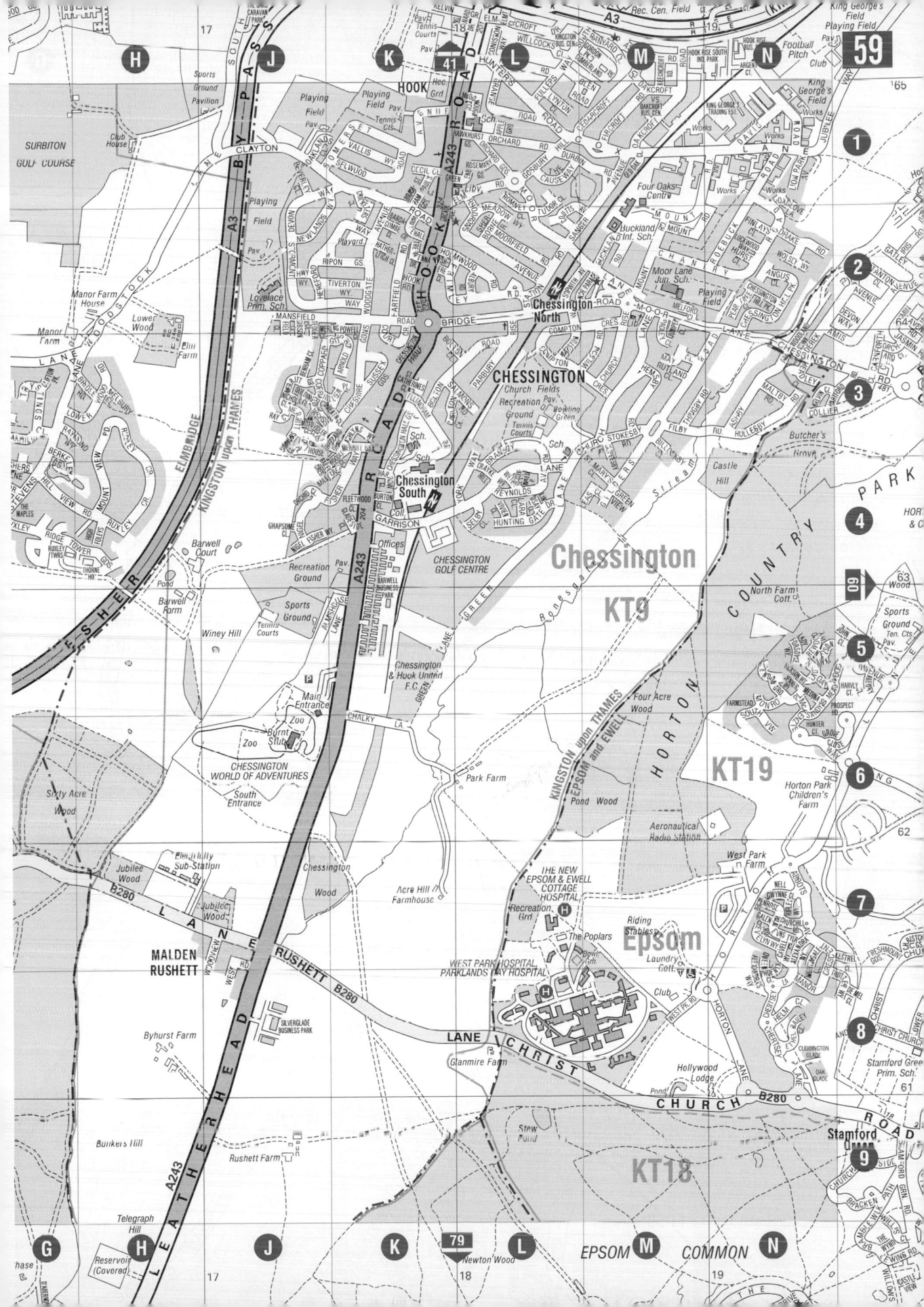

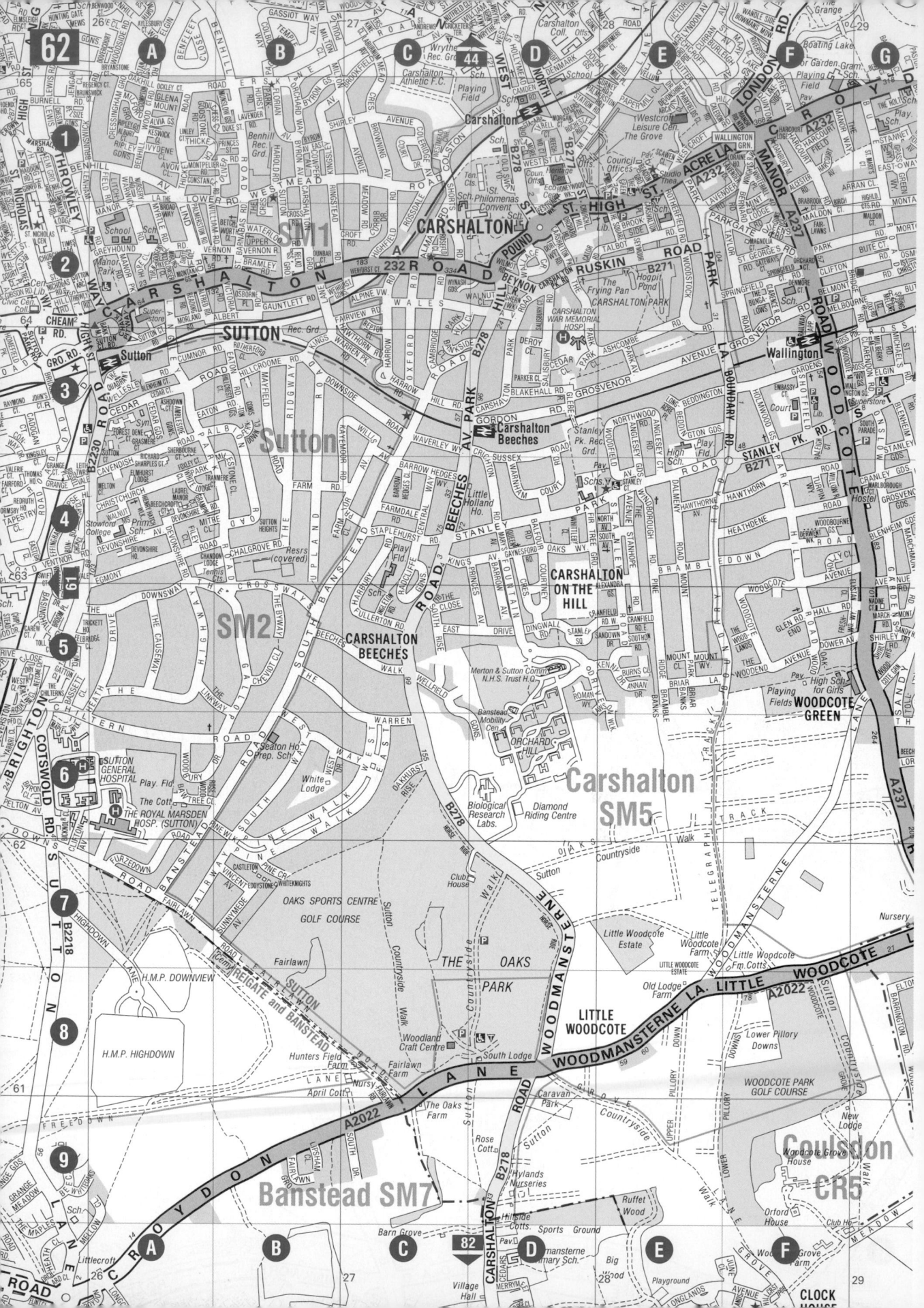

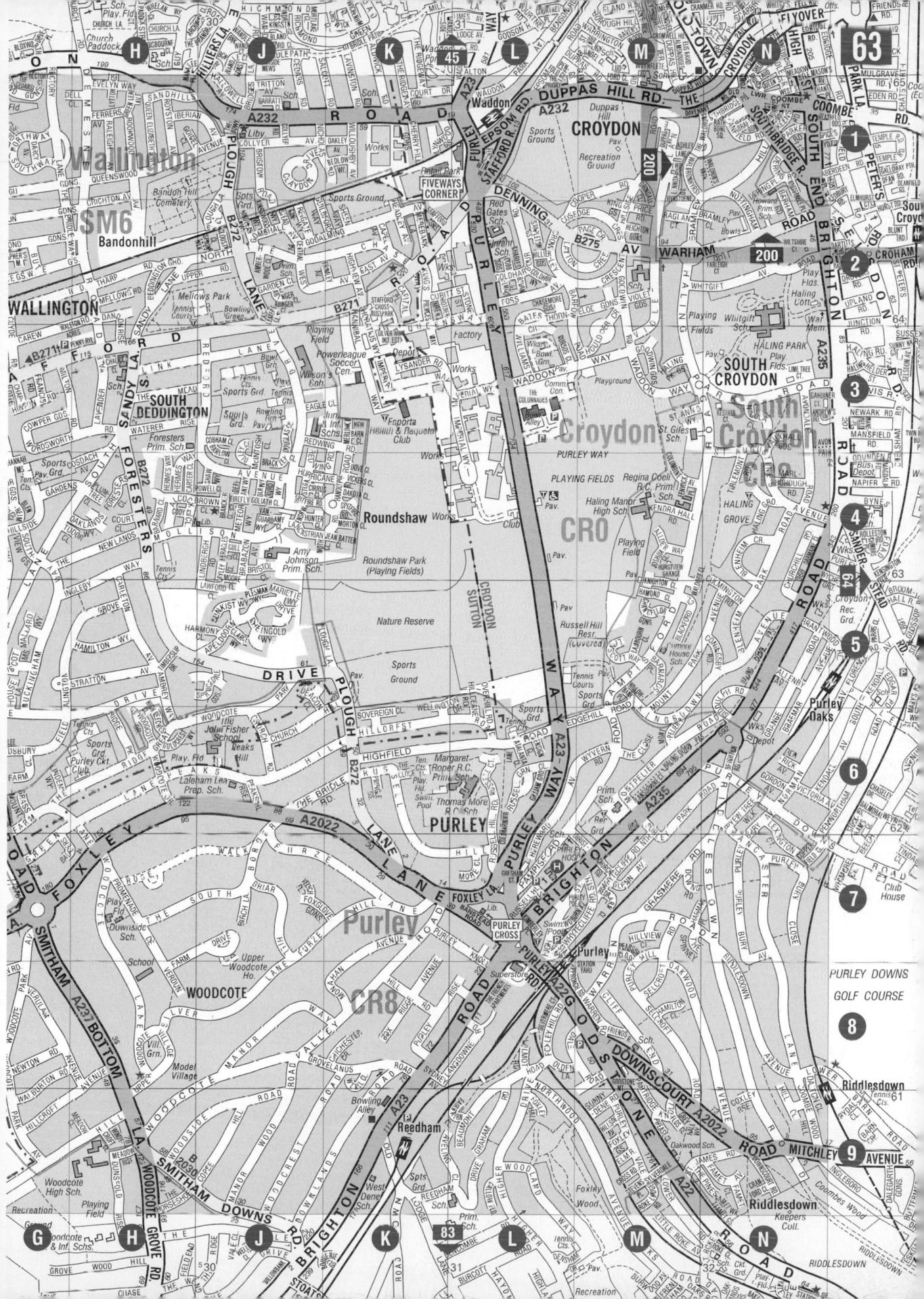

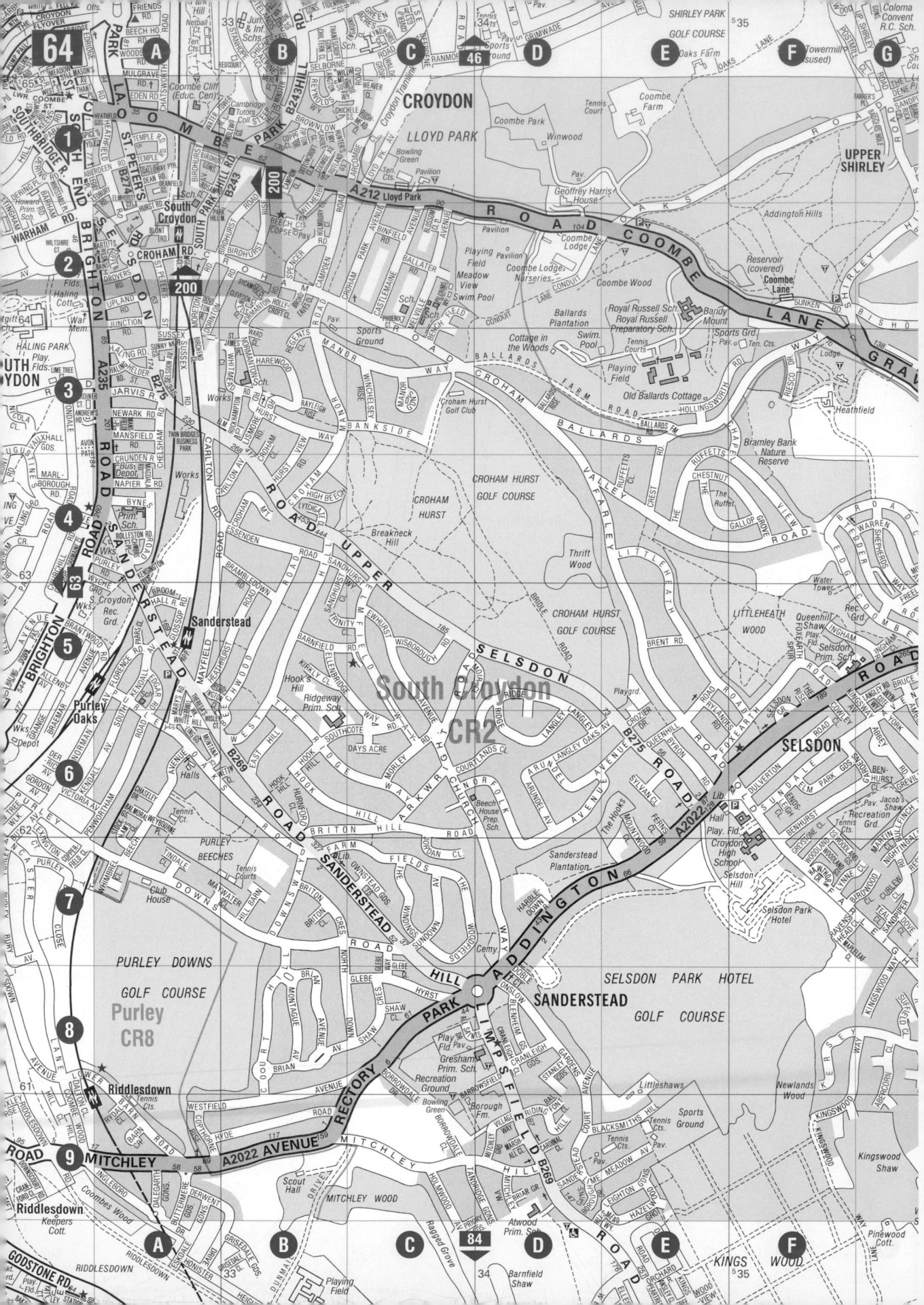

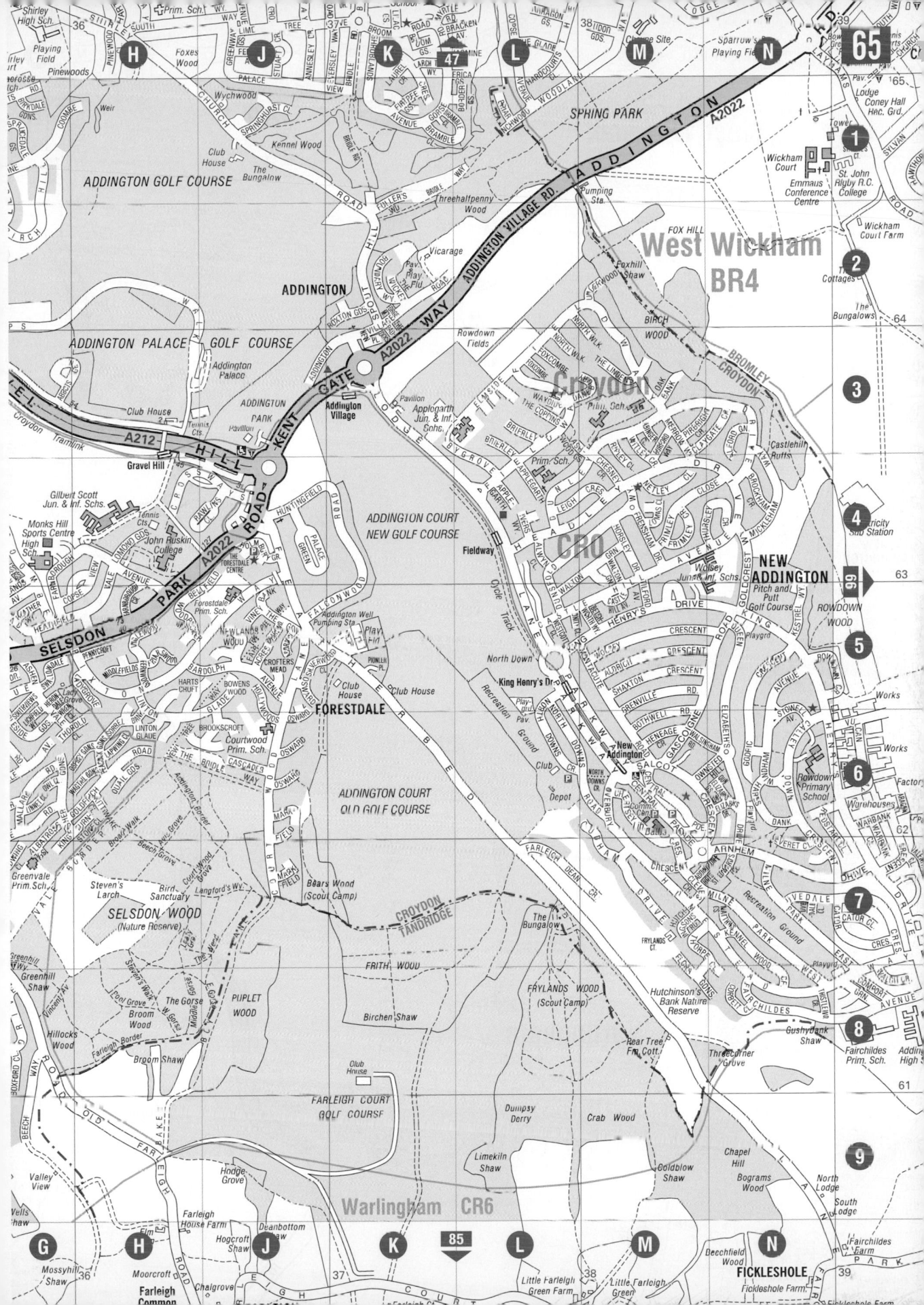

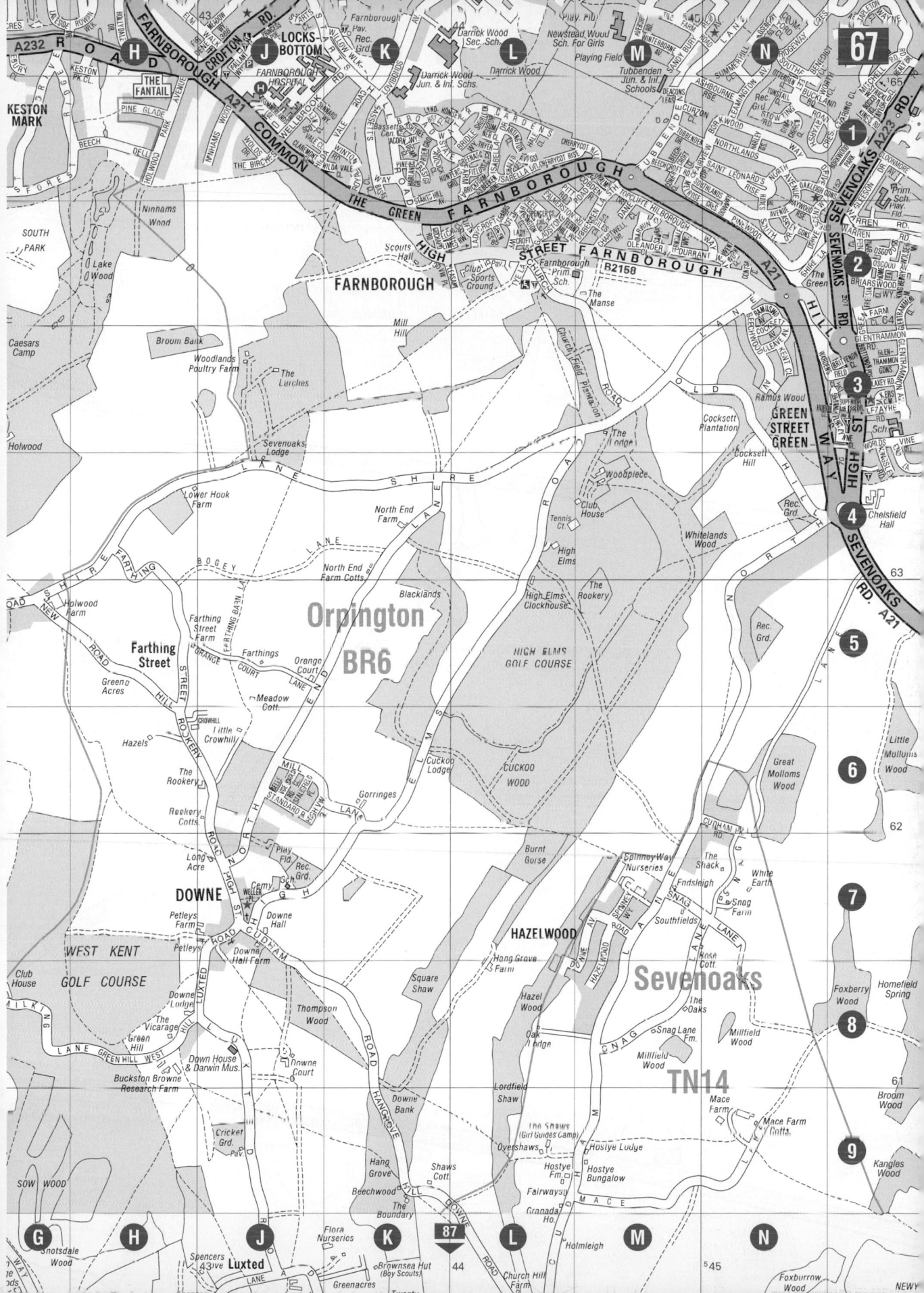

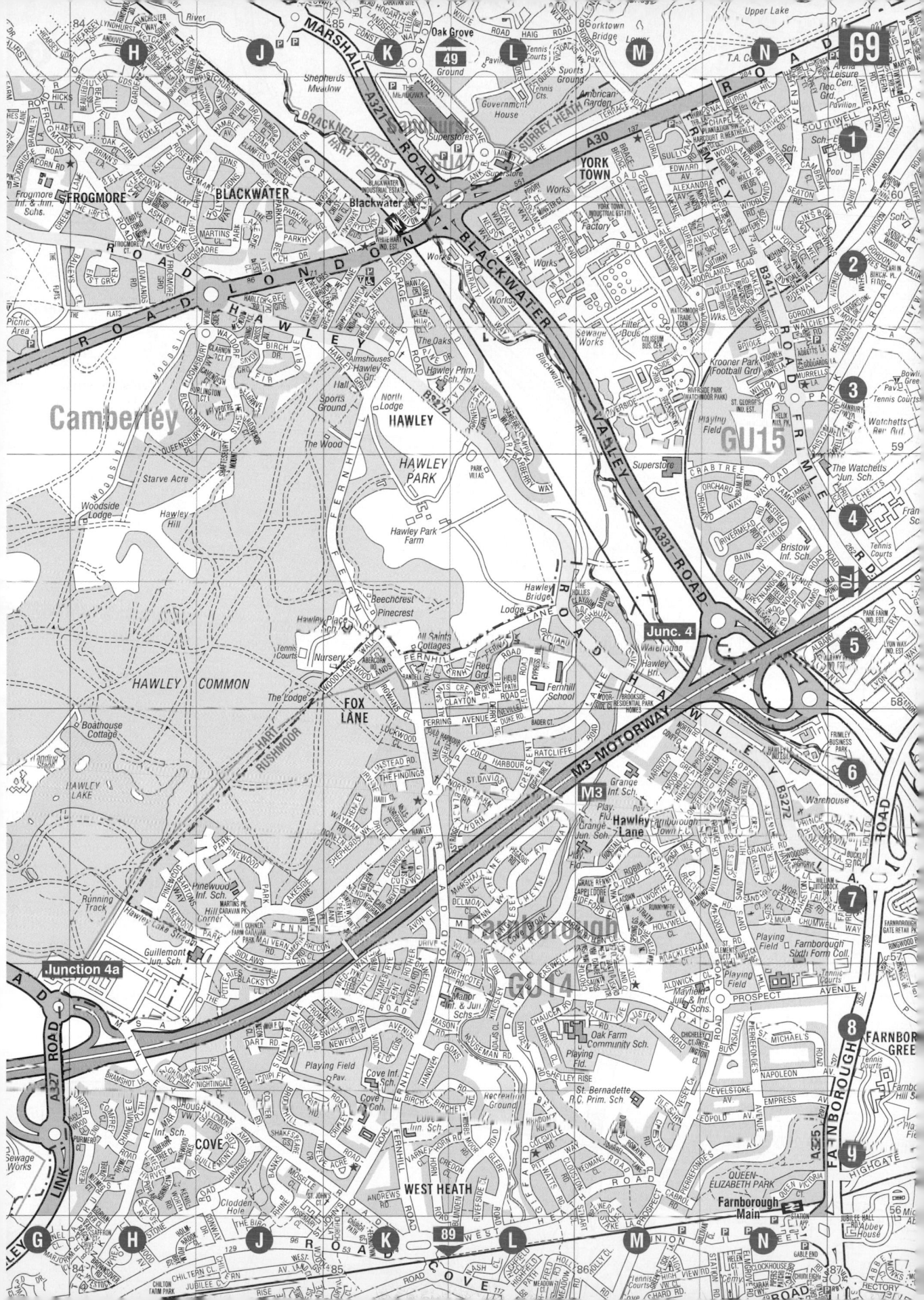

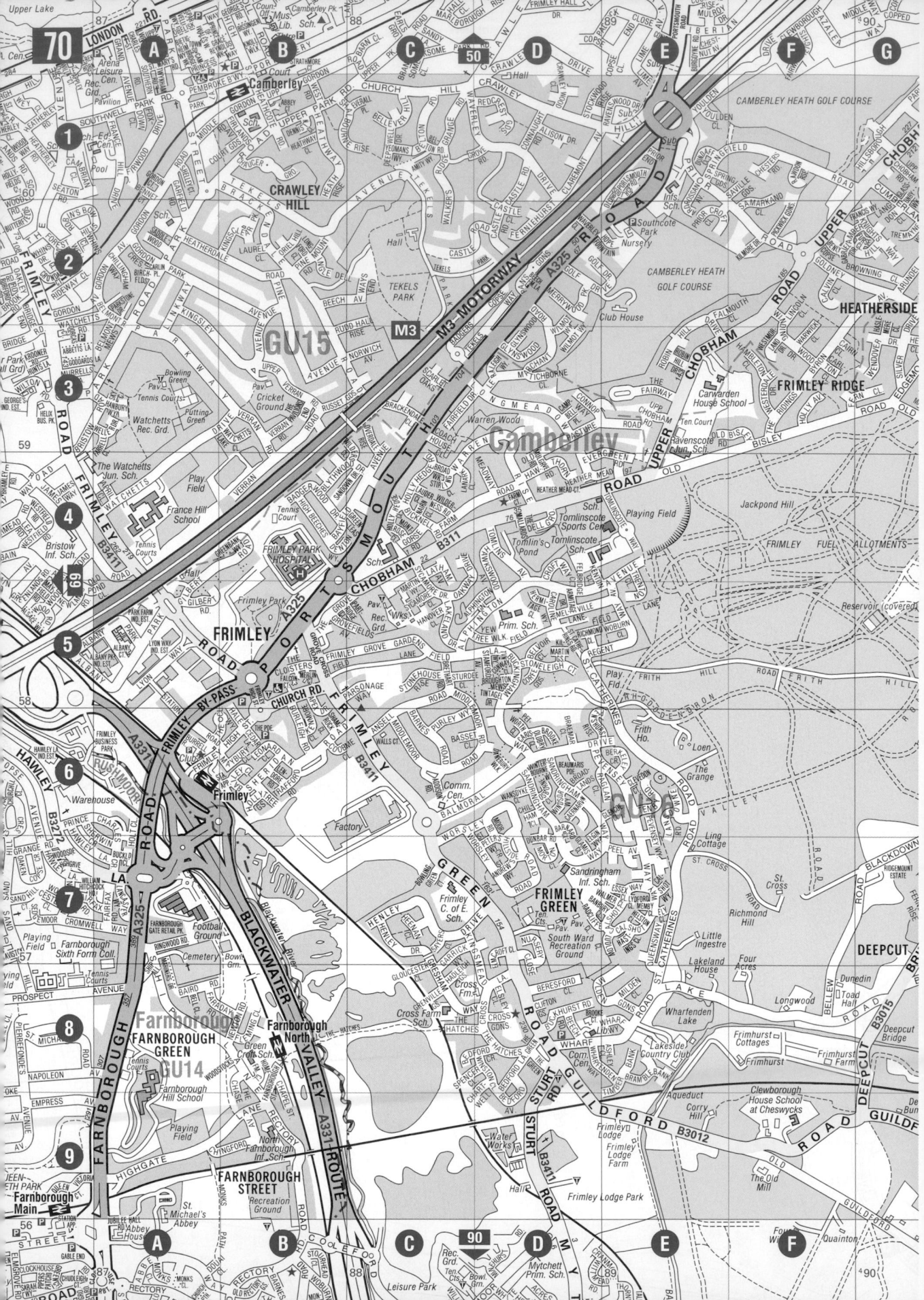

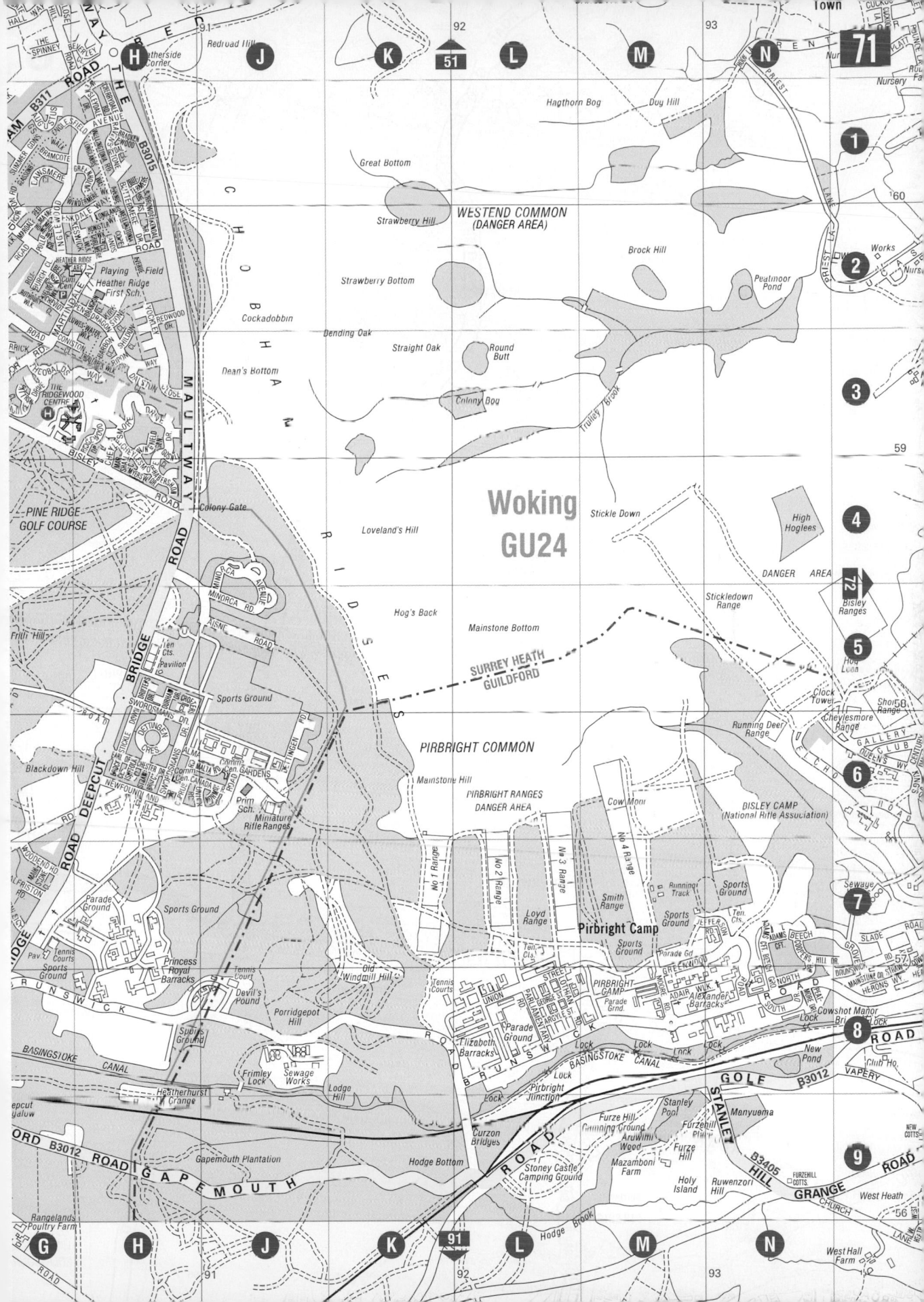

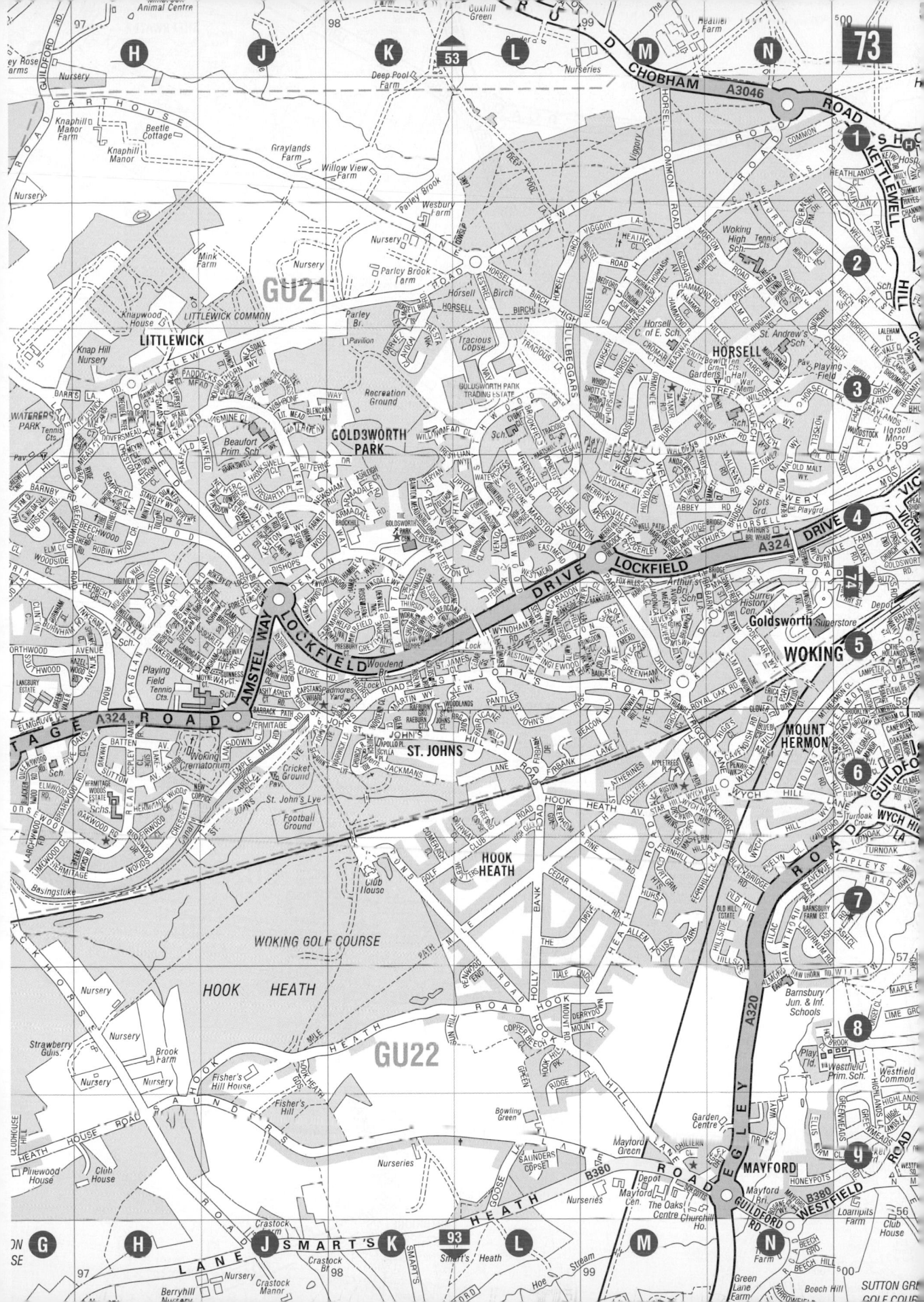

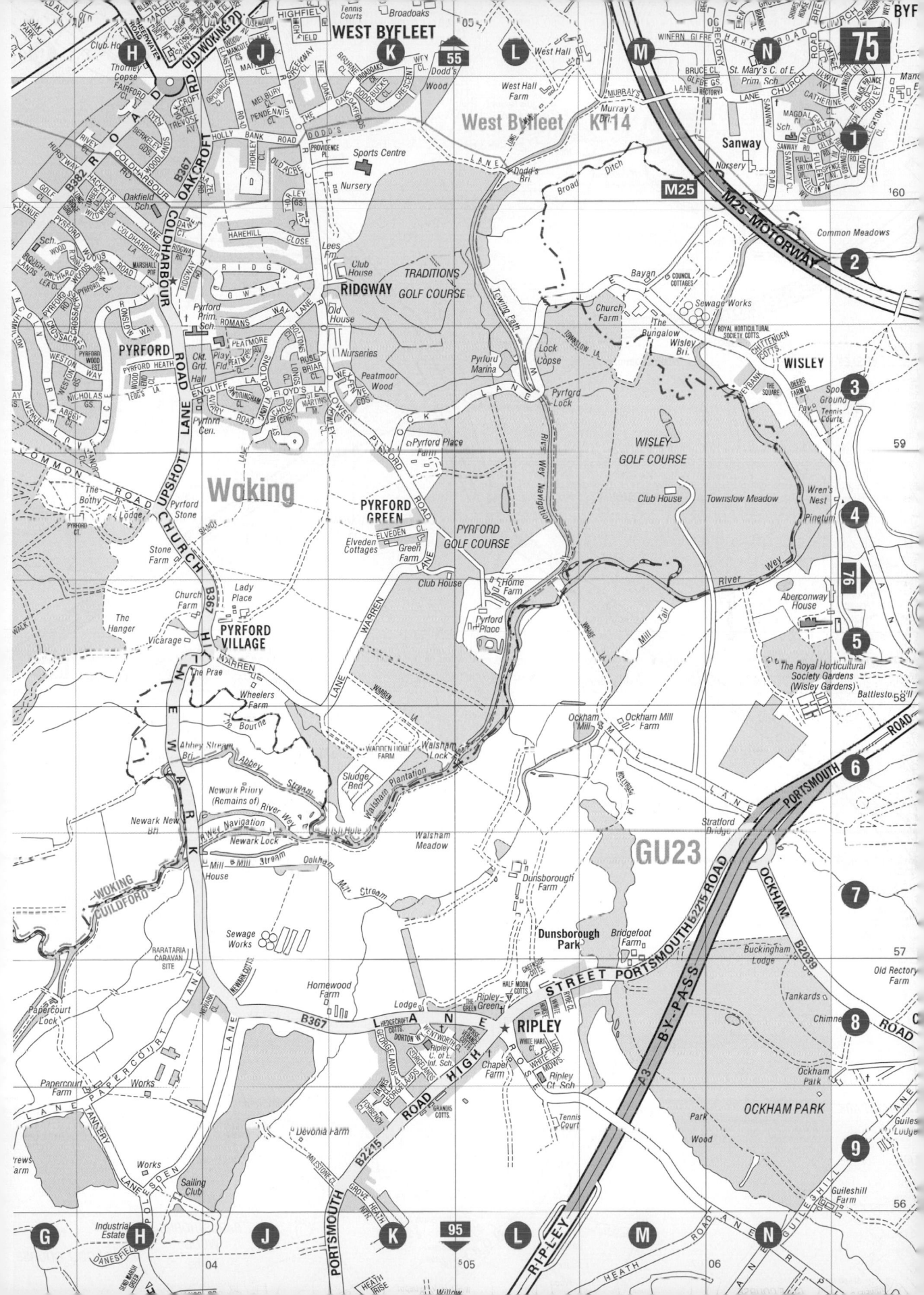

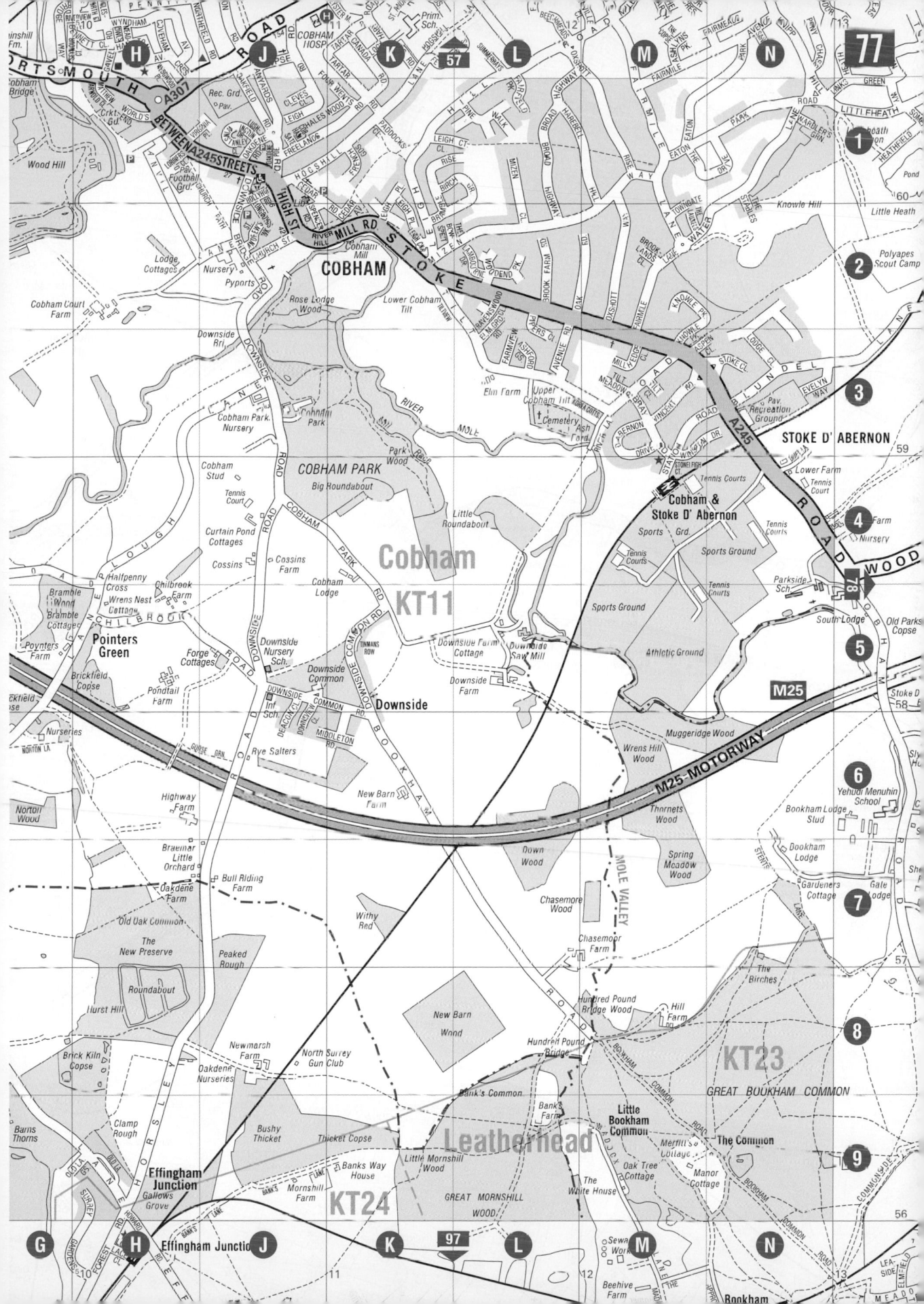

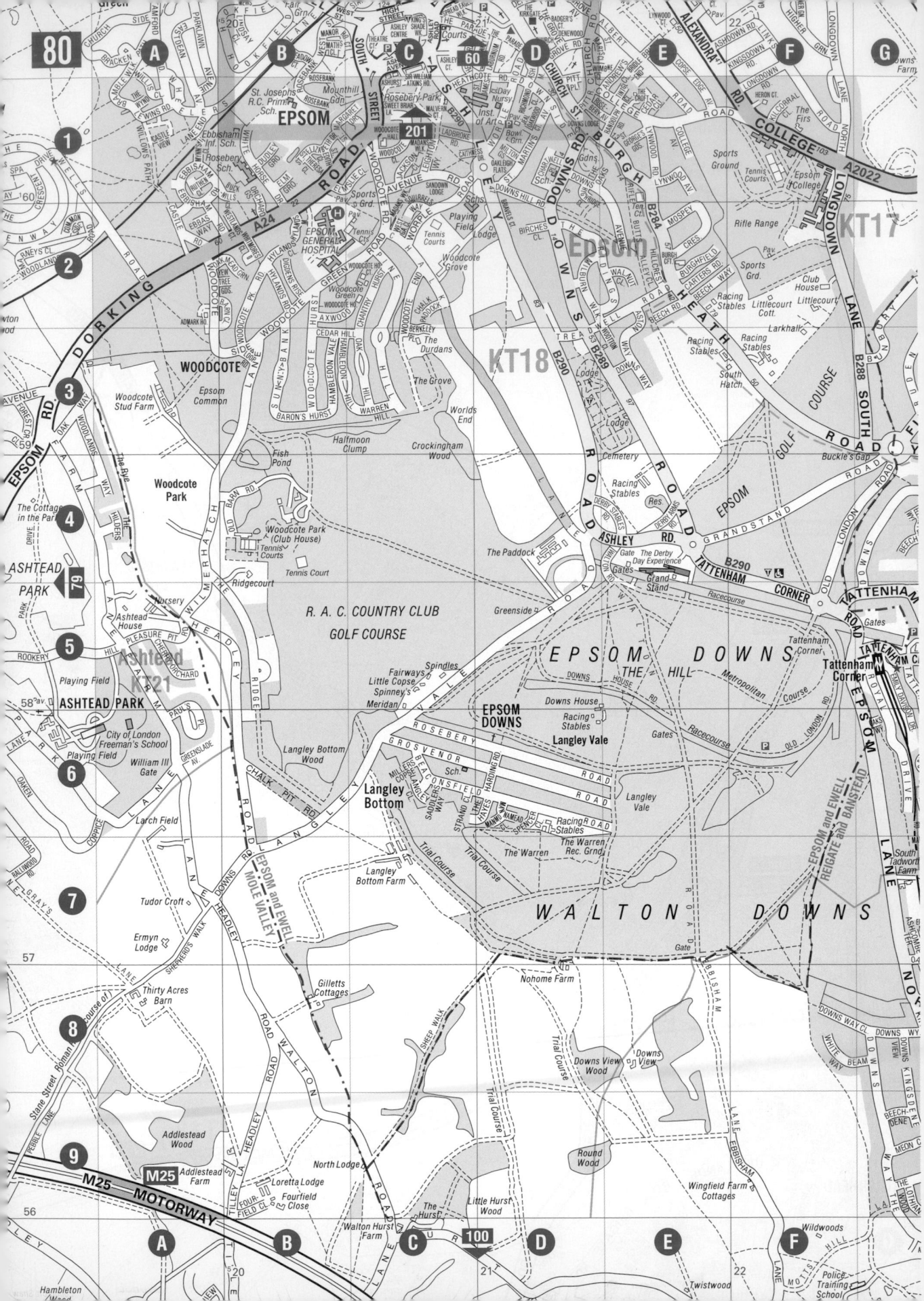

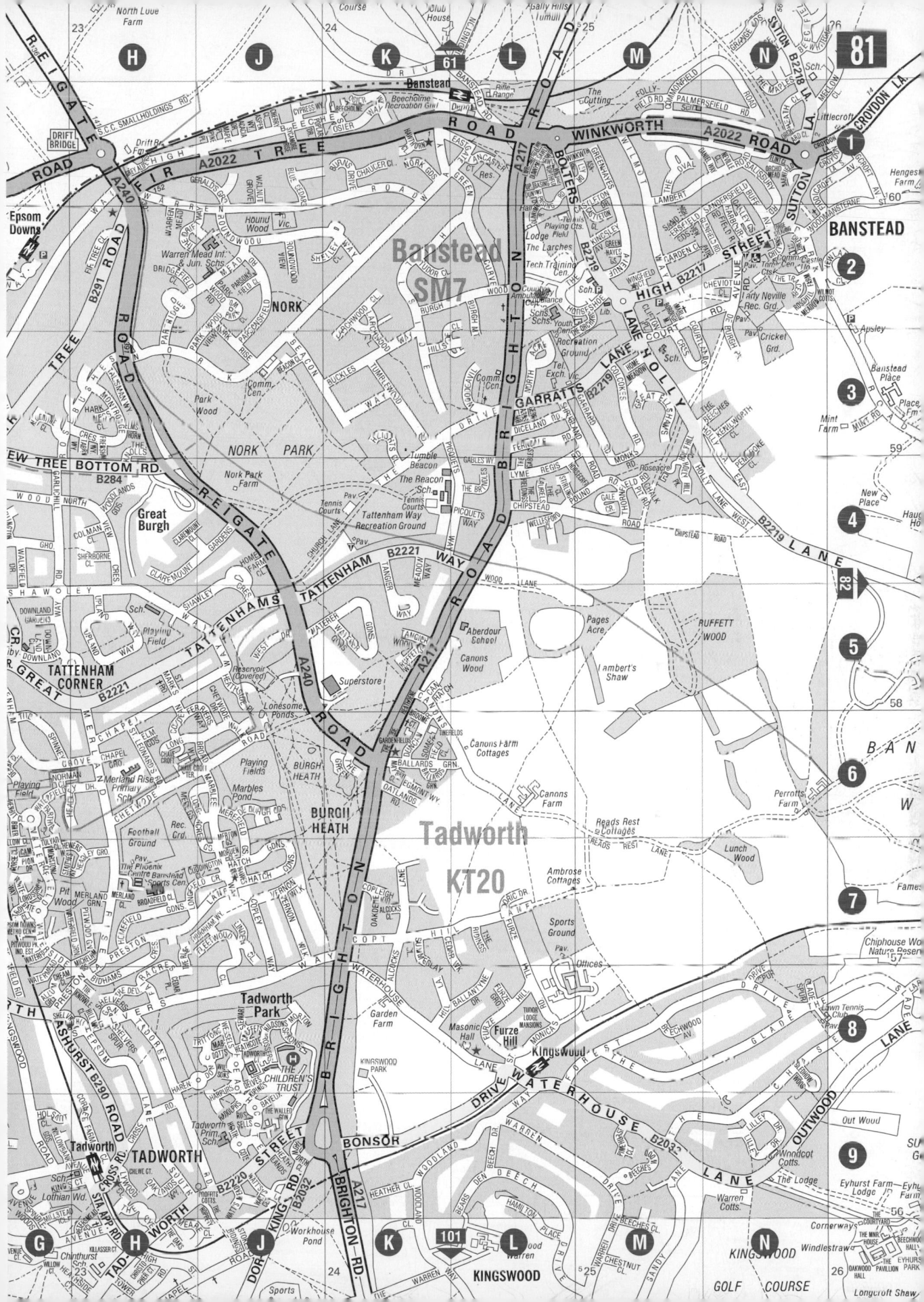

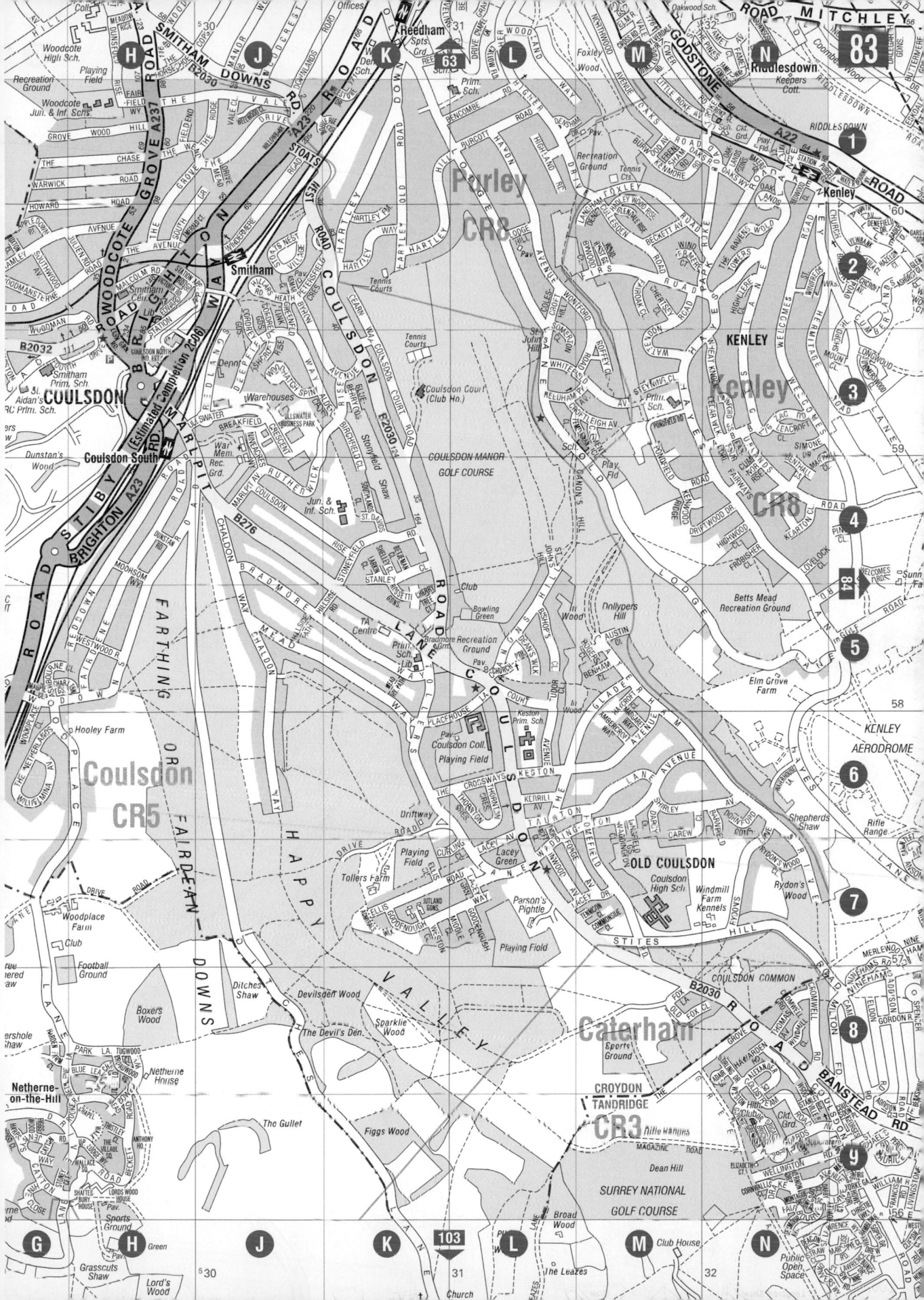

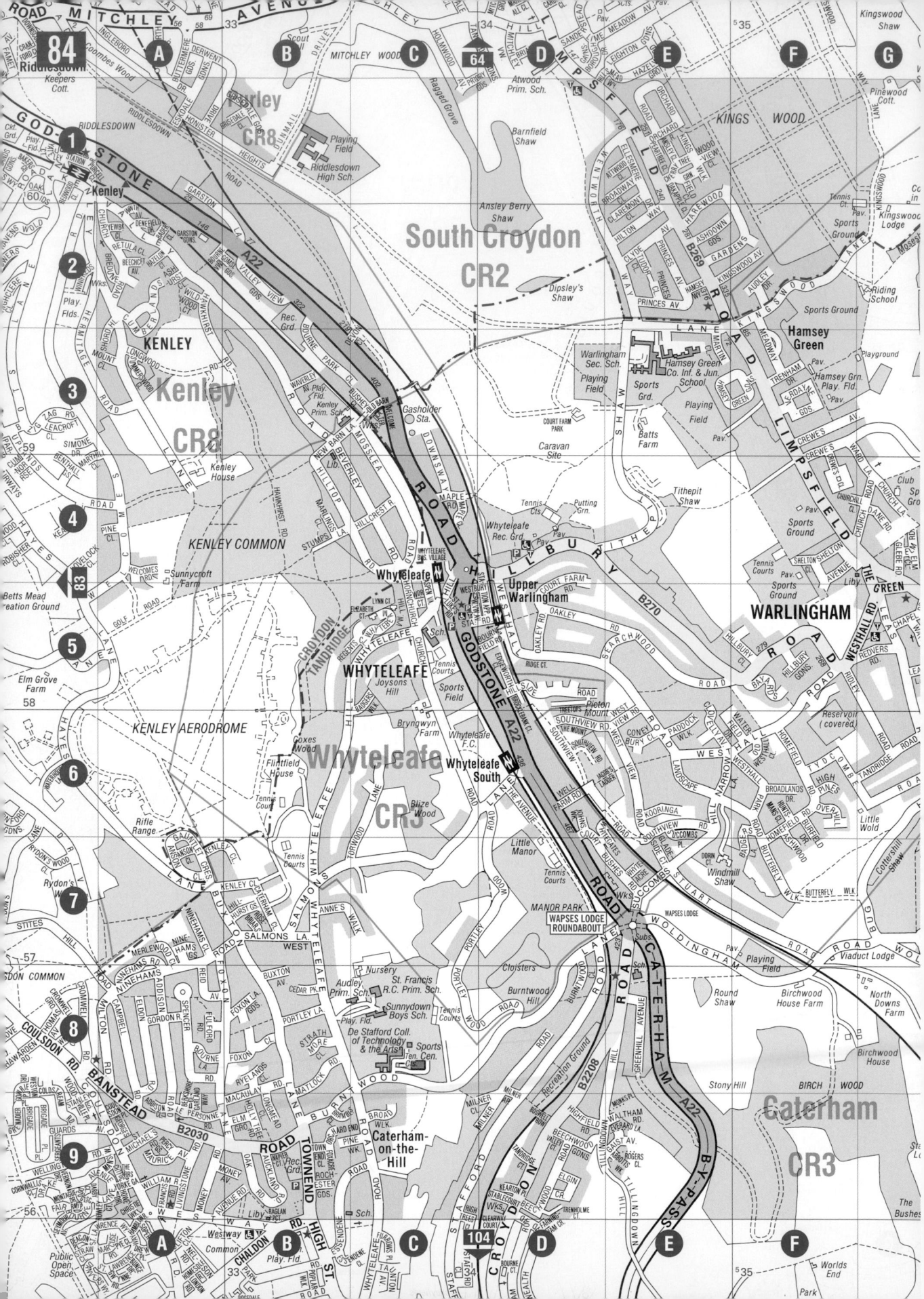

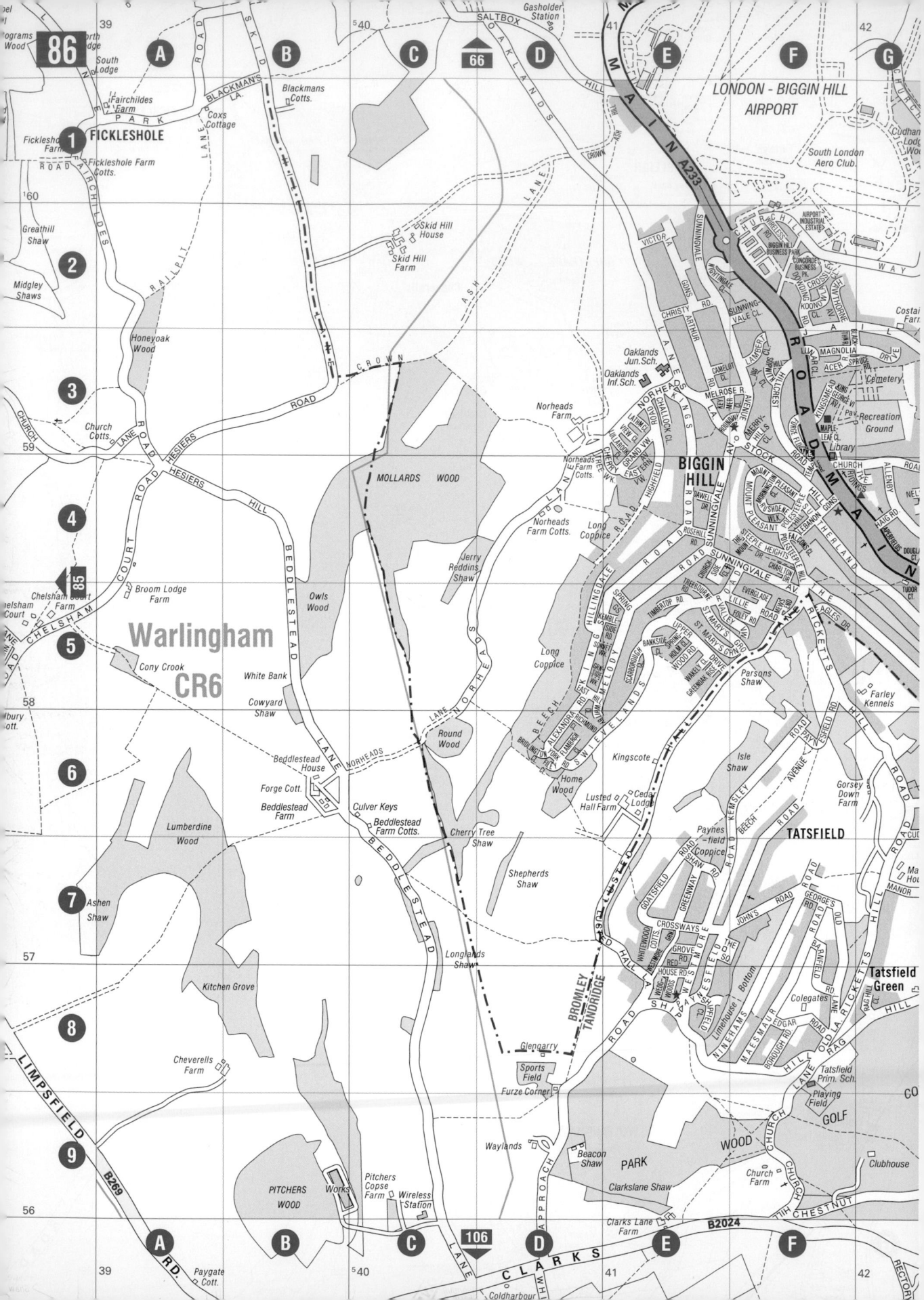

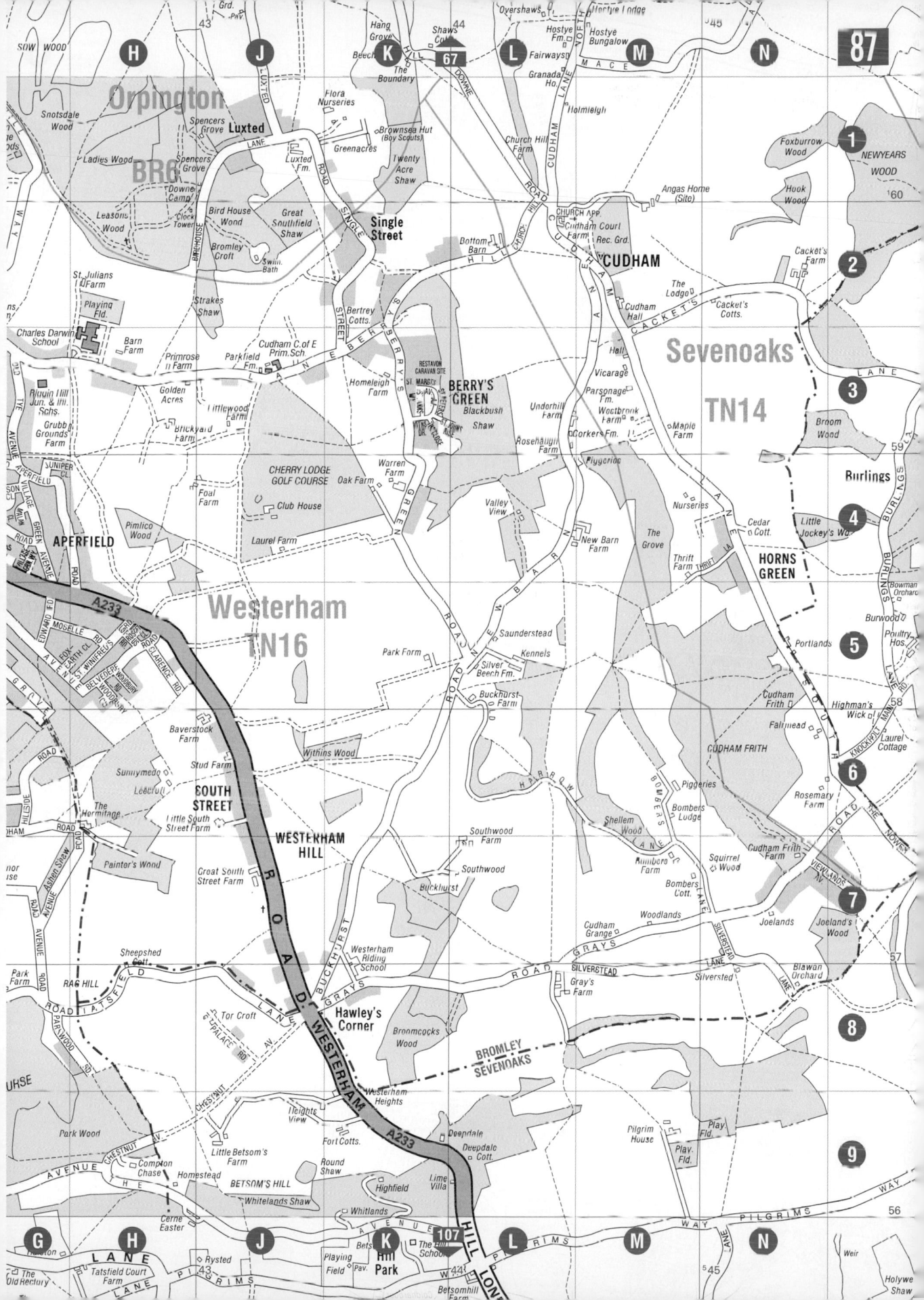

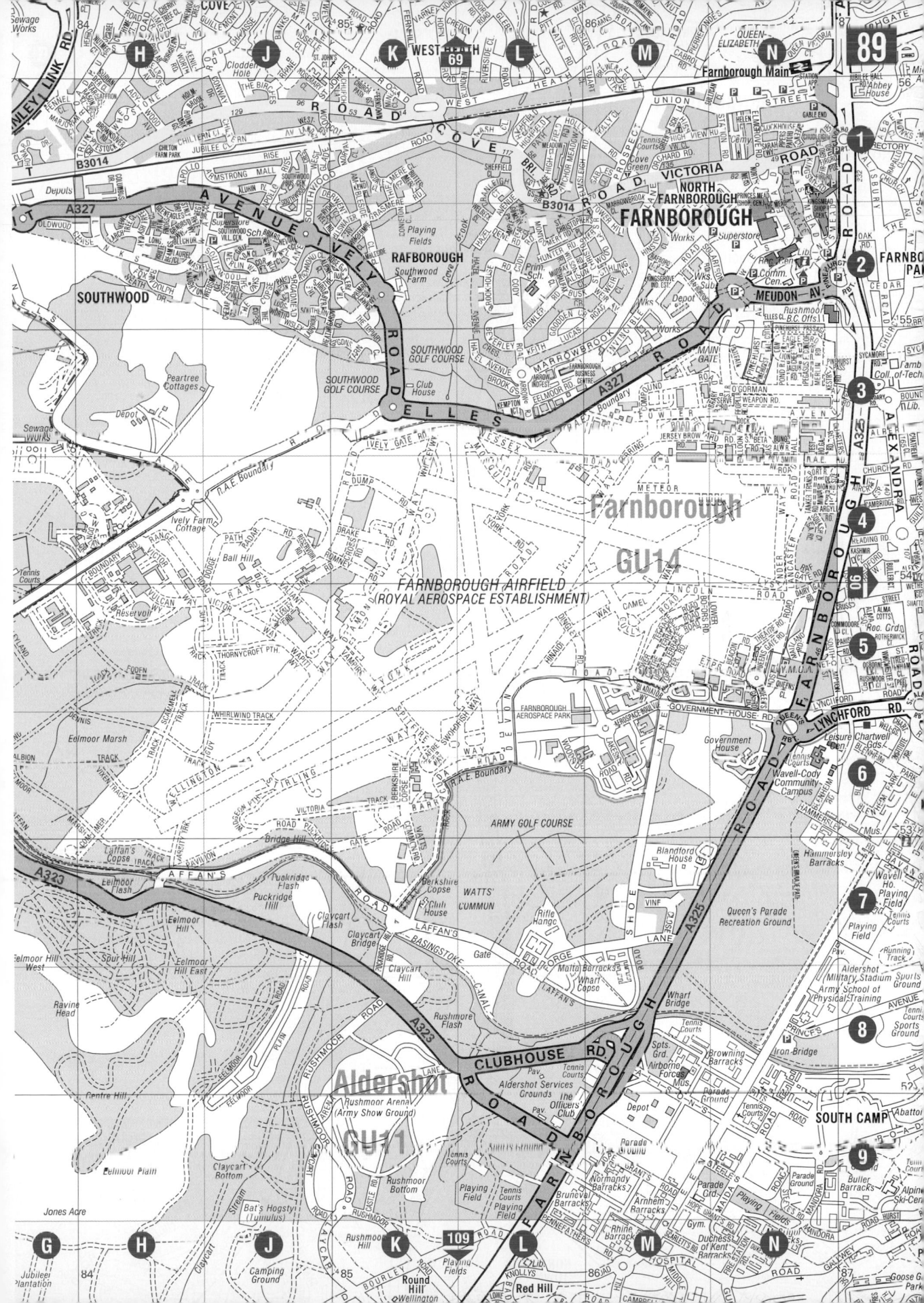

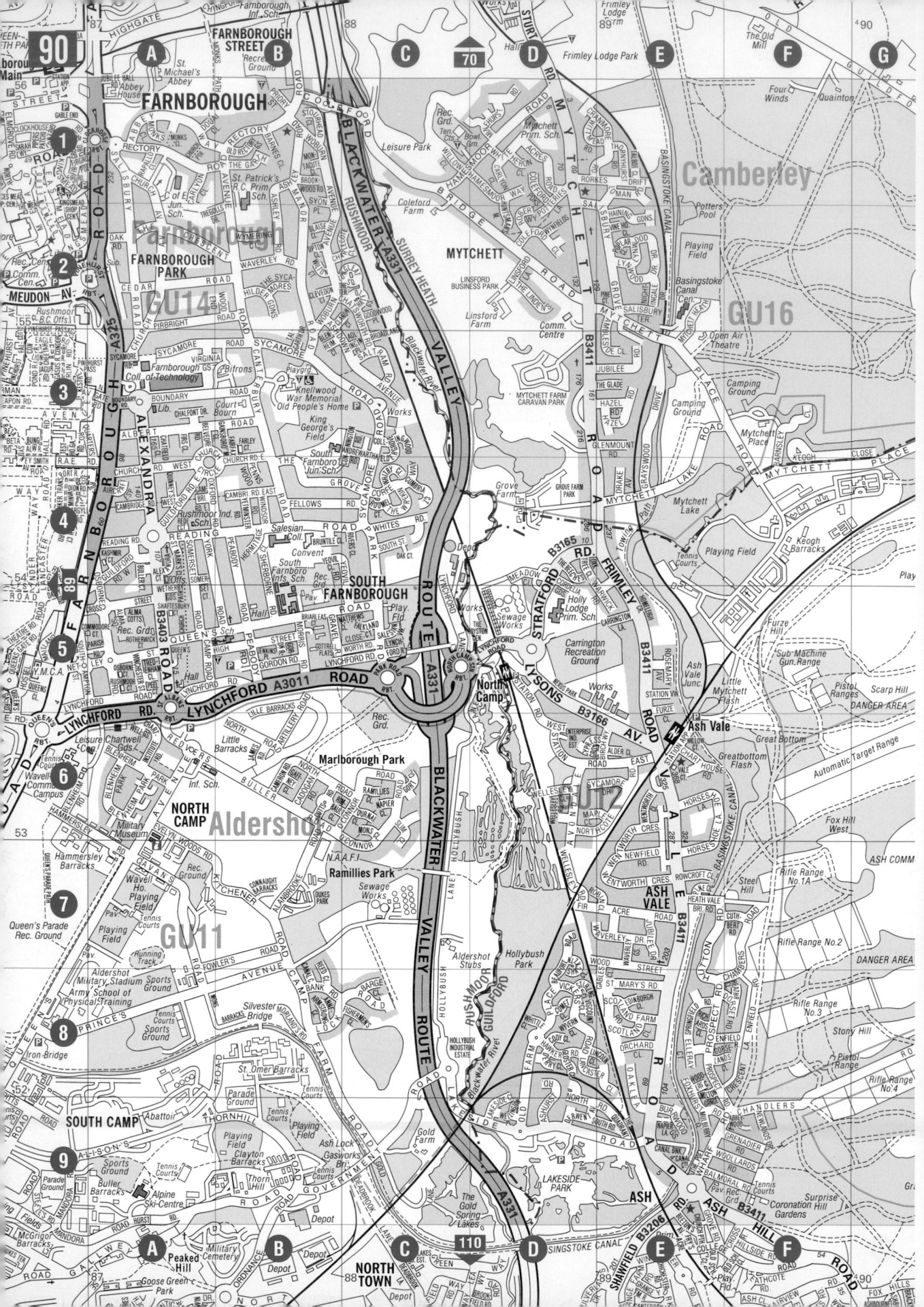

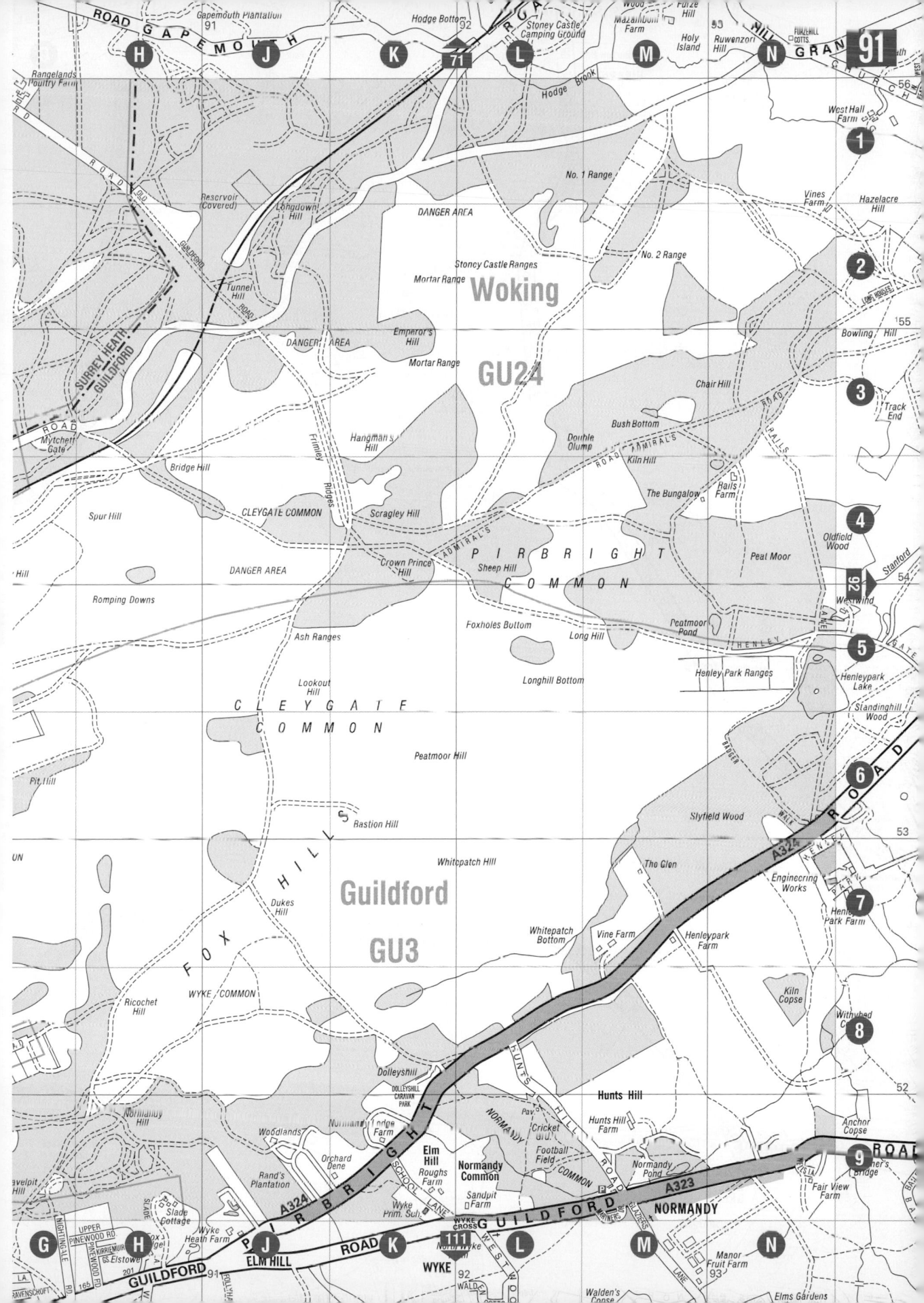

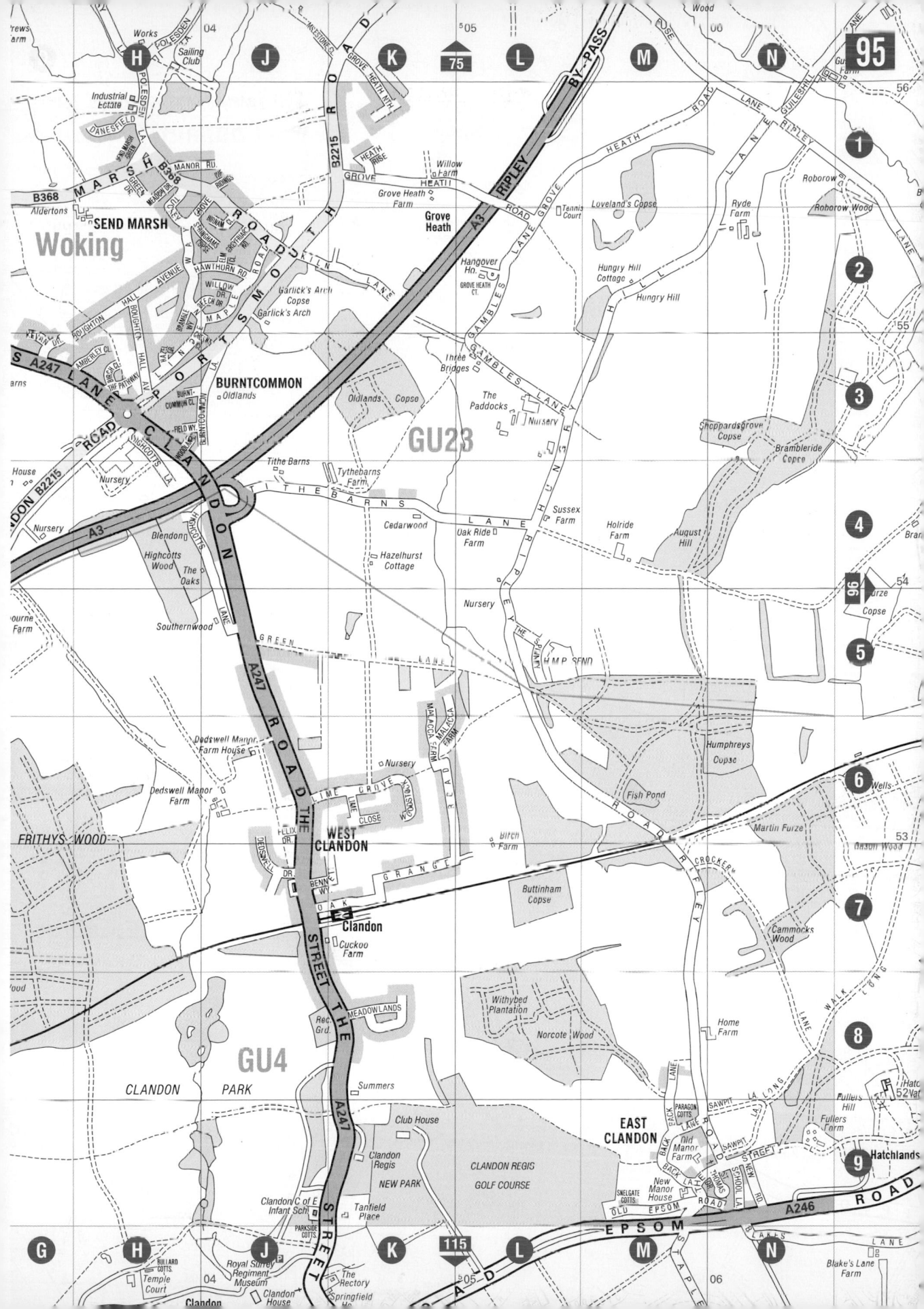

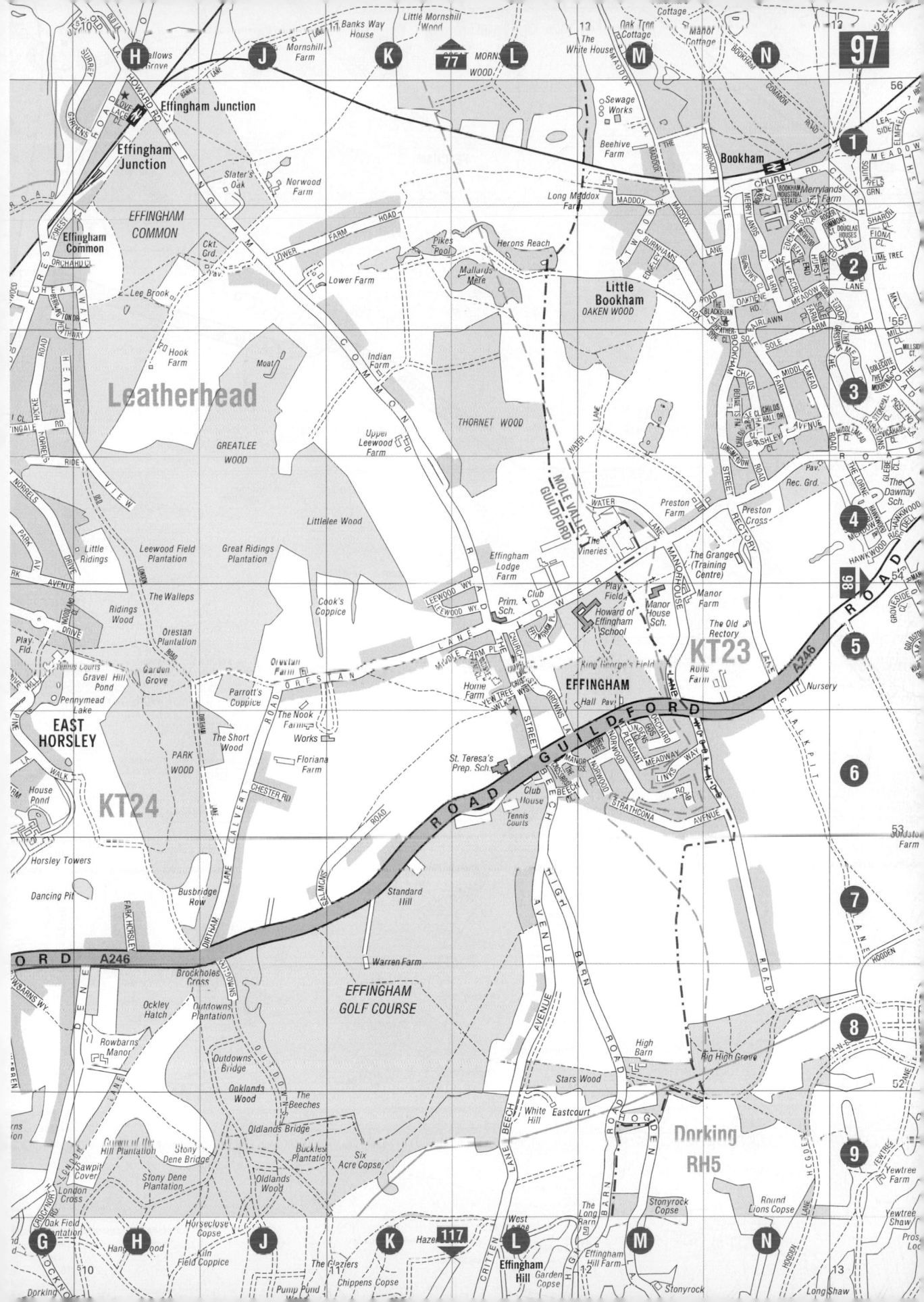

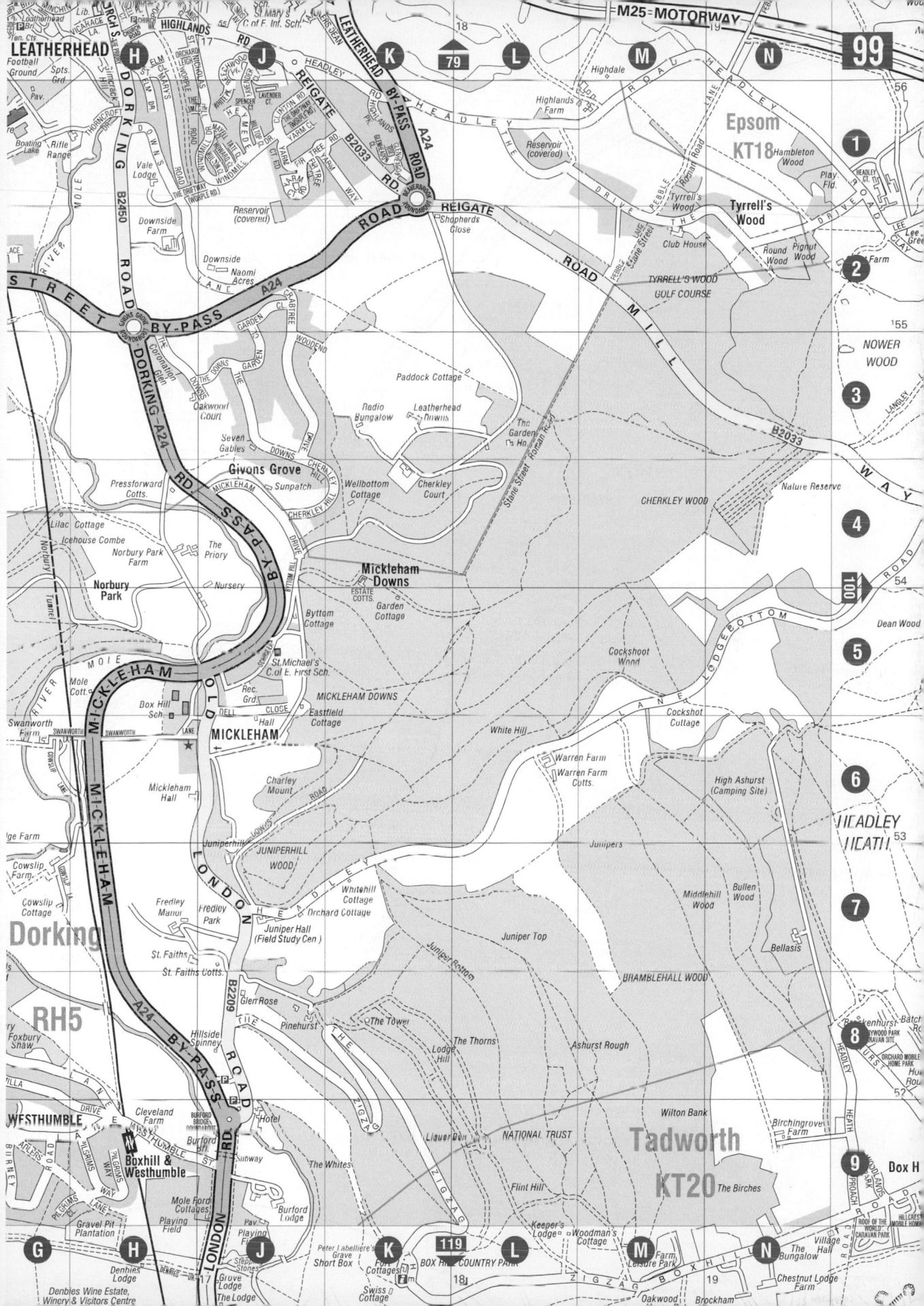

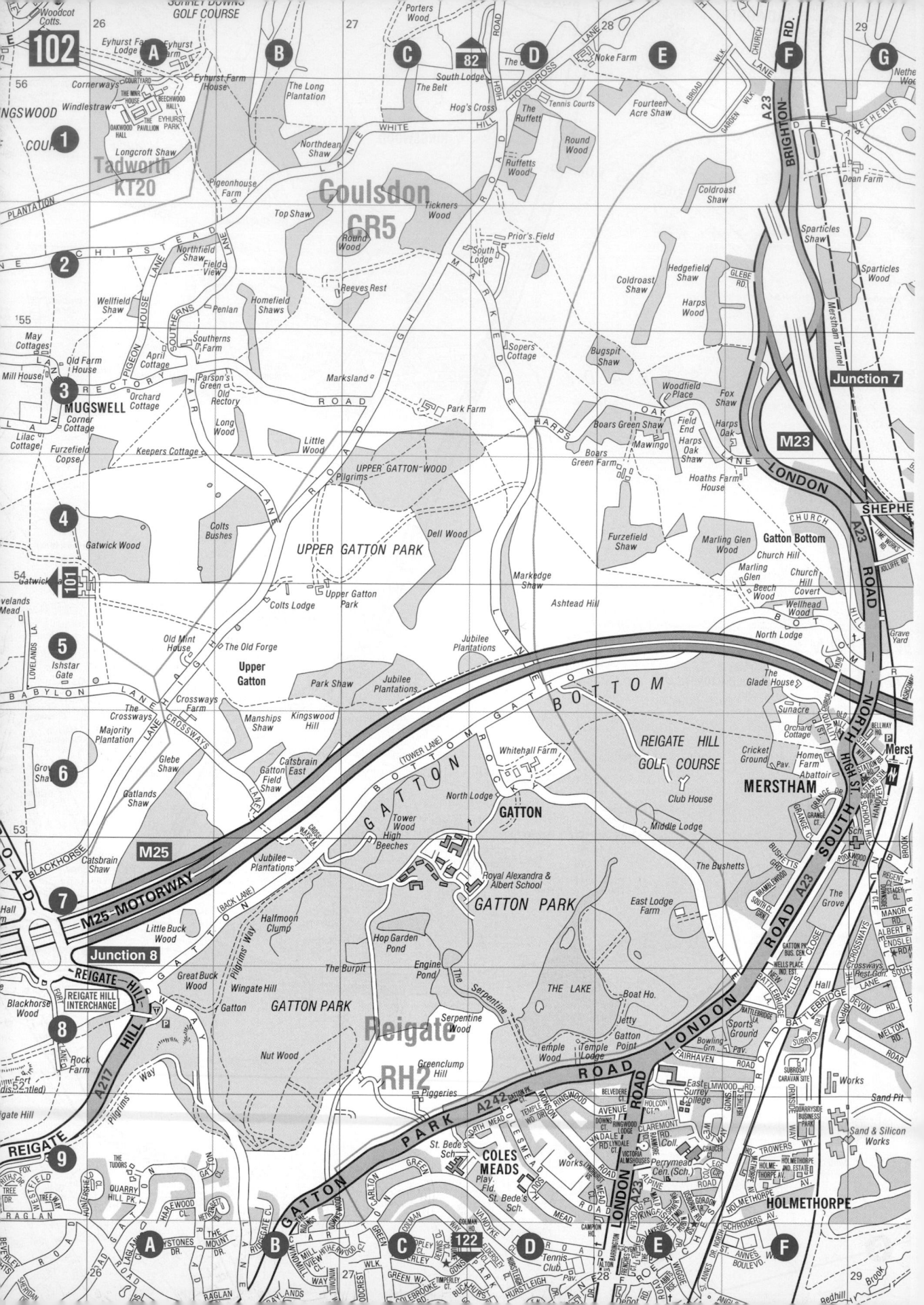

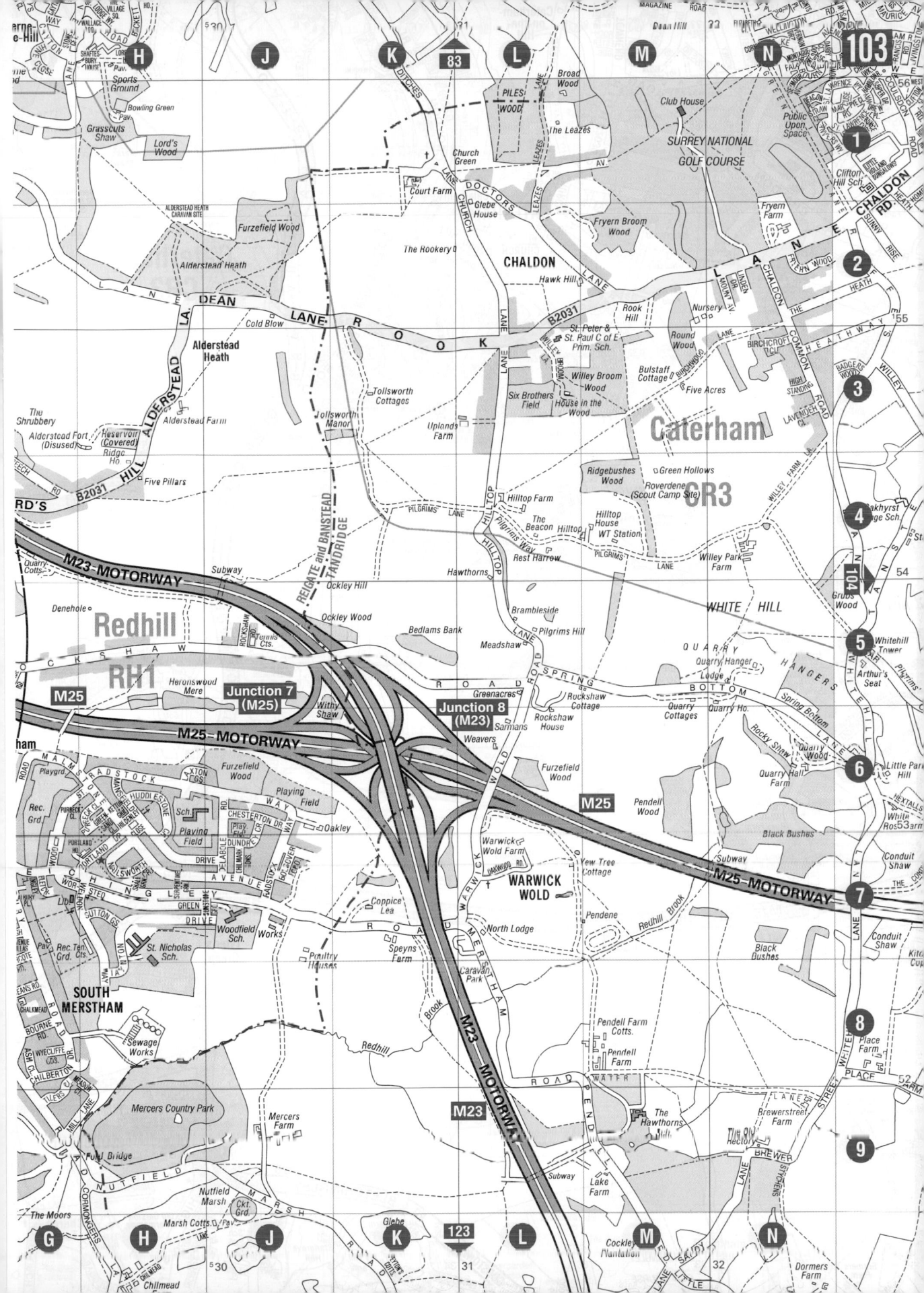

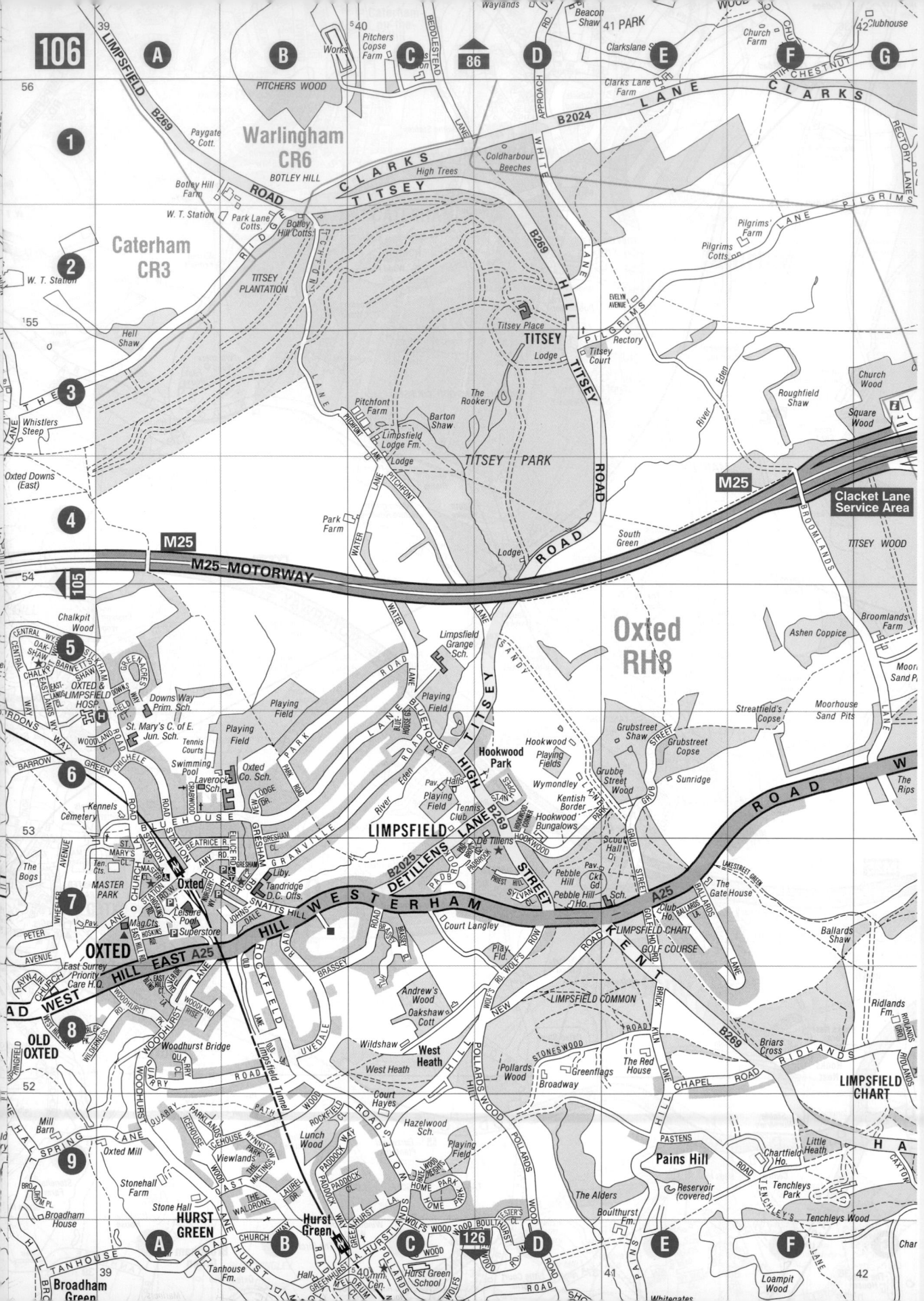

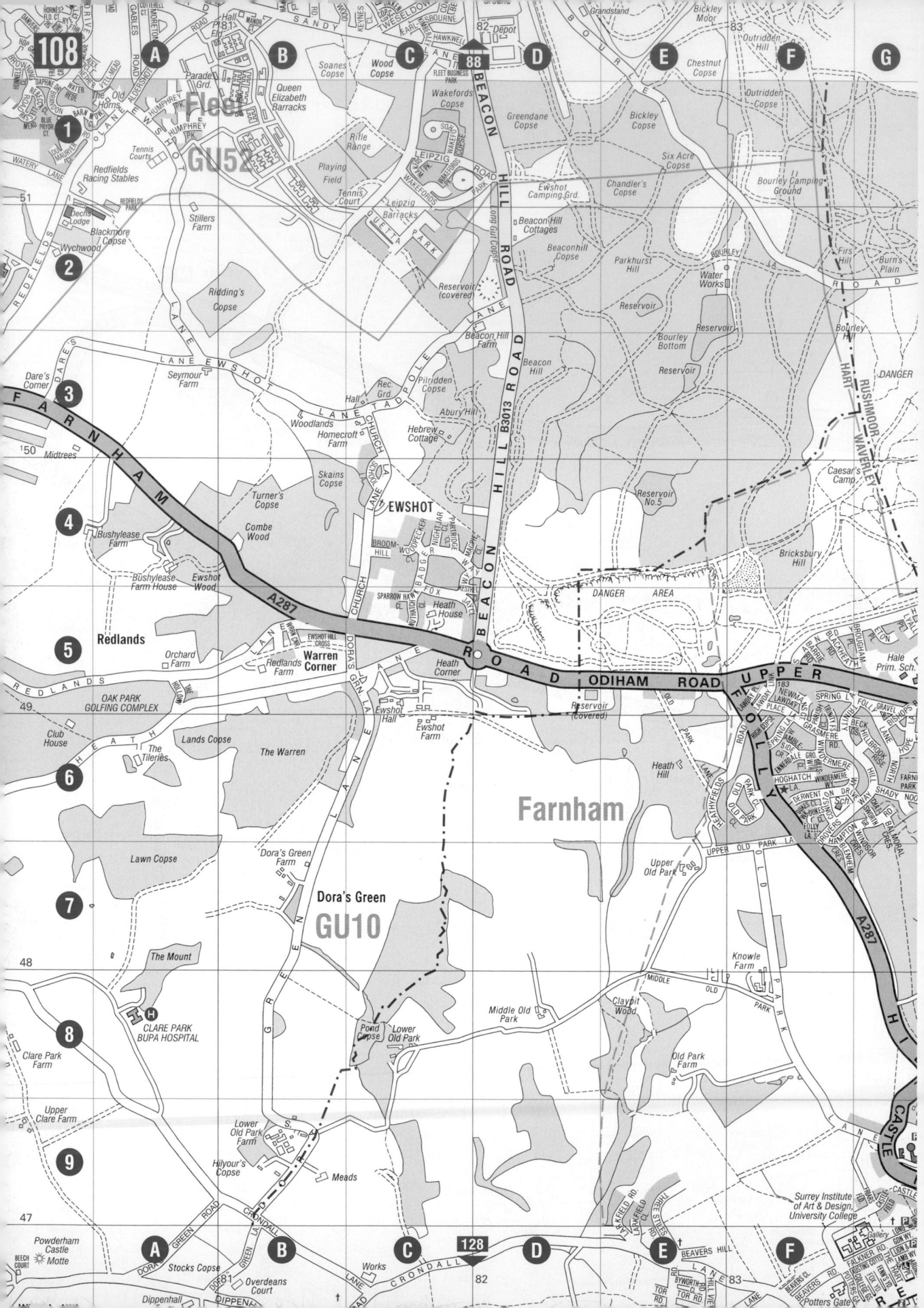

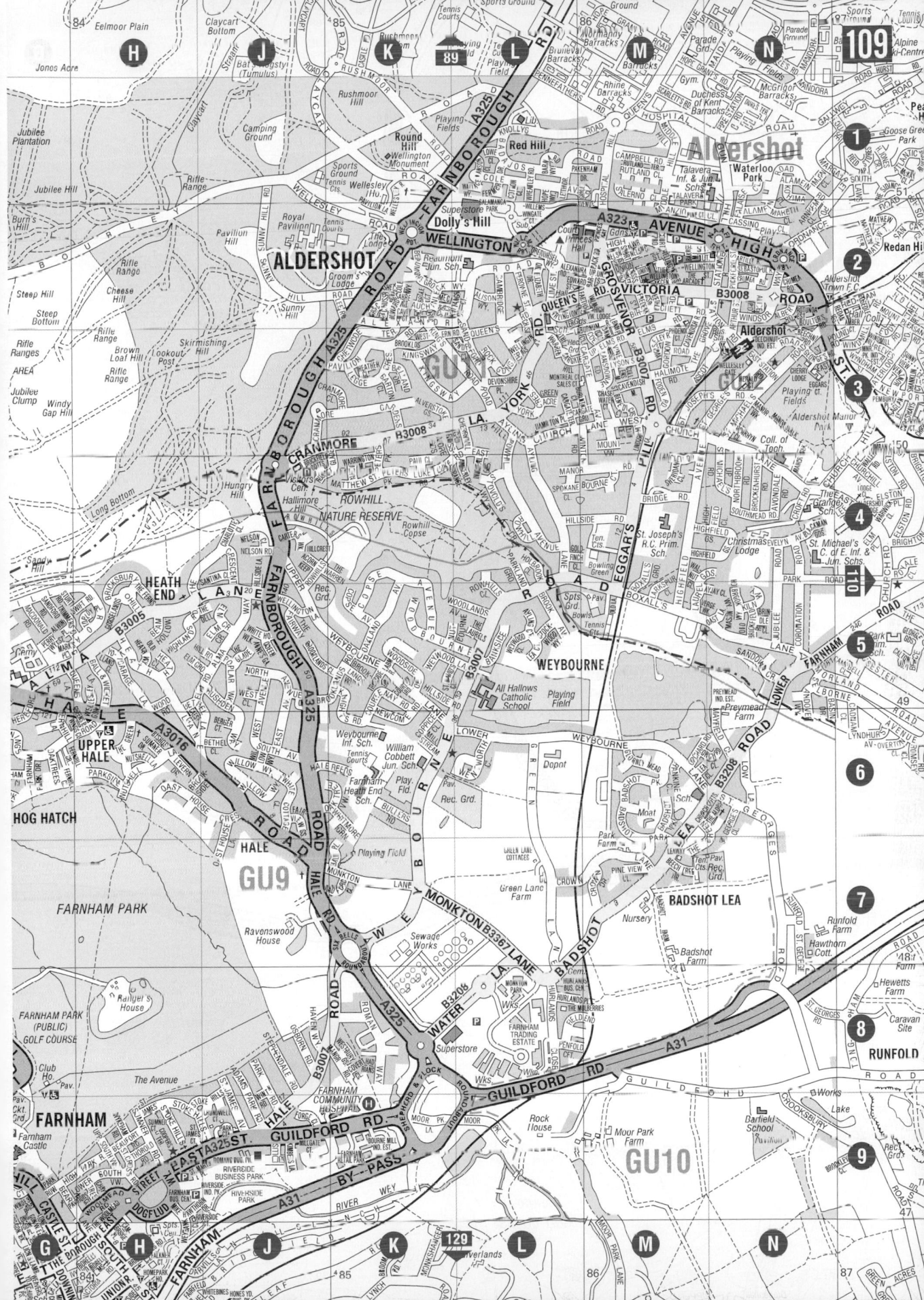

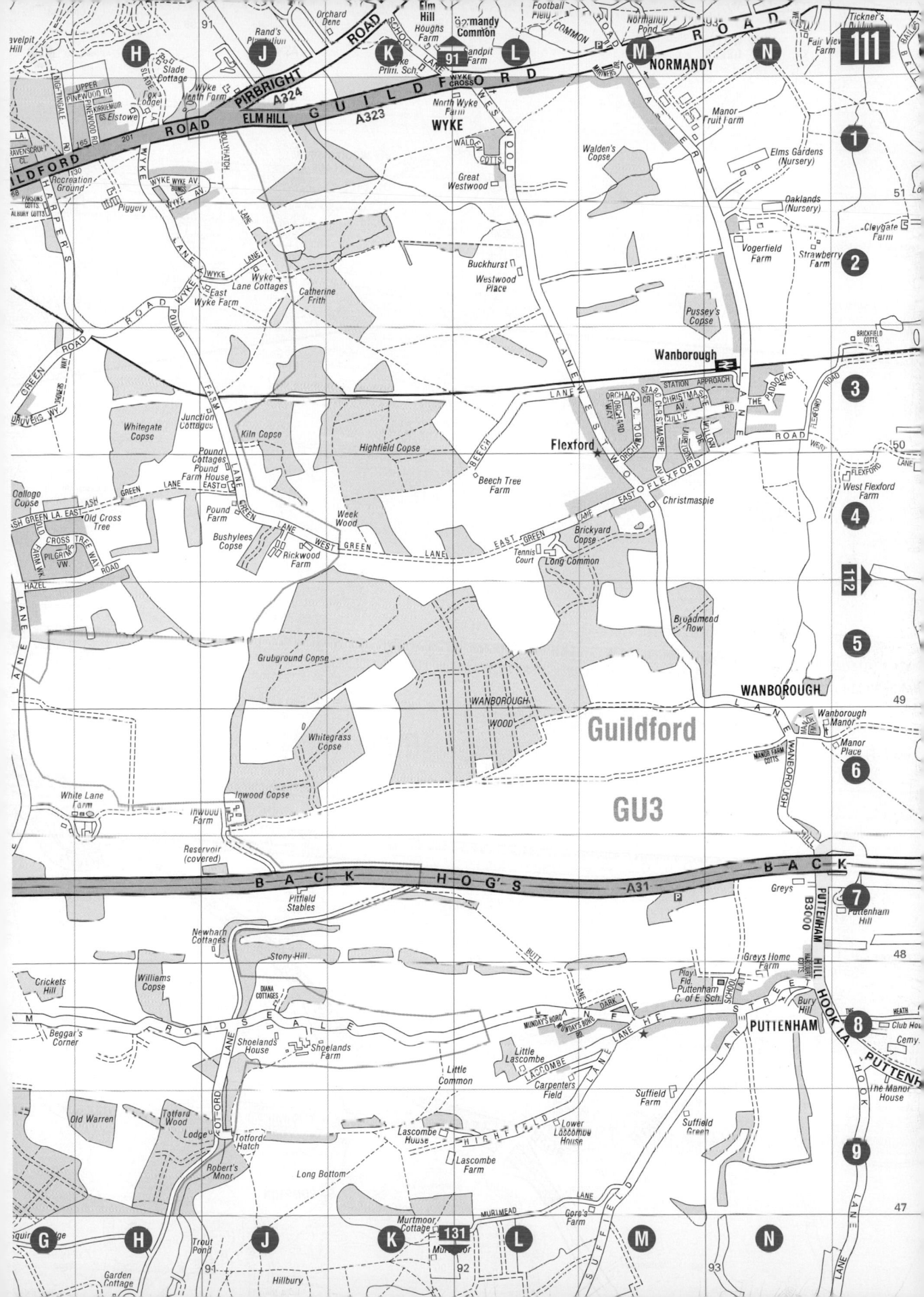

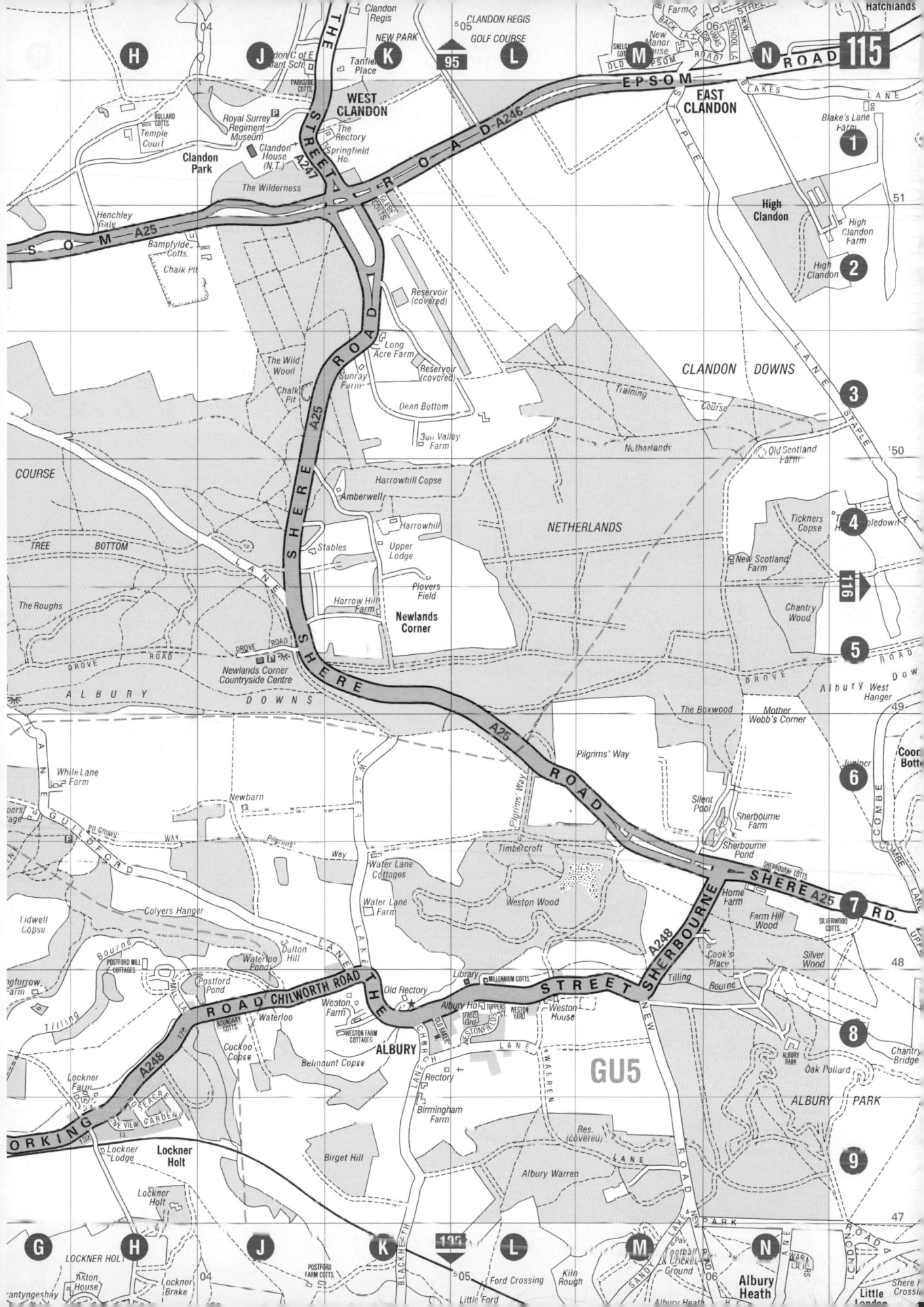

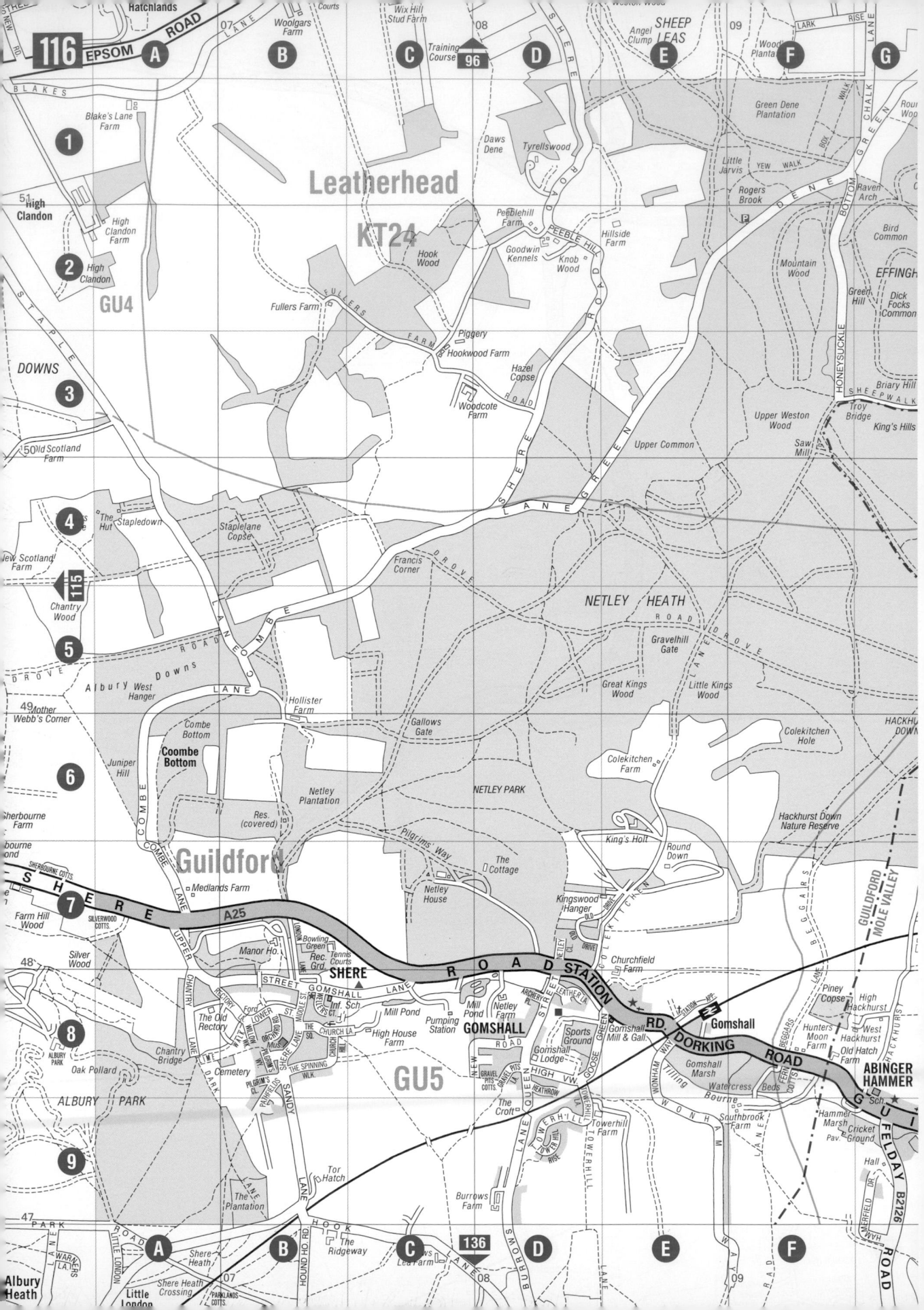

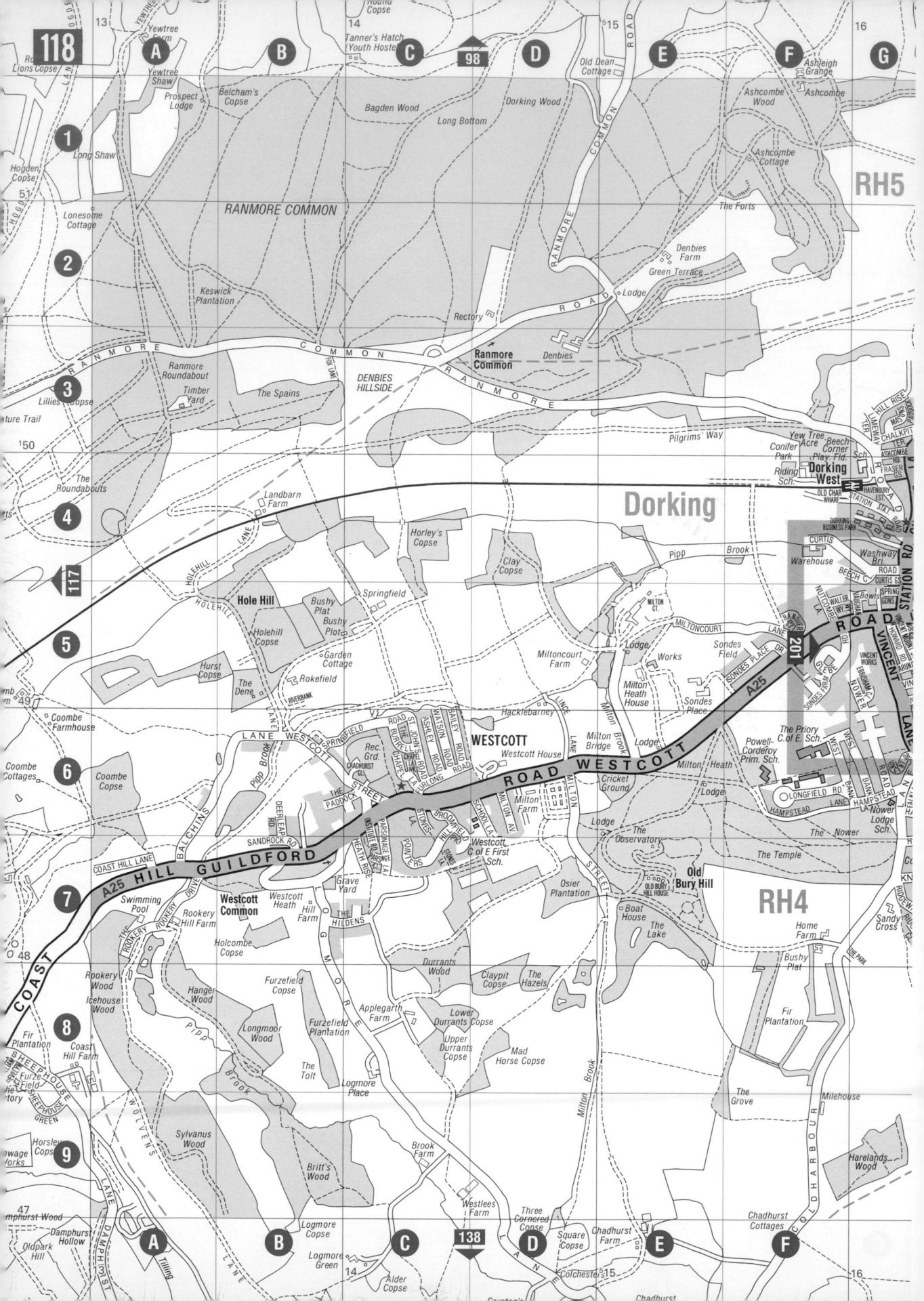

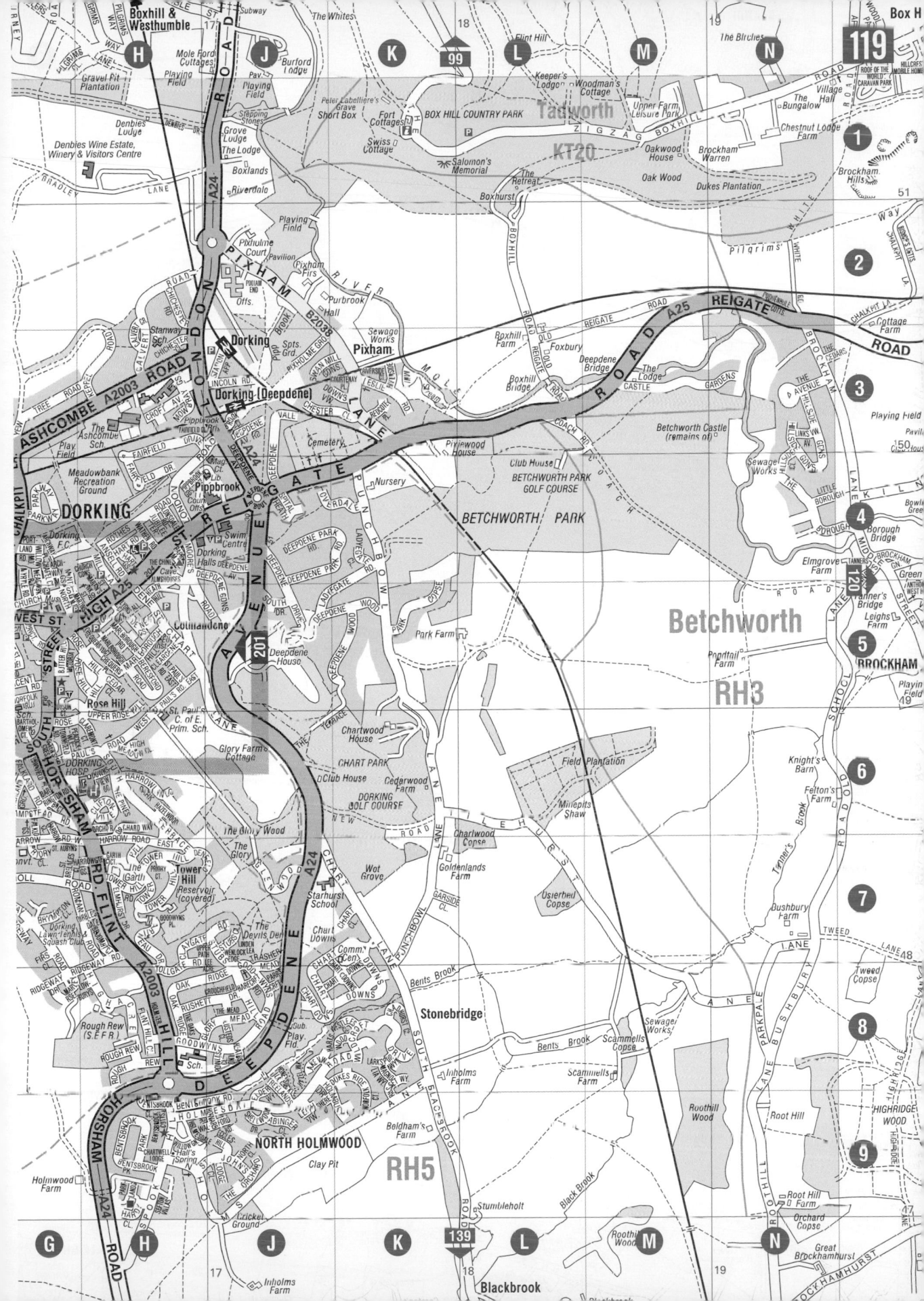

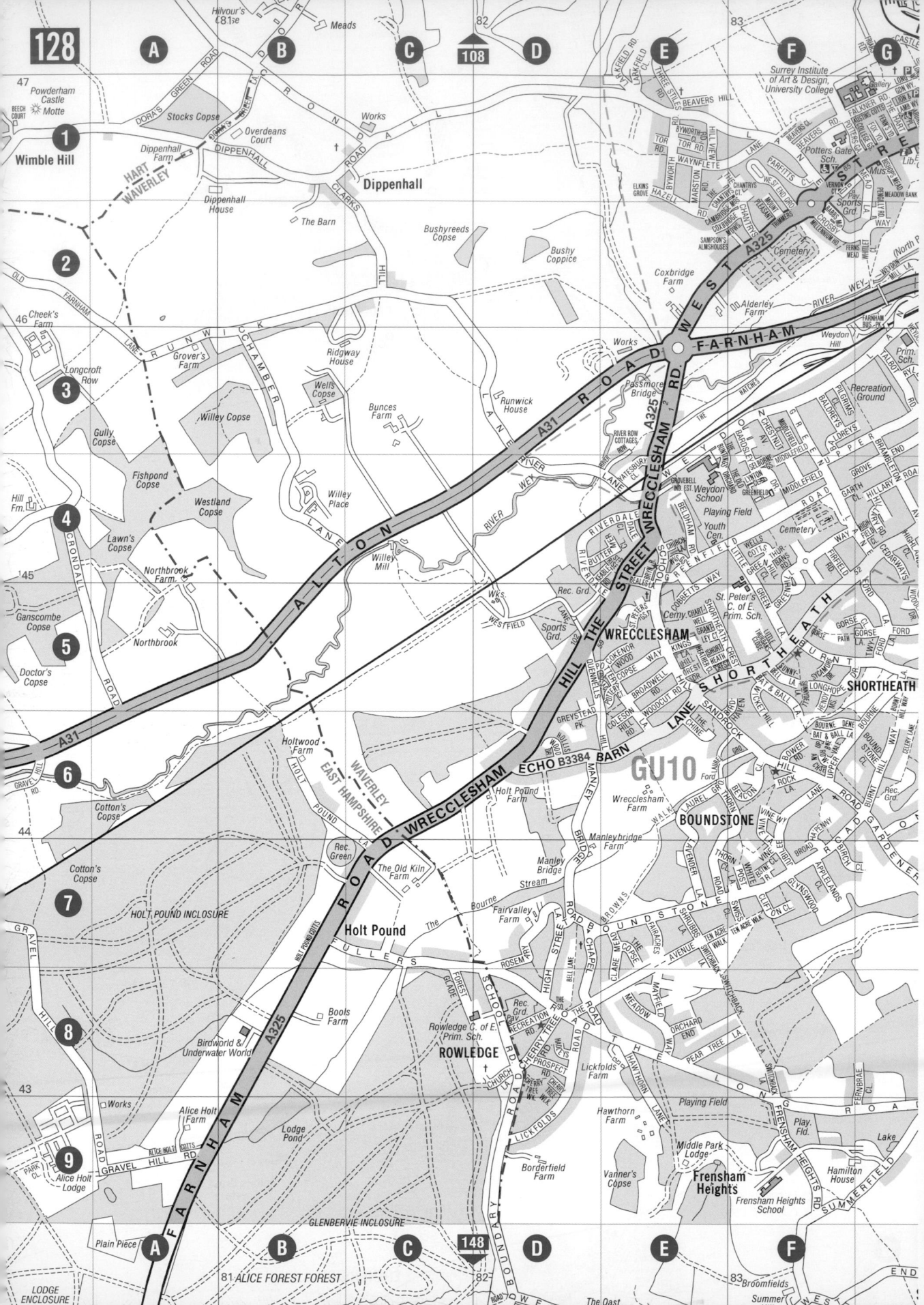

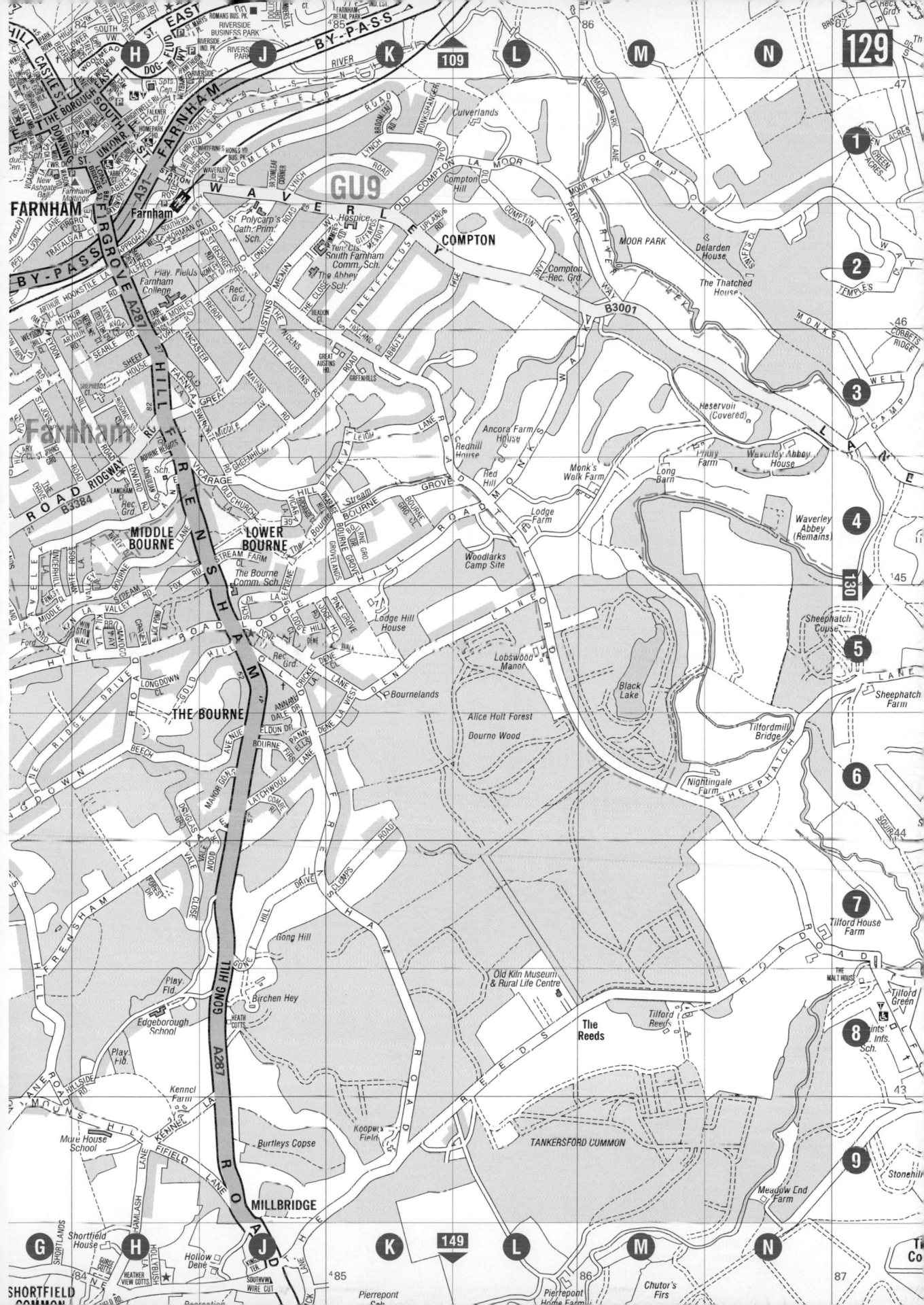

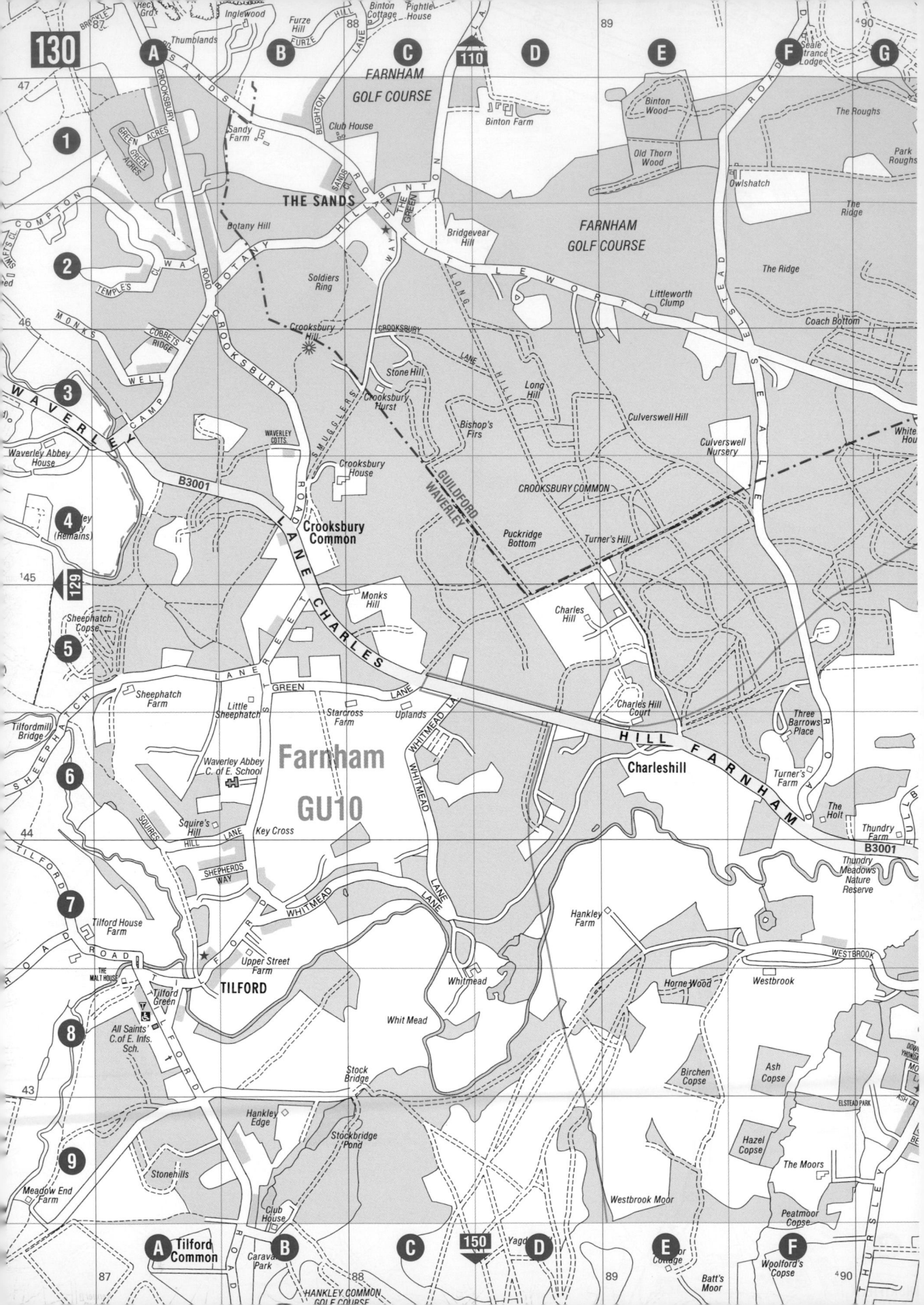

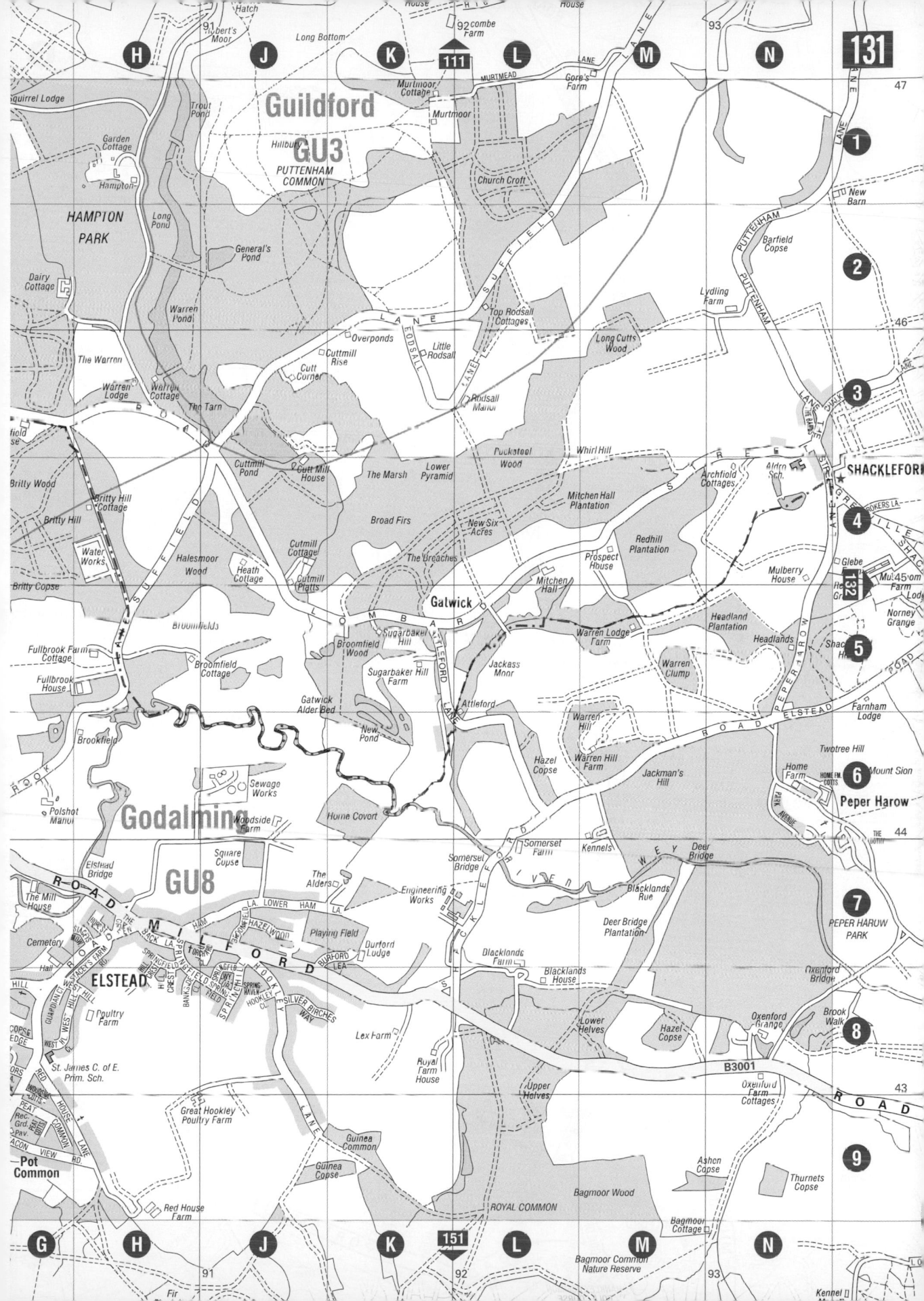

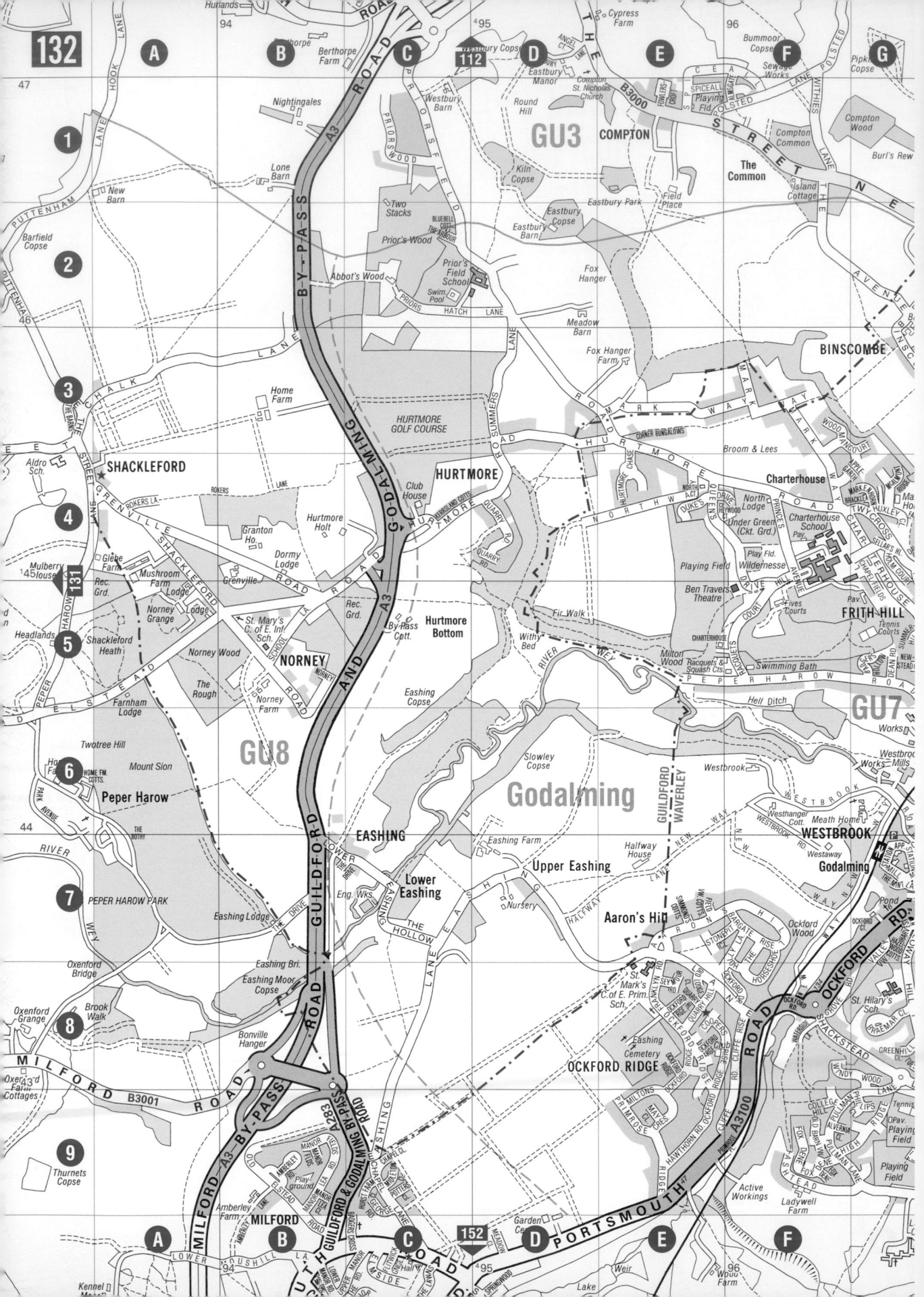

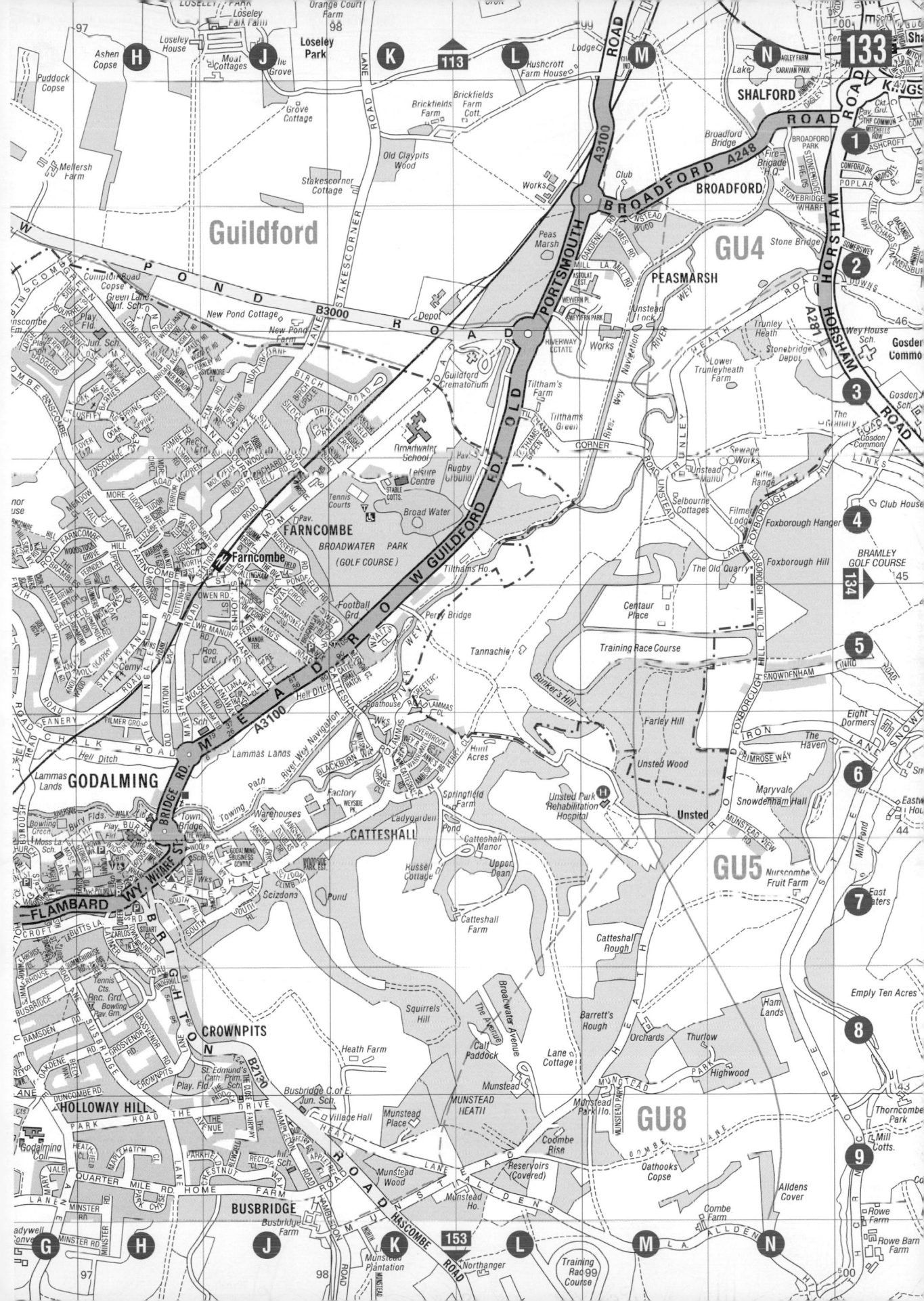

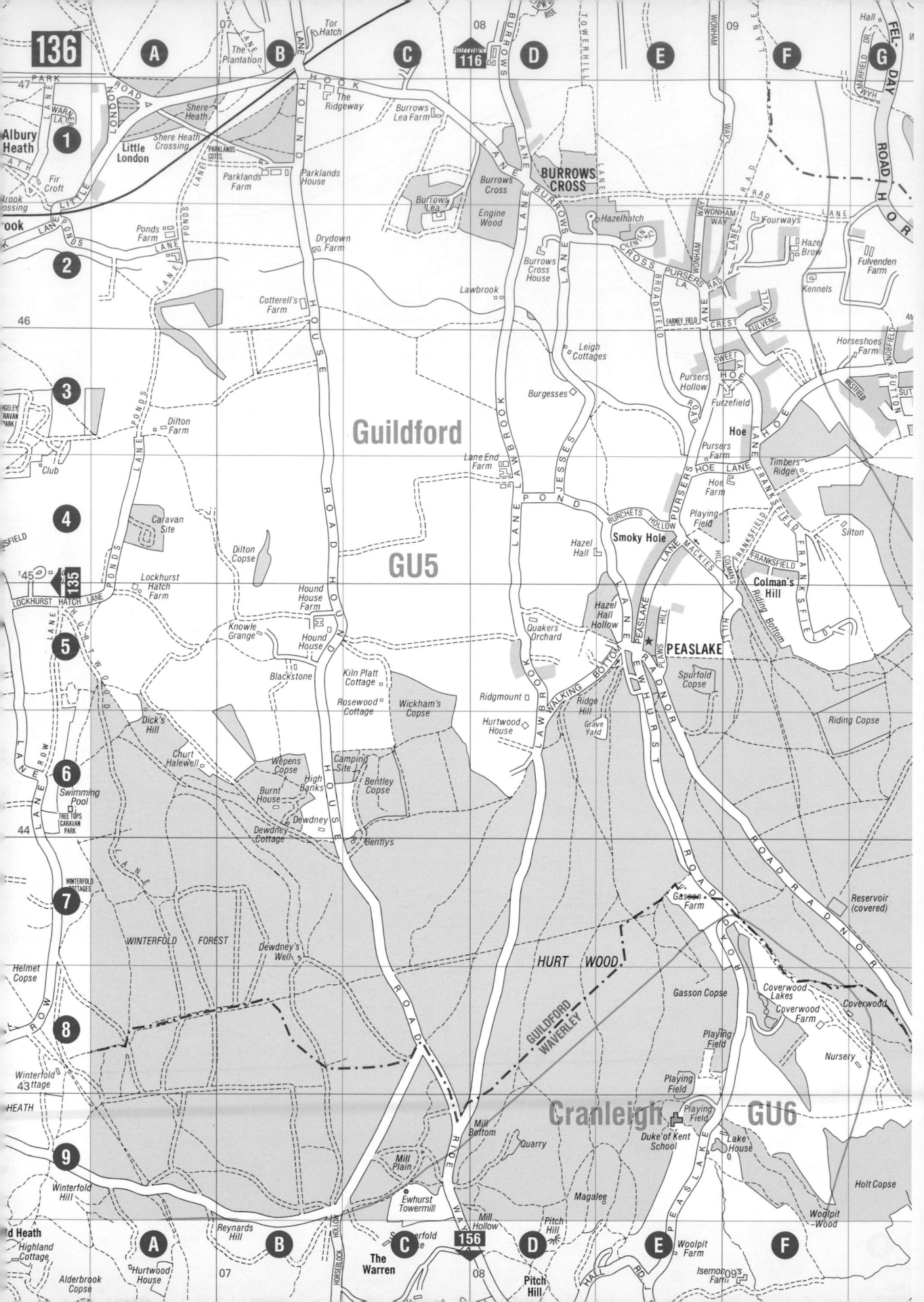

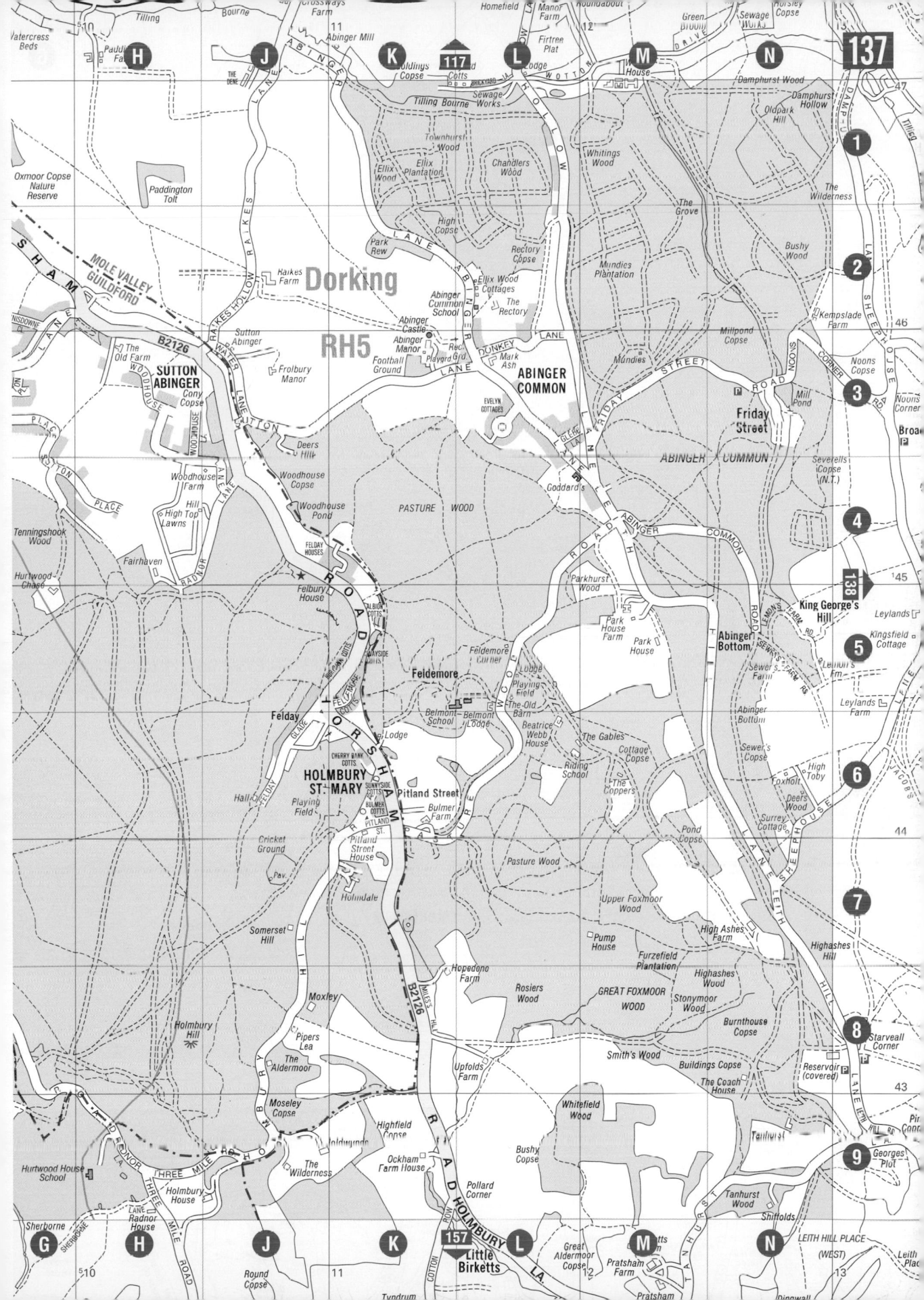

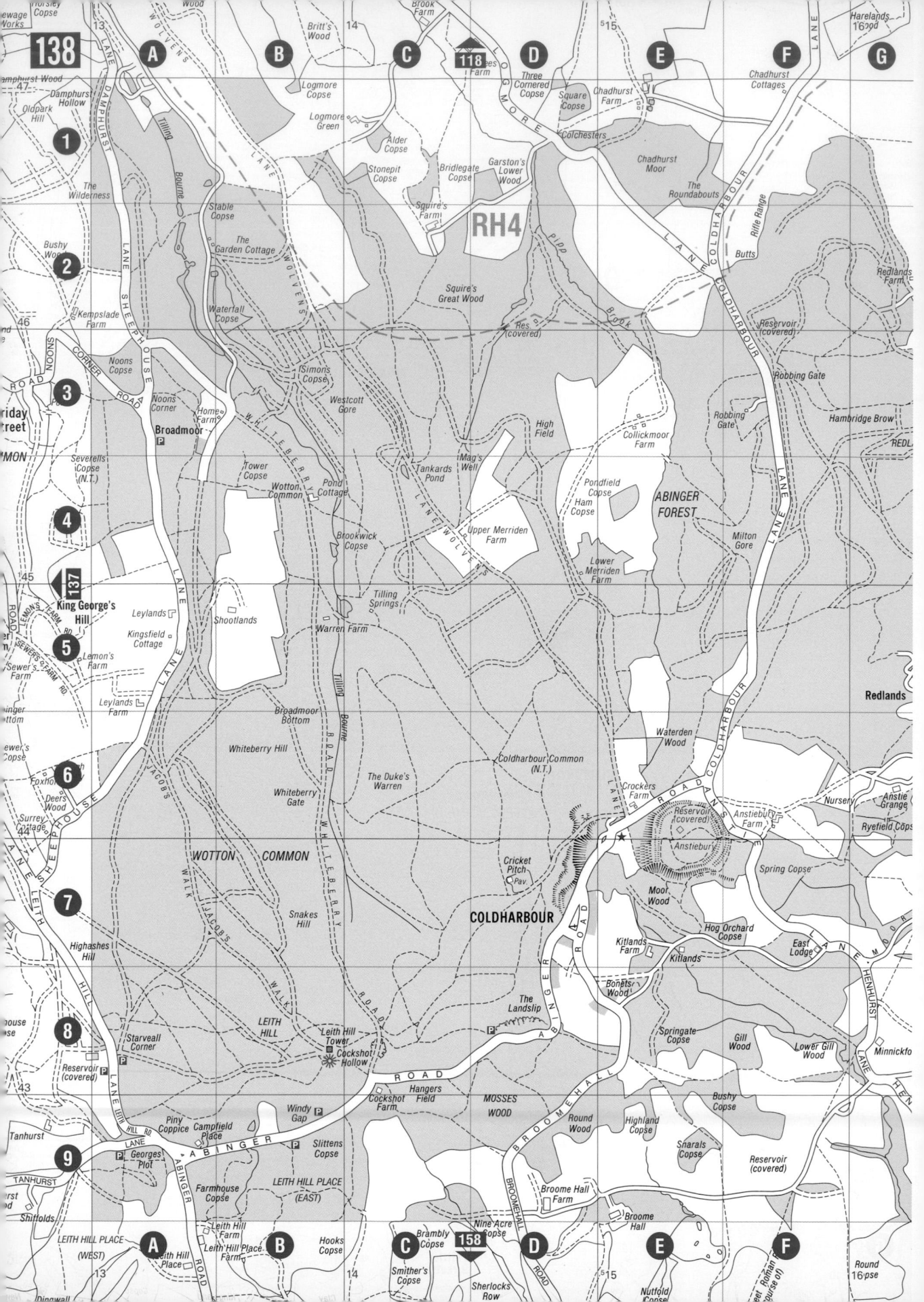

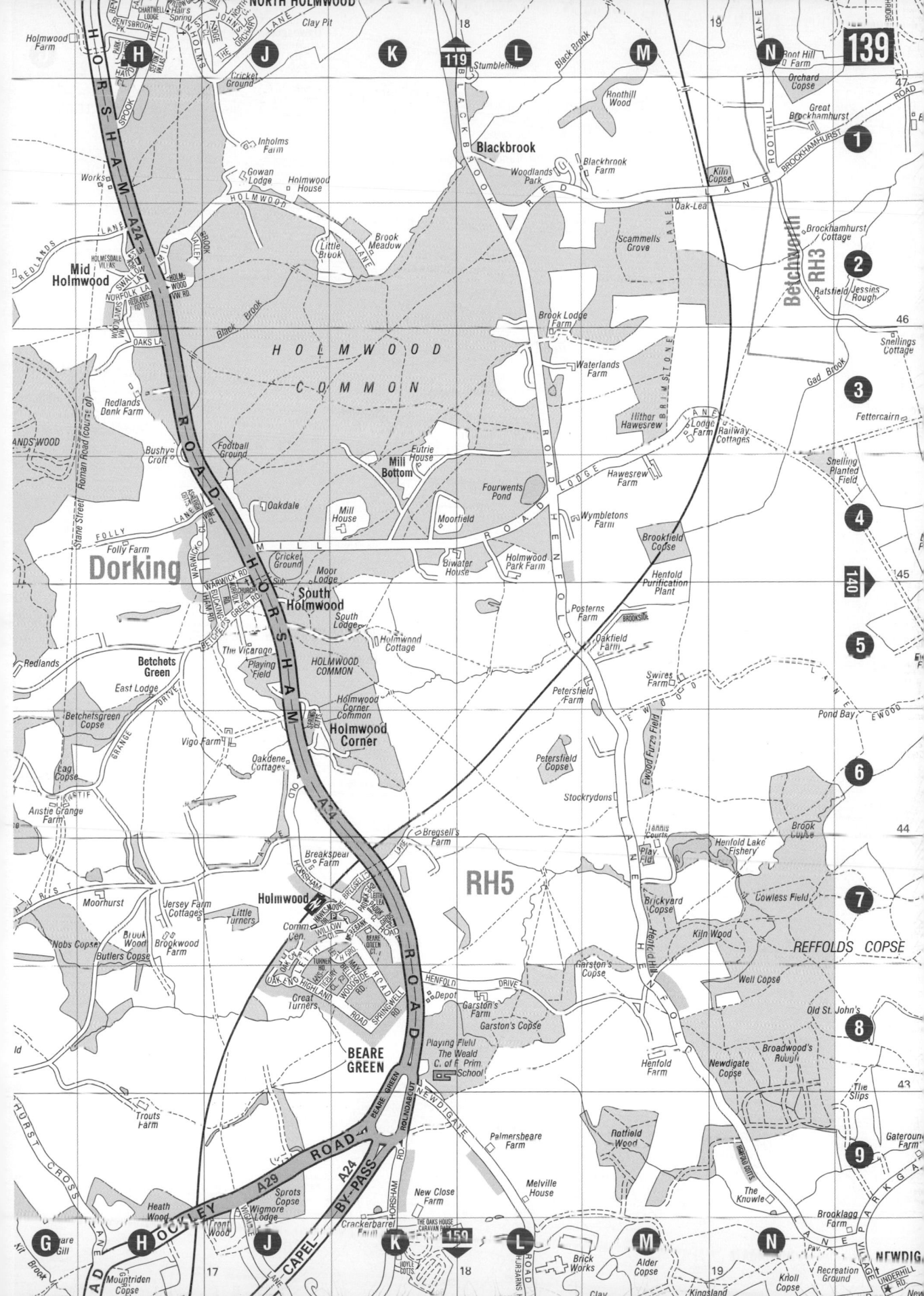

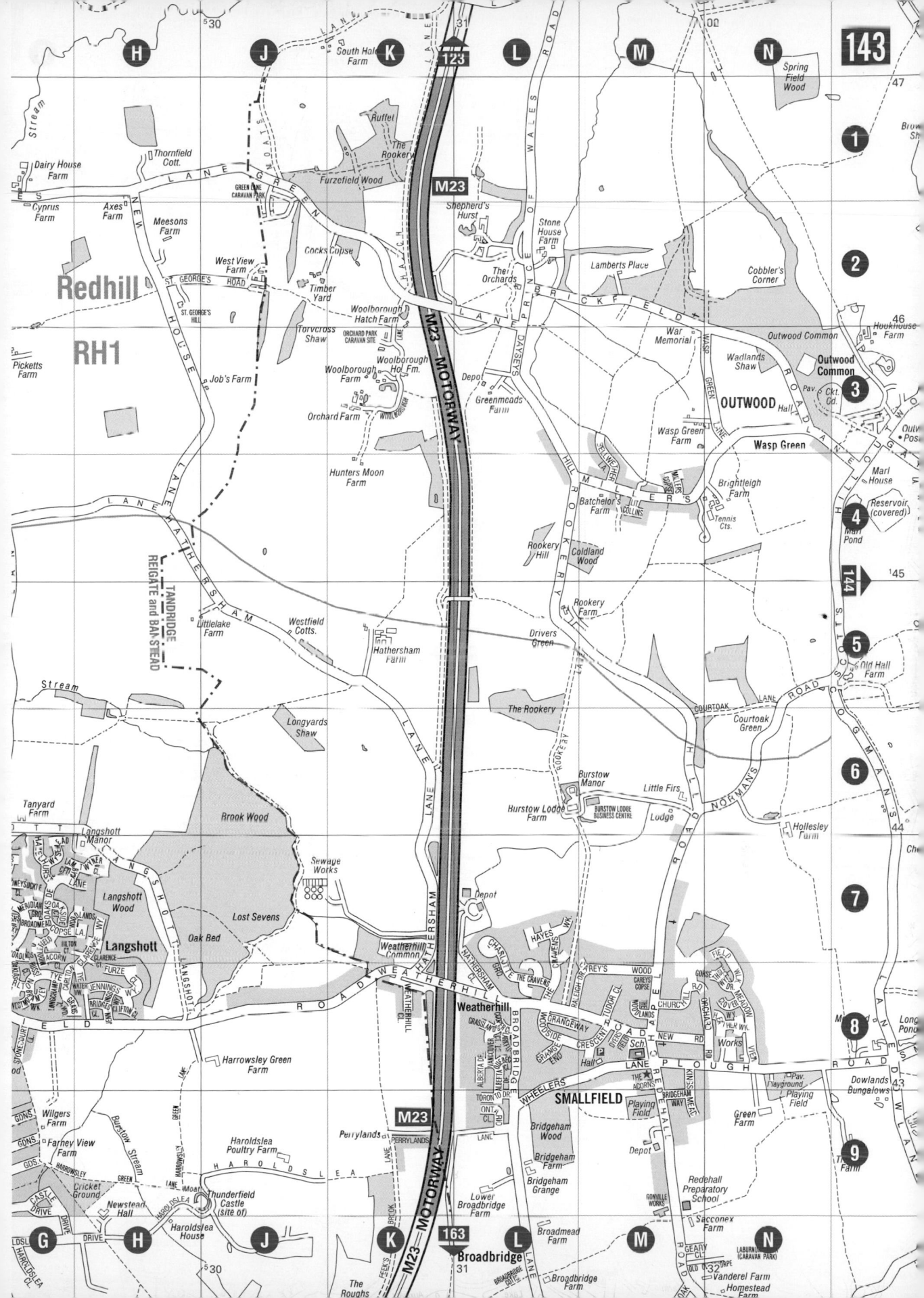

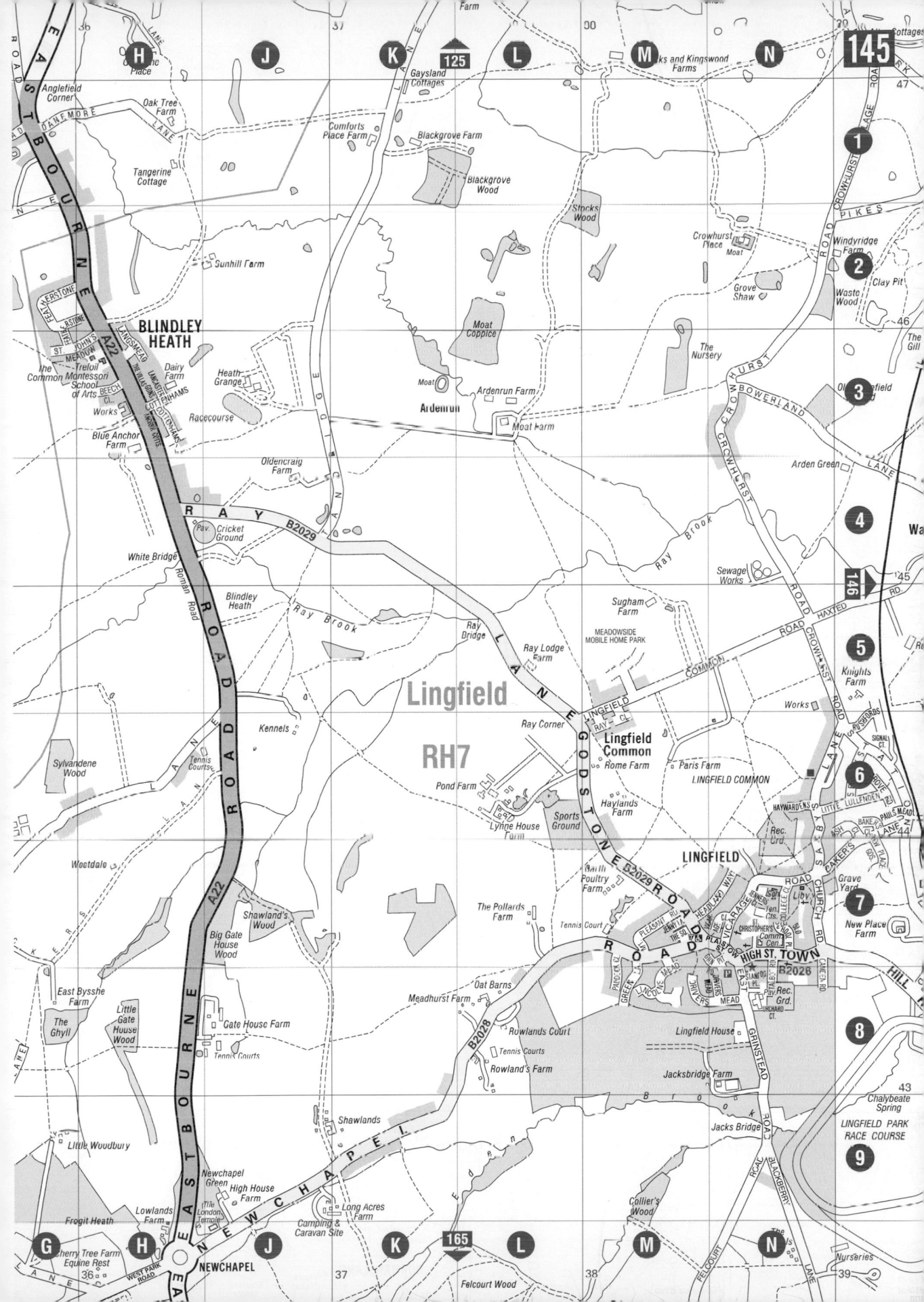

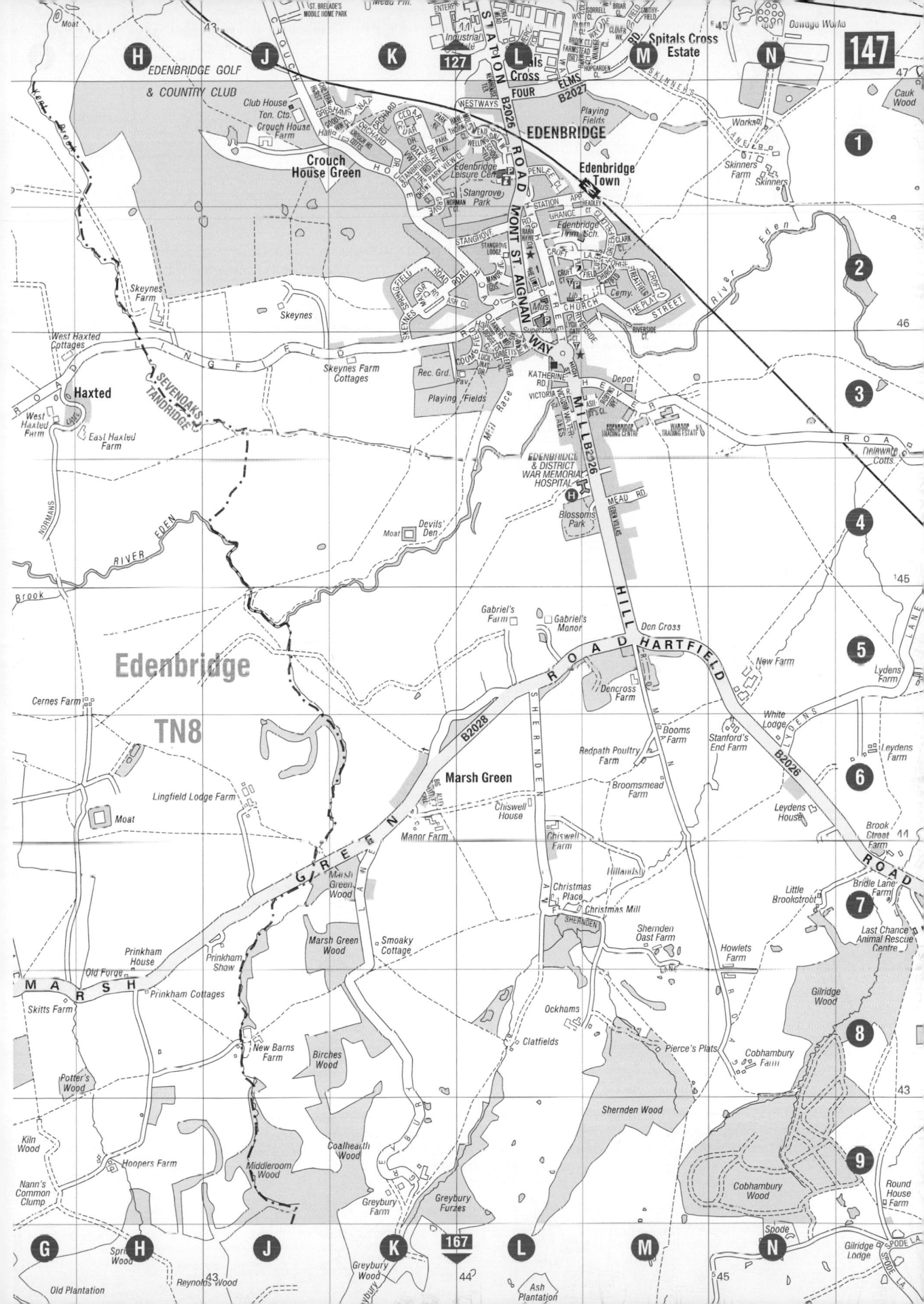

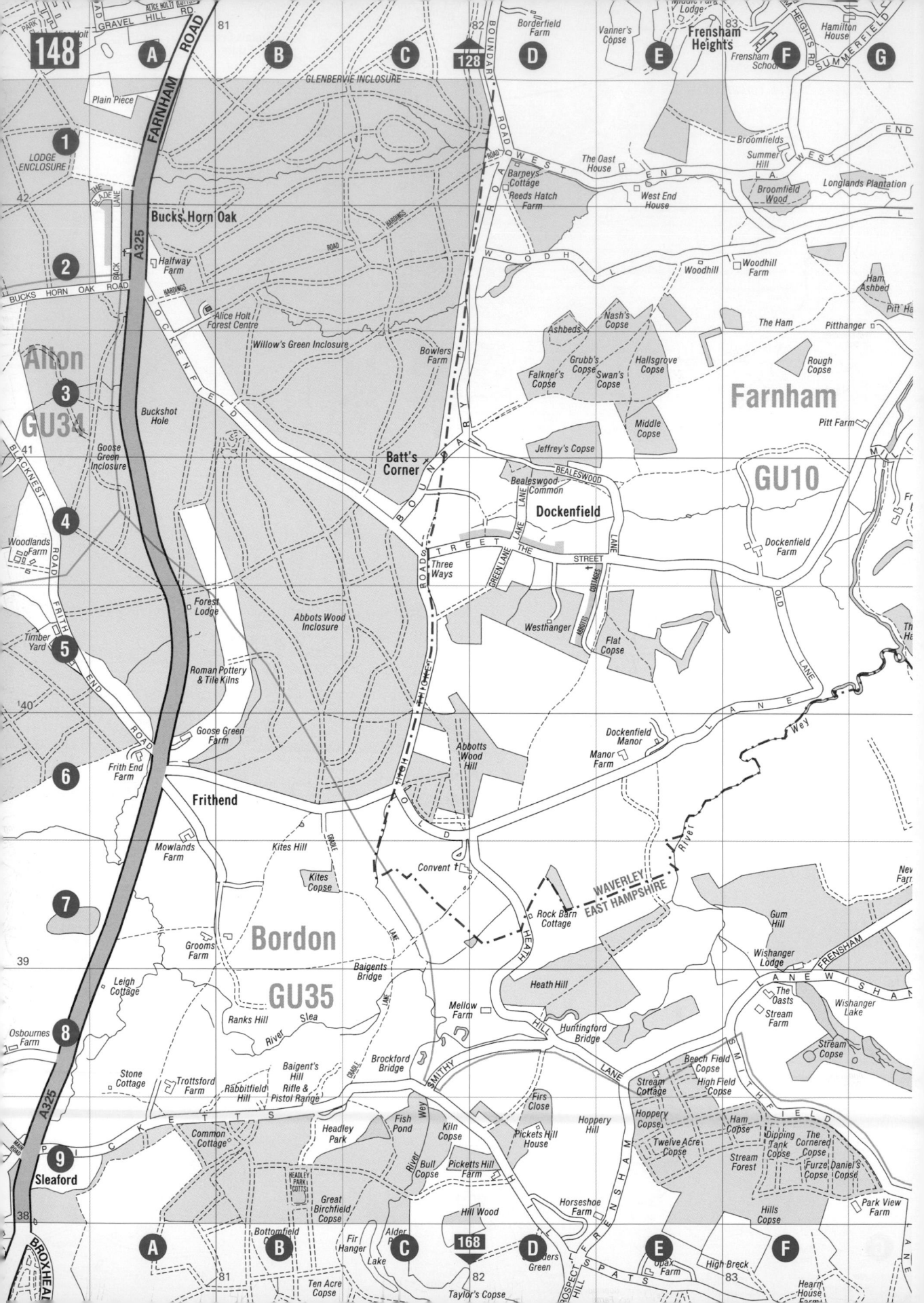

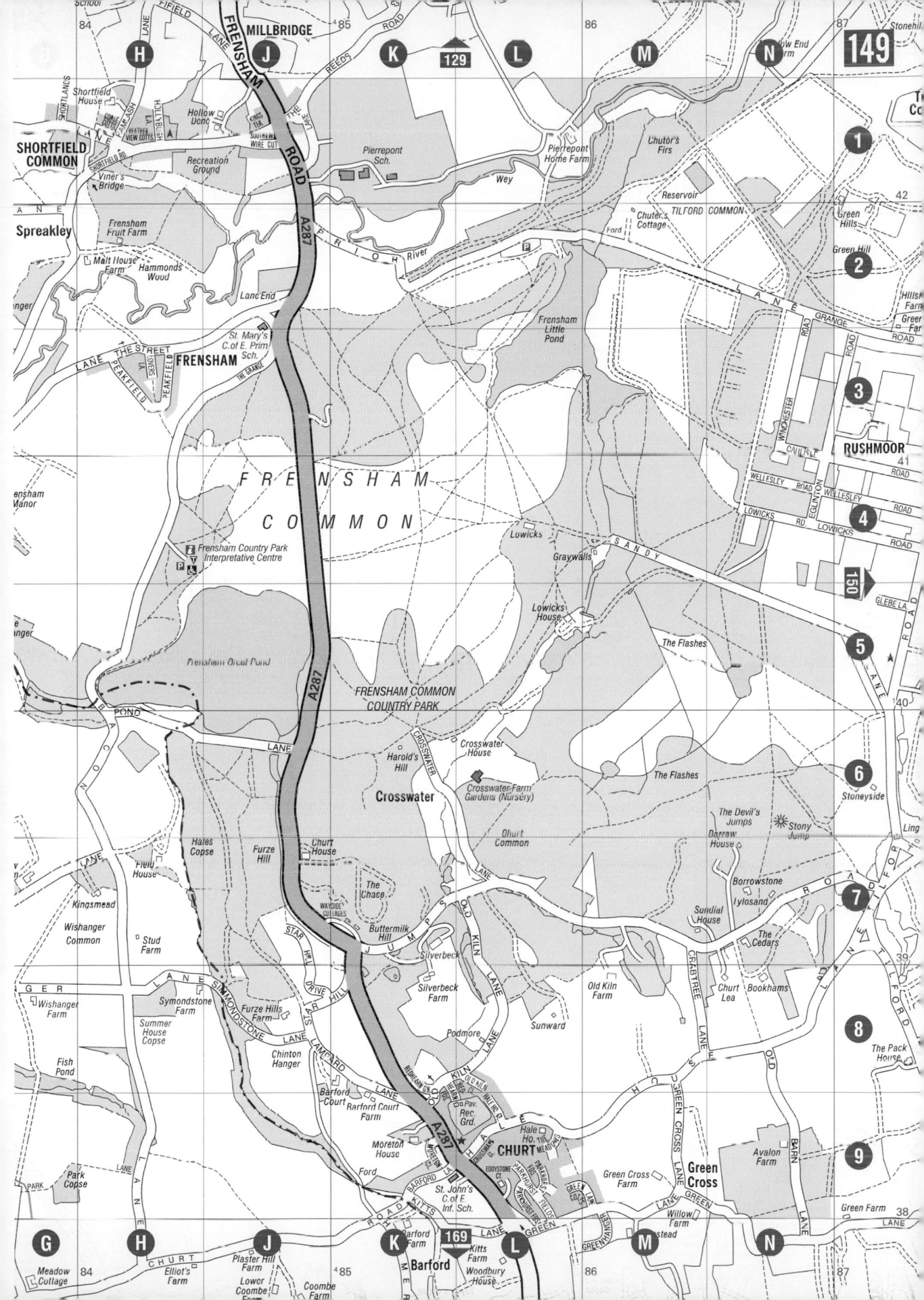

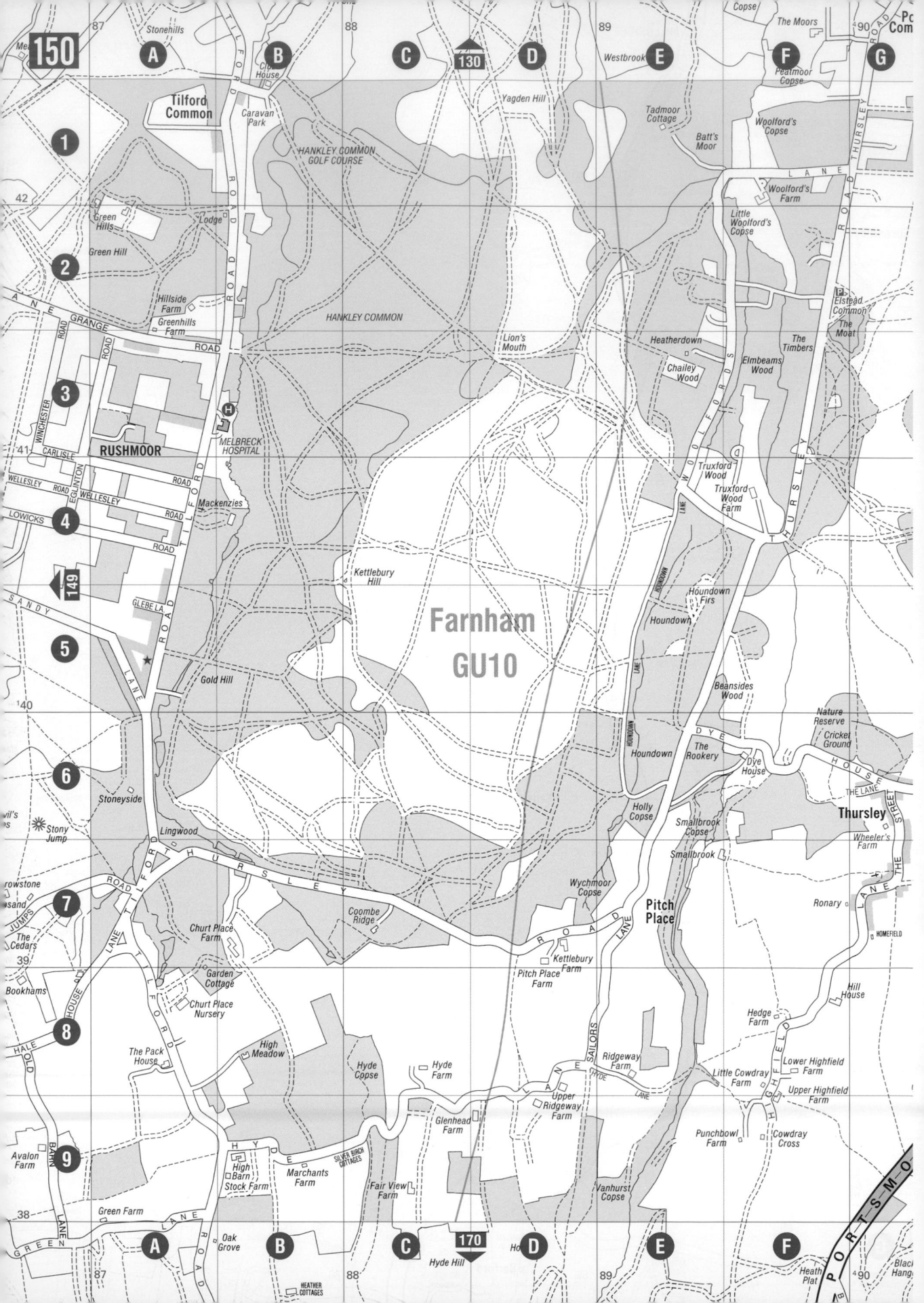

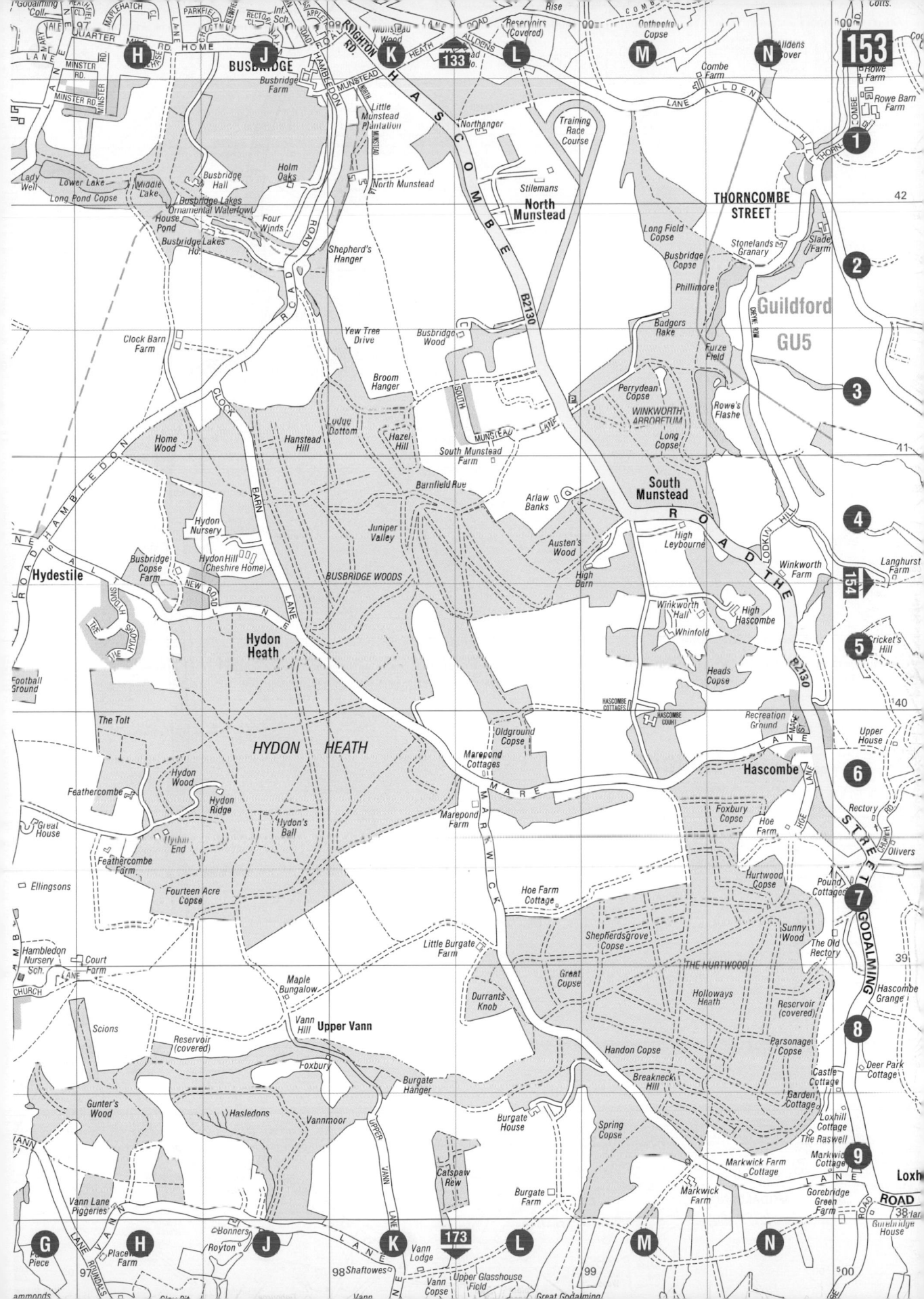

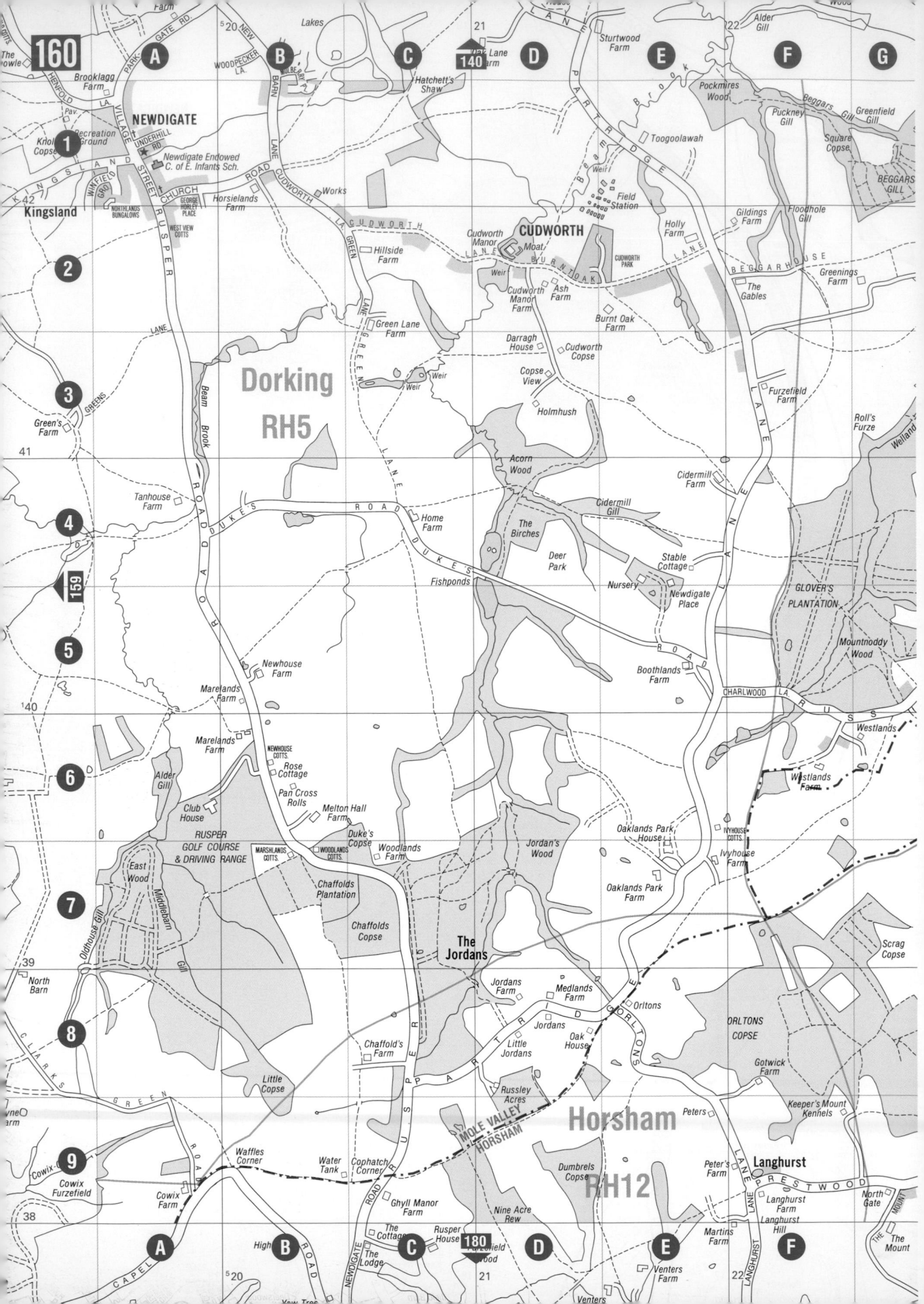

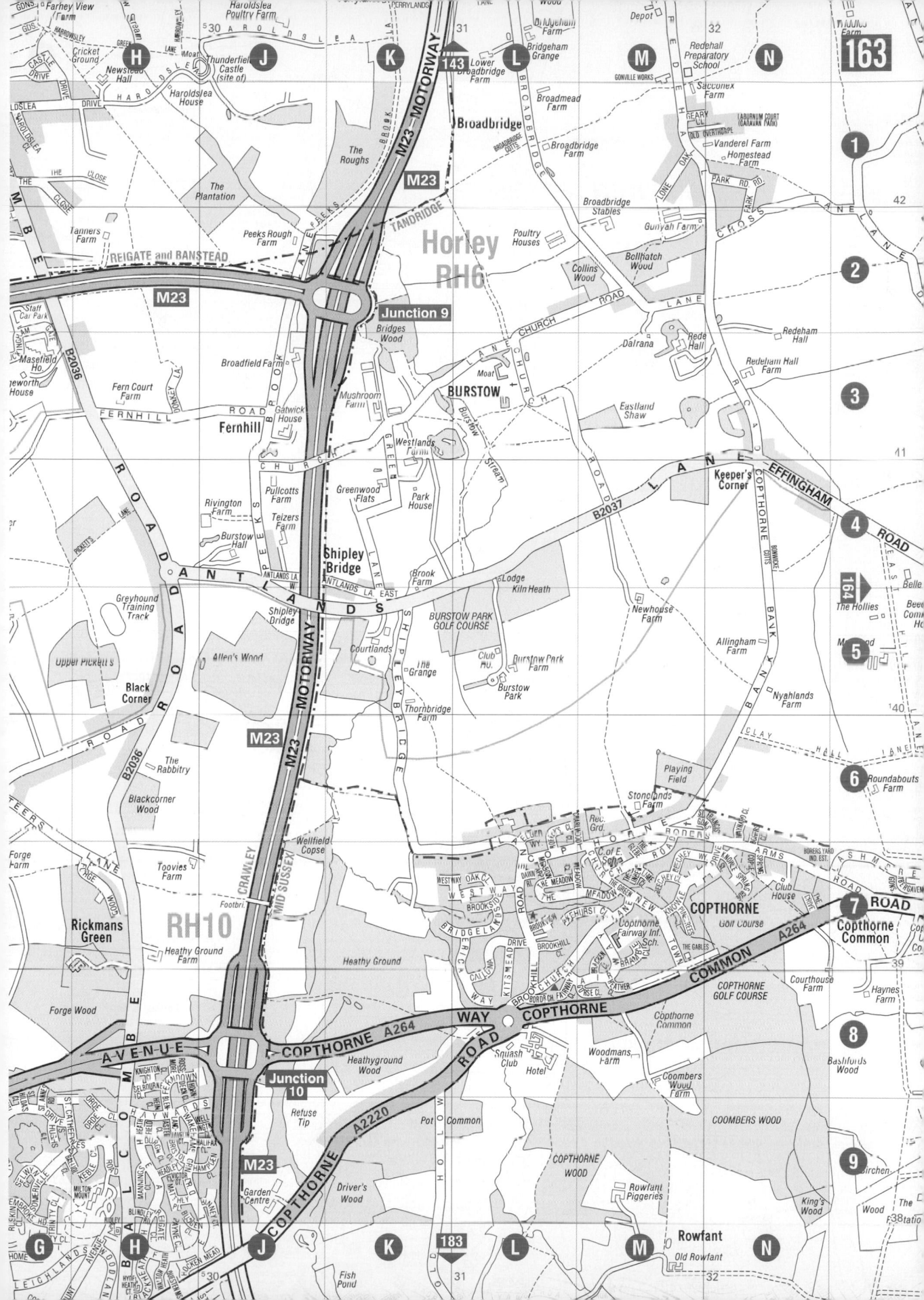

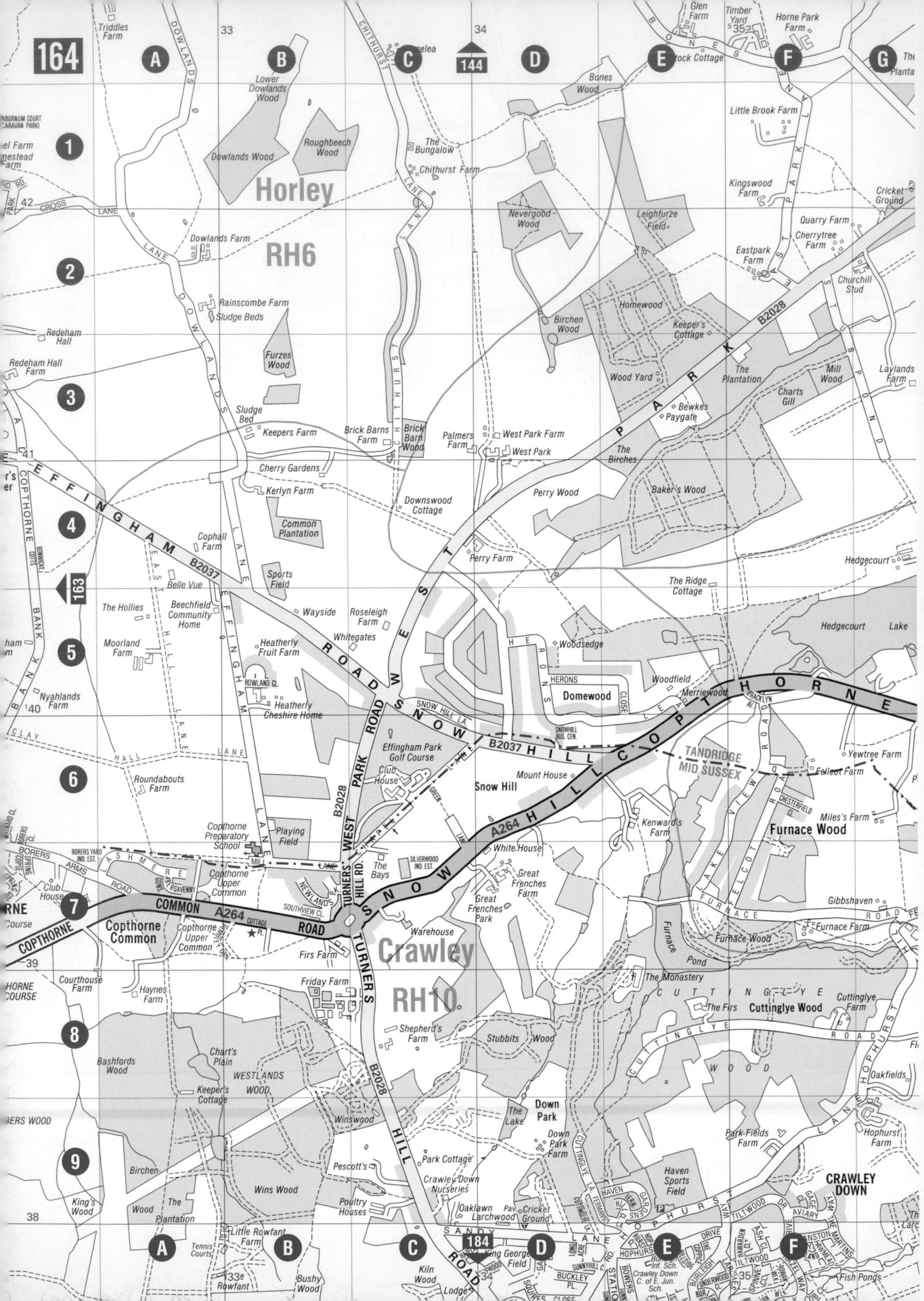

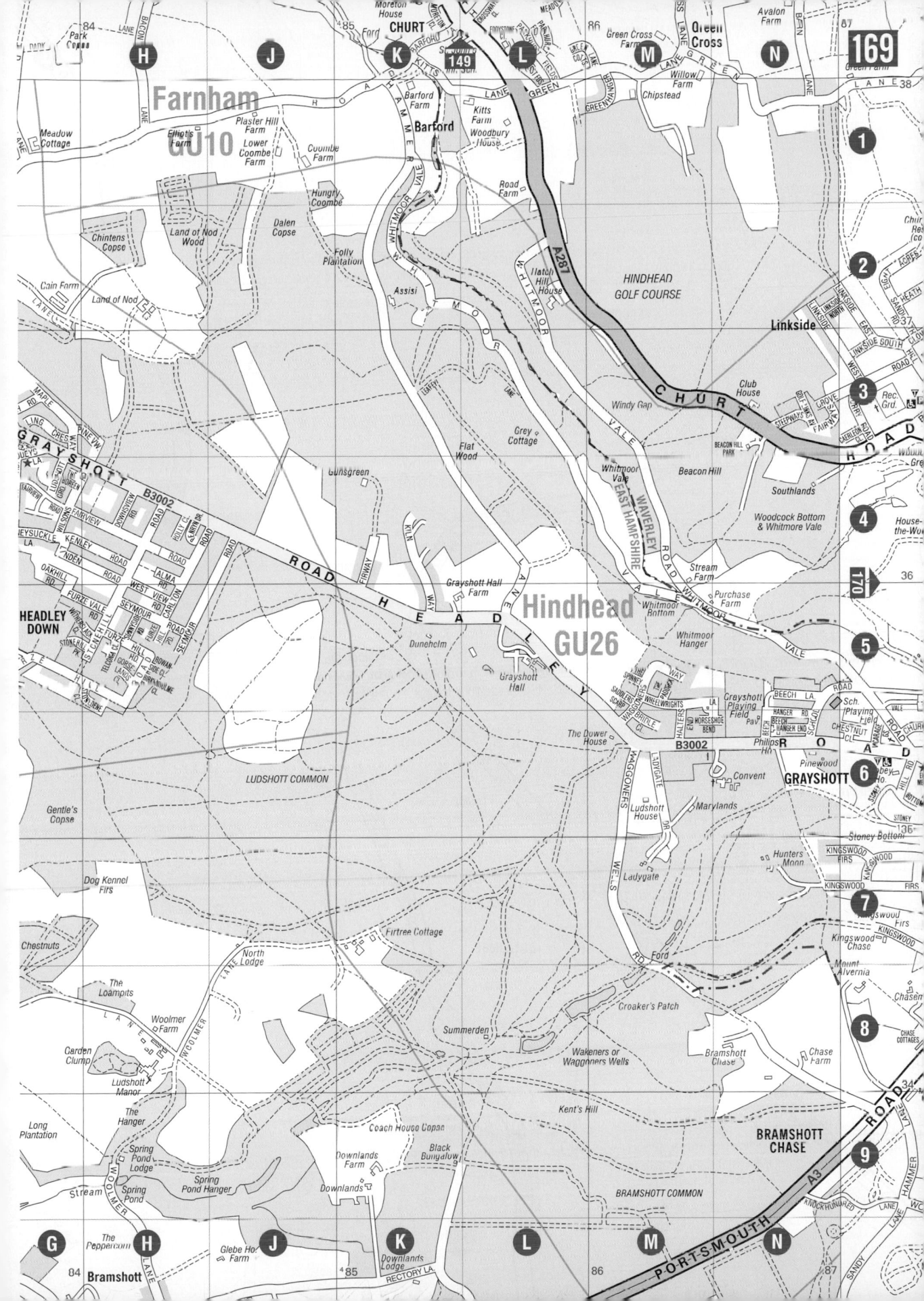

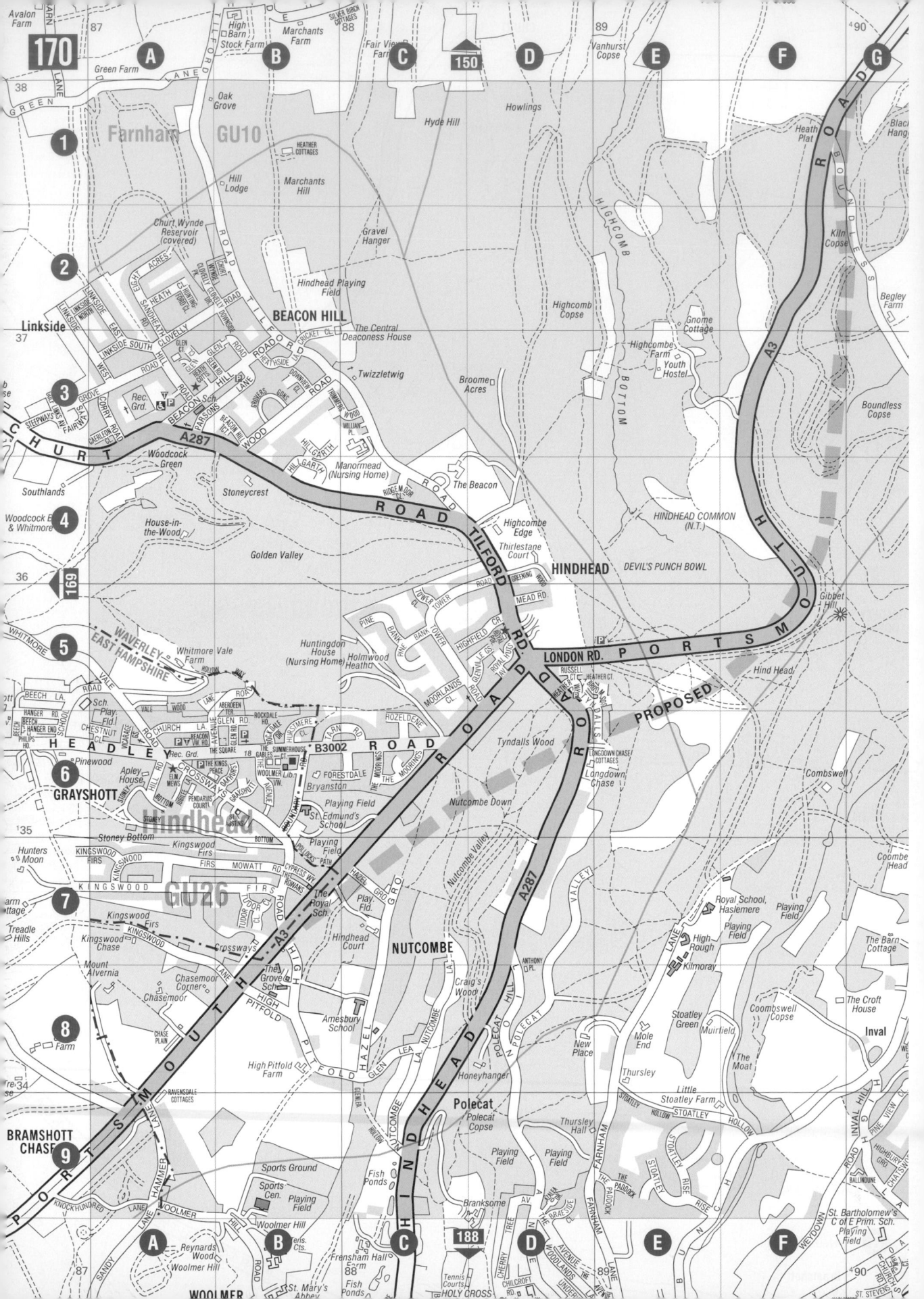

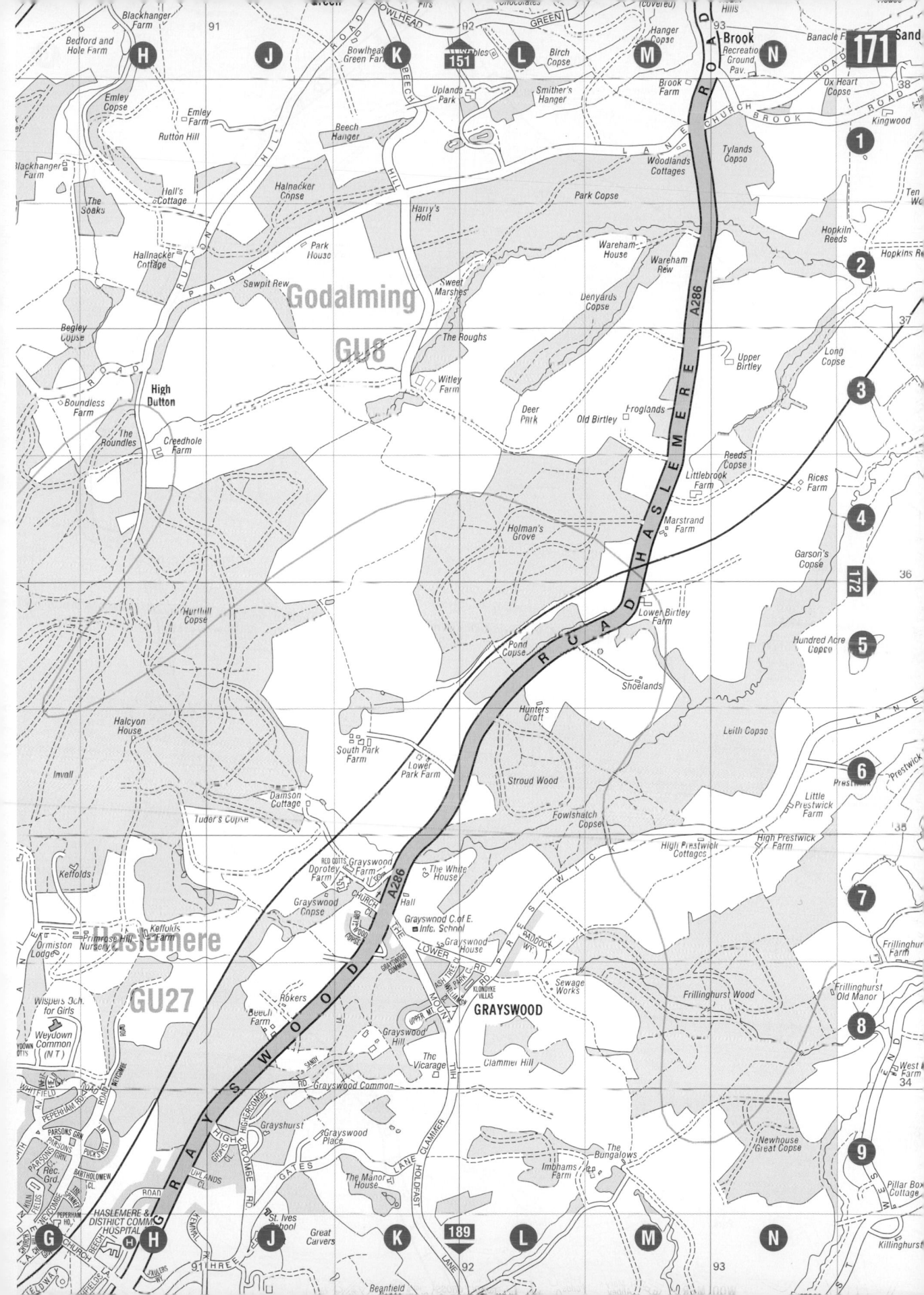

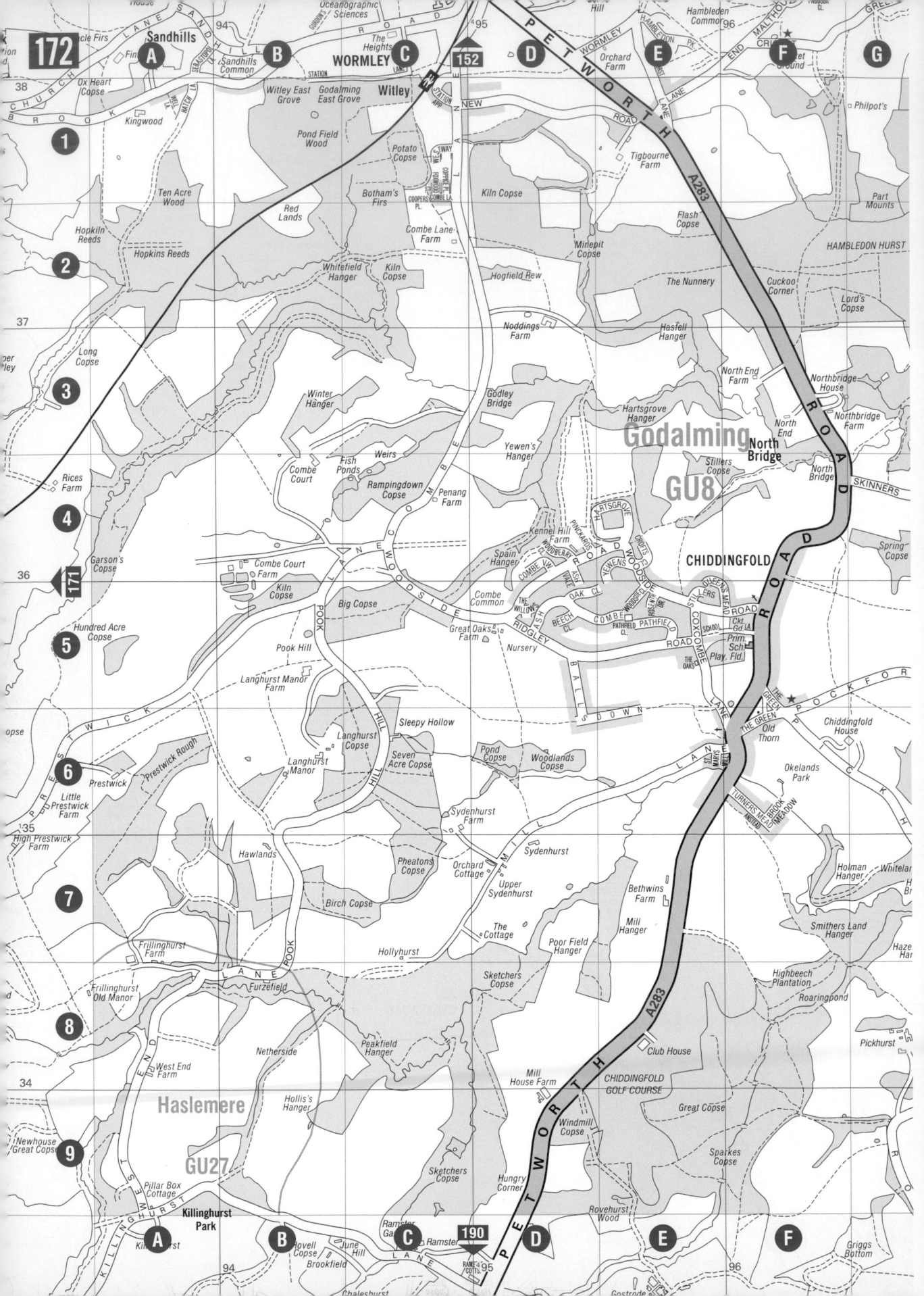

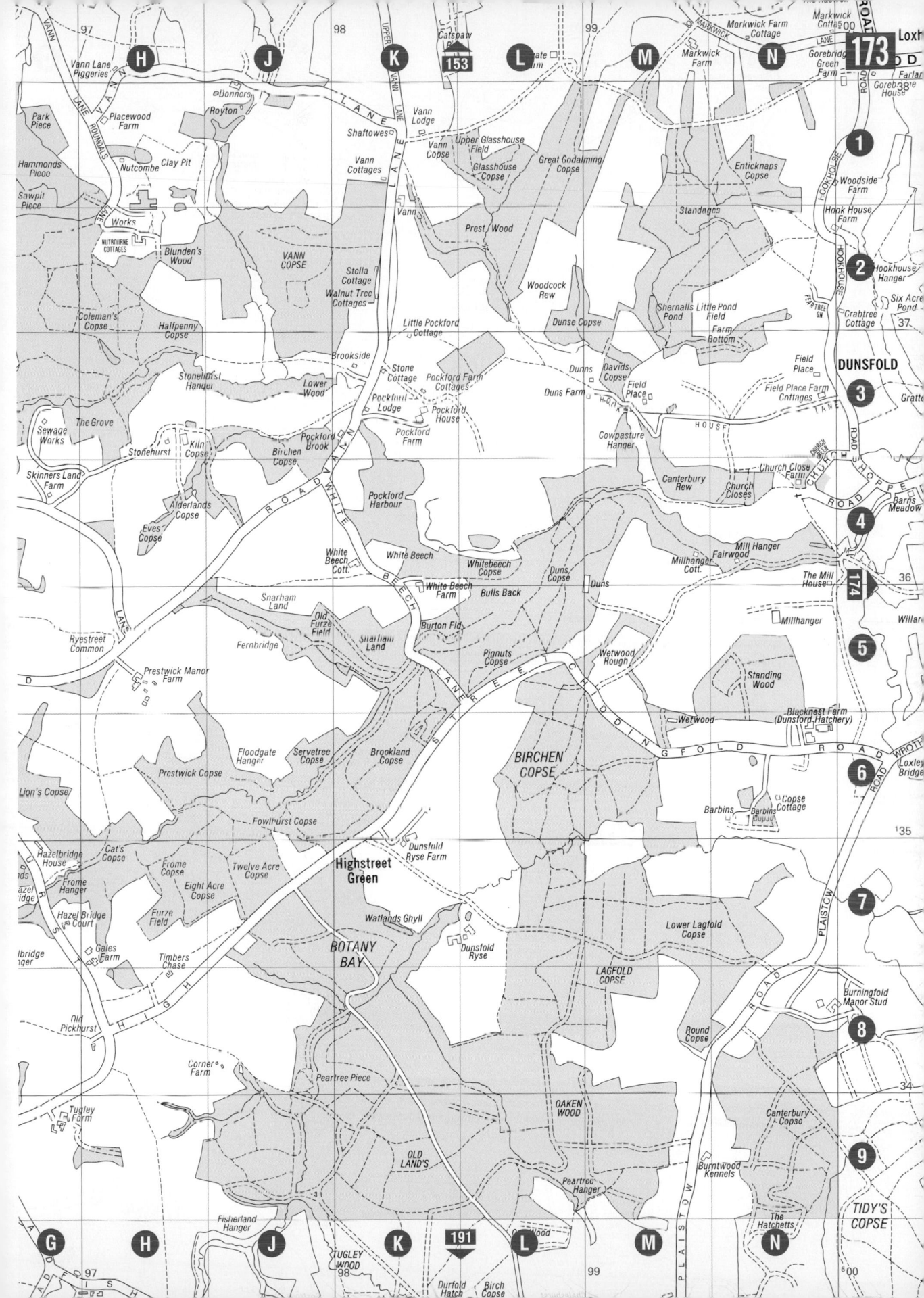

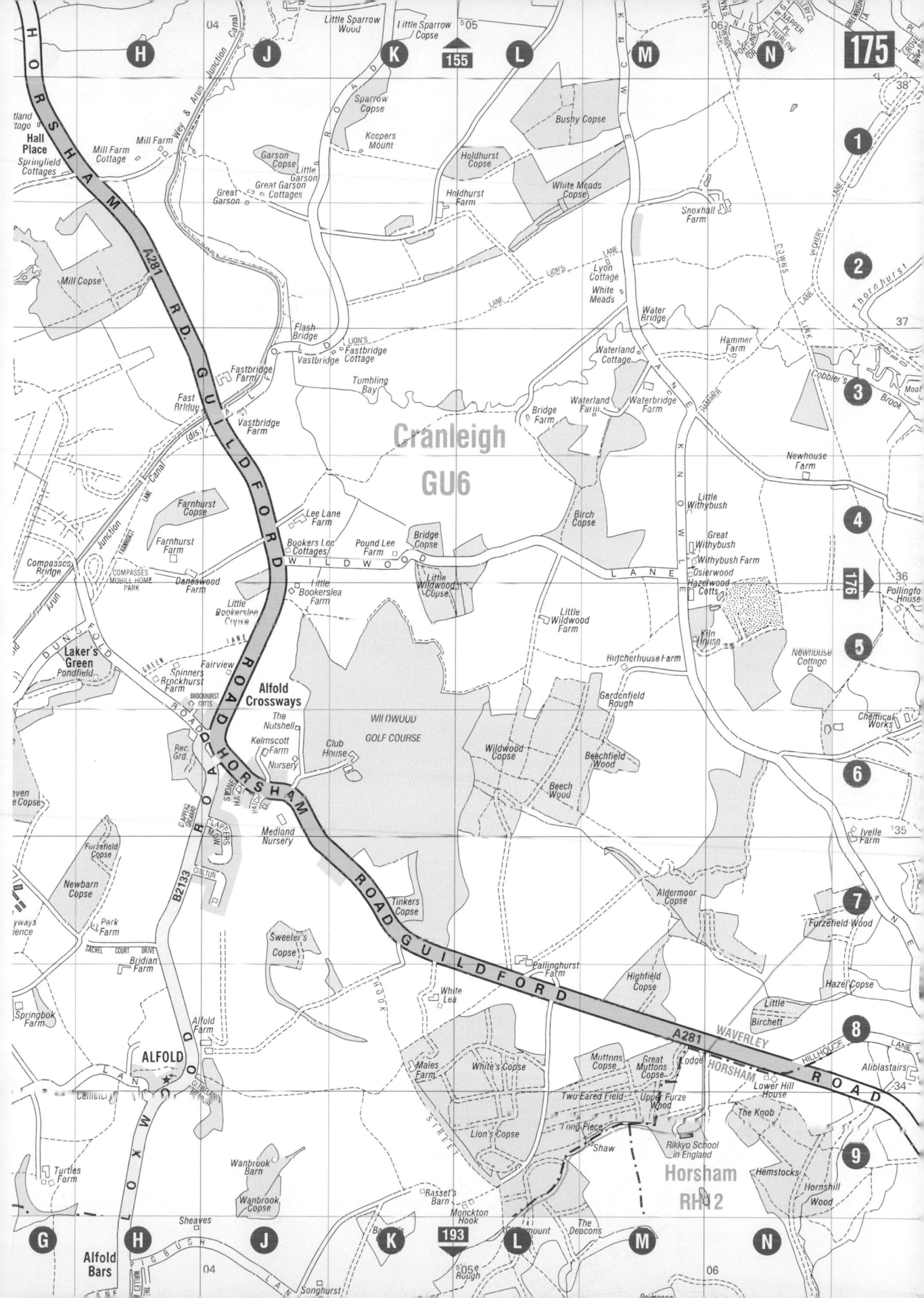

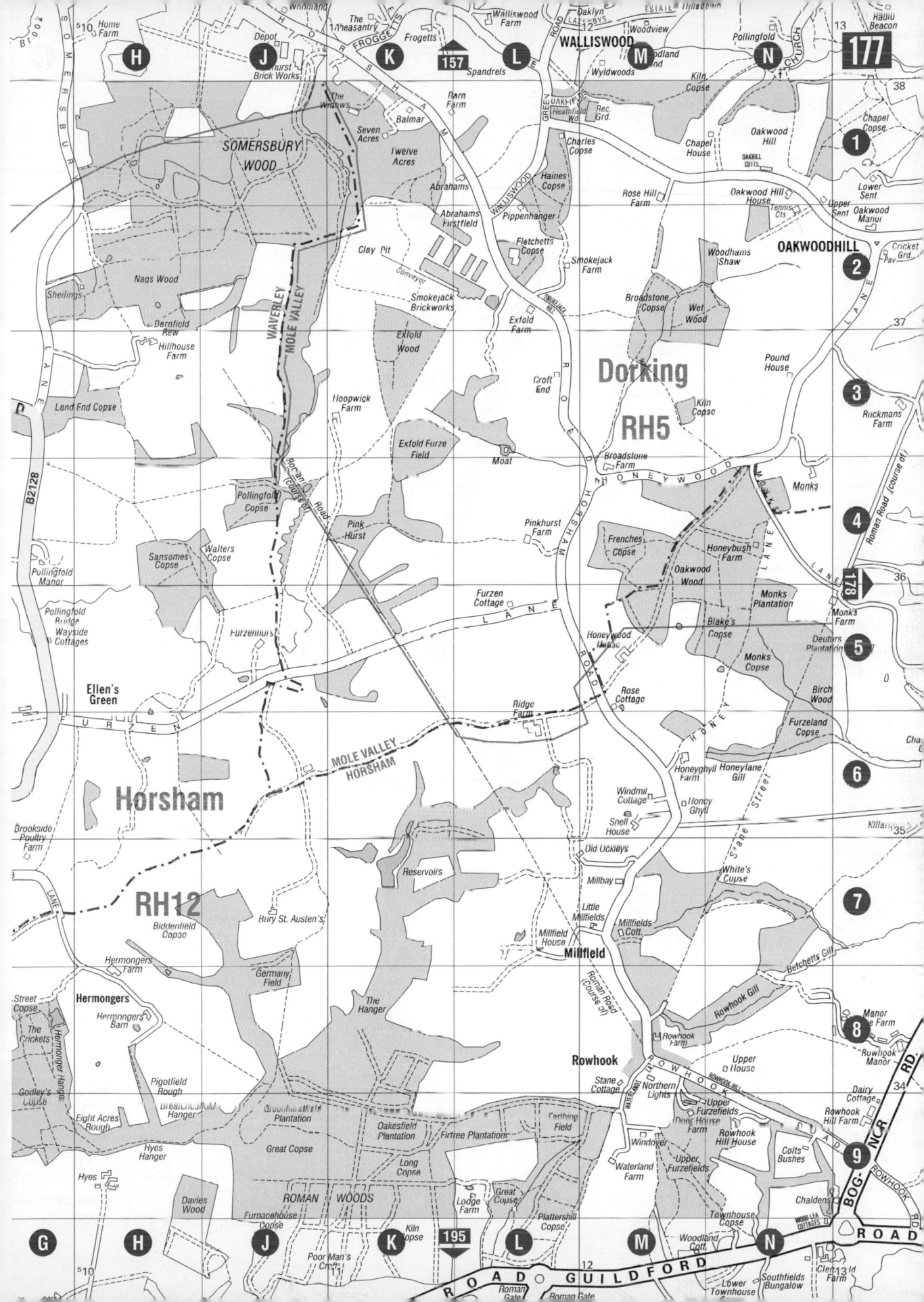

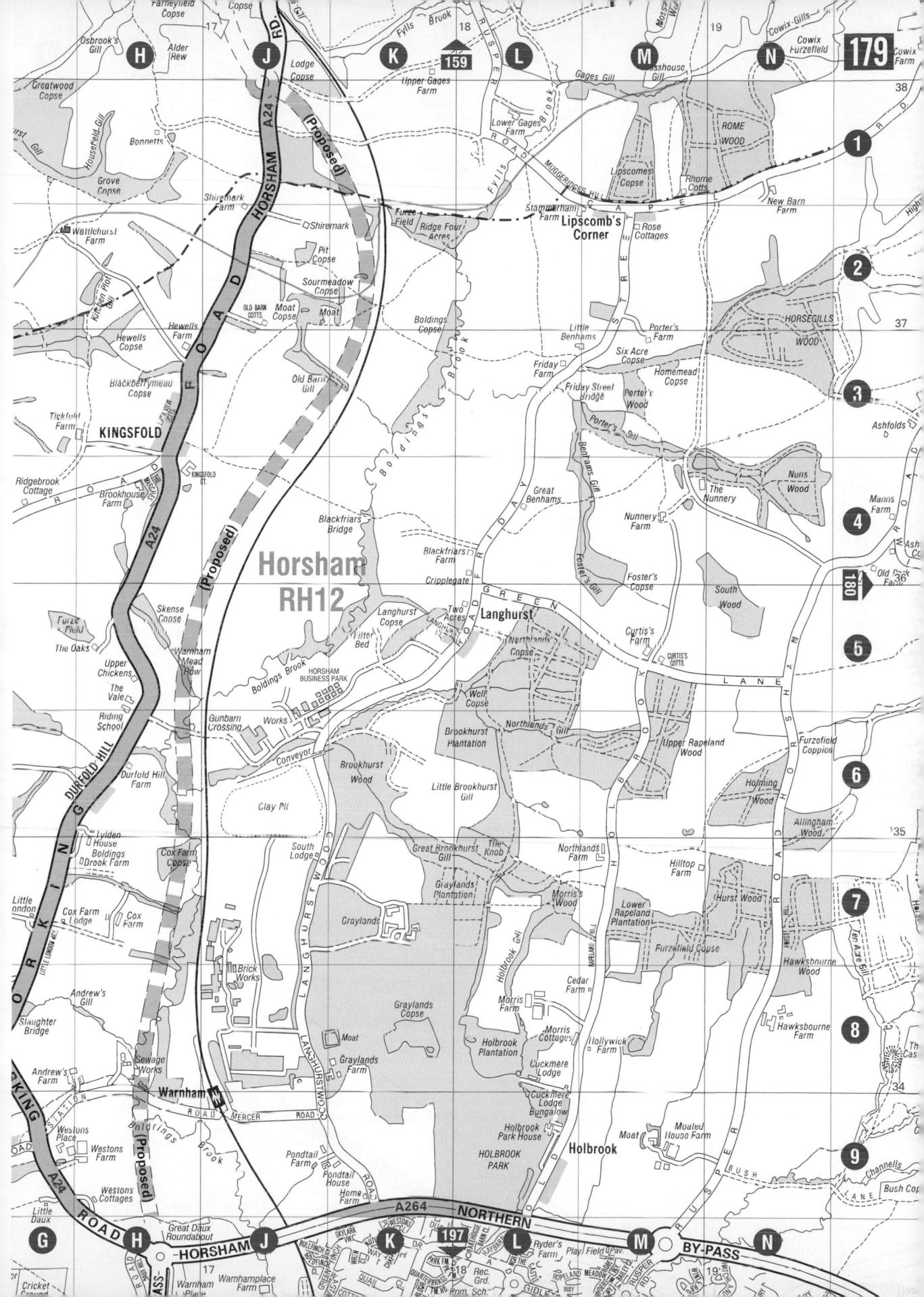

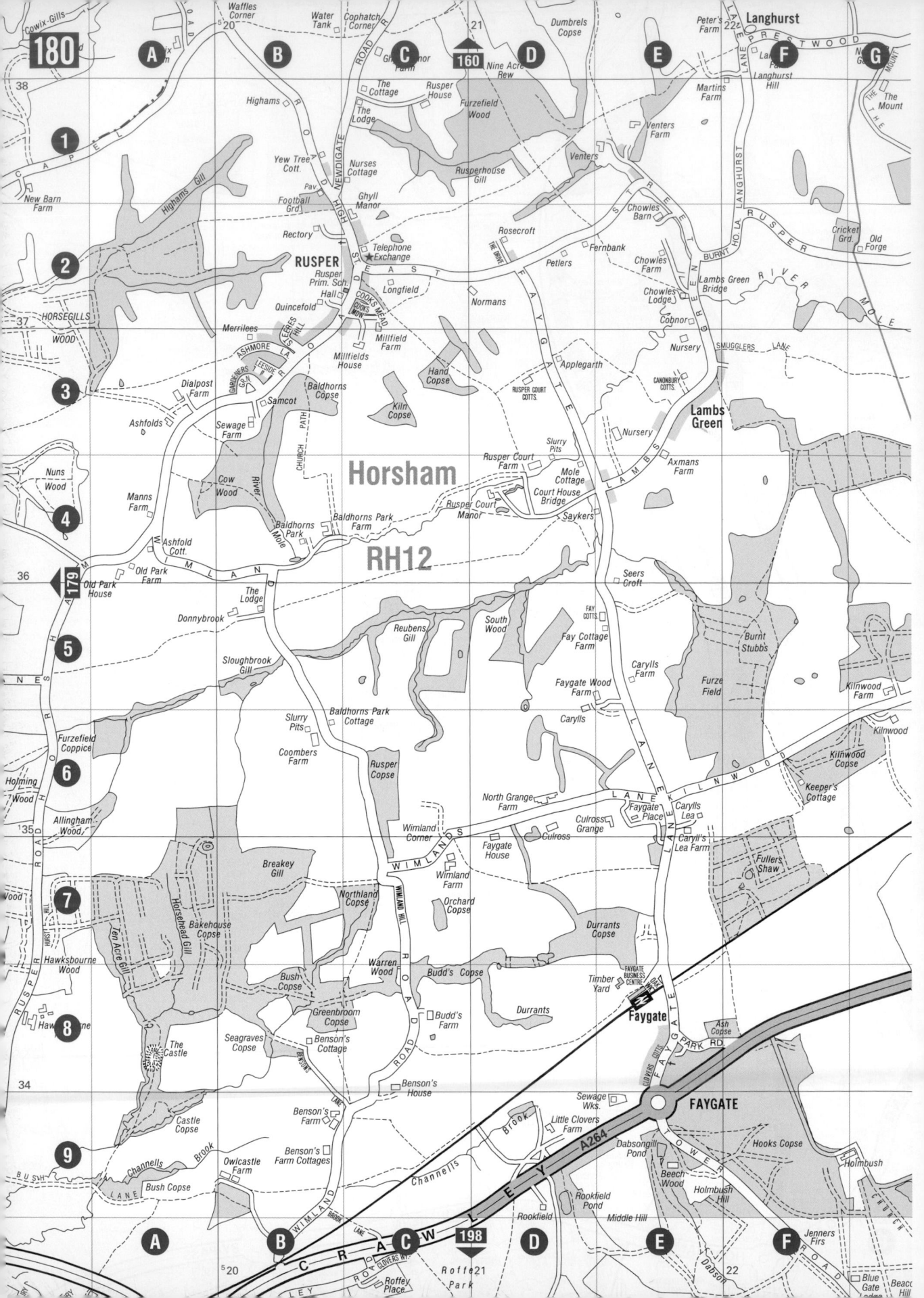

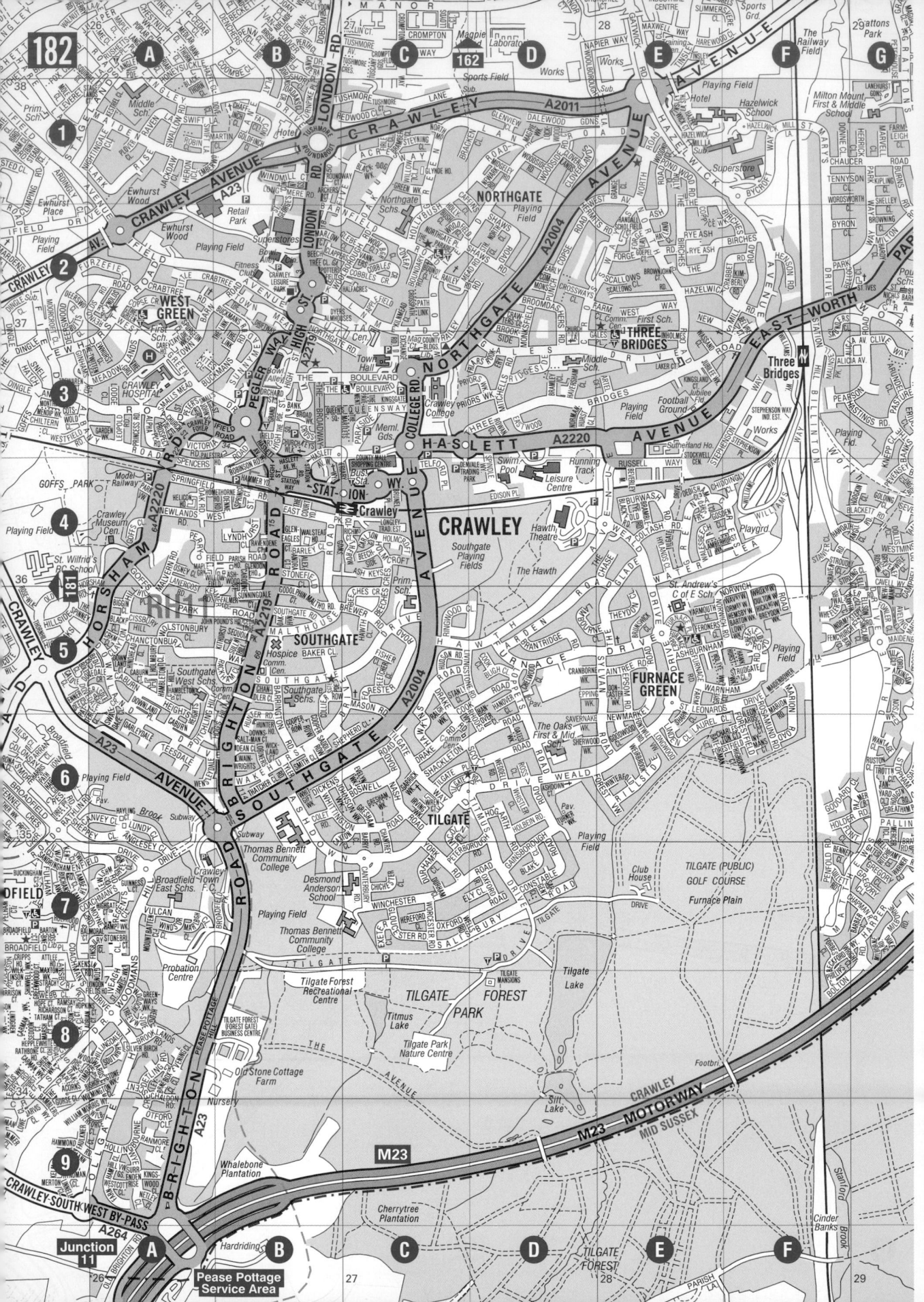

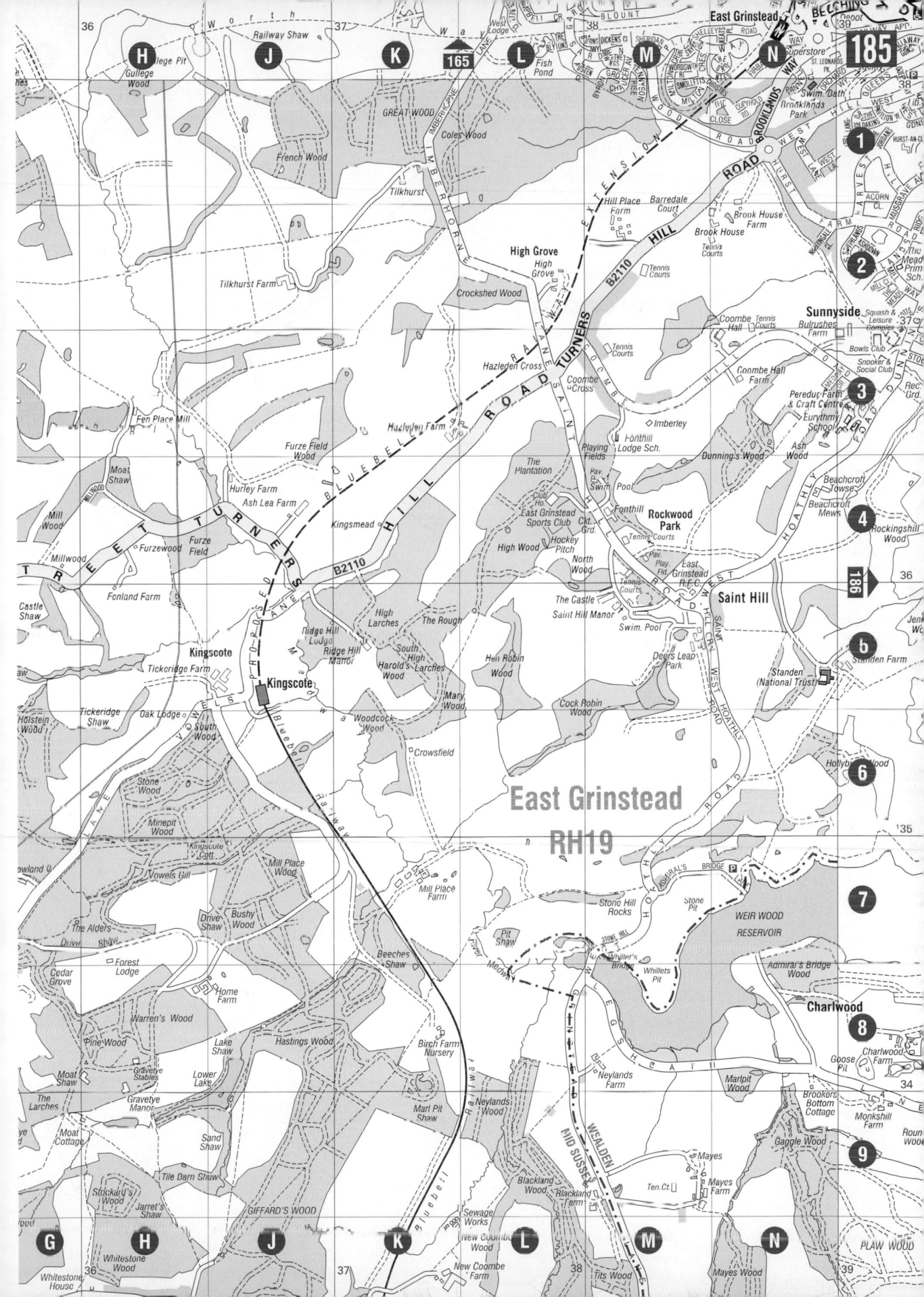

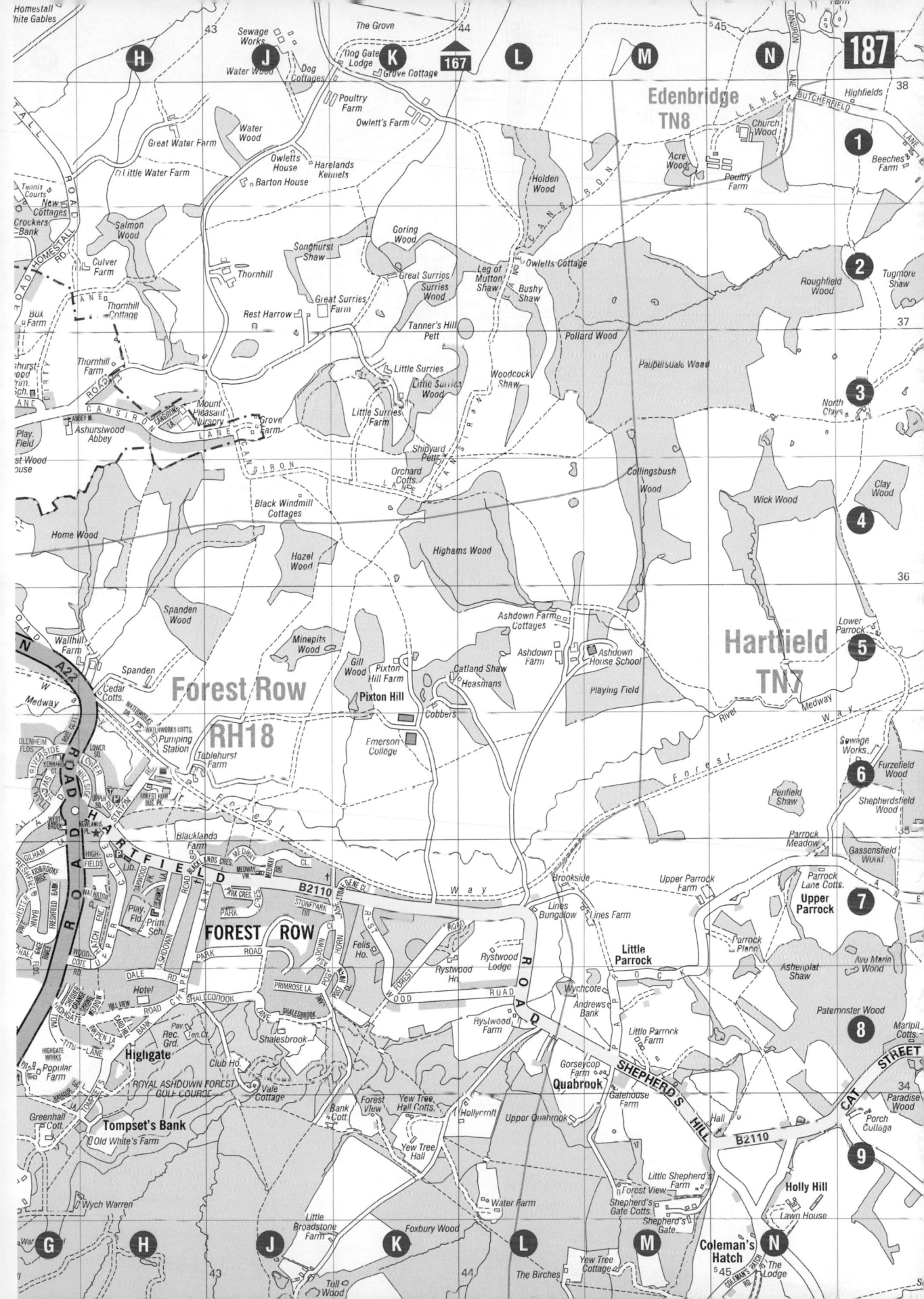

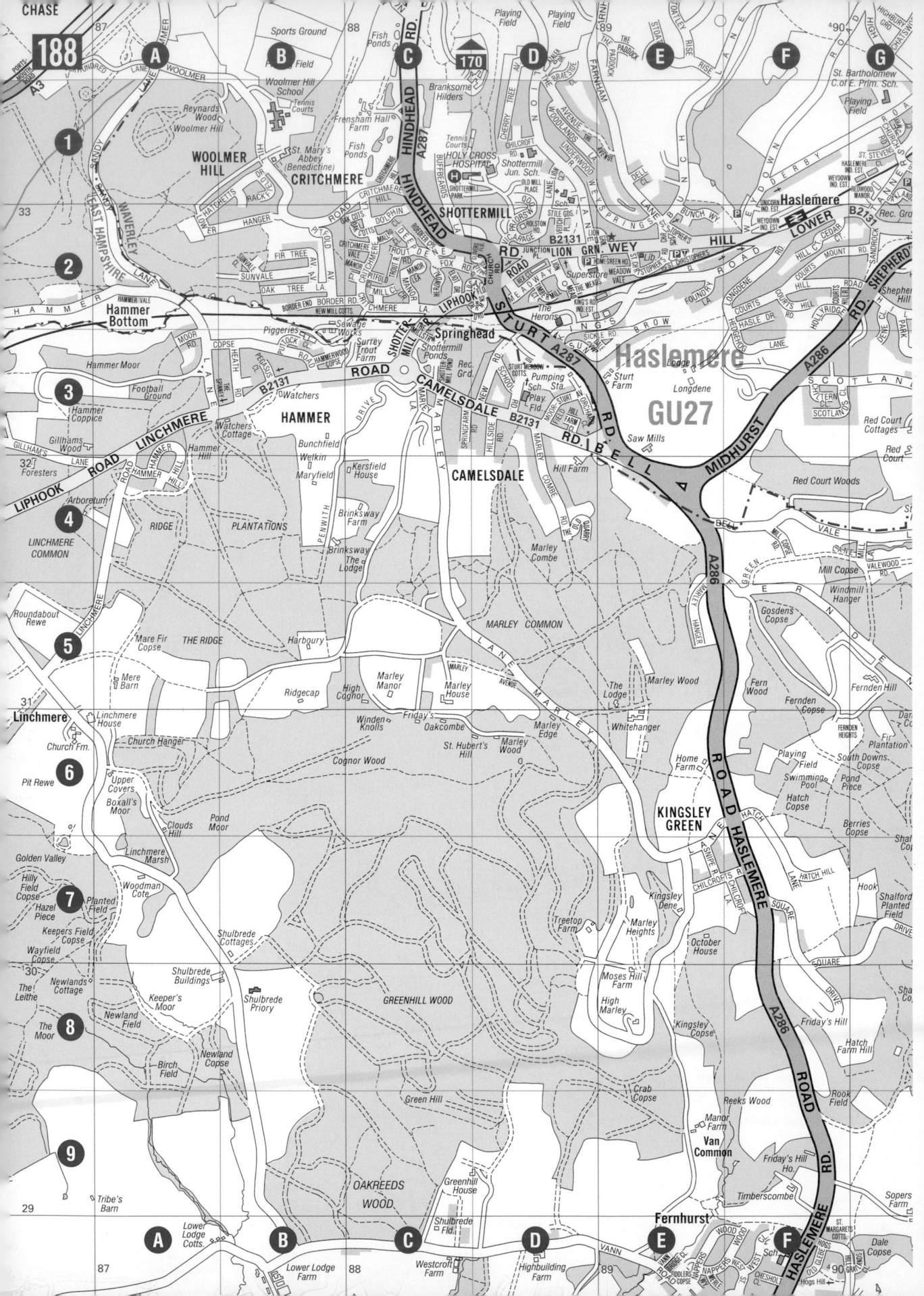

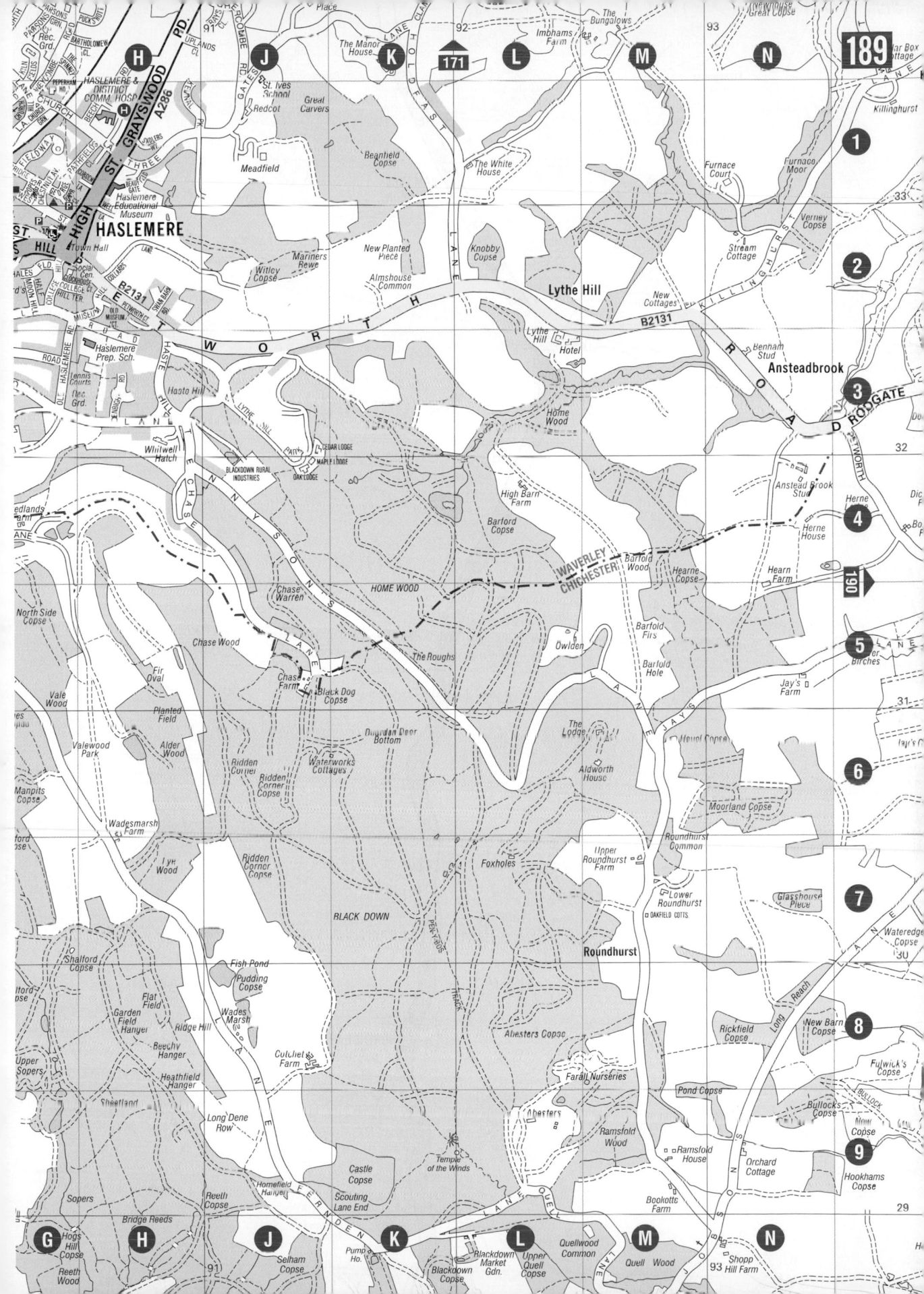

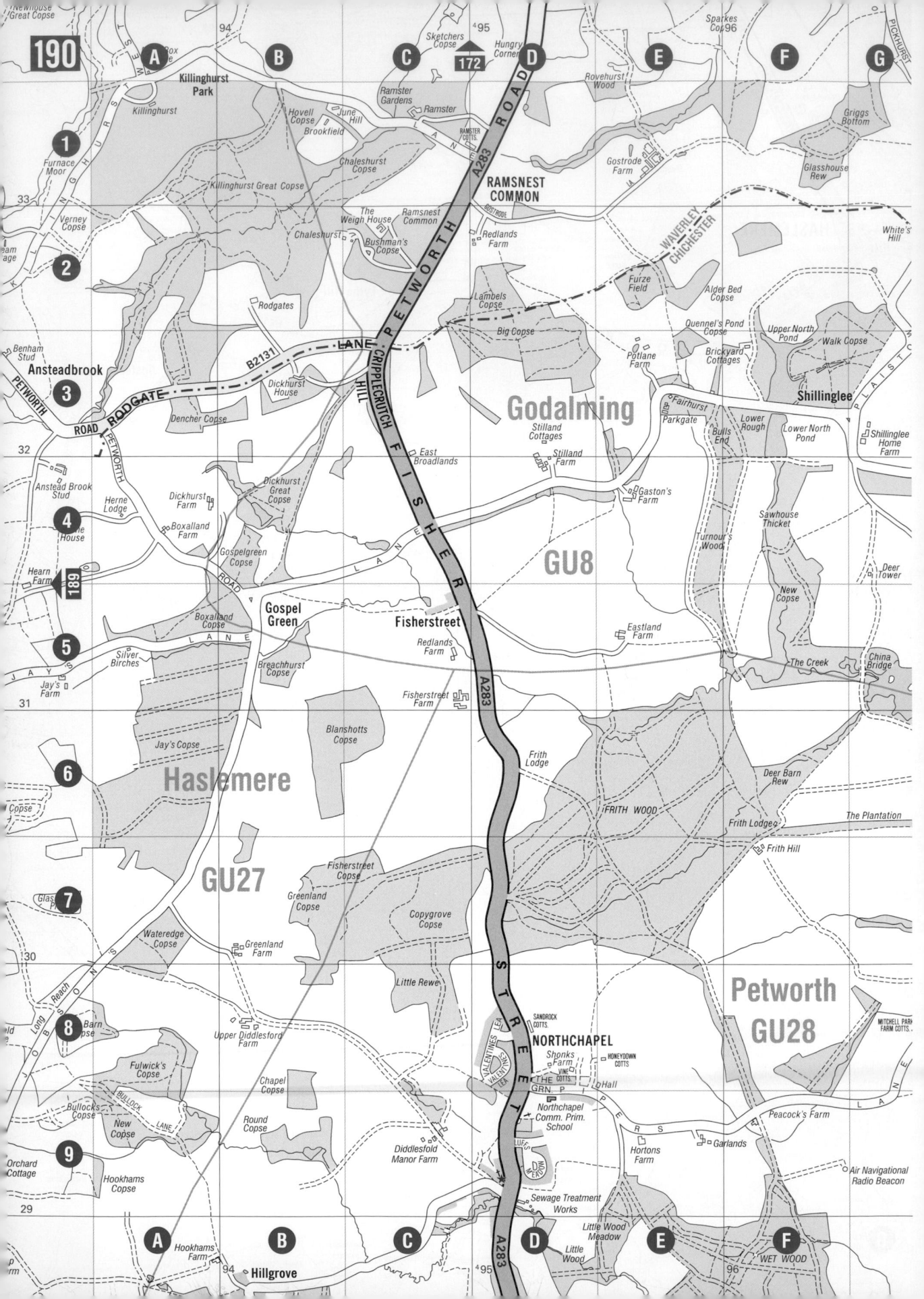

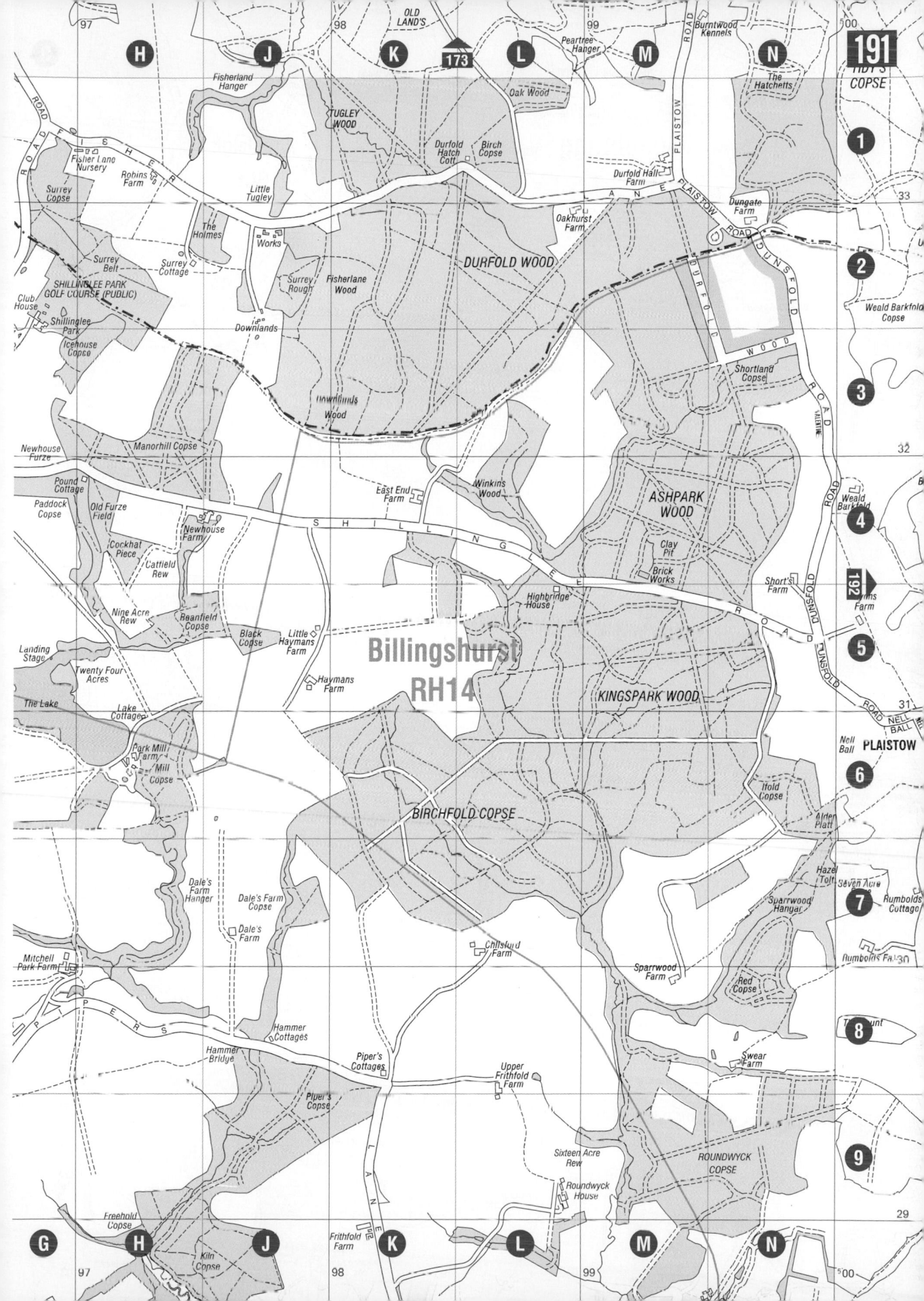

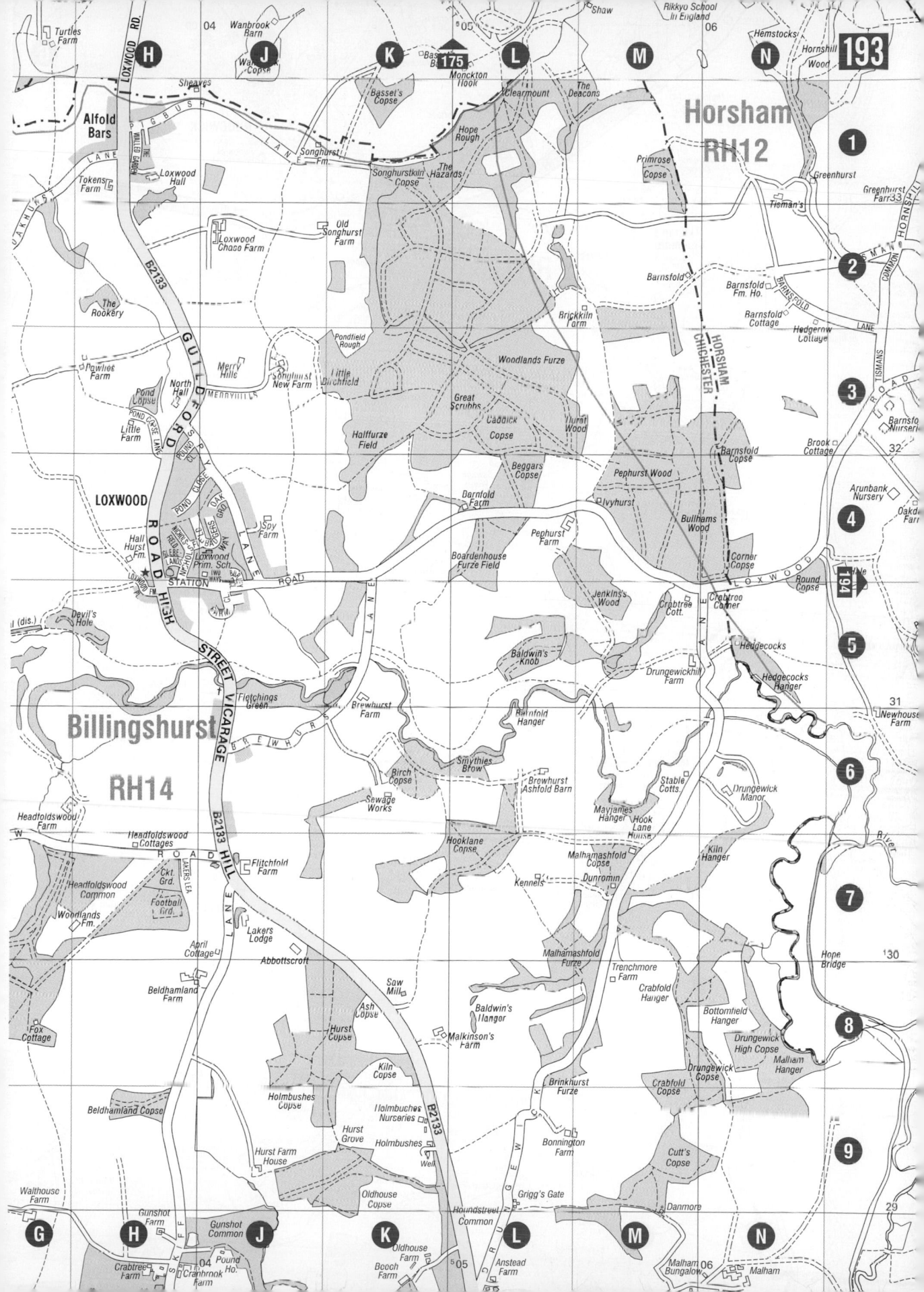

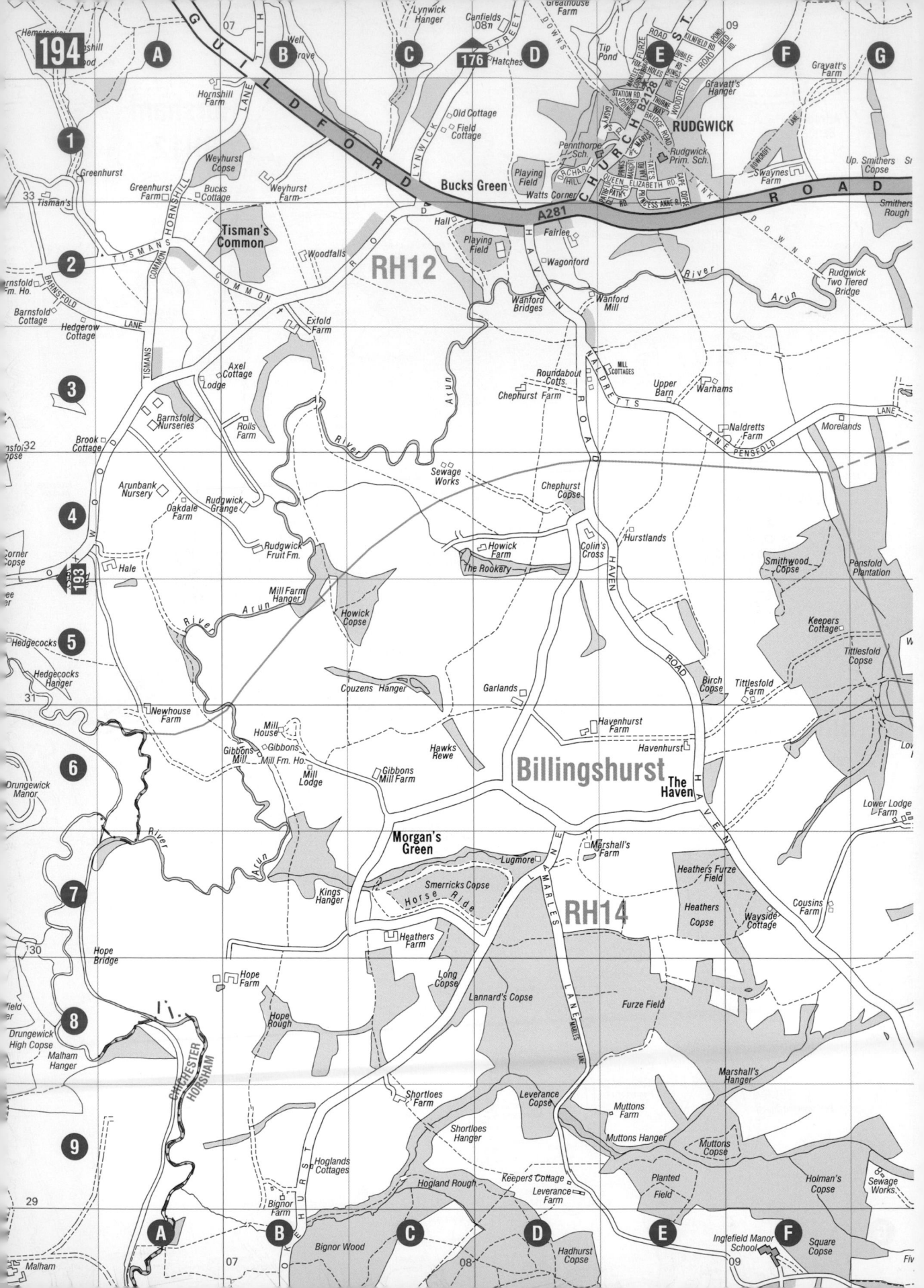

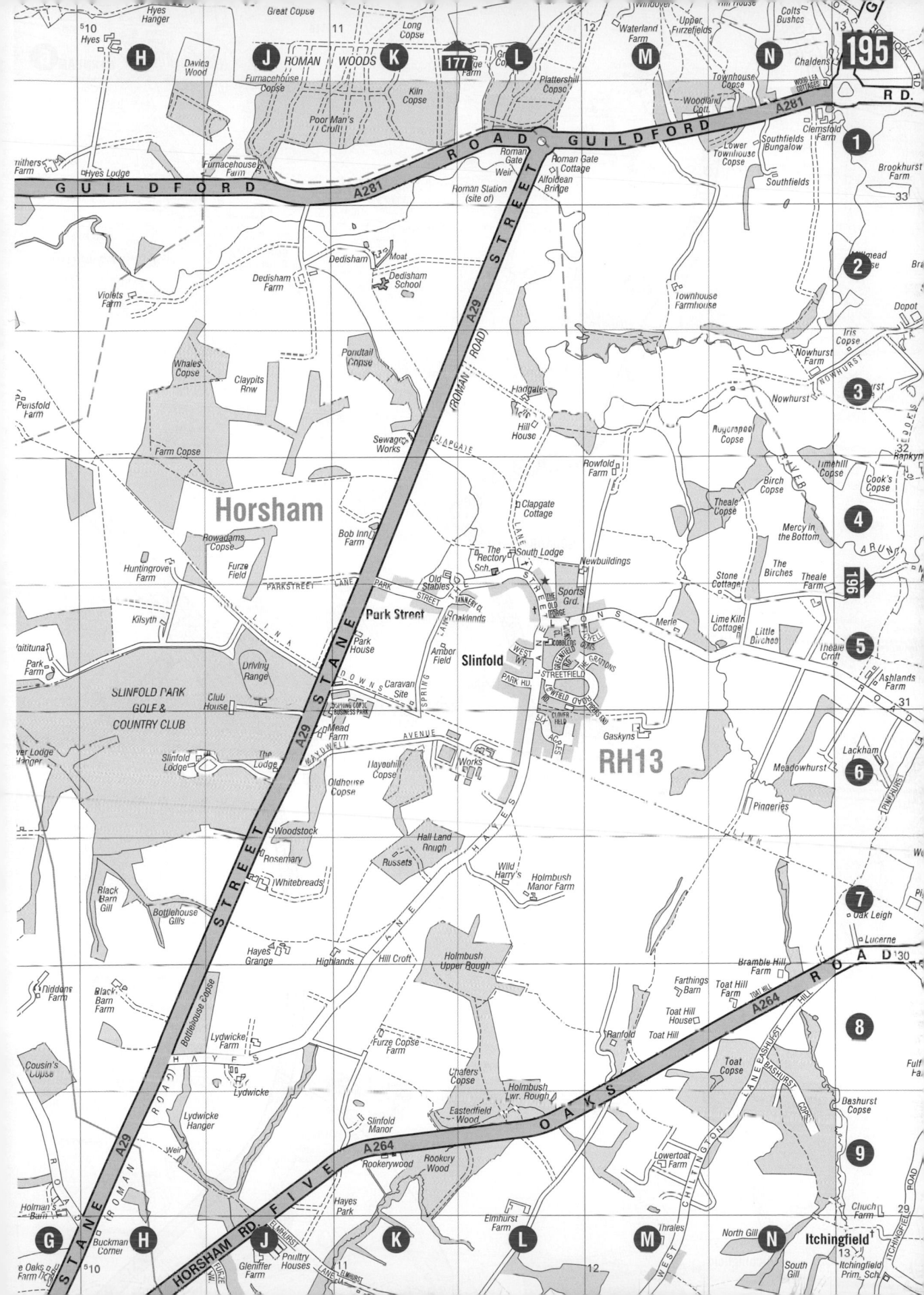

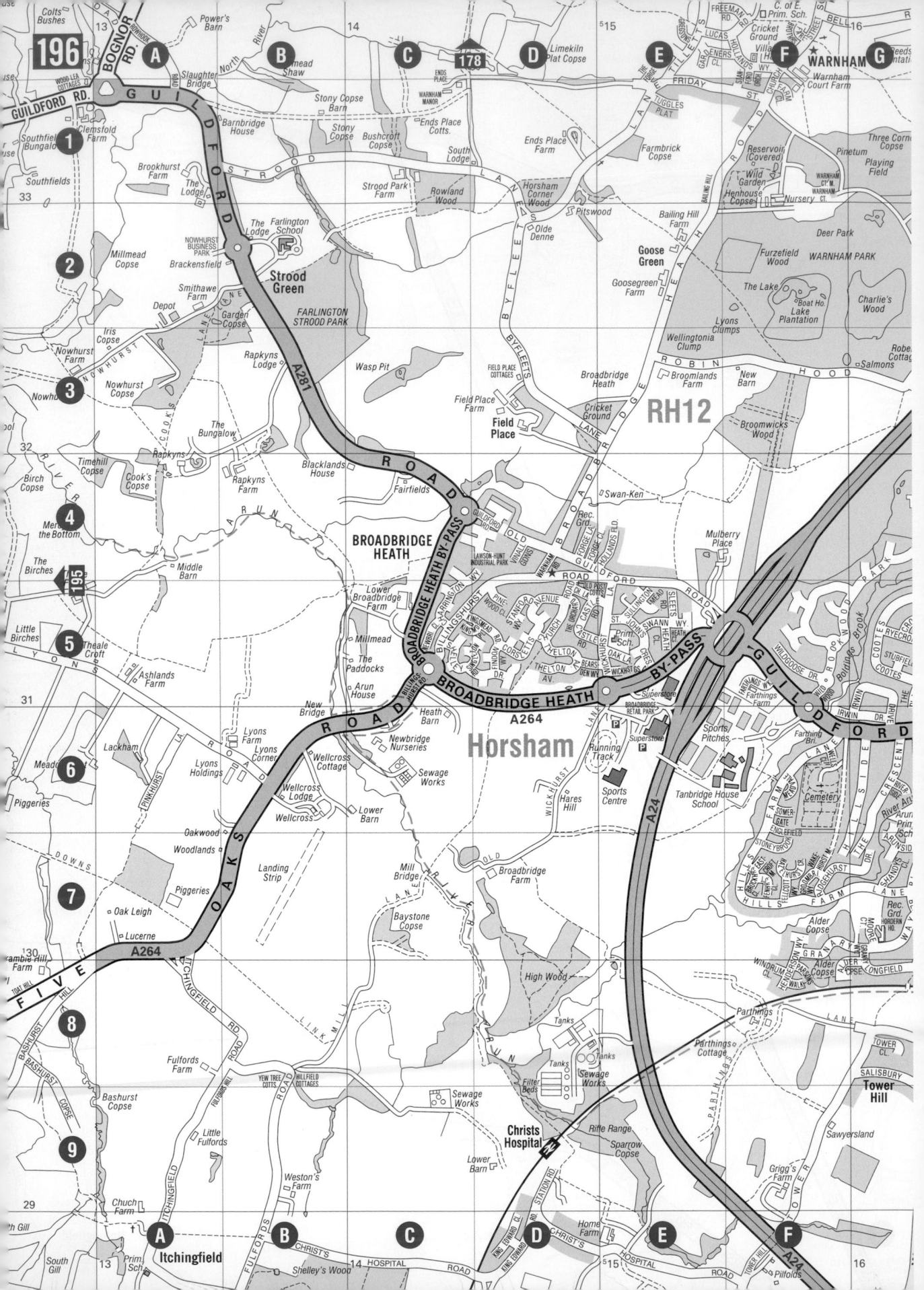

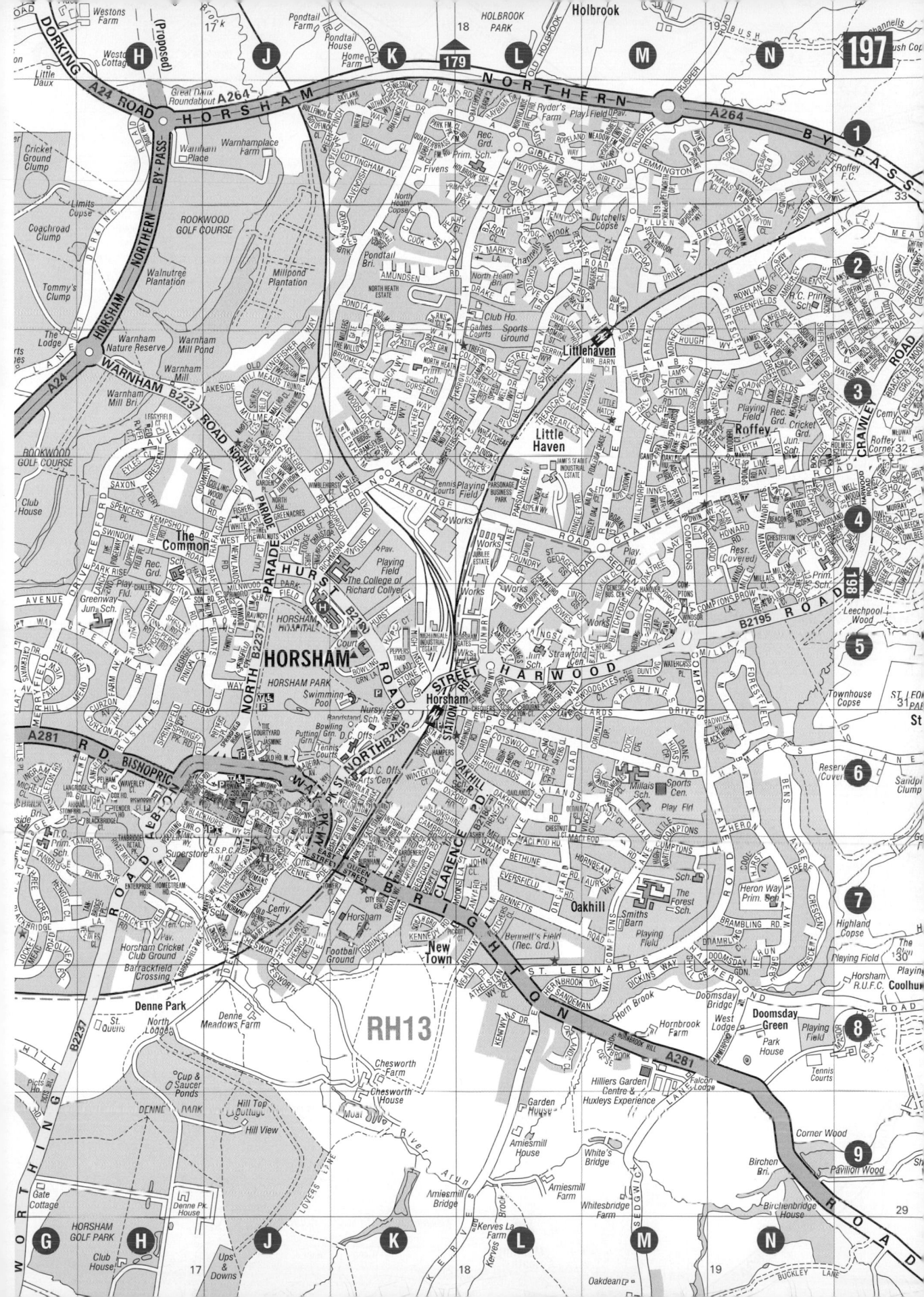

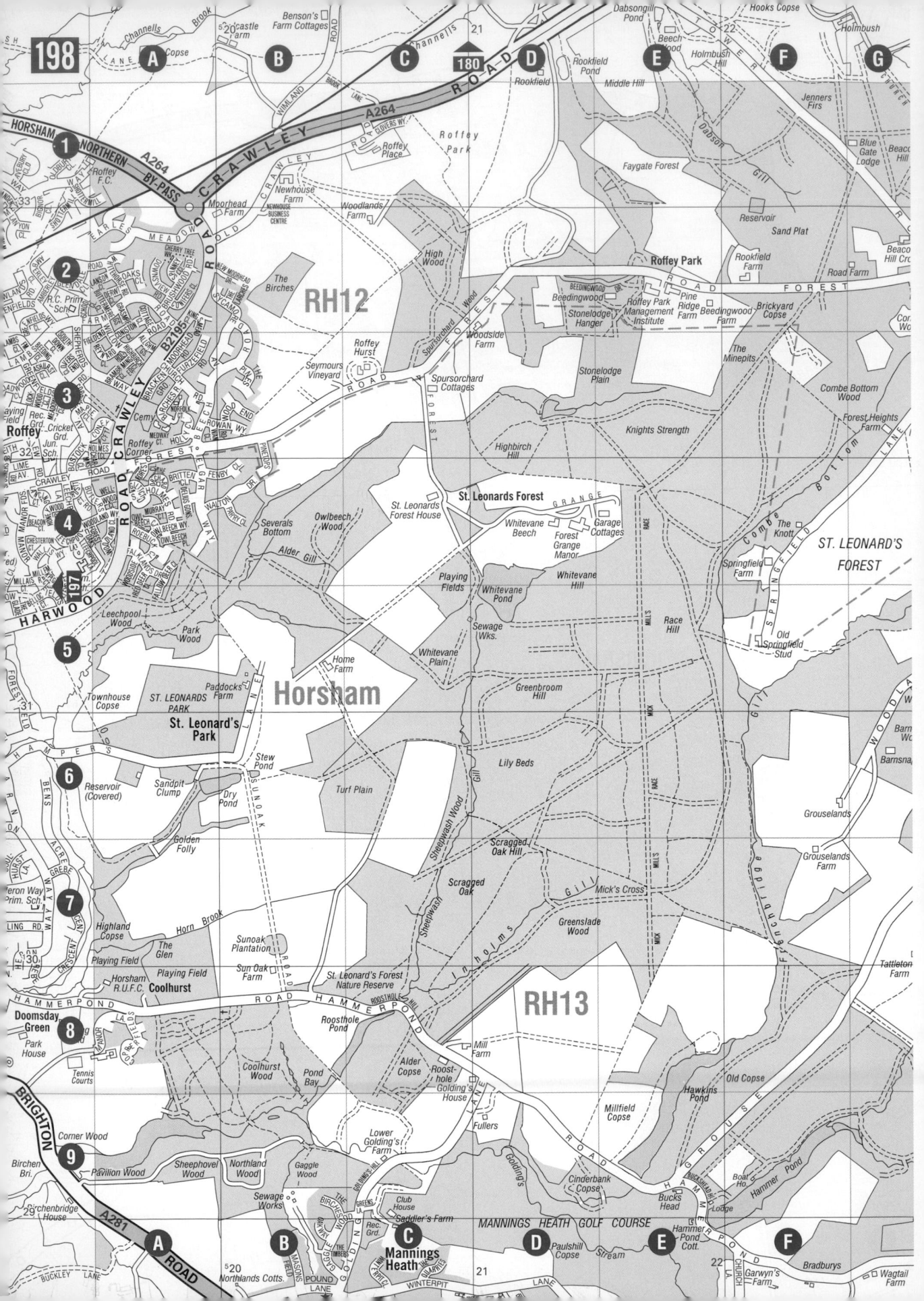

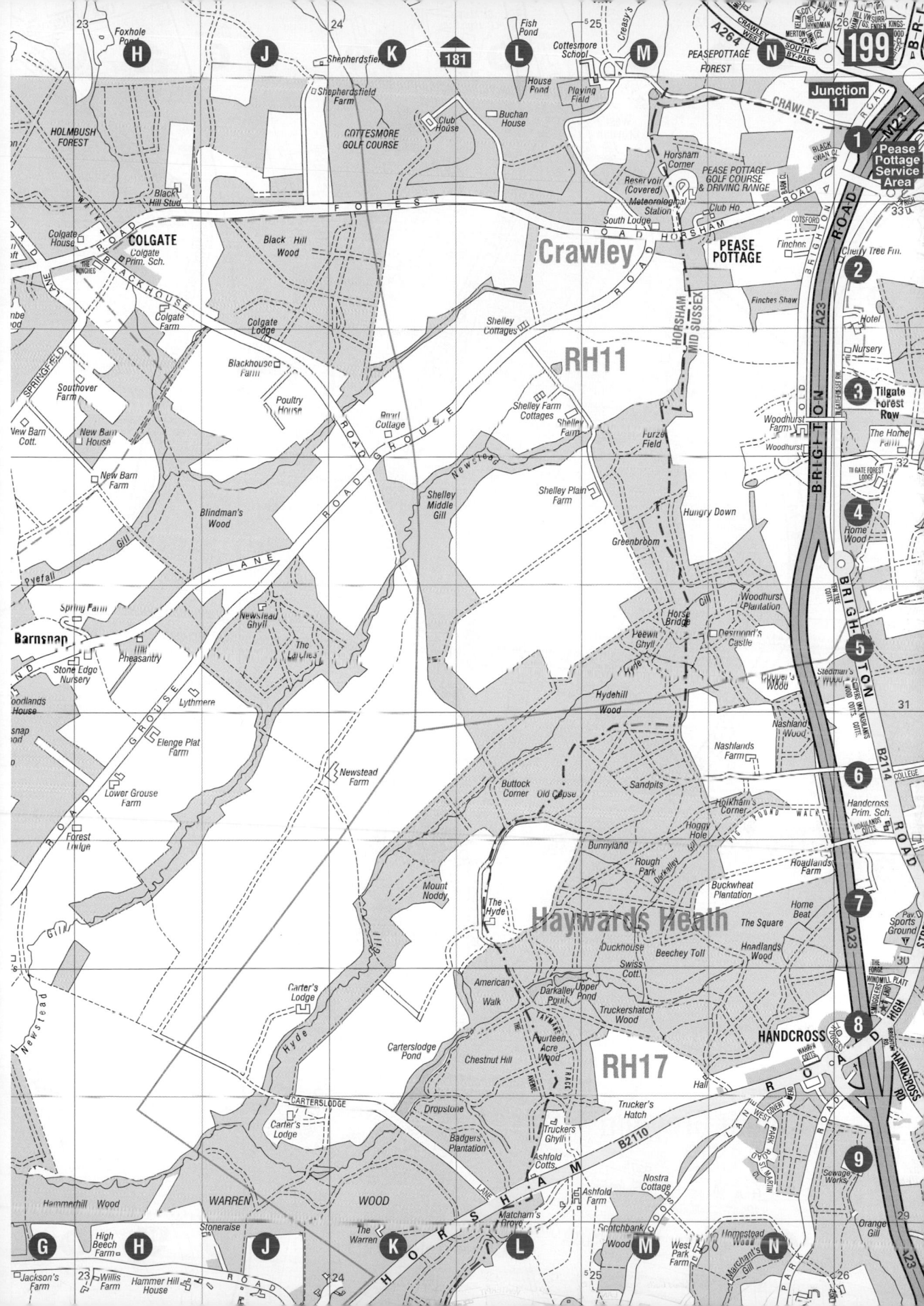

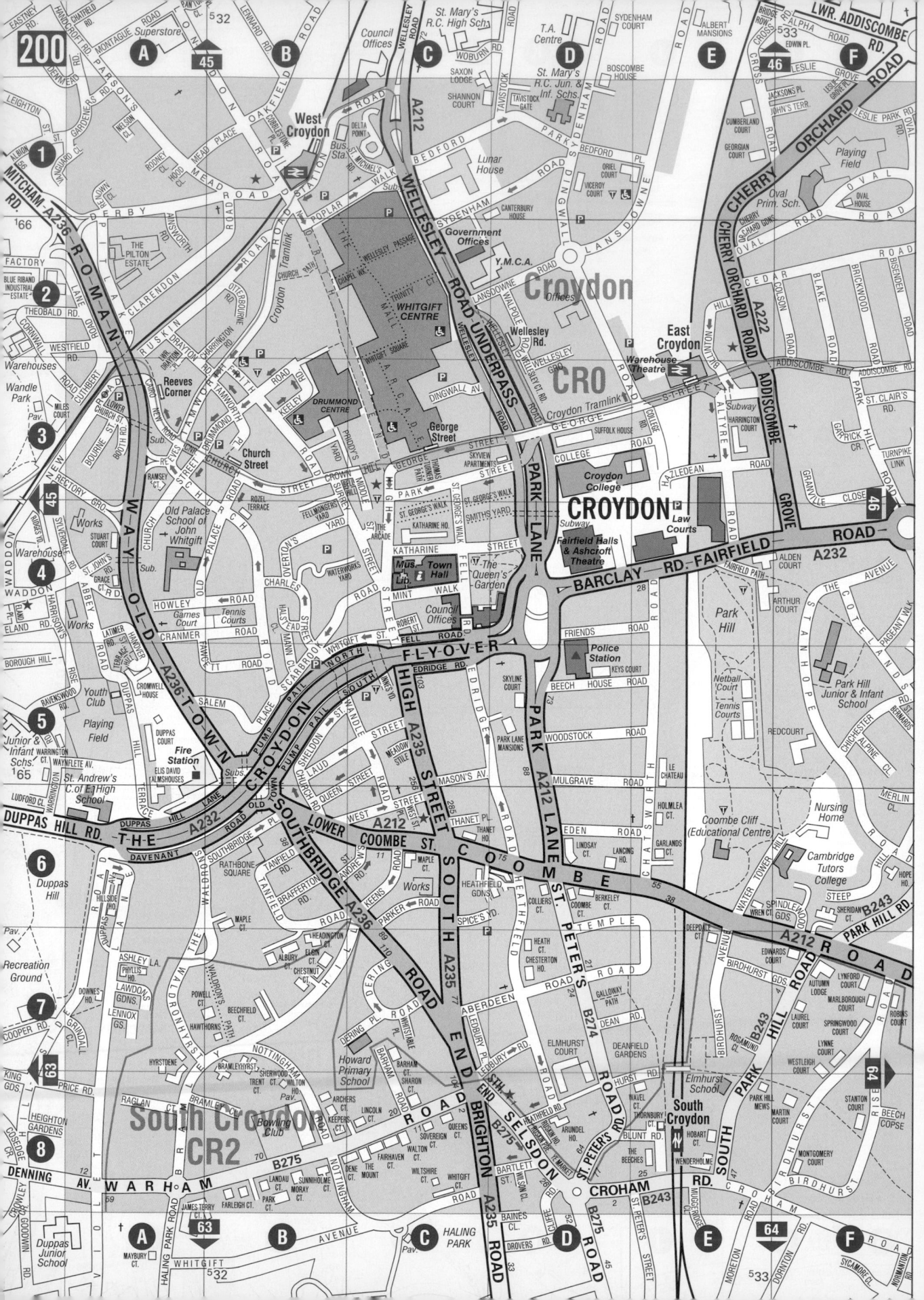

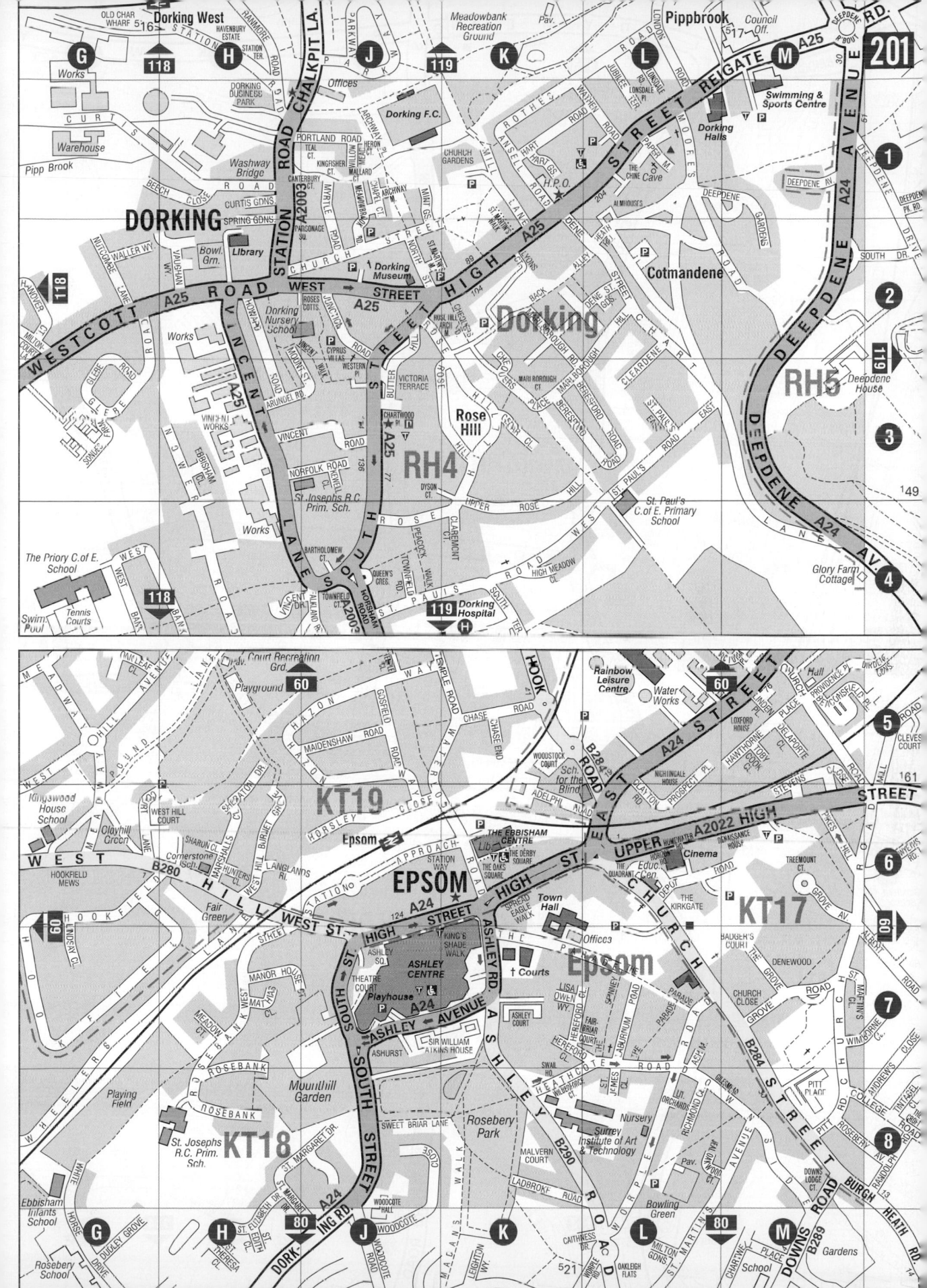

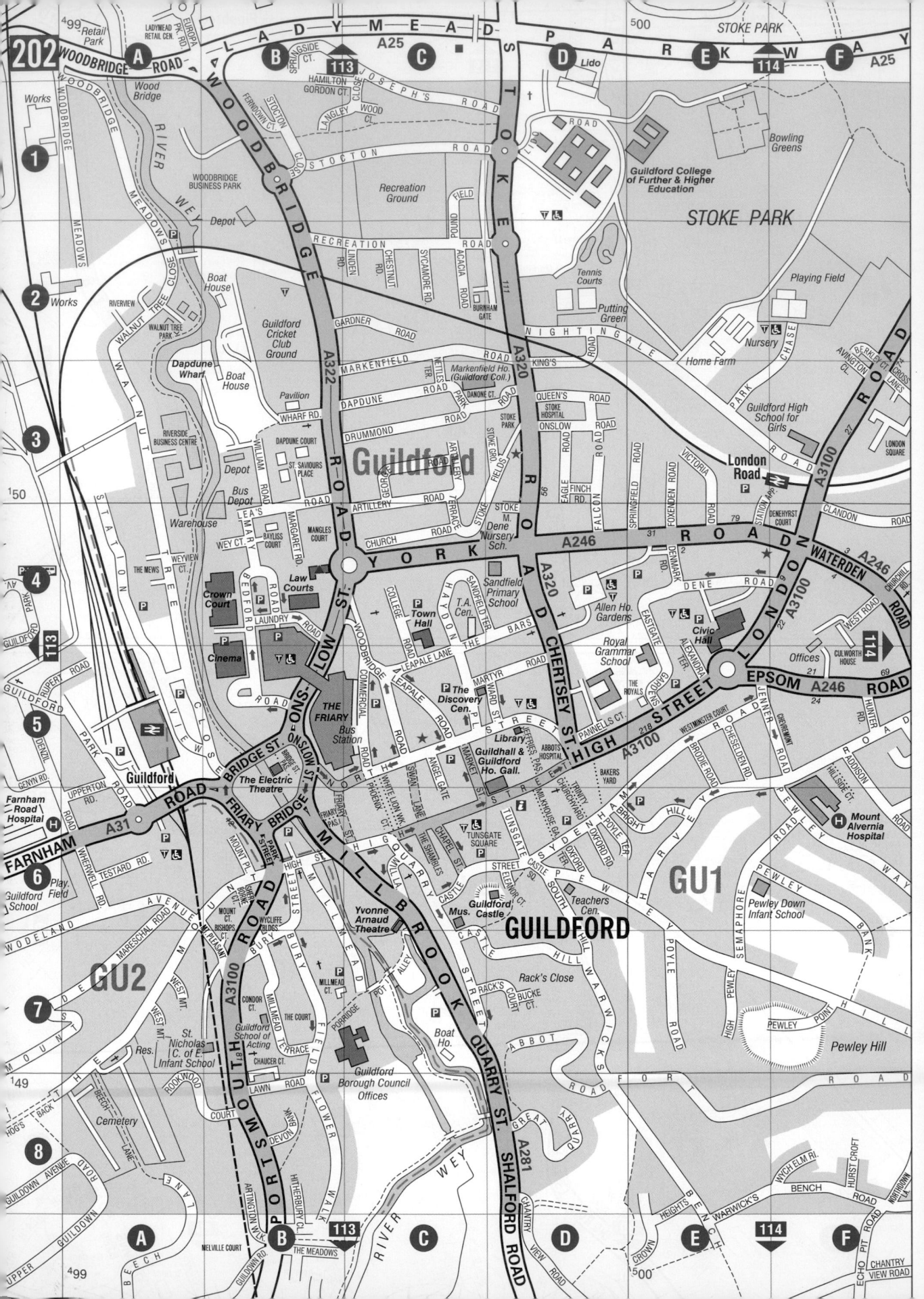

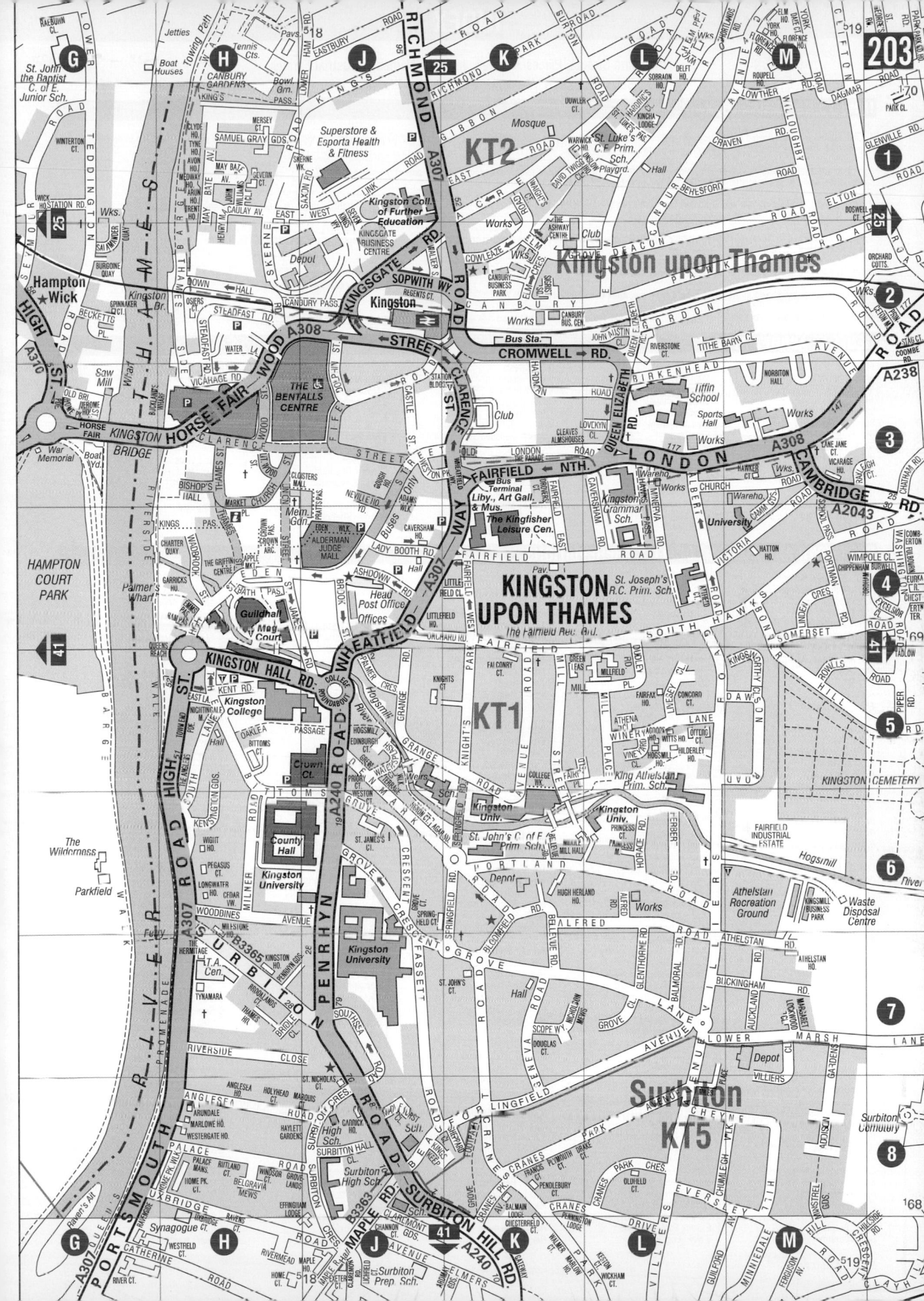

INDEX

Including Streets, Places & Areas, Junction Names, Industrial Estates,
Selected Flats & Walkways and Selected Places of Interest.

HOW TO USE THIS INDEX

1. Each street name is followed by its Posttown or Postal Locality and then by its map reference; e.g. Aaron's Hill *G'ming* ....7E **132** is in the Godalming Posttown and is to be found in square 7E on page **132**. The page number being shown in bold type.

2. A strict alphabetical order is followed in which Av., Rd., St., etc. (though abbreviated) are read in full and as part of the street name; e.g. Abbeyfield Clo. appears after Abbey Dri. but before Abbey Gdns.

3. Streets and a selection of flats and walkways too small to be shown on the maps, appear in the index in *Italics* with the thoroughfare to which it is connected shown in brackets; e.g. *Abbey Pde. SW19 ....8A* **28** *(off Merton High St.)*

4. Places and areas are shown in the index in **blue type** and the map reference is to the actual map square in which the town centre or area is located and not to the place name shown on the map; e.g. **Addlestone** 1K **55**

5. An example of a selected place of interest is Abinger Castle 2K **137**

6. Junction names are shown in the index in **bold type**; e.g. **Apex Corner (Junct.)** 4N **23**

7. Map references shown in brackets; e.g. Abbey Rd. *Croy* ....9M **45** (4A **200**) refer to entries that also appear on the large scale pages **200** -**203**.

GENERAL ABBREVIATIONS

All : Alley	Cir : Circus	Gt : Great	M : Mews	Sq : Square
App : Approach	Clo : Close	Grn : Green	Mt : Mount	Sta : Station
Arc : Arcade	Comn : Common	Gro : Grove	Mus : Museum	St : Street
Av : Avenue	Cotts : Cottages	Ho : House	N : North	Ter : Terrace
Bk : Back	Ct : Court	Ind : Industrial	Pal : Palace	Trad : Trading
Boulevd : Boulevard	Cres : Crescent	Info : Information	Pde : Parade	Up : Upper
Bri : Bridge	Cft : Croft	Junct : Junction	Pk : Park	Va : Vale
B'way : Broadway	Dri : Drive	La : Lane	Pas : Passage	Vw : View
Bldgs : Buildings	E : East	Lit : Little	Pl : Place	Vs : Villas
Bus : Business	Embkmt : Embankment	Lwr : Lower	Quad : Quadrant	Vis : Visitors
Cvn : Caravan	Est : Estate	Mc : Mac	Res : Residential	Wlk : Walk
Cen : Centre	Fld : Field	Mnr : Manor	Ri : Rise	W : West
Chu : Church	Gdns : Gardens	Mans : Mansions	Rd : Road	Yd : Yard
Chyd : Churchyard	Gth : Garth	Mkt : Market	Shop : Shopping	
Circ : Circle	Ga : Gate	Mdw : Meadow	S : South	

POSTTOWN AND POSTAL LOCALITY ABBREVIATIONS

Ab C : Abinger Common	*Busb* : Busbridge	*E Mol* : East Molesey	*Head* : Headley (Bordon)	*Lyne* : Lyne
Ab H : Abinger Hammer	*Byfl* : Byfleet	*Eden* : Edenbridge	*H'ley* : Headley (Epsom)	*M'bowr* : Maidenbower
Add : Addlestone	*Camb* : Camberley	*Eff* : Effingham	*H'row* : Heathrow	*M'head* : Maidenhead
Alb : Albury	*Capel* : Capel	*Eff J* : Effingham Junction	*H'row A* : London Heathrow Airport	*Maid G* : Maidens Green
Alder : Aldershot	*Cars* : Carshalton	*Egh* : Egham	*Head D* : Headley Down	*Man H* : Mannings Heath
Alf : Alfold	*Cat* : Caterham	*Elst* : Elstead	*Hers* : Hersham	*M Grn* : Marsh Green
Adgly : Ardingly	*Charl* : Charlwood	*Elv* : Elvetham	*Hever* : Hever	*Mayf* : Mayford
Art : Artington	*Cheam* : Cheam	*Eng G* : Englefield Green	*Hin W* : Hinchley Wood	*Mers* : Merstham
Asc : Ascot	*Chels* : Chelsfield	*Ent* : Enton	*Hind* : Hindhead	*Mick* : Mickleham
As : Ash	*Chel* : Chelsham	*Eps* : Epsom	*Holm M* : Holmbury St Mary	*Mid H* : Mid Holmwood
Ashf : Ashford	*Cher* : Chertsey	*Esh* : Esher	*Holmw* : Holmwood	*Milf* : Milford
Ash G : Ash Green	*Chess* : Chessington	*Eton* : Eton	*Holt P* : Holt Pound	*Mitc* : Mitcham
Asht : Ashtead	*C'fold* : Chiddingfold	*Eton C* : Eton College	*Hkwd* : Hookwood	*Mit J* : Mitcham Junction
Ash W : Ashurst Wood	*Chil* : Chilworth	*Eton W* : Eton Wick	*Horl* : Horley	*Mord* : Morden
Ash V : Ash Vale	*Chips* : Chipstead	*Eve* : Eversley	*Horne* : Horne	*Myt* : Mytchett
Bad L : Badshot Lea	*Chob* : Chobham	*Ewe* : Ewell	*Hors* : Horsell	*New Ad* : New Addington
Bag : Bagshot	*C Hosp* : Christs Hospital	*Ewh* : Ewhurst	*H'ham* : Horsham	*Newc* : Newchapel
Bans : Banstead	*C Crook* : Church Crookham	*Ews* : Ewshot	*Hort* : Horton	*Newd* : Newdigate
B'ham : Barkham	*Churt* : Churt	*F'boro* : Farnborough (Kent)	*Houn* : Hounslow	*New H* : New Haw
Bear G : Beare Green	*Clar P* : Claremont Park	*Farnb* : Farnborough (Hampshire)	*Hurst* : Hurst	*N Mald* : New Malden
Beck : Beckenham	*Clay* : Claygate	*Farnc* : Farncombe	*Hurt* : Hurtmore	*Norm* : Normandy
Bedd : Beddington	*Cobh* : Cobham	*Farnh* : Farnham	*Hyde* : Hydestile	*N Asc* : North Ascot
Bedf : Bedfont	*Cold* : Coldharbour	*Fay* : Faygate	*If'd* : Ifield	*N'chap* : Northchapel
Belm : Belmont	*Cole H* : Colemans Hatch	*Felb* : Felbridge	*Iswth* : Isleworth	*N Holm* : North Holmwood
B'ley : Bentley	*Colg* : Colgate	*Felc* : Felcourt	*Itch* : Itchingfield	*Nutf* : Nutfield
Berr G : Berrys Green	*Col T* : College Town	*Felt* : Feltham	*Iver* : Iver	*Ock* : Ockham
Bet : Betchworth	*Coln* : Colnbrook	*Fern* : Fernhurst	*Jac* : Jacob's Well	*Ockl* : Ockley
Bew : Bewbush	*Comp* : Compton	*Fet* : Fetcham	*Kenl* : Kenley	*Oke H* : Okewood Hill
Big H : Biggin Hill	*Copt* : Copthorne	*Finch* : Finchampstead	*Kes* : Keston	*Old Win* : Old Windsor
Bil : Billingshurst	*Coul* : Coulsdon	*Fleet* : Fleet	*Kew* : Kew	*Old Wok* : Old Woking
Binf : Binfield	*Cowd* : Cowden	*F Grn* : Forest Green	*Kingf* : Kingfield	*Onsl* : Onslow Village
Bisl : Bisley	*Cowf* : Cowfold	*F Row* : Forest Row	*K'fold* : Kingsfold	*Orp* : Orpington
B'hth : Blackheath	*Cran* : Cranford	*Four E* : Four Elms	*K'ley* : Kingsley	*Ott* : Ottershaw
B'nest : Blacknest	*Cranl* : Cranleigh	*Fren* : Frensham	*K Grn* : Kingsley Green	*Out* : Outwood
B'water : Blackwater	*Craw* : Crawley	*Frim* : Frimley	*King T* : Kingston Upon Thames	*Owl* : Owlsmoor
Blet : Bletchingley	*Craw D* : Crawley Down	*Frim G* : Frimley Green	*Kgswd* : Kingswood	*Oxs* : Oxshott
Blind H : Blindley Heath	*Crock H* : Crockham Hill	*Gat A* : London Gatwick Airport	*Kird* : Kirdford	*Oxt* : Oxted
Bookh : Bookham	*Cron* : Crondall	*G'ming* : Godalming	*Knap* : Knaphill	*Pass* : Passfield
Bord : Bordon	*Crow* : Crowhurst	*God* : Godstone	*Knock* : Knockholt	*Peas P* : Pease Pottage
Bourne : Bourne, The	*Crowt* : Crowthorne	*Gom* : Gomshall	*Lale* : Laleham	*Peasl* : Peaslake
Brack : Bracknell	*Croy* : Croydon	*Gray* : Grayshott	*Langl* : Langley	*P'mrsh* : Peasmarsh
Brmly : Bramley	*Cud* : Cudham	*G'wood* : Grayswood	*Lea* : Leatherhead	*Pep H* : Peper Harow
Bram : Bramshott	*Dat* : Datchet	*G Str* : Green Street Green	*Leigh* : Leigh	*Pirb* : Pirbright
Bram C : Bramshott Chase	*Deep* : Deepcut	*Guild* : Guildford	*Lei H* : Leith Hill	*Plais* : Plaistow
Bras : Brasted	*Dipp* : Dippenhall	*Hack* : Hackbridge	*Light* : Lightwater	*Purl* : Purley
Bren : Brentford	*Dit H* : Ditton Hill	*Ham* : Ham	*Limp* : Limpsfield	*P'ham* : Puttenham
Broad H : Broadbridge Heath	*Dock* : Dockenfield	*Hamb* : Hambledon	*Limp C* : Limpsfield Chart	*Pyr* : Pyrford
Broadf : Broadfield	*Dork* : Dorking	*Hamm* : Hammerwood	*Lind* : Lindford	*Ran C* : Ranmore Common
Brock : Brockham	*D'land* : Dormansland	*Hamp* : Hampton	*Ling* : Lingfield	*Read* : Reading
Brom : Bromley	*Dor P* : Dormans Park	*Hamp H* : Hampton Hill	*Lip* : Liphook	*Red* : Redhill
Brook : Brook	*Dor* : Dorney	*Hamp W* : Hampton Wick	*L Sand* : Little Sandhurst	*Reig* : Reigate
Bro I : Brooklands Ind. Est.	*Dow* : Downe	*Hand* : Handcross	*Longc* : Longcross	*Rich* : Richmond
Bro P : Brooklands Ind. Pk.	*D'side* : Downside	*Hanw* : Hanworth	*Lwr Bo* : Lower Bourne	*Rip* : Ripley
Brkwd : Brookwood	*Duns* : Dunsfold	*Harm* : Harmondsworth	*Lwr E* : Lower Eashing	*Rowf* : Rowfant
Buck : Buckland	*Earl* : Earlswood	*Hartf* : Hartfield	*Lwr K* : Lower Kingswood	*Rowh* : Rowhook
Bucks H : Bucks Horn Oak	*E Clan* : East Clandon	*Hasc* : Hascombe	*Low H* : Lowfield Heath	*Rowl* : Rowledge
Burp : Burpham	*E Grin* : East Grinstead	*Hasl* : Haslemere	*Loxh* : Loxhill	*Rud* : Rudgwick
Burs : Burstow	*E Hor* : East Horsley	*Hay* : Hayes	*Loxw* : Loxwood	*Runf* : Runfold

Rusp : Rusper
St G : St Georges Hill
St J : St Johns
Salf : Salfords
Sand : Sandhurst
Seale : Seale
Send : Send
Shack : Shackleford
Shalf : Shalford
Sham G : Shamley Green
Sheer : Sheerwater
Shep : Shepperton
Shere : Shere
Ship B : Shipley Bridge
Short : Shortlands
Shot : Shottermill
Shur R : Shurlock Row
Slea : Sleaford
Slin : Slinfold
Slou : Slough
Sly I : Slyfield Ind. Est.
Small : Smallfield
S'hall : Southall
S Asc : South Ascot
S Croy : South Croydon
S God : South Godstone
S Nut : South Nutfield
S Pk : South Park
Stai : Staines
Stand : Standford
Stanw : Stanwell
Stoke D : Stoke D'Abernon
S'leigh : Stoneleigh
Str G : Strood Green
Sun : Sunbury-on-Thames
S'dale : Sunningdale
S'hill : Sunninghill
Surb : Surbiton
Sur R : Surrey Research Park
Sutt : Sutton
Sut G : Sutton Green
Tad : Tadworth
Tand : Tandridge
Tap : Taplow
Tats : Tatsfield
Tedd : Teddington
Th Dit : Thames Ditton
T Hth : Thornton Heath
Thur : Thursley
Tilf : Tilford
Tin G : Tinsley Green
T'sey : Titsey
Tong : Tongham
Turn H : Turners Hill
Twic : Twickenham
Up Har : Upper Hartfield
Vir W : Virginia Water
Wall : Wallington
Wal W : Wallis Wood
W on T : Walton-on-Thames
Wanb : Wanborough
Warf : Warfield
Warf P : Warfield Park
Warl : Warlingham
Warn : Warnham
Wel C : Wellington College
Well : Welling
W Byf : West Byfleet
W Cla : West Clandon
Westc : Westcott
W Dray : West Drayton
W End : West End
W'ham : Westerham
W Ewe : West Ewell
W Hoa : West Hoathly
W Hor : West Horsley
Westh : Westhumble
W Mol : West Molesey
W Wick : West Wickham
Wey : Weybridge
W'hill : Whitehill
W Vil : Whiteley Village
Whit : Whitton
Whyt : Whyteleafe
W'sham : Windlesham
Wind : Windsor
Wind C : Windsor Castle
Wink : Winkfield
Wink R : Winkfield Row
Winn : Winnersh
Wis G : Wisborough Green
Wis : Wisley
Witl : Witley
Wok : Woking
Wokgm : Wokingham
Wold : Woldingham
Won : Wonersh
Wdhm : Woodham
Wood S : Wood Street Village
Wor Pk : Worcester Park
Wmly : Wormley
Worp : Worplesdon
Worp H : Worplesdon Hill
Worth : Worth
Wott : Wotton
Wray : Wraysbury
Wrec : Wrecclesham
Yat : Yateley

A

Aaron's Hill 7E **132**
Aaron's Hill. *G'ming* 7E **132**
Abbess Clo. *SW2* 2M **29**
Abbetts La. *Camb* 3N **69**
Abbey Chase. *Cher* 6K **37**
Abbey Clo. *Brack* 4B **32**
Abbey Clo. *Cranl* 8H **155**
Abbey Clo. *Wok* 3G **75**
Abbey Clo. *Wokgm* 1B **30**
Abbey Ct. *Camb* 1B **70**
Abbey Ct. *Cher* 6K **37**
Abbey Ct. *Farnh* 1H **129**
Abbey Ct. *Hamp* 8A **24**
Abbey Ct. *Stai* 3L **37**
Abbey Dri. *SW17* 6E **28**
Abbey Dri. *Stai* 3L **37**
Abbeyfield Clo. *Mitc* 1C **44**
Abbey Gdns. *W6* 2K **13**
Abbey Gdns. *Cher* 5J **37**
Abbey Grn. *Cher* 5J **37**
Abbey Ind. Est. *Mitc* 4D **44**
Abbey M. *Ash W* 3H **187**
Abbey M. *Stai* 3L **37**
Abbey Pde. SW19 8A **28**
(off Merton High St.)
Abbey Pl. *Cher* 2J **37**
Abbey Rd. *SW19* 8A **28**
Abbey Rd. *Cher* 6K **37**
Abbey Rd. *Croy* 9M **45** (4A **200**)
Abbey Rd. *Shep* 7B **38**
Abbey Rd. *S Croy* 6G **64**
Abbey Rd. *Vir W* 4N **35**
Abbey Rd. *Wok* 4M **73**
Abbey St. *Farnh* 1H **129**
Abbey Wlk. *W Mol* 2B **40**
Abbey Way. *Farnb* 1A **90**
Abbeywood. *Ash V* 9F **90**
Abbeywood. *S'dale* 6D **34**
Abbot Clo. *Byfl* 9M **55**
Abbot Clo. *Stai* 8M **21**
Abbot Rd. *Guild* 5N **113** (7D **202**)
Abbots Av. *Eps* 7N **59**
Abbotsbury. *Brack* 4L **31**
Abbotsbury Ct. *H'ham* 5L **197**
Abbotsbury Rd. *Mord* 4N **43**
Abbots Clo. *Fleet* 4B **88**
Abbot's Clo. *Guild* 6H **113**
Abbots Dri. *Vir W* 4L **35**
Abbotsfield Rd. *If'd* 4J **181**
Abbotsford Clo. *Wok* 4C **74**
Abbots Grn. *Croy* 3G **65**
Abbots Hospital. *Guild* 5D **202**
Abbots La. *Kenl* 3N **83**
Abbotsleigh Clo. *Sutt* 4N **61**
Abbotsleigh Rd. *SW16* 5G **28**
Abbots Mead. *Rich* 5K **25**
Abbotsmede Clo. *Twic* 3F **24**
Abbots Pk. *SW2* 2L **29**
Abbot's Ride. *Farnh* 3K **129**
Abbots Ri. *Red* 1E **122**
Abbotstone Rd. *SW15* 6H **13**
Abbots Wlk. *Wind* 5B **4**
Abbots Way. *Cher* 6H **37**
Abbots Way. *Guild* 2F **114**
Abbotswood 1B **114**
Abbotswood. *Guild* 1B **114**
Abbotswood Clo. *Guild* 9B **94**
Abbotswood Dri. *Wey* 6F **56**
Abbotswood Rd. *SW16* 4H **29**
Abbott Av. *SW20* 9J **27**
Abbott Clo. *Hamp* 7M **23**
Abbotts Cotts. *Dock* 5D **148**
Abbotts Rd. *Mitc* 3G **45**
(in two parts)
Abbotts Rd. *Sutt* 1K **61**
Abbott's Tilt. *W on T* 9M **39**
Abbotts Wlk. *Cat* 9E **84**
Abelia Clo. *W End* 9B **52**
Abercairn Rd. *SW16* 8G **28**
Aberconway Rd. *Mord* 3N **43**
Abercorn Clo. *S Croy* 9G **64**
Abercorn Ho. *B'water* 5K **69**
Abercorn M. *Rich* 7M **11**
Abercorn Way. *Wok* 5K **73**
Aberdare Clo. *W Wick* 8M **47**
Aberdeen Rd. *Croy* 1N **63** (7C **200**)
Aberdeen Ter. *Gray* 5B **170**
Aberfoyle Rd. *SW16* 7H **29**
(in two parts)
Abergavenny Gdns. *Copt* 7A **164**
Abingdon. W14 1L **13**
(off Kensington Village)
Abingdon Clo. *SW19* 7A **28**
Abingdon Clo. *Brack* 4C **32**
Abingdon Clo. *Wok* 5M **73**
Abingdon Rd. *SW16* 1J **45**
Abingdon Rd. *Sand* 7H **49**
Abinger Av. *Sutt* 5H **61**
Abinger Bottom 5N **137**
Abinger Castle 2K **137**
Abinger Clo. *New Ad* 3M **65**
Abinger Clo. *N Holm* 9J **119**
Abinger Clo. *Wall* 2J **63**
Abinger Common 3L **137**
Abinger Comn. Rd. *Ab C* 4M **137**
Abinger Ct. *Wall* 2J **63**
Abinger Dri. *Red* 5C **122**
Abinger Gdns. *Iswth* 6E **10**
Abinger Hammer 8G **116**
Abinger Keep. Horl 7G **142**
(off Langshott La.)
Abinger La. *Ab H* 9J **117**
Abinger Rd. *Lei H* 9A **138**
Abinger Roughs 8J **117**
Abinger Way. *Guild* 7D **94**
Aboyne Dri. *SW20* 1F **43**
Aboyne Rd. *SW17* 4B **28**
Abrahams Rd. *Craw* 8M **181**
Abury La. *Brack* 5E **32**
Acacia Av. *Bren* 3H **11**
Acacia Av. *Owl* 6J **49**
Acacia Av. *Shep* 4B **38**
Acacia Av. *Wok* 7N **73**
Acacia Av. *Wray* 7A **6**
Acacia Clo. *SE20* 1D **46**
Acacia Clo. *Wdhm* 6H **55**
Acacia Ct. *Brack* 3N **31**
Acacia Dri. *Bans* 1J **81**
Acacia Dri. *Sutt* 7M **43**
Acacia Dri. *Wdhm* 6H **55**
Acacia Gdns. *W Wick* 8M **47**
Acacia Gro. *SE21* 3N **29**
Acacia Gro. *N Mald* 2C **42**
Acacia M. *W Dray* 2M **7**
Acacia Rd. *SW16* 9J **29**
Acacia Rd. *Beck* 2J **47**
Acacia Rd. *Guild* 3N **113** (2C **202**)
Acacia Rd. *Hamp* 7A **24**
Acacia Rd. *Mitc* 1E **44**
Acacia Rd. *Stai* 6K **21**
(in two parts)
Academy Clo. *Camb* 7C **50**
Academy Gdns. *Croy* 7C **46**
Academy Pl. *Sand* 8K **49**
Accommodation La. *W Dray* 2L **7**
(Moor La.)
Accommodation La. *W Dray* 4J **7**
(Old Bath Rd.)
Accommodation Rd. *Eps* 2F **60**
Accommodation Rd. *Longc* 9N **35**
A.C. Court. *Th Dit* 5G **40**
Ace Pde. *Chess* 9L **41**
Acer Dri. *W End* 9C **52**
Acer Rd. *Big H* 3F **86**
Acfold Rd. *SW6* 4N **13**
Acheulian Clo. *Farnh* 4H **129**
Achilles Pl. *Wok* 4M **73**
Ackmar Rd. *SW6* 4M **13**
Ackrells Mead. *Sand* 6E **48**
Acorn Clo. *E Grin* 1A **186**
Acorn Clo. *Hamp* 7B **24**
Acorn Clo. *Horl* 7G **143**
Acorn Dri. *Wokgm* 1B **30**
Acorn Gdns. *SE19* 1C **46**
Acorn Gro. *Hay* 3G **9**
Acorn Gro. *Tad* 2L **101**
Acorn Gro. *Wok* 8A **74**
Acorn Keep. *Farnh* 4J **109**
Acorn M. *Farnb* 7M **69**
Acorn Rd. *B'water* 1G **69**
Acorns. *H'ham* 4N **197**
Acorns, The. *Craw* 8N **181**
Acorns, The. *Small* 8M **143**
Acorns Way. *Esh* 2C **58**
Acorn Way. *Beck* 4M **47**
Acorn Way. *Orp* 1K **67**
Acre La. *Cars & Wall* 1E **62**
Acre Pas. *Wind* 4G **4**
Acre Rd. *SW19* 7B **28**
Acre Rd. *King T* 9L **25** (1K **203**)
Acres Gdns. *Tad* 6J **81**
Acres Platt. *Cranl* 6A **156**
Acris St. *SW18* 8N **13**
Acropolis Ho. *King T* 5L **203**
Acton La. *W3 & W4* 1B **12**
(in three parts)
Acuba Rd. *SW18* 3N **27**
Adair Clo. *SE25* 2E **46**
Adair Wlk. *Brkwd* 8M **71**
Adams Clo. *Farnb* 8L **69**
Adams Clo. *Surb* 5M **41**
Adams Cft. *Brkwd* 7N **71**
Adams Dri. *Fleet* 4D **88**
Adamson Ct. *Craw* 8N **181**
Adams Pk. Rd. *Farnh* 8J **109**
Adams Rd. *Beck* 4H **47**
Adams Wlk. *King T* 1L **41** (3J **203**)
Adams Way. *Croy* 5C **46**
Adam Wlk. *SW6* 3H **13**
Adare Wlk. *SW16* 4K **29**
Addington 2K **65**
Addington Clo. *Wind* 6D **4**
Addington Ct. *SW14* 6C **12**
Addington Heights. *New Ad* 7M **65**
Addington Rd. *Croy* 7L **45**
Addington Rd. *S Croy* 7D **64**
Addington Rd. *W Wick* 1M **65**
Addington Village Rd. *Croy* 3J **65**
(in two parts)
Addiscombe 7D **46**
Addiscombe Av. *Croy* 7D **46**
Addiscombe Ct. Rd. *Croy* 7B **46**
Addiscombe Gro. *Croy* 8B **46** (3E **200**)
Addiscombe Rd. *Crowt* 3H **49**
Addiscombe Rd. *Croy* 8B **46** (3F **200**)
Addison Av. *Houn* 4C **10**
Addison Clo. *Cat* 9A **84**
Addison Ct. *Guild* 5B **114**
Addison Gdns. *Surb* 3M **41** (8M **203**)
Addison Pl. *SE25* 3D **46**
Addison Rd. *SE25* 3D **46**
Addison Rd. *Cat* 8A **84**
Addison Rd. *Frim* 6C **70**
Addison Rd. *Guild* 5A **114** (5F **202**)
Addison Rd. *Tedd* 7H **25**
Addison Rd. *Wok* 4B **74**
Addisons Clo. *Croy* 8J **47**
Addison Ter. W4 1B **12**
(off Chiswick Rd.)
Addlestone 1K **55**
Addlestone Moor 8J **37**
Addlestone Moor. *Add* 8L **37**
Addlestone Pk. *Add* 2K **55**
Addlestone Rd. *Add & Wey* 1N **55**
Adecroft Way. *W Mol* 2C **40**
Adela Av. *N Mald* 4G **42**
Adela Ho. W6 1H **13**
(off Queen Caroline St.)
Adelaide Clo. *Craw* 9B **162**
Adelaide Clo. *H'ham* 4M **197**
Adelaide Pl. *Wey* 1E **56**
Adelaide Rd. *Ashf* 6M **21**
Adelaide Rd. *SW18* 8M **13**
Adelaide Rd. *Houn* 4M **9**
Adelaide Rd. *Rich* 7M **11**
Adelaide Rd. *Surb* 4L **41**
Adelaide Rd. *Tedd* 7F **24**
Adelaide Rd. *W on T* 9H **39**
Adelaide Rd. *Wind* 4J **5**
Adelaide Sq. *Wind* 6G **4**
Adelaide Ter. *Bren* 1K **11**
Adelina M. *SW12* 2H **29**
Adelphi Clo. *M'bowr* 5H **183**
Adelphi Ct. *W4* 2C **12**
Adelphi Rd. *Eps* 9C **60** (6K **201**)
Adeney Clo. *W6* 2J **13**
Adlers La. *Westh* 9G **99**
Adlington Pl. *Farnb* 3C **90**
Admark Ho. *Eps* 2A **80**
Admiral Ct. *Cars* 7C **44**
Admiral Ho. *Tedd* 5G **25**
Admiral Kepple Ct. *Asc* 8J **17**
Admiral Rd. *Craw* 6M **181**
Admiral's Bri. La. *E Grin* 7M **185**
Admirals Ct. *Guild* 2D **114**
Admirals Rd. *Bookh & Fet* 6C **98**
Admiral's Rd. *Pirb* 4K **91**
Admiral Stirling Ct. *Wey* 1A **56**
Admirals Wlk. *Coul* 7K **83**
Admiral's Wlk. *Dork* 8B **98**
Admiralty Rd. *Tedd* 7F **24**
Admiralty Way. *Camb* 2L **69**
Admiralty Way. *Tedd* 7F **24**
Adrian Ct. *Craw* 8N **181**
Adrian M. *SW10* 2N **13**
Advance Rd. *SE27* 5N **29**
Aerodrome Way. *Houn* 2K **9**
Aerospace Boulevd. *Farnb* 6M **89**
Agar Clo. *Surb* 8M **41**
Agar Cres. *Brack* 8N **15**
Agar Ho. *King T* 6J **203**
Agars Pl. *Dat* 2K **5**
Agate La. *H'ham* 3L **197**
Agates La. *Asht* 5K **79**
Agincourt. *Asc* 2N **33**
Agnes Scott Ct. Wey 9C **38**
(off Palace Dri.)
Agraria Rd. *Guild* 4L **113**
Ailsa Av. *Twic* 8G **11**
Ailsa Clo. *Craw* 6N **181**
Ailsa Rd. *Twic* 8H **11**
Ainger Clo. *Alder* 1B **110**
Ainsdale Way. *Wok* 5K **73**
Ainslie Wlk. *SW12* 1F **28**
Ainsworth Rd. *Croy* 7M **45** (2A **200**)
Aintree Clo. *Coln* 4G **6**
Aintree Est. SW6 3K **13**
(off Aintree St.)
Aintree Rd. *Craw* 5E **182**
Aintree St. *SW6* 3K **13**
Airborne Forces Mus. 8M **89**
Airbourne Ho. Wall 1G **62**
(off Maldon Rd.)
Aircraft Esplanade. *Farnb* 4A **90**
Airedale Av. *W4* 1E **12**
Airedale Av. S. *W4* 1F **12**
Airedale Rd. *SW12* 1D **28**
Air Forces Memorial 5N **19**
Airlinks Ind. Est. *Houn* 1K **9**
Air Pk. Way. *Felt* 3J **23**
Airport Ind. Est. *Big H* 2F **86**
Airport Way. *Gat A* 2E **162**
Airport Way. *Stai* 7H **7**
Aisgill Av. *W14* 1L **13**
(in two parts)
Aisne Rd. *Deep* 5J **71**
Aitken Clo. *Mitc* 6D **44**
Akabusi Clo. *Croy* 5D **46**
Akehurst Clo. *Copt* 7L **163**
Akehurst St. *SW15* 9F **12**
Akerman Rd. *Surb* 5J **41**
Alamein Rd. *Alder* 2N **109**
Alanbrooke Clo. *Knap* 5F **72**
Alanbrooke Rd. *Alder* 7B **90**
Alan Hilton Ct. Ott 3F **54**
(off Cheshire Clo.)
Alan Rd. *SW19* 6K **27**
Alan Turing Rd. *Sur R* 3G **113**
Albain Cres. *Ashf* 3N **21**
Albany Clo. *SW14* 7A **12**
Albany Clo. *Esh* 5A **58**
Albany Clo. *Fleet* 5C **88**
Albany Clo. *Reig* 9M **101**
Albany Ct. *Camb* 5A **70**
Albany Ct. *Fleet* 4C **88**
Albany Cres. *Clay* 3E **58**
Albany M. *King T* 7K **25**
Albany M. *Sutt* 2N **61**
Albany Pde. *Bren* 2L **11**
Albany Pk. *Camb* 5A **70**
Albany Pk. *Coln* 4F **6**
Albany Pk. Ind. Est. *Camb* 5A **70**
Albany Pk. Rd. *King T* 7K **25**
Albany Pk. Rd. *Lea* 6G **78**
Albany Pas. *Rich* 8L **11**
Albany Pl. *Egh* 5D **20**
Albany Reach. *Th Dit* 4F **40**
Albany Rd. *SW19* 6N **27**
Albany Rd. *Bren* 2K **11**
Albany Rd. *Craw* 3N **181**
Albany Rd. *Fleet* 5B **88**
Albany Rd. *N Mald* 3C **42**
Albany Rd. *Old Win* 8K **5**
Albany Rd. *Rich* 8M **11**
Albany Rd. *W on T* 1L **57**
Albany Rd. *Wind* 5G **4**
Albany Ter. Rich 8M **11**
(off Albany Pas.)
Albatross Gdns. *S Croy* 7G **65**
Albemarle. *SW19* 3J **27**
Albemarle Av. *Twic* 2N **23**
Albemarle Gdns. *N Mald* 3C **42**
Albemarle Pk. *Beck* 1L **47**
Albemarle Rd. *Beck* 1L **47**
Alben Rd. *Binf* 6H **15**
Alberta Av. *Sutt* 1K **61**
Alberta Dri. *Small* 8L **143**
Albert Av. *Cher* 2J **37**
Albert Carr Gdns. *SW16* 6J **29**
Albert Crane Ct. *Craw* 1M **181**
Albert Dri. *SW19* 3K **27**
Albert Dri. *Stai* 6J **21**
Albert Dri. *Wok* 2E **74**
Albert Gro. *SW20* 9J **27**
Albertine Clo. *Eps* 3G **81**
Albert Mans. *Croy* 1E **200**
Albert M. *Red* 6E **122**

Albert Pl.—Anderson Pl.

Albert Pl. Eton W 1D 4
Albert Rd. Ashf. 6A 22
Albert Rd. Farnb. 3A 90
Albert Rd. SE25 3D 46
Albert Rd. Add. 1M 55
Albert Rd. Alder 2N 109
Albert Rd. Asht 5M 79
Albert Rd. Bag 6J 51
Albert Rd. Brack. 9N 15
Albert Rd. Crowt 2G 49
Albert Rd. Eng G 7N 19
Albert Rd. Eps 9E 60 (7M 201)
Albert Rd. Hamp H. 6C 24
Albert Rd. Horl 7E 142
Albert Rd. Houn 7A 10
Albert Rd. King T 1M 41 (3L 203)
Albert Rd. Mitc. 2D 44
Albert Rd. N Mald. 3E 42
Albert Rd. Red 7G 102
Albert Rd. Rich. 8L 11
Albert Rd. Sutt. 2B 62
Albert Rd. Tedd. 7F 24
Albert Rd. Twic. 2F 24
Albert Rd. Warl. 4J 85
Albert Rd. Wind & Old Win 6G 5
Albert Rd. Wokgm 3A 30
Albert Rd. N. Reig 2L 121
Albert St. Fleet 5A 88
Albert St. Wind. 4E 4
Albert Wlk. Crowt. 2G 49
Albery Clo. H'ham 4H 197
Albion Clo. Craw 4H 183
Albion Cotts. Holm M. 5K 137
Albion Ct. W6. 1G 13
(off Albion Pl.)
Albion Ho. Slou 1D 6
Albion Ho. Wok 4B 74
Albion M. W6. 1G 13
Albion Pl. SE25 2D 46
Albion Pl. W6. 1G 13
Albion Pl. Wind 5D 4
Albion Rd. Houn. 7A 10
Albion Rd. King T. 9B 26
Albion Rd. Reig 4A 122
Albion Rd. Sand. 8G 49
Albion Rd. Sutt. 3B 62
Albion Rd. Twic 2E 24
Albion St. Croy. 7M 45 (1A 200)
Albion Way. Eden. 9K 127
Albion Way. H'ham 6H 197
Albury. 8K 115
Albury Av. Iswth 3F 10
Albury Av. Sutt. 5H 61
Albury Clo. Eps 5A 60
Albury Clo. Hamp. 7B 24
Albury Clo. Longc 9K 35
Albury Cotts. As. 2G 111
Albury Ct. Mitc. 1B 44
Albury Ct. S Croy. 7B 200
Albury Ct. Sutt. 1A 62
Albury Heath. 1M 135
Albury Ho. Guild 5B 114
Albury Keep. Horl 8F 142
(off Langshott La.)
Albury Park. 9N 115
Albury Pk. Alb 8N 115
Albury Pl. Red 7G 103
Albury Rd. Chess 2L 59
Albury Rd. Guild 4B 114
Albury Rd. Red 7G 102
Albury Rd. W on T. 3F 56
Alcester Rd. Wall 1F 62
Alcock Clo. Wall. 4H 63
Alcock Rd. Houn 3L 9
Alcocks Clo. Tad. 7K 81
Alcocks La. Kgswd. 8K 81
Alcorn Clo. Sutt. 8M 43
Alcot Clo. Crowt. 3G 48
Alcott Clo. Felt 2G 22
Alden Ct. Croy 9B 46 (4F 200)
Aldenham Ter. Brack 5A 32
Aldenholme. Wey 3F 56
Alden Vw. Wind 4A 4
Alderbrook Clo. Crowt 3D 48
Alderbrook Farm Cotts. Cranl 3M 155
Alderbrook Rd. SW12. 1F 28
Alderbrook Rd. Cranl 2K 155
Alderbury Rd. SW13 2F 12
Alder Clo. Ash V. 6E 90
Alder Clo. Craw D. 1E 184
Alder Clo. Eng G. 6A 20
Aldercombe La. Cat 5B 104
Alder Copse. H'ham 8F 196
Aldercroft. Coul 3K 83
Alder Gro. Yat. 1B 68
Aldergrove Gdns. Houn. 5M 9
Alder Lodge. SW6 4H 13
Alderman Judge Mall. King T 1L 41 (4J 203)
Alderman Willey Clo. Wokgm 2A 30
Alderney Av. Houn 3B 10
Alder Rd. Hdly D 3G 168
Alder Rd. SW14. 6C 12
Alders Av. E Grin 7N 165
Aldersbrook Dri. King T. 7M 25
Aldersey Rd. Guild. 3B 114
Alders Gro. E Mol 4D 40
Aldershot. 2M 109
Aldershot Lodge. Alder 4A 110
Aldershot Military Mus. 6A 90
Aldershot Rd. As 3C 110
Aldershot Rd. C Crook. 9A 88
Aldershot Rd. Fleet. 5B 88
Aldershot Rd. Norm & Guild 8B 92
Aldershot Rd. Pirb 5A 92
Aldershot Town Football Club. 2A 110
Alderside Wlk. Eng G. 6A 20
Aldersmead Av. Croy 5G 47
Alders Rd. Reig 1N 121
Alderstead Heath. 3H 103
Alderstead La. Red. 3H 103
Alders, The. SW16. 5G 29
Alders, The. Bad L 6N 109
Alders, The. Felt 5M 23
Alders, The. Houn 2N 9
Alders, The. W Byf 8L 55
Alders, The. W Wick. 7L 47
Alders Vw. Dri. E Grin 7A 166
Alderton Rd. Croy 6C 46
Alderville Rd. SW6. 5L 13
Alderwick Dri. Houn. 6D 10
Alderwood Clo. Cat 3B 104
Aldingbourne Clo. If'd 2L 181
Aldis M. SW17. 6C 28
Aldis St. SW17. 6C 28
Aldren Rd. SW17. 4A 28
Aldrich Cres. New Ad 5M 65
Aldrich Gdns. Sutt 9L 43
Aldrich Ter. SW18 3A 28
Aldridge Pk. Wink R 7F 16
Aldridge Ri. N Mald 6D 42
Aldrington Rd. SW16. 6G 29
Aldrin Pl. Farnb. 1J 89
Aldwick Clo. Farnb 8M 69
Aldwick Rd. Croy 9K 45
Aldworth Clo. Brack 3M 31
Aldworth Gdns. Crowt 2F 48
Aldwych Clo. M'bowr. 5H 183
Aldwyn Ct. Eng G. 7L 19
Alexa Ct. Sutt 3M 61
Alexander Clo. Twic 3E 24
Alexander Ct. Beck. 1N 47
Alexander Godley Clo. Asht 6M 79
Alexander Rd. Coul. 2F 82
Alexander Rd. Egh. 6D 20
(in two parts)
Alexander Rd. Reig 6M 121
Alexanders Wlk. Cat. 4C 104
Alexander Wlk. Brack. 4N 31
Alexandra Av. W4. 3C 12
Alexandra Av. Camb 1M 69
Alexandra Av. Sutt. 9M 43
Alexandra Av. Warl 4J 85
Alexandra Clo. Ashf 8E 22
Alexandra Clo. Stai 7M 21
Alexandra Clo. W on T. 8H 39
Alexandra Ct. Ashf 7E 22
Alexandra Ct. Farnb 4A 90
Alexandra Ct. Craw. 4B 182
Alexandra Ct. Houn 5B 10
Alexandra Ct. Wokgm 3B 30
Alexandra Dri. Surb 6N 41
Alexandra Gdns. W4 3D 12
Alexandra Gdns. Cars. 4E 62
Alexandra Gdns. Houn. 5B 10
Alexandra Gdns. Knap 5F 72
Alexandra Ho. W6 1H 13
(off Queen Caroline St.)
Alexandra Mans. Eps 9E 60
(off Alexandra Rd.)
Alexandra M. SW19. 7L 27
Alexandra Pl. SE25. 4A 46
Alexandra Pl. Croy. 7B 46
Alexandra Pl. Guild. 5B 114
Alexandra Rd. Ashf. 8E 22
Alexandra Rd. Farnb. 3A 90
Alexandra Rd. SW14 6C 12
Alexandra Rd. SW19 7L 27
Alexandra Rd. Add 1M 55
(in two parts)
Alexandra Rd. Alder. 2K 109
(in two parts)
Alexandra Rd. As. 3D 110
Alexandra Rd. Big H. 6D 86
Alexandra Rd. Bren 2K 11
Alexandra Rd. Croy 7B 46 (1F 200)
Alexandra Rd. Eng G. 7M 19
Alexandra Rd. Eps 9E 60
Alexandra Rd. Houn. 5B 10
Alexandra Rd. King T. 8N 25
Alexandra Rd. Mitc. 8C 28
Alexandra Rd. Rich 5M 11
Alexandra Rd. Th Dit 4F 40
Alexandra Rd. Twic. 9J 11
Alexandra Rd. Warl. 4J 85
Alexandra Rd. Wind. 5G 4
Alexandra Sq. Mord 4M 43
Alexandra Ter. Guild 4A 114 (4E 202)
Alexandra Way. Eps 7N 59
Alfold. 8H 175
Alfold Bars. 1H 193
Alfold Crossways. 5J 175
Alfold Rd. Cranl 7K 155
Alfold Rd. Duns 5B 174
Alfonso Clo. Alder 4A 110
Alford Clo. Guild. 9B 94
Alford Grn. New Ad 3N 65
Alfred Clo. W4 1C 12
Alfred Clo. Worth 4J 183
Alfred Rd. SE25 4D 46
Alfred Rd. Farnh. 2H 129
Alfred Rd. Felt 3K 23
Alfred Rd. King T 2L 41 (6K 203)
Alfred Rd. Sutt. 2A 62
Alfreton Clo. SW19. 4J 27
Alfriston. Surb. 5M 41
Alfriston Av. Croy 6J 45
Alfriston Clo. Surb. 4M 41
Alfriston Rd. Deep 7G 71
Algar Clo. Iswth 6G 10
Algar Rd. Iswth 6G 11
Algarve Rd. SW18. 2N 27
Alice Gilliatt Ct. W14 2L 13
(off Star Rd.)
Alice Gough Homes. Brack 2N 31
Alice Holt Cotts. Holt P 9A 128
Alice Holt Forest Cen. 2B 148
Alice M. Tedd 6F 24
Alice Rd. Alder. 2N 109
Alice Ruston Pl. Wok 6M 73
Alice Way. Houn. 7B 10
Alicia Av. Craw 3F 182
Alington Gro. Wall 5G 63
Alison Clo. Farnb 2L 89
Alison Clo. Croy. 7G 46
Alison Clo. Wok 2A 74
Alison Dri. Camb 1D 70
Alison's Rd. Alder 8M 89
Alison Way. Alder. 2L 109
Alkerden Rd. W4 1D 12
Allan Clo. N Mald 4C 42
Allbrook Clo. Tedd 6E 24
Allcard Clo. H'ham 4K 197
Allcot Clo. Craw 6K 181
Allden Av. Alder 5B 110
Allden Cotts. G'ming 7E 132
(off Aaron's Hill)
Allden Gdns. Alder. 5B 110
Alldens Hill. G'ming & Brmly 1N 153
Alldens La. G'ming. 9L 133
Allder Way. S Croy 4M 63
Allenby Av. S Croy. 5N 63
Allenby Rd. Big H. 4G 86
Allenby Rd. Camb 9M 49
Allen Clo. Mitc 9F 28
Allen Clo. Sun. 9J 23
Allendale Clo. Sand. 5F 48
Allenford Ho. SW15. 9E 12
(off Tunworth Cres.)
Allen Ho. Pk. Wok 7M 73
Allen Rd. Beck 1G 46
Allen Rd. Bookh 4B 98
Allen Rd. Croy 7L 45
Allen Rd. Sun 9J 23
Allen's Clo. Ash W 3F 186
Allestree Rd. SW6 3K 13
Alleyn Pk. S'hall 1A 10
Allfarthing La. SW18 9N 13 & 1A 28
Allgood Clo. Mord 5J 43
Allingham Ct. G'ming 4J 133
Allingham Gdns. H'ham. 3A 198
Allingham Rd. Reig. 6M 121
Allington Av. Shep 2F 38
Allington Clo. SW19. 6J 27
Allkins Ct. Wind. 5G 5
Alloway Clo. Wok. 5L 73
All Saints Clo. Wokgm 1B 30
All Saints Ct. Houn. 4L 9
(off Springwell Rd.)
All Saints Cres. Farnb. 6K 69
All Saints Dri. S Croy. 8C 64
All Saints Pas. SW18 8M 13
All Saints Ri. Warf 8B 16
All Saints Rd. SW19. 8A 28
(in two parts)
All Saints Rd. Light 6N 51
All Saints Rd. Sutt. 9N 43
Allsmoor La. Brack 2D 32
All Souls Rd. Asc 3L 33
Allum Gro. Tad. 8G 81
Allyington Way. Worth. 4H 183
Allyn Clo. Stai 7H 21
Alma Clo. Alder 2B 110
Alma Clo. Knap 4H 73
Alma Cotts. Farnb 5A 90
Alma Ct. Cat. 8N 83
(off Coulsdon Rd.)
Alma Cres. Sutt 2K 61
Alma Gdns. Deep. 6H 71
Alma Ho. Bren 2L 11
Alma La. Farnh 5G 109
Alma Pl. T Hth 4L 45
Alma Rd. Hdly D 4H 169
Alma Rd. SW18. 7N 13
Alma Rd. Bord 6A 168
Alma Rd. Cars 2C 62
Alma Rd. Esh. 7E 40
Alma Rd. Eton W. 1C 4
Alma Rd. Reig 2N 121
Alma Rd. Wind. 5F 4
Alma Sq. Farnb 5A 90
Alma Ter. SW18 1B 28
Alma Way. Farnh 5J 109
Almer Rd. SW20 8F 26
Almners Rd. Lyne 7C 36
(in two parts)
Almond Av. Cars 8D 44
Almond Av. Wok 8N 73
Almond Clo. Farnb 7M 69
Almond Clo. Craw. 4M 181
Almond Clo. Eng G. 7L 19
Almond Clo. Felt 2H 23
Almond Clo. Guild 9N 93
Almond Clo. Shep 1D 38
Almond Clo. Wind 5E 4
Almond Ct. C Crook. 7C 88
Almond Gro. Bren 3H 11
Almond Rd. Eps. 7C 60
Almond Way. Mitc 4H 45
Almorah Rd. Houn. 4L 9
Almsgate. Comp. 1F 132
Alms Heath. Ock 8C 76
Almshouse La. Chess. 5J 59
Almshouses. Cher 6J 37
Almshouses. Dork 4H 119 (1L 201)
Almshouses. Wrec. 5D 128
Alnwick Gro. Mord. 3N 43
Aloes, The. Fleet 5C 88
Alphabet Gdns. Cars 5B 44
Alpha Pl. Mord. 7J 43
Alpha Rd. Chob 6J 53
Alpha Rd. Craw 3A 182
Alpha Rd. Croy 7B 46 (1F 200)
Alpha Rd. Surb 5M 41
Alpha Rd. Tedd 6D 24
Alpha Rd. Wok. 3D 74
Alpha Way. Egh 9E 20
Alphea Clo. SW19 8C 28
Alphington Av. Frim 5C 70
Alphington Grn. Frim 5C 70
Alpine Av. Surb 8B 42
Alpine Clo. Farnb 2J 89
Alpine Clo. Asc. 5A 34
Alpine Clo. Croy 9B 46 (5F 200)
Alpine Rd. Red. 9E 102
Alpine Rd. W on T. 6H 39
Alpine Vw. Cars 2C 62
Alresford Rd. Guild 4K 113
Alric Av. N Mald. 2D 42
Alsace Wlk. Camb 5N 69
Alsford Clo. Light. 8K 51
Alsom Av. Wor Pk 1F 60
Alston Clo. Surb 6H 41
Alston Rd. SW17. 5B 28
Alterton Clo. Wok. 4K 73
Alt Gro. SW19 8L 27
Althea St. SW6 5N 13
Althorne Rd. Red. 5E 122
Althorp Rd. SW17. 2D 28
Alton Clo. Iswth 5F 10
Alton Ct. Stai 9G 21
Alton Gdns. Twic 1D 24
Alton Ho. Red. 1E 122
Alton Ride. B'water 9H 49
Alton Rd. SW15 2F 26
Alton Rd. Croy. 9L 45
Alton Rd. Farnh 5B 128
Alton Rd. Fleet. 4D 88
Alton Rd. Rich 7L 11
Altyre Clo. Beck 4J 47
Altyre Rd. Croy 8A 46 (3E 200)
Altyre Way. Beck 4J 47
Alvernia Clo. G'ming. 9F 132
Alverstoke Gdns. Alder 3K 109
Alverstone Av. SW19 3M 27
Alverstone Rd. N Mald. 3E 42
Alverston Gdns. SE25 4B 46
Alvia Gdns. Sutt. 1A 62
Alway Av. Eps 2C 60
Alwin Pl. Farnh 5G 109
Alwyn Av. W4. 1C 12
Alwyn Clo. New Ad. 4L 65
Alwyne Ct. Wok 3A 74
Alwyne Rd. SW19 7L 27
Alwyns Clo. Cher 5J 37
Alwyns La. Cher. 5H 37
Amalgamated Dri. Bren 2G 11
Ambarrow Cres. Sand 6E 48
Ambarrow La. Sand. 5C 48
Ambassador. Brack 4L 31
Ambassador Clo. Houn. 5M 9
Amber Ct. Alder. 2A 110
Ambercroft Way. Coul. 6M 83
Amber Hill. Camb. 2F 70
Amberley Clo. Craw. 3G 183
Amberley Clo. H'ham. 2N 197
Amberley Clo. Send. 3H 95
Amberley Ct. Craw. 7B 162
(off County Oak La.)
Amberley Dri. Wdhm. 6H 55
(in two parts)
Amberley Gdns. Eps 1E 60
Amberley Grange. Alder. 4L 109
Amberley Gro. Croy. 6C 46
Amberley La. Milf 1B 152
Amberley Pl. Wind. 4G 4
Amberley Rd. H'ham 2N 197
Amberley Rd. Milf 9B 132
Amberley Way. Houn 8K 9
Amberley Way. Mord 6L 43
Amberside Clo. Iswth 9D 10
Amberwood Clo. Wall 2J 63
Amberwood Dri. Camb 8D 50
Amberwood Ri. N Mald 5D 42
Amblecote. Cob 8L 57
Ambleside. G'ming 6K 133
Ambleside Av. SW16. 5H 29
Ambleside Av. Beck. 4H 47
Ambleside Av. W on T. 7K 39
Ambleside Clo. Farnb. 1K 89
Ambleside Clo. If'd. 4J 181
Ambleside Clo. Myt 3E 90
Ambleside Clo. Red 8F 122
Ambleside Cres. Farnh. 6F 108
Ambleside Dri. Felt 2G 22
Ambleside Gdns. SW16. 6H 29
Ambleside Gdns. S Croy 5G 64
Ambleside Gdns. Sutt 3A 62
Ambleside Rd. Light 7K 51
Ambleside Way. Egh 8D 20
Ambrey Way. Wall 5H 63
Ambrose Clo. Orp 1N 67
Amelia Ho. W6 1H 13
(off Queen Caroline St.)
Amen Corner. 2J 31
Amen Corner. SW17 7D 28
Amen Corner Bus. Pk. Brack 2J 31
(Beehive Rd.)
Amen Corner Bus. Pk. Brack 1K 31
(Cain Rd.)
Amenity Way. Mord. 6H 43
American International University of London, The. 1L 25
(in Richmond University)
Amerland Rd. SW18 8L 13
Amersham Rd. Croy 5N 45
Amesbury Av. SW2 3J 29
Amesbury Clo. Wor Pk 7H 43
Amesbury Rd. Felt. 3L 23
Amey Dri. Bookh 2C 98
Amhurst Gdns. Iswth 5G 10
Amis Av. Eps 3A 60
Amis Av. New H. 6J 55
Amis Rd. Wok 6H 73
Amity Gro. SW20 9G 27
Amity Way. Camb 1C 70
Amlets La. Cranl. 5M 155
Ampere Way. Croy. 6J 45
(in two parts)
Amstel Way. Wok. 5J 73
Amundsen Rd. H'ham 2K 197
Amyand Cotts. Twic. 9H 11
Amyand La. Twic. 1H 25
Amyand Pk. Gdns. Twic. 1H 25
Amyand Pk. Rd. Twic 1G 25
Amy Clo. Wall. 4J 63
Amy Rd. Oxt 7A 106
Ancaster Cres. N Mald. 5F 42
Ancaster Dri. Asc 9J 17
Ancaster M. Beck 2G 47
Ancaster Rd. Beck. 2G 46
Ancells Bus. Pk. Fleet 1D 88
(Ancells Rd.)
Ancells Bus. Pk. Fleet 9C 68
(Harvest Cres.)
Ancells Rd. Fleet 1C 88
Anchor. SW18 7N 13
Anchorage Clo. SW19. 6M 27
Anchor Bus. Cen. Croy. 9J 45
Anchor Cotts. Blind H 3H 145
Anchor Ct. H'ham. 7J 197
Anchor Cres. Knap 4G 72
Anchor Hill. Knap 4G 72
Anchor Mdw. Farnb 1L 89
Anchor M. SW12 1F 28
Ancill Clo. W6 2K 13
Andermans. Wind 4A 4
Anders Corner. Brack. 9L 15
Anderson Clo. Eps. 8A 60
Anderson Clo. Sutt 7M 43
Anderson Dri. Ashf 5D 22
Anderson Pl. Bag 3J 51

Anderson Pl.—Ashdown Dri.

Anderson Pl. *Houn* . . . 7B **10**
Anderson Rd. *Wey* . . . 9E **38**
Andover Clo. *Eps* . . . 7C **60**
Andover Clo. *Felt* . . . 2G **23**
Andover Rd. *B'water* . . . 9H **49**
Andover Rd. *Twic* . . . 2D **24**
Andover Way. *Alder* . . . 5N **109**
Andreck Ct. *Beck* . . . 1L **47**
Andrewartha Rd. *Farnb* . . . 3C **90**
Andrew Clo. *Wokgm* . . . 3D **30**
Andrewes Ho. *Sutt* . . . 1M **61**
Andrews Clo. *C Crook* . . . 7B **88**
Andrew's Clo. *Eps* . . . 1E **80** (8M **201**)
Andrews Clo. *Wor Pk* . . . 8J **43**
Andrew's Ho. *S Croy* . . . 3N **63**
Andrews Rd. *Farnb* . . . 9K **69**
Andromeda Clo. *Bew* . . . 5K **181**
Anerley. . . . 1E **46**
Anerley Rd. *SE19 & SE20* . . . 1E **46**
Anfield Clo. *SW12* . . . 1G **28**
Angas Ct. *Wey* . . . 2D **56**
Angel Ct. *Comp* . . . 9D **112**
Angel Ct. *G'mlng* . . . 7G **133**
Angelfield. *Houn* . . . 7D **10**
Angel Ga. *Guild* . . . 4N **113** (5C **202**)
Angel Hill. *Sutt* . . . 9N **43**
(in two parts)
Angel Hill Dri. *Sutt* . . . 9N **43**
Angelica Gdns. *Croy* . . . 7G **46**
Angelica Rd. *Bisl* . . . 2D **72**
Angelica Rd. *Guild* . . . 8K **93**
Angell Clo. *M'bowr* . . . 4G **182**
Angel M. *SW15* . . . 1F **26**
Angel Pl. *Binf* . . . 7H **15**
Angel Rd. *Th Dit* . . . 6G **41**
Angel Wlk. *W6* . . . 1H **13**
Angers Clo. *Camb* . . . 8G **50**
Anglers Clo. *Rich* . . . 5J **25**
Anglers Reach. *Surb* . . . 4K **41**
Anglers, The. *King T* . . . 5H **203**
Anglesea Ho. *King T* . . . 8H **203**
Anglesea Rd. *King T* . . . 3K **41** (8H **203**)
Anglesey Av. *Farnb* . . . 7L **69**
Anglesey Clo. *Ashf* . . . 4B **22**
Anglesey Clo. *Craw* . . . 6A **182**
Anglesey Ct. Rd. *Cars* . . . 3F **62**
Anglesey Gdns. *Cars* . . . 3F **62**
Anglesey Rd. *Alder* . . . 3B **110**
Angles Rd. *SW16* . . . 6J **29**
Anglo Way. *Red* . . . 1F **122**
Angora Way. *Fleet* . . . 1C **88**
Angus Clo. *Chess* . . . 2N **59**
Angus Clo. *H'ham* . . . 4K **197**
Angus Ho. *SW2* . . . 1H **29**
Anlaby Rd. *Tedd* . . . 6E **24**
Annadale Ct. Red . . . *2D 122*
(off Warwick Rd.)
Annandale Dri. *Lwr Bo* . . . 5J **129**
Annandale Rd. *W4* . . . 1D **12**
Annandale Rd. *Croy* . . . 8D **46**
Annandale Rd. *Guild* . . . 5L **113**
Annan Dri. *Cars* . . . 5E **62**
Anne Armstrong Clo. *Alder* . . . 8B **90**
Anne Boleyn's Wlk. *King T* . . . 6L **25**
Anne Boleyn's Wlk. *Sutt* . . . 4J **61**
Anne Case M. *N Mald* . . . 2C **42**
Anneforde Pl. *Brack* . . . 8M **15**
Anners Clo. *Egh* . . . 2E **36**
Annesley Dri. *Croy* . . . 9J **47**
Anne's Wlk. *Cat* . . . 7B **84**
Annes Way. *C Crook* . . . 7C **88**
Annett Clo. *Shep* . . . 3F **38**
Annettes Cft. *C Crook* . . . 9A **88**
Annett Rd. *W on T* . . . 6H **39**
Anne Way. *W Mol* . . . 3B **40**
Annie Brookes Clo. *Stai* . . . 4F **20**
Anningsley Park. . . . 6E **54**
Anningsley Pk. *Ott* . . . 6D **54**
Annisdowne Clo. *Ab H* . . . 2G **137**
Annsworthy Av. *T Hth* . . . 2A **46**
Annsworthy Cres. *SE25* . . . 1A **46**
Ansell Gro. *Cars* . . . 7E **44**
Ansell Rd. *SW17* . . . 4C **28**
Ansell Rd. *Dork* . . . 4H **119** (1K **201**)
Ansell Rd. *Frim* . . . 6C **70**
Anselm Clo. *Croy* . . . 9C **46**
Anselm Rd. *SW6* . . . 2M **13**
Ansley Clo. *S Croy* . . . 1E **84**
Anson Clo. *Alder* . . . 1L **109**
Anson Clo. *Kenl* . . . 7A **84**
Anstead. *C'fold* . . . 9F **172**
Ansteadbrook. . . . 3N **189**
Anstice Clo. *W4* . . . 3D **12**
Anstiebury Clo. *Bear G* . . . 8J **139**
Anstie Grange Dri. *Holmw* . . . 6G **139**
Anstie La. *Cold* . . . 6E **138**
Anston Ct. *Guild* . . . 3H **113**
Anthony Rd. *SE25* . . . 5D **46**
Anthonys. . . . **8C 54**
Anthony Wall. *Warf* . . . 9D **16**
Anthony W. Ho. *Brock* . . . 5A **120**
Antlands La. *Ship B* . . . 4J **163**
Antlands La. E. *Ship B* . . . 4K **163**
Antlands La. W. *Ship B* . . . 4J **163**
Anton Cres. *Sutt* . . . 9M **43**
Antrobus Clo. *Sutt* . . . 2L **61**
Anvil Clo. *SW16* . . . 8G **28**
Anvil La. *Cob* . . . 1H **77**
Anvil Rd. *Sun* . . . 2H **39**
Anyards Rd. *Cob* . . . 9J **57**
Anzio Clo. *Alder* . . . 2M **109**
Apeldoorn Dri. *Wall* . . . 5J **63**
Aperdele Rd. *Lea* . . . 5G **79**
Aperfield. . . . 4G **87**
Aperfield Rd. *Big H* . . . 4G **87**
Aperfields. *Big H* . . . 4G **86**
Apers Av. *Wok* . . . 8B **74**
Apex Clo. *Wey* . . . 9F **38**
Apex Corner. (Junct.) . . . **4N 23**
Apex Dri. *Frim* . . . 5B **70**
Apex Retail Pk. *Felt* . . . 4N **23**
Apley Rd. *Reig* . . . 6M **121**
Aplin Way. *Isw th* . . . 4F **10**
Aplin Way. *Light* . . . 7L **51**
Apollo Dri. *Bord* . . . 7A **168**
Apollo Pl. *St J* . . . 6K **73**
Apollo Ri. *Farnb* . . . 1H **89**
Apostle Way. *T Hth* . . . 1M **45**
Apperlie Dri. *Horl* . . . 1G **162**
Appleby Clo. *Twic* . . . 3D **24**
Appleby Gdns. *Felt* . . . 2G **22**
Appleby Ho. *Eps* . . . 7C **60**
Appledore. *Brack* . . . 5L **31**
Appledore Clo. *SW17* . . . 3D **28**
Appledore M. *Farnb* . . . 7M **69**
Appledown Ri. *Coul* . . . 2G **83**
Applefield. *Craw* . . . 2C **182**
Apple Gth. *Bren* . . . 1K **11**
Applegarth. *Clay* . . . 2F **58**
Applegarth. *G'ming* . . . 4G **132**
Applegarth. *New Ad* . . . 4L **65**
(in two parts)
Applegarth Av. *Guild* . . . 3G **112**
Apple Gro. *Chess* . . . 1L **59**
Applelands Clo. *Wrec* . . . 7F **128**
Apple Mkt. *King T* . . . 1K **41** (4H **203**)
Appleton Gdns. *N Mald* . . . 5F **42**
Appleton Sq. *Mitc* . . . 9C **28**
Apple Tree Clo. *Fet* . . . 2C **98**
Appletree Clo. *G'ming* . . . 9J **133**
Appletree Ct. *Guild* . . . 9F **94**
Appletree Pl. *Brack* . . . 9M **15**
Appletrees Pl. *Wok* . . . 6M **73**
Apple Tree Way. *Owl* . . . 6J **49**
Appley Ct. *Camb* . . . 1N **69**
Appley Dri. *Camb* . . . 9N **49**
Approach Rd. *Ashf* . . . 7D **22**
Approach Rd. *SW20* . . . 1H **43**
Approach Rd. *Farnh* . . . 2H **129**
Approach Rd. *Purl* . . . 8L **63**
Approach Rd. *Tats* . . . 1D **106**
Approach Rd. *W Mol* . . . 4A **40**
Approach, The. *Bookh* . . . 1M **97**
Approach, The. *Dor P* . . . 4B **166**
April Clo. *Asht* . . . 5M **79**
April Clo. *Camb* . . . 4A **70**
April Clo. *Felt* . . . 4H **23**
April Clo. *H'ham* . . . 4J **197**
Aprilwood Clo. *Wdhm* . . . 7H **55**
Apsey Ct. *Binf* . . . 8K **15**
Apsley Ct. *Craw* . . . 5L **181**
Apsley Ho. *Houn* . . . 7N **9**
Apsley Rd. *SE25* . . . 3E **46**
Apsley Rd. *N Mald* . . . 2B **42**
Aquarius. *Twic* . . . 2H **25**
Aquarius Ct. *Craw* . . . 5K **181**
Aquila Clo. *Lea* . . . 8L **79**
Arabella Dri. *SW15* . . . 7D **12**
Aragon Av. *Eps* . . . 6G **60**
Aragon Av. *Th Dit* . . . 4F **40**
Aragon Clo. *New Ad* . . . 6A **66**
Aragon Clo. *Sun* . . . 7G **22**
Aragon Ct. *Brack* . . . 3A **32**
Aragon Ct. *E Mol* . . . 3C **40**
Aragon Rd. *King T* . . . 6L **25**
Aragon Rd. *Mord* . . . 5J **43**
Aragon Rd. *Yat* . . . 2B **68**
Aragon Wlk. *Byfl* . . . 9A **56**
Aram Ct. *Wok* . . . 2E **74**
Aran Ct. *Wey* . . . 8E **38**
Arbor Clo. *Beck* . . . 1L **47**
Arborfield Clo. *SW2* . . . 2K **29**
Arbour Clo. *Fet* . . . 1F **98**
Arbour, The. *Hurt* . . . 2C **132**
Arbrook Chase. *Esh* . . . 3C **58**
Arbrook Hall. *Clay* . . . 3F **58**
Arbrook La. *Esh* . . . 3C **58**
Arbury Ct. *SE20* . . . 1E **46**
Arbutus Clo. *Red* . . . 5A **122**
Arbutus Rd. *Red* . . . 6A **122**
Arcade. *Croy* . . . 8N **45** (3C **200**)
Arcade Pde. *Chess* . . . 2K **59**
Arcade, The. *Alder* . . . 2M **109**
Arcade, The. *Croy* . . . 4C **200**
Arcade, The. *Wokgm* . . . 2B **30**
Arcadia Clo. *Cars* . . . 1E **62**
Archbishop's Pl. *SW2* . . . 1K **29**
Archdale Pl. *King T* . . . 2A **42**
Archel Rd. *W14* . . . 2L **13**
Archeological Cen. . . . **3J 51**
Archer Clo. *King T* . . . 8L **25**
Archer M. *Hamp H* . . . 7C **24**
Archer Rd. *SE25* . . . 3E **46**
Archers Ct. *Craw* . . . 1B **182**
Archers Ct. *S Croy* . . . 8B **200**
Archery Pl. *Gom* . . . 8D **116**
Arches, The. Wind . . . *4F 4*
(off Goswell Rd.)
Arch Rd. *W on T* . . . 9L **39**
Archway Clo. *SW19* . . . 4N **27**
Archway Clo. *Wall* . . . 9H **45**
Archway M. SW15 . . . *7K 13*
(off Putney Bri. Rd.)
Archway M. *Dork* . . . 4G **119** (1J **201**)
Archway Pl. *Dork* . . . 4G **119** (1J **201**)
Archway St. *SW13* . . . 6D **12**
Arcturus Rd. *Craw* . . . 6K **181**
Arden Clo. *Brack* . . . 1D **32**
Arden Clo. *Reig* . . . 7N **121**
Arden Gro. *Orp* . . . 1K **67**
Ardon Rd. *Craw* . . . 5D **182**
Ardenrun. . . . **3L 145**
Ardent Clo. *SE25* . . . 2B **46**
Ardesley Wood. *Wey* . . . 1F **56**
Ardfern Av. *SW16* . . . 2L **45**
Ardingly. *Brack* . . . 5M **31**
Ardingly Clo. *Craw* . . . 1N **181**
Ardingly Clo. *Croy* . . . 9G **47**
Ardingly Rd. *W Hoa* . . . 9E **184**
Ardleigh Gdns. *Sutt* . . . 6M **43**
Ardlui Rd. *SE27* . . . 3N **29**
Ardmay Gdns. *Surb* . . . 4L **41** (8J **203**)
Ardmore Av. *Guild* . . . 1L **113**
Ardmore Ho. *Guild* . . . 1L **113**
Ardmore Way. *Guild* . . . 1L **113**
Ardrossan Av. *Camb* . . . 2E **70**
Ardrossan Gdns. *Wor Pk* . . . 9F **42**
Ardshiel Clo. *SW15* . . . 6J **13**
Ardshiel Dri. *Red* . . . 5C **122**
Ardwell Clo. *Crowt* . . . 2D **48**
Ardwell Rd. *SW2* . . . 3J **29**
Arena La. *Alder* . . . 9J **89**
Arenal Dri. *Crowt* . . . 4G **49**
Arethusa Way. *Bisl* . . . 3C **72**
Arford. . . . **3E 168**
Arford Comn. *Hdly* . . . 3E **168**
Arford Rd. *Hdly* . . . 4F **168**
Argent Clo. *Egh* . . . 7E **20**
Argent Ct. *Chess* . . . 9N **41**
Argente Clo. *Fleet* . . . 1C **88**
Argent Ter. *Col T* . . . 7K **49**
Argon M. *SW6* . . . 3M **13**
Argosy Gdns. *Stai* . . . 7H **21**
Argosy La. *Stanw* . . . 1M **21**
Argus Wlk. *Craw* . . . 6M **181**
Argyle Av. *Houn* . . . 9A **10**
(in two parts)
Argyle Pl. *W6* . . . 1G **13**
Argyle Rd. *Houn* . . . 8B **10**
Argyle St. *Brkwd* . . . 8L **71**
Ariel Way. *Houn* . . . 6J **9**
Arkell Gro. *SE19* . . . 8M **29**
Arkendale. *Felb* . . . 6K **165**
Arklow M. *Surb* . . . 8L **41**
Ark, The. W6 . . . *1J 13*
(off Talgarth Rd.)
Arkwright Dri. *Brack* . . . 1J **31**
Arkwright Ho. SW2 . . . *1J 29*
(off Streatham Pl.)
Arkwright Rd. *Coln* . . . 5G **6**
Arkwright Rd. *S Croy* . . . 6C **64**
Arlesey Clo. *SW15* . . . 8K **13**
Arlington Bus. Pk. *Brack* . . . 1M **31**
Arlington Clo. *Brack* . . . 9M **15**
Arlington Clo. *Sutt* . . . 8M **43**
Arlington Clo. *Twic* . . . 9J **11**
Arlington Ct. *Hay* . . . 1F **8**
Arlington Ct. *Reig* . . . 1N **121**
Arlington Dri. *Cars* . . . 8D **44**
Arlington Gdns. *W4* . . . 1B **12**
Arlington Lodge. *Wey* . . . 1C **56**
Arlington M. *Twic* . . . 9H **11**
Arlington Pk. Mans. W4 . . . *1B 12*
(off Sutton La. N.)
Arlington Pas. *Tedd* . . . 5F **24**
Arlington Rd. *Ashf* . . . 6A **22**
Arlington Rd. *Rich* . . . 3K **25**
Arlington Rd. *Surb* . . . 5K **41**
Arlington Rd. *Tedd* . . . 5F **24**
Arlington Rd. *Twic* . . . 9J **11**
Arlington Sq. *Brack* . . . 1M **31**
Arlington Ter. *Alder* . . . 2L **109**
Armadale Rd. *SW6* . . . 3M **13**
Armadale Rd. *Felt* . . . 8H **9**
Armadale Rd. *Wok* . . . 4K **73**
Armfield Clo. *W Mol* . . . 4N **39**
Armfield Cres. *Mitc* . . . 1D **44**
Armistice Gdns. *SE25* . . . 2D **46**
Armitage Ct. *Asc* . . . 5N **33**
Armitage Dri. *Frim* . . . 5D **70**
Armoury Way. *SW18* . . . 8M **13**
Armstrong Clo. *W on T* . . . 5H **39**
Armstrong Mall. *Farnb* . . . 1J **89**
Armstrong Rd. *Eng G* . . . 7M **19**
Armstrong Rd. *Felt* . . . 6M **23**
Armstrong Way. *Farnb* . . . 4G **88**
Army Medical Services Mus. . . . **4F 90**
(in Keogh Barracks)
Army Physical Training Corps Mus. . . . ***8N 89***
(off Queen's Av.)
Armytage Rd. *Houn* . . . 3L **9**
Arnal Cres. *SW18* . . . 1K **27**
Arncliffe. *Brack* . . . 4M **31**
Arndale Wlk. *SW18* . . . 8N **13**
Arndale Way. *Egh* . . . 6C **20**
Arne Clo. *Craw* . . . 6L **181**
Arne Gro. *Horl* . . . 6C **142**
Arnewood Clo. *SW15* . . . 2F **26**
Arnewood Clo. *Oxs* . . . 1B **78**
Arneys La. *Mitc* . . . 5E **44**
Arnfield Clo. *If'd* . . . 4K **181**
Arnhem Clo. *Alder* . . . 2N **109**
Arnhem Dri. *New Ad* . . . 7N **65**
Arnison Rd. *E Mol* . . . 3D **40**
Arnold Cres. *Isw th* . . . 8D **10**
Arnold Dri. *Chess* . . . 3K **59**
Arnold Mans. W14 . . . *2L 13*
(off Queen's Club Gdns.)
Arnold Rd. *SW17* . . . 8D **28**
Arnold Rd. *Stai* . . . 8L **21**
Arnold Rd. *Wok* . . . 2D **74**
Arnott Clo. *W4* . . . 1C **12**
Arnulls Rd. *SW16* . . . 7M **29**
Arodene Rd. *SW2* . . . 1K **29**
Arosa Rd. *Twic* . . . 9K **11**
(in two parts)
Arragon Gdns. *SW16* . . . 8J **29**
Arragon Gdns. *W Wick* . . . 9L **47**
Arragon Rd. *SW18* . . . 2M **27**
Arragon Rd. *Twic* . . . 1G **24**
Arran Clo. *Craw* . . . 6N **181**
Arran Clo. *Wall* . . . 1F **62**
Arran Ct. *H'ham* . . . 6G **197**
Arran Way. *Esh* . . . 8B **40**
Arras Av. *Mord* . . . 4A **44**
Arreton Mead. *Hors* . . . 1B **74**
Arrivals Rd. Gat A . . . *2D 162*
(off Gatwick Way)
Arrol Rd. *Beck* . . . 2F **46**
Arrow Ct. SW5 . . . *1M 13*
(off W. Cromwell Rd.)
Arrow Ind. Est. *Farnb* . . . 3L **89**
Arrow Rd. *Farnb* . . . 3L **89**
Artel Cft. *Craw* . . . 3E **182**
Arterberry Rd. *SW20* . . . 8H **27**
Arthur Clo. *Bag* . . . 6J **51**
Arthur Clo. *Farnh* . . . 2G **129**
Arthur Ct. *Croy* . . . 4F **200**
Arthur Henderson Ho. SW6 . . . *5L 13*
(off Fulham Rd.)
Arthur Rd. *SW19* . . . 6L **27**
Arthur Rd. *Big H* . . . 2E **86**
Arthur Rd. *Farnh* . . . 2G **129**
(in two parts)
Arthur Rd. *H'ham* . . . 7K **197**
Arthur Rd. *If'd* . . . 3K **181**
Arthur Rd. *King T* . . . 8N **25**
Arthur Rd. *N Mald* . . . 4G **43**
Arthur Rd. *Wind* . . . 4F **4**
Arthur's Bri. Rd. *Wok* . . . 4M **73**
Arthur's Bri. Wharf. *Wok* . . . 4N **73**
Arthurstone Birches. *Binf* . . . 6J **15**
Arthur St. *Alder* . . . 2N **109**
Artillery Rd. *Alder* . . . 2N **109**
(High St.)
Artillery Rd. *Alder* . . . 6B **90**
(North Rd.)
Artillery Rd. *Guild* . . . 4N **113** (4C **202**)
Artillery Ter. *Guild* . . . 3N **113** (3C **202**)
Artington. . . . **8M 113**
Artington Clo. *Orp* . . . 1L **67**
Artington Wlk. *Guild* . . . 6M **113** (8B **202**)
Artslink Theatre. . . . **9B 50**
Arun Ct. *SE25* . . . 4D **46**
Arundale. *King T* . . . 8H **203**
Arundel Av. *Eps* . . . 6G **60**
Arundel Av. *Mord* . . . 3L **43**
Arundel Av. *S Croy* . . . 6D **64**
Arundel Clo. *Craw* . . . 3G **182**
Arundel Clo. *Croy* . . . 9M **45**
Arundel Clo. *Fleet* . . . 5C **88**
Arundel Clo. *Hamp H* . . . 6B **24**
Arundel Clo. *Pass* . . . 9C **168**
Arundel Ct. SW13 . . . *2G 13*
(off Arundel Ter.)
Arundel Ct. *Brom* . . . 1N **47**
Arundel Ho. *Croy* . . . 8D **200**
Arundel Mans. SW6 . . . *4L 13*
(off Kelvedon Rd.)
Arundel Pl. *Farnh* . . . 1K **129**
Arundel Rd. *Camb* . . . 2G **70**
Arundel Rd. *Croy* . . . 5A **46**
Arundel Rd. *Dork* . . . 5G **118** (3H **201**)
Arundel Rd. *Houn* . . . 6K **9**
Arundel Rd. *King T* . . . 1A **42**
Arundel Rd. *Sutt* . . . 4L **61**
Arundel Ter. *SW13* . . . 2G **13**
Arun Ho. *King T* . . . 9K **25** (1H **203**)
Arunside. *H'ham* . . . 7G **196**
Arun Way. *H'ham* . . . 7L **197**
Aschurch Rd. *Croy* . . . 6C **46**
Ascot. . . . **2L 33**
Ascot Ct. *Alder* . . . 3M **109**
Ascot Heath. . . . **1K 33**
Ascot M. *Wall* . . . 5G **63**
Ascot Pk. *Asc* . . . 2H **33**
Ascot Racecourse. . . . **1L 33**
Ascot Rd. *SW17* . . . 7E **28**
Ascot Rd. *Felt* . . . 2B **22**
Ascot Rd. *M'head & Warf* . . . 1B **16**
Ascot Wood Pl. *Asc* . . . 2L **33**
Ash. . . . **9E 90**
Ashbourne. *Brack* . . . 5L **31**
Ashbourne Clo. *As* . . . 1G **110**
Ashbourne Clo. *Coul* . . . 5G **83**
Ashbourne Ct. *As* . . . 1G **110**
Ashbourne Gro. *W4* . . . 1D **12**
Ashbourne Ri. *Orp* . . . 1M **67**
Ashbourne Rd. *Mitc* . . . 8E **28**
Ashbourne Ter. *SW19* . . . 8L **27**
Ash Bri. Cvn. Pk. *As* . . . 4C **110**
Ashbrook Rd. *Old Win* . . . 1L **19**
Ashburnham Ct. *Beck* . . . 1M **47**
Ashburnham Pk. *Esh* . . . 1C **58**
Ashburnham Rd. *SW10* . . . 3N **13**
Ashburnham Rd. *Craw* . . . 5F **182**
Ashburnham Rd. *Rich* . . . 4H **25**
Ashburn Pl. *SW7* . . . 1N **13**
Ashburton Av. *Croy* . . . 7E **46**
Ashburton Clo. *Croy* . . . 7D **46**
Ashburton Enterprise Cen. *SW15* . . . 9H **13**
Ashburton Gdns. *Croy* . . . 8D **46**
Ashburton Memorial Homes. *Croy* . . . 6E **46**
Ashburton Rd. *Croy* . . . 8D **46**
Ashbury Cres. *Guild* . . . 1E **114**
Ashbury Dri. *B'water* . . . 5M **69**
Ashbury Pl. *SW19* . . . 7A **28**
Ashby Av. *Chess* . . . 3N **59**
Ashby Ct. *H'ham* . . . 6L **197**
Ashby's Clo. *Eden* . . . 3M **147**
Ashby Wlk. *Croy* . . . 5N **45**
Ashby Way. *W Dray* . . . 3B **8**
Ash Church Rd. *As* . . . 2F **110**
Ash Clo. *SE20* . . . 1F **46**
Ash Clo. *As* . . . 1F **110**
Ash Clo. *B'water* . . . 1H **69**
Ash Clo. *Cars* . . . 8D **44**
Ash Clo. *Craw D* . . . 1F **184**
Ash Clo. *Eden* . . . 2K **147**
Ash Clo. *Ling* . . . 6A **146**
Ash Clo. *N Mald* . . . 1C **42**
Ash Clo. *Pyr* . . . 2J **75**
Ash Clo. *Red* . . . 8G **103**
Ash Clo. *Tad* . . . 9D **100**
Ash Clo. *Wok* . . . 7A **74**
Ash Combe. *C'fold* . . . 5D **172**
Ashcombe Av. *Surb* . . . 6K **41**
Ashcombe Dri. *Eden* . . . 8K **127**
Ashcombe Rd. *SW19* . . . 6M **27**
Ashcombe Rd. *Cars* . . . 3E **62**
Ashcombe Rd. *Dork* . . . 3G **118**
Ashcombe Rd. *Red* . . . 5G **102**
Ashcombe Sq. *N Mald* . . . 2B **42**
Ashcombe St. *SW6* . . . 5N **13**
Ashcombe Ter. *Tad* . . . 7G **80**
Ash Ct. *SW19* . . . 8K **27**
Ash Ct. *Add* . . . 2K **55**
Ash Ct. *Eps* . . . 1B **60**
Ash Ct. *Wokgm* . . . 2B **30**
Ashcroft. *Shalf* . . . 1A **134**
Ashcroft Pk. *Cob* . . . 8M **57**
Ashcroft Ri. *Coul* . . . 3J **83**
Ashcroft Rd. *Chess* . . . 9M **41**
Ashcroft Sq. *W6* . . . 1H **13**
Ashcroft Theatre. . . . **9A 46 (4D 200)**
Ashdale. *Bookh* . . . 4C **98**
Ashdale Clo. *Stai* . . . 3N **21**
Ashdale Clo. *Twic* . . . 1C **24**
Ashdale Pk. *Finch* . . . 1B **48**
Ashdale Way. *Twic* . . . 1B **24**
Ashdene Clo. *Ashf* . . . 9D **22**
Ashdene Cres. *As* . . . 1E **110**
Ashdene Rd. *As* . . . 1E **110**
Ashdown Av. *Farnb* . . . 2B **90**
Ashdown Clo. *Beck* . . . 1L **47**
Ashdown Clo. *Brack* . . . 1E **32**
Ashdown Clo. *F Row* . . . 7J **187**
Ashdown Clo. *Reig* . . . 7N **121**
Ashdown Ct. *Craw* . . . 6D **182**
Ashdown Ct. *Sutt* . . . 3A **62**
Ashdown Dri. *Craw* . . . 6B **182**

Branksome Clo.—Brockbridge Ho.

Branksome Clo. *Tedd* 5D 24
Branksome Clo. *W on T* 8L 39
Branksome Ct. *Fleet* 4A 88
Branksome Hill Rd. *Col T* 8K 49
Branksome Pk. Rd. *Camb* 9C 50
Branksome Rd. *SW19* 9M 27
Branksome Way. *N Mald* 9B 26
Branksomewood Rd. *Fleet* 3A 88
Bransby Rd. *Chess* 3L 59
Branson Rd. *Bord* 6A 168
Branstone Rd. *Rich* 4M 11
Brantridge Rd. *Craw* 5D 182
Brants Bri. *Brack* 1C 32
Brantwood Av. *Iswth* 7G 10
Brantwood Clo. *W Byf* 9J 55
Brantwood Ct. W Byf 9H 55 (off Brantwood Dri.)
Brantwood Dri. *W Byf* 9H 55
Brantwood Gdns. *W Byf* 9H 55
Brantwood Rd. *S Croy* 5N 63
Brasenose Dri. *SW13* 2H 13
Brassey Clo. *Felt* 2H 23
Brassey Clo. *Oxt* 7C 106
Brassey Hill. *Oxt* 7C 106
Brassey Rd. *Oxt* 8B 106
Brasted Clo. *Sutt* 6M 61
Brasted Rd. *W'ham & Bras* 4M 107
Brathway Rd. *SW18* 1M 27
Bratten Ct. *Croy* 5A 46
Bravington Clo. *Shep* 4A 38
Braxted Pk. *SW16* 7K 29
Braybourne Dri. *Iswth* 3F 10
Braybrooke Rd. *Brack* 8N 15
Bray Clo. *M'bowr* 6H 183
Bray Ct. *SW16* 6J 29
Braycourt Av. *W on T* 6J 39
Braye Clo. *Sand* 6H 49
Bray Gdns. *Wok* 3G 74
Bray Rd. *Guild* 4L 113
Bray Rd. *Stoke D* 3M 77
Braywood Av. *Egh* 7B 20
Braziers La. *Wink R* 6H 17
Brazil Clo. *Bedd* 6J 45
Breakfield. *Coul* 3J 83
Breamore Clo. *SW15* 2F 26
Breamwater Gdns. *Rich* 4H 25
Breasley Clo. *SW15* 7G 13
Brecon Clo. *Farnb* 7J 69
Brecon Clo. *Mitc* 2J 45
Brecon Clo. *Wor Pk* 8H 43
Brecon Rd. *W6* 2K 13
Brecons, The. *Wey* 1E 56
Bredon Rd. *Croy* 6C 46
Bredune. *Kenl* 2A 84
Breech La. *Tad* 2F 100
Breech, The. *Col T* 8K 49
Breer St. *SW6* 6N 13
Breezehurst Dri. *Craw* 6K 181
Bregsells La. *Bear G* 7K 139
Bremer Rd. *Stai* 4J 21
Bremner Av. *Horl* 7D 142
Brenda Rd. *SW17* 3D 28
Brende Gdns. *W Mol* 3B 40
Brendon Clo. *Esh* 3C 58
Brendon Clo. *Hay* 3D 8
Brendon Ct. *S'hall* 1B 10
Brendon Dri. *Esh* 3C 58
Brendon Rd. *Farnb* 7J 69
Brenley Clo. *Mitc* 2E 44
Brentford. 2K 11
Brentford Bus. Cen. *Bren* 3J 11
Brentford End. 3H 11
Brentford F.C. (Griffin Pk.) 2K 11
Brentford Ho. *Twic* 1H 25
Brentford Musical Mus. 2L 11
Brent Lea. *Bren* 3J 11
Brentmoor Rd. *W End* 9N 51
Brent Rd. *Bren* 2J 11
Brent Rd. *S Croy* 5E 64
Brent Side. *Bren* 2J 11
Brentside Executive Cen. *Bren* 2H 11
Brentwaters Bus. Pk. *Bren* 3J 11
Brent Way. *Bren* 3K 11
Brentwick Gdns. *Bren* 1L 11
Brentwood Ct. *Add* 1K 55
Brethart Rd. *Frim* 5C 70
Bretlands Rd. *Cher* 8G 36
Brettgrave. *Eps* 6B 60
Brett Ho. Clo. *SW15* 1J 27
Brettingham Clo. *Craw* 6K 181
Brewer Rd. *Craw* 5C 182
Brewers Clo. *Farnb* 9M 69
Brewers La. *Rich* 8K 11
Brewer St. *Blet* 9N 103
Brewery La. *Byfl* 9N 55
Brewery La. *Twic* 1F 24
Brewery M. Cen. *Iswth* 6G 10
Brewery Rd. *Wok* 4N 73
Brew Ho. Rd. *Str G & Brock* 7B 120
Brewhouse St. *SW15* 6K 13
Brewhurst La. *Loxw* 6J 193 (in two parts)
Breydon Wlk. *Craw* 5F 182
Brian Av. *S Croy* 8B 64
Briane Rd. *Eps* 6B 60
Briar Av. *SW16* 8K 29
Briar Av. *Light* 8K 51
Briar Banks. *Cars* 5E 62
Briar Clo. *Craw* 9A 162
Briar Clo. *Eden* 9M 127
Briar Clo. *Hamp* 6N 23
Briar Clo. *Iswth* 8F 10
Briar Clo. *W Byf* 7K 55
Briar Ct. *SW15* 7G 13
Briar Ct. *Sutt* 1H 61
Briar Gro. *S Croy* 9D 64
Briar Hill. *Purl* 7J 63
Briar La. *Cars* 5E 62
Briar La. *Croy* 1L 65
Briarleas Ct. *Farnb* 5B 90
Briar Patch. *G'ming* 5G 133
Briar Rd. *SW16* 2J 45
Briar Rd. *Send* 2D 94
Briar Rd. *Shep* 4A 38
Briar Rd. *Twic* 2E 24
Briars Clo. *Farnb* 2J 89
Briars Ct. *Oxs* 1D 78
Briars, The. *As* 3F 110
Briars, The. *Slou* 1B 6
Briars, The. *Stai* 8J 7
Briars Wood. *Horl* 7G 142
Briarswood Clo. *Craw* 1H 183
Briarswood Way. *Orp* 2N 67
Briar Wlk. *SW15* 7G 13
Briar Wlk. *W Byf* 8J 55
Briar Way. *Guild* 8D 94
Briarwood Clo. *Felt* 5F 22
Briarwood Ct. Wor Pk 7F 42 (off Avenue, The)
Briarwood Rd. *Eps* 3F 60
Briarwood Rd. *Wok* 6G 73
Briavels Ct. *Eps* 2D 80
Brickbarn Clo. SW10 3N 13 (off King's Barn)
Brickbat All. *Lea* 8H 79
Brick Farm Clo. *Rich* 4A 12
Brickfield Clo. *Bren* 3J 11
Brickfield Cotts. *Alder* 4J 109
Brickfield Cotts. *Crowt* 4E 48
Brickfield Cotts. *Norm* 3A 112
Brickfield Farm Gdns. *Orp* 1L 67
Brickfield La. *Hay* 2E 8
Brickfield Rd. *SW19* 5N 27
Brickfield Rd. *Out* 2L 143
Brickfield Rd. *T Hth* 9M 29
Brickfields Ind. Pk. *Brack* 1L 31
Brick Hill. 1F 52
Brickhouse La. *S God & Newc* 4F 144
Brick Kiln La. *Oxt* 8E 106
Bricklands. *Craw D* 2E 184
Brick La. *Fleet* 3A 88
Bricksbury Hill. *Farnh* 5H 109
Brickwood Rd. *Croy* 8B 46 (2F 200)
Brickyard Copse. *Ockl* 6C 158
Brickyard La. *Craw D* 1E 184
Brickyard La. *Wott* 1L 137
Brideake Clo. *Craw* 6M 181
Bridge Av. *W6* 1H 13
Bridge Av. Mans. W6 1H 13 (off Bridge Av.)
Bridge Barn La. *Wok* 5N 73
Bridge Clo. *Byfl* 8A 56
Bridge Clo. *Stai* 5G 20
Bridge Clo. *Tedd* 5F 24
Bridge Clo. *W on T* 6G 38
Bridge Clo. *Wok* 4M 73
Bridge Ct. *Wey* 1C 56
Bridge Ct. *Wok* 4N 73
Bridge End. 7C 76
Bridge End. *Camb* 2N 69
Bridgefield. *Farnh* 1J 129
Bridgefield Clo. *Bans* 2H 81
Bridgefield Rd. *Sutt* 3M 61
Bridgefoot. *Sun* 9G 23
Bridge Gdns. *Ashf* 8D 22
Bridge Gdns. *E Mol* 3D 40
Bridgeham Clo. *Wey* 2B 56
Bridgeham Way. *Small* 9M 143
Bridgehill Clo. *Guild* 1K 113
Bridge Ho. Sutt 3N 61 (off Bridge Rd.)
Bridge Ind. Est. *Horl* 8F 142
Bridgelands. *Copt* 7L 163
Bridge La. *Vir W* 4A 36
Bridgeman Dri. *Wind* 5D 4
Bridgeman Rd. *Tedd* 7G 24
Bridgemead. Frim 6A 70 (off Frimley High St.)
Bridge Mead. *Pirb* 4C 92
Bridge M. *G'ming* 7H 133
Bridge M. *St J* 4N 73
Bridge M. *Tong* 5D 110
Bridgend Rd. *SW18* 7N 13
Bridgepark. *SW18* 8M 13
Bridge Pk. *Guild* 9E 94
Bridge Pl. *Croy* 7A 46
Bri. Retail Pk. *Wokgm* 3A 30
Bridge Rd. *Farnb* 1L 89
Bridge Rd. *Alder* 4M 109
Bridge Rd. *Asc* 4A 34
Bridge Rd. *Bag* 4J 51
Bridge Rd. *Camb* 3N 69
Bridge Rd. *Cher* 6K 37
Bridge Rd. *Chess* 2L 59
Bridge Rd. *Cranl* 8N 155
Bridge Rd. *E Mol* 3D 40
Bridge Rd. *Eps* 8E 60
Bridge Rd. *G'ming* 6H 133
Bridge Rd. *Hasl* 1G 189
Bridge Rd. *Houn & Isw th* 6D 10
Bridge Rd. *Rud* 1E 194
Bridge Rd. *Sutt* 3N 61
Bridge Rd. *Twic* 9H 11
Bridge Rd. *Wall* 2F 62
Bridge Rd. *Wey* 1A 56
Bridge Row. *Croy* 7A 46 (1E 200)
Bridges Clo. *Horl* 8H 143
Bridges Ct. *H'ham* 3M 197
Bridges La. *Croy* 1J 63
Bridges Pl. *SW6* 4L 13
Bridge Sq. *Farnh* 1H 129
Bridges Rd. *SW19* 7N 27
Bridges Rd. M. *SW19* 7N 27
Bridge St. *W4* 1C 12
Bridge St. *Coln* 3F 6
Bridge St. *G'ming* 7H 133
Bridge St. *Guild* 4M 113 (5B 202)
Bridge St. *Lea* 9G 79
Bridge St. *Rich* 8K 11
Bridge St. *Stai* 5G 21
Bridge St. *W on T* 7F 38
Bridge St. Pas. *Guild* 5B 202
Bridge Vw. *W6* 1H 13
Bridge Vw. *S'dale* 6E 34
Bridge Wlk. *Yat* 8C 48
Bridgewater Ct. *Slou* 1C 6
Bridgewater Rd. *Wey* 3E 56
Bridgewater Ter. *Wind* 4G 4
Bridgewater Way. *Wind* 4G 4
Bridge Way. *Cob* 9G 57
Bridge Way. *Coul* 6C 82
Bridge Way. *Twic* 1C 24
Bridge Wharf. *Cher* 6L 37
Bridge Wharf Rd. *Isw th* 6H 11
Bridgewood Rd. *SW16* 8H 29
Bridgewood Rd. *Wor Pk* 1F 60
Bridgford St. *SW18* 4A 28
Bridle Clo. *Eps* 2C 60
Bridle Clo. *Gray* 6M 169
Bridle Clo. *King T* 3K 41 (7H 203)
Bridle Clo. *Sun* 2H 39
Bridle Ct. *Alder* 2K 109
Bridle End. *Eps* 9E 60
Bridle La. *Stoke D & Oxs* 2B 78
Bridle La. *Twic* 9H 11
Bridle Path. *Croy* 9J 45 (in two parts)
Bridle Path, The. *Eps* 6H 61
Bridlepath Way. *Felt* 2F 22
Bridle Rd. *Clay* 3H 59
Bridle Rd. *Croy* 9K 47 (in two parts)
Bridle Rd. *Eps* 9E 60
Bridle Rd. *S Croy* 5D 64
Bridle Rd., The. *Purl* 6J 63
Bridle Way. *Craw* 2H 183
Bridle Way. *Croy* 1K 65
Bridle Way. *Orp* 1L 67
Bridleway Clo. *Eps* 6H 61
Bridle Way, The. *Croy* 6H 65
Bridleway, The. *Wall* 2G 63
Bridlington Clo. *Big H* 6D 86
Bridport Rd. *T Hth* 2L 45
Brier Lea. *Lwr K* 4L 101
Brierley. *New Ad* 3L 65 (in two parts)
Brierley Clo. *SE25* 3D 46
Brierley Rd. *SW12* 3G 28
Brierly Clo. *Guild* 1K 113
Brier Rd. *Tad* 6G 81
Brigade Pl. *Cat* 9N 83
Briggs Clo. *Mitc* 9F 28
Bright Hill. *Guild* 5A 114 (6D 202)
Brightlands Rd. *Reig* 1A 122
Brightman Rd. *SW18* 2B 28
Brighton Clo. *Add* 2L 55
Brighton Rd. *Add* 2L 55
Brighton Rd. *Alder* 4A 110
Brighton Rd. *Coul & Purl* 5G 83
Brighton Rd. *G'ming* 7H 133
Brighton Rd. *Hand* 8N 199
Brighton Rd. *Horl* 9D 142
Brighton Rd. *H'ham* 7K 197
Brighton Rd. *Kgswd & Lwr K* 9K 81
Brighton Rd. *Mers & Coul* 1F 102
Brighton Rd. *Peas P & Hand* 5N 199
Brighton Rd. *Purl & S Croy* 7L 63
Brighton Rd. *Red* 4D 122
Brighton Rd. *Salf* 1E 142
Brighton Rd. *S Croy* 2N 63 (8C 200)
Brighton Rd. *Surb* 5J 41
Brighton Rd. *Sutt* 7M 61
Brighton Rd. *Tad & Bans* 8K 81
Brighton Ter. *Red* 4D 122
Brightside Av. *Stai* 8L 21
Brightwell Clo. *Croy* 7L 45
Brightwell Cres. *SW17* 6D 28
Brightwells Rd. *Farnh* 1H 129
Brigstock Rd. *Coul* 2F 82
Brigstock Rd. *T Hth* 4L 45
Brimshot La. *Chob* 5H 53
Brimstone La. *Holmw* 3M 139
Brind Cotts. *Chob* 6J 53
Brindle Clo. *Alder* 5N 109
Brindles, The. *Bans* 4L 81
Brinkley Rd. *Wor Pk* 8G 42
Brinksway. *Fleet* 4B 88
Brinn's La. *B'water* 1H 69
Brinsworth Clo. *Twic* 2D 24
Brinsworth Ho. *Twic* 3D 24
Brisbane Av. *SW19* 9N 27
Brisbane Clo. *Craw* 9B 162
Briscoe Rd. *SW19* 7B 28
Brisson Clo. *Esh* 2N 57
Bristol Clo. *Craw* 9H 163
Bristol Clo. *Stanw* 9N 7
Bristol Clo. *Wall* 4J 63
Bristol Ct. *Stanw* 9N 7
Bristol Gdns. *SW15* 1H 27
Bristol Rd. *Mord* 4A 44
Bristow Rd. *Camb* 3N 69
Bristow Rd. *Croy* 1J 63
Bristow Rd. *Houn* 6C 10
Britannia Clo. *Bord* 6A 168
Britannia Ind. Est. *Coln* 5G 6
Britannia La. *Twic* 1C 24
Britannia Rd. *SW6* 3N 13 (in two parts)
Britannia Rd. *Surb* 6M 41
Britannia Way. SW6 3N 13 (off Britannia Rd.)
Britannia Way. *Stanw* 1M 21
British Gro. *W4* 1E 12
British Gro. Pas. *W4* 1E 12
British Gro. S. W4 1E 12 (off British Gro. Pas.)
Briton Clo. *S Croy* 7B 64
Briton Cres. *S Croy* 7B 64
Briton Hill Rd. *S Croy* 6B 64
Brittain Ct. *Sand* 8H 49
Brittain Rd. *W on T* 2L 57
Britten Clo. *As* 2F 110
Britten Clo. *Craw* 6L 181
Britten Clo. *H'ham* 4A 198
Brittenden Clo. *Orp* 3N 67
Brittenden Pde. *G Str* 3N 67
Brittens Clo. *Guild* 7K 93
Brittleware Cotts. *Charl* 8L 141
Brixton Hill. *SW2* 1J 29
Brixton Hill Pl. *SW2* 1J 29
Broadacre. *Stai* 6J 21
Broad Acres. *G'ming* 3H 133
Broadacres. *Guild* 1H 113
Broadbridge. 1L 163
Broadbridge Cotts. *Small* 1L 163
Broadbridge Heath. 5D 196
Broadbridge Heath By-Pass. *Broad H* 5C 196
Broadbridge Heath Rd. *Broad H & Warn* 4D 196
Broadbridge La. *Small* 8L 143
Broadbridge Retail Pk. *Broad H* 5E 196
Broad Clo. *W on T* 9L 39
Broadcommon Rd. *Hurst* 2A 14
Broadcoombe. *S Croy* 4F 64
Broadeaves Clo. *S Croy* 2B 64
Broadfield. 7N 181
Broadfield Barton. *Craw* 7N 181
Broadfield Clo. *Croy* 8K 45
Broadfield Clo. *Tad* 7H 81
Broadfield Dri. *Craw* 6N 181
Broadfield Pk. *Craw* 7B 182
Broadfield Pl. *Craw* 7N 181
Broadfield Rd. *Peasl* 2E 136
Broadfields. *E Mol* 5E 40
Broadford. 1N 133
Broadford La. *Chob* 8H 53
Broadford Pk. *Shalf* 1N 133
Broadford Rd. *P'rmsh & Shalf* 2M 133
Broadgates Rd. *SW18* 2B 28
Broad Green. 6M 45
Broad Grn. Av. *Croy* 6M 45
Broadham Green. 1N 125
Broadham Grn. Rd. *Oxt* 1N 125
Broadham Pl. *Oxt* 9N 105
Broad Ha'penny. *Wrec* 7F 128
Broad Highway. *Cob* 1L 77
Broadhurst. *Farnb* 1H 89
Broadhurst. *Asht* 3L 79
Broadhurst Clo. *Rich* 8M 11
Broadhurst Gdns. *Reig* 6N 121
Broadlands. *Farnb* 3C 90
Broadlands. *Frim* 6D 70
Broadlands. *Hanw* 4A 24
Broadlands. *Horl* 7G 142
Broadlands Av. *SW16* 3J 29
Broadlands Av. *Shep* 5D 38
Broadlands Clo. *SW16* 3J 29
Broadlands Ct. *Brack* 9K 15
Broadlands Ct. Rich 3N 11 (off Kew Gdns. Rd.)
Broadlands Dri. *S Asc* 6N 33
Broadlands Dri. *Warl* 6F 84
Broadlands Way. *N Mald* 5E 42
Broad La. *Brack* 2A 32
Broad La. *Hamp* 8N 23
Broad La. *Newd* 7C 140
Broadley Grn. *W'sham* 4A 52
Broadmead. *Farnb* 2J 89
Broadmead. *W14* 1K 13
Broad Mead. *Asht* 4M 79
Broadmead. *Horl* 7G 143
Broadmead. Mers 6G 102 (off Station Rd.)
Broadmead Av. *Wor Pk* 6F 42
Broadmead Clo. *Hamp* 7A 24
Broadmead Rd. *Send & Old Wok* 9D 74
Broadmeads. *Wok* 9D 74
Broadmoor. 3A 138
Broadmoor Est. *Crowt* 3J 49
Broadoak. *Sun* 7G 23
Broadoaks. *Surb* 8A 42
Broadoaks Cres. *W Byf* 9K 55
Broadpool Cotts. *Asc* 8L 17
Broadrick Heath. *Warf* 8B 16
Broad St. *Guild* 1F 112
Broad St. *Tedd* 7F 24
Broad St. *W End* 9A 52
Broad St. *Wokgm* 2B 30
Broad Street Common. 9G 92
Broad St. Wlk. *Wokgm* 2B 30
Broadview Rd. *SW16* 8H 29
Broad Wlk. *Cat* 9C 84
Broad Wlk. *Coul* 1E 102
Broad Wlk. *Cranl* 9A 156
Broad Wlk. *Craw* 3B 182
Broad Wlk. *Eps* 6J 81
Broad Wlk. *Frim* 4C 70
Broad Wlk. *Houn* 4L 9
Broad Wlk. *Rich* 3M 11
Broad Wlk., The. *E Mol* 3F 40
Broadwater Clo. *W on T* 2H 57
Broadwater Clo. *Wok* 8F 54
Broadwater Clo. *Wray* 1A 20
Broadwater Gdns. *Orp* 1K 67
Broadwater La. *G'ming* 5J 133
Broadwater Pl. *Wey* 8F 38
Broadwater Ri. *Guild* 4C 114
Broadwater Rd. *SW17* 5C 28
Broadwater Rd. N. *W on T* 2G 57
Broadwater Rd. S. *W on T* 2G 57
Broadway. *Brack* 1N 31
Broadway. *Knap* 5E 72
Broadway. *Stai* 6K 21
Broadway. *Wink* 2M 17
Broadway Arc. W6 1H 13 (off Hammersmith B'way.)
Broadway Av. *Croy* 4A 46
Broadway Av. *Twic* 9H 11
Broadway Cen., The. *W6* 1H 13
Broadway Chambers. W6 1H 13 (off Hammersmith B'way)
Broadway Clo. *S Croy* 1E 84
Broadway Ct. *SW19* 7M 27
Broadway Ct. *Beck* 2M 47
Broadway Ct. *Knap* 4F 72
Broadway Gdns. *Mitc* 3C 44
Broadway Ho. *Knap* 5F 72
Broadway Mkt. *SW17* 5D 28
Broadway Pl. *SW19* 7L 27
Broadway Rd. *Light & W'sham* 6N 51
Broadway, The. *SW13* 5D 12
Broadway, The. *SW19* 7L 27
Broadway, The. *Cheam* 3K 61
Broadway, The. *Craw* 3B 182
Broadway, The. *Croy* 1J 63
Broadway, The. *New H* 6J 55
Broadway, The. *Sand* 8G 49
Broadway, The. *Stai* 2L 37
Broadway, The. *Sutt* 2A 62
Broadway, The. *Th Dit* 7E 40
Broadway, The. *Wok* 4B 74
Broadwell Ct. Houn 4L 9 (off Springwell Rd.)
Broadwell Rd. *Wrec* 5E 128
Broadwood Clo. *H'ham* 3N 197
Broadwood Cotts. *Capel* 4L 159
Broadwood Ri. *Broadf* 8M 181
Brocas St. *Eton* 3G 4
Brocas Ter. *Eton* 3G 4
Brockbridge Ho. *SW15* 9E 12

Brock Clo.—Bunce Comn. Rd.

Brock Clo. *Deep* 6H 71
Brockdene Dri. *Kes* 1F 66
Brockenhurst. *W Mol* 4N 39
Brockenhurst Av. *Wor Pk* 7D 42
Brockenhurst Clo. *Wok* 1B 74
Brockenhurst Dri. *Yat* 2C 68
Brockenhurst Rd. *Alder* 4N 109
Brockenhurst Rd. *Asc* 3L 33
Brockenhurst Rd. *Brack* 2D 32
Brockenhurst Rd. *Croy* 6E 46
Brockenhurst Way. *SW16* 1H 45
Brockham 5A 120
Brockham Clo. *SW19* 6L 27
Brockham Cres. *New Ad* 4N 65
Brockham Dri. *SW2* 1K 29
Brockham Grn. *Brock* 4A 120
Brockham Hill. Tad 9B 100
(off Boxhill Rd.)
Brockham Hill Pk. *Tad* 9B 100
Brockham Ho. SW2 1K 29
(off Brockham Dri.)
Brockhamhurst Rd. *Bet* 1N 139
Brockham La. *Brock* 3N 119
Brockham Pk.
(Research Laboratories).
Bet 8B 120
Brock Hill 5E 16
Brockhill. *Wok* 4K 73
Brockhurst Clo. *H'ham* 7F 196
Brockhurst Cotts. *Alf* 5H 175
Brocklands. *Yat* 2A 68
Brocklebank Ct. *Whyt* 5D 84
Brocklebank Rd. *SW18* 1A 28
Brocklesby Rd. *SE25* 3E 46
Brockley Combe. *Wey* 1E 56
Brock Rd. *Craw* 9N 161
Brocks Clo. *G'ming* 6K 133
Brocks Dri. *Guild* 8F 92
Brocks Dri. *Sutt* 9K 43
Brockshot Clo. *Bren* 1K 11
Brock Way. *Vir W* 4M 35
Brockway Clo. *Guild* 2D 114
Brockway Ho. *Slou* 1D 6
Brockwell Pk. Gdns. *SE24* 1L 29
Brockwell Pk. Row. *SW2* 1L 29
Broderick Gro. *Bookh* 4A 98
Brodie Rd. *Guild* 4A 114 (5F 202)
Brodrick Rd. *SW17* 3C 28
Brograve Gdns. *Beck* 1L 47
Broke Ct. *Guild* 9E 94
Broken Furlong. *Eton* 1E 4
Brokes Cres. *Reig* 1M 121
Brokes Rd. *Reig* 1M 121
Bromford Clo. *Oxt* 2C 126
Bromley Gro. *Brom* 1N 47
Bromley Rd. *Beck & Short* 1L 47
Brompton Clo. *SE20* 1D 46
Brompton Clo. *Houn* 8N 9
Brompton Pk. Cres. *SW6* 2N 13
Bronsart Rd. *SW6* 3K 13
Bronson Rd. *SW20* 1J 43
Bronte Ct. Red 2E 122
(off St Anne's Ri.)
Bronte Ho. *SW4* 1G 29
Brontes, The. *E Grin* 9N 165
Brook 9N 151
(Godalming)
Brook 2N 135
(Guildford)
Brook Av. *Farnh* 5L 109
Brook Clo. *SW17* 3E 28
Brook Clo. *SW20* 2G 43
Brook Clo. *As* 1F 110
Brook Clo. *Dork* 3J 119
Brook Clo. *E Grin* 9D 166
Brook Clo. *Eps* 5D 60
Brook Clo. *Fleet* 5B 88
Brook Clo. *Owl* 6K 49
Brook Clo. *Stanw* 1A 22
Brook Cotts. *Yat* 9B 48
Brook Ct. *Eden* 9L 127
Brook Dri. *Brack* 3C 32
Brooke Ct. *Frim G* 8D 70
Brooke Forest. *Guild* 8F 92
Brooke Pl. *Binf* 6J 15
Brookers Clo. *Asht* 4J 79
Brookers Corner. *Crowt* 2H 49
Brookers Row. *Crowt* 1H 49
Brook Farm Rd. *Cob* 2L 77
Brookfield. *G'ming* 3K 133
Brookfield. *Wok* 3L 73
Brookfield Av. *Sutt* 1C 62
Brookfield Clo. *Ott* 3F 54
Brookfield Clo. *Red* 9E 122
Brookfield Gdns. *Clay* 3F 58
Brookfield Rd. *Alder* 1C 110
Brookfields Av. *Mitc* 4C 44
Brook Gdns. *Farnb* 3L 89
Brook Gdns. *SW13* 6E 12
Brook Gdns. *King T* 9B 26
Brook Green 1J 13
Brook Grn. *Brack* 9L 15
(in two parts)
Brook Grn. Chob 6J 53
(off Chertsey Rd.)
Brookham Keep. Horl 7G 142
(off Langshott La.)
Brook Hill. *Alb* 3M 135
Brook Hill. *Oxt* 8M 105
Brookhill Clo. *Copt* 7L 163
Brookhill Rd. *Copt* 8L 163
Brook Ho. W6 1H 13
(off Shepherd's Bush Rd.)
Brook Ho. Cranl 6A 156
(off Park Dri.)
Brook Ho. Farnh 6J 109
(off Fairview Gdns.)
Brookhouse Rd. *Farnb* 2L 89
Brookhurst Fld. *Rud* 9L 179
Brookhurst Rd. *Add* 3K 55
Brookland Ct. *Reig* 1N 121
Brooklands 6A 56
Brooklands. *Alder* 3K 109
Brooklands. *S God* 1E 144
Brooklands Av. *SW19* 3N 27
Brooklands Bus. Pk. *Wey* 7N 55
Brooklands Clo. *Cob* 2M 77
Brooklands Clo. *Farnh* 5J 109
Brooklands Clo. *Sun* 9F 22
Brooklands Ct. *King T* 7H 203
Brooklands Ct. *Mitc* 1B 44
Brooklands Ct. *New H* 6M 55
Brooklands La. *Wey* 3A 56
Brooklands Mus. 5B 56
Brooklands Rd. *Craw* 8A 182
Brooklands Rd. *Farnh* 5K 109
Brooklands Rd. *Th Dit* 7F 40
Brooklands Rd. *Wey* 7B 56
Brooklands, The. *Iswth* 4D 10
Brooklands Way. *E Grin* 1N 185
Brooklands Way. *Farnh* 5K 109
Brooklands Way. *Red* 1C 122
Brook La. *Alb* 2N 135
Brook La. *Chob* 7G 53
Brook La. *Fay* 9B 180
Brook La. *Send* 9G 74
Brook La. Bus. Cen. *Bren* 1K 11
Brook La. N. *Bren* 1K 11
(in three parts)
Brookley Clo. *Farnh* 9A 110
Brookleys. *Chob* 6J 53
Brookly Gdns. *Fleet* 3C 88
Brooklyn Av. *SE25* 3E 46
Brooklyn Clo. *Cars* 8C 44
Brooklyn Clo. *Wok* 6A 74
Brooklyn Ct. *Wok* 6A 74
Brooklyn Gro. *SE25* 3E 46
Brooklyn Rd. *SE25* 3E 46
Brooklyn Rd. *Wok* 5A 74
Brook Mead. *Eps* 3D 60
Brook Mead. *Milf* 2C 152
Brookmead Ct. *Cranl* 8N 155
Brookmead Ct. *Farnh* 2G 128
Brookmead Ind. Est. *Croy* 5G 45
Brook Mdw. *C'fold* 6F 172
Brookmead Rd. *Croy* 5G 45
Brook Rd. *Bag* 5J 51
Brook Rd. *Camb* 2N 69
Brook Rd. *Chil* 1E 134
Brook Rd. *H'ham* 2L 197
Brook Rd. *Mers* 7G 102
Brook Rd. *Red* 4D 122
Brook Rd. *Surb* 8L 41
Brook Rd. *T Hth* 3N 45
Brook Rd. *Twic* 9G 11
Brook Rd. *Wmly* 1N 171
Brook Rd. S. *Bren* 2K 11
Brooksby Clo. *B'water* 1G 68
Brooks Clo. *Wey* 6B 56
Brookscroft. *Croy* 6J 65
Brookside 7K 17
Brookside. *Dear G* 5M 139
Brookside. *Cars* 2E 62
Brookside. *Cher* 6G 37
Brookside. *Coln* 3E 6
Brookside. *Copt* 7L 163
Brookside. *Cranl* 7N 155
(Ewhurst Rd.)
Brookside. *Cranl* 9N 155
(Northdowns)
Brookside. *Craw* 2D 182
Brookside. *Craw D* 1E 184
Brookside. *Farnh* 6H 109
Brookside. *Guild* 7N 93
Brookside. *Sand* 8H 49
Brookside. *S God* 7G 124
Brookside Av. *Ashf* 6L 21
Brookside Av. *Wray* 6A 6
Brookside Clo. *Felt* 4H 23
Brookside Cres. *Wor Pk* 7F 42
Brookside Residential Pk. Homes.
Farnb 5M 69
Brookside Way. *Croy* 5G 46
Brooks La. *W4* 2N 11
Brooks Rd. *W4* 1N 11
Brook St. *King T* 1L 41 (4J 203)
Brook St. *Wind* 5G 5
Brook Trad. Est., The. *Alder*
2C 110
Brook Valley. *Mid H* 2H 139
Brookview. *Copt* 7L 163
Brookview Rd. *SW16* 6G 28
Brookville Rd. *SW6* 3L 13
Brook Way. *Lea* 5G 78
Brookwell La. *Brmly* 1C 154
Brookwood 7D 72
Brookwood. *Horl* 7F 142
Brookwood Av. *SW13* 5E 12
Brookwood Lye Rd. *Brkwd* 7E 72
Brookwood Pk. *Horl* 9G 142
Brookwood Rd. *Farnb* 1B 90
Brookwood Rd. *SW18* 2L 27
Brookwood Rd. *Houn* 5B 10
Broom Acres. *Fleet* 7A 88
Broom Acres. *Sand* 7G 48
Broom Clo. *Esh* 2B 58
Broom Clo. *Tedd* 8K 25
Broomcroft Clo. *Wok* 3F 74
Broomcroft Dri. *Wok* 2F 74
Broomdashers Rd. *Craw* 2D 182
Broome Clo. *H'ley* 4B 100
Broome Clo. *H'ham* 3K 197
Broome Clo. *Yat* 8B 48
Broome Ct. *Brack* 2N 31
Broome Ct. *Tad* 8K 81
Broomehall Rd. *Cold* 9D 138
Broome Rd. *Hamp* 8N 23
Broomers La. *Ewh* 5F 156
Broom Farm Est. *Wind* 5A 4
Broomfield. *Elst* 7J 131
Broomfield. *Guild* 2H 113
Broom Fld. *Light* 8L 51
Broomfield. *Stai* 7J 21
Broomfield. *Sun* 9H 23
Broomfield Clo. *Asc* 6E 34
Broomfield Clo. *Guild* 1H 113
Broomfield Ct. *Wey* 3C 56
Broomfield Pk. *Asc* 5E 34
Broomfield Pk. *Westc* 6C 118
Broomfield Ride. *Oxs* 8D 58
Broomfield Rd. *Beck* 2H 47
Broomfield Rd. *New H* 7K 55
Broomfield Rd. *Rich* 4M 11
Broomfield Rd. *Surb* 7M 41
Broomfield Rd. *Tedd* 7J 25
Broomfields. *Esh* 2C 58
Broom Gdns. *Croy* 9K 47
Broomhall 5D 34
Broom Hall. *Oxs* 1D 78
Broomhall End. *Wok* 3A 74
Broomhall La. *Asc* 5D 34
Broomhall La. *Wok* 3A 74
Broomhall Rd. *S Croy* 5A 64
Broomhall Rd. *Wok* 3A 74
Broomhill. *Ews* 4C 108
Broomhill Rd. *Farnb* 9J 69
Broomhill Rd. *SW18* 8M 13
Broomhouse La. *SW6* 5M 13
(in two parts)
Broomhouse Rd. *SW6* 5M 13
Broomhurst Ct. *Dork* 7H 119
Broomlands La. *Oxt* 4F 106
Broom La. *Chob* 5H 53
Broomleaf Corner. *Farnh* 1J 129
Broomleaf Rd. *Farnh* 1J 129
Broomloan La. *Sutt* 8M 43
Broom Lock. *Tedd* 7J 25
Broom Pk. *Tedd* 8K 25
Broom Rd. *Croy* 9K 47
Broom Rd. *Tedd* 6H 25
Broom Squires. *Hind* 5E 170
Broomsquires Rd. *Bag* 5K 51
Broom Water. *Tedd* 7J 25
Broom Water W. *Tedd* 6J 25
Broom Way. *B'water* 2J 69
Broom Way. *Wey* 1F 56
Broomwood Clo. *Croy* 4G 47
Broomwood Way. *Lwr Bo* 5H 129
Broster Gdns. *SE25* 2C 46
Brougham Pl. *Farnh* 5G 108
Brough Clo. *King T* 6K 25
Broughton Av. *Rich* 4H 25
Broughton M. *Frim* 5D 70
Broughton Rd. *SW6* 5N 13
Broughton Rd. *T Hth* 5L 45
Browell Ho. Guild 2F 114
(off Merrow St.)
Browells La. *Felt* 3J 23
(in two parts)
Brown Bear Ct. *Felt* 5L 23
Brown Clo. *Wall* 4J 63
Browngraves Rd. *Hay* 3D 8
Browning Av. *Sutt* 1C 62
Browning Av. *Wor Pk* 7G 42
Browning Clo. *Camb* 2C 70
Browning Clo. *Craw* 2G 182
Browning Clo. *Hamp* 5N 23
Browning Rd. *C Crook* 9A 88
Browning Rd. *Fet* 3D 98
Brownings. *Eden* 8L 127
Brownings, The. *E Grin* 9M 165
Browning Way. *Houn* 4L 9
Brownjohn Ct. *Craw* 2E 182
Brownlow Dri. *Brack* 8A 16
Brownlow Rd. *Croy* 1B 64
Brownlow Rd. *Red* 3C 122
Brownrigg Cres. *Brack* 9C 16
Brownrigg Rd. *Ashf* 5B 22
Brown's Hill. *Out* 1A 144
Browns La. *Eff* 5L 97
Brownsover Rd. *Farnb* 1H 89
Brown's Rd. *Surb* 6M 41
Browns Wlk. *Rowl* 7E 128
Browns Wood. *E Grin* 6A 166
Brow, The. *Red* 8E 122
Brox 4E 54
Broxhead Farm Rd. *Lind* 1A 168
Broxhead Trad. Est. *Lind* 3A 168
Broxholme Ho. SW6 4N 13
(off Harwood Rd.)
Broxholm Rd. *SE27* 4L 29
Brox La. *Ott* 4E 54
Brox Rd. *Ott* 3E 54
Bruce Av. *Shep* 5D 38
Bruce Clo. *Byfl* 9M 55
Bruce Dri. *S Croy* 5G 64
Bruce Hall M. *SW17* 5E 28
Bruce Rd. *SE25* 3A 46
Bruce Rd. *Mitc* 8E 28
Bruce Wlk. *Wind* 5A 4
Brudenell. *Wind* 6C 4
Brudenell Rd. *SW17* 4D 28
Brumana Clo. *Wey* 3C 56
Brumfield Rd. *Eps* 2B 60
Brunel Cen., The. *Craw* 8D 162
Brunel Clo. *Houn* 3J 9
Brunel Dri. *Crowt* 8H 31
Brunel Pl. *Craw* 4C 182
Brunel University 3E 10
(Borough Rd., Isleworth)
Brunel University
(Runnymede Campus)
4M 19
Brunel University 7H 11
(St Margaret's Rd.)
Brunel Wlk. *Twic* 1A 24
Brunswick Ct. *Ott* 2E 54
Brunswick. *Brack* 6M 31
Brunswick Clo. *Craw* 5E 182
Brunswick Clo. *Th Dit* 7F 40
Brunswick Clo. *Twic* 4D 24
Brunswick Clo. *W on T* 8K 39
Brunswick Ct. Craw 5F 182
(off Brunswick Clo.)
Brunswick Ct. *Sutt* 1N 61
Brunswick Dri. *Brkwd* 7A 72
Brunswick Gro. *Cob* 9K 57
Brunswick M. *SW16* 7H 29
Brunswick Rd. *Brkwd* 8L 71
(in two parts)
Brunswick Rd. *Deep* 8G 71
Brunswick Rd. *King T* 9N 25
Brunswick Rd. *Sutt* 1N 61
Bruntile Clo. *Farnb* 4B 90
Brushfield Way. *Knap* 6F 72
Brushwood Rd. *H'ham* 2A 198
Bruton Rd. *Mord* 3A 44
Bruton Way. *Brack* 6C 32
Bryan Clo. *Sun* 8H 23
Bryan's All. *SW6* 5N 13
Bryanston Av. *Twic* 2B 24
Bryanstone Av. *Guild* 8J 93
Bryanstone Clo. *C Crook* 7B 88
Bryanstone Clo. *Guild* 9J 93
Bryanstone Ct. *Sutt* 9A 44
Bryanstone Gro. *Guild* 8J 93
Bryce Clo. *H'ham* 3N 197
Bryce Gdns. *Alder* 5A 110
Bryer Pl. *Wind* 6A 4
Brympton Clo. *Dork* 7G 119
Brynford Clo. *Wok* 2A 74
Bryn Rd. *Wrec* 4E 128
Bryony Ho. *Brack* 9K 15
Bryony Rd. *Guild* 9D 94
Bryony Way. *Sun* 7H 23
Buccleuch Rd. *Dat* 3K 5
Buchan Country Pk. & Info. Cen.
7K 181
Buchan Hill 9M 181
Buchan Pk. *Craw* 7L 181
Buchans Lawn. *Craw* 7N 181
Buchan, The. *Camb* 7E 50
Bucharest Rd. *SW18* 1A 28
Buckfast Rd. *Mord* 3N 43
Buckham Thorns Rd. *W'ham*
4L 107
Buckhold Rd. *SW18* 9M 13
Buckhurst Av. *Cars* 7C 44
Buckhurst Clo. *E Grin* 7M 165
Buckhurst Clo. *Red* 1C 122
Buckhurst Gro. *Wokgm* 3E 30
Buckhurst Hill 9C 18
Buckhurst Hill. *Brack* 3D 32
Buckhurst La. *Asc* 2C 34
Buckhurst Mead. *E Grin* 6M 165
Buckhurst Rd. *Asc* 9C 18
Buckhurst Rd. *Frim G* 8D 70
Buckhurst Rd. *W'ham* 8J 87
Buckhurst Way. *E Grin* 7M 165
Buckingham Av. *Felt* 9J 9
Buckingham Av. *T Hth* 9L 29
Buckingham Av. *W Mol* 1B 40
Buckingham Clo. *Guild* 2B 114
Buckingham Clo. *Hamp* 6N 23
Buckingham Ct. *Craw* 7N 181
Buckingham Ct. *Sutt* 5M 61
Buckingham Dri. *E Grin* 1C 186
Buckingham Gdns. *T Hth* 1L 45
Buckingham Gdns. *W Mol* 1B 40
Buckingham Ga. *Gat A* 3G 162
Buckingham Rd. *Hamp* 5N 23
Buckingham Rd. *Holmw* 5J 139
Buckingham Rd. *King T*
3M 41 (7L 203)
Buckingham Rd. *Mitc* 3J 45
Buckingham Rd. *Rich* 3K 25
Buckingham Way. *Frim* 6D 70
Buckingham Way. *Wall* 5G 63
Buckland 2F 120
Buckland Clo. *Farnb* 7A 70
Buckland Ct. Gdns. *Bet* 2F 120
Buckland Cres. *Wind* 4C 4
Buckland La. *Tad & Buck* 6F 100
Buckland Rd. *Chess* 2M 59
Buckland Rd. *Lwr K* 7L 101
Buckland Rd. *Orp* 1N 67
Buckland Rd. *Reig* 2J 121
Buckland Rd. *Sutt* 6H 61
Bucklands Rd. *Tedd* 7J 25
Buckland's Wharf. *King T*
1K 41 (3G 203)
Buckland Wlk. *Mord* 3A 44
Buckland Way. *Wor Pk* 7H 43
Bucklebury. *Brack* 6M 31
Buckleigh Av. *SW20* 2K 43
Buckleigh Rd. *SW16* 7H 29
Buckle La. *Warf* 3M 15
(in two parts)
Bucklers All. *SW6* 2L 13
(in two parts)
Buckler's Way. *Cars* 9D 44
Buckles Way. *Bans* 3K 81
Buckley La. *H'ham* 9N 197
Buckley Pl. *Craw D* 1D 184
Buckmans Rd. *Craw* 2B 182
Bucknall Way. *Beck* 3L 47
Bucknills Clo. *Eps* 1B 80
Bucks Clo. *W Byf* 1K 75
Bucks Green 1C 194
Buckshead Hill. *Colg* 9F 198
Bucks Horn Oak 2A 148
Bucks Horn Oak Rd. *B'nest*
2A 148
Buckswood Dri. *Craw* 5M 181
Buckthorn Clo. *Wokgm* 1D 30
Buckthorns. *Brack* 8K 15
Budd's All. *Twic* 8J 11
Budebury Rd. *Stai* 6J 21
Budge La. *Mitc* 6D 44
Budgen Clo. *Craw* 9H 163
Budgen Dri. *Red* 9E 102
Budge's Cotts. *Wokgm* 9D 14
Budge's Gdns. *Wokgm* 1C 30
Budge's Rd. *Wokgm* 1C 30
Budham Way. *Brack* 5N 31
Buer Rd. *SW6* 5K 13
Buff Av. *Bans* 1N 81
Buffbeards La. *Hasl* 1C 188
Buffers La. *Lea* 6G 79
Bug Hill. *Wold & Warl* 7G 84
Bulbeggars La. *God* 1F 124
Bulganak Rd. *T Hth* 3N 45
Bulkeley Av. *Wind* 6E 4
Bulkeley Clo. *Eng G* 6M 19
Bullard Cotts. *W Cla* 1H 115
Bullard Rd. *Tedd* 7E 24
Bullbeggars La. *Wok* 3L 73
Bullbrook 1C 32
Bullbrook Dri. *Brack* 9C 16
Bullbrook Row. *Brack* 1C 32
Buller Ct. *Farnb* 4A 90
Buller Rd. *T Hth* 1A 46
Bullers Rd. *Farnb* 6K 109
Bullfinch Clo. *Col T* 7K 49
Bullfinch Clo. *Horl* 7C 142
Bullfinch Clo. *H'ham* 1J 197
Bullfinch Rd. *S Croy* 6G 64
Bull Hill. *Lea* 8G 79
Bull La. *Brack* 9N 15
Bullock La. *Hasl* 9A 190
Bullrush Clo. *Cars* 8C 44
Bullrush Clo. *Croy* 5B 46
Bull's All. *SW14* 5C 12
Bulls Head Row. *God* 9E 104
Bullswater Common 3D 92
Bullswater Comn. Rd. *Pirb* 4D 92
Bulmer Cotts. *Holm M* 6K 137
Bulow Est. SW6 4N 13
(off Pearscroft Rd.)
Bulstrode Av. *Houn* 5N 9
Bulstrode Gdns. *Houn* 6A 10
Bulstrode Rd. *Houn* 6A 10
Bunbury Way. *Eps* 3G 80
Bunce Common 1C 140
Bunce Comn. Rd. *Leigh* 1C 140

Bunce Dri.—Callow Hill

Bunce Dri. *Cat* 1A **104**
Bunce's Clo. *Eton W.* 1E **4**
Bunch La. *Hasl* 1E **188**
Bunch Way. *Hasl* 2E **188**
Bundy's Way. *Stai* 7H **21**
Bungalow Rd. *SE25* 3B **46**
Bungalow Rd. *Ock* 2D **96**
Bungalows, The. *SW16* 8F **28**
Bungalows, The. *Guild* 7J **93**
Bungalows, The. *Wall* 2F **62**
Bunting Clo. *H'ham* 5M **197**
Bunting Clo. *Mitc* 4D **44**
Buntings, The. *Farnh* 3E **128**
Bunyan Clo. *Craw* 6K **181**
Bunyan's La. *Knap* 1F **72**
Bunyard Dri. *Wok* 1E **74**
Burbage Grn. *Brack* 4D **32**
Burbage Rd. *SE21* 1N **29**
Burbeach Clo. *Craw* 6N **181**
Burberry Clo. *N Mald* 1D **42**
Burbidge Rd. *Shep* 3B **38**
Burbury Woods. *Camb* 9C **50**
Burchets Hollow. *Peasl* 4E **136**
Burchetts Way. *Shep* 5C **38**
Burcote. *Wey* 3E **56**
Burcote Rd. *SW18* 1B **28**
Burcott Gdns. *Add* 3L **55**
Burcott Rd. *Purl* 1L **83**
Burden Clo. *Bren* 1J **11**
Burdenshott Av. *Rich* 7A **12**
Burdenshott Hill. *Worp* 3K **93**
Burdenshott Rd. *Worp* 3K **93**
Burden Way. *Guild* 7L **93**
Burdett Av. *SW20* 9F **26**
Burdett Clo. *Worth* 4H **183**
Burdett Rd. *Croy* 5A **46**
Burdett Rd. *Rich* 5M **11**
Burdock Clo. *Craw* 7M **181**
Burdock Clo. *Croy* 7G **47**
Burdock Clo. *Light* 7M **51**
Burdon La. *Sutt* 4K **61**
Burdon Pk. *Sutt* 5L **61**
Burfield Clo. *SW17* 5B **28**
Burfield Dri. *Warl* 6F **84**
Burfield Rd. *Old Win* 9K **5**
Burford Bri. Roundabout. *Dork* 9J **99**
Burford Ct. *Wokgm* 3D **30**
Burford Ho. *Bren* 1K **11**
Burford Ho. *Eps* 7H **61**
Burford La. *Eps* 7H **61**
Burford Lea. *Elst* 7J **131**
Burford Rd. *Bren* 1L **11**
Burford Rd. *Camb* 2N **69**
Burford Rd. *H'ham* 6L **197**
Burford Rd. *Sutt* 8M **43**
Burford Rd. *Wor Pk* 6E **42**
Burford Wlk. *SW6* 3N **13**
Burford Way. *New Ad* 3M **65**
Burges Gro. *SW13* 3G **13**
Burgess Clo. *Felt* 5M **23**
Burgess M. *SW19* 7N **27**
Burgess Rd. *Sutt* 1N **61**
Burges Way. *Stai* 6J **21**
Burgh Clo. *Craw* 9H **163**
Burgh Cft. *Eps* 2E **80**
Burghead Clo. *Col T* 8J **49**
Burghfield. *Eps* 2E **80**
Burgh Heath 6K **81**
Burgh Heath Rd. *Eps* 1E **80** (8M **201**)
Burgh Hill Rd. *Pass* 9E **168**
Burghley Av. *N Mald* 9C **26**
Burghley Hall Clo. *SW19* 2K **27**
Burghley Pl. *Mitc* 4D **44**
Burghley Rd. *SW19* 5J **27**
Burgh Mt. *Bans* 2L **81**
Burgh Wood. *Bans* 2K **81**
Burgos Clo. *Croy* 3L **63**
Burgoyne Rd. *SE25* 3C **46**
Burgoyne Rd. *Camb* 9E **50**
Burgoyne Rd. *Sun* 7G **22**
Burhill 5H **57**
Burhill Rd. *W on T* 5J **57**
Burke Clo. *SW15* 7D **12**
Burket Clo. *S'hall* 1M **9**
Burlands. *Craw* 9M **161**
Burlea Clo. *W on T* 2J **57**
Burleigh 9J **17**
Burleigh Av. *Wall* 9E **44**
Burleigh Clo. *Add* 2K **55**
Burleigh Clo. *Craw D* 1E **184**
Burleigh Gdns. *Ashf* 6D **22**
Burleigh Gdns. *Wok* 4B **74**
Burleigh La. *Asc* 9J **17**
Burleigh La. *Craw D* 2E **184**
Burleigh Pk. *Cob* 8M **57**
Burleigh Pl. *SW15* 8J **13**
Burleigh Rd. *Add* 2K **55**
Burleigh Rd. *Asc* 1J **33**
Burleigh Rd. *Frim* 6B **70**
Burleigh Rd. *Sutt* 7K **43**
Burleigh Way. *Craw D* 1E **184**
Burley Clo. *SW16* 1H **45**
Burley Clo. *Loxw* 4J **193**
Burley Orchard. *Cher* 5J **37**
Burleys Rd. *Craw* 3G **183**
Burley Way. *B'water* 9H **49**
Burlingham Clo. *Guild* 1F **114**
Burlings 4N **87**
Burlings La. *Knock* 4N **87**
Burlings, The. *Asc* 1J **33**
Burlington Av. *Rich* 4N **11**
Burlington Clo. *Felt* 1E **22**
Burlington Ct. *Alder* 3M **109**
Burlington Ct. *B'water* 3J **69**
Burlington Gdns. *SW6* 5K **13**
Burlington Gdns. *W4* 1B **12**
Burlington La. *W4* 3B **12**
Burlington M. *SW15* 8L **13**
Burlington Pl. *SW6* 5K **13**
Burlington Pl. *Reig* 2M **121**
Burlington Rd. *SW6* 5K **13**
Burlington Rd. *W4* 1B **12**
Burlington Rd. *Iswth* 4D **10**
Burlington Rd. *N Mald* 3E **42**
Burlington Rd. *T Hth* 1N **45**
Burlsdon Way. *Brack* 9C **16**
Burma Rd. *Chob* 9J **35**
Burmarsh Ct. *SE20* 1F **46**
Burmester Rd. *SW17* 4A **28**
Burnaby Cres. *W4* 2B **12**
Burnaby Gdns. *W4* 2A **12**
Burnaby St. *SW10* 3N **13**
Burnbury Rd. *SW12* 2G **29**
Burn Clo. *Add* 1M **55**
Burn Clo. *Oxs* 2D **78**
Burne-Jones Dri. *Col T* 9J **49**
Burne Jones Ho. *W14* 1K **13**
Burnell Av. *Rich* 6J **25**
Burnell Rd. *Sutt* 1N **61**
Burnet Av. *Guild* 9D **94**
Burnet Clo. *W End* 9B **52**
Burnet Gro. *Eps* 9B **60** (6H **201**)
Burnetts Rd. *Wind* 4B **4**
Burney Av. *Surb* 4M **41**
Burney Clo. *Fet* 3C **98**
Burney Ct. *Craw* 6M **181**
Burney Rd. *Westh* 9G **99**
Burnfoot Av. *SW6* 4K **13**
Burnham Clo. *Knap* 5G **73**
Burnham Clo. *Wind* 5A **4**
Burnham Dri. *Reig* 2M **121**
Burnham Dri. *Wor Pk* 8J **43**
Burnham Gdns. *Croy* 6C **46**
Burnham Gdns. *Houn* 4J **9**
Burnham Ga. *Guild* 3N **113** (2C **202**)
Burnham Gro. *Brack* 8A **16**
Burnham Pl. *H'ham* 7K **197**
Burnham Rd. *Knap* 5G **73**
Burnham Rd. *Mord* 3N **43**
Burnhams Rd. *Bookh* 2M **97**
Burnham St. *King T* 9N **25**
Burnhill Rd. *Beck* 1K **47**
Burn Moor Chase. *Brack* 6C **32**
Bursall Clo. *Farnb* 8N **69**
Burns Av. *C Crook* 9C **88**
Burns Av. *Felt* 9H **9**
Burns Clo. *Farnb* 8L **69**
Burns Clo. *SW19* 7B **28**
Burns Clo. *Cars* 5E **62**
Burns Clo. *H'ham* 1L **197**
Burns Dri. *Bans* 1K **81**
Burnside. *Asht* 5M **79**
Burnside. *Fleet* 4B **88**
Burnside Clo. *Twic* 9G **10**
Burns Rd. *Craw* 1G **182**
Burns Way. *E Grin* 9M **165**
Burns Way. *Fay* 8H **181**
Burns Way. *Houn* 5L **9**
Burntcommon 3H **95**
Burntcommon Clo. *Rip* 3H **95**
Burntcommon La. *Rip* 3J **95**
Burnt Hill Rd. *Wrec* 5F **128**
Burnt Hill Way. *Wrec* 6G **128**
(in two parts)
Burnt Ho. Gdns. *Warf* 8C **16**
Burnt Ho. La. *Rusp* 2E **180**
Burnthouse Ride. *Brack* 3J **31**
Burnthwaite Rd. *SW6* 3L **13**
Burntoak La. *Newd* 2D **160**
Burnt Pollard La. *Light* 6B **52**
Burntwood Clo. *SW18* 2C **28**
Burntwood Clo. *Cat* 8D **84**
Burntwood Grange Rd. *SW18* 2B **28**
Burntwood La. *SW17* 4A **28**
Burntwood La. *Cat* 9B **84**
Burpham 9D **94**
Burpham Court Farm Pk. 7B **94**
Burpham La. *Guild* 7C **94**
Burrell Clo. *Croy* 5H **47**
Burrell Ct. *Craw* 5L **181**
Burrell Rd. *Frim* 6A **70**
Burrell Row. *Beck* 1K **47**
Burrells, The. *Cher* 7K **37**
Burrell, The. *Westc* 6C **118**
Burr Hill La. *Chob* 5J **53**
Burritt Rd. *King T* 1N **41**
Burrow Hill 5H **53**
(Chobham)
Burrow Hill 9B **72**
(Pirbright)
Burrow Hill Grn. *Chob* 5G **53**
Burrows Clo. *Bookh* 2N **97**
Burrows Clo. *Guild* 2J **113**
Burrows Cross 1D **136**
Burrows Cross. *Gom* 1D **136**
Burrows La. *Gom* 1D **136**
Burrow Wlk. *SE21* 1N **29**
Burr Rd. *SW18* 2M **27**
Burrwood Gdns. *Ash V* 9E **90**
Burstead Clo. *Cob* 8L **57**
Burstock Rd. *SW15* 7K **13**
Burston Gdns. *E Grin* 6N **165**
Burston Rd. *SW15* 8J **13**
Burstow 3L **163**
Burstow Lodge Bus. Cen. *Horl* 6M **143**
Burstow Rd. *SW20* 9K **27**
Burtenshaw Rd. *Th Dit* 6G **41**
Burton Clo. *Chess* 4K **59**
Burton Clo. *Horl* 9E **142**
Burton Clo. *T Hth* 2A **46**
Burton Clo. *W'sham* 3A **52**
Burton Ct. *SE20* 1F **46**
Burton Dri. *Guild* 7D **92**
Burton Gdns. *Houn* 4N **9**
Burton Rd. *King T* 8L **25** (1K **203**)
Burtons Ct. *H'ham* 6J **197**
Burton's Rd. *Hamp H* 5B **24**
Burton Way. *Wind* 6B **4**
Burtwell La. *SE27* 5N **29**
Burwash Rd. *Craw* 4E **182**
Burway Cres. *Cher* 3J **37**
Burwell. *King T* 4M **203**
Burwood Av. *Kenl* 1M **83**
Burwood Clo. *Guild* 2F **114**
Burwood Clo. *Reig* 3B **122**
Burwood Clo. *Surb* 7N **41**
Burwood Clo. *W on T* 3K **57**
Burwood Pde. Cher *6J 37*
(off Guildford St.)
Burwood Park 8H **57**
(Cobham)
Burwood Park 2G **57**
(Walton-on-Thames)
Burwood Pk. Rd. *W on T* 1J **57**
Burwood Rd. *W on T* 4F **56**
Bury Clo. *Wok* 3N **73**
Bury Fields. *Guild* 5M **113** (7B **202**)
Bury Gro. *Mord* 4N **43**
Bury La. *Wok* 3M **73**
Burys, The. *G'ming* 6H **133**
Bury St. *Guild* 5M **113** (7B **202**)
Burywood Hill. *Bear G* 3E **158**
Busbridge 9J **133**
Busbridge Lakes Ornamental Wildfowl 1H **153**
Busbridge La. *G'ming* 8G **133**
Busch Clo. *Iswth* 4H **11**
Busdens Clo. *Milf* 2C **152**
Busdens La. *Milf* 2C **152**
Busdens Way. *Milf* 2C **152**
Bushbury Rd. *Bet* 8N **119**
Bush Clo. *Add* 2L **55**
Bush Cotts. *SW18* 8M **13**
Bushell Clo. *SW2* 3K **29**
Bushetts Gro. *Red* 7F **102**
Bushey Clo. *Kenl* 3C **84**
Bushey Ct. *SW20* 2G **43**
Bushey Cft. *Oxt* 8M **105**
Bushey Down. *SW12* 3F **28**
Bushey La. *Sutt* 1M **61**
Bushey Mead 1J **43**
Bushey Rd. *SW20* 2G **42**
Bushey Rd. *Croy* 8K **47**
Bushey Rd. *Sutt* 1M **61**
Bushey Shaw. *Asht* 4H **79**
Bushey Way. *Beck* 5N **47**
Bushfield. *Plais* 6B **192**
Bushfield Dri. *Red* 8E **122**
Bush La. *H'ham* 9N **179**
Bush La. *Send* 2F **94**
Bushnell Rd. *SW17* 3F **28**
Bush Rd. *Rich* 2M **11**
Bush Rd. *Shep* 4A **38**
Bush Wlk. *Wokgm* 2B **30**
Bushwood Rd. *Rich* 2N **11**
Bushy Ct. King T *9J 25*
(off Up. Teddington Rd.)
Bushy Hill 2F **114**
Bushy Hill Dri. *Guild* 1D **114**
Bushy Pk. Gdns. *Tedd* 6D **24**
Bushy Pk. Rd. *Tedd* 8H **25**
(in two parts)
Bushy Rd. *Fet* 9B **78**
Bushy Rd. *Tedd* 7F **24**
Business Cen., The. *Wokgm* 4A **30**
Business Pk. 5. *Lea* 7F **78**
Busk Cres. *Farnb* 2L **89**
Butcherfield La. *Hartf* 1N **187**
Bute Av. *Rich* 3L **25**
Bute Ct. *Wall* 2G **62**
Bute Gdns. *W6* 1J **13**
Bute Gdns. *Rich* 2L **25**
Bute Gdns. *Wall* 2G **63**
Bute Gdns. W. *Wall* 2G **62**
Bute Rd. *Croy* 7L **45**
Bute Rd. *Wall* 1G **62**
Butler Rd. *Bag* 5K **51**
Butler Rd. *Crowt* 1G **48**
Butlers Clo. *Wind* 4A **4**
Butlers Dene Rd. *Wold* 7J **85**
Butlers Hill. *W Hor* 8C **96**
Butlers Rd. *H'ham* 4N **197**
Butt Clo. *Cranl* 6N **155**
Buttercup Clo. *Lind* 4B **168**
Buttercup Clo. *Wokgm* 2F **30**
Buttercup Sq. *Stanw* 2M **21**
Butterfield. *E Grin* 7L **165**
Butterfield Clo. *Twic* 9F **10**
Butterfields. *Camb* 2N **69**
Butterfly Wlk. *Warl* 7F **84**
(in two parts)
Butter Hill. *Cars* 9E **44**
Butter Hill. *Dork* 5G **119** (3J **201**)
Buttermer Clo. *Wrec* 4D **128**
Buttermere Clo. *Farnb* 1K **89**
Buttermere Clo. *Felt* 2G **22**
Buttermere Clo. *H'ham* 2A **198**
Buttermere Clo. *Mord* 5J **43**
Buttermere Ct. Ash V *9D 90*
(off Lakeside Clo.)
Buttermere Dri. *SW15* 8K **13**
Buttermere Dri. *Camb* 1H **71**
Buttermere Gdns. *Brack* 2A **32**
Buttermere Gdns. *Purl* 9A **64**
Buttermere Way. *Egh* 8D **20**
Buttersteep Ri. *Asc* 7G **33**
Butterwick. *W6* 1J **13**
Butt La. *P'ham* 7L **111**
Butts Clo. *Craw* 2N **181**
Butts Cotts. *Felt* 4M **23**
Butts Cres. *Hanw* 4A **24**
Butts La. *G'ming* 7G **133**
(in two parts)
Butts Rd. *Wok* 4A **74**
Butts, The. *Bren* 2J **11**
Butts, The. *Sun* 2K **39**
Buxton Av. *Cat* 8B **84**
Buxton Cres. *Sutt* 1K **61**
Buxton Dri. *N Mald* 1C **42**
Buxton La. *Cat* 7A **84**
Buxton Rd. *Ashf* 6M **21**
Buxton Rd. *SW14* 6D **12**
Buxton Rd. *T Hth* 4M **45**
Byam St. *SW6* 5N **13**
Byards Cft. *SW16* 9H **29**
Byatt Wlk. *Hamp* 7M **23**
Bychurch End. *Tedd* 6F **24**
Bycroft Way. *Craw* 1F **182**
Byegrove Rd. *SW19* 7B **28**
Byerley Way. *Craw* 2H **183**
Byers La. *Horne* 5D **144**
Byers La. *S God* 4F **144**
Byeways. *Twic* 4B **24**
Byeways, The. *Surb* 4N **41**
Byeway, The. *SW14* 6B **12**
Byfeld Gdns. *SW13* 4F **12**
Byfield Pas. *Iswth* 6G **10**
Byfield Rd. *Iswth* 6G **10**
Byfleet 9A **56**
Byfleet Ind. Est. *Byfl* 7M **55**
Byfleet Rd. *Byfl & Cob* 8B **56**
Byfleet Rd. *New H* 4M **55**
Byfleets La. *Warn* 2D **196**
Byfleet Technical Cen. *Byfl* 7M **55**
Bygrove. *New Ad* 3L **65**
Bylands. *Wok* 6C **74**
Byne Rd. *Cars* 8C **44**
Bynes Rd. *S Croy* 4A **64**
By-Pass Rd. *Lea* 7H **79**
Byrd Rd. *Craw* 6L **181**
Byrefield Rd. *Guild* 9J **93**
Byrne Rd. *SW12* 2F **28**
Byron Av. *Camb* 3F **70**
Byron Av. *Coul* 2J **83**
Byron Av. *Houn* 5H **9**
Byron Av. *N Mald* 4F **42**
Byron Av. *Sutt* 1B **62**
Byron Av. E. *Sutt* 1B **62**
Byron Clo. *SE20* 2E **46**
Byron Clo. *SW16* 7J **29**
Byron Clo. *Craw* 2F **182**
Byron Clo. *Fleet* 5B **88**
Byron Clo. *Hamp* 5N **23**
Byron Clo. *H'ham* 2L **197**
Byron Clo. *Knap* 4H **73**
Byron Clo. *W on T* 7M **39**
Byron Clo. *Yat* 2A **68**
Byron Ct. *Wind* 6D **4**
Byron Dri. *Crowt* 4G **48**
Byron Gdns. *Sutt* 1B **62**
Byron Gro. *E Grin* 1M **185**
Byron Ho. *Slou* 1D **6**
Byron Pl. *Lea* 9H **79**
Byron Rd. *Add* 1N **55**
Byron Rd. *S Croy* 6E **64**
Byron Way. *W Dray* 1A **8**
Byton Rd. *SW17* 7D **28**
Byttom Hill. *Mick* 4J **99**
Byward Av. *Felt* 9K **9**
Byways. *Yat* 1A **68**
Byways, The. *Asht* 5K **79**
Byway, The. *Eps* 1E **60**
Byway, The. *Sutt* 5B **62**
Bywood. *Brack* 6M **31**
Bywood Av. *Croy* 5F **46**
Bywood Clo. *Kenl* 2M **83**
Byworth Clo. *Farnh* 1E **128**
Byworth Rd. *Farnh* 1E **128**

C

Cabbage Hill. *Warf* 6L **15**
Cabbage Hill La. *Binf* 5K **15**
Cabbel Pl. *Add* 1L **55**
Cabell Rd. *Guild* 2G **113**
Caberfeigh Pl. *Red* 3B **122**
Cabin Moss. *Brack* 6C **32**
Cabrera Av. *Vir W* 5M **35**
Cabrera Clo. *Vir W* 5N **35**
Cabrol Rd. *Farnb* 9M **69**
Caburn Ct. *Craw* 5A **182**
Caburn Heights. *Craw* 5A **182**
Caci Ho. W14 *1L 13*
(off Avonmore Rd.)
Cacket's La. *Cud* 2M **87**
Cackstones, The. *Worth* 1H **183**
Cadbury Clo. *Iswth* 4G **11**
Cadbury Clo. *Sun* 8F **22**
Cadbury Rd. *Sun* 8F **22**
Caddy Clo. *Egh* 6C **20**
Cader Rd. *SW18* 9N **13** & 1A **28**
Cadet Way. *C Crook* 9C **88**
Cadman Ct. W4 *1A 12*
(off Chaseley Dri.)
Cadmer Clo. *N Mald* 3D **42**
Cadnam Clo. *Alder* 6A **110**
Cadogan Clo. *Beck* 1N **47**
Cadogan Clo. *Tedd* 6E **24**
Cadogan Ct. *Sutt* 3N **61**
Cadogan Ho. Guild *4B 114*
(off St Lukes Sq.)
Cadogan Rd. *Alder* 6B **90**
Cadogan Rd. *Surb* 4K **41**
Caenshill Rd. *Wey* 4B **56**
Caenswood Hill. *Wey* 6B **56**
Caenwood Clo. *Wey* 3B **56**
Caen Wood Rd. *Asht* 5J **79**
Caerleon Clo. *Hind* 3A **170**
Caernarvon. *Frim* 6D **70**
Caernarvon Clo. *Mitc* 2J **45**
Caesar Ct. *Alder* 2K **109**
Caesars Camp Rd. *Camb* 7D **50**
Caesar's Clo. *Camb* 7D **50**
Caesars Ct. *Farnh* 6H **109**
Caesars Ga. *Warf* 9C **16**
Caesars Wlk. *Mitc* 4D **44**
Caesars Way. *Shep* 5E **38**
Caffins Clo. *Craw* 1C **182**
Cage Yd. *Reig* 3M **121**
Caillard Rd. *Byfl* 7N **55**
Cain Rd. *Brack* 1J **31**
Cain's La. *Felt* 8F **8**
Cairn Clo. *Camb* 3F **70**
Cairn Ct. *Eps* 6E **60**
Cairngorm Clo. *Tedd* 6G **24**
Cairngorm Pl. *Farnb* 7K **69**
Cairo New Rd. *Croy* 8M **45** (3A **200**)
Caistor M. *SW12* 1F **28**
Caistor Rd. *SW12* 1F **28**
Caithness Dri. *Eps* 1C **80** (8K **201**)
Caithness Rd. *Mitc* 8F **28**
Calbourne Rd. *SW12* 1D **28**
Caldbeck Av. *Wor Pk* 8F **42**
Caldbeck Ho. Craw *6L 181*
(off Salvington Rd.)
Caldecote. *King T* 4M **203**
Calder Ct. *Langl* 1B **6**
Calderdale Clo. *Craw* 5N **181**
Calder Rd. *Mord* 4A **44**
Calder Way. *Coln* 6G **7**
Caldwell Ho. SW13 *3H 13*
(off Trinity Chu. Rd.)
Caldwell Rd. *W'sham* 2A **52**
Caledonian Way. *Gat A* 3F **162**
Caledonia Rd. *Stai* 2N **21**
Caledon Pl. *Guild* 9C **94**
Caledon Rd. *Wall* 1E **62**
Calfridus Way. *Brack* 2C **32**
Calidore Clo. *SW2* 1K **29**
California Rd. *N Mald* 3A **42**
Calley Down Cres. *New Ad* 6N **65**
Callis Farm Clo. *Stanw* 9N **7**
Callisto Clo. *Craw* 6K **181**
Callow Fld. *Purl* 9L **63**
Callow Hill. *Vir W* 2M **35**

Calluna Ct.—Castle Rd.

Calluna Ct. Wok . . . 5B 74
Calluna Dri. Copt . . . 8L 163
Calonne Rd. SW19 . . . 5J 27
Calshot Rd. H'row A . . . 5B 8
(in two parts)
Calshot Way. Frim . . . 7E 70
Calshot Way. H'row A . . . 5B 8
(in two parts)
Calthorpe Gdns. Sutt . . . 9A 44
Calthorpe Rd. Fleet . . . 3A 88
Calton Gdns. Alder . . . 5A 110
Calverley Rd. Eps . . . 3F 60
Calvert Clo. Alder . . . 3B 110
Calvert Cres. Dork . . . 3H 119
Calvert Rd. Dork . . . 3H 119
Calvert Rd. Eff . . . 6J 97
Calvin Clo. Camb . . . 2F 70
Calvin Wlk. Craw . . . 6K 181
Camac Rd. Twic . . . 2D 24
Camargue Pl. G'ming . . . 7J 133
Cambalt Rd. SW15 . . . 8J 13
Camber Clo. Craw . . . 3G 183
Camberley. . . . 9B 50
Camberley Av. SW20 . . . 1G 42
Camberley Clo. Sutt . . . 9J 43
Camberley Rd. H'row A . . . 0D 8
Camborne Clo. H'row A . . . 6B 8
Camborne Rd. SW18 . . . 1M 27
Camborne Rd. Croy . . . 6D 46
Camborne Rd. Mord . . . 4J 43
Camborne Rd. Sutt . . . 4M 61
Camborne Way. Houn . . . 4A 10
Cambourne Rd. H'row A . . . 6B 8
Cambourne Wlk. Rich . . . 9K 11
Cambray Rd. SW12 . . . 2G 29
Cambria Clo. Houn . . . 7A 10
Cambria Ct. Felt . . . 1J 23
Cambria Ct. Stai . . . 5G 20
Cambria Gdns. Stai . . . 1N 21
(in two parts)
Cambrian Clo. SE27 . . . 4M 29
Cambrian Clo. Camb . . . 1N 69
Cambrian Rd. Farnb . . . 7J 69
Cambrian Rd. Rich . . . 9M 11
Cambrian Way. Finch . . . 8A 30
Cambria St. SW6 . . . 3N 13
Cambridge Av. N Mald . . . 2D 42
(in two parts)
Cambridge Clo. SW20 . . . 9G 26
Cambridge Clo. Houn . . . 7M 9
Cambridge Clo. W Dray . . . 2M 7
Cambridge Clo. Wok . . . 5J 73
Cambridge Cotts. Rich . . . 2N 11
Cambridge Cres. Tedd . . . 6G 24
Cambridge Gdns. King T . . . 1N 41
Cambridge Gro. Rd. King T . . . 2N 41
(in two parts)
Cambridge Ho. Wind . . . 4F 4
Cambridge Lodge Cvn. Pk. Horl . . . 5E 142
Cambridge Meadows. Farnh . . . 2E 128
Cambridge Pk. Twic . . . 9J 11
Cambridge Pk. Ct. Twic . . . 1K 25
Cambridge Pl. Farnh . . . 1H 129
Cambridge Rd. Ashf . . . 8D 22
Cambridge Rd. SE20 . . . 2E 46
Cambridge Rd. SW13 . . . 5E 12
Cambridge Rd. SW20 . . . 9F 26
Cambridge Rd. Alder . . . 2L 109
Cambridge Rd. Cars . . . 3C 62
Cambridge Rd. Crowt . . . 3H 49
Cambridge Rd. Hamp . . . 8N 23
Cambridge Rd. H'ham . . . 6K 197
Cambridge Rd. Houn . . . 7M 9
Cambridge Rd. King T . . . 1M 41 (3M 203)
Cambridge Rd. Mitc . . . 2G 44
Cambridge Rd. N Mald . . . 3C 42
Cambridge Rd. Owl . . . 6K 49
Cambridge Rd. Rich . . . 3N 11
Cambridge Rd. Tedd . . . 5F 24
Cambridge Rd. Twic . . . 9K 11
Cambridge Rd. W on T . . . 5J 39
Cambridge Rd. W Mol . . . 3N 39
Cambridge Rd. E. Farnb . . . 4A 90
(in two parts)
Cambridge Rd. N. W4 . . . 1A 12
Cambridge Rd. S. W4 . . . 1A 12
Cambridge Rd. W. Farnb . . . 4A 90
(in two parts)
Cambridgeshire Clo. Warf . . . 8D 16
Cambridge Sq. Camb . . . 9A 50
(off Cambridge Wlk.)
Cambridge Wlk. Camb . . . 9A 50
Camden Av. Felt . . . 2K 23
Camden Gdns. Sutt . . . 2N 61
Camden Gdns. T Hth . . . 2M 45
Camden Rd. Cars . . . 1D 62
Camden Rd. Ling . . . 8N 145
Camden Rd. Sutt . . . 2N 61
Camden Wlk. Fleet . . . 4D 88
Camden Way. T Hth . . . 2M 45
Cameford Ct. SW12 . . . 1J 29
Camel Gro. King T . . . 6K 25
Camellia Ct. W End . . . 9C 52
Camellia Pl. Twic . . . 1B 24
Camelot Clo. SW19 . . . 5L 27
Camelot Clo. Big H . . . 3E 86
Camelot Ct. If'd . . . 3K 181
Camelsdale. . . . 3D 188
Camelsdale Rd. Hasl . . . 3C 188
Cameron Clo. Cranl . . . 9N 155
Cameron Rd. Alder . . . 6B 90
Cameron Rd. Croy . . . 5M 45
Cameron Sq. Mitc . . . 9C 28
Camilla Clo. Bookh . . . 3B 98
Camilla Clo. Sun . . . 7G 22
Camilla Dri. Westh . . . 8G 98
Camille Clo. SE25 . . . 2D 46
Camm Av. Wind . . . 6B 4
Camm Gdns. King T . . . 1M 41 (4M 203)
Camm Gdns. Th Dit . . . 6F 40
Camomile Av. Mitc . . . 9D 28
Campana Rd. SW6 . . . 4M 13
Campbell Av. Wok . . . 8B 74
Campbell Clo. SW16 . . . 5H 29
Campbell Clo. Alder . . . 5A 110
Campbell Clo. Fleet . . . 4A 88
Campbell Clo. Twic . . . 2D 24
Campbell Clo. Yat . . . 9E 48
Campbell Cres. E Grin . . . 9L 165
Campbell Pl. Frim . . . 3D 70
Campbell Rd. Alder . . . 1M 109
Campbell Rd. Cat . . . 0A 84
Campbell Rd. Croy . . . 6M 45
Campbell Rd. E Mol . . . 2E 40
Campbell Rd. M'bowr . . . 5G 182
Campbell Rd. Twic . . . 3D 24
Campbell Rd. Wey . . . 4B 56
Campden Rd. S Croy . . . 2B 64
Campen Clo. SW19 . . . 3K 27
Camp End Rd. Wey . . . 8D 56
Camperdown Ho. Wall . . . 3F 62
(off Stanley Pk. Rd.)
Camp Farm Rd. Alder . . . 8B 90
Camp Hill. Farnh . . . 3A 130
Camphill Ct. W Byf . . . 8J 55
Camphill Ind. Est. W Byf . . . 7K 55
Camphill Rd. W Byf . . . 8J 55
Campion Clo. B'water . . . 3L 69
Campion Clo. Lind . . . 5B 168
Campion Clo. S Croy . . . 1B 64
Campion Dri. Tad . . . 7G 81
Campion Ho. Brack . . . 9K 15
Campion Ho. Red . . . 1D 122
Campion Rd. SW15 . . . 7H 13
Campion Rd. H'ham . . . 3L 197
Campion Rd. Iswth . . . 4F 10
Campion Way. Wokgm . . . 9D 14
Camp Rd. Farnb . . . 5A 90
Camp Rd. SW19 . . . 6G 26
(in two parts)
Camp Rd. Wold . . . 7H 85
Camp Vw. SW19 . . . 6G 27
Camrose Av. Felt . . . 5K 23
Camrose Clo. Croy . . . 6H 47
Camrose Clo. Mord . . . 3M 43
Canada Av. Red . . . 7E 122
Canada Dri. Red . . . 7E 122
Canada Rd. Cob . . . 9K 57
Canada Rd. Byfl . . . 7M 55
Canada Rd. Deep . . . 6H 71
Canadian Memorial Av. Asc . . . 1J 35
Canal Bank. Ash V . . . 9E 90
Canal Clo. Alder . . . 8B 90
Canal Cotts. Ash V . . . 9E 90
Canal Wlk. SE25 . . . 5B 46
Canberra Clo. Craw . . . 9B 162
Canberra Clo. Yat . . . 7A 48
Canberra Pl. H'ham . . . 3M 197
Canberra Rd. H'row A . . . 6B 8
Canbury Av. King T . . . 9M 25 (1L 203)
Canbury Bus. Cen. King T . . . 9L 25 (2K 203)
Canbury Bus. Pk. King T . . . 2K 203
Canbury Pk. Rd. King T . . . 9L 25 (2K 203)
Canbury Pas. King T . . . 9K 25 (2H 203)
Candleford Clo. Brack . . . 8A 16
Candler M. Twic . . . 1G 25
Candlerush Clo. Wok . . . 4D 74
Candover Clo. W Dray . . . 3M 7
Candy Cft. Bookh . . . 4B 98
Canes La. Lind . . . 4A 168
Canewden Clo. Wok . . . 6A 74
Canford Dri. Add . . . 8K 37
Canford Gdns. N Mald . . . 5D 42
Canford Pl. Tedd . . . 7J 25
Canham Rd. SE25 . . . 2B 46
Can Hatch. Tad . . . 5K 81
Canmore Gdns. SW16 . . . 8G 29
Canning Rd. Alder . . . 2B 110
Canning Rd. Croy . . . 0D 46
Cannizaro Rd. SW19 . . . 7H 27
Cannon Clo. Col T . . . 7L 49
Cannon Clo. SW20 . . . 2H 43
Cannon Clo. Hamp . . . 7B 24
Cannon Cres. Chob . . . 7H 53
Cannon Gro. Fet . . . 9E 78
Cannon Hill. Brack . . . 5A 32
Cannon Hill La. SW20 . . . 4J 43
Cannonside. Fet . . . 9E 78
Cannon Way. Fet . . . 8E 78
Cannon Way. W Mol . . . 3A 40
Canonbury Cotts. Rusp . . . 3E 180
Canons Clo. Reig . . . 2L 121
Canons Hill. Coul . . . 5L 83
(in two parts)
Canons La. Tad . . . 5K 81
Canon's Wlk. Croy . . . 9G 46
Canopus Way. Stai . . . 1N 21
Cansiron La. Ash W . . . 3H 187
(in five parts)
Cansiron La. Cowd . . . 7N 167
(in three parts)
Cantelupe M. E Grin . . . 9B 166
(off Cantelupe Rd.)
Cantelupe Rd. E Grin . . . 9B 166
Canterbury Ct. Dork . . . 1H 201
Canterbury Gro. SE27 . . . 5L 29
Canterbury Ho. Croy . . . 1D 200
Canterbury M. Oxs . . . 9C 58
Canterbury Rd. Farnb . . . 3B 90
Canterbury Rd. As . . . 1F 110
Canterbury Rd. Craw . . . 7C 182
Canterbury Rd. Croy . . . 6K 45
Canterbury Rd. Felt . . . 3M 23
Canterbury Rd. Guild . . . 1J 113
Canterbury Rd. Mord . . . 6N 43
Canter, The. Craw . . . 2J 183
Cantley. . . . 9A 14
Cantley Cres. Wokgm . . . 9A 14
Cantley Gdns. SE19 . . . 1C 46
Canvey Clo. Craw . . . 6A 182
Cape Copse. Rud . . . 1E 194
Capel. . . . 4K 159
Capel Av. Wall . . . 2K 63
Capel By-Pass. Capel . . . 3H 159
Capel La. Craw . . . 4L 181
Capel Rd. Rusp . . . 2M 179
Capern Rd. SW18 . . . 2A 28
Capital Ind. Est. Mitc . . . 4D 44
Capital Interchange Way. Bren . . . 1N 11
Capital Pk. Wok . . . 8D 74
Capital Pl. Croy . . . 2K 63
Caple Ho. SW10 . . . 3N 13
(off King's Rd.)
Capricorn Clo. Craw . . . 5K 181
Capri Rd. Croy . . . 7C 46
Capsey Rd. If'd . . . 3K 181
Capstans Wharf. St J . . . 5J 73
Caradon Clo. Wok . . . 5L 73
Caraway Clo. Craw . . . 7N 181
Caraway Pl. Guild . . . 7K 93
Caraway Pl. Wall . . . 9F 44
Carbery La. Asc . . . 2M 33
Cardamom Clo. Guild . . . 8K 93
Card Hill. F Row . . . 8H 187
Cardigan Clo. Wok . . . 5H 73
Cardigan Rd. SW13 . . . 5F 12
Cardigan Rd. SW19 . . . 7A 28
Cardigan Rd. Rich . . . 9L 11
Cardinal Av. King T . . . 6L 25
Cardinal Av. Mord . . . 5K 43
Cardinal Clo. Mord . . . 5K 43
Cardinal Clo. S Croy . . . 9D 64
Cardinal Clo. Wor Pk . . . 1F 60
Cardinal Cres. N Mald . . . 1B 42
Cardinal Dri. W on T . . . 7L 39
Cardinal Pl. SW15 . . . 7J 13
Cardinal Rd. Felt . . . 2J 23
Cardinals, The. . . . 5E 110
Cardinals, The. Brack . . . 3N 31
Cardinals Wlk. Hamp . . . 8C 24
Cardinals Wlk. Sun . . . 7F 22
Cardingham. Wok . . . 4K 73
Cardington Rd. H'row A . . . 6C 8
Cardington Sq. Houn . . . 7L 9
Cardwell Cres. Asc . . . 4N 33
Cardwells Keep. Guild . . . 9K 93
Carew Clo. Coul . . . 6M 83
Carew Ct. Sutt . . . 5N 61
Carew Manor & Dovecote. . . . 9G 45
Carew Mnr. Cotts. Wall . . . 9H 45
Carew Rd. Ashf . . . 7D 22
Carew Rd. Mitc . . . 1E 44
Carew Rd. T Hth . . . 3M 45
Carew Rd. Wall . . . 3G 63
Carey Clo. Wind . . . 6E 4
Carey Ho. Craw . . . 3A 182
Carey Rd. Wokgm . . . 3B 30
Careys Copse. Small . . . 8M 143
Carey's Wood. Small . . . 8M 143
Carfax. H'ham . . . 6J 197
Carfax Av. Tong . . . 4D 110
Carfax Rd. Hay . . . 1G 9
Cargate Av. Alder . . . 3M 109
Cargate Gro. Alder . . . 3M 109
Cargate Hill. Alder . . . 3L 109
Cargate Ter. Alder . . . 3L 109
Cargill Rd. SW18 . . . 2N 27
Cargo Forecourt Rd. Gat A . . . 3B 162
Cargo Rd. Gat A . . . 2B 162
Cargreen Pl. SE25 . . . 3C 46
Cargreen Rd. SE25 . . . 3C 46
Carina M. SE27 . . . 5N 29
Carisbrooke. Frim . . . 6D 70
Carisbrooke Ct. Cheam . . . 4L 61
Carisbrooke Rd. Mitc . . . 3H 45
Carleton Av. Wall . . . 5H 63
Carleton Clo. Esh . . . 7D 40
Carlingford Gdns. Mitc . . . 8D 28
Carlingford Rd. Mord . . . 5J 43
Carlin Pl. Camb . . . 2A 70
Carlinwark Dri. Camb . . . 8D 50
Carlisle Clo. King T . . . 9N 25
Carlisle M. King T . . . 9N 25
Carlisle Rd. Rush . . . 3N 149
Carlisle Rd. Hamp . . . 8B 24
Carlisle Rd. Sutt . . . 3L 61
Carlisle Way. SW17 . . . 6E 28
Carlos St. G'ming . . . 7H 133
Carlson Ct. SW15 . . . 7L 13
Carlton Av. Felt . . . 0K 9
Carlton Av. Hay . . . 1F 8
Carlton Av. S Croy . . . 4B 64
Carlton Clo. Camb . . . 3F 70
Carlton Clo. Chess . . . 3K 59
Carlton Clo. Craw . . . 4C 182
Carlton Clo. Wok . . . 1B 74
Carlton Ct. SE20 . . . 1E 46
Carlton Ct. Horl . . . 0L 142
Carlton Ct. Stai . . . 6J 21
Carlton Cres. C Crook . . . 7C 88
Carlton Cres. Sutt . . . 1K 61
Carlton Dri. SW15 . . . 8J 13
Carlton Grn. Red . . . 9C 102
Carlton Ho. Felt . . . 9G 8
Carlton Ho. Houn . . . 9A 10
Carlton Pk. Av. SW20 . . . 1J 43
Carlton Rd. SW14 . . . 6B 12
Carlton Rd. Head D . . . 5H 169
Carlton Rd. N Mald . . . 1D 42
Carlton Rd. Reig & Red . . . 1B 122
Carlton Rd. S Croy . . . 3A 64
Carlton Rd. S God . . . 1F 144
Carlton Rd. Sun . . . 8G 22
Carlton Rd. W on T . . . 6J 39
Carlton Rd. Wok . . . 1C 74
Carlton Tye. Horl . . . 8G 142
Carlwell St. SW17 . . . 6C 28
Carlyle Clo. W Mol . . . 1B 40
Carlyle Ct. SW6 . . . 4N 13
(off Imperial Rd.)
Carlyle Ct. Crowt . . . 3H 49
Carlyle Pl. SW15 . . . 7J 13
Carlyle Rd. W5 . . . 1J 11
Carlyle Rd. Croy . . . 8D 46
Carlyle Rd. Stai . . . 8J 21
Carlyon Clo. Farnb . . . 1A 90
Carlyon Clo. Myt . . . 1D 90
Carlys Clo. Beck . . . 1G 47
Carmalt Gdns. SW15 . . . 7H 13
Carmalt Gdns. W on T . . . 2K 57
Carman Wlk. Craw . . . 8N 181
Carmarthen Clo. Farnb . . . 7L 69
Carmel Clo. Wok . . . 5A 74
Carmichael Ct. SW13 . . . 5E 12
(off Grove Rd.)
Carmichael M. SW18 . . . 1B 28
Carmichael Rd. SE25 . . . 4C 46
Carminia Rd. SW17 . . . 3F 28
Carnac St. SE27 . . . 5N 29
Carnation Clo. Crowt . . . 8G 30
Carnation Dri. Wink R . . . 7E 16
Carnegie Clo. Surb . . . 8M 41
Carnegie Pl. SW19 . . . 4J 27
Carnforth Clo. Eps . . . 3A 60
Carnforth Rd. SW16 . . . 8H 29
Carnie Hall. SW17 . . . 4F 28
Carnival Sq. Fleet . . . 4A 88
Carnoustie. Brack . . . 6K 31
Carnwath Rd. SW6 . . . 6M 13
Carolina Rd. T Hth. . . . 1M 45
Caroline Clo. SW16 . . . 4K 29
Caroline Clo. Croy . . . 1B 64
Caroline Clo. Iswth . . . 3D 10
Caroline Ct. Ashf . . . 7C 22
Caroline Ct. Craw . . . 4B 182
Caroline Ho. W6 . . . 1H 13
(off Queen Caroline St.)
Caroline Pl. Hay . . . 3F 8
Caroline Rd. SW19 . . . 8L 27
Caroline Wlk. W6 . . . 2K 13
(off Lillie Rd.)
Caroline Way. Frim . . . 5D 70
Carolyn Clo. Wok . . . 6J 73
Carpenter Clo. Eps . . . 5E 60
Carpenters Ct. Twic . . . 3E 24
Carrara Wharf. SW6 . . . 6K 13
Carriage Pl. SW16 . . . 6G 29
Carrick Clo. Iswth . . . 6G 10
Carrick Ga. Esh . . . 0C 40
Carrick La. Yat . . . 9D 48
Carrington Av. Houn . . . 8B 10
Carrington Clo. Croy . . . 6H 47
Carrington Clo. King T . . . 6B 26
Carrington Clo. Red . . . 2D 122
Carrington La. Ash V . . . 5E 90
Carrington Pl. Esh . . . 2C 58
Carrington Rd. Rich . . . 7N 11
Carroll Av. Guild . . . 3D 114
Carroll Cres. Asc . . . 4K 33
Carrow Rd. W on T . . . 9L 39
Carshalton. . . . 1E 62
Carshalton Athletic F.C. . . . 9C 44
Carshalton Beeches. . . . 5C 62
Carshalton Gro. Sutt . . . 1B 62
Carshalton on the Hill. . . . 4E 62
Carshalton Pk. Rd. Cars . . . 2D 62
Carshalton Pl. Cars . . . 2F 62
Carshalton Rd. Bans . . . 1D 82
Carshalton Rd. Camb . . . 6E 50
Carshalton Rd. Mitc . . . 3E 44
Carshalton Rd. Sutt & Cars . . . 2A 62
Carslake Rd. SW15 . . . 9H 13
Carson Rd. SE21 . . . 3N 29
Cartbridge. . . . 9D 74
Cartbridge Clo. Send . . . 1D 94
Carter Clo. Wall . . . 4H 63
Carter Clo. Wind . . . 5D 4
Carterdale Cotts. Capel . . . 5J 159
Carter Rd. SW19 . . . 7B 28
Carter Rd. M'bowr . . . 6H 183
Carters Clo. Guild . . . 8A 94
Carters Clo. Wor Pk . . . 8J 43
Carter's Cotts. Red . . . 5C 122
Carter's Hill. Wokgm & Binf . . . 5F 14
Carters Hill Pk. Wokgm . . . 5E 14
Carters La. Wok . . . 7E 74
Carterslodge La. Hand . . . 9J 199
Cartersmeade Clo. Horl . . . 7F 142
Carters Rd. Eps . . . 2E 80
Carters Wlk. Farnh . . . 4J 109
Carter's Yd. SW18 . . . 8M 13
Carthona Dri. Fleet . . . 6A 88
Carthouse Cotts. Guild . . . 9E 94
Carthouse La. Wok . . . 1H 73
Cartmel Clo. Reig . . . 1C 122
Cartmel Gdns. Mord . . . 4A 44
Cartwright Way. SW13 . . . 3G 13
Carville Cres. Bren . . . 1L 11
Cascades. Croy . . . 6J 65
Caselden Clo. Add . . . 2L 55
Casewick Rd. SE27 . . . 6L 29
Cashar Rd. M'bowr . . . 6G 183
Cassidy Rd. SW6 . . . 3M 13
(in two parts)
Casslis Rd. Twic . . . 8H 11
Cassino Clo. Alder . . . 2N 109
Cassiobury Av. Felt . . . 1G 22
Cassland Rd. T Hth . . . 3A 46
Cassocks Sq. Shep . . . 6E 38
Castello Av. SW15 . . . 8H 13
Castelnau. . . . 2G 12
Castelnau. SW13 . . . 4F 12
Castelnau Gdns. SW13 . . . 2G 13
Castelnau Mans. SW13 . . . 2G 13
(off Castelnau, in two parts)
Castelnau Row. SW13 . . . 2G 12
Castle Av. Dat . . . 2K 5
Castle Av. Eps . . . 6F 60
Castle Clo. SW19 . . . 4J 27
Castle Clo. Blet . . . 2N 123
Castle Clo. Brom . . . 2N 47
Castle Clo. Camb . . . 2D 70
Castle Clo. Reig . . . 7N 121
Castle Clo. Sun . . . 8F 22
Castlecombe Dri. SW19 . . . 1J 27
Castle Ct. Farnh . . . 9G 108
Castlecraig Ct. Col T . . . 8J 49
Castle Dri. Horl . . . 1G 162
Castle Dri. Reig . . . 7M 121
Castle Fld. Farnh . . . 9G 108
Castlefield Ct. Reig . . . 3N 121
Castlefield Rd. Reig . . . 3M 121
Castle Gdns. Dork . . . 3M 119
Castlegate. Rich . . . 6M 11
Castle Green. . . . 9G 53
Castle Grn. Wey . . . 9F 38
Castle Gro. Rd. Chob . . . 9G 53
Castle Hill. Farnh . . . 9G 108
Castle Hill. Guild . . . 5N 113 (7C 202)
Castle Hill. Wind . . . 4G 5
Castle Hill Av. New Ad . . . 5L 65
Castle Hill Rd. Egh . . . 5L 19
Castlemaine Av. Eps . . . 5G 61
Castlemaine Av. S Croy . . . 2C 64
Castle Pde. Eps . . . 4F 60
Castle Pl. W4 . . . 1D 12
Castle Rd. Alder . . . 9K 89
Castle Rd. Broad H . . . 5D 196
Castle Rd. Camb . . . 2C 70
Castle Rd. Coul . . . 7C 82
Castle Rd. Eps . . . 2A 80
Castle Rd. Iswth . . . 5F 10
Castle Rd. Wey . . . 9E 38
Castle Rd. Wok . . . 1B 74

Castle Row—Chard Rd.

Castle Row. W4 1C 12
Castle Sq. Blet 2N 123
Castle Sq. Guild 5N 113 (6D 202)
Castle St. Blet 2M 123
Castle St. Farnh 9G 109
Castle St. Fleet 6A 88
Castle St. Guild 5N 113 (6C 202)
Castle St. King T 1L 41 (3J 203)
Castle, The. H'ham 1L 197
Castleton. Cars 7B 62
Castleton Clo. Bans 2M 81
Castleton Clo. Croy 5H 47
Castleton Dri. Bans 2M 81
Castleton Rd. Mitc 3H 45
(in two parts)
Castletown Rd. W14 1K 13
Castle Vw. Eps 1A 80
Castleview Rd. Slou 1M 5
Castle Vw. Rd. Wey 1C 56
Castle Wlk. Reig 3M 121
Castle Wlk. Sun 2K 39
Castle Way. SW19 4J 27
Castle Way. Eps 6F 60
Castle Way. Felt 5K 23
Castle Yd. Rich 8K 11
Castor Ct. C Crook 8C 88
Castor Ct. Yat 8A 48
Caswall Clo. Binf 7H 15
Caswall Ride. Yat 1D 68
Caswell Clo. Farnb 8L 69
Catalina Rd. H'row A 5C 8
Catalpa Clo. Guild 1M 113
Catena Ri. Light 6L 51
Caterfield La. Crow & Oxt 1B 146
Cater Gdns. Guild 1J 113
Caterham 2D 104
Caterham By-Pass. Cat 8E 84
Caterham Clo. Cat 7B 84
(in two parts)
Caterham Clo. Pirb 8B 72
Caterham Dri. Coul 5M 83
Caterham-on-the-Hill 9C 84
Caterways. H'ham 5G 197
Catesby Gdns. Yat 1A 68
Cathcart Rd. SW10 2N 13
Cathedral Clo. Guild 4L 113
Cathedral Ct. Guild 3K 113
Cathedral Hill Ind. Est. Guild 2K 113
Cathedral Precinct. Guild 4K 113
Cathedral Vw. Guild 3J 113
Catherine Clo. Byfl 1N 75
Catherine Ct. SW19 6L 27
Catherine Dri. Rich 7L 11
Catherine Dri. Sun 7G 22
Catherine Gdns. Houn 7D 10
Catherine Howard Ct. Wey 9C 38
(off Old Palace Rd.)
Catherine Rd. Surb 4K 41 (8G 203)
Catherine Wheel Rd. Bren 3K 11
Cat Hill. Ockl 7B 158
Cathill La. Ockl 7B 158
Cathles Rd. SW12 1F 28
Catlin Cres. Shep 4E 38
Catlin Gdns. God 8E 104
Cator Clo. New Ad 7A 66
Cator Cres. New Ad 7A 66
Cator La. Beck 1J 47
Cator Rd. Cars 2D 62
Cato's Hill. Esh 1B 58
Cat St. Up Har 8N 187
Catteshall 6K 133
Catteshall Hatch. G'ming 5K 133
Catteshall La. G'ming 7H 133
Catteshall Rd. G'ming 5K 133
(in two parts)
Catteshall Ter. G'ming 6K 133
(off Catteshall Rd.)
Caudwell Ter. SW18 1B 28
Causeway Ct. Wok 5J 73
Causeway Est. Stai 5D 20
Causewayside. Hasl 1H 189
(off High St.)
Causeway, The. SW18 8N 13
(in two parts)
Causeway, The. SW19 6H 27
Causeway, The. Cars 9E 44
Causeway, The. Chess 1L 59
Causeway, The. Clay 4F 58
Causeway, The. Felt & Houn 7H 9
Causeway, The. H'ham 7J 197
Causeway, The. Stai 5E 20
Causeway, The. Sutt 5A 62
Causeway, The. Tedd 7F 24
Cavalier Ct. Surb 5M 41
Cavalier Way. E Grin 2B 186
Cavalry Ct. Alder 2K 109
Cavalry Cres. Houn 7L 9
Cavalry Cres. Wind 6F 4
Cavalry Gdns. SW15 8L 13
Cavan's Rd. Alder 7A 90
Cavell Ho. Ott 3F 54
Cavell Way. Eps 7N 59
Cavell Way. Knap 6F 72
Cavell Way. M'bowr 4G 182
Cavendish Av. N Mald 4F 42
Cavendish Clo. H'ham 1K 197
Cavendish Clo. Sun 7G 22
Cavendish Ct. B'water 3J 69
Cavendish Ct. Cher 7J 37
(off Victory Rd.)
Cavendish Ct. Coln 4G 6
Cavendish Ct. Sun 7G 22
Cavendish Dri. Clay 2E 58
Cavendish Gdns. SW4 1G 29
Cavendish Gdns. C Crook 8A 88
Cavendish Gdns. Red 2E 122
Cavendish Meads. Asc 5A 34
Cavendish M. Alder 3M 109
Cavendish Pde. Houn 5M 9
Cavendish Pk. Cvn. Site. Sand 9K 49
Cavendish Rd. SW12 1G 28
Cavendish Rd. SW19 8B 28
Cavendish Rd. W4 4B 12
Cavendish Rd. Alder 3M 109
Cavendish Rd. C Crook 9A 88
Cavendish Rd. Croy 7M 45
Cavendish Rd. N Mald 3E 42
Cavendish Rd. Red 3E 122
Cavendish Rd. Sun 7G 22
Cavendish Rd. Sutt 4A 62
Cavendish Rd. Wey 5C 56
Cavendish Rd. Wok 6N 73
Cavendish Ter. Felt 3H 23
Cavendish Way. W Wick 7L 47
Cavenham Clo. Wok 6A 74
Caverleigh Way. Wor Pk 7F 42
Cave Rd. Rich 5J 25
Caversham Av. Sutt 8K 43
Caversham Ho. King T 4J 203
Caversham Rd. King T 1M 41 (3L 203)
Caves Farm Clo. Sand 7F 48
Cawcott Dri. Wind 4B 4
Cawsey Way. Wok 4A 74
Caxton Av. Add 3J 55
Caxton Clo. Craw 6B 182
Caxton Gdns. Guild 2L 113
Caxton La. Oxt 9G 106
Caxton M. Bren 2K 11
Caxton Ri. Red 2E 122
Caxton Rd. SW19 6A 28
Cayley Clo. Wall 4J 63
Cayton Rd. Coul 9G 83
Cearn Way. Coul 2K 83
Cecil Clo. Ashf 8D 22
Cecil Clo. Chess 1K 59
Cecil Ct. SW10 2N 13
(off Fawcett St.)
Cecil Pl. Mitc 4D 44
Cecil Rd. Ashf 8D 22
Cecil Rd. SW19 8N 27
Cecil Rd. Croy 5J 45
Cecil Rd. Houn 5C 10
Cecil Rd. Sutt 3L 61
Cedar Av. Cob 2K 77
Cedar Av. B'water 1J 69
Cedar Av. Twic 9B 10
Cedar Clo. SE21 2N 29
Cedar Clo. SW15 5C 26
Cedar Clo. Alder 4C 110
Cedar Clo. Bag 4J 51
Cedar Clo. Binf 7J 15
Cedar Clo. Cars 3D 62
Cedar Clo. Craw 9A 162
Cedar Clo. Dork 5H 119 (3K 201)
Cedar Clo. E Mol 3E 40
Cedar Clo. Eps 1E 80
Cedar Clo. Esh 3N 57
Cedar Clo. H'ham 5H 197
Cedar Clo. Reig 5A 122
Cedar Clo. Stai 2L 37
Cedar Clo. Warl 6H 85
Cedar Clo. Wokgm 2B 30
Cedar Ct. SW19 4J 27
Cedar Ct. Bren 2J 11
Cedar Ct. Egh 5C 20
Cedar Ct. Hasl 2F 188
Cedar Ct. Lea 9G 78
Cedar Ct. Sutt 3A 62
Cedar Ct. Wind 5D 4
Cedar Cres. Brom 1G 66
Cedarcroft Rd. Chess 1M 59
Cedar Dri. Asc 3G 35
(Blacknest Rd.)
Cedar Dri. Asc 6D 34
(Broomhall La.)
Cedar Dri. Brack 8A 16
Cedar Dri. Eden 1K 147
Cedar Dri. Fet 1E 98
Cedar Dri. Fleet 4D 88
Cedar Gdns. Sutt 3A 62
Cedar Gdns. Wok 5L 73
Cedar Gro. Bisl 2D 72
Cedar Gro. Wey 1D 56
Cedar Heights. Rich 2L 25
Cedar Hill. Eps 3B 80
Cedar Ho. Guild 1E 114
Cedarland Ter. SW20 8G 27
Cedar La. Frim 6B 70
Cedar Lodge. Craw 5B 182
Cedar Lodge. Hasl 3J 189
Cedarne Rd. SW6 3N 13
Cedar Pk. Cat 8B 84
Cedar Rd. Cob 1J 77
Cedar Rd. Farnb 2A 90
Cedar Rd. Croy 8A 46 (2E 200)
Cedar Rd. E Mol 3E 40
Cedar Rd. Felt 2E 22
Cedar Rd. Houn 5K 9
Cedar Rd. Sutt 3A 62
Cedar Rd. Tedd 6G 24
Cedar Rd. Wey 1B 56
Cedar Rd. Wok 7L 73
Cedars. Bans 1D 82
Cedars. Brack 3D 32
Cedars Av. Mitc 3E 44
Cedars Clo. Sand 7E 48
Cedars Ct. Guild 9C 94
Cedars Rd. SW13 5F 12
Cedars Rd. W4 2B 12
Cedars Rd. Beck 1H 47
Cedars Rd. Croy 9J 45
Cedars Rd. Hamp W 9J 25
Cedars Rd. Mord 3M 43
Cedars, The. Brock 3N 119
Cedars, The. Byfl 8A 56
Cedars, The. Fleet 5C 88
Cedars, The. Guild 9C 94
Cedars, The. Lea 8K 79
Cedars, The. Milf 2B 152
Cedars, The. Pirb 9A 72
Cedars, The. Reig 3B 122
Cedars, The. Tedd 7F 24
Cedars, The. Wall 1G 63
Cedar Ter. Rich 7L 11
Cedar Tree Gro. SE27 6M 29
Cedar Vw. King T 6H 203
Cedarville Gdns. SW16 7K 29
Cedar Wlk. Clay 3F 58
Cedar Wlk. Kenl 3N 83
Cedar Wlk. Kgswd 7K 81
Cedar Way. Guild 1M 113
Cedar Way. Slou 1A 6
Cedar Way. Sun 8F 22
Cedarways. Farnh 4G 128
Celandine Clo. Craw 6N 181
Celandine Clo. Crowt 1H 49
Celandine Ct. Yat 8A 48
Celandine Rd. W on T 1M 57
Celery La. Wrec 6G 128
Celia Cres. Ashf 7M 21
Cell Farm Av. Old Win 8L 5
Celtic Av. Brom 2N 47
Celtic Rd. Byfl 1N 75
Cemetery Pales. Brkwd 9C 72
Cemetery Rd. Fleet 6A 88
Centaur Ct. Bren 1L 11
Centaurs Bus. Cen. Iswth 2G 10
Centenary Ct. Red 2D 122
(off Warwick Rd.)
Centennial Ct. Brack 1M 31
Central Av. Houn 7C 10
Central Av. Wall 2J 63
Central Av. W Mol 3N 39
Central Gdns. Mord 4N 43
Central Hill. SE19 6N 29
Central La. Wink 2M 17
Central Pde. Felt 1K 23
Central Pde. Horl 9E 142
Central Pde. Houn 3N 9
Central Pde. New Ad 6M 65
Central Pde. Red 2D 122
Central Pde. Surb 5L 41
Central Pde. W Mol 3N 39
Central Pk. Est. Houn 8L 9
Central Pl. SE25 4D 46
Central Rd. Mord 5M 43
Central Rd. Wor Pk 7F 42
Central School Path. SW14 6B 12
Central Ter. Beck 2G 46
Central Wlk. Wokgm 2B 30
Central Way. Cars 4C 62
Central Way. Felt 8H 9
Central Way. Oxt 5N 105
Central Way. Wink 2M 17
Centre Ct. Shop. Cen. SW19 7L 27
Centre Rd. Wind 3A 4
Centre, The. Felt 3H 23
Centre, The. Houn 6B 10
Centre, The. W on T 7G 39
Centurion Clo. Col T 7J 49
Centurion Ct. Hack 8F 44
Century Ct. Wok 3B 74
Century Ho. SW15 7J 13
Century Rd. Stai 6E 20
Century Way. Brkwd 6A 72
Cerne Rd. Mord 5A 44
Cerotus Pl. Cher 6H 37
Ceylon Ter. Deep 6H 71
(off Swordsmans Dri.)
Chadacre Rd. Eps 3G 60
Chadhurst Clo. N Holm 8K 119
Chadwick Av. SW19 7M 27
Chadwick Clo. SW15 1E 26
Chadwick Clo. Craw 8N 181
Chadwick Clo. Tedd 7G 25
Chadwick Pl. Surb 6J 41
Chadworth Way. Clay 2D 58
Chaffers Mead. Asht 3M 79
Chaffinch Av. Croy 5G 46
Chaffinch Bus. Pk. Beck 3G 47
Chaffinch Clo. Col T 7J 49
Chaffinch Clo. Craw 1B 182
Chaffinch Clo. Croy 4G 46
Chaffinch Clo. H'ham 1K 197
Chaffinch Clo. Surb 9N 41
Chaffinch Rd. Beck 1H 47
Chaffinch Way. Horl 7C 142
Chailey Clo. Craw 6M 181
Chailey Clo. Houn 4L 9
Chailey Pl. W on T 1M 57
Chalcot Clo. Sutt 4M 61
Chalcot M. SW16 4J 29
Chalcott Gdns. Surb 7J 41
Chaldon 2L 103
Chaldon Clo. Red 5C 122
Chaldon Comn. Rd. Cat 2N 103
Chaldon Ct. SE19 9N 29 & 1A 46
Chaldon Rd. SW6 3K 13
Chaldon Rd. Cat 2A 104
Chaldon Rd. Craw 8A 182
Chaldon Way. Coul 4J 83
Chale Rd. SW2 1J 29
Chalet Hill. Bord 6A 168
Chale Wlk. Sutt 5N 61
Chalfont Dri. Farnb 3A 90
Chalfont Rd. SE25 2C 46
Chalford Clo. W Mol 3A 40
Chalgrove Av. Mord 4M 43
Chalgrove Rd. Sutt 4B 62
Chalice Clo. Wall 3H 63
Chalker's Corner. (Junct.) 6A 12
Chalk Hill Rd. W6 1J 13
Chalk La. Asht 6M 79
Chalk La. E Hor 1G 116
Chalk La. Eps 2C 80
(in two parts)
Chalk La. Shack 3A 132
Chalkley Clo. Mitc 1D 44
Chalkmead. Red 8G 103
Chalk Paddock. Eps 2C 80
Chalk Pit Cotts. W Hor 8C 96
Chalkpit La. Bet 2A 120
(in two parts)
Chalkpit La. Bookh 5N 97
Chalkpit La. Dork 4G 119 (1J 201)
Chalkpit La. Oxt 3M 105
(in two parts)
Chalk Pit Rd. Bans 4M 81
Chalk Pit Rd. Eps 6B 80
(in two parts)
Chalkpit Ter. Dork 3G 118
Chalk Pit Way. Sutt 3A 62
Chalkpit Wood. Oxt 5N 105
Chalk Rd. G'ming 6G 133
Chalk Rd. Loxw 6E 192
Chalky La. Chess 6K 59
Challen Ct. H'ham 5H 197
Challenge Ct. Lea 6H 79
Challenge Rd. Ashf 4E 22
Challice Way. SW2 2K 29
Challis Pl. Brack 1K 31
Challis Rd. Bren 1K 11
Challock Clo. Big H 3E 86
Challoner Cres. W14 1L 13
Challoners Clo. E Mol 3D 40
Challoner St. W14 1L 13
Chalmers Clo. Charl 4K 161
Chalmers Rd. Ashf 6C 22
Chalmers Rd. Bans 2B 82
Chalmers Rd. E. Ashf 5C 22
Chalmers Way. Felt 8J 9
Chamberlain Cres. W Wick 7L 47
Chamberlain Gdns. Houn 4C 10
Chamberlain Wlk. Felt 5M 23
(off Swift Rd.)
Chamberlain Way. Surb 6L 41
Chamber La. Farnh 3B 128
Chambers Ind. Pk. W Dray 2B 8
Chambers Pl. S Croy 4A 64
Chambers Rd. Ash V 8F 90
Chambon Pl. W6 1F 12
Chamomile Gdns. Farnb 9H 69
Champion Way. C Crook 8B 88
Champness Clo. SE27 5N 29
Champney Clo. Hort 6C 6
Champneys Clo. Sutt 4L 61
Chancellor Ct. Guild 4G 113
(in two parts)
Chancellor Gdns. S Croy 5M 63
Chancellor Gro. SE21 3N 29
Chancellor's Rd. W6 1H 13
Chancellor's St. W6 1H 13
Chancellors Wharf. W6 1H 13
Chancel Mans. Warf 7A 16
Chancery La. Beck 1L 47
Chancery M. SW17 3C 28
Chanctonbury Chase. Red 3E 122
Chanctonbury Dri. Asc 6B 34
Chanctonbury Gdns. Sutt 4N 61
Chanctonbury Way. Craw 5A 182
Chandler Clo. Craw 5B 182
Chandler Clo. Hamp 9A 24
Chandler Ct. Felt 9H 9
Chandlers Clo. Felt 1G 22
Chandlers La. Yat 8B 48
Chandlers Rd. Ash V 9F 90
Chandlers Way. SW2 1L 29
Chandon Lodge. Sutt 4A 62
Chandos Rd. Stai 6F 20
Channel Clo. Houn 4A 10
Channings. Hors 2A 74
Channon Ct. Surb 8J 203
Chantlers Clo. E Grin 8M 165
Chanton Dri. Sutt 6H 61
Chantrey Rd. Craw 6C 182
Chantry Clo. Asht 6J 79
Chantry Clo. Horl 7D 142
Chantry Clo. Wind 4D 4
Chantry Cotts. Chil 9D 114
Chantry Ct. Cars 9C 44
Chantry Ct. Frim 5B 70
(off Church Rd.)
Chantry Hurst. Eps 2C 80
Chantry Ind. Pk. Art 9M 113
Chantry La. Shere 8A 116
Chantry Rd. Bag 5H 51
Chantry Rd. Cher 6L 37
Chantry Rd. Chess 2M 59
Chantry Rd. Chil 9D 114
Chantrys Ct. Farnh 1F 128
Chantrys, The. Farnh 1E 128
Chantry Vw. Rd. Guild 6N 113 (8D 202)
Chantry Way. Mitc 2B 44
Chapel Av. Add 1K 55
Chapel Clo. Milf 9C 132
Chapel Ct. Dork 4G 119 (1J 201)
Chapel Farm Animal Trail. 8G 98
Chapel Farm Mobile Home Pk. Norm 9B 92
Chapel Fields. G'ming 4G 132
Chapel Gdns. Lind 4A 168
Chapel Green 4B 30
Chapel Gro. Add 1K 55
Chapel Gro. Eps 6H 81
Chapel Hill. Duns 6B 174
Chapel Hill. Eff 5L 97
Chapelhouse Clo. Guild 3H 113
Chapel La. Farnb & B'water 6L 69
Chapel La. Ash W 3F 186
Chapel La. Bag 5H 51
Chapel La. Binf 8H 15
Chapel La. Bookh 6C 98
Chapel La. Craw D 7C 164
Chapel La. F Row 8H 187
Chapel La. Milf 9C 132
Chapel La. Pirb 9D 72
Chapel La. Westc 6C 118
Chapel La. Westh 8E 98
Chapel La. Works. Westc 6C 118
(off Chapel La.)
Chapel Pk. Rd. Add 1K 55
Chapel Rd. SE27 5M 29
Chapel Rd. Camb 1N 69
Chapel Rd. Charl 3K 161
Chapel Rd. Houn 6B 10
Chapel Rd. Oxt 8E 106
Chapel Rd. Red 3D 122
Chapel Rd. Rowl 7D 128
Chapel Rd. Small 8M 143
Chapel Rd. Tad 1H 101
Chapel Rd. Twic 1H 25
Chapel Rd. Warl 5G 84
Chapel Sq. Ryl M 9L 49
Chapel Sq. Vir W 3A 36
Chapel St. Farnb 8B 70
Chapel St. Guild 5N 113 (6C 202)
Chapel St. Wok 4B 74
Chapel Ter. Binf 8H 15
Chapel Vw. S Croy 3F 64
Chapel Wlk. Croy 8N 45 (2B 200)
Chapel Way. Eps 6H 81
Chapel Yd. SW18 8M 13
(off Wandsworth High St.)
Chaplain's Hill. Crowt 3J 49
Chaplin Cres. Sun 7F 22
Chapman Rd. Croy 7L 45
Chapman Rd. M'bowr 7G 182
Chapman's La. E Grin 9L 165
(in four parts)
Chapman Sq. SW19 3J 27
Chapter M. Wind 3G 5
Chapter Way. Hamp 5A 24
Chara Pl. W4 2C 12
Charcot Ho. SW15 9E 12
Chardin Rd. W4 1D 12
Chard Rd. H'row A 5C 8

Chargate Clo.—Chestnut Clo.

Chargate Clo. W on T. 3G 57
Charing Clo. Orp 1N 67
Charing Ct. Brom 1N 47
Chariotts Pl. Wind 4G 4
Charlbury Clo. Brack 3D 32
Charlecote Clo. Farnb 2B 90
Charles Cobb Gdns. Croy 2L 63
Charlesfield Rd. Horl 7D 142
Charles Haller St. SW2 1L 29
Charles Harrod Ct. SW13 2H 13
(off Somerville Av.)
Charleshill 6E 130
Charles Hill. Tilf 5B 130
Charles Ho. Wind 4F 4
Charles Rd. SW19 9M 27
Charles Rd. Stai 7M 21
Charles Sq. Brack 1A 32
Charles St. SW13 5D 12
Charles St. Cher 7H 37
Charles St. Croy 9N 45 (4D 200)
Charles St. Houn 5N 9
Charles St. Wind 4F 4
Charleston Clo. Felt 4H 23
Charleston Ct. Craw 6F 182
Charleville Mans. W14 1K 13
(off Charleville Rd.)
Charleville Rd. W14 1K 13
Charlmont Rd. SW17 7C 28
Charlock Clo. Craw 7M 181
Charlock Way. Guild 9D 94
Charlotte Clo. Farnh 4J 109
Charlotte Ct. Craw 3A 182
(off Leopold Rd.)
Charlotte Ct. Guild 5B 114
Charlotte Gro. Small 7L 143
Charlotte Ho. W6 1H 13
(off Queen Caroline St.)
Charlotte M. Esh 1B 58
(off Heather Pl.)
Charlotte Rd. SW13 4E 12
Charlotte Rd. Wall 3G 63
Charlotte Sq. Rich 9M 11
Charlotteville 5B 114
Charlow Clo. SW6 5N 13
Charlton 2D 38
Charlton. Wind 5A 4
Charlton Av. W on T 1J 57
Charlton Ct. Owl 6J 49
Charlton Dri. Big H 4F 86
Charlton Gdns. Coul 5G 83
Charlton Ho. Bren 2L 11
Charlton Kings. Wey 9F 38
Charlton La. Shep 2D 38
(in two parts)
Charlton Pl. Wind 5A 4
(off Charlton Way)
Charlton Rd. Shep 2D 38
Charlton Row. Wind 5A 4
Charlton Sq. Wind 5A 4
(off Guards Rd.)
Charlton Wlk. Wind 5A 4
Charlton Way. Wind 5A 4
Charlwood 8A 186
(East Grinstead)
Charlwood 3K 161
(Horley)
Charlwood. Croy 5J 65
Charlwood Clo. Bookh 2B 98
Charlwood Clo. Copt 6L 163
Charlwood Dri. Oxs 2D 78
Charlwood La. Newd & Charl 5F 160
Charlwood M. Charl 3K 161
Charlwood Rd. SW15 7J 13
Charlwood Rd. Horl 2A 162
Charlwood Rd. If'd 7K 161
Charlwood Rd. Low H 6N 161
Charlwoods Bus. Pk. E Grin 7N 165
Charlwoods Pl. E Grin 7A 166
Charlwood Sq. Mitc 2B 44
Charlwoods Rd. E Grin 8N 165
Charlwood Ter. SW15 7J 13
Charlwood Wlk. Craw 9N 161
Charman Rd. Red 3C 122
Charmans Clo. H'ham 3A 198
Charm Clo. Horl 7C 142
Charminster Av. SW19 1M 43
Charminster Ct. Surb 6K 41
Charminster Rd. Wor Pk 7J 43
Charmouth Ct. Rich 8M 11
Charnwood. Asc 5C 34
Charnwood Av. SW19 1M 43
Charnwood Clo. N Mald 3D 42
Charnwood Rd. SE25 4A 46
Charrington Rd. Croy 8N 45 (2B 200)
Charrington Way. Broad H 5C 196
Charta Rd. Egh 6E 20
Chart Clo. Croy 5F 46
Chart Clo. Dork 7K 119
Chart Clo. Mitc 3D 44
Chart Downs. Dork 7J 119
Charter Ct. N Mald 2D 42
Charter Cres. Houn 7M 9
Charterhouse 4F 132
Charterhouse. G'ming 5E 132
Charter Ho. Sutt 3N 61
(off Mulgrave Rd.)
Charterhouse Clo. Brack 4C 32
Charterhouse Rd. G'ming 4G 132
Charter Quay. King T 4H 203
Charter Rd. King T 2A 42
Charters Clo. Asc 4A 34
Charters La. Asc 4A 34
Charter Sq. King T 1A 42
Charters Rd. Asc 6A 34
Charters Way. Asc 6C 34
Chartfield Av. SW15 8G 13
Chartfield Pl. Wey 2C 56
Chartfield Rd. Reig 4A 122
Chartfield Sq. SW15 8J 13
Chart Gdns. Dork 8J 119
Chartham Gro. SE27 4M 29
Chartham Rd. SE25 2E 46
Chart Ho. Rd. Ash V 6E 90
Chart La. Dork 5H 119 (2L 201)
Chart La. Reig 3N 121
Chart La. S. Dork 7J 119
Charts Clo. Cranl 8N 155
Chart Way. H'ham 6J 197
Chartway. Reig 2N 121
Chartwell 9N 107
Chartwell. Farnh 5E 128
Chartwell. Frim G 9C 70
Chartwell Clo. Croy 7A 46
Chartwell Dri. Orp 2M 67
Chartwell Gdns. Alder 6A 90
Chartwell Gdns. Sutt 9K 43
Chartwell Lodge. Dork 9H 119
Chartwell Pl. Eps 1D 80 (8M 201)
Chartwell Pl. Sutt 9L 43
Chartwell Way. SE20 1E 46
Chartwood Pl. Dork 3J 201
Char Wood. SW16 5L 29
Charwood Rd. Wokgm 2D 30
Chase Cotts. Gray 8A 170
Chase Ct. Iswth 5G 10
Chase End. Eps 8C 60 (5K 201)
Chasefield Clo. Guild 9C 94
Chasefield Rd. SW17 5D 28
Chase Gdns. Binf 6H 15
Chase Gdns. Twic 1D 24
Chase La. Hasl 4H 189
Chaseley Dri. W4 1A 12
Chaseley Dri. S Croy 6A 64
Chasemore Clo. Mitc 6D 44
Chasemore Gdns. Croy 2L 63
Chasemore Ho. SW6 3K 13
(off Williams Clo.)
Chase Rd. Eps 8C 60 (5K 201)
Chase Rd. Lind 5A 168
Chaseside Av. SW20 9K 27
Chaseside Gdns. Cher 6K 37
Chase, The. Farnb 8B 70
Chase, The. SW16 8K 29
Chase, The. SW20 9K 27
Chase, The. Asht 5J 79
Chase, The. Coul 1G 83
Chase, The. Craw 4E 182
Chase, The. Crowt 1F 48
Chase, The. E Hor 4G 96
Chase, The. Guild 4K 113
Chase, The. Kgswd 9M 81
Chase, The. Oxs 2C 78
Chase, The. Reig 4B 122
Chase, The. Sun 9J 23
Chase, The. Wall 2J 63
Chasewater Ct. Alder 3M 109
Chatelet Clo. Horl 7F 142
Chatfield Clo. Farnb 3A 90
Chatfield Ct. Cat 9A 84
Chatfield Dri. Guild 1E 114
Chatfield Rd. Croy 7M 45 (1A 200)
Chatfields. Craw 5N 181
Chatham Clo. Sutt 6L 43
Chatham Rd. King T 1N 41 (3M 203)
Chathill 6L 125
Chatley Heath Semaphore Tower. 4E 76
Chatsfield. Eps 6F 60
Chatsworth Av. SW20 9K 27
Chatsworth Av. Hasl 9G 170
Chatsworth Clo. W4 2B 12
Chatsworth Cres. Houn 7D 10
Chatsworth Gdns. N Mald 4E 42
Chatsworth Gro. Farnh 6G 108
Chatsworth Heights. Camb 8E 50
Chatsworth Lodge. W4 1C 12
(off Bourne Pl.)
Chatsworth Pl. Mitc 2D 44
Chatsworth Pl. Oxs 9D 58
Chatsworth Pl. Tedd 5G 24
Chatsworth Rd. Farnb 2C 90
Chatsworth Rd. W4 2B 12
Chatsworth Rd. Croy 1A 64 (6E 200)
Chatsworth Rd. Sutt 2J 61
Chatsworth Way. SE27 4M 29
Chattern Hill 5C 22
Chattern Hill. Ashf 5C 22
Chattern Rd. Ashf 5D 22
Chatterton Ct. Rich 5M 11
Chatton Row. Bisl 4D 72
Chaucer Av. E Grin 1M 185
Chaucer Av. Houn 5J 9
Chaucer Av. Rich 6N 11
Chaucer Av. Wey 4B 56
Chaucer Clo. Bans 1K 81
Chaucer Clo. Wind 6G 4
Chaucer Clo. Wokgm 2L 30
Chaucer Ct. Guild 5M 113 (7B 202)
Chaucer Ct. Red 9E 102
Chaucer Gdns. Sutt 9M 43
(in two parts)
Chaucer Grn. Croy 6E 46
Chaucer Gro. Camb 1B 70
Chaucer Ho. Sutt 9M 43
(off Chaucer Gdns.)
Chaucer Mans. W14 2K 13
(off Queen's Club Gdns.)
Chaucer Rd. Ashf 5N 21
Chaucer Rd. Farnb 8L 69
Chaucer Rd. Craw 1F 182
Chaucer Rd. Crowt 4G 48
Chaucer Rd. Sutt 1M 61
Chaucer Way. SW19 7A 28
Chaucer Way. Add 3J 55
Chavasse Way. Farnb 9J 69
Chave Cft. Eps 6H 81
Chave Cft. Ter. Eps 6H 81
Chavey Down 9F 16
Chavey Down Rd. Wink R 6F 16
Chaworth Clo. Ott 3E 54
Chaworth Rd. Ott 3E 54
Chawridge La. Wink 2G 16
Cheam 3K 61
Cheam Clo. Brack 4B 32
Cheam Clo. Tad 8G 81
Cheam Comn. Rd. Wor Pk 8G 43
Cheam Mans. Sutt 4K 61
Cheam Pk. Way. Sutt 3K 61
Cheam Rd. Eps & Ewe 6F 60
Cheam Rd. Sutt 3L 61
Cheam Village. (Junct.) 3K 61
Cheapside 9B 18
Cheapside. Wok 1N 73
Cheapside Rd. Asc 2N 33
Cheeseman Clo. Hamp 7M 23
Cheeseman Clo. Wokgm 1C 30
Cheesemans Ter. W14 1L 13
(in two parts)
Chellows La. Crow 1B 146
Chelmsford Clo. W6 2J 13
Chelmsford Clo. Sutt 5M 61
Chelsea Clo. Hamp H 6C 24
Chelsea Clo. Wor Pk 6F 42
Chelsea F.C. (Stamford Bridge). 3N 13
Chelsea Gdns. Sutt 1K 61
Chelsea Studios. SW6 3N 13
(off Fulham Rd.)
Chelsea Village. SW6 3N 13
(off Fulham Rd.)
Chelsham 4K 85
Chelsham Clo. Warl 6H 85
Chelsham Common 3K 85
Chelsham Comn. Rd. Warl 4K 85
Chelsham Ct. Rd. Warl 5N 85
Chelsham Rd. S Croy 4A 64
Chelsham Rd. Warl 5J 85
Cheltenham Av. Twic 1G 25
Cheltenham Clo. N Mald 2B 42
Cheltenham Vs. Stai 9H 7
Chelverton Rd. SW15 7J 13
Chelwood Clo. Coul 6G 82
Chelwood Clo. Craw 5D 182
Chelwood Clo. Eps 8E 60
Chelwood Dri. Sand 6E 48
Chelwood Gdns. Rich 5N 11
Chelwood Gdns. Pas. Rich 5N 11
Cheney Clo. Binf 7J 15
Chenies Cotts. Oke H 2A 178
Chenies Ho. W4 3E 12
(off Corney Reach Way)
Cheniston Clo. W Byf 9J 55
Cheniston Ct. S'dale 6D 34
Chennells Brook Cotts. H'ham 1M 197
(off Giblets La.)
Chennells Way. H'ham 3K 197
Chepstow Clo. SW15 9K 13
Chepstow Clo. Craw 3J 183
Chepstow Ri. Croy 9B 46
Chepstow Rd. Croy 9B 46
Chequer Grange. F Row 8G 187
Chequer Rd. E Grin 9B 166
Chequers Clo. Horl 7E 142
Chequers Clo. Tad 3F 100
Chequers Ct. H'ham 5L 197
Chequers Dri. Horl 7E 142
Chequers La. Tad 3F 100
Chequers Pl. Dork 5H 119 (3K 201)
Chequers Yd. Dork 5H 119 (2K 201)
Chequer Tree Clo. Knap 3H 73
Cherberry Clo. Fleet 1C 88
Cherbury Clo. Brack 2C 32
Cherimoya Gdns. W Mol 2B 40
Cherington Way. Asc 1J 33
Cheriton Ct. W on T 7K 39
Cheriton Sq. SW17 3E 28
Cheriton Way. B'water 1J 69
Cherkley Hill. Lea 4J 99
Cherrimans Orchard. Hasl 2D 188
Cherry Bank Cotts. Holm M 6K 137
Cherry Clo. SW2 1L 29
Cherry Clo. Bans 1J 81
Cherry Clo. Cars 8D 44
Cherry Clo. Mord 3K 43
Cherrycot Hill. Orp 1L 67
Cherrycot Ri. Orp 1L 67
Cherry Cotts. Tad 2G 100
Cherry Ct. H'ham 7K 197
Cherry Cres. Bren 3H 11
Cherrydale Rd. Camb 1H 71
Cherry Gth. Bren 1K 11
Cherry Grn. Clo. Red 5F 122
Cherry Hill Gdns. Croy 1K 63
Cherryhill Gro. Alder 3L 109
Cherryhurst. Hamb 9E 152
Cherry La. Craw 9A 162
Cherry Laurel Wlk. SW2 1K 29
Cherry Lodge. Alder 3N 109
Cherry Orchard. Asht 5A 80
Cherry Orchard. Stai 6J 21
Cherry Orchard Gdns. Croy 7A 46 (2E 200)
Cherry Orchard Gdns. W Mol 2N 39
Cherry Orchard Rd. Croy 8A 46 (1E 200)
Cherry Orchard Rd. W Mol 2A 40
Cherry St. Wok 5A 74
Cherry Tree Av. Guild 3J 113
Cherry Tree Av. Hasl 1D 188
Cherry Tree Av. Stai 7K 21
Cherry Tree Clo. Farnb 9H 69
Cherry Tree Clo. Farnh 9H 109
Cherry Tree Clo. Owl 6J 49
Cherry Tree Clo. Worth 1H 183
Cherry Tree Ct. Coul 5K 83
Cherrytree Dri. SW16 4J 29
Cherry Tree Dri. Brack 2B 32
Cherry Tree Farm Equine Dept. 1G 165
Cherry Tree Grn. S Croy 1E 84
Cherry Tree La. G'ming 3G 133
Cherry Tree Rd. Milf 1B 152
Cherry Tree Rd. Rowl 8D 128
Cherry Tree Wlk. Beck 3J 47
Cherry Tree Wlk. Big H 4E 86
Cherry Tree Wlk. H'ham 2A 198
Cherry Tree Wlk. Rowl 8D 128
(in two parts)
Cherry Tree Wlk. W Wick 1B 66
Cherry Way. Eps 3C 60
Cherry Way. Hort 6E 6
Cherry Way. Shep 3E 38
Cherrywood Av. Eng G 8L 19
Cherry Wood Clo. King T 8N 25
Cherrywood Ct. Tedd 6G 24
Cherrywood Dri. SW15 8J 13
Cherrywood La. Mord 3K 43
Cherrywood Rd. Farnb 7M 69
Chertsey 6J 37
Chertsey Abbey (Remains of). 5J 37
Chertsey Bri. Rd. Cher 6M 37
Chertsey Clo. Kenl 2M 83
Chertsey Ct. SW14 6A 12
Chertsey Cres. New Ad 6M 65
Chertsey Dri. Sutt 8K 43
Chertsey La. Eps 8N 59
Chertsey La. Stai 6G 20
Chertsey Lock 6L 37
Chertsey Meads 7N 37
Chertsey Mus. 5J 37
(off Windsor St.)
Chertsey Rd. Ashf & Sun 8E 22
Chertsey Rd. Add 8K 37
(in two parts)
Chertsey Rd. Byfl 7M 55
Chertsey Rd. Chob 6J 53
Chertsey Rd. Felt 6F 22
Chertsey Rd. Shep 6N 37
Chertsey Rd. Twic 3B 24
Chertsey Rd. W'sham 3A 52
Chertsey Rd. Wok 4B 74
Chertsey South 9G 36
Chertsey St. SW17 6E 28
Chertsey St. Guild 4N 113 (5D 202)
Chertsey Wlk. Cher 6J 37
Chervil Clo. Felt 4H 23
Cherwell Clo. Slou 2D 6
Cherwell Ct. Eps 1B 60
Cherwell Wlk. Craw 4L 181
Cheryls Clo. SW6 4N 13
Cheselden Rd. Guild 4A 114 (6E 202)
Chesfield Rd. King T 8L 25
Chesham Clo. Sutt 6K 61
Chesham Cres. SE20 1F 46
Chesham M. Guild 4A 114
Chesham Rd. SE20 1F 46
Chesham Rd. SW19 6B 28
Chesham Rd. Guild 4B 114
Chesham Rd. King T 1N 41
Cheshire Clo. Mitc 2J 45
Cheshire Clo. Ott 3E 54
Cheshire Gdns. Chess 3K 59
Cheshire Ho. Mord 6N 43
Cheshire Ho. Ott 3F 54
(off Cheshire Clo.)
Cheshire Pk. Warf 7C 16
Cheshalt Clo. Fern 9F 188
Chesilton Cres. C Crook 8B 88
Chesilton Rd. SW6 4L 13
Chesney Cres. New Ad 4M 65
Chessell Clo. T Hth 3M 45
Chessholme Rd. Ashf 7D 22
Chessington 2M 59
Chessington Clo. Eps 3B 60
Chessington Hall Gdns. Chess 4K 59
Chessington Hill Pk. Chess 2N 59
Chessington Ho. Eps 5E 60
(off Spring St.)
Chessington Pde. Chess 3K 59
Chessington Rd. Eps & Ewe 3N 59
Chessington Way. W Wick 8L 47
Chessington World of Adventures. 6J 59
Chesson Rd. W14 2L 13
Chester Av. Rich 9M 11
Chester Av. Twic 2N 23
Chesterblade La. Brack 6B 32
Chester Clo. Ashf 6E 22
Chester Clo. SW13 6G 13
Chester Clo. As 2F 110
Chester Clo. Dork 3J 119
Chester Clo. Guild 1J 113
Chester Clo. Rich 9M 11
Chester Clo. Sutt 8M 43
Chesterfield Clo. Felb 6F 164
Chesterfield Ct. Surb 8K 203
Chesterfield Dri. Esh 8G 40
Chesterfield M. Ashf 5N 21
Chesterfield Rd. Ashf 5N 21
Chesterfield Rd. W4 2B 12
Chesterfield Rd. Eps 4C 60
Chester Gdns. Mord 5A 44
Chesterman Ct. W4 3D 12
(off Corney Reach Way)
Chester Rd. SW19 7H 27
Chester Rd. As 1F 110
Chester Rd. Eff 6J 97
Chester Rd. Houn 6J 9
Chester Rd. H'row A 6B 8
Chesters. Horl 6C 142
Chesters Rd. Camb 1F 70
Chesters, The. N Mald 9D 26
Chesterton Clo. SW18 8M 13
Chesterton Clo. E Grin 2B 186
Chesterton Ct. H'ham 4N 197
Chesterton Dri. Red 6J 103
Chesterton Dri. Stai 2A 22
Chesterton Ho. Croy 7D 200
Chesterton Sq. W8 1M 13
Chesterton Ter. King T 1N 41 (4M 203)
Chester Way. Tong 6D 110
Chestnut All. SW6 2L 13
Chestnut Av. SW14 6C 12
Chestnut Av. Alder 5C 110
Chestnut Av. Bren 1K 11
Chestnut Av. Camb 9E 50
Chestnut Av. E Mol & Tedd 2F 40
Chestnut Av. Eps 1D 60
Chestnut Av. Esh 6D 40
Chestnut Av. Farnh 3F 128
Chestnut Av. Guild 6M 113
Chestnut Av. Hamp 8A 24
Chestnut Av. Hasl 1G 189
Chestnut Av. Vir W 3J 36
Chestnut Av. W'ham 9F 86
Chestnut Av. W Wick 2A 66
Chestnut Av. Wey 4D 56
Chestnut Av. W Vill 5F 56
Chestnut Clo. Ashf 5C 22
Chestnut Clo. SW16 5L 29
Chestnut Clo. Add 2M 55
Chestnut Clo. B'water 2K 69
Chestnut Clo. Cars 7D 44
Chestnut Clo. E Grin 9C 166
Chestnut Clo. Eden 1K 147
Chestnut Clo. Eng G 7L 19
Chestnut Clo. Fleet 1D 88
Chestnut Clo. Gray 6A 170

Church Rd.—Cline Rd.

Church Rd. *Broad H* 5D **196**
Church Rd. *Burs.* 3L **163**
Church Rd. *Byfl* 1N **75**
Church Rd. *Cat.* 1C **104**
Church Rd. *Clay* 3F **58**
Church Rd. *Copt* 7M **163**
Church Rd. *Croy* 9N **45** (3A **200**)
(in two parts)
Church Rd. *Duns* 4N **173**
Church Rd. *E Mol* 3D **40**
Church Rd. *Egh* 6B **20**
Church Rd. *Eps* 8D **60** (5M **201**)
Church Rd. *F'boro* 2L **67**
Church Rd. *Felt* 6L **23**
Church Rd. *Fleet* 3A **88**
Church Rd. *Frim.* 5B **70**
Church Rd. *Guild*
. . . . 4N **113** (4C **202**)
Church Rd. *Ham & Rich* 5K **25**
Church Rd. *Hasc* 7A **154**
Church Rd. *Hasl.* 1G **188**
(Derby Rd.)
Church Rd. *Hasl.* 2D **188**
(Hindhead Rd.)
Church Rd. *Horl.* 9D **142**
(in two parts)
Church Rd. *Horne* 5C **144**
Church Rd. *Hors* 2A **74**
Church Rd. *H'ham* 3A **198**
Church Rd. *Houn* 1J **9**
(High St.)
Church Rd. *Houn* 3A **10**
(Up. Sutton La.)
Church Rd. *Iswth.* 4D **10**
Church Rd. *Kenl.* 2A **84**
Church Rd. *Kes* 4F **66**
Church Rd. *King T*
. . . . 1M **41** (3L **203**)
Church Rd. *Lea* 9H **79**
Church Rd. *Ling.* 7N **145**
Church Rd. *Low H* 5C **162**
Church Rd. *Milf* 2C **152**
Church Rd. *Newd.* 1A **160**
Church Rd. *Old Win* 8L **5**
Church Rd. *Owl* 6K **49**
Church Rd. *Purl* 6J **63**
Church Rd. *Red* 5C **122**
Church Rd. *Reig* 5M **121**
Church Rd. *Rich.* 7L **11**
Church Rd. *St J* 6K **73**
Church Rd. *Sand* 6E **48**
Church Rd. *Shop* 6C **38**
Church Rd. *Short.* 2N **47**
Church Rd. *Surb.* 7J **41**
Church Rd. *Sutt* 3K **61**
Church Rd. *Tedd* 5E **24**
Church Rd. *Turn H.* 6C **184**
Church Rd. *Wall.* 9H **45**
Church Rd. *Warl* 4G **84**
Church Rd. *W End* 8C **52**
Church Rd. *W Ewe.* 4C **60**
Church Rd. *Whyt.* 5C **84**
Church Rd. *W'sham* 3M **51**
Church Rd. *Wold* 9G **85**
Church Rd. *Wor Pk* 7D **42**
Church Rd. *Worth & M'bowr*
. . . . 3J **183**
Church Rd. E. *Farnb.* 4B **90**
Church Rd. E. *Crowt* 2G **49**
Church Rd. Ind. Est. *Low H*
. . . . 5D **162**
Church Rd. Trad. Est. *Low H*
. . . . 5C **162**
Church Rd. W. *Farnb* 4A **90**
Church Rd. W. *Crowt.* 3G **48**
Church Side. *Eps* 9A **60**
Churchside Clo. *Big H* 4E **86**
Church Sq. *Shep* 6C **38**
Church St. *Cob* 2J **77**
Church St. *W4* 2E **12**
Church St. *Alder.* 2L **109**
Church St. *Bet* 4D **120**
Church St. *Craw.* 3A **182**
Church St. *Crowt.* 2G **48**
Church St. *Croy* 9M **45** (4A **200**)
Church St. *Dork* . . . 5G **119** (2J **201**)
Church St. *Eden* 2L **147**
Church St. *Eff.* 5L **97**
Church St. *Eps* 5F **60**
Church St. *Esh* 1B **58**
Church St. *Ewe* 9D **60** (6L **201**)
Church St. *G'ming* 7G **132**
Church St. *Hamp* 9C **24**
Church St. *Iswth* 6H **11**
Church St. *King T* . . . 1K **41** (3H **203**)
Church St. *Lea* 9H **79**
(in two parts)
Church St. *Old Wok* 8E **74**
Church St. *Reig* 3M **121**
Church St. *Rud* 1D **194**
Church St. *Stai* 5F **20**
Church St. *Sun* 2J **39**
Church St. *Sutt* 2N **61**
Church St. *Twic* 2G **25**
Church St. *W on T* 7H **39**
Church St. *Warn* 1F **196**
Church St. *Wey* 1B **56**
Church St. *Wind* 4G **5**
Church St. E. *Wok* 4B **74**
Church St. W. *Wok.* 4A **74**
Church Stretton Rd. *Houn* 8C **10**
Church Ter. *Holmw.* 5J **139**
Church Ter. *Rich.* 8K **11**
Church Ter. *Wind* 5B **4**
Church Town. **1G 124**
Church Vw. *As* 2E **110**
(in two parts)
Church Vw. *Rich.* 8L **11**
Church Vw. *Yat.* 8C **48**
Churchview Clo. *Horl.* 9D **142**
Churchview Rd. *Twic* 2D **24**
Church Wlk. *SW13* 4F **12**
Church Wlk. *SW15* 8G **13**
Church Wlk. *SW16* 1G **45**
Church Wlk. *SW20* 2H **43**
Church Wlk. *Blet* 2A **124**
Church Wlk. *Bren* 2J **11**
(in two parts)
Church Wlk. *Cat.* 2D **104**
Church Wlk. *Cher* 5J **37**
Church Wlk. *Craw* 3B **182**
Church Wlk. *Fay.* 9G **180**
Church Wlk. *G'ming* 5J **133**
(in two parts)
Church Wlk. *Horl* 9D **142**
Church Wlk. *Lea* 9H **79**
Church Wlk. *Reig.* 3N **121**
(in two parts)
Church Wlk. *Rich* 8K **11**
Church Wlk. *Th Dit* 5F **40**
Church Wlk. *W on T* 7H **39**
Church Wlk. *Wey* 9B **38**
Churchward Ho. W14 . . . . *1L* **13**
(off Ivatt Pl.)
Church Way. *Oxt* 1B **126**
Church Way. *S Croy* 6C **64**
Churston Clo. *SW2* 2L **29**
Churston Dri. *Mord* 4J **43**
Churt. **9L 149**
Churt Rd. *Hdly D* 3F **168**
Churt Rd. *Churt & Hind.* 3M **169**
Churt Wynde. *Hind.* 2B **170**
Chuters Clo. *Byfl* 8N **55**
Chuters Gro. *Eps* 8E **60**
Cicada Rd. *SW18.* 9N **13**
Cinder Path. *Wok* 9M **73**
Cinnamon Clo. *Croy* 6J **45**
Cinnamon Clo. *Wind* 4C **4**
Cinnamon Gdns. *Guild* 7K **93**
Circle Gdns. *SW19* 1M **43**
Circle Gdns. *Byfl* 9A **56**
Circle Hill Rd. *Crowt* 2H **49**
Circle Rd. *W Vill* 5F **56**
Circle, The. *G'ming* 5J **133**
Circuit Cen., The. *Bro I* 6N **55**
Circus, The. Lea *7H* **79**
(off Kingston Rd.)
Cirrus Clo. *Wall* 4J **63**
Cissbury Clo. *H'ham* 2N **197**
Cissbury Hill. *Craw.* 5A **182**
City Bus. Cen. *H'ham* 7K **197**
City Bus. Cen., The. *Craw* . . . 8B **162**
City Ho. Wall *7E* **44**
(off Corbet Clo.)
Clacket La. *W'ham.* 2G **107**
Clacy Grn. *Brack* 8M **15**
Claireville Ct. *Reig* 3B **122**
Clairvale Rd. *Houn* 4L **9**
Clairview Rd. *SW16* 6F **28**
Clammer Hill Rd. *G'wood.* 9K **171**
Clancarty Rd. *SW6* 5M **13**
Clandon Av. *Egh* 8E **20**
Clandon Clo. *Eps* 3E **60**
Clandon Ct. *Farnb* 2B **90**
Clandon Ho. *Guild* 5C **114**
Clandon House & Pk. **1J 115**
Clandon Park. **1J 115**
Clandon Rd. *Guild*
. . . . 4A **114** (4F **202**)
Clandon Rd. *Send* 3H **95**
Clandon Ter. *SW20.* 1J **43**
Clanfield Ride. *B'water* 1J **69**
Clapgate La. *Slin* 3K **195**
Clapham Pk. Est. *SW4.* 1H **29**
Clappers Ga. *Craw.* 2B **182**
Clappers La. *Chob* 7F **52**
Clappers Mdw. *Alf* 6J **175**
Clappers Orchard. *Alf.* 6H **175**
Clare Av. *Wokgm* 1B **30**
Clare Clo. *Craw* 9G **162**
Clare Clo. *W Byf* 9J **55**
Clare Cotts. *Blet* 2M **123**
Clare Ct. *Fleet.* 4B **88**
Clare Ct. *Wold* 1K **105**
Clare Cres. *Lea.* 5G **79**
Claredale. *Wok.* 6A **74**
Clarefield Ct. *Asc* 6D **34**
Clare Gdns. *Egh* 6C **20**
Clare Hill. *Esh.* 3B **58**
Clare Lawn Av. *SW14.* 8B **12**
Clare Mead. *Rowl.* 8E **128**
Clare M. *SW6.* 3N **13**
Claremont. *Shep* 5C **38**
Claremont Av. *Camb* 1D **70**
Claremont Av. *Esh* 3N **57**
Claremont Av. *N Mald.* 4F **42**
Claremont Av. *Sun* 9J **23**
Claremont Av. *W on T* 1L **57**
Claremont Av. *Wok* 6A **74**
Claremont Clo. *SW2.* 2J **29**
Claremont Clo. *Orp.* 1J **67**
Claremont Clo. *S Croy* 2F **84**
Claremont Clo. *W on T.* 2K **57**
Claremont Ct. *Dork*
. . . . 6H **119** (4K **201**)
Claremont Dri. *Esh.* 3B **58**
Claremont Dri. *Wok* 6A **74**
Claremont End. *Esh* 3B **58**
Claremont Gdns. *Surb*
. . . . 4L **41** (8J **203**)
Claremont Gro. *W4* 3D **12**
Claremont Landscape Garden.
. . . . **4A 58**
Claremont La. *Esh* 2B **58**
Claremont Park. **4A 58**
Claremont Pk. Rd. *Esh.* 3B **58**
Claremont Rd. *Clay* 4E **58**
Claremont Rd. *Croy.* 7D **46**
Claremont Rd. *Red.* 9E **102**
Claremont Rd. *Stai* 8F **20**
Claremont Rd. *Surb*
. . . . 4L **41** (8J **203**)
Claremont Rd. *Tedd* 6F **24**
Claremont Rd. *Twic* 1H **25**
Claremont Rd. *W Byf* 8J **55**
Claremont Rd. *Wind.* 5F **4**
Claremont Ter. *Th Dit.* 6H **41**
Claremount Clo. *Eps* 4H **81**
Claremount Gdns. *Eps.* 4H **81**
Clarence Av. *SW4* 1H **29**
Clarence Av. *N Mald.* 1B **42**
Clarence Clo. *Alder.* 2A **110**
Clarence Clo. *W on T* 1J **57**
Clarence Ct. W6 . . . . *1G* **13**
(off Cambridge Gro.)
Clarence Ct. Egh. *6B* **20**
(off Clarence St.)
Clarence Ct. *Horl* 7H **143**
Clarence Ct. *Wind.* 4E **4**
Clarence Cres. *SW4* 1H **29**
Clarence Cres. *Wind* 4F **4**
Clarence Dri. *Camb.* 8F **50**
Clarence Dri. *E Grin* 2B **186**
Clarence Dri. *Eng G.* 5M **19**
Clarence La. *SW15* 9D **12**
Clarence M. *SW12* 1F **28**
Clarence Rd. *SW19* 7N **27**
Clarence Rd. *W4* 1N **11**
Clarence Rd. *Big H.* 5H **87**
Clarence Rd. *Croy* 6A **46**
Clarence Rd. *Fleet* 5A **88**
Clarence Rd. *H'ham* 7K **197**
Clarence Rd. *Red.* 6B **122**
Clarence Rd. *Rich* 4M **11**
Clarence Rd. *Sutt.* 2N **61**
Clarence Rd. *Tedd* 7F **24**
Clarence Rd. *Wall.* 2F **62**
Clarence Rd. *W on T* 1J **57**
Clarence Rd. *Wind.* 5D **4**
Clarence St. *Egh.* 7B **20**
Clarence St. *King T*
. . . . 1K **41** (3H **203**)
(in three parts)
Clarence St. *Rich* 7L **11**
Clarence St. *Stai* 5G **21**
Clarence Ter. *Houn.* 7B **10**
Clarence Wlk. *Red* 6B **122**
Clarence Way. *Horl* 7H **143**
Clarendon Ct. Beck. *1L* **47**
(off Albemarle Rd.)
Clarendon Ct. *B'water.* 3J **69**
Clarendon Ct. *Fleet.* 4A **88**
Clarendon Ct. *Houn.* 4H **9**
Clarendon Ct. *Rich* 4M **11**
Clarendon Ct. *Wind* 4E **4**
Clarendon Cres. *Twic.* 4D **24**
Clarendon Dri. *SW15.* 7H **13**
Clarendon Ga. *Ott.* 3F **54**
Clarendon Gro. *Mitc.* 2D **44**
Clarendon Rd. *Ashf* 5A **22**
Clarendon Rd. *SW19.* 8C **28**
Clarendon Rd. *Croy*
. . . . 8M **45** (2A **200**)
Clarendon Rd. *Red.* 2D **122**
Clarendon Rd. *Wall* 3G **62**
Clare Pl. *SW15.* 1E **26**
Clare Rd. *Houn* 6N **9**
Clare Rd. *Stanw* 2M **21**
Clares, The. *Cat* 2D **104**
Claret Gdns. *SE25* 2B **46**
Clareville Rd. *Cat.* 2D **104**
Clare Wood. *Lea* 5H **79**
Clarewood Dri. *Camb.* 9C **50**
Clarice Way. *Wall* 5J **63**
Claridge Ct. *SW6* 5L **13**
Claridge Gdns. *D'land* 9C **146**
Claridges Mead. *D'land* 9C **146**
Clarke Cres. *Ryl M* 8K **49**
Clarkes Av. *Wor Pk.* 7J **43**
Clark Pl. *Cranl* 8H **155**
Clark Rd. *Farnb* 9N **69**
Clark Rd. *Craw* 8M **181**
Clark's Green. **6J 159**
Clarks Grn. Rd. *Capel* 8N **159**
Clarks Hill. *Farnh* 1B **128**
Clarks La. *T'sey & Tats.* 1C **106**
Clarks La. *W'ham.* 1F **106**
Clark Way. *Houn.* 3L **9**
Claudia Pl. *SW19* 2K **27**
Claverdale Rd. *SW2* 1K **29**
Claverdon. *Brack* 6M **31**
Claver Dri. *Asc* 3A **34**
Clavering Av. *SW13* 2G **13**
Clavering Clo. *Twic* 5G **24**
Claverton. *Asht.* 4L **79**
Claxton Gro. *W6.* 1J **13**
Clay Av. *Mitc* 1F **44**
Claybrook Rd. *W6* 2J **13**
Claycart Rd. *Alder.* 9J **89**
(in two parts)
Clay Clo. Add *2K* **55**
(off Monks Cres.)
Clay Corner. *Cher.* 7K **37**
Claydon Dri. *Croy* 1J **63**
Claydon Gdns. *B'water* 5M **69**
Claydon Rd. *Wok.* 9K **73**
Clayford. *D'land.* 9C **146**
Claygate. **3F 58**
Claygate Cres. *New Ad* 3M **65**
Claygate La. *Esh* 8G **40**
(in two parts)
Claygate La. *Th Dit.* 7G **40**
Claygate Lodge Clo. *Clay* 4E **58**
Claygate Rd. *Dork* 7H **119**
Clay Hall La. *Copt* 6N **163**
Clayhall La. *Old Win* 8J **5**
Clayhall La. *Reig.* 7J **121**
Clayhanger. *Guild* 1E **114**
Clayhill. *Surb* 4N **41** (8M **203**)
Clayhill Clo. *Brack* 2D **32**
Clayhill Clo. *Leigh.* 1F **140**
Clayhill Rd. *Leigh.* 3D **140**
Clay La. *Guild.* 6N **93**
Clay La. *H'ley* 2A **100**
Clay La. *Newc* 9G **144**
Clay La. *S Nut* 4G **123**
Clay La. *Stanw* 1A **22**
Clay La. *Wokgm.* 2E **30**
Claymore Clo. *Mord* 6M **43**
Claypole Dri. *Houn* 4M **9**
Clayponds Av. *W5 & Bren* 1L **11**
Clayponds Gdns. *W5* 1K **11**
(in two parts)
Clayponds La. *Bren* 1L **11**
(in two parts)
Clays Clo. *E Grin* 1A **186**
Clayton Cres. *Bren.* 1K **11**
Clayton Dri. *Guild.* 9J **93**
Clayton Gro. *Brack.* 9C **16**
Clayton Hill. *Craw.* 5A **182**
Clayton Ho. SW13. . . . . *3H* **13**
(off Trinity Chu. Rd.)
Clayton Mead. *God* 8E **104**
Clayton Rd. *Farnb.* 5L **69**
Clayton Rd. *Chess* 1J **59**
Clayton Rd. *Eps* 8D **60** (6L **201**)
Clayton Rd. *Iswth.* 6E **10**
Cleardene. *Dork* . . . 5H **119** (3L **201**)
Cleardown. *Wok.* 5D **74**
Clears Cotts. *Reig* 1K **121**
Clearsprings. *Light.* 6L **51**
Clears, The. *Reig* 1K **121**
Clearwater Pl. *Surb* 5J **41**
Clearway Ct. *Cat* 9D **84**
Cleave Av. *Hay* 1F **8**
Cleave Av. *Orp* 3N **67**
Cleaveland Rd. *Surb.* 4K **41**
Cleave Prior. *Coul.* 6C **82**
Cleaverholme Clo. *SE25* 5E **46**
Cleaves Almshouses. *King T*
. . . . 3K **203**
Cleeve Ct. *Felt* 2F **22**
Cleeve Rd. *Lea* 7F **78**
Cleeves Ct. Red *2E* **122**
(off St Anne's Mt.)
Cleeve, The. *Guild* 3C **114**
Cleeve Way. *SW15* 1E **26**
Clem Attlee Ct. *SW6.* 2L **13**
Clem Attlee Pde. SW6 . . . . *2L* **13**
(off N. End Rd.)
Clement Clo. *Purl* 3M **83**
Clement Gdns. *Hay.* 1F **8**
Clement Rd. *SW19* 6K **27**
Clement Rd. *Beck* 1G **47**
Clements Ct. *Houn* 7L **9**
Clements Mead. *Lea* 6G **78**
Clements Pl. *Bren* 1K **11**
Clements Rd. *W on T.* 8J **39**
Clensham Ct. *Sutt* 8M **43**
Clensham La. *Sutt.* 8M **43**
Cleopatra Pl. *Warf* 8C **16**
Clerics Wlk. *Shop.* 6E **38**
Clerks Cft. *Blet.* 2A **124**
Clevedon. *Wey* 2E **56**
Clevedon Ct. *Farnb* 2B **90**
Clevedon Ct. *Frim* 6E **70**
Clevedon Ct. *S Croy.* 2B **64**
Clevedon Gdns. *Houn* 4J **9**
Clevedon Rd. *SE20* 1G **46**
Clevedon Rd. *King T* 1N **41**
Clevedon Rd. *Twic* 9K **11**
(in two parts)
Cleve Ho. *Brack.* 3C **32**
Cleveland Av. *SW20.* 1L **43**
Cleveland Av. *W4* 1E **12**
Cleveland Av. *Hamp.* 8N **23**
Cleveland Clo. *W on T* 9J **39**
Cleveland Dri. *Stai* 1K **37**
Cleveland Gdns. *SW13* 5E **12**
Cleveland Gdns. *Wor Pk*
. . . . 8D **42**
Cleveland Pk. *Stai* 9N **7**
Cleveland Ri. *Mord.* 6J **43**
Cleveland Rd. *SW13* 5E **12**
Cleveland Rd. *Iswth.* 7G **10**
Cleveland Rd. *N Mald* 3D **42**
Cleveland Rd. *Wor Pk* 8D **42**
Cleves Av. *Eps.* 5G **61**
Cleves Clo. *Cob* 1J **77**
Cleves Ct. *Eps* 8E **60** (5M **201**)
Cleves Ct. *Wind* 6C **4**
Cleves Cres. *New Ad.* 7M **65**
Cleves Rd. *Rich* 4J **25**
Cleves Way. *Hamp* 8N **23**
Cleves Way. *Sun* 7G **22**
Cleves Wood. *Wey* 1F **56**
Clewborough Dri. *Camb.* 9F **50**
Clewer Av. *Wind* 5D **4**
Clewer Ct. Rd. *Wind.* 3E **4**
Clewer Fields. *Wind* 4F **4**
Clewer Green. **5C 4**
Clewer Hill. **6B 4**
Clewer Hill Rd. *Wind* 5B **4**
Clewer New Town. **5E 4**
Clewer New Town. *Wind* 5D **4**
Clewer Pk. *Wind* 3D **4**
Clewer St Andrew. **3D 4**
Clewer St Stephen. **3E 4**
Clewer Village. **4D 4**
Clewer Within. **4F 4**
Clew's La. *Bisl* 3D **72**
Clifden Rd. *Bren* 2K **11**
Clifden Rd. *Twic* 2F **24**
Cliff End. *Purl.* 8M **63**
Cliffe Ri. *G'ming.* 8F **132**
Cliffe Rd. *G'ming* 9E **132**
Cliffe Rd. *S Croy.* . . . 2A **64** (8D **200**)
Cliffe Wlk. Sutt. *2A* **62**
(off Greyhound Rd.)
Clifford Av. *SW14* 6A **12**
(in two parts)
Clifford Av. *Wall.* 1G **62**
Clifford Gro. *Ashf.* 5B **22**
Clifford Haigh Ho. *SW6* 3J **13**
Clifford Ho. W14 . . . . *1L* **13**
(off Edith Vs.)
Clifford Mnr. Rd. *Guild.* 7A **114**
Clifford Rd. *SE25* 3D **46**
Clifford Rd. *Houn.* 6L **9**
Clifford Rd. *Rich* 3K **25**
Clifton Av. *Felt* 4K **23**
Clifton Av. *Sutt* 7N **61**
Clifton Clo. *Add* 8K **37**
Clifton Clo. *Cat.* 1A **104**
Clifton Clo. *Horl.* 8H **143**
Clifton Clo. *Orp* 2L **67**
Clifton Clo. *Wrec* 7F **128**
Clifton Ct. *Stanw* 9N **7**
Clifton Gdns. *W4* 1C **12**
(in two parts)
Clifton Gdns. *Frim G* 8D **70**
Clifton Pde. *Felt.* 5K **23**
Clifton Pk. Av. *SW20.* 1H **43**
Clifton Pl. *Bans* 2M **81**
Clifton Ri. *Wind.* 4A **4**
Clifton Rd. *SE25* 3B **46**
Clifton Rd. *SW19* 7J **27**
Clifton Rd. *Coul* 2F **82**
Clifton Rd. *Craw* 4G **183**
Clifton Rd. *Iswth* 5E **10**
Clifton Rd. *King T*
. . . . 8M **25** (1M **203**)
Clifton Rd. *Tedd.* 5E **24**
Clifton Rd. *Wall* 2F **62**
Clifton Rd. *Wokgm* 1A **30**
Clifton's La. *Reig* 1J **121**
Clifton Ter. Dork. *6H* **119**
(off Cliftonville)
Cliftonville. *Dork* 6H **119**
Clifton Wlk. W6 . . . . *1G* **13**
(off King St.)
Clifton Way. *H'row A* 6C **8**
Clifton Way. *Wok* 4J **73**
Climping Rd. *Craw* 1N **181**
Cline Rd. *Guild.* 5B **114**

Clinton Av.—Common, The

Clinton Av. E Mol 3C 40
Clinton Clo. Knap 5G 73
Clinton Clo. Wey 8C 38
Clinton Hill. D'land 1C 166
Clinton Rd. Lea 1J 99
Clintons Grn. Brack 9M 15
Clippesby Clo. Chess 3M 59
Clipstone Rd. Houn 6A 10
Clitherow Ct. Bren 1J 11
Clitherow Gdns. Craw 4C 182
Clitherow Pas. Bren 1J 11
Clitherow Rd. Bren 1H 11
Cliveden Pl. Shep 5D 38
Cliveden Rd. SW19 . . . . 9L 27
Clive Grn. Brack 4N 31
(in two parts)
Clive Rd. SE21 . . . . 4N 29
Clive Rd. SW19 . . . . 7C 28
Clive Rd. Alder 3B 110
Clive Rd. Esh 1B 58
Clive Rd. Felt 9H 9
Clive Rd. Twic 5F 24
Clive Way. Craw 3G 182
Clock Barn La. Busb & G'ming 3J 153
Clock House 1F 82
Clockhouse Clo. SW19 . . . . 3H 27
Clock Ho. Clo. Byfl 8A 56
Clock Ho. Cotts. Capel 8J 159
Clockhouse Ct. Beck 1H 47
Clockhouse Ct. Guild 8M 93
Clockhouse Ct. Hasl 2G 189
Clockhouse La. Ashf & Felt 5B 22
Clockhouse La. Brmly 5B 134
Clockhouse La. E. Egh 8D 20
Clockhouse La. W. Egh 8C 20
Clock Ho. Mead. Oxs 1B 78
Clockhouse Pl. SW15 . . . . 9K 13
Clockhouse Rd. Farnb 1N 89
Clock Ho. Rd. Beck 2H 47
Clockhouse Roundabout. (Junct.) 2D 22
Clockhouse Roundabout. Farnb 1N 89
Clock Tower Ind. Est. Iswth 6F 10
Clock Tower Rd. Iswth 6F 10
Clodhouse Hill. Wok 9G 73
Cloister Clo. Tedd 6H 25
Cloister Gdns. SE25 . . . . 5E 46
Cloisters Mall. King T 1L 41 (3H 203)
Cloisters, The. Frim 5B 70
Cloisters, The. Wok 8D 74
Cloncurry St. SW6 . . . . 5J 13
Clonmel Rd. SW6 . . . . 3L 13
Clonmel Rd. Tedd 5D 24
Clonmore St. SW18 . . . . 2L 27
Cloonmore Av. Orp 1N 67
Close, The. Col T 7K 49
Close, The. SE25 . . . . 5D 46
Close, The. Asc 1H 33
Close, The. Beck 3H 47
Close, The. Berr G 3K 87
Close, The. Brack 3A 32
Close, The. Cars 5C 62
Close, The. E Grin 1N 185
Close, The. Farnh 2J 129
Close, The. Frim 6A 70
Close, The. G'ming 8J 133
Close, The. Horl 1G 163
Close, The. Iswth 5D 10
Close, The. Light 6L 51
Close, The. Loxw 5F 192
Close, The. Mitc 3D 44
Close, The. N Mald 1B 42
Close, The. Purl 6M 63
(Pampisford Rd.)
Close, The. Purl 6K 63
(Russell Hill)
Close, The. Reig 4N 121
Close, The. Rich 6A 12
Close, The. Str G 7A 120
Close, The. Surb 5L 41
Close, The. Sutt 6L 43
Close, The. Vir W 4N 35
Close, The. W Byf 9J 55
Close, The. Won 4D 134
Closeworth Rd. Farnb 5C 90
Cloudesdale Rd. SW17 . . . . 3F 28
Clouston Clo. Wall 2J 63
Clouston Rd. Farnb 9L 69
Clovelly Av. Warl 6E 84
Clovelly Dri. Hind 2A 170
Clovelly Pk. Hind 2A 170
Clovelly Rd. Hind 3A 170
Clovelly Rd. Houn 5A 10
Clover Clo. Lind 4B 168
Clover Clo. Wokgm 1D 30
Clover Ct. Wok 5N 73
Clover Fld. Slin 6L 195
Cloverfields. Horl 7F 142
Clover Hill. Coul 8F 82
Cloverlands. Craw 1D 182
Clover La. Yat 9A 48
Clover Lea. G'ming 3H 133
Clover Rd. Guild 2H 113
Clovers Cotts. Fay 8E 180
Clovers End. H'ham 3N 197
Clovers Way. Fay 1C 198
Clover Wlk. Eden 9M 127
Clover Way. Small 8N 143
Clover Way. Wall 7E 44
Clowser Clo. Sutt 2A 62
Clubhouse Rd. Alder 8L 89
Club La. Crowt 2J 49
Club Row. Brkwd 6A 72
Clump Av. Tad 9B 100
Clumps Rd. Lwr Bo 7K 129
Clumps, The. Ashf 5E 22
Clunbury Av. S'hall 1N 9
Cluny M. SW5 . . . . 1M 13
Clyde Av. S Croy 2E 84
Clyde Clo. Red 2E 122
Clyde Flats. SW6 . . . . 3L 13
(off Rhylston Rd.)
Clyde Ho. King T 9K 25 (1H 203)
Clyde Rd. Croy 8C 46
Clyde Rd. Stai 2M 21
Clyde Rd. Sutt 2M 61
Clyde Rd. Wall 3G 63
Clydesdale Clo. Iswth 6F 10
Clydesdale Gdns. Rich 7A 12
Clymping Dene. Felt 1J 23
Clyve Way. Stai 9G 21
Coach Ho. Clo. Frim 3C 70
Coach Ho. Gdns. Fleet 2B 88
Coach Ho. La. SW19 . . . . 5J 27
Coach Ho. M. Red 4D 122
Coach Ho. Yd. SW18 . . . . 7N 13
Coachlads Av. Guild 3J 113
Coachman's Dri. Craw 7N 181
Coachmans Gro. Sand 8G 49
Coach Rd. Asc 8J 17
Coach Rd. Brock 3L 119
(in two parts)
Coach Rd. Ott 3E 54
Coaldale Wlk. SE21 . . . . 1N 29
Coalecroft Rd. SW15 . . . . 7H 13
Coast Hill. Westc 8N 117
Coast Hill La. Westc 7A 118
Coates Wlk. Bren 2L 11
Coatham Pl. Cranl 7A 156
Cobb Clo. Dat 4N 5
Cobbett Clo. Craw 1G 183
Cobbett Hill Rd. Norm 6B 92
Cobbett Rd. Guild 2J 113
Cobbett Rd. Twic 2A 24
Cobbetts Clo. Norm 7C 92
Cobbetts Clo. Wok 4L 73
Cobbetts Hill. Wey 3C 56
Cobbett's La. Yat & B'water 1E 68
Cobbetts M. Farnh 1G 128
Cobbetts Wlk. Bisl 2D 72
Cobbetts Way. Eden 3L 147
Cobbetts Way. Farnh 5E 128
Cobblers. Slin 5L 195
Cobblers Wlk. Hamp & Tedd 9C 24
(in two parts)
Cobbles Cres. Craw 2C 182
Cobblestone Pl. Croy 7N 45 (1B 200)
Cobb's Hall. SW6 . . . . 2J 13
(off Fulham Pal. Rd.)
Cobb's Rd. Houn 7N 9
Cob Clo. Craw D 1F 184
Cobden La. Hasl 1H 189
Cobden Rd. SE25 . . . . 4D 46
Cobden Rd. Orp 1M 67
Cobham 1J 77
Cobham Av. N Mald 4F 42
Cobham Bus Mus. 8D 56
Cobham Clo. Wall 3J 63
Cobham Ct. Mitc 1B 44
Cobham Ga. Cob 1J 77
Cobham Mill 2K 77
Cobham Pk. Rd. D'side 4J 77
Cobham Rd. Houn 3K 9
Cobham Rd. King T 1N 41
Cobham Rd. Stoke D 5A 78
Cobham Way. Craw 6F 162
Cobham Way. E Hor 4F 96
Cobner Clo. Craw 5L 181
Cobs Way. New H 6L 55
Coburg Cres. SW2 . . . . 2K 29
Cob Wlk. Craw 3M 181
Cochrane Pl. W'sham 2A 52
Cochrane Rd. SW19 . . . . 8K 27
Cock-A-Dobby. Sand 6F 48
Cockcrow Hill 7K 41
Cock La. Fet 9C 78
Cockpit Path. Wokgm 3B 30
Cocks Cres. N Mald 3E 42
Cocksett Av. Orp 3N 67
Cockshot Hill. Reig 4N 121
Cockshot Rd. Reig 4N 121
Cock's La. Warf 3E 16
Coda Cen., The. SW6 . . . . 3K 13
Codrington Ct. Wok 5J 73
Cody Clo. Ash V 8D 90
Cody Clo. Wall 4H 63
Cody Rd. Farnb 2L 89
Coe Av. SE25 . . . . 5D 46
Coe Clo. Alder 3M 109
Cogman's La. Out & Small 6A 144
Cokenor Wood. Wrec 5E 128
Cokers La. SE21 . . . . 2N 29
Colbeck. C Crook 9C 88
Colbeck M. SW7 . . . . 1N 13
Colborne Way. Wor Pk 9H 43
Colbred Corner. Fleet 1D 88
Colburn Av. Cat 2C 104
Colburn Cres. Guild 9C 94
Colburn Way. Sutt 9B 44
Colby Rd. W on T 7H 39
Colchester Va. F Row 7G 186
Colcokes Rd. Bans 3M 81
Cold Blows. Mitc 2D 44
Coldharbour 7D 138
Coldharbour Clo. Egh 2E 36
Coldharbour Common 6D 138
Cold Harbour La. Farnb 6K 69
(in two parts)
Coldharbour La. Blet 3C 124
Coldharbour La. Dork & Cold 2E 138
Coldharbour La. Egh 2E 36
Coldharbour La. Purl 7L 63
Coldharbour La. W End 7C 52
Coldharbour La. Wok 2H 75
Coldharbour Rd. Croy 2L 63
Coldharbour Rd. W Byf 1H 75
Coldharbour Way. Croy 2L 63
Coldshott. Oxt 2C 126
Coldstream Gdns. SW18 . . . . 9L 13
Coldstream Rd. Cat 8N 83
Cole Av. Alder 1L 109
Colebrook. Ott 3F 54
Colebrook Clo. SW15 . . . . 1J 27
Colebrooke Ri. Brom 1N 47
Colebrooke Rd. Red 1C 122
Colebrook Pl. Ott 4D 54
Colebrook Rd. SW16 . . . . 9J 29
Cole Clo. Craw 8N 181
Cole Ct. Twic 1G 24
Coleford Bri. Rd. Myt 1B 90
Coleford Clo. Myt 2D 90
Coleford Paddocks. Myt 1D 90
Coleford Rd. SW18 . . . . 8N 13
Cole Gdns. Houn 3H 9
Coleherne Ct. SW5 . . . . 1N 13
Coleherne Mans. SW5 . . . . 1N 13
(off Old Brompton Rd.)
Coleherne M. SW10 . . . . 1N 13
Coleherne Rd. SW10 . . . . 1N 13
Colehill Gdns. SW6 . . . . 5K 13
Colehill La. SW6 . . . . 4K 13
Colekitchen La. Gom 7E 116
Coleman Clo. SE25 . . . . 1D 46
Coleman Rd. Alder 3B 110
Colemans Hatch Rd. Cole H 9N 187
Colenorton Cres. Eton W 1B 4
Cole Park 9G 11
Cole Pk. Gdns. Twic 8G 10
Cole Pk. Rd. Twic 8G 10
Cole Pk. Vw. Twic 9G 11
Coleridge Av. Sutt 1C 62
Coleridge Av. Yat 1D 68
Coleridge Clo. Crowt 3H 49
Coleridge Clo. H'ham 2L 197
Coleridge Cres. Coln 4G 6
Coleridge Rd. Ashf 5N 21
Coleridge Rd. Croy 6F 46
Coleridge Way. W Dray 1A 8
Cole Rd. Twic 9G 10
Colesburg Rd. Beck 2J 47
Colescroft Hill. Purl 2L 83
Coleshill Rd. Tedd 7E 24
Cole's La. Capel & Ockl 4E 158
Colesmead Rd. Red 9D 102
Coles Meads 9D 102
Coleson Hill Rd. Wrec 6E 128
Colet Ct. W6 . . . . 1J 13
(off Hammersmith Rd.)
Colet Gdns. W14 . . . . 1J 13
Colet Rd. Craw 6B 182
Coleville Rd. Farnb 9L 69
Coley Av. Wok 5C 74
Colgate 2H 199
Colgate Clo. Craw 1N 181
Colin Clo. Croy 9J 47
Colin Clo. W Wick 1B 66
Colinette Rd. SW15 . . . . 7H 13
Colin Rd. Cat 1D 104
Coliseum Bus. Cen. Camb 3M 69
Coliston Pas. SW18 . . . . 1M 27
Coliston Rd. SW18 . . . . 1M 27
Collamore Av. SW18 . . . . 2C 28
Collards La. Hasl 2H 189
College Av. Egh 7D 20
College Av. Eps 1E 80
College Clo. Add 9M 37
College Clo. Camb 7B 50
College Clo. E Grin 9B 166
College Clo. Hand 6N 199
College Clo. Ling 7N 145
College Clo. Twic 2D 24
College Ct. W6 . . . . 1H 13
(off Queen Caroline St.)
College Cres. Col T 7K 49
College Cres. Red 9E 102
College Cres. Wind 5E 4
College Dri. Th Dit 6E 40
College Fields Bus. Cen. SW19 . . . . 9B 28
College Gdns. SW17 . . . . 3C 28
(in three parts)
College Gdns. Farnh 1G 128
College Gdns. N Mald 4E 42
College Hill. G'ming 9F 132
College Hill. Hasl 2G 189
College Hill Ter. Hasl 2G 189
College La. E Grin 9B 166
College La. Wok 6M 73
College M. SW18 . . . . 8N 13
College Pl. SW10 . . . . 3N 13
(off Hortensia Rd.)
College Ride. Bag 6E 50
(in two parts)
College Ride. Camb 8B 50
College Rd. Col T 8K 49
College Rd. SW19 . . . . 7B 28
College Rd. As & Ash V 1E 110
College Rd. Brack 3A 32
College Rd. Craw 3C 182
College Rd. Croy 8A 46 (3D 200)
College Rd. Eps 1E 80 (8M 201)
College Rd. Guild 4N 113 (4C 202)
College Rd. Iswth 4F 10
College Rd. Wok 3D 74
College Roundabout. King T 2L 41 (5J 203)
College Town 9K 49
College Wlk. King T 2L 41 (5K 203)
College Way. Ashf 5A 22
Collendean La. Horl 7K 141
Collens Fld. Pirb 2C 92
Collett's All. H'ham 6J 197
(off Carfax)
Colley La. Reig 2K 121
Colley Mnr. Dri. Reig 2J 121
Colley Way. Reig 9K 101
Collier Clo. Farnb 9J 69
Collier Clo. Eps 3N 59
Collier Row. Craw 5B 182
Colliers. Cat 3D 104
Colliers Clo. Wok 4L 73
Colliers Ct. Croy 6D 200
Colliers Shaw. Kes 2F 66
Colliers Water La. T Hth 4L 45
Collier's Wood 8B 28
Colliers Wood. (Junct.) 8B 28
Collier Way. Guild 1F 114
Collingdon. Cranl 9A 156
Collingham Gdns. SW5 . . . . 1N 13
Collingham Pl. SW5 . . . . 1N 13
Collingham Rd. SW5 . . . . 1N 13
Collingsbourne. Add 1L 55
Collingwood. Farnb 3C 90
Collingwood Av. Surb 7B 42
Collingwood Clo. E Grin 2B 186
Collingwood Clo. Horl 7F 142
Collingwood Clo. H'ham 4J 197
Collingwood Clo. Twic 1A 24
Collingwood Cres. Guild 2C 114
Collingwood Grange Clo. Camb 7F 50
Collingwood Pl. W on T 9H 39
Collingwood Ri. Camb 8E 50
Collingwood Rd. Craw 4H 183
Collingwood Rd. H'ham 4J 197
Collingwood Rd. Mitc 2C 44
Collingwood Rd. Sutt 9M 43
Collins Gdns. As 2F 110
Collins Path. Hamp 7N 23
Collins Rd. Bew 5K 181
Collis All. Twic 2E 24
Collyer Av. Croy 1J 63
Collyer Rd. Croy 1J 63
Colman Clo. Eps 4H 81
Colman Ho. Red 1D 122
Colman's Hatch 9N 187
Colman's Hill 4F 136
Colman's Hill. Peasl 4F 136
Colman Way. Red 1C 122
Colmer Rd. SW16 . . . . 9J 29
Coln Bank. Hort 6E 6
Colnbrook 3F 6
Colnbrook By-Pass. Coln & W Dray 2E 6
Colnbrook Ct. Coln 4H 7
Colndale Rd. Coln 5G 6
Colnebridge Clo. Stai 5G 21
Colne Ct. Eps 1B 60
Colne Dri. W on T 9L 39
Colne Pk. Cvn. Site. W Dray 1L 7
Colne Reach. Stai 8H 7
Colne Rd. Twic 2E 24
Colne Wlk. Craw 5L 181
Colne Way. As 3E 110
Colne Way. Stai 3D 20
Coln Trad. Est. Coln 4H 7
Colonel's La. Cher 5J 37
Colonial Av. Twic 9C 10
Colonial Dri. W4 . . . . 1B 12
Colonial Rd. Felt 1F 22
Colonnades, The. Croy 3L 63
Colonsay Rd. Craw 6N 181
Colson Rd. Croy 8B 46 (2F 200)
Colson Way. SW16 . . . . 5G 29
Colston Av. Cars 1C 62
Colston Ct. Cars 1D 62
(off West St.)
Colston Rd. SW14 . . . . 7B 12
Coltash Rd. Craw 4E 182
Coltsfoot Dri. Guild 9C 94
Coltsfoot Dri. H'ham 3L 197
Coltsfoot La. Oxt 2B 126
Coltsfoot Rd. Lind 4B 168
Columbia Av. Wor Pk 6E 42
Columbia Cen., The. Brack 1N 31
Columbia Sq. SW14 . . . . 7B 12
Columbine Av. S Croy 4M 63
Columbus Dri. Sth B 1H 89
Colville Gdns. Light 7N 51
Colvin Rd. T Hth 4L 45
Colwith Rd. W6 . . . . 2H 13
Colwood Gdns. SW19 . . . . 8B 28
Colworth Rd. Croy 7D 46
Colwyn Clo. SW16 . . . . 6G 28
Colwyn Clo. Craw 5L 181
Colwyn Clo. Yat 9B 48
Colwyn Cres. Houn 4C 10
Colyton Clo. Wok 5M 73
Combe La. Farnb 8M 69
Combe La. Brmly & Shere 6A 116
Combe La. C'fold & Wmly 4C 172
Combe La. G'ming & Wmly 9M 133
Combe La. Wmly 1C 172
Combemartin Rd. SW18 . . . . 1K 27
Combe Ri. Lwr Bo 6J 129
Combermere Clo. Wind 5E 4
Combermere Rd. Mord 5N 43
Combe Rd. G'ming 3H 133
Comberton. King T 4M 203
Comeragh Clo. Wok 7K 73
Comeragh M. W14 . . . . 1K 13
Comeragh Rd. W14 . . . . 1K 13
Comet Clo. Ash V 8D 90
Comet Rd. Stanw 1M 21
Comforts Farm Av. Oxt 2B 126
Comfrey Clo. Farnb 9H 69
Comfrey Clo. Wokgm 9D 14
Commerce Rd. Bren 2J 11
Commerce Way. Croy 8K 45
Commerce Way. Eden 9L 127
Commercial Rd. Alder 4A 110
Commercial Rd. Guild 4N 113 (5C 202)
Commercial Rd. Stai 7J 21
Commercial Way. Wok 4A 74
Commodore Ct. Farnb 5A 90
Common Clo. Wok 1N 73
Commondale. SW15 . . . . 6H 13
Commonfield La. SW17 . . . . 6C 28
Commonfield Rd. Bans 1M 81
Commonfields. W End 8D 52
Common La. Clay 4G 58
Common La. Eton C 1F 4
Common La. New H 5L 55
Common Rd. SW13 . . . . 6G 12
Common Rd. Clay 3G 58
Common Rd. Dor 1A 4
Common Rd. Eton W 1C 4
Common Rd. Red 5D 122
Common Rd. Slou 1C 6
Commonside. Bookh 9A 78
(in two parts)
Common Side. Eps 2N 79
Commonside. Kes 1E 66
Commonside Clo. Coul 7M 83
Commonside Clo. Sutt 7N 61
Commonside E. Mitc 2E 44
(in two parts)
Commonside W. Mitc 2D 44
Common, The 9N 77
(Cobham)
Common, The 1F 132
(Compton)
Common, The 5C 174
(Dunsfold)
Common, The 4H 197
(Horsham)
Common, The. Asht 3K 79
Common, The. Cranl 7L 155
Common, The. Shalf 1A 134
(in two parts)
Common, The. S'hall 1L 9
Common, The. W Dray 1L 7
Common, The. Won 3D 134

Commonwealth Rd.—Cotterill Rd.

Commonwealth Rd. *Cat* 1D **104**
Community Clo. *Houn* 4J **9**
Community Way. *Esh* 1C **58**
Compasses Mobile Home Pk. *Alf* 4H **175**
Compass Hill. *Rich* 9K **11**
Compass Ho. *SW18* 7N **13**
Compassion Clo. *Bew* 4K **181**
Comper Clo. *Craw* 5K **181**
Comport Grn. *New Ad* 8A **66**
Compton. 1K 129 (Farnham)
Compton. 9D 112 (Guildford)
Compton Clo. *Brack* 5K **31**
Compton Clo. *C Crook* 8C **88**
Compton Clo. *Esh* 3D **58**
Compton Clo. *Sand* 6H **49**
Compton Ct. *Guild* 4B **114**
Compton Ct. *Sutt* 1A **62**
Compton Cres. *W4* 2B **12**
Compton Cres. *Chess* 2L **59**
Compton Gdns. Add 2K **55** *(off Monks Cres.)*
Compton Heights. *Guild* 6G **112**
Compton Pl. Bus. Cen. Camb 2M **69** *(off Surrey Av.)*
Compton Rd. *SW19* 7L **27**
Compton Rd. *C Crook* 8C **88**
Compton Rd. *Croy* 7E **46**
Compton St Nicholas Church 1D 132
Comptons Brow La. *H'ham* 5N **197**
Comptons Ct. *H'ham* 5M **197**
Comptons La. *H'ham* 4M **197**
Compton Way. *Farnh* 1M **129**
Comsaye Wlk. *Brack* 4A **32**
Conaways Clo. *Eps* 6F **60**
Concord Ct. *King T* 5L **203**
Concorde Bus. Pk. *Big H* 2F **86**
Concorde Clo. *Houn* 5B **10**
Conde Way. *Bord* 7A **168**
Condor Ct. *Guild* 5M **113** (7B **202**)
Condor Rd. *Stai* 2K **37**
Conduit La. *Dat* 2A **6**
Conduit La. *S Croy* 2D **64** (in two parts)
Conduit, The. *Blet* 7A **104**
Coney Acre. *SE21* 2N **29**
Coneyberry. *Reig* 7A **122**
Coneybury. *Blet* 3B **124**
Coneybury Clo. *Warl* 6E **84**
Coney Clo. *Craw* 1N **181**
Coney Cft. *H'ham* 3A **198**
Coney Grange. *Warf* 7N **15**
Coney Hall. 1A 66
Coneyhurst La. *Ewh* 3D **156**
Conford. 9D 168
Conford Dri. *Shalf* 1A **134**
Coniers Way. *Guild* 9D **94**
Conifer Clo. *C Crook* 8A **88**
Conifer Clo. *Orp* 1M **67**
Conifer Clo. *Reig* 1M **121**
Conifer Dri. *Camb* 9E **50**
Conifer Gdns. *SW16* 4J **29**
Conifer Gdns. *Sutt* 8N **43**
Conifer La. *Egh* 6E **20**
Conifer Pk. *Eps* 7D **60**
Conifers. *Wey* 1F **56**
Conifers Clo. *H'ham* 2A **198**
Conifers Clo. *Tedd* 8H **25**
Conifers, The. *Crowt* 9F **30**
Coniger Rd. *SW6* 5M **13**
Coningsby. *Brack* 3A **32**
Coningsby Rd. *S Croy* 5N **63**
Conista Ct. *Wok* 3J **73**
Coniston Clo. *Farnb* 2K **89**
Coniston Clo. *SW13* 3E **12**
Coniston Clo. *SW20* 5J **43**
Coniston Clo. *W4* 3B **12**
Coniston Clo. *Camb* 3G **71**
Coniston Clo. *H'ham* 3A **198**
Coniston Clo. *If'd* 5J **181**
Coniston Ct. Ash V 9D **90** *(off Lakeside Clo.)*
Coniston Ct. *Light* 6M **51**
Coniston Ct. *Wey* 3C **56**
Coniston Dri. *Farnh* 6F **108**
Coniston Gdns. *Sutt* 3B **62**
Coniston Rd. *Coul* 3G **82**
Coniston Rd. *Croy* 6D **46**
Coniston Rd. *Twic* 9B **10**
Coniston Rd. *Wok* 7D **74**
Coniston Way. *Chess* 9L **41**
Coniston Way. *C Crook* 8A **88**
Coniston Way. *Egh* 8D **20**
Coniston Way. *Reig* 2C **122**
Connaught Av. *Ashf* 5N **21**
Connaught Av. *SW14* 6B **12**
Connaught Av. *Houn* 7M **9**
Connaught Barracks. *Alder* 7B **90**
Connaught Bus. Cen. *Mitc* 4D **44**
Connaught Clo. *Crowt* 4E **48**
Connaught Clo. *Sutt* 8B **44**
Connaught Clo. *Yat* 9A **48**
Connaught Cres. *Brkwd* 7C **72**
Connaught Dri. *Wey* 7D **56**
Connaught Gdns. *Craw* 1B **182**
Connaught Gdns. *Mord* 3A **44**
Connaught M. *SW6* 4K **13**
Connaught Rd. *Alder* 2A **110**
Connaught Rd. *Bag* 4G **51**
Connaught Rd. *Brkwd* 8D **72**
Connaught Rd. *Camb* 1D **70**
Connaught Rd. *Fleet* 5A **88**
Connaught Rd. *N Mald* 3D **42**
Connaught Rd. *Rich* 8M **11**
Connaught Rd. *Sutt* 8B **44**
Connaught Rd. *Tedd* 6D **24**
Connicut La. *Bookh* 6B **98**
Connolly Ct. *Vir W* 3A **36**
Connolly Pl. *SW19* 7A **28**
Connop Way. *Frim* 3D **70**
Conquest Rd. *Add* 2J **55**
Conrad Dri. *Wor Pk* 7H **43**
Consfield Av. *N Mald* 3F **42**
Consort Ct. Wok 5A **74** *(off York Rd.)*
Consort Dri. *Camb* 8G **50**
Consort Ho. *Horl* 8E **142**
Consort M. *Iswth* 8D **10**
Consort Way. *Horl* 8E **142**
Consort Way E. *Horl* 9F **142**
Constable Ct. W4 1A **12** *(off Chaseley Dri.)*
Constable Gdns. *Iswth* 8D **10**
Constable Rd. *Craw* 7D **182**
Constable Way. *Col T* 9K **49**
Constance Rd. *Croy* 6M **45**
Constance Rd. *Sutt* 1A **62**
Constance Rd. *Twic* 1B **24**
Constantius Ct. C Crook 9A **88** *(off Brandon Rd.)*
Constant Rd. *Farnb* 3F **88**
Constitution Hill. *Wok* 6A **74**
Contessa Clo. *Orp* 2N **67**
Control Tower Rd. *Gat A* 4B **162**
Control Tower Rd. *H'row A* 6B **8**
Convent Gdns. *W5* 1J **11**
Convent Hill. *SE19* 7N **29**
Convent La. *Cob* 7F **56**
Convent Lodge. *Ashf* 6C **22**
Convent Rd. *Ashf* 6B **22**
Convent Rd. *Wind* 5C **4**
Convent Way. *S'hall* 1K **9**
Conway Clo. *Frim* 5D **70**
Conway Dri. *Ashf* 7D **22**
Conway Dri. *Farnb* 1J **89**
Conway Dri. *Sutt* 3N **61**
Conway Gdns. *Mitc* 3J **45**
Conway Rd. *SW20* 9H **27**
Conway Rd. *Felt* 6L **23**
Conway Rd. *Houn* 1N **23**
Conway Rd. *H'row A* 6C **8**
Conway Wlk. *Hamp* 7N **23**
Conyers Clo. *W on T* 2L **57**
Conyer's Rd. *SW16* 6H **29**
Cook Cres. *H'ham* 6M **197**
Cooke Ri. *Warf* 7A **16**
Cookes La. *Sutt* 3K **61**
Cookham Clo. *Sand* 9H **49**
Cookham Rd. *Brack* 1K **31**
Cook Rd. *Craw* 5C **182**
Cook Rd. *H'ham* 2K **197**
Cooks Hill. *Rud* 8A **176**
Cook's La. *Broad H* 3A **196**
Cooks Mead. *Rusp* 2C **180**
Cooks Mdw. *Rusp* 2C **180**
Coolarne Ri. *Camb* 9E **50**
Coolgardie Rd. *Ashf* 6D **22**
Coolham Ct. *Craw* 3L **181**
Coolhurst. 8A 198
Coolhurst La. *H'ham* 7N **197**
Coombe. 8C 26
Coombe Av. *Croy* 1B **64**
Coombe Bank. *King T* 9D **26**
Coombe Bottom. 6A 116
Coombe Clo. *Craw* 9B **162**
Coombe Clo. *Frim* 6B **70**
Coombe Clo. *Houn* 7A **10**
Coombe Ct. *Croy* 6D **200**
Coombe Cres. *Hamp* 8N **23**
Coombe Dri. *Add* 3H **55**
Coombe Dri. *Fleet* 4D **88**
Coombe End. *King T* 8C **26**
Coombefield Clo. *N Mald* 4D **42**
Coombe Gdns. *SW20* 1F **42**
Coombe Gdns. *N Mald* 3E **42**
Coombe Hill Ct. *Wind* 6A **4**
Coombe Hill Glade. *King T* 8D **26**
Coombe Hill Rd. *E Grin* 3M **185**
Coombe Hill Rd. *King T* 8D **26**
Coombe Ho. Chase. *N Mald* 9C **26**
Coombelands La. *Add* 3J **55**
Coombe Lane. (Junct.) 8E 26
Coombe La. *SW20* 9E **26**
Coombe La. *Asc* 3N **33**
Coombe La. *Croy* 2E **64**
Coombe La. *W Vill* 5G **56**
Coombe La. *Worp* 7F **92** (in two parts)
Coombe La. Flyover. *SW20* 9E **26**
Coombe La. W. *King T* 9A **26**
Coombe Neville. *King T* 8C **26**
Coombe Pk. *King T* 6B **26**
Coombe Pine. *Brack* 5B **32**
Coomber Ho. SW6 6N **13** *(off Wandsworth Bri. Rd.)*
Coombe Ridings. *King T* 6B **26**
Coombe Ri. *King T* 9B **26**
Coombe Rd. *W4* 1D **12**
Coombe Rd. *Croy* 1A **64** (6C **200**)
Coombe Rd. *Hamp* 7N **23**
Coombe Rd. *King T* 9N **25** (2M **203**)
Coombe Rd. *N Mald* 1D **42**
Coombe Rd. *Yat* 8A **48**
Coomber Way. *Croy* 6H **45** (in two parts)
Coombes, The. *Brmly* 6C **134**
Coombe, The. *Bet* 9C **100**
Coombe Vw. *C'fold* 4D **172**
Coombe Wlk. *Sutt* 9N **43**
Coombe Way. *Byfl* 8A **56**
Coombe Wood Hill. *Purl* 9N **63**
Coombewood Rd. *King T* 6B **26**
Coombfield. *Eden* 3L **147**
Coomer M. *SW6* 2L **13**
Coomer Pl. *SW6* 2L **13**
Coomer Rd. *SW6* 2L **13**
Cooper Clo. *Small* 8L **143**
Cooper Cres. *Cars* 9D **44**
Cooper Ho. *Houn* 6N **9**
Cooper Rd. *Croy* 1M **63**
Cooper Rd. *Guild* 5B **114**
Cooper Rd. *W'sham* 3A **52**
Cooper Row. *Craw* 6B **182**
Coopers Clo. *Stai* 6G **21**
Coopers Ct. Iswth 5F **10** *(off Woodlands Rd.)*
Coopers Hill Dri. *Brkwd* 7N **71**
Coopers Hill La. *Eng G* 4M **19** (in three parts)
Cooper's Hill Rd. *Nutf & S Nut* 3L **123**
Coopers Pl. *Wmly* 1C **172**
Coopers Ri. *G'ming* 8E **132**
Coopers Ter. *Farnh* 9H **109**
Coopers Wood. *Hand* 5N **199**
Coos La. *Hand* 9M **199**
Cootes Av. *H'ham* 5G **196**
Copelands Clo. *Camb* 2H **71**
Copenhagen Wlk. *Crowt* 3G **49**
Copenhagen Way. *W on T* 9J **39**
Copgate Path. *SW16* 7K **29**
Copleigh Dri. *Tad* 7K **81**
Copley Clo. *Red* 1C **122**
Copley Clo. *Wok* 6H **73**
Copley Pk. *SW16* 7K **29**
Copley Way. *Tad* 7J **81**
Copnall Way. *H'ham* 6J **197**
Coppard Gdns. *Chess* 3J **59**
Copped Hall Dri. *Camb* 9G **50**
Copped Hall Way. *Camb* 9G **50**
Copper Beech Clo. *Wind* 4A **4**
Copper Beech Clo. *Wok* 8L **73**
Copper Beeches Ct. *Iswth* 4D **10**
Copperfield Av. *Owl* 5K **49**
Copperfield Clo. *S Croy* 7N **63**
Copperfield Ct. *Lea* 8G **79**
Copperfield Pl. *H'ham* 4H **197**
Copperfield Ri. *Add* 2H **55**
Copperfields. *Fet* 9C **78**
Copperfields. *H'ham* 8A **198**
Copper Mill Dri. *Iswth* 5F **10**
Copper Mill La. *SW17* 5A **28**
Coppermill Rd. *Wray* 9C **6**
Coppice Clo. *SW20* 2H **43**
Coppice Clo. *Beck* 3L **47**
Coppice Clo. *Farnh* 6K **109**
Coppice Clo. *Guild* 2G **113**
Coppice Dri. *SW15* 9G **12**
Coppice Dri. *Wray* 1N **19**
Coppice End. *Wok* 3G **74**
Coppice Gdns. *Crowt* 2E **48**
Coppice Gdns. *Yat* 1B **68**
Coppice Grn. *Brack* 8L **15** (in two parts)
Coppice La. *Reig* 1L **121**
Coppice Pl. *Wmly* 1C **172**
Coppice Rd. *H'ham* 3N **197**
Coppice, The. *Ashf* 7C **22**
Coppice, The. *Craw D* 1E **184**
Coppice Wlk. *Craw* 2E **182**
Coppid Beech La. *Wokgm* 2F **30**
Copping Clo. *Croy* 1B **64**
Coppins, The. *New Ad* 3L **65**
Coppsfield. *W Mol* 2A **40**
Copse Av. *Farnh* 5K **109**
Copse Av. *W Wick* 9L **47**
Copse Clo. *Camb* 9E **50**
Copse Clo. *Chil* 1E **134**
Copse Clo. *Craw D* 1E **184**
Copse Clo. *E Grin* 7C **166**
Copse Clo. *H'ham* 2M **197**
Copse Cres. *Craw* 2A **182**
Copse Dri. *Wokgm* 1A **30**
Copse Edge. *Cranl* 6A **156**
Copse Edge. *Elst* 8G **131**
Copse Edge Av. *Eps* 9E **60**
Copse End. *Camb* 9D **50**
Copse Glade. *Surb* 6K **41**
Copse Hill. 8G 26
Copse Hill. *SW20* 9F **26**
Copse Hill. *Purl* 9J **63**
Copse Hill. *Sutt* 4N **61**
Copse La. *C Crook* 8A **88**
Copse La. *Eve* 7A **48**
Copse La. *Horl* 7G **143**
Copsem Dri. *Esh* 3B **58**
Copsem La. *Esh & Oxs* 3B **58**
Copsem Way. *Esh* 4C **58**
Copsem Wood. *Oxs* 7C **58**
Copse Rd. *Cob* 9J **57**
Copse Rd. *Hasl* 3B **188**
Copse Rd. *Red* 5A **122**
Copse Rd. *Wok* 5J **73**
Copse Side. *G'ming* 3G **133**
Copse, The. *Farnb* 2J **89**
Copse, The. *Row* 7E **128**
Copse, The. *Brack* 2B **32**
Copse, The. *Cat* 4D **104**
Copse, The. *Fet* 1B **98**
Copse, The. *S Nut* 5J **123**
Copse, The. *Wink* 2L **17**
Copse Vw. *S Croy* 5G **65**
Copse Way. *Wrec* 5F **128**
Copsleigh Av. *Red* 1E **142**
Copsleigh Clo. *Salf* 9E **122**
Copsleigh Way. *Red* 9E **122**
Copthall Gdns. *Twic* 2F **24**
Copthall Way. *New H* 6H **55**
Copt Hill La. *Tad* 7K **81**
Copthorne. 7L 163
Copthorne Av. *SW12* 1H **29**
Copthorne Bank. *Copt* 4N **163**
Copthorne Chase. *Ashf* 5A **22**
Copthorne Clo. *Shep* 5D **38**
Copthorne Common. 7A 164
Copthorne Comn. Rd. *Copt* 8L **163**
Copthorne Ct. *Lea* 9G **79**
Copthorne Dri. *Light* 6M **51**
Copthorne Ri. *S Croy* 9A **64**
Copthorne Rd. *Copt & Felb* 6E **164**
Copthorne Rd. *Craw* 1H **183**
Copthorne Rd. *Lea* 7H **79**
Copthorne Way. *Craw* 8J **163**
Copyhold Rd. *E Grin* 1N **185**
Coram Ho. W4 1D **12** *(off Wood St.)*
Corban Rd. *Houn* 6A **10**
Corbet Clo. *Wall* 7E **44**
Corbet Rd. *Eps* 6D **60**
Corbett Clo. *Croy* 8N **65**
Corbett Dri. *Light* 8K **51**
Corbett Ho. SW10 2N **13** *(off Cathcart Rd.)*
Corbiere Ct. *SW19* 7J **27**
Corby Clo. *Bew* 6K **181**
Corby Clo. *Eng G* 7M **19**
Corby Dri. *Eng G* 7L **19**
Cordelia Cft. *Warf* 9C **16**
Cordelia Gdns. *Ash V* 4D **90**
Cordelia Gdns. *Stai* 1N **21**
Cordelia Rd. *Stai* 1N **21**
Corderoy Pl. *Cher* 5G **37**
Cordrey Gdns. *Coul* 2J **83** (in two parts)
Cordrey Ho. *Add* 8J **37**
Cordwalles Rd. *Camb* 7D **50**
Corelli Ct. SW5 1M **13** *(off W. Cromwell Rd.)*
Coresbrook Way. *Knap* 5D **72**
Corfe Clo. *Asht* 5J **79**
Corfe Gdns. *Frim* 5D **70**
Corfe Way. *Farnb* 4C **90**
Coriander Clo. *Farnb* 9H **69**
Coriander Cres. *Guild* 7K **93**
Corinthian Way. *Stanw* 1M **21**
Corkran Rd. *Surb* 6K **41**
Corkscrew Hill. *W Wick* 8M **47**
Cork Tree Ho. SE27 6M **29** *(off Lakeview Rd.)*
Cormongers La. *Nutf* 9H **103**
Cormorant Pl. *Col T* 8J **49**
Cormorant Pl. *Sutt* 2L **61**
Cornbunting Clo. *Col T* 7J **49**
Corn Cft. *Warf* 8B **16**
Cornelia Clo. *Farnb* 2J **89**
Cornelia Ho. Twic 9K **11** *(off Denton Rd.)*
Corner Bungalows. *G'ming* 3E **132**
Cornercroft. Sutt 2J **61** *(off Wickham Av.)*
Corner Farm Clo. *Tad* 9H **81**
Corner Fielde. *SW2* 2K **29**
Cornerside. *Ashf* 8D **22**
Cornerstone Ho. *Croy* 6N **45**
Corner, The. *W Byf* 9J **55**
Corney Reach Way. *W4* 3D **12**
Corney Rd. *W4* 2D **12**
Cornfield Rd. *Reig* 4A **122**
Cornfields. *G'ming* 3J **133**
Cornfields. *Yat* 2A **68**
Cornflower La. *Croy* 7G **47**
Cornford Gro. *SW12* 3F **28**
Cornhill Clo. *Add* 8K **37**
Cornish Ho. *Bren* 1M **11**
Cornwall Av. *Byfl* 1A **76**
Cornwall Av. *Clay* 4F **58**
Cornwall Clo. *Camb* 8D **50**
Cornwall Clo. *Eton W* 1B **4**
Cornwall Clo. *Warf* 7D **16**
Cornwall Gdns. *SE25* 3C **46**
Cornwall Gdns. *E Grin* 1B **186**
Cornwall Gro. *W4* 1D **12**
Cornwallis Clo. *Cat* 9N **83**
Cornwall Rd. *Croy* 8M **45** (2A **200**)
Cornwall Rd. *Sutt* 4L **61**
Cornwall Rd. *Twic* 1G **25**
Cornwall Way. *Stai* 7G **20**
Cornwell Rd. *Old Win* 9K **5**
Coronation Av. *Wind* 5K **5**
Coronation Rd. *Alder* 5N **109**
Coronation Rd. *Asc* 6L **33**
Coronation Rd. *E Grin* 2A **186**
Coronation Rd. *Hay* 1G **9**
Coronation Rd. *Yat* 8D **48**
Coronation Sq. *Wokgm* 1C **30**
Coronation Wlk. *Twic* 2A **24**
Coronet Clo. *Craw* 2J **183**
Coronet, The. *Horl* 1G **162**
Corporate Dri. *Felt* 4J **23**
Corporation Av. *Houn* 7M **9**
Corrib Dri. *Sutt* 2C **62**
Corrie Gdns. *Vir W* 6M **35**
Corrie Rd. *Add* 1M **55**
Corrie Rd. *Wok* 7D **74**
Corrigan Av. *Coul* 2E **82**
Corringway. *C Crook* 7C **88**
Corry Rd. *Hind* 3A **170**
Corsair Clo. *Stai* 1M **21**
Corsair Rd. *Stai* 1N **21**
Corscombe Clo. *King T* 6B **26**
Corsehill St. *SW16* 7G **28**
Corsham Way. *Crowt* 2G **48**
Corsletts Av. *Broad H* 5D **196**
Corston Hollow. Red 4D **122** *(off Woodlands Rd.)*
Cortayne Ct. *Twic* 3E **24**
Cortayne Rd. *SW6* 5L **13**
Cortis Rd. *SW15* 9G **13**
Cortis Ter. *SW15* 9G **13**
Corunna Dri. *H'ham* 6M **197**
Cosdach Av. *Wall* 4H **63**
Cosedge Cres. *Croy* 2L **63** (8A **200**)
Cosford Rd. *Thur* 6J **151**
Costells Mdw. *W'ham* 4M **107**
Coteford St. *SW17* 5D **28**
Cotelands. *Croy* 9B **46** (4F **200**)
Cotford Rd. *T Hth* 3N **45**
Cotherstone. *Eps* 6C **60**
Cotherstone Rd. *SW2* 2K **29**
Cotland Acres. *Red* 5B **122**
Cotman Clo. *SW15* 9J **13**
Cotmandene. 5H 119 (2L 201)
Cotsford. *Peas P* 2N **199**
Cotsford Av. *N Mald* 4B **42**
Cotswold Clo. *Farnb* 7K **69**
Cotswold Clo. *Craw* 3N **181**
Cotswold Clo. *Hin W* 8F **40**
Cotswold Clo. *King T* 7B **26**
Cotswold Clo. *Stai* 6J **21**
Cotswold Ct. *Fleet* 4A **88**
Cotswold Ct. *H'ham* 6L **197**
Cotswold Rd. *Hamp* 6A **24**
Cotswold Rd. *Sand* 6E **48**
Cotswold Rd. *Sutt* 6N **61**
Cotswold St. *SE27* 5M **29**
Cotswold Way. *Wor Pk* 8H **43**
Cottage Clo. *H'ham* 2A **198**
Cottage Clo. *Ott* 3E **54**
Cottage Farm Way. *Egh* 2E **36**
Cottage Gdns. *Farnb* 1L **89**
Cottage Gro. *Surb* 5K **41**
Cottage Pl. *Copt* 7B **164**
Cottage Rd. *Eps* 4D **60**
Cottenham Dri. *SW20* 8G **27**
Cottenham Pde. *SW20* 1G **43**
Cottenham Park. 9G 27
Cottenham Pk. Rd. *SW20* 9F **26** (in two parts)
Cottenham Pl. *SW20* 8G **27**
Cottenhams. *Blind H* 3H **145**
Cotterell Clo. *Brack* 8N **15**
Cotterell Ct. *C Crook* 9A **88**
Cotterill Rd. *Surb* 9L **41**

A-Z Surrey 223

Denmead Rd.—Dowding Rd.

Denmead Rd. *Croy* 7M **45** (1A **200**)
Denmore Ct. *Wall* 2F **62**
Dennan Rd. *Surb* 7M **41**
Dennard Way. *F'boro* 1J **67**
Denne Pde. *H'ham* 7J **197**
Denne Park. 8H 197
Denne Rd. *Craw* 4B **182**
Denne Rd. *H'ham* 7J **197**
Dennett Rd. *Croy* 7L **45**
Dennettsland Rd. *Crock H* . . . 3L **127**
Denning Av. *Croy* . . . 1L **63** (8A **200**)
Denning Clo. *Fleet* 6A **88**
Denning Clo. *Hamp* 6N **23**
Denningtons, The. *Wor Pk* . . . 8D **42**
Dennis Clo. *Ashf* 8E **22**
Dennis Clo. *Red* 1C **122**
Dennis Ho. *Sutt* 1M **61**
Dennis Pk. Cres. *SW20* 9K **27**
Dennis Reeve Clo. *Mitc* 9D **28**
Dennis Rd. *E Mol* 3C **40**
Dennistoun Clo. *Camb* 1B **70**
Dennisville. 4K 113
Dennis Way. *Guild & Sly I* . . . 7A **94**
Denny Rd. *Slou* 1B **6**
Den Rd. *Brom* 2N **47**
Densham Dri. *Purl* 1L **83**
Denton Clo. *Red* 8E **122**
Denton Gro. *W on T* 8M **39**
Denton Rd. *Twic* 9K **11**
Denton Rd. *Wokgm* 2B **30**
Denton St. *SW18* 9N **13**
Denton Way. *Frim* 4B **70**
Denton Way. *Wok* 4J **73**
Dents Gro. *Tad* 6L **101**
Dents Rd. *SW11* 1D **28**
Denvale Trad. Pk. *Craw* 4C **182**
Denvale Wlk. *Wok* 5K **73**
Denzil Rd. *Guild* . . . 4L **113** (5A **202**)
Deodar Rd. *SW15* 7K **13**
Departures Rd. Gat A 2D 162
(off Gatwick Way)
Depot Rd. *Craw* 9B **162**
Depot Rd. *Eps* 9D **60** (6L **201**)
Depot Rd. *H'ham* 6L **197**
Depot Rd. *Houn* 6D **10**
Derby Arms Rd. *Eps* 4E **80**
Derby Clo. *Eps* 6G **81**
Derby Day Experience, The. 4E 80
Derby Rd. *SW14* 7A **12**
Derby Rd. *SW19* 8M **27**
Derby Rd. *Croy* 7M **45** (1A **200**)
Derby Rd. *Guild* 3J **113**
Derby Rd. *Hasl* 1F **188**
Derby Rd. *Houn* 7B **10**
Derby Rd. *Surb* 7N **41**
Derby Rd. *Sutt* 3L **61**
Derbyshire Grn. *Warf* 8D **16**
Derby Sq., The. *Eps* 8K **201**
Derby Stables Rd. *Eps* 4E **80**
Derek Av. *Eps* 3N **59**
Derek Av. *Wall* 1F **62**
Derek Clo. *Ewe* 2A **60**
Derek Horn Ct. *Camb* 9N **49**
Derleene Clo. *Stanw* 9N **7**
Dering Pl. *S Croy* . . . 1N **63** (7C **200**)
Dering Rd. *Croy* . . . 1N **63** (7C **200**)
Derinton Rd. *SW17* 5D **28**
Deronda Est. *SW2* 2M **29**
Deronda Rd. *SE24* 2M **29**
De Ros Pl. *Egh* 7C **20**
Deroy Clo. *Cars* 3D **62**
Derrick Av. *S Croy* 6N **63**
Derrick Rd. *Beck* 2J **47**
Derry Clo. *Ash V* 8D **90**
Derrydown. *Wok* 8M **73**
Derry Rd. *Farnb* 6L **69**
Derry Rd. *Croy* 9J **45**
Derwent Av. *SW15* 5D **26**
Derwent Av. *Ash V* 9D **90**
Derwent Clo. *Farnb* 1K **89**
Derwent Clo. *Add* 2M **55**
Derwent Clo. *Clay* 3F **58**
Derwent Clo. *Craw* 4L **181**
Derwent Clo. *Farnh* 6F **108**
Derwent Clo. *Felt* 2G **22**
Derwent Clo. *H'ham* 2A **198**
Derwent Dri. *Purl* 9A **64**
Derwent Ho. SE20 . . . . . 1E 46
(off Derwent Rd.)
Derwent Lodge. *Iswth* 5D **10**
Derwent Lodge. *Wor Pk* 8G **42**
Derwent Rd. *SE20* 1D **46**
Derwent Rd. *SW20* 4J **43**
Derwent Rd. *Egh* 8D **20**
Derwent Rd. *Light* 7M **51**
Derwent Rd. *Twic* 9B **10**
Derwent Wlk. *Wall* 4F **62**
Desborough Clo. *Shep* 7B **38**
Desborough Ho. W14 . . . . . 2L 13
(off N. End Rd.)
Desford Ct. *Ashf* 3B **22**
Desford Way. *Ashf* 3A **22**
Detillens La. *Oxt* 7C **106**
Detling Rd. *Craw* 8A **182**
Dettingen Barracks. *Deep* 5H **71**
Dettingen Cres. *Deep* 6H **71**
Dettingen Rd. *Deep* 6J **71**
Devana End. *Cars* 9D **44**
Devas Rd. *SW20* 9H **27**
Devenish Clo. *S'hill* 5A **34**
Devenish La. *Asc* 7A **34**
Devenish Rd. *Asc* 5N **33**
Devereux La. *SW13* 3G **12**
Devereux Rd. *SW11* 1D **28**
Devereux Rd. *Wind* 5G **4**
Devey Clo. *King T* 8E **26**
Devil's Highway, The. *Crowt* 2D **48**
Devil's Jumps, The. 6N 149
Devil's La. *Egh & Stai* 7E **20**
(in three parts)
Devil's Punchbowl 4E 170
De Vitre Grn. *Wokgm* 1E **30**
Devitt Clo. *Asht* 3N **79**
Devoil Clo. *Guild* 8D **94**
Devoke Way. *W on T* 8L **39**
Devon Av. *Twic* 2C **24**
Devon Bank. *Guild* 6M **113** (8B **202**)
Devon Chase. *Warf* 7C **16**
Devon Clo. *Col T* 8J **49**
Devon Clo. *Fleet* 1C **88**
Devon Clo. *Kenl* 3C **84**
Devon Ct. *Hamp* 8A **24**
Devon Cres. *Red* 3D **122**
Devoncroft Gdns. *Twic* 1G **25**
Devon Ho. *Cat* 2C **104**
Devonhurst Pl. *W4* 1C **12**
Devon Rd. *Red* 8G **102**
Devon Rd. *Sutt* 5K **61**
Devon Rd. *W on T* 1K **57**
Devonshire Av. *Sutt* 4A **62**
Devonshire Av. *Wok* 1E **74**
Devonshire Dri. *Camb* 8D **50**
Devonshire Dri. *Surb* 7K **41**
Devonshire Gdns. *W4* 3B **12**
Devonshire Ho. *Sutt* 4A **62**
Devonshire M. *W4* 1D **12**
Devonshire Pas. *W4* 1D **12**
Devonshire Pl. *Alder* 3L **109**
Devonshire Rd. *SW19* 8C **28**
Devonshire Rd. *W4* 1D **12**
Devonshire Rd. *Cars* 1E **62**
Devonshire Rd. *Croy* 6A **46**
Devonshire Rd. *Felt* 4M **23**
Devonshire Rd. *H'ham* 6K **197**
Devonshire Rd. *Sutt* 4A **62**
Devonshire Rd. *Wey* 1B **56**
Devonshire St. *W4* 1D **12**
Devonshire Way. *Croy* 8H **47**
Devon Way. *Chess* 2J **59**
Devon Way. *Eps* 2A **60**
Devon Waye. *Houn* 3N **9**
Dewar Clo. *If'd* 4K **181**
Dewey St. *SW17* 6D **28**
Dewlands. *God* 9F **104**
(in two parts)
Dewlands Clo. *Cranl* 7N **155**
Dewlands La. *Cranl* 7N **155**
Dewlands Rd. *God* 9F **104**
Dewsbury Ct. *W4* 1B **12**
Dewsbury Gdns. *Wor Pk* 9F **42**
Dexter Dri. *E Grin* 1A **186**
Dexter Way. *Fleet* 1C **88**
Diamedes Av. *Stanw* 1M **21**
Diamond Ct. Red 2E 122
(off St Anne's Mt.)
Diamond Est. *SW17* 4C **28**
Diamond Hill. *Camb* 8C **50**
Diamond Ridge. *Camb* 8B **50**
Diana Cotts. *Seale* 8J **111**
Diana Gdns. *Surb* 8M **41**
Diana Ho. *SW13* 4E **12**
Diana Wlk. Horl 8F 142
(off High St.)
Dianthus Clo. *Cher* 6G **37**
Dianthus Ct. *Wok* 5N **73**
Dianthus Pl. *Wink R* 7F **16**
Dibdene La. *Sham G* 7H **135**
Dibdin Clo. *Sutt* 9M **43**
Dibdin Rd. *Sutt* 9M **43**
Diceland Rd. *Bans* 3L **81**
Dickens Clo. *E Grin* 9M **165**
Dickens Clo. *Hay* 1F **8**
Dickens Clo. *Rich* 3L **25**
Dickens Ct. *Wokgm* 2A **30**
Dickens Dri. *Add* 3J **55**
Dickenson Rd. *Felt* 6K **23**
Dickensons La. *SE25* 4D **46**
(in two parts)
Dickensons Pl. *SE25* 5D **46**
Dickens Rd. *Craw* 6B **182**
Dickens Way. *Yat* 1B **68**
Dickenswood Clo. *SE19* 8M **29**
Dickerage La. *N Mald* 2B **42**
Dickerage Rd. *King T* 9B **26**
Dickins Way. *H'ham* 8M **197**
Dick Turpin Way. *Felt* 7G **9**
Digby Mans. W6 . . . . . 1G 13
(off Hammersmith Bri. Rd.)
Digby Pl. *Croy* 9C **46**
Digby Way. *Byfl* 8A **56**
Digdens Ri. *Eps* 2B **80**
Dighton Rd. *SW18* 8N **13**
Dillon Cotts. *Guild* 7E **94**
Dilston Rd. *Lea* 6G **79**
Dilton Gdns. *SW15* 2F **26**
Dimes Pl. *W6* 1G **13**
Dingle Clo. *Craw* 2N **181**
Dingle Rd. *Ashf* 6C **22**
Dingle, The. *Craw* 3N **181**
Dingley La. *SW16* 3H **29**
Dingwall Av. *Croy & New Ad* 8N **45** (3C **200**)
Dingwall Rd. *SW18* 1A **28**
Dingwall Rd. *Cars* 5D **62**
Dingwall Rd. *Croy* 7A **46** (1D **200**)
Dinorben Av. *Fleet* 6A **88**
Dinorben Beeches. *Fleet* 6A **88**
Dinorben Clo. *Fleet* 6A **88**
Dinsdale Clo. *Wok* 5C **74**
Dinsdale Gdns. *SE25* 4B **46**
Dinsmore Rd. *SW12* 1F **28**
Dinton Rd. *SW19* 7B **28**
Dinton Rd. *King T* 8M **25**
Dione Wlk. *Bew* 6K **181**
Dippenhall. 1B 128
Dippenhall Rd. *Dipp* 1B **128**
Dirdene Clo. *Eps* 8E **60**
Dirdene Gdns. *Eps* 9E **60** (5M **201**)
Dirdene Gro. *Eps* 8D **60**
Dirtham La. *Eff* 6J **97**
(in two parts)
Dirty La. *Ash W* 3G **187**
Disbrowe Rd. *W6* 2K **13**
Discovery Pk. *Craw* 7E **162**
Disraeli Ct. *Coln* 2D **6**
Disraeli Gdns. *SW15* 7L **13**
Disraeli Rd. *SW15* 7K **13**
Distillery La. *W6* 1H **13**
Distillery Rd. *W6* 1H **13**
Distillery Wlk. *Bren* 2L **11**
Ditches Grn. Cotts. *Ockl* 8M **157**
Ditches La. *Coul & Cat* 7J **83**
Ditchling. *Brack* 6M **31**
Ditchling Hill. *Craw* 6A **182**
Ditton Clo. *Th Dit* 6G **40**
Dittoncroft Clo. *Croy* 1B **64**
Ditton Grange Clo. *Surb* 7K **41**
Ditton Grange Dri. *Surb* 7K **41**
Ditton Hill. *Surb* 7J **41**
Ditton Hill Rd. *Surb* 7J **41**
Ditton Lawn. *Th Dit* 7G **40**
Ditton Pk. Rd. *Slou* 2A **6**
Ditton Reach. *Th Dit* 5H **41**
Ditton Rd. *Dat* 4N **5**
Ditton Rd. *Slou* 1B **6**
Ditton Rd. *S'hall* 1N **9**
Ditton Rd. *Surb* 8K **41**
Divis Way. SW15 . . . . . 9G 13
(off Dover Pk. Dri.)
Dixon Dri. *Wey* 6A **56**
Dixon Pl. *W Wick* 7L **47**
Dixon Rd. *SE25* 2D **46**
Dobbins Pl. *If'd* 4J **181**
Doble Ct. *S Croy* 8D **64**
Dobson Rd. *Craw* 9B **162**
Dockenfield. 4D 148
Dockenfield St. *Dock* 2A **148**
Dockett Eddy. *Cher* 7N **37**
Dockett Eddy La. *Shep* 7A **38**
Dock Rd. *Bren* 3K **11**
Dockwell Clo. *Felt* 7H **9**
Doctor Johnson Av. *SW17* 4F **28**
Doctors La. *Cat* 1L **103**
Dodbrooke Rd. *SE27* 4L **29**
Dodds Cres. *W Byf* 1K **75**
Dodd's La. *Wok* 1J **75**
(in two parts)
Dodds Pk. *Brock* 5A **120**
Doel Clo. *SW19* 8A **28**
Dogflud Way. *Farnh* 9H **109**
Doggetts Clo. *Eden* 3L **147**
Doghurst Av. *Hay* 3C **8**
Doghurst Dri. *W Dray* 3C **8**
Doghurst La. *Coul* 7D **82**
Dogkennel Green. 3L 117
Dogkennel Grn. *Ran C* 3L **117**
Dolby Rd. *SW6* 5L **13**
Dolby Ter. *Charl* 4K **161**
Dollary Pde. King T 2A 42
(off Kingston Rd.)
Dolleyshill Cvn. Pk. *Norm* 8K **91**
Dollis Clo. *M'bowr* 4G **182**
Dollis Dri. *Farnh* 9J **109**
Dolly's Hill. 2L 109
Dolman Rd. *W4* 1C **12**
Dolphin Clo. *Hasl* 2C **188**
Dolphin Clo. *Surb* 4K **41**
Dolphin Ct. *Brack* 3A **32**
Dolphin Ct. *Stai* 4J **21**
Dolphin Ct. N. *Stai* 4J **21**
Dolphin Est. *Sun* 9F **22**
Dolphin Ho. *SW18* 7N **13**
Dolphin Rd. *Sun* 9F **22**
Dolphin Rd. N. *Sun* 9F **22**
Dolphin Rd. S. *Sun* 9F **22**
Dolphin Rd. W. *Sun* 9F **22**
Dolphin Sq. *W4* 3D **12**
Dolphin St. *King T* . . . 1L **41** (3J **203**)
Doman Rd. *Camb* 2L **69**
Dome Hill. *Cat* 5B **104**
Dome Hill Peak. *Cat* 4B **104**
Dome, The. *Red* 2D **122**
Dome Way. *Red* 2D **122**
Domewood. 5D 164
Dominica Ter. Deep 6H 71
(off Cyprus Rd.)
Dominion Rd. *Croy* 6C **46**
Donald Rd. *Croy* 6K **45**
Donald Woods Gdns. *Surb* . . . 8A **42**
Doncaster Wlk. *Craw* 5E **182**
Doncastle Rd. *Brack* 2K **31**
Doneraile St. *SW6* 5J **13**
Donkey La. *Ab C* 3L **137**
Donkey La. *Horl* 3H **163**
Donkey La. *W Dray* 1L **7**
Donkey Town. 9A 52
Donlan Dri. *Farnb* 4H **89**
Donnafields. *Bisl* 3D **72**
Donne Clo. *Craw* 1F **182**
Donne Ct. *SE24* 1N **29**
Donne Gdns. *Wok* 2C **74**
Donnelly Ct. SW6 . . . . . 3K 13
(off Dawes Rd.)
Donne Pl. *Mitc* 3F **44**
Donnington Clo. *Camb* 2N **69**
Donnington Ct. *Craw* 6L **181**
Donnington Rd. *Wor Pk* 8F **42**
Donnybrook. *Brack* 6M **31**
Donnybrook Rd. *SW16* 8G **29**
Donovan Clo. *Eps* 6C **60**
Doods Pk. Rd. *Reig* 2A **122**
Doods Pl. *Reig* 2B **122**
Doods Rd. *Reig* 2A **122**
Doods Way. *Reig* 2B **122**
Doomsday Garden. *H'ham* 7N **197**
Doomsday Green. 8N 197
Doone Clo. *Tedd* 7G **24**
Doral Way. *Cars* 2D **62**
Doran Ct. *Red* 3B **122**
Doran Dri. *Red* 3B **122**
Doran Gdns. *Red* 3B **122**
Dora Rd. *SW19* 6M **27**
Dora's Green. 7B 108
Dora's Grn. La. *Ews & Dipp* 5C **108**
Dora's Grn. Rd. *Dipp* 1A **128**
Dorcas Ct. *Camb* 3N **69**
Dorchester Ct. *Reig* 2B **122**
Dorchester Ct. *Stai* 6J **21**
Dorchester Ct. *Wok* 3C **74**
Dorchester Dri. *Felt* 9F **8**
Dorchester Gro. *W4* 1D **12**
Dorchester M. *N Mald* 3C **42**
Dorchester M. *Twic* 9J **11**
Dorchester Rd. *Mord* 6N **43**
Dorchester Rd. *Wey* 9C **38**
Dorchester Rd. *Wor Pk* 7H **43**
Doreen Clo. *Farnb* 7K **69**
Dore Gdns. *Mord* 0N **40**
Dorian Dri. *Asc* 9B **18**
Doria Rd. *SW6* 5L **13**
Doric Dri. *Tad* 7L **81**
Dorien Rd. *SW20* 1J **43**
Dorin Ct. *Warl* 7E **84**
Dorincourt. *Wok* 2G **74**
Doris Rd. *Ashf* 7E **22**
Dorking. 4H 119 (2J 201)
Dorking Bus. Pk. *Dork* 4F **118** (1H **201**)
Dorking Clo. *Wor Pk* 8J **43**
Dorking Football Club 4G 119 (1J 201)
Dorking Halls 4H 119 (1L 201)
Dorking Mus. 5G 119 (2J 201)
Dorking Rd. *Bookh* 4B **98**
Dorking Rd. *Chil* 9G **114**
Dorking Rd. *Eps* 3N **79** (8H **201**)
Dorking Rd. *Gom & Ab H* 0E **116**
Dorking Rd. *Lea* 9H **79**
Dorking Rd. *Tad* 7D **100**
Dorking Rd. *Warn & K'fold* 8G **178**
Dorking Vs. *Knap* 1G **70**
Dorlcote. *Witl* 5B **152**
Dorlcote Rd. *SW18* 1C **28**
Dorling Dri. *Eps* 8E **60**
Dorly Clo. *Shep* 4F **38**
Dormans. *Craw* 4M **181**
Dormans Av. *D'land* 9C **146**
Dormans Clo. *D'land* 2C **166**
Dormans Gdns. *Dor P* 4A **166**
Dormans High St. *D'land* 2C **166**
Dormansland. 1C 166
Dormans Park. 4A 166
Dormans Pk. Rd. *Dor P* 3A **166**
Dormans Pk. Rd. *E Grin* 7N **165**
Dormans Rd. *D'land* 9C **146**
Dormans Sta. Rd. *D'land* 3B **166**
Dormay St. *SW18* 8N **13**
Dormer Clo. *Crowt* 2F **48**
Dormers Clo. *G'ming* 4G **133**
Dorncliffe Rd. *SW6* 5K **13**
Dorney Gro. *Wey* 8C **38**
Dorney Way. *Houn* 8M **9**
Dornford Gdns. *Coul* 6N **83**
Dornton Rd. *SW12* 3F **28**
Dornton Rd. *S Croy* 3A **64** (8F **200**)
Dorothy Pettingell Ho. Sutt . . . 9N 43
(off Angel Hill)
Dorrien Wlk. *SW16* 3H **29**
Dorrington Ct. *SE25* 1B **46**
Dorrit Cres. *Guild* 1H **113**
Dorset Av. *E Grin* 7M **165**
Dorset Ct. *Camb* 7D **50**
Dorset Ct. *Eps* 8E **60**
Dorset Dri. *Wok* 4D **74**
Dorset Gdns. *E Grin* 7M **165**
Dorset Gdns. *Mitc* 3K **45**
Dorset Rd. *Ashf* 4M **21**
Dorset Rd. *SW19* 9M **27**
Dorset Rd. *Ash V* 8F **90**
Dorset Rd. *Beck* 2G **46**
Dorset Rd. *Mitc* 1C **44**
Dorset Rd. *Sutt* 6M **61**
Dorset Rd. *Wind* 5F **4**
Dorset Sq. *Eps* 6C **60**
Dorset Vs. *Warf* 7C **16**
Dorset Way. *Byfl* 6M **55**
Dorset Way. *Twic* 2D **24**
Dorset Waye. *Houn* 3N **9**
Dorsten Pl. *Craw* 6K **181**
Dorsten Sq. *Craw* 6L **181**
Dorton Vs. *W Dray* 3B **8**
Dorton Way. *Rip* 8K **75**
Douai Clo. *Farnb* 1A **90**
Douai Gro. *Hamp* 9C **24**
Doughty Ho. SW10 . . . . . 2N 13
(off Netherton Gro.)
Douglas Av. *N Mald* 3G **42**
Douglas Clo. *Guild* 6N **93**
Douglas Clo. *Wall* 3J **63**
Douglas Ct. *Big H* 4G **86**
Douglas Ct. *Cat* 9N **83**
Douglas Ct. *King T* 7K **203**
Douglas Dri. *Croy* 9K **47**
Douglas Dri. *G'ming* 6J **133**
Douglas Gro. *Lwr Bo* 6H **129**
Douglas Ho. *Reig* 2M **121**
Douglas Ho. *Surb* 7M **41**
Douglas Houses. *Bookh* 2A **98**
Douglas Johnstone Ho. SW6 . . . . . 2L 13
(off Clem Attlee Ct.)
Douglas La. *Wray* 8B **6**
Douglas Mans. *Houn* 6B **10**
Douglas Pl. *Farnb* 9M **69**
Douglas Rd. *Add* 9K **37**
Douglas Rd. *Esh* 8B **40**
Douglas Rd. *Houn* 6B **10**
Douglas Rd. *King T* 1A **42**
Douglas Rd. *Reig* 2M **121**
Douglas Rd. *Stanw* 9M **7**
Douglas Rd. *Surb* 8M **41**
Douglas Robinson Ct. SW16 . . . . . 8J 29
(off Streatham High Rd.)
Douglas Sq. *Mord* 5M **43**
Doultons, The. *Stai* 8J **21**
Dounesforth Gdns. *SW18* 2N **27**
Dove Clo. *Craw* 1B **182**
Dove Clo. *S Croy* 7G **64**
Dove Clo. *Wall* 4K **63**
Dove Cote Clo. *Wey* 9C **38**
Dovecote Gdns. *SW14* 6C **12**
Dovedale Clo. *Guild* 9C **94**
Dovedale Clo. *Owl* 5J **49**
Dovedale Cres. *Craw* 5N **181**
Dovedale Ri. *Mitc* 8D **28**
Dovehouse Grn. *Wey* 9E **38**
Dove M. *SW5* 1N **13**
Dover Ct. *Cranl* 7B **156**
Dovercourt Av. *T Hth* 4L **45**
Dovercourt La. *Sutt* 9A **44**
Doverfield Rd. *SW2* 1J **29**
Doverfield Rd. *Guild* 9C **94**
Dover Gdns. *Cars* 9D **44**
Dover Ho. Rd. *SW15* 7F **12**
Dover Pk. Dri. *SW15* 9G **12**
Doversgreen. 7N 121
Dovers Grn. Rd. *Reig* 6N **121**
Doversmead. *Knap* 3H **73**
Dover Ter. Rich 5M 11
(off Sandycombe Rd.)
Doveton Rd. *S Croy* 2A **64**
Dowdeswell Clo. *SW15* 7D **12**
Dowding Ct. *Crowt* 1H **49**
Dowding Rd. *Big H* 2F **86**

Dower Av.—Eardley Cres.

Dower Av. Wall 5F 62
Dower Pk. Wind 7B 4
Dower Wlk. Craw 4M 181
Dowes Ho. SW16 4J 29
Dowlands La. Small & Copt 8A 144
Dowlans Clo. Bookh 5A 98
Dowlans Rd. Bookh 5B 98
Dowler Ct. King T 1K 203
Dowlesgreen 1D 30
Dowman Clo. SW19 9N 27
Downbury M. SW18 8M 13
Downe 7J 67
Downe Av. Cud 8M 67
Downe Clo. Horl 6C 142
Downer Mdw. G'ming 3H 133
Downe Rd. Cud 9L 67
Downe Rd. Kes 5G 66
Downe Rd. Mitc 1D 44
Downes Clo. Twic 9H 11
Downes Ho. Croy 7A 200
Downe Ter. Rich 9L 11
Downfield. Wor Pk 7E 42
Down Hall Rd. King T 9K 25 (2H 203)
Down House Mus. 8J 67
Downhurst Rd. Ewh 4F 156
Downing Av. Guild 4J 113
Downing St. Farnh 1G 129
Downland Clo. Eps 5G 81
Downland Ct. Craw 5A 182
Downland Dri. Craw 5A 182
Downland Gdns. Eps 5G 81
Downland Pl. Craw 5A 182
Downlands Clo. Coul 1F 82
Downlands Rd. Purl 9J 63
Downland Way. Eps 5G 81
Down La. Comp 9E 112
Downmill Rd. Brack 1L 31
Down Park 9D 164
Down Pl. W6 1G 13
Down Rd. Guild 3D 114
Down Rd. Tedd 7H 25
Downs Av. Eps 1D 80
Downsbridge Rd. Beck 1N 47
Downs Ct. Red 9E 102
Downscourt Rd. Purl 8M 63
Downs Hill Rd. Eps 1D 80
Downshire Way. Brack 1M 31 (in two parts)
Downs Ho. Rd. Eps 5D 80
Downside 5J 77
Downside. Brack 2N 31
Downside. Cher 7H 37
Downside. Eps 1D 80 (8L 201)
Downside. Hind 2B 170
Downside. Sun 9H 23
Downside. Twic 4F 24
Downside Bri. Rd. Cob 1J 77
Downside Clo. SW19 7A 28
Downside Comn. Rd. D'side 5J 77
Downside Ct. Mers 7G 102
Downside Ind. Est. Cher 7H 37
Downside Orchard. Wok 4C 74
Downside Rd. D'side 3J 77
Downside Rd. Guild 4D 114
Downside Rd. Sutt 3B 62
Downside Wlk. Bren 2K 11 (off Windmill Rd.)
Downs La. Lea 1H 99
Downs Link. Brmly 3B 134
Downs Link. Brmly & Sham G 6C 134
Downs Link. Chil 8F 114
Downs Link. Cranl 4H 155
Downs Link. Rud 6B 176
Downs Link. Shalf 2A 134
Downs Link. Slin 8D 176
Downs Link. Won & Chil 2D 134
Downs Lodge Ct. Eps 1D 80 (8M 201)
Downsman Ct. Craw 6B 182
Downs Residential Site, The. Cat 5E 104
Downs Rd. Beck 1L 47 (in two parts)
Downs Rd. Coul 5G 83
Downs Rd. Eps 1D 80 (8M 201) (Epsom)
Downs Rd. Eps 7A 80 (Langley Bottom)
Downs Rd. Mick 6J 99
Downs Rd. Purl 7M 63
Downs Rd. Sutt 6N 61
Downs Rd. T Hth 9N 29
Downs Side. Sutt 7L 61
Downs, The. SW20 8J 27
Downs, The. Lea 3H 99
Down St. W Mol 4A 40
Downs Vw. Dork 3K 119
Downs Vw. Iswth 4F 10
Downs Vw. Tad 8G 80
Downsview Av. Wok 8B 74
Downsview Clo. D'side 6J 77
Downsview Ct. Guild 8M 93
Downsview Gdns. SE19 8M 29
Downsview Gdns. Dork 6H 119
Downsview Rd. Hdly D 4H 169
Downsview Rd. SE19 8N 29
Downs Vw. Rd. Bookh 5C 98
Downsview Rd. H'ham 2A 198
Downs Way. Bookh 4C 98
Downs Way. Eps 3E 80
Downsway. Guild 3G 114
Downsway. Orp 2N 67
Downs Way. Oxt 5A 106
Downsway. S Croy 7B 64
Downs Way. Tad 8G 80
Downsway. Whyt 3C 84
Downs Way Clo. Tad 8F 80
Downsway, The. Sutt 5A 62
Downs Wood. Eps 4G 80
Downswood. Reig 9B 102
Downton Av. SW2 3J 29
Downview Clo. Hind 3B 170
Down Yhonda. Elst 8G 131
Doyle Gdns. Yat 2B 68
Doyle Ho. SW13 3H 13 (off Trinity Chu. Rd.)
Doyle Rd. SE25 3D 46
D'Oyly Carte Island. Wey 7C 38
Draco Ga. SW15 6H 13
Dragon La. Wey 7B 56
Dragoon Ct. Alder 2K 109
Drake Av. Cat 9N 83
Drake Av. Myt 4E 90
Drake Av. Slou 1N 5
Drake Av. Stai 6H 21
Drake Clo. Brack 4N 31
Drake Clo. H'ham 2L 197
Drake Ct. Surb 8K 203
Drakefield Rd. SW17 4E 28
Drake Rd. Chess 2N 59
Drake Rd. Craw 6C 182
Drake Rd. Croy 6K 45
Drake Rd. Horl 8C 142
Drake Rd. Mitc 5E 44
Drakes Clo. Cranl 7N 155
Drake's Clo. Esh 1A 58
Drakes Way. Wok 9N 73
Drakewood Rd. SW16 8H 29
Draper Clo. Iswth 5D 10
Drax Av. SW20 8F 26
Draxmont. SW19 7K 27
Draxmont. SW19 7K 27
Draycot Rd. Surb 7N 41
Draycott. Brack 4C 32
Dray Ct. Guild 4L 113
Dray Ct. Wor Pk 7E 42
Drayhorse Dri. Bag 5J 51
Draymans Way. Iswth 6F 10
Drayton Clo. Brack 1B 32
Drayton Clo. Fet 2E 98
Drayton Clo. Houn 8N 9
Drayton Gdns. SW10 1N 13
Drayton Rd. Croy 8M 45 (2A 200)
Dresden Way. Wey 2D 56
Drew Ho. SW16 4J 29
Drewitts Ct. W on T 7G 39
Drew Pl. Cat 1A 104
Drewstead Rd. SW16 3H 29
Drift Bridge. (Junct.) 1H 81
Drifters Dri. Deep 5H 71
Drift La. Stoke D 3N 77
Drift Rd. E Hor 2E 96
Drift Rd. M'head & Wink 1L 17
Drift Rd. Wink 1L 17
Drift, The. Brom 1F 66
Drift Way. Coln 4E 6
Driftway, The. Bans 2H 81
Driftway, The. Craw 2B 182
Driftway, The. Lea 1H 99 (in two parts)
Driftway, The. Mitc 9E 28
Driftwood Dri. Kenl 4M 83
Drill Hall Rd. Cher 6J 37
Drive Mans. SW6 5K 13 (off Fulham Rd.)
Drive Mead. Coul 1J 83
Drive Rd. Coul 7H 83
Drivers Mead. Ling 8M 145
Drive Spur. Tad 8N 81
Drive, The. Ashf 8E 22
Drive, The. Cob 1M 77
Drive, The. SW6 5K 13
Drive, The. SW16 2K 45
Drive, The. SW20 8H 27
Drive, The. Bans 4K 81
Drive, The. Beck 1K 47
Drive, The. Copt 7N 163
Drive, The. Coul 1J 83
Drive, The. Cranl 8N 155
Drive, The. Dat 4L 5
Drive, The. Eps 3E 60
Drive, The. Esh 7C 40
Drive, The. Felt 1K 23
Drive, The. Fet 9E 78
Drive, The. G'ming 9H 133
Drive, The. Guild 3J 113 (Beech Gro.)
Drive, The. Guild 5J 113 (Farnham Rd.)
Drive, The. Guild 7L 113 (Sandy La.)
Drive, The. Horl 9F 142
Drive, The. Houn & Isw th 5D 10
Drive, The. King T 8B 26
Drive, The. Lea 1L 99
Drive, The. Loxw 5F 192
Drive, The. Mord 4A 44
Drive, The. Pep H 7B 132 (in two parts)
Drive, The. Rusp 2D 180
Drive, The. Surb 6L 41
Drive, The. Sutt 8L 61
Drive, The. T Hth 3A 46
Drive, The. Vir W 4B 36
Drive, The. Wall 6G 62
Drive, The. W Wick 6N 47
Drive, The. Wok 7L 73
Drive, The. Won 5D 134
Drive, The. Wray 8N 5
Drodges Clo. Brmly 3B 134
Droitwich Clo. Brack 2B 32
Dromore Rd. SW15 9K 13
Drove Rd. Alb 5N 115
Drove Rd. Guild 5H 115 (in two parts)
Drove Rd. W Hor & Ran C 4C 116
Drovers Ct. King T 3K 203
Drovers End. Fleet 1D 88
Drovers Rd. S Croy 2A 64 (8D 200)
Drovers Way. Ash G 3G 111 (in two parts)
Drovers Way. Brack 2D 32
Drovers Way. Farnh 6F 108
Druce Wood. Asc 9J 17
Druids Clo. Asht 7M 79
Druids Way. Brom 3N 47
Drumaline Ridge. Wor Pk 8D 42
Drummond Cen., The. Croy 8N 45 (3B 200)
Drummond Clo. Brack 9D 16
Drummond Gdns. Eps 7B 60
Drummond Pl. Twic 1H 25
Drummond Rd. Croy 8N 45 (3B 200) (in two parts)
Drummond Rd. Guild 3N 113 (3C 202)
Drummond Rd. If'd 4K 181
Drungewick La. Loxw 9L 193
Drury Clo. M'bowr 5H 183
Drury Cres. Croy 8L 45
Dryad St. SW15 6J 13
Dry Arch Rd. Asc 5C 34
Dryburgh Rd. SW15 6G 13
Dryden. Brack 6M 31
Dryden Mans. W14 2K 13 (off Queen's Club Gdns.)
Dryden Rd. Farnb 8L 69
Dryden Rd. SW19 7A 28
Drynham Pk. Wey 9F 38
Du Cane Ct. SW17 2E 28
Ducavel Ho. SW2 2K 29
Duchess Clo. Crowt 9G 30
Duchess Clo. Sutt 1A 62
Ducklands. Bord 7A 168
Ducks Wlk. Twic 8J 11
Dudley. Brack 6B 32
Dudley Clo. Add 9L 37
Dudley Ct. C Crook 7B 88
Dudley Dri. Mord 7K 43
Dudley Gro. Eps 1B 80 (8G 201)
Dudley Rd. Ashf 6A 22
Dudley Rd. SW19 7M 27
Dudley Rd. Felt 2D 22
Dudley Rd. King T 2M 41 (5L 203)
Dudley Rd. Rich 5M 11
Dudley Rd. W on T 5H 39
Dudset La. Houn 4H 9
Duffield Rd. Tad 2G 100
Duffins Orchard. Ott 4E 54
Dugdale Ho. Egh 6E 20 (off Pooley Grn. Rd.)
Duke Clo. M'bowr 7G 182
Duke of Cambridge Clo. Twic 9D 10
Duke of Cornwall Av. Camb 6B 50
Duke of Edinburgh Rd. Sutt 8B 44
Duke Rd. W4 1C 12
Duke's Av. W4 1C 12
Dukes Av. Houn 7M 9
Dukes Av. N Mald 2D 42
Dukes Av. Rich 5J 25
Dukes Clo. Ashf 5D 22
Dukes Clo. Cranl 8B 156
Dukes Clo. Farnh 6F 108
Dukes Clo. Hamp 6N 23
Dukes Ct. Wok 4B 74
Dukes Covert. Bag 1J 51
Duke's Dri. G'ming 4E 132
Dukes Ga. W4 1B 12
Dukes Grn. Av. Felt 8H 9
Dukes Head Pas. Hamp 8C 24
Dukes Hill. Wold 7H 85 (in two parts)
Dukeshill Rd. Brack 9N 15
Dukes La. Asc & Wind 8D 18
Dukes Pk. Alder 7B 90
Duke's Ride. Crowt 3D 48
Dukes Ride. N Holm 8K 119
Duke's Rd. Newd 4A 160 (in two parts)
Dukes Rd. W on T 2L 57
Dukes Ter. Alder 1N 109
Duke St. Rich 7K 11
Duke St. Sutt 1B 62
Duke St. Wind 3F 4
Duke St. Wok 4B 74
Dukes Wlk. Farnh 6F 108
Duke's Warren, The. 6C 138
Dukes Way. W Wick 9N 47
Dukes Wood. Crowt 2G 49 (in two parts)
Dulverton Rd. S Croy 6F 64
Dumas Clo. Yat 1B 68
Du Maurier Clo. C Crook 1A 108
Dumbarton Ct. SW2 1J 29
Dumbarton Rd. SW2 1J 29
Dumbleton Clo. King T 9A 26
Dumsey Eyot. Cher 6N 37
Dumville Dri. God 9E 104
Dunally Pk. Shep 6E 38
Dunbar Av. SW16 1L 45
Dunbar Av. Beck 3H 47
Dunbar Ct. Sutt 2B 62
Dunbar Ct. W on T 7K 39
Dunbar Rd. Frim 7D 70
Dunbar Rd. N Mald 3B 42
Dunbar St. SE27 4N 29
Dunboe Pl. Shep 6D 38
Dunbridge Ho. SW15 9E 12 (off Highcliffe Dri.)
Duncan Dri. Guild 2C 114
Duncan Dri. Wokgm 3C 30
Duncan Gdns. Stai 7J 21
Duncannon Cres. Wind 6A 4
Duncan Rd. Rich 7L 11
Duncan Rd. Tad 6K 81
Duncans Yd. W'ham 4M 107
Duncombe Rd. G'ming 9G 133
Duncroft. Stai 5G 20
Duncroft. Wind 6C 4
Duncroft Clo. Reig 3L 121
Duncton Clo. Craw 1N 181
Dundaff Clo. Camb 1E 70
Dundas Clo. Brack 3N 31
Dundas Gdns. W Mol 2B 40
Dundee Rd. SE25 4E 46
Dundela Gdns. Wor Pk 1G 61
Dundonald Rd. SW19 8K 27 (in two parts)
Dundrey Cres. Red 7J 103
Dunedin Dri. Cat 3B 104
Dunelm Gro. SE27 4N 29
Dunfee Way. W Byf 8N 55
Dunford Pl. Binf 8K 15
Dungarvan Av. SW15 7F 12
Dungates La. Buck 2F 120
Dungells Farm Clo. Yat 2C 68
Dungells La. Yat 2B 68
Dunheved Clo. T Hth 5L 45
Dunheved Rd. N. T Hth 5L 45
Dunheved Rd. S. T Hth 5L 45
Dunheved Rd. W. T Hth 5L 45
Dunkeld Rd. SE25 3A 46
Dunkirk St. SE27 5N 29
Dunleary Clo. Houn 1N 23
Dunley Dri. New Ad 4L 65
Dunlin Clo. Red 8C 122
Dunlin Ri. Guild 1F 114
Dunmall Dri. Purl 1B 84
Dunmore. Guild 2G 113
Dunmore Rd. SW20 9H 27
Dunmow Clo. Felt 4M 23
Dunmow Hill. Fleet 3B 88
Dunmow Ho. Byfl 9N 55
Dunnets. Knap 4H 73
Dunning's Rd. E Grin 3A 186
Dunnymans Rd. Bans 2L 81
Dunottar Clo. Red 5B 122
Dunraven Av. Red 1F 142
Dunsborough Park. 7L 75
Dunsbury Clo. Sutt 5N 61
Dunsdon Av. Guild 4L 113
Dunsfold. 4B 174
Dunsfold Aerodrome. 4F 174
Dunsfold Clo. Craw 4M 181
Dunsfold Comn. Duns 5B 174
Dunsfold Ri. Coul 9H 63
Dunsfold Rd. Alf 5E 174
Dunsfold Rd. Loxh & Cranl 1C 174
Dunsfold Rd. Plais 2N 191
Dunsfold Way. New Ad 5L 65
Dunsford Way. SW15 9G 13
Dunsmore Gdns. Yat 1A 68
Dunsmore Rd. W on T 5J 39
Dunstable Rd. Rich 7L 11
Dunstable Rd. W Mol 3N 39
Dunstall Pk. Farnb 7M 69
Dunstall Rd. SW20 7G 27
Dunstall Way. W Mol 2B 40
Dunstan Rd. Coul 4H 83
Dunster Av. Mord 7J 43
Dunton Clo. Surb 7L 41
Duntshill Rd. SW18 2N 27
Dunvegan Clo. W Mol 3B 40
Dunvegan Ho. Red 3D 122
Dupont Rd. SW20 1J 43
Duppas Av. Croy 1M 63 (7A 200)
Duppas Clo. Shep 4E 38
Duppas Ct. Croy 5A 200
Duppas Hill La. Croy 1M 63 (6A 200)
Duppas Hill Rd. Croy 1L 63 (6A 200)
Duppas Hill Ter. Croy 9M 45 (5A 200)
Duppas Rd. Croy 9L 45
Durand Clo. Cars 7D 44
Durban Rd. SE27 5N 29
Durban Rd. Beck 1J 47
Durbin Rd. Chess 1L 59
Durfold Dri. Reig 3A 122
Durfold Hill. Warn 6H 179
Durfold Rd. H'ham 1K 197
Durfold Wood. Plais 2M 191
Durford Cres. SW15 2G 26
Durham Av. Houn 1N 9
Durham Clo. SW20 1G 43
Durham Clo. Craw 7C 182 (in two parts)
Durham Clo. Guild 1J 113
Durham Ct. Tedd 5E 24
Durham Dri. Deep 5H 71
Durham Rd. SW20 9G 27
Durham Rd. Felt 1K 23
Durham Rd. Owl 5K 49
Durham Wharf. Bren 3J 11
Durkins Rd. E Grin 7N 165 (in two parts)
Durleston Pk. Dri. Bookh 3C 98
Durley Mead. Brack 4D 32
Durlston Rd. King T 7L 25
Durning Pl. Asc 2M 33
Durning Rd. SE19 6N 29
Durnsford Av. SW19 3M 27
Durnsford Av. Fleet 6B 88
Durnsford Rd. SW19 3M 27
Durnsford Way. Cranl 8A 156
Durrant Way. Orp 2M 67
Durrell Rd. SW6 4L 13
Durrell Way. Shep 5E 38
Durrington Av. SW20 8H 27
Durrington Pk. Rd. SW20 9H 27
Dutch Barn Clo. Stanw 9M 7
Dutchells Copse. H'ham 2L 197
Dutch Elm Av. Wind 3J 5
Dutch Gdns. King T 7A 26
Dutch Yd. SW18 8M 13
Duval Pl. Bag 4J 51
Duxberry Av. Felt 4K 23
Duxhurst La. Reig 5N 141
Dwelly La. Eden 6D 126
Dye Ho. Rd. Thur 6F 150
Dyer Ho. Hamp 9B 24
Dyer Rd. Wokgm 1D 30
Dyers Almhouses. Craw 2B 182
Dyers Fld. Small 8M 143
Dyers La. SW15 7G 13
Dykes Path. Wok 2E 74
Dymchurch Clo. Orp 1N 67
Dymes Path. SW19 3J 27
Dymock St. SW6 6N 13
Dynevor Pl. Guild 8F 92
Dynevor Rd. Rich 8L 11
Dysart Av. King T 6J 25
Dyson Clo. Wind 6E 4
Dyson Ct. Dork 5G 119 (3J 201)
Dyson Wlk. Craw 8N 181

E

Eady Clo. H'ham 6M 197
Eagle Clo. Crowt 9F 30
Eagle Clo. Wall 3J 63
Eagle Hill. SE19 7N 29
Eaglehurst Cotts. Binf 6H 15
Eagle Rd. Guild 3N 113 (3D 202)
Eagles Dri. Tats 5F 86 (in two parts)
Eagles Nest. Sand 6F 48
Eagle Trad. Est. Mitc 5D 44
Ealing Pk. Gdns. W5 1J 11
Ealing Rd. Bren 1K 11
Ealing Rd. Trad. Est. Bren 1K 11
Eardley Cres. SW5 1M 13

Eardley Rd.—Ellen's Green

Eardley Rd. *SW16* . . . 6G **29**
Earldom Rd. *SW15* . . . 7H **13**
Earle Cft. *Warf* . . . 8A **16**
Earle Gdns. *King T* . . . 8L **25**
Earles Mdw. *H'ham* . . . 2A **198**
Earleswood. *Cob* . . . 8M **57**
Earleydene. *Asc* . . . 7M **33**
Earl of Chester Dri. *Deep* . . . 6H **71**
Earl Rd. *SW14* . . . 7B **12**
Earlsbourne. *C Crook* . . . 9C **88**
Earlsbrook Rd. *Red* . . . 5D **122**
Earl's Court. . . . **1M 13**
Earl's Court Exhibition Building. . . . **1M 13**
Earls Ct. Gdns. *SW5* . . . 1N **13**
Earls Ct. Rd. *W8 & SW5* . . . 1M **13**
Earl's Ct. Sq. *SW5* . . . 1N **13**
Earlsfield. . . . **2A 28**
Earlsfield Rd. *SW18* . . . 2A **28**
Earls Gro. *Camb* . . . 9C **50**
Earlsthorpe M. *SW12* . . . 1E **28**
Earlswood. . . . **5D 122**
Earlswood. *Brack* . . . 6N **31**
Earlswood Av. *T Hth* . . . 4L **45**
Earlswood Clo. *H'ham* . . . 4M **197**
Earlswood Ct. *Red* . . . 5D **122**
Earlswood Rd. *Red* . . . 4D **122**
Early Commons. *Craw* . . . 2D **182**
(in two parts)
Easby Cres. *Mord* . . . 5N **43**
Eashing. . . . **7C 132**
Eashing Bridge. . . . **8B 132**
Eashing La. *Milf & G'ming* . . . 9C **132**
Easington Pl. *Guild* . . . 4B **114**
East Av. *Farnh* . . . 6J **109**
East Av. *Wall* . . . 2K **63**
East Av. *W Vill* . . . 6G **56**
Eastbank Rd. *Hamp H* . . . 6C **24**
East Bedfont. . . . **1F 22**
Eastbourne Gdns. *SW14* . . . 6B **12**
Eastbourne Rd. *SW17* . . . 7E **28**
Eastbourne Rd. *W4* . . . 2B **12**
Eastbourne Rd. *Bren* . . . 1J **11**
Eastbourne Rd. *Felb* . . . 4J **165**
Eastbourne Rd. *Felt* . . . 3L **23**
Eastbourne Rd. *God* . . . 1F **124**
Eastbourne Rd. *Newc & Ling* . . . 9H **145**
Eastbourne Rd. *S God & Blind H* . . . 9G **125**
Eastbrook Clo. *Wok* . . . 3C **74**
Eastbury Ct. *Brack* . . . 8L **15**
Eastbury Gro. *W4* . . . 1D **12**
Eastbury La. *Comp* . . . 9D **112**
Eastbury Rd. *King T* . . . 8L **25** (1J **203**)
Eastchurch Rd. *H'row A* . . . 5F **8**
East Clandon. . . . **9M 95**
Eastcote Av. *W Mol* . . . 4N **39**
Eastcote Ho. *Eps* . . . 8D **60**
East Ct. *E Grin* . . . 8B **166**
East Cres. *Wind* . . . 4C **4**
Eastcroft Ct. *Guild* . . . 4C **114**
Eastcroft M. *H'ham* . . . 7F **196**
Eastcroft Rd. *Eps* . . . 4D **60**
Eastdean Av. *Eps* . . . 9A **60**
East Dri. *Cars* . . . 5C **62**
East Dri. *Vir W* . . . 6K **35**
Eastern Av. *Cher* . . . 2J **37**
Eastern Industrial Area, Bracknell . . . **1B 32**
Eastern La. *Crowt* . . . 2K **49**
Eastern Perimeter Rd. *H'row A* . . . 5G **8**
Eastern Rd. *Alder* . . . 2B **110**
Eastern Rd. *Brack* . . . 1B **32**
Eastern Vw. *Big H* . . . 4E **86**
Easter Way. *S God* . . . 6H **125**
East Ewell. . . . **6H 61**
Eastfield Rd. *Red* . . . 4G **122**
Eastfields. *Witl* . . . 5C **152**
Eastfields Rd. *Mitc* . . . 1E **44**
E. Flexford La. *Wanb* . . . 5C **112**
East Gdns. *SW17* . . . 7C **28**
East Gdns. *Wok* . . . 4E **74**
Eastgate. *Bans* . . . 1L **81**
Eastgate Gdns. *Guild* . . . 4A **114** (4C **202**)
East Grn. *B'water* . . . 2H **69**
East Grinstead. . . . **1B 186**
E. Grinstead Rd. *Ling* . . . 8N **145**
East Grinstead Town Mus. . . . **8B 166**
Easthampstead. . . . **4N 31**
Easthampstead Mobile Home Pk. *Wokgm* . . . 8H **31**
Easthampstead Pk. Crematorium. *Wokgm* . . . 6J **31**
Easthampstead Rd. *Brack* . . . 1M **31**
Easthampstead Rd. *Wokgm* . . . 3C **30**
Eastheath. . . . **5A 30**
Eastheath Av. *Wokgm* . . . 4A **30**
Eastheath Gdns. *Wokgm* . . . 5A **30**
East Hill. *SW18* . . . 8N **13**
East Hill. *Big H* . . . 5D **86**
East Hill. *Dor P* . . . 4A **166**
East Hill. *Oxt* . . . 7A **106**
East Hill. *S Croy* . . . 6B **64**
East Hill. *Wok* . . . 3E **74**
E. Hill Ct. *Oxt* . . . 8A **106**
E. Hill La. *Copt* . . . 4A **164**
E. Hill Rd. *Oxt* . . . 7A **106**
East Horsley. . . . **7G 98**
Eastlands Clo. *Oxt* . . . 5N **105**
Eastlands Way. *Oxt* . . . 5N **105**
East La. *King T* . . . 2K **41** (5H **203**)
East La. *W Hor* . . . 4D **96**
Eastleigh Clo. *Sutt* . . . 4N **61**
Eastleigh Rd. *H'row A* . . . 6G **8**
Eastleigh Wlk. *SW15* . . . 1F **26**
Eastleigh Way. *Felt* . . . 2H **23**
Eastly End. . . . **2F 36**
East Mall. Stai . . . *5H **21***
(off Elmsleigh Shop. Cen.)
Eastman Ho. *SW4* . . . 1G **29**
Eastmead. *Farnb* . . . 1N **89**
Eastmead. *Wok* . . . 4L **73**
East Meads. *Guild* . . . 4J **113**
Eastmearn Rd. *SE27* . . . 3N **29**
East M. *H'ham* . . . 6J **197**
East Molesey. . . . **3D 40**
Eastmont Rd. *Esh* . . . 8E **40**
Eastney Rd. *Croy* . . . 7M **45** (1A **200**)
Eastnor Clo. *Reig* . . . 5L **121**
Eastnor Pl. *Reig* . . . 5M **121**
Eastnor Rd. *Reig* . . . 6M **121**
East Pk. *Craw* . . . 4B **182**
E. Park La. *Newc* . . . 2F **164**
East Pl. *SE27* . . . 5N **29**
East Ramp. *H'row A* . . . 4C **8**
East Ring. *Tong* . . . 5E **110**
East Rd. *SW19* . . . 7A **28**
East Rd. *Felt* . . . 1E **22**
East Rd. *King T* . . . 9L **25** (1K **203**)
East Rd. *Reig* . . . 2L **121**
East Rd. *Wey* . . . 4E **56**
East Shalford. . . . **9C 114**
E. Shalford La. *Guild* . . . 8A **114**
East Sheen. . . . **7B 12**
E. Sheen Av. *SW14* . . . 8C **12**
East Sta. Rd. *Alder* . . . 3N **109**
E. Stratton Clo. *Brack* . . . 4D **32**
East St. *Bookh* . . . 3B **98**
East St. *Bren* . . . 3J **11**
East St. *Eps* . . . 9D **60** (6L **201**)
East St. *Farnh* . . . 9H **109**
East St. *H'ham* . . . 7J **197**
East St. *Rusp* . . . 2C **180**
East St. *Turn H* . . . 5D **184**
East Surrey Mus. . . . **2C 104**
E. View Cotts. *Cranl* . . . 7L **155**
E. View La. *Cranl* . . . 7L **155**
East Wlk. *Reig* . . . 3N **121**
East Way. *Croy* . . . 8H **47**
Eastway. *Eps* . . . 7C **60**
Eastway. *Guild* . . . 3J **113**
Eastway. *Gat A* . . . 3F **162**
Eastway. *Mord* . . . 4J **43**
Eastway. *Wall* . . . 1G **62**
E. W. Link Rd. *King T* . . . 9K **25** (1H **203**)
E. Whipley La. *Sham G* . . . 3H **155**
Eastwick Dri. *Bookh* . . . 1A **98**
Eastwick Pk. Av. *Bookh* . . . 2B **98**
Eastwick Rd. *Bookh* . . . 3B **98**
Eastwick Rd. *W on T* . . . 3J **57**
Eastwood. *Craw* . . . 3D **182**
Eastwood Lodge. *Brmly* . . . 4B **134**
Eastwood Rd. *Brmly* . . . 4B **134**
Eastwood St. *SW16* . . . 7G **28**
Eastworth. . . . **7K 37**
Eastworth Rd. *Cher* . . . 7J **37**
Eaton Ct. *Guild* . . . 1C **114**
Eaton Dri. *King T* . . . 8N **25**
Eaton Ho. Guild . . . *5B **114***
(off St Lukes Sq.)
Eaton Pk. *Cob* . . . 1M **77**
Eaton Pk. Rd. *Cob* . . . 1M **77**
Eaton Rd. *Camb* . . . 2N **69**
Eaton Rd. *Houn* . . . 7D **10**
Eaton Rd. *Sutt* . . . 3A **62**
Eatonville Rd. *SW17* . . . 3D **28**
Eatonville Vs. *SW17* . . . 3D **28**
Ebbage Ct. *Wok* . . . 5A **74**
Ebbas Way. *Eps* . . . 2A **80**
Ebbisham Cen. *Eps* . . . 9C **60**
Ebbisham Clo. *Dork* . . . 5G **118** (3H **201**)
Ebbisham La. *Tad* . . . 8E **80**
(in two parts)
Ebbisham Rd. *Eps* . . . 1A **80**
Ebbisham Rd. *Wor Pk* . . . 8H **43**
Ebenezer Wlk. *SW16* . . . 9G **28**
Ebner St. *SW18* . . . 8N **13**
Ebor Cotts. *SW15* . . . 4D **26**
Ebury Clo. *Kes* . . . 1G **67**
Ebury M. *SE27* . . . 4M **29**
Ecclesbourne Rd. *T Hth* . . . 4N **45**
Eccleshill. *N Holm* . . . 9J **119**
Echelforde Dri. *Ashf* . . . 5B **22**
Echo Barn La. *Wrec* . . . 6D **128**
Echo Pit Rd. *Guild* . . . 7A **114** (8F **202**)
Ecob Clo. *Guild* . . . 8J **93**
Ecton Rd. *Add* . . . 1K **55**
Eddeys Clo. *Hdly D* . . . 3G **169**
Eddeys La. *Hdly D* . . . 3G **168**
Eddington Hill. *Craw* . . . 8N **181**
Eddington Rd. *Brack* . . . 5K **31**
Eddiscombe Rd. *SW6* . . . 5L **13**
Eddy Rd. *Alder* . . . 3A **110**
Eddystone. *Cars* . . . 7B **62**
Eddystone Ct. *Churt* . . . 9L **149**
Eddystone Wlk. *Stai* . . . 1N **21**
Ede Clo. *Houn* . . . 6N **9**
Edenbridge. . . . **2L 147**
Edenbridge Trad. Cen. *Eden* . . . 3M **147**
Eden Brook. *Ling* . . . 7A **146**
Eden Clo. *New H* . . . 6K **55**
Eden Clo. *Slou* . . . 1C **6**
Edencourt Rd. *SW16* . . . 7F **28**
Edencroft. *Brmly* . . . 4B **134**
Edenfield Gdns. *Wor Pk* . . . 9E **42**
Eden Gro. Rd. *Byfl* . . . 9N **55**
Edenhurst Av. *SW6* . . . 6L **13**
Eden M. *SW17* . . . 4A **28**
Eden Park. . . . **4K 47**
Eden Pk. Av. *Beck* . . . 3H **47**
(in two parts)
Eden Rd. *SE27* . . . 5M **29**
Eden Rd. *Beck* . . . 3H **47**
Eden Rd. *Craw* . . . 5L **181**
Eden Rd. *Croy* . . . 1A **64** (6D **200**)
Edenside Rd. *Bookh* . . . 2N **97**
Edensor Gdns. *W4* . . . 3D **12**
Edensor Rd. *W4* . . . 3D **12**
Eden St. *King T* . . . 1K **41** (4H **203**)
Eden Va. *E Grin* . . . 7N **165**
(in two parts)
Edenvale Clo. *Mitc* . . . 8E **28**
Edenvale Rd. *Mitc* . . . 8E **28**
Edenvale St. *SW6* . . . 5N **13**
Eden Wlk. *King T* . . . 1L **41** (4J **203**)
Eden Way. *Beck* . . . 4J **47**
Eden Way. *Warl* . . . 5H **85**
Ederline Av. *SW16* . . . 2K **45**
Edes Fld. *Reig* . . . 5K **121**
Edgar Clo. *Worth* . . . 3J **183**
Edgar Ct. *N Mald* . . . 1D **42**
Edgarley Ter. *SW6* . . . 4K **13**
Edgar Rd. *Houn* . . . 1N **23**
Edgar Rd. *S Croy* . . . 5A **64**
Edgar Rd. *Tats* . . . 8F **86**
Edgbarrow Ct. *Crowt* . . . 4F **48**
Edgbarrow Ri. *Sand* . . . 5F **48**
Edgbarrow Woods Nature Reserve. . . . **5G 49**
Edgcumbe Pk. Dri. *Crowt* . . . 2F **48**
Edgeborough Ct. *Guild* . . . 4B **114**
Edge Clo. *Wey* . . . 4B **56**
Edgecoombe. *S Croy* . . . 4F **64**
Edgecoombe Clo. *King T* . . . 8C **26**
Edgedale Clo. *Crowt* . . . 3G **49**
Edgefield Clo. *Cranl* . . . 6L **155**
Edgefield Clo. *Red* . . . 8F **122**
Edge Hill. *SW19* . . . 8J **27**
Edge Hill. *Guild* . . . 4B **114**
Edge Hill Ct. *SW19* . . . 8J **27**
Edgehill Ct. *W on T* . . . 7K **39**
Edgehill Rd. *Mitc* . . . 9F **28**
Edgehill Rd. *Purl* . . . 6L **63**
Edgeley. *Bookh* . . . 2M **97**
Edgeley Cvn. Pk. *Alb* . . . 3N **135**
Edgell Clo. *Vir W* . . . 2B **36**
Edgell Rd. *Stai* . . . 6H **21**
Edgel St. *SW18* . . . 7N **13**
Edgemoor Rd. *Frim* . . . 3G **70**
Edgepoint Clo. *SE27* . . . 6M **29**
Edgewood Clo. *Crowt* . . . 9F **30**
Edgewood Grn. *Croy* . . . 7G **47**
Edgeworth Clo. *Whyt* . . . 5D **84**
Edgington Rd. *SW16* . . . 7H **29**
Edinburgh Clo. *Ash V* . . . 8E **90**
Edinburgh Ct. *SW20* . . . 4J **43**
Edinburgh Ct. Alder . . . *2L **109***
(off Queen Elizabeth Dri.)
Edinburgh Ct. *King T* . . . 5J **203**
Edinburgh Dri. *Stai* . . . 7M **21**
Edinburgh Gdns. *Wind* . . . 5G **5**
Edinburgh Rd. *Sutt* . . . 8A **44**
Edinburgh Way. *E Grin* . . . 2B **186**
Edison Pl. *Craw* . . . 4D **102**
Edith Gdns. *Surb* . . . 6A **42**
Edith Gro. *SW10* . . . 2N **13**
Edith Ho. W6 . . . *1H **13***
(off Queen Caroline St.)
Edith Rd. *SE25* . . . 4A **46**
Edith Rd. *SW19* . . . 7N **27**
Edith Rd. *W14* . . . 1K **13**
Edith Row. *SW6* . . . 4N **13**
Edith Summerskill Ho. SW6 . . . *3L **13***
(off Clem Attlee Est.)
Edith Ter. *SW10* . . . 3N **13**
Edith Vs. *W14* . . . 1L **13**
Edmonds Ct. *Brack* . . . 9A **16**
Edmund Rd. *Mitc* . . . 2C **44**
Edna Rd. *SW20* . . . 1J **43**
Edney Clo. *C Crook* . . . 7C **88**
Edrich Rd. *Broadf* . . . 8M **181**
Edridge Rd. *Croy* . . . 9N **45** (5C **200**)
Edward Av. *Camb* . . . 1M **69**
Edward Av. *Mord* . . . 4B **44**
Edward Clo. *Hamp H* . . . 6C **24**
Edward Ct. *Stai* . . . 7L **21**
Edward Ct. *Wokgm* . . . 3A **30**
Edward Rd. *Big H* . . . 5G **87**
Edward Rd. *Coul* . . . 2H **83**
Edward Rd. *Croy* . . . 6C **46**
Edward Rd. *Farnh* . . . 4H **129**
Edward Rd. *Felt* . . . 8E **8**
Edward Rd. *Hamp H* . . . 6C **24**
Edward Rd. *W'sham* . . . 3A **52**
Edwards Clo. *Wor Pk* . . . 8J **43**
Edwards Ct. *S Croy* . . . 7E **200**
Edward II Av. *Byfl* . . . 1A **76**
Edward St. *Alder* . . . 2L **109**
Edward Way. *Ashf* . . . 3A **22**
Edwin Clo. *W Hor* . . . 3E **96**
Edwin Pl. *Croy* . . . 1E **200**
Edwin Rd. *Twic* . . . 2E **24**
(in two parts)
Edwin Rd. *W Hor* . . . 3D **96**
Edwinstray Ho. *Felt* . . . 3A **24**
Eelmoor Plain Rd. *Alder* . . . 9J **89**
Eelmoor Rd. *Farnb* . . . 3L **89**
Eelmoor Rd. *Alder* . . . 8J **89**
Effie Pl. *SW6* . . . 3M **13**
Effie Rd. *SW6* . . . 3M **13**
Effingham. . . . **5L 97**
Effingham Clo. *Sutt* . . . 4N **61**
Effingham Common. . . . **2H 97**
Effingham Comn. Rd. *Eff* . . . 1H **97**
Effingham Ct. Wok . . . *6A **74***
(off Constitution Hill)
Effingham Hill. . . . **1L 117**
Effingham Junction. . . . **1H 97**
Effingham La. *Copt* . . . 5B **164**
Effingham Lodge. *King T* . . . 3K **41** (8H **203**)
Effingham Pl. *Eff* . . . 5L **97**
Effingham Rd. *Burs & Copt* . . . 4N **163**
Effingham Rd. *Croy* . . . 6K **45**
Effingham Rd. *Reig* . . . 4N **121**
Effingham Rd. *Surb* . . . 6H **41**
Effort St. *SW17* . . . 6C **28**
Effra Clo. *SW19* . . . 7N **27**
Effra Rd. *SW19* . . . 7N **27**
Egbury Ho. SW15 . . . *9E **12***
(off Tangley Gro.)
Egerton Ct. *Guild* . . . 3H **113**
Egerton Pl. *Wey* . . . 3D **56**
Egerton Rd. *SE25* . . . 2B **46**
Egerton Rd. *Camb* . . . 9L **49**
Egerton Rd. *Guild* . . . 3H **113**
Egerton Rd. *N Mald* . . . 3E **42**
Egerton Rd. *Twic* . . . 1E **24**
Egerton Rd. *Wey* . . . 3D **56**
Egerton Way. *Hay* . . . 3C **8**
Eggars Ct. *Alder* . . . 9N **109**
Eggar's Hill. *Alder* . . . 4M **109**
Eggleton Clo. *C Crook* . . . 8A **88**
Egham. . . . **6C 20**
Egham Bus. Village. *Egh* . . . 9E **20**
Egham By-Pass. *Egh* . . . 6B **20**
Egham Clo. *SW19* . . . 3K **27**
Egham Clo. *Sutt* . . . 8K **43**
Egham Cres. *Sutt* . . . 9K **43**
Egham Hill. *Egh* . . . 7N **19**
Egham Hythe. . . . **6G 21**
Egham Mus. . . . **6C 20**
Egham Roundabout. *Stai* . . . 6G **20**
Egham Wick. . . . **8K 19**
Eglantine Rd. *SW18* . . . 8N **13**
Egleston Rd. *Mord* . . . 5N **43**
Egley Dri. *Wok* . . . 9N **73**
Egley Rd. *Wok* . . . 9N **73**
(in two parts)
Eglinton Rd. *Rush* . . . 4N **149**
Eglise Rd. *Warl* . . . 4H **85**
Egliston M. *SW15* . . . 6H **13**
Egliston Rd. *SW15* . . . 6H **13**
Egmont Av. *Surb* . . . 7M **41**
Egmont Pk. Rd. *Tad* . . . 3F **100**
Egmont Rd. *N Mald* . . . 3E **42**
Egmont Rd. *Surb* . . . 7M **41**
Egmont Rd. *Sutt* . . . 4A **62**
Egmont Rd. *W on T* . . . 6J **39**
Egmont Way. *Tad* . . . 6K **81**
Egremont Rd. *SE27* . . . 4L **29**
Eight Acres. *Hind* . . . 2A **170**
Eighteenth Rd. *Mitc* . . . 3J **45**
Eileen Rd. *SE25* . . . 4A **46**
Eindhoven Clo. *Cars* . . . 7E **44**
Eland Pl. *Croy* . . . 9M **45** (4A **200**)
Eland Rd. *Alder* . . . 3B **110**
Eland Rd. *Croy* . . . 9M **45** (4A **200**)
Elberon Av. *Croy* . . . 5G **45**
Elbe St. *SW6* . . . 5N **13**
Elborough Rd. *SE25* . . . 4D **46**
Elborough St. *SW18* . . . 2M **27**
Elbow Mdw. *Coln* . . . 4H **7**
Elcho Rd. *Brkwd* . . . 6N **71**
Elderberry Gro. *SE27* . . . 5N **29**
Elderberry Rd. *Lind* . . . 5B **168**
Elder Clo. *Guild* . . . 9C **94**
Elderfield Pl. *SW17* . . . 5F **28**
Elder Gdns. *SE27* . . . 6N **29**
Eldergrove. *Farnb* . . . 4C **90**
Elder Oak Clo. *SE20* . . . 1E **46**
Elder Rd. *SE27* . . . 5N **29**
Elder Rd. *Bisl* . . . 2D **72**
Eldersley Clo. *Red* . . . 1D **122**
Elderslie Clo. *Beck* . . . 4K **47**
Eldertree Pl. *Mitc* . . . 9G **28**
Eldertree Way. *Mitc* . . . 9G **28**
Elder Way. *N Holm* . . . 9J **119**
Elderwood Pl. *SE27* . . . 6N **29**
Eldon Av. *Croy* . . . 8F **46**
Eldon Av. *Houn* . . . 3A **10**
Eldon Dri. *Lwr Bo* . . . 6J **129**
Eldon Pk. *SE25* . . . 3E **46**
Eldon Rd. *Cat* . . . 8A **84**
Eldrick Ct. *Felt* . . . 2E **22**
Eldridge Clo. *Felt* . . . 2H **23**
Eleanora Ter. Sutt . . . *2A **62***
(off Lind Rd.)
Eleanor Av. *Eps* . . . 6C **60**
Eleanor Clo. *Pass* . . . 9C **168**
Eleanor Ct. *Guild* . . . 5N **113** (6D **202**)
Eleanor Gro. *SW13* . . . 6D **12**
Eleanor Ho. W6 . . . *1H **13***
(off Queen Caroline St.)
Electric Pde. *Surb* . . . 5K **41**
Electric Theatre, The. . . . **4M 113 (5B 202)**
Elfin Gro. *Tedd* . . . 6F **24**
Elgal Clo. *Orp* . . . 2K **67**
Elgar Av. *SW16* . . . 2J **45**
Elgar Av. *Crowt* . . . 9G **30**
Elgar Av. *Surb* . . . 7N **41**
Elgar Way. *H'ham* . . . 4A **198**
Elger Way. *Copt* . . . 6L **163**
Elgin Av. *Ashf* . . . 7D **22**
Elgin Clo. *H'ham* . . . 5M **197**
Elgin Ct. *S Croy* . . . 7D **200**
Elgin Cres. *Cat* . . . 9D **84**
Elgin Cres. *H'row A* . . . 5F **8**
Elgin Gdns. *Guild* . . . 2C **114**
Elgin Pl. *Wey* . . . 3D **56**
Elgin Rd. *Croy* . . . 8C **46**
Elgin Rd. *Sutt* . . . 9A **44**
Elgin Rd. *Wall* . . . 3G **62**
Elgin Rd. *Wey* . . . 2B **56**
Elgin Way. *Frim* . . . 6D **70**
Eliot Clo. *Camb* . . . 8F **50**
Eliot Dri. *Hasl* . . . 2C **188**
Eliot Gdns. *SW15* . . . 7F **12**
Elis David Almshouses. *Croy* . . . 9M **45** (5A **200**)
Elizabethan Clo. *Stanw* . . . 1M **21**
Elizabethan Way. *Craw* . . . 4G **183**
Elizabethan Way. *Stanw* . . . 1M **21**
Elizabeth Av. *Bag* . . . 5K **51**
Elizabeth Av. *Stai* . . . 7L **21**
Elizabeth Barnes Ct. SW6 . . . *5N **13***
(off Marinefield Rd.)
Elizabeth Clo. *Brack* . . . 3A **32**
Elizabeth Clo. *Sutt* . . . 1L **61**
Elizabeth Cotts. *Kew* . . . 4M **11**
Elizabeth Ct. Alder . . . *2L **109***
(off Queen Elizabeth Dri.)
Elizabeth Ct. *G'ming* . . . 4H **133**
Elizabeth Ct. *Horl* . . . 8E **142**
Elizabeth Ct. *Tedd* . . . 6E **24**
Elizabeth Ct. *Wey* . . . 1F **56**
Elizabeth Ct. *Whyt* . . . 5C **84**
Elizabeth Ct. *Wokgm* . . . 2A **30**
Elizabeth Cres. *E Grin* . . . 7B **166**
Elizabeth Dri. *C Crook* . . . 8B **88**
Elizabeth Fry Ho. *Hay* . . . 1G **8**
Elizabeth Fry Ho. Ott . . . *3F **54***
(off Vernon Clo.)
Elizabeth Gdns. *Asc* . . . 4M **33**
Elizabeth Gdns. *Sun* . . . 2K **39**
Elizabeth Ho. W6 . . . *1H **13***
(off Queen Caroline St.)
Elizabeth Rd. *G'ming* . . . 4H **133**
Elizabeth Rd. *Wokgm* . . . 2C **30**
Elizabeth Way. *SE19* . . . 8N **29**
Elizabeth Way. *Felt* . . . 5K **23**
Elkins Gdns. *Guild* . . . 9C **94**
Elkins Gro. *Farnh* . . . 1E **128**
Ellaline Rd. *W6* . . . 2J **13**
Elland Rd. *W on T* . . . 8L **39**
Ellenborough Clo. *Brack* . . . 9B **16**
Ellenborough Pl. *SW15* . . . 7F **12**
Ellenbridge Way. *S Croy* . . . 5B **64**
Ellen Dri. *Fleet* . . . 1D **88**
Ellen's Green. . . . **6H 177**

A-Z Surrey 229

Ellen Wilkinson Ho.—Eswyn Rd.

Ellen Wilkinson Ho. SW6 . . . . . 2L 13
(off Clem Attlee Ct.)
Elleray Ct. Ash V. 8E 90
Elleray Rd. Tedd 7F 24
Ellerby St. SW6 . . . . 4J 13
Ellerdine Rd. Houn 7C 10
Ellerker Gdns. Rich. 9L 11
Ellerman Av. Twic. 2N 23
Ellerton Rd. SW13 . . . . 4F 12
Ellerton Rd. SW18 . . . . 2B 28
Ellerton Rd. SW20 . . . . 8F 26
Ellerton Rd. Surb. 8M 41
Ellery Clo. Cranl 9N 155
Ellery Rd. SE19 . . . . 8N 29
Elles Av. Guild 3E 114
Elles Clo. Farnb 2N 89
Ellesfield Av. Brack. 3K 31
Ellesmere Av. Beck 1L 47
Ellesmere Ct. W4 . . . . 1C 12
Ellesmere Dri. S Croy 1E 84
Ellesmere Pl. W on T 2F 56
Ellesmere Rd. W4 . . . . 2B 12
Ellesmere Rd. Twic. 9J 11
Ellesmere Rd. Wey 4F 56
Elles Rd. Farnb. 3K 89
Elleswood Ct. Surb. 6K 41
Ellice Rd. Oxt 7B 106
Ellie M. Ashf. 3N 21
Ellingham. Wok 6A 74
Ellingham Rd. Chess 3K 59
Ellington Rd. Felt 5G 22
Ellington Rd. Houn. 5B 10
Ellington Way. Eps. 4G 81
Elliot Clo. M'bowr 4G 182
Elliott Gdns. Shep 3B 38
Elliott Pk. Ind. Est. Alder 2C 110
Elliott Ri. Asc 1H 33
Elliott Rd. W4. . . . . 1D 12
Elliott Rd. T Hth. 3M 45
Ellis Av. Onsl. 5J 113
Ellis Clo. Coul. 7K 83
Ellis Farm Clo. Wok 9N 73
Ellisfield Dri. SW15. . . . . 1F 26
Ellison Clo. Wind 6C 4
Ellison Rd. SW13. . . . . 5E 12
Ellison Rd. SW16. . . . . 8H 29
Ellison Way. Tong 5D 110
Ellison Way. Wokgm 2A 30
Ellis Rd. Coul 7K 83
Ellis Rd. Crowt 1F 48
Ellis Rd. Mitc 5D 44
Ellman Rd. Craw. 5L 181
Ellora Rd. SW16 . . . . 6H 29
Ellson Clo. M'bowr. 5G 182
Ellwood Pl. Craw 3L 181
Elm Av. Ashf 3N 21
Elm Bank. Yat. 8B 48
Elmbank Av. Eng G. 7L 19
Elmbank Av. Guild 4K 113
Elm Bank Gdns. SW13. . . . . 5D 12
Elmbourne Rd. SW17. . . . . 4E 28
Elmbridge Av. Surb 4A 42
Elmbridge Cotts. Cranl 7J 155
Elm Bri. Est. Wok. 6B 74
Elmbridge La. Wok. 6B 74
Elmbridge Mus. 1B 56
Elmbridge Rd. Cranl. 8G 154
Elmbridge Village. Cranl. 8H 155
(off Essex Dri.)
Elmbrook Clo. Sun 9J 23
Elmbrook Rd. Sutt 1L 61
Elm Clo. SW20. . . . . 3H 43
Elm Clo. Bord. 6A 168
Elm Clo. Cars. 7D 44
Elm Clo. Lea. 9H 79
Elm Clo. Rip 2J 95
Elm Clo. S Croy 3B 64
Elm Clo. Stanw 2M 21
Elm Clo. Surb. 6B 42
Elm Clo. Tad. 8B 100
Elm Clo. Twic. 3B 24
Elm Clo. Warl. 4G 84
Elm Clo. Wok. 2N 73
Elm Corner. 6B 76
Elm Cotts. Eden 8K 127
Elm Cotts. Mitc 1D 44
Elm Ct. Knap 4G 73
Elm Ct. Sand 5K 49
Elm Ct. W Mol 3B 40
Elmcourt Rd. SE27 . . . . 3M 29
Elm Cres. Farnh 5J 109
Elm Cres. King T. . . . 9L 25 (2K 203)
Elmcroft. Bookh 2A 98
Elm Cft. Dat. 4M 5
Elmcroft Clo. Chess 9L 41
Elmcroft Clo. Felt. 9G 9
Elmcroft Clo. Frim G 7D 70
Elmcroft Dri. Ashf 6B 22
Elmcroft Dri. Chess 9L 41
Elmdene. Surb 7B 42
Elmdene Clo. Beck 5J 47
Elmdon Rd. Houn. 5L 9
Elmdon Rd. H'row A 6G 8
Elm Dri. Chob. 6J 53
Elm Dri. E Grin. 9C 166
Elm Dri. Lea. 1H 99
Elm Dri. Sun. 1K 39
Elm Dri. Wink 3M 17
Elmer Cotts. Fet 1G 98
Elmer Gdns. Iswth 6D 10
Elmer M. Fet 9G 78
Elmers Dri. Tedd 7H 25
Elmers End. 3H 47
Elmers End Rd. SE20 & Beck
. . . . 1F 46
Elmerside Rd. Beck 3H 47
Elmers Rd. SE25 . . . . 6D 46
Elmers Rd. Ockl 6C 158
Elmfield. Bookh 1A 98
Elmfield Av. Mitc 9E 28
Elmfield Av. Tedd 6F 24
Elm Fld. Cotts. Wood S 2D 112
Elmfield Ct. Lind. 4A 168
(off Liphook Rd.)
Elmfield Ho. Guild 1E 114
Elmfield Rd. SW17. . . . . 3E 28
Elmfield Way. S Croy 5C 64
Elm Gdns. Clay. 3F 58
Elm Gdns. Eps 6H 81
Elm Gdns. Mitc 3H 45
Elmgate Av. Felt 4J 23
Elm Gro. SW19 . . . . 8K 27
Elm Gro. Bisl 3D 72
Elm Gro. Cat. 9B 84
Elm Gro. Eps 1B 80
Elm Gro. Farnh. 5H 109
Elm Gro. H'ham 7L 197
Elm Gro. King T. 9L 25 (2K 203)
Elm Gro. Sutt. 1N 61
Elmgrove Clo. Wok 6G 73
Elm Gro. Pde. Wall. 9E 44
Elm Gro. Rd. Cob 3L 77
Elmgrove Rd. Farnb. 1N 89
Elm Gro. Rd. SW13 . . . . 4F 12
Elmgrove Rd. Croy. 6E 46
Elmgrove Rd. Wey 1B 56
Elm Hill. 9K 91
Elm Hill. Norm 1J 111
Elm Ho. King T 1M 203
Elmhurst Av. Mitc. 8F 28
Elmhurst Ct. Croy . . . 1A 64 (7D 200)
Elmhurst Ct. Guild 4B 114
Elmhurst Dri. Dork. 7H 119
Elmhurst La. Slin 9J 195
(in two parts)
Elmhurst Lodge. Sutt. 4A 62
Elm La. Ock 6B 76
Elm La. Tong 4D 110
Elm Lodge. SW6 . . . . 4H 13
Elm M. Gray. 6A 170
Elmore Rd. Coul. 8D 82
Elm Pk. SW2 . . . . 1K 29
Elm Pk. Cranl 7J 155
Elm Pk. S'dale 7B 34
Elm Pk. Gdns. S Croy. 6F 64
Elm Pk. Rd. SE25. . . . . 2C 46
Elm Pl. Alder 4A 110
Elm Rd. SW14. . . . . 6B 12
Elm Rd. Beck 1J 47
Elm Rd. Chess 1L 59
Elm Rd. Clay. 3F 58
Elm Rd. Eps 3E 60
Elm Rd. Farnh. 5J 109
Elm Rd. Felt 2E 22
Elm Rd. G'ming 3J 133
Elm Rd. King T. 9M 25 (2L 203)
Elm Rd. Lea 9H 79
Elm Rd. N Mald 1C 42
Elm Rd. Purl 9M 63
Elm Rd. Red. 3C 122
Elm Rd. T Hth 3A 46
Elm Rd. Wall 7E 44
Elm Rd. Warl 4G 84
Elm Rd. W'ham 3N 107
Elm Rd. Wind. 6E 4
Elm Rd. Wok 5N 73
(Kingsway)
Elm Rd. Wok 2B 74
(Woodham Ri.)
Elm Rd. W. Sutt 6L 43
Elms Cres. SW4. . . . . 1G 29
Elmshaw Rd. SW15 . . . . 8F 12
Elmshorn. Eps 3H 81
Elmside. Guild 4K 113
Elmside. Milf 1C 152
Elmside. New Ad 3L 65
Elmsleigh Ct. Sutt 9N 43
Elmsleigh Ho. Twic 3D 24
(off Staines Rd.)
Elmsleigh Rd. Farnb 1L 89
Elmsleigh Rd. Stai 6H 21
Elmsleigh Rd. Twic 3D 24
Elmsleigh Shop. Cen. Stai 5H 21
Elmslie Clo. Eps 1B 80
Elms Rd. Alder 3M 109
Elms Rd. Fleet 4D 88
Elms Rd. Wokgm 3A 30
Elmstead Clo. Eps 2D 60
Elmstead Gdns. Wor Pk 9F 42
Elmstead Rd. W Byf 9J 55
Elms, The. SW13 . . . . 6E 12
Elms, The. B'water. 2K 69
Elms, The. Clay. 4F 58
Elms, The. Croy 7N 45
(off Tavistock Rd.)
Elms, The. Tong. 4D 110
Elms, The. Warf P 7E 16
Elmstone Rd. SW6 . . . . 4M 13
Elmsway. Ashf 6B 22
Elmswood. Bookh 2N 97
Elmsworth Av. Houn 5B 10
Elm Tree Av. Esh 6D 40
Elm Tree Clo. Ashf 6C 22
Elmtree Clo. Byfl 9N 55
Elm Tree Clo. Cher. 8G 37
Elm Tree Clo. Horl 7E 142
Elmtree Rd. Tedd 5E 24
Elm Vw. As. 1F 110
Elm Vw. Ho. Hay 1E 8
Elm Wlk. SW20 . . . . 3H 43
Elm Wlk. Orp 1H 67
Elm Way. Eps. 2C 60
Elm Way. Wor Pk. 9H 43
Elmwood Av. Felt 3H 23
Elmwood Clo. Asht. 4K 79
Elmwood Clo. Eps 4F 60
Elmwood Clo. Wall 8F 44
Elmwood Ct. Asht 4K 79
Elmwood Dri. Eps. 3F 60
Elmwood Rd. W4. . . . . 2B 12
Elmwood Rd. Croy 6M 45
Elmwood Rd. Mitc 2D 44
Elmwood Rd. Red 8E 102
Elmwood Rd. Wok. 6G 73
Elmworth Gro. SE21 . . . . 3N 29
Elphinstone Clo. Brkwd 8C 72
Elphinstone Ct. SW16. . . . . 7J 29
Elsa Ct. Beck. 1J 47
Elsdon Rd. Wok 5K 73
Elsenham St. SW18 . . . . 2L 27
Elsenwood Cres. Camb 8E 50
Elsenwood Dri. Camb. 8E 50
Elsinore Av. Stai 1N 21
Elsinore Ho. W6 . . . . 1J 13
(off Fulham Pal. Rd.)
Elsinore Way. Rich 6A 12
Elsley Clo. Frim G 8D 70
Elsrick Av. Mord 4M 43
Elstan Way. Croy 6H 47
Elstead. 7H 131
Elstead Ct. Sutt 7K 43
Elstead Ho. SW2 . . . . 1K 29
(off Redlands Way)
Elstead Pk. Elst. 9F 130
Elstead Rd. Seale 7E 110
Elstead Rd. Shack 5N 131
Elsted Clo. Craw. 1N 181
Elston Pl. Alder 4A 110
Elston Rd. Alder. 4A 110
Elswick St. SW6. . . . . 5N 13
Elsworth Clo. Felt 2F 22
Elsworthy. Th Dit 5E 40
Elthiron Rd. SW6 . . . . 4M 13
Elthorne Ct. Felt. 2K 23
Elton Clo. King T. 8J 25
Elton Rd. King T . . . 9M 25 (1M 203)
Elton Rd. Purl 8G 62
Eltringham St. SW18. . . . . 7N 13
Elveden Clo. Wok. 4K 75
Elvedon Rd. Cob. 7J 57
Elvetham Clo. Fleet. 2B 88
Elvetham Pl. Fleet. 2A 88
Elvetham Rd. Fleet. 2N 88
Elwell Clo. Egh 7C 20
Elwill Way. Beck 3M 47
Ely Clo. Craw 7C 182
Ely Clo. Frim. 7E 70
Ely Clo. N Mald. 1E 42
Ely Pl. Guild 1J 113
Ely Rd. Croy. 4A 46
Ely Rd. Houn 6K 9
Ely Rd. H'row A 5G 8
Elysium Pl. SW6. . . . . 5L 13
(off Elysium St.)
Elysium St. SW6 . . . . 5L 13
Elystan Clo. Wall 4G 62
Emanuel Dri. Hamp 6N 23
Embankment. SW15. . . . . 5J 13
(in three parts)
Embankment, The. Twic. 2G 25
Embankment, The. Wray. 1M 19
Embassy Ct. Wall 3F 62
Ember Cen. W on T. 8M 39
Ember Clo. Add. 2M 55
Embercourt Rd. Th Dit 5E 40
Ember Farm Av. E Mol 5D 40
Ember Farm Way. E Mol 5D 40
Ember Gdns. Th Dit 6E 40
Ember La. Esh & E Mol 6D 40
Emberwood. Craw 1A 182
Embleton Rd. Hdly D 3G 168
Embleton Wlk. Hamp 6N 23
Emden St. SW6. . . . . 4N 13
Emerald Ct. Coul 2H 83
Emerson Ct. Crowt. 2G 49
Emerton Rd. Fet. 8C 78
Emery Down Clo. Brack 2E 32
Emily Davison Dri. Eps 5G 80
Emley Rd. Add 9J 37
Emlyn La. Lea 9G 79
Emlyn Rd. Horl 7C 142
Emlyn Rd. Red. 5E 122
Emmanuel Clo. Guild 9K 93
Emmanuel Rd. SW12 . . . . 2G 28
Emmets Nest. Binf. 7H 15
Emmets Pk. Binf 7H 15
Emmetts Clo. Wok. 4N 73
Emms Pas. King T
. . . . 1K 41 (4H 203)
Empire Vs. Red 4E 142
Empress Av. Farnb. 9N 69
Empress Pl. SW6 . . . . 1M 13
Empress State Building. W14
. . . . 1M 13
Emsworth Clo. M'bowr 6G 183
Emsworth Ct. SW16. . . . . 4J 29
Emsworth St. SW2 . . . . 3K 29
Ena Rd. SW16 . . . . 2J 45
Enborne Gdns. Brack. 8B 16
Endale Clo. Cars 8D 44
Endeavour Way. SW19 . . . . 5N 27
Endeavour Way. Croy. 6J 45
Endlesham Rd. SW12 . . . . 1E 28
Endsleigh Clo. S Croy. 6F 64
Endsleigh Gdns. Surb. 5J 41
Endsleigh Gdns. W on T 2K 57
Endsleigh Rd. Red. 7G 102
Ends Pl. Warn 9C 178
End Way. Surb. 6N 41
Endymion Rd. SW2 . . . . 1K 29
Enfield Rd. Ash V. 8F 90
Enfield Rd. Bren. 1K 11
Enfield Rd. Craw 7N 181
Enfield Rd. H'row A 5F 8
Enfield Wlk. Bren 1K 11
Engadine Clo. Croy 9C 46
Engadine St. SW18 . . . . 2L 27
Engalee. E Grin 8M 165
England Way. N Mald 3A 42
Englefield. H'ham 6F 196
Englefield Clo. Croy. 5N 45
Englefield Clo. Eng G 7M 19
Englefield Green. 6M 19
Englefield Rd. Knap 4F 72
Engleheart Dri. Felt 9G 9
Englehurst. Eng G. 7M 19
Englemere Pk. Asc. 3H 33
Englemere Pk. Oxs. 9B 58
Englemere Rd. Brack 8L 15
Englesfield. Camb 1G 71
Englewood Rd. SW12 . . . . 1G 28
Engliff La. Wok. 3J 75
English Gdns. Wray. 7N 5
Enmore Av. SE25. . . . . 4D 46
Enmore Gdns. SW14 . . . . 8C 12
Enmore Rd. SE25 . . . . 4D 46
Enmore Rd. SW15. . . . . 7H 13
Ennerdale. Brack. 3M 31
Ennerdale Clo. Craw 5N 181
Ennerdale Clo. Felt. 2G 22
Ennerdale Clo. Sutt 1L 61
Ennerdale Gro. Farnh 6F 108
Ennerdale Rd. Rich 5M 11
Ennismore Av. W4. . . . . 1E 12
Ennismore Av. Guild 3B 114
Ennismore Gdns. Th Dit. 5E 40
Ennor Ct. Sutt 1H 61
Ensign Clo. Purl. 6L 63
Ensign Clo. Stanw. 2M 21
Ensign Way. Stanw 2M 21
Ensign Way. Wall 4J 63
Enterdent Cotts. God 2G 124
Enterdent Rd. God 3F 124
Enterdent, The. God. 2G 124
Enterprise Clo. Croy. 7L 45
Enterprise Ct. Craw 8B 162
Enterprise Ct. Red 4D 122
(off Mill St.)
Enterprise Est. Guild 8A 94
Enterprise Ho. H'ham 7H 197
Enterprise Ind. Est. Ash V 6D 90
Enterprise Way. SW18 . . . . 7M 13
Enterprise Way. Eden. 9K 127
Enterprise Way. Tedd 7F 24
Enton Green. 4E 152
Enton La. Ent. 7D 152
Envis Way. Guild 8F 92
Eothen Clo. Cat 2D 104
Epirus M. SW6 . . . . 3M 13
Epirus Rd. SW6 . . . . 3L 13
Epping Wlk. Craw 5D 182
Epping Way. Brack. 3D 32
Epple Rd. SW6. . . . . 4L 13
Epsom. 9C 60 (6K 201)
Epsom Bus. Pk. Eps 7D 60
Epsom Clo. Camb 7A 50
Epsom Downs. 6D 80
Epsom Downs Metro Cen. Tad
. . . . 7G 81
Epsom Downs Racecourse. . . 5E 80
Epsom Gap. Lea 2H 79
Epsom La. N. Eps 5G 80
Epsom La. S. Tad 8H 81
Epsom Pl. Cranl. 7A 156
Epsom Playhouse. 7J 201
Epsom Rd. Asht 5M 79
Epsom Rd. Craw 5E 182
Epsom Rd. Croy. 1L 63
Epsom Rd. E Clan & W Hor
. . . . 9N 95
Epsom Rd. Eps 7E 60
Epsom Rd. Guild
. . . . 4A 114 (5E 202)
Epsom Rd. Lea 8H 79
Epsom Rd. Sutt. 6L 43
Epsom Sq. H'row A. 5G 8
Epworth Rd. Iswth. 3H 11
Eresby Dri. Beck 7K 47
Erfstadt Ct. Wokgm 3B 30
Erica Clo. W End 9B 52
Erica Ct. Wok. 5N 73
Erica Dri. Wokgm. 3C 30
Erica Gdns. Croy 9L 47
Erica Way. Copt 7L 163
Erica Way. H'ham. 3K 197
Ericcson Clo. SW18 . . . . 8M 13
Eridge Clo. Craw 3G 182
Eriswell Cres. W on T. 3F 56
Eriswell Rd. W on T. 1G 57
Erkenwald Clo. Cher 6G 37
Ermine Clo. Houn 5K 9
Ermyn Clo. Lea 8K 79
Ermyn Cotts. Horne. 5D 144
Ermyn Way. Lea. 8K 79
Erncroft Way. Twic 9F 10
Ernest Av. SE27 . . . . 5M 29
Ernest Clo. Beck 4K 47
Ernest Clo. Lwr Bo 5G 129
Ernest Cotts. Eps 4E 60
Ernest Gdns. W4 . . . . 2A 12
Ernest Gro. Beck 4J 47
Ernest Rd. King T 1A 42
Ernest Sq. King T. 1A 42
Ernle Rd. SW20. . . . . 8G 27
Ernshaw Pl. SW15. . . . . 8K 13
Erpingham Rd. SW15 . . . . 6H 13
Erridge Rd. SW19. . . . . 1M 43
Errington Dri. Wind 4D 4
Errol Gdns. N Mald 3F 42
Erskine Clo. Craw 7K 181
Erskine Clo. Sutt 9C 44
Erskine Rd. Sutt. 1B 62
Esam Way. SW16. . . . . 6L 29
Escombe Dri. Guild 7L 93
Escot Rd. Sun 8G 22
Escott Pl. Ott 3E 54
Esher. 1B 58
Esher Av. Sutt 9J 43
Esher Av. W on T. 6H 39
Esher By-Pass. Cob & Esh 9G 57
Esher By-Pass. Clay & Chess
. . . . 5H 59
Esher Clo. Esh 2B 58
Esher Common. (Junct.) 5C 58
Esher Cres. H'row A 5G 8
Esher Gdns. SW19. . . . . 3J 27
Esher Grn. Esh. 1B 58
Esher Green Dri. Esh 9B 40
Esher M. Mitc 2E 44
Esher Pk. Av. Esh. 1B 58
Esher Pl. Av. Esh 1A 58
Esher Rd. Camb. 6E 50
Esher Rd. E Mol 5D 40
Esher Rd. W on T 2L 57
Eskdale Ct. Ash V 8D 90
(off Lakeside Clo.)
Eskdale Gdns. Purl 1A 84
Eskdale Way. Camb 2G 71
Esmond St. SW15 . . . . 7K 13
Esparto St. SW18 . . . . 1N 27
Essame Clo. Wokgm 2C 30
Essendene Clo. Cat 1B 104
Essendene Rd. Cat. 1B 104
Essenden Rd. S Croy. 4B 64
Essex Av. Iswth 6E 10
Essex Clo. Add. 1L 55
Essex Clo. Frim 7E 70
Essex Clo. Mord. 6J 43
Essex Ct. SW13. . . . . 5E 12
Essex Dri. Cranl. 8H 155
Essex Pl. W4 . . . . 1B 12
(in two parts)
Essex Pl. Sq. W4. . . . . 1C 12
Essex Ri. Warf. 8D 16
Essex Rd. W4 . . . . 1C 12
(in two parts)
Estate Cotts. Mick 5K 99
Estcots Dri. E Grin 9B 166
Estcourt Rd. SE25 . . . . 5E 46
Estcourt Rd. SW6 . . . . 3L 13
Estella Av. N Mald 3G 43
Estoria Clo. SW2 . . . . 1L 29
Estreham Rd. SW16 . . . . 7H 29
Estridge Clo. Houn. 7A 10
Eswyn Rd. SW17. . . . . 5D 28

Eternit Wlk.—Farm Fields

Eternit Wlk. SW6 4H 13
Ethel Bailey Clo. Eps 8N 59
Ethelbert Rd. SW20 9J 27
Ethelbert St. SW12 2F 28
Ethel Rd. Ashf 6N 21
Etherley Hill. Ockl 3A 158
Etherstone Grn. SW16 5L 29
Etherstone Rd. SW16 5L 29
Eton. 2G 4
Eton Av. Houn 2N 9
Eton Av. N Mald 4C 42
Eton Clo. SW18 1N 27
Eton Clo. Dat 2K 5
Eton Ct. Eton 3G 4
Eton Ct. Stai 6H 21
Eton Pl. Farnh 5G 108
Eton Rd. Dat 1J 5
Eton Rd. Hay 3G 8
Eton Sq. Eton 3G 4
Eton St. Rich 8L 11
Eton Wick. 1C 4
Eton Wick Rd. Eton W & Eton 1B 4
Etwell Pl. Surb 5M 41
Eureka Rd. King T 1N 41 (4M 203)
Europa Pk. Rd. Guild 2M 113 (1A 202)
Eustace Cres. Wokgm 9C 14
Eustace Rd. SW6 3M 13
Eustace Rd. Guild 1F 114
Euston Rd. Croy 7L 45
Evans Clo. M'bowr 4H 183
Evans Gro. Felt 9A 24
Evans Ho. Felt 3A 24
Evedon. Brack 6N 31
Eveline Rd. Mitc 9D 28
Evelyn Av. Alder 4N 109
Evelyn Av. T'sey 2E 106
Evelyn Clo. Felb 6H 165
Evelyn Clo. Twic 1B 24
Evelyn Clo. Wok 7N 73
Evelyn Cotts. Ab C 3L 137
Evelyn Cotts. God 6H 125
Evelyn Cres. Sun 9G 22
Evelyn Gdns. God 8F 104
Evelyn Gdns. Rich 7L 11
Evelyn Mans. W14 2K 13
(off Queen's Club Gdns.)
Evelyn Rd. SW19 6N 27
Evelyn Rd. Ham 4J 25
Evelyn Rd. Rich 6L 11
Evelyn Ter. Rich 6L 11
Evelyn Wlk. Craw 6C 182
Evelyn Way. Eps 7N 59
Evelyn Way. Stoke D 3N 77
Evelyn Way. Sun 9G 22
Evelyn Way. Wall 1H 63
Evelyn Woods Rd. Alder 6A 90
Evendon's Clo. Wokgm 5A 30
Evenlode Way. Sand 7H 49
Evenwood Clo. SW15 8K 13
Everard La. Cat 9E 84
Everatt Clo. SW18 9L 13
Everdon Rd. SW13 2F 12
Everest Ct. Wok 3H 73
Everest Rd. Camb 7B 50
Everest Rd. Crowt 1G 49
Everest Rd. Stanw 1M 21
Everglade. Big H 6F 86
Evergreen Ct. Stai 1M 21
Evergreen Oak Av. Wind 6K 5
Evergreen Rd. Frim 4D 70
Evergreen Way. Stanw 1M 21
Everington St. W6 2J 13
(in two parts)
Everlands Clo. Wok 5A 74
Eve Rd. Iswth 7G 11
Eve Rd. Wok 2D 74
Eversfield Rd. H'ham 7L 197
Eversfield Rd. Reig 3N 121
Eversfield Rd. Rich 5M 11
Eversley Cres. Iswth 4D 10
Eversley Pk. SW19 7G 26
Eversley Rd. SE19 8N 29
Eversley Rd. Surb 3M 41 (8L 203)
Eversley Rd. Yat 8A 48
Eversley Way. Croy 1K 65
Eversley Way. Egh 1E 36
Everton Rd. Croy 7D 46
Evesham Clo. Reig 2L 121
Evesham Clo. Sutt 4M 61
Evesham Ct. Rich 9M 11
Evesham Grn. Mord 5N 43
Evesham Rd. Mord 5N 43
Evesham Rd. Reig 2L 121
Evesham Rd. N. Reig 2L 121
Evesham Ter. Surb 5K 41
Evesham Wlk. Owl 6J 49
Ewald Rd. SW6 5L 13
Ewelands. Horl 7G 142
Ewell. 5E 60
Ewell By-Pass. Eps 4F 60
Ewell Ct. Av. Eps & Ewe 2D 60
Ewell Downs Rd. Eps 7F 60
Ewell Ho. Gro. Eps & Ewe 6E 60
Ewell Pk. Gdns. Eps 4F 60
Ewell Pk. Way. Ewe 3F 60
Ewell Rd. Surb 6H 41
(Effingham Rd.)
Ewell Rd. Surb 5L 41
(Surbiton Hill Rd.)
Ewell Rd. Sutt 4J 61
Ewen Cres. SW2 1L 29
Ewhurst. 5F 156
Ewhurst Av. S Croy 5C 64
Ewhurst Clo. Craw 3A 182
Ewhurst Clo. Sutt 5H 61
Ewhurst Ct. Mitc 2B 44
Ewhurst Green. 6F 156
Ewhurst Rd. Cranl 7N 155
Ewhurst Rd. Craw 3N 181
Ewhurst Rd. Peasl & Ewh 5E 136
Ewhurst Towermill. 9C 136
Ewins Clo. As 2E 110
Ewood La. Newd 5M 139
(in three parts)
Ewshot. 4C 108
Ewshot Hill Cross. Ews 5B 108
Ewshot La. C Crook & Ews 1A 108
Excalibur Clo. If'd 4K 181
Excelsior Clo. King T 1N 41 (4M 203)
Exchange Rd. Asc 4N 33
Exchange Rd. Craw 3C 182
Exeforde Av. Ashf 5B 22
Exeter Clo. Craw 7C 182
Exeter Ct. Surb 8J 203
Exeter Gdns. Yat 8A 48
Exeter Ho. Felt 3N 23
(off Watermill Way)
Exeter M. SW6 3M 13
Exeter Pl. Guild 1J 113
Exeter Rd. As 1E 110
Exeter Rd. Croy 6B 46
Exeter Rd. Felt 4N 23
Exeter Rd. H'row A 6F 8
Exeter Way. H'row A 5F 8
Explorer Av. Stai 2N 21
Eyebright Clo. Croy 7G 47
Eyhurst Clo. Kgswd 1L 101
Eyhurst Pk. Tad 1A 102
Eyhurst Spur. Tad 2L 101
Eyles Clo. H'ham 4H 197
Eylewood Rd. SE27 6N 29
Eyot Gdns. W6 1E 12
Eyot Grn. W4 1E 12
Eyston Dri. Wey 6B 56

F

Fabian Rd. SW6 3L 13
Facade, The. Reig 2M 121
Factory La. Croy 7L 45 (2A 200)
Factory Sq. SW16 7J 29
(off Streatham High Rd.)
Fagg's Rd. Felt 7G 8
Fairacre. N Mald 2D 42
Fairacres. Cob 8L 57
Fairacres. Row 7E 128
Fairacres. SW15 7E 12
Fair Acres. Croy 5J 65
Fairacres. Tad 8H 81
Fairacres Ind. Est. Wind 5A 4
Fairbairn Clo. Purl 9L 63
Fairborne Way. Guild 9K 93
Fairbourne. Cob 9L 57
Fairbourne Clo. Wok 5K 73
Fairbourne La. Cat 9N 83
Fairbriar Ct. Eps 7L 201
Fairburn Ct. SW15 8K 13
Fairburn Ho. W14 1L 13
(off Ivatt Pl.)
Fairchildes Av. New Ad 8N 65
Fairchildes Rd. Warl 1N 85
Faircroft Ct. Tedd 7G 25
Faircross. Brack 2N 31
Fairdale Gdns. SW15 7G 13
Fairdene Rd. Coul 5H 83
Fairfax. Brack 9M 15
Fairfax Av. Eps & Ewe 5G 60
Fairfax Av. Red 2C 122
Fairfax Clo. W on T 7J 39
Fairfax Ho. King T 5L 203
Fairfax Ind. Est. Alder 2C 110
Fairfax M. Farnb 3B 90
Fairfax M. SW15 7H 13
Fairfax Rd. Farnb 7N 69
Fairfax Rd. Tedd 7G 25
Fairfax Rd. Wok 7D 74
Fairfield. 8H 79
Fairfield App. Wray 9N 5
Fairfield Av. Dat 3M 5
Fairfield Av. Horl 9E 142
Fairfield Av. Stai 5H 21
Fairfield Av. Twic 2B 24
Fairfield Clo. Dat 3N 5
Fairfield Clo. Dork 3H 119
Fairfield Clo. Ewe 2D 60
Fairfield Clo. Guild 2K 113
Fairfield Clo. Mitc 8C 28
Fairfield Cotts. Bookh 3B 98
Fairfield Ct. Lea 8H 79
(off Linden Rd.)
Fairfield Dri. SW18 8N 13
Fairfield Dri. Dork 3H 119
Fairfield Dri. Frim 3C 70
Fairfield E. King T 1L 41 (3K 203)
Fairfield Halls. 9A 46 (4D 200)
Fairfield Ind. Est. King T 2M 41 (6M 203)
Fairfield La. W End 8D 52
Fairfield Lodge. Guild 2K 113
Fairfield N. King T 1L 41 (3K 203)
Fairfield Pk. Cob 1L 77
Fairfield Path. Croy 9A 46 (4E 200)
Fairfield Pl. King T 2L 41 (5K 203)
Fairfield Ri. Guild 2J 113
Fairfield Rd. Beck 1K 47
Fairfield Rd. Croy 9A 46 (4E 200)
Fairfield Rd. E Grin 1B 186
Fairfield Rd. King T 1L 41 (4K 203)
Fairfield Rd. Lea 8H 79
Fairfield Rd. Wray 9N 5
Fairfields. Cher 7J 37
Fairfield S. King T 1L 41 (4K 203)
Fairfields Rd. Houn 6C 10
Fairfield St. SW18 8N 13
Fairfield, The. Farnh 1H 129
(in two parts)
Fairfield Wlk. Lea 8H 79
(off Fairfield Rd.)
Fairfield Way. Coul 1H 83
Fairfield Way. Eps 2D 60
Fairfield W. King T 1L 41 (4K 203)
Fairford Av. Croy 4G 47
Fairford Clo. Croy 4H 47
Fairford Clo. Reig 1A 122
Fairford Clo. W Byf 1H 75
Fairford Ct. Sutt 4N 61
Fairford Gdns. Wor Pk 8E 42
Fairgreen Rd. T Hth 4M 45
Fairhaven. Egh 6B 20
Fairhaven Av. Croy 5G 46
Fairhaven Ct. Egh 6B 20
Fairhaven Ct. S Croy 8C 200
Fairhaven Rd. Red 8L 102
Fairholme. Felt 1F 22
Fairholme Cres. Asht 4J 79
Fairholme Gdns. Farnh 2H 129
Fairholme Rd. Ashf 6N 21
Fairholme Rd. W14 1K 13
Fairholme Rd. Croy 6L 45
Fairholme Rd. Sutt 3L 61
Fairland Clo. Fleet 5C 88
Fairlands. 8F 92
Fairlands Av. Guild 8F 92
Fairlands Av. Sutt 8M 43
Fairlands Av. T Hth 3K 45
Fairlands Ct. Guild 8F 92
Fairlands Rd. Guild 7F 92
Fair La. Coul 3A 102
Fairlawn. Bookh 2N 97
Fairlawn. Wey 2F 56
Fair Lawn Clo. Clay 3F 58
Fairlawn Clo. Felt 5N 23
Fairlawn Clo. King T 7B 26
Fairlawn Cres. E Grin 8L 165
Fairlawn Dri. E Grin 8L 165
Fairlawn Dri. Red 5C 122
Fairlawn Gro. Bans 9B 62
Fairlawn Pk. Wind 7B 4
Fairlawn Pk. Wok 1A 74
Fairlawn Rd. SW19 8L 27
Fairlawn Rd. Sutt 7A 62
(in three parts)
Fairlawns. Add 2K 55
Fairlawns. Guild 3E 114
Fairlawns. Horl 9F 142
Fairlawns. Sun 2G 39
Fairlawns. Twic 9J 11
Fairlawns. Wall 2F 62
Fairlawns. Wdhm 7H 55
Fairlawns Clo. Stai 7K 21
Fairlight Av. Wind 5G 4
Fairlight Clo. Wor Pk 1H 61
Fairlight Rd. SW17 5B 28
Fairline Ct. Beck 1M 47
Fairlop Wlk. Cranl 8H 155
Fairmead. Surb 7A 42
Fairmead. Wok 5M 73
Fairmead Clo. Col T 8K 49
Fairmead Clo. Houn 3L 9
Fairmead Clo. N Mald 2C 42
Fairmead Ct. Rich 5A 12
Fairmead Rd. Croy 6K 45
Fairmead Rd. Eden 7L 127
Fairmeads. Cob 9N 57
Fairmile. 8M 57
Fairmile. Fleet 7A 88
Fairmile Av. Cob 9M 57
Fairmile Av. SW16 6H 29
Fairmile Ct. Cob 8M 57
Fairmile Ho. Tedd 5G 25
Fairmile La. Cob 8L 57
Fairmile Pk. Copse. Cob 9N 57
Fairmile Pk. Rd. Cob 9N 57
Fairoak Clo. Kenl 2M 83
Fairoak Clo. Oxs 8D 58
Fairoak La. Oxs & Chess 8C 58
Fairoaks Airport. 6A 54
Fairoaks Cvn. Pk. Guild 7D 92
Fairoaks Ct. Add 2K 55
(off Lane Clo.)
Fairs Rd. Lea 6G 79
Fairstone Ct. Horl 7F 142
Fair St. Houn 6C 10
Fairview. Eps 7H 61
Fair Vw. H'ham 5G 197
Fairview Av. Wok 5A 74
Fairview Clo. Wok 5B 74
Fairview Ct. Ashf 6B 22
Fairview Ct. Stai 7J 21
Fairview Dri. Orp 1M 67
Fairview Dri. Shep 4A 38
Fair Vw. Gdns. Farnh 6J 109
Fairview Ho. SW2 1K 29
Fairview Ind. Est. Oxt 2C 126
Fairview Pl. SW2 1K 29
Fairview Rd. Hdly D 4G 169
Fairview Rd. SW16 9K 29
Fairview Rd. As 1F 110
Fairview Rd. Eps 7E 60
Fairview Rd. Sutt 2D 62
Fairview Rd. Wokgm 3B 30
Fairview Ter. Hdly 3F 168
Fairwater Dri. New H 5M 55
Fairwater Ho. Tedd 5G 25
Fairway. SW20 2H 43
Fairway. Cars 7A 62
Fairway. Cher 7K 37
Fairway. Copt 8M 163
Fairway. Guild 2F 114
Fairway. If'd 4J 181
Fairway. Vir W 5M 35
Fairway Clo. Copt 8L 163
Fairway Clo. Croy 4H 47
Fairway Clo. Eps 1B 60
Fairway Clo. Houn 8K 9
Fairway Clo. Wok 6L 73
Fairway Gdns. Beck 5N 47
Fairway Heights. Camb 9F 50
Fairways. Ashf 7C 22
Fairways. Hind 3N 169
Fairways. Iswth 4D 10
Fairways. Kenl 4N 83
Fairways. Tedd 8K 25
Fairways, The. Red 6B 122
Fairway, The. Farnb 4F 88
Fairway, The. Camb 3E 70
Fairway, The. Farnh 5J 109
Fairway, The. G'ming 9J 133
Fairway, The. Lea 5G 79
Fairway, The. N Mald 9C 26
Fairway, The. W Mol 2B 40
Fairway, The. Wey 7B 56
Fairway, The. Worp 2F 92
Fairwell La. W Hor 6C 96
Faithfull Clo. Warf 7N 15
Fakenham Way. Owl 6J 49
Falaise. Egh 6A 20
Falaise Clo. Alder 2N 109
Falcon Clo. W4 2B 12
Falcon Clo. Craw 1B 182
Falcon Clo. Light 7K 51
Falcon Ct. Frim 5B 70
Falcon Ct. Wok 9E 54
Falcon Dri. Stanw 9M 7
Falconhurst. Oxs 2D 78
Falcon Rd. Guild 4N 113 (4D 202)
(in two parts)
Falcon Rd. Hamp 8N 23
Falconry Ct. King T 5K 203
Falcons Clo. Big H 4F 86
Falcon Way. Felt 8J 9
Falcon Way. Sun 1F 38
Falcon Way. Yat 9A 48
Falconwood. E Hor 2G 96
Falconwood. Egh 6A 20
Falcon Wood. Lea 7F 78
Falconwood Rd. Croy 5J 65
Falcourt Clo. Sutt 2N 61
Falkland Ct. Farnh 5C 90
Falkland Gdns. Dork 6G 119
Falkland Gro. Dork 6G 118
Falkland Ho. W14 1L 13
(off Edith Vs.)
Falkland Pk. Av. SE25 2B 46
Falkland Rd. Dork 6G 119 (4J 201)
Falklands Dri. H'ham 4A 198
Falkner Ct. Farnh 1H 129
Falkner Rd. Farnh 1G 128
Falkners Clo. Fleet 1D 88
Fallow Deer Clo. H'ham 5A 198
Fallowfield. Fleet 1D 88
Fallowfield. Yat 8A 48
Fallowfield Way. Horl 7F 142
Fallsbrook Rd. SW16 7F 28
Falmer Clo. Craw 5B 182
Falmouth Clo. Camb 2E 70
Falmouth Rd. W on T 1K 57
Falstaff M. Hamp H 6D 24
(off Parkside)
Falstone. Wok 5L 73
Famet Av. Purl 9N 63
Famet Clo. Purl 9N 63
Famet Gdns. Kenl 9N 63
Famet Wlk. Purl 9N 63
Fanes Clo. Brack 9L 15
Fane St. W14 2L 13
Fangrove Pk. Lyne 7C 36
Fanshawe Rd. Rich 5J 25
Fantail, The. (Junct.) 1H 67
Fanthorpe St. SW15 6H 13
Faraday Av. E Grin 3B 186
Faraday Cen., The. Craw 9D 162
Faraday Ct. Craw 8C 162
Faraday Mans. W14 2K 13
(off Queen's Club Gdns.)
Faraday Rd. Farnb 8A 70
Faraday Rd. SW19 7M 27
Faraday Rd. Craw 8D 162
Faraday Rd. W Mol 3A 40
Faraday Way. Croy 7K 45
Farcrosse Clo. Sand 7H 49
Farebrothers. Warn 9F 178
Fareham Dri. Yat 9A 48
Fareham Rd. Felt 1K 23
Farewell Pl. Mitc 9C 28
Farhalls Cres. H'ham 3M 197
Faringdon Clo. Sand 6H 49
Faringdon Dri. Brack 4B 32
Farington Acres. Wey 9E 38
Faris Barn Dri. Wdhm 8H 55
Faris La. Wdhm 7H 55
Farleigh. 1J 85
Farleigh Common. 1H 85
Farleigh Ct. Guild 3H 113
Farleigh Ct. S Croy 2N 63 (8B 200)
Farleigh Ct. Rd. Warl 1J 85
Farleigh Dean Cres. Croy 7L 65
Farleigh Rd. New H 7J 55
Farleigh Rd. Warl 5G 85
Farleton Clo. Wey 3E 56
Farley Copse. Brack 9K 15
Farley Ct. Farnb 3D 90
Farleycroft. W'ham 4L 107
Farley Green. 3M 135
Farley Heath. 4L 135
Farley Heath Rd. Alb 7J 135
Farley La. W'ham 4K 107
Farley Nursery. W'ham 5L 107
Farley Pk. Oxt 8N 105
Farley Pl. SE25 3D 46
Farley Rd. S Croy 4E 64
Farleys Clo. W Hor 4D 96
Farley Wood. 1J 31
Farlington Pl. SW15 1G 26
Farlow Rd. SW15 6J 13
Farlton Rd. SW18 2N 27
Farm Av. SW16 5J 29
Farm Av. H'ham 5H 197
Farm Clo. SW6 3M 13
Farm Clo. Asc 4N 33
Farm Clo. Brack 9L 15
Farm Clo. Byfl 8A 56
Farm Clo. Coul 7D 82
Farm Clo. Craw 2E 182
Farm Clo. Crowt 9H 31
Farm Clo. E Grin 1D 186
Farm Clo. E Hor 6G 96
Farm Clo. Fet 2D 98
Farm Clo. Guild 9N 93
Farm Clo. Loxw 5J 193
Farm Clo. Lyne 5C 36
Farm Clo. Shep 6B 38
Farm Clo. Stai 6G 20
Farm Clo. Sutt 4B 62
Farm Clo. Wall 6G 63
Farm Clo. Warn 1F 196
Farm Clo. W Wick 1B 66
Farm Clo. Worp 7F 92
Farm Clo. Yat 1C 68
Farm Cotts. Wokgm 9A 14
Farm Ct. Frim 4D 70
Farmdale Rd. Cars 4C 62
Farm Dri. Croy 8J 47
Farm Dri. Fleet 1C 88
Farm Dri. Old Win 9L 5
Farm Dri. Purl 8H 63
Farmers Rd. Stai 6G 20
Farmet Ct. E Grin 7M 165
(off Halsford La.)
Farmfield Cotts. Horl 3N 161
Farmfield Dri. Charl 2N 161
Farm Fields. S Croy 7B 64

Farm Ho. Clo.—Fir Gro.

Farm Ho. Clo. Wok 2F 74
Farmhouse Rd. SW16 8G 29
Farmington Av. Sutt 9B 44
Farm La. SW6 2M 13
Farm La. Add 4J 55
Farm La. Asht 3N 79
Farm La. Croy 8J 47
Farm La. E Hor 6G 96
Farm La. Purl 6G 63
Farm La. Send 2E 94
Farm La. Trad. Est. SW6 2M 13
Farmleigh Clo. Craw 1G 182
Farmleigh Gro. W on T 2G 56
Farm M. Mitc 1F 44
Farm Rd. Alder 1C 110
Farm Rd. Esh 7B 40
Farm Rd. Frim 4C 70
Farm Rd. Houn 2M 23
Farm Rd. Mord 4N 43
Farm Rd. Stai 7K 21
Farm Rd. Sutt 4B 62
Farm Rd. Warl 6H 85
Farm Rd. Wok 7D 74
Farmstead. Eps 5N 59
Farmstead Dri. Eden 9L 127
Farmview. Cob 3L 77
Farm Vw. Lwr K 5L 101
Farm Vw. Yat 1C 68
Farm Wlk. Ash G 4G 111
Farm Wlk. Guild 5J 113
Farm Wlk. Horl 8D 142
Farm Way. Stai 9H 7
Farm Way. Wor Pk 9H 43
Farm Yd. Wind 3G 5
Farnan Rd. SW16 6J 29
Farnborough. 2N 89
(Aldershot)
Farnborough. 2L 67
(Orpington)
Farnborough Aerospace Pk. Farnb 5L 89
Farnborough Airfield. 5K 89
Farnborough Av. S Croy 5G 65
Farnborough Bus. Cen. Farnb 3L 89
Farnborough Comn. Orp 1H 67
Farnborough Cres. S Croy 5H 65
Farnborough Ga. Retail Pk. Farnb 7A 70
Farnborough Green. 8A 70
Farnborough Hill. Orp 2M 67
Farnborough Park. 2A 90
Farnborough Rd. Farnb 5N 89
Farnborough Rd. Alder 2K 109
Farnborough Rd. Farnh & Alder 4J 109
Farnborough Street. 1B 90
Farnborough St. Farnb 8B 70
Farnborough Way. Orp 2L 67
Farncombe. 4H 133
Farncombe Hill. G'ming 4G 132
(in two parts)
Farncombe St. G'ming 4H 133
Farnell M. SW5 1N 13
Farnell M. Wey 9C 38
Farnell Rd. Iswth 6D 10
Farnell Rd. Stai 4J 21
Farney Fld. Peasl 2E 136
Farnham. 1H 129
Farnham Bus. Cen. Farnh 9H 109
Farnham Bus. Pk. Farnh 2G 128
Farnham By-Pass. Farnh 3E 128
Farnham Castle. 9G 108
Farnham Clo. Brack 1B 32
Farnham Clo. Craw 9A 182
Farnham Ct. Sutt 3K 61
Farnham Gdns. SW20 1G 42
Farnham La. Hasl 9E 170
Farnham Maltings. 1H 129
Farnham Mus. 1G 128
Farnham Pk. Clo. Farnh 6G 108
Farnham Pk. Dri. Farnh 6G 109
Farnham Retail Pk. Farnh 9K 109
Farnham Rd. Elst 6E 130
Farnham Rd. Ews 3A 108
Farnham Rd. Fleet 4E 88
Farnham Rd. Guild 6G 112 (6A 202)
Farnham Rd. Holt P 1A 148
Farnham Trad. Est. Farnh 8L 109
Farnhurst La. Alf 4H 175
Farningham. Brack 5C 32
Farningham Ct. SW16 8H 29
Farningham Cres. Cat 1D 104
Farningham Rd. Cat 1D 104
Farnley. Wok 4J 73
Farnley Rd. SE25 3A 46
Farquhar Rd. SW19 4M 27
Farquharson Rd. Croy 7N 45
Farrell Clo. Camb 3A 70
Farrer Ct. Twic 1K 25
Farrer's Pl. Croy 1G 64
Farrier Clo. Sun 2H 39
Farriers Clo. Eps 8D 60
Farriers Rd. Eps 8D 60
Farriers, The. Brmly 6C 134
Farrier Wlk. SW10 2N 13
Farthing Barn La. Orp 5J 67
Farthing Fields. Hdly 4D 168
Farthingham La. Ewh 4F 156
Farthings. Knap 3H 73
Farthings Hill. H'ham 5F 196
(off Guildford Rd.)
Farthings, The. King T 9N 25
Farthing Street. 5H 67
Farthing St. Orp 4H 67
Farthings Wlk. H'ham 5F 196
Fassett Rd. King T 3L 41 (7J 203)
Fauconberg Ct. W4 2B 12
(off Fauconberg Rd.)
Fauconberg Rd. W4 2B 12
Faulkner Clo. Craw 9N 181
Faulkner Pl. Bag 3J 51
Faulkners Rd. W on T 2K 57
Favart Rd. SW6 4M 13
Faversham Rd. Beck 1J 47
Faversham Rd. Mord 5N 43
Faversham Rd. Owl 6J 49
Fawcett Clo. SW16 6L 29
Fawcett Rd. Croy 9N 45 (5A 200)
Fawcett Rd. Wind 4E 4
Fawcett St. SW10 2N 13
Fawcus Clo. Clay 3E 58
Fawe Pk. M. SW15 7L 13
Fawe Pk. Rd. SW15 7L 13
Fawler Mead. Brack 3D 32
Fawley Clo. Cranl 8A 156
Fawns Mnr. Clo. Felt 2D 22
Fawns Mnr. Rd. Felt 2E 22
Fawsley Clo. Coln 3G 6
Fay Cotts. Fay 5D 180
Faygate. 8E 180
Faygate Bus. Cen. Fay 8E 180
Faygate La. Rusp & Fay 2D 180
Faygate La. S God 9H 125
Faygate Rd. SW2 3K 29
Fayland Av. SW16 6G 28
Fay Rd. H'ham 3J 197
Fearn Clo. E Hor 7F 96
Fearnley Cres. Hamp 6M 23
Featherbed La. Croy & Warl 4J 65
Feathers La. Wray 3C 20
Featherstone. Blind H 2G 145
Fee Farm Rd. Clay 4F 58
Felbridge. 6K 165
Felbridge Av. Craw 2H 183
Felbridge Cen., The. E Grin 7K 165
Felbridge Clo. SW16 5L 29
Felbridge Clo. E Grin 7M 165
Felbridge Clo. Frim 4D 70
Felbridge Clo. Sutt 5N 61
Felbridge Ct. Felb 6K 165
Felbridge Ct. Felt 2J 23
(off High St.)
Felbridge Ct. Hay 2E 8
Felbridge Rd. Felb 7G 164
Felcot Rd. Felb 7F 164
Felcott Clo. W on T 9K 39
Felcott Rd. W on T 9K 39
Felcourt. 2M 165
Felcourt La. Felc 2L 165
Felcourt Rd. Felc & Ling 3M 165
Felday. 6J 137
Felday Glade. Holm M 6J 137
Felday Houses. Holm M 4J 137
Felday Rd. Ab H 9G 116
Feldemore. 5K 137
Feldemore Cotts. Holm M 5K 137
Felden St. SW6 4L 13
Feld, The. Felb 7K 165
Felgate M. W6 1G 12
Felix Dri. W Cla 6J 95
Felix La. Shep 5F 38
Felix Rd. W on T 5H 39
Felland Way. Reig 7B 122
Fellbrook. Rich 4H 25
Fellcott Way. H'ham 7F 196
Fellmongers Yd. Croy 4B 200
Fellowes Rd. Cars 9C 44
Fellow Grn. W End 9C 52
Fellow Grn. Rd. W End 9C 52
Fellows Rd. Farnb 4B 90
Fell Rd. Croy 9N 45 (4C 200)
(in two parts)
Felmingham Rd. SE20 1F 46
Felsberg Rd. SW2 1J 29
Felsham M. SW15 6J 13
(off Felsham Rd.)
Felsham Rd. SW15 6H 13
Felstead Rd. Eps 7C 60
Feltham. 3H 23
Feltham Av. E Mol 3E 40
Felthambrook Ind. Est. Felt 4J 23
Felthambrook Way. Felt 4J 23
Feltham Bus. Complex. Felt 3J 23
Felthamhill. 6G 23
Feltham Hill Rd. Ashf 6B 22
Felthamhill Rd. Felt 5H 23
Feltham Rd. Ashf 5B 22
Feltham Rd. Mitc 1D 44
Feltham Rd. Red 8D 122
Feltham Wlk. Red 8D 122
Felwater Ct. E Grin 7K 165
Fenby Clo. H'ham 4A 198
Fenchurch Rd. M'bowr 5F 182
Fencote. Brack 5B 32
Fendall Rd. Eps 2B 60
Fender Ho. H'ham 6H 197
Fenelon Pl. W14 1L 13
Fengates Rd. Red 3C 122
Fenhurst Clo. H'ham 7F 196
Fennel Clo. Farnb 1G 89
Fennel Clo. Croy 7G 47
Fennel Clo. Guild 9D 94
Fennel Cres. Craw 7N 181
Fennells Mead. Eps 5E 60
Fenn Ho. Iswth 4H 11
Fennscombe Ct. W End 9B 52
Fenns La. W End 9B 52
Fenns Way. Wok 2A 74
Fenn's Yd. Farnh 1G 128
Fenton Av. Stai 7L 21
Fenton Clo. Red 3E 122
Fenton Ho. Houn 2A 10
Fenton Rd. Red 3E 122
Fentum Rd. Guild 1K 113
Fenwick Clo. Wok 5L 73
Fenwick Pl. S Croy 4M 63
Ferbies. Fleet 7B 88
Ferguson Av. Surb 4M 41 (8M 203)
Ferguson Clo. Brom 2N 47
Fermandy La. Craw D 9D 164
Fermor Dri. Alder 1L 109
Fern Av. Mitc 3H 45
Fernbank Av. W on T 6M 39
Fernbank Cres. Asc 9H 17
Fernbank M. SW12 1F 28
Fernbank Pl. Asc 9G 17
Fernbank Rd. Add 2J 55
Fernbank Rd. Asc 2G 33
Fernbrae Clo. Rowl 8G 128
Fern Clo. Crowt 9G 30
Fern Clo. Frim 3F 70
Fern Clo. Warl 5H 85
Fern Cotts. Ab H 8F 116
Fern Ct. As 3D 110
Ferndale. Guild 1H 113
Ferndale Av. Cher 9G 36
Ferndale Av. Houn 6M 9
Ferndale Rd. Ashf 6M 21
Ferndale Rd. SE25 4E 46
Ferndale Rd. Bans 3L 81
Ferndale Rd. C Crook 9A 88
Ferndale Rd. Wok 3B 74
Ferndale Way. Orp 2M 67
Fernden Heights. Hasl 6F 188
Fernden La. Hasl 5F 188
Fernden Ri. G'ming 4H 133
Ferndown. Craw 8H 163
Ferndown. Horl 6E 142
Ferndown Clo. Guild 4C 114
Ferndown Clo. Sutt 3B 62
Ferndown Ct. Guild 2M 113 (1B 202)
Ferndown Gdns. Cob 9K 57
Ferndown Gdns. Farnb 1K 89
Fern Dri. C Crook 7A 88
Fernery, The. Stai 6G 21
Ferney Ct. Byfl 8M 55
Ferney Meade Way. Iswth 5G 11
Ferney Rd. Byfl 8M 55
Fern Gro. Felt 1J 23
Fernham Rd. T Hth 2N 45
Fernhill. 3J 163
Fern Hill. Oxs 1D 78
Fernhill Clo. B'water 5L 69
Fernhill Clo. Brack 8L 15
Fernhill Clo. Craw D 9E 164
Fernhill Clo. Farnh 6G 109
Fernhill Clo. Wok 7M 73
Fernhill Dri. Farnh 6G 109
Fernhill Gdns. King T 6K 25
Fernhill La. B'water 5K 69
Fernhill La. Farnh 6G 109
Fernhill La. Wok 7M 73
(in two parts)
Fernhill Pk. Wok 7M 73
Fern Hill Pl. Orp 2L 67
Fernhill Rd. B'water & Farnb 4K 69
Fernhill Rd. Horl 3H 163
Fernhill Wlk. B'water 5L 69
Fernhurst. 9F 188
Fernhurst Clo. Craw 1N 181
Fernhurst Rd. Ashf 5D 22
Fernhurst Rd. SW6 4K 13
Fernhurst Rd. Croy 6E 46
Ferniehurst. Camb 2D 70
Fernihough Clo. Wey 6B 56
Fernlands Clo. Cher 9G 37
Fern La. Houn 1N 9
Fernlea. Bookh 2B 98
Fernlea Rd. SW12 2F 28
Fernlea Rd. Mitc 1E 44
Fernleigh Clo. Croy 1L 63
Fernleigh Clo. W on T 9J 39
Fernleigh Ri. Deep 7G 71
Fernley Ho. G'ming 3H 133
Fern Rd. G'ming 5J 133
Ferns Clo. S Croy 6E 64
Fernshaw Clo. SW10 2N 13
Fernshaw Rd. SW10 2N 13
Fernside Av. Felt 5J 23
Fernside Rd. SW12 2D 28
Ferns Mead. Farnh 2F 128
Ferns, The. Farnh 5H 109
Fernthorpe Rd. SW16 7G 28
Fern Towers. Cat 3D 104
Fern Wlk. Ashf 6M 21
Fern Way. H'ham 3K 197
Fernwood. Croy 5H 65
Fernwood Av. SW16 5H 29
Feroners Clo. Craw 5E 182
Feroners Ct. Craw 5E 182
(off Feroners Clo.)
Ferrard Clo. Asc 9H 17
Ferraro Clo. Houn 2A 10
Ferrers Av. Wall 1H 63
Ferrers Rd. SW16 6H 29
Ferrier Ind. Est. SW18 7N 13
(off Ferrier St.)
Ferrier St. SW18 7N 13
Ferriers Way. Eps 5H 81
Ferring Clo. Craw 2N 181
Ferris Av. Croy 9J 47
Ferry Av. Stai 8G 21
Ferry La. SW13 2E 12
Ferry La. Bren 2L 11
Ferry La. Cher 4J 37
(in two parts)
Ferry La. Guild 7M 113
Ferry La. Rich 2M 11
Ferry La. Shep 7B 38
Ferry La. Wray 3D 20
Ferrymoor. Rich 4H 25
Ferry Quays. Bren 3K 11
(in two parts)
Ferry Rd. SW13 3F 12
Ferry Rd. Tedd 6H 25
Ferry Rd. Th Dit 5H 41
Ferry Rd. Twic 2H 25
Ferry Rd. W Mol 2A 40
Ferry Sq. Bren 3L 11
Ferry Sq. Shep 6C 38
Festing Rd. SW15 6J 13
Festival Ct. M'bowr 5G 183
Festival Wlk. Cars 2D 62
Fetcham. 1D 98
Fetcham Comn. La. Fet 8B 78
Fetcham Downs. 4D 98
Fetcham Pk. Dri. Fet 1E 98
Fettes Rd. Cranl 7B 156
Fickleshole. 1N 85
Fiddicroft Av. Bans 1N 81
Fiddlers Copse. Fern 9E 188
Field Clo. Chess 2J 59
Field Clo. Guild 1F 114
Field Clo. Hay 3D 8
Field Clo. Houn 4J 9
Field Clo. S Croy 1E 84
Field Clo. W Mol 4B 40
Fieldcommon. 6N 39
Fieldcommon La. W on T 7M 39
Field Ct. SW19 4M 27
Field Ct. Oxt 5A 106
Field Dri. Eden 9M 127
Field End. Coul 1H 83
Field End. Farnh 8L 109
Fieldend. H'ham 3A 198
Field End. Twic 5F 24
Field End. W End 9C 52
Fieldend Rd. SW16 9G 29
Fielden Pl. Brack 1B 32
Fielders Grn. Guild 3C 114
Fieldfare Av. Yat 9A 48
Fieldgate La. Mitc 1C 44
Field Ho. Clo. Asc 7L 33
Fieldhouse Rd. SW12 2G 29
Fieldhouse Vs. Bans 2C 82
Fieldhurst. Slou 1B 6
Fieldhurst Clo. Add 2K 55
Fielding Av. Twic 4C 24
Fielding Gdns. Crowt 3G 48
Fielding Ho. W4 2D 12
(off Devonshire Rd.)
Fielding M. SW13 2G 12
(off Jenner Pl.)
Fielding Rd. Col T 9K 49
Fieldings, The. Bans 4L 81
Fieldings, The. Horl 7F 142
Fieldings, The. Wok 3J 73
Field La. Bren 3J 11
Field La. Frim 5B 70
(in five parts)
Field La. G'ming 4J 133
Field La. Tedd 6G 24
Field Pk. Brack 9B 16
Field Path. Farnb 5L 69
Field Place. 3D 196
Field Pl. G'ming 4H 133
Field Pl. N Mald 5E 42
Field Pl. Cotts. Broad H 3D 196
Field Rd. Farnb 5L 69
Field Rd. W6 1K 13
Field Rd. Felt 9J 9
Fieldsend Rd. Sutt 2K 61
Fieldside Clo. Orp 1L 67
Field Stores App. Alder 1A 110
Fieldview. SW18 2B 28
Field Vw. Egh 6E 20
Field Vw. Felt 5E 22
Fieldview. Horl 7F 142
Fld. View Cotts. G'ming 7E 132
Fieldview Ct. Stai 7J 21
Field Wlk. Horl 8D 142
(off Ct. Lodge Rd.)
Field Wlk. Small 7N 143
Field Way. Alder 1C 110
Fieldway. Hasl 1G 189
Fieldway. New Ad 4L 65
Field Way. Rip 3H 95
Field Way. Tong 5D 110
Fifehead Clo. Ashf 7N 21
Fife Rd. SW14 8B 12
Fife Rd. King T 1L 41 (3J 203)
(in two parts)
Fife Way. Bookh 3A 98
Fifield La. Fren 9H 129
Fifth Cross Rd. Twic 3D 24
Figges Rd. Mitc 8E 28
Figgswood. Coul 8H 83
Filbert Cres. Craw 3M 181
Filby Rd. Chess 3M 59
Filey Clo. Big H 6D 86
Filey Clo. Craw 5L 181
Filey Clo. Sutt 4A 62
Filmer Gro. G'ming 6H 133
Filmer Rd. SW6 4K 13
Filmer Rd. Wind 5A 4
Finborough Ho. SW10 2N 13
(off Finborough Rd.)
Finborough Rd. SW10 1N 13
Finborough Rd. SW17 7D 28
Finborough Theatre, The. 2N 13
(off Finborough Rd.)
Fincham End Dri. Crowt 3E 48
Finchampstead Ridges. 4A 48
Finchampstead Rd. Finch & Wokgm 8A 30
Finch Av. SE27 5N 29
Finch Clo. Knap 4F 72
Finch Cres. Turn H 4F 184
Finchdean Ho. SW15 1E 26
Finch Dri. Felt 1L 23
Finches Ri. Guild 1D 114
Finch Rd. Guild 3N 113 (3D 202)
Findhorn Clo. Col T 8J 49
Findings, The. Farnb 6K 69
Findlay Dri. Guild 8J 93
Findon Clo. SW18 9M 13
Findon Ct. Add 2H 55
Findon Rd. Craw 1N 181
Findon Way. Broad H 5D 196
Finlay Gdns. Add 1L 55
Finlays Clo. Chess 2N 59
Finlay St. SW6 4J 13
Finmere. Brack 6A 32
Finnart Clo. Wey 1D 56
Finnart Ho. Dri. Wey 1D 56
Finney Dri. W'sham 3A 52
Finney La. Iswth 4G 11
Finsbury Clo. Craw 7A 182
Finstock Grn. Brack 3D 32
Fintry Pl. Farnb 7K 69
Fintry Wlk. Farnb 7K 69
Fiona Clo. Bookh 2A 98
Fir Acre Rd. Ash V 7D 90
Firbank Dri. Wok 6L 73
Firbank La. Wok 6L 73
Firbank Pl. Eng G 7L 19
Firbank Way. E Grin 9N 165
Fir Clo. Fleet 5A 88
Fir Clo. W on T 6H 39
Fircroft. Fleet 4A 88
Fircroft Clo. Wok 5B 74
Fircroft Ct. Wok 5B 74
Fircroft Rd. SW17 3D 28
Fircroft Rd. Chess 1M 59
Fircroft Way. Eden 9L 127
Fir Dene. Orp 1H 67
Firdene. Surb 7B 42
Fir Dri. B'water 3J 69
Fireball Hill. Asc 6A 34
Fire Bell La. Surb 5L 41
Firefly Clo. Wall 4J 63
Fire Sta. M. Beck 1K 47
Fire Sta. Rd. Alder 1N 109
Fire Thorn Clo. Fleet 6B 88
Firfield Rd. Add 1J 55
Firfield Rd. Farnh 4F 128
Firfields. Wey 3C 56
Firglen Dri. Yat 8C 48
Fir Grange Av. Wey 2C 56
Fir Gro. N Mald 5E 42

Firgrove—Foxon Clo.

Firgrove. *Wok* 6L **73**
Firgrove Ct. *Farnb* 1N **89**
Firgrove Ct. *Farnh* 2G **129**
Firgrove Hill. *Farnh* 2H **129**
Firgrove Pde. *Farnb* 1N **89**
Firgrove Rd. *Farnb* 1N **89**
Firgrove Rd. *Yate* 9A **48**
Firlands. *Brack* 4A **32**
Firlands. *Horl* 7F **142**
Firlands. *Wey* 3F **56**
Firlands Av. *Camb* 1B **70**
Firle Clo. *Craw* 1C **182**
Firle Ct. *Eps* 8F **60**
Fir Rd. *Felt* 6L **23**
Fir Rd. *Sutt* 7L **43**
Firs Av. *SW14* 7B **12**
Firs Av. *Brmly* 5C **134**
Firs Av. *Wind* 6C **4**
Firsby Av. *Croy* 7G **47**
Firs Clo. *Farnb* 8A **90**
Firs Clo. *Clay* 3E **58**
Firs Clo. *Dork* 7G **119**
Firs Clo. *Mitc* 9F **28**
Firs Dene Clo. *Ott* 3F **54**
Firs Dri. *Houn* 3J **9**
Firs La. *Sham G* 7F **134**
Firs Rd. *Kenl* 2M **83**
First Av. *SW14* 6D **12**
First Av. *Eps* 5D **60**
First Av. Tad *3K 101*
(off Holly Lodge Mobile Home Pk.)
First Av. *W on T* 5J **39**
First Av. *W Mol* 3N **39**
First Clo. *W Mol* 2C **40**
First Cross Rd. *Twic* 3E **24**
Firs, The. *Bisl* 3D **72**
Firs, The. *Bookh* 2C **98**
Firs, The. *Brack* 4D **32**
Firs, The. *Byfl* 8M **55**
Firs, The. *Cat* 9A **84**
Firs, The. *Guild* 7L **113**
First Quarter Ind. Pk. *Eps* 7D **60**
First Slip. *Lea* 5G **79**
Firstway. *SW20* 1H **43**
Firsway. *Guild* 2J **113**
Firswood Av. *Eps* 2D **60**
Firth Gdns. *SW6* 4K **13**
Fir Tree Av. *Hasl* 2B **188**
Firtree Av. *Mitc* 1E **44**
Firtree Clo. *SW16* 6G **29**
Fir Tree Clo. *Asc* 6L **33**
Fir Tree Clo. *Craw* 9N **161**
Fir Tree Clo. *Eps* 2H **81**
Fir Tree Clo. *Esh* 2C **58**
Firtree Clo. *Ewe* 1E **60**
Fir Tree Clo. *Lea* 1J **99**
Firtree Clo. *Sand* 6E **48**
Firtree Gdns. *Croy* 1K **65**
Fir Tree Gro. *Cars* 4D **62**
Fir Tree Pl. *Ashf* 6B **22**
Fir Tree Rd. *Bans* 1H **81**
Fir Tree Rd. *Eps* 3G **80**
Fir Tree Rd. *Guild* 9M **93**
Fir Tree Rd. *Houn* 7M **9**
Fir Tree Rd. *Lea* 1J **99**
Fir Tree Wlk. *Reig* 3B **122**
Fir Tree Way. *Fleet* 5C **88**
Fir Wlk. *Sutt* 3J **61**
Firway. *Gray* 4K **169**
Firwood Clo. *Wok* 6H **73**
Firwood Dri. *Camb* 1A **70**
Firwood Rd. *Vir W* 5H **35**
Fisher Clo. *Craw* 5C **182**
Fisher Clo. *Croy* 7C **46**
Fisher Clo. *W on T* 1J **57**
Fisher Grn. *Binf* 7G **15**
Fisher La. *C'fold & Duns* 1G **191**
Fisherman Clo. *Rich* 5H **25**
Fisherman's Pl. *W4* 2E **12**
Fishermen's Clo. *Alder* 8C **90**
Fisher Rowe Clo. *Brmly* 5C **134**
Fishers. *Horl* 7G **142**
Fisher's Clo. *SW16* 4H **29**
Fishers Ct. *H'ham* 4J **197**
Fishers Dene. *Clay* 4G **58**
Fisher's La. *W4* 1C **12**
Fisherstreet. **5C 190**
Fisher St. *C'fold* 4C **190**
Fishers Wood. *Asc* 7F **34**
Fishponds Clo. *Wokgm* 4A **30**
Fishponds Rd. *SW17* 5C **28**
Fishponds Rd. *Kes* 2F **66**
Fishponds Rd. *Wokgm* 4A **30**
Fiske Ct. *Yat* 9D **48**
Fitchet Clo. *Craw* 1N **181**
Fitzalan Ho. *Ewe* 6E **60**
Fitzalan Rd. *Clay* 4E **58**
Fitzalan Rd. *H'ham* 4N **197**
Fitzgeorge Av. *W14* 1K **13**
Fitzgeorge Av. *N Mald* 9C **26**
Fitzgerald Av. *SW14* 6D **12**
Fitzgerald Rd. *SW14* 6C **12**
Fitzgerald Rd. *Th Dit* 5G **40**
Fitzhugh Gro. *SW18* 1B **28**
Fitzjames Av. *W14* 1K **13**
Fitzjames Av. *Croy* 8D **46**
Fitzjohn Clo. *Guild* 9E **94**
Fitzrobert Pl. *Egh* 7C **20**
Fitzroy Clo. *Brack* 5M **31**
Fitzroy Ct. *Croy* 6A **46**
Fitzroy Cres. *W4* 3C **12**
Fitzwilliam Av. *Rich* 5M **11**
Fitzwilliam Ho. *Rich* 7K **11**
Fitzwygram Clo. *Hamp H* 6C **24**
Fiveacre Clo. *T Hth* 5L **45**
Five Acres. *Craw* 1C **182**
Five Acres Clo. *Lind* 4A **168**
Five Elms Rd. *Brom* 1E **66**
Five Oaks. *Add* 3H **55**
Five Oaks Clo. *Wok* 6G **73**
Five Oaks Rd. *Slin* 9J **195**
Five Ways Bus. Cen. *Felt* 4J **23**
Fiveways Corner. (Junct.) **1K 63**
Flag Clo. *Croy* 7G **47**
Flambard Way. *G'ming* 7G **133**
Flamborough Clo. *Big H* 6D **86**
Flamsteed Heights. *Craw* 8N **181**
Flanchford Rd. *Leigh* 9E **120**
Flanchford Rd. *Reig* 5H **121**
Flanders Ct. *Egh* 6E **20**
Flanders Cres. *SW17* 8D **28**
Flats, The. *B'water* 2G **69**
Flaxley Rd. *Mord* 6N **43**
Flaxman Ho. W4 *1D 12*
(off Devonshire St.)
Fleece Rd. *Surb* 7J **41**
Fleet. **4A 88**
Fleet Bus. Pk. *C Crook* 9C **88**
Fleet Clo. *W Mol* 4N **39**
Fleet La. *W Mol* 5N **39**
Fleet Rd. *Alder* 6F **88**
Fleet Rd. *Fleet & Farnb* 2E **88**
(Cove Rd.)
Fleet Rd. *Fleet* 5A **88**
(Reading Rd. N.)
Fleetside. *W Mol* 4N **39**
Fleetway. *Egh* 2E **36**
Fleetwood Clo. *Chess* 4K **59**
Fleetwood Clo. *Croy* 9C **46**
Fleetwood Clo. *Tad* 7J **81**
Fleetwood Ct. *Stanw* 9M **7**
Fleetwood Ct. *W Byf* 9J **55**
Fleetwood Rd. *King T* 2A **42**
Fleetwood Sq. *King T* 2A **42**
Fleming Cen., The. *Craw* 8C **162**
Fleming Clo. *Farnb* 8B **70**
Fleming Ct. *Croy* 2L **63**
Fleming Mead. *Mitc* 8C **28**
Fleming Wlk. *E Grin* 3B **186**
Fleming Way. *Craw* 8C **162**
Fleming Way. *Iswth* 7F **10**
Fleming Way Ind. Cen. *Craw* 7D **162**
Flemish Fields. *Cher* 6J **37**
Flemish Pl. *Brack* 8B **16**
Fletcher Clo. *Craw* 5C **182**
Fletcher Clo. *Ott* 3G **54**
Fletcher Gdns. *Brack* 9J **15**
Fletcher Rd. *Ott* 3F **54**
Fletchers Clo. *H'ham* 7L **197**
Fleur Gates. *SW19* 1J **27**
Flexford. **3M 111**
Flexford Grn. *Brack* 5K **31**
Flexford Rd. *Norm* 4M **111**
(in two parts)
Flexlands La. *W End* 6E **52**
Flint Clo. *Bans* 1N **81**
Flint Clo. *Bookh* 4C **98**
Flint Clo. *G Str* 3N **67**
Flint Clo. *M'bowr* 6F **182**
Flint Clo. *Red* 2D **122**
Flint Cotts. Lea *8H 79*
(off Gravel Hill)
Flintgrove. *Brack* 9B **16**
Flint Hill. *Dork* 7H **119**
Flint Hill Clo. *Dork* 8H **119**
Flintlock Clo. *Stai* 7J **7**
Flitwick Grange. *Milf* 1C **152**
Flock Mill Pl. *SW18* 2N **27**
Flood La. *Twic* 2G **25**
Flora Gdns. *Croy* 7M **65**
Floral Ct. *Asht* 5J **79**
Floral Ho. Cher *7H 37*
(off Fox La. S.)
Florence Av. *Mord* 4A **44**
Florence Av. *New H* 7J **55**
Florence Clo. *W on T* 6J **39**
Florence Clo. *Yat* 9B **48**
Florence Ct. *SW19* 7K **27**
Florence Ct. *Knap* 5F **72**
Florence Gdns. *W4* 2B **12**
Florence Gdns. *Stai* 8K **21**
Florence Ho. *King T* 1M **203**
Florence Rd. *Col T* 8J **49**
Florence Rd. *SW19* 7N **27**
Florence Rd. *Beck* 1H **47**
Florence Rd. *Felt* 2J **23**
Florence Rd. *Fleet* 7B **88**
Florence Rd. *King T* 8M **25** (1M **203**)
Florence Rd. *S Croy* 5A **64**
Florence Rd. *W on T* 6J **39**
Florence Ter. *SW15* 4D **26**
Florence Way. *SW12* 2D **28**
Florence Way. *Knap* 5F **72**
Florian Av. *Sutt* 1B **62**
Florian Rd. *SW15* 7K **13**
Florida Ct. *Stai* 5J **21**
Florida Rd. *Shalf* 9A **114**
Florida Rd. *T Hth* 9M **29**
Floss St. *SW15* 5H **13**
Flower Cres. *Ott* 3D **54**
Flower La. *God* 8G **105**
Flowersmead. *SW17* 3E **28**
Flower Wlk. *Guild* 6M **113** (8B **202**)
Floyd's La. *Wok* 3J **75**
Flyers Way, The. *W'ham* 4M **107**
Foden Rd. *Alder* 3M **109**
Folder's La. *Brack* 8A **16**
Foley M. *Clay* 3E **58**
Foley Rd. *Big H* 5F **86**
Foley Rd. *Clay* 4E **58**
Folkestone Ct. *Slou* 1C **6**
Follett Clo. *Old Win* 9L **5**
Folly Clo. *Fleet* 6B **88**
Follyfield Rd. *Bans* 1M **81**
Follyhatch La. *As* 1J **111**
Folly Hill. *Farnh* 6F **108**
Folly La. *Holmw* 4H **139**
Folly La. N. *Farnh* 5G **108**
Folly La. S. *Farnh* 6F **108**
Folly, The. *Light* 8M **51**
Fontaine Rd. *SW16* 8K **29**
Fontana Clo. *Worth* 4H **183**
Fontenoy Rd. *SW12* 3F **28**
Fonthill Clo. *SE20* 1D **46**
Fontley Way. *SW15* 1F **26**
Fontmell Clo. *Ashf* 6B **22**
Fontmell Pk. *Ashf* 6A **22**
Fontwell Clo. *Alder* 2B **110**
Fontwell Rd. *Craw* 6E **182**
Footpath, The. *SW15* 9F **12**
Forbench Clo. *Rip* 9K **75**
Forbes Chase. *Col T* 8J **49**
Forbes Clo. *M'bowr* 7F **182**
Forbe's Ride. *Wind* 1L **17**
Force Green. **2M 107**
Force Grn. La. *W'ham* 2M **107**
Fordbridge Cvn. Pk. *Sun* 5G **38**
Fordbridge Clo. *Cher* 7K **37**
Fordbridge Ct. *Ashf* 7N **21**
Fordbridge Rd. *Ashf* 7N **21**
Fordbridge Rd. *Sun* 5F **38**
Fordbridge Roundabout. (Junct.) **7N 21**
Ford Clo. *Ashf* 7N **21**
Ford Clo. *Shep* 3B **38**
Ford Clo. *T Hth* 4M **45**
Fordham. *King T* 4M **203**
Fordingbridge Clo. *H'ham* 7J **197**
Ford La. *Wrec* 5G **128**
Ford Mnr. Cotts. *D'land* 1D **166**
Ford Mnr. Rd. *D'land* 9D **146**
Ford Rd. *Ashf* 5A **22**
Ford Rd. *Bisl* 1B **72**
Ford Rd. *Cher* 7K **37**
Ford Rd. *Chob* 6F **52**
Ford Rd. *Wok* 7D **74**
Fordwater Rd. *Cher* 7K **37**
Fordwater Trad. Est. *Cher* 7L **37**
Fordwells Dri. *Brack* 3D **32**
Foreman Ct. *Twic* 2F **24**
Foreman Pk. *As* 2F **110**
Foreman Rd. *Ash G* 3F **110**
Forest Clo. *Asc* 2G **33**
Forest Clo. *Craw D* 1E **184**
Forest Clo. *E Hor* 3G **96**
Forest Clo. *H'ham* 4A **198**
Forest Clo. *Wok* 2F **74**
Forest Cres. *Asht* 3N **79**
Forestdale. **5J 65**
Forestdale. *Hind* 6B **170**
Forestdale Cen., The. *Croy* 4J **65**
Forest Dean. *Fleet* 1D **88**
Forest Dene Ct. *Sutt* 3A **62**
Forest Dri. *Kes* 1G **66**
Forest Dri. *Kgswd* 8L **81**
Forest Dri. *Lwr Bo* 7H **129**
Forest Dri. *Sun* 8G **22**
Forest End. *Fleet* 7A **88**
Forest End. *Sand* 6E **48**
Forest End Rd. *Sand* 6E **48**
Forester Rd. *Craw* 5C **182**
Foresters Clo. *Wall* 4H **63**
Foresters Clo. *Wok* 5J **73**
Foresters Dri. *Wall* 4H **63**
Foresters Sq. *Brack* 2C **32**
Foresters Way. *Crowt* 9K **31**
Forestfield. *Craw* 6E **182**
Forestfield. *H'ham* 5N **197**
Forest Glade. *Rowl* 8C **128**
Forest Grange. *H'ham* 3C **198**
Forest Green. **3M 157**
Forest Grn. *Brack* 9B **16**
Forest Grn. Rd. *Ockl* 3C **158**
Forest Hills. *Camb* 2N **69**
Forest La. *E Hor* 2G **97**
Forest La. *Lind* 3B **168**
Forest Lodge. *E Grin* 1B **186**
Forest Oaks. *H'ham* 4A **198**
Forest Park. **5D 32**
Forest Ridge. *Beck* 2K **47**
Forest Ridge. *Kes* 1G **67**
Forest Rd. *Colg* 2K **199**
Forest Rd. *Crowt* 2H **49**
Forest Rd. *E Hor* 4G **96**
Forest Rd. *Eff J* 2G **97**
Forest Rd. *Felt* 3K **23**
Forest Rd. *F Row* 8K **187**
Forest Rd. *H'ham & Craw* 4A **198**
Forest Rd. *Rich* 3N **11**
Forest Rd. *Sutt* 7M **43**
Forest Rd. *Warf & Asc* 6C **16**
Forest Rd. *Wind* 2A **18**
(Cranbourne)
Forest Rd. *Wind* 5A **4**
(Windsor)
Forest Rd. *Wok* 2F **74**
Forest Rd. *Wokgm & Binf* 7A **14**
Forest Rd., The. *Loxw* 5D **192**
Forest Row. **6H 187**
Forest Row Bus. Pk. *F Row* 6H **187**
Forest Side. *Wor Pk* 7E **42**
Forest Vw. *Craw* 6E **182**
Forest Vw. Rd. *E Grin* 3A **186**
Forest Wlk. *Cranl* 8H **155**
Forest Way. *Asht* 4M **79**
Forest Way. *Warf P* 8D **16**
Forge Av. *Coul* 7L **83**
Forgebridge La. *Coul* 9F **82**
Forge Clo. *Broad H* 4D **196**
Forge Clo. *Farnh* 9J **109**
Forge Clo. *Hay* 2E **8**
Forge Cotts. Broad H *4E 196*
(off Forge La.)
Forge Cft. *Eden* 2L **147**
Forge Dri. *Clay* 4G **58**
Forge End. *Wok* 4A **74**
Forge Fld. *Big H* 3F **86**
Forge La. *Alder* 7L **89**
Forge La. *Broad H* 4D **196**
Forge La. *Craw* 2E **182**
Forge La. *Felt* 6M **23**
Forge La. *Sun* 2H **39**
Forge La. *Sutt* 4K **61**
Forge M. *Croy* 2K **65**
Forge Rd. *Craw* 2E **182**
Forge Steading. *Bans* 2N **81**
Forge, The. *Hand* 7N **199**
Forge, The. *Warn* 9E **178**
Forge Wood. *Craw* 7H **163**
Forge Wood Ind. Est. *Craw* 8F **162**
Forrest Gdns. *SW16* 2K **45**
Forster Rd. *SW12* 1J **29**
Forster Rd. *Beck* 2H **47**
Forsyte Cres. *SE19* 1B **46**
Forsythia Pl. *Guild* 1M **113**
Forsyth Path. *Wok* 9F **54**
Forsyth Rd. *Wok* 1E **74**
Fortescue Av. *Twic* 4C **24**
Fortescue Rd. *SW19* 8B **28**
Fortescue Rd. *Wey* 1A **56**
Forth Clo. *Farnb* 8J **69**
Fort La. *Reig* 8N **101**
Fort Narrien. *Col T* 8K **49**
Fort Rd. *Guild* 6A **114** (8E **202**)
Fort Rd. *Tad* 9A **100**
Fortrose Clo. *Col T* 8J **49**
Fortrose Gdns. *SW2* 2J **29**
Fortune Dri. *Cranl* 9N **155**
Forty Footpath. *SW14* 6B **12**
Forty Foot Rd. *Lea* 8J **79**
(in two parts)
Forum, The. *W Mol* 3B **40**
Forval Clo. *Mitc* 4D **44**
Foskett Rd. *SW6* 5L **13**
Foss Av. *Croy* 2L **63**
Fosseway. *Crowt* 2E **48**
Fosse Way. *W Byf* 9H **55**
Fossewood Dri. *Camb* 7B **50**
Foss Rd. *SW17* 5B **28**
Foster Av. *Wind* 6B **4**
Fosterdown. *God* 7E **104**
Foster Rd. *W4* 1C **12**
Fosters Gro. *W'sham* 1M **51**
Fosters La. *Knap* 4F **72**
Foster's Way. *SW18* 2N **27**
Foulser Rd. *SW17* 4D **28**
Foulsham Rd. *T Hth* 2N **45**
Founders Gdns. *SE19* 8N **29**
Foundry Clo. *H'ham* 4L **197**
Foundry Ct. *Cher* 6J **37**
Foundry La. *Hasl* 2E **188**
Foundry La. *H'ham* 5L **197**
Foundry La. *Hort* 6D **6**
Foundry M. Cher *6J 37*
(off Gogmore La.)
Foundry Pl. *SW18* 1N **27**
Fountain Dri. *Cars* 4D **62**
Fountain Gdns. *Wind* 6G **4**
Fountain Rd. *SW17* 6B **28**
Fountain Rd. *Red* 5C **122**
Fountain Rd. *T Hth* 2N **45**
Fountain Roundabout. *N Mald* 3D **42**
Fountains Av. *Felt* 4N **23**
Fountains Clo. *Craw* 5M **181**
Fountains Clo. *Felt* 3N **23**
(in two parts)
Fountains Gth. *Brack* 2M **31**
Four Acres. *Cob* 9M **57**
Four Acres. *Guild* 1E **114**
Four Elms Rd. *Eden & Four E* 1L **147**
Fourfield Clo. *Eps* 9B **80**
Four Seasons Cres. *Sutt* 8L **43**
Four Sq. Ct. *Houn* 9A **10**
Fourth Cross Rd. *Twic* 3D **24**
Fourth Dri. *Coul* 3G **83**
Four Wents. *Cob* 1K **77**
Fowler Clo. *M'bowr* 5G **182**
Fowler Rd. *Farnb* 2L **89**
Fowler Rd. *Mitc* 1E **44**
Fowlerscroft. *Comp* 1E **132**
Fowlers La. *Brack* 9N **15**
Fowlers Mead. *Chob* 5H **53**
Fowler's Rd. *Alder* 7A **90**
Foxacre. *Cat* 9B **84**
Foxborough Clo. *Slou* 1C **6**
Foxborough Hill. *Brmly* 4N **133**
Foxborough Hill Rd. *Brmly* 4N **133**
Foxbourne Rd. *SW17* 3E **28**
Foxbridge La. *Kird* 8D **192**
Foxburrows Av. *Guild* 3J **113**
Foxburrows Ct. *Guild* 2J **113**
Fox Clo. *Craw* 9N **161**
Fox Clo. *Wey* 2E **56**
Fox Clo. *Wok* 2F **74**
Foxcombe. *New Ad* 3L **65**
(in two parts)
Foxcombe Rd. *SW15* 2F **26**
Fox Corner. **3F 92**
Foxcote. *Finch* 9A **30**
Fox Covert. *Fet* 2D **98**
Fox Covert. *Light* 7L **51**
Fox Covert Clo. *Asc* 4N **33**
Foxcroft. *C Crook* 8B **88**
Fox Dene. *G'ming* 9F **132**
Foxdown Clo. *Camb* 1A **70**
Fox Dri. *Yat* 8C **48**
Foxearth Clo. *Big H* 5G **87**
Foxearth Rd. *S Croy* 6F **64**
Foxearth Spur. *S Croy* 5F **64**
Foxenden Rd. *Guild* 4A **114** (4E **202**)
Foxes Dale. *Brom* 2N **47**
Foxes Path. *Sut G* 4B **94**
Foxglove Av. *H'ham* 2L **197**
Foxglove Clo. *Eden* 9M **127**
Foxglove Clo. *Stanw* 2M **21**
Foxglove Clo. *Wink R* 7E **16**
Foxglove Gdns. *Guild* 1E **114**
Foxglove Gdns. *Purl* 7J **63**
Foxglove La. *Chess* 1N **59**
Foxglove Wlk. *Craw* 6N **181**
Foxglove Way. *Wall* 7F **44**
Fox Gro. *W on T* 6J **39**
Foxgrove Dri. *Wok* 2C **74**
Foxhanger Gdns. *Wok* 3C **74**
Fox Heath. *Farnb* 2H **89**
Foxheath. *Brack* 4C **32**
Fox Hill. *Kes* 2E **66**
Foxhill Cres. *Camb* 7F **50**
Fox Hills. *Wok* 4M **73**
Foxhills Clo. *Ott* 3D **54**
Fox Hills La. *As* 1C **110**
Foxhills Rd. *Ott* 1C **54**
Foxholes. *Rud* 9E **176**
Foxholes. *Wey* 2E **56**
Foxhurst Rd. *Ash V* 8E **90**
Foxlake Rd. *Byfl* 8A **56**
Fox Lane. **6K 69**
Fox La. *Bookh* 2M **97**
Fox La. *Cat* 8M **83**
Fox La. *Kes* 2D **66**
Fox La. *Ran C* 3B **118**
Fox La. *Reig* 9N **101**
Fox La. N. *Cher* 7H **37**
Fox La. S. *Cher* 7H **37**
Foxleigh Chase. *H'ham* 4M **197**
Foxley Clo. *B'water* 1H **69**
Foxley Clo. *Red* 8E **122**
Foxley Ct. *Sutt* 4A **62**
Foxley Gdns. *Purl* 9M **63**
Foxley Hall. *Purl* 9L **63**
Foxley Hill Rd. *Purl* 8L **63**
Foxley La. *Binf* 7G **14**
Foxley La. *Purl* 7G **63**
Foxley Rd. *Kenl* 1M **83**
Foxley Rd. *T Hth* 3M **45**
Foxon Clo. *Cat* 8B **84**

Foxon La.—Gardener Gro.

Foxon La. Cat. 8A 84
Foxon La. Gdns. Cat. 8B 84
Fox Rd. Brack. 3A 32
Fox Rd. Hasl. 2C 188
Fox Rd. Lwr Bo 4H 129
Fox's Path. Mitc 1C 44
Foxton Gro. Mitc 1B 44
Foxwarren. Clay 5F 58
Fox Way. Ews. 5C 108
Foxwood. Fleet. 2D 88
Foxwood Clo. Felt. 4J 23
Foxwood Clo. Wmly. 1C 172
Fox Yd. Farnh. 1G 128
Foye La. C Crook 8C 88
Frailey Clo. Wok. 3D 74
Frailey Hill. Wok. 3D 74
Framfield Clo. Craw. 1M 181
Framfield Rd. Mitc 8E 28
Frampton Clo. Sutt 4M 61
Frampton Rd. Houn. 8M 9
France Hill Dri. Camb. 1A 70
Frances Rd. Wind. 6F 4
Franche Ct. Rd. SW17 4A 28
Francis Av. Felt. 4H 23
Francis Barber Clo. SW16 6K 29
Franciscan Rd. SW17 6D 28
Francis Chichester Clo. Asc 4M 33
Francis Clo. Eps 1C 60
Francis Clo. Shep 3B 38
Francis Ct. Guild. 1L 113
Francis Ct. Surb 8K 203
Francis Edwards Way. Craw 7K 181
Francis Gdns. Warf 8B 16
Francis Gro. SW19 7L 27 (in two parts)
Francis Rd. Cat. 9A 84
Francis Rd. Croy 6M 45
Francis Rd. Houn 5L 9
Francis Rd. Wall. 3G 63
Francis Way. Camb 2G 70
Frank Beswick Ho. SW6 2L 13 (off Clem Attlee Ct.)
Franklands Dri. Add. 4H 55
Franklin Clo. SE27 4M 29
Franklin Clo. King T 2N 41
Franklin Ct. Guild 3J 113 (off Derby Rd.)
Franklin Cres. Mitc 3G 45
Franklin Rd. M'bowr 4G 183
Franklin Sq. W14 1L 13
Franklin Way. Croy 6J 45
Franklyn Cres. Wind. 6A 4
Franklyn Rd. G'ming. 8E 132
Franklyn Rd. W on T 5H 39
Franks Av. N Mald 3B 42
Franksfield. Peasl 4F 136 (in two parts)
Frank Soskice Ho. SW6 2L 13 (off Clem Attlee Ct.)
Franks Rd. Guild 9K 93
Frank Towell Ct. Felt. 1H 23
Frant Field. Eden 2M 147
Frant Rd. T Hth 4M 45
Fraser Gdns. Dork 4G 118
Fraser Ho. Bren. 1M 11
Fraser Mead. Col T. 9K 49
Fraser Rd. Brack 9N 15
Fraser St. W4. 1D 12
Frederick Clo. Sutt 1L 61
Frederick Gdns. Croy. 5M 45
Frederick Gdns. Sutt. 1L 61
Frederick Pl. Wokgm 2A 30
Frederick Rd. Sutt 2L 61
Frederick Sanger Rd. Sur R 4G 113
Frederick St. Alder. 2M 109
Freeborn Way. Brack 9C 16
Freedown La. Sutt 9N 61
Freehold Ind. Est. Houn 8K 9
Freelands Av. S Croy 5G 64
Freelands Dri. C Crook 8A 88
Freelands Rd. Cob 1J 77
Freeman Clo. Shep 3F 38
Freeman Dri. W Mol. 3N 39
Freeman Rd. Mord 4B 44
Freeman Rd. Warn 9F 178
Freemantle Clo. Bag 3J 51
Freemantle Rd. Bag 4K 51
Freemasons Rd. Croy. 7B 46
Free Prae Rd. Cher 7J 37
Freesia Clo. Orp 2N 67
Freesia Dri. Bisl 3D 72
Freestone Yd. Coln 3F 6 (off Park St.)
French Apartments, The. Purl 8L 63
Frenchaye. Add. 1L 55
Frenches Ct. Red 1E 122
Frenches Rd. Red. 1E 122
Frenches, The. Red 1E 122
French Gdns. Cob 1K 77
French Gdns. B'water 2J 69
Frenchlands Hatch. E Hor. 5F 96
French La. Thur 6K 151
Frenchmans Creek. C Crook 9A 88
French Street. 7N 107
French St. Sun 1K 39
French St. W'ham 6N 107
French's Wells. Wok. 4L 73
Frensham. 3H 149
Frensham. Brack 5B 32
Frensham Av. Fleet. 4D 88
Frensham Clo. Yat 9A 48
Frensham Common. 4J 149
Frensham Common Country Pk. 5K 149
Frensham Country Pk. Interpretative Cen. 4J 149
Frensham Dri. SW15 4E 26 (in two parts)
Frensham Dri. New Ad 4M 65
Frensham Heights 9F 128
Frensham Heights Rd. Rowl 9F 128
Frensham La. Hdly & Churt 1D 168
Frensham La. Lind 3B 168
Frensham Little Pond. 2L 149
Frensham Rd. Crowt 1G 49
Frensham Rd. Farnh & Fren 3H 129
Frensham Rd. Kenl 1M 83
Frensham Va. Lwr Bo 7G 129
Frensham Way. Eps 3H 81
Frere Av. Fleet 6A 88
Freshborough Ct. Guild 4B 114
Freshfield Bank. F Row 7G 186
Freshfield Clo. Craw 4E 182
Freshfield Flats. Lwr K 5L 101
Freshfields. Croy. 7J 47
Freshford St. SW17 4A 28
Freshmount Gdns. Eps. 7A 60
Freshwater Clo. SW17 7E 28
Freshwater Pde. H'ham 6H 197 (off Bishopric)
Freshwater Rd. SW17 7E 28
Freshwood Clo. Beck 1L 47
Freshwood Dri. Yat. 2C 68
Freshwood Way. Wall 5F 62
Frewin Rd. SW18 2B 28
Friar M. SE27 4M 29
Friars Av. SW15 4E 26
Friars Fld. Farnh. 9G 108
Friar's Ga. Guild 5K 113
Friars Keep. Brack 3N 31
Friars La. Rich 8K 11
Friars Orchard. Fet. 8D 78
Friars Ri. Wok 5C 74
Friars Rd. Vir W. 3N 35
Friars Rookery. Craw 3D 182
Friars Stile Pl. Rich. 9L 11
Friars Stile Rd. Rich 9L 11
Friars Way. Cher. 5J 37
Friarswood. Croy 5H 65
Friary Bri. Guild 5M 113 (6B 202)
Friary Ct. Wok. 5J 73
Friary Island. 9M 5
Friary Island. Wray 9M 5
Friary Pas. Guild 5M 113 (6B 202)
Friary Rd. Asc. 5L 33
Friary Rd. Wray. 1M 19 (in two parts)
Friary St. Guild 5N 113 (6B 202)
Friary, The. Guild 4M 113 (5B 202)
Friary, The. Old Win 9M 5
Friary Way. Craw 4B 182
Friday Rd. Mitc 8D 28
Friday Street. 3M 137
Friday St. Ockl 6D 158
Friday St. Rusp. 4L 179
Friday St. Warn 1E 196
Friday St. Rd. Ab C 3M 137
Friend Av. Alder 3B 110
Friends Clo. Craw. 9B 162
Friendship Way. Brack 2N 31
Friends Rd. Croy. 9A 46 (4D 200)
Friends Rd. Purl 8M 63
Friends Wlk. Stai 6H 21
Friesian Clo. Fleet. 1C 88
Frimley. 6A 70
Frimley Aqueduct. 9E 70
Frimley Av. Wall 2J 63
Frimley Bus. Pk. Frim. 6A 70
Frimley By-Pass. Frim 6A 70
Frimley Clo. SW19. 3K 27
Frimley Clo. New Ad 4M 65
Frimley Cres. New Ad 4M 65
Frimley Gdns. Mitc. 2C 44
Frimley Green. 8D 70
Frimley Grn. Rd. Frim & Frim G 5B 70
Frimley Gro. Gdns. Frim. 5B 70
Frimley Hall Dri. Camb. 9D 50
Frimley High St. Frim. 6A 70
Frimley Ridge. 3F 70
Frimley Rd. Ash V 4E 90
Frimley Rd. Camb & Frim 1M 69
Frimley Rd. Chess 2K 59
Frinton Rd. SW17. 7E 28
Friston St. SW6 5N 13
Friston Wlk. Craw 1M 181
Fritham Clo. N Mald 5D 42
Frithend. 6A 148
Frith End Rd. Bord 5A 148
Frith Hill. 5G 132
Frith Hill Rd. Frim. 5E 70
Frith Hill Rd. G'ming 4G 133
Frith Knowle. W on T 3J 57
Frith Pk. E Grin. 7A 166
Frith Rd. Croy 8N 45 (3B 200)
Friths Dri. Reig. 9N 101
Frithwald Rd. Cher 6H 37
Frobisher. Brack. 6A 32
Frobisher Clo. Kenl 4N 83
Frobisher Ct. Sutt. 4K 61
Frobisher Cres. Stai 1N 21
Frobisher Gdns. Guild 2C 114
Frobisher Gdns. Stai 1N 21
Frodsham Way. Owl. 5K 49
Froggetts La. Wal W 9K 157
Frog Gro. La. Wood S 1C 112
Frog Hall Dri. Wokgm 2D 30
Froghole. 1M 127
Froghole La. Eden 1M 127
Frog La. Brack. 2M 31
Frog La. Sut G 3A 94
Frogmore. 1H 69 (Camberley)
Frogmore. 6J 5 (Windsor)
Frogmore. SW18. 8M 13
Frogmore Border. Wind 6H 5
Frogmore Clo. Sutt. 9J 43
Frogmore Ct. B'water 2H 69
Frogmore Ct. S'hall 1N 9
Frogmore Dri. Wind. 4H 5
Frogmore Gdns. Sutt 1K 61
Frogmore Gro. B'water 2H 69
Frogmore Ho. 6J 5
Frogmore Pk. Dri. B'water 2H 69
Frogmore Rd. B'water 1G 69
Frome Clo. Farnb 8J 69
Fromondes Rd. Sutt. 2K 61
Fromow Gdns. W'sham 3A 52
Froxfield Down. Brack 4D 32
Fruen Rd. Felt 1G 23
Fry Clo. Craw. 8N 181
Fryern Wood. Cat. 2N 103
Frylands Ct. New Ad 7M 65
Frymley Vw. Wind 4A 4
Fry Rd. Ashf 5M 21
Fry's Acre. As. 1E 110
Fry's La. Yat 8D 48
Fryston Av. Coul 1F 82
Fryston Av. Croy 8D 46
Fuchsia Pl. Brack 1B 32
Fuchsia Way. W End 9B 52
Fugelmere Rd. Fleet. 3D 88
Fugelmere Wlk. Fleet 3D 88
Fulbourn. King T 4M 203
Fulbourne Clo. Red 1C 122
Fulbrook Av. New H 7J 55
Fulford Ho. Eps 4C 60
Fulford Rd. Cat. 8A 84
Fulford Rd. Eps 4C 60
Fulfords Hill. Itch 9A 196
Fulfords Rd. Itch 9B 196
Fulham. 5K 13
Fulham Broadway. (Junct.) 3M 13
Fulham B'way. SW6 3M 13
Fulham Clo. Craw. 7N 181
Fulham Ct. SW6 4M 13
Fulham F.C. (Craven Cottage). 4J 13
Fulham High St. SW6. 5K 13
Fulham Pal. Rd. W6 & SW6 1H 13
Fulham Pk. Gdns. SW6 5L 13
Fulham Pk. Rd. SW6 5L 13
Fulham Rd. SW6,SW10 & SW3 5K 13 (in two parts)
Fullbrook La. Elst. 6G 130
Fullbrooks Av. Wor Pk 7E 42
Fullers Av. Surb. 8M 41
Fullers Farm Rd. W Hor. 2B 116
Fuller's Griffin Brewery & Vis. Cen. 2E 12
Fullers Hill. W'ham 4M 107
Fullers Rd. Rowl. 7B 128
Fullers Va. Hdly D. 4E 168
Fullers Way N. Surb 9M 41
Fullers Way S. Chess 1L 59
Fuller's Wood. Croy 2K 65
Fullers Wood La. S Nut 4G 123
Fullerton Clo. Byfl. 1A 76
Fullerton Ct. Tedd. 7G 25
Fullerton Dri. Byfl. 1N 75
Fullerton Rd. SW18 8N 13
Fullerton Rd. Byfl. 1N 75
Fullerton Rd. Cars 5C 62
Fullerton Rd. Croy 6C 46
Fullerton Way. Byfl. 1N 75
Fuller Way. Hay 1G 8
Fullmer Way. Wdhm 6H 55
Fulmar Clo. If'd. 4J 181
Fulmar Ct. Surb. 5M 41
Fulmar Dri. E Grin 7C 166
Fulmead St. SW6. 4N 13
Fulmer Clo. Hamp 6M 23
Fulstone Clo. Houn 7N 9
Fulvens. Peasl 2F 136
Fulwell. 5D 24
Fulwell Pk. Av. Twic 3B 24
Fulwell Rd. Tedd 5D 24
Fulwood Gdns. Twic 9F 10
Fulwood Wlk. SW19 2K 27
Furlong Clo. Wall 7F 44
Furlong Rd. Westc. 6C 118
Furlong Way. Gat A 2D 162 (off Gatwick Way)
Furlough, The. Wok 3C 74
Furmage St. SW18 1N 27
Furnace Dri. Craw 5D 182
Furnace Farm Rd. Craw 5E 182
Furnace Green. 5E 182
Furnace Pde. Craw. 5E 182
Furnace Pl. Craw 5E 182
Furnace Rd. Felb 7E 164
Furnace Wood. 6F 164
Furneaux Av. SE27 6M 29
Furness. Wind 5A 4
Furness Pl. Wind 5A 4
Furness Rd. SW6. 5N 13
Furness Rd. Mord 5N 43
Furness Row. Wind 5A 4
Furness Sq. Wind 5A 4
Furness Wlk. Wind. 5A 4 (off Furnace Sq.)
Furness Way. Wind 5A 4
Furniss Ct. Cranl 8H 155
Furnival Clo. Vir W. 5N 35
Furrows Pl. Cat 1C 104
Furrows, The. W on T 8K 39
Furse Clo. Camb 2G 70
Furtherfield. Cranl 6N 155
Furtherfield Clo. Croy 5L 45
Further Vell-Mead. C Crook 9A 88
Furzebank. Asc 3A 34
Furze Clo. Ash V. 5E 90
Furze Clo. Horl. 8H 143
Furze Clo. Red. 2D 122
Furzedown. 6F 28
Furzedown Clo. Egh. 7A 20
Furzedown Dri. SW17 6F 28
Furzedown Rd. SW17 6F 28
Furzedown Rd. Sutt. 7A 62
Furzefield. Craw. 2N 181
Furze Fld. Oxs 9D 58
Furzefield Chase. Dor P 4A 166
Furzefield Cres. Reig 5A 122
Furzefield Rd. E Grin 6N 165
Furzefield Rd. H'ham 3A 198
Furzefield Rd. Reig 5A 122
Furze Gro. Tad 8L 81
Furze Hill. 8L 81
Furze Hill. Farnh. 9B 110
Furze Hill. Kgswd 7L 81
Furze Hill. Purl 7J 63
Furze Hill. Red 2C 122
Furzehill Cotts. Pirb 9N 71
Furze Hill Cres. Crowt 3H 49
Furze Hill Rd. Head D 5G 168 (in two parts)
Furze La. E Grin 6L 165
Furze La. G'ming 3J 133
Furze La. Purl. 7J 63
Furzemoors. Brack 4N 31
Furzen La. Rud & Oke H 6H 177
Furze Rd. Add 3H 55
Furze Rd. Rud 9E 176
Furze Rd. T Hth 2N 45
Furze Va. Rd. Head D 5G 169
Furzewood. Sun. 9H 23
Fuzzens Wlk. Wind. 5B 4
Fydler's Clo. Wink 7M 17
Fyfield Clo. B'water. 1J 69
Fyfield Clo. Brom. 3N 47

G

Gable Ct. Red 2E 122 (off St Anne's Mt.)
Gable End. Farnb 1N 89
Gables. Gray 6B 170
Gables Av. Ashf 6A 22
Gables Clo. Farnb 1M 89
Gables Clo. Ash V 8E 90
Gables Clo. Dat 2K 5
Gables Clo. Kingf 7B 74 (in two parts)
Gables Ct. Kingf 7B 74
Gables Rd. C Crook 9A 88
Gables, The. Bans 4L 81
Gables, The. Copt 7M 163
Gables, The. Horl 9E 142
Gables, The. H'ham 4K 197
Gables, The. Oxs 8C 58
Gables Way. Bans 4L 81
Gabriel Clo. Felt 5M 23
Gabriel Dri. Camb. 2F 70
Gabriel Rd. M'bowr 7G 183
Gadbridge La. Ewh. 6F 156
Gadbrook Rd. Bet 9B 120
Gadd Clo. Wokgm 1E 30
Gadesden Rd. Eps 3B 60 (in two parts)
Gaffney Clo. Alder 6B 90
Gage Clo. Craw D. 9F 164
Gage Ridge. F Row 7G 187
Gaggle Wood. Man H. 9B 198
Gainsborough. Brack. 5A 32
Gainsborough Clo. Farnb. 3B 90
Gainsborough Clo. Camb 8D 50
Gainsborough Clo. Esh 7E 40
Gainsborough Ct. W4 1A 12 (off Chaseley Dri.)
Gainsborough Ct. Fleet 4B 88
Gainsborough Ct. W on T 1H 57
Gainsborough Dri. Asc 2H 33
Gainsborough Dri. S Croy 9D 64
Gainsborough Gdns. Iswth 8D 10
Gainsborough Mans. W14 2K 13 (off Queen's Club Gdns.)
Gainsborough Rd. Craw 7D 182
Gainsborough Rd. Eps. 6B 60
Gainsborough Rd. N Mald 5C 42
Gainsborough Rd. Rich 5M 11
Gainsborough Ter. Sutt 4L 61 (off Belmont Ri.)
Gaist Av. Cat 9E 84
Galahad Rd. If'd. 3K 181
Galata Rd. SW13 3F 12
Galba Ct. Bren 3K 11
Gale Clo. Hamp 7M 23
Gale Clo. Mitc 2B 44
Gale Cres. Bans 4M 81
Gale Dri. Light 6L 51
Galena Ho. W6 1G 12 (off Galena Rd.)
Galena Rd. W6 1G 13
Galen Clo. Eps 7N 59
Galesbury Rd. SW18 9N 13 & 1A 28
Gales Clo. Guild 9F 94
Gales Dri. Craw 3D 182
Gales Pl. Craw 3E 182
Galgate Clo. SW19. 2J 27
Galleries, The. Alder 2M 109 (off High St.)
Gallery Ct. SW10. 2N 13 (off Gunter Gro.)
Gallery Rd. Brkwd 6A 72
Galleymead Rd. Coln 4H 7
Gallop, The. S Croy 4E 64
Gallop, The. Sutt 5B 62
Gallop, The. Wind. 1F 18
Gallop, The. Yat. 8C 48
Galloway Clo. Fleet 1D 88
Galloway Path. Croy 1A 64 (7D 200)
Gallwey Rd. Alder 1N 109
Gally Hill Rd. C Crook 8A 88
Gallys Rd. Wind. 5A 4
Galpin's Rd. T Hth 4J 45
Galsworthy Rd. Cher 6J 37
Galsworthy Rd. King T. 8A 26
Galton Rd. Asc. 5C 34
Galvani Way. Croy 7K 45
Galveston Rd. SW15 8L 13
Galvins Clo. Guild 9K 93
Galway Rd. Yat 2B 68
Gambles La. Rip 2L 95
Gambole Rd. SW17. 5C 28
Gamlen Rd. SW15 7J 13
Gander Grn. Cres. Hamp 9A 24
Gander Grn. La. Sutt 8K 43
Gangers Hill. God & Wold 6H 105
Ganghill. Guild. 1C 114
Ganymede Ct. Craw 6K 181
Gapemouth Rd. Pirb 9H 71
Gap Rd. SW19 6M 27
Garbetts Way. Tong 6D 110
Garbrand Wlk. Eps. 5E 60
Garden Av. Mitc 8F 28
Garden Clo. Ashf 7D 22
Garden Clo. Farnb 2K 89
Garden Clo. SW15 1H 27
Garden Clo. Add 1M 55
Garden Clo. Bans 2M 81
Garden Clo. E Grin 2B 186
Garden Clo. Hamp 6N 23
Garden Clo. Lea 2J 99
Garden Clo. Sham G 7F 134
Garden Clo. Wall 2J 63
Garden Ct. Croy 8C 46
Garden Ct. Hamp 6N 23
Garden Ct. Rich 4M 11
Gardener Gro. Felt 3N 23

Gardeners Clo.—Glenmill

Gardeners Clo. Warn 9E 178
Gardeners Ct. H'ham 7K 197
Gardeners Green 6E 30
Gardeners Grn. Rusp 3B 180
Gardener's Hill Rd. Wrec & Lwr Bo 6G 120
Gardeners Rd. Croy 7M 45 (1A 200)
Gardeners Rd. Wink R 7E 16
Gardener's Wlk. Bookh 4B 98
Gardenfields. Tad 0K 01
Garden Ho. La. E Grin 2B 186
Gardenia Dri. W End 9C 52
Garden La. SW2 2K 29
Garden Pl. H'ham 4J 197
Garden Rd. SE20 1F 46
Garden Rd. Rich 6N 11
Garden Rd. W on T 5J 39
Gardens, The. Cob 6D 76
Gardens, The. Beck 1M 47
Gardens, The. Esh 1A 58
Gardens, The. Felt 8E 8
Gardens, The. Pirb 9C 72
Gardens, The. Tong 5D 110
Garden Wlk. Beck 1J 47
Garden Wlk. Coul 1E 102
Garden Wlk. Craw 3A 182
Garden Wlk. H'ham 4J 197
Garden Wood Rd. E Grin 9L 165
Gardiner Ct. S Croy 3N 63
Gardner Ho. Felt 3N 23
Gardner La. Craw D 1D 184
Gardner Rd. Guild 3N 113 (2C 202)
Garendon Gdns. Mord 6N 43
Garendon Rd. Mord 6N 43
Gareth Clo. Wor Pk 8J 43
Gareth Ct. SW16 4H 29
Garfield Pl. Wind 5G 4
Garfield Rd. SW19 6A 28
Garfield Rd. Add 2L 55
Garfield Rd. Camb 1A 70
Garfield Rd. Twic 2G 25
Garibaldi Rd. Red 4D 122
Garland Rd. E Grin 8N 165
Garlands Ct. Croy 6E 200
Garlands Rd. Lea 8H 79
Garlands Rd. Red 4D 122
Garland Way. Cat 9A 84
Garlichill Rd. Eps 4G 81
Garnet Fld. Yat 1A 68
Garnet Rd. T Hth 3N 45
Garrad's Rd. SW16 4H 29
Garrard Rd. Bans 0M 01
Garratt Clo. Croy 1J 63
Garratt Ct. SW18 1N 27
Garratt La. SW18 & SW17 9N 13
Garratts La. Bans 3L 81
Garratt Ter. SW17 5C 28
Garraway Ct. SW13 3H 13
(off Wyatt Dri.)
Garrett Clo. M'bowr 5G 183
Garrick Clo. Rich 8K 11
Garrick Clo. Stai 8J 21
Garrick Clo. W on T 1J 57
Garrick Cres. Croy 8B 46 (3F 200)
Garrick Gdns. W Mol 2A 40
Garrick Ho. W4 2D 12
Garrick Ho. King T 8J 203
Garrick Rd. Rich 5N 11
Garricks Ho. King T 4H 203
Garrick Wlk. Craw 6C 182
Garrick Way. Frim G 7C 70
Garrison Clo. Houn 8N 9
Garrison La. Chess 4K 59
Garrones, The. Craw 2H 183
Garsdale Ter. W14 1L 13
(off Aisgill Av.)
Garside Clo. Dork 7K 119
Garside Clo. Hamp 7B 24
Garson Clo. Esh 3N 57
Garson La. Wray 1N 19
Garson's La. Warf 2E 16
Garston Gdns. Kenl 2A 84
Garston La. Kenl 1A 84
Garstons, The. Bookh 3A 98
Garswood. Brack 5B 32
Garth Clo. W4 1C 12
Garth Clo. Farnh 4F 128
Garth Clo. King T 6M 25
Garth Clo. Mord 6J 43
Garth Ct. W4 1C 12
Garth Ct. Dork 7H 119
Garth Hunt Cotts. Brack 7N 15
Garth Rd. W4 1C 12
Garth Rd. King T 6M 25
Garth Rd. Mord 5H 43
Garth Rd. Ind. Est. Mord 7J 43
Garthside. Ham 6L 25
Garth Sq. Brack 8N 15
Garth, The. Cob 9M 57
Garth, The. Farnb 1B 90
Garth, The. As 3D 110
Garth, The. Hamp 7B 24
Gartmoor Gdns. SW19 2L 27
Garton Clo. If'd 4K 181
Garton Pl. SW18 9N 13 & 1A 28
Gascoigne Rd. New Ad 6M 65
Gascoigne Rd. Wey 9C 38
Gasden Copse. Witl 5A 152
Gasden Dri. Witl 4A 152
Gasden La. Witl 4A 152
Gaskarth Rd. SW12 1F 28
Gaskyns Clo. Rud 1E 194
Gassiot Rd. SW17 5D 28
Gassiot Way. Sutt 9B 44
Gasson Wood Rd. Craw 5K 181
Gastein Rd. W6 2J 13
Gaston Bell Clo. Rich 6M 11
Gaston Bri. Rd. Shep 5E 38
Gaston Rd. Mitc 2E 44
Gaston Way. Shep 4E 38
Gate Cen., The. Bren 3G 11
Gateford Dri. H'ham 2M 197
Gatehouse Clo. King T 8B 26
Gatehouse Clo. Wind 7E 4
Gates Clo. M'bowr 7G 182
Gatesden Clo. Fet 1C 98
Gatesden Rd. Fet 9C 78
Gates Grn. Rd. W Wick & Kes 1B 66
Gateside Rd. SW17 4D 28
Gate St. Brmly 1C 154
(in two parts)
Gateway. Wey 9C 38
Gateways. Guild 3C 114
Gateways. Surb 8K 203
Gateways Ct. Wall 2F 62
Gateways, The. Rich 7K 11
(off Park La.)
Gateway, The. Wok 1D 74
Gatfield Gro. Felt 3A 24
Gatfield Ho. Felt 3N 23
Gatley Av. Eps 2A 60
Gatley Dri. Guild 9B 94
Gatton 6D 102
Gatton Bottom 4F 102
Gatton Bottom. Reig & Red 8A 102
Gatton Clo. Reig 9A 102
Gatton Clo. Sutt 5N 61
Gatton Pk. Bus. Cen. Red 7F 102
Gatton Pk. Ct. Red 8D 102
Gatton Pk. Rd. Reig & Red 1B 122
Gatton Rd. SW17 5C 28
Gatton Rd. Reig 1A 122
Gatwick 5K 131
Gatwick Airport 3E 162
Gatwick Airport Spectator Gallery 3E 162
Gatwick Bus. Pk. Gat A 6F 162
Gatwick Ga. Low H 5C 162
Gatwick Ga. Ind. Est. Low H 5C 162
Gatwick International Distribution Cen. Craw 6F 162
Gatwick Metro Cen. Horl 8F 142
Gatwick Rd. SW18 1L 27
Gatwick Rd. Craw 9E 162
Gatwick Way. Gat A 2D 162
Gatwick Zoo & Aviaries 4H 161
Gauntlet Cres. Kenl 7A 84
Gauntlett Rd. Sutt 2B 62
Gavell Rd. Cob 9H 57
Gaveston Clo. Byfl 9A 56
Gaveston Rd. Lea 7G 78
Gavina Clo. Mord 4C 44
Gayfere Rd. Eps 2F 60
Gayhouse La. Out 3A 144
Gayler Clo. Blet 2C 124
Gaynesford Rd. Cars 4D 62
Gay St. SW15 6J 13
Gayton Clo. Asht 5L 79
Gayton Ct. Reig 2M 121
Gayville Rd. SW11 1D 28
Gaywood Clo. SW2 2K 29
Gaywood Rd. Asht 5M 79
Geary Clo. Small 1M 163
Geffers Ride. Asc 1J 33
Gemini Clo. Craw 5K 181
Genesis Bus. Cen. H'ham 5M 197
Genesis Bus. Pk. Wok 2F 74
Genesis Clo. Stanw 2A 22
Geneva Clo. Shep 1F 38
Geneva Rd. King T 3L 41 (8K 203)
Geneva Rd. T Hth 4N 45
Genoa Av. SW15 8H 13
Genoa Rd. SE20 1F 46
Gentles La. Pass & Head 8F 168
Genyn Rd. Guild 4L 113 (5A 202)
George Denyer Clo. Hasl 1G 189
George Eliot Clo. Witl 5C 152
George Gdns. Alder 5A 110
George Gro. Rd. SE20 1D 46
Georgeham Rd. Owl 5J 49
George Horley Pl. Newd 1A 160
Georgelands. Rip 8K 75
George Lindgren Ho. SW6 3L 13
(off Clem Attlee Ct.)
George Pinion Ct. H'ham 5H 197
George Rd. Fleet 4C 88
George Rd. G'ming 4H 133
George Rd. Guild 3N 113 (3C 202)
George Rd. King T 8A 26
(in two parts)
George Rd. Milf 9C 132
George Rd. N Mald 3F 42
George Sq. SW19 2M 43
George's Rd. Tats 7F 86
George's Sq. SW6 2L 13
(off N. End Rd.)
Georges Ter. Cat 9A 84
George St. Brkwd 8L 71
George St. Croy 8N 45 (3C 200)
George St. Houn 5N 9
George St. Rich 8K 11
George St. Stai 5H 21
George Wyver Clo. SW19 1K 27
Georgian Clo. Camb 8C 50
Georgian Clo. Craw 4H 183
Georgian Clo. Stai 5K 21
Georgian Ct. SW16 5J 29
Georgian Ct. Croy 1E 200
Georgia Rd. N Mald 3B 42
Georgia Rd. T Hth 9M 29
Georgina Ct. Fleet 4B 88
Gerald Ct. H'ham 6L 197
Geraldine Rd. SW18 8N 13
Geraldine Rd. W4 2N 11
Gerald's Gro. Bans 1J 81
Geranium Clo. Crowt 8G 30
Gerard Av. Houn 1A 24
Gerard Rd. SW13 4E 12
Germander Dri. Bisl 2D 72
Gerrards Mead. Bans 3L 81
Gervis Ct. Houn 3C 10
Ghyll Cres. H'ham 8M 197
Giant Arches Rd. SE24 1N 29
Gibbet La. Camb 7E 50
Gibbins La. Warf 6B 16
(in two parts)
Gibbon Rd. King T 9L 25 (1K 203)
Gibbons Clo. M'bowr 6G 183
Gibbons Clo. Sand 8H 49
Gibbon Wlk. SW15 7F 12
Gibb's Acre. Pirb 1C 92
Gibbs Av. SE19 6N 29
Gibbs Brook La. Oxt 5N 125
Gibbs Clo. SE19 6N 29
Gibbs Grn. W14 1L 13
(in two parts)
Gibbs Grn. Clo. W14 1L 13
Gibbs Sq. SE19 6N 29
Gibbs Way. Yat 2A 68
Giblets La. H'ham 1M 197
Giblets Way. H'ham 1L 197
Gibraltar Cres. Eps 6D 60
Gibson Clo. Chess 2J 59
Gibson Clo. Iswth 6E 10
Gibson Ct. Dat 1B 6
Gibson Ct. Esh 8F 40
Gibson Ho. Sutt 1M 61
Gibson M. Twic 9J 11
Gibson Pl. Stanw 9L 7
Gibson Rd. Sutt 2N 61
Gibsons Hill. SW16 8L 29
Gidd Hill. Coul 3E 82
Giffard Dri. Farnb 9L 69
Giffards Clo. E Grin 9B 166
Giffards Mdw. Farnh 2K 129
Giffard Way. Guild 9K 93
Giggshill 6G 40
Giggshill Gdns. Th Dit 7G 40
Giggshill Rd. Th Dit 6G 40
Gilbert Clo. SW19 8N 27
(off High Path)
Gilbert Ho. SW13 3G 13
(off Trinity Chu. Rd.)
Gilbert Rd. SW19 8A 28
Gilbert Rd. Camb 5A 70
Gilbert St. Houn 6C 10
Gilbert Way. Croy 8K 45
Gilbey Rd. SW17 5C 28
Gilders Rd. Chess 4M 59
Gilesmead. Eps 8L 201
Giles Travers Clo. Egh 2E 36
Gilham La. F Row 7G 187
Gilhams Av. Bans 8J 61
Gill Av. Guild 4H 113
Gillespie Ho. Vir W 3A 36
(off Holloway Dri.)
Gillett Ct. H'ham 4A 198
Gillette Corner. (Junct.) 3G 10
Gillett Rd. T Hth 3A 46
Gillham's La. Hasl 3A 188
Gilliam Gro. Purl 6L 63
Gillian Av. Alder 4A 110
Gillian Clo. Alder 4B 110
Gillian Pk. Rd. Sutt 7L 43
Gilliat Dri. Guild 1F 114
Gilligan Clo. H'ham 6H 197
Gill Ri. Warf 7A 16
Gilmais. Bookh 3C 98
Gilman Cres. Wind 6A 4
Gilmore Cres. Ashf 6B 22
Gilpin Av. SW14 7C 12
Gilpin Clo. Mitc 1C 44
Gilpin Cres. Twic 1B 24
Gilpin Way. Hay 3E 8
Gilsland Rd. T Hth 3A 46
Gilstead Rd. SW6 5N 13
Gilston Rd. SW10 1N 13
Gingers Clo. Cranl 8A 156
Ginhams Rd. Craw 3N 181
Gipsy La. SW15 6G 12
Gipsy La. Brack 1B 32
(in two parts)
Gipsy La. Wey 8C 38
Gipsy La. Wokgm 3B 30
Gipsy Rd. SE27 5N 29
Gipsy Rd. Gdns. SE27 5N 29
Girdwood Rd. SW18 1K 27
Girling Way. Felt 6H 9
Gironde Rd. SW6 3L 13
Girton Clo. Owl 6K 49
Girton Gdns. Croy 9K 47
Gisbourne Clo. Wall 9H 45
Givons Grove 4J 99
Givons Gro. Roundabout. Lea 2H 99
Glade Clo. Surb 8K 41
Glade Gdns. Croy 6H 47
Gladeside. Croy 5G 46
Gladeside Clo. Chess 4K 59
Gladeside Ct. Warl 7E 84
Glade Spur. Tad 8N 81
Glades, The. E Grin 9D 166
Glade, The. Asc 4N 33
Glade, The. Bucks H 1A 148
Glade, The. Coul 6L 83
Glade, The. Craw 5E 182
Glade, The. Croy 5H 47
Glade, The. Eps 3F 60
Glade, The. Farnh 5J 109
Glade, The. Fet 9A 78
Glade, The. H'ham 5N 197
Glade, The. Myt 3E 90
Glade, The. Stai 7K 21
Glade, The. Sutt 5K 61
Glade, The. Tad 0M 81
Glade, The. W Byf 9G 54
Glade, The. W Wick 9L 47
Gladiator Way. Farnb 5M 89
Gladioli Clo. Hamp 7A 24
Gladsmuir Clo. W on T 8K 39
Gladstone Av. Felt 9H 9
Gladstone Av. Twic 2D 24
Gladstone Gdns. Houn 4C 10
Gladstone Pl. E Mol 4E 40
Gladstone Rd. SW19 8M 27
Gladstone Rd. Asht 5K 79
Gladstone Rd. Croy 6A 46
Gladstone Rd. H'ham 5K 197
Gladstone Rd. King T 2N 41
Gladstone Rd. Orp 2L 67
Gladstone Rd. Surb 8K 41
Gladstone Ter. SE27 6N 29
(off Bentons La.)
Gladwyn Rd. SW15 6J 13
Glamis Clo. Frim 7D 70
Glamorgan Clo. Mitc 2J 45
Glamorgan Rd. King T 8J 25
Glanfield Rd. Beck 3J 47
Glanty 5E 20
Glanty, The. Egh 5D 20
Glanville Wlk. Craw 6M 181
Glasbrook Av. Twic 2N 23
Glasford St. SW17 7D 28
Glassonby Wlk. Camb 1G 70
(in two parts)
Glastonbury Rd. Mord 6M 43
Glayshers Hill. Hdly D 3F 168
Glazbury Rd. W14 1K 13
Glazebrook Clo. SE21 3N 29
Glazebrook Rd. Tedd 8F 24
Glaziers La. Norm 1M 111
Gleave Clo. E Grin 8C 166
Glebe Av. Mitc 1C 44
Glebe Clo. W4 1D 12
Glebe Clo. Bookh 4A 98
Glebe Clo. Craw 2C 182
Glebe Clo. Light 6N 51
Glebe Clo. S Croy 7C 64
Glebe Cotts. Felt 4A 24
Glebe Cotts. W Cla 1K 115
Glebe Ct. Fleet 4A 88
Glebe Ct. Guild 3B 114
Glebe Ct. Mitc 2D 44
Glebe Gdns. Byfl 1M 75
Glebe Gdns. N Mald 6D 42
Glebe Hyrst. S Croy 8C 64
Glebeland Gdns. Shep 5D 38
Glebeland Rd. Camb 2L 69
Glebelands. Clay 5F 58
Glebelands. Craw D 2D 184
Glebelands. Loxw 4H 193
Glebelands. W Mol 4B 40
Glebelands Mdw. Alf 8H 175
Glebelands Rd. Felt 2H 23
Glebelands Rd. Wokgm 1B 30
Glebe La. Rush 5A 150
Glebe La. Ab C 3L 137
Glebe Path. Mitc 2D 44
Glebe Rd. Farnb 9L 69
Glebe Rd. Hdly 4D 168
Glebe Rd. SW13 5F 12
Glebe Rd. Asht 5K 79
Glebe Rd. Cars 3D 62
Glebe Rd. Cranl 7M 155
Glebe Rd. Dork 5F 110 (3G 201)
Glebe Rd. Egh 6F 20
Glebe Rd. Old Win 8L 5
Glebe Rd. Red 2F 102
Glebe Rd. Stai 6K 21
Glebe Rd. Sutt 5K 61
Glebe Rd. Warl 4G 84
Glebe Side. Twic 9F 10
Glebe Sq. Mitc 2D 44
Glebe St. W4 1D 12
Glebe Ter. W4 1D 12
Glebe, The. SW16 5H 29
Glebe, The. B'water 2K 69
Glebe, The. Copt 7M 163
Glebe, The. Ewh 4F 156
Glebe, The. Felb 6K 165
Glebe, The. Horl 8D 142
Glebe, The. Leigh 1F 140
Glebe, The. Wor Pk 7E 42
Glebe Way. Hanw 4A 24
Glebe Way. W Croy 0O 04
Glebe Way. W Wick 8M 47
Glebewood. Brack 4A 32
Gledhow Gdns. SW5 1N 13
Gledhow Wood. Tad 8N 81
Gledstanes Rd. W14 1K 13
Gleeson Dri. Orp 2N 67
Gleeson M. Add 1L 55
Glegg Pl. SW15 7J 13
Glen Albyn Rd. SW19 3J 27
Glenallan Ho. W14 1L 13
(off N. End Cres.)
Glena Mt. Sutt 1A 62
Glen Av. Ashf 5B 22
Glenavon Clo. Clay 3G 58
Glenavon Ct. Wor Pk 8G 43
Glenavon Gdns. Yat 2C 68
Glenbuck Rd. Surb 5K 41
Glenburnie Rd. SW17 4D 28
Glencairn Rd. SW16 9J 29
Glen Clo. Hind 3A 170
Glen Clo. Kgswd 1K 101
Glen Clo. Shep 3B 38
Glencoe Clo. Frim 6E 70
Glencoe Rd. Wey 9B 38
Glen Ct. Add 2H 55
Glen Ct. Hind 3A 170
Glen Ct. St J 6K 73
Glendale Clo. H'ham 2N 197
Glendale Clo. Wok 5M 73
Glendale Clo. Wokgm 5A 30
Glendale Dri. SW19 6L 27
Glendale Dri. Guild 9E 94
Glendale M. Beck 1L 47
Glendale Ri. Kenl 2M 83
Glendarvon St. SW15 6J 13
Glendene Av. E Hor 4F 06
Glendon Ho. Craw 4D 182
Glendower Gdns. SW14 6C 12
Glendower Rd. SW14 6C 12
Glendyne Clo. E Grin 1C 186
Glendyne Way. E Grin 1C 186
Gleneagle M. SW16 6H 29
Gleneagle Rd. SW16 6H 29
Gleneagles Clo. Stanw 9L 7
Gleneagles Ct. Craw 4B 182
Gleneagles Dri. Farnb 2H 09
Gleneagles Ho. Brack 5K 31
(off St Andrews)
Gleneldon M. SW16 5J 29
Gleneldon Rd. SW16 5J 29
Glenfield Clo. Brock 7A 120
Glenfield Cotts. Charl 3J 161
Glenfield Ho. Brack 3A 32
Glenfield Rd. Ashf 7C 22
Glenfield Rd. SW12 2G 29
Glenfield Rd. Bans 2N 81
Glenfield Rd. Brock 6A 120
Glen Gdns. Croy 9L 45
Glenheadon Clo. Lea 1K 99
Glenheadon Ri. Lea 1K 99
Glenhurst. W'sham 1L 51
Glenhurst Clo. B'water 2K 69
Glenhurst Ri. SE19 8N 29
Glenhurst Rd. Bren 2J 11
Gleninnes. Col T 6L 49
Glenister Pk. Rd. SW16 8H 29
Glenlea. Gray 8C 170
Glenlea Hollow. Gray 9C 170
(in two parts)
Glenmill. Hamp 6N 23

Grange, The—Gresham Rd.

Grange, The. Wor Pk 1C 60
Grange Va. Sutt 4N 61
Grangeway. Small 8L 143
Grangewood Dri. Sun 8G 22
Grangewood Ter. SE25 1A 46
Gransden Clo. Ewh 5F 156
Grantchester. King T 1N 41
(off St Peters Rd.)
Grant Clo. Shep 5C 38
Grantham Clo. Owl 6K 49
Grantham Ct. King T 6K 25
Grantham Rd. W4 3D 12
Grantley Av. Won 5D 134
Grantley Clo. Shalf 1A 134
Grantley Ct. Farnh 5E 128
Grantley Dri. Fleet 6A 88
Grantley Gdns. Guild 2K 113
Grantley Rd. Guild 2K 113
Grantley Rd. Houn 5K 9
Granton Rd. SW16 9G 29
Grant Pl. Croy 7C 46
Grant Rd. Crowt 4H 49
Grant Rd. Croy 7C 46
Grants La. Oxt & Eden 1E 126
Grant Wlk. Asc 7B 34
Grant Way. Iswth 2G 10
Grantwood Clo. Red 8E 122
Granville Av. Felt 3H 23
Granville Av. Houn 8A 10
Granville Clo. Byfl 9A 56
Granville Clo. Croy 8B 46 (3F 200)
Granville Clo. Wey 3D 56
Granville Gdns. SW16 9K 29
Granville Pl. SW6 3N 13
Granville Rd. SW18 1L 27
Granville Rd. SW19 8M 27
Granville Rd. Oxt 7B 106
Granville Rd. W'ham 4L 107
Granville Rd. Wey 4D 56
Granville Rd. Wok 7B 74
Granwood Ct. Iswth 4E 10
Grapsome Clo. Chess 4J 59
Grasholm Way. Slou 1E 6
Grasmere Av. SW15 5C 26
Grasmere Av. SW19 2M 43
Grasmere Av. Houn 9B 10
Grasmere Clo. Egh 8D 20
Grasmere Clo. Felt 2G 22
Grasmere Clo. Guild 2D 114
Grasmere Ct. SW13 2F 12
(off Verdun Rd.)
Grasmere Ct. Sutt 3A 62
Grasmere Gdns. H'ham 2A 198
Grasmere Rd. Farnb 2K 89
Grasmere Rd. SE25 5E 46
Grasmere Rd. SW16 6K 29
Grasmere Rd. Farnh 6F 108
Grasmere Rd. Light 6M 51
Grasmere Rd. Purl 7M 63
Grasmere Way. Byfl 8A 56
Grassfield Clo. Coul 6F 82
Grasslands. Small 8L 143
Grassmere. Horl 7G 142
Grassmount. Purl 6G 63
Grass Way. Wall 1G 62
Gratton Dri. Wind 7B 4
Grattons Dri. Craw 9G 162
Grattons, The. Slin 5M 195
Gravel Hill. Croy 3G 64
Gravel Hill. Lea 8H 79
Gravel Hill Rd. B'ley 6A 128
Gravel Hill Rd. Holt P 7A 128
Gravelly Hill. Cat 6C 104
Gravel Pits Cotts. Gom 8D 116
Gravel Pits La. Gom 8D 116
Gravel Rd. Farnb 5D 90
Gravel Rd. C Crook 7C 88
Gravel Rd. Farnh 5G 108
Gravel Rd. Twic 2E 24
Gravenel Gdns. SW17 6C 28
(off Nutwell St.)
Graveney Rd. SW17 5C 28
Graveney Rd. M'bowr 4G 182
Gravetts La. Guild 8H 93
Gravetye Clo. Craw 5E 182
Gray Clo. Add 2K 55
Grayham Cres. N Mald 3C 42
Grayham Rd. N Mald 3C 42
Graylands. Wok 3A 74
Graylands Clo. Wok 3A 74
Graylands Ct. Guild 4B 114
Gray Pl. Ott 3F 54
Grays Clo. Hasl 9J 171
Grayscroft Rd. SW16 8H 29
Grayshot Dri. B'water 1H 69
Grayshott 6A 170
Grayshott. Gray 6B 170
Grayshott Laurels. Lind 4B 168
Grayshott Rd. Hdly D 3G 169
Grays La. Ashf 5C 22
Gray's La. Asht 6M 79
(in two parts)
Grays Rd. G'ming 4J 133
Grays Rd. W'ham 8K 87
Grayswood 7K 171
Grays Wood. Horl 8G 143
Grayswood Comn. G'wood 8K 171
Grayswood Copse. G'wood 7K 171
Grayswood Dri. Myt 4E 90
Grayswood Gdns. SW20 1G 42
Grayswood Rd. Hasl & G'wood 1H 189
Great Austins. Farnh 3J 129
Gt. Austins Ho. Farnh 3J 129
Great Benty. W Dray 1N 7
Great Bookham 4B 98
Great Bookham Common 8N 77
Great Burgh 4H 81
Gt. Chertsey Rd. W4 5B 12
Gt. Chertsey Rd. Felt & Twic 4N 23
Gt. Church La. W6 1J 13
Great Cockcrow Railway 7F 36
Great Ellshams. Bans 3M 81
Great Enton 6D 152
Greatfield Clo. Farnb 6N 69
Greatfield Rd. Farnb 6M 69
Greatford Dri. Guild 3F 114
Gt. Gatton Clo. Croy 6H 47
Gt. George St. G'ming 7H 133
Gt. Goodwin Dri. Guild 1D 114
Greatham Rd. M'bowr 6G 182
Greatham Wlk. SW15 2F 26
Greathed Manor 1E 166
Great Hollands 5L 31
Gt. Hollands Rd. Brack 5K 31
Gt. Hollands Sq. Brack 5L 31
Great Ho. Ct. E Grin 1B 186
Greathurst End. Bookh 2N 97
Greatlake Ct. Horl 7F 142
(off Tanyard Way)
Gt. Mead. Eden 9L 127
Gt. Oaks Pk. Guild 7D 94
Great Quarry. Guild 6N 113 (8D 202)
Gt. South W. Rd. Bedf & Felt 1D 22
Great Tattenhams. Eps 5G 81
Gt. West Rd. W4 & W6 1E 12
Gt. West Rd. Houn 5L 9
Gt. West Rd. Iswth & Bren 3E 10
Gt. West Trad. Est. Bren 2H 11
Greatwood Clo. Ott 5E 54
Gt. Woodcote Dri. Purl 6H 63
Gt. Woodcote Pk. Purl 6H 63
Greaves Pl. SW17 5C 28
Grebe Ct. Sutt 2L 61
Grebe Cres. H'ham 7N 197
Grebe Ter. King T 2L 41 (5J 203)
Grecian Cres. SE19 7M 29
Green Acre. Alder 3L 109
Green Acre. Knap 3H 73
Greenacre. Wind 5B 4
Greenacre Ct. Eng G 7M 19
Greenacre Pl. Hack 8F 44
Greenacres. Bookh 2B 98
Greenacres. Bord 5A 168
Greenacres. Craw 4E 182
Green Acres. Croy 9C 46
Greenacres. H'ham 4J 197
Greenacres. Oxt 5A 106
Green Acres. Runf 1A 130
Greenacres Clo. Orp 1L 67
Grn. Bank Cotts. F Grn 3M 157
Greenbank Way. Camb 1B 70
Greenbush La. Cranl 9A 156
Green Bus. Cen., The. Stai 5E 20
Green Clo. Brom 2N 47
Green Clo. Cars 8D 44
Green Clo. Felt 6M 23
Greencourt Av. Croy 8E 46
Greencourt Gdns. Croy 7E 46
Greencroft. Farnb 1N 89
Greencroft. Guild 3D 114
Green Cft. Wokgm 9D 14
Greencroft Rd. Houn 4N 9
Green Cross 9M 149
Grn. Cross La. Churt 9M 149
Green Curve. Bans 1L 81
Green Dene. E Hor 4D 116
Grn. Dragon La. Bren 1L 11
Green Dri. Rip 1H 95
Green Dri. Slou 1A 6
(in two parts)
Green Dri. Wokgm 4D 30
Greene Fielde End. Stai 8M 21
Green End. Chess 1L 59
Green End. Yat 8C 48
Grn. Farm Clo. Orp 3N 67
Grn. Farm Rd. Bag 4K 51
Greenfield. Eden 2M 147
Greenfield. Farnh 4F 128
Greenfield Av. Surb 6A 42
Greenfield Link. Coul 2J 83
Greenfield Rd. Farnh 4E 128
Greenfield Rd. Slin 5L 195
Greenfields Clo. Horl 6C 142
Greenfields Clo. H'ham 2N 197
Greenfields Pl. Bear G 7K 139
Greenfields Rd. Horl 6D 142
Greenfields Rd. H'ham 3N 197
Greenfields Way. H'ham 2N 197
Greenfield Way. Crowt 9F 30
Grn. Finch Clo. Crowt 1E 48
Greenfinch Way. H'ham 1J 197
Greenford Rd. Sutt 1N 61
(in two parts)
Green Gdns. Orp 2L 67
Green Glades. C Crook 8A 88
Greenham Ho. Houn 6D 10
Greenham Wlk. Wok 5M 73
Greenham Wood. Brack 5A 32
Greenhanger. Churt 1M 169
Greenhaven. Yat 1A 68
Greenhayes Av. Bans 1M 81
Grn. Hayes Clo. Reig 3A 122
Greenhayes Gdns. Bans 2M 81
Green Hedge. Twic 8J 11
Grn. Hedges Av. E Grin 8N 165
Grn. Hedges Clo. E Grin 8N 165
Greenheys Pl. Wok 5B 74
Green Hill. Orp 8H 67
Greenhill. Sutt 8A 44
Greenhill Av. Cat 8E 84
Greenhill Clo. Camb 9G 51
Greenhill Clo. Farnh 4F 128
Greenhill Clo. G'ming 8G 132
Greenhill Gdns. Guild 1E 114
Grn. Hill La. Warl 4H 85
Green Hill Rd. Camb 9G 51
Greenhill Rd. Farnh 4J 129
Greenhills. Farnh 3K 129
Greenhill Way. Farnh 6F 128
Greenholme. Camb 1H 71
Greenhow. Brack 2M 31
Greenhurst La. Oxt 1B 126
Greenhurst Rd. SE27 6L 29
Greenlake Ter. Stai 8J 21
Greenlands. Ott 9E 36
Greenlands Rd. Camb 5N 69
Greenlands Rd. Stai 5J 21
Greenlands Rd. Wey 9C 38
Green La. Cob 8M 57
Green La. SW16 & T Hth 8K 29
Green La. Alf 5H 175
Green La. Asc 9B 18
Green La. Asht 4J 79
Green La. Bad L 6L 109
Green La. Bag 5K 51
Green La. Bear G 1H 159
Green La. D'water 2K 69
(Hawley Rd.)
Green La. D'water 2G 69
(Reading Rd.)
Green La. Blet 9B 104
Green La. Byfl 8A 56
Green La. Cat 9N 83
Green La. Cher & Add 8G 36
Green La. Chess 5K 59
(in two parts)
Green La. Chob 6J 53
Green La. Churt 1L 169
Green La. Craw 1C 182
Green La. Craw D 6C 164
Green La. Crowt & Bag 9F 32
Green La. Dat 4L 5
Green La. Dock 4D 148
Green La. Egh 5D 20
(in two parts)
Green La. Egh & Stai 1E 36
(in two parts)
Green La. Farnh 3F 128
Green La. Felt 6M 23
Green La. G'ming 2G 133
Green La. Guild 3D 114
Green La. Hasl 4F 188
Green La. H'ham 5L 179
Green La. Houn 6J 9
Green La. Lea 8K 79
(in two parts)
Green La. Leigh 3D 140
Green La. Ling 8M 145
Green La. Lwr K & Coul 4L 101
Green La. Milf 2B 152
Green La. Mord 6H 43
(Battersea Cemetery)
Green La. Mord 5M 43
(Morden)
Green La. Newd 2C 160
(in two parts)
Green La. N Mald 4B 42
Green La. Ock 2C 96
Green La. Ockl 7M 157
Green La. Out 1J 143
Green La. Purl 7G 63
Green La. Red 1C 122
(Carlton Rd.)
Green La. Red 8E 122
(Spencer's Way)
Green La. Reig 3L 121
Green La. Sand 8H 49
Green La. Sham G 5H 135
Green La. Shep 5D 38
Green La. Ship B 3K 163
Green La. Sun 8G 22
Green La. Tilf 5B 130
Green La. W on T 3J 57
Green La. Warl 3H 85
Green La. W Cla 5J 95
Green La. W Mol 4B 40
Green La. Wind 5D 4
Green La. Wok 8L 73
Green La. Wokgm 6F 14
Green La. Wood S 1D 112
Green La. Wor Pk 7F 42
Green La. Worth 3H 183
(in two parts)
Green La. Yat 9A 48
Green La. Av. W on T 2K 57
Green La. Cvn. Pk. Red 1J 143
Green La. Clo. Byfl 8A 56
Green La. Clo. Camb 8A 50
Green La. Clo. Cher 8G 36
Green La. Cotts. Churt 9L 149
Green La. Cotts. Farnh 7L 109
Green La. E. Norm 4K 111
(Avenue, The, in two parts)
Green La. Gdns. T Hth 1N 45
Green Lanes. Eps 5D 60
(Ten Acre La., in two parts)
Green La. W. Ash G 4J 111
Green La. W. W Hor 3B 96
Greenlaw Gdns. N Mald 6F 42
Grn. Leaf Av. Wall 1H 63
Greenleaf Clo. SW2 1L 29
Greenleas. Frim 4C 70
Green Leas. King T 5K 203
Green Leas. Sun 7G 23
Grn. Leas Clo. Sun 7G 23
Greenleas Clo. Yat 8B 48
Greenleaves Ct. Ashf 7C 22
Green Leys. C Crook 9A 88
Grn. Man La. Felt 7H 9
(Faggs Rd.)
Grn. Man La. Felt 7J 9
(Heron Way)
Green Mead. Esh 3N 57
Greenmead Clo. SE25 4D 46
Greenmeads. Wok 9A 74
Greenoak Ri. Big H 5E 86
Greenoak Way. SW19 5J 27
Greenock Rd. SW16 9H 29
Greeno Cres. Shep 4B 38
Green Pde. Houn 8D 10
Green Pk. Stai 4G 20
Green Ride. Brack 6D 32
Green Rd. Egh 4B 36
Greensand Clo. Red 6H 103
Greensand Rd. Red 2E 122
Greenside. Crowt 2E 48
Greenside Clo. Guild 1E 114
Greenside Cotts. Rip 8L 75
Greenside Rd. Croy 6L 45
Greenside Wlk. Big H 5D 86
Greenslade Av. Asht 6A 80
Greens La. Man H 9C 198
Greens La. Newd 3N 159
Green's School La. Farnb 1M 89
(in two parts)
Greenstead Gdns. SW15 8G 12
Greenstede Av. E Grin 7B 166
Green St. Sun 9H 23
Green Street Green 3N 67
Green, The 9C 72
Green, The. Ashf 6M 21
Green, The. SW19 6J 27
Green, The. Bad L 7M 109
Green, The. B'water 2H 69
Green, The. Brack 3N 31
Green, The. Buck 2F 120
Green, The. Cars 1E 62
Green, The. C'fold 5F 172
Green, The. Clay 3F 58
Green, The. Copt 7M 163
Green, The. Craw 2A 182
Green, The. Croy 5J 65
Green, The. Dat 3L 5
Green, The. Duns 3B 174
Green, The. Elst 7H 131
Green, The. Eng G 5M 19
Green, The. Eps 7F 60
Green, The. Ewh 5F 156
Green, The. Farnh 6H 109
Green, The. Felt 3J 23
Green, The. Fet 2D 98
Green, The. Frim G 8D 70
Green, The. God 1E 124
Green, The. Hers 2K 57
Green, The. Houn 2A 10
Green, The. Mord 3K 43
Green, The. N Mald 2C 42
Green, The. N'chap 8D 190
Green, The. Ockl 5D 158
Green, The. Orp 1K 67
Green, The. Rich 8K 11
Green, The. Rip 8L 75
Green, The. Seale 2C 130
Green, The. Sham G 6F 134
Green, The. Shep 3F 38
Green, The. Sutt 9N 43
Green, The. Tad 6K 81
Green, The. Twic 2E 24
Green, The. Warl 4G 84
Green, The. W'ham 4M 107
Green, The. W Vill 6F 56
Green, The. Wold 1K 105
Green, The. Wray 9A 6
Green, The. Yat 9A 48
Greenvale Rd. Knap 5G 73
Green Vw. Chess 4M 59
Green Vw. God 9E 104
Greenview Av. Beck 5H 47
Greenview Av. Croy 5H 47
Greenview Ct. Ashf 5A 22
Green Wlk. Craw 1C 182
Green Wlk. Hamp 7N 23
Green Wlk. S'hall 1A 10
Greenway. SW20 3H 43
Green Way. Alder 1C 110
Greenway. Bookh 1B 98
Greenway. H'ham 5H 197
Green Way. Red 1C 122
Green Way. Sun 3H 39
Greenway. Tats 7E 86
Green Way. Wall 1G 62
Greenway Clo. W Byf 9J 55
Greenway Dri. Stai 9M 21
Greenway Gdns. Croy 9J 47
Greenways. Beck 2K 47
Greenways. Egh 6A 20
Greenways. Esh 1E 58
Greenways. Fleet 7A 88
Greenways. Sand 6G 49
Greenways. Tad 3G 100
Greenways Dri. Asc 7B 34
Greenways, The. Twic 9G 11
Greenways Wlk. Craw 8A 182
Greenway, The. Eps 1N 79
Greenway, The. Houn 7N 9
Greenway, The. Oxt 2D 126
Greenwell Clo. God 8E 104
Greenwich Clo. Craw 7A 182
Green Wood. Asc 9G 17
Greenwood Bus. Cen. Croy 6C 46
Greenwood Clo. Mord 3K 43
Greenwood Clo. Th Dit 7G 41
Greenwood Clo. Wdhm 7H 55
Greenwood Cotts. Asc 5F 34
Greenwood Ct. Craw 8N 181
Greenwood Dri. Red 8E 122
Greenwood Gdns. Cat 3D 104
Greenwood La. Hamp H 6B 24
Greenwood Pk. King T 8D 26
Greenwood Rd. Brkwd 8M 71
Greenwood Rd. Crowt 1F 48
Greenwood Rd. Croy 6M 45
Greenwood Rd. Iswth 6F 10
Greenwood Rd. Mitc 2H 45
Greenwood Rd. Th Dit 7G 41
Greenwood Rd. Wok 7H 73
Greenwood, The. Guild 2C 114
Grn. Wrythe Cres. Cars 7C 44
Grn. Wrythe La. Cars 5B 44
Gregory Clo. M'bowr 7G 182
Gregory Clo. Wok 4M 73
Gregory Dri. Old Win 9L 5
Gregsons. Warn 9E 178
Grenaby Av. Croy 6A 46
Grenaby Rd. Croy 6A 46
Grenadier Pl. Cat 9N 83
Grenadier Rd. Ash V 9F 90
Grenadiers Way. Farnb 2H 89
Grena Gdns. Rich 7M 11
Grena Rd. Rich 7M 11
Grendon Clo. Horl 6D 142
Grenehurst Pk. Capel 6J 159
Grenfell Rd. SW17 7D 28
Grennell Clo. Sutt 8B 44
Grennell Rd. Sutt 8A 44
Grenside Rd. Wey 9C 38
Grenville Clo. Cob 9L 57
Grenville Clo. Surb 7B 42
Grenville Dri. C Crook 7A 88
Grenville Gdns. Frim G 8C 70
Grenville M. SW7 1N 13
(off Harrington Gdns.)
Grenville M. Hamp 6B 24
Grenville Pl. Brack 1A 32
(off Ring, The)
Grenville Rd. New Ad 5M 65
Grenville Rd. Shack 1A 132
Gresham Av. Warl 5H 85
Gresham Clo. Oxt 7B 106
Gresham Ct. Purl 7L 63
Gresham Ind. Est. Alder 2C 110
Gresham Pl. Oxt 7B 106
Gresham Rd. SE25 3D 46
Gresham Rd. Beck 1H 47
Gresham Rd. Hamp 7A 24
Gresham Rd. Houn 4C 10
Gresham Rd. Oxt 6B 106

Hall Rd.—Harvard La.

Hall Rd. Iswth . . . 8D 10
Hall Rd. Wall . . . 5F 62
Halls Farm Clo. Knap . . . 4G 73
Hallsland. Craw D . . . 1F 184
Hallsland Way. Oxt . . . 2B 126
Hall Way. Purl . . . 9M 63
Halnaker Wlk. Craw . . . 6L 181
Halsford Cft. E Grin . . . 7L 165
Halsford Grn. E Grin . . . 7L 165
Halsford La. E Grin . . . 8L 165
Halsford Pk. Rd. E Grin . . . 8M 165
Halstead Clo. Croy . . . 9N 45 (4B 200)
Halters End. Gray . . . 6M 169
Ham. . . . 4J 25
Hamble Av. B'water . . . 1J 69
Hamble Clo. Wok . . . 4K 73
Hambleden Ct. Brack . . . 3C 32
Hambledon. . . . 9F 152
Hambledon Gdns. SE25 . . . 2C 46
Hambledon Hill. Eps . . . 3B 80
Hambledon Pk. Hamb . . . 9E 152
Hambledon Pl. Bookh . . . 1A 98
Hambledon Rd. SW18 . . . 1L 27
Hambledon Rd. Busb & G'ming . . . 9J 133 (in two parts)
Hambledon Rd. Cat . . . 1A 104
Hambledon Rd. Hamb & Hyde . . . 7G 153
Hambledon Va. Eps . . . 3B 80
Hamblehyrst. Beck . . . 1L 47
Hamble St. SW6 . . . 6N 13
Hambleton Clo. Frim . . . 3F 70
Hambleton Clo. Wor Pk . . . 8H 43
Hambleton Ct. Craw . . . 5A 182
Hambleton Hill. Craw . . . 5A 182
Hamble Wlk. Wok . . . 5K 73
Hambridge Way. SW2 . . . 1L 29
Hambrook Rd. SE25 . . . 2E 46
Hambro Rd. SW16 . . . 7H 29
Ham Clo. Rich . . . 4J 25 (in two parts)
Ham Comn. Rich . . . 4K 25
Hamesmoor Rd. Myt . . . 1C 90
Hamesmoor Way. Myt . . . 1D 90
Ham Farm Rd. Rich . . . 5K 25
Hamfield Clo. Oxt . . . 5M 105
Ham Ga. Av. Rich . . . 4K 25
Hamhaugh Island. Shep . . . 8B 38
Ham House. . . . 2J 25
Hamilton Av. Cob . . . 9H 57
Hamilton Av. Surb . . . 8N 41
Hamilton Av. Sutt . . . 8K 43
Hamilton Av. Wok . . . 2G 75
Hamilton Clo. Bag . . . 4J 51
Hamilton Clo. Bord . . . 5A 168
Hamilton Clo. Cher . . . 7J 37
Hamilton Clo. Eps . . . 8B 60
Hamilton Clo. Felt . . . 6G 22
Hamilton Clo. Guild . . . 7K 93
Hamilton Clo. Purl . . . 8M 63
Hamilton Ct. SW15 . . . 6K 13
Hamilton Ct. Bookh . . . 3B 98
Hamilton Ct. Croy . . . 7D 46
Hamilton Cres. Houn . . . 8B 10
Hamilton Dri. Asc . . . 6B 34
Hamilton Dri. Guild . . . 7K 93
Hamilton Gordon Ct. Guild . . . 2M 113 (1B 202)
Hamilton Ho. W4 . . . 2D 12
Hamilton M. SW18 . . . 2M 27
Hamilton M. SW19 . . . 8M 27
Hamilton Pde. Felt . . . 5G 23
Hamilton Pl. Alder . . . 3L 109
Hamilton Pl. Guild . . . 7K 93
Hamilton Pl. Kgswd . . . 9L 81
Hamilton Pl. Sun . . . 8J 23
Hamilton Rd. SE27 . . . 5N 29
Hamilton Rd. SW19 . . . 8N 27
Hamilton Rd. Bren . . . 2K 11
Hamilton Rd. C Crook . . . 7C 88
Hamilton Rd. Felt . . . 5G 22
Hamilton Rd. H'ham . . . 6H 197
Hamilton Rd. T Hth . . . 2A 46
Hamilton Rd. Twic . . . 2E 24
Hamilton Rd. M. SW19 . . . 8N 27
Hamilton Way. Wall . . . 5H 63
Ham Island. . . . 7N 5
Ham La. Elst . . . 7H 131
Ham La. Eng G . . . 5L 19
Ham La. Old Win . . . 8M 5 (in two parts)
Hamlash La. Fren . . . 1H 149
Hamlet Gdns. W6 . . . 1F 12
Hamlet St. Warf . . . 9C 16
Hamm Ct. Wey . . . 8N 37
Hammer. . . . 3B 188
Hammer Bottom. . . . 2A 188
Hammerfield Dri. Ab H . . . 1G 136
Hammer Hill. Hasl . . . 4A 188
Hammer La. Bram C . . . 9A 170
Hammer La. Churt . . . 1K 169
Hammer La. Cranl . . . 3M 175
Hammer La. Hasl . . . 2A 188
Hammer Pond Cotts. Thur . . . 4K 151
Hammerpond Rd. Colg . . . 9E 198
Hammerpond Rd. H'ham & Man H . . . 7M 197
Hammersley Rd. Alder . . . 6N 89
Hammersmith. . . . 1H 13
Hammersmith Bri. SW13 & W6 . . . 2G 13
Hammersmith Bri. Rd. W6 . . . 1H 13
Hammersmith B'way. W6 . . . 1H 13
Hammersmith Flyover. (Junct.) . . . 1H 13
Hammersmith Ind. Est. W6 . . . 2H 13
Hammersmith Rd. W6 & W14 . . . 1J 13
Hammersmith Ter. W6 . . . 1F 12
Hammer Va. Hasl . . . 2A 188
Hammerwood. . . . 7K 167
Hammerwood Copse. Hasl . . . 3B 188
Hammerwood Pk. . . . 8L 167
Hammerwood Rd. Ash W . . . 3F 186
Hammer Yd. Craw . . . 4B 182
Hamm Moor La. Add . . . 2N 55
Hammond Av. Mitc . . . 1F 44
Hammond Clo. Hamp . . . 9A 24
Hammond Clo. Wok . . . 2M 73
Hammond Ct. Brack . . . 9M 15 (off Crescent Rd.)
Hammond Rd. Craw . . . 9N 181
Hammond Rd. Wok . . . 2M 73
Hammond Way. Light . . . 6M 51
Ham Moor. . . . 1N 55
Hamond Clo. S Croy . . . 5M 63
Hampden Av. Beck . . . 1H 47
Hampden Clo. Craw . . . 9J 163
Hampden Rd. Beck . . . 1H 47
Hampden Rd. King T . . . 2N 41
Hampers Ct. H'ham . . . 6K 197
Hamper's La. H'ham . . . 6N 197
Hampshire Clo. Alder . . . 5B 110
Hampshire Ct. Add . . . 2L 55
Hampshire Hog La. W6 . . . 1G 12
Hampshire Ri. Warf . . . 7D 16
Hampshire Rd. Camb . . . 7D 50
Hampstead La. Dork . . . 6F 118
Hampstead Rd. Dork . . . 6G 118
Hampstead Wlk. Craw . . . 7A 182
Hampton. . . . 9B 24
Hampton & Richmond Borough F.C. . . . 9B 24
Hampton Clo. SW20 . . . 8H 27
Hampton Clo. C Crook . . . 9B 88
Hampton Court. . . . 3E 40
Hampton Court. (Junct.) . . . 2E 40
Hampton Ct. Av. E Mol . . . 5D 40
Hampton Ct. Bri. E Mol . . . 3E 40
Hampton Ct. Cres. E Mol . . . 2D 40
Hampton Court Palace. . . . 3F 40
Hampton Ct. Pde. E Mol . . . 3E 40
Hampton Ct. Rd. E Mol & King T . . . 2F 40
Hampton Ct. Rd. Hamp & E Mol . . . 1C 40
Hampton Ct. Way. Th Dit & E Mol . . . 8E 40
Hampton Farm Ind. Est. Felt . . . 4M 23
Hampton Gro. Eps . . . 7E 60
Hampton Hill. . . . 6C 24
Hampton La. Felt . . . 5M 23
Hampton Rd. Croy . . . 5N 45
Hampton Rd. Farnh . . . 6F 108
Hampton Rd. Red . . . 8D 122
Hampton Rd. Tedd . . . 6D 24
Hampton Rd. Twic . . . 4D 24
Hampton Rd. Wor Pk . . . 8F 42
Hampton Rd. E. Felt . . . 5N 23
Hampton Rd. W. Felt . . . 4M 23
Hampton Way. E Grin . . . 2B 186
Hampton Wick . . . 9J 25 (1G 203)
Ham Ridings. Rich . . . 6M 25
Hamsey Green. . . . 3E 84
Hamsey Grn. Gdns. Warl . . . 3E 84
Hamsey Way. S Croy . . . 2E 84
Ham St. Rich . . . 2H 25
Ham, The. Bren . . . 3J 11
Ham Vw. Croy . . . 5H 47
Hanah Ct. SW19 . . . 8J 27
Hanbury Dri. Big H . . . 9D 66
Hanbury Path. Wok . . . 1F 74
Hanbury Rd. If'd . . . 4K 181
Hanbury Way. Camb . . . 3A 70
Hancock Rd. SE19 . . . 7N 29
Hancocks Mt. Asc . . . 5A 34
Hancombe Rd. Sand . . . 6F 48
Handcroft Rd. Croy . . . 6M 45 (1A 200)
Handcross. . . . 8N 199
Handcross Rd. Hand . . . 8N 199
Handel Mans. SW13 . . . 3H 13
Handford La. Yat . . . 1C 68
Handinhand La. Tad . . . 8B 100
Handley Page Rd. Wall . . . 4K 63
Handside Clo. Wor Pk . . . 7J 43
Hanford Clo. SW18 . . . 2M 27
Hanford Row. SW19 . . . 7H 27
Hangerfield Clo. Yat . . . 1B 68
Hanger Hill. Wey . . . 3C 56
Hanger, The. Hdly . . . 2D 168
Hangrove Hill. Orp . . . 9K 67
Hanley Clo. Wind . . . 4A 4
Hannah Clo. Beck . . . 2M 47
Hannah M. Wall . . . 4G 63
Hannah Peschar Gallery Garden. . . . 8A 158
Hannay Wlk. SW16 . . . 3H 29
Hannell Rd. SW6 . . . 3K 13
Hannen Rd. SE27 . . . 4M 29
Hannibal Rd. Stanw . . . 1M 21
Hannibal Way. Croy . . . 2K 63
Hanover Av. Felt . . . 2H 23
Hanover Clo. Craw . . . 5D 182 (in two parts)
Hanover Clo. Eng G . . . 7L 19
Hanover Clo. Frim . . . 5C 70
Hanover Clo. Red . . . 6G 102
Hanover Clo. Rich . . . 3N 11
Hanover Clo. Sutt . . . 1K 61
Hanover Clo. Wind . . . 4C 4
Hanover Clo. Yat . . . 8C 48
Hanover Ct. SW15 . . . 7E 12
Hanover Ct. Dork . . . 5F 118 (2G 201)
Hanover Ct. Guild . . . 1N 113
Hanover Ct. H'ham . . . 5M 197
Hanover Ct. Wok . . . 6A 74
Hanover Dri. Fleet . . . 1D 88
Hanover Gdns. Farnb . . . 8K 69
Hanover Gdns. Brack . . . 6L 31
Hanover Rd. SW19 . . . 8A 28
Hanover St. Croy . . . 9M 45 (4A 200)
Hanover Ter. Iswth . . . 4G 11
Hanover Wlk. Wey . . . 9E 38
Hanover Way. Wind . . . 5C 4
Hansler Gro. E Mol . . . 3D 40
Hanson Clo. SW12 . . . 1F 28
Hanson Clo. SW14 . . . 6B 12
Hanson Clo. Camb . . . 8F 50
Hanson Clo. Guild . . . 9B 94
Hanworth. . . . 6M 31 (Bracknell)
Hanworth. . . . 6M 23 (Feltham)
Hanworth Clo. Brack . . . 5A 32
Hanworth La. Cher . . . 7H 37
Hanworth Rd. Brack . . . 7M 31
Hanworth Rd. Felt . . . 2J 23
Hanworth Rd. Hamp . . . 6N 23
Hanworth Rd. Houn . . . 2M 23
Hanworth Rd. Red . . . 8D 122
Hanworth Rd. Sun . . . 8H 23 (in two parts)
Hanworth Ter. Houn . . . 7B 10
Hanworth Trad. Est. Cher . . . 7J 37
Hanworth Trad. Est. Felt . . . 4M 23
Harberson Rd. SW12 . . . 2F 28
Harbledown Rd. SW6 . . . 4M 13
Harbledown Rd. S Croy . . . 7D 64
Harbord St. SW6 . . . 4J 13
Harborough Rd. SW16 . . . 5K 29
Harbour Av. SW10 . . . 4N 13
Harbour Clo. Farnb . . . 6M 69
Harbourfield Rd. Bans . . . 2N 81
Harbridge Av. SW15 . . . 1E 26
Harbury Rd. Cars . . . 5C 62
Harcourt Av. Wall . . . 1F 62
Harcourt Clo. Egh . . . 7E 20
Harcourt Clo. Iswth . . . 6G 11
Harcourt Cotts. P'ham . . . 8N 111
Harcourt Fld. Wall . . . 1F 62
Harcourt Lodge. Wall . . . 1F 62
Harcourt M. Wray . . . 9A 6
Harcourt Rd. SW19 . . . 8M 27
Harcourt Rd. Brack . . . 5N 31
Harcourt Rd. Camb . . . 1M 69
Harcourt Rd. T Hth . . . 5K 45
Harcourt Rd. Wall . . . 1F 62
Harcourt Rd. Wind . . . 4B 4
Harcourt Ter. SW10 . . . 1N 13
Harcourt Way. S God . . . 6H 125
Hardcastle Clo. Croy . . . 5D 46
Hardcourts Clo. W Wick . . . 9L 47
Hardell Clo. Egh . . . 6C 20
Hardel Ri. SW2 . . . 2M 29
Hardel Wlk. SW2 . . . 1L 29
Harden Farm Clo. Coul . . . 8G 83
Hardham Clo. Craw . . . 1M 181
Harding Clo. Croy . . . 9C 46
Harding Ho. SW13 . . . 2G 13 (off Wyatt Dri.)
Harding Rd. Eps . . . 6D 80
Harding's Clo. King T . . . 9M 25 (1L 203)
Hardings Rd. Dock . . . 2A 148
Hardman Rd. King T . . . 1L 41 (3K 203)
Hardwell Way. Brack . . . 3C 32
Hardwick Clo. Oxs . . . 2C 78
Hardwicke Av. Houn . . . 4A 10
Hardwicke Rd. Reig . . . 2M 121
Hardwicke Rd. Rich . . . 5J 25
Hardwick La. Lyne . . . 6E 36
Hardwick Rd. Red . . . 5B 122
Hardwicks Way. SW18 . . . 8M 13
Hardy Av. Yat . . . 2B 68
Hardy Clo. Craw . . . 2G 182
Hardy Clo. Horl . . . 8C 142
Hardy Clo. H'ham . . . 4H 197
Hardy Clo. N Holm . . . 9H 119
Hardy Grn. Crowt . . . 3G 49
Hardy Ho. SW4 . . . 1G 29
Hardy Rd. SW19 . . . 8N 27
Hardys Clo. E Mol . . . 3E 40
Harebell Hill. Cob . . . 1L 77
Harecroft. Dork . . . 8J 119
Harecroft. Fet . . . 2B 98
Harefield. Esh . . . 9E 40
Harefield Av. Sutt . . . 5K 61
Harefield Rd. SW16 . . . 8K 29
Hare Hill. Add . . . 3G 55
Harehill Clo. Pyr . . . 2J 75
Harelands Clo. Wok . . . 4M 73
Harelands La. Wok . . . 5M 73 (in two parts)
Hare La. Clay . . . 2D 58
Hare La. Craw . . . 9N 161
Hare La. G'ming . . . 5J 133
Hare La. Ling . . . 7F 144
Harendon. Tad . . . 8H 81
Hares Bank. New Ad . . . 6N 65
Harestone Dri. Cat . . . 2C 104
Harestone Hill. Cat . . . 4C 104
Harestone La. Cat . . . 3B 104 (in two parts)
Harestone Valley Rd. Cat . . . 4B 104
Hareward Rd. Guild . . . 1E 114
Harewood Clo. Craw . . . 9C 162
Harewood Clo. Reig . . . 9A 102
Harewood Gdns. S Croy . . . 2E 84
Harewood Rd. SW19 . . . 7C 28
Harewood Rd. Iswth . . . 3F 10
Harewood Rd. S Croy . . . 3B 64
Harfield Rd. Sun . . . 1L 39
Harkness Clo. Eps . . . 3H 81
Harland Av. Croy . . . 9C 46
Harland Clo. SW19 . . . 2N 43
Harlands Gro. Orp . . . 1K 67
Harlech Gdns. Houn . . . 2K 9
Harlech Rd. B'water . . . 2J 69
Harlequin Av. Bren . . . 2G 11
Harlequin Cen. S'hall . . . 1K 9
Harlequin Clo. Iswth . . . 8F 10
Harlequin Rd. Tedd . . . 8H 25
Harlequins R.U.F.C. (Stoop Memorial Ground). . . . 1E 24
Harlequin Theatre. . . . 2D 122
Harley Gdns. Orp . . . 1N 67
Harlington. . . . 2E 8
Harlington Cen., The. Fleet . . . 4A 88 (off Fleet Rd.)
Harlington Clo. Hay . . . 3D 8
Harlington Corner. (Junct.) . . . 4E 8
Harlington Rd. E. Felt . . . 1J 23
Harlington Rd. W. Felt . . . 9J 9
Harlington Way. Fleet . . . 4A 88
Harlow Ct. Reig . . . 3B 122 (off Wray Comn. Rd.)
Harman Pl. Purl . . . 7M 63
Harmans Dri. E Grin . . . 9D 166
Harmans Mead. E Grin . . . 9D 166
Harmanswater. . . . 3B 32
Harman's Water Rd. Brack . . . 4A 32
Harmar Clo. Wokgm . . . 2D 30
Harmondsworth. . . . 2M 7
Harmondsworth La. W Dray . . . 2N 7
Harmondsworth Rd. W Dray . . . 1N 7
Harmony Clo. Bew . . . 5K 181
Harmony Clo. Wall . . . 5H 63
Harms Gro. Guild . . . 9E 94
Harold Rd. SE19 . . . 8N 29
Harold Rd. Sutt . . . 1B 62
Harold Rd. Worth . . . 3J 183
Haroldslea. Horl . . . 1H 163 (in two parts)
Haroldslea Clo. Horl . . . 1G 163
Haroldslea Dri. Horl . . . 1G 162
Harold Wilson Ho. SW6 . . . 2L 13 (off Clem Attlee Ct.)
Harpenden Rd. SE27 . . . 4M 29
Harper Dri. M'bowr . . . 7G 182
Harper M. SW17 . . . 4A 28
Harper's Rd. As . . . 1G 111
Harpesford Av. Vir W . . . 4L 35
Harps Oak La. Red . . . 3D 102
Harpton Clo. Yat . . . 8C 48
Harpton Pde. Yat . . . 8C 48
Harpurs. Tad . . . 9J 81
Harrier Clo. Cranl . . . 6N 155
Harrier Ct. Craw . . . 9H 163 (off Bristol Clo.)
Harrier Ct. Houn . . . 6M 9
Harriet Gdns. Croy . . . 8D 46
Harriet Ho. SW6 . . . 3N 13 (off Wandon Rd.)
Harriet Tubman Clo. SW2 . . . 1K 29
Harrington Clo. Croy . . . 8J 45
Harrington Clo. Leigh . . . 1F 140
Harrington Clo. Wind . . . 7C 4
Harrington Ct. Croy . . . 8A 46 (3E 200)
Harrington Gdns. SW7 . . . 1N 13
Harrington Rd. SE25 . . . 3D 46
Harriott's Clo. Asht . . . 7J 79
Harriott's La. Asht . . . 6J 79
Harris Clo. Craw . . . 6N 181
Harris Clo. Houn . . . 4A 10
Harrison Clo. Reig . . . 4N 121
Harrison Ct. Shep . . . 4C 38
Harrison's Ri. Croy . . . 9M 45 (4A 200)
Harris Path. Craw . . . 6N 181
Harris Way. Sun . . . 9F 22
Harrogate Ct. Slou . . . 1C 6
Harrow Bottom Rd. Vir W . . . 5B 36
Harrow Clo. Add . . . 8K 37
Harrow Clo. Chess . . . 4K 59
Harrow Clo. Dork . . . 6G 119
Harrow Clo. Eden . . . 9L 127
Harrowdene. Cranl . . . 6N 155
Harrowdene Gdns. Tedd . . . 7G 25
Harrow Gdns. Warl . . . 3J 85
Harrowgate Gdns. Dork . . . 7H 119
Harrowlands Pk. Dork . . . 6H 119
Harrow La. G'ming . . . 4H 133
Harrow Rd. Cars . . . 3C 62
Harrow Rd. Felt . . . 3B 22
Harrow Rd. Warl . . . 2J 85
Harrow Rd. E. Dork . . . 7H 119
Harrow Rd. W. Dork . . . 7G 118
Harrowsley Ct. Horl . . . 7F 142
Harrowsley Grn. La. Horl . . . 9G 143
Harrow Way. Shep . . . 1D 38
Hart Cen., The. Fleet . . . 4A 88
Hart Clo. Farnb . . . 6K 69
Hart Clo. Blet . . . 2B 124
Hart Clo. Brack . . . 8M 15
Hart Dene Ct. Bag . . . 4J 51
Hart Dyke Clo. Wokgm . . . 6A 30
Harte Rd. Houn . . . 5N 9
Hartfield Cres. SW19 . . . 8L 27
Hartfield Cres. W Wick . . . 1C 66
Hartfield Rd. SW19 . . . 8L 27
Hartfield Rd. Chess . . . 2K 59
Hartfield Rd. F Row . . . 6H 187
Hartfield Rd. M Grn . . . 6M 147
Hartfield Rd. W Wick . . . 1C 66
Hartford Ri. Camb . . . 9B 50
Hartford Rd. Eps . . . 3A 60
Hart Gdns. Dork . . . 4H 119 (1K 201)
Hartham Clo. Iswth . . . 4G 10
Hartham Rd. Iswth . . . 4F 10
Harting Ct. Craw . . . 6L 181
Hartington Clo. F'boro . . . 2L 67
Hartington Ct. W4 . . . 3A 12
Hartington Pl. Reig . . . 1M 121
Hartington Rd. W4 . . . 3A 12
Hartington Rd. Twic . . . 1H 25
Hartismere Rd. SW6 . . . 3L 13
Hartland Clo. New H . . . 6L 55
Hartland Pl. Farnb . . . 8M 69
Hartland Rd. Add . . . 4J 55
Hartland Rd. Hamp H . . . 5B 24
Hartland Rd. Iswth . . . 6G 11
Hartland Rd. Mord . . . 6M 43
Hartlands, The. Houn . . . 2J 9
Hartland Way. Croy . . . 9H 47
Hartland Way. Mord . . . 6L 43
Hartley Clo. B'water . . . 1G 69
Hartley Copse. Old Win . . . 9K 5
Hartley Down. Purl . . . 2K 83
Hartley Farm. Purl . . . 2K 83
Hartley Hill. Purl . . . 2K 83
Hartley Old Rd. Purl . . . 2K 83
Hartley Rd. Croy . . . 6N 45
Hartley Rd. W'ham . . . 3M 107
Hartley Way. Purl . . . 2K 83
Hartop Point. SW6 . . . 3K 13 (off Pellant Rd.)
Hart Rd. Byfl . . . 9N 55
Hart Rd. Dork . . . 4H 119 (1K 201)
Harts Cft. Croy . . . 5H 65
Harts Gdns. Guild . . . 9L 93
Hartsgrove. C'fold . . . 4E 172
Harts Hill. Guild . . . 2G 113
Hartshill Wlk. Wok . . . 3L 73
Harts La. S God . . . 5G 124
Hartsleaf Clo. Fleet . . . 5A 88
Harts Leap Clo. Sand . . . 6G 48
Harts Leap Rd. Sand . . . 7F 48
Hartsplece Rd. Red . . . 5E 122
Hartswood. N Holm . . . 8J 119
Hartswood Av. Reig . . . 7M 121
Harts Yd. Farnh . . . 1G 129
Harts Yd. G'ming . . . 7H 133
Hart, The. Farnh . . . 1G 128
Harvard Hill. W4 . . . 2A 12
Harvard La. W4 . . . 1B 12

Harvard Rd.—Heatherdene

Harvard Rd. W4 . . . 1A 12
Harvard Rd. Iswth . . . 4E 10
Harvard Rd. Owl . . . 6K 49
Harvest Bank Rd. W Wick . . . 1B 66
Harvest Clo. Yat . . . 2A 68
Harvest Ct. Esh . . . 8A 40
Harvest Ct. Shep . . . 3B 38
Harvest Cres. Fleet . . . 9C 68
Harvester Rd. Eps . . . 6C 60
Harvesters. H'ham . . . 4K 197
Harvesters Clo. Iswth . . . 8D 10
Harvest Hill. E Grin . . . 1A 186
Harvest Hill. G'ming . . . 7G 132
Harvest La. Th Dit . . . 5G 40
Harvest Ride. Brack . . . 7M 15
(in two parts)
Harvest Rd. Eng G . . . 6N 19
Harvest Rd. Felt . . . 5H 23
Harvest Rd. M'bowr . . . 5G 183
Harvestside. Horl . . . 7G 142
Harvey Clo. Craw . . . 8M 181
Harvey Ct. Eps . . . 5A 60
Harvey Dri. Hamp . . . 9B 24
Harvey Ho. Bren . . . 1L 11
Harvey Rd. Farnb . . . 9H 69
Harvey Rd. Guild . . . 5A 114 (6E 202)
Harvey Rd. Houn . . . 1N 23
Harvey Rd. W on T . . . 6G 39
Harwood Av. Mitc . . . 2C 44
Harwood Ct. SW15 . . . 7H 13
Harwood Gdns. Old Win . . . 1L 19
Harwood M. SW6 . . . 3M 13
Harwood Pk. Red . . . 3E 142
Harwood Rd. SW6 . . . 3M 13
Harwood Rd. H'ham . . . 5L 197
Harwoods Clo. E Grin . . . 2B 186
Harwoods La. E Grin . . . 2B 186
Harwood Ter. SW6 . . . 4N 13
Hascombe . . . 6N 153
Hascombe Cotts. Hasc . . . 5M 153
Hascombe Ct. Craw . . . 4M 181
Hascombe Ct. Hasc . . . 6M 153
Hascombe Rd. Cranl . . . 9E 154
Hascombe Rd. G'ming . . . 1K 153
Haslam Av. Sutt . . . 7K 43
Hasle Dri. Hasl . . . 2F 188
Haslemere . . . 2G 189
Haslemere and Heathrow Est., The. Houn . . . 5J 9
Haslemere Av. SW18 . . . 3N 27
Haslemere Av. Houn . . . 5K 9
Haslemere Av. Mitc . . . 1B 44
Haslemere Clo. Frim . . . 3G 70
Haslemere Clo. Hamp . . . 6N 23
Haslemere Clo. Wall . . . 2J 63
Haslemere Educational Mus. . . . 1H 189
Haslemere Ind. Est. SW18 . . . 3N 27
Haslemere Ind. Est. Hasl . . . 1G 188
Haslemere Rd. Brook & Wmly . . . 4M 171
Haslemere Rd. Fern . . . 7F 188
Haslemere Rd. T Hth . . . 4M 45
Haslemere Rd. Wind . . . 4D 4
Haslemere Rd. Witl & Milf . . . 6N 151
Haslett Av. E. Craw . . . 3C 182
Haslett Av. W. Craw . . . 3B 182
Haslett Rd. Shep . . . 1F 38
Hassocks Ct. Craw . . . 6L 181
Hassocks Rd. SW16 . . . 9H 29
Hassock Wood. Kes . . . 1F 66
Haste Hill. Hasl . . . 3H 189
Hastings Clo. Frim . . . 7E 70
Hastings Ct. Tedd . . . 6D 24
Hastings Dri. Surb . . . 5J 41
Hastings Rd. Craw . . . 3G 182
Hastings Rd. Croy . . . 7C 46
Hatch Clo. Add . . . 9K 37
Hatch Clo. Alf . . . 6J 175
Hatch End. F Row . . . 7H 187
Hatch End. W'sham . . . 3N 51
Hatches, The. Farnh . . . 3E 128
Hatches, The. Frim G . . . 8B 70
(in two parts)
Hatchet La. Asc & Wink . . . 6L 17
Hatchett Rd. Felt . . . 2D 22
Hatchetts Dri. Hasl . . . 2A 188
Hatch Farm M. Add . . . 9L 37
Hatchford . . . 6F 76
Hatchford End . . . 6D 76
Hatch Gdns. Tad . . . 7J 81
Hatchgate. Horl . . . 9D 142
Hatchgate Copse. Brack . . . 5K 31
Hatch Hill. Hasl . . . 7F 188
Hatchlands . . . 9A 96
Hatchlands. Capel . . . 5J 159
Hatchlands. H'ham . . . 1N 197
Hatchlands Pk. . . . 8A 96
Hatchlands Rd. Red . . . 3C 122
Hatch La. Coul . . . 2D 82
Hatch La. Hasl . . . 6F 188
Hatch La. Ock . . . 5C 76
(Elm La.)
Hatch La. Ock . . . 7C 76
(Ockham La.)
Hatch La. Out . . . 2K 143
Hatch La. W Dray . . . 3M 7
Hatch La. Wind . . . 6D 4
Hatch La. Wmly . . . 1A 172
Hatch Pl. King T . . . 6M 25
Hatch Ride. Crowt . . . 9G 31
Hatch Rd. SW16 . . . 1J 45
Hatfield Clo. Mitc . . . 3B 44
Hatfield Clo. Sutt . . . 5N 61
Hatfield Clo. W Byf . . . 8K 55
Hatfield Gdns. Farnb . . . 2C 90
Hatfield Mead. Mord . . . 4M 43
Hatfield Rd. Asht . . . 6M 79
Hatfield Wlk. Craw . . . 6K 181
Hathaway Ct. Red . . . 2E 122
(off St Anne's Ri.)
Hathaway Rd. Croy . . . 6M 45
Hatherleigh Clo. Chess . . . 2K 59
Hatherleigh Clo. Mord . . . 3M 43
Hatherley Rd. Rich . . . 4M 11
Hatherop Rd. Hamp . . . 8N 23
Hathersham Clo. Small . . . 7L 143
Hathersham La. Small . . . 4H 143
Hatherwood. Lea . . . 8K 79
Hatherwood. Yat . . . 1E 68
Hatton . . . 7G 8
Hatton Ct. Wind . . . 5F 4
Hatton Cross. (Junct.) . . . 6G 8
Hatton Gdns. Mitc . . . 4D 44
Hatton Grn. Felt . . . 7H 9
Hatton Hill. W'sham . . . 1M 51
Hatton Ho. King T . . . 4M 203
Hatton Rd. Croy . . . 7L 45
Hatton Rd. Felt . . . 1D 22
Hatton Rd. S. Felt . . . 7G 8
Havana Rd. SW19 . . . 3M 27
Havelock Rd. SW19 . . . 6A 28
Havelock Rd. Croy . . . 8C 46
Havelock Rd. Wokgm . . . 2A 30
Havelock St. Wokgm . . . 2A 30
Havenbury Est. Dork . . . 4G 118 (1H 201)
Haven Clo. SW19 . . . 4J 27
Haven Ct. Beck . . . 1M 47
Haven Ct. Surb . . . 5M 41
Haven Gdns. Craw D . . . 9E 164
Havengate. H'ham . . . 3M 197
Haven Rd. Ashf . . . 4C 22
Haven Rd. Rud & Bil . . . 2D 194
Haven, The . . . 6E 194
Haven, The. Rich . . . 6N 11
Haven, The. Sun . . . 8H 23
Haven Way. Farnh . . . 8J 109
Haverfield Gdns. Rich . . . 3N 11
Haverhill Rd. SW12 . . . 2G 28
Havers Av. W on T . . . 2L 57
Haversham Clo. Craw . . . 3D 182
Haversham Clo. Twic . . . 9K 11
Haversham Dri. Brack . . . 5N 31
Havisham Pl. SE19 . . . 8M 29
Hawarden Clo. Craw D . . . 1F 184
Hawarden Gro. SE24 . . . 1N 29
Hawarden Rd. Cat . . . 8N 83
Hawes La. W Wick . . . 7M 47
Hawes Rd. Tad . . . 7J 81
Haweswater Ct. Ash V . . . 8D 90
(off Lakeside Clo.)
Hawker Ct. King T . . . 3M 203
Hawker Rd. Ash V . . . 8D 90
Hawkesbourne Rd. H'ham . . . 3M 197
Hawkesbury Rd. SW15 . . . 8G 12
Hawkes Leap. W'sham . . . 1M 51
Hawkesley Clo. Twic . . . 5G 24
Hawkesmoor Rd. Craw . . . 5K 181
Hawkes Rd. Felt . . . 1H 23
Hawkes Rd. Mitc . . . 9D 28
Hawkesworth Dri. Bag . . . 6H 51
Hawkewood Rd. Sun . . . 2H 39
Hawkfield Ct. Iswth . . . 5E 10
Hawkhirst Rd. Kenl . . . 2A 84
Hawkhurst. Cob . . . 1A 78
Hawkhurst Gdns. Chess . . . 1L 59
Hawkhurst Rd. SW16 . . . 9H 29
Hawkhurst Rd. Kenl . . . 4B 84
Hawkhurst Wlk. Craw . . . 5F 182
Hawkhurst Way. N Mald . . . 4C 42
Hawkhurst Way. W Wick . . . 8L 47
Hawkins Clo. Brack . . . 1E 32
Hawkins Rd. Craw . . . 6C 182
Hawkins Rd. Tedd . . . 7H 25
Hawkins Way. Fleet . . . 5D 88
Hawkins Way. Wokgm . . . 2D 30
Hawk La. Brack . . . 3B 32
Hawkley Gdns. SE27 . . . 3M 29
Hawkridge Ct. Brack . . . 3C 32
Hawksbrook La. Beck . . . 5L 47
(in two parts)
Hawkshaw Clo. SW2 . . . 1J 29
Hawk's Hill. Lea . . . 1F 98
Hawkshill Clo. Esh . . . 3A 58
Hawks Hill Clo. Fet . . . 1F 98
Hawk's Hill Ct. Fet . . . 1F 98
Hawkshill Pl. Esh . . . 3A 58
Hawkshill Way. Esh . . . 3N 57
Hawksmoore Dri. Bear G . . . 7J 139
Hawksmoor St. W6 . . . 2J 13
Hawks Pas. King T . . . 3L 203
Hawks Rd. King T . . . 1M 41 (4M 203)
Hawksview. Cob . . . 9N 57
Hawks Way. Stai . . . 4H 21
Hawkswell Clo. Wok . . . 4J 73
Hawkswell Wlk. Wok . . . 4J 73
Hawkswood Av. Frim . . . 4D 70
Hawkswood Ho. Brack . . . 9K 15
Hawkwell. C Crook . . . 9C 88
Hawkwood Dell. Bookh . . . 4A 98
Hawkwood Ri. Bookh . . . 4A 98
Hawley . . . 3K 69
Hawley Clo. Hamp . . . 7N 23
Hawley Ct. Farnb . . . 6K 69
Hawley Grn. B'water . . . 3K 69
Hawley Lane . . . 6N 69
Hawley La. Farnb . . . 5M 69
(in three parts)
Hawley La. Ind. Est. Farnb . . . 6N 69
Hawley Rd. B'water . . . 2J 69
Hawley's Corner . . . 8K 87
Hawley Way. Ashf . . . 6B 22
Hawmead. Craw D . . . 1F 184
Haworth Rd. M'bowr . . . 4F 182
Haws La. Stai . . . 9J 7
Hawth Av. Craw . . . 5C 182
Hawth Clo. Craw . . . 5C 182
Hawthorn Clo. Alder . . . 4C 110
Hawthorn Clo. Bans . . . 1K 81
Hawthorn Clo. Brack . . . 9M 15
Hawthorn Clo. Craw . . . 9A 162
Hawthorn Clo. Eden . . . 1K 147
Hawthorn Clo. Hamp . . . 6A 24
Hawthorn Clo. H'ham . . . 4J 197
Hawthorn Clo. Houn . . . 3J 9
Hawthorn Clo. Red . . . 8E 122
Hawthorn Clo. Wok . . . 7A 74
Hawthorn Ct. Rich . . . 4A 12
Hawthorn Cres. SW17 . . . 6E 28
Hawthorn Cres. S Croy . . . 7F 64
Hawthorn Dri. W Wick . . . 1A 66
Hawthorne Av. Big H . . . 2F 86
Hawthorne Av. Cars . . . 4E 62
Hawthorne Av. Mitc . . . 1B 44
Hawthorne Av. T Hth . . . 9M 29
Hawthorne Av. Wink . . . 3M 17
Hawthorne Clo. Sutt . . . 8A 44
Hawthorne Ct. Stanw . . . 1M 21
(off Hawthorne Way)
Hawthorne Cres. B'water . . . 2K 69
Hawthorne Dri. Wink . . . 3M 17
Hawthorne Pl. Eps . . . 8D 60 (5M 201)
Hawthorne Rd. Stai . . . 6E 20
Hawthorne Way. Guild . . . 8D 94
Hawthorne Way. Stanw . . . 1M 21
Hawthorne Way. Wink . . . 2M 17
Hawthorn Hatch. Bren . . . 3H 11
Hawthorn Hill . . . 1B 16
Hawthorn La. Rowl . . . 8E 128
Hawthorn La. Wind . . . 1C 16
Hawthorn Rd. Bren . . . 3H 11
Hawthorn Rd. Frim . . . 4D 70
Hawthorn Rd. G'ming . . . 9E 132
Hawthorn Rd. Rip . . . 2J 95
Hawthorn Rd. Sutt . . . 3C 62
Hawthorn Rd. Wall . . . 4F 62
Hawthorn Rd. Wok . . . 7N 73
Hawthorns. S Croy . . . 7A 200
Hawthorns, The. Coln . . . 4H 7
Hawthorns, The. Eps . . . 4E 60
Hawthorns, The. Oxt . . . 2C 126
Hawthorn Way. Bisl . . . 3D 72
Hawthorn Way. New H . . . 6L 55
Hawthorn Way. Red . . . 4F 122
Hawthorn Way. Shep . . . 3E 38
Hawth Theatre . . . 4D 182
Hawtrey Rd. Wind . . . 5F 4
Haxted . . . 3G 147
Haxted Mill & Mus. . . . 3F 146
Haxted Rd. Ling & Eden . . . 5A 146
Haybarn Dri. H'ham . . . 1L 197
Haycroft Clo. Coul . . . 5M 83
Haycroft Rd. Surb . . . 8K 41
Hayden Ct. New H . . . 7K 55
Haydn Av. Purl . . . 1L 83
Haydon Pk. Rd. SW19 . . . 6M 27
Haydon Pl. Guild . . . 4N 113 (4C 202)
Haydon Pl. Yat . . . 9D 48
Haydons Rd. SW19 . . . 6N 27
Hayes Barton. Wok . . . 3F 74
Hayes Chase. W Wick . . . 5N 47
Hayes Ct. SW2 . . . 2J 29
Hayes Cres. Sutt . . . 1J 61
Hayes Hill. Brom . . . 7N 47
Hayes La. Beck . . . 2M 47
Hayes La. Kenl . . . 3M 83
Hayes La. Slin . . . 8H 195
Hayes, The. Eps . . . 6D 80
Hayes Wlk. Small . . . 7L 143
Hayes Way. Beck . . . 3M 47
Hayfields. Horl . . . 7F 142
Haygarth Pl. SW19 . . . 6J 27
Haygreen Clo. King T . . . 7A 26
Haylett Gdns. King T . . . 3K 41 (8H 203)
Hayley Grn. Warf . . . 6D 16
Hayling Av. Felt . . . 4H 23
Hayling Ct. Craw . . . 6A 182
Hayling Ct. Sutt . . . 1H 61
Haymeads Dri. Esh . . . 3C 58
Haymer Gdns. Wor Pk . . . 9F 42
Hayne Rd. Beck . . . 1J 47
Haynes Clo. Rip . . . 9K 75
Haynes Clo. Slou . . . 1B 6
Haynt Wlk. SW20 . . . 2K 43
Hays Bri. Bus. Cen. S God . . . 5F 144
Hays Bri. Houses. God . . . 4E 144
Hayse Hill. Wind . . . 4A 4
Haysleigh Gdns. SE20 . . . 1D 46
Hays Wlk. Sutt . . . 6J 61
Haywain. Oxt . . . 8N 105
Hayward Clo. SW19 . . . 8N 27
Haywardens. Ling . . . 6N 145
Hayward Gdns. SW15 . . . 9H 13
Hayward Rd. Th Dit . . . 7F 40
Haywards. Craw . . . 9H 163
Haywards Mead. Eton W . . . 1C 4
Haywood. Brack . . . 6A 32
Haywood Dri. Fleet . . . 6B 88
Haywood Ri. Orp . . . 2N 67
Hazel Av. Farnb . . . 2L 89
(in three parts)
Hazel Av. Guild . . . 8M 93
Hazel Bank. SE25 . . . 1B 46
Hazel Bank. Surb . . . 7B 42
Hazelbank Ct. Cher . . . 7L 37
Hazelbank Rd. Cher . . . 7L 37
Hazelbourne Rd. SW12 . . . 1F 28
Hazelbury Clo. SW19 . . . 1M 43
Hazel Clo. Bren . . . 3H 11
Hazel Clo. Craw . . . 9A 162
Hazel Clo. Craw D . . . 1F 184
Hazel Clo. Croy . . . 6G 46
Hazel Clo. Eng G . . . 7L 19
Hazel Clo. Mitc . . . 3H 45
Hazel Clo. Reig . . . 5A 122
Hazel Clo. Twic . . . 1C 24
Hazel Ct. Guild . . . 8N 93
Hazel Dene. Add . . . 2L 55
Hazeldene Ct. Kenl . . . 2A 84
Hazel Dri. Rip . . . 3H 95
Hazel Gro. Felt . . . 2H 23
Hazel Gro. Hind . . . 7C 170
Hazel Gro. Stai . . . 7K 21
Hazelhurst. Beck . . . 1N 47
Hazelhurst. Horl . . . 7G 143
Hazelhurst Clo. Guild . . . 7D 94
Hazelhurst Cres. H'ham . . . 7F 196
Hazelhurst Dri. Worth . . . 3J 183
Hazelhurst Rd. SW17 . . . 5A 28
Hazel La. Rich . . . 3L 25
Hazell Hill. Brack . . . 2A 32
Hazell Rd. Farnh . . . 1E 128
Hazel Mead. Eps . . . 6F 60
Hazelmere Clo. Felt . . . 9F 8
Hazelmere Clo. Lea . . . 6H 79
Hazelmere Ct. SW2 . . . 2K 29
Hazel Pde. Fet . . . 9C 78
Hazel Rd. Ash G . . . 5G 111
Hazel Rd. Myt . . . 3E 90
Hazel Rd. Reig . . . 5A 122
Hazel Rd. W Byf . . . 1J 75
Hazel Wlk. N Holm . . . 8J 119
Hazel Way. Coul . . . 6D 82
Hazel Way. Craw D . . . 1F 184
Hazel Way. Fet . . . 9C 78
Hazelwick Av. Craw . . . 1E 182
Hazelwick Ct. Craw . . . 1E 182
Hazelwick Mill La. Craw . . . 1E 182
(in two parts)
Hazelwick Rd. Craw . . . 2E 182
Hazelwood . . . 7M 67
Hazelwood. Craw . . . 3M 181
Hazelwood. Dork . . . 6H 119
Hazelwood. Elst . . . 7J 131
Hazelwood Av. Mord . . . 3N 43
Hazelwood Clo. Craw D . . . 1C 184
Hazelwood Cotts. G'ming . . . 7G 132
Hazelwood Ct. Surb . . . 5L 41
Hazelwood Gro. S Croy . . . 9E 64
Hazelwood Heights. Oxt . . . 9C 106
Hazelwood Houses. Short . . . 2N 47
Hazelwood La. Binf . . . 1M 15
(in four parts)
Hazelwood La. Coul . . . 5C 82
Hazelwood Rd. Cud . . . 8M 67
Hazelwood Rd. Knap . . . 5H 73
Hazelwood Rd. Oxt . . . 1D 126
Hazlebury Rd. SW6 . . . 5N 13
Hazledean Rd. Croy . . . 8A 46 (3E 200)
Hazledene Rd. W4 . . . 2B 12
Hazlemere Gdns. Wor Pk . . . 7F 42
Hazlewell Rd. SW15 . . . 8H 13
Hazlitt Clo. Felt . . . 5M 23
Hazon Way. Eps . . . 8B 60 (5H 201)
Headcorn Pl. T Hth . . . 3K 45
Headcorn Rd. T Hth . . . 3K 45
Headington Clo. Wokgm . . . 9C 14
Headington Ct. Croy . . . 7B 200
Headington Dri. Wokgm . . . 9C 14
Headington Rd. SW18 . . . 3A 28
Headlam Rd. SW4 . . . 1H 29
(in two parts)
Headland Way. Ling . . . 7M 145
Headley . . . 4D 168
(Bordon)
Headley . . . 3B 100
(Epsom)
Headley Av. Wall . . . 2K 63
Headley Clo. Craw . . . 9H 163
Headley Clo. Eps . . . 3N 59
Headley Comn. Rd. H'ley . . . 5C 100
Headley Ct. Eden . . . 1M 147
Headley Ct. H'ley . . . 1A 100
Headley Down . . . 5H 169
Headley Dri. Eps . . . 6G 81
Headley Dri. New Ad . . . 4L 65
Headley Fields. Hdly . . . 4D 168
Headley Gro. Tad . . . 7H 81
Headley Heath . . . 6A 100
Headley Heath App. Tad . . . 8A 100
Headley Hill Rd. Hdly . . . 4E 168
Headley La. Mick . . . 7J 99
Headley La. Pass . . . 8D 168
Headley Pk. Cotts. Hdly . . . 9B 148
Headley Rd. Eps . . . 5A 80
(in two parts)
Headley Rd. Gray . . . 5K 169
Headley Rd. Lea & Eps . . . 9J 79
Headley Rd. Lind . . . 4B 168
Headon Ct. Farnh . . . 2J 129
Headway Clo. Rich . . . 5J 25
Headway, The. Eps . . . 5E 60
Healy Dri. Orp . . . 1N 67
Hearmon Clo. Yat . . . 9D 48
Hearn . . . 1F 168
Hearne Rd. W4 . . . 2N 11
Hearn Va. Hdly D . . . 2F 168
Hearnville Rd. SW12 . . . 2E 28
Hearn Wlk. Brack . . . 9C 16
Hearsey Gdns. B'water . . . 9G 49
(in two parts)
Heathacre. Coln . . . 4G 6
Heatham Pk. Twic . . . 1F 24
Heathbridge. Wey . . . 4B 56
Heathbridge App. Wey . . . 3B 56
Heath Bus. Cen. Houn . . . 7C 10
Heath Bus. Cen. Salf . . . 4F 142
Heath Clo. Bans . . . 1N 81
Heath Clo. Broad H . . . 5E 196
Heath Clo. Farnh . . . 5H 109
Heath Clo. Hay . . . 3E 8
Heath Clo. Hind . . . 2A 170
Heath Clo. Stanw . . . 9L 7
Heath Clo. Vir W . . . 3N 35
Heath Clo. Wokgm . . . 4A 30
Heathcote. Tad . . . 8J 81
Heathcote Clo. Ash V . . . 1E 110
(off Church Path)
Heathcote Dri. E Grin . . . 8L 165
Heathcote Rd. As . . . 1F 110
Heathcote Rd. Camb . . . 1B 70
Heathcote Rd. Eps . . . 1C 80 (8K 201)
Heathcote Rd. Twic . . . 9H 11
Heath Cotts. Hind . . . 3A 170
Heath Cotts. Lwr Bo . . . 8J 129
Heath Ct. Bag . . . 4J 51
Heath Ct. Broad H . . . 5E 196
Heath Ct. Croy . . . 7D 200
Heath Ct. Houn . . . 7N 9
Heathcroft Av. Sun . . . 8G 22
Heathdale Av. Houn . . . 6M 9
Heathdene. Tad . . . 5K 81
Heathdene Rd. SW16 . . . 8K 29
Heathdene Rd. Wall . . . 4F 62
Heathdown Rd. Wok . . . 2F 74
Heath Dri. SW20 . . . 3H 43
Heath Dri. Brkwd . . . 7D 72
Heath Dri. Send . . . 9D 74
Heath Dri. Sutt . . . 5A 62
Heath Dri. Tad . . . 3F 100
Heath End . . . 5H 109
Heather Clo. Alder . . . 3K 109
Heather Clo. Ash V . . . 8F 90
Heather Clo. Copt . . . 8M 163
Heather Clo. Farnh . . . 5E 128
Heather Clo. Guild . . . 2L 113
Heather Clo. Hamp . . . 9N 23
Heather Clo. H'ham . . . 3K 197
Heather Clo. Iswth . . . 8D 10
Heather Clo. New H . . . 6K 55
Heather Clo. Red . . . 9F 102
Heather Clo. Tad . . . 9K 81
Heather Clo. Wok . . . 2M 73
Heather Cotts. Hind . . . 1B 170
Heather Ct. Hind . . . 5D 170
Heatherdale Clo. King T . . . 7N 25
Heatherdale Rd. Camb . . . 2A 70
Heatherdene. W Hor . . . 3E 96

Heatherdene Av.—High Dri.

Heatherdene Av. Crowt 3D 48
Heatherdene Clo. Mitc 3B 44
Heather Dri. Asc 6F 34
Heather Dri. C Crook 8A 88
Heather Dri. Lind 4A 168
Heatherfields. New H 6K 55
Heather Gdns. Farnb 3J 89
Heather Gdns. Sutt 3M 61
Heatherlands. Horl 7F 142
(in two parts)
Heatherlands. Sun 7H 23
Heatherley Clo. Camb 1N 69
Heatherley Rd. Camb 1N 69
Heather Mead. Frim 4D 70
Heather Mead Ct. Frim 4D 70
Heathermount. Brack 3C 32
Heathermount Dri. Crowt 1E 48
Heathermount Gdns. Crowt 1E 48
Heather Pl. Esh 1B 58
Heather Ridge Arc. Camb 2G 71
Heatherset Clo. Esh 2C 58
Heatherset Gdns. SW16 8K 29
Heatherside 2G 71
Heatherside Clo. Bookh 3N 97
Heatherside Dri. Vir W 5K 35
Heatherside Rd. Eps 4C 60
Heathersland. Dork 8J 119
Heathers, The. Stai 1A 22
Heathervale Cvn. Pk. New H
6L 55
Heathervale Rd. New H 6K 55
Heathervale Way. New H 6L 55
Heather Vw. Cotts. Fren 1H 149
Heather Wlk. Brkwd 8A 72
Heather Wlk. Craw 6N 181
Heather Wlk. Small 8N 143
Heather Wlk. Twic 1A 24
(off Stephenson Rd.)
Heather Wlk. W Vill 6F 56
Heather Way. Chob 4H 53
Heatherway. Crowt 2F 48
Heatherway. Felb 3J 165
Heather Way. Hind 5D 170
Heather Way. S Croy 5G 65
Heathfield. Cob 1A 78
Heathfield. Craw 9H 163
(in two parts)
Heathfield Av. SW18 1B 28
Heathfield Av. Asc 4B 34
Heathfield Clo. G'ming 9H 133
Heathfield Clo. Kes 2E 66
Heathfield Clo. Wok 5C 74
Heathfield Ct. W4 1C 12
Heathfield Ct. Fleet 6A 88
Heathfield Dri. Mitc 9C 28
Heathfield Dri. Red 8C 122
Heathfield Gdns. W4 1B 12
Heathfield Gdns. Croy
1A 64 (6C 200)
Heathfield N. Twic 1E 24
Heathfield Rd. SW18 1B 28
Heathfield Rd. Croy
1A 64 (6D 200)
Heathfield Rd. Kes 2E 66
Heathfield Rd. W on T 1M 57
Heathfield Rd. Wok 5C 74
Heathfields Clo. Lea 5J 79
Heathfields Ct. Houn 8M 9
Heathfield S. Twic 1F 24
Heathfield Sq. SW18 1B 28
Heathfield Ter. W4 1B 12
Heathfield Va. S Croy 5G 65
Heath Gdns. Twic 2F 24
Heath Gro. Sun 8G 23
Heath Hill. Dock 7D 148
Heath Hill. Dork 5H 119 (2L 201)
Heath Hill Rd. N. Crowt 2G 48
Heath Hill Rd. S. Crowt 2G 49
Heath Ho. Rd. Wok 9G 73
Heathhurst Rd. S Croy 5A 64
Heathlands. Brack 3M 31
Heathlands. Tad 9J 81
Heathlands Clo. Sun 1H 39
Heathlands Clo. Twic 3F 24
Heathlands Clo. Wok 1A 74
Heathlands Ct. Wokgm 8E 30
Heathlands Ct. Yat 2D 68
Heathlands Rd. Wokgm 5E 30
Heathland St. Alder 2M 109
Heathlands Way. Houn 8M 9
Heathland Vis. Cen. 6K 51
(Lightwater Country Pk.)
Heath La. Alb 1N 135
Heath La. Cron & Ews 6A 108
Heath La. Farnh 5H 109
Heath La. G'ming 9K 133
Heathmans Rd. SW6 4L 13
Heath Mead. SW19 4J 27
Heath Mill La. Worp 3E 92
(in two parts)
Heathmoors. Brack 4A 32
Heathpark Dri. W'sham 3B 52
Heath Pl. Bag 4J 51
Heath Ride. Finch & Crowt 1A 48
Heath Ridge Grn. Cob 9A 58
Heath Ri. SW15 9J 13
Heath Ri. Camb 1B 70
Heath Ri. Rip 1K 95
Heath Ri. Vir W 3N 35
Heath Ri. Westc 7C 118
Heath Rd. Bag 4J 51
Heath Rd. Cat 1A 104
Heath Rd. Hasl 3B 188
Heath Rd. Houn 7B 10
Heath Rd. Oxs 8C 58
Heath Rd. T Hth 2N 45
Heath Rd. Twic 2F 24
Heath Rd. Wey 1B 56
Heath Rd. Wok 2B 74
Heathrow. Gom 8D 116
Heathrow Airport 6C 8
Heathrow Boulevd. W Dray 3A 8
(in two parts)
Heathrow Causeway Cen. Houn
6H 9
Heathrow Clo. W Dray 4K 7
Heathrow Corporate Pk. Houn
6K 9
Heathrow International Trad. Est.
Houn 6J 9
Heathside. Esh 9E 40
Heathside. Houn 1N 23
Heathside. Wey 2C 56
Heathside Clo. Esh 9E 40
Heathside Ct. Tad 1G 101
Heathside Cres. Wok 4B 74
Heathside Gdns. Wok 4C 74
Heathside La. Hind 3B 170
Heathside Pk. Camb 8C 50
Heathside Pk. Rd. Wok 5B 74
Heathside Pl. Eps 5J 81
Heathside Rd. Wok 5B 74
Heath, The 3C 56
Heath, The. Cat 2N 103
Heath, The. P'ham 8A 112
Heath Va. Bri. Rd. Ash V 7E 90
Heath Vw. E Hor 3G 97
Heathview Gdns. SW15 1H 27
Heathview Rd. Milf 3B 152
Heathview Rd. T Hth 3L 45
Heathway. Asc 9J 17
Heathway. Camb 1B 70
Heathway. Cat 3N 103
Heathway. Croy 9J 47
Heathway. E Hor 2G 97
Heath Way. H'ham 3K 197
Heathway Clo. Camb 1B 70
Heathwood Clo. Yat 8C 48
Heathyfields Rd. Farnh 6E 108
Heaton Rd. Mitc 8E 28
Hebbecastle Down. Warf 7N 15
Hebdon Rd. SW17 4C 20
Heber Mans. W14 2K 13
(off Queen's Club Gdns.)
Heckets Ct. Esh 6C 58
Heckfield Pl. SW6 3M 13
Heddon Clo. Iswth 7G 10
Heddon Wlk. Farnb 7M 69
Hedgecourt Pl. Felb 6H 165
Hedge Cft. Yat 9A 48
Hedgecroft Cotts. Rip 8K 75
Hedgehog La. Hasl 2F 188
Hedgerley Ct. Wok 4M 73
Hedger's Almshouses. Guild
2F 114
(off Wykeham Rd.)
Hedgeside. Craw 8A 182
Hedgeway. Guild 5K 113
Hedingham Clo. Horl 7G 142
Hedley Rd. Twic 1A 24
Heenan Clo. Frim G 7C 70
Heidegger Cres. SW13 3G 13
Heighton Gdns. Croy
2M 63 (8A 200)
Heights Clo. SW20 8G 27
Heights Clo. Bans 3K 81
Heights, The. Wey 6B 56
Helby Rd. SW4 1H 29
Heldor St. S Croy 3A 64
Heldmann Clo. Houn 7D 10
Helena Rd. Wind 5G 4
Helen Av. Felt 1J 23
Helen Clo. W Mol 3B 40
Helen Ct. Farnb 1N 89
Helford Wlk. Wok 5K 73
Helgiford Gdns. Sun 8F 22
Helicon Ho. Craw 4A 182
Helix Bus. Pk. Camb 3N 69
Helix Rd. SW2 1K 29
Helm Clo. Eps 8N 59
Helme Clo. SW19 6L 27
Helmsdale. Brack 4R 32
Helmsdale. Wok 5L 73
Helmsdale Rd. SW16 9H 29
Helston Clo. Frim 7E 70
Helston La. Wind 4E 4
Helvellyn Clo. Egh 8D 20
Hemingford Rd. Sutt 1H 61
Hemlock Clo. Kgswd 1K 101
Hemming Clo. Hamp 9A 24
Hemmyng Corner. Warf 7A 16
Hempshaw Av. Bans 3D 82
Hemsby Rd. Chess 3M 59
Hemsby Wlk. Craw 5F 182
Hemsley Ct. Guild 9K 93
Hemwood Rd. Wind 6A 4
Henbane Ct. Craw 7M 181
Henbit Clo. Tad 6G 81
Henchley Dene. Guild 9F 94
Henderson Av. Guild 8L 93
Henderson Rd. SW18 1C 28
Henderson Rd. Big H 8E 66
Henderson Rd. Craw 8N 181
Henderson Rd. Croy 5A 46
Henderson Way. H'ham 8F 196
Hendham Rd. SW17 3C 28
Hendon Gro. Eps 5N 59
Hendon Way. Stanw 9M 7
Hendrick Av. SW12 1D 28
Hendy M. Wrec 5F 128
Heneage Cres. New Ad 6M 65
Henfield Rd. SW19 9L 27
Henfold Cotts. Newd 9N 139
Henfold Dri. Bear G 8K 139
Henfold La. Holmw 4L 139
Henfold La. Newd 7M 139
Hengelo Gdns. Mitc 3B 44
Hengist Clo. H'ham 7G 197
Hengist Way. Brom 3N 47
Hengrove Cres. Ashf 4M 21
Henhurst Cross La. Cold 8G 138
Henhurst La. Cold 8G 138
Henley Av. Sutt 9K 43
Henley Bank. Guild 5K 113
Henley Clo. Farnb 6K 69
Henley Clo. Iswth 4F 10
Henley Clo. M'bowr 6H 183
Henley Ct. Wok 7D 74
Henley Dri. Frim G 7C 70
Henley Dri. King T 8E 26
Henley Fort Bungalows. Guild
6K 113
Henley Gdns. Yat 1C 68
Henley Ga. Norm & Pirb 5N 91
Henley Pk. Norm 7N 91
Henley Way. Felt 6L 23
Henlow Pl. Rich 3K 25
Henlys Roundabout. (Junct.)
5K 9
Hennessey Ct. Wok 9E 54
Henrietta Ct. Twic 1J 25
(off Richmond Rd.)
Henrietta Ho. W6 1H 13
(off Queen Caroline St.)
Henry Doulton Dri. SW17 5E 28
Henry Hatch Wlk. Sutt 4A 62
Henry Jackson Rd. SW15 6J 13
Henry Macaulay Av. King T
9K 25 (2H 203)
Henry Peters Dri. Tedd 6E 24
(off Somerset Gdns.)
Henry Tate M. SW16 6L 29
Henshaw Clo. Craw 5L 181
Henslow Way. Wok 1F 74
Henson Rd. Craw 2F 182
Hensworth Rd. Ashf 6M 21
Henty Clo. Craw 6K 181
Henty Wlk. SW15 8G 12
Hepple Clo. Iswth 5H 11
Hepplestone Clo. SW15 9G 13
Hepplewhite Clo. Craw 8N 181
Hepworth Ct. Sutt 7M 43
Hepworth Cft. Col T 9K 49
Hepworth Rd. SW16 8J 29
Hepworth Way. W on T 7G 39
Heracles Clo. Wall 4J 63
Herald Ct. Alder 3N 109
Herald Gdns. Wall 8F 44
Herbert Clo. Brack 4N 31
Herbert Cres. Knap 5H 73
Herbert Gdns. W4 2A 12
Herbert Morrison Ho. SW6 2L 13
(off Clem Attlee Ct.)
Herbert Rd. SW19 8L 27
(in two parts)
Herbert Rd. King T
2M 41 (6L 203)
Herbs End. Farnb 9H 69
Hereford Clo. Craw 7C 182
Hereford Clo. Eps 9C 60 (7K 201)
Hereford Clo. Guild 1J 113
Hereford Clo. Stai 9K 21
Hereford Copse. Wok 6L 73
Hereford Ct. Sutt 4M 61
Hereford Gdns. Twic 2C 24
Hereford Ho. SW10 3N 13
(off Fulham Rd.)
Hereford La. Farnh 6G 109
Hereford Mead. Fleet 1C 88
Hereford Rd. Felt 2K 23
Hereford Sq. SW7 1N 13
Hereford Way. Chess 2J 59
Hereward Av. Purl 7L 63
Hereward Rd. SW17 5D 20
Heriot Rd. Cher 6J 37
Heritage Hill. Kes 2E 66
Heritage Lawn. Horl 7G 142
Herlwyn Gdns. SW17 5D 28
Herm Clo. Craw 7M 181
Herm Clo. Iswth 3C 10
Hermes Clo. Fleet 4D 88
Hermes Way. Wall 4H 63
Hermitage Bri. Cotts. Wok 6F 72
Hermitage Clo. Farnb 4B 90
Hermitage Clo. Clay 3G 58
Hermitage Clo. Frim 5D 70
Hermitage Clo. Shep 3B 38
Hermitage Dri. Asc 1J 33
Hermitage Gdns. SE19 8N 29
Hermitage Grn. SW16 9J 29
Hermitage La. SE25 5D 46
(in two parts)
Hermitage La. SW16 8K 29
Hermitage La. E Grin 1B 186
Hermitage La. Wind 6D 4
Hermitage Pde. Asc 2M 33
Hermitage Path. SW16 9J 29
Hermitage Rd. SE19 8N 29
Hermitage Rd. E Grin 7N 165
Hermitage Rd. Kenl 2N 83
Hermitage Rd. Wok 6G 72
Hermitage, The. SW13 4E 12
Hermitage, The. Felt 4G 23
Hermitage, The. King T
3K 41 (7H 203)
Hermitage, The. Rich 8L 11
Hermitage, The. Warf 6B 16
Hermitage Woods Cres. Wok
6H 73
Hermitage Woods Est. Wok 6H 73
Hermits Rd. Craw 2D 182
Hermongers 8H 177
Hermonger's La. Rud 7G 176
Hernbrook Dri. H'ham 8L 197
Herndon Clo. Egh 5C 20
Herndon Rd. SW18 8N 13
Herne Rd. Surb 8K 41
Heron Clo. Asc 9H 17
Heron Clo. C Crook 7D 88
Heron Clo. Craw 1A 182
Heron Clo. Eden 9L 127
Heron Clo. Guild 9L 93
Heron Clo. Myt 1D 90
Heron Clo. Sutt 2L 61
Heron Ct. Dork 1J 201
Heron Ct. Eps 1F 80
Heron Ct. King T 2L 41 (6J 203)
Heron Dale. Add 2M 55
Herondale. Brack 6A 32
Herondale. Hasl 2C 188
Herondale. S Croy 5G 65
Herondale Av. SW18 2B 28
Heronfield. Eng G 7M 19
Heron Pl. E Grin 1B 186
Heron Rd. Croy 8B 46
Heron Rd. Twic 7G 11
Heronry, The. W on T 3H 57
Heronsbrook. Asc 1B 34
Herons Clo. Copt 5D 164
Herons Ct. Light 7N 51
Herons Cft. Wey 3D 56
Heron Shaw. Cranl 9N 155
Herons Lea. Copt 5D 164
Heron's Pl. Iswth 6H 11
Heron Sq. Rich 8K 11
Herons Way. Brkwd 8A 72
Heron's Way. Wokgm 1D 30
Herons Wood Ct. Horl 7F 142
Herontye Dri. E Grin 1B 186
Heron Wlk. Wok 1E 74
Heron Way. Felt 7H 9
Heron Way. H'ham 6N 197
Heron Wood Rd. Alder 4B 110
Herretts Gdns. Alder 3B 110
Herrett St. Alder 4B 110
Herrick Clo. Craw 1G 182
Herrick Clo. Frim 3G 70
Herrings La. Cher 5J 37
Herrings La. W'sham 2A 52
Herriot Ct. Yat 2B 68
Herschel Grange. Warf 6B 16
Herschel Wlk. Craw 8N 181
Hersham 2L 57
Hersham By Pass. W on T 2J 57
Hersham Clo. SW15 1F 26
Hersham Gdns. W on T 1J 57
Hersham Green 2L 57
Hersham Grn. Shop. Cen. W on T
2L 57
Hersham Pl. W on T 2L 57
Hersham Rd. W on T 7H 39
Hersham Trad. Est. W on T 8M 39
Hershell Ct. SW14 7A 12
Hertford Av. SW14 8C 12
Hertford Sq. Mitc 3J 45
Hertford Way. Mitc 3J 45
Hesiers Hill. Warl 4A 86
Hesiers Rd. Warl 3A 86
Hesketh Clo. Cranl 7N 155
Heslop Rd. SW12 2D 28
Hesper M. SW5 1N 13
Hessle Gro. Eps 7E 60
Hestercombe Av. SW6 5K 13
Hesterman Way. Croy 7K 45
Hester Ter. Rich 6N 11
Heston 3A 10
Heston Av. Houn 2M 9
Heston Cen., The. Houn 1K 9
Heston Grange. Houn 2N 9
Heston Grange La. Houn 2N 9
Heston Ind. Cen. Houn 2K 9
Heston Ind. Mall. Houn 3N 9
Heston Rd. Houn 3A 10
Heston Rd. Red 7D 122
Heston Wlk. Red 7D 122
Hetherington Rd. Shep 1D 38
Hethersett Clo. Reig 9A 102
Hever Rd. Eden 3M 147
Hevers Av. Horl 7D 142
Hevers Corner. Horl 7D 142
Hewers Way. Tad 7G 81
Hewitt Clo. Croy 9K 47
Hewitts Ind. Est. Cranl 7K 155
Hewlett Pl. Bag 4K 51
Hexham Clo. Owl 5J 49
Hexham Clo. Worth 3J 183
Hexham Gdns. Iswth 3G 11
Hexham Rd. SE27 3N 29
Hexham Rd. Mord 7N 43
Hextalls La. Blet 6A 104
Heybridge Av. SW16 8J 29
Heyford Av. SW20 2L 43
Heyford Rd. Mitc 1C 44
Heymede. Lea 1J 99
Heythorpe Clo. Wok 4J 73
Heythorp St. SW18 2L 27
Heywood Ct. G'ming 4F 132
Heywood Dri. Bag 5G 51
Hibbert's All. Wind 4G 4
Hibernia Gdns. Houn 7A 10
Hibernia Rd. Houn 7A 10
Hibiscus Gro. Bord 7A 168
Hickey's Almshouses. Rich 7M 11
Hickling Wlk. Craw 5F 182
Hickmans Clo. God 1F 124
Hicks La. B'water 1G 69
Hidcote Clo. Wok 3D 74
Hidcote Gdns. SW20 2G 42
Higgins Wlk. Hamp 7M 23
(off Abbott Clo.)
Higgs La. Bag 4H 51
(in two parts)
Highacre. Dork 8H 119
Highams Hill. Craw 4L 181
Highams Hill. Warl 8C 66
Highams La. Chob 3D 52
High Barn Rd. Eff & Ran C 7L 97
Highbarrow Rd. Croy 7D 46
High Beech. Brack 3D 32
High Beech. S Croy 4B 64
High Beeches. Bans 1H 81
High Beeches. Frim 4B 70
High Beeches Clo. Purl 6H 63
Highbirch Clo. H'ham 3A 198
High Broom Cres. W Wick 6L 47
Highbury Av. T Hth 1L 45
Highbury Clo. N Mald 3B 42
Highbury Clo. W Wick 8L 47
Highbury Cres. Camb 8E 50
Highbury Gro. Hasl 9G 170
Highbury Rd. SW19 8K 27
High Button 3H 171
High Cedar Dri. SW20 8H 27
High Clandon 2N 115
Highclere. Asc 4A 34
Highclere. Guild 1C 114
Highclere Clo. Brack 1C 32
Highclere Clo. Kenl 2N 83
Highclere Ct. Knap 4F 72
Highclere Dri. Camb 8E 50
Highclere Gdns. Knap 4F 72
Highclere Rd. Alder 4B 110
Highclere Rd. Knap 4F 72
Highclere Rd. N Mald 2C 42
Highcliffe Dri. SW15 9E 12
(in two parts)
High Coombe Pl. King T 7C 26
High Copse. Farnh 6F 108
Highcotts La. Send 3H 95
(in two parts)
Highcroft. Milf 2B 152
Highcroft. Sham G 7G 134
Highcroft Ct. Bookh 1A 98
Highcroft Dri. Rud 8F 176
Highcross Way. SW15 2F 26
High Curley 8J 51
Highdaun Dri. SW16 3K 45
Highdown. Fleet 3B 88
Highdown. Wor Pk 8D 42
Highdown Ct. Craw 6F 182
Highdown La. Sutt 7N 61
Highdown Rd. SW15 9G 12
Highdown Way. H'ham 2M 197
High Dri. N Mald 9B 26
High Dri. Oxs 1D 78

Hoadlands Cotts.—Hopgarden Clo.

Hoadlands Cotts. *Hand* 6N **199**
Hoadly Rd. *SW16* 4H **29**
Hobart Ct. *S Croy* 8E **200**
Hobart Gdns. *T Hth* 2A **46**
Hobart Pl. *Rich* 1M **25**
Hobart Rd. *Wor Pk* 9G **42**
Hobbes Wlk. *SW15* 8G **12**
Hobbs Clo. *W Byf* 9K **55**
Hobbs Ind. Est. *Newc* 2H **165**
Hobbs Rd. *SE27* 5N **29**
Hobbs Rd. *Broadf* 7M **181**
Hobill Wlk. *Surb* 5M **41**
Hocken Mead. *Craw* 1H **183**
Hockering Est. *Wok* 5D **74**
Hockering Gdns. *Wok* 5C **74**
Hockering Rd. *Wok* 5C **74**
Hockford Clo. *Pirb* 4E **92**
Hodge La. *Wink* 6L **17**
(in two parts)
Hodges Clo. *Bag* 6H **51**
Hodgkin Clo. *M'bowr* 4G **182**
Hodgson Gdns. *Guild* 9C **94**
Hoe. **3F 136**
Hoebrook Clo. *Wok* 8N **73**
Hoe La. *Hasc* 6N **153**
Hoe La. *Peasl & Ab H* 3F **136**
Hoffman Clo. *Brack* 7B **16**
Hogarth Av. *Ashf* 7D **22**
Hogarth Bus. Cen. *W4* 2D **12**
Hogarth Clo. *Col T* 9K **49**
Hogarth Ct. *Houn* 3M **9**
Hogarth Cres. *SW19* 9B **28**
Hogarth Cres. *Croy* 6N **45**
Hogarth Gdns. *Houn* 3A **10**
Hogarth La. *W4* 2D **12**
Hogarth Pl. SW5 1N **13**
(off Hogarth Rd.)
Hogarth Rd. *SW5* 1N **13**
Hogarth Rd. *Craw* 6D **182**
Hogarth Roundabout. (Junct.) **2E 12**
Hogarth's House. ***2D 12***
(off Hogarth La.)
Hogarth Ter. *W4* 2D **12**
Hogarth Way. *Hamp* 9C **24**
Hogden Clo. *Tad* 3L **101**
Hogden La. *Ran C* 9M **97**
(in four parts)
Hog Hatch. **6F 108**
Hoghatch La. *Farnh* 6F **108**
Hog's Back. *Guild* 6H **113**
Hog's Back. *P'ham* 7K **111**
Hog's Back. *Seale* 8B **110**
Hog's Back Brewery. **7D 110**
Hogscross La. *Coul* 1D **102**
Hog's Hill. *Craw* 6B **182**
Hogs Hill. *Fern* 9F **188**
Hogshill La. *Cob* 1J **77**
(in three parts)
Hogsmill Ho. *King T* 5L **203**
Hogsmill Wlk. *King T* 5J **203**
Hogsmill Way. *Eps* 2B **60**
Hogtrough La. *God* 5K **105**
(in two parts)
Hogtrough La. *S Nut* 4G **123**
Hogwood Rd. *Loxw* 5E **192**
Holbeach M. *SW12* 2F **28**
Holbeche Clo. *Yat* 1A **68**
Holbeck. *Brack* 5L **31**
Holbein Rd. *Craw* 6D **182**
Holborn Way. *Mitc* 1D **44**
Holbreck Pl. *Wok* 5B **74**
Holbrook. **9L 179**
Holbrook Clo. *Farnh* 4L **109**
Holbrooke Pl. *Rich* 8K **11**
Holbrook Mdw. *Egh* 7E **20**
Holbrook School La. *H'ham* 1L **197**
Holbrook Way. *Alder* 5N **109**
Holcombe Clo. *W'ham* 4M **107**
Holcombe St. *W6* 1G **13**
Holcon Ct. *Red* 9E **102**
Holcroft Ct. *E Grin* 6B **166**
Holden Brook La. *Ockl* 7M **157**
Holdernesse Clo. *Iswth* 4G **10**
Holdernesse Rd. *SW17* 4D **28**
Holderness Way. *SE27* 6M **29**
Holder Rd. *Alder* 3C **110**
Holder Rd. *M'bowr* 6F **182**
Holdfast La. *Hasl* 9K **171**
Hole Hill. **5B 118**
Holehill La. *Westc* 4A **118**
Hole La. *Eden* 5H **127**
Holford Rd. *Guild* 3E **114**
Holland. **2C 126**
Holland Av. *SW20* 9E **26**
Holland Av. *Sutt* 5M **61**
Holland Clo. *Farnh* 3K **129**
Holland Clo. *Red* 3D **122**
Holland Ct. *Surb* 6K **41**
Holland Cres. *Oxt* 2C **126**
Holland Gdns. *Egh* 1H **37**
Holland Gdns. *Fleet* 5B **88**
Holland La. *Oxt* 2C **126**
Holland Pines. *Brack* 6L **31**
Holland Rd. *SE25* 4D **46**
Holland Rd. *Oxt* 2C **126**
Hollands Fld. *Broad H* 4E **196**
Hollands, The. *Felt* 5L **23**
Hollands, The. *Wok* 5A **74**
Hollands, The. *Wor Pk* 7E **42**
Hollands Way. *E Grin* 6C **166**
Hollands Way. *Warn* 9F **178**
Hollerith Ri. *Brack* 5N **31**
Holles Clo. *Hamp* 7A **24**
Hollies Av. *W Byf* 9H **55**
Hollies Clo. *SW16* 7L **29**
Hollies Clo. *Twic* 3F **24**
Hollies Ct. *Add* 2L **55**
Hollies, The. Add 2L **55**
(off Crockford Pk. Rd.)
Hollies, The. *B'water* 5M **69**
Hollies Way. *SW12* 1E **28**
Hollin Ct. *Craw* 9C **162**
Hollingbourne Cres. *Craw* 9A **182**
Hollingsworth Ct. *Surb* 6K **41**
Hollingsworth Rd. *Croy* 3E **64**
Hollington Cres. *N Mald* 5E **42**
Hollingworth Clo. *W Mol* 3N **39**
Hollingworth Way. *W'ham* 4M **107**
Hollis Row. *Red* 5D **122**
Hollis Wood Dri. *Wrec* 6D **128**
Hollman Gdns. *SW16* 7M **29**
Holloway Clo. *W Dray* 1N **7**
Holloway Dri. *Vir W* 3A **36**
Holloway Hill. **9H 133**
Holloway Hill. *G'ming* 7G **133**
Holloway Hill. *Ott* 9E **36**
Holloway La. *W Dray* 2M **7**
Holloway St. *Houn* 6B **10**
Hollow Clo. *Guild* 4L **113**
Hollow La. *Hdly* 3D **168**
Hollow La. *D'land & E Grin* 1D **166**
Hollow La. *Vir W* 2M **35**
Hollow La. *Wott* 9L **117**
Hollows, The. *Bren* 2M **11**
Hollow, The. *Craw* 4L **181**
Hollow, The. *Ews* 5A **108**
Hollow, The. *Lwr E* 7C **132**
Hollow Way. *Gray* 5A **170**
Holly Acre. *Yat* 1C **68**
Holly Av. *Frim* 3F **70**
Holly Av. *New H* 6J **55**
Holly Av. *W on T* 7L **39**
Hollybank. *W End* 9C **52**
Hollybank Clo. *Hamp* 6A **24**
Holly Bank Rd. *W Byf* 1J **75**
Holly Bank Rd. *Wok* 8L **73**
Hollybrook Pk. *Bord* 6A **168**
Hollybush Clo. *Craw* 2C **182**
Hollybush Ind. Est. *Alder* 8C **90**
Hollybush La. *Alder* 8C **90**
Hollybush La. *Fren* 1H **149**
Holly Bush La. *Hamp* 8N **23**
Hollybush La. *Rip* 6M **75**
Hollybush Ride. *Finch* 3B **48**
(in two parts)
Hollybush Ride. *W'sham* 9K **33**
Hollybush Rd. *Craw* 2C **182**
Hollybush Rd. *King T* 6L **25**
Holly Clo. *Farnb* 1M **89**
Holly Clo. *Hdly* 4H **169**
Holly Clo. *Alder* 2A **110**
Holly Clo. *Beck* 3M **47**
Holly Clo. *Craw* 1E **182**
Holly Clo. *Eng G* 7L **19**
Holly Clo. *Felt* 6M **23**
Holly Clo. *H'ham* 3A **198**
Holly Clo. *Longc* 9K **35**
Holly Clo. *Wall* 4F **62**
Holly Clo. *Wok* 6L **73**
Hollycombe. *Eng G* 5M **19**
Holly Ct. Cher 7H **37**
(off King St.)
Holly Ct. *Crowt* 3D **48**
Holly Ct. *Sutt* 4M **61**
Holly Cres. *Beck* 4J **47**
Holly Cres. *Wind* 5A **4**
Hollycroft Clo. *S Croy* 2B **64**
Hollycroft Clo. *W Dray* 2B **8**
Hollycroft Gdns. *W Dray* 2B **8**
Hollydale Dri. *Brom* 1H **67**
Holly Dri. *Old Win* 8H **5**
Holly Farm Rd. *S'hall* 1M **9**
Hollyfield Rd. *Surb* 6M **41**
Hollyfields Clo. *Camb* 1N **69**
Holly Grn. *Wey* 1E **56**
Hollygrove Clo. *Houn* 7N **9**
Holly Hedge Clo. *Frim* 4C **70**
Hollyhedge Rd. *Cob* 1J **77**
Holly Hedge Rd. *Frim* 4C **70**
Holly Hill. **9N 187**
Holly Hill Dri. *Bans* 4M **81**
Hollyhock Dri. *Bisl* 2D **72**
Hollyhook Clo. *Crowt* 1F **48**
Holly Ho. *Brack* 5N **31**
Holly Ho. *Iswth* 2J **11**
Holly La. *Bans* 3M **81**
Holly La. *G'ming* 7F **132**
Holly La. *Worp* 7F **92**
Holly La. E. *Bans* 3N **81**
Holly La. W. *Bans* 4M **81**
Holly Lea. *Guild* 6N **93**
Holly Lodge Mobile Home Pk. *Tad* 4K **101**
Hollymead. *Cars* 9D **44**
Hollymead Rd. *Coul* 5E **82**
Hollymeoak Rd. *Coul* 6F **82**
Hollymoor La. *Eps* 6C **60**
Holly Pde. Cob 1J **77**
(off Hollyhedge Rd.)
Hollyridge. *Hasl* 2F **188**
Holly Rd. *Farnb* 1L **89**
Holly Rd. *W4* 1C **12**
Holly Rd. *Alder* 2A **110**
Holly Rd. *Hamp* 7C **24**
Holly Rd. *Houn* 7B **10**
Holly Rd. *Reig* 5N **121**
Holly Rd. *Twic* 2G **25**
Holly Spring Cotts. *Brack* 8B **16**
Holly Spring La. *Brack* 9A **16**
Holly Tree Clo. *SW19* 2J **27**
Hollytree Gdns. *Frim* 6B **70**
Holly Tree Rd. *Cat* 9B **84**
Holly Wlk. *Wind* 5D **18**
Hollywater. **8A 168**
Hollywater Rd. *Bord* 8A **168**
Hollywater Rd. *Pass* 9A **168**
Holly Way. *B'water* 2J **69**
Holly Way. *Mitc* 3H **45**
Hollywood M. *SW10* 2N **13**
Hollywood Rd. *SW10* 2N **13**
Hollywoods. *Croy* 5J **65**
Holman Clo. *Craw* 9N **181**
Holman Ct. *Eps* 5F **60**
Holman Hunt Ho. W6 1K **13**
(off Field Rd.)
Holman Rd. *Eps* 2B **60**
Holmbank Dri. *Shep* 3F **38**
Holmbrook Clo. *Farnb* 1H **89**
Holmbrook Gdns. *Farnb* 1H **89**
Holmbury Av. *Crowt* 9F **30**
Holmbury Clo. *Craw* 5A **182**
Holmbury Ct. *SW17* 4D **28**
Holmbury Ct. *S Croy* 2B **64**
Holmbury Dri. *N Holm* 8J **119**
Holmbury Gro. *Croy* 4J **65**
Holmbury Hill Rd. *Holm M* 9J **137**
Holmbury Keep. Horl 7G **142**
(off Maize Cft.)
Holmbury La. *Holm M* 1L **157**
Holmbury St Mary. **6K 137**
Holmbush Clo. *H'ham* 2K **197**
Holmbush Ct. *Fay* 8G **181**
Holmbush Potteries Ind. Est. *Fay* 8H **181**
Holmbush Rd. *SW15* 9K **13**
Holm Clo. *Wdhm* 8G **55**
Holm Ct. *G'ming* 4G **132**
Holmcroft. *Craw* 4C **182**
Holmcroft. *Tad* 3G **101**
Holmdene Clo. *Beck* 1M **47**
Holmead Rd. *SW6* 3N **13**
Holme Chase. *Wey* 3D **56**
Holme Clo. *Crowt* 9F **30**
Holme Green. **5E 30**
Holmes Clo. *Asc* 5N **33**
Holmes Clo. *Wok* 8B **74**
Holmesdale Av. *SW14* 6A **12**
Holmesdale Clo. *SE25* 2C **46**
Holmesdale Clo. *Guild* 2D **114**
Holmesdale Pk. *Nutf* 3K **123**
Holmesdale Rd. *Croy & SE25* 4A **46**
Holmesdale Rd. *N Holm* 9H **119**
Holmesdale Rd. *Reig* 2M **121**
Holmesdale Rd. *Rich* 4M **11**
Holmesdale Rd. *S Nut* 5K **123**
Holmesdale Rd. *Tedd* 8J **25**
Holmesdale Ter. *N Holm* 9H **119**
Holmesdale Vs. *Mid H* 2H **139**
Holmes Rd. *SW19* 8A **28**
Holmes Rd. *Twic* 3F **24**
Holmethorpe. **9F 102**
Holmethorpe Av. *Red* 9F **102**
Holmethorpe Ind. Est. *Red* 9F **102**
Holmewood Clo. *Wokgm* 6A **30**
Holmewood Gdns. *SW2* 1K **29**
Holmewood Rd. *SE25* 2B **46**
Holmewood Rd. *SW2* 1J **29**
Holming End. *H'ham* 3A **198**
Holmlea Ct. *Croy* 6E **200**
Holmlea Rd. *Dat* 4N **5**
Holmlea Wlk. *Dat* 4M **5**
Holmoak Clo. *SW15* 9L **13**
Holmoaks Ho. *Beck* 1M **47**
Holmside Rd. *SW12* 1E **28**
Holmsley Clo. *N Mald* 5E **42**
Holmsley Ho. SW15 1E **26**
(off Tangley Gro.)
Holm Ter. *Dork* 8H **119**
Holmwood Av. *S Croy* 9C **64**
Holmwood Clo. *Add* 2J **55**
Holmwood Clo. *E Hor* 6F **96**
Holmwood Clo. *Sutt* 5J **61**
Holmwood Common. **3J 139**
Holmwood Corner. **6K 139**
Holmwood Gdns. *Wall* 3F **62**
Holmwood Rd. *Chess* 2K **59**
Holmwood Rd. *Sutt* 5H **61**
Holmwood Vw. Rd. *Mid H* 2H **139**
Holne Chase. *Mord* 5L **43**
Holroyd Clo. *Clay* 5F **58**
Holroyd Rd. *SW15* 7H **13**
Holroyd Rd. *Clay* 5F **58**
Holsart Clo. *Tad* 9G **81**
Holstein Av. *Wey* 1B **56**
Holst Mans. *SW13* 2H **13**
Holsworthy Way. *Chess* 2J **59**
Holt Clo. *Farnb* 7A **70**
Holt La. *Wokgm* 1A **30**
Holton Heath. *Brack* 3D **32**
Holt Pound. **7C 128**
Holt Pound Cotts. *Row* 7B **128**
Holt Pound La. *Holt P* 6B **128**
Holt, The. *Mord* 3M **43**
Holt, The. *Wall* 1G **62**
Holtwood Rd. *Oxs* 9C **58**
Holtye. **7N 167**
Holtye Av. *E Grin* 7D **166**
Holtye Common. **6N 167**
Holtye Rd. *E Grin* 8B **166**
Holtye Wlk. *Craw* 5E **182**
Holwood Clo. *W on T* 8K **39**
Holwood Pk. Av. *Orp* 1H **67**
Holybourne Av. *SW15* 1F **26**
Holyhead Ct. *King T* 8H **203**
Holyoake Av. *Wok* 4M **73**
Holyoake Cres. *Wok* 4M **73**
Holyport Rd. *SW6* 3J **13**
Holyrood. *E Grin* 2C **186**
Holyrood Pl. *Craw* 7N **181**
Holywell Clo. *Farnb* 7M **69**
Holywell Clo. *Stai* 2N **21**
Holywell Way. *Stai* 2N **21**
Hombrook Dri. *Brack* 9K **15**
Hombrook Ho. *Brack* 9K **15**
Homebeech Ho. Wok 5A **74**
(off Mt. Hermon Rd.)
Home Clo. *Cars* 8D **44**
Home Clo. *Craw* 1G **183**
Home Clo. *Fet* 8D **78**
Home Clo. *Vir W* 5N **36**
Home Ct. *Surb* 4K **41** (8H **203**)
Home Farm Clo. *Farnb* 8B **70**
Home Farm Clo. *Bet* 4D **120**
Home Farm Clo. *Eps* 4J **81**
Home Farm Clo. *Esh* 3B **58**
Home Farm Clo. *Ott* 4C **54**
Home Farm Clo. *Shep* 3F **38**
Home Farm Clo. *Th Dit* 6F **40**
Home Farm Cotts. *Pep H* 6N **131**
Home Farm Gdns. *W on T* 8K **39**
Home Farm Rd. *G'ming* 9H **133**
Homefield. *Mord* 3M **43**
Homefield. *Thur* 7G **150**
Homefield Av. *W on T* 1L **57**
Homefield Clo. *Horl* 7F **142**
Homefield Clo. *Lea* 8J **79**
Homefield Clo. *Wdhm* 8G **55**
Homefield Ct. *SW16* 4J **29**
Homefield Gdns. *Mitc* 1A **44**
Homefield Gdns. *Tad* 7H **81**
Homefield Pk. *Sutt* 3N **61**
Homefield Rd. *SW19* 7J **27**
Homefield Rd. *W4* 1E **12**
Homefield Rd. *Coul & Cat* 6M **83**
Homefield Rd. *W on T* 6M **39**
Homefield Rd. *Warl* 6F **84**
Homegreen Ho. *Hasl* 2E **188**
Homeland Dri. *Sutt* 5N **61**
Homelands. *Lea* 8J **79**
Home La. *Orp* 2N **67**
Homelea Clo. *Farnb* 6N **69**
Homeleigh Cres. *Ash V* 5E **90**
Home Mdw. *Bans* 3M **81**
Homemead Rd. *Croy* 5G **45**
Home Pk. *Oxt* 9C **106**
Home Pk. Clo. *Brmly* 5B **134**
Home Pk. Ct. *King T* 8H **203**
Homepark Ho. *Farnh* 1H **129**
Home Pk. Pde. *King T* 3G **203**
Home Pk. Rd. *SW19* 5L **27**
Home Pk. Rd. *Yat* 9C **48**
Home Pk. Ter. *King T* 3G **203**
Home Pk. Wlk. *King T* 3K **41** (8H **203**)
Homer Rd. *Croy* 5G **47**
Homersham Rd. *King T* 1N **41**
Homers Rd. *Wind* 4A **4**
Homesdale Rd. *Cat* 1A **104**
Homestall. *Guild* 3G **113**
Homestall Rd. *Ash W* 9G **166**
Homestead. *Cranl* 6A **156**
Homestead & Middle Vw. Mobile Home Pk. *Norm* 9B **92**
Homestead Gdns. *Clay* 2E **58**
Homestead Rd. *SW6* 3L **13**
Homestead Rd. *Cat* 1A **104**
Homestead Rd. *Eden* 7K **127**
Homestead Rd. *Stai* 7K **21**
Homestead Way. *New Ad* 7M **65**
Homestream Ho. *H'ham* 7H **197**
Homethorne Ho. *Craw* 4A **182**
Home Vs. *Alb* 3L **135**
Homewater Ho. *Eps* 9D **60** (6L **201**)
Homewaters Av. *Sun* 9G **23**
Homewood. *Cranl* 7B **156**
Homewood Clo. *Hamp* 7N **23**
Homewoods. *SW12* 1G **28**
Homeworth Ho. Wok 5A **74**
(off Mt. Hermon Rd.)
Hone Hill. *Sand* 7G **48**
Hones Yd. Bus. Pk. *Farnh* 1J **129**
Honeybrook Rd. *SW12* 1G **28**
Honeycrock Ct. *Red* 1E **142**
Honeycrock La. *Red* 1E **142**
Honeydown Cotts. *N'chap* 8E **190**
Honey Hill. *Wokgm* 6E **30**
Honeyhill Rd. *Brack* 9M **15**
Honey La. *Rowh & Oke H* 6M **177**
Honeypot La. *Eden* 8F **126**
Honeypots Rd. *Wok* 9N **73**
Honeysuckle Bottom. *E Hor* 3F **116**
Honeysuckle Clo. *Crowt* 9F **30**
Honeysuckle Clo. *Horl* 7G **143**
Honeysuckle Clo. *Yat* 9A **48**
Honeysuckle Gdns. *Croy* 6G **46**
Honeysuckle La. *Hdly D* 4G **168**
Honeysuckle La. *Craw* 9A **162**
Honeysuckle La. *N Holm* 8J **119**
Honeysuckle Wlk. *H'ham* 3N **197**
Honeywood Heritage Cen. **1D 62**
Honeywood La. *Oke H* 4M **177**
Honeywood Rd. *H'ham* 4N **197**
Honeywood Rd. *Iswth* 7G **10**
Honeywood Wlk. *Cars* 1D **62**
Honister Gdns. *Fleet* 3D **88**
Honister Heights. *Purl* 1A **84**
Honister Wlk. *Camb* 2H **71**
Honnor Gdns. *Iswth* 5D **10**
Honnor Rd. *Stai* 8M **21**
Hood Av. *SW14* 8B **12**
Hood Clo. *Croy* 7M **45** (1A **200**)
Hood Rd. *SW20* 8E **26**
Hook. **2K 59**
Hooke Rd. *E Hor* 3G **97**
Hookfield. *Eps* 9B **60** (7G **201**)
Hookfield M. *Eps* 9B **60** (6G **201**)
Hook Heath. **8L 73**
Hook Heath Av. *Wok* 6L **73**
Hook Heath Gdns. *Wok* 8J **73**
Hook Heath Rd. *Wok* 8H **73**
Hook Hill. *S Croy* 6B **64**
(in two parts)
Hook Hill La. *Wok* 8L **73**
Hook Hill Pk. *Wok* 8L **73**
Hook Ho. La. *Duns* 3M **173**
Hookhouse Rd. *Duns* 1N **173**
Hook Junction. (Junct.) **9K 41**
Hook La. *Bisl* 9N **51**
Hook La. *P'ham* 8N **111**
Hook La. *Shere* 1B **136**
Hookley Clo. *Elst* 8J **131**
Hookley La. *Elst* 8J **131**
Hook Mill La. *Light* 5A **52**
Hook Ri. Bus. Cen. *Chess* 9N **41**
Hook Ri. N. *Surb* 9L **41**
Hook Ri. S. *Surb* 9L **41**
Hook Ri. S. Ind. Pk. *Chess* 9M **41**
Hook Rd. *Chess & Surb* 2K **59**
Hook Rd. *Eps* 4B **60** (5K **201**)
Hookstile La. *Farnh* 2H **129**
Hookstone La. *W End* 7C **52**
Hook St. *Alf* 8K **175**
Hookwood. **9B 142**
Hookwood Corner. *Oxt* 6D **106**
Hookwood Park. **6D 106**
Hookwood Pk. *Oxt* 7D **106**
Hooley. **8F 82**
Hooley La. *Red* 4D **122**
Hope Av. *Brack* 6C **32**
Hope Clo. *Bren* 1L **11**
Hope Clo. *Sutt* 2A **62**
Hope Cotts. *Brack* 2A **32**
Hope Ct. *Craw* 8N **181**
Hope Fountain. *Camb* 2E **70**
Hope Grant's Rd. *Alder* 9M **89**
(in two parts)
Hope Ho. *Croy* 6F **200**
Hope La. *Farnh* 6G **108**
Hopeman Clo. *Col T* 7J **49**
Hopes Clo. *Houn* 2A **10**
Hope St. *Elst* 7H **131**
Hope Way. *Alder* 1L **109**
Hopfield. *Hors* 3A **74**
Hopfield Av. *Byfl* 8N **55**
Hop Garden. *C Crook* 9A **88**
Hopgarden Clo. *Eden* 9M **127**

Hophurst Clo.—Ilex Clo.

Hophurst Clo. Craw D 1E 184
Hophurst Dri. Craw D 1E 184
Hophurst Hill. Craw D 8G 164
Hophurst La. Craw D 1E 184
Hopkins Ct. Craw 8N 181
Hopper Va. Brack 5M 31
Hoppety, The. Tad 9J 81
Hoppingwood Av. N Mald 2D 42
Hopton Ct. Guild 3H 113 (off Pk. Barn Dri.)
Hopton Gdns. N Mald 5F 42
Hopton Rd. SW16 6J 29
Hopwood Clo. SW17 4A 28
Horace Rd. King T 2M 41 (6L 203)
Horatio Av. Warf 9C 16
Horatio Ho. W6 1J 13 (off Fulham Pal. Rd.)
Horatio Pl. SW19 9M 27
Horatius Way. Croy 2K 63
Hordern Ho. H'ham 7G 196
Horder Rd. SW6 4K 13
Horewood Rd. Brack 5N 31
Horizon Ho. Eps 9D 60 (6L 201)
Horley. 8F 142
Horley Lodge La. Red 3D 142
Horley Rd. Charl 4L 161
Horley Rd. Red 5D 122
Horley Row. Horl 7D 142
Hormer Clo. Owl 6J 49
Hornbeam Clo. Farnb 9H 69
Hornbeam Clo. H'ham 7M 197
Hornbeam Clo. Owl 6J 49
Hornbeam Cres. Bren 3H 11
Hornbeam Rd. Guild 9M 93
Hornbeam Rd. Reig 6N 121
Hornbeam Ter. Cars 7C 44
Hornbeam Wlk. Rich 3M 25
Hornbeam Wlk. W Vill 6F 56
Hornbrook Copse. H'ham 8M 197
Hornbrook Hill. H'ham 8M 197
Hornby Av. Brack 6B 32
Hornchurch Clo. King T 5K 25
Hornchurch Hill. Whyt 5C 84
Horndean Clo. SW15 2F 26
Horndean Clo. Craw 8H 163
Horndean Rd. Brack 5D 32
Horne. 6C 144
Horne Ct. Hill. Horne 4C 144
Horner La. Mitc 1B 44
Horne Rd. Shep 3B 38
Horne Way. SW15 5H 13
Hornhatch. Chil 9D 114
Hornhatch Clo. Chil 9D 114 (in two parts)
Hornhatch La. Guild 9C 114
Horn Rd. Farnb 9K 69
Horns Green. 4N 87
Hornshill La. Rud 2A 194
Horse & Groom Cvn. Site. Brack 3A 32
Horseblock Hollow. Cranl 3B 156
Horsebrass Dri. Bag 5J 51
Horsecroft. Bans 4L 81
Horse Fair. King T 1K 41 (3G 203)
Horsegate Ride. Asc 5L 33 (Coronation Rd.)
Horsegate Ride. Asc 4F 32 (Swinley Rd.)
Horse Hill. Horl 6M 141
Horsell. 3M 73
Horsell Birch. Hors & Wok 2K 73 (in three parts)
Horsell Comn. Rd. Wok 1M 73
Horsell Ct. Cher 6K 37
Horsell Moor. Wok 4N 73
Horsell Pk. Wok 3N 73
Horsell Pk. Clo. Wok 3N 73
Horsell Ri. Wok 2N 73
Horsell Ri. Clo. Wok 2N 73
Horsell Va. Wok 3A 74
Horsell Way. Wok 3M 73
Horse Ride. Cars 6C 62
Horseshoe Bend. Gray 6M 169
Horseshoe Clo. Camb 7D 50
Horseshoe Clo. Craw 2H 183
Horseshoe Cres. Bord 6A 168
Horseshoe Cres. Camb 7D 50
Horse Shoe Grn. Sutt 8N 43
Horseshoe La. Ash V 6E 90
Horseshoe La. Cranl 6L 155
Horseshoe La. E. Guild 2D 114
Horseshoe La. W. Guild 2D 114
Horseshoe, The. Bans 2L 81
Horseshoe, The. Coul 9H 63
Horseshoe, The. G'ming 8F 132
Horsham. 6J 197
Horsham Arts Cen. 6K 197
Horsham Bus. Pk. K'fold 5J 179
Horsham Gates. H'ham 5L 197
Horsham Mus. 7J 197
Horsham Northern By-Pass. Warn 2H 197
Horsham Rd. Ab H & Holm M 2G 136
Horsham Rd. Alf 6J 175
Horsham Rd. Bear G 2K 159
Horsham Rd. Brmly & Cranl 1E 154 (Brooks Hill)
Horsham Rd. Brmly & Shalf 2N 133 (Trunley Heath Rd.)
Horsham Rd. Capel 2J 179
Horsham Rd. Cowf & Slin 9J 195
Horsham Rd. Cranl & Rud 8N 155
Horsham Rd. Craw 7K 181
Horsham Rd. Dork 6G 119 (4J 201)
Horsham Rd. Ewh & Wal W 6F 156
Horsham Rd. Felt 9D 8
Horsham Rd. F Grn 5M 157
Horsham Rd. Hand 9K 199
Horsham Rd. Holmw & Bear G 4J 139
Horsham Rd. N Holm & Mid H 9H 119
Horsham Rd. Owl 6J 49
Horsham Rd. Peas P 2M 199
Horsham Rd. Rusp 6N 179
Horsley Clo. Eps 9C 60 (6J 201)
Horsley Dri. King T 6K 25
Horsley Dri. New Ad 4M 65
Horsley Rd. Eff J & D'side 9H 77
Horsnape Gdns. Binf 7G 15
Horsneile La. Brack 8N 15
Hortensia Ho. SW10 3N 13 (off Hortensia Rd.)
Hortensia Rd. SW10 3N 13
Horticultural Pl. W4 1C 12
Horton. 6C 6 **(Colnbrook)**
Horton. 7B 60 **(Ewell)**
Horton Country Pk. 6M 59
Horton Footpath. Eps 7B 60
Horton Gdns. Eps 7B 60
Horton Gdns. Hort 6B 6
Horton Hill. Eps 7B 60
Horton Ho. W6 1K 13 (off Field Rd.)
Horton La. Eps 7N 59
Horton Pk. Children's Farm 6N 59
Horton Pl. W'ham 4M 107
Horton Rd. Coln 6G 6
Horton Rd. Dat 3L 5
Horton Rd. Hort & Coln 5C 6
Horton Rd. Stai 7H 7
Hortons Way. W'ham 4M 107 (in two parts)
Horton Trad. Est. Hort 6E 6
Horton Way. Croy 4G 46
Horvath Clo. Wey 1E 56
Hosack Rd. SW17 3E 28
Hosey Comn. La. W'ham 7N 107
Hosey Comn. Rd. Eden & W'ham 2L 127
Hosey Hill. 6N 107
Hosey Hill. W'ham 5M 107
Hoskins Clo. Hay 1G 8
Hoskins Pl. E Grin 6C 166
Hoskins Rd. Oxt 7A 106 (in two parts)
Hoskins Wlk. Oxt 7A 106 (off Station Rd. W.)
Hospital Bri. Rd. Twic 1B 24
Hospital Bridge Roundabout. (Junct.) 3B 24
Hospital Hill. Alder 1M 109
Hospital Rd. Alder 1M 109
Hospital Rd. Houn 6A 10
Hostel Rd. Farnb 5N 89
Hotham Clo. W Mol 2A 40
Hotham Rd. SW15 6H 13
Hotham Rd. SW19 8A 28
Hotham Rd. M. SW19 8A 28
Houblon Rd. Rich 8L 11
Houghton Clo. Hamp 7M 23
Houghton Rd. M'bowr 6G 182
Houlder Cres. Croy 3M 63
Houlton Ct. Bag 5J 51
Hound Ho. Rd. Shere 1B 136
Houndown La. Thur 6E 150
Hounslow. 6B 10
Hounslow Av. Houn 8B 10
Hounslow Bus. Pk. Houn 7A 10
Hounslow Cen. Houn 6B 10
Hounslow Gdns. Houn 8B 10
Hounslow Rd. Felt 2J 23
Hounslow Rd. Hanw 5L 23
Hounslow Rd. Twic 9B 10
Hounslow Urban Farm. 8H 9
Hounslow West. 5M 9
Household Cavalry Mus. 6F 4
Houseman Rd. Farnb 8L 69
Houston Pl. Esh 7D 40
Houston Rd. Surb 5H 41
Houston Way. Crowt 2C 48
Houstoun Ct. Houn 3N 9
Hove Gdns. Sutt 7N 43
Howard Av. Eps 6F 60
Howard Clo. Asht 5M 79
Howard Clo. Fleet 4D 88
Howard Clo. Hamp 8C 24
Howard Clo. Lea 1J 99
Howard Clo. Sun 7G 22
Howard Clo. Tad 3E 100
Howard Clo. W Hor 3E 96
Howard Cole Way. Alder 2K 109
Howard Ct. Reig 2A 122
Howard Dri. Farnb 1G 89
Howard Gdns. Guild 2C 114
Howard M. Reig 1M 121
Howard Ridge. Burp 8C 94
Howard Rd. Ashf 5M 21
Howard Rd. SE25 4D 46
Howard Rd. Bookh 5B 98
Howard Rd. Coul 2G 83
Howard Rd. Craw 7K 181
Howard Rd. Dork 5G 118 (2H 201)
Howard Rd. Eff J 1H 97
Howard Rd. H'ham 4N 197
Howard Rd. Iswth 6F 10
Howard Rd. N Mald 2D 42
Howard Rd. N Holm 9J 119
Howard Rd. Reig 4N 121
Howard Rd. Surb 5M 41
Howard Rd. Wokgm 3B 30
Howards Clo. Wok 7C 74
Howards Crest Clo. Beck 1M 47
Howards Ho. Reig 2N 121
Howard's La. SW15 7G 13
Howards La. Add 3H 55
Howards Rd. Wok 7B 74
Howard St. Th Dit 6H 41
Howberry Rd. T Hth 9N 29 & 1A 46
Howden Ho. Houn 1M 23
Howden Rd. SE25 1C 46
Howe Dri. Cat 9A 84
Howe La. Binf 1K 15
Howell Clo. Warf 7A 16
Howell Hill Clo. Eps 7H 61
Howell Hill Gro. Eps 6H 61
Howes Gdns. C Crook 7A 88
Howe, The. Farnb 4F 88
Howgate Rd. SW14 6C 12
Howitts Clo. Esh 3A 58
Howland Ho. SW16 4J 29
How La. Coul 4E 82
Howley Rd. Croy 9M 45 (4A 200)
Howorth Ct. Brack 3C 32
Howsman Rd. SW13 2F 12
Howson Ter. Rich 9L 11
Hoylake Clo. If'd 4J 181
Hoylake Gdns. Mitc 2G 44
Hoyland Ho. Craw 3L 181
Hoyle Cotts. Bear G 1K 159
Hoyle Rd. SW17 6C 28
Hubbard Dri. Chess 3K 59
Hubbard Rd. SE27 5N 29
Hubberholme. Brack 2M 31
Hubert Clo. SW19 9A 28 (off Nelson Gro. Rd.)
Huddington Glade. Yat 1A 68
Huddlestone Cres. Red 6H 103
Hudson Ct. Guild 3J 113
Hudson Rd. Craw 5C 182
Hudson Rd. Hay 2E 8
Hudsons. Tad 8J 81
Huggins Pl. SW2 2K 29
Hugh Dalton Av. SW6 2L 13
Hughenden Rd. Wor Pk 6F 42
Hughes Rd. Ashf 7D 22
Hughes Rd. Wokgm 1C 30
Hughes Wlk. Croy 6N 45
Hugh Gaitskell Clo. SW6 2L 13
Hugh Herland Ho. King T 2L 41 (6K 203)
Hugon Rd. SW6 6N 13
Huguenot Pl. SW18 8N 13
Hullbrook La. Sham G 7F 134
Hullmead. Sham G 7G 134
Hulton Clo. Lea 1J 99
Hulverston Clo. Sutt 6N 61
Humber Clo. Sand 7J 49
Humber Way. Sand 7J 49
Humber Way. Slou 1C 6
Humbolt Clo. Guild 3J 113
Humbolt Rd. W6 2K 13
Hummer Rd. Egh 5C 20
Humphrey Clo. Fet 9C 78
Humphrey Pk. C Crook 1A 108 (in two parts)
Humphries Yd. Brack 3A 32
Hungerford Clo. Sand 7H 49
Hungerford Sq. Wey 1E 56
Hungry Hill La. Send 4L 95
Hunnels Clo. C Crook 1A 108
Hunstanton Clo. Coln 3E 6
Hunstanton Clo. If'd 4J 181
Hunston Rd. Mord 7N 43
Hunter Clo. Wall 4J 63
Hunter Ct. Eps 6N 59
Hunter Ho. SW5 1M 13 (off Old Brompton Rd.)
Hunter Ho. Craw 6B 182
Hunter Rd. Farnb 2L 89
Hunter Rd. SW20 9H 27
Hunter Rd. Craw 6B 182
Hunter Rd. Guild 4A 114 (5F 202)
Hunter Rd. T Hth 2A 46
Hunters Chase. S God 6J 125
Hunters Clo. SW12 2E 28
Hunters Clo. Eps 9B 60 (6H 201)
Hunters Ct. Rich 8K 11
Huntersfield Clo. Reig 9N 101
Hunters Gro. Orp 1K 67
Hunters M. Wind 4F 4
Hunter's Rd. Chess 9L 41
Hunter's Way. Croy 1B 64
Hunting Clo. Esh 1A 58
Huntingdon Clo. Mitc 2J 45
Huntingdon Gdns. W4 3B 12
Huntingdon Gdns. Wor Pk 9H 43
Huntingdon Rd. Red 3D 122
Huntingdon Rd. Wok 4J 73
Huntingfield. Croy 4J 65
Huntingfield Rd. SW15 7F 12
Huntingfield Way. Egh 8F 20
Huntingford Clo. Hind 2A 170
Hunting Ga. Dri. Chess 4L 59
Hunting Ga. M. Sutt 9N 43
Hunting Ga. M. Twic 2E 24
Huntley Way. SW20 1F 42
Huntly Rd. SE25 3B 46
Hunts Clo. Guild 2G 112
Huntsgreen Ct. Brack 1A 32
Hunts Hill. 9M 91
Hunts Hill Rd. Norm 8L 91
Hunts La. Camb 3N 69
Huntsmans Clo. Felt 5J 23
Huntsmans Clo. Fet 2D 98
Huntsmans Clo. Warl 6F 84
Huntsmans Ct. Cat 8N 83 (off Coulsdon Rd.)
Huntsmans Mdw. Asc 9K 17
Huntsman's M. Myt 2D 90
Huntsmoor Rd. Eps 2C 60
Huntspill St. SW17 4A 28
Hurland La. Head 5E 168
Hurlands Bus. Cen. Farnh 8L 109
Hurlands Clo. Farnh 8L 109
Hurlands La. Duns 7B 174
Hurlands Pl. Farnh 8M 109
Hurley Clo. W on T 8J 39
Hurley Ct. Brack 3C 32
Hurley Gdns. Guild 9C 94
Hurlford. Wok 4K 73
Hurlingham. 6M 13
Hurlingham Bus. Pk. SW6 6M 13
Hurlingham Club, The 6M 13
Hurlingham Ct. SW6 6L 13
Hurlingham Gdns. SW6 6L 13
Hurlingham Retail Pk. SW6 6N 13
Hurlingham Rd. SW6 5L 13
Hurlingham Sq. SW6 6M 13
Hurlstone Rd. SE25 4B 46
Hurn Ct. Houn 5L 9
Hurn Ct. Rd. Houn 5L 9
Hurnford Clo. S Croy 6B 64
Huron Clo. G Str 3N 67
Huron Rd. SW17 3E 28
Hurricane Rd. Wall 4J 63
Hurricane Way. Slou 1D 6
Hurst-an-Clays. E Grin 1A 186
Hurst Av. H'ham 5K 197
Hurstbourne. Clay 3F 58
Hurstbourne Ho. SW15 9E 12 (off Tangley Gro.)
Hurst Clo. Brack 4M 31
Hurst Clo. Chess 2N 59
Hurst Clo. Craw 5L 181
Hurst Clo. H'ley 2B 100
Hurst Clo. Wok 7M 73
Hurst Ct. H'ham 5K 197
Hurstcourt Rd. Sutt 8N 43
Hurst Cft. Guild 6A 114 (8F 202)
Hurstdene Av. Stai 7K 21
Hurst Dri. Tad 4F 100
Hurst Farm Clo. Milf 9C 132
Hurst Farm Rd. E Grin 1N 185
Hurstfield Rd. W Mol 2A 40
Hurst Green. 1B 126
Hurst Grn. Clo. Oxt 1C 126
Hurst Grn. Rd. Oxt 1B 126
Hurst Gro. W on T 7G 38
Hurst Hill. Rusp 7N 179
Hurst Hill Cotts. Brmly 6C 134
Hurstlands. Oxt 1C 126
Hurst La. E Mol 3C 40
Hurst La. Egh 1C 36
Hurst La. H'ley 2B 100
Hurstleigh Clo. Red 1D 122
Hurstleigh Dri. Red 1D 122
Hurst Lodge. Wey 3E 56
Hurstmere Clo. Gray 6B 170
Hurst Park. 1C 40
Hurst Rd. Farnb 6N 69
Hurst Rd. Alder 9A 90
Hurst Rd. Croy 2A 64 (8D 200)
Hurst Rd. Eps 7C 60
Hurst Rd. H'ley & Tad 1C 100
Hurst Rd. Horl 7C 142
Hurst Rd. H'ham 4J 197
Hurst Rd. W on T & W Mol 4K 39
Hurstview Grange. S Croy 4M 63
Hurst Vw. Rd. S Croy 4B 64
Hurstway. Pyr 1G 75
Hurst Way. S Croy 3B 64
Hurstwood. Asc 5L 33
Hurtbank Cotts. Holm M 5K 137
Hurtmore. 4C 132
Hurtmore Bottom. 5C 132
Hurtmore Chase. Hurt 4E 132
Hurtmore Rd. Hurt 4C 132
Hurtwood La. Alb 5N 135
Hurtwood Rd. W on T 6N 39
Huson Rd. Warf 7A 16
Hussar Ct. Alder 2K 109
Hussars Clo. Houn 6M 9
Hutchingsons Rd. New Ad 7M 65
Hutchins Way. Horl 6D 142
Hutsons Clo. Wokgm 9C 14
Hutton Clo. W'sham 4A 52
Hutton Rd. Ash V 7E 90
Huxley Clo. G'ming 4G 132
Huxley Rd. Sur R 3G 113
Huxleys Experience. 9M 197
Hyacinth Clo. Hamp 7A 24
Hyacinth Rd. SW15 2F 26
Hyde Clo. Ashf 7F 22
Hyde Dri. Craw 4K 181
Hyde Farm M. SW12 2H 29
Hyde Heath Ct. Craw 1H 183
Hyde La. Churt & Thur 9B 150
Hyde La. Ock 7C 76
Hyde Rd. Rich 8M 11
Hyde Rd. S Croy 9B 64
Hydestile. 4G 153
Hydestile Cotts. Hamb 5G 152
Hyde Ter. Ashf 7F 22
Hydethorpe Rd. SW12 2G 28
Hyde Wlk. Mord 6M 43
Hydon Heath. 5J 153
Hydon Heath. 6J 153
Hydons, The. Hyde 5H 153
Hylands Clo. Craw 4E 182
Hylands Clo. Eps 2B 80
Hylands M. Eps 2B 80
Hylands Rd. Eps 2B 80
Hylle Clo. Wind 4B 4
Hyndman Clo. Craw 9N 181
Hyperion Ct. Bew 5K 181
Hyperion Ho. SW2 1K 29
Hyperion Pl. Eps 5C 60
Hyperion Wlk. Horl 1F 162
Hyrstdene. S Croy 1M 63 (7A 200)
Hythe Clo. Brack 4C 32
Hythe End. 3D 20
Hythe End Rd. Wray 3B 20
Hythe Fld. Av. Egh 7F 20
Hythe Pk. Rd. Egh 6E 20
Hythe Rd. Stai 6F 20
Hythe Rd. T Hth 1A 46
Hythe, The. Stai 6G 20

I

Iberian Av. Wall 1H 63
Iberian Way. Camb 9E 50
Ibis La. W4 4B 12
Ibsley Gdns. SW15 2F 26
Icehouse Wood. Oxt 9A 106
Icklesham Ho. Craw 6L 181 (off Salvington Rd.)
Icklingham Ga. Cob 8K 57
Icklingham Rd. Cob 8K 57
Idlecombe Rd. SW17 7E 28
Idmiston Rd. SE27 4N 29
Idmiston Rd. Wor Pk 6E 42
Idmiston Sq. Wor Pk 6E 42
Ifield. 2M 181
Ifield Av. Craw 9M 161
Ifield Clo. Red 5C 122
Ifield Dri. Craw 2L 181
Ifield Green. 1M 181
Ifield Grn. If'd 9M 161
Ifield Pk. Craw 3L 181
Ifield Rd. SW10 2N 13
Ifield Rd. Charl 6K 161
Ifield Rd. Craw 2N 181
Ifield St. If'd 1L 181
Ifield Watermill. 4K 181
Ifieldwood. 9J 161
Ifield Wood. If'd 2H 181
Ifold. 6E 192
Ifold Bri. La. Loxw 4E 192
Ifoldhurst. Loxw 6E 192
Ifold Rd. Red 5E 122
Ikona Ct. Wey 2D 56
Ilex Clo. Eng G 8L 19

Ilex Clo.—Keble Clo.

Ilex Clo. *Sun.* 1K 39
Ilex Clo. *Yat* 9A 48
Ilex Ho. *Wdhm* 6J 55
Ilex Way. *SW16* 6L 29
Ilford Ct. *Cranl* 8H 155
Illingworth. *Wind* 6B 4
Illingworth Clo. *Mitc* 2B 44
Illingworth Gro. *Brack* 9D 16
Imadene Clo. *Lind* 5A 168
Imadene Cres. *Lind* 5A 168
Imber Clo. *Esh* 7D 40
Imber Ct. Trad. Est. *E Mol* 5D 40
Imber Cross. *Th Dit* 5F 40
Imber Gro. *Esh* 6D 40
Imberhorne Bus. Cen. *E Grin* 8L 165
Imberhorne La. *E Grin* 7L 165
Imberhorne Way. *E Grin* 7L 165
Imber Pk. Rd. *Esh* 7D 40
Imjin Clo. *Alder* 1N 109
Impact Ct. *SE20* 1E 46
Imperial Ct. *Wind* 6D 4
Imperial Gdns. *Mitc* 2F 44
Imperial Rd. *SW6* 4N 13
Imperial Rd. *Felt* 1F 22
Imperial Rd. *Wind* 6D 4
Imperial Sq. *SW6* 4N 13
Imperial Way. *Croy* 3K 63
Imran Ct. *Alder* 3A 110
Ince Rd. *W on T* 3F 56
Inchwood. *Brack* 7A 32
Inchwood. *Croy* 1L 66
Independent Bus. Pk., The. *E Grin* 7K 165
Ingatestone Rd. *SE25* 3E 46
Ingham Clo. *S Croy* 5G 64
Ingham Rd. *S Croy* 5F 64
Ingleboro Dri. *Purl* 9A 64
Ingleby Way. *Wall* 5H 63
Ingle Dell. *Camb* 2B 70
Inglehurst. *New H* 6K 55
Inglemere Rd. *Mitc* 8D 28
Ingleside. *Coln* 4G 7
Inglethorpe St. *SW6* 4J 13
Ingleton. *Brack* 2M 31
Ingleton Rd. *Cars* 5C 62
Inglewood. *Cher* 9H 37
Inglewood. *Croy* 5H 65
Inglewood. *Wok* 5L 73
Inglewood Av. *Camb* 2G 71
Inglis Rd. *Croy* 7C 46
Ingram Clo. *H'ham* 6G 197
Ingram Rd. *T Hth* 9N 29
Ingrams Clo. *W on T* 2K 57
Ingress St. *W4* 1D 12
Inholmes. *Craw* 3C 182
Inholms La. *N Holm* 9H 119
Inkerman Rd. *Eton W* 1C 4
Inkerman Rd. *Knap* 5H 73
Inkerman Way. *Wok* 5H 73
Inkpen La. *F Row* 8H 187
Ink, The. *Yat* 8B 48
Inman Rd. *SW18* 1A 28
Inner Pk. Rd. *SW19* 2J 27
Inner Ring E. *H'row A* 6C 8
Inner Ring W. *H'row A* 6B 8
Innes Clo. *SW20* 1K 43
Innes Gdns. *SW15* 9G 13
Innes Rd. *H'ham* 4M 197
Innes Yd. *Croy* 9N 45 (5C 200)
Innings La. *Warf* 9D 16
Innisfail Gdns. *Alder* 4L 109
Institute Rd. *Alder* (GU11) 6A 90
Institute Rd. *Alder* (GU12) 3B 110
Institute Rd. *Westc* 6C 118
Institute Wlk. *E Grin* 9A 166
Instow Gdns. *Farnb* 7M 69
Interface Ho. Houn 6A 10
(off Staines Rd.)
International Av. *Houn* 1K 9
Inval. 8G 170
Inval Hill. *Hasl* 9G 170
Inveresk Gdns. *Wor Pk* 9F 42
Inverness Rd. *Houn* 7N 9
Inverness Rd. *Wor Pk* 7J 43
Inverness Way. *Col T* 8J 49
Invicta Clo. *Felt* 2G 22
Invincible Rd. *Farnb* 3M 89
Inwood Av. *Coul* 7L 83
Inwood Av. *Houn* 6C 10
Inwood Clo. *Croy* 8H 47
Inwood Ct. *W on T* 8K 39
Inwood Rd. *Houn* 7B 10
Iona Clo. *Craw* 6N 181
Iona Clo. *Mord* 6N 43
Ipswich Rd. *SW17* 7E 28
Irene Rd. *SW6* 4M 13
Irene Rd. *Stoke D* 1B 78
Ireton Av. *W on T* 8F 38
Iris Clo. *Croy* 7G 46
Iris Clo. *Surb* 6M 41
Iris Dri. *Bisl* 2D 72
Iris Rd. *Bisl* 2D 72
Iris Rd. *W Ewe* 2A 60
Iron La. *Brmly* 6N 133
Iron Mill Pl. *SW18* 9N 13
Iron Mill Rd. *SW18* 9N 13
Irons Bottom. 3L 141
Irons Bottom Rd. *Leigh* 3L 141
Irvine Dri. *Farnb* 6K 69
Irvine Pl. *Vir W* 4A 36
Irving Mans. W14 2K 13
(off Queen's Club Gdns.)
Irving Wlk. *Craw* 6C 182
Irwin Dri. *H'ham* 5G 196
Irwin Rd. *Guild* 4K 113
Isabel Hill Clo. *Hamp* 1B 40
Isabella Ct. Rich 9M 11
(off Kings Mead)
Isabella Dri. *Orp* 1L 67
Isabella Ho. W6 1H 13
(off Queen Caroline St.)
Isabella Plantation. 5A 26
Isbells Dri. *Reig* 4N 121
Isham Rd. *SW16* 1J 45
Isis Clo. *SW15* 7H 13
Isis Ct. *W4* 3A 12
Isis St. *SW18* 3A 28
Isis Way. *Sand* 7J 49
Island Clo. *Stai* 5G 20
Island Farm Av. *W Mol* 4N 39
Island Farm Rd. *W Mol* 4N 39
Island Rd. *Mitc* 8D 28
Islandstone La. *Hurst* 3A 14
Island, The. *Th Dit* 5G 40
Island, The. *W Dray* 3L 7
Island, The. *Wey* 3N 55
Island, The. *Wray* 4C 20
Islay Gdns. *Houn* 8L 9
Isleworth. 6G 11
Isleworth Bus. Complex. *Iswth* 5F 10
Isleworth Promenade. *Twic* 7H 11
Itchingfield. 9A 196
Itchingfield Rd. *Slin & Itch* 8A 196
Itchingwood Comn. Rd. *Oxt* 2E 126
Ivanhoe Clo. *Craw* 9B 162
Ivanhoe Rd. *Houn* 6L 9
Ivatt Pl. *W14* 1L 13
Iveagh Clo. *Craw* 8A 182
Iveagh Ct. *Beck* 2M 47
Iveagh Ct. *Brack* 4B 32
Iveagh Ho. SW10 3N 13
(off King's Rd.)
Iveagh Rd. *Guild* 4L 113
Iveagh Rd. *Wok* 5J 73
Ively Rd. *Farnb* 2K 89
(in two parts)
Iverna Gdns. *Felt* 8E 8
Ivers Way. *New Ad* 4L 65
Ives Clo. *Yat* 8A 48
Ivor Clo. *Guild* 4B 114
Ivory Ct. *Felt* 3H 23
Ivory Wlk. *Craw* 5K 181
Ivybank. *G'ming* 5H 133
Ivybridge Clo. *Twic* 1G 24
Ivy Bri. Retail Pk. *Iswth* 8F 10
Ivy Clo. *Sun* 1K 39
Ivydale Rd. *Cars* 8D 44
Ivyday Gro. *SW16* 4K 29
Ivydene. *Knap* 5F 72
Ivydene. *W Mol* 4N 39
Ivydene Clo. *Red* 8F 122
Ivydene Clo. *Sutt* 1A 62
Ivy Dene La. *Ash W* 3F 186
Ivy Dri. *Light* 8L 51
Ivy Gdns. *Mitc* 2H 45
Ivyhouse Cotts. *Newd* 6F 160
Ivy La. *Farnh* 1G 129
Ivy La. *Houn* 7N 9
Ivy La. *Wok* 4D 74
Ivy Mill Clo. *God* 1E 124
Ivy Mill La. *God* 1D 124
Ivymount Rd. *SE27* 4L 29
Ivy Rd. *SW17* 6C 28
Ivy Rd. *Alder* 2B 110
Ivy Rd. *Houn* 7B 10
Ivy Rd. *Surb* 7N 41

J

Jacaranda Clo. *N Mald* 2D 42
Jackass La. *Kes* 2D 66
Jackass La. *Tand* 9J 105
Jackdaw Clo. *Craw* 1A 182
Jackdaw La. *H'ham* 3L 197
Jack Goodchild Way. *King T* 2A 42
Jackmans La. *Wok* 6K 73
(in two parts)
Jackson Clo. *Brack* 4N 31
Jackson Clo. *Cranl* 8H 155
Jackson Clo. *Eps* 1C 80
Jackson Rd. *Craw* 9N 181
Jacksons Pl. *Croy* 7A 46 (1E 200)
Jackson's Way. *Croy* 9K 47
Jackson Way. *Eps* 5N 59
Jacob Clo. *Brack* 1J 31
Jacob Clo. *Wind* 4B 4
Jacobean Clo. *Craw* 4G 183
Jacob Rd. *Col T* 8M 49
Jacob's Ladder. *Warl* 6D 84
Jacob's Wlk. *Ab C* 6A 138
Jacobs Well. 6N 93
Jacob's Well Rd. *Guild* 7N 93
Jaffray Pl. *SE27* 5M 29
Jaggard Way. *SW12* 1D 28
Jail La. *Big H* 3F 86
Jamaica Rd. *T Hth* 5M 45
James Boswell Clo. *SW16* 5K 29
James Est. *Mitc* 1D 44
James Hockey Gallery 1G 128
James Rd. *Alder* 6B 90
James Rd. *Camb* 4N 69
James Rd. *P'mrsh* 2M 133
James's Cotts. *Rich* 3N 11
James Searle Ind. Est. *H'ham* 4L 197
James St. *Houn* 6D 10
James St. *Wind* 4G 4
James Ter. SW14 6C 12
(off Church Path)
James Terry Ct. *S Croy* 8B 200
Jameston. *Brack* 7A 32
James Watt Way. *Craw* 7E 162
James Way. *Camb* 4N 69
Jamieson Ho. *Houn* 9N 9
Jamnagar Clo. *Stai* 7H 21
Janoway Hill La. *Wok* 6M 73
Japonica Clo. *Wok* 5M 73
Japonica Ct. *As* 3D 110
Jarrett Clo. *SW2* 2M 29
Jarrow Clo. *Mord* 4N 43
Jarvis Clo. *Craw* 9N 181
Jarvis Rd. *S Croy* 3A 64
Jasmine Clo. *Red* 8E 122
Jasmine Clo. *Wok* 3J 73
Jasmine Ct. *SW19* 6M 27
Jasmine Ct. *H'ham* 6J 197
Jasmine Gdns. *Croy* 9L 47
Jasmine Way. *E Mol* 3E 40
Jasmin Rd. *Eps* 2A 60
Jason Clo. *Red* 8C 122
Jason Clo. *Wey* 2D 56
Jasons Dri. *Guild* 9E 94
Javelin Ct. *Craw* 9H 163
Jay Av. *Add* 9N 37
Jay Clo. *Ews* 5C 108
Jay's La. *Hasl* 6M 189
Jays Nest Clo. *B'water* 2J 69
Jay Wlk. *Turn H* 4F 184
Jeal Oakwood Ct. *Eps* 1D 80 (8L 201)
Jealott's Hill. 2N 15
Jean Batten Clo. *Wall* 4K 63
Jean Orr Ct. *C Crook* 8B 88
Jeans Ct. *Craw* 8N 181
Jebb Av. *SW2* 1J 29
(in two parts)
Jeddere Cotts. *D'land* 9C 146
Jefferson Clo. *Slou* 1C 6
Jefferson Rd. *Brkwd* 7N 71
Jeffries Pas. *Guild* 4N 113 (5D 202)
Jeffries Rd. *W Hor* 9C 96
Jeffs Clo. *Hamp* 7B 24
Jeffs Rd. *Sutt* 1L 61
Jemmett Clo. *King T* 9A 26
Jengar Clo. *Sutt* 1N 61
Jenkins Hill. *Bag* 5H 51
Jenkins Pl. *Farnb* 5B 90
Jenner Dri. *W End* 9D 52
Jenner Pl. *SW13* 2G 12
Jenner Rd. *Craw* 7D 162
Jenner Rd. *Guild* 4A 114 (5E 202)
Jenners Clo. *Ling* 7N 145
Jenner Way. *Eps* 5N 59
Jennett Rd. *Croy* 9L 45
Jennings Clo. *Surb* 6J 41
Jennings Clo. *Wdhm* 5L 55
Jennings Way. *Horl* 8H 143
Jenny La. *Ling* 7M 145
Jennys Wlk. *Yat* 9D 48
Jennys Way. *Coul* 9G 83
Jephtha Rd. *SW18* 9M 13
Jeppos La. *Mitc* 3D 44
Jepson Ho. SW6 4N 13
(off Pearscroft Rd.)
Jerdan Pl. *SW6* 3M 13
Jerome Corner. *Crowt* 4H 49
Jerome Ho. *Hamp W* 3G 203
Jersey Clo. *Cher* 9H 37
Jersey Clo. *Fleet* 1C 88
Jersey Clo. *Guild* 7D 94
Jersey Rd. *SW17* 7F 28
Jersey Rd. *Craw* 7M 181
Jersey Rd. *Houn & Iswth* 4B 10
Jerviston Gdns. *SW16* 7L 29
Jesmond Clo. *Mitc* 2F 44
Jesmond Rd. *Croy* 6C 46
Jessamy Rd. *Wey* 8C 38
Jesse Clo. *Yat* 1E 68
Jessel Mans. W14 2K 13
(off Queen's Club Gdns.)
Jesses La. *Peasl* 4D 136
Jessett Dri. *C Crook* 9A 88
Jessiman Ter. *Shep* 4B 38
Jessop Av. *S'hall* 1N 9
Jessops Way. *Croy* 5G 45
Jevington. *Brack* 7A 32
Jewels Hill. *Big H* 8C 66
Jewel Wlk. *Craw* 6M 181
Jew's Row. *SW18* 7N 13
Jeypore Pas. *SW18* 9N 13 & 1A 28
Jeypore Rd. *SW18* 1A 28
Jig's La. N. *Warf* 7C 16
Jig's La. S. *Warf* 9C 16
Jillian Clo. *Hamp* 8A 24
Jim Griffiths Ho. SW6 2L 13
(off Clem Attlee Ct.)
Joanna Ho. W6 1H 13
(off Queen Caroline St.)
Jobson's La. *Hasl & C'fold* 9M 189
Jocelyn Rd. *Rich* 6L 11
Jockey Mead. *H'ham* 7G 197
Jock's La. *Brack* 9K 15
Jodrell Clo. *Iswth* 4G 10
Joe Hunte Ct. *SE27* 6M 29
John Austin Clo. *King T* 9M 25 (2L 203)
John Clo. *Alder* 1K 109
John Cobb Rd. *Wey* 4B 56
John F. Kennedy Memorial. 3M 19
John Gale Ct. Eps 6E 60
(off West St.)
John Goddard Way. *Felt* 3J 23
John Knight Lodge. *SW6* 3M 13
John Nike Way. *Brack* 1H 31
John Pound Ho. *SW18* 1N 27
John Pound's Ho. *Craw* 5A 182
John Russell Clo. *Guild* 9K 93
John's Clo. *Ashf* 5D 22
John's Ct. *Sutt* 3N 61
Johnsdale. *Oxt* 7B 106
John's La. *Mord* 4A 44
John Smith Av. *SW6* 3L 13
Johnson Dri. *Finch* 9A 30
Johnson Mans. W14 2K 13
(off Queen's Club Gdns.)
Johnson Rd. *Croy* 6A 46
Johnson Rd. *Houn* 3K 9
Johnsons Clo. *Cars* 8D 44
Johnson's Common. 1K 161
Johnsons Dri. *Hamp* 9C 24
Johnson Wlk. *Craw* 6C 182
Johnson Way. *C Crook* 8B 88
John's Rd. *Tats* 7F 86
John's Ter. *Croy* 7B 46 (1F 200)
Johnston Grn. *Guild* 8K 93
Johnston Wlk. *Guild* 8K 93
John Strachey Ho. SW6 2L 13
(off Clem Attlee Ct.)
John St. *SE25* 3D 46
John St. *Houn* 5M 9
Johns Wlk. *Whyt* 6D 84
John Watkin Clo. *Eps* 5A 60
John Wesley Ct. *Twic* 2G 24
John Wheatley Ho. SW6 2L 13
(off Clem Attlee Ct.)
John Williams Clo. *King T* 9K 25 (1H 203)
John Wiskar Dri. *Cranl* 7M 155
Joinville Pl. *Add* 1M 55
Jolesfield Ct. *Craw* 6L 181
Jolive Ct. *Guild* 4C 114
Jolliffe Rd. *Mers* 4G 102
Jones Corner. *Asc* 9J 17
Jones M. *SW15* 7K 13
Jones Wlk. *Rich* 9M 11
Jonquil Gdns. *Hamp* 7A 24
Jonson Clo. *Mitc* 3F 44
Jordan Clo. *S Croy* 7C 64
Jordans Clo. *Craw* 1B 182
Jordans Clo. *Guild* 2C 114
Jordans Clo. *Iswth* 4E 10
Jordans Clo. *Red* 8E 122
Jordans Clo. *Stanw* 1L 21
Jordans Cres. *Craw* 9B 162
Jordans M. *Twic* 3E 24
Jordans, The. 7C 160
Jordans, The. *E Grin* 1A 186
Joseph Ct. *Warf* 7C 16
Josephine Av. *Tad* 4L 101
Josephine Clo. *Tad* 5L 101
Joseph Locke Way. *Esh* 8A 40
Joseph Powell Clo. *SW12* 1F 28
Joseph's Rd. *Guild* 2N 113 (1C 202)
Joshua Clo. *S Croy* 4M 63
Jourdelays Pas. *Wind* 2G 4
Jubilee Arch. *Wind* 4G 4
Jubilee Av. *Asc* 9J 17
Jubilee Av. *Twic* 2C 24
Jubilee Av. *Wokgm* 1A 30
Jubilee Clo. *Farnb* 1J 89
Jubilee Clo. *Asc* 9J 17
Jubilee Clo. *King T* 9J 25
Jubilee Clo. *Stanw* 1L 21
Jubilee Ct. *Brack* 2A 32
Jubilee Ct. Houn 6C 10
(off Bristow Rd.)
Jubilee Ct. *Stai* 6J 21
Jubilee Cres. *Add* 2M 55
Jubilee Dri. *Ash V* 7E 90
Jubilee Est. *H'ham* 4L 197
Jubilee Hall Rd. *Farnb* 1A 90
Jubilee La. *Gray* 6A 170
Jubilee La. *Wrec* 7F 128
Jubilee Rd. *Alder* 5N 109
Jubilee Rd. *Myt* 3E 90
Jubilee Rd. *Rud* 9E 176
Jubilee Rd. *Sutt* 4J 61
Jubilee Ter. *Dork* 4H 119 (1L 201)
Jubilee Ter. *Str G* 7B 120
Jubilee Vs. *Esh* 7D 40
Jubilee Wlk. *Craw* 3E 182
Jubilee Way. *SW19* 9N 27
Jubilee Way. *Chess* 1N 59
Jubilee Way. *Felt* 2H 23
Judge's Ter. *E Grin* 1A 186
Judge Wlk. *Clay* 3F 58
Jug Hill. *Big H* 3F 86
Jugshill La. *Oke H* 2B 178
Julian Clo. *Wok* 5M 73
Julian Hill. *Wey* 4B 56
Julien Rd. *Coul* 2H 83
Juliet Gdns. *Warf* 9D 16
Julius Hill. *Warf* 9D 16
Jumps Rd. *Churt* 7K 149
Junction Pl. *Hasl* 2D 188
Junction Rd. *Ashf* 6D 22
Junction Rd. *W5* 1J 11
Junction Rd. *Dork* 5G 119 (2J 201)
Junction Rd. *Light* 6M 51
Junction Rd. *S Croy* 2A 64
June Clo. *Coul* 1F 82
June La. *Red* 1F 142
Junewood Clo. *Wdhm* 7H 55
Juniper. *Brack* 7A 32
Juniper Clo. *Big H* 4G 87
Juniper Clo. *Chess* 2M 59
Juniper Clo. *Guild* 7L 93
Juniper Clo. *Reig* 5A 122
Juniper Ct. Houn 7B 10
(off Grove Rd.)
Juniper Dri. *Bisl* 2D 72
Juniper Gdns. *SW16* 9G 28
Juniper Gdns. *Sun* 7G 23
Juniper Pl. *Shalf* 1N 133
Juniper Rd. *Farnb* 9H 69
Juniper Rd. *Craw* 9A 162
Juniper Rd. *Reig* 5A 122
Juniper Wlk. *Brock* 5B 120
Jura Clo. *Craw* 6N 181
Justin Clo. *Bren* 3K 11
Jutland Gdns. *Coul* 7K 83
Jutland Pl. *Egh* 6E 20
Juxon Clo. *Craw* 5L 181

K

Kalima Cvn. Site. *Chob* 6L 53
Karenza Ct. *H'ham* 5L 197
Kashmir Clo. *New H* 5M 55
Kashmir Ct. *Farnb* 4A 90
Katharine Ho. *Croy* 4C 200
Katharine St. *Croy* 9N 45 (4C 200)
Katherine Clo. *Add* 3J 55
Katherine Rd. *Eden* 3L 147
Katherine Rd. *Twic* 2G 24
Kathleen Godfree Ct. *SW19* 7M 27
Kay Av. *Add* 9N 37
Kay Cres. *Hdly D* 3F 168
Kaye Ct. *Guild* 9M 93
Kaye Don Way. *Wey* 6B 56
Kayemoor Rd. *Sutt* 3B 62
Kaynes Pk. *Asc* 9J 17
Keable Rd. *Wrec* 4E 128
Kean Ho. Twic 9K 11
(off Arosa Rd.)
Kearton Clo. *Kenl* 4N 83
Kearton Pl. *Cat* 9D 84
Keates Grn. *Brack* 9N 15
Keates La. *Eton C* 2F 4
Keats Av. *Red* 1E 122
Keats Clo. *SW19* 7B 28
Keats Clo. *H'ham* 1M 197
Keats Gdns. *Fleet* 4C 88
Keats Pl. *E Grin* 9N 165
Keats Way. *Crowt* 9G 30
Keats Way. *Croy* 5F 46
Keats Way. *W Dray* 1A 8
Keats Way. *Yat* 2A 68
Keble Clo. *Craw* 9H 163
Keble Clo. *Wor Pk* 7E 42

Keble Pl.—Kingscroft La.

Keble Pl. SW13 2G 13
Keble St. SW17 5A 28
Keble Way. Owl 5K 49
Kedeston Ct. Sutt 7N 43
Keeler Clo. Wind 6B 4
Keeley Rd. Croy 8N 45 (2B 200)
Keens Clo. SW16 6H 29
Keens La. Guild 8J 93
Keens Pk. Rd. Guild 8J 93
Keens Rd. Croy 1N 63 (6C 200)
Keepers Clo. Guild 9F 94
Keepers Coombe. Brack 5B 32
Keeper's Corner. 4N 163
Keepers Ct. S Croy 8B 200
Keepers Farm Clo. Wind 5B 4
(in two parts)
Keepers M. Tedd 7J 25
Keepers Wlk. Vir W 4N 35
Keephatch Rd. Wokgm 9D 14
Keep, The. King T 7M 25
Keevil Dri. SW19 1J 27
Keir Hardie Ho. W6 2J 13
(off Fulham Pal. Rd.)
Keir Hardie Ho. Craw 8N 181
Keir, The. SW19 6H 27
Keith Lucas Rd. Farnb 3L 89
Keith Pk. Cres. Big H 8D 66
Keldholme. Brack 2M 31
Kelling Gdns. Croy 6M 45
Kellino St. SW17 5D 28
Kelly Clo. Shep 1F 38
Kelmscott Ri. Craw 9N 181
Kelsall Pl. Asc 6M 33
Kelsey Clo. Horl 8D 142
Kelsey Ga. Beck 1L 47
Kelsey Gro. Yat 1D 68
Kelsey La. Beck 1K 47
(in two parts)
Kelsey Pk. Av. Beck 1L 47
Kelsey Pk. Rd. Beck 1K 47
Kelsey Sq. Beck 1K 47
Kelsey Way. Beck 2K 47
Kelso Clo. Worth 2J 183
Kelso Rd. Cars 6A 44
Kelvedon Av. W on T 4F 56
Kelvedon Clo. King T 7N 25
Kelvedon Rd. SW6 3L 13
Kelvin Av. Lea 6F 78
Kelvin Av. Tedd 7E 24
Kelvinbrook. W Mol 2B 40
Kelvin Bus. Cen. Craw 9D 162
Kelvin Clo. Eps 3N 59
Kelvin Ct. Iswth 5E 10
Kelvin Dri. Twic 9H 11
Kelvin Gdns. Croy 6J 45
Kelvin Gro. Chess 9K 41
Kelvington Clo. Croy 6H 47
Kelvin La. Craw 8D 162
Kelvin Way. Craw 8D 162
Kemble Clo. Wey 1E 56
Kemble Cotts. Add 1J 55
Kemble Rd. Croy 9M 45
Kembleside Rd. Big H 5E 86
Kemerton Rd. Beck 1L 47
Kemerton Rd. Croy 6C 46
Kemishford. Wok 1K 93
Kemnal Pk. Hasl 1H 189
Kemp Ct. Bag 5K 51
Kempe Clo. Slou 1E 6
Kemp Gdns. Croy 5N 45
Kempsford Gdns. SW5 1M 13
Kempshott Rd. SW16 8H 29
Kempshott Rd. H'ham 4H 197
Kempson Rd. SW6 4M 13
Kempton Av. Sun 9J 23
Kempton Ct. Farnb 3L 89
Kempton Ct. Sun 9J 23
Kempton Pk. Racecourse. 8K 23
Kempton Rd. Hamp 1N 39
(in three parts)
Kempton Wlk. Croy 5H 47
Kemsing Clo. T Hth 3N 45
Kemsley Rd. Tats 6F 86
Kendal Clo. Farnb 1K 89
Kendal Clo. Felt 2G 22
Kendal Clo. Reig 2B 122
Kendale Clo. M'bowr 7G 183
Kendal Gdns. Sutt 8A 44
Kendal Gro. Camb 2H 71
Kendal Ho. SE20 1D 46
(off Derwent Rd.)
Kendall Av. Beck 1H 47
Kendall Av. S Croy 5A 64
Kendall Av. S. S Croy 6N 63
Kendall Ct. SW19 7B 28
Kendall Rd. Beck 1H 47
Kendall Rd. Iswth 5G 10
Kendal Pl. SW15 8L 13
Kendor Av. Eps 7B 60
Kendra Hall Rd. S Croy 4M 63
Kendrey Gdns. Twic 1E 24
Kendrick Clo. Wokgm 3B 30
Kenilford Rd. SW12 1F 28
Kenilworth Av. SW19 6M 27
Kenilworth Av. Brack 9A 16
Kenilworth Av. Stoke D 1B 78
Kenilworth Clo. Bans 3N 81
Kenilworth Clo. Craw 7N 181
Kenilworth Cres. Fleet 3D 88
Kenilworth Dri. W on T 9L 39
Kenilworth Gdns. Stai 6L 21
Kenilworth Rd. Ashf 4M 21
Kenilworth Rd. Farnb 9H 69
Kenilworth Rd. Eps 2F 60
Kenilworth Rd. Fleet 4C 88
(in two parts)
Kenley. 1N 83
Kenley Clo. Cat 7A 84
(in two parts)
Kenley Ct. Kenl 2M 83
Kenley Gdns. T Hth 3M 45
Kenley La. Kenl 1N 83
Kenley Rd. Hdly D 4G 169
Kenley Rd. SW19 1M 43
Kenley Rd. King T 1A 42
Kenley Rd. Twic 9H 11
Kenley Wlk. Sutt 1J 61
Kenlor Rd. SW17 6B 28
Kenmara Clo. Craw 9E 162
Kenmara Ct. Craw 8E 162
Kenmare Dri. Mitc 8D 28
Kenmare Rd. T Hth 5L 45
Kenmore Clo. C Crook 8C 88
Kenmore Clo. Frim 6B 70
Kenmore Clo. Rich 3N 11
Kenmore Rd. Kenl 1M 83
Kennard Ct. F Row 6G 187
Kenneally. Wind 5A 4
Kenneally Clo. Wind 5A 4
Kenneally Pl. Wind 5A 4
Kenneally Row. Wind 5A 4
(off Liddell Sq.)
Kenneally Wlk. Wind 5A 4
(off Guards Rd.)
Kennedy Av. E Grin 7N 165
Kennedy Clo. Mitc 9E 28
Kennedy Ct. Beck 5J 47
Kennedy Rd. H'ham 7K 197
Kennel Av. Asc 9K 17
Kennel Clo. Asc 7K 17
Kennel Clo. Fet 2C 98
Kennel Grn. Asc 9J 17
Kennel La. Brack 8N 15
Kennel La. Fet 9B 78
(in two parts)
Kennel La. Fren 9H 129
Kennel La. Hkwd 9B 142
Kennel La. W'sham 2N 51
Kennel Ride. Asc 9K 17
Kennels La. Farnb 2G 88
Kennel Wood. Asc 9K 17
Kennel Wood Cres. New Ad 7N 65
Kennet Clo. Farnb 8K 69
Kennet Clo. As 3E 110
Kennet Clo. Craw 4L 181
Kenneth Rd. Bans 2B 82
Kenneth Younger Ho. SW6 2L 13
(off Clem Attlee Ct.)
Kennet Rd. Iswth 6F 10
Kennet Sq. SW19 9B 28
Kennett Ct. W4 3A 12
Kenny Dri. Cars 5E 62
Kenrick Sq. Blet 2B 124
Kensington Av. T Hth 9L 29
Kensington Gdns. King T
2K 41 (6H 203)
(in two parts)
Kensington Hall Gdns. W14 1L 13
Kensington Mans. SW5 1M 13
(off Trebovir Rd., in two parts)
Kensington Rd. Craw 7N 181
Kensington Ter. S Croy 4A 64
Kensington Village. W14 1L 13
Kent Clo. Mitc 3J 45
Kent Clo. Orp 3N 67
Kent Clo. Stai 7M 21
Kent Dri. Tedd 6E 24
Kent Folly. Warf 7D 16
Kent Ga. Way. Croy 3J 65
Kent Hatch. 9K 107
Kent Hatch Rd. Oxt 7E 106
Kent Ho. W4 1D 12
(off Devonshire St.)
Kentigern Dri. Crowt 2J 49
Kenton Av. Sun 1L 39
Kenton Clo. Brack 1B 32
Kenton Clo. Frim 4D 70
Kenton Ct. Twic 9K 11
Kentone Ct. SE25 3E 46
Kentons La. Wind 5B 4
Kenton Way. Wok 4J 73
Kent Rd. E Mol 3C 40
Kent Rd. Fleet 4C 88
Kent Rd. King T 2K 41 (5H 203)
Kent Rd. Rich 3N 11
Kent Rd. W Wick 7L 47
Kent Rd. W'sham 2A 52
Kent Rd. Wok 3D 74
Kent's Pas. Hamp 9N 23
Kent Way. Surb 9L 41
Kentwode Grn. SW13 3F 12
Kentwyns Dri. H'ham 8L 197
Kentwyns Ri. S Nut 4K 123
Kenward Ct. Str G 7B 120
Kenway Rd. SW5 1N 13
Kenwith Av. Fleet 4D 88
Kenwood Clo. W Dray 2B 8
Kenwood Dri. Beck 2M 47
Kenwood Dri. W on T 3J 57
Kenwood Pk. Wey 3E 56
Kenwood Ridge. Kenl 4M 83
Kenworth Gro. Light 6L 51
Kenwyn Rd. SW20 9H 27
Kenya Ct. Horl 7D 142
Kenyngton Ct. Sun 6H 23
Kenyngton Dri. Sun 6H 23
Kenyon Mans. W14 2K 13
(off Queen's Club Gdns.)
Kenyons. W Hor 6C 96
Kenyon St. SW6 4J 13
Keogh Clo. Ash V 3F 90
Keppel Rd. Dork 3H 119
Keppel Spur. Old Win 1L 19
Kepple Pl. Bag 4J 51
Kepple St. Wind 5G 5
Kerria Way. W End 9B 52
Kerrill Av. Coul 6L 83
Kerry Clo. Fleet 1C 88
Kerry Ter. Wok 3D 74
Kersey Dri. S Croy 8F 64
Kersfield Rd. SW15 9J 13
Kershaw Clo. SW18 1B 28
Kersland Cotts. G'ming 4C 132
Kerves La. H'ham 9K 197
Keston. 2E 66
Keston Av. Coul 6L 83
Keston Av. Kes 2E 66
Keston Av. New H 7J 55
Keston Ct. Surb 8L 203
Keston Gdns. Kes 1E 66
Keston Mark. 1G 67
Keston Mark. (Junct.) 1F 67
Keston Pk. Clo. Kes 1H 67
Keston Rd. T Hth 5L 45
Kestrel Av. Stai 4H 21
Kestrel Clo. Craw 1A 182
Kestrel Clo. Eden 9L 127
Kestrel Clo. Eps 7A 60
Kestrel Clo. Ews 5C 108
Kestrel Clo. Guild 1F 114
Kestrel Clo. H'ham 3L 197
Kestrel Clo. King T 5K 25
Kestrel Ct. S Croy 3N 63
Kestrel Wlk. Turn H 4F 184
Kestrel Way. New Ad 5N 65
Kestrel Way. Wok 2L 73
Keswick Av. SW15 6D 26
Keswick Av. SW19 1M 43
Keswick Av. Shep 2F 38
Keswick Clo. Camb 2H 71
Keswick Clo. If'd 5J 181
Keswick Clo. Sutt 1A 62
Keswick Dri. Light 7M 51
Keswick Rd. SW15 8K 13
Keswick Rd. Bookh 3B 98
Keswick Rd. Egh 8D 20
Keswick Rd. Fet 2C 98
Keswick Rd. Twic 9C 10
Keswick Rd. W Wick 8N 47
Keswick Rd. Witl 4A 152
Ketcher Grn. Binf 5H 15
Kettering St. SW16 7G 28
Kettlewell Clo. Wok 1N 73
Kettlewell Dri. Wok 1A 74
Kettlewell Hill. Wok 1A 74
Ketton Grn. Red 6H 103
Kevan Dri. Send 3G 95
Kevin Clo. Houn 5L 9
Kevins Dri. Yat 8D 48
Kevins Gro. Fleet 4C 88
Kew. 3N 11
Kew Bridge. (Junct.) 2N 11
Kew Bri. Bren 2M 11
Kew Bri. Arches. Rich 1N 11
Kew Bri. Ct. W4 1N 11
Kew Bri. Distribution Cen. Bren
1M 11
Kew Bri. Rd. Bren 2M 11
Kew Bridge Steam Mus. 1M 11
Kew Cres. Sutt 9K 43
Kew Foot Rd. Rich 7L 11
Kew Gardens Plants & People
Exhibition. 3M 11
Kew Gdns. Rd. Rich 3M 11
Kew Green. (Junct.) 3M 11
Kew Grn. Rich 2M 11
Kew Mdw. Path. Rich 5B 12
(Thames Bank)
Kew Mdw. Path. Rich 4A 12
(W. Park Av.)
Kew Palace. 3L 11
Kew Retail Pk. Rich 4A 12
Kew Rd. Rich 2N 11
Keymer Clo. Big H 3E 86
Keymer Rd. SW2 3K 29
Keymer Rd. Craw 5A 182
Keynes Clo. C Crook 9C 88
Keynsham Rd. Mord 7N 43
Keynsham Wlk. Mord 7N 43
Keynsham Way. Owl 5J 49
Keys Ct. Croy 5D 200
Keysham Av. Houn 4H 9
Keywood Dri. Sun 7H 23
Khama Rd. SW17 5C 28
Khartoum Rd. SW17 5B 28
Khartoum Rd. Witl 4B 152
Kibble Grn. Brack 5A 32
Kidborough Down. Bookh 5A 98
Kidborough Rd. Craw 4L 181
Kidbrooke Park. 8F 186
Kidbrooke Pk. & Repton Grounds.
8F 186
Kidbrooke Ri. F Row 7G 187
Kidderminster Pl. Croy 7M 45
Kidderminster Rd. Croy 7M 45
Kidmans Clo. H'ham 3M 197
Kidworth Clo. Horl 6D 142
Kielder Wlk. Camb 2G 71
Kier Pk. Asc 2N 33
Kilberry Clo. Iswth 4D 10
Kilburns Mill Clo. Wall 8F 44
Kilcorral Clo. Eps 1F 80
Kilkie St. SW6 5N 13
Killarney Rd. SW18
9N 13 & 1A 28
Killasser Ct. Tad 1H 101
Killester Gdns. Wor Pk 1G 61
Killick Ho. Sutt 1N 61
Killicks. Cranl 6A 156
Killieser Av. SW2 3J 29
Killinghurst La. Hasl & C'fold
2N 189
Killinghurst Park. 1A 190
Killy Hill. Chob 4H 53
Kilmaine Rd. SW6 3K 13
Kilmarnock Pk. Reig 2N 121
Kilmartin Av. SW16 2L 45
Kilmartin Gdns. Frim 5D 70
Kilmington Clo. Brack 6C 32
Kilmington Rd. SW13 2F 12
Kilmiston Av. Shep 5D 38
Kilmore Dri. Camb 2F 70
Kilmorey Gdns. Twic 8H 11
Kilmorey Rd. Twic 7H 11
Kilmuir Clo. Col T 8J 49
Kiln Clo. Craw D 2E 184
Kiln Clo. Hay 2E 8
Kiln Copse. Cranl 6N 155
Kiln Cotts. Newd 7C 140
Kilnfield Rd. Rud 9E 176
Kiln Fields. Hasl 9G 171
Kiln La. Asc 4D 34
Kiln La. Bisl 4E 72
Kiln La. Brack 1M 31
Kiln La. Brock 4A 120
Kiln La. Eps 7D 60
Kiln La. Horl 6E 142
Kiln La. Lwr Bo 5G 129
Kiln La. Rip 2J 95
Kiln La. Wink 7M 17
Kilnmead. Craw 2C 182
Kilnmead Clo. Craw 2C 182
Kiln Meadows. Guild 8F 92
Kiln M. SW17 6B 28
Kiln Ride. Finch 8A 30
Kiln Ride Extension. Finch 1A 48
Kiln Rd. Craw D 2E 184
Kilnside. Clay 4G 58
Kiln Wlk. Red 8E 122
Kiln Way. Alder 5N 109
Kiln Way. Gray 4K 169
Kilnwood La. Fay 6E 180
Kilross Rd. Felt 2E 22
Kilrue La. W on T 1G 57
Kilrush Ter. Wok 3C 74
Kilsha Rd. W on T 5K 39
Kimbell Gdns. SW6 4K 13
Kimber Clo. Wind 6D 4
Kimber Ct. Guild 1F 114
Kimberley. Brack 7A 32
Kimberley. C Crook 9C 88
Kimberley Clo. Horl 8C 142
Kimberley Clo. Slou 1B 6
Kimberley Pl. Purl 7L 63
Kimberley Ride. Cobh 9B 58
Kimberley Rd. Beck 1G 47
Kimberley Rd. Craw 2F 182
Kimberley Rd. Croy 5M 45
Kimberley Wlk. W on T 6J 39
Kimber Rd. SW18 1M 27
Kimbers La. Farnh 9J 109
Kimble Rd. SW19 7B 28
Kimmeridge. Brack 5C 32
Kimpton Ind. Est. Sutt 8L 43
Kimpton Rd. Sutt 8L 43
Kinburn Dri. Egh 6A 20
Kincha Lodge. King T 1L 203
Kindersley Clo. E Grin 7D 166
Kinfauns Rd. SW2 3L 29
King Acre Ct. Stai 4G 20
King Charles Cres. Surb 6M 41
King Charles Ho. SW6 3N 13
(off Wandon Rd.)
King Charles Rd. Surb 4M 41
King Charles Wlk. SW19 2K 27
Kingcup Clo. Croy 6G 46
Kingcup Dri. Bisl 2D 72
King Edward Clo. C Hosp 9D 196
King Edward Ct. Wind 4G 4
King Edward Dri. Chess 9L 41
King Edward M. SW13 4F 12
King Edward Rd. C Hosp 9D 196
King Edward's Clo. Asc 9J 17
King Edward VII Av. Wind 3H 5
King Edwards Gro. Tedd 7H 25
King Edwards Mans. SW6 3M 13
(off Fulham Rd.)
King Edward's Ri. Asc 8J 17
King Edward's Rd. Asc 9J 17
Kingfield. 7C 74
Kingfield Clo. Wok 7B 74
Kingfield Dri. Wok 7B 74
Kingfield Gdns. Wok 7B 74
Kingfield Green. 7B 74
Kingfield Rd. Wok 7A 74
Kingfisher Clo. Farnb 8H 69
Kingfisher Clo. Bord 7A 168
Kingfisher Clo. C Crook 8B 88
Kingfisher Clo. Craw 8E 162
Kingfisher Clo. W on T 2M 57
Kingfisher Ct. SW19 3J 27
Kingfisher Ct. Dork 1J 201
Kingfisher Ct. Houn 8B 10
Kingfisher Ct. Wok 1E 74
Kingfisher Dri. Guild 1E 114
Kingfisher Dri. Red 9E 102
Kingfisher Dri. Rich 5H 25
Kingfisher Dri. Stai 5H 21
Kingfisher Dri. Yat 9A 48
Kingfisher Gdns. S Croy 7G 65
Kingfisher La. Turn H 4F 184
Kingfisher Ri. E Grin 1B 186
Kingfisher Wlk. As 1D 110
Kingfisher Way. Beck 4G 46
Kingfisher Way. H'ham 3J 197
King Gdns. Croy 2M 63 (8A 200)
King George Av. E Grin 7M 165
King George Av. W on T 7L 39
King George Clo. Sun 6F 22
King George's Dri. New H 6J 55
King George's Hill. 5N 137
King George VI Av. Big H 3F 86
King George VI Av. Mitc 3D 44
King George Sq. Rich 9M 11
King George's Trad. Est. Chess
1N 59
Kingham Clo. SW18 1A 28
King Henry M. Orp 2N 67
King Henry's Dri. New Ad 5L 65
King Henry's Reach. W6 2H 13
King Henry's Rd. King T 2A 42
King John's Clo. Wray 8N 5
Kinglake Ct. Wok 5H 73
Kingpost Pde. Guild 9D 94
Kings Acre. S Nut 6K 123
Kings Arbour. S'hall 1M 9
King's Arms All. Bren 2K 11
Kings Arms Way. Cher 7H 37
Kings Av. SW12 & SW4 2H 29
King's Av. Brkwd 6A 72
Kings Av. Byfl 8M 55
King's Av. Cars 4C 62
Kings Av. Houn 4B 10
Kings Av. N Mald 3D 42
Kings Av. Red 5C 122
King's Av. Sun 6G 23
Kings Av. Tong 4C 110
Kingsbridge Cotts. Wokgm 9C 30
Kingsbridge Rd. Mord 5J 43
Kingsbridge Rd. S'hall 1N 9
Kingsbridge Rd. W on T 6J 39
Kingsbrook. Lea 5G 79
Kingsbury Cres. Stai 5F 20
Kingsbury Dri. Old Win 1K 19
Kings Chase. E Mol 2C 40
Kingsclear Pk. Camb 2B 70
Kingsclere Clo. SW15 1F 26
Kingscliffe Gdns. SW19 2L 27
Kings Clo. Stai 8M 21
Kings Clo. Th Dit 5G 41
Kings Clo. W on T 7J 39
Kings Copse. E Grin 1B 186
Kingscote. 5J 185
Kingscote Hill. Craw 5N 181
Kingscote Rd. Croy 6E 46
Kingscote Rd. N Mald 2C 42
Kings Ct. W6 1F 12
Kings Ct. Byfl 7M 55
King's Ct. H'ham 5L 197
King's Ct. Tad 9G 81
Kings Ct. Tong 4C 110
Kingscourt Rd. SW16 4H 29
King's Cres. Camb 7A 50
Kingscroft. Fleet 5B 88
Kingscroft La. Warf 3D 16

Kingscroft Rd.—Lagham Pk.

Kingscroft Rd. *Bans* 2B **82**
Kingscroft Rd. *Lea* 7H **79**
Kings Cross La. *S Nut* 5H **123**
Kingsdene. *Tad* 8G **80**
Kingsdown Av. *S Croy* 6M **63**
Kingsdowne Rd. *Surb* 6L **41**
Kingsdown Rd. *Eps* 9F **60**
Kingsdown Rd. *Sutt* 2K **61**
Kings Dri. *Surb* 6N **41**
Kings Dri. *Tedd* 6D **24**
Kings Dri. *Th Dit* 6H **41**
Kings Dri. *W on T* 5G **57**
Kings Farm Av. *Rich* 7N **11**
Kingsfield. *Alb* 4N **135**
Kingsfield. *Wind* 4A **4**
Kingsfold 3H 179
Kingsfold Ct. *K'fold* 4H **179**
Kingsgate. *Craw* 3C **182**
Kings Ga. G'ming 5J **133**
(off King's Rd.)
Kingsgate Bus. Cen. *King T* 2J **203**
Kingsgate Rd. *King T* 9L **25** (2J **203**)
Kingsgrove Ind. Est. *Farnb* 2M **89**
Kings Head La. *Byfl* 7M **55**
Kingshill Av. *Wor Pk* 6F **42**
Kings Keep. *SW15* 8J **13**
Kings Keep. *Fleet* 7B **88**
Kings Keep. *King T* 3L **41** (8J **203**)
King's Keep. *Sand* 6G **49**
Kingsland 2N 159
Kingsland. *Newd* 2N **159**
Kingsland Ct. *Craw* 3E **182**
Kings La. *Eng G* 6A **20**
(Egham)
Kings La. *Eng G* 6K **19**
(Englefield Green)
Kings La. *Sutt* 3B **62**
Kings La. *W'sham* 2B **52**
Kings La. *Wrec* 5E **128**
Kingslawn Clo. *SW15* 8G **13**
Kingslea. *H'ham* 5L **197**
Kingslea. *Lea* 7G **79**
Kingsleigh Pl. *Mitc* 2D **44**
Kingsley Av. *Bans* 2M **81**
Kingsley Av. *Camb* 2A **70**
Kingsley Av. *Eng G* 7L **19**
Kingsley Av. *Houn* 5C **10**
Kingsley Av. *Sutt* 1B **62**
Kingsley Clo. *Crowt* 4G **49**
Kingsley Clo. *Horl* 6D **142**
Kingsley Ct. *Sutt* 4N **61**
Kingsley Ct. Wor Pk 8E **42**
(off Avenue, The)
Kingsley Dri. *Wor Pk* 8E **42**
Kingsley Green 6E 188
Kingsley Gro. *Reig* 6M **121**
Kingsley Mans. W14 2K **13**
(off Greyhound Rd.)
Kingsley Rd. *Farnb* 8L **69**
Kingsley Rd. *SW19* 6N **27**
Kingsley Rd. *Craw* 6M **181**
Kingsley Rd. *Croy* 7L **45**
Kingsley Rd. *Horl* 6D **142**
Kingsley Rd. *Houn* 4B **10**
Kingsley Rd. *Orp* 4N **67**
Kingslyn Cres. *SE19* 1B **46**
Kings Mall. *W6* 1H **13**
Kingsmead. *Farnb* 1N **89**
Kingsmead. *Big H* 3F **86**
Kings Mead. *Cranl* 7N **155**
Kingsmead. *Frlm G* 7C **70**
Kings Mead. *Rich* 9M **11**
Kings Mead. *Small* 8M **143**
Kingsmead. *S Nut* 5J **123**
Kingsmead. *Wok* 3C **74**
Kingsmead Av. *Mitc* 2G **45**
Kingsmead Av. *Sun* 1K **39**
Kingsmead Av. *Surb* 8N **41**
Kingsmead Av. *Wor Pk* 8G **42**
Kingsmead Clo. *Eps* 4C **60**
Kingsmead Clo. *H'ham* 2A **198**
Kingsmead Clo. *Tedd* 7H **25**
Kings Mead Pk. *Clay* 4E **58**
Kingsmead Pl. *Broad H* 5C **196**
Kingsmead Rd. *SW2* 3L **29**
Kingsmead Rd. *Broad H* 5D **196**
Kingsmead Shop. Cen. *Farnb* 1N **89**
Kingsmere Clo. *SW15* 6J **13**
Kingsmere Rd. *SW19* 3J **27**
Kingsmere Rd. *Brack* 9L **15**
Kingsmill Bus. Pk. *King T* 2M **41** (6M **203**)
Kings Mill La. *Red & S Nut* 8F **122**
Kingsnympton Pk. *King T* 8A **26**
King's Paddock. *Hamp* 9C **24**
King's Pde. Cars 9D **44**
(off Wrythe La.)
Kings Pde. *Fleet* 3B **88**
Kings Pas. *King T* (KT1) 1K **41** (4H **203**)
King's Pas. *King T* (KT2) 9K **25** (1H **203**)
Kings Peace, The. *Gray* 6A **170**
King's Pl. *W4* 1B **12**
King's Ride. *Asc* 4G **32**
King's Ride. *Camb* 6B **50**
(in two parts)
Kings Ride Ga. *Rich* 7N **11**
Kingsridge. *SW19* 3K **27**
Kings Rd. *SE25* 2D **46**
King's Rd. *SW6,SW10 & SW3* 3N **13**
Kings Rd. *SW14* 6C **12**
Kings Rd. *SW19* 7M **27**
King's Rd. *Alder* 3K **109**
King's Rd. *Asc* 4A **34**
Kings Rd. *Big H* 3E **86**
Kings Rd. *Cranl* 8N **155**
Kings Rd. *Crowt* 3G **49**
Kings Rd. *Egh* 5C **20**
Kings Rd. *Felt* 2K **23**
Kings Rd. *Fleet* 3B **88**
King's Rd. *G'ming* 5J **133**
King's Rd. *Guild* 3N **113** (3D **202**)
Kings Rd. *Hasl* 2D **188**
Kings Rd. *Horl* 8E **142**
King's Rd. *H'ham* 5L **197**
King's Rd. *King T* 9L **25** (1J **203**)
Kings Rd. *Mitc* 2E **44**
Kings Rd. *New H* 6K **55**
King's Rd. *Orp* 1N **67**
Kings Rd. *Rich* 9M **11**
Kings Rd. *Rud* 9F **176**
Kings Rd. *Shalf* 1A **134**
King's Rd. *Surb* 7J **41**
King's Rd. *Sutt* 6M **61**
Kings Rd. *Tedd* 6D **24**
Kings Rd. *Twic* 9H **11**
Kings Rd. *W on T* 8J **39**
King's Rd. *W End* 1D **72**
King's Rd. *Wind* 7G **4**
Kings Rd. *Wok* 3C **74**
Kings Rd. Ind. Est. *Hasl* 2D **188**
King's Shade Wlk. *Eps* 9C **60** (7K **201**)
Kingstable St. *Eton* 3G **4**
Kings Ter. *Fren* 1J **149**
King's Ter. *Iswth* 7G **11**
Kingston Av. *E Hor* 4F **96**
Kingston Av. *Felt* 9F **8**
Kingston Av. *Lea* 8H **79**
Kingston Av. *Sutt* 9K **43**
Kingston Bri. *King T* 1K **41** (3G **203**)
Kingston Bus. Cen. *Chess* 9L **41**
Kingston By-Pass. *SW15 & SW20* 5D **26**
Kingston By-Pass. *N Mald* 4D **42**
Kingston By-Pass. *Surb* 9K **41**
Kingston By-Pass Rd. *Esh & Surb* 8E **40**
Kingston Clo. *Tedd* 7H **25**
Kingston Cres. *Ashf* 6L **21**
Kingston Cres. *Beck* 1J **47**
Kingston Gdns. *Croy* 9J **45**
Kingston Hall Rd. *King T* 2K **41** (5H **203**)
Kingston Hill. *King T* 9N **25**
Kingston Hill Pl. *King T* 5B **26**
Kingston Ho. *King T* 7H **203**
Kingston Ho. Est. *Surb* 5H **41**
Kingston Ho. Gdns. *Lea* 8H **79**
Kingstonian F.C. 2A 42
Kingston La. *Tedd* 6G **25**
Kingston La. *W Hor* 5B **96**
Kingston Ri. *New H* 6J **55**
Kingston Rd. *SW15 & SW19* 3F **26**
Kingston Rd. *SW20 & SW19* 1J **43**
Kingston Rd. *Camb* 7D **50**
Kingston Rd. *Eps* 5E **60**
Kingston Rd. *King T & N Mald* 2A **42**
Kingston Rd. *Lea* 8G **79**
(in two parts)
Kingston Rd. *Stai & Ashf* 5J **21**
(in two parts)
Kingston Rd. *Surb & Eps* 8A **42**
Kingston Rd. *Tedd* 6H **25**
Kingstons Ind. Est. *Alder* 2C **110**
Kingston University 3L 41 (6C 203)
(Grange Rd.)
Kingston University 6C 26
(Kingston Hill)
Kingston University. 3L 41 (7L 203)
(Penrhyn Rd.)
Kingston Upon Thames 1K 41 (4J 203)
Kingston upon Thames Crematorium. *King T* 2N **41**
Kingston upon Thames Library, Art Gallery and Mus. 1L 41 (3K 203)
Kingston Vale 5D 26
Kingston Va. *SW15* 5C **26**
King St. *W6* 1F **12**
King St. *Cher* 7J **37**
King St. *E Grin* 9A **166**
King St. *Rich* 8K **11**
King St. *Twic* 2G **24**
King St. Cloisters. W6 1G **13**
(off King St.)
King St. Pde. Twic 2G **24**
(off King St.)
King's Wlk. *Col T* 9L **49**
Kings Wlk. *S Croy* 1E **84**
Kings Warren. *Oxs* 7C **58**
Kingsway. *SW14* 6A **12**
Kingsway. *Alder* 3K **109**
Kingsway. *B'water* 1J **69**
King's Way. *Croy* 2K **63**
Kingsway. *N Mald* 3H **43**
Kingsway. *Stai* 2M **21**
Kingsway. *W Wick* 1A **66**
Kingsway. *Wok* 5N **73**
Kingsway Av. *S Croy* 5F **64**
Kingsway Av. *Wok* 5N **73**
Kingsway Bus. Pk. *Hamp* 9N **23**
Kingsway Rd. *Sutt* 4K **61**
Kingsway Ter. *Wey* 5B **56**
Kingsway, The. *Eps* 7D **60**
Kingswey Bus. Pk. *Wok* 1E **74**
Kingswick Clo. *Asc* 3D **34**
Kingswick Dri. *Asc* 3A **34**
Kingswood 1L 101
Kingswood Av. *Brom* 2N **47**
Kingswood Av. *Hamp* 7B **24**
Kingswood Av. *Houn* 4N **9**
Kingswood Av. *S Croy* 2E **84**
Kingswood Av. *T Hth* 4L **45**
Kingswood Bus. Cen. *Red* 4E **122**
Kingswood Clo. *Broadf* 9A **182**
Kingswood Clo. *Eng G* 5N **19**
Kingswood Clo. *Guild* 2E **114**
Kingswood Clo. *N Mald* 5E **42**
Kingswood Clo. *Surb* 6L **41**
Kingswood Clo. *Wey* 4C **56**
Kingswood Ct. *Hors* 3A **74**
Kingswood Ct. *Kgswd* 2K **101**
Kingswood Creek. *Wray* 8N **5**
Kingswood Dri. *Cars* 7D **44**
Kingswood Dri. *Sutt* 5N **61**
Kingswood Firs. *Gray* 7N **169**
Kingswood La. *Hind* 7A **170**
Kingswood La. *Warl* 2F **84**
(in two parts)
Kingswood Pk. *Tad* 8K **81**
Kingswood Ri. *Eng G* 6N **19**
Kingswood Rd. *SW2* 1J **29**
Kingswood Rd. *SW19* 8L **27**
Kingswood Rd. *Brom* 3N **47**
Kingswood Rd. *Tad* 8G **80**
Kingswood Way. *S Croy* 9F **64**
(in two parts)
Kingswood Way. *Wall* 2J **63**
Kingsworth Clo. *Beck* 4H **47**
Kingsworthy Clo. *King T* 2M **41** (5M **203**)
Kings Yd. SW15 6H **13**
(off Lwr. Richmond Rd.)
Kings Yd. *Asc* 3J **33**
Kingwood Rd. *SW6* 4K **13**
Kinloss Rd. *Cars* 6A **44**
Kinnaird Av. *W4* 3B **12**
Kinnersley Wlk. *Reig* 8M **121**
Kinnibrugh Dri. *D'land* 1C **166**
Kinnoul Rd. *W6* 2K **13**
Kinross Av. *Asc* 4K **33**
Kinross Av. *Wor Pk* 8F **42**
Kinross Clo. *Sun* 6G **23**
Kinross Ct. *Asc* 4K **33**
Kinross Dri. *Sun* 6G **22**
Kinsella Gdns. *SW19* 6G **26**
Kintyre Clo. *SW16* 1K **45**
Kintyre Ct. *SW2* 1J **29**
Kipings. *Tad* 8J **81**
Kipling Clo. *Craw* 1G **182**
Kipling Clo. *Yat* 2B **68**
Kipling Ct. *H'ham* 4N **197**
Kipling Ct. *Wind* 5E **4**
Kipling Dri. *SW19* 7B **28**
Kipling Way. *E Grin* 9M **165**
Kirby Clo. *Eps* 2E **60**
Kirby Rd. *Wok* 4M **73**
Kirby Way. *W on T* 5K **39**
Kirdford Clo. *Craw* 1M **181**
Kirkefields. *Guild* 9K **93**
Kirkgate, The. *Eps* 9D **60** (6L **201**)
Kirkham Clo. *Owl* 5J **49**
Kirk Knoll. *Hdly* 4E **168**
Kirkland Av. *Wok* 3H **73**
Kirkleas Rd. *Surb* 7L **41**
Kirklees Rd. *T Hth* 4L **45**
Kirkley Rd. *SW19* 9M **27**
Kirkly Clo. *S Croy* 5B **64**
Kirk Ri. *Sutt* 9N **43**
Kirkstall Gdns. *SW2* 2J **29**
Kirkstall Rd. *SW2* 2H **29**
Kirksted Rd. *Mord* 7N **43**
Kirkstone Clo. *Camb* 2H **71**
Kirrane Clo. *N Mald* 4E **42**
Kirriemuir Gdns. *As* 1H **111**
Kirton Lodge. *SW18* 9N **13**
Kitchener Rd. *Alder* 7B **90**
Kitchener Rd. *T Hth* 2A **46**
Kites Clo. *Craw* 3A **182**
Kithurst Clo. *Craw* 5B **182**
Kitley Gdns. *SE19* 1C **46**
Kitsmead. *Copt* 8L **163**
Kitsmead La. *Longc* 7M **35**
Kitson Rd. *SW13* 4F **12**
Kittiwake Clo. *If'd* 5J **181**
Kittiwake Clo. *S Croy* 6H **65**
Kittiwake Pl. *Sutt* 2L **61**
Kitts La. *Churt* 9K **149**
Klondyke Vs. *G'wood* 8L **171**
Knaphill 4G 72
Knapp Rd. *Ashf* 5A **22**
Knapton M. *SW17* 7E **28**
Knaresborough Dri. *SW18* 2N **27**
Kneller Gdns. *Iswth* 9D **10**
Kneller Rd. *N Mald* 6D **42**
Kneller Rd. *Twic* 9C **10**
Knepp Clo. *Craw* 3G **182**
Knighton Clo. *Craw* 8H **163**
Knighton Clo. *S Croy* 5M **63**
Knighton Rd. *Red* 5E **122**
Knightons La. *Duns* 5B **174**
Knightsbridge Cres. *Stai* 7K **21**
Knightsbridge Gro. *Camb* 8C **50**
Knightsbridge Ho. Guild 4B **114**
(off St Lukes Sq.)
Knightsbridge Rd. *Camb* 8C **50**
Knights Clo. *Egh* 7F **20**
Knights Clo. *Wind* 4A **4**
Knights Ct. *King T* 2L **41** (5J **203**)
Knights Hill. *SE27* 6M **29**
Knight's Hill Sq. *SE27* 5M **29**
Knight's Pk. *King T* 2L **41** (5K **203**)
Knights Pl. *Red* 2E **122**
Knight's Pl. *Twic* 2E **24**
Knights Pl. *Wind* 6F **4**
Knights Rd. *Farnh* 5K **109**
Knights Way. *Camb* 2G **70**
Knightswood. *Brack* 7N **31**
Knightswood. *Wok* 5J **73**
Knightwood Clo. *Reig* 5M **121**
Knightwood Cres. *N Mald* 5D **42**
Knipp Hill. *Cob* 9N **57**
Knivet Rd. *SW6* 2M **13**
Knobfield. *Ab H* 3G **136**
Knob Hill. *Warn* 9F **178**
Knockholt Clo. *Sutt* 6N **61**
Knockholt Main Rd. *Knock* 6N **87**
Knockhundred La. *Bram C* 9N **169**
Knole Clo. *Croy* 5F **46**
Knole Clo. *Worth* 2H **183**
Knole Gro. *E Grin* 7M **165**
Knole Wood. *Asc* 7B **34**
Knoll Clo. *Fleet* 3B **88**
Knoll Ct. *Fleet* 2B **88**
Knoll Farm Rd. *Capel* 7G **159**
Knollmead. *Surb* 7B **42**
Knoll Pk. Rd. *Cher* 7H **37**
Knoll Quarry. *G'ming* 5H **133**
Knoll Rd. *SW18* 8N **13**
Knoll Rd. *Camb* 9B **50**
Knoll Rd. *Dork* 7G **118**
Knoll Rd. *Fleet* 3B **88**
Knoll Rd. *G'ming* 5G **133**
Knoll Roundabout. (Junct.) 8J 79
Knolls Clo. *Wor Pk* 9G **42**
Knolls, The. *Eps* 3H **81**
Knoll, The. *Cob* 9A **58**
Knoll, The. *Beck* 1L **47**
Knoll, The. *Cher* 7H **37**
Knoll, The. *Lea* 8J **79**
Knoll Wlk. *Camb* 9B **50**
Knoll Wood. *G'ming* 5G **133**
Knollys Clo. *SW16* 4L **29**
Knollys Rd. *SW16* 4K **29**
Knollys Rd. *Alder* 1L **109**
Knook, The. *Col T* 8J **49**
Knowle Clo. *Copt* 7N **163**
Knowle Dri. *Copt* 7M **163**
Knowle Gdns. *W Byf* 9H **55**
Knowle Green 6K 21
Knowle Grn. *Stai* 6J **21**
Knowle Gro. *Vir W* 6M **35**
Knowle Gro. Clo. *Vir W* 6M **35**
Knowle Hill 6M 35
Knowle Hill. *Vir W* 6L **35**
Knowle La. *Cranl & Rud* 8M **155**
Knowle Pk. *Cob* 3M **77**
Knowle Pk. Av. *Stai* 7K **21**
Knowle Rd. *Twic* 2E **24**
Knowles Av. *Crowt* 2E **48**
Knowle, The. *Tad* 8H **81**
Knowl Hill. *Wok* 6D **74**
Knox Grn. *Binf* 6H **15**
Knox Rd. *Guild* 7L **93**
Kohat Ct. *Alder* 2L **109**
Kohat Rd. *SW19* 6N **27**
Kohima Clo. *Alder* 1N **109**
Koonowla Clo. *Big H* 2F **86**
Kooringa. *Warl* 6E **84**
Korda Clo. *Shep* 2A **30**
Korea Cotts. *Cob* 3L **77**
Kotan Dri. *Stai* 5E **20**
Kramer M. *SW5* 1M **13**
Kreisel Wlk. *Rich* 2M **11**
Kristina Ct. Sutt 3M **61**
(off Overton Rd.)
Krooner Rd. *Camb* 3N **69**
Kuala Gdns. *SW16* 9K **29**
Kyle Clo. *Brack* 2N **31**
Kynaston Av. *T Hth* 4N **45**
Kynaston Ct. *Cat* 3B **104**
Kynaston Cres. *T Hth* 4N **45**
Kynaston Rd. *T Hth* 4N **45**
Kynnersley Clo. *Cars* 9D **44**

L

Laburnum Av. *Sutt* 9C **44**
Laburnum Clo. *Alder* 3M **109**
Laburnum Clo. *Guild* 9M **93**
Laburnum Ct. *SE19* 1C **46**
Laburnum Ct. (Cvn. Pk.). *Small* 1N **163**
Laburnum Cres. *Sun* 9J **23**
Laburnum Gdns. *C Crook* 8C **88**
Laburnum Gdns. *Croy* 6G **46**
Laburnum Gro. *Houn* 7N **9**
Laburnum Gro. *N Mald* 1C **42**
Laburnum Gro. *Slou* 2D **6**
Laburnum Ho. *Short* 1N **47**
Laburnum Pas. *Alder* 2M **109**
Laburnum Pl. *Eng G* 7L **19**
Laburnum Rd. *SW19* 8A **28**
Laburnum Rd. *Alder* 3M **109**
Laburnum Rd. *Cher* 7J **37**
Laburnum Rd. *Eps* 9D **60** (7L **201**)
Laburnum Rd. *Farnh* 5K **109**
Laburnum Rd. *Hay* 1H **9**
Laburnum Rd. *Mitc* 1E **44**
Laburnum Rd. *Wok* 7N **73**
Laburnums, The. *B'water* 1G **68**
Laburnum Way. *Stai* 2A **22**
Lacey Av. *Coul* 7L **83**
Lacey Clo. *Egh* 8F **20**
Lacey Dri. *Coul* 7L **83**
Lacey Dri. *Hamp* 9N **23**
Lacey Grn. *Coul* 7L **83**
Lackford Rd. *Coul* 5D **82**
Lacock Clo. *SW19* 7A **28**
Lacrosse Way. *SW16* 9H **29**
Lacy Rd. *SW15* 7J **13**
(in two parts)
Ladas Rd. *SE27* 5N **29**
Ladbroke Cotts. Red 2E **122**
(off Ladbroke Rd.)
Ladbroke Ct. *Red* 1E **122**
Ladbroke Gro. *Red* 2E **122**
Ladbroke Hurst. *D'land* 1C **166**
Ladbroke Rd. *Eps* 1C **80** (8K **201**)
Ladbroke Rd. *Horl* 6F **142**
Ladbroke Rd. *Red* 2E **122**
Ladbrook Rd. *SE25* 3A **46**
Ladderstile Ride. *King T* 6A **26**
Ladybank. *Brack* 7N **31**
Lady Booth Rd. *King T* 1L **41** (4J **203**)
Ladycroft Gdns. *Orp* 2L **67**
Ladycroft Way. *Orp* 2L **67**
Ladycross. *Milf* 2B **152**
Ladyegate Clo. *Dork* 4K **119**
Ladyegate Rd. *Dork* 5J **119**
Lady Elizabeth Ho. *SW14* 6B **12**
Lady Forsdyke Way. *Eps* 5N **59**
Ladygate Dri. *Gray* 6M **169**
Ladygrove. *Croy* 5H **65**
Ladygrove Dri. *Guild* 7C **94**
Lady Harewood Way. *Eps* 5N **59**
Lady Hay. *Wor Pk* 8E **42**
Lady Margaret Rd. *Asc* 7C **34**
Lady Margaret Rd. *Craw* 2M **181**
Lady Margaret Wlk. *Craw* 2M **181**
Ladymead. *Guild* 2M **113** (1B **202**)
Ladymead Clo. *M'bowr* 6G **183**
Ladymead Retail Cen. *Guild* 2M **113** (1A **202**)
Ladythorpe Clo. *Add* 1K **55**
Ladywood Av. *Farnb* 1H **89**
Ladywood Rd. *Surb* 8N **41**
Laffan's Rd. *Alder* 7H **89**
Lafone Av. *Felt* 3K **23**
Lagham Pk. *S God* 6H **125**

Lavender Way—Lincoln Rd.

Lavender Way. Croy 5G 47
Lavengro Rd. SE27 3N 29
Lavenham Rd. SW18 3L 27
Laverstoke Gdns. SW15 1E 26
Laverton M. SW5 1N 13
Laverton Pl. SW5 1N 13
Lavington Clo. Craw 2L 181
Lavington Rd. Croy 9K 45
Lawbrook La. Peasl & Gom 6D 136
Lawday Link. Farnh 5F 108
Lawday Pl. Farnh 5F 108
Lawday Pl. La. Farnh 5F 108
Lawdons Gdns. Croy 1M 63 (7A 200)
Lawford Clo. Wall 5J 63
Lawford Cres. Yat 9C 48
Lawford Gdns. Kenl 3N 83
Lawford Rd. W4 3B 12
Lawford's Hill Clo. Worp 2F 92
Lawford's Hill Rd. Worp 2F 92
Lawley Ho. Twic 9K 11
Lawn Clo. Dat 3M 5
Lawn Clo. N Mald 1D 42
Lawn Cres. Rich 5N 11
Lawn Rd. Guild 6M 113 (8B 202)
Lawnsmead. Won 4D 134
Lawnsmead Cotts. Won 4D 134
Lawns Rd. Rud 6B 176
Lawns, The. Farnb 2K 89
Lawns, The. SE19 9N 29 & 1A 46
Lawns, The. SW19 6L 27
Lawns, The. Asc 2H 33
Lawns, The. Coln 4G 7
Lawns, The. Milf 1C 152
Lawns, The. Sutt 4K 61
Lawn, The. S'hall 1A 10
Lawnwood Cotts. G'ming 6K 133 (off Catteshall La.)
Lawrence Av. N Mald 5C 42
Lawrence Clo. Guild 7D 94
Lawrence Clo. Wokgm 2C 30
Lawrence Ct. Wind 5F 4
Lawrence Cres. W'sham 3A 52
Lawrence Est. Houn 7K 9
Lawrence Gro. Binf 9J 15
Lawrence La. Buck 1G 120
Lawrence Pde. Iswth 6H 11 (off Lower Sq.)
Lawrence Rd. SE25 3C 46
Lawrence Rd. Fleet 5A 88
Lawrence Rd. Hamp 8N 23
Lawrence Rd. Houn 7K 9
Lawrence Rd. Rich 5J 25
Lawrence Rd. W Wick 1C 66
Lawrence Way. Camb 2L 69
Lawrence Weaver Clo. Mord 5M 43
Laws Clo. If'd 4K 181
Lawson Clo. SW19 4J 27
Lawson Ct. Surb 6K 41
Lawson-Hunt Ind. Pk. Broad H 4D 196
Lawson Wlk. Cars 5C 62
Lawson Way. Asc 5F 34
Laws Ter. Alder 1A 110
Laxey Rd. Orp 3N 67
Laxton Gdns. Red 6H 103
Layard Rd. T Hth 1A 46
Layburn Cres. Slou 2D 6
Layhams Rd. Warl & Kes 8B 66
Layhams Rd. W Wick & Kes 9N 47
Layton Ct. Bren 1K 11
Layton Ct. Wey 1C 56
Layton Cres. Croy 2L 63
Layton Pl. Kew 4N 11
Layton Rd. Bren 1K 11
Layton Rd. Houn 7B 10
Layton's La. Sun 1G 38
Lazenbys Est. Wal W 9L 157
Leach Gro. Lea 9J 79
Lea Clo. As 3E 110
Lea Clo. Bad L 6M 109
Lea Clo. Craw 4L 181
Lea Clo. Twic 1N 23
Lea Coach Rd. Thur 5L 151
Lea Ct. Farnh 5L 109
Leacroft. Asc 4D 34
Lea Cft. Crowt 1G 49
Leacroft. Stai 6J 21
Leacroft Av. SW12 1D 28
Leacroft Clo. Kenl 3N 83
Leacroft Clo. Stai 5K 21
Leaf Clo. Th Dit 4E 40
Leafey La. Gray 3K 169
Leaf Gro. SE27 6L 29
Leafield Clo. SW16 7M 29
Leafield Clo. Wok 5M 73
Leafield Copse. Brack 3D 32
Leafield Rd. SW20 2L 43
Leafield Rd. Sutt 8M 43
Leafy Gro. Kes 2E 66
Leafy Way. Croy 8C 46
Lea La. Fleet 6A 88
Leamington Av. Mord 3K 43
Leamington Av. Orp 1N 67
Leamington Clo. Houn 8C 10
Leamore St. W6 1H 13
Leander Ct. Surb 6K 41
Leander Rd. SW2 1K 29
Leander Rd. T Hth 3K 45
Leapale La. Guild 4N 113 (5C 202)
Leapale Rd. Guild 4N 113 (5C 202)
Lea Rd. Beck 1K 47
Lea Rd. Camb 4N 69
Lea Rd. S'hall 1M 9
Leas Clo. Chess 4M 59
Leaside. Bookh 1A 98
Leas La. Warl 5G 84
Lea's Rd. Guild 4M 113 (4B 202)
Leas Rd. Warl 5G 84
Lea, The. Egh 8E 20
Lea, The. Wok 6A 80
Leather Clo. Eden 3L 147
Leather Clo. Mitc 1E 44
Leatherhead 9H 79
Leatherhead Common 6G 79
Leatherhead Ind. Est. Lea 8F 78
Leatherhead Mus. of Local History 9H 79
Leatherhead Rd. Bookh 4B 98
Leatherhead Rd. Chess 1H 79
Leatherhead Rd. Lea & Asht 8K 79
Leatherhead Rd. Oxs 1D 78
Leather La. Gom 8D 116
Leaveland Clo. Beck 3K 47
Leavesden Rd. Wey 2C 56
Leaves Green 7F 66
Leaves Grn. Brack 5B 32
Leaves Grn. Cres. Kes 7E 66
Leaves Grn. Rd. Kes 7F 66
Lea Way. Alder 1D 110
Leaway. Bad L 7M 109
Leawood Rd. Fleet 6A 88
Leazes Av. Cat 1L 103
Leazes La. Cat 1L 103
Lebanon Av. Felt 6L 23
Lebanon Dri. Cob 9A 58
Lebanon Gdns. SW18 9M 13
Lebanon Gdns. Big H 4F 86
Lebanon Pk. Twic 1H 25
Lebanon Rd. SW18 8M 13
Lebanon Rd. Croy 7B 46
Le Chateau. Croy 5C 200
Lechford Rd. Horl 9E 142
Leckford Rd. SW18 3A 28
Leckhampton Pl. SW2 1L 29
Leconfield Av. SW13 6E 12
Ledbury Pl. Croy 1N 63 (7C 200)
Ledbury Rd. Croy 1A 64 (8C 200)
Ledbury Rd. Reig 3M 121
Ledger Clo. Guild 1D 114
Ledger Dri. Add 2H 55
Ledgers La. Warl 4L 85
Ledgers Rd. Warl 3K 85
Lee Acre. Dork 7J 119
Leechcroft Rd. Wall 9E 44
Leech La. Dork & H'ley 4A 100
Leechpool La. H'ham 4N 197
Lee Ct. Alder 4A 110
Leegate Clo. Wok 3L 73
Lee Grn. La. H'ley 2A 100
Leehurst. Milf 1B 152
Lee Rd. SW19 9N 27
Lee Rd. Alder 2K 109
Leeside. Rusp 3B 180
Leeson Gdns. Eton W 1B 4
Leeson Ho. Twic 1H 25
Lees, The. Croy 8J 47
Lee St. Horl 8C 142
Leeward Gdns. SW19 6K 27
Leeways, The. Sutt 3K 61
Leewood Way. Eff 5K 97
Lefroy Pk. Fleet 4A 88
Leger Clo. C Crook 8A 88
Legge Cres. Alder 3K 109
Leggyfield Ct. H'ham 3H 197
Legion Ct. Mord 5M 43
Legoland 8A 4
Legrace Av. Houn 5L 9
Legsheath La. E Grin 8M 185
Leicester. Brack 6C 32
Leicester Av. Mitc 3J 45
Leicester Clo. Wor Pk 1H 61
Leicester Ct. Craw 3H 183
Leicester Ct. Twic 9K 11 (off Clevedon Rd.)
Leicester Rd. Croy 6B 46
Leigh 1F 140
Leigham Av. SW16 4J 29
Leigham Clo. SW16 4K 29
Leigham Ct. Rd. SW16 3J 29
Leigham Dri. Iswth 3F 10
Leigham Hall Pde. SW16 4J 29 (off Streatham High Rd.)
Leigham Va. SW16 & SW2 4K 29
Leigh Clo. Add 4H 55
Leigh Clo. N Mald 3B 42
Leigh Clo. Ind. Est. N Mald 3C 42
Leigh Corner. Cob 2K 77
Leigh Ct. Clo. Cob 1K 77
Leigh Cres. New Ad 4L 65
Leigh Hill Rd. Cob 2K 77
Leighlands. Craw 1G 183
Leigh La. Farnh 3K 129
Leigh Orchard Clo. SW16 4K 29
Leigh Pk. Dat 3L 5
Leigh Pl. Cob 2K 77
Leigh Pl. Cotts. Leigh 9F 120
Leigh Pl. La. God 1G 125
Leigh Pl. Rd. Leigh 9F 120
Leigh Rd. Cob 1J 77
Leigh Rd. Bet 9B 120
Leigh Rd. Houn 7D 10
Leigh Sq. Wind 5A 4
Leighton Gdns. Croy 7M 45
Leighton Gdns. S Croy 9E 64
Leighton Mans. W14 2K 13 (off Greyhound Rd.)
Leighton St. Croy 7M 45
Leighton Way. Eps 1C 80 (8K 201)
Leinster Av. SW14 6B 12
Leipzig Rd. C Crook 1C 108
Leisure La. W Byf 8K 55
Leisure West. Felt 3J 23
Leith Clo. Crowt 9F 30
Leithcote Gdns. SW16 5K 29
Leithcote Path. SW16 4K 29
Leith Dri. Alder 1L 109
Leith Gro. Bear G 7K 139
Leith Hill La. Ab C 4M 137
Leith Hill Place (East) 9B 138
Leith Hill Place (West) 1N 157
Leith Hill Rd. Holm M 9A 138
Leith Hill Tower 8B 138
Leith Lea. Bear G 7K 139
Leith Rd. Bear G 8J 139
Leith Rd. Eps 8D 60
Leith Towers. Sutt 4N 61
Leith Va. Cotts. Ockl 7A 158
Leith Vw. N Holm 9J 119
Leith Vw. Cotts. K'fold 3H 179
Leith Vw. Rd. H'ham 3N 197
Lela Av. Houn 5K 9
Le Marchant Rd. Frim & Cam 3D 70
Le May Clo. Horl 7E 142
Lemington Gro. Brack 5N 31
Lemmington Way. H'ham 1M 197
Lemon Gro. Felt 2H 23
Lemon's Farm Rd. Ab C 5N 137
Lemuel St. SW18 9N 13 & 1A 28
Lendore Rd. Frim 6B 70
Lenelby Rd. Surb 7N 41
Leney Clo. Wokgm 9C 14
Len Freeman Pl. SW6 2L 13
Lenham Rd. Sutt 1N 61
Lenham Rd. T Hth 1A 46
Lennard Av. W Wick 8N 47
Lennard Rd. Croy 7N 45 (1B 200)
Lennel Gdns. C Crook 7D 88
Lennox Ct. Red 2E 122 (off St Anne's Ri.)
Lennox Gdns. Croy 1M 63 (7A 200)
Lennox Ho. Twic 9K 11 (off Clevedon Rd.)
Lenten Clo. Peasl 2E 136
Lenton Ri. Rich 6L 11
Leo Ct. Bren 3K 11
Leominster Rd. Mord 5A 44
Leominster Wlk. Mord 5A 44
Leonard Av. Mord 4A 44
Leonard Clo. Frim 6B 70
Leonard Rd. SW16 9G 28
Leonardslee Ct. Craw 5F 182
Leonard Way. H'ham 6M 197
Leopold Av. Farnb 9N 69
Leopold Av. SW19 6L 27
Leopold Rd. SW19 5L 27
Leopold Rd. Craw 3A 182
Leopold Ter. SW19 6L 27
Le Personne Homes. Cat 9A 84 (off Banstead Rd.)
Le Personne Rd. Cat 9A 84
Leppington. Brack 7N 31
Leret Way. Lea 8H 79
Lerry Clo. W14 2L 13
Lesbourne Rd. Reig 4N 121
Leslie Dunne Ho. Wind 5B 4
Leslie Gdns. Sutt 3M 61
Leslie Gro. Croy 7B 46 (1E 200)
Leslie Gro. Pl. Croy 7B 46 (1F 200)
Leslie Pk. Rd. Croy 7B 46 (1F 200)
Leslie Rd. Chob 6H 53
Leslie Rd. Dork 3K 119
Lessingham Av. SW17 5D 28
Lessness Rd. Mord 5A 44
Lestock Way. Fleet 4D 88
Letchworth Av. Felt 1G 22
Letchworth Ct. Bew 6K 181
Letchworth St. SW17 5D 28
Letcombe Sq. Brack 3C 32
Letterstone Rd. SW6 3L 13
Lettice St. SW6 4L 13
Levana Clo. SW19 2K 27
Levehurst Ho. SE27 6N 29
Leveret Clo. New Ad 7N 65
Leveret La. Craw 1N 181
Leverkusen Rd. Brack 2N 31
Levern Dri. Farnh 6H 109
Leverson St. SW16 7G 28
Levett Rd. Lea 7H 79
Levylsdene. Guild 3E 114
Levylsdene Ct. Guild 3F 114
Lewes Clo. Craw 3G 183
Lewesdon Clo. SW19 2J 27
Lewes Rd. E Grin & F Row 1B 186
Lewes Rd. F Row 9F 186
Lewin Rd. SW14 6C 12
Lewin Rd. SW16 7H 29
Lewins Rd. Eps 1A 80
Lewis Clo. Add 1L 55
Lewisham Clo. Craw 7A 182
Lewisham Way. Owl 6J 49
Lewis Ho. Brack 5N 31
Lewis Rd. Mitc 1B 44 (in two parts)
Lewis Rd. Rich 8K 11
Lewis Rd. Sutt 1N 61
Leworth Pl. Wind 4G 4
Lexden Rd. Mitc 3H 45
Lexington Ct. Purl 6N 63
Lexton Gdns. SW12 2H 29
Leybourne Pk. Rich 4N 11
Leybourne Av. Byfl 9A 56
Leybourne Clo. Byfl 9A 56
Leybourne Clo. Craw 8A 182
Leyburn Gdns. Croy 8B 46
Leycester Clo. W'sham 1M 51
Leyfield. Wor Pk 7D 42
Leylands La. Stai 7H 7 (in two parts)
Ley Rd. Farnb 6M 69
Leyside. Crowt 2F 48
Leys Rd. Oxs 8D 58
Leys, The. W on T 1N 57
Leyton Rd. SW19 8A 28
Lezayre Rd. Orp 3N 67
Liberty Av. SW19 9A 28
Liberty Hall Rd. Add 2J 55
Liberty La. Add 2J 55
Liberty M. SW12 1F 28
Liberty Ri. Add 3J 55
Library Way. Twic 1C 24
Lichfield Ct. Rich 7L 11
Lichfield Ct. Surb 8J 203
Lichfield Gdns. Rich 7L 11
Lichfield Rd. Houn 6K 9
Lichfield Rd. Rich 4M 11
Lichfields. Brack 1C 32
Lichfield Ter. Rich 8L 11
Lichfield Way. S Croy 6G 65
Lickey Ho. W14 2L 13 (off N. End Rd.)
Lickfolds Rd. Rowl 9D 128
Liddell. Wind 6A 4
Liddell Pl. Wind 5A 4
Liddell Sq. Wind 5A 4
Liddell Way. Asc 4K 33
Liddell Way. Wind 6A 4
Liddington Hall Dri. Guild 9H 93
Liddington New Rd. Guild 9H 93
Lidiard Rd. SW18 3A 28
Lido Rd. Guild 2N 113 (1D 202)
Lidsey Clo. M'bowr 5G 183
Lidstone Clo. Wok 4L 73
Lifetimes Mus. 9N 45 (4C 200) (off High St.)
Liffords Pl. SW13 5E 12
Lifford St. SW15 7J 13
Lightermans Wlk. SW18 7M 13
Lightwater 6L 51
Lightwater By-Pass. Light 5L 51
Lightwater Mdw. Light 7M 51
Lightwater Rd. Light 7M 51
Lightwood. Brack 5B 32
Lilac Av. Wok 7N 73
Lilac Clo. Guild 8M 93
Lilac Ct. Tedd 5F 24
Lilac Gdns. Croy 9K 47
Lilian Rd. SW16 9G 28
Lille Barracks. Alder 5B 90
Lilleshall Rd. Mord 5B 44
Lilley Ct. Crowt 3G 49
Lilley Dri. Kgswd 9N 81
Lillian Rd. SW13 2F 12
Lillie Mans. SW6 2K 13 (off Lillie Rd.)
Lillie Rd. SW6 2K 13
Lillie Rd. Big H 5F 86
Lillie Yd. SW6 2M 13
Lilliot's La. Lea 6G 79
Lily Clo. W14 1J 13 (in two parts)
Lily Ct. Wokgm 2A 30
Lilyfields Chase. Ewh 6F 156
Lily Hill Dri. Brack 1C 32
Lily Hill Rd. Brack 1C 32
Lilyville Rd. SW6 4L 13
Lime Av. Asc 5F 32
Lime Av. Camb 9E 50
Lime Av. H'ham 4N 197
Lime Av. Wind 4J 5 (Windsor)
Lime Av. Wind 4C 18 (Windsor Great Park)
Limebush Clo. New H 5L 55
Lime Clo. Cars 8D 44
Lime Clo. Copt 7M 163
Lime Clo. Craw 9A 162
Lime Clo. Reig 6N 121
Lime Clo. W Cla 6K 95
Lime Ct. Mitc 1B 44
Lime Cres. As 2F 110
Lime Cres. Sun 1K 39
Limecroft. Yat 1B 68
Limecroft Clo. Eps 4C 60
Limecroft Rd. Knap 4E 72
Lime Dri. Fleet 1D 88
Lime Gro. Add 1J 55
Lime Gro. Guild 8L 93
Lime Gro. N Mald 2C 42
Lime Gro. Twic 9F 10
Lime Gro. Warl 6H 85
Lime Gro. W Cla 6J 95
Lime Gro. Wok 8A 74
Lime Mdw. Av. S Croy 9D 64
Limerick Clo. SW12 1G 28
Limerick Clo. Brack 9M 15
Lime Rd. Rich 7M 11
Limes Av. SW13 5E 12
Limes Av. Cars 7D 44
Limes Av. Croy 9L 45
Limes Av. Horl 9F 142
Limes Clo. Ashf 6B 22
Limes Fld. Rd. SW14 6D 12
Limes Gdns. SW18 9M 13
Limes M. Egh 6B 20
Limes Pl. Croy 6A 46
Limes Rd. Farnb 9H 69
Limes Rd. Beck 1L 47
Limes Rd. Croy 5A 46
Limes Rd. Egh 6B 20
Limes Rd. Wey 1D 56
Limes Row. F'boro 2K 67
Limes, The. SW18 9M 13
Limes, The. E Mol 3B 40
Limes, The. Eden 2L 147
Limes, The. Felb 5K 165
Limes, The. Lea 1H 99
Limes, The. Wind 4A 4
Limes, The. Wok 2N 73
Lime St. Alder 2L 109
Lime Tree Av. Esh 7D 40
Limetree Clo. SW2 2K 29
Lime Tree Clo. Bookh 2A 98
Lime Tree Ct. Asht 5L 79
Lime Tree Ct. S Croy 3N 63
Lime Tree Gro. Croy 9J 47
Lime Tree Pl. Mitc 9F 28
Lime Tree Rd. Houn 4B 10
Limetree Wlk. SW17 6E 28
Lime Tree Wlk. Vir W 3A 36
Lime Tree Wlk. W Wick 1B 66
Lime Wlk. Brack 3A 32
Lime Wlk. Shere 8A 116
Limeway Ter. Dork 3G 118
Limewood Clo. Beck 4M 47
Limewood Clo. Wok 7G 73
Lime Works Rd. Mers 4G 102
Limpsfield 7D 106
Limpsfield Av. SW19 3J 27
Limpsfield Av. T Hth 4K 45
Limpsfield Chart 8G 107
Limpsfield Common 8D 106
Limpsfield Rd. S Croy 8D 64
Linacre Ct. W6 1J 13
Linacre Dri. Rud & Cranl 7D 176
Lince La. Westc 5D 118
Linchfield Rd. Dat 4M 5
Linchmere 6A 188
Linchmere Pl. Craw 2M 181
Linchmere Rd. Hasl 5A 188
Lincoln Av. SW19 4J 27
Lincoln Av. Twic 3C 24
Lincoln Clo. SE25 5D 46
Lincoln Clo. Ash V 8D 90
Lincoln Clo. Camb 2F 70
Lincoln Clo. Craw 6C 182
Lincoln Clo. Horl 9E 142
Lincoln Ct. S Croy 8C 200
Lincoln Dri. Wok 2G 74
Lincoln M. SE21 3N 29
Lincoln Rd. SE25 2E 46
Lincoln Rd. Dork 3J 119
Lincoln Rd. Felt 4N 23

Lincoln Rd.—London Rd.

Lincoln Rd. Guild 1J 113
Lincoln Rd. Mitc. 4J 45
Lincoln Rd. N Mald 2B 42
Lincoln Rd. Wor Pk 7G 42
Lincolnshire Gdns. Warf 8C 16
Lincolns Mead. Ling 8M 145
Lincoln Wlk. Eps 6C 60
(in two parts)
Lincoln Way. Sun 9F 22
Lincombe Ct. Add 2K 55
Lindale Clo. Vir W. 3J 35
Lindbergh Rd. Wall. 4J 63
Linden. Brack. 4D 32
Linden Av. Coul 3F 82
Linden Av. E Grin 8M 165
Linden Av. Houn. 8B 10
Linden Av. T Hth 3M 45
Linden Clo. Craw 6E 182
Linden Clo. H'ham 4L 197
Linden Clo. New H 7J 55
Linden Clo. Tad. 7J 81
Linden Clo. Th Dit. 6F 40
Linden Ct. Camb 8D 50
Linden Ct. Eng G 7L 19
Linden Ct. Lea 8H 79
Linden Cres. King T
1M 41 (4M 203)
Linden Dri. Cat. 2N 103
Linden Gdns. W4. 1D 12
Linden Gdns. Lea 8J 79
Linden Gro. N Mald 2D 42
Linden Gro. Tedd 6F 24
Linden Gro. W on T. 8G 39
Linden Gro. Warl 5H 85
Lindenhill Rd. Brack. 9L 15
Linden Ho. Hamp 7A 24
Linden Ho. Slou 1D 6
Linden Lea. Dork 7J 119
Linden Leas. W Wick. 8N 47
Linden Pit Path. Lea 7J 79
(Linden Gdns.)
Linden Pit Path. Lea. 8H 79
(Linden Rd.)
Linden Pl. E Hor 4F 96
Linden Pl. Eps 8D 60 (5M 201)
Linden Pl. Mitc. 3C 44
Linden Pl. Stai 5J 21
Linden Rd. Hdly D 4G 169
Linden Rd. Guild. 3N 113 (2C 202)
Linden Rd. Hamp. 8A 24
Linden Rd. Lea. 8H 79
Linden Rd. Wey. 5D 56
Lindens Clo. Eff. 6M 97
Lindens, The. W4. 4B 12
Lindens, The. Copt 7M 163
Lindens, The. Farnh 2J 129
Lindens, The. Myt 2D 90
Lindens, The. New Ad 3M 65
Linden Way. Purl 6G 63
Linden Way. Rip. 3H 95
Linden Way. Shep 4D 38
Linden Way. Wok. 8B 74
Lindfield Gdns. Guild 2B 114
Lindfield Rd. Croy 5C 46
Lindford. 4A 168
Lindford Chase. Lind 4A 168
Lindford Rd. Lind. 3A 168
Lindford Wey. Lind. 4A 168
Lindgren Wlk. Craw. 8N 181
Lindisfarne Rd. SW20 8F 26
Lindley Ct. King T. 9J 25
Lindley Pl. Kew 4N 11
Lindley Rd. God 8F 104
Lindley Rd. W on T 9L 39
Lindores Rd. Cars 6A 44
Lind Rd. Sutt. 2A 62
Lindrop St. SW6 5N 13
Lindsay Clo. Chess. 4L 59
Lindsay Clo. Eps. 9B 60 (7G 201)
Lindsay Clo. Stanw 8M 7
Lindsay Ct. Croy 6D 200
Lindsay Dri. Shep. 5E 38
Lindsay Rd. Hamp H 5B 24
Lindsay Rd. New H. 6J 55
Lindsay Rd. Wor Pk. 8G 43
Lindsey Clo. Mitc 3J 45
Lindsey Gdns. Felt 1E 22
Lindum Clo. Alder. 3M 109
Lindum Dene. Alder 3M 109
Lindum Rd. Tedd 8J 25
Lindway. SE27. 6M 29
Linersh Dri. Brmly 5C 134
Linersh Wood Clo. Brmly. 6C 134
Linersh Wood Rd. Brmly 5C 134
Lines Rd. Hurst 4A 14
Linfield Clo. W on T. 2J 57
Ling Cres. Hdly D. 3G 169
Ling Dri. Light 8K 51
Lingfield. 7N 145
Lingfield Av. King T
3L 41 (8K 203)
Lingfield Common. 6M 145
Lingfield Comn. Rd. Ling 6M 145
Lingfield Dri. Worth 2J 183
Lingfield Gdns. Coul 6M 83
Lingfield Pk. Racecourse. 9A 146
Lingfield Rd. SW19 6J 27
Lingfield Rd. E Grin 6N 165
Lingfield Rd. Eden 3H 147
Lingfield Rd. Wor Pk 9H 43
Lingmala Gro. C Crook. 8C 88
Lings Coppice. SE21 3N 29
Lingwell Rd. SW17 4C 28
Lingwood. Brack 5A 32
Lingwood Gdns. Iswth 3E 10
Link Av. Wok 2F 74
Linkfield. W Mol. 2B 40
Linkfield Corner. Red 3B 122
(Hatchlands Rd.)
Linkfield Corner. Red 3C 122
(Linkfield St.)
Linkfield Gdns. Red 3C 122
Linkfield La. Red 2C 122
Linkfield Rd. Iswth 5F 10
Linkfield St. Red. 3C 122
Link La. Wall 3H 63
Link Rd. Add 1N 55
Link Rd. Dat 4M 5
Link Rd. Felt. 1G 23
Link Rd. Wall 7E 44
Links Av. Mord 3M 43
(in two parts)
Links Brow. Fet 2E 98
Links Clo. Asht 4J 79
Links Clo. Ewh 4F 156
Linkscroft Av. Ashf. 7C 22
Links Gdns. SW16 8L 29
Links Grn. Way. Cob 1A 78
Linkside. 2N 169
Linkside. N Mald 1D 42
Linkside E. Hind. 2A 170
Linkside N. Hind 2N 169
Linkside S. Hind. 3A 170
Linkside W. Hind 2N 169
Links Pl. Asht. 4K 79
Links Rd. Ashf 6N 21
Links Rd. SW17. 7E 28
Links Rd. Asht 5J 79
Links Rd. Brmly. 4A 134
Links Rd. Eps. 9F 60
Links Rd. W Wick 7M 47
Links, The. Asc. 1J 33
Links, The. W on T 8H 39
Links Vw. Av. Brock 3N 119
Links Vw. Ct. Hamp 5D 24
Links Vw. Rd. Croy 9K 47
Links Vw. Rd. Hamp H. 6C 24
Links Way. Farnb 2H 89
Links Way. Beck. 5K 47
Links Way. Bookh 6M 97
Link, The. Craw 3B 182
(in two parts)
Link, The. Tedd. 7F 24
Linkway. SW20. 3G 43
Linkway. Camb. 2A 70
Linkway. Crowt. 2E 48
Linkway. Fleet. 7A 88
Linkway. Guild 2J 113
Linkway. Rich. 3H 25
Link Way. Stai 7K 21
Linkway. Wok. 4E 74
Linkway Pde. Fleet. 7A 88
Linkway, The. Sutt 5A 62
Linley Ct. Sutt 1A 62
Linnell Clo. Craw 9N 181
Linnell Rd. Red. 4E 122
Linnet Clo. S Croy 6G 65
Linnet Clo. Turn H 4F 184
Linnet Gro. Guild 1F 114
Linnet M. SW12. 1E 28
Linsford Bus. Pk. Myt 2C 90
Linsford La. Myt 2D 90
Linslade Clo. Houn 8M 9
Linstead Rd. Farnb. 6K 69
Linstead Way. SW18 1K 27
Linsted La. Hdly. 2C 168
Lintaine Clo. W6. 2K 13
Linton Clo. Mitc 6D 44
Linton Glade. Croy. 5H 65
(in two parts)
Linton Gro. SE27. 6M 29
Lintons La. Eps 8D 60
Lintott Ct. Stanw. 9M 7
Lintott Gdns. H'ham. 5L 197
Linver Rd. SW6. 5M 13
Lion & Lamb Way. Farnh. 1G 128
Lion & Lamb Yd. Farnh 1G 129
Lion Av. Twic 2F 24
Lion Clo. Hasl 1D 188
Lion Clo. Shep. 2N 37
Lionel Rd. N. Bren 1L 11
Lionel Rd. S. Bren. 1M 11
Lion Ga. Gdns. Rich 6M 11
Lion Gate M. SW18. 1M 27
Liongate M. E Mol 2F 40
Lion Grn. Hasl 2D 188
Lion Grn. Rd. Coul. 3H 83
Lion La. Gray & Hasl 8D 170
Lion La. Red 2D 122
Lion La. Turn H 5D 184
Lion Mead. Hasl. 2D 188
Lion Pk. Av. Chess. 1N 59
Lion Retail Pk. Wok 3D 74
Lion Rd. Croy. 4N 45
Lion Rd. Twic. 2F 24
Lion's La. Alf 3K 175
(in two parts)
Lion Way. Bren. 3K 11
Lion Way. C Crook 8C 88
Lion Wharf Rd. Iswth 6H 11
Lipcombe Cotts. Alb. 3L 135
Liphook Rd. Hasl 2C 188
Liphook Rd. Head & Pass 6D 168
Liphook Rd. Lind 4A 168
Liphook Rd. W'hill 9A 168
Lipscomb's Corner. 1M 179
Lipsham Clo. Bans. 9B 62
Lisbon Av. Twic 3C 24
Liscombe. Brack 6N 31
Liscombe Ho. Brack. 6N 31
Lisgar Ter. W14 1L 13
Liskeard Dri. Farnb 8M 69
Lisle Clo. SW17 5F 28
Lismore. SW19 6L 27
(off Woodside)
Lismore Clo. Iswth. 5G 10
Lismore Cres. Craw. 6N 181
Lismore Rd. S Croy 3B 64
Lismoyne Clo. Fleet 3A 88
Lissoms Rd. Coul. 5E 82
Lister Av. E Grin. 3A 186
Lister Clo. Mitc. 9C 28
Listergate Ct. SW15. 7H 13
Lister Ho. Hay. 1F 8
Litchfield Av. Mord. 6L 43
Litchfield Rd. Sutt 1A 62
Litchfield Way. Guild. 5J 113
Lithgow's Rd. H'row A 7F 8
Little Acre. Beck. 2K 47
Lit. Austins Rd. Farnh. 3J 129
Little Benty. W Dray 1M 7
Lit. Birch Clo. New H. 5M 55
Little Birketts. 1L 157
Lit. Boltons, The. SW5 & SW10
1N 13
Little Bookham. 2N 97
Little Bookham Common 9M 77
Lit. Bookham St. Bookh 1N 97
Little Borough. Brock. 4N 119
Littlebrook Clo. Croy 5G 47
Lit. Browns La. Eden 8G 127
Little Buntings. Wind 6C 4
Little Collins. Out. 4M 143
Littlecombe Clo. SW15. 9J 13
Lit. Common La. Blet 1M 123
Little Comptons. H'ham 6M 197
Little Copse. Fleet. 6A 88
Little Copse. Yat. 8C 48
Littlecote Clo. SW19 1K 27
Little Ct. W Wick 8N 47
Little Crabtree. Craw 2A 182
Lit. Cranmore La. W Hor 6C 96
Little Cft. Yat 1C 68
Littlecroft Rd. Egh 6B 20
Littledale Clo. Brack 2C 32
Little Dimocks. SW12. 3F 28
Little Elms. Hay 3E 8
Lit. Ferry Rd. Twic 2H 25
Littlefield Clo. As 3E 110
Littlefield Clo. Guild 8G 92
Littlefield Clo. King T
1L 41 (4K 203)
Littlefield Common. 7E 92
Littlefield Gdns. As. 3E 110
Littlefield Ho. King T. 4J 203
Littlefield Way. Guild. 8F 92
Littleford La. B'hth & Sham G
2G 134
Little Fryth. Finch 1B 48
Little Grebe. H'ham. 3J 197
Little Grn. Rich. 7K 11
Lit. Green La. Cher. 9G 36
Lit. Green La. Farnh 4F 128
Lit. Green La. Farm Est. Cher
1F 54
Little Gro. Dork. 7J 119
(off Stubs Hill)
Little Halliards. W on T 5H 39
Little Hatch. H'ham. 3M 197
Little Haven. 3M 197
Lit. Haven La. H'ham. 3M 197
Littleheath La. Cob. 1A 78
Lit. Heath Rd. Chob 5H 53
Littleheath Rd. S Croy 4E 64
Little Hide. Guild 1D 114
Lit. Holland Bungalows. Cat
1A 104
Little Kiln. G'ming 3H 133
Lit. King St. E Grin. 9A 166
Little Kings Wood. 5E 116
Little London. 1A 136
Little London. Alb 1N 135
Little London. Witl 5B 152
Lit. London Hill. Warn 8G 179
Lit. Lullenden. Ling 6N 145
Lit. Manor Gdns. Cranl 8M 155
Little Mead. Cranl. 8K 155
Littlemead. Esh 1D 58
Little Mead. Wok 3J 73
Lit. Mead Ind. Est. Cranl 7K 155
Little Moor. Sand. 6H 49
Lit. Moreton Clo. W Byf. 8K 55
Little Orchard. Wok 1C 74
Little Orchard. Wdhm. 7J 55
Little Orchards. Eps 8L 201
Lit. Orchard Way. Shalf 1A 134
Little Paddock. Camb. 7E 50
Lit. Park Dri. Felt. 3M 23
Little Parrock. 8M 187
Little Platt. Guild 2G 112
Lit. Queen's Rd. Tedd. 7F 24
Little Ringdale. Brack. 3C 32
Lit. Roke Av. Kenl 1M 83
Lit. Roke Rd. Kenl 1N 83
Littlers Clo. SW19 9A 28
Lit. St Leonard's. SW14. 6B 12
Little Sandhurst. 6F 48
Little St. Guild 8L 93
Lit. Sutton La. Slou 1E 6
Little Thatch. G'ming 5J 133
Lit. Thurbans Clo. Farnh. 5F 128
Littleton. 8K 113
(Guildford)
Littleton. 2B 38
(Shepperton)
Littleton Common. 8D 22
Littleton La. Guild 8K 113
Littleton La. Reig 5J 121
Littleton La. Shep 5M 37
Littleton Rd. Ashf. 8D 22
Littleton St. SW18 3A 28
Lit. Tumners Ct. G'ming. 4H 133
Little Vigo. Yat. 2A 68
Lit. Warkworth Ho. Iswth. 5H 11
Lit. Warren Clo. Guild 5D 114
Lit. Wellington St. Alder 2M 109
Littlewick. 3H 73
Littlewick Rd. Knap & Wok 3H 73
Littlewood. Cranl 7A 156
Little Woodcote. 7E 62
Lit. Woodcote Est. Cars 7E 62
Lit. Woodcote La. Cars. 8F 62
Little Woodlands. Wind 6C 4
Lit. Wood St. King T
1K 41 (3H 203)
Littleworth Av. Esh. 2D 58
Littleworth Comn. Rd. Esh 9D 40
Littleworth La. Esh. 1D 58
Littleworth Pl. Esh 1D 58
Littleworth Rd. Esh 2D 58
Littleworth Rd. Seale 2C 130
Liverpool Rd. King T. 8N 25
Liverpool Rd. T Hth 2N 45
Livesey Clo. King T
2M 41 (5L 203)
Livingstone Mans. W14. 2K 13
(off Queen's Club Gdns.)
Livingstone Rd. Cat. 9A 84
Livingstone Rd. Craw. 5C 182
Livingstone Rd. H'ham 7K 197
Livingstone Rd. Houn 7C 10
Livingstone Rd. T Hth 1N 45
Llanaway Clo. G'ming. 5J 133
Llanaway Rd. G'ming 5J 133
Llangar Gro. Crowt. 2F 48
Llanthony Rd. Mord. 4B 44
Llanvair Clo. Asc 5L 33
Llanvair Dri. Asc 5K 33
Lloyd Av. SW16 9J 29
Lloyd Av. Coul 1E 82
Lloyd Pk. Av. Croy 1C 64
Lloyd Rd. Wor Pk 9H 43
Lloyds Ct. Craw 9C 162
Lloyds Way. Beck 4H 47
Lobelia Rd. Bisl 2D 72
Locarno Ct. SW16 6G 29
Lochaline St. W6 2H 13
Lochinvar St. SW12 1F 28
Lochinver. Brack 6N 31
Lock Clo. Wdhm 8G 55
Locke King Clo. Wey 4B 56
Locke King Rd. Wey 4B 56
Lockesley Sq. Surb 5K 41
Lockestone. Wey 3A 56
Lockestone Clo. Wey 3A 56
Lockets Clo. Wind 4A 4
Locke Way. Wok 4B 74
Lockfield Dri. Knap 3H 73
Lockfield Dri. Wok 4M 73
Lockhart Rd. Cob. 9K 57
Lockhurst Hatch La. Alb 5N 135
Lockie Pl. SE25 2D 46
Lock La. Wok. 3K 75
Lockner Holt. 9H 115
Lock Path. Dor. 2A 4
(in two parts)
Lock Rd. Alder. 8B 90
Lock Rd. Guild. 9N 93
Lock Rd. Rich. 5J 25
Locksbottom. 1J 67
Locks La. Mitc 9E 28
Locksley Dri. Wok 4J 73
Locksmeade Rd. Rich 5J 25
Locks Mdw. D'land 1C 166
Locks Ride. Asc 9F 16
Lockswood. Brkwd 7E 72
Lockton Chase. Asc. 2H 33
Lockwood Clo. Farnb. 6K 69
Lockwood Clo. H'ham 3N 197
Lockwood Ct. Craw 1D 182
Lockwood Path. Wok. 9F 54
Lockwood Way. Chess. 2N 59
Lockyer Ho. SW15 6J 13
Locomotive Dri. Felt 2H 23
Loddon Clo. Camb. 9E 50
Loddon Rd. Farnb 8J 69
Loddon Way. As. 3E 110
Loder Clo. Wok 9F 54
Lodge Av. SW14 6D 12
Lodge Av. Croy 9L 45
Lodgebottom Rd. Mick 5N 99
Lodge Clo. Alder 4A 110
Lodge Clo. Craw 3A 182
Lodge Clo. E Grin 9M 165
Lodge Clo. Eng G 6N 19
Lodge Clo. Eps 6H 61
Lodge Clo. Fet. 9D 78
Lodge Clo. Iswth. 4H 11
Lodge Clo. N Holm. 9J 119
Lodge Clo. Stoke D 3N 77
Lodge Clo. Wall 7E 44
Lodge Gdns. Beck 4J 47
Lodge Gro. Yat. 9E 48
Lodge Hill. Purl 2L 83
Lodge Hill Clo. Lwr Bo. 5J 129
Lodge Hill Rd. Lwr Bo 5J 129
Lodge La. Holmw. 4L 139
Lodge La. New Ad 3K 65
Lodge La. Red 3C 142
Lodge La. W'ham. 5L 107
Lodge Pl. Sutt 2N 61
Lodge Rd. Croy. 5M 45
Lodge Rd. Fet 9C 78
Lodge Rd. Wall. 2F 62
Lodge Wlk. Horl 8D 142
(off Thornton Pl.)
Lodge Way. Ashf 3N 21
Lodge Way. Shep 1D 38
Lodge Way. Wind 6B 4
Lodkin Hill. Hasc 4N 153
Lodsworth. Farnb 2J 89
Loft Ho. Pl. Chess 3J 59
Logan Clo. Houn 6N 9
Logmore La. Westc & Dork
7B 118
Lois Dri. Shep 4C 38
Lollesworth La. W Hor 4D 96
(in two parts)
Loman Rd. Myt 1E 90
Lomas Clo. Croy. 4M 65
Lombard Bus. Pk. Croy 6K 45
Lombard Rd. SW19. 1N 43
Lombard Roundabout. (Junct.)
6K 45
Lombard St. Shack 5K 131
Lombardy Clo. Wok 4J 73
Lomond Gdns. S Croy. 4H 65
Loncin Mead Av. New H. 5L 55
London Biggin Hill Airport.
8F 66
London Broncos Rugby League Football Club (Brentford F.C.)
2K 11
London Butterfly House. 4H 11
London Fields Ho. Craw 8A 182
London Gatwick Airport, North Terminal 2C 162
London Gatwick Airport, South Terminal. 3E 162
London Heathrow Airport 6C 8
London La. E Hor 9G 97
London La. Shere 7B 116
London Rd. SW16. 9K 29
London Rd. SW17 & Mitc. 8D 28
London Rd. Asc 2M 33
(Winkfield Rd.)
London Rd. Asc & Vir W 4F 34
(Broomhall La.)
London Rd. Binf & Brack 1G 31
London Rd. B'water & Camb
2J 69
London Rd. Brack & Asc. 1B 32
London Rd. Camb & Bag. 9A 50
London Rd. Cat. 1A 104
London Rd. Craw. 2B 182
London Rd. Dat 3L 5
(in two parts)
London Rd. Dork
4H 119 (1L 201)
London Rd. E Grin. 6K 165
London Rd. Ewe & Sutt. 5E 60
London Rd. F Row 5G 186
London Rd. Guild & Send
4A 114 (4E 202)
(in two parts)

Lydden Rd.—Manor Gdns.

Lydden Rd. *SW18* 1N **27**
Lydele Clo. *Wok* 2B **74**
Lydens La. *Hever* 6N **147**
Lydford Clo. *Farnb* 7M **69**
Lydford Clo. *Frim* 7E **70**
Lydhurst Av. *SW2* 3K **29**
Lydney. *Brack* 6N **31**
Lydney Clo. *SW19* 3K **27**
Lydon Ho. *Craw* 9B **162**
Lye Copse Av. *Farnb* 6N **69**
Lyefield La. *F Grn* 4K **157**
Lyell Pl. E. *Wind* 6A **4**
Lyell Pl. W. *Wind* 6A **4**
Lyell Rd. *Wind* 6A **4**
Lyell Wlk. E. *Wind* 6A **4**
Lyell Wlk. W. *Wind* 6A **4**
Lye, The. *Tad* 9H **81**
Lyfield. *Oxs* 1B **78**
Lyford Rd. *SW18* 1B **28**
Lygon Ho. SW6 4K 13 (off Fulham Pal. Rd.)
Lyham Clo. *SW2* 1J **29**
Lyham Rd. *SW2* 1J **29**
Lyle Clo. *Mitc* 6E **44**
Lymbourne Clo. *Sutt* 6M **61**
Lymden Gdns. *Reig* 4N **121**
Lyme Regis Rd. *Bans* 4L **81**
Lymescote Gdns. *Sutt* 8M **43**
Lyminge Gdns. *SW18* 2C **28**
Lymington Av. *Yat* 1A **68**
Lymington Clo. *SW16* 1H **45**
Lymington Ct. *Sutt* 9N **43**
Lymington Gdns. *Eps* 2E **60**
Lynchborough Rd. *Pass* 9C **168**
Lynchen Clo. *Houn* 4J **9**
Lynchford La. *Farnb* 5C **90**
Lynchford Rd. *Farnb* 6N **89** (in two parts)
Lynchford Rd. *Ash V* 5D **90**
Lynch Rd. *Farnh* 1J **129**
Lyncroft Gdns. *Eps* 5E **60**
Lyncroft Gdns. *Houn* 8C **10**
Lyndale. *Th Dit* 6E **40**
Lyndale Ct. *Red* 9E **102**
Lyndale Ct. *W Byf* 9J **55**
Lyndale Dri. *Fleet* 4E **88**
Lyndale Rd. *Red* 9D **102**
Lynde Ho. *W on T* 5K **39**
Lynden Hyrst. *Croy* 8C **46**
Lyndford Ter. *Fleet* 6A **88**
Lyndhurst Av. *SW16* 1H **45**
Lyndhurst Av. *Alder* 6A **110**
Lyndhurst Av. *B'water* 9H **49**
Lyndhurst Av. *Sun* 2H **39**
Lyndhurst Av. *Surb* 7A **42**
Lyndhurst Av. *Twic* 2N **23**
Lyndhurst Clo. *Brack* 2E **32**
Lyndhurst Clo. *Craw* 4B **182**
Lyndhurst Clo. *Croy* 9C **46**
Lyndhurst Clo. *Orp* 1K **67**
Lyndhurst Clo. *Wok* 2N **73**
Lyndhurst Ct. Sutt. 4M 61 (off Grange Rd.)
Lyndhurst Dri. *N Mald* 6D **42**
Lyndhurst Farm Clo. *Felb* 6G **165**
Lyndhurst Rd. *Asc* 3L **33**
Lyndhurst Rd. *Coul* 3E **82**
Lyndhurst Rd. *Reig* 6M **121**
Lyndhurst Rd. *T Hth* 3L **45**
Lyndhurst Vs. *Red* 9D **102**
Lyndhurst Way. *Cher* 9G **36**
Lyndhurst Way. *Sutt* 5M **61**
Lyndon Av. *Wall* 9E **44**
Lyndsey Clo. *Farnb* 1G **88**
Lyndum Pl. *Lind* 4A **168**
Lyndwood Dri. *Old Win* 9K **5**
Lyne. **5C 36**
Lyne Clo. *Vir W* 5B **36**
Lyne Crossing Rd. *Lyne* 5C **36**
Lynegrove Av. *Ashf* 6D **22**
Lyneham Rd. *Crowt* 2G **48**
Lyne La. *Vir W & Lyne* 5C **36** (in two parts)
Lyne Rd. *Vir W* 5N **35**
Lynford Ct. *Croy* 7F **200**
Lynmead Clo. *Eden* 8K **127**
Lynmouth Av. *Mord* 5J **43**
Lynmouth Gdns. *Houn* 3L **9**
Lynn Clo. *Ashf* 6E **22**
Lynn Ct. *Whyt* 5C **84**
Lynne Clo. *Orp* 3N **67**
Lynne Clo. *S Croy* 7F **64**
Lynne Ct. *S Croy* 7F **200**
Lynne Wlk. *Esh* 2C **58**
Lynn Rd. *SW12* 1F **28**
Lynn Wlk. *Reig* 6N **121**
Lynn Way. *Farnb* 7L **69**
Lynscott Way. *S Croy* 5M **63**
Lynstead Ct. *Beck* 1H **47**
Lynton Clo. *Chess* 1L **59**
Lynton Clo. *E Grin* 8B **166**
Lynton Clo. *Farnh* 4F **128**
Lynton Clo. *Iswth* 7F **10**
Lynton Pk. Av. *E Grin* 8B **166**
Lynton Rd. *Croy* 5L **45**
Lynton Rd. *N Mald* 4C **42**
Lynwick St. *Rud* 1C **194**
Lynwood. *Guild* 4L **113**
Lynwood Av. *Coul* 2F **82**
Lynwood Av. *Egh* 7A **20**
Lynwood Av. *Eps* 1E **80**
Lynwood Chase. *Brack* 8A **16**
Lynwood Clo. *Lind* 4B **168**
Lynwood Clo. *Wok* 9F **54**
Lynwood Ct. *Eps* 9E **60**
Lynwood Ct. *H'ham* 5J **197**
Lynwood Ct. *King T* 1A **42**
Lynwood Cres. *Asc* 5B **34**
Lynwood Dri. *Myt* 2E **90**
Lynwood Dri. *Wor Pk* 8F **42**
Lynwood Gdns. *Croy* 1K **63**
Lynwood Rd. *SW17* 4D **28**
Lynwood Rd. *Eps* 1E **80**
Lynwood Rd. *Red* 1E **122**
Lynwood Rd. *Th Dit* 8F **40**
Lynx Hill. *E Hor* 6G **96**
Lyon Clo. *M'bowr* 7G **183**
Lyon Ct. *H'ham* 6L **197**
Lyon Oaks. *Warf* 7N **15**
Lyon Rd. *SW19* 9A **28**
Lyon Rd. *Crowt* 1H **49**
Lyon Rd. *W on T* 8M **39**
Lyons Clo. *Slin* 5L **195**
Lyons Ct. *Dork* 5H **119** (2K **201**)
Lyonsdene. *Tad* 5L **101**
Lyons Dri. *Guild* 7K **93**
Lyons Rd. *Slin* 5L **195**
Lyon Way. *Frim* 5A **70**
Lyon Way Ind. Est. *Frim* 5A **70**
Lyric Clo. *M'bowr* 5H **183**
Lyric Rd. *SW13* 4E **12**
Lyric Theatre. **1H 13**
Lysander Gdns. *Surb* 5M **41**
Lysander Rd. *Croy* 3K **63**
Lysia Ct. SW6 3J 13 (off Lysia St.)
Lysias Rd. *SW12* 1F **28**
Lysia St. *SW6* 3J **13**
Lysons Av. *Ash V* 5D **90**
Lyson's Rd. *Alder* 3M **109**
Lysons Wlk. *SW15* 7F **12**
Lyster M. *Cob* 9K **57**
Lytchgate Clo. *S Croy* 4B **64**
Lytcott Dri. *W Mol* 2N **39**
Lytham. *Brack* 5K **31**
Lytham Ct. *S'hill* 4N **33**
Lythe Hill. **2L 189**
Lythe Hill Pk. *Hasl* 3J **189**
Lytton Dri. *Craw* 2H **183**
Lytton Gdns. *Wall* 1H **63**
Lytton Gro. *SW15* 8J **13**
Lytton Pk. *Cob* 8N **57**
Lytton Rd. *Wok* 3D **74**
Lyveden Rd. *SW17* 7D **28**
Lywood Clo. *Tad* 9H **81**

M

Mabbotts. *Tad* 8J **81**
Mabel St. *Wok* 5N **73**
Maberley Rd. *Beck* 2G **46**
Mablethorpe Rd. *SW6* 3K **13**
Macadam Av. *Crowt* 9H **31**
McAlmont Ridge. *G'ming* 4G **132**
Macaulay Av. *Esh* 8F **40**
Macaulay Rd. *Cat* 9B **84**
Macbeth Ct. *Warf* 9C **16**
Macbeth St. *W6* 1G **13**
McCarthy Rd. *Felt* 6L **23**
Macclesfield Rd. *SE25* 4F **46**
MacDonald Rd. *Farnh* 5G **109**
Macdonald Rd. *Light* 8K **51**
McDonalds Almshouses. *Farnh* 2F **128**
McDonough Clo. *Chess* 1L **59**
Mace La. *Cud* 9M **67**
Macfarlane La. *Iswth* 2F **10**
McIndoe Rd. *E Grin* 7N **165**
McIntosh Clo. *Wall* 4J **63**
McIver Clo. *Felb* 6J **165**
McKay Clo. *Alder* 1A **110**
McKay Rd. *SW20* 8G **27**
McKay Trad. Est. *Coln* 5G **7**
Mackenzie Rd. *Beck* 1F **46**
McKenzie Way. *Eps* 5N **59**
McKernan Ct. *Sand* 7E **48**
Mackie Rd. *SW2* 1L **29**
Mackies Hill. *Peasl* 4E **136**
Mackrells. *Red* 6A **122**
Maclaren M. *SW15* 7H **13**
Macleod Rd. *H'ham* 7L **197**
Macmillan Way. *SW17* 5F **28**
MacNaghten Woods. *Camb* 9C **50**
McNaughton Clo. *Farnb* 2H **89**
Macphail Clo. *Wokgm* 9D **14**
McRae La. *Mitc* 6D **44**
Macrae Rd. *Yat* 9B **48**
Madan Rd. *W'ham* 3M **107**
Madans Wlk. *Eps* 2C **80** (8K **201**) (in two parts)
Maddison Clo. *Tedd* 7F **24**
Maddox La. *Bookh* 9M **77** (in two parts)
Maddox Pk. *Bookh* 1M **97**
Madehurst Ct. *Craw* 6L **181**
Madeira Av. *H'ham* 6J **197**
Madeira Clo. *W Byf* 9J **55**
Madeira Cres. *W Byf* 9H **55**
Madeira Rd. *SW16* 6J **29**
Madeira Rd. *Mitc* 3D **44**
Madeira Rd. *W Byf* 9H **55**
Madeira Wlk. *Reig* 2B **122**
Madeira Wlk. *Wind* 4G **5**
Madeley Rd. *C Crook* 7C **88**
Madgehole La. *Sham G* 7J **135**
Madingley. *Brack* 7N **31**
Madox Brown End. *Col T* 8K **49**
Madrid Rd. *SW13* 4F **12**
Madrid Rd. *Guild* 4L **113**
Maesmaur Rd. *Tats* 8F **86**
Mafeking Av. *Bren* 2L **11**
Mafeking Rd. *Wray* 3D **20**
Magazine Pl. *Lea* 9H **79**
Magazine Rd. *Cat* 9M **83**
Magdala Rd. *Iswth* 6G **11**
Magdala Rd. *S Croy* 4A **64**
Magdalen Clo. *Byfl* 1N **75**
Magdalen Cres. *Byfl* 1N **75**
Magdalene Clo. *Craw* 9G **162**
Magdalene Rd. *Owl* 5L **49**
Magdalene Rd. *Shep* 3A **38**
Magdalen Rd. *SW18* 2A **28**
Magellan Ter. *Craw* 8E **162**
Magna Carta La. *Wray* 2N **19**
Magna Carta Monument. **3N 19**
Magna Rd. *Eng G* 7L **19**
Magnolia Clo. *King T* 7A **26**
Magnolia Clo. *Owl* 6J **49**
Magnolia Ct. *Felt* 2H **23**
Magnolia Ct. *Horl* 8E **142**
Magnolia Ct. *Rich* 4A **12**
Magnolia Ct. Sutt 4M 61 (off Grange Rd.)
Magnolia Ct. *Wall* 2F **62**
Magnolia Dri. *Big H* 3F **86**
Magnolia Pl. *Guild* 9M **93**
Magnolia Rd. *W4* 2A **12**
Magnolia St. *W Dray* 1M **7**
Magnolia Way. *Eps* 2B **60**
Magnolia Way. *Fleet* 6B **88**
Magnolia Way. *N Holm* 8K **119**
Magpie Clo. *Bord* 7A **168**
Magpie Clo. *Coul* 5G **83**
Magpie Clo. *Ews* 4C **108**
Magpie Grn. *Eden* 9L **127**
Magpie Wlk. *Craw* 1D **182**
Maguire Dri. *Frim* 3G **71**
Maguire Dri. *Rich* 5J **25**
Mahonia Clo. *W End* 9C **52**
Maida Rd. *Alder* 9N **89**
Maidenbower. **5G 183**
Maidenbower Dri. *M'bowr* 5G **182**
Maidenbower La. *M'bowr* 5F **182** (in two parts)
Maidenbower Pl. *M'bowr* 5G **183**
Maidenbower Sq. *M'bowr* 5G **183**
Maidenhead Rd. *Binf* 3N **15**
Maidenhead Rd. *Wind* 3A **4**
Maidenhead Rd. *Wokgm* 6D **14**
Maiden La. *Craw* 1A **182**
Maiden's Green. **3F 16**
Maiden's Grn. *Wink* 3F **16**
Maidenshaw Rd. *Eps* 8C **60** (5J **201**)
Maids of Honour Row. *Rich* 8K **11**
Main Dri. *Brack* 8D **16**
Mainprize Rd. *Brack* 9C **16**
Main Rd. *Big H & Kes* 9E **66**
Main Rd. *Crock H & Eden* 6K **127**
Main Rd. *K'ley* 9A **148**
Main Rd. *Wind* 3A **4**
Mainstone Clo. *Deep* 7G **71**
Mainstone Cres. *Brkwd* 8A **72**
Mainstone Rd. *Bisl* 3C **72**
Main St. *Add* 9N **37**
Main St. *Felt* 6L **23**
Main St. *Yat* 8C **48**
Maisie Webster Clo. *Stanw* 1L **21**
Maisonettes, The. *Sutt* 2L **61**
Maitland Clo. *Houn* 6N **9**
Maitland Clo. *W on T* 8M **39**
Maitland Clo. *W Byf* 9J **55**
Maitland Rd. *Farnb* 5N **89**
Maitlands Clo. *Tong* 6C **110**
Maize Cft. *Horl* 7G **142**
Maize La. *Warf* 7B **16**
Majestic Way. *Mitc* 1D **44**
Majors Farm Rd. *Dat* 3M **5**
Major's Hill. *Worth* 4N **183**
Makepiece Rd. *Brack* 8N **15**
Malacca Farm. *W Cla* 5K **95**
Malan Clo. *Big H* 4G **87**
Malbrook Rd. *SW15* 7G **13**
Malcolm Dri. *Surb* 7K **41**
Malcolm Gdns. *Hkwd* 1B **162**
Malcolm Rd. *SE25* 5D **46**
Malcolm Rd. *SW19* 7K **27**
Malcolm Rd. *Coul* 2H **83**
Malden Av. *SE25* 3E **46**
Malden Ct. *N Mald* 2G **42**
Malden Green. **7F 42**
Malden Grn. Av. *Wor Pk* 7E **42**
Malden Hill. *N Mald* 2E **42**
Malden Hill Gdns. *N Mald* 2E **42**
Malden Junction. (Junct.) **4D 42**
Malden Pk. *N Mald* 5E **42**
Malden Rd. *N Mald* 4D **42**
Malden Rd. *Sutt* 1H **61**
Malden Rushett. **7J 59**
Malden Way. *N Mald* 5C **42**
Maldon Ct. *Wall* 2G **62**
Maldon Rd. *Wall* 2F **62**
Malet Clo. *Egh* 7F **20**
Maley Av. *SE27* 3M **29**
Malham Clo. *M'bowr* 6G **183**
Malham Fell. *Brack* 3M **31**
Mallard Clo. *As* 1D **110**
Mallard Clo. *Hasl* 2C **188**
Mallard Clo. *Horl* 6E **142**
Mallard Clo. *H'ham* 3J **197**
Mallard Clo. *Red* 9E **102**
Mallard Clo. *Twic* 1A **24**
Mallard Ct. *Dork* 1J **201**
Mallard Pl. *E Grin* 1B **186**
Mallard Pl. *Twic* 4G **24**
Mallard Rd. *S Croy* 6G **65**
Mallards Reach. *Wey* 8E **38**
Mallards, The. *Frim* 4D **70**
Mallards, The. *Stai* 1K **37**
Mallards Way. *Light* 7L **51**
Mallard Wlk. *Beck* 4G **47**
Mallard Way. *Eden* 9L **127**
Mallard Way. *Wall* 5G **63**
Mallard Way. *Yat* 9A **48**
Malling Clo. *Croy* 5F **46**
Malling Gdns. *Mord* 5A **44**
Mallinson Rd. *Croy* 9H **45**
Mallow Clo. *Croy* 7G **46**
Mallow Clo. *H'ham* 2L **197**
Mallow Clo. *Lind* 4B **168**
Mallow Clo. *Tad* 7G **81**
Mallow Cres. *Guild* 9D **94**
Mallowdale Rd. *Brack* 6C **32**
Mall Rd. *W6* 1G **13**
Mall, The. *SW14* 8B **12**
Mall, The. *Bren* 2K **11**
Mall, The. *Croy* 8N **45** (2B **200**)
Mall, The. *Surb* 4K **41**
Mall, The. *W on T* 2L **57**
Malmains Clo. *Beck* 3N **47**
Malmains Way. *Beck* 3M **47**
Malmesbury Rd. *Mord* 6A **44**
Malmstone Av. *Red* 6G **103**
Malta Rd. *Deep* 6J **71**
Maltby Rd. *Chess* 3N **59**
Malt Hill. *Egh* 6A **20**
Malt Hill. *Warf* 5C **16**
Malthouse Clo. *C Crook* 8A **88**
Malt Ho. Clo. *Old Win* 1L **19**
Malthouse Ct. *W End* 8C **52**
Malthouse Dri. *W4* 2E **12**
Malthouse Dri. *Felt* 6L **23**
Malthouse La. *Hamb* 9F **152**
Malthouse La. *W End* 1E **92** (Chapel La., in two parts)
Malthouse La. *W End* 9C **52** (Commonfields)
Malthouse Mead. *Witl* 5C **152**
Malthouse Pas. SW13 5E 12 (off Maltings Clo.)
Malthouse Rd. *Craw* 5B **182**
Malthouses, The. *Cranl* 7N **155**
Malt Ho., The. *Tilf* 8A **130**
Maltings. *W4* 1N **11**
Maltings Clo. *SW13* 5E **12**
Maltings Lodge. W4 2D 12 (off Corney Reach Way)
Maltings Pl. *SW6* 4N **13**
Maltings, The. *Byfl* 9A **56**
Maltings, The. *Oxt* 9B **106**
Maltings, The. *Stai* 5G **20**
Malting Way. *Iswth* 6F **10**
Malus Clo. *Add* 4H **55**
Malus Dri. *Add* 4H **55**
Malva Clo. *SW18* 8N **13**
Malvern Clo. *SE20* 1D **46**
Malvern Clo. *Mitc* 2G **44**
Malvern Clo. *Ott* 3E **54**
Malvern Clo. *Surb* 7L **41**
Malvern Ct. *Coln* 2C **6**
Malvern Ct. *Eps* 1C **80** (8K **201**)
Malvern Ct. *Sutt* 4M **61**
Malvern Dri. *Felt* 6L **23**
Malvern Rd. *Farnb* 7J **69**
Malvern Rd. *Craw* 4A **182**
Malvern Rd. *Hamp* 8A **24**
Malvern Rd. *Hay* 3F **8**
Malvern Rd. *Surb* 8L **41**
Malvern Rd. *T Hth* 3L **45**
Malwood Rd. *SW12* 1F **28**
Malyons, The. *Shep* 5E **38**
Manatee Pl. *Wall* 9H **45**
Manawey Bus. Units. *Alder* 3C **110**
Manbre Rd. *W6* 2H **13**
Manchester Rd. *T Hth* 2N **45**
Mandeville Clo. *SW20* 8K **27**
Mandeville Clo. *Guild* 9K **93**
Mandeville Ct. *Egh* 5C **20**
Mandeville Dri. *Surb* 7K **41**
Mandeville Rd. *Iswth* 5G **10**
Mandeville Rd. *Shep* 4B **38**
Mandora Rd. *Alder* 9N **89**
Mandrake Rd. *SW17* 4D **28**
Manfield Pk. *Cranl* 5K **155**
Manfield Rd. *As* 2E **110**
Manfred Rd. *SW15* 8L **13**
Mangles Ct. *Guild* 4M **113** (4B **202**)
Mangles Rd. *Guild* 1N **113**
Manitoba Gdns. *G Str* 3N **67**
Manley Bri. Rd. *Rowl* 6D **128**
Mannamead. *Eps* 6D **80**
Mannamead Clo. *Eps* 6D **80**
Mann Clo. *Craw* 9N **181**
Mann Clo. *Croy* 9N **45** (4B **200**)
Manning Clo. *E Grin* 7N **165**
Manning Pl. *Rich* 9M **11**
Mannings Clo. *Craw* 9H **163**
Mannings Heath. **9C 198**
Mannings Hill. *Cranl* 4M **155**
Manningtree Clo. *SW19* 2K **27**
Mann's Clo. *Iswth* 8F **10**
Manny Shinwell Ho. SW6 2L 13 (off Clem Attlee Ct.)
Manoel Rd. *Twic* 4C **24**
Manor Av. *Cat* 2B **104**
Manor Av. *Houn* 6L **9**
Manor Chase. *Wey* 2C **56**
Manor Circus. (Junct.) **6M 11**
Manor Clo. *Brack* 8M **15**
Manor Clo. *E Hor* 6F **96**
Manor Clo. *Hasl* 2C **188**
Manor Clo. *Horl* 8D **142**
Manor Clo. *Tong* 5D **110**
Manor Clo. *Warl* 4H **85**
Manor Clo. *Wok* 4H **75**
Manor Clo. *Wor Pk* 7D **42**
Manor Ct. *SW6* 4N **13**
Manor Ct. *SW16* 4J **29**
Manor Ct. *W3* 1N **11**
Manor Ct. *C Crook* 9B **88**
Manor Ct. *Craw* 9D **162**
Manor Ct. *H'ham* 3N **197**
Manor Ct. *King T* 9N **25**
Manor Ct. *Twic* 3C **24**
Manor Ct. *W Mol* 3A **40**
Manor Ct. *W Wick* 7L **47**
Manor Ct. *Wey* 1C **56**
Manor Cres. *Brkwd* 7A **72**
Manor Cres. *Byfl* 9A **56**
Manor Cres. *Eps* 8N **59**
Manor Cres. *Guild* 1L **113**
Manor Cres. *Hasl* 2C **188**
Manor Cres. *Surb* 5N **41**
Manorcrofts Rd. *Egh* 7C **20**
Manordene Clo. *Th Dit* 7G **40**
Manor Dri. *Eps* 3D **60**
Manor Dri. *Esh* 8F **40**
Manor Dri. *Felt* 6L **23**
Manor Dri. *Horl* 8D **142**
Manor Dri. *New H* 6J **55**
Manor Dri. *Sun* 1H **39**
Manor Dri. *Surb* 5M **41**
Manor Dri. N. *N Mald & Wor Pk* 6C **42**
Manor Dri., The. *Wor Pk* 7D **42**
Manor Farm. *Wanb* 6N **111**
Mnr. Farm Av. *Shep* 5C **38**
Mnr. Farm Bus. Cen. *Tong* 7D **110**
Mnr. Farm Clo. *As* 3D **110**
Mnr. Farm Clo. *Wind* 6C **4**
Mnr. Farm Clo. *Wor Pk* 7D **42**
Mnr. Farm Cotts. *Wanb* 6N **111**
Mnr. Farm Ct. *Egh* 6C **20**
Manor Farm Estate. **1M 19**
Mnr. Farm La. *Egh* 6C **20**
Mnr. Farm Rd. *SW16* 1L **45**
Manor Fields. *SW15* 9J **13**
Manorfields. *Craw* 7J **181**
Manor Fields. *H'ham* 4N **197**
Manor Fields. *Milf* 9B **132**
Manor Fields. *Seale* 7F **110**
Manor Gdns. *SW20* 1L **43**
Manor Gdns. *W4* 1D **12**
Manor Gdns. *Eff* 6L **97**
Manor Gdns. *G'ming* 4H **133**
Manor Gdns. *Guild* 1L **113**
Manor Gdns. *Hamp* 8B **24**
Manor Gdns. *Lwr Bo* 6J **129**
Manor Gdns. *Rich* 7M **11**
Manor Gdns. *S Croy* 3C **64**

Manor Gdns.—Mason Rd.

Manor Gdns. *Sun* 9H **23**
Manorgate Rd. *King T* 9N **25**
Manor Grn. *Milf* 1B **152**
Mnr. Green Rd. *Eps* 9A **60**
Manor Gro. *Beck* 1L **47**
Manor Gro. *Rich* 7N **11**
Manor Hill. *Bans* 2D **82**
Manor Ho. Ct. *Eps* 9B **60** (7H **201**)
Manor Ho. Ct. *Shep* 6C **38**
Manor Ho. Dri. *Asc* 8L **17**
Manor Ho. Flats. *Tong* 6C **110**
Manor Ho. Gdns. *Eden* 2L **147**
Manorhouse La. *Bookh* 4M **97**
Manor Ho. La. *Dat* 3L **5**
Manor Ho., The. *Kgswd* 1A **102**
Manor Ho. Way. *Iswth* 6H **11**
Manor La. *Felt* 3H **23**
Manor La. *Hay* 2E **8**
Manor La. *H'ham* 8A **198**
Manor La. *Sham G.* 8G **134**
Manor La. *Sun* 1H **39**
Manor La. *Sutt* 2A **62**
Manor La. *Tad* 7M **101**
Manor Lea. *Hasl* 2C **188**
Manor Lea Clo. *Milf* 9B **132**
Manor Lea Rd. *Milf* 9B **132**
Manor Leaze. *Egh* 6D **20**
Manor Lodge. *Guild* 1L **113**
Manor Pk. *Rich* 7M **11**
Mnr. Park Clo. *W Wick* 7L **47**
Manor Pk. Dri. *Yat* 1C **68**
Manor Pk. Ind. Est. *Alder* 3A **110**
Mnr. Park Rd. *Sutt* 2A **62**
Mnr. Park Rd. *W Wick* 7L **47**
Manor Pl. *Bookh* 4A **98**
Manor Pl. *Felt* 2H **23**
Manor Pl. *Mitc* 2G **45**
Manor Pl. *Stai* 6K **21**
Manor Pl. *Sutt* 1N **61**
Manor Pl. W on T 6H **39**
(off Thames St., in two parts)
Manor Rd. *Ashf* 6A **22**
Manor Rd. *Farnb* 1B **90**
Manor Rd. *SE25* 3D **46**
Manor Rd. *SW20* 1L **43**
Manor Rd. *Alder* 4L **109**
Manor Rd. *Beck* 1L **47**
Manor Rd. *E Grin* 8M **165**
Manor Rd. *E Mol* 3D **40**
Manor Rd. *Eden* 2K **147**
Manor Rd. *Farnh* 8K **109**
Manor Rd. *Guild* 1L **113**
Manor Rd. *H'ham* 3N **197**
Manor Rd. *Mitc* 3G **44**
Manor Rd. *Red* 7G **102**
Manor Rd. *Reig* 1L **121**
Manor Rd. *Rich* 7N **11**
Manor Rd. *Rip* 1H **95**
Manor Rd. *Shur R* 1F **14**
Manor Rd. *Sutt* 4L **61**
Manor Rd. *Tats* 7G **86**
Manor Rd. *Tedd* 6G **25**
(in two parts)
Manor Rd. *Tong* 5D **110**
Manor Rd. *Twic* 3C **24**
Manor Rd. *Wall* 1F **62**
Manor Rd. *W on T* 6G **39**
Manor Rd. *W Wick* 8L **47**
Manor Rd. *Wind* 5B **4**
Manor Rd. *Wok* 3M **73**
Manor Rd. *Wokgm* 6A **30**
Manor Rd. N. *Esh* 9F **40**
Manor Rd. N. *Wall* 1F **62**
Manor Rd. S. *Esh* 1E **58**
Manor Royal. *Craw* 9C **162**
Mnr. Royal Ind. Est. *Craw* 8C **162**
Manor Ter. *G'ming* 5J **133**
Manor, The. *Milf* 1C **152**
Manor Va. *Bren* 1J **11**
Manor Wlk. *Alder* 3N **109**
(in two parts)
Manor Wlk. Horl 8D **142**
(off Manor Dri.)
Manor Wlk. *Wey* 2C **56**
Manor Way. *Bag* 5J **51**
Manor Way. *Bans* 3D **82**
Manor Way. *Beck* 1K **47**
Manor Way. *Egh* 7B **20**
Manor Way. *Guild* 6H **113**
Manor Way. *Mitc* 2G **44**
Manor Way. *Old Wok* 8D **74**
Manor Way. *Oxs* 2C **78**
Manor Way. *Purl* 8J **63**
Manor Way. *S Croy* 3B **64**
Manor Way. *Wor Pk* 7D **42**
Manor Way, The. *Wall* 1F **62**
Mnr. Wood Rd. *Purl* 9J **63**
Mansard Beeches. *SW17* 6E **28**
Manse Clo. *Hay* 2E **8**
Mansel Clo. *Guild* 7L **93**
Mansell Clo. *Wind* 4B **4**
Mansell Way. *Cat* 9A **84**
Mansel Rd. *SW19* 7K **27**
Mansfield Clo. *Asc* 9H **17**
Mansfield Cres. *Brack* 5N **31**
Mansfield Dri. *Red* 6H **103**
Mansfield Pl. *Asc* 1H **33**
Mansfield Pl. *S Croy* 3A **64**
Mansfield Rd. *Chess* 2J **59**
Mansfield Rd. *S Croy* 3A **64**
Manship Rd. *Mitc* 8E **28**
Mansions, The. *SW5* 1N **13**
Manston Av. *S'hall* 1A **10**
Manston Clo. *SE20* 1F **46**
Manston Dri. *Brack* 5A **32**
Manston Gro. *King T* 6K **25**
Manston Rd. *Guild* 8C **94**
Mantilla Rd. *SW17* 5E **28**
Mantlet Clo. *SW16* 8G **29**
Manville Gdns. *SW17* 4F **28**
Manville Rd. *SW17* 3E **28**
Manygate La. *Shep* 6D **38**
Manygate Mobile Home Est. Shep 5E **38**
(off Mitre Clo.)
Manygates. *SW12* 3F **28**
Maori Rd. *Guild* 3B **114**
Maple Clo. *Ash V* 6D **90**
Maple Clo. *B'water* 1H **69**
Maple Clo. *Craw* 9A **162**
Maple Clo. *Hamp* 7M **23**
Maple Clo. *H'ham* 3N **197**
Maple Clo. *Mitc* 9F **28**
Maple Clo. *Sand* 6E **48**
Maple Clo. *Whyt* 4C **84**
Maple Ct. *Brack* 3D **32**
Maple Ct. *Croy* 6C **200**
Maple Ct. *Croy* 6B **200**
Maple Ct. *Eng G* 7L **19**
Maple Ct. *Horo* 0M **70**
Maple Ct. *N Mald* 2C **42**
Mapledale Av. *Croy* 8D **46**
Mapledrakes Clo. *Ewh* 5F **156**
Mapledrakes Rd. *Ewh* 5F **156**
Maple Dri. *Crowt* 9H **31**
Maple Dri. *E Grin* 9C **166**
Maple Dri. *Light* 7K **51**
Maple Dri. *Red* 9D **122**
Maple Gdns. *Stai* 3N **21**
Maple Gdns. *Yat* 1C **68**
Maplegreen. *Craw* 4A **182**
Maple Gro. *Bren* 3H **11**
Maple Gro. *Guild* 1N **113**
Maple Gro. *Wok* 8A **74**
Maple Gro. Bus. Cen. *Houn* 7K **9**
Maplehatch Clo. *G'ming* 9H **133**
Maple Ho. *King T* 8J **203**
Maplehurst. *Brom* 1N **47**
Maplehurst. *Lea* 1D **98**
Maplehurst Clo. *King T* 3L **41** (8J **203**)
Maple Ind. Est. *Felt* 4H **23**
Maple Leaf Clo. *Farnb* 2L **89**
Maple Leaf Clo. *Big H* 3F **86**
Mapleleaf Clo. *S Croy* 7F **64**
Maple Lodge. *Hasl* 4J **189**
Maple M. *SW16* 6K **29**
Maple Pl. *Bans* 1J **81**
Maple Rd. *SE20* 1E **46**
Maple Rd. *Asht* 6K **79**
Maple Rd. *Red* 7D **122**
Maple Rd. *Rip* 2J **95**
Maple Rd. *Surb* 5K **41** (8J **203**)
Maple Rd. *Whyt* 4C **84**
Maplestead Rd. *SW2* 1K **29**
Maples, The. *Bans* 1N **81**
Maples, The. *Clay* 4G **59**
Maples, The. *King T* 8J **25**
Maples, The. *Ott* 3D **54**
Maplethorpe Rd. *T Hth* 3L **45**
Mapleton Cres. *SW18* 9N **13**
Mapleton Rd. *SW18* 9M **13**
(in two parts)
Mapleton Rd. *W'ham* 8N **107**
Maple Wlk. *Alder* 4B **110**
Maple Wlk. *Sutt* 6N **61**
Maple Way. *Hdly D* 3G **169**
Maple Way. *Coul* 8F **82**
Maple Way. *Felt* 4H **23**
Marbeck Clo. *Wind* 4A **4**
Marble Hill Clo. *Twic* 1H **25**
Marble Hill Gdns. *Twic* 1H **25**
Marble Hill House. 1J **25**
Marbles Way. *Tad* 6J **81**
Marbull Way. *Warf* 7N **15**
Marchbank Rd. *W14* 2L **13**
March Ct. *SW15* 7G **12**
Marcheria Clo. *Brack* 5N **31**
Marches Rd. *Warn & K'fold* 6D **170**
Marches, The. *K'fold* 4H **179**
Marchmont Rd. *Rich* 8M **11**
Marchmont Rd. *Wall* 4G **62**
March Rd. *Twic* 1G **24**
March Rd. *Wey* 2B **56**
Marchside Clo. *Houn* 4L **9**
Marcuse Rd. *Cat* 1A **104**
Marcus St. *SW18* 9N **13**
Marcus Ter. *SW18* 9N **13**
Mardale. *Camb* 2G **71**
Mardell Rd. *Croy* 4G **46**
Marden Cres. *Croy* 5K **45**
Marden Park. 1H **105**
Marden Rd. *Croy* 5K **45**
Mardens, The. *Craw* 2N **181**
Mare La. *Binf* 1K **15**
(in two parts)
Mare La. *Hasc* 6L **153**
Mareschal Rd. *Guild* 5M **113** (7A **202**)
Mares Fld. *Croy* 9B **46**
Maresfield Ho. Guild 2F **114**
(off Merrow St.)
Mareshall Av. *Warf* 7N **15**
Mare St. *Hasc* 6N **153**
Mareth Clo. *Alder* 2N **109**
Marfleet Clo. *Cars* 8C **44**
Margaret Clo. *Stai* 8M **21**
Margaret Herbison Ho. SW6 2L **13**
(off Clem Attlee Ct.)
Margaret Ho. W6 1H **13**
(off Queen Caroline St.)
Margaret Ingram Clo. SW6 2L **13**
(off Rylston Rd.)
Margaret Lockwood Clo. *King T* 3M **41** (7M **203**)
Margaret Rd. *Guild* 4M **113** (4B **202**)
Margaret Way. *Coul* 6M **83**
Margery. 7M **101**
Margery Gro. *Tad* 7K **101**
Margery La. *Lwr K & Tad* 7L **101**
Margery Wood La. *Lwr K & Reig* 7L **101**
Margin Dri. *SW19* 6J **27**
Margravine Gdns. *W6* 1J **13**
Margravine Rd. *W6* 1J **13**
Marham Gdns. *SW18* 2C **28**
Marham Gdns. *Mord* 5A **44**
Marian Ct. *Sutt* 2N **61**
Marian Rd. *SW16* 9G **29**
Maria Theresa Clo. *N Mald* 4C **42**
Mariette Way. *Wall* 5J **63**
Marigold Clo. *Crowt* 9E **30**
Marigold Ct. *Guild* 9A **94**
Marigold Dri. *Bisl* 2D **72**
Marigold Way. *Croy* 7G **46**
Marina Av. *N Mald* 4G **42**
Marina Clo. *Cher* 7L **37**
Marina Way. *Tedd* 8K **25**
Marinefield Rd. *SW6* 5N **13**
Mariner Gdns. *Rich* 4J **25**
Mariners Dri. *Farnb* 8A **70**
Mariners Dri. *Norm* 9M **91**
Marion Av. *Shep* 4C **38**
Marion Rd. *Craw* 5F **182**
Marion Rd. *T Hth* 4N **45**
Marius Pas. *SW17* 3E **28**
Marius Rd. *SW17* 3E **28**
Marjoram Clo. *Farnb* 1G **89**
Marjoram Clo. *Guild* 8K **93**
Marke Clo. *Kes* 1G **66**
Markedge La. *Coul* 2C **102**
Markenfield Rd. *Guild* 3N **113** (3C **202**)
Markenhorn. *G'ming* 4G **132**
Market Cen., The. *S'hall* 1J **9**
Marketfield Rd. *Red* 3D **122**
Marketfield Way. *Red* 3D **122**
Market Pde. *Felt* 4M **23**
Market Pl. *Brack* 1N **31**
Market Pl. *Bren* 3J **11**
Market Pl. *Coln* 3E **6**
Market Pl. *King T* 1K **41** (3H **203**)
Market Pl. *Wokgm* 2B **30**
Market Rd. *Rich* 6N **11**
Market Sq. *H'ham* 7J **197**
Market Sq. *Stai* 6G **21**
Market Sq. *W'ham* 4M **107**
Market Sq. *Wok* 4A **74**
Market St. *Brack* 1N **31**
Market St. *Guild* 4N **113** (5C **202**)
Market St. *Wind* 4G **5**
Market Ter. Bren 2L **11**
(off Albany Rd.)
Market, The. *Sutt* 7A **44**
Market Way. *W'ham* 4M **107**
Markfield. *Croy* 6J **65**
(in three parts)
Markfield Rd. *Cat* 4E **104**
Markham Ct. *Camb* 9B **50**
Markham M. *Wokgm* 2A **30**
Markham Rd. *Capel* 5J **159**
Markhole Clo. *Hamp* 8N **23**
Mark Oak La. *Fet* 9A **78**
Marksbury Av. *Rich* 6N **11**
Marks Rd. *Warl* 5H **85**
Marks Rd. *Wokgm* 9A **14**
Marks St. *Reig* 2N **121**
Markville Gdns. *Cat* 3D **104**
Mark Way. *G'ming* 3E **132**
Markway. *Sun* 1K **39**
Markwick La. *Loxh* 6L **153**
Marlborough Clo. *SW19* 7C **28**
Marlborough Clo. *Craw* 7A **182**
Marlborough Clo. *Fleet* 5E **88**
Marlborough Clo. *H'ham* 3K **197**
Marlborough Clo. *W on T* 9L **39**
Marlborough Ct. *Dork* 5H **119** (3K **201**)
Marlborough Ct. *S Croy* 7F **200**
Marlborough Ct. *Wall* 4G **62**
Marlborough Ct. W'ham 5L **107**
(off Croydon Rd.)
Marlborough Ct. *Wokgm* 1C **30**
Marlborough Cres. *Hay* 3E **8**
Marlborough Dri. *Wey* 9D **38**
Marlborough Gdns. *Surb* 6K **41**
Marlborough Hill. *Dork* 5H **119** (3K **201**)
Marlborough M. *Bans* 2M **81**
Marlborough Park 6B **90**
Marlborough Ri. *Camb* 9C **50**
Marlborough Rd. *Ashf* 6M **21**
Marlborough Rd. *SW19* 7C **28**
Marlborough Rd. *W4* 1B **12**
Marlborough Rd. *Dork* 5H **119** (2K **201**)
Marlborough Rd. *Felt* 3L **23**
Marlborough Rd. *Hamp* 7A **24**
Marlborough Rd. *Iswth* 4H **11**
Marlborough Rd. *Rich* 9M **11**
Marlborough Rd. *Slou* 1N **5**
Marlborough Rd. *S Croy* 4N **63**
Marlborough Rd. *Sutt* 9M **43**
Marlborough Rd. *Wok* 3C **74**
Marlborough Vw. *Farnb* 9H **69**
Marld, The. *Asht* 5M **79**
Marles La. *Bil* 7D **194**
(in two parts)
Marlet Corner. *Rud* 1E **194**
Marley Av. *Hasl* 5C **188**
Marley Clo. *Add* 3H **55**
Marley Combe Rd. *Hasl* 3D **188**
Marley Common & Wood. **5D** 188
Marley Hanger. *Hasl* 5E **188**
Marley La. *Hasl* 3C **188**
Marley Ri. *Dork* 8G **119**
Marlfield Clo. *Wor Pk* 7F **42**
Marlhurst. *Eden* 8K **127**
Marlin Clo. *Sun* 7F **22**
Marlingdene Clo. *Hamp* 7A **24**
Marlings Clo. *Whyt* 4B **84**
Marlins Clo. *Sutt* 2A **62**
Marlow Clo. *SE20* 2E **46**
Marlow Ct. *Craw* 2D **182**
Marlow Cres. *Twic* 9F **10**
Marlow Dri. *Sutt* 8J **43**
Marlowe Ho. *King T* 8H **203**
Marlowe Sq. *Mitc* 3G **44**
Marlowe Way. *Croy* 8J **45**
Marlow Ho. *Surb* 8K **203**
Marlow Ho. *Tedd* 5G **25**
Marlow Rd. *SE20* 2E **46**
Marlpit Av. *Coul* 6J **83**
Marlpit Clo. *E Grin* 7A **166**
Marlpit Clo. *Eden* 8L **127**
Marlpit Hill. 8K **127**
Marlpit La. *Coul* 3H **83**
Marl Rd. *SW18* 7N **13**
Marlyns Clo. *Guild* 9C **94**
Marlyns Dri. *Guild* 8C **94**
Marmot Rd. *Houn* 6L **9**
Marnell Way. *Houn* 6L **9**
Marneys Clo. *Eps* 2N **79**
Marnfield Cres. *SW2* 2L **29**
Marnham Pl. *Add* 1L **55**
Marqueen Towers. *SW16* 8K **29**
Marquis Ct. *King T* 8H **203**
Marrick Clo. *SW15* 7F **12**
Marriott Clo. *Felt* 9E **8**
Marriott Lodge Clo. *Add* 1L **55**
Marrowbrook Clo. *Farnb* 2M **89**
Marrowbrook La. *Farnb* 3L **89**
Marrowells. *Wey* 9G **38**
Marryat Clo. *Houn* 7N **9**
Marryat Pl. *SW19* 5K **27**
Marryat Rd. *SW19* 6J **27**
Marryat Sq. *SW6* 4K **13**
Marshall Clo. *Farnb* 7L **69**
Marshall Clo. *SW18* 9N **13** & 1A **28**
Marshall Clo. *Frim* 4H **71**
Marshall Clo. *Houn* 8N **9**
Marshall Clo. *S Croy* 9D **64**
Marshall Pde. *Wok* 2H **75**
Marshall Pl. *New H* 5L **55**
Marshall Rd. *Col T* 8J **49**
Marshall Rd. *G'ming* 9H **133**
Marshall Rd. *M'bowr* 5G **182**
Marshalls Clo. *Eps* 9B **60** (6H **201**)
Marshall's Rd. *Sutt* 1N **61**
Marsham Ho. *Brack* 8N **15**
Marsh Av. *Eps* 6D **60**
Marsh Av. *Mitc* 1D **44**
Marsh Clo. *Bord* 6A **168**
Marsh Ct. *Craw* 8N **181**
Marsh Farm Rd. *Twic* 2F **24**
Marshfield. *Dat* 4M **5**
Marsh Green. 6L **147**
Marsh Grn. Rd. *M Grn* 8G **147**
Marshlands Cotts. *Newd* 7B **160**
Marsh La. *Add* 1K **55**
Marshwood Rd. *Light* 7A **52**
Marston. *Eps* 7B **60**
Marston Av. *Chess* 3L **59**
Marston Ct. *W on T* 7K **39**
Marston Dri. *Farnb* 7N **69**
Marston Dri. *Warl* 5H **85**
Marston Rd. *Farnh* 1E **128**
Marston Rd. *Tedd* 6H **25**
Marston Rd. *Wok* 4L **73**
Marston Way. *SE19* 8M **29**
Marston Way. *Asc* 1J **33**
Martel Clo. *Camb* 8G **50**
Martell Rd. *SE21* 4N **29**
Martens Pl. *G'ming* 5H **133**
Martin Clo. *Craw* 1B **182**
Martin Clo. *S Croy* 7G **64**
Martin Clo. *Warl* 3E **84**
Martin Clo. *Wind* 4A **4**
Martin Ct. *S Croy* 8F **200**
Martin Cres. *Croy* 7L **45**
Martindale. *SW14* 8B **12**
Martindale Av. *Camb* 2G **71**
Martindale Clo. *Guild* 1F **114**
Martindale Rd. *SW12* 1F **28**
Martindale Rd. *Houn* 6M **9**
Martindale Rd. *Wok* 5K **73**
Martineau Clo. *Esh* 1D **58**
Martineau Dri. *Dork* 7H **119**
Martingale Clo. *Sun* 3H **39**
Martingale Ct. *Alder* 2K **109**
Martingales Clo. *Rich* 4K **25**
Martin Gro. *Mord* 2M **43**
Martin Rd. *Guild* 1K **113**
Martins Clo. *B'water* 2J **69**
Martins Clo. *Guild* 2E **114**
Martins Clo. *W Wick* 7N **47**
Martin's Dri. *Wokgm* 9A **14**
Martin's Heron. 2D **32**
Martin's La. *Brack* 2C **32**
Martins Pk. Cvn. Pk. *Farnb* 7J **69**
Martins, The. *Craw D* 1F **184**
Martins Wood. *Milf* 3B **152**
Martinsyde. *Wok* 4E **74**
Martin Way. *SW20 & Mord* 1J **43**
Martin Way. *Frim* 5C **70**
Martin Way. *Wok* 5K **73**
Martlets Clo. *H'ham* 3J **197**
Martlets, The. *Craw* 3C **182**
Marts, The. *Rud* 1E **194**
Martyns Pl. *E Grin* 1B **186**
Martyr Rd. *Guild* 4N **113** (5C **202**)
Martyrs Av. *Craw* 9A **162**
Martyr's Green. 7C **76**
Martyr's La. *Wok* 8D **54**
Marvell Clo. *Craw* 1G **182**
Marville Rd. *SW6* 3L **13**
Marwell. *W'ham* 4K **107**
Mary Adelaide Clo. *SW15* 5D **26**
Mary Drew Almshouses. *Egh* 7N **19**
Mary Flux Ct. SW5 1N **13**
(off Bramham Gdns.)
Maryhill Clo. *Kenl* 4N **83**
Mary Ho. W6 1H **13**
(off Queen Caroline St.)
Maryland Rd. *T Hth* 9M **29**
Maryland Way. *Sun* 1H **39**
Mary Macarthur Ho. *W6* 2K **13**
Mary Mead. *Warf* 7B **16**
Mary Rd. *Guild* 4M **113** (4B **202**)
Mary Rose Clo. *Hamp* 9A **24**
Mary Smith Ct. SW5 1M **13**
(off Trebovir Rd.)
Mary's Ter. *Twic* 1G **24**
(in two parts)
Mary Va. *G'ming* 9G **133**
Marzena Ct. *Houn* 9C **10**
Masault Ct. Rich 7L **11**
(off Kew Foot Rd.)
Mascotte Rd. *SW15* 7J **13**
Masefield Ct. *Surb* 6K **41**
Masefield Gdns. *Crowt* 4G **48**
Masefield Rd. *Craw* 6K **181**
Masefield Rd. *Hamp* 5N **23**
Masefield Way. *Stai* 2A **22**
Maskall Clo. *SW2* 2L **29**
Maskani Wlk. *SW16* 8G **29**
Maskell Rd. *SW17* 4A **28**
Maskell Way. *Farnb* 2H **89**
Mason Clo. *E Grin* 8A **166**
Mason Clo. *Hamp* 9N **23**
Mason Clo. *Yat* 1D **68**
Masonettes. Eps 6C **60**
(off Sefton Rd.)
Masonic Hall Rd. *Cher* 5H **37**
Mason Pl. *Sand* 7E **48**
Mason Rd. *Farnb* 8K **69**

Merling Clo.—Mitcham La.

Merling Clo. *Chess* 2J **59**
Merlin Gro. *Beck* 3J **47**
Merlins Clo. *Farnh* 2H **129**
Merlin Way. *Farnb* 2J **89**
Merlin Way. *E Grin* 7C **166**
Merredene St. *SW2* 1K **29**
Merrilands Rd. *Wor Pk* 7H **43**
Merrilyn Clo. *Clay* 3G **58**
Merrington Rd. *SW6* 2M **13**
Merritt Gdns. *Chess* 3J **59**
Merrivale Gdns. *Wok* 4M **73**
Merron Clo. *Yat* 1B **68**
Merrow. 2D **114**
Merrow Bus. Cen. *Guild* 9F **94**
Merrow Chase. *Guild* 3E **114**
Merrow Comn. Rd. *Guild* 9E **94**
Merrow Copse. *Guild* 2D **114**
Merrow Ct. *Guild* 3F **114**
Merrow Ct. *Mitc* 1B **44**
Merrow Cft. *Guild* 2E **114**
Merrow Downs. 4F **114**
Merrow La. *Guild* 7E **94**
Merrow Pl. *Guild* 1F **114**
Merrow Rd. *Sutt* 5J **61**
Merrow St. *Guild* 1F **114**
Merrow Way. *Guild* 2F **114**
Merrow Way. *New Ad* 3M **65**
Merrow Woods. *Guild* 1D **114**
Merryacres. *Witl* 4B **152**
Merryfield Dri. *H'ham* 5G **197**
Merryhill Rd. *Brack* 8M **15**
Merryhills Clo. *Big H* 3F **86**
Merryhills La. *Loxw* 3J **193**
Merrylands. *Cher* 9G **37**
Merrylands Rd. *Bookh* 1N **97**
Merryman Dri. *Crowt* 1F **48**
Merrymeet. *Bans* 1D **82**
Merryweather Ct. *N Mald* 4D **42**
Merrywood Gro. *Tad* 8K **101**
Merrywood Pk. *Camb* 2D **70**
Merrywood Pk. *Reig* 1N **121**
Merrywood Pk. Cvn. Site. *Tad* 8A **100**
Merryworth Clo. *As* 3D **110**
Mersey Ct. *King T* 9K **25** (1H **203**)
Mersham Rd. *T Hth* 2A **46**
Merstham. 6G **102**
Merstham Rd. *Mers* 7L **103**
Merthyr Ter. *SW13* 2G **13**
Merton. 8A **28**
Merton Av. *W4* 1F **12**
Merton Clo. *Owl* 5L **49**
Merton Gdns. *Tad* 6J **81**
Merton Hall Gdns. *SW20* 9K **27**
Merton Hall Rd. *SW19* 8K **27**
Merton High St. *SW19* 8N **27**
Merton Ind. Pk. *SW19* 9N **27**
Merton Mans. *SW20* 1J **43**
Merton Park. 1M **43**
Merton Pk. Pde. *SW19* 9L **27**
Merton Pl. SW19 9A **28** *(off Nelson Gro. Rd.)*
Merton Rd. *SE25* 4D **46**
Merton Rd. *SW18* 9M **13**
Merton Rd. *SW19* 8N **27**
Merton Rd. *Craw* 9N **181**
Merton Wlk. *Lea* 5G **79**
Merton Way. *Lea* 6G **79**
Merton Way. *W Mol* 3B **40**
Mervyn Rd. *Shep* 6D **38**
Merwin Way. *Wind* 5A **4**
Metana Ho. *Craw* 7E **162**
Metcalf Rd. *Asht* 6C **22**
Metcalf Wlk. *Felt* 5M **23**
Metcalf Way. *Craw* 8B **162**
Meteor Way. *Wall* 4J **63**
Metro Ind. Cen. *Iswth* 5E **10**
Meudon Av. *Farnb* 2N **89**
Mews Ct. *E Grin* 3B **186**
Mews End. *Big H* 5F **86**
Mews, The. Broad H 4D **196** *(off Old Guildford Rd.)*
Mews, The. *Charl* 3K **161**
Mews, The. *Duns* 4B **174**
Mews, The. *Guild* 4M **113** (4A **202**)
Mews, The. *Reig* 2N **121**
Mews, The. *Twic* 9H **11**
Mexfield Rd. *SW15* 8L **13**
Meyrick Clo. *Knap* 3H **73**
Michael Cres. *Horl* 1E **162**
Michael Fields. *F Row* 7G **186**
Michaelmas Clo. *SW20* 2H **43**
Michaelmas Clo. *Yat* 2C **68**
Michael Rd. *SE25* 2B **46**
Michael Rd. *SW6* 4N **13**
Michael Stewart Ho. SW6 2L **13** *(off Clem Attlee Ct.)*
Micheldever Way. *Brack* 5D **32**
Michelet Clo. *Light* 6M **51**
Michelham Gdns. *Tad* 7H **81**
Michelham Gdns. *Twic* 4F **24**
Michell Clo. *H'ham* 6G **197**
Michelsdale Dri. *Rich* 7L **11**
Michel's Row. Rich 7L **11** *(off Michelsdale Dri.)*
Mickleham. 5J **99**
Mickleham By-Pass. *Mick* 6H **99**
Mickleham Downs. 4K **99**
Mickleham Downs. 5K **99**
Mickleham Dri. *Mick* 4J **99**
Mickleham Gdns. *Sutt* 3K **61**
Mickleham Way. *New Ad* 4N **65**
Mickle Hill. *Sand* 6F **48**
Micklethwaite Rd. *SW6* 2M **13**
Mick Mill's Race. *H'ham* 7E **198**
Midas Metropolitan Ind. Est. *Mord* 6H **43**
Middle Av. *Farnh* 3J **129**
Middle Bourne. 4H **129**
Middle Bourne La. *Lwr Bo* 5G **129**
Middle Church La. *Farnh* 1G **129**
Middle Clo. *Camb* 9F **50**
Middle Clo. *Coul* 7L **83**
Middle Clo. *Eps* 8D **60**
Middle Farm Clo. *Eff* 5L **97**
Middle Farm Pl. *Eff* 5K **97**
Middlefield. *Farnh* 4F **128** (in two parts)
Middlefield. *Horl* 7G **143**
Middlefield Clo. *Farnh* 3F **128**
Middlefields. *Croy* 5H **65**
Middle Gordon Rd. *Camb* 1A **70**
Middle Grn. *Brock* 5A **120**
Middle Grn. *Stai* 8M **21**
Middle Grn. Clo. *Surb* 5M **41**
Middle Hill. *Alder* 1M **109**
Middle Hill. *Egh* 5M **19**
Middle La. *Eps* 8D **60**
Middle La. *Tedd* 7F **24**
Middlemarch. *Witl* 5B **152**
Middlemead Clo. *Bookh* 3A **98**
Middlemead Rd. *Bookh* 3N **97**
Middle Mill Hall. *King T* 2M **41** (6K **203**)
Middlemoor Rd. *Frim* 5C **70**
Middle Old Pk. *Farnh* 8E **108**
Middle Rd. *SW16* 1H **45**
Middle Rd. *Lea* 8H **79**
Middle Row. *E Grin* 1B **186**
Middlesex Ct. *W4* 1E **12**
Middlesex Ct. Add 2L **55** *(off Marnham Pl.)*
Middlesex Rd. *Mitc* 4J **45**
Middle St. *Brock & Str G* 4A **120**
Middle St. *Croy* 8N **45** (3C **200**) (in two parts)
Middle St. *H'ham* 6J **197**
Middle St. *Shere* 8B **116**
Middleton Gdns. *Farnb* 8K **69**
Middleton Rd. *Camb* 9C **50**
Middleton Rd. *D'side* 6J **77**
Middleton Rd. *Eps* 6C **60**
Middleton Rd. *H'ham* 6G **197**
Middleton Rd. *Mord* 5N **43**
Middleton Rd. *N Mald* 2B **42**
Middleton Way. *If'd* 4K **181**
Middle Wlk. *Wok* 4A **74**
Middle Way. *SW16* 1H **45**
Midgarth Clo. *Oxs* 1C **78**
Midgeley Rd. *Craw* 1D **182**
Midholm Rd. *Croy* 9H **47**
Mid Holmwood. 2H **139**
Mid Holmwood La. *Mid H* 2H **139**
Midhope Clo. *Wok* 6A **74**
Midhope Gdns. *Wok* 6A **74**
Midhope Rd. *Wok* 6A **74**
Midhurst Av. *Croy* 6L **45**
Midhurst Clo. *Craw* 2M **181**
Midhurst Rd. *Hasl* 4E **188**
Midleton Clo. *Milf* 9C **132**
Midleton Ind. Est. *Guild* 3L **113**
Midleton Ind. Est. Rd. *Guild* 2L **113**
Midleton Rd. *Guild* 2L **113**
Midmoor Rd. *SW12* 2G **29**
Midmoor Rd. *SW19* 9J **27**
Mid St. *S Nut* 6K **123**
Midsummer Av. *Houn* 7N **9**
Midsummer Wlk. *Wok* 3N **73**
Midway. *Sutt* 6L **43**
Midway. *W on T* 8J **39**
Midway Av. *Cher* 2J **37**
Midway Av. *Egh* 2D **36**
Midway Clo. *Stai* 4K **21**
Miena Way. *Asht* 4K **79**
Mike Hawthorn Dri. *Farnh* 9H **109**
Milbanke Ct. *Brack* 1L **31**
Milbanke Way. *Brack* 1L **31**
Milborne Rd. *M'bowr* 7G **182**
Milbourne La. *Esh* 3C **58**
Milbrook. *Esh* 3C **58**
Milburn Wlk. *Eps* 2D **80**
Milbury Grn. *Warl* 5N **85**
Milcombe Clo. *Wok* 5M **73**
Milden Clo. *Frim G* 8E **70**
Milden Gdns. *Frim G* 8D **70**
Mile Path. *Wok* 8J **73** (in two parts)
Mile Rd. *Wall* 7F **44**
Miles Ct. *Croy* 3A **200**
Miles La. *Cob* 9M **57**
Miles La. *Tand* 5J **125**
Miles Pl. *Light* 8K **51**
Miles Pl. *Surb* 3M **41** (8L **203**)
Miles Rd. *As* 1F **110**
Miles Rd. *Eps* 8C **60**
Miles Rd. *Mitc* 2C **44**
Miles's Hill. *Holm M* 8K **137**
Milestone Clo. *Rip* 9J **75**
Milestone Clo. *Sutt* 4B **62**
Milestone Green. (Junct.) 7C **12**
Milestone Ho. *King T* 6H **203**
Milford. 1C **152**
Milford By-Pass Rd. *Milf* 2A **152**
Milford Gdns. *Croy* 4F **46**
Milford Gro. *Sutt* 1A **62**
Milford Heath Rd. *Milf* 2B **152**
Milford Lodge. *Milf* 2C **152**
Milford M. *SW16* 4K **29**
Milford Rd. *Elst* 7H **131**
Milkhouse Ga. *Guild* 5N **113** (6D **202**)
Milking La. *Kes* 7F **66** (in two parts)
Millais. *H'ham* 5N **197**
Millais Clo. *Craw* 7L **181**
Millais Ct. *H'ham* 4N **197**
Millais Rd. *N Mald* 6D **42**
Millais Way. *Eps* 1B **60**
Millan Clo. *New H* 6K **55**
Millbank, The. *Craw* 3L **181**
Millbay La. *H'ham* 7H **197**
Mill Bottom. 4K **139**
Millbourne Rd. *Felt* 5M **23**
Millbridge. 9J **129**
Mill Bri. Rd. *Yat* 7A **48**
Millbrook. *Guild* 5N **113** (6B **202**)
Millbrook. *Wey* 1F **56**
Millbrook Way. *Coln* 5G **7**
Mill Chase Rd. *Bord* 5A **168**
Mill Clo. *Bag* 4H **51**
Mill Clo. *Bookh* 2A **98**
Mill Clo. *Cars* 8E **44**
Mill Clo. *E Grin* 2A **186**
Mill Clo. *Hasl* 2C **188**
Mill Clo. *Horl* 7C **142**
Mill Copse Rd. *Hasl* 4F **188**
Mill Corner. *Fleet* 1D **88**
Mill Cotts. *E Grin* 2A **186**
Mill Cotts. *Rud* 3E **194**
Mill Ct. *Red* 9G **103**
Millennium Cotts. *Alb* 8L **115**
Millennium Ho. Bew 6L **181** *(off Meridian Clo.)*
Millennium Ho. *Farnh* 2F **128**
Miller Clo. *Mitc* 6D **44**
Miller Rd. *SW19* 7B **28**
Miller Rd. *Croy* 7K **45**
Miller Rd. *Guild* 9E **94**
Millers Clo. *Stai* 6K **21**
Millers Copse. *Eps* 6C **80**
Millers Copse. *Out* 4M **143**
Miller's Ct. *W4* 1E **12**
Millers Ct. *Egh* 7F **20**
Millers Ga. *H'ham* 3K **197**
Miller's La. *Old Win* 9J **5**
Miller's La. *Out* 4M **143**
Mill Farm Av. *Sun* 8F **22**
Mill Farm Bus. Pk. *Houn* 1M **23**
Mill Farm Cres. *Houn* 2M **23**
Mill Farm Rd. *H'ham* 4N **197**
Millfield. 7M **177**
Mill Fld. *Bag* 4H **51**
Millfield. *King T* 2M **41** (5L **203**)
Millfield. *Sun* 9E **22**
Millfield La. *Tad* 3L **101**
Millfield Rd. *Houn* 2M **23**
Millford. *Wok* 4L **73**
Millgate Ct. *Farnh* 9J **109**
Mill Grn. *Binf* 8K **15**
Mill Grn. *Mitc* 6E **44**
Mill Grn. Bus. Pk. *Mitc* 6E **44**
Mill Grn. Rd. *Mitc* 6E **44**
Millhedge Clo. *Cob* 3M **77**
Mill Hill. *SW13* 5F **12**
Mill Hill. *Brock* 4B **120**
Mill Hill. *Eden* 3L **147**
Mill Hill La. *Brock* 3A **120**
Mill Hill Rd. *SW13* 5F **12**
Millholme Wlk. *Camb* 2G **71**
Mill Ho. La. *Egh & Cher* 3D **36**
Millhouse Pl. *SE27* 5M **29**
Millins Clo. *Owl* 6K **49**
Mill La. *Asc* 1C **34**
Mill La. *Brack* 3L **31**
Mill La. *Brmly* 5B **134**
Mill La. *Byfl* 9A **56**
Mill La. *Cars* 1D **62**
Mill La. *C'fold* 7D **172**
Mill La. *Chil* 8H **115**
Mill La. *Copt* 7B **164**
Mill La. *Cron* 3G **148**
Mill La. *Croy* 9K **45**
Mill La. *Dork* 4H **119** (1K **201**)
Mill La. *Duns* 4A **174**
Mill La. *Egh* 3E **36**
Mill La. *Eps* 5E **60**
Mill La. *Felb* 5H **165**
Mill La. *Fet* 9B **78**
Mill La. *F Grn* 3L **157**
Mill La. *G'ming* 7G **132**
Mill La. *Guild* 5N **113** (6C **202**)
Mill La. *Hasl* 4G **188**
Mill La. *Hkwd* 8B **142**
Mill La. *Hort* 6D **6**
Mill La. *If'd* 1M **181**
Mill La. *Itch* 8B **196**
Mill La. *Limp C* 9H **107**
Mill La. *Lind* 5B **168**
Mill La. *Ling* 1B **166**
Mill La. *Newd* 7C **140** (in two parts)
Mill La. *Orp* 6J **67**
Mill La. *Oxt* 1B **126**
Mill La. *P'rmsh* 2M **133**
Mill La. *Pirb* 2A **92**
Mill La. *Red* 9G **103**
Mill La. *Rip* 6M **75**
Mill La. *W'ham* 5L **107**
Mill La. *Wind* 3D **4**
Mill La. *Witl* 5C **152**
Mill La. *Yat & Sand* 7C **48**
Millmead. *Byfl* 8A **56**
Millmead. *Esh* 8A **40**
Millmead. *Guild* 5M **113** (6B **202**)
Mill Mead. *Stai* 5H **21**
Millmead Ct. *Guild* 5M **113** (7B **202**)
Millmead Ter. *Guild* 5M **113** (7B **202**)
Millmere. *Yat* 8C **48**
Mill Pl. *Dat* 5N **5**
Mill Pl. *King T* 2M **41** (5K **203**)
Mill Pl. Cvn. Pk. *Dat* 5N **5**
Mill Plat. *Iswth* 5G **11** (in two parts)
Mill Plat Av. *Iswth* 5G **10**
Millpond Ct. *Add* 2N **55**
Mill Pond Rd. *W'sham* 1M **51**
Mill Ride. *Asc* 9G **17**
Mill Rd. *Cob* 2K **77**
Mill Rd. *SW19* 8A **28**
Mill Rd. *Craw* 2F **182**
Mill Rd. *Eps* 8E **60** (5M **201**)
Mill Rd. *Esh* 8A **40**
Mill Rd. *Holmw* 4J **139**
Mill Rd. *P'rmsh* 2M **133**
Mill Rd. *Tad* 1J **101**
Mill Rd. *Twic* 3C **24**
Mill Shaw. *Oxt* 1B **126**
Millshot Clo. *SW6* 4H **13**
Millside. *Cars* 8D **44**
Millside Ct. *Bookh* 3A **98**
Millside Pl. *Iswth* 5H **11**
Mills Rd. *W on T* 2K **57**
Mills Row. *W4* 1C **12**
Mills Spur. *Old Win* 1L **19**
Millstead Clo. *Tad* 9G **81**
Mill Stream. *Farnh* 6K **109**
Millstream, The. *Hasl* 3C **188**
Mill St. *Coln* 3F **6**
Mill St. *King T* 2L **41** (5K **203**)
Mill St. *Red* 4C **122**
Mill St. *W'ham* 5M **107**
Millthorpe Rd. *H'ham* 4M **197**
Mill Vw. Clo. *Ewe* 4E **60**
Mill Vw. Clo. *Reig* 1B **122**
Mill Vw. Gdns. *Croy* 9G **46**
Mill Way. *Dork* 2M **99**
Mill Way. *E Grin* 2A **186**
Mill Way. *Felt* 8J **9**
Mill Way. *Reig* 3B **122**
Millwood. *Turn H* 4H **185**
Millwood Rd. *Houn* 8C **10**
Milman Clo. *Brack* 1E **32**
Milne Clo. *Craw* 6K **181**
Milne Pk. E. *New Ad* 7N **65**
Milne Pk. W. *New Ad* 7N **65**
Milner App. *Cat* 8D **84**
Milner Clo. *Cat* 9C **84**
Milner Dri. *Cob* 8N **57**
Milner Dri. *Twic* 1D **24**
Milner Pl. *Cars* 1E **62**
Milner Rd. *SW19* 9N **27**
Milner Rd. *Cat* 9D **84**
Milner Rd. *King T* 2K **41** (6H **203**)
Milner Rd. *Mord* 4B **44**
Milner Rd. *T Hth* 2A **46**
Milnthorpe Rd. *W4* 2C **12**
Milnwood Rd. *H'ham* 5J **197**
Milton Av. *Croy* 6A **46**
Milton Av. *Sutt* 9B **44**
Milton Av. *Westc* 6D **118**
Milton Clo. *Brack* 5N **31**
Milton Clo. *Hort* 6C **6**
Milton Clo. *Sutt* 9B **44**
Milton Ct. *SW18* 8M **13**
Milton Ct. *Dork* 5E **118**
Milton Ct. *Twic* 4E **24**
Milton Ct. *Wokgm* 1A **30**
Miltoncourt La. *Dork* 5E **118** (2G **201**)
Milton Cres. *E Grin* 1M **185**
Milton Dri. *Shep* 3N **37**
Milton Dri. *Wokgm* 1A **30**
Milton Gdns. *Eps* 1D **80** (8L **201**)
Milton Gdns. *Stai* 2A **22**
Milton Gdns. *Wokgm* 2A **30**
Milton Grange. *Ash V* 8E **90**
Milton Ho. *Sutt* 9M **43**
Milton Lodge. *Twic* 1F **24**
Milton Mans. W14 2K **13** *(off Queen's Club Gdns.)*
Milton Mt. *Craw* 9H **163**
Milton Mt. Av. *Craw* 1G **183**
Milton Rd. *SW14* 6C **12**
Milton Rd. *SW19* 7A **28**
Milton Rd. *Add* 3J **55**
Milton Rd. *Cat* 8A **84**
Milton Rd. *Craw* 2G **182**
Milton Rd. *Croy* 7A **46**
Milton Rd. *Egh* 6B **20**
Milton Rd. *Hamp* 8A **24**
Milton Rd. *H'ham* 5J **197**
Milton Rd. *Mitc* 8F **28**
Milton Rd. *Sutt* 9M **43**
Milton Rd. *Wall* 3G **63**
Milton Rd. *W on T* 9L **39**
Milton Rd. *Wokgm* 9A **14**
Miltons Cres. *G'ming* 9E **132**
Milton St. *Westc* 6D **118**
Miltons Yd. Witl 6C **152** *(off Petworth Rd.)*
Milton Way. *Fet* 1C **98**
Milton Way. *W Dray* 1A **8**
Milward Gdns. *Binf* 1H **31**
Mimbridge. 9K **53**
Mimosa Clo. *Lind* 4B **168**
Mimosa St. *SW6* 4L **13**
Mina Rd. *SW19* 9M **27**
Minchin Clo. *Lea* 9G **79**
Minchin Grn. *Binf* 6H **15**
Mincing La. *Chob* 4J **53**
Mindelheim Av. *E Grin* 8D **166**
Minden Rd. *Sutt* 8L **43**
Minehead Rd. *SW16* 6K **29**
Minehurst Rd. *Myt* 1D **90**
Minerva Clo. *Stai* 8J **7**
Minerva Rd. *King T* 1M **41** (3L **203**)
Minimax Clo. *Felt* 9H **9**
Mink Ct. *Houn* 5K **9**
Minley. 5D **68**
Minley Clo. *Farnb* 1K **89**
Minley Ct. *Reig* 2M **121**
Minley Gro. *Fleet* 2C **88**
Minley La. *Yat* 4C **68**
Minley Link Rd. *Farnb* 1G **88**
Minley Rd. *B'water & Farnb* 6E **68** (Farnborough, in two parts)
Minley Rd. *B'water & Fleet* 7B **68** (Fleet)
Minniedale. *Surb* 4M **41** (8M **203**)
Minorca Av. *Deep* 4J **71**
Minorca Rd. *Deep* 5J **71**
Minorca Rd. *Wey* 1B **56**
Minoru Pl. *Binf* 6J **15**
Minstead Clo. *Brack* 2D **32**
Minstead Dri. *Yat* 1B **68**
Minstead Gdns. *SW15* 1E **26**
Minstead Way. *N Mald* 5D **42**
Minster Av. *Sutt* 8M **43**
Minster Ct. *Camb* 2L **69**
Minster Dri. *Croy* 1B **64**
Minster Gdns. *W Mol* 3N **39**
Minsterley Av. *Shep* 3F **38**
Minster Rd. *G'ming* 9H **133**
Minstrel Gdns. *Surb* 3M **41** (8M **203**)
Mint Gdns. *Dork* 4G **119** (1J **201**)
Mint La. *Lwr K* 7M **101**
Mint Rd. *Bans* 3A **82**
Mint Rd. *Wall* 1F **62**
Mint St. *G'ming* 7G **133**
Mint, The. *G'ming* 7G **132**
Mint Wlk. *Croy* 9N **45** (4C **200**)
Mint Wlk. *Knap* 4H **73**
Mint Wlk. *Warl* 4G **85**
Mirabel Rd. *SW6* 3L **13**
Miranda Wlk. *Bew* 5K **181**
Misbrooks Grn. Rd. *Bear G & Capel* 1L **159**
Missenden Clo. *Felt* 2G **23**
Missenden Gdns. *Mord* 5A **44**
Mission Sq. *Bren* 2L **11**
Mistletoe Clo. *Croy* 7G **46**
Mistletoe Rd. *Yat* 2C **68**
Misty's Fld. *W on T* 7K **39**
Mitcham. 2D **44**
Mitcham Garden Village. *Mitc* 4E **44**
Mitcham Ind. Est. *Mitc* 9F **28**
Mitcham La. *SW16* 7G **28**

Mitcham Pk.—Mount Way

Mitcham Pk. Mitc. 3C 44
Mitcham Rd. SW17 6D 28
Mitcham Rd. Camb 6E 50
Mitcham Rd. Croy 5J 45 (1A 200)
Mitchell Gdns. Slin. 5L 195
Mitchell Pk. Farm Cotts. N'chap 8G 191
Mitchell Rd. Orp. 1N 67
Mitchells Clo. Shalf 9A 114
Mitchells Rd. Craw. 3D 182
Mitchells Row. Shalf 1A 134
Mitchener's La. Blet 3A 124
Mitchley Av. Purl & S Croy 9A 64
Mitchley Gro. S Croy 9D 64
Mitchley Hill. S Croy 9C 64
Mitchley Vw. S Croy. 9D 64
Mitford Clo. Chess 3J 59
Mitford Wlk. Craw. 6M 181
Mitre Clo. Shep 5E 38
Mitre Clo. Sutt 4A 62
Mitre Pl. Warf 7N 15
Mixbury Gro. Wey 3E 56
Mixnams La. Cher 2J 37
Mizen Clo. Cob 1L 77
Mizen Way. Cob 2K 77
Moat Ct. Asht 4L 79
Moated Farm Dri. Add 4L 55
Moat Rd. E Grin 8A 166
Moat Side. Felt 5K 23
Moats La. S Nut 1J 143
Moat, The. N Mald 9D 26
Moat Wlk. Craw 2G 183
Moberley Rd. SW4 1H 29
Modder Pl. SW15 7J 13
Model Cotts. SW14 7B 12
Model Cotts. Pirb 8A 72
Moffat Ct. SW19 6M 27
Moffat Rd. SW17 5D 28
Moffat Rd. T Hth 1N 45
Moffats Clo. Sand 7F 48
Mogador. 6K 101
Mogador Rd. Lwr K 6K 101
Mogden La. Iswth 8F 10
Moir Clo. S Croy 5D 64
Mole Abbey Gdns. W Mol 2B 40
Mole Bus. Pk. Lea 8F 78
Mole Clo. Farnb 8J 69
Mole Clo. Craw 1N 181
Mole Ct. Eps 1B 60
Molember Ct. E Mol 3E 40
Molember Rd. E Mol 4E 40
Mole Rd. Fet 8D 78
Mole Rd. W on T 2L 57
Moles Clo. Wokgm 3C 30
Molesey Av. W Mol 4N 39
Molesey Clo. W on T 1M 57
Molesey Dri. Sutt 8K 43
Molesey Pk. Av. W Mol 4B 40
Molesey Pk. Clo. E Mol 4C 40
Molesey Pk. Rd. W Mol 4B 40
Molesey Rd. W on T & W Mol 2L 57
Molesford Rd. SW6 4M 13
Molesham Clo. W Mol 2B 40
Molesham Way. W Mol 2B 40
Moles Hill. Oxs 7D 58
Moles Mead. Eden 1L 147
Mole St. Ockl 3A 158
Molesworth Rd. Cob 9H 57
Mole Valley Pl. Asht 6K 79
Molins Ct. Craw 6M 181 (off Brideake Clo.)
Mollison Dri. Wall 4H 63
Molloy Ct. Wok 3C 74
Molly Huggins Clo. SW12 1G 28
Molly Millars Bri. Wokgm 4A 30
Molly Millars Clo. Wokgm 4A 30
Molly Millars La. Wokgm 3A 30
Molyneux Dri. SW17 5F 28
Molyneux Rd. G'ming 4J 133
Molyneux Rd. Wey 2B 56
Molyneux Rd. W'sham 3A 52
Monahan Av. Purl 8K 63
Monarch Clo. Craw 6M 181
Monarch Clo. Felt 1F 22
Monarch Clo. W Wick 1B 66
Monarch M. SW16 6L 29
Monarch Pde. Mitc 1D 44
Monaveen Gdns. W Mol 2B 40
Moncks Row. SW18 9L 13
Mondial Way. Hay 3D 8
Money Av. Cat 9B 84
Money Rd. Cat 9A 84
Mongers La. Eps 6E 60 (in two parts)
Mongomery Ct. W4 3B 12
Monkleigh Rd. Mord 2K 43
Monks All. Binf 6G 14
Monks Av. W Mol 4N 39
Monks Clo. Farnb 1A 90 (in two parts)
Monks Clo. Asc 5M 33
Monks Ct. Reig 3N 121
Monks Cres. Add 2K 55
Monks Cres. W on T 7J 39
Monksdene Gdns. Sutt 9N 43
Monks Dri. Asc 5M 33
Monksfield. Craw 3D 182
Monks Grn. Fet 8C 78
Monks Gro. Comp 8B 112
Monkshanger. Farnh 1K 129
Monks Hood Clo. Wokgm 1D 30
Monks La. Eden 6F 126
Monks La. Oke H 4N 177
Monks Orchard. 6H 47
Monks Orchard Rd. Beck 7K 47
Monks Path. Farnb 9B 70
Monks Pl. Cat 9E 84
Monks Rd. Bans 4M 81
Monks Rd. Vir W 3N 35
Monks Rd. Wind 5A 4
Monks Wlk. Asc 5M 33
Monk's Wlk. Egh 2F 36
Monk's Wlk. Farnh 4L 129
Monk's Wlk. Reig 3N 121
Monks Way. Beck 5K 47
Monks Way. Stai 8M 21
Monks Way. W Dray 2N 7
Monks Well. Farnh 2N 129
Monkswell La. Coul 2N 101
Monkton La. Farnh 7K 109
Monkton Pk. Farnh 8L 109
Monmouth Av. King T 8J 25
Monmouth Clo. Mitc 3J 45
Monmouth Gro. W5 1L 11
Mono La. Felt 3J 23
Monro Dri. Guild 9K 93
Monroe Dri. SW14 8A 12
Monro Pl. Eps 5N 59
Mons Barracks. Alder 8A 90
Mons Clo. Alder 6C 90
Monsell Gdns. Stai 6G 21
Monson Rd. Red 9D 102
Mons Wlk. Egh 6E 20
Montacute Clo. Farnb 1B 90
Montacute Rd. Mord 5B 44
Montacute Rd. New Ad 5M 65
Montague Av. S Croy 8B 64
Montague Clo. Camb 1N 69
Montague Clo. Light 6L 51
Montague Clo. W on T 6J 39
Montague Clo. Wokgm 9D 14
Montague Dri. Cat 9N 83
Montague Rd. SW19 8N 27
Montague Rd. Croy 7M 45 (1A 200)
Montague Rd. Houn 6B 10
Montague Rd. Rich 9L 11
Montagu Gdns. Wall 1G 62
Montagu Rd. Dat 4L 5
Montana Clo. S Croy 6A 64
Montana Gdns. Sutt 2A 62
Montana Rd. SW17 4E 28
Montana Rd. SW20 9H 27
Monteagle La. Yat 1A 68
Montem Rd. N Mald 3D 42
Montford Rd. Sun 3H 39
Montfort Pl. SW19 2J 27
Montfort Ri. Red 2D 142
Montgomerie Dri. Guild 7K 93
Montgomery Av. Esh 8E 40
Montgomery Clo. Mitc 3J 45
Montgomery Clo. Sand 7G 49
Montgomery Ct. S Croy 8F 200
Montgomery of Alamein Ct. Brack 9B 16
Montgomery Path. Farnb 2L 89
Montgomery Rd. Farnb 2L 89
Montgomery Rd. Wok 5A 74
Montholme Rd. SW11 1D 28
Montolieu Gdns. SW15 8G 13
Montpelier Ct. Wind 5F 4
Montpelier Rd. Purl 6M 63
Montpelier Rd. Sutt 1A 62
Montpelier Row. Twic 1J 25
Montreal Ct. Alder 3L 109
Montrell Rd. SW2 2J 29
Montreux Ct. Craw 3N 181
Montrose Av. Dat 3M 5
Montrose Av. Twic 1B 24
Montrose Clo. Ashf 7D 22
Montrose Clo. Fleet 5C 88
Montrose Clo. Frim 4C 70
Montrose Gdns. Mitc 1D 44
Montrose Gdns. Oxs 8D 58
Montrose Gdns. Sutt 8N 43
Montrose Rd. Felt 9E 8
Montrose Wlk. Wey 9C 38
Montrose Way. Dat 4N 5
Montrouge Cres. Eps 3H 81
Montserrat Rd. SW15 7K 13
Mont St. Aignan Way. Eden 3L 147
Monument Bri. Ind. Est. E. Wok 2D 74
Monument Bri. Ind. Est. W. Wok 2C 74
Monument Grn. Wey 9C 38
Monument Hill. Wey 1C 56
Monument Rd. Wey 1C 56
Monument Rd. Wok 1C 74
Monument Way E. Wok 2D 74
Monument Way W. Wok 2C 74
Moon Hall Rd. Ewh 1D 156
Moons Hill. Fren 9G 129
Moon's La. D'land 3F 166
Moons La. H'ham 7L 197
Moor Clo. Owl 6K 49
Moorcroft Clo. Craw 2N 181
Moorcroft Rd. SW16 4J 29
Moordale Av. Brack 9K 15
Moore Clo. SW14 6B 12
Moore Clo. Add 2K 55
Moore Clo. C Crook 8B 88
Moore Clo. Mitc 1F 44
Moore Clo. Tong 4D 110
Moore Clo. Wall 4J 63
Moore Ct. H'ham 7G 196
Moore Gro. Cres. Egh 7B 20
Moore Pk. Ct. SW6 3N 13 (off Fulham Rd.)
Moore Pk. Rd. SW6 3M 13
Moore Rd. SE19 7N 29
Moore Rd. Brkwd 8M 71
Moore Rd. C Crook 8B 88
Moores Grn. Wokgm 9D 14
Moores La. Eton W 1C 4
Moore's Rd. Dork 4H 119 (1L 201)
Moore Way. Sutt 5M 61
Moorfield. Hasl 3D 188
Moorfield Cen., The. Sly I 8N 93
Moorfield Rd. Chess 2L 59
Moorfield Rd. Guild & Sly I 8N 93
Moorfields Clo. Stai 9G 21
Moorhayes Dri. Stai 2L 37
Moorhead Rd. H'ham 3A 198
Moorholme. Wok 6A 74
Moorhouse. 5H 107
Moorhouse Bank. 6J 107
Moorhouse Rd. Oxt & W'ham 9H 107
Moorhurst La. Holmw 7G 138
Moorings. Bookh 3A 98
Moorings, The. Felb 7K 165
Moorings, The. Hind 6C 170
Moor Junction. (Junct.) 3K 7
Moorland Clo. Twic 1A 24
Moorland Rd. M'bowr 6G 183
Moorland Rd. W Dray 2L 7
Moorlands Clo. Fleet 5C 88
Moorlands Clo. Hind 5C 170
Moorlands Pl. Camb 1M 69
Moorlands Rd. Camb 2M 69
Moorlands, The. Wok 8B 74
Moor La. Brack 2H 31
Moor La. Chess 1L 59
Moor La. D'land & M Grn 9D 146
Moor La. Stai 2F 20
Moor La. W Dray 2L 7
Moor La. Wok 9A 74
Moormead Dri. Eps 2D 60
Moor Mead Rd. Twic 9G 11
Moormede Cres. Stai 5H 21
Moor Pk. Horl 9F 142 (off Aurum Clo.)
Moor Pk. Cres. If'd 4J 181
Moor Pk. Gdns. King T 8D 26
Moor Pk. Ho. Brack 5K 31 (off St Andrews)
Moor Pk. La. Farnh 9K 109 (in two parts)
Moor Pk. Way. Farnh 1L 129
Moor Pl. E Grin 8N 165
Moor Pl. W'sham 2M 51
Moor Rd. Farnb 6M 69
Moor Rd. Frim 6D 70
Moor Rd. Hasl 3A 188
Moorside Clo. Farnb 5M 69
Moors La. Elst 8G 130
Moorsom Way. Coul 4H 83
Moors, The. Tong 5C 110
Moor, The. 3F 20
Moray Av. Col T 7J 49 (in two parts)
Moray Ct. S Croy 8B 200
Morcote Clo. Shalf 1A 134
Mordaunt Dri. Wel C 4G 48
Morden. 2N 43
Morden Clo. Brack 3D 32
Morden Clo. Tad 7J 81
Morden Ct. Mord 3N 43
Morden Ct. Pde. Mord 3N 43
Morden Gdns. Mitc 3B 44
Morden Hall Rd. Mord 2N 43
Morden Park. 5K 43
Morden Rd. SW19 9N 27
Morden Rd. Mord & Mitc. 3A 44
Morden Way. Sutt 6M 43
More Circ. G'ming 4H 133
More Clo. W14 1J 13
More Clo. Purl 7L 63
Morecombe Clo. Craw 5L 181
Morecoombe Clo. King T 8A 26
Moreland Av. Coln 3E 6
Moreland Clo. Coln 3E 6
More La. Esh 9B 40
Morella Clo. Vir W 3N 35
Morella Rd. SW12 1D 28
More Rd. G'ming 4H 133
Moresby Av. Surb 6A 42
Moretaine Rd. Ashf 4M 21
Moreton Almshouses. W'ham 4M 107
Moreton Av. Iswth 4E 10
Moreton Clo. C Crook 9A 88
Moreton Clo. Churt 9K 149
Moreton Rd. S Croy 2A 64 (8E 200)
Moreton Rd. Wor Pk 8F 42
Morgan Ct. Ashf 6C 22
Morgan Ct. Cars 1D 62
Morgan Rd. Tedd 7E 24
Morgan's Green. 7C 194
Morgan Wlk. Beck 3L 47
Morie St. SW18 8N 13
Moring Rd. SW17 5E 28
Morland Av. Croy 7B 46
Morland Clo. Hamp 6N 23
Morland Clo. Mitc 2C 44
Morland Rd. Alder 5N 109
Morland Rd. Croy 7B 46
Morland Rd. Sutt 2A 62
Morland's Rd. Alder 8B 90
Morley Clo. Yat 1A 68
Morley Ct. Fet 8D 78
Morley Rd. Farnh 2H 129
Morley Rd. S Croy 6C 64
Morley Rd. Sutt 7L 43
Morley Rd. Twic 9K 11
Morningside Rd. Wor Pk 8G 43
Mornington Av. W14 1L 13
Mornington Clo. Big H 4F 86
Mornington Cres. Houn 4J 9
Mornington Rd. Ashf 6D 22
Mornington Wlk. Rich 5J 25
Morrell Av. H'ham 3M 197
Morris Clo. Croy 4H 47
Morris Gdns. SW18 1M 27
Morrish Rd. SW2 1J 29
Morrison Ct. Craw 8N 181
Morris Rd. Farnb 5B 90
Morris Rd. Iswth 6F 10
Morris Rd. S Nut 5J 123
Morston Clo. Tad 7G 81
Morten Clo. SW4 1H 29
Morth Gdns. H'ham 7J 197
Mortimer Clo. SW16 3H 29
Mortimer Cres. Wor Pk 9C 42
Mortimer Ho. W14 1K 13 (off N. End Rd.)
Mortimer Rd. Big H 8E 66
Mortimer Rd. Capel 4K 159
Mortimer Rd. Mitc 9D 28
Mortlake. 6C 12
Mortlake Clo. Croy 9J 45
Mortlake Crematorium. Rich 5B 12
Mortlake Dri. Mitc 9C 28
Mortlake High St. SW14 6C 12
Mortlake Rd. Rich 3N 11
Mortlake Ter. Rich 3N 11 (off Mortlake Rd.)
Morton. Tad 8J 81
Morton Clo. Craw 9N 181
Morton Clo. Frim 7D 70
Morton Clo. Wall 4K 63
Morton Clo. Wok 2M 73
Morton Gdns. Wall 2G 62
Morton M. SW5 1N 13
Morton Rd. E Grin 2A 186
Morton Rd. Mord 4B 44
Morton Rd. Wok 2N 73
Morval Clo. Farnb 1K 89
Morven Rd. SW17 4D 28
Moselle Clo. Farnb 9J 69
Moselle Rd. Big H 5G 87
Mosford Clo. Horl 6D 142
Mospey Cres. Eps 2E 80
Moss End. 3N 15
Mossfield. Cob 9H 57
Moss Gdns. Felt 3H 23
Moss Gdns. S Croy 4G 64
Moss La. G'ming 7G 133
Mosslea Rd. Whyt 3C 84
Mossville Gdns. Mord 2L 43
Moston Clo. Hay 1G 8
Mostyn Ho. Brack 8N 15 (off Merryhill Rd.)
Mostyn Rd. SW19 9L 27
Mostyn Ter. Red 4E 122
Moth Clo. Wall 4J 63
Motspur Park. 5F 42
Motspur Pk. N Mald 5E 42
Motts Hill La. Tad 1F 100
Mouchotte Clo. Big H 8D 66
Moulsham Copse La. Yat 8A 48
Moulsham Grn. Yat 8A 48
Moulsham La. Yat 8A 48
Moulton Av. Houn 5M 9
Mt. Angelus Rd. SW15 1E 26
Mt. Ararat Rd. Rich 8L 11
Mount Arlington. Brom 1N 47 (off Park Hill Rd.)
Mount Av. Cat 2N 103
Mountbatten Clo. Craw 7A 182
Mountbatten Ct. Alder 2M 109 (off Birchett Rd.)
Mountbatten Gdns. Beck 3H 47
Mountbatten M. SW18 1A 28
Mountbatten Ri. Sand 6E 48
Mountbatten Sq. Wind 4F 4
Mount Clo. Cars 5E 62
Mount Clo. Craw 2H 183
Mount Clo. Ewh 5F 156
Mount Clo. Fet 1E 98
Mount Clo. Kenl 3A 84
Mount Clo. Wok 8M 73
Mount Clo., The. Vir W 5N 35
Mountcombe Clo. Surb 6L 41
Mount Cotts. If'd 2H 181
Mount Ct. SW15 6K 13
Mount Ct. Guild 5M 113 (6B 202)
Mount Ct. W Wick 8N 47
Mount Dri., The. Reig 1B 122
Mountearl Gdns. SW16 4K 29
Mt. Ephraim La. SW16 4H 29
Mt. Ephraim Rd. SW16 4H 29
Mount Felix. W on T 7G 38
Mount Hermon. 6N 73
Mt. Hermon Clo. Wok 6N 73
Mt. Hermon Rd. Wok 6N 73
Mount La. Brack 2A 32
Mount La. Turn H 5D 184
Mount Lee. Egh 6B 20
Mount M. Hamp 9B 24
Mt. Nod Rd. SW16 4K 29
Mount Pk. Cars 4E 62
Mt. Park Av. S Croy 5M 63
Mount Pl. Guild 5M 113 (6B 202)
Mount Pleasant. SE27 5N 29
Mount Pleasant. Big H 4F 86
Mount Pleasant. Brack. 2A 32 (in three parts)
Mount Pleasant. Eff 6M 97
Mount Pleasant. Eps 6E 60
Mount Pleasant. Farnh 2F 128
Mount Pleasant. Guild 5M 113 (7B 202)
Mount Pleasant. Sand 6F 48
Mount Pleasant. W Hor 7C 96
Mount Pleasant. Wey. 9B 38
Mount Pleasant. Wokgm 2A 30
Mt. Pleasant Clo. Light 6L 51
Mt. Pleasant Rd. Alder 2A 110
Mt. Pleasant Rd. Cat 1D 104
Mt. Pleasant Rd. Lind 4A 168
Mt. Pleasant Rd. Ling 7M 145
Mt. Pleasant Rd. N Mald 2B 42
Mount Ri. Red 5B 122
Mount Rd. SW19 3M 27
Mount Rd. Chess 2M 59
Mount Rd. Chob 8L 53
Mount Rd. Cranl 8N 155
Mount Rd. Felt 4M 23
Mount Rd. Mitc 1B 44
Mount Rd. N Mald 2C 42
Mount Rd. Wok 8L 73
Mountsfield Clo. Stai 9J 7
Mounts Hill. Wink 3N 17
Mountside. Guild 5L 113 (7A 202)
Mt. Side Pl. Wok 5B 74
Mount St. Dork 5G 118 (2H 201)
Mount, The. Hdly 3F 168
Mount, The. Coul 2E 82
Mount, The. Cranl 8N 155
Mount, The. Craw 1G 180
Mount, The. Eps. 6E 60
Mount, The. Esh 3A 58
Mount, The. Ewh 4F 156
Mount, The. Fet 1E 98
Mount, The. Fleet. 3B 88
Mount, The. G'wood 7K 171
Mount, The. Guild 5M 113 (8A 202)
Mount, The. Knap. 6F 72
Mount, The. N Mald 2E 42
Mount, The. S Croy 8C 200
Mount, The. Tad. 4L 101
Mount, The. Vir W. 5N 35
Mount, The. Warl. 6D 84
Mount, The. Wey 8F 38
Mount, The. Wok. 6K 73 (off St John's Hill Rd.)
Mount, The. Wok. 5N 73 (off Elm Rd.)
Mount, The. Wor Pk 1G 61
Mount Vw. Alder. 3M 109
Mount Vw. S'hall 1L 9
Mountview Clo. Red 5C 122
Mountview Dri. Red. 5C 122
Mount Vw. Rd. Clay. 4H 59
Mount Vs. SE27 4M 29
Mount Way. Cars 5E 62

Mount Wood—New Rd.

Mount Wood. W Mol 2B 40
Mountwood Clo. S Croy 6E 64
Moushill La. Milf 2B 152
Mowat Ct. Wor Pk 8E 42
(off Avenue, The)
Mowatt Rd. Gray 7B 170
Mowbray Av. Byfl. 9N 55
Mowbray Cres. Egh 6C 20
Mowbray Dri. Craw 5L 181
Mowbray Gdns. Dork. 3H 119
Mowbray Rd. Rich 4J 25
Mower Clo. Wokgm 1E 30
Mower Pl. Cranl. 6N 155
Mowshurst 8M 127
Moylan Rd. W6 2K 13
Moyne Ct. Wok 5J 73
Moyne Rd. Craw 7A 182
Moys Clo. Croy 5J 45
Moyser Rd. SW16 6F 28
Muchelney Rd. Mord 5A 44
Muckhatch La. Egh 2D 36
Muggeridge Clo. S Croy 2A 64 (8E 200)
Muggeridges Hill. Rusp 1L 179
Mugswell 3N 101
Muirdown Av. SW14 7C 12
Muirfield Clo. If'd 4J 181
Muirfield Ho. Brack 5K 31
(off St Andrews)
Muirfield Rd. Wok 5K 73
Mulberries, The. Farnh 8L 109
Mulberry Av. Stai 2N 21
Mulberry Av. Wind 6J 5
Mulberry Bus. Pk. Wokgm 4A 30
Mulberry Clo. SW16 5G 28
Mulberry Clo. Ash V 9E 90
Mulberry Clo. Crowt 3H 49
Mulberry Clo. H'ham 3J 107
Mulberry Clo. Owl 7J 49
Mulberry Clo. Wey 9C 38
Mulberry Clo. Wok 1A 74
Mulberry Ct. Brack 4C 32
Mulberry Ct. Guild 1F 114
Mulberry Ct. Surb 6K 41
Mulberry Ct. Twic 4F 24
Mulberry Ct. Wokgm 2B 30
Mulberry Cres. Bren 3H 11
Mulberry Dri. Slou 1A 6
Mulberry Ho. Brack 8N 15
Mulberry Ho. Short 1N 47
Mulberry La. Croy 7C 46
Mulberry M. Wall 3G 62
Mulberry Pl. W6 1F 12
Mulberry Pl. Newd 9B 140
Mulberry Rd. Craw 9N 161
Mulberry Trees. Shep 6E 38
Mulgrave Ct. Sutt 3N 61
(off Mulgrave Rd.)
Mulgrave Rd. SW6 2L 10
Mulgrave Rd. Croy 9A 46 (5D 200)
Mulgrave Rd. Frim 4D 70
Mulgrave Rd. Sutt 4L 61
Mulgrave Way. Knap 5H 73
Mulholland Clo. Mitc 1F 44
Mullards Clo. Mitc 7D 44
Mullein Wlk. Craw 7M 181
Mullens Rd. Egh 6D 20
Muller Rd. SW4 1H 29
Mullins Path. SW14 6C 12
Mulroy Dri. Camb 9E 50
Multon Rd. SW18 1B 28
Muncaster Clo. Ashf 5B 22
Muncaster Rd. Ashf 6C 22
Munday Ct. Binf 8K 15
Munday's Boro. P'ham 8L 111
Munday's Boro Rd. P'ham 8L 111
Munden St. W14 1K 13
Mund St. W14 1L 13
Mundy Ct. Eton 2G 4
Munnings Dri. Col T 9J 49
Munnings Gdns. Iswth 8D 10
Munslow Gdns. Sutt 1B 62
Munstead Heath Rd. G'ming & Brmly 1K 153
Munstead Pk. G'ming 8M 133
Munstead Vw. Guild 7L 113
Munstead Vw. Rd. Brmly 6N 133
Munster Av. Houn 8M 9
Munster Ct. SW6 5L 13
Munster Ct. Tedd 7J 26
Munster M. SW6 3K 13
Munster Rd. SW6 3K 13
Munster Rd. Tedd 7H 25
Murdoch Clo. Stai 6J 21
Murdoch Rd. Wokgm 3B 30
Murfett Clo. SW19 3K 27
Murray Av. Houn 8B 10
Murray Ct. Asc 5N 33
Murray Ct. Craw 8M 181
Murray Ct. H'ham 4A 198
Murray Ct. Twic 3D 24
Murray Grn. Wok 1E 74
Murray Ho. Ott 3E 54
Murray Rd. Farnb 2L 89
Murray Rd. SW19 7J 27
Murray Rd. W5 1J 11
Murray Rd. Ott 3E 54
Murray Rd. Rich 3H 25
Murray Rd. Wokgm 2A 30
Murray's La. W Byf 1M 75
Murrellhill La. Binf 8H 15
Murrell Rd. As 1E 110
Murrells La. Camb 3N 69
Murrell's Wlk. Bookh 1A 98
Murreys Ct. Asht 5K 79
Murreys, The. Asht 5J 79
Murtmead La. P'ham 9L 111
Musard Rd. W6 2K 13
Muscal. W6 2K 13
(off Field Rd.)
Muschamp Rd. Cars 8C 44
Museum Hill. Hasl 2H 189
Mus. of Eton Life 2G 4
Mus. of Fulham Palace 5K 13
Mus. of Richmond 8K 11
(off Whittaker Av.)
Mus. of Rugby, The 9E 10
Musgrave Av. E Grin 2A 186
Musgrave Cres. SW6 3M 13
Musgrave Rd. Iswth 4F 10
Mushroom Castle. Wink R 7F 16
Musquash Way. Houn 5K 9
Mustard Mill Rd. Stai 5H 21
Mustow Pl. SW6 5L 13
Mutton Hill. Brack 9H 15
Mutton Hill. D'land 3C 166
Mutton Oaks. Binf 1J 31
Muybridge Rd. N Mald 1B 42
Myers Way. Frim 4H 71
Mylne Clo. W6 1F 12
Mylne Sq. Wokgm 2C 30
Mylor Clo. Wok 1A 74
Mynn's Clo. Eps 1A 80
Mynthurst 4G 141
Mynthurst. Leigh 4G 141
Myrke 1J 5
Myrke, The. Dat 1J 5
Myrna Clo. SW19 8C 28
Myrtle Av. Felt 8F 8
Myrtle Clo. Coln 4G 6
Myrtle Clo. Light 7M 51
Myrtle Dri. B'water 1J 69
Myrtle Gro. N Mald 1B 42
Myrtle Rd. Croy 9K 47
Myrtle Rd. Dork 4G 119 (1J 201)
Myrtle Rd. Hamp H 7C 24
Myrtle Rd. Houn 5C 10
Myrtle Rd. Sutt 2A 62
Mytchett 1D 90
Mytchett Farm Cvn. Pk. Myt 3D 90
Mytchett Heath. Myt 3F 90
Mytchett Lake Rd. Myt 4E 90
Mytchett Pl. Rd. Myt & Ash V 2E 90
Mytchett Rd. Myt 1D 90
Myton Rd. SE21 4N 29

N

Naafi Roundabout. Alder 2N 109
Nadine Ct. Wall 5G 62
Nailsworth Cres. Red 7H 103
Nairn Clo. Frim 4C 70
Nalderswood 4H 141
Naldrett Clo. H'ham 4M 197
Naldretts La. Rud 3E 194
Nallhead Rd. Felt 6K 23
Namba Roy Clo. SW16 5K 29
Namton Dri. T Hth 3K 45
Napier Av. SW6 6L 13
Napier Clo. Alder 6C 90
Napier Clo. Crowt 2H 49
Napier Ct. SW6 6L 13
(off Ranelagh Gdns.)
Napier Ct. Cat 9B 84
Napier Dri. Camb 8E 50
Napier Gdns. Guild 2D 114
Napier La. Ash V 9E 90
Napier Rd. Ashf 8E 22
Napier Rd. SE25 3E 46
Napier Rd. Crowt 3H 49
Napier Rd. Iswth 7G 10
Napier Rd. H'row A 4M 7
Napier Rd. S Croy 4A 64
Napier Wlk. Ashf 8E 22
Napier Way. Craw 9E 162
Napoleon Av. Farnb 8N 69
Napoleon Rd. Twic 1H 25
Napper Clo. Asc 1G 33
Napper Pl. Cranl 9N 155
Nappers Wood. Fern 9E 188
Narborough St. SW6 5N 13
Narrow La. Warl 6E 84
Naseby. Brack 7N 31
Naseby Clo. Iswth 4E 10
Naseby Ct. W on T 8K 39
Nash 3C 66
Nash Clo. Farnb 1L 89
Nash Clo. Sutt 9B 44
Nash Dri. Red 1D 122
Nash Gdns. Asc 1J 33
Nash Gdns. Red 1D 122
Nashlands Cotts. Hand 6N 199
Nash La. Kes 4C 66
Nash Pk. Binf 7G 15
Nash Rd. Craw 6C 182
Nash Rd. Slou 1B 6
Nassau Rd. SW13 4E 12
Nasturtium Dri. Bisl 2D 72
Natalie Clo. Felt 1E 22
Natalie M. Twic 4D 24
Natal Rd. SW16 7H 29
Natal Rd. T Hth 2A 46
Neale Clo. E Grin 7L 165
Neale Ho. F Grin 9A 166
Neath Gdns. Mord 5A 44
Neb La. Oxt 9M 105
Needham Clo. Wind 4B 4
Needles Bank. God 9E 104
(in two parts)
Needles Clo. H'ham 7H 197
Neil Clo. Ashf 6D 22
Neil Wates Cres. SW2 2L 29
Nella Rd. W6 2J 13
Nell Ball. Plais 6A 192
Nell Gwynne Av. Asc 3A 34
Nell Gwynne Av. Shep 5E 38
Nell Gwynne Clo. Asc 3A 34
Nell Gwynne Clo. Eps 7N 59
Nello James Gdns. SE27 5N 29
Nelson Clo. Alder 3A 110
Nelson Clo. Big H 4G 86
Nelson Clo. Brack 9C 16
Nelson Clo. Croy 7M 45 (1A 200)
Nelson Clo. Farnh 4J 109
Nelson Clo. Felt 2G 23
Nelson Clo. M'bowr 4G 183
Nelson Clo. W on T 7J 39
Nelson Ct. Cher 7J 37
Nelson Gdns. Guild 2C 114
Nelson Gdns. Houn 9A 10
Nelson Gro. Rd. SW19 9A 28
Nelson Ind. Est. SW19 9N 27
Nelson Rd. Ashf 6N 21
Nelson Rd. SW19 8N 27
Nelson Rd. Cat 1A 104
Nelson Rd. Farnh 4J 109
Nelson Rd. H'ham 5H 197
Nelson Rd. Houn & Twic 9A 10
Nelson Rd. H'row A 4A 8
Nelson Rd. N Mald 4C 42
Nelson Rd. Wind 6C 4
Nelson Rd. M. SW19 8N 27
Nelson's La. Hurst 4A 14
Nelson St. Alder 2M 109
Nelson Wlk. Eps 5N 59
Nelson Way. Camb 2L 69
Nene Gdns. Felt 3N 23
Nene Rd. H'row A 4C 8
Nene Rd. Roundabout. (Junct.) 4C 8
Nepean St. SW15 9F 12
Neptune Clo. Bew 5K 181
Neptune Rd. Bord 7A 168
Neptune Rd. H'row A 4D 8
Nero Ct. Bren 3K 11
Nesbit Ct. Craw 6K 181
Netheravon Rd. W4 1E 12
Netheravon Rd. S. W4 1E 12
Netherby Pk. Wey 2F 56
Nethercote Av. Wok 4J 73
Netherfield Rd. SW17 4E 28
Netherlands, The. Coul 6G 83
Netherleigh Pk. S Nut 6J 123
Nether Mt. Guild 5L 113
Nethern Ct. Rd. Wold 1K 105
Netherne Dri. Coul 8F 82
Netherne La. Coul 1G 102
(in two parts)
Netherne-on-the-Hill 9G 83
Netherton. Brack 3M 31
Netherton Gro. SW10 2N 13
Netherton Rd. Twic 8G 11
Nether Vell-Mead. C Crook 9A 88
Netherwood. Craw 5N 181
Netley Clo. Cheam 2J 61
Netley Clo. Craw 9A 182
Netley Clo. Gom 7D 116
Netley Clo. New Ad 4M 65
Netley Dri. W on T 6N 39
Netley Gdns. Mord 6A 44
Netley Pk 8D 116
Netley Rd. Bren 2L 11
Netley Rd. Mord 6A 44
Netley St. Farnb 5N 89
Nettlecombe. Brack 5B 32
Nettlecombe Clo. Sutt 5N 61
Nettlefold Pl. SE27 4M 29
Nettles Ter. Guild 3N 113 (3C 202)
Nettleton Rd. H'row A 4C 8
Nettlewood Rd. SW16 8H 29
Neuman Cres. Brack 5M 31
Nevada Clo. Farnb 2J 89
Nevada Clo. N Mald 3B 42
Nevelle Clo. Binf 9J 15
Nevern Mans. SW5 1M 13
(off Warwick Rd.)
Nevern Pl. SW5 1M 13
Nevern Rd. SW5 1M 13
Nevern Sq. SW5 1M 13
Nevile Clo. Craw 6M 181
Neville Av. N Mald 9C 26
Neville Clo. Bans 1N 81
Neville Clo. Esh 3N 57
Neville Clo. Houn 5B 10
Neville Duke Rd. Farnb 6L 69
Neville Gill Clo. SW18 9M 13
Neville Ho. Yd. King T 1L 41 (3J 203)
Neville Rd. Croy 6A 46
Neville Rd. King T 1N 41
Neville Rd. Rich 4J 25
Neville Wlk. Cars 6C 44
Nevis Rd. SW17 3E 28
New Addington 6M 65
Newall Rd. H'row A 4D 8
Newark Clo. Guild 7D 94
Newark Clo. Rip 8J 75
Newark Cotts. Rip 8J 75
Newark Ct. W on T 7K 39
Newark La. Wok & Rip 6H 75
Newark Rd. Craw 1D 182
Newark Rd. S Croy 3A 64
Newark Rd. W'sham 1M 51
New Ashgate Gallery 1G 129
New Barn Clo. Wall 3K 63
New Barn La. Newd 9B 140
New Barn La. Ockl 7A 158
Newbarn La. W'ham & Cud 5L 87
New Barn La. Whyt 3B 84
New Barns Av. Mitc 3H 45
(in two parts)
New Battlebridge La. Red 8F 102
Newberry Cres. Wind 5A 4
New Berry La. W on T 2L 57
Newbolt Av. Sutt 2H 61
Newborough Grn. N Mald 3C 42
Newbridge Clo. Broad H 5C 196
New Bridge Cotts. Cranl 7K 155
(off Elmbridge Rd.)
Newbridge Ct. Cranl 7K 155
New B'way. Hamp H 6D 24
Newbury Gdns. Eps 1E 60
Newbury Rd. Craw 3H 183
Newbury Rd. H'row A 4A 8
New Causeway. Reig 6N 121
Newchapel 1H 165
Newchapel Rd. Ling 1J 165
New Chapel Sq. Felt 2J 23
New Clo. SW19 2A 44
New Clo. Felt 6M 23
New Colebrooke Ct. Cars 4E 62
(off Stanley Rd.)
Newcombe Gdns. SW16 5J 29
Newcombe Gdns. Houn 7N 9
Newcome Pl. Alder 5B 110
Newcome Rd. Farnh 6K 109
New Coppice. Wok 6H 73
New Cotts. Pirb 9A 72
New Cotts. Turn H 5D 184
New Ct. Add 9L 37
New Cross Rd. Guild 1K 113
New Dawn Clo. Farnb 2J 89
Newdigate 1A 160
Newdigate Rd. Bear G 9K 139
Newdigate Rd. Leigh 1D 140
Newdigate Rd. Rusp 1B 180
Newell Green 6B 16
Newell Grn. Warf 6A 16
New England Hill. W End 8A 52
Newenham Rd. Bookh 4A 98
New Farthingdale. D'land 2C 166
Newfield Av. Farnb 8K 69
Newfield Clo. Hamp 9A 24
Newfield Rd. Ash V 7E 90
New Forest Ride. Brack 3D 32
Newfoundland Rd. Deep 6H 71
Newgate. Croy 7N 45
Newgate Clo. Felt 3M 23
Newhache. D'land 1C 166
Newhall Gdns. W on T 8K 39
Newhaven Cres. Ashf 6E 22
Newhaven Rd. SE25 4A 46
New Haw 4L 55
New Haw Rd. Add 3L 55
New Heston Rd. Houn 3N 9
New Horizons Ct. Bren 2J 11
Newhouse Bus. Cen. Fay 1B 198
Newhouse Clo. N Mald 6D 42
Newhouse Cotts. Newd 6B 160
New Ho. Farm La. Wood S 2F 112
New Ho. La. Red 2H 143
Newhouse Wlk. Mord 6A 44
Newhurst Gdns. Warf 6B 16
New Inn La. Guild 8D 94
New Kelvin Av. Tedd 7E 24
New Kings Rd. SW6 5L 13
Newlands. Fleet 7B 88
Newlands Av. Th Dit 7E 40
Newlands Av. Wok 8B 74
Newlands Clo. Horl 6D 142
Newlands Clo. S'hall 1M 9
Newlands Clo. W on T 1M 57
Newlands Clo. Yat 1C 68
Newlands Corner 5J 115
Newlands Corner Countryside Cen. 5J 115
Newlands Ct. Add 2K 55
(off Addlestone Pk.)
Newlands Ct. Cat 8N 83
(off Coulsdon Rd.)
Newlands Cres. E Grin 8N 165
Newlands Cres. Guild 5B 114
Newlands Dri. Ash V 9F 90
Newlands Dri. Coln 6G 7
Newlands Est. Witl 5C 152
Newlands Pk. Copt 7B 164
Newlands Pl. F Row 6H 187
Newlands Rd. SW16 1J 45
Newlands Rd. Camb 5N 69
Newlands Rd. Craw 4A 182
Newlands Rd. H'ham 4J 197
Newlands, The. Wall 4G 63
Newlands Way. Chess 2J 59
Newlands Wood. Croy 5J 65
New La. Wok & Sut G 9A 74
New Lodge Dri. Oxt 6B 106
New Malden 3D 42
Newman Clo. M'bowr 5G 182
Newman Rd. Croy 7K 45
Newman Rd. Ind. Est. Croy 6K 45
Newmans Ct. Farnh 5F 108
Newmans La. Surb 5K 41
Newmans Pl. S'dale 6E 34
Newmarket Rd. Craw 6E 182
New Mdw. Asc 9H 17
New Mile Rd. Asc 1M 33
New Mill Cotts. Hasl 2B 188
Newminster Rd. Mord 5A 44
New Moorhead Dri. H'ham 2B 198
Newnes Path. SW15 7G 12
Newnet Clo. Cars 7D 44
Newnham Clo. T Hth 1N 45
New N. Rd. Reig 6L 121
New Pde. Ashf 5A 22
New Pk. Pde. SW2 1J 29
(off New Pk. Rd.)
New Pk. Rd. Ashf 6D 22
New Pk. Rd. SW2 2H 29
New Pk. Rd. Cranl 7N 155
New Pl. Croy 3K 65
New Pl. Gdns. Ling 7A 146
New Pond Rd. Comp & G'ming 1G 132
New Poplars Ct. As 3E 110
Newport Dri. Warf 7N 15
Newport Rd. SW13 4F 12
Newport Rd. Alder 3A 110
Newport Rd. H'row A 4B 8
New Rd. Alb 8M 115
New Rd. Asc 8J 17
New Rd. Bag & W'sham 4K 51
New Rd. Bedf 2J 23
New Rd. B'water 2K 60
New Rd. Brack 1B 32
New Rd. Bren 2K 11
New Rd. Chil 1D 134
New Rd. C Crook 7C 88
New Rd. Crowt 2H 49
New Rd. Dat 4N 5
New Rd. Dork 6K 119
New Rd. E Clan 9N 95
New Rd. Esh 9C 40
New Rd. Felt 9E 8
New Rd. F Grn 4M 157
New Rd. Gom 8D 116
New Rd. Hanw 6M 23
New Rd. Hasl 3D 188
New Rd. Hay 3D 8
New Rd. Houn 7B 10
New Rd. Hyde 4H 153
New Rd. King T 8N 25
New Rd. Limp 8D 106
New Rd. Milf 1B 152
New Rd. Mitc 7D 44
New Rd. Oxs 7F 58
New Rd. Rich 5J 25
New Rd. Sand 7F 48
New Rd. Shep 2B 38
New Rd. Small 8M 143
New Rd. Stai 6E 20
New Rd. Tad 1H 101
New Rd. Tand 5K 125
New Rd. Tong 6D 110
New Rd. W Mol 3A 40
New Rd. Wey 2D 56
New Rd. Won 3D 134
New Rd. Wmly 1C 172

A-7 Surrey 257

Nova Rd.—Oil Mill La.

Nova Rd. *Croy.* 7M 45
Novello St. *SW6* 4M 13
Nowell Rd. *SW13* 2F 12
Nower Rd. *Dork* 5G 118 (3H 201)
Nower, The. *Knock* 6N 87
Nowhurst Bus. Pk. *Broad H* 2A 196
Nowhurst La. *Broad H* 3N 195
Noyna Rd. *SW17* 4D 28
Nuffield Ct. *Houn* 3N 9
Nuffield Dri. *Owl* 6L 49
Nugee Ct. *Crowt* 2G 49
Nugent Clo. *Duns* 3B 174
Nugent Rd. *SE25* 2C 46
Nugent Rd. *Sur R* 3G 112
Numa Ct. *Bren* 3K 11
Nunappleton Way. *Oxt* 1C 126
Nuneaton. *Brack* 5C 32
Nunns Fld. *Capel* 5J 159
Nuns Wlk. *Dork* 8B 98
Nuns Wlk. *Vir W* 4N 35
Nuptown 2D 16
Nuptown La. *Warf* 2D 16
Nursery Av. *Croy* 8G 46
Nursery Clo. *SW15* 7J 13
Nursery Clo. *Capel* 4J 159
Nursery Clo. *Croy* 8G 46
Nursery Clo. *Eps* 6D 60
Nursery Clo. *Felt* 1J 23
(in two parts)
Nursery Clo. *Fleet* 5E 88
Nursery Clo. *Frim G* 7D 70
Nursery Clo. *Tad* 3G 100
Nursery Clo. *Wok* 3M 73
Nursery Clo. *Wdhm* 8H 55
Nursery Gdns. *Chil* 9D 114
Nursery Gdns. *Hamp* 5N 23
Nursery Gdns. *Houn* 8N 9
Nursery Gdns. *Stai* 7K 21
Nursery Gdns. *Sun* 1G 39
Nursery Hill. *Sham G* 6F 134
Nurserylands. *Craw* 3M 181
Nursery La. *Asc* 9J 17
Nursery La. *Hkwd* 9B 142
Nursery Pl. *Old Win* 9L 5
Nursery Rd. *SW19* 1N 43
(Merton)
Nursery Rd. *SW19* 8K 27
(Wimbledon)
Nursery Rd. *G'ming* 4J 133
Nursery Rd. *Knap* 4G 73
Nursery Rd. *Sun* 1F 38
Nursery Rd. *Sutt* 1A 62
Nursery Rd. *Tad* 3F 100
Nursery Rd. *T Hth* 3A 46
Nursery Way. *Oxt* 7A 106
Nursery Way. *Wray* 9N 5
Nutbourne. *Farnh* 5K 109
Nutbourne Cotts. *Hamb* 2H 173
Nutcombe 7C 170
Nutcombe Down 6C 170
Nutcombe La. *Dork* 5F 118 (2G 201)
Nutcombe La. *Hind* 9C 170
Nutcroft Gro. *Fet* 8E 78
Nutfield 2K 123
Nutfield Clo. *Cars* 9C 44
Nutfield Ct. *Nutf* 1K 123
Nutfield Marsh Rd. *Nutf* 9H 103
Nutfield Park 6L 123
Nutfield Rd. *Coul* 3E 82
Nutfield Rd. *Mers* 7G 102
Nutfield Rd. *Red & Nutf* 3F 122
Nutfield Rd. *T Hth* 3M 45
Nuthatch Clo. *Ews* 5C 108
Nuthatch Clo. *Stai* 2A 22
Nuthatch Gdns. *Reig* 7A 122
Nuthatch Way. *H'ham* 1K 197
Nuthatch Way. *Turn H* 4F 184
Nuthurst. *Brack* 4C 32
Nuthurst Av. *SW2* 3K 29
Nuthurst Av. *Cranl* 7N 155
Nuthurst Clo. *Craw* 2M 181
Nutley. *Brack* 7M 31
Nutley Clo. *Yat* 1C 68
Nutley Ct. Reig 3L 121
(off Nutley La.)
Nutley Gro. *Reig* 3M 121
Nutley La. *Reig* 2L 121
Nutmeg Ct. *Farnb* 9H 69
Nutshell La. *Farnh* 6H 109
Nutty La. *Shep* 2D 38
Nutwell St. *SW17* 6C 28
Nutwood. G'ming 5G 133
(off Frith Hill Rd.)
Nutwood Av. *Brock* 4B 120
Nutwood Clo. *Brock* 4B 120
Nye Bevan Ho. SW6 3L 13
(off St Thomas's Way)
Nyefield Pk. *Tad* 4F 100
Nylands Av. *Rich* 4N 11
Nymans Clo. *H'ham* 1N 197
Nymans Ct. *Craw* 6F 182
Nymans Gdns. *SW20* 2G 42

O

Oakapple Clo. *Craw* 8N 181
Oakapple Clo. *S Croy* 1E 84
Oak Av. *Croy* 7K 47
Oak Av. *Egh* 8E 20
Oak Av. *Hamp* 6M 23
Oak Av. *Houn* 3L 9
Oak Av. *Owl* 6J 49
Oakbank. *Fet* 1C 98
Oak Bank. *New Ad* 3M 65
Oakbank. *Wok* 6A 74
Oakbank Av. *W on T* 6N 39
Oakbury Rd. *SW6* 5N 13
Oak Clo. *C'fold* 5D 172
Oak Clo. *Copt* 7L 163
Oak Clo. *G'ming* 3H 133
Oak Clo. *Sutt* 8A 44
Oak Clo. *Tad* 8A 100
Oakcombe Clo. *N Mald* 9D 26
Oak Corner. *Bear G* 7J 139
Oak Cottage Clo. *Wood S* 2F 112
Oak Cotts. *Hand* 5N 199
Oak Cotts. *Hasl* 2C 188
(in two parts)
Oak Ct. *Farnb* 4C 90
Oak Ct. *Craw* 8B 162
Oak Ct. *Farnh* 2G 129
Oak Cft. *E Grin* 1C 186
Oakcroft Bus. Cen. *Chess* 1M 59
Oakcroft Clo. *W Byf* 1H 75
Oakcroft Rd. *Chess* 1M 59
Oakcroft Rd. *W Byf* 1H 75
Oakcroft Vs. *Chess* 1M 59
Oakdale. *Brack* 5B 32
Oakdale La. *Crock H* 2L 127
Oakdale Rd. *SW16* 6J 29
Oakdale Rd. *Eps* 5C 60
Oakdale Rd. *Wey* 9B 38
Oakdale Way. *Mitc* 6E 44
Oak Dell. *Craw* 2G 183
Oakdene. *Asc* 5C 34
Oakdene. *Chob* 6J 53
Oakdene. *Tad* 7K 81
Oakdene Av. *Th Dit* 7G 40
Oakdene Clo. *Bookh* 5C 98
Oakdene Clo. *Brock* 5B 120
Oakdene Ct. *W on T* 9J 39
Oakdene Dri. *Surb* 6B 42
Oakdene M. *Sutt* 7L 43
Oakdene Pde. *Cob* 1J 77
Oakdene Rd. *Cob* 1J 77
Oakdene Rd. *Bookh* 2N 97
Oakdene Rd. *Brock* 5A 120
Oakdene Rd. *G'ming* 8G 133
Oakdene Rd. *P'mrsh* 2M 133
Oakdene Rd. *Red* 3D 122
Oak Dri. *Tad* 8A 100
Oake Ct. *SW15* 8K 13
Oaken Coppice. *Asht* 6N 79
Oaken Copse. *C Crook* 9C 88
Oaken Copse Cres. *Farnb* 7N 69
Oak End. *Bear G* 8J 139
Oaken Dri. *Clay* 3F 58
Oak End Way. *Wdhm* 8G 55
Oakengates. *Brack* 7M 31
Oaken La. *Clay* 1E 58
Oakenshaw Clo. *Surb* 6L 41
Oakey Dri. *Wokgm* 3A 30
Oak Farm Clo. *B'water* 1H 69
Oakfield. *Plais* 6A 192
Oakfield. *Wok* 4H 73
Oakfield Clo. *N Mald* 4E 42
Oakfield Clo. *Wey* 1D 56
Oakfield Cotts. *Hasl* 7M 189
Oakfield Ct. Horl 8E 142
(off Consort Way)
Oakfield Dri. *Reig* 1M 121
Oakfield Gdns. *Beck* 4L 47
Oakfield Gdns. *Cars* 7C 44
Oakfield Glade. *Wey* 1D 56
Oakfield La. *Kes* 1E 66
Oakfield Rd. *Ashf* 6C 22
Oakfield Rd. *Cob* 1J 77
Oakfield Rd. *SW19* 4J 27
Oakfield Rd. *Asht* 4K 79
Oakfield Rd. *B'water* 2K 60
Oakfield Rd. *Croy* 7N 45 (1B 200)
Oakfield Rd. *Eden* 7K 127
Oakfields. *Camb* 1N 69
Oakfields. *Guild* 1H 113
Oakfields. *Wal W* 1L 177
Oakfields. *W on T* 7H 39
Oakfields. *W Byf* 1K 75
Oakfields. *Worth* 1H 183
Oakfield St. *SW10* 2N 13
Oakfield Way. *E Grin* 7B 166
Oak Gdns. *Croy* 8K 47
Oak Glade. *Eps* 8N 59
Oak Grange Rd. *W Cla* 7K 95
Oak Grove 9K 49
Oak Gro. *Cranl* 9A 156
Oak Gro. *Loxw* 4J 193
Oak Gro. *Sun* 8J 23
Oak Gro. *W Wick* 7M 47
Oak Gro. Cres. *Col T* 9K 49
Oak Gro. Rd. *SE20* 1F 46
Oakhall Dri. *Sun* 6G 22
Oakhaven. *Craw* 5B 182
Oakhill 7M 197
Oak Hill. *Burp* 7E 94
Oakhill. *Clay* 3G 58
Oak Hill. *Eps* 3C 80
Oakhill. *Surb* 6L 41
Oak Hill. *Wood S* 1E 112
Oakhill Clo. *Asht* 5J 79
Oakhill Cotts. *Oke H* 1N 177
Oakhill Ct. *SW19* 8J 27
Oakhill Cres. *Surb* 6L 41
Oakhill Dri. *Surb* 6L 41
Oakhill Gdns. *Wey* 8F 38
Oakhill Gro. *Surb* 5L 41
Oakhill Path. *Surb* 5L 41
Oakhill Pl. *SW15* 8M 13
Oakhill Rd. *Hdly D* 4G 169
Oakhill Rd. *SW15* 8L 13
Oakhill Rd. *SW16* 9J 29
Oakhill Rd. *Add* 3H 55
Oakhill Rd. *Asht* 5J 79
Oakhill Rd. *Beck* 1M 47
Oakhill Rd. *H'ham* 6L 197
Oakhill Rd. *Reig* 4N 121
Oakhill Rd. *Surb* 5L 41
Oakhill Rd. *Sutt* 9N 43
Oakhurst. *Chob* 5H 53
Oakhurst. *Gray* 6B 170
Oakhurst Clo. *Tedd* 6E 24
Oakhurst Gdns. *E Grin* 8M 165
Oakhurst La. *Loxw* 2G 193
Oakhurst Ri. *Cars* 6C 62
Oakhurst Rd. *Eps* 3B 60
Oakington Av. *Hay* 1E 8
Oakington Dri. *Sun* 1K 39
Oakland Av. *Farnh* 5K 109
Oakland Ct. *Add* 9K 37
Oaklands. *Cranl* 9M 155
Oaklands. *Fet* 2D 98
Oaklands. *Hasl* 1G 188
Oaklands. *Horl* 8G 143
Oaklands. *H'ham* 6L 197
Oaklands. *Kenl* 1N 83
Oaklands. *S God* 6H 125
Oaklands. *Yat* 9C 48
Oaklands Av. *Esh* 7D 40
Oaklands Av. *Iswth* 2F 10
Oaklands Av. *T Hth* 3L 45
Oaklands Av. *W Wick* 9L 47
Oaklands Bus. Cen. *Wokgm* 5A 30
Oaklands Clo. *Asc* 8K 17
Oaklands Clo. *Chess* 1J 59
Oaklands Clo. *H'ham* 8L 197
Oaklands Clo. *Shalf* 2A 134
Oaklands Dri. *Asc* 8K 17
Oaklands Dri. *Red* 5F 122
Oaklands Dri. *Twic* 1C 24
Oaklands Dri. *Wokgm* 3A 30
Oaklands Est. *SW4* 1G 29
Oaklands Gdns. *Kenl* 1N 83
Oaklands La. *Big H* 0D 66
Oaklands La. *Crowt* 1F 48
(in two parts)
Oaklands Pk. *Wokgm* 4A 30
Oaklands Rd. *SW14* 6C 12
Oaklands Way. *Tad* 9H 81
Oaklands Way. *Wall* 4H 63
Oakland Way. *Eps* 3D 60
Oak La. *Broad H* 5E 196
Oak La. *Eng G* 4M 19
Oak La. *Iswth* 7E 10
Oak La. *Twic* 1G 25
Oak La. *Wind* 4D 4
Oak La. *Wok* 3D 74
Oaklawn Rd. *Lea* 5E 78
Oaklea. *Ash V* 8E 90
Oak Leaf Clo. *Eps* 8B 60 (5G 201)
Oak Leaf Clo. *Guild* 2G 113
Oak Leaf Ct. *As* 9H 17
Oaklea Pas. *King T* 2K 41 (5H 203)
Oakleigh. *God* 8F 104
Oakleigh Av. *Surb* 7N 41
Oakleigh Flats. *Eps* 1D 80 (8L 201)
Oakleigh Gdns. *Orp* 1N 67
Oakleigh Rd. *H'ham* 4M 197
Oakleigh Way. *Mitc* 9F 28
Oakleigh Way. *Surb* 7N 41
Oakley Av. *Croy* 1K 63
Oakley Clo. *Add* 1M 55
Oakley Clo. *E Grin* 2D 186
Oakley Clo. *Iswth* 4D 10
Oakley Ct. Red 2E 122
(off St Anne's Ri.)
Oakley Dell. *Guild* 1E 114
Oakley Dri. *Brom* 1G 66
Oakley Dri. *Fleet* 5B 88
Oakley Gdns. *Bans* 2N 81
Oakley Ho. *G'ming* 3H 133
Oakley M. *Wind* 5B 4
Oakley Rd. *SE25* 4E 46
Oakley Rd. *Brom* 1G 66
Oakley Rd. *Camb* 2N 69
Oakley Rd. *Warl* 5D 84
Oakley Wlk. *W6* 2J 13
Oak Lodge. *Crowt* 2H 49
Oak Lodge. *Hasl* 4J 189
Oak Lodge Clo. *W on T* 2K 57
Oaklodge Dri. *Red* 2E 142
Oak Lodge Dri. *W Wick* 6L 47
Oak Lodge La. *W'ham* 3M 107
Oak Mead. *G'ming* 3G 133
Oakmead Grn. *Eps* 2B 80
Oakmead Pl. *Mitc* 9C 28
Oakmead Rd. *SW12* 2E 28
Oakmead Rd. *Croy* 5H 45
Oakmede Pl. *Binf* 7H 15
Oak Pk. *W Byf* 9G 55
Oak Pk. Gdns. *SW19* 2J 27
Oak Pl. *SW18* 8N 13
Oak Ridge. *Dork* 8H 119
Oakridge. *W End* 9C 52
Oak Rd. *Cob* 2L 77
Oak Rd. *Farnb* 2A 90
Oak Rd. *Cat* 9B 84
Oak Rd. *Craw* 4A 182
Oak Rd. *Lea* 5G 79
Oak Rd. *N Mald* 1C 42
Oak Rd. *Reig* 2N 121
Oak Rd. *W'ham* 3M 107
Oak Row. *SW16* 1G 45
Oaks Av. *Felt* 3M 23
Oaks Av. *Wor Pk* 9G 40
Oaks Cvn. Pk., The. *Chess* 9J 41
Oaks Clo. *H'ham* 2A 198
Oaks Clo. *Lea* 8G 79
Oakshade Rd. *Oxs* 1C 78
Oakshaw. *Oxt* 5N 105
Oakshaw Rd. *SW18* 1N 27
Oaks Ho. Cvn. Pk., The. *Bear G* 1K 159
Oakside Ct. *Horl* 7G 143
Oakside La. *Horl* 7G 143
Oaks La. *Croy* 9F 46
(in two parts)
Oaks La. *Mid H* 3H 139
Oaks Rd. *Croy* 2E 64
Oaks Rd. *Kenl* 1M 83
Oaks Rd. *Reig* 2B 122
Oaks Rd. *Stanw* 9M 7
Oaks Rd. *Wok* 4A 74
Oaks Sq., The. *Eps* 6K 201
Oaks, The. *Farnb* 2J 89
Oaks, The. *Brack* 1B 32
Oaks, The. *C'fold* 5E 172
Oaks, The. *Dork* 8H 119
Oaks, The. *E Grin* 1C 186
Oaks, The. *Eps* 1D 80
Oaks, The. *Mord* 3K 43
Oaks, The. *Stai* 5H 21
Oaks, The. *Tad* 1H 101
Oaks, The. *W Byf* 1J 75
Oaks, The. *Yat* 1C 68
Oaks Track. *Cars* 7D 62
Oaks Way. *Cars* 4D 62
Oaks Way. *Eps* 6G 80
Oaks Way. *Kenl* 1N 83
Oaksway. *Surb* 7K 41
Oak Tree Clo. *Alder* 4C 110
Oak Tree Clo. *Ash V* 4D 90
Oak Tree Clo. *Burp* 7E 94
Oak Tree Clo. *Guild* 6N 93
Oak Tree Clo. *Head* 5E 168
Oak Tree Clo. *Knap* 5E 72
Oak Tree Clo. *Vir W* 5N 35
Oak Tree Dri. *Eng G* 6M 19
Oak Tree Dri. *Guild* 8M 93
Oak Tree La. *Hasl* 2B 188
Oak Tree M. *Brack* 2B 32
Oak Tree Rd. *Knap* 5E 72
Oak Tree Rd. *Milf* 1B 152
Oaktrees. *As* 3D 110
Oaktrees. *Farnh* 6G 109
Oaktrees Ct. As 3D 110
(off Oaktrees)
Oak Tree Vw. *Farnh* 6K 109
Oaktree Way. *H'ham* 4M 197
Oaktree Way. *Sand* 6F 48
Oak Vw. *Eden* 1K 147
Oak Vw. *Wokgm* 4A 30
Oakview Gro. *Croy* 7H 47
Oak Wlk. *Fay* 8E 180
Oak Way. *SW20* 3H 43
Oakway. *Alder* 4C 110
Oak Way. *Asht* 3N 79
Oakway. *Brom* 1N 47
Oak Way. *Craw* 2C 182
Oak Way. *Croy* 5G 47
Oak Way. *Felt* 2F 22
Oak Way. *Man H* 9B 198
Oak Way. *Reig* 4B 122
Oakway. *Wok* 6H 73
Oakway Dri. *Frim* 5C 70
Oakwood. *C Crook* 9B 88
Oakwood. *Guild* 7K 93
Oakwood. *Wall* 5F 62
Oakwood Av. *Beck* 1M 47
Oakwood Av. *Eps* 5N 59
Oakwood Av. *Mitc* 1B 44
Oakwood Av. *Purl* 8M 63
Oakwood Clo. *E Hor* 5F 96
Oakwood Clo. *Red* 3E 122
Oakwood Clo. *S Nut* 5K 123
Oakwood Ct. *Bisl* 3D 72
Oakwood Dri. *E Hor* 5F 96
Oakwood Gdns. *Knap* 5D 72
Oakwood Gdns. *Sutt* 8M 43
Oakwood Hall. *Kgswd* 1A 102
Oakwoodhill 1N 177
Oakwood Ind. Pk. *Craw* 8E 162
Oakwood Pk. *F Row* 7H 187
Oakwood Pl. *Croy* 5L 45
Oakwood Ri. *Cat* 3D 104
Oakwood Rd. *SW20* 9F 26
Oakwood Rd. *Brack* 1C 32
Oakwood Rd. *Croy* 5L 45
Oakwood Rd. *Horl* 7E 142
Oakwood Rd. *Mers* 7L 103
Oakwood Rd. *Vir W* 4M 35
Oakwood Rd. *W'sham* 3B 52
Oakwood Rd. *Wok* 6H 73
Oareborough. *Brack* 3C 32
Oarsman Pl. *E Mol* 3E 40
Oast Ho. Clo. *Wray* 1A 20
Oast Ho. Cres. *Farnh* 6H 109
Oast Ho. Dri. *Fleet* 1D 88
Oast Ho. La. *Farnh* 7J 109
Oast La. *Alder* 5N 109
Oast Lodge. W4 3D 12
(off Corney Reach Way)
Oast Rd. *Oxt* 9B 106
Oates Clo. *Brom* 2N 47
Oates Wlk. *Craw* 6D 182
Oatfield Rd. *Tad* 7G 80
Oatlands. *Craw* 4M 181
Oatlands. *Horl* 7G 142
Oatlands Av. *Wey* 2E 56
Oatlands Chase. *Wey* 9F 38
Oatlands Clo. *Wey* 1D 56
Oatlands Dri. *Wey* 1D 56
Oatlands Grn. *Wey* 9E 38
Oatlands Mere. *Wey* 9E 38
Oatlands Park 9F 38
Oatlands Rd. *Tad* 6K 81
Oatsheaf Pde. *Fleet* 5A 88
Oban Rd. *SE25* 3A 46
Obelisk Way. *Camb* 9A 50
(in two parts)
Oberon Way. *Craw* 6K 181
Oberon Way. *Shep* 2N 37
Oberursel Way. *Alder* 2L 109
Observatory Rd. *SW14* 7B 12
Observatory Wlk. *Red* 3D 122
Occam Rd. *Sur R* 3G 112
Occupation Rd. *Eps* 4C 60
Ocean Ho. *Brack* 1N 31
Ockenden Clo. *Wok* 5B 74
Ockenden Gdns. *Wok* 5B 74
Ockenden Rd. *Wok* 5B 74
Ockfields. *Milf* 1C 152
Ockford Ct. *G'ming* 7G 132
Ockford Dri. *G'ming* 8F 132
Ockford Ridge 8E 132
Ockford Ridge. *G'ming* 8E 132
Ockford Rd. *G'ming* 8F 132
Ockham 8C 76
Ockham Dri. *W Hor* 2E 96
Ockham La. *Ock & D'side* 8B 76
Ockham Rd. N. *Ock & E Hor* 7N 75
Ockham Rd. S. *E Hor* 4F 96
Ockley 5D 158
Ockley Ct. *Guild* 7D 94
Ockley Ct. *Sutt* 1A 62
Ockley Rd. *SW16* 5J 29
Ockley Rd. *Bear G* 1H 159
Ockley Rd. *Croy* 6K 45
Ockley Rd. *Ewh & Bear G* 4F 156
Ockleys Mead. *God* 7F 104
O'Connor Rd. *Alder* 6C 90
Octagon Rd. *W Vill* 5F 56
Octavia. *Brack* 7M 31
Octavia Clo. *Mitc* 4C 44
Octavia Rd. *Iswth* 6E 10
Octavia Way. *Stai* 7J 21
Odard Rd. *W Mol* 3A 40
Odiham Rd. *Farnh* 5E 108
Offers Ct. *King T* 2M 41 (5L 203)
Offley Pl. *Iswth* 5D 10
Off Up. Manor Rd. G'ming 4H 133
(off Up. Manor Rd.)
Ogden Ho. *Felt* 4M 23
Ogden Pk. *Brack* 2C 32
Oglethorpe Ct. G'ming 7G 133
(off High St.)
Oil Mill La. *W6* 1F 12

Okeburn Rd.—Ormonde Rd.

Okeburn Rd. SW17 6E 28
Okehurst La. Bil 9B 194
Okingham Clo. Owl 5J 49
Oldacre. W End 8C 52
Old Acre. Wok 1J 75
Oldacre M. SW12 1E 28
Old Av. W Byf 9G 55
Old Av. Wey 4D 56
Old Av. Clo. W Byf 9G 54
Old Bakery M. Alb 8K 115
Old Barn Clo. Sutt 4K 61
Old Barn Cotts. K'fold 2J 179
Old Barn Dri. Capel 4K 159
Old Barn La. Churt 8N 149
Old Barn La. Kenl 3C 84
Old Barn Rd. Eps 4B 80
Old Barn Vw. G'ming 9F 132
Old Bath Rd. Coln & W Dray 4G 6
Old Bisley Rd. Frim 4E 70
Old Bracknell Clo. Brack 2N 31
Old Bracknell La. E. Brack 2N 31
Old Bracknell La. W. Brack 2M 31
Old Brentford. 3K 11
Old Brickfield Rd. Alder 5N 109
Old Bri. St. Hamp W
1K 41 (3G 203)
Old Brighton Rd. Peas P
3N 199 & 9A 182
Old Brighton Rd. S. Low H
6C 162
Old Brompton Rd. SW5 & SW7
1M 13
Oldbury. Brack 2L 31
Oldbury Clo. Frim 6D 70
Oldbury Clo. H'ham 1N 197
Old Bury Hill. 7E 118
Old Bury Hill Ho. Westc 7E 118
Oldbury Rd. Cher 6G 36
Old Chapel La. As 2E 110
Old Charlton Rd. Shep 4D 38
Old Char Wharf. Dork
4F 118 (1G 201)
Old Chertsey Rd. Chob 6L 53
Old Chestnut Av. Clar P 3A 58
Old Chiswick Yd. W4 2D 12
(off Pumping Sta. Rd.)
Old Church La. Farnh 4J 129
Old Church Path. Esh 1C 58
Old Claygate La. Clay 3G 58
Old Coach Rd. Cher 4F 36
Old Common. 9J 57
Old Comn. Rd. Cob 9J 57
Old Compton La. Farnh 1K 129
Old Convent. E Grin 8A 166
Oldcorne Hollow. Yat 1A 68
Old Corn M. G'ming 5J 133
Old Cote Dri. Houn 2A 10
Old Coulsdon. 7L 83
Old Ct. Asht 6L 79
Old Ct. Rd. Guild 4K 113
Old Cove Rd. Fleet 2C 88
Old Crawley Rd. Fay 2B 198
Old Cross Tree Way. Ash G
4G 111
Old Dairy M. SW12 2E 28
Old Dean Rd. Camb 8B 50
Old Deer Pk. Gdns. Rich 6L 11
Old Denne Gdns. H'ham 7J 197
Old Devonshire Rd. SW12 1F 28
Old Dock Clo. Rich 2N 11
Old Dorking Rd. Warn 2H 197
Old Dri. Gom 7D 116
Olde Farm Dri. B'water 9G 48
Old Elstead Rd. Milf 9B 132
Olden La. Purl 8L 63
Old Epsom Rd. E Clan 9M 95
Old Esher Clo. W on T 2L 57
Old Esher Rd. W on T 2L 57
Old Farleigh Rd. S Croy & Warl
6F 64
Old Farm Clo. SW17 3C 28
Old Farm Clo. Houn 7N 9
Old Farm Dri. Brack 8A 16
Old Farm Ho. Dri. Oxs 2D 78
Old Farm Pas. Hamp 9C 24
Old Farm Pl. Ash V 9D 90
Old Farm Rd. Guild 9N 93
Old Farm Rd. Hamp 7N 23
(in two parts)
Old Farnham La. Farnh
(GU10) 2A 128
Old Farnham La. Farnh
(GU9) 3H 129
Old Ferry Dri. Wray 9M 5
Oldfield Clo. Horl 1D 162
Oldfield Ct. Surb 8L 203
Oldfield Gdns. Asht 6K 79
Oldfield Ho. W4 1D 12
(off Devonshire Rd.)
Oldfield Rd. SW19 7K 27
Oldfield Rd. Hamp 9N 23
Oldfield Rd. Horl 1D 162
Oldfields Rd. Sutt 9L 43
Oldfields Trad. Est. Sutt 9M 43
Oldfieldwood. Wok 4D 74
Old Forge Ct. Shalf 9B 114
Old Forge Cres. Shep 5C 38
Old Forge End. Sand 8G 49
Old Forge, The. Slin 5L 195
Old Fox Clo. Cat 8M 83
Old Frensham Rd. Lwr Bo 5J 129
Old Glebe. Fern 9F 188
Old Grn. La. Camb 8A 50
Old Guildford Rd. Broad H 4D 196
Old Guildford Rd. Frim G 9F 70
Old Harrow La. W'ham 5L 87
Old Haslemere Rd. Hasl 3G 189
Old Heath Way. Farnh 5H 109
Old Hill. Orp 3M 67
Old Hill. Wok 7N 73
Old Hill Est. Wok 7N 73
Old Holbrook. H'ham 9L 179
Old Hollow. Worth 3K 183
Old Horsham Rd. Bear G 6J 139
Old Horsham Rd. Craw 5N 181
Old Hospital Clo. SW17 2D 28
Old Ho. Clo. SW19 6K 27
Old Ho. Clo. Eps 6E 60
Old Ho. Gdns. Twic 9J 11
Oldhouse La. Bisl 1D 72
Oldhouse La. W'sham 4M 51
Old Ho. M. H'ham 6J 197
Old Isleworth. 6H 11
Old Kiln Clo. Churt 8L 149
Old Kiln La. Brock 3B 120
Old Kiln La. Churt 7L 149
Old Kiln Mus. & Rural Life Cen.
8L 129
Old Kingston Rd. Wor Pk 8B 42
Old Lands Hill. Brack 9B 16
Old La. Alder (GU11) 5M 109
Old La. Alder (GU12) 1C 110
Old La. Dock 5F 148
Old La. Ock & Cobh 4C 76
Old La. Oxt 7B 106
(in two parts)
Old La. Tats 7F 86
Old La. Gdns. Cob 9H 77
Old Lodge Clo. G'ming 8E 132
Old Lodge La. Purl 9K 63
Old Lodge Pl. Twic 9H 11
Old London Rd. E Hor 4H 97
Old London Rd. Eps 6F 80
(in two parts)
Old London Rd. King T
1L 41 (3K 203)
Old London Rd. Mick 5J 99
Old Malden. 7D 42
Old Malden La. Wor Pk 8C 42
Old Malt Way. Wok 4N 73
Old Mnr. Clo. Craw 1M 181
Old Mnr. Ct. Craw 1M 181
Old Mnr. Dri. Iswth 9C 10
Old Manor Gdns. Chil 9E 114
Old Mnr. Ho. M. Shep 2B 38
Old Mnr. La. Chil 9E 114
Old Mnr. Yd. SW5 1N 13
Old Martyrs. Craw 9B 162
Old Merrow St. Guild 9F 94
Old Mill La. Red 6F 102
Old Millmeads. H'ham 3J 197
Old Mill Pl. Hasl 1D 188
Old Mill Pl. Wray 9D 6
Old Monteagle La. Yat 9A 48
Old Museum Ct. Hasl 2H 189
Old Nursery Pl. Ashf 6C 22
Old Oak Av. Coul 6C 82
Old Oak Clo. Chess 1M 59
Old Orchard. Byfl 8A 56
Old Orchard. Sun 1K 39
Old Orchards. M'bowr 3J 183
Old Orchard, The. Farnh 4E 128
Old Overthorpe. Small 1M 163
Old Oxted. 8N 105
Old Pal. La. Rich 8J 11
Old Pal. Rd. Croy 9M 45 (4A 200)
Old Pal. Rd. Guild 4K 113
Old Pal. Rd. Wey 9C 38
Old Pal. Ter. Rich 8K 11
Old Pal. Yd. Rich 8J 11
Old Pk. Av. SW12 1E 28
Old Pk. Clo. Farnh 6F 108
Old Pk. La. Farnh 5E 108
(in two parts)
Old Pk. M. Houn 3N 9
Old Parvis Rd. W Byf 8L 55
Old Pasture Rd. Frim 4D 70
Old Pharmacy Ct. Crowt 3G 49
Old Pond Clo. Camb 5A 70
Old Portsmouth Rd. Camb 1E 70
Old Portsmouth Rd.
G'ming & P'mrsh 3L 133
Old Portsmouth Rd. Thur 6H 151
Old Post Cotts. Broad H 5D 196
Old Pottery Clo. Reig 5N 121
Old Pound Clo. Iswth 5G 10
Old Pound Cotts. If'd 2J 181
Old Priory La. Warf 7B 16
Old Pump Ho. Clo. Fleet 3D 88
Old Quarry, The. Hasl 4D 188
Old Rectory Clo. Brmly 5B 134
Old Rectory Clo. Tad 2F 100
Old Rectory Dri. As 2F 110
Old Rectory Gdns. Farnb 1B 90
Old Rectory Gdns. G'ming 9J 133
Old Rectory La. E Hor 4F 96
Old Redstone Dri. Red 4E 122
Old Reigate Rd. Bet 3A 120
Old Reigate Rd. Dork 3L 119
Oldridge Rd. SW12 1E 28
Old Rd. Add 4H 55
Old Rd. Buck 3D 120
Old Rd. E Grin 9B 166
Old Row Ct. Wokgm 2B 30
Old St Mary's. W Hor 7C 96
Old Sawmill La. Crowt 1H 49
Old School Clo. SW19 1M 43
Old School Clo. As 1E 110
(in two parts)
Old School Clo. Beck 1G 47
Old School Clo. Fleet 4B 88
Old School Ct. Wray 1A 20
Old School Ho. Eden 2L 147
Old School La. Brock 6A 120
Old School La. Yat 9B 48
Old School M. Stai 6F 20
Old School M. Wey 1E 56
Old School Pl. Ling 7N 145
Old School Pl. Wok 8A 74
Old Schools La. Eps 5E 60
Old School Sq. Th Dit 5F 40
Old School Ter. Fleet 4B 88
(off Old School Clo.)
Old Slade La. Iver 1H 7
Old Sta. App. Lea 8G 78
Old Sta. Clo. Craw D 2E 184
Old Sta. Gdns. Tedd 7G 24
(off Victoria Rd.)
Old Sta. Way. G'ming 6H 133
Oldstead. Brack 4B 32
Old Surrey Hall. 6G 166
Old Swan Yd. Cars 1D 62
Old Thorn. 6F 172
Old Tilburstow Rd. God 3F 124
Old Town. Croy 9M 45 (4A 200)
Old Tye Av. Big H 3G 87
Old Welmore. Yat 1D 68
Old Westhall Clo. Warl 6F 84
Old Wharf Way. Wey 1A 56
Old Wickhurst La. Broad H
7D 196
Old Windsor. 9K 5
Old Windsor Lock. Old Win 8M 5
Old Woking. 8D 74
Old Wokingham Rd.
Wokgm & Crowt 6G 31
Old Woking Rd. W Byf 9H 55
Old Woking Rd. Wok 6D 74
Oldwood Chase. Farnb 2G 89
Old York Rd. SW18 8N 13
Oleander Clo. Crowt 9E 30
Oleander Clo. Orp 2M 67
Oliver Av. SE25 2C 46
Oliver Clo. W4 2A 12
Oliver Clo. Add 1K 55
Oliver Gro. SE25 3C 46
Olive Rd. SW19 8A 28
Oliver Rd. Asc 3L 33
Oliver Rd. H'ham 7G 197
Oliver Rd. N Mald 1B 42
Oliver Rd. Sutt 1B 62
Olivette St. SW15 6J 13
Olivia Ct. Wokgm 2A 30
Olivier Rd. M'bowr 4H 183
Ollerton. Brack 7M 31
Olley Clo. Wall 4J 63
Olveston Wlk. Cars 5B 44
O'Mahoney Ct. SW17 4A 28
Omega Rd. Wok 3C 74
Omega Way. Egh 9E 20
Omnibus Building. Reig 4N 121
One Tree Hill Rd. Guild 4D 114
Ongar Clo. Add 3H 55
Ongar Hill. Add 3J 55
Ongar Pde. Add 3J 55
Ongar Pl. Add 3J 55
Ongar Rd. SW6 2M 13
Ongar Rd. Add 2J 55
Onslow Av. Rich 8L 11
Onslow Av. Sutt 6L 61
Onslow Clo. Th Dit 7E 40
Onslow Clo. Wok 4C 74
Onslow Cres. Wok 4C 74
Onslow Dri. Asc 8L 17
Onslow Gdns. S Croy 8D 64
Onslow Gdns. Th Dit 7E 40
Onslow Gdns. Wall 3G 62
Onslow Ho. King T 1L 203
Onslow M. Cher 5H 37
Onslow Rd. Asc 6E 34
Onslow Rd. Croy 6K 45
Onslow Rd. Guild
3N 113 (3D 202)
Onslow Rd. N Mald 3F 42
Onslow Rd. Rich 8L 11
Onslow Rd. W on T 1G 57
Onslow St. Guild
4M 113 (5B 202)
Onslow Village. 5J 113
Onslow Way. Th Dit 7E 40
Onslow Way. Wok 2H 75
Ontario Clo. Small 9L 143
Openfields. Hdly 4D 168
Openview. SW18 2A 28
Ophelia Ho. W6 1J 13
(off Fulham Pal. Rd.)
Opladen Way. Brack 4A 32
Opossum Way. Houn 6K 9
Opus Pk. Sly I 8N 93
Oracle Cen. Brack 1A 32
Orange Ct. La. Orp 5J 67
Orangery, The. Rich 3J 25
Orbain Rd. SW6 3K 13
Orchard Av. Ashf 7D 22
Orchard Av. Croy 8H 47
Orchard Av. Felt 8E 8
Orchard Av. Houn 3M 9
Orchard Av. Mitc 7E 44
Orchard Av. N Mald 1D 42
Orchard Av. Th Dit 7G 41
Orchard Av. Wind 4D 4
Orchard Av. Wdhm 7H 55
Orchard Bus. Cen. Red 3E 142
Orchard Clo. Ashf 7D 22
Orchard Clo. SW20 3H 43
Orchard Clo. Ash V 8E 90
Orchard Clo. Bad L 6N 109
Orchard Clo. Bans 1N 81
Orchard Clo. B'water 5L 69
Orchard Clo. E Hor 2G 97
Orchard Clo. Eden 1K 147
Orchard Clo. Egh 6D 20
Orchard Clo. Elst 7H 131
Orchard Clo. Fet 9D 78
Orchard Clo. Guild 3D 114
Orchard Clo. Hasl 3D 188
Orchard Clo. Horl 7D 142
Orchard Clo. Lea 6F 78
Orchard Clo. Norm 3M 111
Orchard Clo. Surb 7H 41
Orchard Clo. W on T 6J 39
Orchard Clo. W End 9A 52
Orchard Clo. W Ewe 3A 60
Orchard Clo. Wok 3D 74
Orchard Clo. Wokgm 2C 30
Orchard Cotts. Charl 3L 161
Orchard Cotts. Chil 9G 114
Orchard Cotts. King T
9M 25 (2M 203)
Orchard Ct. Brack 1A 32
Orchard Ct. Iswth 3D 10
Orchard Ct. Ling 8N 145
Orchard Ct. Twic 3D 24
Orchard Ct. Wall 2F 62
Orchard Ct. W Dray 3L 7
Orchard Ct. Wor Pk 7F 42
Orchard Dene. W Byf 9J 55
(off Madeira Rd.)
Orchard Dri. Asht 7K 79
Orchard Dri. Eden 1K 147
Orchard Dri. Shep 3F 38
Orchard Dri. Wok 2A 74
Orchard End. Cat 9B 84
Orchard End. Fet 2C 98
Orchard End. Rowl 8E 128
Orchard End. Wey 8F 38
Orchard Fld. Rd. G'ming 4J 133
Orchard Fields. Fleet 4A 88
Orchard Gdns. Alder 4A 110
Orchard Gdns. Chess 1L 59
Orchard Gdns. Cranl 8A 156
Orchard Gdns. Eff 6M 97
Orchard Gdns. Eps 1B 80
Orchard Gdns. Sutt 2M 61
Orchard Ga. Esh 7D 40
Orchard Ga. Sand 7G 49
Orchard Gro. Croy 6H 47
Orchard Hill. Cars 2D 62
Orchard Hill. Rud 1D 194
Orchard Hill. W'sham 4A 52
Orchard Ho. SW6 3L 13
(off Varna Rd.)
Orchard Ho. Guild 2F 114
(off Merrow St.)
Orchard Ho. Tong 5D 110
Orchard La. SW20 9G 27
Orchard La. E Mol 5D 40
Orchard Lea Clo. Wok 2G 75
Orchard Leigh. Lea 9H 79
Orchard Mains. Wok 6M 73
Orchard Mobile Home Pk.
Tad 8A 100
Orchard Pk. Cvn. Site. Out 3K 143
Orchard Pl. Kes 5E 66
Orchard Pl. Wokgm 2B 30
Orchard Ri. Croy 7H 47
Orchard Ri. King T 9B 26
Orchard Ri. Rich 7A 12
Orchard Rd. Farnb 1M 89
Orchard Rd. Bad L 6M 109
Orchard Rd. Bren 2J 11
Orchard Rd. Chess 1L 59
Orchard Rd. Dork 6H 119
Orchard Rd. F'boro 2K 67
Orchard Rd. Felt 2H 23
Orchard Rd. Guild 8D 94
Orchard Rd. Hamp 8N 23
Orchard Rd. H'ham 7L 197
Orchard Rd. Houn 8N 9
Orchard Rd. King T
1L 41 (4J 203)
Orchard Rd. Mitc 7E 44
Orchard Rd. Old Win 9L 5
Orchard Rd. Onsl 5J 113
Orchard Rd. Reig 3N 121
Orchard Rd. Rich 6N 11
Orchard Rd. Shalf 9A 114
Orchard Rd. Shere 8B 116
Orchard Rd. Small 8N 143
Orchard Rd. S Croy 1E 84
Orchard Rd. Sun 8J 23
Orchard Rd. Sutt 2M 61
Orchard Rd. Twic 8G 11
Orchards Clo. W Byf 1J 75
Orchard Sq. W14 1L 13
Orchards, The. H'ham 3M 197
Orchards, The. If'd 4J 181
Orchard St. Craw 3B 182
Orchard, The. Bans 2M 81
Orchard, The. Broad H 5D 196
Orchard, The. Eps 4E 60
(Meadow Wlk.)
Orchard, The. Eps 6E 60
(Tayles Hill)
Orchard, The. Horl 8E 142
Orchard, The. H'ham 4A 198
Orchard, The. Houn 5C 10
Orchard, The. Light 7L 51
Orchard, The. N Holm 9J 119
Orchard, The. Vir W 4A 36
Orchard, The. Wey 1C 56
Orchard, The. Wok 9A 74
Orchard Way. Ashf 3A 22
Orchard Way. Add 2K 55
Orchard Way. Alder 4A 110
Orchard Way. Camb 4N 69
Orchard Way. Croy 7H 47
Orchard Way. Dork 6H 119
Orchard Way. E Grin 1N 185
Orchard Way. Esh 3C 58
Orchard Way. Norm 3M 111
Orchard Way. Oxt 2C 126
Orchard Way. Reig 6N 121
Orchard Way. Send 3E 94
Orchard Way. Sutt 1B 62
Orchard Way. Tad 4L 101
Orchid Clo. Chess 4J 59
Orchid Ct. Egh 5D 20
Orchid Dri. Bisl 2D 72
Orchid Mead. Bans 1N 81
Orde Clo. Craw 9H 163
Ordnance Clo. Felt 3H 23
Ordnance Rd. Alder 2N 109
Ordnance Roundabout. Alder
2N 109
Oregano Way. Guild 7K 93
Oregon Clo. N Mald 3B 42
Orestan La. Eff 5J 97
Orewell Gdns. Reig 5N 121
Orford Ct. SE27 3M 29
Orford Gdns. Twic 3F 24
Organ Crossroads. (Junct.)
4F 60
Oriel Clo. Craw 9G 162
Oriel Clo. Mitc 3H 45
Oriel Ct. Croy 7A 46 (1D 200)
Oriel Dri. SW13 2H 13
Oriel Hill. Camb 2B 70
Oriental Clo. Wok 4B 74
Oriental Rd. Asc 3A 34
Oriental Rd. Wok 4B 74
Orion. Brack 7M 31
Orion Cen., The. Croy 8J 45
Orion Ct. Bew 5J 181
Orlando Gdns. Eps 6C 60
Orleans Clo. Esh 8D 40
Orleans Ct. Twic 1H 25
Orleans House Gallery. 2H 25
Orleans Rd. Twic 1H 25
Orltons La. Rusp 8E 160
Ormathwaites Corner. Warf 8C 16
Ormeley Rd. SW12 2F 28
Orme Rd. King T 1A 42
Ormerod Gdns. Mitc 1E 44
Ormesby Wlk. Craw 5F 182
Ormond Av. Hamp 9B 24
Ormond Av. Rich 8K 11
Ormond Cres. Hamp 9B 24
Ormond Dri. Hamp 8B 24
Ormonde Av. Eps 6C 60
Ormonde Ct. SW15 7H 13
Ormonde Rd. SW14 6B 12
Ormonde Rd. G'ming 5H 133
Ormonde Rd. Wok 3M 73
Ormonde Rd. Wokgm 3A 30

Pembroke Pl.—Pitchfont La.

Pembroke Pl. Iswth 5E 10
Pembroke Rd. SE25 . . . . . 3B 46
Pembroke Rd. Craw 9G 163
Pembroke Rd. Mitc 1E 44
Pembroke Rd. Wok 5C 74
Pembroke Vs. Rich 7K 11
Pembury Av. Wor Pk 7F 42
Pembury Clo. Coul 1E 82
Pembury Ct. Hay 2E 8
Pembury Pl. Alder 3A 110
Pembury Rd. SE25 . . . . . 3D 46
Pemdevon Rd. Croy 6L 45
Pemerich Clo. Hay 1G 8
Penates. Esh 1D 58
Penbury Rd. S'hall 1N 9
Pendarves Rd. SW20 . . . . . 9H 27
Pendarvis Ct. Gray 6A 170
Pendell Av. Hay 3G 8
Pendell Rd. Blet 9M 103
Pendennis Clo. W Byf 1J 75
Pendennis Rd. SW16 . . . . . 5J 29
Penderel Rd. Houn 8A 10
Pendine Pl. Brack 4N 31
Pendlebury. Brack 6M 31
Pendlebury Ct. Surb 8K 203
Pendle Rd. SW16 . . . . . 7F 28
Pendleton Clo. Red 4D 122
Pendleton Rd. Reig 6A 122
Pendragon Way. Camb 2H 71
Pendry's La. Binf 1M 15
Penfold Clo. Croy 9L 45
Penfold Cft. Farnh 8L 109
(in two parts)
Penfold Rd. M'bowr 7F 182
Penge Rd. SE25 & SE20 . . . . . 2D 46
Pengilly Rd. Farnh 2G 128
Penhurst. Wok 1D 74
Peninsular Clo. Camb 8F 50
Peninsular Clo. Felt 9E 8
Penistone Rd. SW16 . . . . . 8J 29
Penlee Clo. Eden 1L 147
Pennards, The. Sun 2K 39
Penn Clo. Craw 9B 162
Penn Ct. Craw 3L 181
Pennefather's Rd. Alder 1L 109
Penner Clo. SW19 . . . . . 3K 27
Penners Gdns. Surb 6L 41
Pennine Clo. Craw 3N 181
Pennine Way. Farnb 7J 69
Pennine Way. Hay 3E 8
Pennings Av. Guild 1J 113
Pennington Clo. SE27 . . . . . 5N 29
Pennington Dri. Wey 9F 38
Pennington Lodge. Surb 8K 203
Penn Rd. Dat 4N 5
Penns Wood. Farnb 4D 90
Pennycroft. Croy 5H 65
Penny Dri. Wood S 2E 112
Pennyfield. Cob 9H 57
Penny Hill Cvn. Pk. B'water 4B 68
Pennyhill Park. 5F 50
Penny La. Shep 6F 38
Pennymead Dri. E Hor 5G 96
Pennymead Ri. E Hor 5G 96
Penny M. SW12 . . . . . 1F 28
Penny Pot. 8F 52
Pennypot La. Chob 9E 52
Penny Royal. Wall 3H 63
Penrhyn Clo. Alder 9N 109
Penrhyn Cres. SW14 . . . . . 7B 12
Penrhyn Gdns. King T
. . . . . 3K 41 (7H 203)
Penrhyn Rd. King T
. . . . . 3L 41 (7J 203)
Penrith Clo. SW15 . . . . . 8K 13
Penrith Clo. Reig 2C 122
Penrith Pl. SE27 . . . . . 3M 29
Penrith Rd. N Mald 3C 42
Penrith Rd. T Hth 1N 45
Penrith St. SW16 . . . . . 7G 28
Penrose Ct. Egh 7N 19
(in two parts)
Penrose Dri. Eps 7N 59
Penrose Rd. Fet 9C 78
Penryn Dri. Hdly D 4H 169
Pensfold La. Rud 3F 194
Pensford Av. Rich 5N 11
Pensford Clo. Crowt 9G 30
Penshurst Clo. Craw 2H 183
Penshurst Ri. Frim 6D 70
Penshurst Rd. T Hth 4M 45
Penshurst Way. Sutt 4M 61
Pentelow Gdns. Felt 9H 9
Pentland Av. Shep 4B 38
Pentland Gdns. SW18 . . . . . 9N 13
Pentland Pl. Farnb 7K 69
Pentlands Clo. Mitc 2F 44
Pentland St. SW18
. . . . . 9N 13 & 1A 20
Pentlow St. SW15 . . . . . 6H 13
Pentney Rd. SW12 . . . . . 2G 28
Pentney Rd. SW19 . . . . . 9K 27
Penton Av. Stai 8H 21
Penton Hall. Stai 9J 21
Penton Hall Dri. Stai 9J 21
Penton Hook Rd. Stai 8J 21
Penton Pk. (Cvn. Site). Cher
. . . . . 2K 37
Penton Rd. Stai 8H 21
Pentreath Av. Guild 4J 113
Penwerris Av. Iswth 3C 10
Penwerris Ct. Houn 3C 10
Penwith Dri. Hasl 4B 188
Penwith Rd. SW18 . . . . . 3M 27
Penwith Wlk. Wok 6N 73
Penwood End. Wok 8L 73
Penwood Gdns. Brack 5J 31
Penwood Ho. SW15 . . . . . 9E 12
Penwortham Rd. SW16 . . . . . 7F 28
Penwortham Rd. S Croy 6N 63
Pen-y-Bos Track. Hasl 7K 189
Penywern Rd. SW5 . . . . . 1M 13
Peperham Ho. Hasl 1G 189
Peperham Rd. Hasl 9G 171
Peper Harow. 6N 131
Peperharow La. Shack 5N 131
Peperharow Rd. G'ming 5E 132
Peppard Rd. M'bowr 6H 183
Pepperbox La. Brmly 5F 154
Pepper Clo. Cat 3B 104
Peppercorn Clo. T Hth 1A 46
Peppermint Clo. Croy 6J 45
Peppers Yd. H'ham 5K 197
Pepys Clo. Asht 4N 79
Pepys Clo. Slou 2D 6
Pepys Rd. SW20 . . . . . 9H 27
Percheron Clo. Iswth 6F 10
Percheron Dri. Knap 6H 72
Percival Clo. Oxs 7B 58
Percival Rd. SW14 . . . . . 7B 12
Percival Rd. Felt 3G 22
Percival Way. Eps 1C 60
Percy Av. Ashf 6B 22
Percy Bryant Rd. Sun 8F 22
Percy Gdns. Iswth 6G 11
Percy Gdns. Wor Pk 7D 42
Percy Pl. Dat 4L 5
Percy Rd. SE20 . . . . . 1G 46
Percy Rd. SE25 . . . . . 4D 46
Percy Rd. Guild 1L 113
Percy Rd. Hamp 8A 24
Percy Rd. H'ham 5H 197
Percy Rd. Iswth 7G 11
Percy Rd. Mitc 6E 44
Percy Rd. Twic 2B 24
Percy Way. Twic 2C 24
Peregrine Clo. Brack 4N 31
Peregrine Clo. Cranl 6N 155
Peregrine Ct. SW16 . . . . . 5K 29
Peregrine Gdns. Croy 8H 47
Peregrine Rd. Sun 1G 38
Peregrine Way. SW19 . . . . . 8H 27
Perham Rd. W14 . . . . . 1K 13
Perifield. SE21 . . . . . 2N 29
Perimeter Rd. E. Gat A 3F 162
Perimeter Rd. N. Gat A 2B 162
(Cargo Rd., in two parts)
Perimeter Rd. N. Gat A 3B 162
(Larkins Rd.)
Perimeter Rd. S. Gat A 5A 162
Periwinkle Clo. Lind 4B 168
Perkin Clo. Houn 7A 10
Perkins Ct. Ashf 6A 22
Perkstead Ct. Craw 6M 181
(off Waddington Clo.)
Perleybrooke La. Wok 4K 73
Perowne St. Alder 2L 109
Perran Rd. SW2 . . . . . 2M 29
Perran Wlk. Bren 1L 11
Perrin Clo. Ashf 6A 22
Perrin Ct. Wok 2D 74
Perring Av. Farnb 6K 69
Perrior Rd. G'ming 4H 133
Perry Av. E Grin 7A 166
Perry Clo. G'ming 6K 133
Perrycroft. Wind 6B 4
Perryfield Rd. Craw 4A 182
Perryfield Way. Rich 4H 25
Perry Hill. Worp 5H 93
(in two parts)
Perryhill Dri. Sand 6E 48
Perry How. Wor Pk 7E 42
Perrylands. Charl 3L 161
Perrylands La. Charl 9K 143
Perrymead St. SW6 . . . . . 4M 13
Perryn Ct. Twic 9G 10
Perry Oaks. Brack 1C 32
Perry Oaks Dri. W Dray & H'row A
. . . . . 5K 7
Perry Way. Brack 1C 32
Perry Way. Farnh 5G 109
Perry Way. Head 5E 168
Perry Way. Light 8K 51
Perrywood Bus. Pk. Red 2F 142
Perseverance Cotts. Rip 8L 75
Perseverance Pl. Rich 7L 11
Persfield Clo. Eps 6E 60
Persfield M. Eps 6E 60
Pershore Gro. Cars 5B 44
Perth Clo. SW20 . . . . . 1E 42
Perth Clo. Craw 9B 162
Perth Rd. Beck 1M 47
Perth Way. H'ham 4M 197
Petavel Rd. Tedd 7E 24
Peter Av. Oxt 7N 105
Peterborough M. SW6 . . . . . 5M 13
Peterborough Rd. SW6 . . . . . 5M 13
Peterborough Rd. Cars 5C 44
Peterborough Rd. Craw 7C 182
Peterborough Rd. Guild 1J 113
Peterborough Vs. SW6 . . . . . 4N 13
Petergate. SW11 . . . . . 7N 13
Peterhead M. Langl 1C 6
Peterhouse Clo. Owl 5L 49
Peterhouse Pde. Craw 9G 162
Peterlee Wlk. Bew 7K 181
**Peter Scott Vis. Cen., The.
. . . . . 4G 12**
Petersfield Av. Stai 6L 21
Petersfield Cres. Coul 2J 83
Petersfield Ri. SW15 . . . . . 2G 26
Petersfield Rd. Stai 6L 21
Petersham. 2L 25
Petersham Av. Byfl 8N 55
Petersham Clo. Byfl 8N 55
Petersham Clo. Rich 3K 25
Petersham Clo. Sutt 2L 61
Petersham Rd. Rich 9K 11
Petersham Ter. Croy 9J 45
(off Richmond Grn.)
Petersmead Clo. Tad 1H 101
Peterstow Clo. SW19 . . . . . 3K 27
Peterswood. Capel 5J 159
Peterwood Pk. Croy 8K 45
Peterwood Way. Croy 8K 45
Petley Rd. W6 . . . . . 2J 13
Petridge Rd. Red 8D 122
**Petridge Wood Common.
. . . . . 8D 122**
Petters Rd. Asht 3M 79
Pettiward Clo. SW15 . . . . . 7H 13
Petts La. Shep 3B 38
Petworth Clo. Coul 6G 82
Petworth Clo. Frim 6D 70
Petworth Ct. Craw 6L 181
Petworth Ct. Hasl 2H 189
Petworth Dri. H'ham 1M 197
Petworth Gdns. SW20 . . . . . 2G 42
Petworth Rd. C'fold 2C 190
Petworth Rd. Hasl & C'fold
. . . . . 2H 189
Petworth Rd. Milf & Witl 3B 152
Petworth Rd. Wmly 8C 152
Pevensey Clo. Craw 4G 182
Pevensey Clo. Iswth 3C 10
Pevensey Rd. SW17 . . . . . 5B 28
Pevensey Rd. Felt 2M 23
Pevensey Way. Frim 6D 70
Peverel Rd. If'd 4K 181
Peveril Dri. Tedd 6D 24
Pewley Bank. Guild
. . . . . 5A 114 (6F 202)
Pewley Hill. Guild
. . . . . 5N 113 (6D 202)
Pewley Point. Guild
. . . . . 5A 114 (7F 202)
Pewley Way. Guild
. . . . . 5A 114 (6F 202)
Pewsey Va. Brack 4D 32
Peyton's Cotts. Nutf 1K 123
Pharaoh Clo. Mitc 6D 44
Pharaoh's Island. Shep 8A 38
Pheasant Clo. Purl 9M 63
Phelps Way. Hay 1G 9
Philanthropic Rd. Red 4E 122
Philbeach Gdns. SW5 . . . . . 1L 13
Philip Gdns. Croy 8J 47
Philip Rd. Stai 7M 21
Philips Clo. Cars 7E 44
Phillips Copse. Brack 6B 32
Phillips Clo. Hdly 4E 168
Phillips Clo. G'ming 9G 132
Phillips Clo. M'bowr 8F 182
Phillips Clo. Tong 6C 110
Phillips Cres. Hdly 4E 168
Phillips Hatch. Won 3E 134
Phillip's Quad. Wok 5A 74
Philpot La. Chob 9L 53
Philpot Sq. SW6 . . . . . 6N 13
Phipps Bri. Rd. SW19 . . . . . 1A 44
Phoenix Bus. Pk. Brack 1H 31
Phoenix Clo. Eps 8N 59
Phoenix Clo. W Wick 8N 47
Phoenix Ct. Alder 3M 109
Phoenix Ct. Guild
. . . . . 5N 113 (6C 202)
Phoenix Ct. Houn 8L 9
Phoenix Ct. S Croy 2C 64
Phoenix Dri. Kes 1F 66
Phoenix Ho. Sutt 1N 61
Phoenix La. Ash W 3G 186
Phoenix Trad. Pk. Bren 1K 11
Phoenix Way. Houn 2L 9
Phyllis Av. N Mald 4G 42
Phyllis Ho. Croy 7A 200
Piccards, The. Guild 7M 113
Pickering. Brack 3M 31
Pickering Gdns. Croy 5C 46
Picket Post Clo. Brack 2D 32
Pickets St. SW12 . . . . . 1F 28
Picketts Hill. Slea 9A 140
Pickett's La. Horl 4H 163
Picketts La. Red 2G 142
Pickford St. Alder 2N 109
Pickhurst La. W Wick & Brom
. . . . . 4N 47
Pickhurst Ri. W Wick 6M 47
Pickhurst Rd. C'fold 6F 172
Pickins Piece. Hort 5C 6
Pickwick Clo. Houn 8M 9
Pickwick Gdns. Camb 2F 70
Picquets Way. Bans 3K 81
Picton Clo. Camb 8G 50
Picts Hill. H'ham 9G 197
Pierrefonde's Av. Farnb 9M 69
Pier Rd. Felt 8J 9
Pierson Rd. Wind 4A 4
Pier Ter. SW18 . . . . . 7N 13
Pigbush La. Loxw 1H 193
Pigeon Ho. La. Coul 3A 102
Pigeonhouse La. Wink 4H 17
Pigeon La. Hamp 5A 24
Pigeon Pass. Turn H 4F 184
Piggott Ct. H'ham 7K 197
Piggott Rd. Wokgm 9C 14
Pig Pound Wlk. Hand 6N 199
Pike Clo. Alder 3A 110
Pikemans Ct. SW5 . . . . . 1M 13
(off W. Cromwell Rd.)
Pikes Hill. Eps 9D 60 (6M 201)
Pikes La. Crow 2A 146
Pilgrim Clo. Mord 6N 43
Pilgrim Ct. Milf 2C 152
Pilgrim Hill. SE27 . . . . . 5N 29
Pilgrims Clo. Farnh 3F 128
Pilgrim's Clo. Shere 8B 116
Pilgrims Clo. Westh 9G 99
Pilgrims' La. Cat 4K 103
Pilgrims La. T'sey & W'ham
. . . . . 3D 106
Pilgrims Pl. Reig 1M 121
Pilgrims Vw. As 4G 111
Pilgrims Way. Hdly 4D 168
Pilgrim's Way. Bisl 3D 72
Pilgrims Way. Guild 7N 113
(in two parts)
Pilgrim's Way. Reig 1L 121
Pilgrim's Way. Shere 8B 116
Pilgrims' Way. Shere 9H 115
Pilgrims Way. S Croy 2C 64
Pilgrims Way. W'ham 1H 107
Pilgrims Way. Westh 9H 99
Pilgrims Way Cotts. Bet 2B 120
Pilsden Clo. SW19 . . . . . 2J 27
Pilton Est., The. Croy
. . . . . 8M 45 (2A 200)
Pimms Clo. Guild 8C 94
Pinckards. C'fold 4D 172
Pincott La. W Hor 7C 96
Pincott Rd. SW19 . . . . . 8A 28
Pine Av. Camb 2B 70
Pine Av. W Wick 7L 47
Pine Bank. Hind 5C 170
Pine Clo. Ryl M 9K 49
Pine Clo. Ash V 7E 90
Pine Clo. Bord 7A 168
Pine Clo. Craw 9A 162
Pine Clo. Kenl 4A 84
Pine Clo. New H 7K 55
Pine Clo. Wok 3M 73
Pine Coombe. Croy 1G 64
Pinecote Dri. Asc 6C 34
Pine Ct. Alder 2M 109
Pine Ct. Brack 3C 32
Pine Ct. Myt 2E 90
Pine Cres. Cars 7B 62
Pinecrest Gdns. Orp 1K 67
Pine Cft. Rd. Wokgm 6A 30
Pine Dean. Bookh 3B 98
Pine Dri. B'water 3K 69
Pinefields. Add 1K 55
(off Church Rd.)
Pinefields Clo. Crowt 2G 48
Pine Gdns. Horl 9E 142
Pine Gdns. Surb 5N 41
Pine Glade. Orp 1H 67
Pine Gro. SW19 . . . . . 6L 27
Pine Gro. C Crook 8C 88
(in two parts)
Pine Gro. E Grin 7L 165
Pine Gro. Eden 1K 147
Pine Gro. Lwr Bo 6K 129
Pine Gro. Wey 2C 56
Pine Gro. W'sham 3A 52
Pine Gro. M. Wey 2D 56
Pine Hill. Eps 2C 80
Pinehill Ri. Sand 7H 49
Pinehill Rd. Crowt 3G 49
Pinehurst. H'ham 4J 197
Pinehurst. S'hill 4A 34
Pinehurst Av. Farnb 3N 89
Pinehurst Clo. Kgswd 9M 81
Pinehurst Cotts. Farnb 3N 89
Pinehurst Roundabout. Farnb
. . . . . 2N 89
Pinel Clo. Vir W 3A 36
Pine Mt. Rd. Camb 2B 70
Pine Pl. Bans 1J 81
Pine Ridge. Cars 4E 62
Pine Ridge Dri. Lwr Bo 6G 129
Pine Rd. Wok 7M 73
Pines Bus. Pk., The. Guild 1H 113
Pine Shaw. Craw 2H 183
Pines Rd. Fleet 3A 88
Pines, The. SE19 . . . . . 8M 29
Pines, The. Coul 5F 82
Pines, The. Dork 6H 119
Pines, The. H'ham 3B 198
Pines, The. Purl 9N 63
Pines, The. Sun 2H 39
Pines, The. Wok 1B 74
Pinetops. H'ham 3B 198
Pine Tree Clo. Houn 4J 9
Pine Tree Hill. Wok 3F 74
Pine Trees Bus. Pk. Stai 6G 20
Pinetrees Clo. Copt 7M 163
Pine Vw. Hdly D 3H 169
Pine Vw. Clo. Bad L 7M 109
Pine Vw. Clo. Chil 9H 115
Pine Vw. Clo. Hasl 9G 170
Pine Wlk. Cob 1L 77
Pine Wlk. Bans 4D 82
Pine Wlk. Bookh 3B 98
Pine Wlk. Cars 6B 62
Pine Wlk. Cat 9D 84
Pine Wlk. E Hor 6G 97
Pine Wlk. Surb 5N 41
Pine Wlk. E. Cars 7B 62
Pine Wlk. W. Cars 6B 62
Pine Way. Eng G 7L 19
Pine Way Clo. E Grin 2A 186
Pinewood. 9G 31
Pine Wood. Sun 9H 23
Pinewood Av. Crowt 1H 49
Pinewood Av. New H 5L 55
Pinewood Cvn. Pk. Wokgm 8H 31
Pinewood Clo. Broad H 5D 196
Pinewood Clo. Croy 9H 47
Pinewood Clo. Sand 7E 48
Pinewood Clo. Wok 2C 74
Pinewood Ct. Add 1M 55
Pinewood Ct. Fleet 3B 88
Pinewood Cres. Farnb 9H 69
Pinewood Dri. Orp 2N 67
Pinewood Dri. Stai 6J 21
Pinewood Gdns. Bag 4G 50
Pinewood Gro. New H 6K 55
Pinewood Hill. Fleet 3B 88
Pinewood M. Stai 9M 7
Pinewood Pk. Farnb 7H 69
Pinewood Pk. New H 7K 55
Pinewood Pl. Eps 1C 60
Pinewood Rd. As 1H 111
Pinewood Rd. Felt 4J 23
Pinewood Rd. Vir W 3K 35
Piney Copse. 8F 116
Pinfold Rd. SW16 . . . . . 5J 29
Pinglestone Clo. W Dray 3N 7
Pinkcoat Clo. Felt 4J 23
Pinkerton Pl. SW16 . . . . . 5H 29
Pinkham Mans. W4 . . . . . 1N 11
Pinkhurst La. Slin 6A 196
Pinks Hill. 2F 112
Pioneer Pl. Croy 5K 65
Pioneers Ind. Pk. Croy 7J 45
Piper Rd. King T 2N 41 (5M 203)
Pipers Clo. Cob 2L 77
Pipers Cft. C Crook 9B 88
Pipers End. Slin 5M 195
Piper's End. Vir W 2N 35
Piper's Gdns. Croy 6H 47
Pipers La. N'chap 8D 190
Pipers Patch. Farnb 1N 89
Pipewell Rd. Cars 5C 44
Pippbrook. 4J 119 (1L 201)
Pippbrook Gdns. Dork 4H 119
Pippin Clo. Croy 7J 47
Pippins Ct. Ashf 7C 22
Pipson La. Yat 1C 68
Pipsons Clo. Yat 9C 48
Piquet Rd. SE20 . . . . . 1F 46
Pirbright. 1C 92
Pirbright Camp. 8M 71
Pirbright Cres. New Ad 3M 65
Pirbright Grn. Pirb 1C 92
Pirbright Rd. Farnb 2A 90
Pirbright Rd. SW18 . . . . . 2L 27
Pirbright Rd. Norm 1J 111
Pirbright Ter. Pirb 1C 92
Piries Pl. H'ham 6J 197
(off East St.)
Pisley La. Ockl 6N 157
Pitcairn Rd. Mitc 8D 28
Pitchfont La. Oxt 2B 106
(in three parts)

Primrose Ct.—Queens Pine

Primrose Ct. As 2E 110
Primrose Dri. Bisl 2D 72
Primrose Gdns. Farnb 2K 89
Primrose La. Croy 7F 46
Primrose La. F Row 8J 187
Primrose Pl. G'ming 9E 132
Primrose Ridge. G'ming 9E 132
Primrose Rd. W on T 2K 57
Primrose Wlk. Brack 4A 32
Primrose Wlk. Eps 4E 60
Primrose Wlk. Fleet 3A 88
Primrose Wlk. Yat 9A 48
Primrose Way. Brmly 6N 133
Primrose Way. Sand 6G 49
Primula Rd. Bord 6A 168
Prince Albert Dri. Asc 3H 33
Prince Albert Sq. Red 8D 122
Prince Albert's Wlk. Wind 4K 5
Prince Andrew Way. Asc 1H 33
Prince Charles Cres. Farnb 6N 69
Prince Charles Way. Wall 9F 44
Prince Consort Cotts. Wind 5G 4
Prince Consort Dri. Asc 3H 33
Prince Consort's Dri. Wind 9C 4
(in two parts)
Prince Dri. Sand 6F 48
Prince George's Av. SW20 1H 43
Prince George's Rd. SW19 9B 28
Prince of Wales Ct. Alder 2L 109
(off Queen Elizabeth Dri.)
Prince of Wales Rd. Out 2L 143
Prince of Wales Rd. Sutt 8B 44
Prince of Wales Ter. W4 1D 12
Prince of Wales Wlk. Camb 9A 50
Prince Regent Rd. Houn 6C 10
Prince Rd. SE25 4B 46
Prince's Av. Alder 0N 89
Princes Av. Cars 4D 62
Prince's Av. G'ming 4F 132
Princes Av. S Croy 2E 84
Princes Av. Surb 7N 41
Princes Clo. Eton W 1C 4
Princes Clo. S Croy 2E 84
Prince's Clo. Tedd 5D 24
Prince's Dri. Oxs 8E 58
Princes Mead (Shop. Cen.). Farnb 1N 89
Princes M. W6 1G 13
(off Down Pl.)
Princes M. Houn 7A 10
Princes Rd. Ashf 6A 22
Princes Rd. SW14 6C 12
Prince's Rd. SW19 7M 27
Princes Rd. Egh 7B 20
Princes Rd. Felt 3G 22
Princes Rd. Kew 4M 11
Princes Rd. King T 8N 25
Prince's Rd. Red 5D 122
Princes Rd. Rich 8M 11
Prince's Rd. Tedd 5D 24
Princes Rd. Wey 2C 56
Princess Anne Rd. Rud 1E 194
Princess Av. Wind 6E 4
Princess Ct. King T 6L 203
Princess Gdns. Wok 3D 74
Princess Ho. Red 2E 122
Princess Margaret Rd. Rud 1E 194
Princess Marys Rd. Add 1L 55
Princess M. King T 2M 41 (6L 203)
Princess Pde. Orp 1J 67
Princess Precinct. Horl 8E 142
(off High St.)
Princess Rd. Craw 3A 182
Princess Rd. Croy 5N 45
Princess Rd. Wok 3D 74
Princess Sq. Brack 1N 31
Princes St. Rich 7L 11
Princes St. Sutt 1B 62
Princess Way. Camb 9A 50
Princess Way. Red 2E 122
Princes Way. SW19 1J 27
Princes Way. Alder 2M 109
Princes Way. Bag 6J 51
Princes Way. Croy 2K 63
Princes Way. W Wick 1B 66
Princeton Ct. SW15 6J 13
Princeton M. King T 9N 25 (2M 203)
Pringle Gdns. SW16 5G 28
(in two parts)
Pringle Gdns. Purl 6K 63
Prior Av. Sutt 4C 62
Prior Cft. Clo. Camb 2E 70
Prior End. Camb 1E 70
Prioress Rd. SE27 4M 29
Prior Rd. Camb 1E 70
Priors Clo. Farnb 6M 69
Priors Ct. As 3D 110
Priors Ct. Wok 5K 73
Prior's Cft. Wok 7C 74
Priorsfield Rd. Comp & Hurt 9C 112
Priors Hatch La. Hurt 2C 132
Priors Keep. Fleet 5C 88
Prior's La. B'water 1F 68
Priors Mead. Bookh 3C 98
Priors Rd. Wind 6A 4
Priors, The. Asht 6K 79
Priors Wlk. Craw 3C 182
Priorswood. Comp 1C 132
Priors Wood. Crowt 3C 48
Priorswood. Hasl 2D 188
Priory Av. Sutt 1J 61
Priory Clo. SW19 9N 27
Priory Clo. Asc 6D 34
Priory Clo. Beck 2H 47
Priory Clo. Dork 7G 119
Priory Clo. Hamp 9N 23
Priory Clo. Horl 7D 142
Priory Clo. Sun 8H 23
Priory Clo. W on T 9H 39
Priory Clo. Wok 9F 54
Priory Ct. Camb 1L 69
Priory Ct. Dork 7H 119
Priory Ct. Eps 5E 60
Priory Ct. Guild 7M 113
Priory Ct. Houn 6B 10
Priory Ct. King T 5J 203
Priory Ct. Sutt 1K 61
Priory Cres. SE19 8N 29
Priory Cres. Sutt 1J 61
Priory Dri. Reig 5M 121
Priory Gdns. Ashf 6E 22
Priory Gdns. SE25 3C 46
Priory Gdns. SW13 6E 12
Priory Gdns. Hamp 8N 23
Priory Grn. Stai 6K 21
Priory La. SW15 9D 12
Priory La. Brack 8A 16
Priory La. Fren 2K 149
Priory La. Rich 3N 11
Priory La. W Mol 3B 40
Priory M. Stai 6K 21
Priory Pk. Fleet 4A 88
Priory Pl. W on T 9H 39
Priory Rd. SW19 8B 28
Priory Rd. Asc 9F 16
Priory Rd. Chess 9L 41
Priory Rd. Croy 6L 45
Priory Rd. F Row 9D 186
Priory Rd. Hamp 8N 23
Priory Rd. Houn 8C 10
Priory Rd. Reig 5M 121
Priory Rd. Rich 2N 11
Priory Rd. S'dale 6D 34
Priory Rd. Sutt 1J 61
Priory St. Farnb 1B 90
Priory Ter. Sun 8H 23
Priory, The. Croy 1L 63
Priory, The. God 9E 104
Priory, The. Lea 9H 79
Priory Wlk. Brack 3D 32
Priory Way. Dat 3L 5
Priory Way. W Dray 2N 7
Privet Rd. Lind 4B 168
Probyn Rd. SW2 3M 29
Proctor Clo. M'bowr 5G 183
Proctor Clo. Mitc 9E 28
Proctor Gdns. Bookh 3B 98
Proctors Clo. Felt 2H 23
Proctors Rd. Wokgm 2E 30
Proffits Cotts. Tad 9J 81
Profumo Rd. W on T 2L 57
Progress Bus. Pk., The. Croy 8K 45
Progress Way. Croy 8K 45
Promenade App. Rd. W4 3D 12
Promenade de Verdun. Purl 7H 63
Promenade, The. W4 5D 12
Prospect Av. Farnb 8N 69
Prospect Clo. Houn 4N 9
Prospect Cotts. SW18 7M 13
Prospect Cres. Twic 9C 10
Prospect Hill. Hdly 1D 168
Prospect Ho. Eps 5A 60
Prospect La. Eng G 6K 19
Prospect Pl. SW20 8G 27
Prospect Pl. W4 1C 12
Prospect Pl. Craw 3A 182
Prospect Pl. Egh 6A 20
Prospect Pl. Eps 8D 60 (6L 201)
Prospect Pl. Stai 6H 21
Prospect Quay. SW18 7M 13
(off Lightermans Wlk.)
Prospect Rd. Farnb 1M 89
Prospect Rd. Ash V 8E 90
Prospect Rd. Rowl 8D 128
Prospect Rd. Surb 5J 41
Prossers. Tad 8J 81
Prothero Rd. SW6 3K 13
Providence La. Hay 3E 8
Providence Pl. Eps 8D 60 (5M 201)
Providence Pl. W Byf 1J 75
Providence Ter. Turn H 5D 184
Prune Hill. Eng G 8N 19
Prunus Clo. W End 9B 52
Public Record Office 3A 12
Puckridge Hill Rd. Alder 7K 89
Puckshill. Knap 4G 73
Puckshott Way. Hasl 9H 171
Puddenhole Cotts. Brock 2N 119
Pudding La. Charl 2K 161
Puffin Clo. Beck 4G 46
Puffin Hill. Turn H 4F 184
Puffin Rd. If'd 4J 181
Pulborough Rd. SW18 1L 27
Pulborough Way. Houn 7K 9
Pullman Ct. SW2 2J 29
Pullman Gdns. SW15 9H 13
Pullman La. G'ming 9F 132
Pullmans Pl. Stai 6J 21
Pulton Pl. SW6 3M 13
Pump All. Bren 3K 11
Pumping Sta. Rd. W4 3D 12
Pump La. Asc 9B 18
Pump Pail N. Croy 9N 45 (5B 200)
Pump Pail S. Croy 9N 45 (5B 200)
Punchbowl La. Dork 4K 119
Punch Copse Rd. Craw 2D 182
Punnetts Ct. Craw 6L 181
Purbeck Av. N Mald 5E 42
Purbeck Clo. Red 6H 103
(in two parts)
Purbeck Ct. Guild 3H 113
Purbeck Dri. Wok 1B 74
Purberry Gro. Eps 6E 60
Purbrook Ct. Brack 5C 32
Purcell Clo. Kenl 1N 83
Purcell Cres. SW6 3J 13
Purcell Mans. W14 2K 13
(off Queen's Club Gdns.)
Purcell Rd. Craw 6L 181
Purcell Rd. Crowt 9G 30
Purcell's Clo. Asht 5M 79
Purdy Ct. Wor Pk 8F 42
Purley 7L 63
Purley Bury Av. Purl 7N 63
Purley Bury Clo. Purl 7N 63
Purley Clo. M'bowr 6H 183
Purley Cross. (Junct.) 8L 63
Purley Downs Rd. Purl 6N 63
Purley Hill. Purl 8M 63
Purley Knoll. Purl 7K 63
Purley Oaks Rd. S Croy 5A 64
Purley Pde. Purl 7L 63
Purley Pk. Rd. Purl 6M 63
Purley Ri. Purl 8K 63
Purley Rd. Purl 7L 63
Purley Rd. S Croy 4A 64
Purley Va. Purl 9M 63
Purley Vw. Ter. S Croy 4A 64
(off Sanderstead Rd.)
Purley Way. Croy 6K 45
Purley Way. Frim 6C 70
Purley Way Cen., The. Croy 8L 45
Purley Way Corner. Croy 6K 45
Purley Way Cres. Croy 6K 45
Purmerend Clo. Farnb 9H 69
Purser Ho. SW2 1L 29
(off Tulse Hill)
Pursers Cross Rd. SW6 4L 13
(in two parts)
Pursers La. Peasl 2E 136
Purslane. Wokgm 3C 30
Purton Rd. H'ham 4H 197
Putney 7K 13
Putney Bri. SW15 & SW6 6K 13
Putney Bri. App. SW6 6K 13
Putney Bri. Rd. SW15 & SW18 7K 13
Putney Comn. SW15 6H 13
Putney Exchange Shop. Cen. SW15 7J 13
Putney Heath 9H 13
Putney Heath. SW15 1G 26
Putney Heath La. SW15 9J 13
Putney High St. SW15 7J 13
Putney Hill. SW15 1J 27
(in two parts)
Putney Pk. Av. SW15 7F 12
Putney Pk. La. SW15 7G 12
(in two parts)
Putney Vale 4F 26
Putney Vale Crematorium. SW15 3F 26
Puttenham 8N 111
Puttenham Heath Rd. P'ham & Comp. 8A 112
Puttenham Hill. P'ham 7N 111
Puttenham La. Shack 2N 131
Puttenham Rd. Seale 8F 110
Puttock Clo. Hasl 3B 188
Pye Clo. Cat 1A 104
Pyecombe Ct. Craw 6L 181
Pyegrove Chase. Brack 6C 32
Pyestock 4G 88
Pyestock Cres. Farnb 1H 89
Pyke Clo. Wokgm 2C 30
Pylbrook Rd. Sutt 9M 43
Pyle Hill 2N 93
Pyle Hill. Wok 2N 93
Pylon Way. Croy 7J 45
Pymers Mead. SE21 2N 29
Pyne Rd. Surb 7N 41
Pyramid Ho. Houn 5M 9
Pycroft La. Wey 2C 56
Pyrcroft Rd. Cher 6G 36
Pyrford 2H 75
Pyrford Comn. Rd. Wok 3F 74
Pyrford Ct. Wok 4G 75
Pyrford Green 4K 75
Pyrford Heath. Wok 3H 75
Pyrford Rd. W Byf 9J 55
Pyrford Village 5J 75
Pyrford Wood Est. Wok 3H 75
Pyrford Woods Clo. Wok 2H 75
Pyrford Woods Rd. Wok 2G 75
Pyrland Rd. Rich 9M 11
Pyrmont Gro. SE27 4M 29
Pyrmont Rd. W4 2N 11
Pytchley Cres. SE19 7N 29

Q

Quabrook 8L 187
Quadrangle, The. SW6 3K 13
Quadrangle, The. Guild 4K 113
Quadrant Ct. Brack 2C 32
Quadrant Rd. Rich 7K 11
Quadrant Rd. T Hth 3M 45
Quadrant, The. SW20 9K 27
Quadrant, The. Ash V 9E 90
Quadrant, The. Eps 9D 60 (6L 201)
Quadrant, The. Rich 7K 11
Quadrant, The. Sutt 3A 62
Quadrant, The. Wey 1B 56
Quadrant Way. Wey 1B 56
Quail Clo. H'ham 1K 197
Quail Gdns. S Croy 6H 65
Quain Mans. W14 2K 13
(off Queen's Club Gdns.)
Quakers La. Iswth 3G 10
(in three parts)
Quakers Way. Guild 8F 92
Qualitas. Brack 7L 31
Quality St. Red 6F 102
Quantock Clo. Craw 3N 181
Quantock Clo. Hay 3E 8
Quantock Clo. Slou 1C 6
Quantock Dri. Wor Pk 8H 43
Quarrendon St. SW6 5M 13
Quarries, The. Man H 9C 198
Quarr Rd. Cars 5B 44
Quarry Bank. Light 7L 51
Quarry Clo. H'ham 2M 197
Quarry Clo. Lea 8K 79
Quarry Clo. Oxt 8A 106
Quarry Cotts. Reig 9N 101
Quarry Gdns. Lea 8K 79
Quarry Hill. G'ming 8E 132
Quarry Hill Pk. Reig 9A 102
Quarry La. Yat 1D 68
Quarry Pk. Rd. Sutt 3L 61
Quarry Path. Oxt 9A 106
Quarry Ri. E Grin 7C 166
Quarry Ri. Sutt 3L 61
Quarry Rd. God 6F 104
Quarry Rd. Hurt 4D 132
Quarry Rd. Oxt 0A 106
Quarryside Bus. Pk. Red 9F 102
Quarry St. Guild 5N 113 (6C 202)
Quarry, The. Bet 1C 120
Quarterbrass Farm Rd. H'ham 1K 197
Quartermaine Av. Wok 9B 74
Quarter Mile Rd. G'ming 9H 133
Quarters Rd. Farnb 3N 89
Quebec Av. W'ham 4M 107
Quebec Clo. Small 8L 143
Quebec Cotts. W'ham 5M 107
Quebec Gdns. B'water 2J 69
Quebec House 4M 107
Quebec Sq. W'ham 4M 107
Queen Adelaide's Ride. Wind 9A 4
Queen Alexandra's Ct. SW19 6L 27
Queen Alexandra's Royal Army Nursing Corps Mus. 2J 109
(in Royal Pavilion)
Queen Alexandra's Way. Eps 7N 59
Queen Anne Dri. Clay 4E 58
Queen Anne's Clo. Twic 4D 24
Queen Anne's Clo. Wind 4E 18
Queen Anne's Gdns. Lea 8H 79
Queen Anne's Gdns. Mitc 2D 44
Queen Anne's Ga. Farnh 5J 109
Queen Anne's Ride. Asc & Wind 6D 18
Queen Anne's Rd. Wind 7F 4
(in two parts)
Queen Anne's Ter. Lea 8H 79
Queen Ann's Ct. Wind 4G 4
(off Peascod St.)
Queen Caroline St. W6 1H 13
(in two parts)
Queen Catherine Ho. SW6 3N 13
(off Wandon Rd.)
Queen Charlotte's Cottage 5K 11
Queen Charlotte St. Wind 4G 5
(off High St.)
Queendale Ct. Wok 3J 73
Queen Eleanor's Rd. Guild 4J 113
Queen Elizabeth Clo. As 2E 110
Queen Elizabeth Dri. Alder 2L 109
Queen Elizabeth Gdns. Mord 3M 43
Queen Elizabeth Ho. SW12 1E 28
Queen Elizabeth Park 8K 93
Queen Elizabeth Rd. Camb 6B 50
Queen Elizabeth Rd. King T 1M 41 (3L 203)
Queen Elizabeth Rd. Rud 1E 194
Queen Elizabeth's Dri. New Ad 5N 65
Queen Elizabeth's Gdns. New Ad 6N 65
Queen Elizabeth's Wlk. Wall 1H 63
Queen Elizabeth's Wlk. Wind 5H 5
Queen Elizabeth Wlk. SW13 4F 12
(in two parts)
Queen Elizabeth Way. Wok 6B 74
Queenhill Rd. S Croy 6E 64
Queenhythe Rd. Guild 8N 93
Queen Mary Av. Camb 1M 69
Queen Mary Av. Mord 4J 43
Queen Mary Clo. Fleet 2A 88
Queen Mary Clo. Surb 9A 42
Queen Mary Clo. Wok 3E 74
Queen Mary Rd. SE19 7M 29
Queen Mary Rd. Shep 1D 38
Queen Mary's Av. Cars 4D 62
Queen Mary's Dri. New H 6H 55
Queens Acre. Sutt 4J 61
Queens Acre. Wind 7G 4
Queen's Av. Alder 1M 109
Queen's Av. Byfl 8M 55
Queens Av. Felt 5K 23
Queensbridge Pk. Iswth 8E 10
Queensbury Ho. Rich 8J 11
Queensbury Pl. B'water 3H 69
Queens Clo. Farnb 5N 89
Queen's Clo. Asc 9J 17
Queens Clo. Bisl 3D 72
Queen's Clo. Esh 1B 58
Queen's Clo. Old Win 8K 5
Queens Clo. Tad 2F 100
Queens Clo. Wall 2F 62
Queen's Club Gdns. W14 2K 13
Queen's Club (Tennis) 1K 13
Queen's Ct. Farnb 5A 90
Queen's Ct. Belm 7M 61
Queen's Ct. Eden 2M 147
Queen's Ct. Horl 8E 142
Queens Ct. Red 2E 122
(off St Anne's Mt.)
Queens Ct. Rich 9M 11
Queens Ct. S Croy 8C 200
Queens Ct. Wey 2E 56
Queens Ct. Wok 5B 74
Queens Ct. Ride. Cob 9H 57
Queen's Cres. Dork 6G 119 (4J 201)
Queen's Cres. Rich 8M 11
Queen's Dri. G'ming 4E 132
Queens Dri. Guild 9K 93
Queen's Dri. Oxs 7C 58
Queen's Dri. Surb 6N 41
Queen's Dri. Th Dit 5G 41
Queensfield Ct. Sutt 1H 61
Queen's Gdns. Houn 4M 9
Queensgate. Cob 8L 57
Queen's Ga. Gat A 3E 162
Queens Ga. Gdns. SW15 7G 13
Queen's Ga. Rd. Farnb 5N 89
Queens Hill Ri. Asc 2N 33
Queens Ho. Tedd 7F 24
Queen's Keep. Twic 9J 11
Queensland Av. SW19 9N 27
Queens La. Asht 5A 22
Queens La. Farnh 5H 109
Queensmead. Farnb 1N 89
Queen's Mead. C'fold 5E 172
Queensmead. Dat 3L 5
Queensmead. Oxs 7C 58
Queensmead Av. Eps 6G 61
Queensmere Clo. SW19 3J 27
Queensmere Ct. SW13 3E 12
Queensmere Rd. SW19 3J 27
Queensmill Rd. SW6 3J 13
Queens Pde. H'ham 7K 197
(off Queen St.)
Queen's Pde. Path. Alder 7N 89
Queen's Pk. Gdns. Felt 4G 23
Queen's Pk. Rd. Cat 1B 104
Queens Pine. Brack 5C 32

Queens Pl.—Redclose Av.

Queens Pl. *Asc.* 2L **33**
Queens Pl. *Mord* 3M **43**
Queen's Promenade. *King T* 3K **41** (8G **203**)
Queens Reach. *E Mol* 3E **40**
Queens Reach. *King T* 1K **41** (4G **203**)
Queens Ride. *SW13 & SW15* 6F **12**
Queens Ride. *Crowt* 9F **30**
Queens Ri. *Rich* 9M **11**
Queen's Rd. *Farnb* 5A **90**
Queen's Rd. *SW14* 6C **12**
Queens Rd. *SW19* 7L **27**
Queen's Rd. *Alder* 3L **109**
Queen's Rd. *Asc.* 4A **34**
Queens Rd. *Beck* 1H **47**
Queens Rd. *Bisl* 7B **72**
Queens Rd. *Camb* 2N **69**
Queens Rd. *Croy* 5M **45**
Queen's Rd. *Dat* 3L **5**
Queen's Rd. *E Grin* 1A **186**
Queen's Rd. *Egh* 6B **20**
Queens Rd. *Eton W* 1C **4**
Queens Rd. *Farnh* 6H **109**
Queen's Rd. *Felt* 2J **23**
Queen's Rd. *Fleet* 6B **88**
Queen's Rd. *Guild* 3N **113** (3D **202**)
Queen's Rd. *Hamp H* 5B **24**
Queen's Rd. *Horl* 8E **142**
Queen's Rd. *Houn* 6B **10**
Queens Rd. *King T* 8N **25**
Queen's Rd. *Knap* 5F **72**
Queens Rd. *Mord* 3M **43**
Queens Rd. *N Mald* 3E **42**
Queen's Rd. *Rich* 1M **25**
Queen's Rd. *Sutt* 6M **61**
Queen's Rd. *Tedd* 7F **24**
Queen's Rd. *Th Dit* 4F **40**
Queens Rd. *Twic* 2G **24**
Queens Rd. *Wall* 2F **62**
Queen's Rd. *Wey & W on T* 1C **56**
Queen's Rd. *Wind* 5F **4**
Queen's Roundabout. *Farnb* 6N **89**
Queen's Sq. *Craw* 3B **182**
Queens Ter. *Iswth* 7G **11**
Queen St. *Alder* 2B **110**
Queen St. *Cher* 7J **37**
Queen St. *Croy* 1N **63** (6B **200**)
Queen St. *G'ming* 7H **133**
Queen St. *Gom* 8D **116**
Queen St. *H'ham* 7K **197**
Queensville Rd. *SW12* 1H **29**
Queen's Wlk. *Ashf* 5M **21**
Queens Wlk. *E Grin* 9A **166**
Queensway. *Brack* 9L **15**
Queen's Way. *Brkwd* 6A **72**
Queensway. *Cranl* 8A **156**
Queensway. *Craw* 3C **182**
Queensway. *Croy* 3K **63**
Queensway. *E Grin* 9A **166**
Queens Way. *Felt* 5K **23**
Queensway. *Frim G* 7E **70**
Queensway. *H'ham* 7J **197**
Queensway. *Red* 2D **122**
Queensway. *Sun* 1J **39**
Queensway. *W Wick* 1A **66**
Queensway N. *W on T* 1K **57** (in two parts)
Queensway S. *W on T* 2K **57** (in two parts)
Queens Wharf. *W6* 1H **13**
Queenswood Av. *Hamp* 7B **24**
Queenswood Av. *Houn* 5N **9**
Queenswood Av. *T Hth* 4L **45**
Queenswood Av. *Wall* 1H **63**
Queenswood Rd. *Wok* 6G **73**
Queen Victoria. (Junct.) **9H 43**
Queen Victoria Ct. *Farnb* 9N **69**
Queen Victoria Rd. *Brkwd* 6A **72**
Queen Victoria's Wlk. *Col T* 9L **49**
Queen Victoria Wlk. *Wind* 4H **5**
Quell La. *Hasl* 9L **189**
Quelmans Head Ride. *Wind* 3A **18**
Quelm La. *Binf* 7N **15**
Quelm La. *Brack* 8N **15**
Quennell Clo. *Asht* 6M **79**
Quennells Hill. *Wrec* 5D **128**
Quentins Dri. *Berr G* 3K **87**
Quentin Way. *Vir W* 3L **35**
Querrin St. *SW6* 5N **13**
Questen M. *Craw* 1H **183**
Quetta Pk. *C Crook* 2C **108**
Quick Rd. *W4* 1D **12**
Quicks Rd. *SW19* 8N **27**
Quiet Clo. *Add* 1J **55**
Quiet Nook. *Brom* 1F **66**
Quill La. *SW15* 7J **13**
Quillot, The. *W on T* 2G **56**
Quince Clo. *Asc* 3N **33**
Quince Dri. *Bisl* 2E **72**
Quincy Rd. *Egh* 6C **20**
Quinney's. *Farnb* 4A **90**
Quintilis. *Brack* 7L **31** (in two parts)
Quintin Av. *SW20* 9L **27**
Quinton Clo. *Beck* 2M **47**
Quinton Clo. *Houn* 3J **9**
Quinton Clo. *Wall* 1F **62**
Quinton Rd. *Th Dit* 7G **41**
Quinton St. *SW18* 3A **28**
Quintrell Clo. *Wok* 4L **73**

R

Rabbit La. *W on T* 4H **57**
Rabies Heath Rd. *Blet* 2B **124**
Raby Rd. *N Mald* 3C **42**
Raccoon Way. *Houn* 5K **9**
Racecourse Rd. *Ling & D'land* 8A **146**
Racecourse Rd. Gat A 2D **162** *(off Gatwick Way)*
Rachael's Lake Vw. *Warf* 8C **16**
Rackfield. *Hasl* 1B **188**
Rackham Clo. *Craw* 5B **182**
Rackham M. *SW16* 7G **29**
Rack's Ct. *Guild* 5N **113** (7D **202**)
Rackstraw Rd. *Sand* 6H **49**
Racquets Ct. Hill. *G'ming* 5F **132**
Racton Rd. *SW6* 2M **13**
Radbourne Rd. *SW12* 1G **29**
Radbroke. *Lea* 9J **79**
Radcliffe Clo. *Frim* 7D **70**
Radcliffe Gdns. *Cars* 5C **62**
Radcliffe M. *Hamp H* 6C **24**
Radcliffe Rd. *Croy* 8C **46**
Radcliffe Sq. *SW15* 9J **13**
Radcliffe Way. *Brack* 9K **15**
Radford Clo. *Farnh* 7K **109**
Radford Rd. *Tin G* 6F **162**
Radipole Rd. *SW6* 4L **13**
Radius Pk. *Felt* 7G **9**
Rad La. *Peasl* 2E **136** (in two parts)
Radley Clo. *Felt* 2G **23**
Radnor Clo. *Mitc* 3J **45**
Radnor Ct. *Red* 3C **122**
Radnor Gdns. *Twic* 3F **24**
Radnor La. *Holm M* 4H **137** (Horsham Rd.)
Radnor La. *Holm M* 9H **137** (Three Mile Rd.)
Radnor Rd. *Brack* 2D **32**
Radnor Rd. *Peasl* 5E **136**
Radnor Rd. *Twic* 2F **24**
Radnor Rd. *Wey* 9B **38**
Radnor Ter. *Sutt* 4M **61**
Radnor Wlk. *Croy* 5H **47**
Radnor Way. *Slou* 1A **6**
Radolphs. *Tad* 9J **81**
Radstock Way. *Red* 6H **103**
Radstone Ct. *Wok* 5B **74**
Raeburn Av. *Surb* 7A **42**
Raeburn Clo. *King T* 8K **25** (1G **203**)
Raeburn Ct. *Wok* 6K **73**
Raeburn Gro. *Wok* 5K **73**
Raeburn Way. *Col T* 9J **49**
Rafborough. **2L 89**
Rafborough Footpath. *Farnb* 2M **89**
Rag Hill Clo. *Tats* 8G **86**
Rag Hill Rd. *Tats* 8F **86**
Raglan Clo. *Alder* 3A **110**
Raglan Clo. *Frim* 6E **70**
Raglan Clo. *Houn* 8N **9**
Raglan Clo. *Reig* 1B **122**
Raglan Ct. *S Croy* 2M **63** (8A **200**)
Raglan Precinct. *Cat* 9B **84**
Raglan Rd. *Knap* 5H **73**
Raglan Rd. *Reig* 9N **101**
Raikes Hollow. *Ab H* 2J **137**
Raikes La. *Ab H* 2J **137**
Railey Rd. *Craw* 2C **182**
Railpit La. *Warl* 2A **86**
Railshead Rd. *Iswth* 7H **11**
Rails La. *Pirb* 3N **91**
Railton Rd. *Guild* 8L **93**
Railway App. *Cher* 7H **37**
Railway App. *E Grin* 9A **166**
Railway App. *Twic* 1G **24**
Railway App. *Wall* 2F **62**
Railway Cotts. *SW19* 5N **27**
Railway Cotts. *Bag* 3J **51**
Railway Cotts. *Twic* 9A **10**
Railway Pas. *Tedd* 7G **24**
Railway Pl. *SW19* 7L **27**
Railway Rd. *Tedd* 5E **24**
Railway Side. *SW13* 6D **12** (in two parts)
Railway Ter. Coul 2H **83** *(off Station App.)*
Railway Ter. *Felt* 2H **23**
Railway Ter. *Stai* 6F **20**
Railway Ter. *W'ham* 3M **107**
Rainbow Ct. *Wok* 3H **73**
Rainville Rd. *W6* 2H **13**
Rake La. *Milf* 3C **152**
Rakers Ridge. *H'ham* 3K **197**
Raleigh Av. *Wall* 1H **63**
Raleigh Ct. *Craw* 7E **162**
Raleigh Ct. *Stai* 5J **21**
Raleigh Ct. *Wall* 3F **62**
Raleigh Dri. *Clay* 2D **58**
Raleigh Dri. *Small* 8L **143**
Raleigh Dri. *Surb* 7B **42**
Raleigh Gdns. *Mitc* 2D **44** (in two parts)
Raleigh Rd. *Felt* 4G **22**
Raleigh Rd. *Rich* 6M **11**
Raleigh Rd. *S'hall* 1M **9**
Raleigh Wlk. *Craw* 5C **182**
Raleigh Way. *Felt* 6K **23**
Raleigh Way. *Frim* 3D **70**
Ralliwood Rd. *Asht* 6N **79**
Ralph Perring Ct. *Beck* 3K **47**
Ralph's Ride. *Brack* 2C **32** (in two parts)
Rama Clo. *SW16* 8J **29**
Rambler Clo. *SW16* 5G **28**
Ramblers Way. *Craw* 9N **181**
Rame Clo. *SW17* 6E **28**
Ramillies Clo. *Alder* 6C **90**
Ramillies Park. **7B 90**
Ramin Ct. *Guild* 9M **93**
Ramones Ter. *Mitc* 3J **45**
Ramornie Clo. *W on T* 2N **57**
Ram Pas. *King T* 1K **41** (4H **203**)
Ramsay Clo. *Camb* 8F **50**
Ramsay Ct. *Craw* 8N **181**
Ramsay Rd. *W'sham* 2B **52**
Ramsbury Clo. *Brack* 5K **31**
Ramsdale Rd. *SW17* 6E **28**
Ramsden Rd. *SW12* 1E **28**
Ramsden Rd. *G'ming* 8G **133**
Ramsey Clo. *Horl* 8D **142**
Ramsey Clo. *H'ham* 3K **197**
Ramsey Ct. *Croy* 3A **200**
Ramsey Pl. *Cat* 9N **83**
Ramsey Rd. *T Hth* 5K **45**
Ramslade Cotts. *Brack* 2A **32**
Ramslade Rd. *Brack* 3B **32**
Rams La. *Duns* 7C **174**
Ramsnest Common. **1D 190**
Ramster Cotts. *C'fold* 1C **190**
Ramster Gardens. **1C 190**
Ram St. *SW18* 8N **13**
Ramuswood Av. *Orp* 2N **67**
Ranald Ct. *Asc* 7K **17**
Rances La. *Wokgm* 2D **30**
Randal Cres. *Reig* 5M **121**
Randall Clo. *Slou* 1B **6**
Randall Farm La. *Lea* 6G **79**
Randall Mead. *Binf* 7G **15**
Randall Scholfield Ct. *Craw* 2E **182**
Randalls Cres. *Lea* 7G **78**
Randalls Pk. Av. *Lea* 7G **78**
Randalls Pk. Crematorium. *Lea* 7E **78**
Randalls Pk. Dri. *Lea* 8G **78**
Randalls Rd. *Lea* 6E **78**
Randalls Way. *Lea* 8G **78**
Randell Clo. *B'water* 5K **69**
Randell Ho. *B'water* 5K **69**
Randle Rd. *Rich* 5J **25**
Randolph Clo. *King T* 6B **26**
Randolph Clo. *Knap* 4H **73**
Randolph Clo. *Stoke D* 2A **78**
Randolph Dri. *Farnb* 2H **89**
Randolph Rd. *Eps* 1E **80** (8M **201**)
Randolph's La. *W'ham* 4K **107**
Ranelagh. *Wink* 3M **17**
Ranelagh Av. *SW6* 6L **13**
Ranelagh Av. *SW13* 5F **12**
Ranelagh Cres. *Asc* 9G **17**
Ranelagh Dri. *Brack* 2A **32**
Ranelagh Dri. *Twic* 7H **11**
Ranelagh Gdns. *SW6* 6K **13** (in two parts)
Ranelagh Gdns. *W4* 3B **12**
Ranelagh Gdns. Mans. SW6 6K **13** *(off Ranelagh Gdns.)*
Ranelagh Pl. *N Mald* 4D **42**
Ranelagh Rd. *Red* 3C **122**
Ranfurly Rd. *Sutt* 8M **43**
Range Ride. *Ryl M* 8L **49**
Range Rd. *Finch* 9A **30**
Ranger Wlk. *Add* 2K **55**
Range, The. *Brmly* 7C **134**
Range Vw. *Col T* 7K **49**
Range Way. *Shep* 6B **38**
Rankine Clo. *Bad L* 6M **109**
Ranmere St. *SW12* 2F **28**
Ranmore Av. *Croy* 9C **46**
Ranmore Clo. *Craw* 9A **182**
Ranmore Clo. *Red* 9E **102**
Ranmore Common. **3D 118**
Ranmore Common. **2B 118**
Ranmore Comn. Rd. *Westh* 3M **117**
Ranmore Pl. Wey 2D **56** *(off Princes Rd.)*
Ranmore Rd. *Dork* 3C **118** (1H **201**)
Ranmore Rd. *Sutt* 5J **61**
Rannoch Rd. *W6* 2H **13**
Ransome Clo. *Craw* 6K **181**
Ranyard Clo. *Chess* 9M **41**
Rapallo Clo. *Farnb* 1A **90**
Rapeland Hill. *H'ham* 7M **179**
Raphael Dri. *Th Dit* 6F **40**
Rapley Clo. *Camb* 7D **50**
Rapley Grn. *Brack* 5A **32**
Rapley's Fld. *Pirb* 1B **92**
Rapsley La. *Knap* 5E **72**
Rashleigh Ct. *C Crook* 9C **88**
Rassett Mead. *C Crook* 1A **108**
Rastell Av. *SW2* 3H **29**
Ratcliffe Rd. *Farnb* 6L **69**
Rathbone Ho. *Craw* 8N **181**
Rathbone Sq. *Croy* 1N **63** (6B **200**)
Rathgar Clo. *Red* 8E **122**
Rathlin Rd. *Craw* 6N **181**
Rathmell Dri. *SW4* 1H **29**
Raven Clo. *H'ham* 2L **197**
Raven Clo. *Turn H* 4F **184**
Raven Clo. *Yat* 9A **48**
Ravendale Rd. *Sun* 1G **38**
Ravendene Ct. *Craw* 4B **182**
Ravenfield. *Eng G* 7M **19**
Ravenfield Rd. *SW17* 4D **28**
Raven La. *Craw* 1A **182**
Ravenna Rd. *SW15* 8J **13**
Ravensbourne Av. *Brom* 1N **47**
Ravensbourne Av. *Stai* 2N **21**
Ravensbourne Rd. *Twic* 9J **11**
Ravensbury Av. *Mord* 4A **44**
Ravensbury Ct. Mitc 3B **44** *(off Ravensbury Gro.)*
Ravensbury Gro. *Mitc* 3B **44**
Ravensbury La. *Mitc* 3B **44**
Ravensbury Path. *Mitc* 3B **44**
Ravensbury Rd. *SW18* 3M **27**
Ravensbury Ter. *SW18* 3N **27**
Ravenscar Rd. *Surb* 8M **41**
Ravens Clo. *Knap* 3F **72**
Ravens Clo. *Red* 2D **122**
Ravens Clo. *Surb* 5K **41**
Ravens Ct. *King T* 8H **203**
Ravenscourt. *Sun* 9G **23**
Ravenscourt Av. *W6* 1F **12**
Ravenscourt Pk. *W6* 1F **12**
Ravenscourt Pl. *W6* 1G **12**
Ravenscourt Rd. *W6* 1G **12** (in two parts)
Ravenscroft Clo. *As* 1G **111**
Ravenscroft Ct. *H'ham* 5J **197**
Ravenscroft Rd. *Beck* 1F **46**
Ravenscroft Rd. *Wey* 7D **56**
Ravensdale Cotts. *Bram C* 9A **170**
Ravensdale M. *Stai* 7K **21**
Ravensdale Rd. *Asc* 4L **33**
Ravensdale Rd. *Houn* 6M **9**
Ravensfield Gdns. *Eps* 2D **60**
Ravenshead Clo. *S Croy* 7F **64**
Ravenside. *King T* 8G **203**
Ravenslea Rd. *SW12* 1D **28**
Ravensmede Way. *W4* 1E **12**
Ravenstone Rd. *Camb* 1H **71**
Ravenstone St. *SW12* 2E **28**
Ravens Wold. *Kenl* 2N **83**
Ravenswood Av. *Crowt* 2D **48**
Ravenswood Av. *Surb* 8M **41**
Ravenswood Av. *W Wick* 7M **47**
Ravenswood Clo. *Cob* 2L **77**
Ravenswood Ct. *King T* 7A **26**
Ravenswood Ct. *Wok* 5B **74**
Ravenswood Cres. *W Wick* 7M **47**
Ravenswood Dri. *Camb* 1E **70**
Ravenswood Gdns. *Iswth* 4E **10**
Ravenswood Rd. *SW12* 1F **28**
Ravenswood Rd. *Croy* 9M **45** (5A **200**)
Ravensworth Ct. SW6 3M **13** *(off Fulham Rd.)*
Rawchester Clo. *SW18* 2L **27**
Rawdon Ri. *Camb* 1F **70**
Rawlins Clo. *S Croy* 4H **65**
Rawlinson Rd. *Camb* 9L **49**
Rawnsley Av. *Mitc* 4B **44**
Raworth Clo. *M'bowr* 5F **182**
Rawsthorne Ct. *Houn* 7N **9**
Raybell Ct. *Iswth* 5F **10**
Ray Clo. *Chess* 3J **59**
Ray Clo. *Ling* 6M **145**
Ray La. *Ling* 4J **145**
Rayleigh Av. *Tedd* 7E **24**
Rayleigh Ct. *King T* 1N **41** (3M **203**)
Rayleigh Ri. *S Croy* 3B **64**
Rayleigh Rd. *SW19* 9L **27**
Raymead Av. *T Hth* 4L **45**
Raymead Clo. *Fet* 9E **78**
Raymead Way. *Fet* 9E **78**
Raymer Wlk. *Horl* 7G **142**
Raymond Clo. *Coln* 4G **7**
Raymond Ct. *Sutt* 3N **61**
Raymond Cres. *Guild* 4J **113**
Raymond Rd. *SW19* 7K **27**
Raymond Rd. *Beck* 3H **47**
Raymond Way. *Clay* 3G **59**
Raynald Ho. *SW16* 4J **29**
Rayners Clo. *Coln* 3E **6**
Rayners Rd. *SW15* 8K **13**
Raynes Park. **3H 43**
Raynes Pk. Bri. *SW20* 1H **43**
Ray Rd. *W Mol* 4B **40**
Ray's Av. *Wind* 3C **4**
Rays Rd. *W Wick* 6M **47**
Raywood Clo. *Hay* 3D **8**
Read Clo. *Th Dit* 6G **40**
Readens, The. *Bans* 3C **82**
Reading Arch Rd. *Red* 3D **122**
Reading Rd. *Farnb* 4A **90**
Reading Rd. *Eve* 8A **48**
Reading Rd. *Sutt* 2A **62**
Reading Rd. *Winn* 1A **30**
Reading Rd. *Yat & B'water* 8A **48**
Reading Rd. N. *Fleet* 4A **88**
Reading Rd. S. *Fleet & C Crook* 5A **88**
Read Rd. *Asht* 4K **79**
Reads Rest La. *Tad* 7M **81**
Reapers Clo. *H'ham* 3K **197**
Reapers Way. *Iswth* 8D **10**
Rebecca Clo. *C Crook* 1A **108**
Reckitt Rd. *W4* 1D **12**
Recovery St. *SW17* 6C **28**
Recreation Clo. *Farnb* 5L **69**
Recreation Rd. *Guild* 3N **113** (2B **202**)
Recreation Rd. *Rowl* 8D **128**
Recreation Way. *Mitc* 2H **45**
Rectory Clo. *SW20* 2H **43**
Rectory Clo. *Asht* 6M **79**
Rectory Clo. *Brack* 3A **32**
Rectory Clo. *Byfl* 9M **55**
Rectory Clo. *Ewh* 5F **156**
Rectory Clo. *G'ming* 9J **133**
Rectory Clo. *Guild* 1F **114**
Rectory Clo. *Ockl* 7C **158**
Rectory Clo. *Sand* 7E **48**
Rectory Clo. *Shep* 2B **38**
Rectory Clo. *Surb* 7J **41**
Rectory Clo. *Wind* 4D **4**
Rectory Clo. *Wokgm* 2B **30**
Rectory Ct. *Felt* 5K **23**
Rectory Ct. *Wall* 1G **63**
Rectory Flats. *If'd* 1L **181**
Rectory Garden. *Cranl* 7M **155**
Rectory Grn. *Beck* 1J **47**
Rectory Gro. *Croy* 8M **45** (3A **200**)
Rectory Gro. *Hamp* 5N **23**
Rectory La. *SW17* 7E **28**
Rectory La. *Asht* 6M **79**
Rectory La. *Bans* 1D **82**
Rectory La. *Bookh* 4N **97**
Rectory La. *Brack* 4N **31**
Rectory La. *Bram* 9K **169**
Rectory La. *Buck* 9E **100**
Rectory La. *Byfl* 9N **55**
Rectory La. *Charl* 3J **161**
Rectory La. *If'd* 1L **181**
Rectory La. *Shere* 8B **116**
Rectory La. *Surb* 7H **41**
Rectory La. *Wall* 1G **63**
Rectory La. *W'ham* 1G **106**
Rectory La. *W'sham* 3N **51**
Rectory Orchard. *SW19* 5K **27**
Rectory Pk. *S Croy* 9B **64**
Rectory Rd. *Farnb* 1A **90**
Rectory Rd. *SW13* 5F **12**
Rectory Rd. *Beck* 1K **47**
Rectory Rd. *Coul* 3A **102**
Rectory Rd. *Houn* 5K **9**
Rectory Rd. *Kes* 4F **66**
Rectory Rd. *Sutt* 9M **43**
Rectory Rd. *Wokgm* 2B **30**
Rectory Row. *Brack* 3N **31**
Red Admiral St. *H'ham* 3L **197**
Redan Gdns. *Alder* 2A **110**
Redan Hill. **2A 110**
Redan Hill Ind. Est. *Alder* 2A **110**
Redan Rd. *Alder* 2A **110**
Redbarn Clo. *Purl* 7M **63**
Redcliffe Clo. SW5 1N **13** *(off Old Brompton Rd.)*
Redcliffe Gdns. *SW5 & SW10* 1N **13**
Redcliffe Gdns. *W4* 3A **12**
Redcliffe M. *SW10* 1N **13**
Redcliffe Pl. *SW10* 2N **13**
Redcliffe Rd. *SW10* 1N **13**
Redcliffe Sq. *SW10* 1N **13**
Redcliffe St. *SW10* 2N **13**
Redclose Av. *Mord* 4M **43**

Ringley Pk. Av.—Rosedale

Ringley Pk. Av. Reig. 4B 122
Ringley Pk. Rd. Reig 3A 122
Ringley Rd. H'ham 4L 197
Ringmead. Brack 4K 31
(in two parts)
Ringmer Av. SW6. . . . . 4K 13
Ringmore Dri. Guild 9E 94
Ringmore Rd. W on T 9K 39
Ring Rd. N. Gat A 2F 162
Ring Rd. S. Gat A 3G 162
Ringstead Rd. Sutt. 1B 62
Ring, The. Brack 1N 31
Ringway. S'hall. 1L 9
Ringwood. Brack 6L 31
Ringwood Av. Croy. 6J 45
Ringwood Av. Red 9D 102
Ringwood Clo. Asc 3M 33
Ringwood Clo. Craw 5C 182
Ringwood Gdns. SW15 . . . . 2F 26
Ringwood Lodge. Red 9E 102
Ringwood Rd. Farnb 7A 70
Ringwood Rd. B'water. 9H 49
Ringwood Way. Hamp H 5A 24
Ripley. 8L 75
Ripley Av. Egh 7A 20
Ripley By-Pass. Rip 1L 95
Ripley Clo. New Ad 3M 65
Ripley Ct. Mitc 1B 44
Ripley Gdns. SW14 . . . . 6C 12
Ripley Gdns. Sutt. 1A 62
Ripley La. Ock & W Hor. 1N 95
Ripley Rd. Hamp 8A 24
Ripley Rd. Send 4L 95
Ripley Springs. 7A 20
Ripley Way. Eps 7N 59
Ripon Clo. Camb 3H 71
Ripon Clo. Guild. 1J 113
Ripon Gdns. Chess 2K 59
Ripplesmere. Brack 3B 32
Ripplesmore Clo. Sand 7G 48
Ripston Rd. Ashf 6E 22
Risborough Dri. Wor Pk. 6F 42
Rise Rd. Asc 4B 34
Rise, The. Craw 3G 183
Rise, The. Crowt. 2E 48
Rise, The. E Grin 1B 186
Rise, The. E Hor 4F 96
Rise, The. Eps 6E 60
Rise, The. S Croy 5F 64
Rise, The. S'dale 5B 34
Rise, The. Tad 7H 81
Rise, The. Wokgm 1A 30
Ritchie Clo. M'bowr 7G 182
Ritchie Rd. Croy. 5E 46
Ritherdon Rd. SW17 . . . . 3E 28
River Ash Estate. 6G 39
River Av. Th Dit 6G 41
River Bank. E Mol. 2E 40
Riverbank. Stai. 7H 21
River Bank. Th Dit 4F 40
Riverbank. Westc 5B 118
River Bank. W Mol. 2A 40
Riverbank, The. Wind. 3E 4
Riverbank Way. Bren 2J 11
River Ct. Surb 8G 203
River Ct. Wok. 1E 74
Rivercourt Rd. W6. . . . . 1G 12
River Crane Way. Felt. 3N 23
(off Watermill Way)
Riverdale. Wrec 4D 128
Riverdale Dri. SW18 . . . . 2N 27
Riverdale Dri. Wok. 8B 74
Riverdale Gdns. Twic 9J 11
Riverdale Rd. Felt 5M 23
Riverdale Rd. Twic 9J 11
Riverdene Ind. Est. W on T . . . 2L 57
Riverfield Rd. Stai 7H 21
River Gdns. Cars 8E 44
River Gdns. Felt 8J 9
River Gdns. Bus. Cen. Felt 8J 9
River Gro. Pk. Beck 1J 47
Riverhead Dri. Sutt 6N 61
River Hill. Cob 2J 77
Riverhill. Wor Pk 8C 42
Riverholme Dri. Eps. 5C 60
River Island Clo. Fet. 8D 78
River La. Farnh 4D 128
River La. Fet. 8D 78
(in two parts)
River La. Rich 1K 25
River La. Stoke D 3M 77
Rivermead. Byfl 9A 56
Rivermead. E Mol. 2C 40
River Mead. H'ham 7H 197
River Mead. If'd 9M 161
Rivermead. King T. . . 4K 41 (8H 203)
Rivermead Clo. Add 4L 55
Rivermead Clo. Tedd 6H 25
Rivermead Ct. SW6 . . . . 6L 13
Rivermead Rd. Camb. 4N 69
River Meads Av. Twic. 4A 24
Rivermede. Bord 5A 168
River Mole Bus. Pk. Esh 8A 40
River Mt. W on T. 6G 38
Rivermount Gdns. Guild 6M 113
Rivernook Clo. W on T. 4K 39
River Pk. Av. Stai 5F 20
River Reach. Tedd 6J 25
River Rd. Stai. 9H 21
River Rd. Wind. 3A 4
River Rd. Yat 7A 48
River Row. Farnh 4E 128
River Row Cotts. Farnh 3E 128
Rivers Clo. Farnb 4C 90
Riversdale Rd. Th Dit. 4G 40
Riversdell Clo. Cher. 6H 37
Rivers Ho. W4 . . . . 1N 11
(off Chiswick High Rd.)
Riverside. Cher. 1J 37
Riverside. Dork 3K 119
Riverside. Eden 2L 147
Riverside. Egh 4C 20
Riverside. F Row 6G 187
Riverside. Guild 1N 113
Riverside. Horl 1E 162
Riverside. H'ham 6G 196
Riverside. Rich. 8K 11
Riverside. Shep 6F 38
Riverside. Stai 9H 21
(Laleham Rd.)
Riverside. Stai 6H 21
(Temple Gdns.)
Riverside. Sun 1L 39
Riverside. Twic. 2H 25
Riverside. Wray. 1M 19
Riverside Av. E Mol 4D 40
Riverside Av. Light 7N 51
Riverside Bus. Cen. SW18. . . . 2N 27
Riverside Bus. Cen. Guild
. . . . 3M 113 (3A 202)
Riverside Bus. Pk. Farnh 9J 109
Riverside Clo. Farnb. 9L 69
Riverside Clo. Brkwd 7C 72
Riverside Clo. King T
. . . . 3K 41 (7H 203)
Riverside Clo. Stai 9H 21
Riverside Clo. Wall. 9F 44
Riverside Ct. Dork 3K 119
Riverside Ct. Eden. 2M 147
Riverside Ct. Farnh 9H 109
Riverside Ct. Felt 1F 22
Riverside Ct. Fet. 9G 78
Riverside Ct. Iswth 5F 10
(off Woodlands Rd.)
Riverside Dri. W4. . . . . 3C 12
Riverside Dri. Brmly. 4C 134
Riverside Dri. Esh 1A 58
Riverside Dri. Mitc 4C 44
Riverside Dri. Rich. 4H 25
Riverside Dri. Stai 6G 21
(Chertsey La.)
Riverside Dri. Stai 8H 21
(Wheatsheaf La.)
Riverside Gdns. W6. . . . . 1G 13
Riverside Gdns. Old Wok. 8D 74
Riverside Ind. Pk. Farnh. 9J 109
Riverside M. Croy. 9J 45
Riverside Pk. Add 2N 55
Riverside Pk. Coln 5G 6
Riverside Pk. Farnh 9J 109
Riverside Pk. (Watchmoor Pk.)
Camb 3M 69
Riverside Pl. Stanw. 9M 7
Riverside Rd. SW17. . . . . 5N 27
Riverside Rd. Stai 2F 36
Riverside Rd. Stanw 8M 7
(in two parts)
Riverside Rd. W on T 1M 57
Riverside, The. E Mol. 2D 40
Riverside Wlk. SW6. . . . . 6K 13
Riverside Wlk. W4 . . . . 2E 12
(off Chiswick Wharf)
Riverside Wlk. G'ming 6G 133
Riverside Wlk. Iswth 6E 10
Riverside Wlk. King T
. . . . 2K 41 (3G 203)
Riverside Wlk. W Wick. 7L 47
Riverside Wlk. Wind 3G 5
(off Thames Side)
Riverside Way. Camb 3M 69
Riverstone Ct. King T
. . . . 9M 25 (2L 203)
River St. Wind 3G 4
River Ter. W6. . . . . 1H 13
River Vw. Add 2L 55
Riverview. Guild. . . 3M 113 (2A 202)
Riverview Gdns. Cob 9G 57
Riverview Gdns. SW13 . . . . . . 2G 13
River Vw. Gdns. Twic 3F 24
Riverview Gro. W4. . . . . 2A 12
Riverview Rd. W4 . . . . 3A 12
Riverview Rd. Eps 1B 60
River Wlk. W6 . . . . 5H 13
River Wlk. W on T. 5H 39
River Way. Eps. 2C 60
Riverway. Stai 9K 21
River Way. Twic 3B 24
Riverway Est. P'mrsh. 3L 133
Riverwood Ct. Guild 1M 113
Rives Av. Yat 1A 68
Rivett Drake Rd. Guild 8K 93
Rivey Clo. W Byf 1H 75
Rd. House Est. Old Wok. 8C 74
Roakes Av. Add 8K 37
Roasthill La. Eton W 2A 4
Robert Clo. W on T. 2J 57
Robert Gentry Ho. W14 . . . . . . 1K 13
(off Gledstanes Rd.)
Robert Owen Ho. SW6. . . . . . . 4J 13
Robertsbridge Rd. Cars 7A 44
Roberts Clo. Stanw 9L 7
Roberts Clo. Sutt 4J 61
Robertson Ct. Wok 5H 73
Robertson Way. As 3D 110
Roberts Rd. Alder 3A 110
Roberts Rd. Camb. 9M 49
Robert St. Croy. . . . 9N 45 (4C 200)
Roberts Way. Eng G 8M 19
Robert Way. H'ham. 1M 197
Robert Way. Myt 2D 90
Robin Clo. Add 2M 55
Robin Clo. Ash V 7E 90
Robin Clo. Craw. 1A 182
Robin Clo. E Grin 8B 166
Robin Clo. Hamp. 6M 23
Robin Gdns. Red 1E 122
Robin Gro. Bren 2J 11
Robin Hill. G'ming 4G 133
Robin Hill Dri. Camb 3E 70
Robin Hood. (Junct.) 4D 26
Robin Hood Clo. Farnb 7M 69
Robinhood Clo. Mitc 2G 45
Robin Hood Clo. Wok. 5J 73
Robin Hood Cres. Knap 4H 73
Robin Hood La. SW15. . . . . 4D 26
Robinhood La. Mitc 2G 45
Robin Hood La. Sutt 2M 61
Robin Hood La. Sut G 2B 94
Robin Hood La. Warn. 3E 196
Robin Hood Rd. SW19 & SW15
. . . . 6F 26
Robin Hood Rd. Knap & Wok
. . . . 4G 73
(in two parts)
Robin Hood Way. SW15 & SW20
. . . . 4D 26
Robin Hood Works. Knap 4H 73
(off Robin Hood Rd.)
Robin La. Sand 7G 49
(in two parts)
Robin Row. Turn H. 4F 184
Robin's Bow. Camb 2N 69
Robin's Ct. Beck. 1N 47
Robins Ct. S Croy. 7F 200
Robins Dale. Knap 4F 72
Robins Gro. W Wick 1C 66
Robins Gro. Cres. Yat 9A 48
Robinson Rd. SW17 & SW19
. . . . 7C 28
Robinson Rd. Craw 4B 182
Robinson Way. Bord 7A 168
Robinsway. W on T 1K 57
Robinswood Ct. H'ham 4M 197
Robin Way. Guild 8L 93
Robin Way. Stai 4H 21
Robin Willis Way. Old Win. 9K 5
Robinwood Pl. SW15. . . . . 5C 26
Robson Rd. SE27 . . . . 4M 29
Roby Dri. Brack 6B 32
Robyns Way. Eden 3M 147
Roche Rd. SW16. . . . . 9K 29
Rochester Av. Felt 3G 23
Rochester Clo. SW16. . . . . 8J 29
Rochester Gdns. Cat 9B 84
Rochester Gdns. Croy 9B 46
Rochester Gro. Fleet 5B 88
Rochester Pde. Felt 3H 23
Rochester Rd. Cars 1D 62
Rochester Rd. Stai. 7F 20
Rochester Wlk. Reig 8M 121
Roche Wlk. Cars 5B 44
Rochford Way. Croy. 5J 45
Rock Av. SW14 . . . . 6C 12
Rock Clo. Mitc 1B 44
Rockdale Dri. Gray. 6B 170
Rockery, The. Farnb 2J 89
Rockfield Clo. Oxt 9B 106
Rockfield Rd. Oxt. 7B 106
Rockfield Way. Col T 7J 49
Rock Gdns. Alder. 3L 109
Rockhampton Clo. SE27 . . . . . 5L 29
Rockhampton Rd. SE27. . . . . . 5L 29
Rockhampton Rd. S Croy 3B 64
Rock Hill. Hamb. 8G 152
Rockingham Clo. SW15 . . . . . . 7E 12
Rockland Rd. SW15. . . . . 7K 13
Rock La. Wrec 6F 128
Rockshaw Rd. Red 5G 102
Rocks La. SW13. . . . . 4F 12
Rocks, The. Ash W. 3E 186
Rockwood Park. 4M 185
Rocky La. Reig. 6D 102
Rocque Ho. SW6 . . . . 3L 13
(off Estcourt Rd.)
Rodale Mans. SW18 . . . . 9N 13
Rodborough Hill Cotts. Milf
. . . . 3N 151
Roden Gdns. Croy 5B 46
Rodenhurst Rd. SW4. . . . . 1G 29
Rodgate La. Hasl 3A 190
Rodgers Ho. SW4 . . . . 1H 29
(off Clapham Pk. Est.)
Roding Clo. Cranl 8H 155
Rodmel Ct. Farnb. 4C 90
Rodmill La. SW2 . . . . 1J 29
Rodney Clo. Croy. . . 7M 45 (1A 200)
Rodney Clo. N Mald. 4D 42
Rodney Clo. W on T. 7K 39
Rodney Gdns. W Wick. 1C 66
Rodney Grn. W on T 8K 39
Rodney Pl. SW19. . . . . 9A 28
Rodney Rd. Mitc 2C 44
Rodney Rd. N Mald 4D 42
Rodney Rd. Twic 9A 10
Rodney Rd. W on T. 8K 39
Rodney Way. Coln 4G 7
Rodney Way. Guild 2C 114
Rodona Rd. Wey 7E 56
Rodsall La. P'ham 3K 131
Rodway Rd. SW15. . . . . 1F 26
Rodwell Ct. Add 1L 55
Roebuck Clo. Asht 7L 79
Roebuck Clo. Felt. 5J 23
Roebuck Clo. H'ham 4A 198
Roebuck Clo. Reig 3M 121
Roebuck Est. Binf 8H 15
Roebuck Rd. Chess 2N 59
Roedean Cres. SW15. . . . . 9D 12
Roedeer Copse. Hasl 2C 188
Roehampton. 1F 26
Roehampton Clo. SW15. . . . . . . 7F 12
Roehampton Ga. SW15. . . . . . 9D 12
Roehampton High St. SW15
. . . . 1F 26
Roehampton Lane. (Junct.)
. . . . 2G 27
Roehampton La. SW15 . . . . . . 7F 12
Roehampton Va. SW15 . . . . . . 4E 26
Roffe's La. Cat 2A 104
Roffey. 4N 197
Roffey Clo. Horl. 8D 142
Roffey Clo. Purl. 3M 83
Roffey Park. 2E 198
Roffey's Clo. Copt 6L 163
Roffords. Wok 4L 73
Roffye Ct. H'ham 4N 197
Rogers Clo. Cat 9E 84
Rogers Clo. Coul. 5M 83
Roger Simmons Ct. Bookh . . . 2N 97
Rogers La. Warl 5J 85
Rogers Mead. God. 1E 124
Rogers Rd. SW17 . . . . 5B 28
Rokeby Clo. Brack 9B 16
Rokeby Ct. Wok 4J 73
Rokeby Pl. SW20. . . . . 8G 27
Roke Clo. Kenl. 1N 83
Roke Clo. Witl 5B 152
Roke La. Witl. 6N 151
Roke Lodge Rd. Kenl 9M 63
Roke Rd. Kenl 2N 83
Rokers La. Shack. 4A 132
(in two parts)
Rokes Pl. Yat 9A 48
Roland Way. Wor Pk 8E 42
Rolinsden Way. Kes 2F 66
Rollesby Rd. Chess 3N 59
Rolleston Rd. S Croy 4A 64
Rollit Cres. Houn 8A 10
Rolston Ho. Hasl 2D 188
Romana Ct. Stai 5J 21
Romanby Ct. Red 4D 122
Roman Clo. Felt. 8K 9
Romanfield Rd. SW2 . . . . 1K 29
Romanhurst Av. Brom 3N 47
Romanhurst Gdns. Brom. 3N 47
Roman Ind. Est. Croy 6B 46
Roman Ride. Crowt 2C 48
Roman Rd. Dork 7G 119
Roman Rd. M Grn. 5M 147
Romans Bus. Pk. Farnh 9J 109
Romans Way. Wok. 2J 75
Roman Way. Cars 5D 62
Roman Way. Croy
. . . . 8M 45 (2A 200)
Roman Way. Farnh 8K 109
Roman Way. Warf 9D 16
Romany Gdns. Sutt. 6M 43
Romany Rd. Knap 2F 72
Romany, The. Farnb 4F 88
Roma Read Clo. SW15 . . . . . . 1G 26
Romayne Clo. Farnb 9M 69
Romberg Rd. SW17. . . . . 4E 28
Romeo Hill. Warf. 9D 16
Romeyn Rd. SW16 . . . . 4K 29
Romily Ct. SW6. . . . . 5L 13
Romley Ct. Farnh 2J 129
Rommany Rd. SE27 . . . . 5N 29
(in two parts)
Romney Clo. Ashf 6D 22
Romney Clo. Chess 1L 59
Romney Ho. Brack. 3C 32
Romney Lock Rd. Wind 3G 5
Romney Rd. N Mald 5C 42
Romola Rd. SE24 . . . . 2M 29
Romsey Clo. Alder. 6A 110
Romsey Clo. B'water. 9H 49
Romsey Clo. Orp 1K 67
Romulus Ct. Bren 3K 11
Rona Clo. Craw 6N 181
Ronald Clo. Beck 3J 47
Ronelean Rd. Surb 8M 41
Ronneby Clo. Wey 9F 38
Roof of the World Cvn. Pk. Tad
. . . . 9A 100
Rookeries Clo. Felt. 4J 23
Rookery Clo. Fet 2E 98
Rookery Dri. Westc 7A 118
Rookery Hill. Asht 5N 79
Rookery Hill. Out & Small . . . 4L 143
Rookery La. Small 6L 143
Rookery Mead. Coul 9H 83
Rookery Rd. Orp 6H 67
Rookery Rd. Stai 6K 21
Rookery, The. Westc 7A 118
Rookery Way. Lwr K 5L 101
Rook La. Cat 3K 103
Rookley Clo. Sutt. 5N 61
Rooks Hill. Brmly 9D 134
Rooksmead Rd. Sun 1G 39
Rooks Nest. 8H 105
Rookstone Rd. SW17 . . . . 6D 28
Rookswood. Brack 8N 15
Rook Way. H'ham 2M 197
Rookwood Av. N Mald 3F 42
Rookwood Av. Owl 5K 49
Rookwood Av. Wall 1H 63
Rookwood Clo. Red 7F 102
Rookwood Ct. Guild
. . . . 6M 113 (8A 202)
Rookwood Pk. H'ham 5F 196
Roosthole Hill. Man H 8C 198
Roothill La. Bet 1N 139
Ropeland Way. H'ham 1L 197
Ropers Wlk. SW2 . . . . 1L 29
Roper Way. Mitc 1E 44
Rope Wlk. Sun. 2K 39
Rorkes Drift. Myt. 1D 90
Rosa Av. Ashf 5B 22
Rosalind Franklin Clo. Guild
. . . . 4H 113
Rosaline Rd. SW6 . . . . 3K 13
Rosaline Ter. SW6 . . . . 3K 13
(off Rosaline Rd.)
Rosamund Clo. S Croy
. . . . 1A 64 (7E 200)
Rosamund Rd. Craw 5F 182
Rosamun St. S'hall. 1M 9
Rosary Clo. Houn 5M 9
Rosary Gdns. Ashf. 5C 22
Rosary Gdns. SW7 . . . . 1N 13
Rosary Gdns. Yat. 9C 48
Rosaville Rd. SW6. . . . . 3L 13
Roseacre. Oxt 3C 126
Roseacre Clo. Shep 4B 38
Roseacre Gdns. Chil 9H 115
Rose & Crown Pas. Iswth 4G 10
Rose Av. Mitc 9D 28
Rose Av. Mord. 4A 44
Rosebank. SW6. . . . . 3H 13
Rosebank. Eps 1B 80 (8H 201)
Rosebank Clo. Tedd. 7G 25
Rose Bank Cotts. Wok. 9A 74
Rosebay. Wokgm 9D 14
Roseberry Av. T Hth 1N 45
Roseberry Gdns. Orp. 1N 67
Rosebery Av. Eps . . 1D 80 (8M 201)
Rosebery Av. N Mald 1E 42
Rosebery Clo. Mord 5J 43
Rosebery Cres. Wok 7B 74
Rosebery Gdns. Sutt. 1N 61
Rosebery Rd. SW2. . . . . 1J 29
Rosebery Rd. Eps 6C 80
Rosebery Rd. Houn 8C 10
Rosebery Rd. King T. 1A 42
Rosebery Rd. Sutt 3L 61
Rosebery Sq. King T 1A 42
Rosebine Av. Twic 1D 24
Rosebriar Clo. Wok 3J 75
Rosebriars. Cat 7B 84
Rosebriars. Esh 2C 58
(in two parts)
Rosebury Dri. Bisl 2D 72
Rosebury Rd. SW6 . . . . 5N 13
Rosebushes. Eps. 3G 81
Rose Cotts. Fay 9H 181
Rose Cotts. F Row. 6G 187
Rose Cotts. Kes 7E 66
Rose Cotts. Rusp 2M 179
Rose Cotts. Wmly 8D 152
Rose Ct. Wokgm 2B 30
Rosecourt Rd. Croy 5K 45
Rosecroft Clo. Big H 5H 87
Rosecroft Gdns. Twic 2D 24
Rosedale. Alder 2A 110
Rosedale. Asht. 5J 79

Rosedale—Russell Yd.

Rosedale. *Binf* 6H **15**
Rosedale. *Cat.* 1B **104**
Rosedale Clo. *Craw* 5M **181**
Rosedale Gdns. *Brack* 4M **31**
Rosedale Pl. *Croy* 6G **47**
Rosedale Rd. *Eps* 2F **60**
Rosedale Rd. *Rich* 6L **11**
Rosedene Av. *SW16* 4K **29**
Rosedene Av. *Croy* 6J **45**
Rosedene Av. *Mord* 4M **43**
Rosedene Gdns. *Fleet* 3A **88**
Rosedene La. *Col T* 9J **49**
Rosedew Rd. *W6* 2J **13**
Rose End. *Wor Pk* 7J **43**
Rosefield Clo. *Cars* 2C **62**
Rosefield Gdns. *Ott* 3F **54**
Rosefield Rd. *Stai* 5J **21**
Rose Gdns. *Farnb* 2K **89**
Rose Gdns. *Felt* 3H **23**
Rose Gdns. *Stanw* 1M **21**
Rose Gdns. *Wokgm* 2B **30**
Roseheath Rd. *Houn* 8N **9**
Rose Hill. **5G 119 (3K 201)** **(Dorking)**
Rosehill. **7A 44** **(Sutton)**
Rose Hill. *Binf* 6H **15**
Rosehill. *Clay* 3G **58**
Rose Hill. *Dork* 5G **119** (3J **201**)
Rosehill. *Hamp* 9A **24**
Rosehill. *Sutt* 8N **43**
Rose Hill Arch M. *Dork* 2K **201**
Rosehill Av. *Cars* 7A **44**
Rosehill Av. *Wok* 3M **73**
Rosehill Ct. Mord 6A **44** *(off St Helier Av.)*
Rosehill Ct. Pde. Mord 6A **44** *(off St Helier Av.)*
Rosehill Farm Mdw. *Bans* 2N **81**
Rosehill Gdns. *Sutt* 8N **43**
Rosehill Pk. W. *Sutt* 7A **44**
Rosehill Rd. *SW18* 9N **13**
Rosehill Rd. *Big H* 4E **86**
Rose Hill Roundabout. (Junct.) **6A 44**
Rose La. *Rip* 8L **75**
Roseleigh Clo. *Twic* 9K **11**
Rosemary Av. *Ash V* 5E **90**
Rosemary Av. *Houn* 5L **9**
Rosemary Av. *W Mol* 2A **40**
Rosemary Clo. *Farnb* 9J **69**
Rosemary Clo. *Croy* 5J **45**
Rosemary Clo. *Oxt* 2C **126**
Rosemary Ct. *Hasl* 1G **188**
Rosemary Ct. *Horl* 7C **142**
Rosemary Cres. *Guild* 8J **93**
Rosemary Gdns. *SW14* 6B **12**
Rosemary Gdns. *B'water* 1H **69**
Rosemary Gdns. *Chess* 1L **59**
Rosemary La. *SW14* 6B **12**
Rosemary La. *Alf* 9E **174**
Rosemary La. *B'water* 9H **49**
Rosemary La. *Charl* 3K **161** (in two parts)
Rosemary La. *Egh* 2D **36**
Rosemary La. *Horl* 9F **142**
Rosemary La. *Rowl* 7D **128**
Rosemary Rd. *SW17* 4A **28**
Rosemead. *Cher* 6K **37**
Rosemead Av. *Felt* 3G **22**
Rosemead Av. *Mitc* 2G **45**
Rosemead Clo. *Red* 5B **122**
Rosemont Rd. *N Mald* 2B **42**
Rosemont Rd. *Rich* 9L **11**
Rosemount Av. *W Byf* 9J **55**
Rosendale Rd. *SE24 & SE21* 1N **29**
Roseneath Dri. *C'fold* 5E **172**
Rose Pk. Cvn. Site. *Wdhm* 5G **54**
Rosery, The. *Croy* 5G **46**
Rosery, The. *Egh* 1G **36**
Rose's Cotts. Dork 5G **119** (2J **201**) *(off Junction Rd.)*
Roses La. *Wind* 5A **4**
Rose St. *Wokgm* 2D **30**
Rosethorn Clo. *SW12* 1H **29**
Rosetrees. *Guild* 4C **114**
Rose Vw. *Add* 2L **55**
Roseville Av. *Houn* 8A **10**
Roseville Rd. *Hay* 1H **9**
Rosevine Rd. *SW20* 9H **27**
Rose Wlk. *Craw* 5N **181**
Rose Wlk. *Fleet* 3A **88**
Rose Wlk. *Purl* 7H **63**
Rose Wlk. *Surb* 4A **42**
Rose Wlk. *W Wick* 8M **47**
Rosewarne Clo. *Wok* 5K **73**
Rosewood. *Sutt* 6A **62**
Rosewood. *Th Dit* 8G **40**
Rosewood. *Wok* 6C **74**
Rosewood Dri. *Shep* 4A **38**
Rosewood Gro. *Sutt* 8A **44**
Rosewood Rd. *Lind* 4B **168**
Rosewood Way. *W End* 9B **52**
Roshni Ho. *SW17* 7C **28**
Roskell Rd. *SW15* 6J **13**
Roslan Ct. *Horl* 9F **142**
Roslyn Clo. *Mitc* 1B **44**
Roslyn Ct. *Wok* 5K **73**
Ross Clo. *Craw* 6D **182**
Rossdale. *Sutt* 2C **62**
Rossdale Rd. *SW15* 7H **13**
Rossett Clo. *Brack* 3N **31**
Rossetti Gdns. *Coul* 5K **83**
Rossignol Gdns. *Cars* 8E **44**
Rossindel Rd. *Houn* 8A **10**
Rossiter Lodge. *Guild* 4C **114**
Rossiter Rd. *SW12* 2F **28**
Rosslare Clo. *W'ham* 3M **107**
Rosslea. *W'sham* 1L **51**
Rosslyn Av. *SW13* 6D **12**
Rosslyn Av. *Felt* 9H **9**
Rosslyn Clo. *Sun* 7F **22**
Rosslyn Pk. *Wey* 1E **56**
Rosslyn Park R.U.F.C. **7E 12**
Rosslyn Rd. *Twic* 9J **11**
Rossmore Clo. *Craw* 8H **163**
Rossmore Gdns. *Alder* 3K **109**
Ross Pde. *Wall* 3F **62**
Ross Rd. *Cob* 9K **57**
Ross Rd. *SE25* 2A **46**
Ross Rd. *Twic* 2B **24**
Ross Rd. *Wall* 2G **62**
Rosswood Gdns. *Wall* 3G **62**
Rostella Rd. *SW17* 5B **28**
Rostrevor Gdns. *S'hall* 1M **9**
Rostrevor M. *SW6* 4L **13**
Rostrevor Rd. *SW6* 4L **13**
Rostrevor Rd. *SW19* 6M **27**
Rothbury Gdns. *Iswth* 3G **10**
Rothbury Wlk. *Camb* 2G **71**
Rother Clo. *Sand* 7H **49**
Rother Cres. *Craw* 4L **181**
Rotherfield Rd. *Cars* 1E **62**
Rotherhill Av. *SW16* 7H **29**
Rothermere Rd. *Croy* 2K **63**
Rother Rd. *Farnb* 8K **69**
Rothervale. *Horl* 5E **142**
Rotherwick Ct. *Farnb* 5A **90**
Rotherwood Clo. *SW20* 9K **27**
Rotherwood Rd. *SW15* 6J **13**
Rothesay Av. *SW20* 1K **43**
Rothesay Av. *Rich* 7A **12**
Rothesay Rd. *SE25* 3A **46**
Rothes Rd. *Dork* 4H **119** (1K **201**)
Rothschild St. *SE27* 5M **29**
Rothwell Ho. *Crowt* 3H **49**
Rothwell Ho. *Houn* 2A **10**
Rotunda Est. *Alder* 2N **109**
Rougemont Av. *Mord* 5M **43**
Roughets La. *Blet* 7B **104**
Roughets, The. **7C 104**
Rough Fld. *E Grin* 6N **165**
Roughgrove Copse. *Binf* 7G **15**
Roughlands. *Wok* 2G **75**
Rough Rew. *Dork* 8H **119**
Rough Rd. *Wok* 9F **72**
Rough Way. *H'ham* 3M **197**
Rounce La. *W End* 9A **52**
Roundacre. *SW19* 3J **27**
Roundals La. *Hamb* 1H **173**
Round Clo. *Yat* 1E **68**
Round Gro. *Croy* 6G **47**
Round Hill. **1K 109**
Roundhill. *Wok* 6D **74**
Roundhill Dri. *Wok* 5D **74**
Roundhill Way. *Cobh* 7B **58**
Roundhill Way. *Guild* 3J **113**
Round House, The. **9C 164**
Roundhurst. **7M 189**
Round Oak Rd. *Wey* 1A **56**
Roundshaw. **4J 63**
Roundshaw Cen. Wall 4J **63** *(off Mollison Dri.)*
Roundshead Dri. *Warf* 9B **16**
Rounds Hill. **9L 15**
Rounds Hill. *Brack* 9K **15**
Roundthorn Way. *Wok* 3J **73**
Roundway. *Big H* 3E **86**
Roundway. *Camb* 9G **50**
Roundway. *Egh* 6E **20**
Roundway Clo. *Camb* 9G **50**
Roundway Ct. *Craw* 1B **182**
Roundway, The. *Clay* 3F **58**
Roundwood Vw. *Bans* 2J **81**
Roundwood Way. *Bans* 2J **81**
Rounton Rd. *C Crook* 7B **88**
Roupell Ho. *King T* 1M **203**
Roupell Rd. *SW2* 2K **29**
Routh Ct. *Felt* 2E **22**
Routh Rd. *SW18* 1C **28**
Rowallan Rd. *SW6* 3K **13**
Rowan. *Brack* 4D **32**
Rowan Av. *Egh* 6E **20**
Rowan Chase. *Wrec* 6F **128**
Rowan Clo. *SW16* 9G **29**
Rowan Clo. *Camb* 7D **50**
Rowan Clo. *Craw* 3D **182**
Rowan Clo. *Fleet* 4D **88**
Rowan Clo. *Guild* 9L **93**
Rowan Clo. *H'ham* 3A **198**
Rowan Clo. *N Mald* 1D **42**
Rowan Clo. *Reig* 5A **122**
Rowan Ct. *SW11* 1D **28**
Rowan Cres. *SW16* 9G **29**
Rowan Dale. *C Crook* 8A **88**
Rowan Dri. *Crowt* 9H **31**
Rowan Gdns. *Croy* 9C **46**
Rowan Grn. *Wey* 1E **56**
Rowan Gro. *Coul* 8F **82**
Rowan Ho. *Short* 1N **47**
Rowan Rd. *SW16* 1G **45**
Rowan Rd. *W6* 1J **13**
Rowan Rd. *Bren* 3H **11**
Rowan Rd. *W Dray* 1M **7**
Rowans Clo. *Farnb* 5K **69**
Rowanside Clo. *Head D* 5H **169**
Rowans, The. *Hind* 7D **170**
Rowans, The. *Sun* 6G **23**
Rowans, The. *Wok* 5A **74**
Rowan Ter. *W6* 1J **13**
Rowan Wlk. *Brom* 1H **67**
Rowan Wlk. *Craw D* 1F **184**
Rowan Way. *H'ham* 3A **198**
Rowbarns Way. *E Hor* 8G **97**
Rowberry Clo. *SW6* 3H **13**
Rowbury. *G'ming* 3K **133**
Rowcroft Clo. *Ash V* 7E **90**
Rowden Rd. *Beck* 1H **47**
Rowden Rd. *Eps* 1A **60**
Rowdown Cres. *New Ad* 6N **65**
Rowe La. *Pirb* 2D **92**
Rowfant. **1M 183**
Rowfant Clo. *Worth* 3J **183**
Rowfant Rd. *SW17* 2E **28**
Rowfield. *Eden* 9M **127**
Rowhill. **3H 55**
Row Hill. *Add* 3H **55**
Rowhill Av. *Alder* 3L **109**
Rowhill Cres. *Alder* 4L **109**
Rowhills. *Farnh* 4J **109**
Rowhills Clo. *Farnh* 5L **109**
Rowhook. **8M 177**
Rowhook Hill. *Rowh* 8N **177**
Rowhook Rd. *Rowh* 8M **177**
Rowhurst Av. *Add* 3K **55**
Rowhurst Av. *Lea* 4F **78**
Rowland Clo. *Copt* 5B **164**
Rowland Clo. *Wind* 6A **4**
Rowland Hill Almshouses. Ashf 6D **22** *(off Feltham Hill Rd.)*
Rowland Rd. *Cranl* 7M **155**
Rowlands Rd. *H'ham* 2N **197**
Rowland Way. *SW19* 9N **27**
Rowland Way. *Ashf* 8E **22**
Row La. *Alb* 8N **135** (in two parts)
Rowledge. **8D 128**
Rowly. **4K 155**
Rowley Clo. *Brack* 2C **32**
Rowley Clo. *Pyr* 3K **75**
Rowley Ct. *Cat* 9A **84**
Rowlls Rd. *King T* 2M **41** (5M **203**)
Rowly Dri. *Cranl* 5J **155**
Rowly Edge. *Cranl* 4J **155**
Rowntree Rd. *Twic* 2E **24**
Rowplatt La. *Felb* 7H **165**
Row, The. *Eden* 8K **127**
Row Town. **4H 55**
Rowtown. *Add* 4H **55**
Roxbee Cox Ct. *Farnb* 3E **88**
Roxborough Av. *Iswth* 3F **10**
Roxburgh Clo. *Camb* 2G **71**
Roxburgh Rd. *SE27* 6M **29**
Roxby Pl. *SW6* 2M **13**
Roxeth Ct. *Ashf* 6B **22**
Roxford Clo. *Shep* 4F **38**
Roxton Gdns. *Croy* 2K **65**
Royal Aerospace Establishment. **5K 89**
Royal Aerospace Establishment Rd. *Farnb* 4N **89**
Royal Army Chaplain's Department Mus. **2H 51** **(in Bagshot Pk.)**
Royal Army Dental Corps Mus. **6A 90**
Royal Av. *Wor Pk* 8D **42**
Royal Botanic Gardens Kew, The. **4L 11**
Royal Cir. *SE27* 4L **29**
Royal Clo. *SW19* 3J **27**
Royal Clo. *Orp* 1K **67**
Royal Clo. *Wor Pk* 8D **42**
Royal Dri. *Eps* 5G **80**
Royal Duchess M. *SW12* 1F **28**
Royal Earlswood Pk. *Red* 6D **122**
Royale Clo. *Alder* 4A **110**
Royal Free Ct. Wind 6G **4** *(off Batchelors Acre)*
Royal Holloway College (University of London). **7N 19**
Royal Horticultural Society Cotts. *Wis* 3N **75**
Royal Horticultural Society Gardens, The. **5N 75** **(Wisley Gardens)**
Royal Huts Av. *Hind* 5D **170**
Royal M. *Wind C* 4G **5**
Royal Oak Clo. *Yat* 9D **48**
Royal Oak Dri. *Crowt* 8G **30**
Royal Oak Rd. *Wok* 5M **73**
Royal Orchard Clo. *SW18* 1K **27**
Royal Pde. *SW6* 3K **13**
Royal Pde. *Hind* 5D **170**
Royal Pde. Rich 4N **11** *(off Layton Pl.)*
Royal Rd. *Tedd* 6D **24**
Royals, The. *Guild* 4N **113** (5E **202**)
Royal Surrey Regiment Mus. **1J 115**
Royal Victoria Gdns. *S Asc* 3L **33**
Royal Wlk. *Wall* 8F **44**
Royal Windsor Racecourse. **2B 4**
Royce Rd. *Craw* 7E **162**
Roycroft Clo. *SW2* 2L **29**
Roydon Ct. *W on T* 1J **57**
Roy Gro. *Hamp* 7B **24**
Roymount Ct. *Twic* 4E **24**
Royston Av. *Byfl* 8N **55**
Royston Av. *Sutt* 9B **44**
Royston Av. *Wall* 1H **63**
Royston Cen., The. *Ash V* 5D **90**
Royston Clo. *Craw* 8E **162**
Royston Clo. *Houn* 4J **9**
Royston Clo. *W on T* 7H **39**
Royston Ct. *SE24* 1N **29**
Royston Ct. *Hin W* 8F **40**
Royston Ct. *Rich* 4M **11**
Royston Gdns. *Wok* 1A **48**
Royston Rd. *SE20* 1G **46**
Royston Rd. *Byfl* 8N **55**
Royston Rd. *Rich* 8L **11**
Roystons, The. *Surb* 4A **42**
Rozeldene. *Hind* 6C **170**
Rozel Ter. *Croy* 3B **200**
Rubus Clo. *W End* 9B **52**
Ruckmans La. *Oke H* 3A **178** (in two parts)
Rudd Hall Ri. *Camb* 3B **70**
Ruddlesway. *Wind* 5A **4** (in three parts)
Ruden Way. *Eps* 3G **80**
Rudge Ri. *Add* 2H **55**
Rudgwick. **1E 194**
Rudgwick Keep. Horl 7G **142** *(off Langshott La.)*
Rudgwick Rd. *Craw* 2L **181**
Rudgwick Two Tiered Bridge. **2F 194**
Rudloe Rd. *SW12* 1G **28**
Rudsworth Clo. *Coln* 4F **6**
Ruffetts Clo. *S Croy* 4E **64**
Ruffetts, The. *S Croy* 4E **64**
Ruffetts Way. *Tad* 5K **81**
Rufford Clo. *Fleet* 7B **88**
Rufwood. *Craw D* 1D **184**
Rugby Clo. *Owl* 6K **49**
Rugby La. *Sutt* 5J **61**
Rugby Rd. *Twic* 8E **10**
Rugglesbrise Rd. *Ashf* 6M **21**
Rugosa Rd. *W End* 9B **52**
Ruislip St. *SW17* 5D **28**
Rumbold Rd. *SW6* 3N **13**
Rumsey Clo. *Hamp* 7N **23**
Run Common. **1G 155**
Runcorn Clo. *Bew* 7K **181**
Runes Clo. *Mitc* 3B **44**
Runfold. **8A 110**
Runfold St George. *Bad L* 7N **109**
Runnemede Rd. *Egh* 5B **20** (in two parts)
Running Horse Yd. *Bren* 2L **11**
Runnymede. **3N 19**
Runnymede. *SW19* 9A **28**
Runnymede Clo. *Twic* 9B **10**
Runnymede Ct. *Farnb* 7M **69**
Runnymede Ct. *SW15* 2F **26**
Runnymede Ct. *Egh* 5C **20**
Runnymede Cres. *SW16* 9H **29**
Runnymede Gdns. *Twic* 9B **10**
Runnymede Ho. Cher 6J **37** *(off Heriot Rd.)*
Runnymede Rd. *Twic* 9B **10**
Runshooke Ct. *Craw* 6M **181**
Runtley Wood La. *Sut G* 3B **94**
Runwick La. *Farnh* 3A **128**
Rupert Ct. W Mol 3A **40** *(off St Peters Rd.)*
Rupert Rd. *Guild* 4M **113** (5A **202**)
Rural Way. *SW16* 8F **28**
Rural Way. *Red* 3E **122**
Ruscoe Dri. *Wok* 4C **74**
Ruscombe Gdns. *Dat* 3K **5**
Ruscombe Way. *Felt* 1G **22**
Rusham Ct. *Egh* 7C **20**
Rusham Pk. Av. *Egh* 7B **20**
Rusham Rd. *SW12* 1D **28**
Rusham Rd. *Egh* 7B **20**
Rushams Rd. *H'ham* 6H **197**
Rushbury Ct. *Hamp* 9A **24**
Rush Comn. M. *SW2* 1K **29**
Rushcroft. *G'ming* 3K **133**
Rushdene Wlk. *Big H* 4F **86**
Rushden Way. *Farnh* 5J **109**
Rushen Wlk. *Cars* 7B **44**
Rushett. **5K 127**
Rushett Clo. *Th Dit* 7H **41**
Rushett Common. **1E 154**
Rushett Dri. *Dork* 8H **119**
Rushett La. *Chess* 7J **59**
Rushett Rd. *Th Dit* 6H **41**
Rushetts Farm. **7A 122**
Rushetts Pl. *Craw* 9A **162**
Rushetts Rd. *Craw* 9N **161**
Rushetts Rd. *Reig* 7A **122**
Rushey Clo. *N Mald* 3C **42**
Rushfords. *Ling* 6A **146**
Rushley Clo. *Kes* 1F **66**
Rushmead. *Rich* 4H **25**
Rushmead Clo. *Croy* 1C **64**
Rushmere Ct. *Wor Pk* 8F **42**
Rushmere Pl. *SW19* 6J **27**
Rushmere Pl. *Eng G* 6A **20**
Rushmon Gdns. *W on T* 9J **39**
Rushmon Pl. *Cheam* 3K **61**
Rushmon Vs. *N Mald* 3E **42**
Rushmoor. **4A 150**
Rushmoor Clo. *Fleet* 6B **88**
Rushmoor Clo. *Guild* 9J **93**
Rushmoor Ct. *Farnb* 5A **90**
Rushmoor Rd. *Alder* 8J **89**
Rusholme Rd. *SW15* 9J **13**
Rush, The. SW19 9L **27** *(off Kingston Rd.)*
Rushton Av. *S God* 7F **124**
Rushworth Rd. *Reig* 2M **121**
Rushy Mdw. La. *Cars* 9C **44**
Ruskin Av. *Felt* 9G **9**
Ruskin Av. *Rich* 3N **11** (in two parts)
Ruskin Clo. *Craw* 9G **163**
Ruskin Ct. *Crowt* 3D **48**
Ruskin Dri. *Wor Pk* 8G **43**
Ruskin Ho. *S Croy* 8D **200**
Ruskin Mans. W14 2K **13** *(off Queen's Club Gdns.)*
Ruskin Pde. *S Croy* 8D **200**
Ruskin Rd. *Cars* 2D **62**
Ruskin Rd. *Croy* 8M **45** (2A **200**)
Ruskin Rd. *Iswth* 6F **10**
Ruskin Rd. *Stai* 7H **21**
Ruskin Way. *SW19* 9B **28**
Rusper. **2C 180**
Rusper Ct. Cotts. *Rusp* 3D **180**
Rusper Rd. *Capel* 6J **159**
Rusper Rd. *H'ham* 4M **197**
Rusper Rd. *Newd* 2A **160**
Rusper Rd. *Rusp & If'd* 2F **180**
Ruspers Keep. *If'd* 2L **181**
Russell Clo. *W4* 2E **12**
Russell Clo. *Beck* 2L **47**
Russell Clo. *Brack* 7B **32**
Russell Clo. *Tad* 3F **100**
Russell Clo. *Wok* 2M **73**
Russell Ct. *SW16* 6K **29**
Russell Ct. *B'water* 1J **69**
Russell Ct. *Guild* 9M **93**
Russell Ct. *Hind* 5D **170**
Russell Ct. *Lea* 9H **79**
Russell Ct. *Purl* 6L **63**
Russell Ct. Wall 2G **63** *(off Ross Rd.)*
Russell Dri. *Stanw* 9M **7**
Russell Gdns. *Rich* 3J **25**
Russell Gdns. *W Dray* 1B **8**
Russell Grn. Clo. *Purl* 6L **63**
Russell Hill. *Purl* 6K **63**
Russell Hill Pl. *Purl* 7L **63**
Russell Hill Rd. *Purl* 7L **63**
Russell Kerr Clo. *W4* 3B **12**
Russell Pl. *Sutt* 4N **61**
Russell Rd. *SW19* 8M **27**
Russell Rd. *Mitc* 2C **44**
Russell Rd. *Shep* 6D **38**
Russell Rd. *Twic* 9F **10**
Russell Rd. *W on T* 5H **39**
Russell Rd. *Wok* 2M **73**
Russells. *Tad* 9J **81**
Russells Cres. *Horl* 9E **142**
Russell's Footpath. *SW16* 6J **29**
Russell St. *Wind* 4G **4**
Russell Wlk. *Rich* 9M **11**
Russell Way. *Craw* 4E **182**
Russell Way. *Sutt* 2N **61**
Russell Yd. *SW15* 7K **13**

A-Z Surrey 269

Russet Av.—St John's Mdw.

Russet Av. Shep 2F 38
Russet Clo. Horl 8G 143
Russet Clo. Stai 9H 7
Russet Clo. Tong 5C 110
Russet Clo. W on T 9L 39
Russet Dri. Croy 7H 47
Russet Gdns. Camb 3B 70
Russet Glade. Alder 4J 109
Russett Ct. Cat 3D 104
Russett Ct. H'ham 4N 197
Russetts Clo. Wok 2B 74
Russetts Dri. Fleet 5B 88
Russet Way. N Holm 8K 119
Russ Hill 5G 161
Russ Hill. Charl 5F 160
Russ Hill Rd. Charl 4J 161
Russington Rd. Shep 5E 38
Russley Grn. Wokgm 7A 30
Rusthall Clo. Croy 5F 46
Rustic Av. SW16 8F 28
Rustic Glen. C Crook 8A 88
Rustington Wlk. Mord 6L 43
Ruston Av. Surb 6A 42
Ruston Clo. M'bowr 6G 182
Ruston Way. Asc 1H 33
Rutford Rd. SW16 6J 29
Ruth Clo. Farnb 9H 69
Ruthen Clo. Eps 1A 80
Rutherford Clo. Sutt 3B 62
Rutherford Clo. Wind 4C 4
Rutherford Way. Craw 7E 162
Rutherford Way Ind. Est. Craw 7E 162
Rutherwick Clo. Horl 8D 142
Rutherwick Ri. Coul 4J 83
Rutherwick Tower. Horl 8D 142
Rutherwyke Clo. Eps 3F 60
Rutherwyk Rd. Cher 6G 36
Rutland Clo. SW14 6A 12
Rutland Clo. SW19 8C 28
Rutland Clo. Alder 1M 109
Rutland Clo. Asht 4L 79
Rutland Clo. Chess 3M 59
Rutland Clo. Eps 6C 60
Rutland Clo. Red 2D 122
Rutland Ct. King T 8H 203
Rutland Dri. Mord 5L 43
Rutland Dri. Rich 2K 25
Rutland Gdns. Croy 1B 64
Rutland Gro. W6 1G 13
Rutland Rd. SW19 8C 28
Rutland Rd. Hay 1E 8
Rutland Rd. Twic 3D 24
Rutland Ter. Alder 1M 109
Rutlish Rd. SW19 9M 27
Rutson Rd. Byfl 1A 76
Rutter Gdns. Mitc 3A 44
Rutton Hill Rd. G'ming 2H 171
Ruvigny Gdns. SW15 6J 13
Ruxbury Rd. Cher 5E 36
Ruxley Clo. Eps 2A 60
Ruxley Ct. Eps 2B 60
Ruxley Cres. Clay 3H 59
Ruxley La. Eps 3A 60
Ruxley M. Eps 2A 60
Ruxley Ridge. Clay 4G 58
Ruxley Towers. Clay 4G 59
Ruxton Clo. Coul 2G 83
Ryan Ct. SW16 8J 29
Ryan Dri. Bren 2G 11
Ryan Mt. Sand 7F 48
Ryarsh Cres. Orp 1N 67
Rybrook Dri. W on T 8K 39
Rycroft. Wind 6C 4
Rydal Clo. Farnb 2J 89
Rydal Clo. Camb 1H 71
Rydal Clo. If'd 5J 181
Rydal Clo. Purl 9A 64
Rydal Dri. C Crook 8A 88
Rydal Dri. W Wick 8N 47
Rydal Gdns. SW15 6D 26
Rydal Gdns. Houn 9B 10
Rydal Pl. Light 7M 51
Rydal Rd. SW16 5H 29
Rydal Way. Egh 8D 20
Ryde Clo. Rip 8L 75
Ryde Ct. Alder 3A 110
Ryde Gdns. Yat 9A 48
Ryde Heron. Knap 4H 73
Ryde Lands. Cranl 6A 156
Rydens 9K 39
Rydens Av. W on T 8J 39
Rydens Clo. W on T 8K 39
Rydens Gro. W on T 1L 57
Rydens Pk. W on T 8L 39
Rydens Rd. W on T 9J 39
Rydens Way. Wok 7C 74
Ryde Pl. Twic 9K 11
Ryders Way. H'ham 1M 197
Rydes Av. Guild 9J 93
Rydes Clo. Wok 7E 74
Rydeshill 1H 113
Ryde's Hill Cres. Guild 8J 93
Ryde's Hill Rd. Guild 1J 113
Ryde, The. Stai 9K 21
Ryde Va. Rd. SW12 3G 28
Rydings. Wind 6C 4
Rydon M. SW19 8H 27
Rydon's La. Coul 7N 83
Rydon's Wood Clo. Coul 7N 83
Rye Ash. Craw 2E 182
(in two parts)
Ryebeck Rd. C Crook 8B 88
Ryebridge Clo. Lea 5G 79
Ryebrook. Lea 7G 79
Ryebrook Rd. Lea 5G 79
Rye Clo. Farnb 8K 69
Rye Clo. Brack 8B 16
Rye Clo. Fleet 9D 68
Rye Clo. Guild 1H 113
Ryecroft Av. Twic 1B 24
Ryecroft Dri. H'ham 5G 196
Ryecroft Gdns. B'water 2K 69
Ryecroft Lodge. SW16 7M 29
Ryecroft Rd. SW16 7L 29
Ryecroft St. SW6 4N 13
Rye Fld. Asht 3K 79
Ryefield Path. SW15 2F 26
Ryefield Rd. SE19 7N 29
Rye Gro. Cranl 7J 155
Rye Gro. Light 4C 52
Ryehurst La. Binf 5K 15
Ryeland Clo. Fleet 1D 88
Ryelands. Craw 4M 181
Ryelands. Horl 7G 142
Ryelands Clo. Cat 8B 84
Ryelands Ct. Lea 5G 79
Ryelands Pl. Wey 9F 38
Ryelaw Rd. C Crook 8B 88
Ryemead La. Wink 4G 17
Ryersh La. Capel 3H 159
Rye Wlk. SW15 8J 13
Ryfold Rd. SW19 4M 27
Ryland Clo. Felt 5G 23
Rylandes Rd. S Croy 5E 64
Ryle Rd. Farnh 3G 128
Rylston Rd. SW6 2L 13
Rymer Rd. Croy 6B 46
Rysted La. W'ham 4L 107
Ryst Wood Rd. F Row 7K 187
Rythe Ct. Th Dit 6G 41
Rythe Rd. Clay 2D 58
Rythe, The. Esh 6B 58

S

Sabah Ct. Ashf 5B 22
Sable Clo. Houn 6K 9
Sabre Ct. Alder 2K 109
Sachel Ct. Dri. Alf 7H 175
Sachel Ct. M. Alf 7G 174
Sachel Ct. Rd. Alf 6F 174
Sachel Hill La. Alf 7F 174
Sackville Clo. E Grin 7M 165
Sackville College 9B 166
Sackville Cotts. Blet 2A 124
Sackville Ct. E Grin 1B 186
Sackville Gdns. E Grin 7M 165
(in two parts)
Sackville Ho. SW16 4J 29
Sackville La. E Grin 7L 165
Sackville Rd. Sutt 4M 61
Saddleback Rd. Camb 7C 50
Saddleback Way. Fleet 1C 88
Saddlebrook Pk. Sun 8F 22
Saddler Corner. Sand 8G 49
Saddler Row. Craw 6B 182
Saddlers Clo. Guild 2F 114
Saddlers M. King T 9J 25
Saddlers Scarp. Gray 5M 169
Saddlers Way. Eps 6C 80
Saddlewood. Camb 2A 70
Sadler Clo. Mitc 1D 44
Sadlers Ride. W Mol 1C 40
Sadlers Way. Hasl 1H 189
Saffron Clo. Craw 6M 181
Saffron Clo. Croy 5J 45
Saffron Clo. Dat 4L 5
Saffron Ct. Farnb 1H 89
Saffron Ct. Felt 1D 22
Saffron Platt. Guild 8K 93
Saffron Rd. Brack 3N 31
Saffron Way. Surb 7K 41
Sage Wlk. Warf 8B 16
Sailmakers Ct. SW6 6N 13
Sailors La. Thur 8D 150
Sainfoin Rd. SW17 3E 28
St Agatha's Dri. King T 7M 25
St Agatha's Gro. Cars 7D 44
St Agnes Rd. E Grin 8A 166
St Albans Av. Felt 6L 23
St Albans Av. Wey 9B 38
St Alban's Clo. Wind 4G 5
St Albans Clo. Wood S 2E 112
St Alban's Gdns. Tedd 6G 25
St Alban's Gro. Cars 6C 44
St Alban's Rd. King T 7L 25
St Alban's Rd. Reig 1M 121
St Alban's Rd. Sutt 1L 61
St Albans Roundabout. Farnb 5A 90
St Alban's St. Wind 4G 5
St Albans Ter. W6 2K 13
St Andrews. Brack 5K 31
St Andrews. Cranl 6K 155
St Andrews. Horl 9F 142
(off Aurum Clo.)
St Andrew's Av. Wind 5C 4
St Andrew's Clo. Crowt 1E 48
St Andrew's Clo. Iswth 4E 10
St Andrew's Clo. Old Win 9K 5
St Andrews Clo. Reig 4N 121
St Andrew's Clo. Shep 3E 38
St Andrews Clo. Wok 4M 73
St Andrew's Clo. Wray 9A 6
St Andrew's Ct. SW18 3A 28
St Andrews Ct. Sutt 9C 44
St Andrew's Cres. Wind 5C 4
St Andrews Gdns. Cob 9K 57
St Andrew's Ga. Wok 5B 74
St Andrews Mans. W14 2K 13
(off St Andrews Rd.)
St Andrews M. SW12 2H 29
St Andrew's Rd. W14 2K 13
St Andrew's Rd. Cars 9C 44
St Andrew's Rd. Coul 3E 82
St Andrew's Rd. Croy 1N 63 (6B 200)
St Andrews Rd. If'd 4J 181
St Andrew's Rd. Surb 5K 41
St Andrew's Sq. Surb 5K 41
St Andrew's Wlk. Cob 2J 77
St Andrew's Way. Frim 7D 70
St Andrews Way. Oxt 9G 107
St Anne's Av. Stanw 1M 21
St Annes Boulevd. Red 1F 122
St Anne's Ct. W Wick 1A 66
St Anne's Dri. Red 2E 122
St Annes Dri. Wokgm 2F 30
St Annes Dri. N. Red 1E 122
St Annes Glade. Bag 4H 51
St Anne's Mt. Red 2E 122
St Anne's Ri. Red 2E 122
St Annes Rd. Craw 9G 163
St Anne's Rd. G'ming 6K 133
St Ann's Clo. Cher 5H 37
St Ann's Ct. Vir W 4B 36
St Ann's Cres. SW18 9N 13
St Ann's Hill. SW18 8N 13 & 1A 28
St Ann's Hill Rd. Cher 5E 36
St Ann's Pk. Rd. SW18 9N 13 & 1A 28
St Ann's Pas. SW13 6D 12
St Ann's Rd. SW13 5E 12
St Ann's Rd. Cher 5G 36
(in two parts)
St Anns Way. Berr G 3K 87
St Ann's Way. S Croy 3M 63
St Anthony's Clo. SW17 3C 28
St Anthonys Clo. Brack 9M 15
St Anthony's Way. Felt 7G 9
St Arvan's Clo. Croy 9B 46
St Aubin Clo. Craw 7L 181
St Aubyns. Dork 7G 119
St Aubyn's Av. SW19 6L 27
St Aubyn's Av. Houn 8A 10
St Augustine's Av. S Croy 3N 63
St Augustine's Clo. Alder 3B 110
St Austins. Gray 6B 170
St Barnabas Clo. Beck 1M 47
St Barnabas Ct. Craw 2G 182
St Barnabas Gdns. W Mol 4A 40
St Barnabas Rd. Mitc 8E 28
St Barnabas Rd. Sutt 2B 62
St Bartholomews Ct. Guild 5B 114
St Benedict's Clo. SW17 6E 28
St Benedicts Clo. Alder 3M 109
St Benet's Clo. SW17 3C 28
St Benet's Gro. Cars 6A 44
St Bernards. Croy 9B 46 (5F 200)
St Bernard's Clo. SE27 5N 29
St Brelades Clo. Dork 7G 119
St Brelades Rd. Craw 7L 181
St Catherines. Wey 9C 38
St Catherines. Wok 6M 73
St Catherines Clo. Chess 3K 59
St Catherine's Clo. SW17 3C 28
St Catherine's Ct. Brmly 4B 134
St Catherines Ct. Felt 2H 23
St Catherines Ct. Stai 5J 21
St Catherine's Cross. Blet 3B 124
St Catherine's Dri. Guild 7L 113
St Catherine's Hill. Guild 7M 113
St Catherines Pk. Guild 5B 114
St Catherines Rd. Craw 9G 163
St Catherines Rd. Frim & Frim G 5D 70
(in two parts)
St Cecilia's Clo. Sutt 7K 43
St Chads Clo. Surb 6J 41
St Charles Pl. Wey 2B 56
St Christopher's. Ling 7N 145
St Christophers Clo. Alder 2B 110
St Christopher's Clo. Hasl 2E 188
St Christopher's Clo. H'ham 4J 197
St Christopher's Clo. Iswth 4E 10
St Christophers Gdns. Asc 9H 17
St Christopher's Gdns. T Hth 2L 45
St Christopher's Grn. Hasl 2E 188
St Christopher's M. Wall 2G 62
St Christopher's Pl. Farnb 2L 89
St Christopher's Rd. Farnb 2M 89
St Christopher's Rd. Hasl 2E 188
St Clair Clo. Oxt 8M 105
St Clair Clo. Reig 3A 122
St Clair Dri. Wor Pk 9G 42
St Claire Cotts. D'land 1D 166
St Clair's Rd. Croy 8B 46 (3F 200)
St Clare Bus. Pk. Hamp 7C 24
St Clement Rd. Craw 7L 181
St Clements Ct. Farnb 7N 69
St Clements Mans. SW6 2J 13
(off Lillie Rd.)
St Cloud Rd. SE27 5N 29
St Crispins Way. Ott 5E 54
St Cross Rd. Farnh 9H 109
St Cross Rd. Frim G 7E 70
St Cuthberts Clo. Eng G 7N 19
St Cyprian's St. SW17 5D 28
St David's. Coul 4K 83
St David's Clo. Farnb 6L 69
St David's Clo. Farnh 5K 109
St David's Clo. Reig 2A 122
St David's Clo. W Wick 6L 47
St David's Dri. Eng G 8M 19
St Denis Rd. SE27 5N 29
St Denys Clo. Knap 5F 72
St Dionis Rd. SW6 5L 13
St Dunstan's. (Junct.) 3L 61
St Dunstan's Clo. Hay 1G 9
St Dunstan's Hill. Sutt 2K 61
St Dunstan's La. Beck 5M 47
St Dunstan's Rd. SE25 3C 46
St Dunstan's Rd. W6 1J 13
St Dunstan's Rd. Felt 4G 23
St Dunstan's Rd. Houn 5J 9
(in two parts)
St Edith Clo. Eps 1B 80 (8H 201)
St Edmund Clo. Craw 9B 162
St Edmund's Clo. SW17 3C 28
St Edmund's La. Twic 1B 24
St Edmunds Sq. SW13 2H 13
St Edmund's Steps. G'ming 7G 133
St Edward's Clo. E Grin 9M 165
St Edward's Clo. New Ad 7N 65
St Elizabeth Dri. Eps 1B 80 (8H 201)
St Faith's Rd. SE21 2M 29
St Francis Gdns. Copt 6M 163
St Francis Wlk. Bew 5K 181
St George's Av. Wey 3C 56
St Georges Bus. Pk. Wey 5B 56
St George's Clo. Bad L 7N 109
St Georges Clo. Horl 8F 142
St George's Clo. Wey 2D 56
St Georges Clo. Wind 4B 4
St George's Ct. SW15 7L 13
St Georges Ct. Add 1L 55
St George's Ct. Craw 2B 182
St Georges Ct. E Grin 7M 165
St Georges Ct. Owl 5K 49
St George's Gdns. Eps 1E 80
St George's Gdns. H'ham 4L 197
St George's Gdns. Surb 8A 42
St George's Gro. SW17 4B 28
St George's Hill 6C 56
St George's Hill. Red 2H 143
St George's Ind. Est. Camb 3N 69
St George's Ind. Est. King T 6K 25
St George's La. Asc 2M 33
(in three parts)
St George's M. Farnh 9G 109
(off Bear La.)
St George's Pl. Twic 2G 25
St George's Rd. SW19 8L 27
(in two parts)
St George's Rd. Add 1L 55
St George's Rd. Alder 3N 109
St George's Rd. Bad L & Farnh 6N 109
(in two parts)
St George's Rd. Beck 1L 47
St George's Rd. Camb 9B 50
St George's Rd. Farnh 2J 129
St George's Rd. Felt 5L 23
St George's Rd. King T 8N 25 (1M 203)
St George's Rd. Mitc 2F 44
St George's Rd. Red 2H 143
St Georges Rd. Rich 6M 11
St George's Rd. Twic 8H 11
St George's Rd. Wall 2F 62
St George's Rd. Wey 3E 56
St George's Rd. E. Alder 3N 109
St George's Sq. N Mald 2D 42
St George's Wlk. Croy 9N 45 (3C 200)
St George's Yd. Farnh 1G 129
(off Castle St.)
St Giles Clo. Orp 2M 67
St Gothard Rd. SE27 5N 29
(in two parts)
St Helens. Th Dit 6F 40
St Helen's Cres. SW16 9K 29
St Helens Cres. Sand 7G 48
St Helen's Rd. SW16 9K 29
St Helier 6C 44
St Helier Av. Mord 6A 44
St Helier Clo. Craw 7M 181
St Helier Clo. Wokgm 5A 30
St Helier's Av. Houn 8A 10
St Hilda's Av. Ashf 6N 21
St Hilda's Clo. SW17 3C 28
St Hilda's Clo. Craw 8G 163
St Hilda's Clo. Horl 8F 142
St Hilda's Clo. Knap 4G 73
St Hilda's Rd. SW13 2G 12
Saint Hill 5M 185
Saint Hill Grn. E Grin 5N 185
Saint Hill Rd. E Grin 3L 185
St Hoathly Rd. E Grin 7M 185
St Hughes Clo. SW17 3C 28
St Hughs Clo. Craw 9G 163
St Ives. Craw 2G 182
St James Av. Eps 7E 60
St James' Av. Farnh 8J 109
St James Av. Sutt 2M 61
St James Clo. Eps 1D 80 (8L 201)
St James Clo. N Mald 4E 42
St James Clo. Wok 5K 73
St James Ct. Asht 4K 79
St James Ct. Farnh 9H 109
St James M. Wey 1C 56
St James Pl. S Croy 3B 64
St James Rd. Cars 9C 44
St James Rd. E Grin 9N 165
St James Rd. Fleet 5A 88
St James Rd. Mitc 8E 28
St James Rd. Purl 9M 63
St James' Rd. Surb 5K 41
St James Rd. Sutt 2M 61
St James's Av. Beck 2H 47
St James's Av. Hamp H 6C 24
St James's Clo. SW17 3D 28
St James's Cotts. Rich 8K 11
St James's Ct. King T 2L 41 (6J 203)
St James's Dri. SW17 & SW12 2D 28
St James's Pk. Croy 6N 45
St James's Pl. Cranl 7L 155
St James's Rd. Croy 6M 45
St James's Rd. Hamp H 6B 24
St James's Rd. King T 1K 41 (4H 203)
St James St. W6 1H 13
St James Ter. SW12 2E 28
St James' Ter. Farnh 9H 109
St James Wlk. Craw 8A 182
St Joan Clo. Craw 9B 162
St John Clo. H'ham 7L 197
St John's 5C 122
(Redhill)
St Johns 6K 73
(Woking)
St John's. N Holm 9J 119
St John's. Red 5C 122
St John's Av. SW15 8J 13
St John's Av. Eps 8F 60
St John's Av. Lea 8H 79
St Johns Chu. Rd. Wott 8N 117
St John's Clo. SW6 3M 13
St John's Clo. E Grin 8A 166
St John's Clo. Guild 4K 113
St John's Clo. Lea 8J 79
St John's Corner. Red 5D 122
(off St John's Rd.)
St John's Ct. Farnb 9J 69
St John's Ct. Brkwd 7C 72
St John's Ct. Egh 6C 20
St John's Ct. Iswth 5F 10
St John's Ct. King T 7K 203
St Johns Ct. S God 7J 125
St John's Ct. Westc 6C 118
(off St John's Rd.)
St Johns Ct. Wok 6K 73
St John's Cres. Broad H 5E 196
St Johns Dri. SW18 2N 27
St John's Dri. W on T 7K 39
St John's Dri. Wind 5D 4
St John's Gro. SW13 5E 12
St John's Gro. Rich 7L 11
St John's Hill. Coul 4L 83
(in two parts)
St John's Hill. Purl 3L 83
St John's Hill Rd. Wok 6K 73
St John's Lye. Wok 6J 73
(in three parts)
St John's Mdw. Blind H 3G 145

St John's M.—Sandrock Hill Rd.

St John's M. Wok. 6K 73
St John's Pas. SW19. 7K 27
St Johns Ri. Berr G. 3K 87
St John's Ri. Wok. 5L 73
St John's Rd. Farnb. 1J 89
St John's Rd. SW19. 8K 27
St John's Rd. Asc. 8K 17
St John's Rd. Cars. 9C 44
St John's Rd. Craw. 3A 182
St John's Rd. Croy. 9M 45 (4A 200)
St John's Rd. E Grin. 8A 166
St John's Rd. E Mol. 3D 40
St John's Rd. Farnh. 3G 129
St John's Rd. Felt. 5M 23
St John's Rd. Guild. 4J 113
St John's Rd. Hamp W. 1J 41
St John's Rd. Iswth. 5F 10
St John's Rd. Lea. 8J 79
St John's Rd. N Mald. 2B 42
St John's Rd. Red. 5D 122
St John's Rd. Rich. 7L 11
St John's Rd. Sand. 8G 49
St John's Rd. Sutt. 8N 43
St John's Rd. Westc. 6C 118
St John's Rd. Wind. 5D 4
St John's Rd. Wok. 6J 73
St Johns St. Crowt. 2G 49
St John's St. G'ming. 5J 133
St John's Ter. SW15. 4D 26 (off Kingston Va.)
St John's Ter. Rd. Red. 5D 122
St John's Way. Cher. 7J 37
St Joseph's Rd. Alder. 3M 109
St Jude's Clo. Eng G. 6M 19
St Judes Rd. Eng G. 5M 19
St Julian's Clo. SW16. 5L 29
St Julian's Farm Rd. SE27. 5L 29
St Katherines Rd. Cat. 3D 104
St Lawrence Bus. Cen. Twic. 3J 23
St Lawrence Ct. Chob. 7H 53
St Lawrence Ho. Chob. 7H 53 (off Bagshot Rd.)
St Lawrence's Way. Reig. 3M 121
St Lawrence Way. Cat. 1N 103
St Leonard's Av. Wind. 5F 4
St Leonards Ct. SW14. 6B 12
St Leonard's Dri. Craw. 5E 182
St Leonards Forest. 4C 198
St Leonard's Gdns. Houn. 4M 9
St Leonard's Hill. Wind. 7A 4
St Leonard's Park. 5A 198
St Leonards Pk. E Grin. 9N 165
St Leonard's Ri. Orp. 1N 67
St Leonard's Rd. SW14. 6A 12
St Leonard's Rd. Clay. 3F 58
St Leonard's Rd. Croy. 9M 45
St Leonard's Rd. Eps. 6H 81
St Leonard's Rd. H'ham. 8L 197
St Leonard's Rd. Surb. 4K 41
St Leonard's Rd. Th Dit. 5G 40
St Leonard's Rd. Wind. 6D 4 (Imperial Rd.)
St Leonard's Rd. Wind. 9A 4 (Queen Adelaide's Ride)
St Leonards Sq. Surb. 4K 41
St Leonard's Wlk. SW16. 8K 29
St Louis Rd. SE27. 5N 29
St Luke's Clo. SE25. 5E 46
St Lukes Ct. Wok. 1E 74
St Luke's Pas. King T. 9M 25 (1L 203)
St Luke's Rd. Old Win. 9K 5
St Luke's Rd. Whyt. 5C 84
St Lukes Sq. Guild. 4B 114
St Margaret Dri. Eps. 1B 80 (8H 201)
St Margarets. 9H 11
St Margaret's. Guild. 3B 114
St Margaret's Av. Ashf. 6C 22
St Margarets Av. Berr G. 3K 87
St Margaret's Av. Dor P. 4A 166
St Margaret's Av. Sutt. 9K 43
St Margarets Bus. Cen. Twic. 9H 11
St Margarets Cotts. Fern. 9F 188
St Margarets Ct. SW15. 7G 12
St Margaret's Cres. SW15. 8G 13
St Margaret's Dri. Twic. 8H 11
St Margaret's Gro. Twic. 9G 11
St Margaret's Rd. Coul. 8F 82
St Margaret's Rd. E Grin. 7B 166
St Margarets Rd. Iswth & Twic. 7H 11
St Margarets Roundabout. (Junct.) 9H 11
St Mark's Clo. Farnb. 4A 90
St Marks Clo. SW6. 4M 13
St Mark's Gro. SW10. 3N 13
St Mark's Hill. Surb. 5L 41
St Mark's La. H'ham. 2L 197
St Mark's Pl. SW19. 7L 27
St Mark's Pl. Farnh. 5G 109
St Marks Pl. Wind. 5F 4
St Mark's Rd. SE25. 3D 46
St Mark's Rd. Binf. 8H 15
St Mark's Rd. Eps. 5H 81
St Marks Rd. Mitc. 1D 44
St Mark's Rd. Tedd. 8H 25
St Marks Rd. Wind. 5F 4
St Martha's Av. Wok. 8B 74
St Marthas Ct. Chil. 9D 114
St Martin Clo. Hand. 9N 199
St Martin's Av. Eps. 1D 80 (8L 201)
St Martins Clo. E Hor. 7F 96
St Martins Clo. Eps. 9D 60 (7M 201)
St Martin's Ct. Ashf. 6L 21
St Martin's Ct. E Hor. 7F 96
St Martins Dri. W on T. 9K 39
St Martins Est. SW2. 2L 29
St Martins La. Beck. 4L 47
St Martins M. Dork. 5G 119 (2J 201)
St Martins M. Pyr. 3J 75
St Martin's Wlk. Dork. 4H 119 (1K 201)
St Martins Way. SW17. 4A 28
St Mary Av. Wall. 9E 44
St Marys. Wey. 9E 38
St Mary's Av. Brom. 2N 47
St Mary's Av. Stanw. 1M 21
St Mary's Av. Tedd. 7F 24
St Mary's Av. Central. S'hall. 1B 10
St Mary's Av. S. S'hall. 1B 10
St Mary's Clo. Chess. 4M 59
St Mary's Clo. Eps. 4E 60
St Mary's Clo. Fet. 1D 98
St Mary's Clo. Oxt. 7A 100
St Mary's Clo. Sand. 7H 49
St Mary's Clo. Stanw. 1M 21
St Mary's Clo. Sun. 3H 39
St Mary's Ct. Wall. 1G 62
St Mary's Ct. W'ham. 4M 107
St Mary's Cres. Iswth. 3D 10
St Mary's Cres. Stanw. 1M 21
St Mary's Dri. Craw. 1F 182
St Mary's Dri. Felt. 1D 22
St Marys Garden. Worp. 5H 93
St Mary's Gdns. Bag. 4J 51
St Mary's Gdns. H'ham. 7J 197
St Mary's Grn. Big H. 5E 86
St Mary's Gro. SW13. 6G 12
St Mary's Gro. W4. 2A 12
St Mary's Gro. Big H. 5E 86
St Mary's Gro. Rich. 7M 11
St Mary's Hill. Asc. 5N 33
St Mary's La. Wink. 4H 17
St Marys M. Rich. 3J 25
St Marys Mill. C'fold. 6E 172
St Mary's Mt. Cat. 2C 104
St Marys Pl. Farnh. 9H 109
St Mary's Rd. SE25. 2B 46
St Mary's Rd. SW19. 6K 27
St Mary's Rd. Asc. 6M 33
St Mary's Rd. Ash V. 8E 90
St Mary's Rd. Camb. 9A 50
St Mary's Rd. Dit H. 6J 41
St Mary's Rd. E Mol. 4D 40
St Mary's Rd. Lea. 9H 79
St Mary's Rd. Reig. 4N 121
St Mary's Rd. S Croy. 6A 64
St Mary's Rd. Surb. 5K 41
St Mary's Rd. Wey. 1E 56
St Mary's Rd. Wok. 4M 73
St Mary's Rd. Wor Pk. 8D 42
St Mary's Wlk. Blet. 2A 124
St Mary's Wlk. H'ham. 7J 197
St Marys Way. Guild. 1H 113
St Matthew's Av. Surb. 7L 41
St Matthew's Rd. Red. 2D 122
St Maur Rd. SW6. 4L 13
St Michael's Av. Guild. 7F 92
St Michaels Clo. Fleet. 5C 88
St Michael's Clo. W on T. 8K 39
St Michael's Clo. Wor Pk. 8E 42
St Michaels Cotts. Wokgm. 8H 31
St Michael's Ct. Wey. 2D 56 (off Princes Rd.)
St Michael's Rd. Ashf. 6B 22
St Michael's Rd. Farnb. 8N 69
St Michael's Rd. Alder. 3N 109
St Michael's Rd. Camb. 1N 69
St Michael's Rd. Cat. 9A 84
St Michael's Rd. Croy. 7N 45 (1C 200)
St Michaels Rd. E Grin. 8A 166
St Michael's Rd. Sand. 7E 48
St Michael's Rd. Wall. 3C 62
St Michael's Rd. Wok. 1F 74
St Mildred's Rd. Guild. 2B 114
St Monicas Rd. Kgswd. 8L 81
St Nazaire Clo. Egh. 6E 20
St Nicholas Av. Bookh. 3B 98
St Nicholas Cen. Sutt. 2N 61
St Nicholas Clo. Fleet. 4A 88
St Nicholas Ct. Craw. 2G 182
St Nicholas Ct. King T. 8J 203
St Nicholas Cres. Pyr. 3J 75
St Nicholas Dri. Shep. 6B 38
St Nicholas Glebe. SW17. 8E 28
St Nicholas Hill. Lea. 9H 79
St Nicholas Rd. Sutt. 2N 61
St Nicholas Rd. Th Dit. 5F 40
St Nicholas Way. Sutt. 1N 61
St Nicolas Av. Cranl. 7N 155
St Nicolas Clo. Cranl. 7N 155
St Normans Way. Eps. 6F 60
St Olaf's Rd. SW6. 3K 13
St Olaves Clo. Stai. 8H 21
St Olaves Wlk. SW16. 1G 45
St Omer Ridge. Guild. 4C 114
St Omer Rd. Guild. 4C 114
St Oswald's Rd. SW16. 9M 29
St Paul's Clo. Ashf. 6D 22
St Paul's Clo. Add. 2J 55
St Paul's Clo. Cars. 7C 44
St Paul's Clo. Chess. 1K 59
St Paul's Clo. Hay. 1E 8
St Paul's Clo. Houn. 5M 9
St Pauls Clo. Tong. 5D 110
St Paul's Ct. Houn. 6M 9
St Paul's Ga. Wokgm. 2A 30
St Paul's Rd. Bren. 2K 11
St Paul's Rd. Rich. 6M 11
St Paul's Rd. Stai. 6F 20
St Paul's Rd. T Hth. 2N 45
St Paul's Rd. Wok. 4C 74
St Paul's Rd. E. Dork. 5H 119 (3L 201)
St Paul's Rd. W. Dork. 6G 119 (4J 201)
St Paul's Studios. W6. 1K 13 (off Talgarth Rd.)
St Paul's Wlk. King T. 8N 25
St Peters Av. Berr G. 3K 87
St Peter's Clo. SW17. 3C 28
St Peter's Clo. Old Win. 8K 5
St Peter's Clo. Stai. 7H 21
St Peter's Clo. Wok. 7E 74
St Peters Ct. W Mol. 3A 40
St Peter's Gdns. SE27. 4L 29
St Peters Gdns. Wrec. 5E 128
St Peter's Gdns. Yat. 9C 48
St Peter's Gro. W6. 1F 12
St Peters Mead. As. 2F 110
St Peters Pk. Alder. 4K 109
St Peter's Rd. W6. 1F 12
St Peter's Rd. Craw. 3A 182
St Peter's Rd. Croy. 1A 64 (6D 200)
St Peter's Rd. King T. 1N 41
St Peters Rd. Old Win. 8K 5
St Peter's Rd. Twic. 8H 11
St Peter's Rd. W Mol. 3A 40
St Peter's Rd. Wok. 8D 74
St Peter's Sq. W6. 1E 12
St Peter's St. S Croy. 2A 64 (8E 200)
St Peter's Ter. SW6. 3L 13
St Peter's Vs. W6. 1F 12
St Peter's Way. Cher & Add. 1F 54
St Peter's Way. Frim. 7D 70
St Peters Way. Hay. 1E 8
St Peter's Wharf. W6. 1F 12
St Philip's Av. Wor Pk. 8G 42
St Philip's Ga. Wor Pk. 8G 43
St Philips Rd. Surb. 5K 41
St Phillips Ct. Fleet. 4B 88
St Pier's La. Ling & M Grn. 8B 146
St Pinnock Av. Stai. 9J 21
St Richard's M. Craw. 3D 182 (off Broomdashers Rd.)
St Sampson Rd. Craw. 7L 181
St Saviour's College. SE27. 5N 29
St Saviours Pl. Guild. 3M 113 (3B 202)
St Saviour's Rd. Croy. 5M 45
Saints Clo. SE27. 5M 29
St Sebastian's Clo. Wokgm. 9D 30
St Simon's Av. SW15. 8H 13
Saints M. Mitc. 2C 44
St Stephen Clo. Craw. 9B 162
St Stephen's Av. Asht. 3L 79
St Stephens Clo. Hasl. 2D 188
St Stephen's Cres. T Hth. 2L 45
St Stephen's Gdns. SW15. 8L 13
St Stephen's Gdns. Twic. 9J 11
St Stephen's Pas. Twic. 9J 11
St Stephen's Rd. Houn. 9A 10
St Stevens Clo. Hasl. 1G 188
St Swithun's Clo. E Grin. 9B 166
St Theresa Clo. Eps. 1B 80 ([illegible] 201)
St Theresa's Rd. Felt. 7C 9
St Thomas Clo. Surb. 7M 41
St Thomas Clo. Wok. 4M 73
St Thomas Dri. E Clan. 9N 95
St Thomas Rd. W4. 2B 12
St Thomas's M. Guild. 5B 114
St Thomas's Way. SW6. 3L 13
St Thomas Wlk. Coln. 3F 6
St Vincent Clo. SE27. 6M 29
St Vincent Clo. Craw. 4H 183
St Vincent Rd. Twic. 9C 10
St Vincent Rd. W on T. 9J 39
St Winifreds. Kenl. 2N 83
St Winifred's Rd. Big H. 5H 87
St Winifred's Rd. Tedd. 7H 25
Salamanca. Crowt. 2D 48
Salamanca Pk. Alder. 1L 109
Salamander Clo. King T. 6J 25
Salamander Quay. King T. 9K 25 (2G 203)
Salbrook Rd. Red. 2E 142
Salcombe Dri. Mord. 7J 43
Salcombe Rd. Ashf. 4N 21
Salcot Cres. New Ad. 6M 65
Salcott Rd. Croy. 9J 45
Sale Garden Cotts. Wokgm. 3B 30
Salehurst Rd. Worth. 3J 183
Salem Pl. Croy. 9N 45 (5B 200)
Salerno Clo. Alder. 1M 109
Sales Ct. Alder. 3L 109
Salesian Gdns. Cher. 7J 37
Salesian Vw. Farnb. 5C 90
Salford Rd. SW2. 2H 29
Salfords. 2E 142
Salfords Ind. Est. Red. 3F 142
Salfords Way. Red. 2E 142
Salisbury Av. Sutt. 3L 61
Salisbury Clo. Wokgm. 6A 30
Salisbury Clo. Wor Pk. 9E 42
Salisbury Ct. Cars. 2D 62
Salisbury Gdns. SW19. 8K 27
Salisbury Gro. Myt. 1D 90
Salisbury M. SW6. 3L 13
Salisbury Pas. SW6. 3L 13 (off Dawes Rd.)
Salisbury Pavement. SW6. 3L 13 (off Dawes Rd.)
Salisbury Pl. W Byf. 7L 55
Salisbury Rd. Farnb. 1A 90
Salisbury Rd. SE25. 5D 46
Salisbury Rd. SW19. 8K 27
Salisbury Rd. As. 1E 110
Salisbury Rd. Bans. 1N 81
Salisbury Rd. B'water. 1H 69
Salisbury Rd. Cars. 3D 62
Salisbury Rd. Craw. 7C 182 (in two parts)
Salisbury Rd. Felt. 2K 23
Salisbury Rd. God. 9F 104
Salisbury Rd. H'ham. 8G 196
Salisbury Rd. Houn. 6K 9
Salisbury Rd. H'row A. 8D 8
Salisbury Rd. N Mald. 2C 42
Salisbury Rd. Rich. 7L 11
Salisbury Rd. Wok. 6A 74
Salisbury Rd. Wor Pk. 1C 60
Salisbury Ter. Myt. 2E 90
Salix Clo. Sun. 8J 23
Salliesfield. Twic. 9D 10
Salmons La. Whyt. 7D 84
Salmons La. W. Cat. 7B 84
Salmons Rd. Chess. 3L 59
Salmons Rd. Eff. 7J 97
Salomons Memorial. 1L 119
Saltash Clo. Sutt. 1L 61
Saltbox Hill. Big H. 9D 66
Salt Box Rd. Worp & Guild. 7J 93
Saltdean Clo. Craw. 6B 182
Salterford Rd. SW17. 7E 28
Salterns Rd. M'bowr. 6G 182
Salter's Hill. SE19. 6N 29
Saltire Gdns. Brack. 9M 15
Salt La. Hyde. 4G 153
Saltram Rd. Farnb. 3C 90
Salvador. SW17. 6D 28
Salvation Pl. Lea. 2G 98
Salvia Ct. Bisl. 3D 72
Salvington Rd. Craw. 6L 181
Salvin Rd. SW15. 6J 13
Salwey Clo. Brack. 5N 31
Samaritan Clo. Bew. 5K 181
Samarkand Clo. Camb. 2F 70
Samels Ct. W6. 1F 12
Samian Pl. Binf. 8K 15
Samos Rd. SE20. 1E 46
Samphire Clo. Craw. 6M 181
Sampleoak La. Chil. 9G 114
Sampson Pk. Binf. 9J 15
Sampson's Almshouses. Farnh. 2E 128
Sampsons Ct. Shep. 4D 38
Samuel Gray Gdns. King T. 9K 25 (1H 203)
Samuel Johnson Clo. SW16. 5K 29
Samuel Lewis Trust Dwellings. SW6. 3M 13 (off Vanston Pl.)
Samuel Lewis Trust Dwellings. W14. 1L 13 (off Lisgar Ter.)
Samuel Richardson Ho. W14. 1L 13 (off N. End Cres.)
San Carlos App. Alder. 2A 110
Sanctuary Rd. H'row A. 9B 8
Sanctuary, The. Mord. 5M 43
Sandal Rd. N Mald. 4C 42
Sandalwood. Guild. 4L 113
Sandalwood Av. Cher. 9G 36
Sandalwood Rd. Felt. 4J 23
Sandbanks. Felt. 2F 22
Sandbourne Av. SW19. 1N 43
Sandcross La. Reig. 6L 121
Sandell's Av. Ashf. 5D 22
Sandeman Way. H'ham. 8L 197
Sanders Clo. Hamp H. 6C 24
Sandersfield Gdns. Bans. 2M 81
Sandersfield Rd. Bans. 2N 81
Sanderstead. 8D 64
Sanderstead Clo. SW12. 1G 29
Sanderstead Ct. Av. S Croy. 9D 64
Sanderstead Hill. S Croy. 7B 64
Sanderstead Rd. S Croy. 4A 64
Sandes Pl. Lea. 5G 79
Sandfield Gdns. T Hth. 2M 45
Sandfield Rd. T Hth. 2M 45
Sandfields. Send. 2F 94
Sandfield Ter. Guild. 4N 113 (4C 202)
Sandford Ct. Alder. 3L 109
Sandford Down. Brack. 4D 32
Sandford Rd. Alder. 3L 109
Sandford Rd. Farnh. 5G 109
Sandford St. SW6. 3N 13
Sandgate La. SW18. 2C 28
Sandhawes Hill. E Grin. 6C 166
Sandheath Rd. Hind. 2A 170
Sand Hill. Farnb. 7N 69
Sand Hill Ct. Farnb. 7N 69
Sandhill La. Craw D. 2E 184
Sandhills. 9A 152
Sandhills. Wall. 1H 63
Sandhills. Wmly. 9A 152 (in two parts)
Sandhills Ct. Vir W. 4A 36
Sandhills La. Vir W. 4A 36
Sandhills Mdw. Shep. 6D 38
Sandhills Rd. Reig. 4M 121
Sandhurst. 8G 49
Sandhurst Av. Surb. 6A 42
Sandhurst Clo. S Croy. 5B 64
Sandhurst La. B'water. 9G 48
Sandhurst Rd. Crowt. 4G 49
Sandhurst Rd. Finch. 8A 30
Sandhurst Rd. Yat. 8E 48
Sandhurst Way. S Croy. 4D 64
Sandiford Rd. Sutt. 8L 43
Sandilands. Croy. 8D 46
Sandilands Rd. SW6. 4N 13
Sandlands Gro. Tad. 1F 100
Sandlands Rd. Tad. 1F 100
Sandon Clo. Esh. 6D 40
Sandown Av. Esh. 2C 58
Sandown Clo. B'water. 1J 69
Sandown Clo. Houn. 4H 9
Sandown Ct. Craw. 3H 183
Sandown Ct. Red. 2C 122 (off Station Rd.)
Sandown Ct. Sutt. 4N 61
Sandown Cres. Alder. 5N 109
Sandown Dri. Cars. 5E 62
Sandown Dri. Frim. 4B 70
Sandown Ga. Esh. 9D 40
Sandown Lodge. Eps. 1C 80
Sandown Pk. Racecourse. 9C 40
Sandown Rd. SE25. 4E 46
Sandown Rd. Coul. 3E 82
Sandown Rd. Esh. 1C 58
Sandpiper Clo. If'd. 5J 181
Sandpiper Rd. S Croy. 7G 64
Sandpiper Rd. Sutt. 2L 61
Sandpit Cotts. Pirb. 9B 72
Sandpit Hall Rd. Chob. 8K 53
Sandpit Heath. Guild. 8G 92
Sandpit La. Knap. 1E 72 (in two parts)
Sandpit Rd. Red. 4C 122
Sandpit Site. Wey. 6B 56
Sandpits Rd. Croy. 1G 64
Sandpits Rd. Rich. 3K 25
Sandra Clo. Houn. 8B 10
Sandringham Av. SW20. 9K 27
Sandringham Clo. SW19. 2J 27
Sandringham Clo. E Grin. 1C 186
Sandringham Clo. Wok. 3J 75
Sandringham Ct. Sutt. 5M 61
Sandringham Dri. Ashf. 5M 21
Sandringham Gdns. Houn. [illegible]
Sandringham Gdns. W Mol. 3A 40
Sandringham Pk. Cob. 8A 58
Sandringham Rd. Craw. 7N 181
Sandringham Rd. H'row A. 8N 7
Sandringham Rd. T Hth. 4N 45
Sandringham Rd. Wor Pk. 9F 42
Sandringham Way. Frim. 6D 70
Sandrock. Hasl. 2G 188
Sandrock Cotts. N'chap. 8D 190
Sandrock Hill Rd. Wrec. 5E 128

Sandrock Pl.—Shaftesbury Ct.

Sandrock Pl. *Croy* 1G 64
Sandrock Rd. *Westc* 7B 118
Sandroyd Way. *Cob* 9A 58
Sands Clo. *Seale* 1B 130
Sands End. 4N 13
Sand's End La. *SW6* 4N 13
Sands Rd. *Farnh & Seale* 9A 110
Sands, The. 2C 130
Sandy Bury. *Orp* 1M 67
Sandy Clo. *Wok* 4E 74
Sandycombe Rd. *Felt* 2H 23
Sandycombe Rd. *Rich* 6M 11
Sandycoombe Rd. *Twic* 9J 11
Sandy Cft. *Eps* 6H 61
Sandy Cross. 8C 110
Sandy Dri. *Cob* 7A 58
Sandy Dri. *Felt* 2F 22
Sandy Hill Rd. *Farnh* 5F 108
Sandy Hill Rd. *Wall* 5G 62
Sandy Holt. *Cob* 9N 57
Sandy La. *Cob & Oxs* 8N 57
Sandy La. *Farnb* 8H 69
Sandy La. *Rush* 4M 149
Sandy La. *Alb* 1L 135
Sandy La. *Asc* 9F 16
(Goaters Hill)
Sandy La. *Asc* 4D 34
(Sunningdale)
Sandy La. *Bet* 4D 120
Sandy La. *Blet* 1M 123
Sandy La. *Brack* 9A 16
Sandy La. *Camb* 9C 50
Sandy La. *Chob* 5H 53
Sandy La. *C Crook* 9B 88
Sandy La. *Comp* 8G 112
Sandy La. *Craw D* 1C 184
Sandy La. *E Grin* 9A 166
Sandy La. *G'ming* 5G 133
Sandy La. *G'wood* 8J 171
Sandy La. *Guild* 8K 113
Sandy La. *Hasl* 1A 188
Sandy La. *Hind* 8D 170
Sandy La. *Kgswd* 2L 101
(in two parts)
Sandy La. *Limp* 5D 106
Sandy La. *Milf* 2B 152
Sandy La. *Mitc* 9E 28
(in two parts)
Sandy La. *Norm* 9B 92
Sandy La. *Oxt* 7M 105
Sandy La. *Pyr & Wok* 4J 75
(in two parts)
Sandy La. *Reig* 4G 120
Sandy La. *Rich* 3J 25
Sandy La. *Sand* 6E 48
Sandy La. *Send* 1E 94
Sandy La. *Shere* 8B 116
Sandy La. *S Nut & Nutf* 4H 123
Sandy La. *Sutt* 4K 61
Sandy La. *Tedd & Hamp W* 8G 24
Sandy La. *Vir W* 3A 36
(in three parts)
Sandy La. *W on T* 5J 39
Sandy La. *W'ham* 3M 107
Sandy La. *Wok* 4D 74
Sandy La. N. *Wall* 2H 63
Sandy La. S. *Wall* 5G 62
Sandy Mead. *Eps* 6N 59
Sandy Ride. *S'hill* 3B 34
Sandy Rd. *Add* 3J 55
Sandy Way. *Cob* 8A 58
Sandy Way. *Croy* 9J 47
Sandy Way. *W on T* 7G 38
Sandy Way. *Wok* 4E 74
San Feliu Ct. *E Grin* 8D 166
Sanger Av. *Chess* 2L 59
Sanger Dri. *Send* 1E 94
Sangers Dri. *Horl* 8D 142
Sangers Wlk. *Horl* 8D 142
Sangley Rd. *SE25* 3B 46
Sankey La. *Fleet* 1E 88
Santina Clo. *Farnh* 4J 109
Santos Rd. *SW18* 8M 13
Sanway. 1N 75
Sanway Clo. *Byfl* 1N 75
Sanway Rd. *Byfl* 1N 75
Saphora Clo. *Orp* 2M 67
Sapphire Cen., The. *Wokgm* 4A 30
Sappho Ct. *Wok* 3H 73
Sapte Clo. *Cranl* 7B 156
Saracen Clo. *Croy* 5A 46
Sarah Way. *Farnb* 1N 89
Sarel Way. *Horl* 6F 142
Sargent Clo. *Craw* 7D 182
Sarjant Path. SW19 3J 27
(off Blincoe Clo.)
Sark Clo. *Craw* 7M 181
Sark Clo. *Houn* 3A 10
Sarsby Dri. *Stai* 3C 20
Sarsen Av. *Houn* 5A 10
Sarsfeld Rd. *SW12* 3D 28
Sarum. *Brack* 7L 31
Sarum Cres. *Wokgm* 1C 30
Sarum Grn. *Wey* 9F 38
Satellite Bus. Village. *Craw* 8C 162
Satis Ct. *Eps* 7E 60
Saturn Clo. *Bew* 5K 181
Saturn Cft. *Wink R* 7F 16
Saunders Clo. *Craw* 3F 182
Saunders Copse. *Wok* 9L 73
Saunders La. *Wok* 9H 73
Saunton Av. *Hay* 3G 8
Saunton Gdns. *Farnb* 8M 69
Savernake Wlk. *Craw* 6D 182
Savernake Way. *Brack* 5C 32
Savery Dri. *Surb* 6J 41
Savile Clo. *N Mald* 4D 42
Savile Clo. *Th Dit* 7F 40
Savile Gdns. *Croy* 8C 46
Saville Cres. *Ashf* 7E 22
Saville Gdns. *Camb* 1F 70
Saville Rd. *Twic* 2F 24
Savill Gdns. *SW20* 2F 42
Savill Garden, The. 7H 19
Savill Ho. *SW4* 1H 29
Savin Lodge. Sutt 4A 62
(off Walnut M.)
Savona Clo. *SW19* 8J 27
Savory Wlk. *Binf* 7G 15
Savoy Av. *Hay* 1F 8
Savoy Gro. *B'water* 3J 69
Sawkins Clo. *SW19* 3K 27
Sawpit La. *E Clan* 9N 95
Sawtry Clo. *Cars* 6C 44
Sawyers Clo. *Wind* 3B 4
Sawyer's Hill. *Rich* 1M 25
Saxby Rd. *SW2* 1J 29
Saxby's La. *Ling* 7N 145
Saxley. *Horl* 7G 142
Saxon Av. *Felt* 3M 23
Saxonbury Av. *Sun* 2J 39
Saxonbury Clo. *Mitc* 2B 44
Saxonbury Gdns. *Surb* 7J 41
Saxon Bus. Cen. *SW19* 1A 44
Saxon Clo. *Surb* 5K 41
Saxon Cres. *H'ham* 4H 197
Saxon Cft. *Farnh* 2H 129
Saxon Dri. *Warf* 9D 16
Saxonfield Clo. *SW2* 2K 29
Saxon Ho. *Felt* 3N 23
Saxon Lodge. *Croy* 1C 200
Saxon Rd. *Ashf* 7E 22
Saxon Rd. *SE25* 4A 46
Saxon Rd. *King T* 9L 25 (1J 203)
Saxon Rd. *W on T* 9L 39
Saxon Rd. *Worth* 4J 183
Saxons. *Tad* 8J 81
Saxon Way. *Old Win* 9L 5
Saxon Way. *Reig* 2L 121
Saxon Way. *W Dray* 2L 7
Saxon Way Ind. Est. *W Dray* 2L 7
Saxony Way. *Yat* 2B 68
Sayers Clo. *Fet* 1C 98
Sayers Clo. *Frim G* 7C 70
Sayers Clo. *H'ham* 6L 197
Sayers, The. *E Grin* 9M 165
Sayer's Wlk. *Rich* 1M 25
Sayes Ct. *Add* 2L 55
Sayes Ct. Farm Dri. *Add* 2K 55
Scallows Clo. *Craw* 2E 182
Scallows Rd. *Craw* 2E 182
Scampton Rd. *H'row A* 9A 8
Scania Wlk. *Wink R* 7F 16
Scarborough Clo. *Big H* 5E 86
Scarborough Clo. *Sutt* 7L 61
Scarborough Rd. *H'row A* 9D 8
Scarbrook Rd. *Croy* 9N 45 (5B 200)
Scarlet Oaks. *Camb* 3C 70
Scarlett Clo. *Wok* 5J 73
Scarlette Mnr. Way. *SW2* 1L 29
Scarlett's Rd. *Alder* 1M 109
Scarth Rd. *SW13* 6E 12
Scawen Clo. *Cars* 1E 62
S.C.C. Smallholdings Rd. *Eps* 1H 81
(in two parts)
Scholars Rd. *SW12* 2G 28
Scholars Wlk. *Guild* 4L 113
School All. *Twic* 2G 25
School Allotment Ride. *Wind* 1M 17
School Clo. *Bisl* 2C 72
School Clo. *Guild* 9N 93
School Clo. *H'ham* 2N 197
School Cotts. *Wok* 9M 73
School Fld. *Eden* 1L 147
School Hill. *Crowt* 3J 49
(in two parts)
School Hill. *Red* 6G 102
School Hill. *Sand* 6F 48
School Hill. *Seale* 8F 110
School Hill. *Warn* 9F 178
School Hill. *Wrec* 4E 128
School Ho. La. *Tedd* 8H 25
School La. *Add* 2J 55
School La. *Asc* 9H 17
School La. *Ash W* 3F 186
School La. *Bag* 5H 51
(in two parts)
School La. *Cat* 4C 104
School La. *C'fold* 5E 172
School La. *E Clan* 9N 95
School La. *Egh* 6C 20
School La. *Ews* 4C 108
School La. *Fet* 9D 78
School La. *F Row* 7H 187
School La. *King T* 9J 25
School La. *Lwr Bo* 5J 129
School La. *Mick* 5J 99
School La. *Norm* 9K 91
School La. *Ock* 9C 76
School La. *Pirb* 9B 72
School La. *P'ham* 8N 111
School La. *Shack* 5B 132
School La. *Shep* 5C 38
School La. *Surb* 7N 41
School La. *Tad* 3F 100
School La. *Westc* 6D 118
School La. *W Hor* 7C 96
School La. *W'sham* 2A 52
School La. *Worp* 6H 93
School La. *Yat* 9A 48
School Pas. *King T* 1M 41 (4M 203)
School Rd. *Ashf* 7C 22
School Rd. *Asc* 4A 34
School Rd. *B'ham* 2C 30
School Rd. *E Mol* 3D 40
School Rd. *Gray* 6N 169
School Rd. *Hamp H* 7C 24
School Rd. *Hasl* 3D 188
School Rd. *Houn* 6C 10
School Rd. *King T* 9J 25
School Rd. *Rowl* 8D 128
School Rd. *W on T* 2G 57
School Rd. *W Dray* 2M 7
School Rd. *W'sham* 1L 51
School Rd. Av. *Hamp H* 7C 24
School Road Junction. (Junct.) 7C 22
School Wlk. *Horl* 8C 142
School Wlk. *Sun* 3G 38
Schroder Ct. *Eng G* 6L 19
Schroders Av. *Red* 1F 122
Schubert Rd. *SW15* 8L 13
Scillonian Rd. *Guild* 4K 113
Scilly Isles. (Junct.) 8E 40
Scizdons Climb. *G'ming* 7J 133
Scoles Cres. *SW2* 2L 29
Scope Way. *King T* 3L 41 (7K 203)
Scory Clo. *Craw* 6M 181
Scotia Rd. *SW2* 1L 29
Scotland Bri. *New H* 7J 55
Scotland Bri. Rd. *New H* 7J 55
Scotland Clo. *Ash V* 8E 90
Scotland Farm Rd. *Ash V* 8E 90
Scotland Hill. *Sand* 6F 48
Scotland La. *Hasl* 3F 188
Scotlands Clo. *Hasl* 3F 188
Scotney Clo. *Orp* 1J 67
Scots Clo. *Stanw* 2M 21
Scotsdale Clo. *Sutt* 4K 61
Scotshall La. *Warl* 2M 85
Scott Clo. *SW16* 9K 29
Scott Clo. *Eps* 2B 60
Scott Clo. *Guild* 1K 113
Scott Clo. *W Dray* 1A 8
Scott Farm Clo. *Th Dit* 7H 41
Scott Gdns. *Houn* 3L 9
Scott Rd. *Craw* 6D 182
Scotts Av. *Brom* 1N 47
Scotts Av. *Sun* 8F 22
Scott's Ct. *Farnb* 7N 69
Scotts Dri. *Hamp* 8B 24
Scotts Farm Rd. *Eps* 3B 60
Scott's Gro. Clo. *Chob* 9G 52
Scott's Gro. Rd. *Chob* 9E 52
Scott's Hill. *Out* 5A 144
Scott's La. *Brom* 2N 47
Scotts La. *W on T* 1L 57
Scotts M. *Asc* 9F 16
Scotts Way. *Sun* 8F 22
Scott Ter. *Brack* 9C 16
Scott Trimmer Way. *Houn* 5M 9
Scrutton Clo. *SW12* 1H 29
Scutley La. *Light & W'sham* 5B 52
Scylla Cres. *H'row A* 9C 8
Scylla Pl. *St J* 6K 73
Scylla Rd. *H'row A* 9C 8
Seabrook Dri. *W Wick* 8N 47
Seaford Ct. *Wokgm* 2C 30
Seaford Rd. *Craw* 8M 181
Seaford Rd. *H'row A* 8M 7
Seaford Rd. *Wokgm* 2C 30
Seaforth Av. *N Mald* 4G 42
Seaforth Gdns. *Eps* 1E 60
Seagrave Lodge. SW6 2M 13
(off Seagrave Rd.)
Seagrave Rd. *SW6* 2M 13
Sealand Rd. *H'row A* 9B 8
Seale. 8F 110
Seale Hill. *Reig* 5M 121
Seale La. *Seale* 8B 110
(in two parts)
Seale La. *Seale & P'ham* 8J 111
Seale Rd. *Seale & Elst* 3F 130
Searchwood Rd. *Warl* 5E 84
Searle Rd. *Farnh* 3H 129
Searle's Vw. *H'ham* 3L 197
Seaton Clo. *SW15* 2G 27
Seaton Clo. *Twic* 9D 10
Seaton Dri. *Ashf* 3N 21
Seaton Rd. *Camb* 1N 69
Seaton Rd. *Mitc* 1C 44
Seaton Rd. *Twic* 9C 10
Sebastopol La. *Wmly* 9A 152
Sebastopol Rd. *Alder* 2N 109
Secombe Theatre. 2N 61
Second Av. *SW14* 6D 12
Second Av. *W on T* 5J 39
Second Clo. *W Mol* 3C 40
Second Cross Rd. *Twic* 3E 24
Seddon Ct. *Craw* 8N 181
Seddon Hill. *Warf* 7N 15
Seddon Rd. *Mord* 4B 44
Sedgefield Clo. *Worth* 2J 183
Sedgemoor. *Farnb* 7N 69
Sedgewick Clo. *Craw* 3G 183
Sedgwick La. *H'ham* 9M 197
Sedleigh Rd. *SW18* 9L 13
Sedlescombe Rd. *SW6* 2M 13
Seebys Oak. *Col T* 9J 49
Seely Rd. *SW17* 7E 28
Seething Wells. 5J 41
Seething Wells La. *Surb* 5J 41
Sefton Clo. *W End* 9C 52
Sefton Ct. *Houn* 4B 10
Sefton Rd. *Croy* 7D 46
Sefton Rd. *Eps* 6C 60
Sefton St. *SW15* 6H 13
Sefton Vs. *N Holm* 9H 119
Segrave Clo. *Wey* 4B 56
Segsbury Gro. *Brack* 3C 32
Sekhon Ter. *Felt* 4A 24
Selborne Av. *Alder* 5N 109
Selborne Clo. *B'water* 9H 49
Selborne Gdns. *Farnh* 4F 128
Selborne Rd. *Croy* 9B 46
Selborne Rd. *N Mald* 1D 42
Selbourne Av. *New H* 5K 55
Selbourne Av. *Surb* 8M 41
Selbourne Clo. *Craw* 8H 163
Selbourne Clo. *New H* 5K 55
Selbourne Rd. *Guild* 9C 94
Selbourne Sq. *God* 8F 104
Selby Clo. *Chess* 4L 59
Selby Grn. *Cars* 6C 44
Selby Rd. *Ashf* 7D 22
Selby Rd. *SE20* 1D 46
Selby Rd. *Cars* 6C 44
Selbys. *Ling* 6A 146
Selby Wlk. *Wok* 5L 73
Selcroft Rd. *Purl* 8M 63
Selham Clo. *Craw* 2M 181
Selhurst. 5A 46
Selhurst Clo. *SW19* 2J 27
Selhurst Clo. *Wok* 2B 74
Selhurst Common. 3C 154
Selhurst New Rd. *SE25* 5B 46
Selhurst Pk. (Crystal Palace F.C. & Wimbledon F.C.) 3B 46
Selhurst Pl. *SE25* 5B 46
Selhurst Rd. *SE25* 5B 46
Selkirk Rd. *SW17* 5C 28
Selkirk Rd. *Twic* 3C 24
Sellar's Hill. *G'ming* 4G 132
Sellincourt Rd. *SW17* 6C 28
Sells, The. *Guild* 5B 114
Selsdon. 6F 64
Selsdon Av. *S Croy* 3A 64
Selsdon Clo. *Surb* 4L 41
Selsdon Cres. *S Croy* 6F 64
Selsdon Pk. Rd. *S Croy & Croy* 5G 65
Selsdon Rd. *SE27* 4L 29
Selsdon Rd. *New H* 7J 55
Selsdon Rd. *S Croy* 2A 64 (8D 200)
Selsey Ct. *Craw* 7N 181
Selsey Rd. *Craw* 7M 181
Selsfield Common. 8E 184
Selsfield Rd. *Turn H & E Grin* 6D 184
Seltops Clo. *Cranl* 8A 156
Selwood Clo. *Stanw* 9L 7
Selwood Gdns. *Stanw* 9L 7
Selwood Rd. *Chess* 1K 59
Selwood Rd. *Croy* 8E 46
Selwood Rd. *Sutt* 7L 43
Selwood Rd. *Wok* 7D 74
Selwoods. *SW2* 1L 29
Selwyn Av. *Rich* 6L 11
Selwyn Clo. *Craw* 9G 163
Selwyn Clo. *Houn* 7M 9
Selwyn Clo. *Wind* 5A 4
Selwyn Dri. *Yat* 9A 48
Selwyn Rd. *N Mald* 4C 42
Semaphore Rd. *Guild* 5A 114 (7E 202)
Semley Rd. *SW16* 1J 45
Semper Clo. *Knap* 4H 73
Sen Clo. *Brack* 7A 16
Send. 2F 94
Send Barns La. *Send* 2F 94
Send Clo. *Send* 1E 94
Send Hill. *Send* 3E 94
Send Marsh. 1H 95
Send Marsh Grn. *Rip* 1H 95
Send Marsh Rd. *Send* 2F 94
Send Pde. Clo. *Send* 1E 94
Send Rd. *Send* 1D 94
Seneca Rd. *T Hth* 3N 45
Senga Rd. *Wall* 7E 44
Senhouse Rd. *Sutt* 9J 43
Sepen Meade. *C Crook* 9A 88
Sequoia Pk. *Craw* 5B 182
Sergeant Ind. Est. *SW18* 9N 13
Sergeants Pl. *Cat* 9N 83
Serpentine Grn. *Red* 7H 103
Serrin Way. *H'ham* 3L 197
Servite Ho. Wor Pk 8E 42
(off Avenue, The)
Servius Ct. *Bren* 3K 11
Setley Way. *Brack* 2D 32
Setter Combe. *Warf* 7B 16
Settrington Rd. *SW6* 5N 13
Sett, The. *Yat* 1A 68
Seven Acres. *Cars* 8C 44
Seven Arches App. *Wey* 4A 56
Seven Hills Clo. *W on T* 5F 56
Seven Hills Rd. *W on T* 5F 56
Seven Hills Rd. S. *Cob* 9F 56
Seven Kings Way. *King T* 9L 25 (1J 203)
Sevenoaks Clo. *Sutt* 6M 61
Sevenoaks Rd. *Grn St & Hals* 4N 67
Sevenoaks Rd. *Orp* 2N 67
Severells Copse. 4N 137
Severn Clo. *Sand* 7H 49
Severn Ct. *King T* 9K 25 (1H 203)
Severn Cres. *Slou* 1D 6
Severn Dri. *Esh* 8G 41
Severn Dri. *W on T* 8L 39
Severn Rd. *Farnb* 8K 69
Severn Rd. *M'bowr* 4G 182
Seward Rd. *Beck* 1G 47
Sewell Av. *Wokgm* 9A 14
Sewer's Farm Rd. *Ab C* 5N 137
Sewill Clo. *Charl* 3L 161
Seymour Av. *Cat* 1N 103
Seymour Av. *Eps* 5G 61
Seymour Av. *Mord* 6J 43
Seymour Clo. *E Mol* 4C 40
Seymour Ct. *Cob* 9G 57
Seymour Ct. *Crowt* 3D 48
Seymour Ct. *Fleet* 3B 88
Seymour Dri. *Camb* 7F 50
Seymour Gdns. *Felt* 5K 23
Seymour Gdns. *Surb* 4M 41
Seymour Gdns. *Twic* 1H 25
Seymour Ho. Sutt 3N 61
(off Mulgrave Rd.)
Seymour M. *Ewe* 6F 60
Seymour Pl. *SE25* 3E 46
Seymour Rd. *SW18* 1L 27
Seymour Rd. *SW19* 4J 27
Seymour Rd. *Cars* 2E 62
Seymour Rd. *Craw* 7M 181
Seymour Rd. *E Mol* 4C 40
Seymour Rd. *G'ming* 8E 132
Seymour Rd. *Hamp H* 6C 24
Seymour Rd. *Head D* 5H 169
Seymour Rd. *King T* 9K 25 (2G 203)
Seymour Rd. *Mitc* 6E 44
Seymour Ter. *SE20* 1E 46
Seymour Vs. *SE20* 1E 46
Seymour Wlk. *SW10* 2N 13
Seymour Way. *Sun* 8G 22
Shackleford. 4A 132
Shackleford Rd. *Elst & Shack* 7L 131
Shackleford Rd. *Shack* 4A 132
Shackleford Rd. *Wok* 7C 74
Shacklegate La. *Tedd* 5E 24
Shackleton Clo. *Ash V* 8D 90
Shackleton Rd. *Craw* 6C 182
Shackleton Wlk. Guild 3H 113
(off Chapelhouse Clo.)
Shackstead La. *G'ming* 8F 132
Shadbolt Clo. *Wor Pk* 8E 42
Shadyhanger. *G'ming* 5H 133
Shady Nook. *Farnh* 6G 108
Shaef Way. *Tedd* 8G 25
Shaftesbury Av. *Felt* 9H 9
Shaftesbury Clo. *Brack* 4B 32
Shaftesbury Ct. *Farnb* 5A 90
Shaftesbury Ct. SW6 4N 13
(off Maltings Pl.)
Shaftesbury Ct. *SW16* 4H 29

Shaftesbury Ct.—Silverwood Ind. Est.

Shaftesbury Ct. Wokgm 1C 30
Shaftesbury Cres. Stai 8M 21
Shaftesbury Ho. Coul 9H 83
Shaftesbury Mt. B'water 4J 69
Shaftesbury Pl. W14 . . . . 1L 13
(off Warwick Rd.)
Shaftesbury Rd. Beck 1J 47
Shaftesbury Rd. Bisl 3C 72
Shaftesbury Rd. Cars 6B 44
Shaftesbury Rd. M'bowr 5H 183
Shaftesbury Rd. Rich 6L 11
Shaftesbury Rd. Wok 4D 74
Shaftesbury Way. Twic 4D 24
Shakespeare Av. Felt 9H 9
Shakespeare Gdns. Farnb 9J 69
Shakespeare Rd. Add 1M 55
Shakespeare Way. Felt 5K 23
Shakespeare Way. Warf 9C 16
Shalbourne Ri. Camb 1B 70
Shalden Ho. SW15 . . . . 9E 12
Shalden Rd. Alder 4B 110
Shaldon Dri. Mord 4K 43
Shaldon Way. W on T 9K 39
Shale Grn. Red 7H 103
Shalesbrook La. F Row 8H 187
(in two parts)
Shalford 9A 114
Shalford Clo. Orp 1L 67
Shalford Mill 8A 114
(Disused)
Shalford Rd. Guild & Shalf
. . . . 6N 113 (8D 202)
Shalstone Rd. SW14 . . . . 6A 12
Shalston Vs. Surb 5M 41
Shambles, The. Guild
. . . . 5N 113 (6C 202)
Shamley Green 7G 134
Shamrock Clo. Fet 8D 78
Shamrock Clo. Frim 6B 70
Shamrock Cotts. Guild 6L 93
Shamrock Rd. Croy 5K 45
Shandys Clo. H'ham 7G 196
Shanklin Ct. Alder 3A 110
Shannon Clo. S'hall 1L 9
Shannon Corner. (Junct.) 3F 42
Shannon Corner Retail Pk. N Mald
. . . . 3F 42
Shannon Ct. Croy 1C 200
Shanti Ct. SW18 . . . . 2M 27
Shap Cres. Cars 7D 44
Sharland Clo. T Hth 5L 45
Sharnbrook Ho. W14 . . . . 2M 13
Sharon Clo. Bookh 2A 98
Sharon Clo. Craw 6E 182
Sharon Clo. Eps 9B 60 (6H 201)
Sharon Clo. Surb 7J 41
Sharon Ct. S Croy 8C 200
Sharon Rd. W4 . . . . 1C 12
Sharp Ho. Twic 9K 11
Sharpthorne Clo. If'd 3L 181
Shaw Clo. Eps 7E 60
Shaw Clo. Ott 3E 54
Shaw Clo. S Croy 8C 64
Shaw Ct. Old Win 0K 5
Shaw Cres. S Croy 8C 64
Shaw Dri. W on T 6K 39
Shaw Farm 7H 5
Shawfield Cotts. As 2D 110
Shawfield La. As 2D 110
Shawfield Rd. As 3D 110
Shawford Ct. SW15 . . . . 1F 26
Shawford Rd. Eps 3C 60
Shawley Cres. Eps 5H 81
Shawley Way. Eps 5G 81
Shaw Pk. Crowt 4G 48
Shaw Rd. Tats 7E 86
Shaws Cotts. Guild 7J 93
(off Worplesdon Rd.)
Shawn Path. Hamp W 9J 25
(off Bennett Clo.)
Shaws Rd. Craw 2D 182
Shaw Way. Wall 4J 63
Shaxton Cres. New Ad 5M 65
Shearing Dri. Cars 6A 44
Shears Ct. Sun 8F 22
Shears, The. (Junct.) 8F 22
Shearwater Ct. If'd 4J 181
(off Stoneycroft Wlk.)
Shearwater Rd. Sutt 2L 61
Sheath's La. Oxs 9B 58
Sheen Comn. Dri. Rich 7N 11
Sheen Ct. Rich 7N 11
Sheen Ct. Rd. Rich 7N 11
Sheendale Rd. Rich 7M 11
Sheen Ga. Gdns. SW14 . . . . . . 7B 12
Sheengate Mans. SW14 . . . . . . 7C 12
Sheen La. SW14 . . . . 8B 12
Sheen Pk. Rich 7M 11
Sheen Rd. Rich 8L 11
Sheen Way. Wall 2K 63
Sheen Wood. SW14 . . . . 8B 12
Sheepbarn La. Warl 8B 66
Sheepcote Clo. Houn 3H 9
Sheepcote Rd. Eton W 1D 4
Sheepcote Rd. Wind 5B 4
Sheepfold Rd. Guild 9J 93
Sheep Green 3C 158
Sheephatch La. Tilf 6N 129
Sheep Ho. Farnh 3H 129
Sheephouse Grn. Wott 9N 117
Sheephouse La. Ab C 7N 137
Sheephouse La. Wott & Ab C
. . . . 8N 117
Sheephouse Way. N Mald 7C 42
Sheeplands Av. Guild 1E 114
Sheep Wlk. Eps 8C 80
Sheep Wlk. Reig 9L 101
Sheep Wlk. Shep 4B 38
Sheepwalk La. E Hor & Ran C
. . . . 3G 116
Sheep Wlk. M. SW19 . . . . 7J 27
Sheep Wlk., The. Shep 0A 38
Sheep Wlk., The. Wok 5F 74
Sheerwater 1F 74
Sheerwater Av. Wdhm 8G 55
Sheerwater Rd. Wok & W Byf
. . . . 8G 54
Sheet's Heath La. Brkwd 6D 72
Sheet St. Wind 5G 5
Sheet St. Rd. Wind 5A 18
Sheffield Clo. Farnb 1L 89
Sheffield Clo. Craw 5F 182
Sheffield Rd. H'row A 9D 8
Sheffield Way. H'row A 8E 8
Shefford Cres. Wokgm 9C 14
Shelburne Dri. Houn 9A 10
Sheldon Clo. Craw 4H 183
Sheldon Clo. Reig 4N 121
Sheldon Ct. Guild 4B 114
Sheldon St. Croy
. . . . 9N 45 (5B 200)
Sheldrick Clo. SW19 . . . . 1B 44
Shelley Av. Brack 1C 32
Shelley Clo. Bans 2J 81
Shelley Clo. Coul 4K 83
Shelley Clo. Craw 1G 182
Shelley Clo. Fleet 5B 88
Shelley Clo. Slou 1C 6
Shelley Ct. Camb 1A 70
Shelley Cres. Houn 4L 9
Shelley Dri. Broad H 5C 196
Shelley Ri. Farnb 8L 69
Shelley Rd. E Grin 9M 165
Shelley Rd. H'ham 5H 197
Shelleys Ct. H'ham 4N 197
Shelley Wlk. Yat 1A 68
Shelley Way. SW19 . . . . 7B 28
Shellfield Clo. Stai 8J 7
Shellwood Cross 4D 140
Shellwood Dri. N Holm 9J 119
Shellwood Rd. Leigh 1B 140
Shelson Av. Felt 4G 22
Shelton Av. Warl 4F 84
Shelton Clo. Guild 7K 93
Shelton Clo. Warl 4F 84
Shelton Rd. SW19 . . . . 9M 27
Shelvers Grn. Tad 8H 81
Shelvers Hill. Tad 8G 81
Shelvers Spur. Tad 8H 81
Shelvers Way. Tad 8H 81
Shenfield Clo. Coul 6G 82
Shenley Rd. Houn 4M 9
Shenston Ct. Wind 4G 4
(off James St.)
Shenstone Clo. Finch 8A 30
Shenstone Pk. S'hill 3B 34
Shepherd & Flock Roundabout.
Farnh 9K 109
Shepherd Clo. Craw 6C 182
Shepherd Clo. Felt 5M 23
Shepherds Chase. Bag 5J 51
Shepherds Clo. Shep 5C 38
Shepherds Ct. Farnh 3H 129
Shepherdsgrove La. Hamm
. . . . 5H 167
Shepherds Hill. Brack 9A 16
Shepherd's Hill. Cole H 8M 187
Shepherd's Hill. Guild 1K 113
Shepherd's Hill. Hasl 2G 188
Shepherd's Hill. Red 4G 102
Shepherd's Hill Bungalows. Hasl
. . . . 2G 189
(off Shepherd's Hill)
Shepherds La. Brack 8M 15
Shepherd's La. Guild 9J 93
Shepherds La. W'sham 2C 52
Shepherds Wlk. Farnh 7K 60
Shepherd's Wlk. Eps 8A 80
Shepherds Way. Crowt 3D 48
Shepherd's Way. Guild 7A 114
(in two parts)
Shepherds Way. H'ham 3N 197
Shepherds Way. S Croy 4G 64
Shepherds Way. Tilf 7A 130
Shepiston La. Hay 1C 8
Shepley Clo. Cars 9E 44
Shepley Dri. Asc 5F 34
Shepley End. Asc 4F 34
Sheppard Clo. King T
. . . . 3L 41 (8K 203)
Sheppard Ho. SW2 . . . . 2L 29
Shepperton 5D 38
Shepperton Bus. Pk. Shep 4D 38
Shepperton Ct. Shep 5C 38
Shepperton Ct. Dri. Shep 4C 38
Shepperton Film Studios 2A 38
Shepperton Green 3B 38
Shepperton Rd. Stai 2L 37
Sheppey Clo. Craw 6N 181
Sheraton Clo. B'water 2K 69
Sheraton Dri. Eps . . . 9B 60 (6H 201)
Sheraton Wlk. Craw 8N 181
Sherborne Clo. Coln 4G 7
Sherborne Clo. Eps 4H 81
Sherborne Ct. Guild
. . . . 5M 113 (6B 202)
Sherborne Cres. Cars 6C 44
Sherborne Gdns. Shep 6F 38
Sherborne La. Peasl 1G 157
Sherborne Rd. Farnb 4B 90
Sherborne Rd. Chess 2L 59
Sherborne Rd. Felt 2E 22
(in two parts)
Sherborne Rd. Sutt 8M 43
Sherborne Wlk. Lea 8J 79
Sherbourne. Alb 8M 115
Sherbourne Cotts. Alb 7N 115
Sherbourne Ct. Sutt 3A 62
Sherbourne Dri. Asc 6J 34
Sherbourne Dri. Wind 7C 4
Sherbrooke Rd. SW6 . . . . 3K 13
Shere 8B 116
Shere Av. Sutt 6H 61
Shere Clo. Chess 2K 59
Shere Clo. N Holm 9J 119
Shere La. Shere 8B 116
Shere Mus 8B 116
Shere Rd. Ewh 2E 156
Shere Rd. W Cla & Shere . . . 4J 115
Shere Rd. W Hor 8C 96
(in two parts)
Sherfield Clo. N Mald 3A 42
Sherfield Gdns. SW15 . . . . 9E 12
Sheridan Clo. Alder 4M 109
Sheridan Ct. Croy 6F 200
Sheridan Ct. Houn 8M 9
Sheridan Dri. Reig 1N 121
Sheridan Grange. Asc 5D 34
Sheridan Pl. SW13 . . . . 6E 12
Sheridan Pl. E Grin 9M 165
Sheridan Pl. Hamp 9B 24
Sheridan Rd. SW19 . . . . 9L 27
Sheridan Rd. Frim 6B 70
Sheridan Rd. Rich 4J 25
Sheridans Rd. Bookh 4C 98
Sheridan Wlk. Cars 2D 62
Sheridan Way. Beck 1J 47
Sheringham Av. Felt 4H 23
Sheringham Av. Twic 2N 23
Sheringham Ct. Felt 4H 23
(off Sheringham Av.)
Sheringham Rd. SE20 . . . . 2F 46
Sherington Clo. Farnb 8N 69
Sherland Rd. Twic 2F 24
Shernden La. M Grn 5L 147
(in two parts)
Sherring Clo. Brack 8A 16
Sherrydon. Cranl 6A 156
Sherwin Cres. Farnb 6N 69
Sherwood Av. SW16 . . . . 8H 29
Sherwood Clo. SW13 . . . . 6G 13
Sherwood Clo. Brack 1E 32
Sherwood Clo. Fet 1C 98
Sherwood Ct. Coln 1B 6
Sherwood Ct. S Croy 8B 200
Sherwood Cres. Reig 7N 121
Sherwood Pk. Rd. Mitc 3G 44
Sherwood Pk. Rd. Sutt 2M 61
Sherwood Rd. SW19 . . . . 8L 27
Sherwood Rd. Coul 3G 82
Sherwood Rd. Croy 6E 46
Sherwood Rd. Hamp H 6C 24
Sherwood Rd. Knap 4H 73
Sherwood Wlk. Craw 6D 182
Sherwood Way. W Wick 8M 47
Shetland Clo. Craw 2J 183
Shetland Clo. Guild 7D 94
Shetland Way. Fleet 1C 88
Shewens Rd. Wey 1E 56
Shey Copse. Wok 4E 74
Shield Dri. Bren 2G 11
Shield Rd. Asht 5D 22
Shilburn Way. Wok 5K 73
Shildon Clo. Camb 3H 71
Shillinglee 3G 190
Shillinglee Rd. Plais 4K 191
Shimmings, The. Guild 2C 114
Shingle End. Bren 3J 11
Shinners Clo. SE25 . . . . 4D 46
Shinwell Wlk. Craw 8N 181
Ship All. Farnb 8A 70
Ship All. W4 . . . . 2N 11
Shipfield Clo. Tats 8E 86
Ship Hill. Tats 8E 86
Shipka Rd. SW12 . . . . 2F 28
Shiplake Ho. Brack 3D 32
Ship La. Farnb 8A 70
Ship La. SW14 . . . . 6B 12
Shipley Bridge 4K 163
Shipleybridge La. Ship B & Copt
. . . . 5K 163
Shipley Rd. Craw 2M 181
Ship St. E Grin 1A 186
Ship Yd. Wey 9C 38
Shire Av. Fleet 1D 88
Shire Clo. Bag 5J 51
Shire Ct. Alder 2K 109
Shire Ct. Eps 4E 60
Shire Horse Way. Iswth 6F 10
Shire La. Kes 5G 67
(in two parts)
Shire La. Orp 2N 67
Shire M. Whit 9C 10
Shire Pde. Craw 2H 183
Shire Pl. SW18 . . . . 1A 28
Shire Pl. Bren 3J 11
Shire Pl. Craw 2H 183
(off Ridings, The)
Shire Pl. Red 5D 122
Shires Clo. Asht 6K 79
Shires Ho. Byfl 9N 55
Shires, The. Ham 5L 25
Shires Way. Yat 8C 48
Shirley 8F 46
Shirley Av. Cheam 5L 61
Shirley Av. Coul 6M 83
Shirley Av. Croy 7F 46
Shirley Av. Red 8D 122
Shirley Av. Sutt 1B 62
Shirley Av. Wind 4C 4
Shirley Chu. Rd. Croy 9F 46
Shirley Clo. Craw 7J 181
Shirley Clo. Houn 8C 10
Shirley Ct. SW16 . . . . 8J 29
Shirley Cres. Beck 3H 47
Shirley Dri. Houn 8C 10
Shirley Heights. Wall 5G 62
Shirley Hills Rd. Croy 2F 64
Shirley Oaks 7G 46
Shirley Oaks Rd. Croy 7G 46
Shirley Pk. Croy 8F 46
Shirley Pk. Rd. Croy 7E 46
Shirley Pl. Knap 4F 72
Shirley Rd. Croy 6E 46
Shirley Rd. Wall 5G 62
Shirley Way. Croy 9H 47
Shoe La. Alder 7M 89
Shophouse La. Alb 4M 135
Shoppe Hill. Dors 4A 174
Shop Rd. Wind 3A 4
Shops, The. Won 3D 134
Shord Hill. Kenl 3A 84
Shore Clo. Felt 1H 23
Shore Clo. Hamp 7M 23
Shore Gro. Felt 3N 23
Shoreham Clo. SW18 . . . . 8N 13
Shoreham Clo. Croy 5F 46
Shoreham Rd. M'bowr 6G 183
Shoreham Rd. E. H'row A 8N 7
Shoreham Rd. W. H'row A 8N 7
Shores Rd. Wok 1A 74
Shorland Oaks. Brack 7A 16
Shorrold's Rd. SW6 . . . . 3L 13
Shortacres. Nutf 2K 123
Short Clo. Craw 9B 162
Shortcroft Rd. Eps 4E 60
Shortdale Rd. Alder 6A 110
Shortfield Common 1H 149
Shortfield Rd. Fren 1H 149
Short Gallop. Craw 2H 183
Shortheath 5F 128
Shortheath Crest. Farnh 5E 128
Shortheath Rd. Farnh 5F 128
Short Hedges. Houn 4A 10
Shortlands 1N 47
Shortlands. W6 . . . . 1J 13
Shortlands. Fren 1G 149
Shortlands. Hay 2E 8
Shortlands Gro. Brom 2N 47
Shortlands Rd. Brom 2N 47
Shortlands Rd. King T
. . . . 8M 25 (1M 203)
Short La. Oxt 1D 126
Short La. Stai 1A 22
Short Rd. W4 . . . . 2D 12
Short Rd. H'row A 9N 7
Shortsfield Clo. H'ham 3J 197
Shorts Rd. Cars 1C 62
Short St. Alder 2M 109
Short Way. Twic 1C 24
Shortwood Av. Stai 4K 21
Shotfield. Wall 3F 62
Shott Clo. Sutt 2A 62
Shottendane Rd. SW6 . . . . . . 4M 13
Shottermill 1D 188
Shottermill. H'ham 1N 197
Shottermill Pk. Hasl 1C 188
Shottermill Pond. Hasl 3C 188
Shottermill Ponds 3C 188
Shottermill Rd. Hasl 3C 188
Shottfield Av. SW14 . . . . 7D 12
Shovelstrode La. F Grin & Ash W
. . . . 1E 186
Shrewsbury Av. SW14 . . . . 7B 12
Shrewsbury Clo. Surb 8L 41
Shrewsbury Ct. Beck 2H 47
Shrewsbury Rd. Cars 6C 44
Shrewsbury Rd. H'row A 9D 8
Shrewsbury Rd. Red 3C 122
Shrewsbury Wlk. Iswth 6G 11
Shrewton Rd. SW17 . . . . 8D 28
Shrivenham Clo. Col T 7J 49
Shropshire Clo. Mitc 3J 45
Shropshire Gdns. Warf 8D 16
Shrubbery Rd. SW16 . . . . 5J 29
Shrubbery, The. Farnb 2J 89
Shrubbery, The. Surb 7L 41
Shrubbs Hill. Chob 5F 52
Shrubbs Hill La. Asc 5F 34
Shrubbs La. Rowl 7E 128
Shrubland Gro. Wor Pk 9H 43
Shrubland Rd. Bans 3L 81
Shrublands Av. Croy 9K 47
Shrublands Dri. Light 7M 51
Shrubs Hill 5F 34
Shulbrede Priory 8B 188
Shurlock Dri. Orp 1L 67
Shurlock Row 1F 14
Shute End. Wokgm 2A 30
Shuters Sq. W14 . . . . 1L 13
Sian Clo. C Crook 8C 88
Sibthorp Rd. Mitc 1D 44
Sibton Rd. Cars 6C 44
Sickle Rd. Hasl 3D 188
Sidbury Clo. Asc 4D 34
Sidbury St. SW6 . . . . 4K 13
Siddeley Dri. Houn 6M 9
Siddons Rd. Croy 9L 45
Sideways La. Hkwd 1A 162
Sidings, The. Alder 1A 110
Sidings, The. Rud 1E 194
Sidings, The. Stai 5K 21
Sidlaws Rd. Farnb 7J 69
Sidlow 1N 141
Sidmouth Av. Iswth 5E 10
Sidney Gdns. Bren 2K 11
Sidney Rd. SE25 . . . . 4D 46
Sidney Rd. Beck 1H 47
Sidney Rd. Stai 5J 21
Sidney Rd. Twic 9G 11
Sidney Rd. W on T 6H 39
Sidney Rd. Wind 6A 4
Sidney Wood 9E 171
Signal Ct. Ling 6A 146
Sigrist Sq. King T . . . 9L 25 (2K 203)
Silbury Av. Mitc 9C 28
Silchester Dri. Craw 6N 181
Silent Pool 6M 115
Silistria Clo. Knap 5F 72
Silkham Rd. Oxt 5N 105
Silkin Wlk. Craw 8M 101
Silkmore La. W Hor 3B 96
(in two parts)
Silo Clo. G'ming 3J 133
Silo Dri. G'ming 3J 133
Silo Rd. G'ming 3J 133
Silver Birch Clo. C Crook 8A 88
Silver Birch Clo. Wdhm 8G 55
Silver Birch Cotts. Churt . . . 9B 150
Silver Birches Way. Elst 8J 131
Silver Birch Ho. Craw 0A 182
Silver Clo. Kgswd 2K 101
Silver Cres. W4 . . . . 1A 12
Silverdale. Fleet 7B 88
Silverdale Av. Oxs 1C 78
Silverdale Av. W on T 8G 38
Silverdale Clo. Brock 7A 120
Silverdale Clo. Sutt 1L 61
Silverdale Ct. Stai 5K 21
Silverdale Dri. Sun 1J 39
Silver Dri. Frim 3G 70
Silverglade Bus. Pk. Chess . . . 8J 59
Silver Glades. Yat 2B 68
Silverhall St. Iswth 6G 11
Silver Hill. Col T 7K 49
Silver Jubilee Way. Houn 5J 9
Silverlands Clo. Ott 9F 36
Silver La. Purl 8H 63
Silver La. W Wick 8N 47
Silverlea Gdns. Horl 9G 142
Silverleigh Rd. T Hth 3K 45
Silvermere Ct. Purl 8L 63
Silver Pk. Clo. C Crook 7C 88
Silversmiths Way. Wok 5M 73
Silverstead La. W'ham 8M 87
Silverstone Clo. Red 1D 122
Silverton Rd. W6 . . . . 2J 13
Silver Tree Clo. W on T 9H 39
Silver Wing Ind. Est. Croy 3K 63
Silverwood. Cranl 4K 155
Silverwood Clo. Croy 5J 65
Silverwood Cotts. Shere 7N 115
Silverwood Dri. Camb 8E 50
Silverwood Ind. Est. Craw D
. . . . 7C 164

Surrey Towers—Telferscot Rd.

Surrey Towers. Add 2L 55
(off Garfield Rd.)
Surrey Way. Guild 2L 113
Surridge Ct. Bag 5J 51
Surridge Gdns. SE19 . . . . 7N 29
Sussex & Surrey Crematorium.
Craw 8H 163
Sussex Av. Iswth 6E 10
Sussex Clo. Knap 5F 72
Sussex Clo. N Mald 3D 42
Sussex Clo. Reig 4B 122
Sussex Clo. Twic 9H 11
Sussex Ct. Add 2L 55
Sussex Ct. Knap 4F 72
Sussex Gdns. Chess 3K 59
Sussex Gdns. Fleet 1C 88
Sussex Lodge. H'ham 4J 197
Sussex Mnr. Bus. Pk. Craw
. . . . 8E 162
Sussex Pl. W6 . . . . 1H 13
Sussex Pl. Knap 5F 72
Sussex Pl. N Mald 3D 42
Sussex Rd. Cars 4D 62
Sussex Rd. Knap 5F 72
Sussex Rd. Mitc 4J 45
Sussex Rd. N Mald 3D 42
Sussex Rd. S Croy 3A 64
Sussex Rd. W Wick 7L 47
Sutherland Av. Big H 4F 86
Sutherland Av. Jac 6A 94
Sutherland Av. Sun 1G 39
Sutherland Chase. Asc 9J 17
Sutherland Dri. SW19 . . . . 9B 28
Sutherland Dri. Burp 9B 94
Sutherland Gdns. SW14 . . . . . 6D 12
Sutherland Gdns. Sun 1G 39
Sutherland Gdns. Wor Pk 7G 42
Sutherland Gro. SW18 . . . . 9K 13
Sutherland Gro. Tedd 6E 24
Sutherland Rd. W4 . . . . 2D 12
Sutherland Rd. Croy 6L 45
Sutton 2N 61
(Cheam)
Sutton 1E 6
(Colnbrook)
Sutton Abinger 3H 137
Sutton Arc. Sutt 2N 61
Sutton Av. Wok 6H 73
Sutton Comn. Rd. Sutt 6L 43
Sutton Ct. W4 . . . . 2B 12
Sutton Ct. Sutt 3A 62
Sutton Ct. Rd. W4 . . . . 3B 12
Sutton Ct. Rd. Sutt 3A 62
Sutton Dene. Houn 4B 10
Sutton Gdns. SE25 . . . . 4C 46
Sutton Gdns. Red 7H 103
Sutton Green 4B 94
Sutton Grn. Rd. Sut G 4A 94
Sutton Gro. Sutt 1B 62
Sutton Hall Rd. Houn 3A 10
Sutton Heights. Sutt 4B 62
Sutton Hill. Guild 7E 94
Sutton La. Ab H & Ab C 3J 137
Sutton La. Houn 6N 9
Sutton La. Slou 2D 6
Sutton La. Sutt & Bans 7N 61
Sutton La. N. W4 . . . . 1B 12
Sutton La. S. W4 . . . . 2B 12
Sutton Park 5B 94
Sutton Pk. Rd. Sutt 3N 61
Sutton Pl. Ab H 3G 136
Sutton Pl. Slou 2D 6
Sutton Rd. Camb 6E 50
Sutton Rd. Houn 4A 10
Sutton Sq. Houn 4N 9
Sutton United F.C. 1M 61
Sutton Way. Houn 4N 9
Swabey Rd. Slou 1C 6
Swaby Rd. SW18 . . . . 2A 28
Swaffield Rd. SW18 . . . . 1N 27
Swail Ho. Eps 7K 201
Swain Clo. SW16 . . . . 7F 28
Swain Rd. T Hth 4N 45
Swains Rd. SW17 . . . . 8D 28
Swaledale. Brack 4M 31
Swaledale Clo. Craw 6A 182
Swaledale Gdns. Fleet 1C 88
Swale Rd. Farnb 8K 69
Swallow Clo. Milf 3B 152
Swallow Clo. Stai 5H 21
Swallow Clo. Yat 9A 48
Swallowdale. S Croy 5G 65
Swallow Fld. D'land 1C 166
Swallowfield. Eng G 7L 19
Swallowfields. Horl 8F 142
(off Rosemary La.)
Swallow Gdns. SW16 . . . . 6H 29
Swallow La. Mid H 2H 139
Swallow Pk. Cvn. Site. Surb
. . . . 9M 41
Swallow Ri. Knap 4F 72
Swallow Rd. Craw 1A 182
Swallow St. Turn H 4F 184
Swallowtail Rd. H'ham 2L 197
Swanage Rd. SW18 . . . . 1A 28
Swan Barn Rd. Hasl 2H 189
Swan Cen., The. SW17 . . . . . . 4N 27
Swan Cen., The. Lea 8H 79
Swan Clo. Croy 6B 46
Swan Clo. Felt 5M 23
Swancote Grn. Brack 4N 31
Swan Ct. SW6 . . . . 3M 13
(off Fulham Rd.)
Swan Ct. Guild 1N 113
Swan Ct. Iswth 6H 11
(off Swan St.)
Swan Ct. Lea 9H 79
Swandon Way. SW18 . . . . 8N 13
Swan La. Charl 3L 161
Swan La. Eden 8L 127
Swan La. Guild 4N 113 (5C 202)
Swan La. Sand 8G 48
Swan M. SW6 . . . . 4L 13
Swan Mill Gdns. Dork 3J 119
Swann Ct. Iswth 6G 11
(off South St.)
Swanns Mdw. Bookh 4A 98
Swann Way. Broad H 5E 196
Swan Pl. SW13 . . . . 5E 12
Swan Ridge. Eden 8M 127
Swan Rd. Felt 6M 23
Swanscombe Rd. W4 . . . . 1D 12
Swansea Rd. H'row A 9D 8
Swans Ghyll. F Row 6G 187
Swan Sq. H'ham 6J 197
Swan St. Iswth 6H 11
Swansway, The. Wey 9B 38
Swan Ter. Wind 3E 4
Swan, The. (Junct.) 7M 47
Swanton Gdns. SW19 . . . . 2J 27
Swan Wlk. H'ham 6J 197
Swan Wlk. Shep 6F 38
Swanwick Clo. SW15 . . . . 1E 26
Swanworth La. Mick 6G 99
Swathling Ho. SW15 . . . . 9E 12
(off Tunworth Cres.)
Swaynesland Rd. Eden 3H 127
Swayne's La. Guild 3G 114
Sweeps Ditch Clo. Stai 9J 21
Sweeps La. Egh 6B 20
Sweetbriar. Crowt 9F 30
Sweet Briar La. Eps
. . . . 1C 80 (8J 201)
Sweet La. Peasl 3F 136
Sweetwater Clo. Sham G 7F 134
Sweetwater La. Sham G 7F 134
Sweetwater La. Wmly 7D 152
Sweetwell Rd. Brack 1K 31
Swievelands Rd. Big H 6D 86
Swift Ct. Sutt 4N 61
Swift La. Bag 4K 51
Swift La. Craw 1A 182
Swift Rd. Farnh 5H 109
Swift Rd. Felt 4M 23
Swift's Clo. Farnh 2N 129
Swift St. SW6 . . . . 4L 13
Swinburne Cres. Croy 5F 46
Swinburne Rd. SW15 . . . . 7F 12
Swindon Rd. H'ham 4H 197
Swindon Rd. H'row A 8D 8
Swinfield Clo. Felt 4M 23
Swingate Rd. Farnh 3J 129
Swinley Rd. Asc 2G 32
Swinley Rd. Bag 1H 51
Swires Shaw. Kes 1F 66
Swiss Clo. Wrec 7F 128
Swissland Hill. Dor P 4N 165
Switchback La. Rowl 7E 128
(in three parts)
Swithin Chase. Warf 8C 16
Swordsmans Dri. Deep 5H 71
Swyncombe Av. W5 . . . . 1H 11
Sybil Thorndike Casson Ho. SW5
. . . . 1M 13
(off Old Brompton Rd.)
Sycamore Av. H'ham 2B 198
Sycamore Clo. Cars 1D 62
Sycamore Clo. Craw 9A 162
Sycamore Clo. Felt 4H 23
Sycamore Clo. Fet 1F 98
Sycamore Clo. Frim 5C 70
Sycamore Clo. Sand 8G 48
Sycamore Clo. S Croy
. . . . 2B 64 (8F 200)
Sycamore Cotts. Camb 3N 69
(off Frimley Rd.)
Sycamore Ct. G'ming 3J 133
Sycamore Ct. Houn 7M 9
Sycamore Ct. N Mald 2D 42
Sycamore Ct. Wind 6F 4
Sycamore Cres. C Crook 7A 88
Sycamore Dri. Ash V 6E 90
Sycamore Dri. E Grin 9C 166
Sycamore Dri. Frim 4C 70
Sycamore Dri. Wrec 5F 128
Sycamore Gdns. Mitc 1B 44
Sycamore Gro. N Mald 2C 42
Sycamore Ho. Short 1N 47
Sycamore Ri. Bans 1J 81
Sycamore Ri. Brack 2B 32
Sycamore Rd. Farnb 3A 90
(in two parts)
Sycamore Rd. SW19 . . . . 7H 27
Sycamore Rd. Guild
. . . . 3N 113 (2C 202)
Sycamores, The. Farnb 2B 90
Sycamores, The. B'water 1G 68
Sycamore Wlk. Eng G 7L 19
Sycamore Wlk. Reig 6A 122
Sycamore Way. Tedd 7J 25
Sycamore Way. T Hth 4L 45
Sydcote. SE21 . . . . 2N 29
Sydenham Ct. Croy 1D 200
Sydenham Pl. SE27 . . . . 4M 29
Sydenham Rd. Croy
. . . . 7N 45 (2C 200)
Sydenham Rd. Guild
. . . . 5N 113 (6D 202)
Sydmondson M. Binf 5H 15
Sydney Av. Purl 8K 63
Sydney Clo. Crowt 9H 31
Sydney Cres. Ashf 7C 22
Sydney Loader Pl. B'water 9F 48
Sydney Pl. Guild 4B 114
Sydney Rd. SW20 . . . . 1J 43
Sydney Rd. Felt 2H 23
Sydney Rd. Guild 4B 114
Sydney Rd. Rich 7L 11
Sydney Rd. Sutt 1M 61
Sydney Rd. Tedd 6F 24
Sykes Dri. Stai 6K 21
Sylvan Clo. Oxt 7D 106
Sylvan Clo. S Croy 6E 64
Sylvan Clo. Wok 4D 74
Sylvan Est. SE19 . . . . 1C 46
Sylvan Gdns. Surb 6K 41
Sylvan Ridge. Sand 6F 48
Sylvan Rd. SE19 . . . . 1C 46
Sylvan Rd. Craw 5E 182
Sylvanus. Brack 6L 31
Sylvan Way. C Crook 8A 88
Sylvan Way. Red 4E 122
(in two parts)
Sylvan Way. W Wick 1A 66
Sylvaways Clo. Cranl 7B 156
Sylverdale Rd. Croy
. . . . 9M 45 (4A 200)
Sylverdale Rd. Purl 9M 63
Sylverns Ct. Warf 8B 16
Sylvestrus Clo. King T 9N 25
Syon Ga. Way. Bren 3G 11
Syon House & Pk. 4J 11
Syon La. Iswth 2F 10
Syon Pk. Gdns. Iswth 3F 10
Syon Pl. Farnb 1B 90
Sythwood. Wok 4L 73
Szabo Cres. Norm 3M 111

T

Tabarin Way. Eps 3H 81
Tabor Ct. Sutt 3K 61
Tabor Gdns. Sutt 3L 61
Tabor Gro. SW19 . . . . 8L 27
Tachbrook Rd. Felt 1G 23
Tadlow. King T 5M 203
Tadmor Clo. Sun 3G 39
Tadorne Rd. Tad 8H 81
Tadpole La. Ews 3C 108
Tadworth 9H 81
Tadworth Av. N Mald 3E 42
Tadworth Clo. Tad 9J 81
Tadworth Ct. Tad 8J 81
Tadworth Park 8J 81
Tadworth St. Tad 1H 101
Taffy's Row. Mitc 2C 44
Tailworth St. Houn 5C 10
Tait Rd. Croy 6B 46
Talavera Pk. Alder 1M 109
Talbot Clo. Myt 1E 90
Talbot Clo. Reig 4N 121
Talbot La. H'ham 7J 197
Talbot Pl. Bag 3J 51
Talbot Pl. Dat 4M 5
Talbot Rd. Ashf 6N 21
Talbot Rd. Cars 2E 62
Talbot Rd. Farnh 3G 128
Talbot Rd. Iswth 7G 11
Talbot Rd. Ling 8N 145
Talbot Rd. T Hth 3A 46
Talbot Rd. Twic 2E 24
Talcott Path. SW2 . . . . 2L 29
Taleworth Clo. Asht 7K 79
Taleworth Pk. Asht 7K 79
Taleworth Rd. Asht 6K 79
Talgarth Dri. Farnb 3B 90
Talgarth Mans. W14 . . . . 1K 13
(off Talgarth Rd.)
Talgarth Rd. W6 & W14 . . . . . . 1J 13
Talina Cen. SW6 . . . . 4N 13
Talisman Clo. Crowt 2C 48
Talisman Way. Eps 3H 81
Tallis Clo. Craw 6L 181
Tall Pines. Eps 7E 60
Tall Trees. SW16 . . . . 2K 45
Tall Trees. Coln 4F 6
Tall Trees. E Grin 1B 186
Tally Rd. Oxt 9G 107
Talma Gdns. Twic 9E 10
Talman Clo. If'd 4K 181
Tamar Clo. M'bowr 4G 182
Tamarind Clo. Guild 7K 93
Tamarind Ct. Egh 6B 20
Tamarisk Ri. Wokgm 1B 30
Tamar Way. Slou 1D 6
Tamerton Sq. Wok 6A 74
Tamesis Gdns. Wor Pk 8D 42
Tamian Ind. Est. Houn 7K 9
Tamian Way. Houn 7K 9
Tamworth. Brack 6B 32
Tamworth Dri. Fleet 1C 88
Tamworth La. Mitc 1F 44
Tamworth Pk. Mitc 3F 44
Tamworth Pl. Croy
. . . . 8N 45 (3B 200)
Tamworth Rd. Croy
. . . . 8M 45 (3A 200)
Tamworth St. SW6 . . . . 2M 13
Tamworth Vs. Mitc 3F 44
Tanbridge Pk. H'ham 7G 197
Tanbridge Pl. H'ham 7H 197
Tanbridge Retail Pk. H'ham
. . . . 7H 197
Tandem Cen. Retail Pk. SW19
. . . . 9B 28
Tandem Way. SW19 . . . . 9B 28
Tandridge 2K 125
Tandridge Ct. Cat 9D 84
Tandridge Gdns. S Croy 9C 64
Tandridge Hill La. God 6J 105
Tandridge La. Tand & Oxt . . . 1K 125
Tandridge Rd. Warl 6G 84
Tanfield Ct. H'ham 6H 197
Tanfield Rd. Croy . . . 1N 63 (6B 200)
Tangier Ct. Alder 2L 109
Tangier Ct. Eton 2G 5
Tangier La. Eton 2G 4
Tangier Rd. Guild 4C 114
Tangier Rd. Rich 7N 11
Tangier Way. Tad 4K 81
Tangier Wood. Tad 5K 81
Tangle Oak. Felb 6H 165
Tanglewood. Finch 9A 30
Tanglewood Clo. Croy 9F 46
Tanglewood Clo. Longc 9L 35
Tanglewood Clo. Wok 3F 74
Tanglewood Ride. W End 8A 52
Tanglewood Way. Felt 4J 23
Tangley Dri. Wokgm 4A 30
Tangley Gro. SW15 . . . . 9E 12
Tangley La. Guild 8J 93
Tangley Pk. Rd. Hamp 6N 23
Tanglyn Av. Shep 4C 38
Tangmere Gro. King T 6K 25
Tangmere Rd. Craw 3L 181
Tanhouse La. Wokgm 3A 30
Tanhouse Rd. Oxt 1N 125
Tanhurst Ho. SW2 . . . . 1K 29
(off Redlands Way)
Tanhurst La. Holm M 2M 157
Tankerton Rd. Surb 8M 41
Tankerton Ter. Croy 5K 45
Tankerville Rd. SW16 . . . . 8H 29
Tank Rd. Sand 1L 69
Tanners Clo. W on T 5J 39
Tanners Ct. Brock 4A 120
Tanners Dean. Lea 9J 79
Tannersfield. Shalf 2A 134
Tanner's Hill. Brock 5A 120
Tanners La. Hasl 1G 188
Tanners Mead. Eden 2L 147
Tanners Mdw. Brock 7A 120
Tanners Yd. Bag 4H 51
Tannery Clo. Beck 4G 46
Tannery Clo. Slin 5L 195
Tannery La. Brmly 3B 134
Tannery La. Send 1F 94
Tannery, The. Red 3D 122
Tansy Clo. Guild 1E 114
Tantallon Rd. SW12 . . . . 2E 28
Tanyard Av. E Grin 1C 186
Tanyard Clo. H'ham 7L 197
Tanyard Clo. M'bowr 6G 182
Tanyard Way. Horl 6F 142
Tapestry Clo. Sutt 4N 61
Taplow Ct. Mitc 3C 44
Tapners Rd. Bet 8E 120
Tara Ct. Beck 1L 47
Tarbat Ct. Col T 7J 49
Target Clo. Felt 9F 8
Target Hill. Warf 8B 16
Tarham Clo. Horl 6C 142
Tarmac Way. W Dray 3K 7
Tarnbrook Way. Brack 6C 32
Tarn Clo. Farnb 3K 89
Tarn Rd. Hind 6B 170
Tarragon Clo. Farnb 1H 89
Tarragon Clo. Brack 8B 16
Tarragon Ct. Guild 8K 93
Tarragon Dri. Guild 7K 93
Tarrant Grn. Warf 8A 16
Tarrington Clo. SW16 . . . . 4H 29
Tartar Hill. Cob 9K 57
Tartar Rd. Cob 9K 57
Tasker Clo. Hay 3D 8
Tasman Ct. Sun 8F 22
Tasso Rd. W6 . . . . 2K 13
Tasso Yd. W6 . . . . 2K 13
(off Tasso Rd.)
Tatchbury Ho. SW15 . . . . 9E 12
(off Tunworth Cres.)
Tate Clo. Lea 1J 99
Tate Rd. Sutt 2M 61
Tate's Way. Rud 1E 194
Tatham Ct. Craw 8N 181
Tatsfield 8E 86
Tatsfield Green 8F 86
Tatsfield La. Tats 8H 87
Tattenham Corner 5G 80
Tattenham Corner Rd. Eps 4E 80
Tattenham Cres. Eps 5F 80
Tattenham Gro. Eps 5G 80
Tattenham Way. Tad 5J 81
Tattersall Clo. Wokgm 3D 30
Taunton Av. SW20 . . . . 1G 42
Taunton Av. Cat 1C 104
Taunton Clo. Craw 2H 183
Taunton Clo. Sutt 7M 43
Taunton La. Coul 6L 83
Tavern Clo. Cars 6C 44
Tavistock Clo. Stai 8M 21
Tavistock Ct. Croy 7A 46
(off Tavistock Rd.)
Tavistock Cres. Mitc 3J 45
Tavistock Gdns. Farnb 7N 69
Tavistock Ga. Croy
. . . . 7A 46 (1D 200)
Tavistock Gro. Croy 6A 46
Tavistock Rd. Cars 7B 44
Tavistock Rd. Croy
. . . . 7A 46 (1D 200)
Tavistock Rd. Well 5A 88
Tavistock Wlk. Cars 7B 44
Tawfield. Brack 6K 31
Tawny Clo. Felt 4H 23
Tawny Cft. Sand 7K 49
Tayben Av. Twic 9E 10
Tay Clo. Farnb 8K 69
Tayles Hill Dri. Eps 6E 60
Taylor Av. Rich 5A 12
Taylor Clo. Eps 7N 59
Taylor Clo. Hamp H 6C 24
Taylor Clo. Houn 4C 10
Taylor Clo. Orp 1N 67
Taylor Ct. SE20 . . . . 1F 46
(off Elmers End Rd.)
Taylor Rd. Asht 4K 79
Taylor Rd. Mitc 8C 28
Taylor Rd. Wall 2F 62
Taylor's Bushes Ride. Wind . . . 3N 17
Taylors Clo. Lind 4A 168
Taylors Ct. Felt 3H 23
Taylors Cres. Cranl 7A 156
Taylors La. Lind 4A 168
Taylor Wlk. Craw 3A 182
Taymans Track. Hand 8L 199
Taynton Dri. Red 8H 103
Teal Clo. H'ham 3J 197
Teal Clo. S Croy 7G 64
Teal Ct. Dork 1J 201
Tealing Dri. Eps 1C 60
Teal Pl. Sutt 2L 61
Teasel Clo. Craw 6N 181
Teasel Clo. Croy 7G 46
Teazlewood Pk. Lea 4G 78
Tebbit Clo. Brack 1B 32
Teck Clo. Iswth 5G 11
Tedder Clo. Chess 2J 59
Tedder Rd. S Croy 4F 64
Teddington 6G 24
Teddington Bus. Pk. Tedd 7F 24
(off Station Rd.)
Teddington Clo. Eps 6C 60
Teddington Pk. Tedd 6F 24
Teddington Pk. Rd. Tedd 5F 24
Tedham La. God 3E 144
Tees Clo. Farnb 8K 69
Teesdale. Craw 6A 182
Teesdale Av. Iswth 4G 11
Teesdale Gdns. SE25 . . . . 1B 46
Teesdale Gdns. Iswth 4G 11
Teevan Clo. Croy 6D 46
Teevan Rd. Croy 7D 46
Tegg's La. Wok 3H 75
Tekels Av. Camb 1B 70
Tekels Pk. Camb 1C 70
Tekels Way. Camb 3C 70
Telconia Clo. Head D 5H 169
Telegraph La. Clay 2F 58
Telegraph Pas. SW2 . . . . 1J 29
Telegraph Rd. SW15 . . . . 1G 27
Telegraph Track. Cars 7E 62
Telephone Pl. SW6 . . . . 2L 13
Telferscot Rd. SW12 . . . . 2H 29

278 A-Z Surrey

Tudor Rd.—Vaughan Almshouses

Tudor Rd. Ashf. 7E 22
Tudor Rd. SE25 4E 46
Tudor Rd. Beck 2M 47
Tudor Rd. G'ming 4H 133
Tudor Rd. Hamp 8A 24
Tudor Rd. Houn 7D 10
Tudor Rd. King T 8N 25
Tudors, The. Reig 9A 102
Tudor Wlk. Lea 7F 78
Tudor Wlk. Wey 9C 38
Tudor Way. C Crook 9B 88
Tudor Way. Wind 4B 4
Tuesley. 1F 152
Tuesley Corner. G'ming 8G 132
Tuesley La. G'ming 8G 133
Tufton Gdns. W Mol 1B 40
Tugela Rd. Croy 5A 46
Tuggles Plat. Warn 1E 196
Tugmutton Clo. Orp 1K 67
Tulip Clo. Croy 7G 46
Tulip Clo. Hamp 7N 23
Tulip Ct. H'ham 4J 197
Tulip Tree Ct. Belm 7M 61
Tullett Rd. M'bowr 7F 182
Tulls La. Stand 7C 168
Tull St. Mitc 6D 44
Tulse Clo. Beck 2M 47
Tulse Hill. 2M 29
Tulse Hill Est. SW2 1L 29
Tulse Ho. SW2 1L 29
Tulsemere Rd. SE27 3N 29
Tulyar Clo. Tad 7G 81
Tumber Clo. As 2F 110
Tumber St. H'ley 3B 100
Tumblewood Rd. Bans 3K 81
Tumbling Bay. W on T 5H 39
Tummons Gdns. SE25 1B 46
Tunbridge La. Bram 8F 168
Tunley Rd. SW17 2E 28
Tunnel Link Rd. H'row A 8B 8
Tunnel Rd. Reig 3M 121
Tunnel Rd. E. H'row A 4C 8
Tunnel Rd. W. H'row A 4B 8
Tunnmeade. If'd 4K 181
Tunsgate. Guild 5N 113 (6D 202)
Tunsgate Sq. Guild 6C 202
Tunstall Clo. Orp 1N 67
Tunstall Rd. Croy 7B 46
Tunstall Wlk. Bren 2L 11
Tunworth Cres. SW15 9E 12
Tuppers Ct. Alb 8L 115
Tupwood La. Cat 4D 104
Tupwood Scrubbs Rd. Cat 6D 104
Turf Hill Rd. Camb 7D 50
Turfhouse La. Chob 6H 53
Turing Dri. Brack 5M 31
Turle Rd. SW16 1J 45
Turle Rd. SW16 1J 45
Turnberry. Brack 5K 31
Turner Av. Mitc 9D 28
Turner Av. Twic 4C 24
Turner Clo. Guild 9B 94
Turner Ct. E Grin 7C 166
Turner Ho. Bear G 7J 139
Turner Ho. Twic 9K 11 (off Clevedon Rd.)
Turner Pl. Col T 9J 49
Turner Rd. Big H 8E 66
Turner Rd. N Mald 6C 42
Turners Clo. Stai 6K 21
Turners Hill. 5D 184
Turners Hill Pk. Turn H 4G 184
Turners Hill Rd. Copt & Craw D 7B 164
Turners Hill Rd. Craw & Worth 3H 183
Turners Hill Rd. E Grin 4J 185
Turners Hill Rd. Turn H 5A 184
Turners La. W on T 3J 57
Turners Mead. C'fold 6F 172
Turners Mdw. Way. Beck 1J 47
Turner's Way. Croy 8L 45
Turner Wlk. Craw 6D 182
Turneville Rd. W14 2L 13
Turney Rd. SE21 1N 29
Turnham Clo. Guild 7M 113
Turnham Green. 1D 12
Turnham Grn. Ter. W4 1D 12
Turnham Grn. Ter. M. W4 1D 12
Turnoak Av. Wok 7A 74
Turnoak La. Wok 7A 74
Turnoak Pk. Wind 7B 4
Turnpike La. Sutt 2A 62
Turnpike Link. Croy 8B 46 (3F 200)
Turnpike Pl. Craw 1B 182
Turnpike Rd. Brack 1J 31
Turnpike Way. Iswth 4G 10
Turnstone Clo. S Croy 6H 65
Turnstone End. Yat 9A 48
Turnville Clo. Light 6L 51
Turpin Rd. Felt 9G 9
Turpins Ri. W'sham 1M 51
Turpin Way. Wall 4F 62
Turtledove Av. Turn H 4F 184
Tuscam Way. Camb 2L 69
Tuscany Gdns. Craw 9C 162
Tuscany Way. Yat 2D 68
Tushmore Av. Craw 9C 162
Tushmore Ct. Craw 1C 182
Tushmore Cres. Craw 9C 162
Tushmore La. Craw 1C 182
Tushmore Roundabout. Craw 1B 182
Tussock Clo. Craw 5M 181
Tuxford Clo. M'bowr 5G 182
Tweed Clo. Farnb 8K 69
Tweeddale Rd. Cars 7B 44
Tweed La. If'd 9L 161
Tweed La. Str G 7N 119 (in two parts)
Tweed Rd. Slou 2D 6
Tweedsmuir Clo. Farnb 2J 89
Twelve Acre Clo. Bookh 2N 97
Twelve Acre Cres. Farnb 9J 69
Tweseldown Rd. C Crook 9C 88
Twickenham. 2G 25
Twickenham Bri. Twic & Rich 8J 11
Twickenham Clo. Croy 9K 45
Twickenham Rd. Felt 4N 23
Twickenham Rd. Iswth 8G 10
Twickenham Rd. Rich 7J 11
Twickenham Rd. Tedd 5G 24 (in two parts)
Twickenham Rugby Union Football Ground. 9E 10
Twickenham Stadium Tours. 9E 10
(Museum of Rugby, Twickenham)
Twickenham Trad. Est. Twic 9F 10
Twilley St. SW18 1N 27
Twin Bridges Bus. Pk. S Croy 3A 64
Twining Av. Twic 4C 24
Twinoaks. Cob 9A 58
Twisell Thorne. C Crook 9A 88
Twitten La. Felb 6H 165
Twitten, The. Craw 3A 182
Two Rivers Retail Pk. Stai 5H 21
Two Ways. Loxw 4J 193
Twycross Rd. G'ming 4G 132
Twycross Rd. Wokgm 1D 30
Twyford La. Wrec 5G 128
Twyford Rd. Binf 1H 15
Twyford Rd. Cars 7B 44
Twyford Rd. Wokgm & Hurst 9A 14
Twyhurst Ct. E Grin 7N 165
Twyne Clo. Craw 5L 181
Twyner Clo. Horl 7H 143
Twynersh Av. Cher 5H 37
Twynham Rd. Camb 1A 70
Tybenham Rd. SW19 2M 43
Tychbourne Dri. Guild 9F 94
Tydcombe Rd. Warl 6F 84
Tye La. H'ley 5D 100
Tye La. Orp 2L 67
Tylden Way. H'ham 2M 197
Tylecroft Rd. SW16 1J 45
Tylehost. Guild 8K 93
Tyle Pl. Old Win 8K 5
Tyler Gdns. Add 1L 55
Tyler Rd. Craw 6B 182
Tylers Clo. God 8E 104
Tylers Ct. Cranl 7M 155 (off Rowland Rd.)
Tyler's Green. 8E 104
Tylers Path. Cars 1D 62
Tymperley Ct. H'ham 5L 197 (off King's Rd.)
Tynamara. King T 7H 203
Tynan Clo. Felt 2H 23
Tyndalls. Hind 5D 170
Tyndalls Wood. 6D 170
Tyne Clo. Farnb 8K 69
Tyne Clo. Craw 4G 183
Tynedale Rd. Str G 7A 120
Tyne Ho. King T 9K 25 (1H 203)
Tynemouth Rd. Mitc 8E 28
Tynemouth St. SW6 5N 13
Tynley Gro. Guild 6N 93
Tyrawley Rd. SW6 4N 13
Tyrell Ct. Cars 1D 62
Tyrell Gdns. Wind 6C 4
Tyrell's Wood. 2N 99
Tyrrell Sq. Mitc 9C 28
Tyrwhitt Av. Guild 8L 93
Tythebarn Clo. Guild 7D 94
Tytherton. Brack 1A 32
Tyting Cotts. Guild 9E 114

U

Uckfield Gro. Mitc 8E 28
Udney Pk. Rd. Tedd 7G 25
Uffington Dri. Brack 3C 32
Uffington Rd. SE27 5L 29
Ujima Ct. SW16 5J 29
Ullathorne Rd. SW16 5G 28
Ullswater. Brack 6K 31
Ullswater Av. Farnb 2K 89
Ullswater Clo. SW15 5C 26
Ullswater Clo. Farnh 6F 108
Ullswater Clo. Light 6M 51
Ullswater Ct. Ash V 8D 90 (off Lakeside Clo.)
Ullswater Cres. SW15 5C 26
Ullswater Cres. Coul 3H 83
Ullswater Rd. SE27 3M 29
Ullswater Rd. SW13 3F 12
Ullswater Rd. Light 6M 51
Ulstan Clo. Wold 1K 105
Ulva Rd. SW15 8J 13
Ulverstone Rd. SE27 3M 29
Ulwin Av. Byfl 9N 55
Umbria St. SW15 9F 12
Underhill Clo. G'ming 8H 133
Underhill La. Lwr Bo 4G 129
Underhill Pk. Rd. Reig 9M 101
Underhill Rd. Newd 1A 160
Underwood. Brack 5K 31
Underwood. New Ad 2M 65
Underwood Av. As 3C 110
Underwood Clo. Craw D 1E 184
Underwood Ct. Binf 7H 15
Underwood Ct. Cat 3B 104
Underwood Rd. Cat 4B 104
Underwood Rd. Hasl 1D 188
Undine St. SW17 6D 28
Unicorn Ind. Est. Hasl 1F 188
Union Clo. Owl 5K 49
Union Ct. Rich 8L 11
Union Rd. Croy 6N 45
Union Rd. Deep 6H 71
Union Rd. Farnh 1H 129
Union St. Farnb 1M 89
Union St. Alder 2M 109
Union St. Brkwd 8L 71
Union St. King T 1K 41 (3H 203)
Union Ter. Alder 2M 109
Unitair Cen. Felt 9D 8
Unity Clo. SE19 6N 29
Unity Clo. New Ad 5L 65
University of Surrey Gallery. 3K 113
University Rd. SW19 7B 28
Unstead La. Brmly 4M 133
Unstead Wood. P'mrsh 2M 133
Unsted. 6M 133
Unwin Av. Felt 8E 8
Unwin Mans. W14 2L 13 (off Queen's Club Gdns.)
Unwin Rd. Iswth 6E 10
Upavon Gdns. Brack 4D 32
Upcerne Rd. SW10 3N 13
Upcroft. Wind 6E 4
Updown Hill. W'sham 3A 52
Upfield. Croy 9E 46
Upfield. Horl 9E 142
Upfield Clo. Horl 1E 162
Upfold Clo. Cranl 4K 155
Upfold La. Cranl 5K 155
Upfolds Grn. Guild 8E 94
Upgrove Mnr. Way. SE24 1L 29
Upham Pk. Rd. W4 1D 12
Upland Rd. Camb 8B 50
Upland Rd. S Croy 2A 64
Upland Rd. Sutt 4B 62
Upland Rd. Wold 7K 85 (in two parts)
Uplands. Asht 7K 79
Uplands. Beck 1K 47
Uplands Clo. SW14 8A 12
Uplands Clo. Hasl 9H 171
Uplands Clo. Sand 7G 48
Uplands Dri. Oxs 1D 78
Uplands Rd. Farnh 2K 129
Uplands Rd. Kenl 3N 83
Upland Way. Eps 5H 81
Uppark Gdns. H'ham 2M 197
Up. Bourne La. Wrec 6F 128
Up. Bourne Va. Wrec 6F 128
Up. Bridge Rd. Red 3C 122
Up. Brighton Rd. Surb 5K 41
Up. Broadmoor Rd. Crowt 2H 49
Up. Butts. Bren 2J 11
Up. Charles St. Camb 9A 50
Up. Chobham Rd. Camb 3E 70
Up. Church La. Farnh 1G 129
Upper Clo. F Row 7H 187
Up. College Ride. Camb 7C 50
Up. Court Rd. Eps 7B 60
Up. Court Rd. Wold 1K 105
Upper Fm. Big H 6E 66
Upper Dunnymans. Bans 1L 81
Upper Eashing. 7D 132
Up. Edgeborough Rd. Guild 4B 114
Upper Elmers End. 4J 47
Up. Elmers End Rd. Beck 3H 47
Up. Elms Rd. Alder 3M 109
Up. Fairfield Rd. Lea 8H 79
Up. Farm Rd. W Mol 3N 39
Upper Gatton. 5B 102
Up. Gordon Rd. Camb 1B 70
Up. Green E. Mitc 2D 44
Up. Green W. Mitc 1D 44 (in two parts)
Up. Grotto Rd. Twic 3F 24
Upper Gro. SE25 3B 46
Up. Guildown Rd. Guild 6L 113 (8A 202)
Upper Hale. 6H 109
Up. Hale Rd. Farnh 5F 108
Upper Halliford. 3F 38
Up. Halliford By-Pass. Shep 4F 38
Up. Halliford Grn. Shep 3F 38
Up. Halliford Rd. Shep 2F 38
Up. Ham Rd. Rich 5K 25
Upper Harestone. Cat 5D 104
Up. High St. Eps 9D 60 (6L 201)
Up. House La. Sham G 2H 155
Upper Ifold. 1B 192
Upper Kiln. Dork 7J 119 (off Stubs Hill)
Upper Mall. W6 1F 12 (in two parts)
Up. Manor Rd. G'ming 4H 133
Up. Manor Rd. Milf 1B 152
Upper Mount. G'wood 8K 171
Up. Mulgrave Rd. Sutt 4K 61
Upper Norwood. 1B 46
Upper Nursery. Asc 4D 34
Up. Old Pk. La. Farnh 7E 108
Up. Palace Rd. E Mol 2C 40
Up. Park Rd. Camb 1B 70
Up. Park Rd. King T 7N 25
Upper Parrock. 7N 187
Upper Path. Dork 7H 119
Up. Pillory Down. Cars 9E 62
Upper Pines. Bans 4D 82
Up. Pinewood Rd. As 1H 111
Up. Queen St. G'ming 7H 133
Up. Richmond Rd. SW15 7E 12
Up. Richmond Rd. W. Rich & SW14 7N 11
Upper Rd. Wall 2H 63
Up. Rose Hill. Dork 6H 119 (4K 201)
Up. St Michael's Rd. Alder 4N 109
Up. Sawley Wood. Bans 1L 81
Up. Selsdon Rd. S Croy 4C 64
Upper Shirley. 1G 64
Up. Shirley Rd. Croy 8F 46
Up. South Vw. Farnh 9H 109
Upper Springfield. Elst 8J 131
Upper Sq. F Row 0H 187
Upper Sq. Iswth 6G 11
Upper Stanford. Pirb 3C 92
Up. Star Post Ride. Crowt 9N 31
Upper St. Fleet 4A 88
Upper St. Shere 7A 116 (in two parts)
Up. Sunbury Rd. Hamp 9M 23
Up. Sutton La. Houn 3A 10
Up. Teddington Rd. King T 8J 25
Upperton Rd. Guild 4M 113 (6A 202)
Upper Tooting. 4D 28
Up. Tooting Pk. SW17 3D 28
Up. Tooting Rd. SW17 5D 28
Up. Tulse Hill. SW2 1K 29
Up. Union St. Alder 2M 109
Up. Union Ter. Alder 2M 109
Upper Vann. 8J 153
Up. Vann La. Hamb 9K 153
Up. Vernon Rd. Sutt 2D 62
Up. Verran Rd. Camb 3B 70
Up. Village Rd. Asc 4N 33
Upper Wlk. Vir W 3A 36
Upper Way. Farnh 4F 128
Up. West St. Reig 3L 121
Up. Weybourne La. Farnh 4J 109
Up. Woodcote Village. Purl 8H 63
Upshire Gdns. Brack 3D 32
Upshott La. Wok 4H 75
Upton. Wok 4L 73
Upton Clo. Farnb 2B 90
Upton Dene. Sutt 4N 61
Upton Rd. Houn 6A 10
Upton Rd. T Hth 1A 46
Upwood Rd. SW16 9J 29
Urmston Dri. SW19 2K 27
Usherwood Clo. Tad 9A 100
Uvedale Clo. New Ad 7N 65
Uvedale Cres. New Ad 7N 65
Uvedale Rd. Oxt 8B 106
Uverdale Rd. SW10 3N 13
Uxbridge Ct. King T 8H 203
Uxbridge Rd. Felt 9K 23
Uxbridge Rd. Hamp H 5A 24
Uxbridge Rd. King T 3K 41 (8G 203)

V

Vachery La. Cranl 2N 175
Vaillant Rd. Wey 1D 56
Vale Border. S Croy 7G 65
Vale Clo. Coul 1J 83
Vale Clo. Lwr Bo 7H 129
Vale Clo. Orp 1J 67
Vale Clo. Twic 4G 24
Vale Clo. Wey 9E 38
Vale Clo. Wok 3A 74
Vale Cotts. SW15 4D 26
Vale Ct. Ash V 6E 90
Vale Ct. Wey 9E 38
Vale Cres. SW15 5D 26
Vale Cft. Clay 5F 58
Vale Dri. H'ham 6H 197
Vale Farm Rd. Wok 4A 74
Valentines. Plais 3N 191
Valentines Lea. N'chap 8D 190
Valentyne Clo. New Ad 7A 66
Vale Pde. SW15 4D 26
Valerie Ct. Sutt 4N 61
Vale Rd. Ash V 6E 90
Vale Rd. Camb 2M 69 (in two parts)
Vale Rd. Clay 5E 58
Vale Rd. Mitc 2H 45
Vale Rd. Sutt 1N 61
Vale Rd. Wey 9E 38
Vale Rd. Wind 3C 4
Vale Rd. Wor Pk & Eps 9E 42
Vale Rd. N. Surb 8L 41
Vale Rd. S. Surb 8L 41
Valery Pl. Hamp 8A 24
Vale St. SE27 4N 29
Vale, The. Coul 1H 83
Vale, The. Croy 8G 47
Vale, The. Felt 9J 9
Vale, The. Houn 2M 9
Vale, The. Sun 7H 23
Va. Wood Dri. Lwr Bo 7J 129
Va. Wood La. Gray 5A 170 (in two parts)
Valewood Rd. Hasl 4G 188
Valley Ct. Cat 9D 84
Valley Cres. Wokgm 9A 14
Valley End. 3D 52
Valley End Rd. Chob 3D 52
Valleyfield Rd. SW16 6K 29
Valley Gardens. 1H 35
Valley Gdns. SW19 8B 28
Valley La. Lwr Bo 5H 129
Valley M. Twic 3F 24
Valley Rd. SW16 6K 29
Valley Rd. Frim 6E 70
Valley Rd. Kenl 2A 84
Valley, The. Guild 7M 113
Valley Vw. Big H 5E 86
Valley Vw. G'ming 7G 132
Valley Vw. Sand 8F 48
Valley Vw. Gdns. Kenl 2B 84
Valley Wlk. Croy 8F 46
Vallis Way. Chess 1K 59
Valnay St. SW17 6D 28
Valonia Gdns. SW18 9L 13
Valroy Clo. Camb 9B 50
Vanbrugh Clo. Craw 6K 181
Vanbrugh Dri. W on T 6K 39
Van Common. 9E 188
Vancouver Clo. Eps 7B 60
Vancouver Ct. Small 8L 143
Vancouver Dri. Craw 9B 162
Vancouver Rd. Rich 5J 25
Vanderbilt Rd. SW18 2N 27
Van Dyck Av. N Mald 6C 42
Vandyke. Brack 5K 31
Vandyke Clo. SW15 1J 27
Vandyke Clo. Red 9D 102
Van Gogh Clo. Iswth 6G 10
Vanguard Clo. Croy 7M 45 (1A 200)
Vanguard Way. H'row A 5F 8
Vanguard Way. Wall 4J 63
Vann Bri. Clo. Fern 9E 188
Vanneck Sq. SW15 8F 12
Vanners. Craw 2C 182
Vanners Pde. Byfl 9N 55
Vann Farm Rd. Ockl 6E 158
Vann Lake. Ockl 6F 158
Vann Lake Rd. Capel & Ockl 7F 158
Vann La. Hamb 9G 152
Vann Rd. Fern 9E 188
Vansittart Est. Wind 3F 4
Vansittart Rd. Wind 4E 4
Vanston Pl. SW6 3M 13
Vantage W. W3 1M 11
Vant Rd. SW17 6D 28
Vapery La. Pirb 8A 72
Varley Way. Mitc 1B 44
Varna Rd. SW6 3K 13
Varna Rd. Hamp 9B 24
Varney Clo. Farnb 9K 69
Varsity Dri. Twic 8E 10
Varsity Row. SW14 5B 12
Vaughan Almshouses. Ashf 6C 22 (off Feltham Hill Rd.)

Vaughan Clo.—Walls Ct.

Vaughan Clo. Hamp . . . 7M 23
Vaughan Gdns. Eton W . . . 1C 4
Vaughan Ho. SW4 . . . 1G 29
Vaughan Rd. Th Dit . . . 6H 41
Vaughan Way. Dork . . . 5G 118 (2H 201)
Vaux Cres. W on T . . . 3J 57
Vauxhall Gdns. S Croy . . . 3N 63
Veals Mead. Mitc . . . 9C 28
Vectis Gdns. SW17 . . . 7F 28
Vectis Rd. SW17 . . . 7F 28
Vector Point. Craw . . . 8D 162
Vegal Cres. Eng G . . . 6L 19
Veitch Clo. Felt . . . 1G 23
Vellum Dri. Cars . . . 9E 44
Velmead Clo. Fleet . . . 6C 88
Velmead Rd. Fleet . . . 6B 88
Vencourt Pl. W6 . . . 1F 12
Ventnor Rd. Sutt . . . 4N 61
Ventnor Ter. Alder . . . 3A 110
Venton Clo. Wok . . . 4L 73
Vera Rd. SW6 . . . 4K 13
Verbania Way. E Grin . . . 9D 166
Verbena Clo. W Dray . . . 1M 7
Verbena Gdns. W6 . . . 1F 12
Verdayne Av. Croy . . . 7G 47
Verdayne Gdns. Warl . . . 3F 84
Verdun Rd. SW13 . . . 2F 12
Vereker Dri. Sun . . . 2H 39
Vereker Rd. W14 . . . 1K 13
Verge Wlk. Alder . . . 5M 109
Vermont Rd. SW18 . . . 9N 13
Vermont Rd. Sutt . . . 9N 43
Verner Clo. Head . . . 5D 168
Verne, The. C Crook . . . 8B 88
Vernon Av. SW20 . . . 1J 43
Vernon Clo. Eps . . . 3B 60
Vernon Clo. H'ham . . . 4N 197
Vernon Clo. Ott . . . 3F 54
Vernon Ct. Farnh . . . 1F 128
Vernon Dri. Asc . . . 1H 33
Vernon Dri. Cat . . . 9N 83
Vernon M. W14 . . . 1K 13
Vernon Rd. SW14 . . . 6C 12
Vernon Rd. Felt . . . 3G 22
Vernon Rd. Sutt . . . 2A 62
Vernon St. W14 . . . 1K 13
Vernon Wlk. Tad . . . 7J 81
Vernon Way. Guild . . . 2J 113
Verona Dri. Surb . . . 8L 41
Veronica Gdns. SW16 . . . 9G 28
Veronica Rd. SW17 . . . 3F 28
Verralls. Wok . . . 4D 74 (in two parts)
Verran Rd. SW12 . . . 1F 28
Verran Rd. Camb . . . 3B 70
Verulam Av. Purl . . . 8G 63
Veryan. Wok . . . 4K 73
Vesey Clo. Farnb . . . 9M 69
Vevers Rd. Reig . . . 6A 122
Vibart Gdns. SW2 . . . 1K 29
Vibia Clo. Stanw . . . 1M 21
Viburnum Ct. W End . . . 9B 52
Vicarage Av. Egh . . . 6D 20
Vicarage Clo. Bookh . . . 3A 98
Vicarage Clo. Farnh . . . 4J 129
Vicarage Clo. Ling . . . 7N 145
Vicarage Clo. Tad . . . 2K 101
Vicarage Clo. Wor Pk . . . 7D 42
Vicarage Ct. Beck . . . 2H 47
Vicarage Ct. Egh . . . 7D 20
Vicarage Ct. Felt . . . 1D 22
Vicarage Cres. Egh . . . 6D 20
Vicarage Dri. SW14 . . . 8C 12
Vicarage Dri. Beck . . . 1K 47
Vicarage Farm Ct. Houn . . . 3N 9
Vicarage Farm Rd. Houn . . . 5M 9
Vicarage Fields. W on T . . . 5K 39
Vicarage Gdns. SW14 . . . 8B 12
Vicarage Gdns. Asc . . . 4L 33
Vicarage Gdns. C Crook . . . 9A 88
Vicarage Gdns. Gray . . . 6A 170
Vicarage Gdns. Mitc . . . 2C 44
Vicarage Ga. Guild . . . 5K 113
Vicarage Hill. Farnh & Lwr Bo . . . 4J 129
Vicarage Hill. Loxw . . . 5J 193
Vicarage Hill. W'ham . . . 4M 107
Vicarage Ho. King T . . . 3M 203
Vicarage La. Bourne . . . 4J 129
Vicarage La. Capel . . . 4K 159
Vicarage La. Crowt & Bag . . . 2E 50
Vicarage La. Eps . . . 5F 60 (in two parts)
Vicarage La. Farnh . . . 1G 129 (Downing St.)
Vicarage La. Farnh . . . 5H 109 (Heath La.)
Vicarage La. Hasl . . . 2D 188
Vicarage La. Horl . . . 7D 142
Vicarage La. Lea . . . 9H 79
Vicarage La. Send . . . 4E 94
Vicarage La. Stai . . . 2L 37
Vicarage La. Wray . . . 2A 20
Vicarage La. Yat . . . 8B 48
Vicarage Rd. SW14 . . . 8B 12
Vicarage Rd. Bag . . . 3G 50 (in two parts)
Vicarage Rd. B'water . . . 2K 69
Vicarage Rd. Chob . . . 7G 53
Vicarage Rd. Craw D . . . 2D 184
Vicarage Rd. Croy . . . 9L 45
Vicarage Rd. Egh . . . 6C 20
Vicarage Rd. Hamp W . . . 9J 25
Vicarage Rd. King T . . . 1K 41 (3H 203)
Vicarage Rd. Ling . . . 7N 145
Vicarage Rd. Stai . . . 4G 20
Vicarage Rd. Sun . . . 6G 23
Vicarage Rd. Sutt . . . 1N 61
Vicarage Rd. Tedd . . . 6G 24
Vicarage Rd. Twic . . . 3E 24 (Green, The)
Vicarage Rd. Twic . . . 9C 10 (Kneller Rd.)
Vicarage Rd. Wok . . . 8B 74
Vicarage Rd. Yat . . . 8A 48
Vicarage Wlk. E Grin . . . 9B 166
Vicarage Wlk. G'ming . . . 6G 132 (off Borough Rd.)
Vicarage Wlk. W on T . . . 6H 39
Vicarage Way. Coln . . . 3E 6
Viceroy Ct. Croy . . . 7A 46 (1D 200)
Vickers Clo. Wall . . . 4K 63
Vickers Dri. N. Bro P . . . 6N 55
Vickers Dri. S. Wey . . . 7N 55
Vickers Rd. Ash V . . . 8D 90
Vickers Way. Houn . . . 8M 9
Victor Ct. Craw . . . 9H 163
Victoria Almshouses. Red . . . 9E 102
Victoria Almshouses. Reig . . . 3A 122
Victoria Av. Camb . . . 1M 69
Victoria Av. Houn . . . 8A 10
Victoria Av. S Croy . . . 6N 63
Victoria Av. Surb . . . 5K 41
Victoria Av. Wall . . . 9E 44
Victoria Av. W Mol . . . 2B 40
Victoria Clo. Eden . . . 3L 147
Victoria Clo. Horl . . . 8E 142
Victoria Clo. W Mol . . . 2A 40
Victoria Clo. Wey . . . 9E 38
Victoria Cotts. Rich . . . 4M 11
Victoria Ct. Bag . . . 6J 51
Victoria Ct. Fleet . . . 4A 88
Victoria Ct. H'ham . . . 6K 197
Victoria Ct. Red . . . 6E 122
Victoria Ct. Shalf . . . 9A 114 (off Station Row)
Victoria Cres. SW19 . . . 8L 27
Victoria Dri. SW19 . . . 1J 27
Victoria Dri. B'water . . . 2H 69
Victoria Gdns. Big H . . . 2E 86
Victoria Gdns. Fleet . . . 4A 88
Victoria Gdns. Houn . . . 4M 9
Victoria Hill Rd. Fleet . . . 4A 88
Victoria La. Hay . . . 1D 8
Victoria M. SW18 . . . 2A 28
Victoria Pde. Rich . . . 4N 11 (off Sandycombe Rd.)
Victoria Pl. Eps . . . 8D 60 (5M 201)
Victoria Pl. Esh . . . 1B 58
Victoria Pl. Rich . . . 8K 11
Victoria Rd. Farnb . . . 1M 89
Victoria Rd. SW14 . . . 6C 12
Victoria Rd. Add . . . 1M 55
Victoria Rd. Alder . . . 2M 109
Victoria Rd. Asc . . . 4L 33
Victoria Rd. Coul . . . 2H 83
Victoria Rd. Cranl . . . 7M 155
Victoria Rd. Craw . . . 3A 182
Victoria Rd. Eden . . . 3L 147
Victoria Rd. Eton W . . . 1B 4
Victoria Rd. Farnh . . . 1H 129
Victoria Rd. Felt . . . 2J 23
Victoria Rd. Fleet . . . 4A 88
Victoria Rd. G'ming . . . 7H 133
Victoria Rd. Guild . . . 3A 114 (3E 202)
Victoria Rd. Horl . . . 8E 142
Victoria Rd. King T . . . 1M 41 (4L 203)
Victoria Rd. Knap . . . 4G 72
Victoria Rd. Mitc . . . 8C 28
Victoria Rd. Owl . . . 6K 49
Victoria Rd. Red . . . 4E 122
Victoria Rd. Stai . . . 4G 20
Victoria Rd. Surb . . . 5K 41
Victoria Rd. Sutt . . . 2B 62
Victoria Rd. Tedd . . . 7G 24
Victoria Rd. Twic . . . 1H 25
Victoria Rd. Wey . . . 9E 38
Victoria Rd. Wok . . . 4A 74
Victoria Sq. Horl . . . 8E 142 (off Consort Way)
Victoria St. Eng G . . . 7M 19
Victoria St. H'ham . . . 6K 197
Victoria St. Wind . . . 4G 4
Victoria Ter. Dork . . . 5G 119 (3J 201)
Victoria Vs. Rich . . . 6M 11
Victoria Way. E Grin . . . 2B 186
Victoria Way. Wey . . . 9E 38
Victoria Way. Wok . . . 4A 74
Victor Rd. Tedd . . . 5E 24
Victor Rd. Wind . . . 6F 4
Victors Dri. Hamp . . . 7M 23
Victory Av. Mord . . . 4A 44
Victory Bus. Cen. Iswth . . . 7F 10
Victory Cotts. Eff . . . 6M 97
Victory Pk. Rd. Add . . . 9L 37 (in two parts)
Victory Rd. SW19 . . . 8A 28
Victory Rd. Cher . . . 7J 37
Victory Rd. H'ham . . . 5H 197
Victory Rd. M. SW19 . . . 8A 28
Victory Way. Houn . . . 1K 9
Vidler Clo. Chess . . . 3J 59
View Clo. Big H . . . 3E 86
Viewfield Rd. SW18 . . . 9L 13
Viewlands Av. W'ham . . . 7N 87
View Ter. D'land . . . 2C 166
Viggory La. Wok . . . 2M 73
Vigo La. Yat . . . 1B 68
Viking. Brack . . . 4K 31
Viking Ct. SW6 . . . 2M 13
Village Clo. Wey . . . 9E 38
Village Gdns. Eps . . . 6E 60
Village Grn. Av. Big H . . . 4G 87
Village Grn. Way. Big H . . . 4G 87
Village Rd. Egh . . . 2E 36
Village Row. Sutt . . . 4M 61
Village St. Newd . . . 1A 160
Village, The. . . . 4D 18
Village, The. Ewh . . . 4E 156
Village Way. Ashf . . . 5A 22
Village Way. Beck . . . 1K 47
Village Way. Cranl . . . 7M 155
Village Way. S Croy . . . 9D 64
Village Way. Yat . . . 8C 48
Villas, The. Blind H . . . 3H 145
Villiers Av. Surb . . . 4M 41 (8L 203)
Villiers Av. Twic . . . 2N 23
Villiers Clo. Surb . . . 3M 41 (8M 203)
Villiers Gro. Sutt . . . 5J 61
Villiers Mead. Wokgm . . . 2A 30
Villiers Path. Surb . . . 4L 41
Villiers Rd. Beck . . . 1G 47
Villiers Rd. Iswth . . . 5E 10
Villiers Rd. King T . . . 3M 41 (7L 203)
Villiers, The. Wey . . . 3E 56
Vinall Gdns. Broad H . . . 4D 196
Vincam Clo. Twic . . . 1A 24
Vincennes Est. SE27 . . . 5N 29
Vincent Av. Cars . . . 7B 62
Vincent Av. Surb . . . 8B 42
Vincent Clo. Cher . . . 6G 37
Vincent Clo. Coul . . . 7D 82
Vincent Clo. Esh . . . 9B 40
Vincent Clo. Fet . . . 1B 98
Vincent Clo. H'ham . . . 6M 197
Vincent Clo. W Dray . . . 2B 8
Vincent Dri. Dork . . . 6G 118 (4H 201)
Vincent Dri. Shep . . . 2F 38
Vincent Grn. Coul . . . 7D 82
Vincent La. Dork . . . 5G 118 (2H 201)
Vincent Ri. Brack . . . 2C 32
Vincent Rd. Cher . . . 6G 37
Vincent Rd. Coul . . . 3G 82
Vincent Rd. Croy . . . 6B 46
Vincent Rd. Dork . . . 5G 118 (3H 201)
Vincent Rd. Houn . . . 5L 9
Vincent Rd. Iswth . . . 4D 10
Vincent Rd. King T . . . 2N 41
Vincent Rd. Stoke D . . . 3M 77
Vincent Row. Hamp H . . . 7C 24
Vincent Sq. Big H . . . 9E 66
Vincent Wlk. Dork . . . 5G 118 (2J 201)
Vincent Works. Dork . . . 3H 201
Vine Clo. Alder . . . 7M 89
Vine Clo. Holmw . . . 4J 139
Vine Clo. Stai . . . 8J 7
Vine Clo. Surb . . . 5M 41
Vine Clo. Sutt . . . 9A 44
Vine Clo. W Dray . . . 1B 8
Vine Clo. Worp . . . 4G 93
Vine Clo. Wrec . . . 7F 128
Vine Cotts. Cranl . . . 7K 155
Vine Cotts. N'chap . . . 8D 190
Vine Farm Cotts. Worp . . . 5G 93
Vine Ho. Clo. Myt . . . 2E 90
Vine La. Wrec . . . 6F 128
Vine Pl. Houn . . . 7B 10
Viner Clo. W on T . . . 5K 39
Vineries Clo. W Dray . . . 2B 8
Vine Rd. SW13 . . . 6E 12
Vine Rd. E Mol . . . 3C 40
Vine Rd. Orp . . . 3N 67
Vine Sq. W14 . . . 1L 13 (off Star Rd.)
Vine St. Alder . . . 3M 109
Vine Way. Wrec . . . 6F 128
Vineyard Clo. King T . . . 2M 41 (5L 203)
Vineyard Hill Rd. SW19 . . . 5L 27
Vineyard Pas. Rich . . . 8L 11
Vineyard Path. SW14 . . . 6C 12
Vineyard Rd. Felt . . . 4H 23
Vineyard Row. Hamp W . . . 9J 25
Vineyards, The. Felt . . . 4H 23 (off High St.)
Vineyards, The. Sun . . . 2H 39
Vineyard, The. Rich . . . 8L 11
Viney Bank. Croy . . . 5J 65
Viola Av. Felt . . . 9K 9
Viola Av. Stai . . . 2M 21
Viola Cft. Warf . . . 9D 16
Violet Clo. Wall . . . 7E 44
Violet Gdns. Croy . . . 2M 63
Violet La. Croy . . . 3M 63 (8A 200)
Virginia Av. Vir W . . . 4M 35
Virginia Beeches. Vir W . . . 2M 35
Virginia Clo. Asht . . . 5K 79
Virginia Clo. N Mald . . . 3B 42
Virginia Clo. Stai . . . 2L 37
Virginia Clo. Wey . . . 3D 56
Virginia Dri. Vir W . . . 4M 35
Virginia Gdns. Farnb . . . 3A 90
Virginia Pk. Vir W . . . 3A 36
Virginia Pl. Cob . . . 1H 77
Virginia Rd. T Hth . . . 9M 29
Virginia Wlk. SW2 . . . 1K 29
Virginia Water. . . . 4A 36
Virginia Water. . . . 2H 35
Viscount Clo. Ash V . . . 8D 90
Viscount Gdns. W Byf . . . 8N 55
Viscount Ind. Est. Coln . . . 6G 6
Viscount Rd. Stanw . . . 2N 21
Viscount Way. H'row A . . . 7F 8 (in two parts)
Vivian Clo. C Crook . . . 7C 88
Vivien Clo. Chess . . . 4L 59
Vivienne Clo. Craw . . . 9B 162
Vivienne Clo. Twic . . . 9K 11
Voewood Clo. N Mald . . . 5E 42
Vogan Clo. Reig . . . 6N 121
Volta Way. Croy . . . 7K 45
Voss Ct. SW16 . . . 7J 29
Vowels La. E Grin . . . 8F 184
Vulcan Clo. Craw . . . 7A 182
Vulcan Clo. Sand . . . 8F 48
Vulcan Ct. Sand . . . 8F 48
Vulcan Way. New Ad . . . 6A 66
Vulcan Way. Sand . . . 8F 48

W

Wadbrook St. King T . . . 1K 41 (4H 203)
Waddington Av. Coul . . . 7L 83
Waddington Clo. Coul . . . 6M 83
Waddington Clo. Craw . . . 6M 181
Waddington Way. SE19 . . . 8N 29
Waddon. . . . 9L 45
Waddon Clo. Croy . . . 9L 45
Waddon Ct. Rd. Croy . . . 9L 45
Waddon Marsh Way. Croy . . . 7K 45
Waddon New Rd. Croy . . . 9M 45 (4A 200)
Waddon Pk. Av. Croy . . . 1L 63
Waddon Rd. Croy . . . 9L 45 (4A 200)
Waddon Way. Croy . . . 3L 63
Wades La. Tedd . . . 6G 24
Wadham. Owl . . . 6L 49
Wadham Clo. Craw . . . 9G 162
Wadham Clo. Shep . . . 6D 38
Wadham Rd. SW15 . . . 7K 13
Wadhurst Clo. SE20 . . . 1E 46
Wadlands Brook Rd. E Grin . . . 5N 165
Wagbullock Ri. Brack . . . 5A 32
Wagg Clo. E Grin . . . 9C 166
Waggon Clo. Guild . . . 2H 113
Waggoners Hollow. Bag . . . 5J 51
Waggoners Roundabout. (Junct.) . . . 4J 9
Waggoners Way. Gray . . . 6M 169
Waggoners Wells Rd. Gray . . . 6M 169
Wagon Yd. Farnh . . . 1G 129
Wagtail Clo. H'ham . . . 1K 197
Wagtail Gdns. S Croy . . . 6H 65
Wagtail Wlk. Beck . . . 4M 47
Waight's Ct. King T . . . 9L 25 (1K 203)
Wain End. H'ham . . . 3K 197
Wainford Clo. SW19 . . . 1J 27
Wainhouse Clo. Eden . . . 9M 127 (in two parts)
Wainscot. Asc . . . 5C 34
Wainwright Clo. Wokgm . . . 2F 30
Wainwright Gro. Iswth . . . 7D 10
Wainwrights. Craw . . . 6B 182
Wake Ct. Guild . . . 9L 93
Wakefield Clo. Byfl . . . 8N 55
Wakefield Rd. Rich . . . 8K 11
Wakefords Copse. C Crook . . . 1C 108
Wakefords Pk. C Crook . . . 1C 108 (in three parts)
Wakehams Grn. Dri. Craw . . . 9H 163
Wakehurst Dri. Craw . . . 6B 182
Wakehurst M. H'ham . . . 7F 196
Wakehurst Path. Wok . . . 1E 74
Wakely Clo. Big H . . . 5E 86
Walburton Rd. Purl . . . 9G 63
Walbury. Brack . . . 3C 32
Waldby Ct. Craw . . . 6M 181
Waldeck Gro. SE27 . . . 4M 29
Waldeck Rd. SW14 . . . 6B 12
Waldeck Rd. W4 . . . 2N 11
Waldeck Ter. SW14 . . . 6B 12 (off Waldeck Rd.)
Waldegrave Av. Tedd . . . 6F 24
Waldegrave Gdns. Twic . . . 3F 24
Waldegrave Pk. Twic . . . 5F 24
Waldegrave Rd. Tedd & Twic . . . 5F 24
Waldegrove. Croy . . . 9C 46
Waldemar Av. SW6 . . . 4K 13
Waldemar Rd. SW19 . . . 6M 27
Walden Cotts. Norm . . . 1L 111
Walden Gdns. T Hth . . . 2K 45
Waldens Pk. Rd. Wok . . . 3M 73
Waldens Rd. Wok . . . 4N 73
Waldo Pl. Mitc . . . 8C 28
Waldorf Clo. S Croy . . . 5M 63
Waldorf Heights. B'water . . . 3J 69
Waldron Gdns. Brom . . . 2N 47
Waldron Hill. Brack . . . 9D 16
Waldronhyrst. S Croy . . . 1M 63 (7A 200)
Waldron Rd. SW18 . . . 4A 28
Waldron's Path. S Croy . . . 1N 63 (7B 200)
Waldrons, The. Croy . . . 1M 63 (7A 200)
Waldrons, The. Oxt . . . 9B 106
Waldy Ri. Cranl . . . 6N 155
Wales Av. Cars . . . 2C 62
Walesbeech. Craw . . . 4E 182
Waleton Acres. Wall . . . 3G 63
Waleys La. Ockl . . . 9E 158
Walford Rd. N Holm . . . 9H 119
Walham Green. . . . 4N 13
Walham Grn. Ct. SW6 . . . 3N 13 (off Waterford Rd.)
Walham Gro. SW6 . . . 3M 13
Walham Ri. SW19 . . . 7K 27
Walham Yd. SW6 . . . 3M 13
Walker Clo. Felt . . . 1G 22
Walker Clo. Hamp . . . 7N 23
Walker Rd. M'bowr . . . 5F 182
Walkerscroft Mead. SE21 . . . 2N 29
Walkers Pl. SW15 . . . 7K 13
Walker's Ridge. Camb . . . 2C 70
Walkfield Dri. Eps . . . 4G 81
Walking Bottom. Peasl . . . 5D 136
Walk, The. Eton W . . . 1D 4
Walk, The. Sun . . . 8G 22
Walk, The. Tand . . . 2K 125
Wallace Clo. Guild . . . 9F 92
Wallace Clo. Shep . . . 3E 38
Wallace Cres. Cars . . . 2D 62
Wallace Fields. Eps . . . 9F 60
Wallace Sq. Coul . . . 9H 83
Wallace Wlk. Add . . . 1L 55
Wallace Wlk. Eton . . . 1J 5
Wallace Way. Alder . . . 1L 109
Wallage La. Rowf . . . 3N 183
Wallbrook Bus. Cen. Houn . . . 6J 9
Wallcroft Clo. Binf . . . 8K 15
Walldown Rd. W'hill . . . 8A 168
Walled Garden, The. Bet . . . 4C 120
Walled Garden, The. Loxw . . . 1H 193
Walled Garden, The. Tad . . . 9J 81
Waller La. Cat . . . 1C 104
Wall Hill. . . . 5G 186
Wall Hill Rd. Ash W & F Row . . . 4F 186
Wallingford Clo. Brack . . . 3C 32
Wallington. . . . 3G 62
Wallington Corner. Wall . . . 1F 62 (off Manor Rd. N.)
Wallington Ct. Wall . . . 3F 62 (off Stanley Pk. Rd.)
Wallington Green. (Junct.) . . . 1F 62
Wallington Rd. Camb . . . 6E 50
Wallington Sq. Wall . . . 3F 62
Wallis Ct. Craw . . . 8D 162
Wallis M. Lea . . . 9G 78
Wallis's Cotts. SW2 . . . 1J 29
Wallis Way. H'ham . . . 4N 197
Walliswood. . . . 9L 157
Walliswood Grn. Rd. Wal W . . . 1L 177
Wallner Way. Wokgm . . . 3D 30
Wallorton Gdns. SW14 . . . 7C 12
Walls Ct. Frim . . . 6C 70

Walmer Clo.—Watson Rd.

Walmer Clo. *Crowt.* 2H **49**
Walmer Clo. *F'boro* 1M **67**
Walmer Clo. *Frim* 7E **70**
Walmer Ct. *Surb* 8K **203**
Walnut Clo. *Alder* 4M **109**
Walnut Clo. *Cars* 2D **62**
Walnut Clo. *Eps* 2E **80**
Walnut Clo. *Yat* 2C **68**
Walnut Dri. *Kgswd* 2K **101**
Walnut Fields. *Eps* 5E **60**
Walnut Gro. *Bans* 1J **81**
Walnut La. *Craw* 9N **161**
Walnut M. *Sutt* 4A **62**
Walnuts, The. *H'ham* 4J **197**
Walnut Tree Av. *Mitc* 2C **44**
Walnut Tree Clo. *SW13* 4E **12**
Walnut Tree Clo. *Bans* 8K **61**
Walnut Tree Clo. *Guild* 3M **113** (2A **202**)
Walnut Tree Clo. *Shep* 2D **38**
Walnut Tree Cotts. *SW19* 6K **27**
Walnut Tree Gdns. *G'ming* 4H **133**
Walnut Tree Ho. SW10 2N **13** *(off Tregunter Rd.)*
Walnut Tree La. *Byfl* 8M **55**
Walnut Tree Pk. *Guild* 3M **113** (2A **202**)
Walnut Tree Rd. *Bren* 2L **11**
Walnut Tree Rd. *Houn* 2N **9**
Walnut Tree Rd. *Shep* 1D **38**
Walpole Av. *Coul* 6D **82**
Walpole Av. *Rich* 5M **11**
Walpole Ct. *Twic* 3E **24**
Walpole Cres. *Tedd* 6F **24**
Walpole Gdns. *W4* 1B **12**
Walpole Gdns. *Twic* 3E **24**
Walpole M. *SW19* 7B **28**
Walpole Pk. *Wey* 4B **56**
Walpole Pl. *Tedd* 6F **24**
Walpole Rd. *SW19* 7B **28**
Walpole Rd. *Croy* 8A **46** (2D **200**)
Walpole Rd. *Old Win* 1L **19**
Walpole Rd. *Surb* 6L **41**
Walpole Rd. *Tedd* 6F **24**
Walpole Rd. *Twic* 3E **24**
Walsham Rd. *Felt* 1J **23**
Walsh Av. *Warf* 8C **16**
Walsh Cres. *New Ad* 8A **66**
Walsingham Gdns. *Eps* 1D **60**
Walsingham Lodge. *SW13* 4F **12**
Walsingham Mans. SW6 3N **13** *(off Fulham Rd.)*
Walsingham Rd. *Mitc* 4D **44**
Walsingham Rd. *New Ad* 6M **65**
Walstead Ho. *Craw* 4D **182**
Walters Mead. *Asht* 4L **79**
Walters Rd. *SE25* 3B **46**
Walter St. *King T* 9L **25** (2J **203**)
Waltham Av. *Guild* 8L **93**
Waltham Clo. *Owl* 6J **49**
Waltham Rd. *Cars* 6B **44**
Waltham Rd. *Cat* 9E **84**
Walton & Hersham F.C. 8H **39**
Walton Av. *N Mald* 3E **42**
Walton Av. *Sutt* 9L **43**
Walton Bri. *Shep & W on T* 6F **38**
Walton Bri. Rd. *Shep* 6F **38**
Walton Clo. *Fleet* 5A **88**
Walton Ct. *S Croy* 8C **200**
Walton Ct. *Wok* 2C **74**
Walton Dri. *Asc* 9K **17**
Walton Dri. *H'ham* 4A **198**
Walton Gdns. *Felt* 5G **22**
Walton Grn. *New Ad* 5L **65**
Walton Heath. 5E **100**
Walton Heath. *Craw* 1H **183**
Walton Heath Golf Course. 5J **101**
Walton La. *Shep* 6E **38**
Walton La. *Wey* 8C **38**
Walton-on-Thames. 7H **39**
Walton on the Hill. 2F **100**
Walton Pk. *W on T* 8L **39**
Walton Pk. La. *W on T* 8L **39**
Walton Rd. *Eps* 8B **80** (Epsom)
Walton Rd. *Eps* 4F **80** (Epsom Downs, in two parts)
Walton Rd. *W on T & W Mol* 4K **39**
Walton Rd. *W Mol* 3N **39**
Walton Rd. *Wok* 3B **74**
Walton St. *Tad* 2F **100**
Walton Ter. *Wok* 2D **74**
Walton Way. *Mitc* 3G **44**
Wanborough. 6N **111**
Wanborough Common. 9C **112**
Wanborough Dri. *SW15* 2G **26**
Wanborough Hill. *Wanb* 6N **111**
Wanborough La. *Cranl* 6B **156**
Wandle Bank. *SW19* 8B **28**
Wandle Bank. *Croy* 9J **45**
Wandle Clo. *As* 3E **110**
Wandle Clo. *M'bowr* 4G **182**
Wandle Ct. *Croy* 9J **45**
Wandle Ct. *Eps* 1B **60**
Wandle Ct. Gdns. *Croy* 9J **45**
Wandle Pk. Trad. Est., The. *Croy* 7M **45**
Wandle Rd. *SW17* 3C **28**
Wandle Rd. *Bedd* 9J **45**
Wandle Rd. *Croy* 9N **45** (6C **200**)
Wandle Rd. *Mord* 3A **44**
Wandle Rd. *Wall* 9F **44**
Wandle Side. *Croy* 9K **45**
Wandle Side. *Wall* 9F **44**
Wandle Way. *SW18* 2N **27**
Wandle Way. *Mitc* 4D **44**
Wandon Rd. *SW6* 3N **13** (in two parts)
Wandsworth. 8L **13**
Wandsworth Bri. *SW6 & SW18* 6N **13**
Wandsworth Common. 2D **28**
Wandsworth Gyratory. (Junct.) 8N **13**
Wandsworth High St. *SW18* 8M **13**
Wandsworth Plain. *SW18* 8N **13**
Wandsworth Shop. Cen. *SW18* 9N **13**
Wanmer Ct. Reig 2M **121** *(off Birkheads Rd.)*
Wansdyke Clo. *Frim* 6D **70**
Wansford Grn. *Wok* 4J **73**
Wanstraw Gro. *Brack* 6C **32**
Wantage Clo. *Brack* 4C **32**
Wantage Clo. *M'bowr* 6G **182**
Wantage Rd. *Col T* 7J **49**
Waplings, The. *Tad* 2G **100**
Wapses Lodge. *Wold* 7E **84**
Wapses Roundabout. (Junct.) 7D **84**
Wapshott Rd. *Stai* 7G **20**
Warbank Clo. *New Ad* 6A **66**
Warbank Cres. *New Ad* 6A **66**
Warbank La. *King T* 8E **26**
Warbler's Grn. *Cob* 1N **77**
Warbleton Ho. Craw 6L **181** *(off Salvington Rd.)*
Warboys App. *King T* 7A **26**
Warboys Rd. *King T* 7A **26**
Warburton Clo. *E Grin* 9C **166**
Warburton Rd. *Twic* 2B **24**
Warbury La. *Knap* 2E **72**
War Coppice Rd. *Cat* 5A **104**
Ward Clo. *S Croy* 3B **64**
Ward Clo. *Wokgm* 9C **14**
Wardens Fld. Clo. *G Str* 3N **67**
Ward La. *Warl* 3F **84**
Wardle Clo. *Bag* 4J **51**
Wardley St. *SW18* 1N **27**
Wardo Av. *SW6* 4K **13**
Ward Rd. *SW19* 9A **28**
Wardrobe, The. Rich 8K **11** *(off Old Pal. Yd.)*
Ward Royal. *Wind* 4F **4**
Ward's Pl. *Egh* 7E **20**
Wards Stone Pk. *Brack* 6C **32**
Ward St. *Guild* 4N **113** (5D **202**)
Ware Ct. *Sutt* 1L **61**
Wareham Clo. *Houn* 7B **10**
Wareham Rd. *Brack* 3D **32**
Warehouse Theatre. 8A **46** (3E **200**)
Warenne Rd. *Fet* 9C **78**
Warfield. 4C **16**
Warfield Park. 8E **16**
Warfield Rd. *Brack* 7A **16**
Warfield Rd. *Felt* 1F **22**
Warfield Rd. *Hamp* 9B **24**
Warfield St. *Warf* 6A **16**
Wargrove Dri. *Col T* 7J **49**
Warham Rd. *S Croy* 2M **63** (8A **200**)
Waring St. *SE27* 5N **29**
Warkworth Gdns. *Iswth* 3G **10**
Warlingham. 5G **84**
Warlingham Rd. *T Hth* 3M **45**
Warltersville Way. *Horl* 1G **162**
Warminster Gdns. *SE25* 1D **46**
Warminster Rd. *SE25* 1C **46**
Warminster Sq. *SE25* 1D **46**
Warminster Way. *Mitc* 9F **28**
Warner Av. *Sutt* 8K **43**
Warner Clo. *Hamp* 6N **23**
Warner Clo. *Hay* 3E **8**
Warner Clo. *M'bowr* 7G **182**
Warner Ct. *Col T* 8K **49**
Warner Pde. *Hay* 3E **8**
Warners La. *Alb* 1N **135**
Warners La. *King T* 5K **25**
Warnford Ho. SW15 9D **12** *(off Tunworth Cres.)*
Warnham. 9F **178**
Warnham Ct. *Warn* 1F **196**
Warnham Ct. M. *Warn* 1F **196**
Warnham Ct. Rd. *Cars* 4D **62**
Warnham Ho. SW2 1K **29** *(off Up. Tulse Hill)*
Warnham Mnr. *Warn* 1C **196**
Warnham Nature Reserve & Vis. Cen. 3H **197**
Warnham Rd. *Broad H* 4D **196**
Warnham Rd. *Craw* 5E **182**
Warnham Rd. *H'ham* 3H **197**
Warramill Rd. *G'ming* 6K **133**
Warren Av. *Orp* 2N **67**
Warren Av. *Rich* 7A **12**
Warren Av. *S Croy* 4G **64**
Warren Av. *Sutt* 6L **61**
Warren Clo. *SE21* 1N **29**
Warren Clo. *Esh* 1B **58**
Warren Clo. *Felb* 7H **165**
Warren Clo. *Fleet* 6C **88**
Warren Clo. *Sand* 7F **48**
Warren Corner. 5B **108**
Warren Corner. *Ews* 5B **108**
Warren Cotts. *Hand* 8N **199**
Warren Ct. *Croy* 7B **46**
Warren Ct. *Wey* 2B **56**
Warren Cutting. *King T* 8C **26**
Warren Down. *Brack* 9K **15**
Warren Dri. *Craw* 2M **181**
Warren Dri. *Kgswd* 9L **81**
Warren Dri. N. *Surb* 7A **42**
Warren Dri. S. *Surb* 7B **42**
Warreners La. *Wey* 4E **56**
Warren Footpath. *Twic* 2J **25**
Warren Hill. *Eps* 3C **80**
Warren Home Farm. *Wok* 6K **75**
Warren Ho. W14 1L **13** *(off Beckford Clo.)*
Warren Ho. Rd. *Wokgm* 9B **14**
Warrenhyrst. *Guild* 4C **114**
Warren La. *Alb* 8L **115**
Warren La. *Oxs* 7C **58**
Warren La. *Oxt* 3C **126**
Warren La. *Wok* 5J **75**
Warren Lodge Dri. *Kgswd* 2K **101**
Warren Mead. *Bans* 2H **81**
Warrenne Heights. *Red* 5B **122**
Warrenne Rd. *Brock* 5B **120**
Warrenne Way. *Reig* 3M **121**
Warren Pk. *King T* 7B **26**
Warren Pk. *Tad* 9B **100**
Warren Pk. *Thur* 5K **151**
Warren Pk. *Warl* 5G **84**
Warren Pk. Rd. *Sutt* 3B **62**
Warren Ri. *Frim* 4C **70**
Warren Ri. *N Mald* 9C **26**
Warren Rd. *Ashf* 8E **22**
Warren Rd. *SW19* 7C **28**
Warren Rd. *Bans* 1H **81**
Warren Rd. *Croy* 7B **46**
Warren Rd. *G'ming* 4H **133**
Warren Rd. *Guild* 4B **114**
Warren Rd. *King T* 7B **26**
Warren Rd. *New H* 6J **55**
Warren Rd. *Orp & Chels* 2N **67**
Warren Rd. *Purl* 8M **63**
Warren Rd. *Reig* 2N **121**
Warren Rd. *Twic* 9C **10**
Warren Row. *Asc* 1H **33**
Warren, The. 3D **32** (Bracknell)
Warren, The. 1C **166** (Ewhurst)
Warren, The. *Alder* 3L **109**
Warren, The. *Asht* 6L **79**
Warren, The. *Brack* 3E **32**
Warren, The. *Cars* 5B **62**
Warren, The. *E Hor* 8G **96**
Warren, The. *Farnh* 4K **109**
Warren, The. *Houn* 3N **9**
Warren, The. *Kgswd* 1K **101**
Warren, The. *Oxs* 8C **58**
Warren, The. *Wor Pk* 1C **60**
Warren Way. *Wey* 2D **56**
Warrington Clo. *Bew* 7K **181**
Warrington Ct. *Croy* 5A **200**
Warrington M. *Alder* 4K **109**
Warrington Rd. *Croy* 9M **45** (6A **200**)
Warrington Rd. *Rich* 8K **11**
Warrington Spur. *Old Win* 1L **19**
Warsop Trad. Est. *Eden* 3M **147**
Warwick. W14 1L **13** *(off Kensington Village)*
Warwick. *Brack* 5C **32**
Warwick Av. *Egh* 9E **20**
Warwick Av. *Stai* 7L **21**
Warwick Clo. *Alder* 4A **110**
Warwick Clo. *Camb* 3F **70**
Warwick Clo. *Hamp* 8C **24**
Warwick Clo. *Holmw* 4H **139**
Warwick Ct. *Brom* 1N **47**
Warwick Deeping. *Ott* 2E **54**
Warwick Dri. *SW15* 6G **12**
Warwick Gdns. *Asht* 4J **79**
Warwick Gdns. *Th Dit* 4F **40**
Warwick Gdns. *T Hth* 2L **45**
Warwick Gro. *Surb* 6M **41**
Warwick Ho. *King T* 1K **203**
Warwick La. *Wok* 6K **73**
Warwick Lodge. *Twic* 4B **24**
Warwick Pl. *Th Dit* 5G **40**
Warwick Quadrant. Red 2F **122** *(off London Rd.)*
Warwick Rd. *Ashf* 6N **21**
Warwick Rd. *SE20* 2E **46**
Warwick Rd. *W14 & SW5* 1L **13**
Warwick Rd. *Ash V* 5E **90**
Warwick Rd. *Coul* 1G **83**
Warwick Rd. *Holmw* 5J **139**
Warwick Rd. *Houn* 6J **9**
Warwick Rd. *King T* 9J **25**
Warwick Rd. *N Mald* 2B **42**
Warwick Rd. *Red* 2D **122**
Warwick Rd. *Sutt* 1A **62**
Warwick Rd. *Th Dit* 4F **40**
Warwick Rd. *T Hth* 2L **45**
Warwick Rd. *Twic* 2E **24**
Warwicks Bench. *Guild* 5N **113** (7D **202**)
Warwick's Bench La. *Guild* 6B **114**
Warwick's Bench Rd. *Guild* 6A **114** (8E **202**)
Warwick Vs. *Egh* 9F **20**
Warwick Wold. 7L **103**
Warwick Wold Rd. *Red* 7L **103**
Wasdale Clo. *Owl* 5J **49**
Washford Clo. *Bord* 5A **168**
Washford La. *Lind* 4A **168**
Washington Clo. *Reig* 1M **121**
Washington Dri. *Wind* 6B **4**
Washington Rd. *SW13* 3F **12**
Washington Rd. *Bew* 6K **181**
Washington Rd. *King T* 1N **41** (4M **203**)
Washington Rd. *Wor Pk* 8G **42**
Washpond La. *Warl* 5M **85**
Wasp Green. 3N **143**
Wasp Grn. La. *Out* 3N **143**
Wassand Clo. *Craw* 3E **182**
Watchetts Dri. *Camb* 4A **70**
Watchetts Lake Clo. *Camb* 3B **70**
Watchetts Rd. *Camb* 2N **69**
Watchfield Ct. *W4* 1B **12**
Watchmoor Point. *Camb* 2M **69**
Watchmoor Rd. *Camb* 3M **69**
Watchmoor Trade Cen. *Camb* 2M **69**
Watcombe Cotts. *Rich* 2N **11**
Watcombe Pl. *SE25* 4E **46**
Watcombe Rd. *SE25* 4E **46**
Watercress Pl. *H'ham* 5M **197**
Watercress Way. *Wok* 4L **73**
Waterden Clo. *Guild* 4B **114**
Waterden Rd. *Guild* 4A **114** (4F **202**)
Waterer Gdns. *Tad* 5J **81**
Waterer Ri. *Wall* 3H **63**
Waterers Ri. *Knap* 4G **72**
Waterfall Clo. *Vir W* 2K **35**
Waterfall Cotts. *SW19* 7B **28**
Waterfall Rd. *SW19* 7B **28**
Waterfall Ter. *SW17* 7C **28**
Waterfield. *Tad* 7G **81** (in two parts)
Waterfield Clo. *H'ham* 5L **197**
Waterfield Dri. *Tad* 6G **81**
Waterfield Dri. *Warl* 6F **84**
Waterfield Gdns. *SE25* 3A **46**
Waterfield Gdns. *Bew* 5K **181**
Waterfield Grn. *Tad* 7G **81**
Waterfields. *Lea* 6H **79**
Waterford Clo. *Cob* 7M **57**
Waterford Rd. *SW6* 3N **13** (in two parts)
Waterford Way. *Wokgm* 2B **30**
Waterfront Bus. Pk. *Fleet* 2C **88**
Watergardens, The. *King T* 7B **26**
Waterham Rd. *Brack* 5N **31**
Waterhouse Clo. *W6* 1J **13**
Waterhouse La. *Blet* 1C **124**
Waterhouse La. *Kenl* 6N **83**
Waterhouse La. *Kgswd* 8K **81**
Waterhouse Mead. *Col T* 8J **49**
Waterlakes. *Eden* 3L **147**
Waterlands La. *Rowh* 9M **177**
Water La. *Cob* 2M **77**
Water La. *Farnb* 7M **69**
Water La. *Ab H* 3J **137**
Water La. *Alb* 6K **115**
Water La. *Bisl* 6D **72**
Water La. *Blet* 8M **103**
Water La. *Bookh* 3L **97** (in two parts)
Water La. *Chob* 5E **52**
Water La. *Eden* 4F **146**
Water La. *Ent* 7D **152**
Water La. *Farnh* 8K **109**
Water La. *King T* 9K **25** (2H **203**)
Water La. *Rich* 8K **11**
Water La. *S God* 7G **124**
Water La. *T'sey* 4C **106** (in two parts)
Water La. *Twic* 2G **25**
Water La. *W'ham* 5M **107**
Water Lea. *Craw* 4E **182**
Waterloo Clo. *Camb* 8F **50**
Waterloo Clo. *Felt* 2G **23**
Waterloo Clo. *Wokgm* 3D **30**
Waterloo Cres. *Wokgm* 3D **30**
Waterloo Park. 1N **109**
Waterloo Pl. Cars 9D **44** *(off Wrythe La.)*
Waterloo Pl. *Crowt* 3G **49**
Waterloo Pl. *Kew* 2N **11**
Waterloo Pl. *Rich* 7L **11**
Waterloo Rd. *Alder* 3A **110**
Waterloo Rd. *Crowt* 3F **48**
Waterloo Rd. *Eps* 8C **60** (5K **201**)
Waterloo Rd. *Sutt* 2B **62**
Waterloo Rd. *Wokgm* 3D **30**
Waterlow Rd. *Reig* 4A **122**
Waterman Clo. *Bord* 7A **168**
Watermans Bus. Pk. *Stai* 5F **20**
Watermans Clo. *King T* 8L **25**
Watermans Ct. Bren 2K **11** *(off High St.)*
Waterman St. *SW15* 6J **13**
Watermead. *Felt* 2F **22**
Watermead. *Tad* 8G **81**
Watermead. *Wok* 3J **73**
Watermead La. *Cars* 6D **44**
Watermeadow La. *SW6* 5N **13**
Watermill Clo. *Rich* 4J **25**
Water Mill Ho. *Felt* 3A **24**
Watermill Way. *SW19* 9B **28**
Watermill Way. *Felt* 3N **23**
Waterperry La. *Chob* 6J **53**
Water Rede. *C Crook* 1A **108**
Waters Dri. *Stai* 4H **21**
Waters Edge. *SW6* 4H **13**
Watersedge. *Eps* 1B **60**
Waterside. 4A **146**
Waterside. *Beck* 1J **47**
Waterside. *E Grin* 9D **166**
Waterside. *Horl* 6E **142**
Waterside. *Tad* 7G **81**
Waterside. *W Dray* 3L **7**
Waterside Bus. Cen. *Iswth* 7H **11**
Waterside Clo. *Bew* 5K **181**
Waterside Clo. *Bord* 5A **168**
Waterside Clo. *G'ming* 6K **133**
Waterside Clo. *Surb* 8L **41**
Waterside Ct. *Fleet* 2C **88**
Waterside Dri. *W on T* 4H **39**
Waterside La. *G'ming* 8F **132**
Waterside M. *Fleet* 2C **88**
Waterside M. *Guild* 1M **113**
Waterside Pk. Ind. Est. *Brack* 1K **31** (Cain Rd.)
Waterside Pk. Ind. Est. *Brack* 9L **15** (Western Rd.)
Waterside Rd. *Guild* 9N **93**
Waterside Trad. Est. *Add* 1N **55**
Waterside Way. *SW17* 5A **28**
Waterside Way. *Wok* 5L **73**
Waterslade. *Red* 3C **122**
Watersmeet Clo. *Guild* 7C **94**
Waters Pl. *SW15* 5H **13**
Watersplash Clo. *King T* 2L **41** (5J **203**)
Watersplash La. *Asc* 9A **18**
Watersplash La. *Hay* 1H **9** (in two parts)
Watersplash La. *Warf* 7N **15**
Watersplash Rd. *Shep* 4B **38**
Waters Rd. *King T* 1A **42**
Waters Sq. *King T* 2A **42**
Water Tower Hill. *Croy* 1A **64** (6F **200**)
Water Vw. *Horl* 8H **143**
Waterway Rd. *Lea* 9G **78**
Waterworks Cotts. *F Row* 6H **187**
Waterworks Dri. *F Row* 5H **187**
Waterworks Yd. *Croy* 9N **45** (4B **200**)
Watery La. *SW20* 1L **43**
Watery La. *Chob* 6G **52**
Watery La. *C Crook* 1A **108**
Watery La. *Hay* 1F **8**
Watery La. *Lyne* 6F **36**
Wates Way. *Mitc* 5D **44**
Watford Clo. *Guild* 3B **114**
Wathen Rd. *Dork* 4H **119** (1L **201**)
Watlings Clo. *Croy* 5H **47**
Watney Cotts. *SW14* 6B **12**
Watney Rd. *SW14* 6B **12**
Watney's Rd. *Mitc* 4H **45**
Watson Av. *Sutt* 8K **43**
Watson Clo. *SW19* 7C **28**
Watson Clo. *M'bowr* 5G **182**
Watson Ho. *Reig* 2M **121**
Watson Rd. *Westc* 6C **118**

West Gdns.—Whither Dale

West Gdns. SW17 . . . 7C 28
West Gdns. Eps . . . 6D 60
Westgate Clo. Eps . . . 2C 80
Westgate Rd. SE25 . . . 3E 46
Westgate Rd. Beck . . . 1L 47
Westgate Ter. SW10 . . . 1N 13
West Glade. Farnb . . . 1J 89
West Green . . . 2A 182
West Grn. Yat . . . 8A 48
West Grn. Dri. Craw . . . 2A 182
West Gro. W on T . . . 2J 57
Westhall Pk. Warl . . . 6F 84
W. Hall Rd. Rich . . . 4A 12
Westhall Rd. Warl . . . 5D 84
Westhatch La. Brack . . . 5N 15
Westhay Gdns. SW14 . . . 8A 12
West Heath . . . 9L 69
(Farnborough)
West Heath . . . 8C 106
(Oxted)
West Heath. Pirb . . . 1A 92
(in two parts)
W. Heath Rd. Farnb . . . 1L 89
West Hill . . . 9L 13
West Hill. SW15 & SW18 . . . 1J 27
West Hill. Dor P . . . 4A 166
West Hill. E Grin . . . 1N 185
West Hill. Elst . . . 8G 131
West Hill. Eps . . . 9A 60 (6G 201)
West Hill. Orp . . . 8H 67
West Hill. Oxt . . . 8N 105
West Hill. S Croy . . . 6B 64
W. Hill Av. Eps . . . 9A 60 (5G 201)
W. Hill Bank. Oxt . . . 8N 105
W. Hill Clo. Brkwd . . . 7E 72
W. Hill Clo. Elst . . . 8G 131
W. Hill Ct. Eps . . . 6C 201
W. Hill Rd. SW18 . . . 9L 13
W. Hill Rd. Wok . . . 6N 73
W. Hoathly Rd. E Grin . . . 4N 185
(in two parts)
Westhorpe Rd. SW15 . . . 6H 13
West Horsley . . . 7C 96
West Ho. Clo. SW19 . . . 2K 27
Westhumble . . . 9H 99
West Humble Chapel . . . 9F 98
(Remains of)
Westhumble St. Westh . . . 9H 99
West Kensington . . . 1L 13
W. Kensington Ct. W14 . . . 1L 13
(off Edith Vs.)
W. Kensington Mans. W14 . . . 1L 13
(off Beaumont Cres.)
Westland Clo. Stanw . . . 9N 7
Westland Ct. Farnb . . . 1J 89
Westlands. H'ham . . . 5L 197
Westlands Ct. Eps . . . 2B 80
Westlands Ter. SW12 . . . 1G 28
Westlands Way. Oxt . . . 5N 105
West La. Ab H . . . 8L 117
West La. E Grin . . . 1N 185
Westleas. Horl . . . 6C 142
Westlees Clo. N Holm . . . 8K 119
West Leigh. E Grin . . . 2A 186
Westleigh Av. SW15 . . . 8G 13
Westleigh Av. Coul . . . 3E 82
Westleigh Ct. S Croy . . . 7F 200
Westley Mill. Binf . . . 1K 15
Westmacott Dri. Felt . . . 2G 22
Westmead. Farnb . . . 2N 89
Westmead. SW15 . . . 9G 12
West Mead. Eps . . . 3D 60
Westmead. Farnh . . . 1G 128
Westmead. Horl . . . 8G 143
Westmead. Wind . . . 6E 4
Westmead. Wok . . . 4L 73
Westmead Corner. Cars . . . 1C 62
Westmead Dri. Red . . . 2E 142
Westmead Rd. Sutt . . . 1B 62
West Meads. Guild . . . 4J 113
Westminster Av. T Hth . . . 1M 45
Westminster Clo. Felt . . . 2H 23
Westminster Clo. Fleet . . . 3B 88
Westminster Clo. Tedd . . . 6G 24
Westminster Ct. Guild
. . . 4A 114 (5E 202)
Westminster Ct. Wok . . . 8D 74
Westminster Rd. M'bowr
. . . 4G 182
Westminster Rd. Sutt . . . 8B 44
West Molesey . . . 3A 40
Westmont Rd. Esh . . . 8E 40
Westmore Grn. Tats . . . 7E 86
Westmoreland Dri. Sutt . . . 4N 61
Westmoreland Rd. SW13 . . . 4E 12
Westmoreland Rd. Brom . . . 4N 47
Westmore Rd. Tats . . . 8E 86
Westmorland Clo. Eps . . . 6D 60
Westmorland Clo. Twic . . . 9H 11
Westmorland Ct. Surb . . . 6K 41
Westmorland Dri. Camb . . . 3F 70
Westmorland Dri. Warf . . . 7D 16
Westmorland Sq. Mitc . . . 4J 45
(off Westmorland Way)
Westmorland Way. Mitc . . . 3H 45
West Mt. Guild . . . 5M 113 (7A 202)
(in two parts)
West Norwood . . . 5N 29
West Norwood Crematorium.
SE27 . . . 4N 29
Weston Av. Add . . . 1K 55
Weston Av. Th Dit . . . 6E 40
Weston Av. W Mol . . . 2M 39
Weston Clo. Coul . . . 7K 83
Weston Clo. G'ming . . . 5H 133
Weston Ct. G'ming . . . 5H 133
Weston Ct. King T . . . 6J 203
Weston Dri. Cat . . . 8N 83
Weston Farm Cotts. Alb . . . 8K 115
Westonfields. Alb . . . 8L 115
Weston Gdns. Isw'th . . . 4E 10
Weston Gdns. Wok . . . 3G 75
Weston Green . . . 7E 40
Weston Grn. Th Dit . . . 8E 40
(in two parts)
Weston Grn. Rd. Esh . . . 7D 40
(in two parts)
Weston Gro. Bag . . . 5K 51
Weston Lea. W Hor . . . 3E 96
Weston Pk. King T . . . 1L 41 (3J 203)
Weston Pk. Th Dit . . . 7E 40
Weston Pk. Clo. Th Dit . . . 7E 40
Weston Rd. Eps . . . 7D 60
Weston Rd. Guild . . . 2K 113
(in two parts)
Weston Rd. Th Dit . . . 7E 40
Westons Clo. H'ham . . . 1K 197
Weston Way. Wok . . . 3G 75
Weston Yd. Alb . . . 8L 115
Westover Clo. Sutt . . . 5N 61
Westover Rd. SW18 . . . 1A 28
Westover Rd. Fleet . . . 4C 88
West Pal. Gdns. Wey . . . 9C 38
West Pde. H'ham . . . 4J 197
W. Park Av. Rich . . . 4N 11
W. Park Clo. Houn . . . 2N 9
W. Park Rd. Copt & Newc . . . 6C 164
(in two parts)
W. Park Rd. Eps . . . 8M 59
W. Park Rd. Hand . . . 9N 199
W. Park Rd. Rich . . . 4N 11
West Pl. SW19 . . . 6H 27
West Ramp. H'row A . . . 4B 8
West Ridge. Seale . . . 7C 110
West Ring. Tong . . . 5D 110
West Rd. Farnb . . . 7N 69
West Rd. Camb . . . 1B 70
West Rd. Chess . . . 8J 59
West Rd. Felt . . . 9F 8
West Rd. Guild . . . 4A 114 (4F 202)
West Rd. King T . . . 9B 26
West Rd. Reig . . . 4N 121
West Rd. Wey . . . 5C 56
West Rd. Wokgm . . . 6G 31
Westrow. SW15 . . . 9H 13
W. Sheen Va. Rich . . . 7M 11
W. Side Comn. SW19 . . . 6H 27
Westside Ct. W End . . . 9B 52
Westside Ho. Red . . . 1F 142
West St. Bren . . . 2J 11
West St. Cars . . . 1D 62
West St. Craw . . . 4B 182
West St. Croy . . . 1N 63 (6C 200)
West St. Dork . . . 5G 119 (2J 201)
West St. D'land . . . 1C 166
West St. E Grin . . . 1A 186
West St. Eps . . . 9B 60 (7H 201)
(in two parts)
West St. Ewe . . . 6D 60
West St. Farnh . . . 1G 128
West St. Hasl . . . 1G 189
West St. H'ham . . . 6J 197
West St. Reig . . . 3K 121
West St. Sutt . . . 2N 61
West St. Wok . . . 4B 74
West St. La. Cars . . . 1D 62
(in two parts)
W. Street Pl. Croy . . . 6C 200
W. Temple Sheen. SW14 . . . 8A 12
West Vw. Felt . . . 1D 22
W. View Av. Whyt . . . 5C 84
Westview Clo. Red . . . 5C 122
W. View Cotts. Newd . . . 2A 160
W. View Gdns. E Grin . . . 1A 186
W. View Rd. Head D . . . 5H 169
W. View Rd. Warl . . . 6E 84
Westville Rd. Th Dit . . . 7G 41
Westward Ho. Guild . . . 1B 114
Westwates Clo. Brack . . . 9B 16
Westway. SW20 . . . 2G 43
West Way. Cars . . . 6B 62
Westway. Cat . . . 9A 84
Westway. Copt . . . 7K 163
West Way. Craw . . . 2E 182
West Way. Croy . . . 8H 47
Westway. Guild . . . 1J 113
West Way. Houn . . . 4N 9
Westway. Gat A . . . 3F 162
West Way. Shep . . . 5E 38
West Way. Slin . . . 5L 195
West Way. W Wick . . . 5N 47
Westway. Wmly . . . 1C 172
Westway Clo. SW20 . . . 2G 43
W. Way Gdns. Croy . . . 8G 47
Westway Gdns. Red . . . 9E 102
Westways. Eden . . . 1L 147
Westways. Eps . . . 1E 60
Westways. W'ham . . . 4L 107
Westwell M. SW16 . . . 7J 29
Westwell Rd. SW16 . . . 7J 29
Westwell Rd. App. SW16 . . . 7J 29
Westwick. King T
. . . 1N 41 (4M 203)
(off Chesterton Ter.)
Westwick Gdns. Houn . . . 5J 9
West Wickham . . . 7M 47
Westwood Av. SE19 . . . 9N 29
Westwood Av. Wdhm . . . 8B 55
Westwood Clo. Esh . . . 9D 40
Westwood Ct. Guild . . . 2J 113
Westwood Gdns. SW13 . . . 6E 12
Westwood La. Norm & Wanb
. . . 1L 111
Westwood Rd. SW13 . . . 6E 12
Westwood Rd. Coul . . . 5H 83
Westwood Rd. W'sham . . . 8B 34
Wetherby Gdns. Farnb . . . 5A 90
Wetherby Gdns. SW5 . . . 1N 13
Wetherby Mans. SW5 . . . 1N 13
(off Earl's Ct. Sq.)
Wetherby M. SW5 . . . 1N 13
Wetherby Pl. SW7 . . . 1N 13
Wetherby Way. Chess . . . 4L 59
Wetlands Cen., The . . . 4G 13
Wettern Clo. S Croy . . . 6B 64
Wetton Pl. Egh . . . 6B 20
Wexfenne Gdns. Wok . . . 3K 75
Wexford Rd. SW12 . . . 1D 28
Wey Av. Cher . . . 2J 37
Weybank. Wis . . . 3N 75
Weybank Clo. Farnh . . . 1H 129
Wey Barton. Byfl . . . 9A 56
Weybourne . . . 6K 109
Weybourne Pl. S Croy . . . 6A 64
Weybourne Rd. Farnh & Alder
. . . 7K 109
Weybourne St. SW18 . . . 3A 28
Weybridge . . . 1B 56
Weybridge Bus. Pk. Add . . . 1N 55
Weybridge Mead. Yat . . . 8D 48
Weybridge Pk. Wey . . . 2B 56
Weybridge Rd. Add . . . 1N 55
Weybridge Rd. T Hth . . . 3L 45
Weybridge Trad. Est. Add . . . 1M 55
Weybrook Dri. Guild . . . 7D 94
Wey Clo. As . . . 3E 110
Wey Clo. Camb . . . 1N 69
Wey Clo. W Byf . . . 9K 55
Weycombe Rd. Hasl . . . 1G 189
(in two parts)
Wey Ct. Eps . . . 1B 60
Wey Ct. G'ming . . . 5K 133
Wey Ct. Guild . . . 4M 113 (4B 202)
Wey Ct. New H . . . 5M 55
Wey Ct. Clo. G'ming . . . 5J 133
Weycrofts. Brack . . . 8L 15
Weydon Farm La. Farnh . . . 3G 128
Weydon Hill Clo. Farnh . . . 3G 129
Weydon Hill Rd. Farnh . . . 3G 129
Weydon La. Farnh . . . 4E 128
Weydon Mill La. Farnh . . . 2G 128
Weydown Clo. SW19 . . . 2K 27
Weydown Clo. Guild . . . 7K 93
Weydown Cotts. Hasl . . . 8G 170
Weydown Ind. Est. Hasl . . . 2F 188
(in two parts)
Weydown La. Guild . . . 7K 93
Weydown Rd. Hasl . . . 2F 188
Wey Hill. Hasl . . . 2E 188
Weylands Clo. W on T . . . 7N 39
Weylands Pk. Wey . . . 3E 56
Weylea Av. Guild . . . 9C 94
Wey Mnr. Rd. New H . . . 5M 55
Weymead Clo. Cher . . . 7L 37
Wey Meadows. Add . . . 2N 55
Weymede. Byfl . . . 8A 56
Weymouth Ct. Sutt . . . 4M 61
Wey Retail Pk. Byfl . . . 8N 55
Wey Rd. G'ming . . . 6K 133
Wey Rd. Wey . . . 9A 38
Weyside. Farnh . . . 1H 129
Weyside Clo. Byfl . . . 8A 56
Weyside Gdns. Guild . . . 1M 113
Weyside Pk. G'ming . . . 6K 133
Weyside Rd. Guild . . . 1L 113
Weysprings. Hasl . . . 1D 188
Weystone Rd. Add . . . 1A 56
Weyvern Pk. P'mrsh . . . 2L 133
Weyvern Pl. P'mrsh . . . 2L 133
Weyview Clo. Guild . . . 1M 113
Wey Vw. Ct. Guild
. . . 4M 113 (4A 202)
Weywood Clo. Farnh . . . 5L 109
Weywood La. Farnh . . . 5K 109
Whaley Rd. Wokgm . . . 9C 14
Wharfedale Gdns. T Hth . . . 3K 45
Wharfedale St. SW10 . . . 1N 13
Wharfenden Way. Frim G . . . 8D 70
Wharf La. Send . . . 5M 75
(Mill La.)
Wharf La. Send . . . 1E 94
(Send Rd.)
Wharf La. Twic . . . 2G 24
Wharf Rd. Ash V . . . 9E 90
Wharf Rd. Frim G . . . 8D 70
Wharf Rd. Guild . . . 3M 113 (3B 202)
Wharf Rd. Wray . . . 1M 19
Wharf St. G'ming . . . 7H 133
Wharf, The. G'ming . . . 6H 133
Wharf Way. Frim G . . . 8E 70
Wharncliffe Gdns. SE25 . . . 1B 46
Wharncliffe Rd. SE25 . . . 1B 46
Whateley Rd. Guild . . . 8L 93
Whatley Av. SW20 . . . 2J 43
Whatley Grn. Brack . . . 5N 31
Whatmore Clo. Stai . . . 9J 7
Wheatash Rd. Add . . . 8K 37
Wheatbutts, The. Eton W . . . 1C 4
Wheatfield Way. Horl . . . 6F 142
Wheatfield Way. King T
. . . 1L 41 (5J 203)
Wheathill Rd. SE20 . . . 2E 46
Wheat Knoll. Kenl . . . 3N 83
Wheatlands. Houn . . . 2A 10
Wheatlands Rd. SW17 . . . 4F 28
Wheatley. Brack . . . 4K 31
Wheatley Ho. SW15 . . . 1F 26
(off Ellisfield Dri.)
Wheatley Rd. Alder . . . 1L 109
Wheatley Rd. Isw'th . . . 6F 10
Wheatsheaf Clo. H'ham . . . 3L 197
Wheatsheaf Clo. Ott . . . 3F 54
Wheatsheaf Clo. Wok . . . 3A 74
Wheatsheaf Ct. Hdly . . . 3E 168
Wheatsheaf La. SW6 . . . 3H 13
Wheatsheaf La. Stai . . . 8H 21
Wheatsheaf Ter. SW6 . . . 3L 13
Wheatstone Clo. Craw . . . 7F 162
Wheatstone Clo. Mitc . . . 9C 28
Wheeler Av. Oxt . . . 7N 105
Wheeler La. Witl . . . 4B 152
Wheeler Rd. M'bowr . . . 5F 182
Wheelers La. Brock . . . 5A 120
Wheelers La. Eps . . . 1A 80 (8G 201)
Wheelers La. Small . . . 9L 143
Wheelerstreet . . . 4C 152
Wheelerstreet. Witl . . . 4C 152
Wheelers Way. Felb . . . 7H 165
Wheelwrights La. Gray . . . 5M 169
Wheelwrights Pl. Coln . . . 3E 6
Whelan Way. Wall . . . 9H 45
Wherwell Rd. Guild
. . . 5M 113 (6A 202)
Whetstone Rd. Farnb . . . 1H 89
Whimbrel Clo. S Croy . . . 7A 64
Whinfell Clo. SW16 . . . 6H 29
Whinn Holt. Fleet . . . 7B 88
Whins Clo. Camb . . . 2N 69
Whins Dri. Camb . . . 2N 69
Whipley Clo. Guild . . . 7D 94
Whistler Clo. Craw . . . 6D 182
Whistler Gro. Col T . . . 9J 49
Whistley Clo. Brack . . . 2C 32
Whitby Clo. Farnb . . . 4C 90
Whitby Clo. Big H . . . 6D 86
Whitby Gdns. Sutt . . . 8B 44
Whitby Rd. Sutt . . . 8B 44
Whitchurch Clo. Alder . . . 6B 110
White Acres Rd. Myt . . . 1D 90
Whitebeam Dri. Reig . . . 6N 121
Whitebeam Gdns. Farnb . . . 2H 89
White Beam Way. Tad . . . 8F 80
White Beech La. C'fold . . . 4K 173
Whiteberry Rd. Ab C . . . 3B 138
Whitebines. Farnh . . . 1J 129
White Bri. Av. Mitc . . . 2B 44
Whitebridge Clo. Felt . . . 9G 9
White Bushes . . . 8E 122
Whitebushes. Red . . . 8E 122
White City. Crowt . . . 2J 49
(in two parts)
White Cottage Clo. Farnh . . . 6J 109
Whitecroft. Horl . . . 7F 142
Whitecroft Clo. Beck . . . 3N 47
Whitecroft Way. Beck . . . 4M 47
White Down La. Ran C . . . 4K 117
Whitefield Av. Purl . . . 3L 83
Whitefield Clo. SW18 . . . 9K 13
White Ga. Wok . . . 7D 74
Whitegates. Whyt . . . 6D 84
Whitegate Way. Tad . . . 7G 81
Whitehall . . . 3K 61
Whitehall Cres. Chess . . . 2K 59
Whitehall Dri. If'd . . . 3K 181
Whitehall Farm La. Vir W . . . 1A 36
(in two parts)
Whitehall Gdns. W4 . . . 2A 12
Whitehall La. Egh . . . 8B 20
Whitehall La. S Pk . . . 7L 121
Whitehall La. Wray . . . 9C 6
Whitehall Pde. E Grin . . . 9A 166
(off London Rd.)
Whitehall Pk. Rd. W4 . . . 2A 12
Whitehall Pl. Wall . . . 1F 62
Whitehall Rd. T Hth . . . 4L 45
White Hart Clo. Hay . . . 2E 8
White Hart Ct. H'ham . . . 4J 197
White Hart Ct. Rip . . . 8L 75
White Hart Ind. Est. B'water
. . . 2K 69
White Hart La. SW13 . . . 6D 12
White Hart La. Wood S . . . 2D 112
White Hart Meadows. Rip . . . 8L 75
White Hart Row. Cher . . . 6J 37
Whitehead Clo. SW18 . . . 1A 28
White Hermitage. Old Win . . . 8M 5
White Heron M. Tedd . . . 7F 24
White Hill. Chips . . . 1C 102
White Hill. S Croy . . . 6A 64
White Hill. W'sham . . . 1M 51
Whitehill Clo. Camb . . . 8B 50
Whitehill La. Cob . . . 1D 96
Whitehill La. Blet . . . 5A 104
Whitehill Pk. W'hill . . . 9A 168
Whitehill Pl. Vir W . . . 4A 36
Whitehill Rd. Stand . . . 8A 168
White Horse Dri. Eps
. . . 1B 80 (8G 201)
Whitehorse La. SE25 . . . 3A 46
White Horse La. Rip . . . 8L 75
Whitehorse Rd. Croy & T Hth
. . . 6N 45
Whitehorse Rd. H'ham . . . 2A 198
White Horse Rd. Wind . . . 6A 4
White Ho. SW4 . . . 1H 29
(off Clapham Pk. Est.)
White House. Add . . . 1L 55
White Ho. Dri. Guild . . . 3D 114
White Ho. Gdns. Yat . . . 8B 48
White Ho. La. Guild . . . 7N 93
(in two parts)
White Ho. Wlk. Farnh . . . 5J 109
Whiteknights. Cars . . . 7B 62
White Knights Rd. Wey . . . 4D 56
White Knobs Way. Cat . . . 3D 104
Whitelands Dri. Asc . . . 9H 17
White La. Ash G & Tong . . . 3G 110
White La. Guild & Shere . . . 5F 114
White La. Tats & T'sey . . . 1D 106
Whiteley. Wind . . . 3B 4
Whiteley's Cotts. W14 . . . 1L 13
Whiteley's Way. Hanw . . . 4A 24
Whiteley Village . . . 5F 56
White Lillies Island. Wind . . . 3D 4
White Lion Ct. Isw'th . . . 6H 11
White Lion Wlk. Guild
. . . 4N 113 (5C 202)
White Lion Way. Yat . . . 8C 48
White Lodge. SE19 . . . 8M 29
White Lodge Clo. Sutt . . . 4A 62
Whitelodge Gdns. Red . . . 2E 142
Whitely Hill . . . 8K 183
Whitely Hill. Turn H . . . 8K 183
Whitemore Rd. Guild . . . 8N 93
White Oak Dri. Beck . . . 1M 47
Whiteoaks. Bans . . . 9N 61
White Post . . . 3C 124
Whitepost Hill. Red . . . 3C 122
(in two parts)
White Post La. Wrec . . . 7F 128
White Rd. Col T . . . 9L 49
White Rd. Brock . . . 2N 119
(in two parts)
White Rose La. Lwr Bo . . . 4G 129
White Rose La. Wok . . . 5B 74
Whites La. Dat . . . 2L 5
Whites La. Pirb . . . 2D 92
(in three parts)
Whites Rd. Farnb . . . 4C 90
Whitestile Rd. Bren . . . 1J 11
Whiteswan M. W4 . . . 1D 12
Whitethorn Av. Coul . . . 2E 82
Whitethorn Clo. As . . . 3F 110
Whitethorn Cotts. Cranl . . . 5K 155
Whitethorn Gdns. Croy . . . 8F 46
Whitewalls. Craw . . . 3L 181
(off Rusper Rd.)
White Way. Bookh . . . 4B 98
Whiteways Ct. Stai . . . 8K 21
Whitewood . . . 5D 144
Whitewood Cotts. Tats . . . 7E 86
Whitewood La. S God . . . 5D 144
Whitfield Clo. Guild . . . 9K 93
Whitfield Clo. Hasl . . . 8G 171
Whitfield Rd. Hasl . . . 9G 171
Whitford Gdns. Mitc . . . 2D 44
Whitgift Av. S Croy
. . . 2M 63 (8A 200)
Whitgift Cen. Croy
. . . 8N 45 (2C 200)
Whitgift Ct. S Croy . . . 8C 200
Whitgift Sq. Croy . . . 8N 45 (3C 200)
Whitgift St. Croy . . . 9N 45 (5B 200)
Whitgift Wlk. Craw . . . 6B 182
Whither Dale. Horl . . . 7C 142

Whitland Rd.—Windmill Clo.

Whitland Rd. Cars 7B 44
Whitlet Clo. Farnh 2G 128
Whitley Clo. Stanw 9N 7
Whitley Rd. Yat 2C 68
Whitlock Dri. SW19 1K 27
Whitmead Clo. S Croy 3B 64
Whitmead La. Tilf 6C 130
Whitmoor La. Guild 4N 93
Whitmoor Rd. Bag 4K 51
Whitmoor Va. Gray 2K 169
Whitmoor Va. Rd. Gray 2L 169
Whitmore Clo. Owl 7J 49
Whitmore Grn. Farnh 6K 109
Whitmore La. Asc 4D 34
Whitmore Rd. Beck 2J 47
Whitmores Clo. Eps 2B 80
Whitmore Way. Horl 7C 142
Whitnell Way. SW15 8H 13
Whitstable Clo. Beck 1J 47
Whitstable Pl. Croy 1N 63 (7C 200)
Whittaker Av. Rich 8K 11
Whittaker Ct. Asht 4K 79
Whittaker Pl. Rich 8K 11 (off Whittaker Av.)
Whittaker Rd. Sutt 9L 43
Whittingham Ct. W4 3D 12
Whittingstall Rd. SW6 4L 13
Whittington Rd. Craw 6B 182
Whittlebury Clo. Cars 4D 62
Whittle Clo. Ash V 8D 90
Whittle Clo. Sand 6F 48
Whittle Cres. Farnb 7L 69
Whittle Rd. Houn 3K 9
Whittle Way. Craw 6E 162
Whitton 1C 24
Whitton Dene. Houn & Iswth 8C 10
Whitton Mnr. Rd. Iswth 9C 10
Whitton Rd. Brack 2D 32
Whitton Rd. Houn 7B 10
Whitton Rd. Twic 9E 10
Whitton Road Roundabout. (Junct.) 9F 10
Whitton Waye. Houn 9A 10
Whitworth Rd. SE25 2B 46
Whitworth Rd. Craw 8B 162
Whopshott Av. Wok 3M 73
Whopshott Clo. Wok 3M 73
Whopshott Dri. Wok 3M 73
Whynstones Rd. Asc 5L 33
Whyteacre. Whyt 7E 84
Whyte Av. Alder 4B 110
Whytebeam Vw. Whyt 5C 84
Whytecliffe Rd. N. Purl 7M 63
Whytecliffe Rd. S. Purl 7L 63
Whytecroft. Houn 3L 9
Whyteleafe 5C 84
Whyteleafe Bus. Village. Whyt 4C 84
Whyteleafe Hill. Whyt 7B 84 (in two parts)
Whyteleafe Rd. Cat 7B 84
Wicket Hill. Wrec 5F 128
Wickets, The. Ashf 5N 21
Wicket, The. Croy 2K 65
Wickham Av. Croy 8H 47
Wickham Av. Sutt 2H 61
Wickham Chase. W Wick 7N 47
Wickham Clo. Bag 1J 51
Wickham Clo. C Crook 7A 88
Wickham Clo. Horl 7D 142
Wickham Clo. N Mald 5E 42
Wickham Ct. C Crook 7A 88
Wickham Ct. Surb 8L 203
Wickham Ct. Rd. W Wick 8M 47
Wickham Cres. W Wick 8M 47
Wickham La. Egh 8C 20
Wickham Pl. C Crook 7A 88
Wickham Rd. Beck 1L 47
Wickham Rd. Camb 7C 50
Wickham Rd. C Crook 7A 88
Wickham Rd. Croy 8F 46
Wickham Va. Brack 5K 31
Wickham Way. Beck 3M 47
Wick Hill 1A 48
Wick Hill La. Finch 1A 48 (in four parts)
Wick Ho. King T 1G 203
Wickhurst Gdns. Broad H 5E 196
Wickhurst La. Broad H 5E 196
Wickland Ct. Craw 6B 182
Wick La. Eng G 7J 19
Wick Rd. Eng G 9K 19
Wick Rd. Tedd 8H 25
Wick's Grn. Binf 5H 15
Wicks La. Shur R 1D 14
Wicksteed Ho. Bren 1M 11
Wide Way. Mitc 2H 45
Widewing Clo. Tedd 8H 25
Widgeon Way. H'ham 3J 197
Widmer Ct. Houn 5M 9
Wient, The. Coln 3E 6
Wiggett Gro. Binf 7H 15
Wiggie La. Red 1E 122
Wiggins La. Rich 3J 25
Wiggins Yd. G'ming 7H 133
Wight Ho. King T 6H 203
Wighton M. Iswth 5E 10
Wigley Rd. Felt 3L 23
Wigmore La. Bear G 9J 139
Wigmore Rd. Cars 8B 44
Wigmore Wlk. Cars 8B 44
Wilberforce Clo. Craw 9A 182
Wilberforce Ct. Eps 8K 201
Wilberforce Way. SW19 7J 27
Wilberforce Way. Brack 4B 32
Wilbury Av. Sutt 6L 61
Wilbury Rd. Wok 4N 73
Wilcot Clo. Bisl 3D 72
Wilcot Gdns. Bisl 3D 72
Wilcox Gdns. Shep 2N 37
Wilcox Rd. Sutt 1N 61
Wilcox Rd. Tedd 5D 24
Wildacre Clo. Loxw 5F 192
Wild Acres. W Byf 7L 55
Wildbank Ct. Wok 5B 74
Wildcroft Dri. N Holm 8K 119
Wildcroft Dri. Wokgm 7A 30
Wildcroft Mnr. SW15 1H 27
Wildcroft Rd. SW15 1H 27
Wildcroft Wood. Witl 4A 152
Wilde Pl. SW18 1B 28
Wilderness Ct. Guild 5J 113
Wilderness Ri. Dor P 5C 166
Wilderness Rd. Frim 4C 70
Wilderness Rd. Guild 5J 113
Wilderness Rd. Oxt 8N 105
Wilderness, The. E Mol 4C 40
Wilderness, The. Hamp 5B 24
Wilders Clo. Brack 8M 15
Wilders Clo. Frim 3C 70
Wilders Clo. Wok 5M 73
Wilderwick Rd. D'land & Dor P 3C 166
Wilderwick Rd. E Grin 6D 166
Wildfield Clo. Wood S 2E 112
Wildgoose Dri. H'ham 5F 196
Wildmoor Heath Nature Reserve. 5H 49
Wildridings 3M 31
Wildridings Rd. Brack 3M 31
Wildridings Sq. Brack 3M 31
Wild Wood. H'ham 5F 196
Wildwood Clo. Cranl 9A 156
Wildwood Clo. E Hor 3G 96
Wildwood Clo. Wok 2H 75
Wildwood Ct. Kenl 2A 84
Wildwood Gdns. Yat 2B 68
Wildwood La. Cranl 4J 175
Wilfred Owen Clo. SW19 7A 28
Wilfred St. Wok 5N 73
Wilhelmina Av. Coul 6G 83
Wilkes Rd. Bren 2L 11
Wilkins Clo. Hay 1G 9
Wilkins Clo. Mitc 9C 28
Wilkinson Ct. SW17 5B 28
Wilkinson Ct. Craw 8N 181
Wilks Gdns. Croy 7H 47
Willats Clo. Cher 5H 37
Willcocks Clo. Chess 9L 41
Willems Av. Alder 2L 109
Willems Roundabout. Alder 2L 109
Willett Pl. T Hth 4L 45
Willett Rd. T Hth 4L 45
Willey Broom La. Cat 3L 103
Willey Farm La. Cat 4N 103
Willey Green 9A 92
Willey La. Cat 3A 104
William Banfield Ho. SW6 5L 13 (off Munster Rd.)
William Dyce M. SW16 5H 29
William Ellis Clo. Old Win 8K 5
William Evans Rd. Eps 7N 59
William Evelyn Ct. Wott 8N 117
William Farm La. SW15 6G 13
William Farthing Clo. Alder 2M 109
William Gdns. SW15 8G 13
William Hitchcock Ho. Farnb 7N 69
William Hunt Mans. SW13 2H 13
William Morris Ho. W6 2J 13
William Morris Way. SW6 6N 13
William Morris Way. Craw 9N 181
William Rd. SW19 8K 27
William Rd. Cat 9A 84
William Rd. Guild 3M 113 (3B 202)
William Rd. Sutt 2A 62
William Russell Ct. Wok 5H 73
Williams Clo. SW6 3K 13
Williams Clo. Add 2K 55
Williams Clo. Ewh 5F 156
Williams Dri. Houn 7A 10
Williams Gro. Surb 5J 41
William Sim Wood. Wink R 7F 16
William's La. SW14 6B 12
Williams La. Mord 4A 44
Williamson Clo. G'wood 8K 171
Williams Rd. S'hall 1M 9
Williams Ter. Croy 3L 63
William St. Cars 9C 44
William St. Wind 4G 4
William's Wlk. Guild 8L 93
Williams Way. Craw 3F 182
Williams Way. Fleet 4D 88
William Pl. Hind 3C 170
Willingham Way. King T 2N 41
Willington Clo. Camb 9N 49
Willis Av. Sutt 3C 62
Willis Clo. Eps 1A 80
Willis Ct. T Hth 5L 45
Willis Rd. Croy 6N 45
Will Miles Ct. SW19 8A 28
Willmore End. SW19 9N 27
Willoughby Av. Croy 1K 63
Willoughby Rd. Brack 2L 31
Willoughby Rd. King T 9M 25 (1M 203)
Willoughby Rd. Twic 8J 11 (in two parts)
Willoughbys, The. SW14 6D 12
Willow Av. SW13 5E 12
Willow Bank. SW6 6K 13
Willowbank. Coul 1J 83
Willow Bank. Rich 4H 25
Willow Bank. Wok 9A 74
Willowbank Gdns. Tad 9G 81
Willowbank Pl. S Croy 5M 63
Willow Brean. Horl 7C 142
Willowbrook. Eton 1G 4
Willowbrook. Hamp H 6B 24
Willowbrook Rd. Stai 3N 21
Willow Bus. Cen., The. Mitc 5D 44
Willow Clo. Bear G 7J 139
Willow Clo. Bord 6A 168
Willow Clo. Bren 2J 11
Willow Clo. Coln 3E 6
Willow Clo. Craw 1C 182
Willow Clo. E Grin 7N 165
Willow Clo. Myt 1C 90
Willow Clo. Wdhm 7H 55
Willow Corner. Charl 3L 161
Willow Cotts. Hanw 4M 23
Willow Cotts. Rich 2N 11
Willow Ct. W4 3D 12 (off Corney Reach Way)
Willow Ct. Ash V 6E 90
Willow Ct. Brack 9M 15
Willow Ct. Frim 5B 70 (off Gro. Cross Rd.)
Willow Ct. Horl 6F 142
Willow Ct. Tad 1G 101
Willow Cres. Farnb 7N 69
Willowdene Clo. Twic 1C 24
Willow Dri. Brack 9A 16
Willow Dri. Norm 3N 111
Willow Dri. Rip 2J 95
Willow End. Surb 7L 41
Willowfield. Craw 4A 182
Willowford. Yat 9C 48
Willow Gdns. Houn 4A 10
Willow Glade. Reig 6A 122
Willow Grn. N Holm 9H 119
Willow Grn. W End 9C 52
Willowhayne Dri. W on T 6J 39
Willowhayne Gdns. Wor Pk 9H 43
Willowherb Clo. Wokgm 1D 30
Willow Ho. Short 1N 47
Willow La. B'water 2J 69
Willow La. Guild 2C 114
Willow La. Mitc 4D 44
Willow Lodge. SW6 4J 13
Willow Mead. Dork 4G 119 (1J 201)
Willow Mead. E Grin 1B 186
Willowmead. Stai 9K 21
Willow Mead. Witl 5B 152
Willowmead Clo. Wok 3K 73
Willow Mere. Esh 1C 58
Willow M. Witl 5C 152
Willow Mt. Croy 9B 46
Willow Pk. As 2D 110
Willow Pl. Eton 2F 4
Willow Ridge. Turn H 6D 184
Willow Rd. Coln 5G 7
Willow Rd. G'ming 3J 133
Willow Rd. H'ham 3A 198
Willow Rd. N Mald 3B 42
Willow Rd. Red 6A 122
Willow Rd. Wall 4F 62
Willow Rd. W End 9C 52
Willows Av. Mord 4N 43
Willows End. Sand 7G 48
Willows Lodge. Wind 3A 4
Willows Mobile Home Pk., The. Norm 9A 92
Willows Path. Eps 1A 80
Willows, The. Beck 1K 47
Willows, The. Brack 3D 32
Willows, The. Byfl 9N 55
Willows, The. C'fold 5D 172
Willows, The. Clay 3E 58
Willows, The. Guild 7K 93 (off Worplesdon Rd.)
Willows, The. Guild 1E 114 (Collier Way)
Willows, The. H'ham 3K 197
Willows, The. Light 6A 52
Willows, The. Red 4D 122
Willows, The. Wey 9B 38
Willows, The. Wind 3A 4
Willow Tree Clo. SW18 2N 27
Willowtree Way. T Hth 9L 29
Willow Va. Fet 1B 98 (in two parts)
Willow Vw. SW19 9B 28
Willow Wlk. Cher 6J 37
Willow Wlk. Eng G 6M 19
Willow Wlk. Orp 1K 67
Willow Wlk. Red 5F 122
Willow Wlk. Shere 8B 116
Willow Wlk. Sutt 9L 43
Willow Wlk. Tad 8A 100
Willow Way. Alder 4C 110
Willow Way. Eps 3C 60
Willow Way. Farnh 6J 109
Willow Way. God 1E 124
Willow Way. Guild 8L 93
Willow Way. Sand 6E 48
Willow Way. Sun 3H 39
Willow Way. Twic 3B 24
Willow Way. W Byf 7L 55
Willow Way. Wok 8A 74
Willow Wood Cres. SE25 5B 46
Wills Cres. Houn 9B 10
Willson Rd. Eng G 6L 19
Wilmar Gdns. W Wick 7L 47
Wilmer Clo. King T 6M 25
Wilmer Cres. King T 6M 25
Wilmerhatch La. Eps 5A 80
Wilmington Av. W4 3C 12
Wilmington Clo. Craw 8N 181
Wilmington Ct. SW16 8J 29
Wilmot Clo. Binf 7H 15
Wilmot Cotts. Bans 2N 81
Wilmot Rd. Cars 2D 62
Wilmot Rd. Purl 8L 63
Wilmots Clo. Reig 2A 122
Wilmot's La. Horne 4A 144 (in three parts)
Wilmot Way. Bans 1M 81
Wilmot Way. Camb 3D 70
Wilna Rd. SW18 1A 28
Wilson Av. Mitc 9C 28 (in two parts)
Wilson Clo. M'bowr 6H 183
Wilson Clo. S Croy 2A 64 (8D 200)
Wilson Dri. Ott 2D 54
Wilson Rd. Farnb 2L 89
Wilson Rd. Alder 3B 110
Wilson Rd. Chess 3M 59
Wilsons. Tad 8J 81
Wilsons Rd. Hdly D 4G 169
Wilson's Rd. W6 1J 13
Wilson Way. Wok 3N 73
Wilstrode Av. Binf 8L 15
Wilton Av. W4 1D 12
Wilton Clo. W Dray 2M 7
Wilton Ct. Farnb 2B 90
Wilton Cres. SW19 8L 27
Wilton Cres. Wind 7A 4
Wilton Gdns. W on T 7L 39
Wilton Gdns. W Mol 2A 40
Wilton Gro. SW19 9L 27
Wilton Gro. N Mald 5E 42
Wilton Ho. S Croy 8B 200
Wilton Pde. Felt 2J 23
Wilton Pl. New H 5M 55
Wilton Rd. SW19 8C 28
Wilton Rd. Camb 3N 69
Wilton Rd. Houn 6L 9
Wilton Rd. Red 4D 122
Wiltshire Av. Crowt 1G 48
Wiltshire Ct. S Croy 2N 63 (8C 200)
Wiltshire Dri. Wokgm 1C 30
Wiltshire Gdns. Twic 2C 24
Wiltshire Gro. Warf 7D 16
Wiltshire Rd. T Hth 2L 45
Wiltshire Rd. Wokgm 9B 14
Wilverley Cres. N Mald 5D 42
Wilwood Rd. Brack 9K 15
Wimbart Rd. SW2 1K 29
Wimbledon 7L 27
Wimbledon (All England Lawn Tennis & Croquet Club). 5K 27
Wimbledon Bri. SW19 7L 27
Wimbledon Clo. SW20 8J 27
Wimbledon Clo. Camb 6D 50
Wimbledon Common 5F 26
Wimbledon Common Postmill & Mus. 3G 27
Wimbledon F.C. (Selhurst Pk.) 3B 46
Wimbledon Greyhound Stadium. 5A 28
Wimbledon Hill Rd. SW19 7K 27
Wimbledon Lawn Tennis Mus. 5K 27 (Centre Court, All England Lawn Tennis & Croquet Club)
Wimbledon Mus. of Local History. 7K 27
Wimbledon Park 4M 27
Wimbledon Pk. Rd. SW19 & SW18 3K 27
Wimbledon Pk. Side. SW19 4J 27
Wimbledon Rd. SW17 5A 28
Wimbledon Rd. Camb 6D 50
Wimbledon Stadium Bus. Cen. SW17 4N 27
Wimble Hill 1A 128
Wimblehurst Ct. H'ham 4J 197
Wimblehurst Rd. H'ham 4J 197
Wimborne Av. Red 8D 122
Wimborne Av. S'hall 1A 10
Wimborne Clo. Eps 9D 60 (7M 201)
Wimborne Clo. Wor Pk 7H 43
Wimborne Ct. SW12 4G 28
Wimborne Way. Beck 2G 47
Wimland Hill. Fay 7C 180
Wimland Rd. Fay 4A 180
Wimlands La. Fay 7C 180
Wimpole Clo. King T 1M 41 (4M 203)
Wimshurst Clo. Croy 7J 45
Wincanton Clo. Craw 2H 183
Wincanton Rd. SW18 1L 27
Winch Clo. Binf 6H 15
Winchcombe Clo. Fleet 5B 88
Winchcombe Rd. Cars 6B 44
Winchelsea Clo. SW15 8J 13
Winchelsea Cres. W Mol 1C 40
Winchelsey Ri. S Croy 3C 64
Winchendon Rd. SW6 4L 13
Winchendon Rd. Tedd 5D 24
Winchester Av. Houn 2N 9
Winchester Clo. Coln 4G 7
Winchester Clo. Esh 1A 58
Winchester Clo. King T 8A 26
Winchester Rd. Rush 3N 149
Winchester Rd. As 1E 110
Winchester Rd. Craw 7C 182
Winchester Rd. Felt 4N 23
Winchester Rd. Hay 3F 8
Winchester Rd. Twic 9H 11
Winchester Rd. W on T 7H 39
Winchester St. Farnb 5A 90
Winchester Way. B'water 9H 49
Winches, The. Colg 2H 199
Winchet Wlk. Croy 5F 46
Winchfield Ho. SW15 9E 12
Winchgrove Rd. Brack 8M 15
Winchstone Clo. Shep 3A 38
Windborough Rd. Cars 4E 62
Windermere Av. SW19 2N 43
Windermere Clo. Farnb 2K 89
Windermere Clo. Egh 8D 20
Windermere Clo. Felt 2G 22
Windermere Clo. Stai 2N 21
Windermere Ct. SW13 2E 12
Windermere Ct. Ash V 9D 90 (off Lakeside Clo.)
Windermere Ct. Cars 9E 44
Windermere Ct. Kenl 2M 83
Windermere Rd. SW15 5D 26
Windermere Rd. SW16 9G 29
Windermere Rd. Coul 2J 83
Windermere Rd. Croy 7C 46
Windermere Rd. Light 6M 51
Windermere Rd. W Wick 8N 47
Windermere Wlk. Camb 1H 71
Windermere Way. Farnh 6F 108
Windermere Way. Reig 2C 122
Windfield. Lea 8H 79
Windgates. Guild 9E 94
Windham Av. New Ad 6N 65
Windham Rd. Rich 6M 11
Windings, The. S Croy 7C 64
Winding Wood Dri. Camb 2F 70
Windlebrook Grn. Brack 9M 15
Windle Clo. W'sham 3A 52
Windlesham 3A 52
Windlesham Ct. W'sham 9N 33
Windlesham Ct. Dri. W'sham 1N 51
Windlesham Gro. SW19 2J 27
Windlesham Rd. Brack 9L 15
Windlesham Rd. Chob 4D 52
Windlesham Rd. W End 7B 52
Windmill Av. Eps 7E 60
Windmill Bridge Ho. Croy 7B 46 (off Freemasons Rd.)
Windmill Bus. Village. Sun 9F 22
Windmill Clo. Cat 8N 83
Windmill Clo. Eps 8E 60
Windmill Clo. Horl 8F 142
Windmill Clo. H'ham 4N 197

Windmill Clo.—Woodland Ct.

Windmill Clo. *Sun* 8F **22**
Windmill Clo. *Surb* 7J **41**
Windmill Clo. *Wind* 5E **4**
Windmill Ct. *Craw* 1B **182**
Windmill Dri. *Hdly D* 3G **168**
Windmill Dri. *Kes* 1E **66**
Windmill Dri. *Lea* 1J **99**
Windmill Dri. *Reig* 1B **122**
Windmill End. *Eps* 8E **60**
Windmill Fld. *W'sham* 3N **51**
Windmill Grn. Shep *6F* ***38***
(off Walton La.)
Windmill Gro. *Croy* 5N **45**
Windmill Hill. *Alder* 3A **110**
Windmill La. *Ash W* 2E **186**
Windmill La. *E Grin* 7N **165**
Windmill La. *Eps* 8E **60**
Windmill La. *S'hall & Iswth* . . . 1E **10**
Windmill La. *Surb* 5H **41**
Windmill M. *W4* 1D **12**
Windmill Pas. *W4* 1D **12**
Windmill Platt. *Hand* 8N **199**
Windmill Ri. *King T* 8A **26**
Windmill Rd. *SW19* 5G **27**
Windmill Rd. *W4* 1D **12**
Windmill Rd. *W5 & Bren* 1J **11**
Windmill Rd. *Alder* 3A **110**
Windmill Rd. *Brack* 9L **15**
Windmill Rd. *Croy* 6N **45**
Windmill Rd. *Hamp H* 6B **24**
Windmill Rd. *Mitc* 4G **44**
Windmill Rd. *Sun* 9F **22**
Windmill Rd. W. *Sun* 1F **30**
Windmill Shott. *Egh* 7B **20**
Windmill Ter. *Shep* 6F **38**
Windmill Way. *Reig* 1B **122**
Windrum Clo. *H'ham* 8F **196**
Windrush. *N Mald* 3A **42**
Windrush Clo. *W4* 4B **12**
Windrush Clo. *Brmly* 5B **134**
Windrush Clo. *Craw* 5L **181**
Windrush Heights. *Sand* 7F **48**
Windsor. 4G 5
Windsor & Eton Relief Rd. *Wind* 4E **4**
Windsor Av. *SW19* 9A **28**
Windsor Av. *N Mald* 4B **42**
Windsor Av. *Sutt* 9K **43**
Windsor Av. *W Mol* 2A **40**
Windsor Brass Rubbing Cen. ***4G 5***
(off High St., Windsor Parish Church)
Windsor Bus. Cen. *Wind* 3F **4**
Windsor Castle. 4H 5
Windsor Clo. *SE27* 5N **29**
Windsor Clo. *Bren* 2H **11**
Windsor Clo. *Craw* 7A **182**
Windsor Clo. *Guild* 5J **113**
Windsor Ct. Alder *2L* ***109***
(off Queen Elizabeth Dri.)
Windsor Ct. *Brack* 3A **32**
Windsor Ct. *Chob* 5H **53**
Windsor Ct. *Fleet* 4B **88**
Windsor Ct. *H'ham* 5M **197**
Windsor Ct. *King T* 8H **203**
Windsor Ct. *Sun* 8H **23**
Windsor Ct. *Whyt* 5C **84**
Windsor Ct. Rd. *Chob* 5H **53**
Windsor Cres. *Farnh* 6G **108**
Windsor Dri. *Asht* 5M **21**
Windsor Gdns. *As* 2D **110**
Windsor Gdns. *Croy* 9J **45**
Windsor Great Pk. 4E 18
Windsor Gro. *SE27* 5N **29**
Windsor Guildhall. 4G 5
Windsor M. SW18 . . . . *1A* ***20***
(off Wilna Rd.)
Windsor Pk. Rd. *Hay* 3G **8**
Windsor Pl. *Cher* 5J **37**
Windsor Pl. *E Grin* 1C **186**
Windsor Ride. *Brack & Asc* . . . 5D **32**
Windsor Ride. *Camb* 7M **49**
(in two parts)
Windsor Ride. *Crowt* 9C **32**
Windsor Rd. *Farnb* 4B **90**
Windsor Rd. *Asc & Wink* 2J **33**
Windsor Rd. *Chob* 1F **52**
Windsor Rd. *Dat* 3K **5**
Windsor Rd. *Houn* 5J **9**
Windsor Rd. *King T* 8L **25**
Windsor Rd. *Lind* 4A **168**
Windsor Rd. *Old Win & Egh* 2M **19**
Windsor Rd. *Rich* 5M **11**
Windsor Rd. *Sun* 7H **23**
Windsor Rd. *Tedd* 6D **24**
Windsor Rd. *T Hth* 1M **45**
Windsor Rd. *Wind* 4A **4**
Windsor Rd. *Wor Pk* 8F **42**
Windsor Rd. *Wray* 9A **6**
Windsor St George's Chapel. 4G 5
Windsor St. *Cher* 5J **37**
Windsor Wlk. *Lind* 4A **168**
Windsor Wlk. *W on T* 7L **39**
Windsor Wlk. *Wey* 2C **56**
Windsor Way. *Alder* 2N **109**
Windsor Way. *Frim* 6D **70**
Windsor Way. *Wok* 3E **74**
Winds Ridge. *Send* 3E **94**
Windways. *Duns* 2B **174**
Windycroft Clo. *Purl* 9H **63**
Windy Gap. 3M 169
Windyridge. *Craw* 4M **181**
Windy Ridge Clo. *SW19* 6J **27**
Windy Wood. *G'ming* 8F **132**
Winern Glebe. *Byfl* 9M **55**
Winery La. *King T* 2M **41** (5L **203**)
Winfield Gro. *Newd* 1N **159**
Winfrith Rd. *SW18* 1A **28**
Wingate Ct. *Alder* 2L **109**
Wingate Cres. *Croy* 5J **45**
Wingfield Clo. *New H* 6K **55**
Wingfield Ct. *Bans* 2M **81**
Wingfield Gdns. *Frim* 3H **71**
Wingfield Rd. *King T* 7M **25**
Wingford Rd. *SW2* 1J **29**
Wingrave Rd. *W6* 2H **13**
Wings Clo. *Farnh* 6G **109**
Wings Clo. *Sutt* 1M **61**
Wings Rd. *Farnh* 6G **109**
Winifred Rd. *SW19* 9M **27**
Winifred Rd. *Coul* 3E **82**
Winifred Rd. *Hamp H* 5A **24**
Winkfield. 4H 17
Winkfield Clo. *Wokgm* 5A **30**
Winkfield La. *Wink* 3F **16**
Winkfield Rd. *Asc* 7L **17**
Winkfield Rd. *Wind* 2N **17**
Winkfield Row. 6F 16
Winkfield Row. *Wink R* 5E **16**
Winkfield Street. 3G 16
Winkfield St. *Wink* 3F **16**
Winkworth Arboretum. 3M 153
Winkworth Pl. *Bans* 1L **81**
Winkworth Rd. *Bans* 1M **81**
Winnards. *Wok* 5K **73**
Winnington Way. *Wok* 5L **73**
Winnipeg Dri. *G Str* 3N **67**
Winscombe. *Brack* 4K **31**
Winslow Rd. *W6* 2H **13**
Winslow Way. *Felt* 4L **23**
Winslow Way. *W on T* 9K **39**
Winstanley Clo. *Cob* 1J **77**
Winstanley Wlk. Cob *1J* ***77***
(off Winstanley Clo.)
Winston Clo. *Frim G* 8D **70**
Winston Dri. *Stoke D* 3M **77**
Winston Wlk. *Lwr Bo* 5H **129**
Winston Way. *Old Wok* 7D **74**
Winterbourne Av. *Orp* 1M **67**
Winterbourne. *H'ham* 1M **197**
Winterbourne Ct. *Brack* 1B **32**
Winterbourne Gro. *Wey* 3D **56**
Winterbourne Rd. *T Hth* 3L **45**
Winterbourne Wlk. *Frim* 6D **70**
Winter Box Wlk. *Rich* 8M **11**
Winterbrook Rd. *SE24* 1N **29**
Winterdown Gdns. *Esh* 3N **57**
Winterdown Rd. *Esh* 3N **57**
Winterfold. *Craw* 6E **182**
Winterfold Clo. *SW19* 3K **27**
Winterfold Cotts. *Alb* 7N **135**
Winterfold Heath. 9N 135
Winterhill Way. *Guild* 8D **94**
Winterpit Clo. *Man H* 9C **198**
Winterpit La. *Man H* 9C **198**
Wintersells Ind. Est. *Byfl* 6N **55**
Wintersells Rd. *Byfl* 6M **55**
Winters Rd. *Th Dit* 6H **41**
Winterton Ct. *SE20* 1D **46**
Winterton Ct. *H'ham* 6K **197**
Winterton Ct. *King T* 1G **203**
Winterton Ct. W'ham *5M* ***107***
(off Market Sq.)
Winthorpe Rd. *SW15* 7K **13**
Winton Cres. *Yat* 1C **68**
Winton Rd. *Alder* 3M **109**
Winton Rd. *Farnh* 9J **109**
Winton Rd. *Orp* 1K **67**
Winton Way. *SW16* 6L **29**
Wire Cut. *Fren* 1J **149**
Wireless Rd. *Big H* 2F **86**
Wire Mill La. *Newc* 2H **165**
Wisbeach Rd. *Croy* 4A **46**
Wisborough Ct. *Craw* 6L **181**
Wisborough Rd. *S Croy* 5C **64**
Wisdom Ct. Iswth *6G* ***11***
(off South St.)
Wise La. *W Dray* 1M **7**
Wiseton Rd. *SW17* 2C **28**
Wishanger La. *Churt* 8F **148**
Wishbone Way. *Wok* 3J **73**
Wishford Ct. *Asht* 5M **79**
Wishmoor Clo. *Camb* 7C **50**
Wishmoor Rd. *Camb* 7C **50**
Wisley. 3N 75
Wisley Common. 3B 76
Wisley Ct. Red *2D* ***122***
(off Clarendon Rd.)
Wisley Ct. *S Croy* 6A **64**
Wisley Gardens. 5N 75
Wisley Gdns. *Farnb* 2J **89**
Wisley Interchange. (Junct.) 3D 76
Wisley La. *Wis* 3L **75**
Wistaria La. *Yat* 1B **68**
Wiston Ct. *Craw* 6L **181**
Witham Ct. *SW17* 4D **28**
Witham Rd. *SE20* 2F **46**
Witham Rd. *Iswth* 4D **10**
Witherby Clo. *Croy* 2B **64**
Withers Clo. *Chess* 3J **59**
Witherslack Clo. *Head D* 5G **169**
Withey Brook. *Hkwd* 1B **162**
Withey Clo. *Wind* 4B **4**
Witheygate Av. *Stai* 7K **21**
Withey Meadows. *Hkwd* 1B **162**
Withies La. *Comp* 1F **132**
Withies, The. *Knap* 4H **73**
Withies, The. *Lea* 7H **79**
Withybed Corner. *Tad* 1G **100**
Withy Clo. *Light* 6N **51**
Withycombe Rd. *SW19* 1J **27**
Withypitts. *Turn H* 6D **184**
Withypitts E. *Turn H* 6D **184**
Witley. 6C 152
Witley Cres. *New Ad* 3M **65**
Witley Ho. *SW2* 1J **29**
Witley Park. 7L 151
Wittenham Rd. *Brack* 9D **16**
Wittering Clo. *King T* 6K **25**
Wittmead Rd. *Myt* 1D **90**
Witts Ho. *King T* 5L **203**
Wivenhoe Ct. *Houn* 7N **9**
Wix Hill. *W Hor* 8C **96**
Wix Hill Clo. *W Hor* 9C **96**
Woburn Av. *Farnb* 1B **90**
Woburn Av. *Purl* 7L **63**
Woburn Clo. *SW19* 7A **28**
Woburn Clo. *Frim* 5E **70**
Woburn Ct. *Croy* 7N **45**
Woburn Hill. *Add* 8L **37**
Woburn Park. 8L 37
Woburn Rd. *Cars* 7C **44**
Woburn Rd. *Craw* 5M **181**
Woburn Rd. *Croy* . . . 7N **45** (1C **200**)
Wodeland Av. *Guild* 5L **113** (7A **202**)
Woffington Clo. *King T* 9J **25**
Woking. 4B 74
Woking Bus. Pk. *Wok* 2D **74**
Woking Clo. *SW15* 7E **12**
Woking Crematorium. *Wok* . . . 6H **73**
Woking F.C. 7B 74
Wokingham 2B 30
Wokingham Rd. *Brack* 9K **15**
Wokingham Rd. *Crowt & Sand* 3D **48**
Wokingham Rd. *Hurst* 3A **14**
Wokingham Theatre. 9A 14
Wokingham Without. 8E 30
Woking Rd. *Guild* 6M **93**
(in five parts)
Wold Clo. *Craw* 5L **181**
Woldhurstlea Clo. *Craw* 5M **181**
Woldingham. 1K 105
Woldingham Garden Village. 7H 85
Woldingham Rd. *Wold* 7E **84**
Wolds Dri. *Orp* 1J **67**
Wold, The. *Wold* 9K **85**
Wolfe Cotts. *W'ham* 5M **107**
Wolfe Rd. *Alder* 3A **110**
Wolfington Rd. *SE27* 5M **29**
Wolf La. *Wind* 6A **4**
Wolf's Hill. *Oxt* 9C **106**
Wolf's Rd. *Oxt* 8D **106**
Wolf's Row. *Oxt* 7D **106**
Wolfs Wood. *Oxt* 1C **126**
Wolseley Av. *SW19* 3M **27**
Wolseley Gdns. *W4* 2A **12**
Wolseley Rd. *Alder* 3M **109**
Wolseley Rd. *G'ming* 5H **133**
Wolseley Rd. *Mitc* 6E **44**
Wolsey Av. *Th Dit* 4F **40**
Wolsey Clo. *SW20* 8G **26**
Wolsey Clo. *Houn* 7C **10**
Wolsey Clo. *King T* 9A **26**
Wolsey Clo. *Wor Pk* 1F **60**
Wolsey Cres. *Mord* 6K **43**
Wolsey Cres. *New Ad* 5M **65**
Wolsey Dri. *King T* 6L **25**
Wolsey Dri. *W on T* 7L **39**
Wolsey Gro. *Esh* 1B **58**
Wolsey M. *Orp* 2N **67**
Wolsey Pl. Shop. Cen. *Wok* . . . 4A **74**
Wolsey Rd. *Ashf* 5N **21**
Wolsey Rd. *E Mol* 3D **40**
Wolsey Rd. *Esh* 1B **58**
Wolsey Rd. *Hamp H* 7B **24**
Wolsey Rd. *Sun* 8G **23**
Wolsey Spring. *King T* 8B **26**
Wolsey Wlk. *Wok* 4A **74**
Wolsey Way. *Chess* 2N **59**
Wolstonbury Clo. *Craw* 5A **182**
Wolvens La. *Dork & Ab C* 9A **118**
Wolverton Av. *King T* 9N **25**
Wolverton Clo. *Horl* 1D **162**
Wolverton Gdns. *W6* 1J **13**
Wolverton Gdns. *Horl* 9D **142**
Wolves Hill. *Capel* 6J **159**
Wondesford Dale. *Binf* 5H **15**
Wonersh. 4D 134
Wonersh Common. 2D 134
Wonersh Comn. Rd. *Won* . . . 2D **134**
Wonersh Pk. *Won* 5D **134**
Wonersh Way. *Sutt* 5J **61**
Wonford Clo. *King T* 9D **26**
Wonford Clo. *Tad* 4F **100**
Wonham La. *Bet* 4D **120**
Wonham Way. *Gom & Peasl* 8E **116**
(in two parts)
Wontford Rd. *Purl* 2L **83**
Wontner Rd. *SW17* 3D **28**
Woodall Clo. *Chess* 3K **59**
Woodbarn, The. *Farnh* 2H **129**
Woodberry Clo. *C'fold* 4D **172**
Woodberry Clo. *Sun* 7H **23**
Woodbine Clo. *Sand* 8H **49**
Woodbine Clo. *Twic* 3D **24**
Woodbine La. *Wor Pk* 9G **43**
Woodbines Av. *King T* 2K **41** (6H **203**)
Woodborough Rd. *SW15* 7G **12**
Woodbourne. *Farnh* 5K **109**
Woodbourne Av. *SW16* 4H **29**
Woodbourne Clo. *SW16* 4J **29**
Woodbourne Clo. *Yat* 9C **48**
Woodbourne Dri. *Clay* 3F **58**
Woodbourne Gdns. *Wall* 4F **62**
Woodbridge Av. *Lea* 5G **79**
Woodbridge Bus. Pk. *Guild* 2M **113** (1B **202**)
Woodbridge Corner. *Lea* 5G **78**
Woodbridge Ct. *H'ham* 3N **197**
Woodbridge Dri. *Camb* 8B **50**
Woodbridge Gro. *Lea* 5G **79**
Woodbridge Hill. 2L 113
Woodbridge Hill. *Guild* 2L **113**
Woodbridge Hill Gdns. *Guild* 2K **113**
Woodbridge Meadows. *Guild* 2M **113** (1A **202**)
Woodbridge Rd. *B'water* 1G **69**
Woodbridge Rd. *Guild* 2M **113** (1A **202**)
(in two parts)
Woodbury Av. *E Grin* 1D **186**
Woodbury Clo. *Big H* 5H **87**
Woodbury Clo. *Croy* 8C **46**
Woodbury Clo. *E Grin* 1C **186**
(in two parts)
Woodbury Dri. *Sutt* 6A **62**
Woodbury Rd. *Big H* 5H **87**
Woodbury St. *SW17* 6C **28**
Woodby Dri. *Asc* 6C **34**
Wood Clo. *Red* 3E **142**
Wood Clo. *Wind* 7F **4**
Woodcock Bottom & Whitmore Vale. 4N 169
Woodcock Dri. *Chob* 4F **52**
Woodcock Hill. *Felb* 4J **165**
Woodcock La. *Chob* 4E **52**
Woodcote. 3B 80
(Epsom)
Woodcote. 8H 63
(Purley)
Woodcote. *Cranl* 6K **155**
Woodcote. G'ming *5G* ***133***
(off Frith Hill Rd.)
Woodcote. *Guild* 7L **113**
Woodcote. *Horl* 7F **142**
Woodcote Av. *T Hth* 3M **45**
Woodcote Av. *Wall* 5F **62**
Woodcote Clo. *Eps* 1C **80** (8J **201**)
Woodcote Clo. *King T* 6M **25**
Woodcote Ct. *Sutt* 3M **61**
Woodcote Dri. *Purl* 6H **63**
Woodcote End. *Eps* 2C **80**
Woodcote Green. 5G 62
Woodcote Grn. *Wall* 5G **62**
Woodcote Grn. Rd. *Eps* 2B **80**
Woodcote Gro. *Cars* 8F **62**
Woodcote Gro. Rd. *Coul* 2H **83**
Woodcote Hall. *Eps* 1C **80** (8J **201**)
Woodcote Ho. *Eps* 2B **80**
Woodcote Ho. Ct. *Eps* 2C **80**
Woodcote Hurst. *Eps* 3B **80**
Woodcote La. *Purl* 7H **63**
Woodcote M. *Wall* 3F **62**
Woodcote Park. 4B 80
Woodcote Pk. Av. *Purl* 8G **63**
Woodcote Pk. Rd. *Eps* 3B **80**
Woodcote Pl. *SE27* 6M **29**
Woodcote Pl. *Asc* 9K **17**
Woodcote Rd. *Eps* 1C **80** (8J **201**)
Woodcote Rd. *F Row* 7G **187**
(in two parts)
Woodcote Rd. *Wall* 3F **62**
Woodcote Side. *Eps* 2A **80**
Woodcote Valley Rd. *Purl* 9H **63**
Woodcot Gdns. *Farnb* 1J **89**
Woodcott Ter. *Alder* 4B **110**
Woodcourt. *Craw* 8A **182**
Wood Crest. Sutt *4A* ***62***
(off Christchurch Pk.)
Woodcrest Rd. *Purl* 9J **63**
Woodcrest Wlk. *Reig* 1C **122**
Woodcroft Rd. *If'd* 5J **181**
Woodcroft Rd. *T Hth* 4M **45**
Woodcut Rd. *Wrec* 5E **128**
Wood End. 7M 17
Wood End. *Farnb* 2B **90**
Woodend. *SE19* 7N **29**
Wood End. *Crowt* 3E **48**
Woodend. *Esh* 8C **40**
Wood End. *H'ham* 3B **198**
Woodend. *Lea* 3J **99**
Woodend. *Sutt* 8A **44**
Woodend Clo. *Asc* 9J **17**
Woodend Clo. *Craw* 1E **182**
Wood End Clo. *Pyr* 3H **75**
Woodend Clo. *Wok* 6K **73**
Woodend Dri. *Asc* 4M **33**
Woodend Pk. *Cob* 2L **77**
Woodend Ride. *Asc & WinK* 8M **17**
Woodend Rd. *Deep* 7G **71**
Woodend, The. *Wall* 5F **62**
Woodenhill. *Brack* 6K **31**
Wooderson Clo. *SE25* 3B **46**
Woodfield. *Asht* 4K **79**
Woodfield Av. *SW16* 4H **29**
Woodfield Av. *Cars* 3E **62**
Woodfield Clo. *SE19* 8N **29**
Woodfield Clo. *Asht* 4K **79**
Woodfield Clo. *Coul* 6G **82**
Woodfield Clo. *Craw* 2C **182**
Woodfield Clo. *Red* 1C **122**
Woodfield Gdns. *N Mald* 4E **42**
Woodfield Gro. *SW16* 4H **29**
Woodfield Hill. *Coul* 6F **82**
Woodfield La. *SW16* 4H **29**
Woodfield La. *Asht* 4L **79**
Woodfield Rd. *Asht* 4K **79**
Woodfield Rd. *Craw* 2C **182**
Woodfield Rd. *Houn* 5J **9**
Woodfield Rd. *Rud* 1E **194**
Woodfield Rd. *Th Dit* 8F **40**
Woodfields, The. *S Croy* 1C **84**
Woodfield Way. *Red* 1C **122**
Woodforde Ct. *Hay* 1E **8**
Woodford Grn. *Brack* 3D **32**
Woodgate. *Fleet* 2D **88**
Woodgate Av. *Chess* 2K **59**
Woodgate Dri. *SW16* 8H **29**
Woodgates Clo. *H'ham* 5M **197**
Woodgavil. *Bans* 3L **81**
Woodger Clo. *Guild* 1E **114**
Woodhall La. *Asc* 8B **34**
Woodham. 6J 55
Woodham Hall Farm. *Wok* 1D **74**
Woodham La. *New H* 5L **55**
Woodham La. *Wok & Wdhm* 1D **74**
Woodham Pk. Rd. *Wdhm* 5H **55**
Woodham Pk. Way. *Wdhm* . . . 7H **55**
Woodham Ri. *Wok* 1B **74**
Woodham Rd. *Wok* 2A **74**
Woodham Waye. *Wok* 9D **54**
Woodhatch. 6N 121
Woodhatch Rd. *Reig & Red* 6N **121**
Woodhatch Spinney. *Coul* 3J **83**
Woodhaw. *Egh* 5D **20**
Woodhayes. *Horl* 7F **142**
Woodhayes Rd. *SW19* 8H **27**
Woodhill. *Send* 4F **94**
Woodhill Ct. *Send* 3F **94**
Woodhill La. *Fren* 2D **148**
Woodhill La. *Sham G* 7G **135**
Woodhouse La. *Holm M* 3H **137**
Woodhouse St. *Binf* 9K **15**
Woodhurst La. *Oxt* 8A **106**
Woodhurst Pk. *Oxt* 8A **106**
Woodhyrst Gdns. *Kenl* 2M **83**
Woodies Clo. *Brack* 8H **15**
Wooding Gro. *Craw* 8N **181**
Woodland Av. *Cranl* 7A **156**
Woodland Av. *Wind* 7C **4**
Woodland Clo. *E Hor* 5G **97**
Woodland Clo. *Eps* 3D **60**
Woodland Clo. *H'ham* 4A **198**
Woodland Clo. *Wey* 1E **56**
Woodland Ct. C Crook *9A* ***88***
(off Brandon Rd.)
Woodland Ct. *Eps* 8E **60**
Woodland Ct. *Oxt* 6N **105**

Woodland Cres.—Wyresdale

Woodland Cres. Brack 8A 16
Woodland Dri. Capel 5G 159
Woodland Dri. Craw D 1E 184
Woodland Dri. E Hor 5G 96
Woodland Dri. Eden 9L 127
Woodland Dri. Wrec 5G 128
Woodland Gdns. Iswth 6E 10
Woodland Gdns. S Croy 7F 64
Woodland Gro. Wey 1E 56
Woodland La. Colg 6G 198
Woodland Ri. C Crook 8A 88
Woodland Ri. Oxt 8A 106
Woodland Rd. T Hth 3L 45
Woodlands. 5E 10
Woodlands. SW20 3H 43
Woodlands. Add 9N 37
Woodlands. Asht 5L 79
Woodlands. Craw 1H 183
Woodlands. Fleet 3A 88
Woodlands. Horl 7G 143
Woodlands. Send 3H 95
Woodlands. Wok 5B 74
Woodlands. Yat 3C 68
Woodlands Av. Farnh 5L 109
Woodlands Av. N Mald 9B 26
Woodlands Av. Red 4D 122
Woodlands Av. W Byf 9H 55
Woodlands Av. Wor Pk 8E 42
Woodlands Cvn. Pk. As 3D 110
Woodlands Clo. Asc 5K 33
Woodlands Clo. Ash V 8E 90
Woodlands Clo. B'water 5K 69
Woodlands Clo. Clay 4F 58
Woodlands Clo. Cranl 7A 156
Woodlands Clo. Craw D 2E 184
Woodlands Clo. Ott 6D 54
Woodlands Copse. Asht 3K 79
Woodlands Cotts. Newd 7B 160
Woodlands Ct. Owl 6L 49
Woodlands Ct. Wok (GU21) 5K 73
Woodlands Ct. Wok (GU22) 6A 74
Woodlands Dri. S God 6H 125
Woodlands Dri. Sun 1K 39
Woodlands Gdns. Eps 4H 81
Woodlands Ga. SW15 8L 13
Woodlands Gro. Coul 4E 82
Woodlands Gro. Iswth 5E 10
Woodlands Ho. Sheer 1E 74
Woodlands La. Hasl 1D 188
Woodlands La. Stoke D 4A 78
Woodlands La. W'sham 3A 52
Woodlands Pde. Ashf 7D 22
Woodlands Pk. Add 2H 55
Woodlands Pk. Guild 2D 114
Woodlands Pk. Tad 9A 100
Woodlands Ride. Asc 5K 33
Woodlands Rd. Farnb 8J 69
Woodlands Rd. SW13 6E 12
Woodlands Rd. Bookh 6M 97
Woodlands Rd. Camb 1N 69
Woodlands Rd. E Grin 6C 166
Woodlands Rd. Eps 2N 79
Woodlands Rd. Guild 8N 93
Woodlands Rd. Hamb 9G 152
Woodlands Rd. Iswth 6D 10
Woodlands Rd. Lea 4D 78 (in two parts)
Woodlands Rd. Red 5D 122
Woodlands Rd. Surb 6K 41
Woodlands Rd. Vir W 3M 35
Woodlands Rd. W Byf 1H 75
Woodlands Rd. E. Vir W 3M 35
Woodlands Rd. W. Vir W 3M 35
Woodlands, The. SE19 8N 29
Woodlands, The. Esh 8C 40
Woodlands, The. Iswth 5F 10
Woodlands, The. Small 8M 143
Woodlands, The. Wall 5F 62
Woodlands Vw. Mid H 2H 139
Woodlands Wlk. B'water 5K 69
Woodlands Way. SW15 8L 13
Woodlands Way. Asht 3N 79
Woodland Vw. G'ming 2H 133
Woodland Wlk. Eps 3N 59
Woodland Way. Cat 6B 104
Woodland Way. Croy 7H 47
Woodland Way. H'ham 4N 197
Woodland Way. Kgswd 8B 100 (Surrey Hills Res. Pk.)
Woodland Way. Kgswd 9K 81 (Waterhouse La.)
Woodland Way. Mitc 8E 28
Woodland Way. Mord 3L 43
Woodland Way. Purl 9L 63
Woodland Way. Surb 8A 42
Woodland Way. W Wick 1L 65
Woodland Way. Wey 2E 56
Wood La. Farnb 2M 89
Wood La. Binf 7J 15
Wood La. Cat 2A 104
Wood La. Fleet 4D 88
Wood La. Iswth 2E 10
Wood La. Knap 5G 72
Wood La. Seale 8F 110
Wood La. Tad 4L 81
Wood La. Wey 5D 56
Woodlark Glade. Camb 8B 50
Woodlawn Clo. SW15 8L 13
Woodlawn Cres. Twic 3B 24
Woodlawn Dri. Felt 3L 23
Woodlawn Gro. Wok 2B 74
Woodlawn Rd. SW6 3J 13
Woodlawns. Eps 4C 60
Wood Lea Cotts. Broad H 1N 195
Woodlee Clo. Vir W 1M 35
Wood Leigh. Fleet 5B 88
Woodleigh Gdns. SW16 4J 29
Woodley Clo. SW17 8D 28
Woodley Ho. G'ming 3H 133
Woodley La. Cars 9C 44
Woodlodge. Asht 4L 79
Wood Lodge La. W Wick 9M 47
Woodmancote Gdns. W Byf 9J 55
Woodmancott Clo. Brack 5D 32
Woodman Ct. Fleet 5A 88
Woodmancourt. G'ming 3F 132
Woodman Rd. Coul 2G 83
Woodmans Hill. Craw 8A 182
Woodmansterne. 2D 82
Woodmansterne La. Bans 2N 81
Woodmansterne La. Cars 8D 62
Woodmansterne Rd. SW16 8G 29
Woodmansterne Rd. Cars 8D 62
Woodmansterne Rd. Coul 2G 83
Woodmansterne St. Bans 2C 82
Woodmere. Brack 3C 32
Woodmere Av. Croy 6F 46
Woodmere Clo. Croy 6G 47
Woodmere Gdns. Croy 6G 46
Woodmere Way. Beck 4N 47
Woodmill Ct. Asc 2H 33
Woodnook Rd. SW16 6F 28
Woodpecker Clo. Cob 8M 57
Woodpecker Clo. Eden 9M 127
Woodpecker Clo. Ews 4C 108
Woodpecker La. Newd 9B 140
Woodpecker Mt. Croy 5H 65
Woodpeckers. Brack 3N 31 (off Crowthorne Rd.)
Woodpeckers. Milf 3B 152
Woodpecker Way. Turn H 4F 184
Woodpecker Way. Wok 2N 93
Woodplace Clo. Coul 6G 83
Woodplace La. Coul 5G 83
Woodridge Clo. Brack 2A 32
Wood Riding. Wok 2G 75
Woodridings. Wey 3B 56
Wood Ri. Guild 1H 113
Wood Rd. Big H 5E 86
Wood Rd. Camb 5N 69
Wood Rd. Farnh 5H 109
Wood Rd. G'ming 4J 133
Wood Rd. Hind 3B 170
Wood Rd. Shep 3B 38
Woodroffe Benton Ho. Craw 3L 181 (off Rusper Rd.)
Woodrough Copse. Brmly 6C 134
Woodrow Dri. Wokgm 2D 30
Woodroyd Av. Horl 9D 142
Woodroyd Gdns. Horl 1D 162
Woodruff Av. Guild 9C 94
Woods Hill Clo. Ash W 3F 186
Woods Hill La. Ash W 3F 186
Woodshore Clo. Vir W 5L 35
Woodside. 5D 46 (Croydon)
Woodside. 6N 17 (Windsor)
Woodside. Farnb 7N 69
Woodside. Ryl M 8L 49
Woodside. SW19 7L 27
Woodside. B'water 4H 69
Woodside. Fet 9B 78
Woodside. H'ham 4A 198
Woodside. Lwr K 6L 101
Woodside. W on T 7H 39
Woodside. W Hor 4D 96
Woodside Av. SE25 5E 46
Woodside Av. Esh 6E 40
Woodside Av. W on T 1J 57
Woodside Clo. Cat 2B 104
Woodside Clo. C'fold 5E 172
Woodside Clo. Knap 4G 73
Woodside Clo. Surb 6B 42
Woodside Cotts. Elst 8G 131
Woodside Ct. Rd. Croy 6D 46
Woodside Cres. Small 8L 143
Woodside Gdns. Fleet 4D 88
Woodside Grn. SE25 5D 46 (in two parts)
Woodside La. Wink 6N 17
Woodside Pk. SE25 5E 46
Woodside Pk. Est. G'ming 7J 133
Woodside Rd. Cob 9A 58
Woodside Rd. Farnb 6L 89
Woodside Rd. SE25 5E 46
Woodside Rd. Bear G 8K 139
Woodside Rd. C'fold 4C 172
Woodside Rd. Craw 1D 182
Woodside Rd. Farnh 5K 109
Woodside Rd. Guild 2J 113
Woodside Rd. King T 8L 25
Woodside Rd. N Mald 1C 42
Woodside Rd. Purl 9H 63
Woodside Rd. Sutt 9A 44
Woodside Rd. Wink 6M 17
Woodside Rd. Flats. C'fold 5E 172 (off Woodside Rd.)
Woodside Way. Croy 5F 46
Woodside Way. Mitc 9F 28
Woodside Way. Red 4E 122 (Old Redstone Dri.)
Woodside Way. Red 9E 122 (West Av.)
Woodside Way. Vir W 2L 35
Woodsome Lodge. Wey 3D 56
Woodspring Rd. SW19 3K 27
Woodstock. E Grin 8M 165
Woodstock. W Cla 6K 95
Woodstock Av. Iswth 8G 10
Woodstock Av. Slou 1N 5
Woodstock Av. Sutt 6L 43
Woodstock Clo. Cranl 9A 156
Woodstock Clo. H'ham 3K 197
Woodstock Clo. Wok 3A 74
Woodstock Ct. Eps 9C 60 (5K 201)
Woodstock Gro. G'ming 4H 133
Woodstock La. N. Surb 8J 41
Woodstock La. S. Clay 2H 59
Woodstock Ri. Sutt 6L 43
Woodstock Rd. Cars 2E 62
Woodstock Rd. Coul 3F 82
Woodstock Rd. Croy 9A 46 (5D 200)
Woodstocks. Farnb 8A 70
Woodstock, The. (Junct.) 6L 43
Woodstock Way. Mitc 1F 44
Woodstone Av. Eps 2F 60
Wood St. W4 1D 12
Wood St. Ash V 7E 90
Wood St. E Grin 9N 165
Wood St. King T 1K 41 (3H 203)
Wood St. Mitc 6E 44
Wood St. Red 7G 103
Wood St. Grn. Wood S 1D 112
Wood Street Village. 1E 112
Woodsway. Oxs 1E 78
Woodthorpe Rd. Ashf 7M 21
Woodthorpe Rd. SW15 7G 13
Woodvale Av. SE25 2C 46
Woodvale Wlk. SE27 6N 29
Woodview. Chess 7J 59
Woodview Clo. SW15 5C 26
Woodview Clo. S Croy 1E 84
Woodville Clo. B'water 1G 68
Woodville Clo. Tedd 5G 24
Woodville Ct. SE19 1C 46
Woodville Gdns. Surb 6K 41
Woodville Pl. Cat 8N 83
Woodville Rd. Mord 3M 43
Woodville Rd. Rich 4H 25
Woodville Rd. T Hth 3N 45
Woodvill Rd. Lea 7H 79
Woodward Clo. Clay 3F 58
Woodwards. Craw 8N 181
Woodward's Footpath. Twic 9C 10
Wood Way. Camb 1N 69
Woodway. Guild 2D 114
Woodyers Clo. Won 4D 134
Woolacombe Way. Hay 1F 8
Woolborough Clo. Craw 2C 182
Woolborough La. Craw 9D 162
Woolborough La. Out 3K 143
Woolborough Rd. Craw 2B 182
Woolf Dri. Wokgm 1A 30
Woolford Clo. Brack 8F 16
Woolfords La. Thur 3E 150
Woolhampton Way. Brack 4B 32
Woolhams. Cat 4D 104
Woollards Rd. Ash V 9F 90
Woolmead Rd. Farnh 9H 109
Woolmead, The. Farnh 9H 109
Woolmead Wlk. Farnh 9H 109 (off Woolmead Rd.)
Woolmer Hill. 1A 188
Woolmer Hill Rd. Hasl 9A 170
Woolmer La. Bram 8F 168 (in two parts)
Woolmer Vw. Gray 6B 170
Woolneigh St. SW6 6N 13
Wool Rd. SW20 7G 27
Woolsack Ct. Guild 9K 93
Woolsack Way. G'ming 7H 133
Wootton Clo. Eps 3E 80
Worbeck Rd. SE20 1E 46
Worcester Clo. Farnb 7N 69
Worcester Clo. Croy 8K 47
Worcester Clo. Mitc 1E 44
Worcester Ct. W on T 8K 39
Worcester Ct. Wor Pk 9D 42
Worcester Dri. Ashf 6C 22
Worcester Gdns. Wor Pk 9D 42
Worcester Park. 7F 42
Worcester Pk. Rd. Wor Pk 9C 42
Worcester Rd. SW19 6L 27
Worcester Rd. Craw 7C 182
Worcester Rd. Guild 1J 113
Worcester Rd. Reig 2L 121
Worcester Rd. Sutt 4M 61
Worcestershire Lea. Warf 8D 16
Wordsworth. Brack 4K 31
Wordsworth Av. Kenl 2A 84
Wordsworth Av. Yat 1A 68
Wordsworth Clo. Craw 1F 182
Wordsworth Dri. Cheam & Sutt 1H 61
Wordsworth Mead. Red 1E 122
Wordsworth Pl. H'ham 1L 197
Wordsworth Ri. E Grin 9M 165
Wordsworth Rd. Add 1M 55
Wordsworth Rd. Hamp 5N 23
Wordsworth Rd. Wall 3G 63
Wordsworth Way. W Dray 1N 7
World Bus. Cen. H'row A 4D 8
World's End. Cob 1H 77
Worlds End Hill. Brack 5D 32
Worlds End La. Orp 3N 67
Worlidge St. W6 1H 13
Wormley. 9C 152
Wormley La. Wmly & Hamb 9D 152
Worple Av. SW19 8J 27
Worple Av. Iswth 8G 10
Worple Av. Stai 7K 21
Worple Rd. SW20 & SW19 1H 43
Worple Rd. Eps 2C 80 (8L 201)
Worple Rd. Iswth 7G 10
Worple Rd. Lea 9H 79 (in three parts)
Worple Rd. Stai 7K 21
Worple Rd. M. SW19 7L 27
Worplesdon. 5H 93
Worplesdon Hill. Wok 9F 72
Worplesdon Rd. Guild 3F 92
Worple St. SW14 6C 12
Worple, The. Wray 9B 6
Worple Way. Rich 8L 11
Worslade Rd. SW17 5B 28
Worsley Rd. Frim 6C 70
Worsted Grn. Red 7G 103
Worsted La. E Grin 1D 186
Worth. 3J 183
Worth Abbey. 8M 183
Worth Clo. Orp 1N 67
Worth Ct. Craw 3H 183
Worth Ct. Turn H 8M 183
Worthfield Clo. Eps 4C 60
Worthing Rd. H'ham 9G 197
Worthing Rd. Houn 2N 9
Worthington Clo. Mitc 3F 44
Worthington Rd. Surb 7M 41
Worth Pk. Av. Craw 2F 182
Worth Rd. Craw 2G 182
Worth Way. Worth 4J 183
Wortley Rd. Croy 6L 45
Worton Ct. Iswth 7E 10
Worton Gdns. Iswth 5D 10
Worton Hall Ind. Est. Iswth 7E 10
Worton Rd. Iswth 7D 10
Worton Way. Iswth 5D 10
Wotton. 8N 117
Wotton Dri. Wott 9L 117
Wotton Way. Sutt 6H 61
Wrabness Way. Stai 9K 21
Wrangthorn Wlk. Croy 1L 63
Wray Clo. Ash W 3F 186
Wray Common. 2B 122
Wray Comn. Rd. Reig 2A 122
Wrayfield Av. Reig 2A 122
Wrayfield Rd. Sutt 9J 43
Wraylands Dri. Reig 1B 122
Wray La. Reig 8A 102
Wraymead. Reig 2N 121
Wraymill Ct. Reig 3B 122
Wray Mill Pk. Reig 1B 122
Wray Pk. Rd. Reig 2N 121
Wray Rd. Sutt 5L 61
Wrays. 7N 141
Wraysbury. 9B 6
Wraysbury Clo. Houn 8M 9
Wraysbury Gdns. Stai 4G 21
Wraysbury Rd. Stai 3D 20
Wrecclesham. 4E 128
Wrecclesham Hill. Wrec 6C 128
Wrecclesham Rd. Wrec & Farnh 4E 128
Wrekin, The. Farnb 4C 90
Wren Clo. H'ham 1K 197
Wren Clo. S Croy 5G 65
Wren Clo. Yat 9A 48
Wren Ct. As 1F 110
Wren Ct. Craw 6C 182
Wren Ct. Croy 6E 200
Wren Cres. Add 2M 55
Wren Ho. Hamp W 1K 41 (3G 203) (off High St.)
Wrenn Ho. SW13 2H 13
Wren's Av. Ashf 5D 22
Wrens Hill. Oxs 2C 78
Wren St. Turn H 4F 184
Wren Way. Farnb 7L 69
Wright. Wind 6A 4
Wright Clo. M'bowr 7F 182
Wright Gdns. Shep 4B 38
Wright Rd. Houn 3K 9
Wrights All. SW19 7H 27
Wright Sq. Wind 6A 4
Wrights Rd. SE25 2B 46
Wrights Row. Wall 1F 62
Wrights Wlk. SW14 6C 12
Wright Way. Wind 6A 4
Wriotsley Way. Add 3J 55
Wrotham Hill. Duns 6A 174
Wroughton Rd. SW11 1D 28
Wroxham. Brack 4L 31
Wroxham Wlk. Craw 5F 182
Wrythe Grn. Cars 9D 44
Wrythe Grn. Rd. Cars 9D 44
Wrythe La. Cars 7A 44
Wrythe, The. 9D 44
Wulwyn Ct. Crowt 2E 48
Wulwyn Side. Crowt 2E 48
Wyatt Clo. Felt 2L 23
Wyatt Dri. SW13 2G 13
Wyatt Ho. Twic 9K 11
Wyatt Pk. Rd. SW2 3J 29
Wyatt Rd. Stai 6J 21
Wyatt Rd. Wind 6A 4
Wyatts Almshouses. G'ming 5K 133 (off Meadrow)
Wyatt's Clo. G'ming 5K 133
Wyche Gro. S Croy 4A 64
Wych Elm Pas. King T 8M 25 (1L 203)
Wych Elm Ri. Guild 6A 114 (8F 202)
Wychelm Rd. Light 7N 51
Wych Hill. Wok 6M 73
Wych Hill La. Wok 6N 73
Wych Hill Pk. Wok 6N 73
Wych Hill Ri. Wok 6M 73
Wych Hill Way. Wok 7N 73
Wychwood. Loxw 5F 192
Wychwood Av. Brack 3D 32
Wychwood Av. T Hth 2N 45
Wychwood Clo. As 2D 110
Wychwood Clo. Sun 7H 23
Wychwood Pl. Camb 6F 50
Wycliffe Bldgs. Guild 6B 202
Wycliffe Ct. Craw 6K 181
Wycliffe Rd. SW19 7N 27
Wycombe Pl. SW18 9N 13
Wydehurst Rd. Croy 6D 46
Wydell Clo. Mord 5J 43
Wyecliffe Gdns. Red 8G 103
Wye Clo. Ashf 5C 22
Wye Clo. Craw 9A 182
Wyeths M. Eps 9E 60
Wyeths Rd. Eps 9E 60 (6M 201)
Wyfold Rd. SW6 3K 13
Wyke. 1L 111
Wyke Av. As 1H 111
Wyke Bungalows. As 1H 111
Wyke Clo. Iswth 2F 10
Wyke Cross. Norm 1L 111
Wykeham Clo. W Dray 1B 8
Wykeham Rd. Farnh 9H 109
Wykeham Rd. Guild 2F 114
Wykehurst La. Ewh 4D 156
Wyke La. As 1H 111
Wyke Rd. SW20 1H 43
Wylam. Brack 4L 31
Wylands Rd. Slou 1C 6
Wyldewoods. Asc 5A 34
Wymering Ct. Farnb 2B 90
Wymond St. SW15 6H 13
Wynash Gdns. Cars 2C 62
Wyncote Way. S Croy 5G 64
Wyndham Av. Cob 9H 57
Wyndham Clo. Sutt 4M 61
Wyndham Clo. Yat 8C 48
Wyndham Cres. Cranl 7J 155
Wyndham Cres. Houn 9A 10
Wyndham Rd. King T 8M 25 (in two parts)
Wyndham Rd. Wok 5L 73
Wyndham St. Alder 3A 110
Wynfields. Myt 2D 90
Wynlea Clo. Craw D 1D 184
Wynne Gdns. C Crook 8C 88
Wynnstow Pk. Oxt 9B 106
Wynsham Way. W'sham 2M 51
Wynton Gdns. SE25 4C 46
Wynton Gro. W on T 9H 39
Wyphurst Rd. Cranl 6M 155
Wyre Gro. Hay 1H 9
Wyresdale. Brack 6C 32

288 A-Z Surrey

HOSPITALS and HOSPICES
covered by this atlas
with their map square reference

N.B. Where Hospitals and Hospices are not named on the map, the reference given is for the road in which they are situated.

ABRAHAM COWLEY UNIT —9F 36
Holloway Hill
Lyne
CHERTSEY
Surrey
KT16 0AE
Tel: 01932 872010

ASHFORD & ST PETER'S HOSPITALS NHS TRUST., THE —9F 36
Guildford Road
CHERTSEY
Surrey
KT16 0PZ
Tel: 01932 872000

ASHFORD HOSPITAL —3N 21
London Road
ASHFORD
Middlesex
TW15 3AA
Tel: 01784 884488

ASHTEAD HOSPITAL —6L 79
The Warren
ASHTEAD
Surrey
KT21 2SB
Tel: 01372 276161

ATKINSON MORLEY'S HOSPITAL —8G 26
31 Copse Hill
LONDON
SW20 0NE
Tel: 020 89467711

BARNES HOSPITAL —6D 12
South Worple Way
LONDON
SW14 8SU
Tel: 020 88784981

BECKENHAM HOSPITAL —1J 47
379 Croydon Road
BECKENHAM
Kent
BR3 3QL
Tel: 020 82896600

BETHLEM ROYAL HOSPITAL, THE —6K 47
Monks Orchard Road
BECKENHAM
Kent
BR3 3BX
Tel: 020 87776611

BRITISH HOME & HOSPITAL FOR INCURABLES —6M 29
Crown Lane
LONDON
SW16 3JB
Tel: 020 86708261

BROADMOOR HOSPITAL —3J 49
Lower Broadmoor Road
CROWTHORNE
Berkshire
RG45 7EG
Tel: 01344 773111

CANE HILL FORENSIC MENTAL HEALTH UNIT —4G 82
Brighton Road
COULSDON
Surrey
CR5 3YL
Tel: 01737 556300

CARSHALTON WAR MEMORIAL HOSPITAL —3D 62
The Park
CARSHALTON
Surrey
SM5 3DB
Tel: 020 86475534

CASSEL HOSPITAL, THE —5K 25
1 Ham Common
RICHMOND
Surrey
TW10 7JF
Tel: 020 89408181

CATERHAM DENE HOSPITAL —1C 104
Church Road
CATERHAM
Surrey
CR3 5RA
Tel: 01883 837500

CHARING CROSS HOSPITAL —2J 13
Fulham Palace Road
LONDON
W6 8RF
Tel: 020 88461234

CHASE CHILDREN'S HOSPICE —8M 113
Old Portsmouth Road
Artington
GUILDFORD
Surrey
GU3 1LP
Tel: 01483 230960

CHELSEA & WESTMINSTER HOSPITAL —2N 13
369 Fulham Road
LONDON
SW10 9NH
Tel: 020 87468000

CHILDREN'S TRUST, THE —8J 81
Tadworth Court
TADWORTH
Surrey
KT20 5RU
Tel: 01737 357171

CLARE PARK BUPA HOSPITAL —8A 108
Crondall Lane
Clare Park
FARNHAM
Surrey
GU10 5XX
Tel: 01252 850216

CLAYPONDS HOSPITAL —1L 11
Sterling Place
LONDON
W5 4RN
Tel: 020 85604011

COBHAM COTTAGE HOSPITAL —9J 57
Portsmouth Road
COBHAM
Surrey
KT11 1HT
Tel: 01932 584200

CRANLEIGH VILLAGE COMMUNITY HOSPITAL —8M 155
6 High Street
CRANLEIGH
Surrey
GU6 8AE
Tel: 01483 782000

CRAWLEY HOSPITAL —3A 182
West Green Drive
CRAWLEY
West Sussex
RH11 7DH
Tel: 01293 600300

DORKING HOSPITAL —6H 119
Horsham Road
DORKING
Surrey
RH4 2AA
Tel: 01737 768511

EAST SURREY HOSPITAL —7E 122
Canada Avenue
REDHILL
RH1 5RH
Tel: 01737 768511

EDENBRIDGE & DISTRICT WAR MEMORIAL HOSPITAL —4L 147
Mill Hill
EDENBRIDGE
Kent
TN8 5DA
Tel: 01732 863164

EPSOM DAY SURGERY UNIT —9E 60 (6M 201)
The Old Cottage Hospital, Alexandra Road
EPSOM
Surrey
KT17 4BL
Tel: 01372 739002

EPSOM GENERAL HOSPITAL —2B 80
Dorking Road
EPSOM
Surrey
KT18 7EG
Tel: 01372 735735

FARNBOROUGH HOSPITAL —1J 67
Farnborough Common
ORPINGTON
Kent
BR6 8ND
Tel: 01689 814000

FARNHAM COMMUNITY HOSPITAL —9K 109
Hale Road
FARNHAM
Surrey
GU9 9QL
Tel: 01483 782000

FARNHAM ROAD HOSPITAL —5L 113
Farnham Road
GUILDFORD
Surrey
GU2 7LX
Tel: 01483 443535

FLEET COMMUNITY HOSPITAL —3A 88
Church Road
FLEET
Hampshire
GU13 8LD
Tel: 01483 782000

FRIMLEY PARK HOSPITAL —4B 70
Portsmouth Road
Frimley
CAMBERLEY
Surrey
GU16 5UJ
Tel: 01276 604604

GATWICK PARK BUPA HOSPITAL —9C 142
Povey Cross Road
HORLEY
Surrey
RH6 0BB
Tel: 01293 785511

GUILDFORD NUFFIELD HOSPITAL, THE —3G 113
Stirling Road
Surrey Research Park
GUILDFORD
Surrey
GU2 7RF
Tel: 01483 555800

HASLEMERE & DISTRICT COMMUNITY HOSPITAL —1H 189
Church Lane
HASLEMERE
Surrey
GU27 2BJ
Tel: 01483 782000

HEATHERWOOD HOSPITAL —2K 33
London Road
ASCOT
Berkshire
SL5 8AA
Tel: 01344 23333

HENDERSON HOSPITAL —5N 61
Homeland Drive
SUTTON
Surrey
SM2 5LY
Tel: 020 86611611

HOLY CROSS HOSPITAL —1C 188
Hindhead Road
HASLEMERE
Surrey
GU27 1NQ
Tel: 01428 643311

HOMEWOOD RESOURCE CENTRE —9E 36
Bournewood House
Guildford Road
CHERTSEY
Surrey
KT16 0QA
Tel: 01932 872010

HORSHAM HOSPITAL —5J 197
Hurst Road
HORSHAM
West Sussex
RH12 2DR
Tel: 01403 227000

HRH PRINCESS CHRISTIAN'S HOSPITAL —4F 4
12 Clarence Road
WINDSOR
Berkshire
SL4 5AG
Tel: 01753 853121

KING EDWARD VII HOSPITAL —6F 4
St Leonard's Road
WINDSOR
Berkshire
SL4 3DP
Tel: 01753 860441

KINGSTON HOSPITAL —9A 26
Galsworthy Road
KINGSTON UPON THAMES
Surrey
KT2 7QB
Tel: 020 85467711

LEATHERHEAD HOSPITAL —9J 79
Poplar Road
LEATHERHEAD
Surrey
KT22 8SD
Tel: 01372 384384

MARIE CURIE CENTRE CATERHAM —3C 104
Harestone Drive
CATERHAM
Surrey
CR3 6YQ
Tel: 01883 342226

MAYDAY UNIVERSITY HOSPITAL —5M 45
Mayday Road
THORNTON HEATH
Surrey
CR7 7YE
Tel: 020 84013000

MEDICAL RECEPTION STATION HOSPITAL —7M 49
Royal Military Academy
Egerton Road
CAMBERLEY
Surrey
GU15 4PH
Tel: 01276 412234

MILFORD HOSPITAL —2F 152
Tuesley Lane
GODALMING
Surrey
GU7 1UF
Tel: 01483 782000

MOLESEY HOSPITAL —4A 40
High Street
WEST MOLESEY
Surrey
KT8 2LU
Tel: 020 89414481

MOUNT ALVERNIA HOSPITAL
—5A **114** (6F **202**)
46 Harvey Road
GUILDFORD
Surrey
GU1 3LX
Tel: 01483 570122

NELSON HOSPITAL —1L **43**
Kingston Road
LONDON
SW20 8DB
Tel: 020 82962000

NEW EPSOM & EWELL COTTAGE HOSPITAL,
THE —7L **59**
West Park Road
EPSOM
Surrey
KT19 8PH
Tel: 01372 734834

NEW VICTORIA HOSPITAL —9D **26**
184 Coombe Lane West
KINGSTON UPON THAMES
Surrey
KT2 7EG
Tel: 020 89499000

NORTH DOWNS HOSPITAL —3D **104**
46 Tupwood Lane
CATERHAM
Surrey
CR3 6DP
Tel: 01883 348981

ORPINGTON HOSPITAL —1N **67**
Sevenoaks Road
ORPINGTON
Kent
BR6 9JU
Tel: 01689 815000

OXTED & LIMPSFIELD HOSPITAL —6N **105**
Eastlands Way
OXTED
Surrey
RH8 0LR
Tel: 01883 714344

PARKLANDS DAY HOSPITAL —8L **59**
West Park Hospital
Horton Lane
EPSOM
Surrey
KT19 8PB
Tel: 01883 388300

PARKSIDE HOSPITAL —4J **27**
53 Parkside
LONDON
SW19 5NX
Tel: 020 89718000

PAUL BEVAN HOSPICE —2J **33**
King's Ride
ASCOT
Berkshire
SL5 7RD
Tel: 01344 877877

PHYLLIS TUCKWELL HOSPICE —2K **129**
Waverley Lane
FARNHAM
Surrey
GU9 8BL
Tel: 01252 729400

PRINCESS ALICE HOSPICE —2A **58**
West End Lane
ESHER
Surrey
KT10 8NA
Tel: 01372 468811

PRINCESS MARGARET HOSPITAL —5G **4**
Osborne Road
WINDSOR
Berkshire
SL4 3SJ
Tel: 01753 743434

PURLEY & DISTRICT WAR MEMORIAL
HOSPITAL —7L **63**
Brighton Road
PURLEY
Surrey
CR8 2YL
Tel: 020 84013000

QUEEN ELIZABETH HOUSE —6M **19**
Torin Court
Englefield Green
EGHAM
Surrey
TW20 0PJ
Tel: 01784 471452

QUEEN MARY'S HOSPITAL FOR CHILDREN
—7A **44**
Wrythe Lane
CARSHALTON
Surrey
SM5 1AA
Tel: 020 82962000

QUEEN MARY'S UNIVERSITY HOSPITAL
—9E **12**
Roehampton Lane
LONDON
SW15 5PN
Tel: 020 87896611

QUEEN VICTORIA HOSPITAL —7B **166**
Holtye Road
EAST GRINSTEAD
West Sussex
RH19 3DZ
Tel: 01342 410210

REDWOOD BUPA HOSPITAL —7E **122**
Canada Drive
REDHILL
RH1 5BY
Tel: 01737 277277

RICHMOND HEALTHCARE HAMLET —6L **11**
Kew Foot Road
RICHMOND
Surrey
TW9 2TE
Tel: 020 89403331

RIDGEWOOD CENTRE, THE —3G **71**
Old Bisley Road
CAMBERLEY
Surrey
GU16 9QE
Tel: 01276 692919

ROEHAMPTON PRIORY HOSPITAL —7E **12**
Priory Lane
LONDON
SW15 5JJ
Tel: 020 88768261

ROYAL HOSPITAL FOR NEURO-DISABILITY
—9K **13**
West Hill
LONDON
SW15 3SW
Tel: 020 87804500

ROYAL MARSDEN HOSPITAL (SUTTON), THE
—6A **62**
Downs Road
SUTTON
Surrey
SM2 5PT
Tel: 020 86426011

ROYAL SURREY COUNTY HOSPITAL, THE
—3H **113**
Egerton Road
GUILDFORD
Surrey
GU2 5XX
Tel: 01483 571122

RUNNYMEDE HOSPITAL, THE —9F **36**
Guildford Road
Ottershaw
CHERTSEY
Surrey
KT16 0RQ
Tel: 01932 877800

ST ANTHONY'S HOSPITAL —8J **43**
London Road
LONDON
SM3 9DW
Tel: 020 83376691

ST CATHERINE'S HOSPICE —5B **182**
Malthouse Road
CRAWLEY
West Sussex
RH10 6BH
Tel: 01293 447333

ST EBBA'S —5B **60**
Hook Road
EPSOM
Surrey
KT19 8QJ
Tel: 01883 388300

ST GEORGE'S HOSPITAL (TOOTING) —8B **28**
Blackshaw Road
LONDON
SW17 0QT
Tel: 020 86721255

ST HELIER HOSPITAL —7A **44**
Wrythe Lane
CARSHALTON
Surrey
SM5 1AA
Tel: 020 82962000

ST JOHN'S AND AMYAND HOUSE —1G **25**
Strafford Road
TWICKENHAM
TW1 3AD
Tel: 020 87449943

ST RAPHAEL'S HOSPICE —7J **43**
St. Anthony's Hospital
London Road
SUTTON
Surrey
SM3 9DW
Tel: 020 83354575

SHIRLEY OAKS HOSPITAL —6F **46**
Poppy Lane
CROYDON
CR9 8AB
Tel: 020 86555500

SLOANE HOSPITAL, THE —1N **47**
125-133 Albemarle Road
BECKENHAM
Kent
BR3 5HS
Tel: 020 84666911

SPRINGFIELD UNIVERSITY HOSPITAL —4C **28**
61 Glenburnie Road
LONDON
SW17 7DJ
Tel: 020 86826000

SURBITON HOSPITAL —5L **41**
Ewell Road
SURBITON
Surrey
KT6 6EZ
Tel: 020 83997111

SUTTON GENERAL HOSPITAL —6N **61**
Cotswold Road
SUTTON
Surrey
SM2 5NF
Tel: 020 82962000

TEDDINGTON MEMORIAL HOSPITAL —7E **24**
Hampton Road
TEDDINGTON
Middlesex
TW11 0JL
Tel: 020 84088210

THAMES VALLEY HOSPICE —6D **4**
Pine Lodge
Hatch Lane
WINDSOR
Berkshire
SL4 3RW
Tel: 01753 842121

TOLWORTH HOSPITAL —8N **41**
Red Lion Road
SURBITON
Surrey
KT6 7QU
Tel: 020 83900102

UNSTED PARK REHABILITATION HOSPITAL
—6M **133**
Munstead Heath Road
GODALMING
Surrey
GU7 1UW
Tel: 01483 892061

WALTON COMMUNITY HOSPITAL —8J **39**
Rodney Road
WALTON-ON-THAMES
Surrey
KT12 3LD
Tel: 01932 220060

WEST MIDDLESEX UNIVERSITY HOSPITAL
—5G **11**
Twickenham Road
ISLEWORTH
Middlesex
TW7 6AF
Tel: 020 85602121

WEST PARK HOSPITAL —8L **59**
Horton Lane
EPSOM
Surrey
KT19 8PB
Tel: 01883 388300

WEYBRIDGE COMMUNITY HOSPITAL —1B **56**
22 Church Street
WEYBRIDGE
Surrey
KT13 8DY
Tel: 01932 852931

WOKING COMMUNITY HOSPITAL —5B **74**
Heathside Road
WOKING
Surrey
GU22 7HS
Tel: 01483 715911

WOKING HOSPICE —5B **74**
5 Hill View Road
WOKING
Surrey
GU22 7HW
Tel: 01483 881750

WOKING NUFFIELD HOSPITAL —1A **74**
Shores Road
WOKING
Surrey
GU21 4BY
Tel: 01483 227800

WOKINGHAM HOSPITAL —2A **30**
41 Barkham Road
WOKINGHAM
Berkshire
RG41 2RE
Tel: 0118 9495000

RAIL, CROYDON TRAMLINK
AND LONDON UNDERGROUND STATIONS

with their map square reference

Addington Village Stop. CT —3K **65**
Addiscombe Stop. CT —7D **46**
Addlestone Station. Rail —1M **55**
Aldershot Station. Rail —3N **109**
Ampere Way Stop. CT —7K **45**
Arena Stop. CT —4F **46**
Ascot Station. Rail —3L **33**
Ashford Station. Rail —5A **22**
Ash Station. Rail —2F **110**
Ashtead Station. Rail —4L **79**
Ash Vale Station. Rail —6E **90**
Avenue Road Stop. CT —1G **47**

Bagshot Station. Rail —3J **51**
Balham Station. Rail & Tube —2F **28**
Banstead Station. Rail —1L **81**
Barnes Bridge Station. Rail —5E **12**
Barnes Station. Rail —6F **12**
Barons Court Station. Tube —1K **13**
Beckenham Road Stop. CT —1H **47**
Beddington Lane Stop. CT —5G **45**
Belgrave Walk Stop. CT —3B **44**
Belmont Station. Rail —6N **61**
Berrylands Station. Rail —3A **42**
Betchworth Station. Rail —1C **120**
Bingham Road Stop. CT —7D **46**
Birkbeck Stop. CT —2F **46**
Blackhorse Lane Stop. CT —6D **46**
Blackwater Station. Rail —2K **69**
Bookham Station. Rail —1N **97**
Boston Manor Station. Tube —1G **11**
Boxhill and Westhumble Station. Rail —9H **99**
Bracknell Station. Rail —2N **31**
Brentford Station. Rail —2J **11**
Brookwood Station. Rail —8D **72**
Byfleet & New Haw Station. Rail —6M **55**

Camberley Station. Rail —1B **70**
Carshalton Beeches Station. Rail —3D **62**
Carshalton Station. Rail —1D **62**
Caterham Station. Rail —2D **104**
Cheam Station. Rail —4K **61**
Chertsey Station. Rail —7H **37**
Chessington North Station. Rail —2L **59**
Chessington South Station. Rail —4K **59**
Chilworth Station. Rail —9G **114**
Chipstead Station. Rail —5D **82**
Chiswick Park Station. Tube —1B **12**
Chiswick Station. Rail —3B **12**
Christs Hospital Station. Rail —9D **196**
Church Street Stop. CT —8N **45** (3B **200**)
Clandon Station. Rail —7K **95**
Clapham South Station. Tube —1F **28**
Claygate Station. Rail —3E **58**
Clock House Station. Rail —1H **47**
Cobham & Stoke D'abernon Station. Rail —4M **77**
Colliers Wood Station. Tube —8B **28**
Coombe Lane Stop. CT —2F **64**
Coulsdon South Station. Rail —3H **83**
Crawley Station. Rail —4C **182**
Crowthorne Station. Rail —3D **48**
Croydon Central Stop. CT —8N **45**

Datchet Station. Rail —4L **5**
Dorking (Deepdene) Station. Rail —3J **119**
Dorking Station. Rail —3J **119**
Dorking West Station. Rail —4F **118** (1H **201**)
Dormans Station. Rail —2B **166**
Dundonald Road Stop. CT —8L **27**

Earl's Court Station. Tube —1N **13**
Earlsfield Station. Rail —2A **28**

Earlswood Station. Rail —5D **122**
East Croydon Station. Rail & CT —8A **46** (3E **200**)
East Grinstead Station. Rail —9N **165**
East Putney Station. Tube —8K **13**

Edenbridge Station. Rail —9K **127**
Edenbridge Town Station. Rail —1M **147**
Eden Park Station. Rail —4K **47**
Effingham Junction Station. Rail —1H **97**
Egham Station. Rail —6C **20**
Elmers End Station. Rail & CT —3G **47**
Epsom Downs Station. Rail —2G **81**
Epsom Station. Rail —9C **60** (6J **201**)
Esher Station. Rail —8D **40**
Ewell East Station. Rail —6G **60**
Ewell West Station. Rail —5D **60**

Farnborough Main Station. Rail —9N **69**
Farnborough North Station. Rail —8B **70**
Farncombe Station. Rail —4J **133**
Farnham Station. Rail —2H **129**
Faygate Station. Rail —8E **180**
Feltham Station. Rail —2J **23**
Fieldway Stop. CT —4L **65**
Fleet Station. Rail —2C **88**
Frimley Station. Rail —6A **70**
Fulham Broadway Station. Tube —3M **13**
Fulwell Station. Rail —5D **24**

Gatwick Airport Station. Rail —3F **162**
George Street Stop. CT —8N **45** (3C **200**)
Godalming Station. Rail —7G **132**
Godstone Station. Rail —7F **124**
Gomshall Station. Rail —8E **116**
Gravel Hill Stop. CT —3H **65**
Guildford Station. Rail —5M **113** (5A **202**)
Gunnersbury Station. Rail & Tube —1A **12**

Hackbridge Station. Rail —8F **44**
Hammersmith Station. Tube —1H **13**
Hampton Court Station. Rail —3E **40**
Hampton Station. Rail —9A **24**
Hampton Wick Station. Rail —9J **25** (2G **203**)
Harrington Road Stop. CT —2F **46**
Haslemere Station. Rail —2F **188**
Hatton Cross Station. Tube —7G **8**
Haydons Road Station. Rail —6A **28**
Heathrow Central Station. Rail —6B **8**
Heathrow Terminal 4 Station. Tube —9D **8**
Heathrow Terminals 1, 2, 3 Station. Tube —6C **8**
Hersham Station. Rail —9M **39**
Hinchley Wood Station. Rail —9F **40**
Holmwood Station. Rail —7J **139**
Horley Station. Rail —9F **142**
Horsham Station. Rail —6K **197**
Horsley Station. Rail —3F **96**
Hounslow Central Station. Tube —6B **10**
Hounslow East Station. Tube —5C **10**
Hounslow Station. Rail —8B **10**
Hounslow West Station. Tube —5M **9**
Hurst Green Station. Rail —1B **126**

Ifield Station. Rail —3M **181**
Isleworth Station. Rail —5F **10**

Kenley Station. Rail —1N **83**
Kew Bridge Station. Rail —1M **11**
Kew Gardens Station. Rail & Tube —4N **11**
King Henry's Drive Stop. CT —5L **65**
Kingscote Station. Rail —5J **185**
Kingston Station. Rail —9L **25** (2J **203**)

Kingswood Station. Rail —8L **81**

Leatherhead Station. Rail —8G **79**
Lebanon Road Stop. CT —8B **46**
Lingfield Station. Rail —7A **146**
Littlehaven Station. Rail —3M **197**
Lloyd Park Stop. CT —1C **64**
London Road Station. Rail —3A **114** (3F **202**)
Longcross Station. Rail —7J **35**

Malden Manor Station. Rail —6D **42**
Martin's Heron Station. Rail —3D **32**
Merstham Station. Rail —6G **102**
Merton Park Stop. CT —9M **27**
Milford Station. Rail —3D **152**
Mitcham Junction Station. Rail & CT —4E **44**
Mitcham Stop. CT —3C **44**
Morden Road Stop. CT —1N **43**
Morden South Station. Rail —4M **43**
Morden Station. Tube —2N **43**
Mortlake Station. Rail —6B **12**
Motspur Park Station. Rail —4G **42**

New Addington Stop. CT —6M **65**
New Malden Station. Rail —2D **42**
Norbiton Station. Rail —9N **25**
Norbury Station. Rail —9K **29**
North Camp Station. Rail —9K **90**
North Sheen Station. Rail —7N **11**
Norwood Junction Station. Rail —3D **46**
Nutfield Station. Rail —5K **123**

Ockley Station. Rail —4G **159**
Osterley Station. Tube —3D **10**
Oxshott Station. Rail —9C **58**
Oxted Station. Rail —7A **106**

Parsons Green Station. Tube —4M **13**
Phipps Bridge Stop. CT —2B **44**
Purley Oaks Station. Rail —5A **64**
Purley Station. Rail —7L **63**
Putney Bridge Station. Tube —6L **13**
Putney Station. Rail —7K **13**

Ravenscourt Park Station. Tube —1G **12**
Raynes Park Station. Rail —1H **43**
Redhill Station. Rail —2E **122**
Reedham Station. Rail —9K **63**
Reeves Corner Stop. CT —8M **45** (3A **200**)
Reigate Station. Rail —6N **121**
Richmond Station. Rail & Tube —7L **11**
Riddlesdown Station. Rail —9N **63**

St Helier Station. Rail —5M **43**
St Margarets Station. Rail —9H **11**
Salfords Station. Rail —2F **142**
Sanderstead Station. Rail —5A **64**
Sandhurst Station. Rail —8F **48**
Sandilands Stop. CT —8C **46**
Selhurst Station. Rail —4B **46**
Shalford Station. Rail —9A **114**
Shepperton Station. Rail —4D **38**
Smitham Station. Rail —2J **83**
South Croydon Station. Rail —2A **64** (8E **200**)
Southfields Station. Tube —2L **27**
South Merton Station. Rail —2L **43**
South Wimbledon Station. Tube —8N **27**
Southfields Station. Tube —2L **27**
Staines Station. Rail —6J **21**
Stoneleigh Station. Rail —2F **60**
Strawberry Hill Station. Rail —4F **24**

Streatham Common Station. Rail —8H **29**
Streatham Hill Station. Rail —3J **29**
Streatham Station. Rail —6H **29**
Sunbury Station. Rail —9H **23**
Sunningdale Station. Rail —6D **34**
Sunnymeads Station. Rail —6A **6**
Surbiton Station. Rail —5L **41**
Sutton Common Station. Rail —8N **43**
Sutton Station. Rail —3A **62**
Syon Lane Station. Rail —3G **11**

Tadworth Station. Rail —9H **81**
Tattenham Corner Station. Rail —5G **80**
Teddington Station. Rail —7G **24**
Thames Ditton Station. Rail —6F **40**
Therapia Lane Stop. CT —6J **45**
Thornton Heath Station. Rail —3N **45**
Three Bridges Station. Rail —3F **182**
Tolworth Station. Rail —8A **42**
Tooting Bec Station. Tube —4E **28**
Tooting Broadway Station. Tube —6C **28**
Tooting Station. Rail —7D **28**
Tulse Hill Station. Rail —3M **29**
Twickenham Station. Rail —1G **24**

Upper Halliford Station. Rail —1F **38**
Upper Warlingham Station. Rail —5D **84**

Virginia Water Station. Rail —4A **36**

Waddon Marsh Stop. CT —8L **45**
Waddon Station. Rail —1L **63**
Wallington Station. Rail —3F **62**
Walton-on-Thames Station. Rail —1H **57**
Wanborough Station. Rail —3N **111**
Wandle Park Stop. CT —8L **45**
Wandsworth Common Station. Rail —2D **28**
Wandsworth Town Station. Rail —7N **13**
Warnham Station. Rail —9J **179**
Wellesley Road Stop. CT —8A **46** (2D **200**)
West Brompton Station. Rail & Tube —2M **13**
West Byfleet Station. Rail —8J **55**
West Croydon Station. Rail & CT —7N **45** (1B **200**)
West Dulwich Station. Rail —3N **29**
West Kensington Station. Tube —1L **13**
West Norwood Station. Rail —5M **29**
West Sutton Station. Rail —1M **61**
West Wickham Station. Rail —6M **47**
Weybridge Station. Rail —3B **56**
Whitton Station. Rail —1C **24**
Whyteleafe South Station. Rail —6D **84**
Whyteleafe Station. Rail —4C **84**
Wimbledon Chase Station. Rail —1K **43**
Wimbledon Park Station. Tube —4M **27**
Wimbledon Station. Rail, CT & Tube —7L **27**
Windsor & Eton Central Station. Rail —4G **4**
Windsor & Eton Riverside Station. Rail —3G **5**
Witley Station. Rail —1C **172**
Wokingham Station. Rail —2A **30**
Woking Station. Rail —4B **74**
Woldingham Station. Rail —9G **85**
Woodmansterne Station. Rail —3F **82**
Woodside Stop. CT —5E **46**
Worcester Park Station. Rail —7F **42**
Worplesdon Station. Rail —2L **93**
Wraysbury Station. Rail —9C **6**

The representation on the maps of a road, track or footpath is no evidence of the existence of a right of way.

The Grid on this map is the National Grid taken from Ordnance Survey mapping with the permission of the Controller of Her Majesty's Stationery Office.

Copyright of Geographers' A-Z Map Co. Ltd.

No reproduction by any method whatsoever of any part of this publication is permitted without the prior consent of the copyright owners.